JUDAISM IN LATE ANTIQUITY

VOLUME TWO

PART THREE

JUDAISM IN LATE ANTIQUITY

EDITED BY

JACOB NEUSNER

AND

ALAN J. AVERY-PECK

PART THREE

WHERE WE STAND: ISSUES AND DEBATES IN ANCIENT JUDAISM

BRILL ACADEMIC PUBLISHERS, INC.
BOSTON • LEIDEN
2001

Judaism in Late Antiquity was originally published as nine hardbound books. This three-volume paperback edition is unabridged and includes all of the information in the original nine books. Each part and each section are paginated separately to match the pagination of the original edition. The paperback edition includes:

Volume 1 – Part One and Part Two
Volume 2 – Part Three, Sections One–Four (In the original edition, Sections One–Four were identified as Volumes One–Four.)
Volume 3 – Part Four and Part Five, Sections One–Two (In the original edition, Sections One–Two were identified as Volumes One–Two.)

Library of Congress Cataloging-in-Publication Data

Judaism in late antiquity/edited by Jacob Neusner.
   p. cm.
   Pt. 3, v. 4 edited by Jacob Neusner and Alan J. Avery-Peck.
   Originally published: Leiden; New York: E.J. Brill, 1995-. Handbuch der Orientalistik, Erste Abteilung, der Nahe und Mittlere Osten, 17. Bd., etc.
   With new introd.
   Contents: pt. 1. The literary and archaeological sources — pt. 2. Historical syntheses — pt. 3. Where we stand: issues and debates in ancient Judaism/ (4 v.) — pt. 4. Death, life-in-death, resurrection, and the world-to-come in the Judaisms of antiquity/edited by Alan J. Avery-Peck and Jacob Neusner — pt. 5. The Judaism of Qumran: a systemic reading of the Dead Sea scrolls/edited by Alan J. Avery-Peck, Jacob Neusner, and Bruce D. Chilton (2 v.).
   Includes bibliographical references and index.
   ISBN 0-391-04153-3
   1. Judaism–History–Post-exilic period, 586 B.C.-210 A.D.—Sources.
I. Neusner, Jacob, 1932- II. Avery-Peck, Alan J. (Alan Jeffery), 1953-
III. Chilton, Bruce.

BM176.J8 2001
296'.09'015–dc21

2001046481

ISBN 0–391–04153–3

PRINTED IN THE UNITED STATES OF AMERICA

JUDAISM IN LATE ANTIQUITY

PART THREE

SECTION ONE

TABLE OF CONTENTS

PREFACE

Why devote so much effort, within the exposition of the state of scholarship, to contemporary debates? It is because the editors place the highest priority upon affording a platform for public discussion of controverted points of learning: facts, methods, interpretations alike. Learning progresses through contentious pursuit of controversy, as hypotheses are put forth, tested against evidence, advocated and criticized. Then public discourse, dense and rich in rigorous argument and explicit discussion, stimulates. Choices present themselves, what is at stake is clarified, knowledge deepens. Those who serve as gatekeepers in scholarship—editors of journals and monograph series, for example—therefore find a place for everything and its opposite. That is their task. They value what is best expressed in the German word *Auseinandersetzungen.*

What the editors, by creating this book and its companions, mean to oppose also comes to expression in a German word uniquely serviceable to scholarship, *Todschweigen,* meaning, to murder through silence (ostracism, suppression, above all, active, ostentatious acts of ignoring views one does not hold). What costs do we aim to avoid? Learning atrophies when political consensus substitutes for criticism and when other than broadly-accepted viewpoints, approaches, and readings find a hearing only with difficulty if at all.

Having presented in Parts I and II of this series some of the main results of contemporary learning on Judaism in late antiquity,[1] we here proceed to portray issues and debates that animate the field. Such an account of contemporary debates, along with a picture of the state of knowledge, is necessary. That is because any responsible account for colleagues of the shape and standing of learning in a given subject must outline not only the present state of pertinent questions but also the contemporary character of debate and discussion. That is especially the case here, for the study of ancient Judaism forms one of the most contentious subjects in the contemporary humanities.

---

[1] *Judaism in Late Antiquity.* Volume One. *Literary and Archaeological Sources. Handbuch der Orientalistik. Judaistik.* Leiden, 1995: E. J. Brill. Volume XVI; *Judaism in Late Antiquity.* Volume Two. *Historical Syntheses.* In the series *Handbuch der Orientalistik. Judaistik.* Leiden, 1995: E. J. Brill. Volume XVII.

What accounts for the highly controverted character of this field of the study of ancient religion, culture, history, and literature? It is not only for the obvious, theological, reason that Judaism and Christianity today have a heavy stake in the results of academic learning about olden times. Many debates come about because of contemporary political or theological considerations, not by reason of issues intrinsic in the sources themselves. But a second fact precipitates quite strong difference of opinion. It is because long-established approaches have been called into question, as new methods and new definitions of critical learning take center-stage. There is a third factor as well: much new information emerges of both a literary and an archaeological character, and, it goes without saying, reasonable people may form different opinions in describing, analyzing, and interpreting facts simply unknown to prior generations of scholars. Not only so, but the state of the contemporary humanities and social sciences bring to the forefront issues hitherto not considered at all. Altogether new perspectives now emerge, new questions deriving from other areas of the humanities than the study of religion, such as women's studies and studies of gender and the social construction of sexuality, emerge, to which even a generation ago no one gave thought. It goes without saying that, in the study of ancient Judaism, all four sources of contention contribute to contemporary debate. Armed with a range of new interests, people turn to that diverse set of kindred religious systems we call "Judaism," rightly anticipating fresh and suggestive answers.

But the nature of the evidence itself—literary and archaeological—makes its own contribution as well. Read even in their own framework, the principal literary sources as well as the main archaeological remains contain many ambiguities. They leave ample space for diverse viewpoints to take shape. Read in one way for nearly half-a-century, the Dead Sea Scrolls, fully available after such a long wait, now require fresh approaches and receive them. An established consensus gives way. Questions not asked at all demand attention, even as diverse answers to long-settled questions are put forth.[2] Not only so, but another principal component of the documentary legacy of

---

[2] In *Judaism in Late Antiquity*. Volume Five. *Judaism at Qumran*, we plan to ask hitherto unasked questions of system and structure of the Judaic religious system adumbrated by the Dead Sea library: what kind of Judaism can have produced this writing? Until now, problems of historical, philological, and archaeological character have predominated, and the religious reading of the writings has been subordinated.

ancient Judaism, the Rabbinic literature, forms the focus of most vigorous debates. And these represent only two among many of the sub-fields of ancient Judaism that today provoke contention.

But academic debates seldom take the form of a public *Auseinander-setzung*, an exchange of opposed views among persons of shared rationality, mutual respect, and good will, an exchange to the point, on a single issue, within a shared consensus of pertinent sources, considerations, and rationalities. Journals automatically reject work that does not conform to the regnant viewpoint of a given set of editors (not seldom appointed for other than scholarly achievement), and university presses and monograph series practice censorship of an other-than-academic character as well. Conferences on a given problem commonly exclude viewpoints not shared by the organizers, and university faculties rarely make certain that their students hear views not shared by the professors of those faculties. Indeed, it is only a small exaggeration to say that, given a list of the conferences a person has attended or the universities at which he or she has lectured, we may easily construct the opinion of that person on the entire agenda of learning in his or her field of specialization.

But debate, discussion, on-going exchanges of views, systematic and sustained criticism—these impart to all fields of academic learning such dynamics as will sustain them over time. Repeating oneself and the views of one's friends and ignoring other positions, not even alluding to them in footnotes or in bibliographies, as though *Tod-schweigen* accomplished its goal—these modes of dealing with difference serve no one. And in this book and its companion, the editors mean to show a better way of doing the work of learning in the study of ancient Judaism.

Here in Part III of the present sub-series, therefore, the editors have invited colleagues systematically to outline their views in an *Auseinandersetzung* with contrary ones. We asked them to tell us how, in broad and sweeping terms, they see the state of learning in their areas of special interest. We wanted sharply-etched state-of-the-question studies, systematic presentations of a distinctive viewpoint and very particular results, and other evidence of how scholarly debate goes forward. We hoped to portray some of the principal issues, to set forth a few of the alternative positions presently maintained about fundamental questions of method and substance. Inviting the leading players in the U.S.A., Europe, and the State of Israel, in the study of ancient Judaism, both in Second Temple times and after 70 C.E., we hoped to find a dozen or so chapters that would adumbrate some of the larger issues. Our hopes were more than met. The responses proved so many that two sizable books are required to set forth the representative sample of debate on a few large questions that we · wished to present here.

We wanted to commence with a thoroughly fresh perspective of a theoretical question, and so accord pride of place to as basic a question as we could imagine, what, in a religion so concerned with social norms and public policy, can we possibly mean by "law" when we speak of law in Judaism. We proceed to three chapters on Second Temple Judaisms, promising further essays on the same topic in part two of this volume, and turn to two on the special subject of the Dead Sea library (with more opinions planned in the successor-book). The two papers in the present part provide an overview of matters and a systematic, critical account of the fading consensus, respectively.

The next set of papers ought to stand as the definitive account of the diverse viewpoints on a basic question of method. Because of the willingness of contending parties to meet one another in a single frame of discourse, we are able to portray with considerable breadth the presently-contending viewpoints concerning the use of Rabbinic literature for historical purposes. A few words of background on what is at issue are called for. While, in the study of ancient Scripture, the Tanakh and the New Testament, for example, critical methods have replaced credulity and paraphrase, until the recent past, it was common to cite a page of the Talmud as evidence for a fact in the life of a person or an event in the history of ancient Judaism and the Jews. If the Talmud said it, it had to be so. That perfect faith in whatever the holy books said characterized scholarly, not theological, accounts of matters is transparent in all work prior to the 1970s in Hebrew, English, and German, and in most, but not all, work in French, on Talmudic history.

One example suffices: the article on Aqiba in the *Encyclopaedia Judaica* (1972) is a pastiche of references to Talmudic stories, all of them set forth as facts about the life of the historical Aqiba, none of them subjected to a trace of critical analysis, e.g., to ask, how do we know that this allegation of what Aqiba is supposed to have said or done is true? Louis Finkelstein's *Akiba,* a generation earlier (1936), followed exactly the same procedures, and his predecessors back to Zechariah Frankel, founder of Talmudic history in the mid-nineteenth century, set the norm: if the text says it, it is true, and there you have your history. "History" meant paraphrase of the rabbinical fables, together with speculation on this, that, and the other thing. But that approach to "Talmudic history" has lost ground. When, in the early 1980s, Finkelstein wrote for his *Cambridge History of Judaism* Volume II the article on the Pharisees, he did not even deign to include in his notes or bibliography any work done after 1936, nor did he address criticism of his own work on the same subject. And the reviews of that volume drew attention to, and condemned, that failure on his part. In that failure, Finkelstein made a considerable, and memorable, contribution to the failure of the entire project—*Cambridge History of Judaism* Volumes III and IV, projected but never published!

The debate on critical method in Talmudic history commenced with publication of the present volume's senior editor's *Development of a Legend. Studies on the Traditions Concerning Yohanan ben Zakkai* (Leiden, 1970: Brill), *The Rabbinic Traditions about the Pharisees before 70* (Leiden, 1971: Brill, 3 vols.), and *Eliezer ben Hyrcanus. The Tradition and the Man* (Leiden, 1973: Brill). *Pharisees* ended with a systematic reading of prior scholarship on the subject, showing the gullible and credulous attitude brought by the scholars to the Rabbinic sources in their portraits of the Pharisees. A syllabus of errors, rare in biblical studies but commonplace in Talmudic studies, was illustrated, chapter and verse, by specific references and citations to the standard accounts of the subject.[3] Not only so, but with the main results recapitulated in *Reading and Believing: Ancient Judaism and Contemporary Gullibility* (Atlanta, 1986: Scholars Press for Brown Judaic Studies), the debate on the requirements of a critical utilization of the Talmudic and other writings has gone forward. Until recent times, the entire critical approach has been ignored, as though in scholarship *Todschweigen* joined to character-assassination of those who hold opposed viewpoints, settles any questions. And in the universities, not only the yeshivas, of the State of Israel, as evidenced by books and journals such as *Tarbis* and *Zion*, it still is.

But a new generation of younger scholars in the State of Israel, joined by counterparts in the U.S. seminary world and in European and American universities, have taken up the issue. Here matters change: the issue is addressed head-on. People will form themselves

---

[3] In Volume Two of this project we shall include much up-to-date scholarship on the Pharisees, which has rendered the senior editor's *Pharisees*, if not obsolete, then at least out of date.

opinions on the state of the question; but now, everything is set forth in a single coherent sequence of statements. The editors are proud to present no fewer than six statements of a systematic character on the issue, covering as far as is possible the full repertoire of opinion on this critical question. Israeli, American-seminary, European, and American academic views all find their place in these pages. The editors take special pleasure in the broad range of viewpoint, in those statements, as questions of theory and method are worked out and the results set on display. The prior generation of Israeli scholars would never have participated in such a project as this, and the mixture of gentiles and Jews—Orthodox and secular, Reform and Conservative—not to mention most nationalities presently engaged in the work, Canadians, Americans, Europeans, and Israelis, attests to the spirit of engagement that has taken over in place of the now-discredited *Todschweigen*. Those who imagine that by ignoring what they do not like and that by vilifying those who hold positions different from their own, they can persuade the scholarly world of their views and prevail here find reality: *Todschweigen* does not and cannot work.

Some may wonder why the vehement espousal of the value of *Auseinandersetzungen* and the equally strong denunciation of *Todschweigen* that this book means to embody. The reason is that when it comes to the study of ancient Judaism, the former is rare, the latter commonplace. A few scholarly journals in the study of religion in general, and of Judaism in particular, best represented by the *Journal of the American Academy of Religion* and the *Journal of Biblical Literature*, sustain and even foster debate. *JAAR* and *JBL* will print not only criticism but rejoinder, not only reviews but replies thereto. They represent the promise of a lively future for learning in religion. When it comes to the study of Judaism in particular, the various monograph series edited by the senior editor of this volume have gladly found a place for numerous studies built upon methods and approaches other than his own.

But much more common in the scholarly communities in which ancient Judaism comes under academic study is the denial of systematic public debate. It is the fact characteristic of universities, university presses, and journals that those who control the media of public discourse close the door on views they do not like. They print violent and *ad hominem* advocacy of one viewpoint but do not permit replies, publish intemperate reviews aimed at nothing short of character-assassination but not answers thereto. Many scholarly journals, university presses, and monograph series take an essentially political position on scholarship, closing off debate and imposing a rigid, orthodoxy upon such learning as they disseminate. They will not even consider articles that bear the wrong names or books or monographs from the camp with which they do not identify.

Certainly, in the English language—German and Hebrew present more blatantly political cases than this one—the most famous example of the Bolshevik-journals is the *Journal of the American Oriental Society*. Unlike *JAAR* and *JBL*, *JAOS* will publish only the viewpoint of those in control of the journal that day (or century). The controlling clique cares nothing for scholarly interchange, even misrepresenting the state of learning in defense of its (imagined) monopoly. As a result, *JAOS* has lost all prominence in the field of the study of ancient Judaism (and not only in that field!), as scholarly discussion has found a more suitable venue for itself. To the American Oriental Society, scholarship makes no difference; to the American Academy of Religion and the Society of Biblical Literature, scholarship makes all the difference.

It remains to express our gratitude to those who have made this project a success. For on-going support of their joint and separate scholarly enterprises, the two editors express thanks to our respective universities and colleges, the University of South Florida and Bard College, for Jacob Neusner, and the College of the Holy Cross, for Alan J. Avery-Peck.

We further thank E.J. Brill and its editors, in particular Drs. Elisabeth Venekamp, for guidance and commitment to this project. We remember with special appreciation the encouragement of Dr. Elisabeth Erdman-Visser, Brill's editor when the project got under way. We call attention to the fact that, of all the scholarly publishers in the U.S.A., Europe, and the State of Israel, none has devoted more effort to opening doors and windows than has E.J. Brill, with whom we are proud to be associated. The senior editor published his first book with Brill in 1962, when Dr. F.C. Wieder, Jr., was the director, and remembers with thanks many editors and directors over the past decades. Brill in this generation has carried forward a great tradition of scholarship, one that has sustained us all.

And, finally, we thank the contributors to this part of Volume III for their prompt and conscientious work. We are proud that so many distinguished scholars have joined in this effort publicly to show where we stand in contemporary issues and debates on ancient Judaism.

Jacob Neusner
Distinguished Research Professor of Religious Studies
University of South Florida, Tampa, FL
and
Professor of Religion
Bard College, Annandale-on-Hudson, NY

Alan J. Avery-Peck
Kraft-Hiatt Professor of Judaic Studies
College of the Holy Cross, Worcester, MA

FUNDAMENTAL QUESTIONS

I. "LAW" IN EARLY JUDAISM

Philip R. Davies
Sheffield University

The problem of "law" in early Judaism (or: in late Second Temple Judaisms and the pre-Mishnaic period) is one of definition above all else: not only of the various words within the same semantic field (*torah, nomos, mitzvah, mishpat, hoq*, etc.) but also of the social and cultural self-understandings and practices into which Jews converted "law," whether as cultic, natural, political, religious, philosophical, or a combination of any of these. However, when Jews of the period referred to their law, they (almost without exception) indicated the divine "law" given to Israel through Moses; and they agreed that this law was contained (if not fully) in the book, or books (scrolls, to be accurate) of Moses. We shall therefore focus on the status and function of the written "law of Moses," without ignoring the fact that "Jewish law" is not simply a matter of Scripture, nor of its exegesis.

Yet there lies an even more fundamental issue, so fundamental that it is scarcely ever addressed. Why did Judaism as a religion based on a Mosaic law (however defined and applied) come into existence in the first place? The scriptures themselves give an answer: it was revealed by God to Moses on Sinai. But this is not a historian's answer. To a large extent this following essay tries to formulate an answer to this question.

The approach to be taken is a literary and not an anthropological or sociological one: dealing with the written texts of early Judaism and not with the practices of early Jewish communities and individuals. The distinction, indeed, between what was written and what was done is extremely important to preserve and comes into play already in the great law-codes of the Semitic ancient Near East. Much later, the distinction remains crucial in understanding the lengthy and incomplete process by which Rabbinic Judaism transformed a scriptural corpus, supplemented by a non-scriptural body of practice and theory, into a systematic statement of Judaism, firstly through the Mishnah (which is still to be regarded as intellectual theory rather than legislation) and the halakhic midrashim, then through the Talmud, and onwards through successive collections of responsa and codifications of Jewish law. For Rabbinic Judaism, the law is the divine will, which has been revealed in a literarily definitive form; and through rational, systematic and intellectually informed exegesis that literary revelation persists through a history of literarily explication. The ideas of law as personified in great figures (e.g., in the book of Jubilees) and as nature (e.g., in 1 Enoch) both have their place in early Judaism and indeed can be found in the Jewish scriptures too (both in the book of Proverbs). But in early Judaism these ideas were, as far as we know, never uncoupled from the written Law of Moses, the Torah.

The study of Jewish law in our period, then, is not a study of judicial practice. The administration of justice at any particular time in the history of the Jewish people is largely a separate matter from this process of creation of Jewish Torah, partly because in the Second Temple period law was administered at different and only partly related levels: by the imperial court, by the Temple authorities, by local elders, priests or communities. Judicial processes continued to be controlled by custom as much if not more than by decree and also varied from place to place, group to group, and from instance to instance. It is therefore a fundamental mistake to *assume* that scriptural laws are necessarily either accurate reflections of actual practice in Israel or Judah, or, indeed, to think that they were intended to serve as such; at best there is a proportion of overlap between what is conceived to be the law and what was currently practiced. Thanks to the activity of the rabbis, Torah has been converted into halakhah (or the two have been accommodated to each other—this question is open to considerable discussion).

To appreciate the intellectual and social challenge that the rabbis faced in creating a halakhic Judaism (as Neusner has it, a Judaism of the *Dual* Torah, scriptural and Mishnaic) that controlled the practice of Judaism and the identity of Israel, we must recognize that in the Second Temple period the Torah of Moses did not function as the constitution of an Israelite society. We can perceive that it was often conceptualized as such, with Moses displayed to the Hellenistic world as the giver of laws to an ancient civilization; but attempts to live a "life according to Torah" emerged only gradually during this period as the chosen lifestyle of certain individuals and sects. Cultic laws might have applied quite directly to priestly practices (although even here some qualification seems necessary), and laws about holiness were adopted by those aspiring to quasi-priestly status (*Haverim*,

Pharisees, groups represented in the Qumran texts). But it cannot be claimed that at any time the law of Moses determined the way Jews even in Judah lived together as a society.

In any case, the five-part Mosaic Torah is not a coherent composition, nor is it purely legal even in the broadest sense. It has been shaped more by historiographical concerns. What we confront in the "books of Moses" is a (many times) edited narrative in which different kinds of law and indeed theories of law are assembled and assigned to a single law-giving event. In this process we can certainly discern a desire to create for the Jewish *ethnos* an ancient divine constitution, just as the narrative gives Israel an ancient ethnic origin. The "law-giving" episode that dominates the five-scroll Mosaic Torah (running from the middle of Exodus to the beginning of Numbers) forms part of an epic that describes the creation of Israel, first anticipated by promise, then given an ancestor, a divine epiphany, a constitution (law), and finally its own land. But we are already at the point at which, in the creation of a national epic, an editing process utilized various collections of laws that were written down earlier. Why were these various "laws" written? What function did they serve at the time of writing? To assume that they simply reflected what "Israel's" legal customs were is naive, though common enough. We cannot begin by attempting to reconstruct the judicial structures or principles of a society from this literature. Rather, it is necessary to deal briefly with the relationship of the writing to the doing, from the beginning.

LAW AS THEORY AND AS PRACTICE

"No direct link necessarily exists between the behavior envisioned by a law and the behavior practiced by members of the community.... It is not even valid to assume, without further evidence, that the law was actually made known to the members of the community." So writes Paul Flesher in his study of the Mishnaic laws of slavery.[1]

This statement appears to contradict the well-known dictum that in law theory follows practice. However, in the case of Second Temple Judaism no less than in the Mishnah, the opposite seems to be the case; Flesher's verdict on the Mishnah, behind which stands a whole

---

[1] *Oxen, Women, or Citizens? Slaves in the System of the Mishnah* (Atlanta, 1988).

program of research dominated by the approach of Jacob Neusner, also holds for earlier Jewish literature. In the case of the Mishnah, of course, the proposition is easier to establish, since the great Rabbinic enterprise represents a conspicuous case of legal theorizing. Though it does no doubt reflect *some* actual practices, its relationship to foregoing or contemporary *realia* is complex and often irretrievable. Its problematic is a theoretical and systemic one, i.e., it derives from the explication of a system based on an ideology of land, people and purity. It is manifestly utopian, its utopia being a land of Israel of a kind that its framers did not occupy and their successors knew even less. Its Israel is not a concrete Jewish society, but an eternal and ideal "people of God." The Mishnah's system, predicated on a people living in the land of Israel and maintaining a Temple cult, subsequently forms the basis for Jewish *halakhah*, which is not utopian at all, but a real way of life. The Mishnah (and its successors) expounds a system of law *subsequently* elaborated by exegesis, made more applicable to everyday life by exegesis and by individual rulings. By the time we come to the literature of *responsa*, we are dealing with practical applications, and we can in most cases deduce practice from them, even though the dynamics of Mishnaic theory continue to exercise a control.[2] But between the Mishnah and the regulations that later govern Jewish life, some considerable distance lies.

The Mishnah is, then, of itself no clear evidence of what was adopted as practice in the times before, or even when, it was formulated and then written. Actual practices have to be carefully sought out in each case, with the aid of archaeological or comparative data. The Mishnah draws on some actual historical practice, offers exegesis of previous literary legal materials (i.e., Scripture) and also introduces complete innovations; it does not reflect legal practice in its own time and place. Yet it *does* determine legal practice in later times and places. Here, therefore, we have a clear case where legal practice follows legal theory.

Does "biblical law" follow a different rule, or should we consider the likelihood that the Mishnah exemplifies a literary and even philo-

---

[2] Since I am focusing here on the Second Temple period, I am taking for granted, rather than arguing, a certain view of the origin and development of Jewish Rabbinic halakhah (i.e., halakhah in the strict sense!). That view has been developed carefully and extensively by Jacob Neusner, but since I take seriously Neusner's insistence that the Rabbinic system be regarded as post-Second Temple, I am not including Rabbinic law in this survey.

sophical tradition that can be traced back to the Second Temple period?

THE NATURE OF BIBLICAL LAWS

Let us apply this insight to an earlier situation, of which we know somewhat less. There are broadly three views that one might take regarding the relationship between the scriptural laws and the actual administration of justice in ancient Israel and Judah. One is to regard the biblical material as descriptive in intent and in effect. This was once a dominant *assumption* of biblical scholarship, so that "Israelite law" and "biblical law" were interchangeable terms, and prescription and practice held to be mutually entailing. If this attitude is probably now regarded by most scholars as naive and obsolete, the assumption is still all to easy to slide into, as a good deal of current scholarship amply demonstrates.

A second view recognizes that the biblical laws are in a form that has been shaped by a process of scribal editing and influenced by wider ideological interest, but that, nevertheless, individual laws by and large do reflect actual social practice. In other words, while the literary law compositions may not be entirely descriptive (or even prescriptive in the sense of being intended to apply directly) in *intent*, individual laws are in fact a reflection of social practices or norms, and thus to an extent the biblical laws may *in effect* be descriptive.

A third view considers that while the evidence of scribal composition, intellectual and theoretical motivation, and literary contextualizing is perfectly obvious in the biblical laws, the relationship between individual prescriptions and actual practice is probably both marginal and also often unprovable, and that these literary creations reflect essentially the reality of their scribal authors' thinking. It was accordingly no part of their program to "describe what was happening," only to theorize on what ought to happen, or ought to have happened, in an ideal world. On this view, law is a mode of social philosophy, or of theocratic theory.

The first view, as already said, is hardly defensible.[3] Still, it shares some elements with the second view, and it may be helpful to ex-

---

[3] But see A. Phillips, *Ancient Israel's Criminal Law* (Oxford, 1985), for the view that the *Book of the Covenant* [the *Mishpatim*] was or contained "ancient Israel's criminal law."

pand, however briefly, on the issues and evidence. Broadly speaking, the two main avenues of research into the "practicality" or "actuality" of biblical laws are (a) ancient law codes and legal documents, and (b) non-legal biblical material such as prophetic and narrative literature. The following comments cannot be adequate, let alone exhaustive, but are intended merely to indicate the shape of the debate.

Since we have very little extra-biblical material *directly* attesting to legal praxis in ancient Israel and Judah, a good deal of weight has come to be attached to ancient Mesopotamian law-codes and their parallels with biblical laws. Certainly there are occasional parallels, the extent of which will remain contested. Different evaluations are possible. On the one hand, scholars such as Paul and Westbrook[4] accept what Westbrook terms the "diffusionist" view of ancient Near Eastern law, whereby a common legislative culture or tradition, facilitated by a range of common economic features, permeated the Fertile Crescent during the second millennium. Such "diffusion" may have taken place through the medium of written sources, but also could have spread through migration and general social and political interaction in the form of basic concepts and practices. Although Westbrook acknowledges that the writing of laws always owes something to scribal discretion, selectivity and ideological bias, he believes (as I understand him) to accept that the range of biblical material relating to legal practice and theory attests a broad social-legal tradition stretching from the Tigris to the borders of Egypt (but not including Egypt, where quite different structures obtained).

However, the theory of such a pattern of praxis must be at the very least tempered by the recognition that the great Mesopotamian law codes are not *prescriptive* legal documents; that is to say, they are not intended to regulate legal praxis in any direct way. "Non-legislative" is Fishbane's neat description of them, and he refers to them as "prototypical collections of cases."[5] Jackson[6] goes a little further in characterizing such codes as "didactic, sapiential, monumental." Legal practice (as evidenced by the extant *mesharum* acts, temporary and

---

[4] S. Paul, *Studies in the Book of the Covenant in the Light of Cuneiform and Biblical Law* (Leiden, 1970), pp. 99-105; R. Westbrook, *Studies in Biblical and Cuneiform Law* (Paris, 1988), p. 12.

[5] M. Fishbane, *Biblical Interpretation in Ancient Israel* (Oxford, 1985), pp. 95-96.

[6] B. Jackson, "Ideas of Law and Legal Administration: A Semiotic Approach," in R.E. Clements, ed., *The World of Ancient Israel* (Cambridge, 1989), p. 186.

specific acts, usually of debt-relief, and corpora of court decisions) was to a great degree unaffected by them.[7] This conclusion is accepted even by some who accept the "diffusionist" view.[8] Put rather simply, *if* there is a "diffusion," is it a broad diffusion of *praxis* or a rather narrower diffusion of a *literary tradition* whereby the scribes of Jerusalem (or wherever) drew upon earlier literary sources in composing their own codes? Indeed, is it necessary to posit a borrowing from early sources (and thus at an early period)? It should be remembered that while the Code of Hammurabi is *in origin* an ancient source, it was still being copied well into the first millennium and can therefore be regarded as a contemporary source even for Second Temple literature (as is true, of course, for much Sumerian and Accadian literature and for Canaanite mythological literature). Literary worlds partake of the synchronic as much as the diachronic.

For Carmichael, the evidence of the Roman legal system is also pertinent. His view that the construction of laws is "an intellectual exercise"[9] appeals, as well as to Mesopotamian law codes, also to the work of the Roman jurists in the late Republic period.[10] But although these jurists did not enact laws, nor participate in court hearings, they did advise on the *interpretations* of law and issued *responsa* on individual matters. They did, therefore, occasionally act within the judicial process. Nevertheless, it is important to note the existence in Rome of a tradition of legal exegesis that operates in formal independence of a tradition of legal judgments. That is to say, on the one hand, we have a body of *theory* being developed, and, on the other, a continuing *practice*, each overlapping, but each practiced by different persons and institutions. Theory, the example of Rome as much as of ancient Babylon shows, is not necessarily or even typically the business of the practitioner, and vice-versa. Such parallels do not, of course, prove anything about the relationship of ancient scriptural laws to judicial practice, but they do pre-empt the assumption that such a connection is to be automatically assumed and demonstrate that, on the contrary, it needs to be argued for.

---

[7] See especially F.R. Krauss, "Ein zentrales Problem des altmesopotamischen Rechts: Was ist der Codex Hammurabi," in *Genava* 8:1960, pp. 283-296.

[8] E.g. Paul, op. cit., pp. 23-25.

[9] C. Carmichael, *The Origins of Biblical Law. The Decalogues and the Book of the Covenant* (Ithaca, 1992), pp. 15-21.

[10] H.F. Jolowitz and B. Nicholas, *Historical Introduction to the Study of Roman Law* (Cambridge, 1972), pp. 91-96; A. Watson, *Law Making in the Later Roman Republic* (Oxford, 1974), pp. 101-110.

Are there grounds for taking the case of ancient Judah as an exception? The exegetical activity in which the Roman jurists engaged brings one to the work of Fishbane, who is quite aware that the biblical legal literature is a product of scribal drafting and interpretation, and indeed emphasizes the exegetical nature of much of it. Nevertheless, he insists that the biblical codes are presented as divine revelations intended to regulate life and notes that Lev. 10:10 (cf., Mal. 2:7) enjoins priests to teach laws, with judges enjoined to follow them (Deut. 16:18-20; 2 Chron. 19:6-10). He thus implies that they have a closer relationship to the practice of justice than the ancient Near Eastern codes: "the *internal traditions of the Hebrew Bible present and regard the covenantal laws as legislative texts*" (his italics). However, it needs to be asked whether this particular device is of a character totally different from, on the one hand, the depiction at the head of the law code of Hammurabi receiving laws from Shamash, or, on the other, the Rabbinic theory that their exegetical work represented oral revelation to Moses on Sinai. On this issue, Jackson has made an especially important and interesting set of observations. Focusing on the semiotics—communicative functions—of law codes, he asks: who are the recipients of these codes' "message"? Apparently not judges. The Mesopotamian law codes contain no instructions that they should be enforced or enacted, nor have there been found separate texts that contain, or allude to, such instructions. The same is true of the biblical laws. They are not directly addressed to judges or elders. Jackson's point is that until a certain stage of social development, law is exercised by means of custom and tradition, not by written documents. In support of his position he cites (p. 188) Deut. 16:18 (cf., 1:16) and 2 Chron. 19:15-7, where commands to judges are general and do not include reference to any written text as a basis for judgment.

A further parallel between Mesopotamian and biblical law codes is that both offer only a selection of legal cases. But they do not, as Fishbane seems to imply, constitute "typical" cases, as one might expect if they are intended to be used for guidance, but unusual and infrequent cases; and they do not cover the entire range of legal matters. They appear, on the contrary, to be almost *ad hoc*. This common feature of the Mesopotamian and Jewish scriptural codes renders unlikely the explanation that the scriptural codes are the product of an editorial selection from a more comprehensive corpus. Not that this explanation serves very well, for the principles on which such a selection might have been undertaken are by no means transparent.

It needs to be asked, then, whether the contents of Exod. 20-24, or Deuteronomy, or Leviticus ever related to legal or judicial practice in the territories of Israel and Judah before the invention of halakhah. Jackson[11] comments that "archaeology has not served well the study of legal institutions of biblical society. We lack 'court' records—using that term in both its legal and politico-administrative sense." He then goes on to make a further point: "what we possess is a rich literature, into which it is *possible*—to put the matter at its highest—that some original sources from the real and administrative milieu may have been incorporated. Certainly we cannot assume without careful argument that the biblical codes come from any such milieu."[12] Whether and how we should argue from silence is, of course, a prime methodological issue. Should the absence of documentation about actual cases support the argument that the biblical literature is not about praxis but theory? Or should such absence permit us to assume that the fuller documentation once existed and that it would have shown the biblical laws to be actually observed? Clearly, *both* positions are inadequate as a basis for argument. But Jackson is not basing his case entirely on silence, as we shall see presently. In any case, the evidence from Babylonian and Assyria does not support the notion that the scriptural law codes lead us directly to judicial administration, to the legal practice of Israel and Judah.

Attempts to infer a social world from biblical laws (and thus to anchor them in historical reality) are not successful, either, for all that can be achieved is a description of the social world (or the ideological world) of the framers of the original documents. An example of the extent and limits of such an approach is Marshall's analysis of the Book of the Covenant.[13] His method is to sketch out the social structures that would have characterized Israelite society before and during the monarchic period, and, building on the theories of K.S. Newman[14] concerning the relationship between law and economics, to assess the likely social setting of the law codes from the implications they offer about the economic basis of society. Marshall's opening discussion of theory is informed and lucid and his working assumptions reasonable (if not always correct): he accepts that laws develop

---

[11] Op. cit., p. 185.

[12] Ibid.

[13] J. Marshall, *Israel and the Book of the Covenant. An Anthropological Approach to Biblical Law* (Atlanta, 1993).

[14] *Law and Economic Organization* (Cambridge, 1983).

over time, that they are multilevelled (i.e., they are mediated by families, elders, and chiefs), and that "law" does not simply equal "custom" but includes scope for rational and improvisatory functions. But he then seeks to extrapolate social structures from the contents of the Book of the Covenant, looking at climate, geology, flora, and fauna to determine the material context of prestate "Israel" and, on this basis, extrapolating the likely legal issues in such society/societies. The next step is to inspect the legal issues dealt with in the Book of the Covenant, and his analysis shows him that Exod. 20:24–22:16 reflects a (dimorphic) pastoral/agrarian society, with free, non-slave, and debt-slave classes. In Exod. 22:17–23:19, however, private ownership and accumulation of wealth appear, implying landowners, landless people, and indentured slaves, plus slightly more developed cultic operations. Marshall's conclusion is that the two law codes, or the two parts of the law code, he discerns in the Book of the Covenant "could have been operative in pre-monarchical Israel" (p. 181).

But there are fatal difficulties of method and preconception here. For his history of the premonarchic period, Marshall relies on archaeology and survey work (especially Finkelstein),[15] while, for the monarchic period, he depends on the Bible. Consistency would require the same data source for both. Reasons could be offered for this choice, but they are not forthcoming: they imply, however, some value-judgments about the nature of each kind of evidence. Then, why does Marshall stop with the monarchic period? He makes no attempt to include social structures in the Persian or Ptolemaic period, for instance, presumably on the grounds that these lie outside the limits of the dates he is prepared to accept. Finally, Marshall also believes that by allowing for the existence of different "legal levels" one can dispense with the need to posit a complex literary history and thus may posit a single "BC [Book of the Covenant] society."

The existence of different "levels" within the "Book of the Covenant," however, is capable of another explanation, which is not considered. That there existed a purposeful relationship between the literature and its application in praxis is taken for granted and a dating assigned accordingly. The possibility that a literary collection of idealized laws might contain reflections of several different social patterns has accordingly not been addressed. Finally, and most important, his thesis does not explain why we have a Book of the

---

[15] I. Finkelstein, *The Archaeology of the Israelite Settlement* (Jerusalem, 1988).

Covenant in the form that it has attained and in the literary setting that it now inhabits. The assumptions that these are socially practicable laws, emanating from a real society that is either pre-monarchic or post-monarchic, so limits the range of his inquiry that it cannot be said to have proved anything much beyond its own premises.

In theory, it remains a valid proposition that the assumptions of even theoretical and idealizing lawmakers (to state the issue as strongly as possible) might be influenced by their authors' own concrete social contexts. The problems is to discern where these contexts are distinctive enough. The importance of elders, the lack of a monarch, the existence of slaves: all these conditions hold for centuries of history. On the other hand, one of the features of utopian legislation is that its vision, its society does *not* exactly mirror the present!

How, then, do we decide whether biblical laws as a whole correspond to a historical pattern of judicial practice?

THE FUNCTION OF BIBLICAL LAW

Quite apart from the hints we receive from the Mishnah, we can start from the recognition that we are confronted with a literary Torah, not an inscription and not a legal document in the strict sense (such as a decree, judgment, or deed). Both the overall literary character and the content of some individual laws permit the hypothesis that we are dealing with literary compositions characterized by clear ideological systems.

Jackson has highlighted the literary features of biblical law codes, proposing a number of cases in which the Book of the Covenant exhibits "chiasmus, thematic reiteration through a sequence of interlocking double-series, and various allusions to the immediate narrative context."[16] Similar observations have emerged from the study by J.M. Sprinkle, who argues that the Book of the Covenant is an "artfully crafted unity, being well-integrated internally and in relation to the Pentateuch of which it is a part."[17] It is not necessary to endorse Sprinkle's conclusion entirely: the arguments he deploys can be

---

[16] Op. cit, p. 198; see his "Biblical Laws of Slavery: A Comparative Approach," in L. Archer, ed., *Slavery and Other Forms of Unfree Labour* (London, 1988), pp. 86-101, for the actual examples.

[17] J.M. Sprinkle, *"The Book of the Covenant:" A Literary Approach* (Sheffield, 1994), p. 206.

added to a number already advanced that raise questions about the existence of an original and retrievable "Book of the Covenant" with a social setting prior to its present literary location in the Torah narrative. The most striking of these observations notes the opening section on slavery, including the law on a runaway slave. It needs no sophisticated literary critic to link this motif to the Exodus narrative, and indeed this link has been noticed often enough. Whether or not one endorses Carmichael's thesis that the biblical laws are responses to problematic narratives in the Torah, the opening of the Book of the Covenant seems to have been composed or editorially placed as a commentary on the Exodus.

This observation does not of itself suggest that the actual laws did not originally comprise a collection reflecting a real society. To counter that possibility we need to look at the *substance* and the ideology of the collections. We can point to abundant evidence that the laws of Deuteronomy and of Lev. 17–26 (or however else it is demarcated) are generated *as a whole* by a theory and not by practice. Thus, while it is entirely possible (and even probable) that *some* of the individual laws reflect practice, a number are entirely impractical. These may be explained as arising from a need to express the logic of a social theory (such as the extermination of Canaanites, since Deuteronomy's utopia has no Canaanites) but may be intended to teach a moral (thus, we might say, are haggadic rather than halakhic in character). Laws of both kinds are easy to find in the Mishnah. An obvious biblical example is the single law about divorce, in Deut. 24.1; this provides for the entirely unlikely case that a husband divorces his wife, she marries another and is divorced by him, then the first husband wishes to remarry her. Why should this one law be included, with nothing else on the whole subject of divorce? It seems plausible that the metaphor of Yahweh and Israel as husband and wife has inspired not only its conclusion but its composition. A nation that has deserted (or been deserted by) its marital deity, follows another spouse-god and then wishes to abandon that god and return to its original spouse-deity cannot do so: the deity will not (*may* not!) receive the wife-nation back. It is not impossible that the same kind of explanation can be given of the absurd law of the rebellious son (Deut. 21:18-21). Could parents of a rebellious son bring him to the elders and would the villagers stone him? (One can easily imagine what a *Monty Python* cast might make of such an incident!) And what of the law (Deut 23:15) that if a slave runs away from his master, he should not be given back? Never mind that Saul/Paul of Tarsus disregards this law in his letter to Philemon about the latter's escaped slave—after all, this writer apparently did not think much of "the Law" (or that is how it appears and how he is often interpreted). But the Deuteronomic law is nothing other than a slave's license to run away! Yet how, in the mind of the framer of this law, could a nation of escaped Egyptian slaves hand back those fortunate enough to do the same? Each of these laws *might* reasonably be considered the product of reflection on wider issues, the disobedience of the nation to its father-god or husband-god or its right to be punished, for instance. Or, conversely, of its right not to go back to Egypt for enslavement. Even the release of all Hebrew slaves after seven years might be a reflection on the interpretation of the exile we find in other biblical texts (Jeremiah: seventy years, Daniel: seventy weeks of years).

Even if this suggested line of interpretation does not offer the only possible explanation, it cannot be denied that the legal stipulations it addresses are impractical and need to be explained as the result of some kind of theorizing or deduction. But if we then assign this kind of motivation to a real historical society, we imagine effectively a utopia. That, unfortunately, has been the virtual effect of much biblical scholarship, for which ancient Israel (or at least its corporate ideals) is indeed the achievement of the divine will on earth. But this is not history, or scholarship, any more than the reconstruction from Mishnah-tractate Sanhedrin of a system of Rabbinic law courts in the Greco-Roman period bereft of rulers or high priests and composed of exactly seventy-one or twenty-three judges, or of the manner of execution by burning, or many of the other details generated by Rabbinic logic and expressed in a narrative in the past tense. It is perhaps already at this stage proper to propose that law collections were the distinctive Jewish genre in which social and political philosophy was expressed.

For many scriptural laws can be explained as a logical outcome of discernible basic premises. Thus, the Deuteronomic laws about holy war are derivable from theories about authorized ownership of land (Yahweh owns it and gives it as a dowry or a bequest to Israel) and conditions of the "covenant" that the writers use as a model for their social philosophy. For Deuteronomy is based on a legal theory that between the deity and the society is a contract, the terms of which include land-possession. That basic theory determines how one treats non-Israelites, justifies the extermination of idolatrous temptations, defines and protects the *ethnos*, and so on. Likewise, Leviticus exhibits a clear ideology of purity based on proximity to the presence of the deity, the world within and without the "camp," and a universe and lifestyle divided into degrees and states of cleanliness. The fact that one cannot identify a Canaanite in one's own society, that one's eye cannot always detect "holiness" (or that one lacks the memory always to recall what state of it one is in) makes "holiness" unenforceable except in some evident cases, and what is the good of that? But of course universal holiness follows very logically from the premise that holy God is encamped in the middle of his people. Legal *praxis* is not the aim of this sort of writing, and thus none of the laws that emanates logically from the theory is self-evidently intended to be enforced by a judicial system. There *are* of course cases in which such laws might shadow practice, or vice-versa; one interesting case is the fallowing of land every seventh year. This may be good agricultural sense, and even followed. But if so, the practice was not necessarily followed *because of a law such as that in Leviticus*. Perhaps the practice, if it were such, inspired the writer of Leviticus, for whom it becomes part of a sabbatical system including the jubilee, and the writer of Deuteronomy, for whom it functions according to a different ideological scheme. But we could not argue *on the basis of either legal system* for a fallow year, or jubilee year, despite the fact that a seven-year agricultural cycle may have been in effect. Equally we cannot argue that adulterers, any more than rebellious sons or runaway slaves were handled according to the theories of the biblical law codes, for whom runaway slaves (Israel) were due for leniency while disobedient children and adulterers (Israel again, according to the writers of the prophetic books) suffered death.

The foregoing discussion is intended to demonstrate the fundamental problem confronting a social-scientific account of law and its institutions in the Second Temple period (as in any other period of Palestinian history). It seems that the investigator must accept (1) that the institutions connected with the *administration* of law and those connected with the generation of the *legal literature* in the Bible are quite distinct and (2) that the social worlds implied by at least Deuteronomy and Leviticus are products of their author's ideologies and related only indirectly, incidentally, and partially to any actual praxis. Indeed, in the area of law, the need for a clear separation of biblical theology and Israelite/Judean history is most vividly illustrated.

WRITTEN LAW GENERATING PRAXIS

During the late Second Temple period, as has been briefly hinted earlier, literary laws *began* to provide the basis for study, and then praxis, within certain Judean societies, sects, and individuals. It was noted earlier that even in the Mishnah we do not have a consistent record of contemporary (or prior) Jewish legal praxis. The process by which scriptural laws became the basis of actual behavior was a long one, extending beyond the Second Temple period and indeed beyond the Mishnah. But the process began to take place much earlier, though only partial or occasionally. In the Gospels (Mark 12:18 and parallels), we have a case in which a legal opinion is sought: the levirate marriage of a woman to seven brothers in turn (a similar dilemma is found in Tobit). Do we infer from these narratives that such laws were enacted? The world of Tobit is clearly a make-believe one, so that here too we cannot be sure whether real or make-believe laws are supposed to apply. In the case of the Gospels, are we dealing with a writer ignorant of Jewish law and wrongly assuming that what is in Scripture is actually done? The New Testament story looks rather like precisely the sort of case that legal theorists might pose for the sake of a debate. Indeed, it is self-evidently theoretical, since it relates to the world to come. Perhaps there is an historical encounter between different schools of thought on a legal opinion, unrelated to realia; such debates are the stuff of Rabbinic halakhic discussion, dealing with extraordinary cases and resulting in a statement of principle (as here). The same is perhaps true of the episode (John 8:1-11) of the adulterous woman, where Jesus is asked to give an opinion on the scriptural ruling that she should be stoned.

It is unwise to conclude that adulterous women were automatically stoned or married their brothers-in-law when occasion required. There is evidence of the institution of a sabbatical year, including debt remission, though we know little of the details. In the case of tithing, or levitical purity, however, we find such laws being adopted by sectarian groups, and, in cases where they applied only to the priesthood, extended beyond the circle of priests. We find, even in the scriptures, the ideal of the righteous man as one who studies "the law" (Ps. 1). That ethic corresponds to the view of the early second century scribe ben Sira (38:34), who also includes wisdom sayings and prophecies as among the studies of the scribe. Ben Sira's comments, taken with Ps. 1, suggest that the Jewish scribe studied the laws for the purpose of obeying them (just as Hos. 14:9 implies that prophecy was recommended to the wise for their consideration). We can therefore show evidence that during the Second Temple period written texts in Hebrew became the basis for the (self-?) education of the Jerusalem elite. And in the Qumran scrolls, such as the *Temple Scroll*, 4QMMT, and the Damascus Document, we have evidence that the written laws were the basis for respectively harmonizing and supplementing, serious disagreement, and regulation of a sectarian lifestyle.[18] It is commonly assumed that we are here dealing with the interpretation of a "Jewish law" that already had some authoritative force but whose implications were still being worked out. This rather oversimplifies the picture. But the Qumran scrolls (and other near-contemporary Judean literature) attest the notion of a "law of Moses" as something that at least some groups regarded as self-evidently authoritative for the way of life of "Israel."

Now, if, as I have suggested, the law codes in Exodus, Deuteronomy, and Leviticus were not originally descriptive of "Israelite law" nor intended to operate as such, how and why, having been edited into a Mosaic Torah, did they come to serve as the inspiration for an educated and pious Jewish lifestyle? When did "Judaism" come to be defined (if only by certain groups at first) as a way of life, obedient to written laws? In this question lies an essential component of the problem of the origins of "Judaism" as an idea, though an idea that found concrete expression in several "Judaisms." Before addressing that gap between the authoring and editing of scriptural law codes and the invention of "Judaism" as a lifestyle based on Torah, it is first necessary to define that gap chronologically. Here some long-established conclusions will be challenged.

The Origins of the "Law Book" Topos

Very little study of the relationship between the literary laws in the Hebrew Bible and ancient social praxis deals with the Second Temple Period. There are several reasons: the classic literary-historical analysis placed both the book of the Covenant and Deuteronomy in the monarchic period (even though the Holiness Code was regarded as post-exilic, a view currently under attack). Moreover, the prevail-

---

[18] On the latter, see P.R. Davies, *Sects and Scrolls. Essays on Qumran and Related Topics* (Atlanta, 1996), pp. 113-126; 163-177.

ing view is that Ezra returned from Babylon and read out a law book, so that the Second Temple period is held to have witnessed only exegetical development and practical application of a body of legislation that already existed.

The current climate of scholarly opinion is rather more favorable to a later dating of biblical literature, although because late dating seems to imply a lower estimate of the historical reliability of the biblical literature, there is a reluctance that goes beyond mere conservatism. But there are sober and persuasive reasons for dating the production of Deuteronomy to the Second Temple period. On the Holiness Code, I do not intend to argue: it clearly refers to an exile and return. (On the "Book of the Covenant," I do not see any clear evidence to indicate a date and confine myself to the occasional observation.) Accordingly, we ought not to entertain the traditional portrait of Jews living in Babylonian exile according to a Mosaic law nor returning bearing Mosaic scrolls and founding a Torah-centered nation in the province of Judah.

Ancient Near Eastern law codes are royal genres, and Deuteronomy is conspicuously not only *not* a royal genre but allows only a minor place for the monarch. While it acknowledges, very faintly, the existence of a king, it has him not writing or making laws but copying a law book in the presence of levitical priests who have presumably given it to him (18:18-20). This is fantasy (constitutional monarchy arrives only centuries later), and while we might speculate whether such a document might have originated in a monarchic system as an anti-monarchic protest, we need not assume that the document was circulated widely, let alone published, under a monarch. It is safer to regard such sentiments as post-monarchic, in an environment in which the fiction of a monarch is lightly maintained. Deuteronomy's formulation of the origin of kingship in 17:14 ("When you have come unto the land which Yahweh your god is giving you, and possess it, and occupy it, and say, 'I will set a king over me, like all the nations that are around me'") is distinctly negative in suggesting that the monarchy is not divinely-ordained and is merely an imitation of the hated neighbors; and the same negative tone is conveyed by 28:36 (if that is to be assigned to the same original composition): "Yahweh will bring you, and your king whom you will set over you, to a nation which neither you nor your ancestors have known; and there you will serve other gods, wood and stone." If chapter 28 *is* an intrinsic part of the Deuteronomic code, of course, its post-monarchic date is unquestionable.

But of course, Deuteronomy is not really a law code in any formal sense. Its presentation as a Mosaic speech (chaps. 1-11) may be secondary, and we shall be safer concentrating on chaps. 12-26 (or 12-28). But even so, it is a paraenetic piece of writing, addressed ostensibly to the people (alternately and puzzlingly singular and plural) who are construed as having a society sustained by a "covenant" between the client people and the patron deity. The ideology assumes a society/nation living amid other nations ("Canaanites") whom the deity has dispossessed and who are therefore to be annihilated before they bring disaster. Since this recommendation makes little sense in a monarchic state in which all those living in the king's territory are equally his subjects, the categories "Israelite" and "Canaanite" are transparently ideological chess pieces, with the Canaanites representing any who, while being in the land, do not conform to the norms and regulations of the ideal Israel and its god. They are, indeed, the "people of the land," and the kind of society envisioned by the writer(s) of Deuteronomy is *one in which religious and social identity can be equated.* The command to have only one sanctuary, to which all members of the society are expected to travel for major festivals also seems to assume a territorially small state; a population such as is nowadays suggested for Persian Yehud (11,000-17,000)[19] makes this provision plausible. Whether Deuteronomy reflected or anticipated the construction of a Persian period Temple in Jerusalem (or even Samaria) is impossible to say.

In view of the style and content and of the implied social and political context, I have very little argument with Weinfeld's[20] account of Deuteronomy's authors: they are a lay scribal elite. I question only his dating to the time of the monarchy, which has no basis other than sentiment for the historicity of 2 Kgs. 22. It is true that there are some clear parallels in the language and ideology of Deuteronomy to not only Assyrian covenant treaties, but also their ideology of warfare; but these parallels provide no more than a *terminus a quo.*

Deuteronomy, then, is a text, in which an ideal "covenant" society is created and defined, over against "Canaanites," by means of paraenesis and individual laws, and, importantly, is set in the past. It deals ostensibly with a constitution of a defunct society, a pre-exilic

---

[19] C. Carter, "The Province of Yehud in the Post-Exilic Period," in T.C. Eskenazi and K.H. Richards, eds., *Second Temple Studies 2. Temple and Community in the Persian Period* (Sheffield, 1994), p. 108.

[20] M. Weinfeld, *Deuteronomy and the Deuteronomic School* (Oxford, 1972)

monarchic "Israel" comprised of a union of Jerusalem and Samaria. In a strikingly similar way, the Mishnah ostensibly deals with a pre-destruction society, with a standing temple and cult, and "Israel" living in the land given to it by its god. But just as the Mishnah represents an intellectual effort to reconstitute Israel, so does Deuteronomy, and this effort marks the beginning of Judaism's tradition of political philosophy. Here is the first Jewish (or "proto-Jewish") treatise on the nature of "Israel" as a social and religious entity. It is hardly the work of a group of deported aristocrats in Babylonia, but rather of the intellectuals of an imperial province aware of the need to create and define a coherent society from among the immigrant and indigenous families and cultures that occupied Judah (and Samaria?).

There are also clues that the author of Deuteronomy regarded priestly authority as legally paramount. One has already been mentioned: the king writes out his copy of the law before the Levites. Another is Deut. 17:8-9: "If a matter arises which is too difficult for you to settle in judgment, between the conflicting families and claims, between injuries on both sides, matters of dispute within your own jurisdiction, then you will leave and come to the place which Yahweh your god will choose, and consult the levitical priests, and the judge that will exist in those days, and seek guidance; and they will give you the decision." So the highest court of appeal is the national judge (who I suspect is a fictitious figure) and the levitical priests (who are not). Note, too that even the book of Deuteronomy does not suggest that these authorities consult a law book (v. 11). What we do find, in Deut. 31:10, is an account of Moses' writing this law and having the Levites deposit it in the ark and then in the Temple. Now, we have seen that 17:8-9 proposed Levites in the one sanctuary as the ultimate legal recourse. However, there was no mention there of a book to be consulted. But now we have an important development of that notion: the authority of these Levites rests on their ability to consult the book, housed in the ark. This law, moreover, is to be read out publicly every seven years. (A similar ritual is also present in Exod. 24:3-9: Moses reads out the laws to the people.) Finally, it is a priest who admonishes the warriors in a time of war, not either king or prophet (20:2). Note that, in keeping with his overall philosophy, the author allows anyone fainthearted to depart before battle begins. Numbers do not matter when Yahweh is fighting; only in the real world does greater manpower tend to win battles. And if one's society is anyway garrisoned not by a royal corps or a militia, but by imperial troops....

Deuteronomy is an example of utopian writing, driven by a clear and simple religio-legal theory, the "covenant," which expresses the kernel of its philosophy. That philosophy we will find to be characteristic of Judean literature from the Persian period onwards, which consistently expresses the notion of a society governed by a single high god who has chosen one nation alone. As for the milieu, Deuteronomy comes from within the apparatus of a ruling elite, almost certainly its scribal officials, whom we might now recognize as the intelligentsia: it expresses several priestly interests, though unlike Leviticus has no clearly priestly ideology. It may well be, as Weinfeld suggests, the invention of a single scribe steeped in ancient Near Eastern legal and wisdom literature. But whatever the identity of the authors, their own society presupposes a single *religious* center, although the administration of justice is carried out locally, by judges and elders; religion and social identity are synonymous.

The idea of a book of written laws, to be read to the people, emerges in the narratives surrounding both Deuteronomy and the "Book of the Covenant." I suggest, following the argument I have just made about Deut. 17:8-9, that this represents a discrete development in the literary history of these two documents. As Jackson insists, these laws are still not represented as having been copied and sent to all the judges and elders in the land. Law is still implied as being enacted according to custom and local tradition, despite the fact that both the Book of the Covenant and Deuteronomy appear to contain quite specific stipulations. But they become at some point embedded in a Mosaic tradition. This embedding presupposes that Moses functions already as the founder of the nation and of its constitution and laws (a clearly Greek notion reflected in Jewish and non-Jewish Greek writers), and thus they become ancient legal texts, constitutional texts, and so inevitably acquire a history of having been read out before.

If, as I am arguing, Deuteronomy is a Second Temple period composition, the legend of the "discovery" of an ancient law book is a subsequent part of the history of the evolution of the literature of post-exilic Judah. We can trace its development in the account of Josiah's finding of the law book in 2 Kgs. 22, where again the contents are read out. I have given reasons elsewhere[21] why I do not believe this story to be historical. Apart from its improbability in the

---

[21] P.R. Davies, *In Search of Ancient Israel* (Sheffield, 1992), pp. 40-41.

monarchical period, it fits too well the process by which Deuteronomy and the Book of the Covenant have been transformed into
ancient Mosaic writings. The added value of the Josiah story is that
the authority as well as antiquity of such a book is reinforced by
association with a pious king. The choice of Josiah, moreover, is
extremely logical. Either history or Judean tradition or both have
him die young, thus explaining why his "reform" did not succeed and
consequently did not avert the Babylonian deportation. His reign
thus lies sufficiently far from the final years preceding that event that
no hint of blame for it attaches to him. His attempted reform, followed by the disasters that his successors invited, teach the classic
lesson that only adherence to this written body of laws will guarantee
security for Israel in the land promised to them. Here we might
recognize a further stage: adherence to the Mosaic laws as the only
guarantee of *national security* (but not yet individual piety).

It remains only to add that the Chronicler also contributed to this
topos. Not content with only a single king utilizing the old law book,
he has the "law of Moses" invoked during the reign of Jehoiada (2
Chron. 23:18), while in the reign of Amaziah (25:4) he refers to "the
book of Moses, where Yahweh commanded...," while Hezekiah acts
according to "Moses the holy man" (30:16). Even Manasseh (33:8)
invokes "the whole law and the statutes and the ordinances by the
agency of Moses." Thus, in the Chronicler's version of events, Josiah,
enforcing the "book of the law of Yahweh given by Moses" merely
repeats the acts of his pious predecessors. From this presentation
emerges the portrait of the ideal king as a follower, or even an en-
forcer, of a national law perhaps already seen, as other writers of the
Hellenistic period present it, as the national constitution of the ancient Jewish race, written down by their founder, the great philoso-
pher-king-prophet-lawgiver. And what neater way to underpin the
continuity of this process from monarchic to post-monarchic times
than to have Jehoshaphat appointing Levites and priests as adminis-
ters of the law of the land (2 Chron. 19:4-7)? Here, of course, Chronicles is only making more explicit what the laws of Deuteronomy
implied: ultimate authority to the priests. But, according to the
Chronicler, this authority is no occasional matter, but an ongoing
responsibility. The Levites are indeed the guardians of the law as well
as of the Temple (and of course its hymn books).

And so the fiction of a society long governed by a law book is
created, and, with it, the authority of that book, once associated with

the support of kings, is vested in the priests, who are presumably the ruling caste of any ideal Israel. What procedures operated for the *actual* administration of justice we do not know, other than assume that they continued as they ever were. Indeed, the claim that a divine law book exists does not automatically lead to the imposition of its contents. Catalysts such as a religiously zealous ruler, the eruption of religious sectarianism, cultural invasion, or perhaps a certain kind of scholarly tradition are to be expected.

The next stage in the movement towards the praxis of scriptural law is perhaps represented by the stories of Ezra and Nehemiah. The historicity of Ezra remains stoutly defended, though it is rather more readily questioned than was once the case. I have argued elsewhere[22] that the Ezra story is a fictitious narrative from several centuries after the events it claims to narrate, and I will not rehearse the arguments here, except to reiterate that Ezra is unheard of by any extant writer until the first century of our era.[23] In the narrative of Ezra, we find a priestly-scribal figure who is placed at the origins of Second Temple Yehud society and who returned from Babylon with a law book. Indeed, even before he appears in Ezra 7, the law book is present in Yehud (it is surprising how many textbooks wrongly claim that he returned *with it*):[24] "Then Jeshua ben Jozadak stood up, and his fellow-priests, and Zerubbabel ben Shealtiel, and his colleagues, and they built the altar of the god of Israel, in order to offer burnt offerings upon it, as written in the law of Moses the holy man" (3:2). Ezra makes his appearance (7:6, 12) as "a scribe fluent in the law of Moses (later of the "law of heaven"), which Yahweh, the god of Israel, had

---

[22] P.R. Davies, "Scenes from Early Judaism," in D.V. Edelman, ed., *The Triumph of Elohim. From Yahwisms to Judaisms* (Kampen, 1995), pp. 145-184, and "Ezra and Nehemiah Revisited," unpublished paper read at the SBL International Meeting, Budapest, 1995.

[23] Note that 4QEzra is not certainly a manuscript of the book of Ezra and does not contain any passage in which Ezra is alluded to. As things stand, the earliest *datable* testimony to Ezra follows the destruction of the Second Temple (4 Ezra and Josephus). This, of course, provides only a *terminus ad quem* for the invention of this character.

[24] The first mention of this law book in Ezra is at Ezra 6:18: "And they set the priests in their divisions, and the Levites in their courses, for the divine service, which is in Jerusalem; as it is written in the book of Moses." Then Neh. 8:1: "And all the people gathered together as one in the street that ran in front of the water gate; and asked Ezra the scribe to bring the book of the law of Moses, which Yahweh had commanded to Israel." Nowhere is it said that Ezra brought the law book from Babylon. Certainly, he was fluent in the "law of Moses" (7:6), but the text gives no hint that this law book was not well known in *both* Palestine *and* Babylonia.

given: and the king granted him all he requested, under the influence of Yahweh his god upon him."

In 10:3, Ezra is addressed by Shecaniah with an appeal to put away foreign wives and children, ending: "let it be done according to the law;" in Neh. 8, the people ask Ezra to bring out and read the law, and as (or after) he does so, the Levites "give the meaning." In Neh. 10, the people take an oath to obey this (written) law. Thus, the relationship between the divine law and the people is now direct, and we find the process of interpretation, which characterizes the scribal tradition of revising and editing and commenting on texts, activity so lucidly exposed by Fishbane, now being applied not to the rewriting of texts but directly to instruction of people. The people are addressed, not just by the law, but by the interpretation; they oblige themselves to keep it, just as Ezra himself had (7:6): "For Ezra had set his heart upon studying the law of Yahweh, and to observe it, and to teach the statutes and ordinances...." Whether or not such a ceremony, or anything like it, ever took place, the scene depicted conveys the belief that the law is to be obeyed by every Judean, who will learn of it directly, and understand it by means of learned exegesis, from the priestly classes. At what point in the Second Temple period do we meet this attitude towards the written law? And from what circles does it emanate? We are certainly not at all distant from the attitude to the Mosaic law expressed in the Damascus Document; and since Nehemiah appears to reflect anti-Samaritan hostility, we may not be much distant in time (the Samaritan temple was destroyed towards the end of the second century B.C.E.; the schism cannot predate the formation of the Pentateuch in more or less its final form, since the Samaritans shared it with Judeans).

CULTIC AND NON-CULTIC LAWS

One characteristic of biblical law also helps to clarify the social context in which it originated and developed. All the biblical law codes combine cultic and non-cultic laws, in varying ratios. It is also clear from subsequent interpreters and students of these laws (the authors of Ezra and Nehemiah, ben Sira, the Pharisees, and "Damascus Covenanters") that no distinction is made between the areas of cult and those outside What happens in the Temple, what the priests do, how the people observe their festivals vitally affects the fabric of the

whole society. This characteristic may reflect the bringing together of
political and cultic authority into a single office, that of high priest,
though the Nehemiah narrative seems either to preserve the memory
of non-priestly authority over Sabbath activities (Neh. 13:15-19) or to
argue for a division of powers between priests and non-priests. Indeed, both Deuteronomy and the Holiness Code develop an ideology
that integrates the sanctuary and its holiness into the political and
social character of the nation. This is a characteristic of priestly legal
theorizing, in which all of human private and social activity is understood in relation to cultic activity, to an overriding divine presence,
whether legal (Deuteronomy) or "holy" (Leviticus). Thus priests (on
their own assessment) sustain the nation by their service.

A society in which temple and economy were in actual fact inextri-
cably bound together, such that priests actually exercised decisive
local political power, is not necessarily implied by these characteristics, though such a context will explain how priestly legal theorizing
came to be preserved and regarded as scriptural. Numerous social
structures exhibiting close connections of temple and society are
known to us throughout the ancient Near East and further afield.[25]
But a good deal of evidence points towards a much greater importance and power for the Jerusalem sanctuary in the Second Temple
period than in the First, when it functioned mainly as a part of the
royal establishment, its religious activities dependent upon the
wishes, and the deity, of the incumbent monarch, and its revenue,
such as it was, subject to royal consent and oversight. The Persians
do not seem to have exercised close oversight of cultic matters; but,
as an imperial collector of taxes, they regarded the Temple as the
focus of economic activity and of tax collecting.

How far, then, do the laws of Deuteronomy and Leviticus reflect
Second Temple praxis? Could they not *derive* from the actual laws of
a Temple society? Weinberg's view[26] is that an initially rather small
society centered on the Temple and enjoying imperial patronage
gradually extended and imposed itself throughout Yehud and beyond. The power of the Jerusalem Temple did no doubt wax considerably, but there are hardly grounds for assuming that the biblical
laws applied once to a *Bürger-Tempel-Gemeinde* and then were imposed

[25] J. Blenkinsopp, "Temple and Society in Achaemenid Judah," in *Second Temple Studies* (1991), pp. 22-53.

[26] J. Weinberg, *The Citizen-Temple Community* (Sheffield, 1993); cf., Blenkinsopp, op. cit.

on the surrounding territory as part of a process whereby the authority, and economic benefit, of the Jerusalem elite was enhanced. Against this suggestion stands the fact that these laws embrace a whole ideal society (Israel) and do not even consistently favor the interests of a *Bürger-Tempel-Gemeinde*. Moreover, there is no evidence that these laws were in fact *imposed* on Judah during the Persian period (the stories of Ezra and Nehemiah having been discussed earlier). The Mishnaic sanhedrins never came to exist in the Second Temple period. No: the merging of cultic and non-cultic laws into a single conception is part of the *earliest* ideology of the biblical codes, *influenced by the configuration of the contemporary social structure, but not intended to govern its life*. The integration of cultic and social in Exodus, Deuteronomy, and Leviticus requires us to date the composition of the law codes, as well as their incorporation into the larger Pentateuchal narrative, *and* the process by which they began to be adopted into various Judean lifestyle, as the work of two to three hundred years. But that seems quite long enough.

LAW AND ETHNICITY

The suggestion above encounters an objection in the widely-held view that, regardless of the precise historicity of Ezra or Nehemiah, Persian policy toward Yehud, as towards other provinces and peoples, was to authorize the production of a more or less autonomous legal system. We must remember that in a multicultural empire, unless there is an imperial law that is universally enforced in all areas, a clear connection between law and ethnicity must develop. The society one is protected by is that whose laws apply to that individual and to which he or she therefore has an ethnic affiliation, or a substitute for one, such as a resident alien status. The Persian empire, as part of its policy of regenerating local economies, encouraged the use of local temples as centers of economic activity. In many cases, these temples had their own land and personnel and their own capital in the form of temple taxes. They were thus able to act as banks and investment houses and would be obvious mechanisms for the collection of imperial taxes too.[27] Concomitantly, the Achaemenids promoted the creation, or reconstitution, of a series of quasi-national

---

[27] Blenkinsopp, op. cit., pp. 23-24.

entities, preserving an indigenous culture and observing its own laws.
The well-known case of the Egyptian Udjahorresnet[28] may be invoked: he seems to have been responsible, under the direction of the
Achaemenid king, for the restoration of at least one cult center in
Egypt, and of the "houses of life," scribal institutions devoted to the
composition and preservation of texts, including especially cultic and
medical. These "houses of life" were generally, though not exclusively, associated with temples. There activities also included teaching.[29]

Blenkinsopp has therefore argued[30] that the mission of Ezra follows closely that of Udjahorresnet: commissioned as a Persian sym-
pathizer, he restores the Temple cult, restores the scribal schools, and
promulgates the local law. The parallel is attractive, and indeed need
not be dismissed, except insofar as it implies that any biblical legislation fits the requirements of the theory. Two difficulties with this
theory should be mentioned. First, the portrait of a law-bringing Ezra
may, as argued earlier, reflect a much later perspective, retrojecting
what was later seen as a law to be interpreted and adopted as the law
of Judah to a written text imposed at the birth of Second Temple
Judaism. The second and more substantial objection lies in the difficulty of matching any particular biblical material with such a law.
Much has been written about this problem, if it is indeed a real
problem (i.e., assuming there was an Ezra), and while a minority of
scholars think of an early Pentateuch, the majority think rather of
something more restricted, such as Deuteronomy or the Priestly
Code. But neither of these is a plausible law for a province or for an
ethnos.

Another problem is: how far is this law presented as having extended? The book of Ezra's decree from Artaxerxes states that Ezra
was to appoint judges throughout the province of Abar-Nahara itself.
This again looks like a reflection of a later situation, when what can
be called a Jewish population was spread beyond Palestine into
Transjordan and Syria. "Jewish" (i.e., "Judean") implies a sort of
ethnic-religious identity by which persons in the Levant could be
defined as "Jewish" or "Judean" even when not living in Judah. If

---

[28] J. Blenkinsopp, "The Mission of Udjahorresnet and Those of Ezra and Nehemiah," in *JBL* 106 (1987), pp. 409-421.
[29] R. Williams, "The Sage in Egyptian Literature," in J.G. Gammie and L.
Perdue, eds., *The Sage in Israel and the Ancient Near East* (Winona Lake, 1990), p. 27.
[30] In his "Mission."

there was a local law governing Yehud, then, it is no longer extant. However, the existence of such an initiative, if accepted, could well have provided the inspiration for the kind of utopian legal theorizing that we find in Deuteronomy and Leviticus.

INTERPRETING SCRIPTURAL LAW

We find among the literature of the Second Temple period successive interpretations and reinterpretations of laws that are at some point along the way of becoming scriptural. The literature comprises material that itself subsequently becomes scriptural, too (Chronicles), and also the Qumran scrolls, the Septuagint, Philo, and Josephus. The relationship between exegesis and praxis is variable. Mostly the interpretations have more to do with the freedom that the writers felt that they had to explain and understand them according to their own preferences than the needs of the writers' own community to know exactly how they should apply "the law." Most of these writers felt, however, that there was a "law" that governed and defined "Judaism," though in the Jewish communities of the Roman Empire it seems that such a belief, insofar as it was held, corresponded with a rather minimal praxis: circumcisions, abstinence from idol worship, Sabbath rest. In one case, however (the *Damascus Document*), we can see the attempt to interpret the law in order to adopt it for the lifestyle of a Jewish sect. The development that comes to its completion in the classic Rabbinic documents is, as we can now see, anticipated in the Second Temple period and betrays a general movement in the direction of turning theory into practice. This is not, however, to affirm some continuous unbroken line between Scripture and Rabbinic Judaism nor to argue for a legally normative "Judaism." It might, nevertheless, be fair to say that among the things that made a Judaism a Judaism was the belief that it was defined by a "law." Here, and here only, I will remark that "law" is not always the most appropriate translation of *torah*. The changing definition of *torah* from "teaching, religious instruction" to "precepts" accompanies the progression from theory to praxis that I have been tracing, though it does not match it precisely. Nor is that changing definition a simply one: rather it remains complex, not least when translated into Greek.

Concluding Observations: The Wider Historical Context

Between the composition of the law codes and their adoption (in theory or practice) as laws binding on each and every Judean's way of life (which is post-Rabbinic) lie several stages. In reconstructing them I do not assume a simple chronological progression nor any absolute datings. But I do suggest that the entire process only begins with the society of the Persian province of Judah.

I have reconstructed, after the writing out of these exercises in legal theory, a process whereby the contents are developed and exegeted. Over time exegesis comes to dominate. But the next stage (I am speaking typologically rather than chronologically, though one implies the other to some degree) these laws come to be seen as a definition of what "Judaism" is, what the national culture is.

This study can go considerably further. I have not here had space to incorporate an analysis of the Elephantine materials, nor begun to consider the impact of the Maccabean wars, for example, and the foundation of a national state under the Hasmoneans, in creating an authoritative definition of what constitutes "Judaism." Nor have I considered the role of Judean education in cultivating the study of Hebrew texts and especially the impact of Greek education in fomenting nationalism. Here I have been essentially concerned with the development of law prior to and while becoming scriptural and not with post-scriptural processes. And I have done little more than clear the way for an agenda of historical investigation. I can do no more here than suggest the contribution of these other factors.

According to my understanding, the production and "scripturing" of Judean literature was part of that cultural movement whereby Yehud and its inhabitants (most of whom were no part of the process) were furnished with a history back to creation, a body of wisdom teaching, and everything else that can form the curriculum of a national scribal educational system. By and by, the student of these laws becomes a practitioner of them; their study and exegesis is not merely an intellectual but a cultural and then a moral and religious imperative. We are witnessing the emergence of "Judaism" *as an idea;* and law is one of its nuclei. The effect of the events of the mid-second century on this development can been discerned through the smoke of propaganda that has surrounded the "Maccabean crisis" from its own times onward. At stake, either before, during, or after this political upheaval, was the meaning and the fate of the national culture, the "traditional laws" that the Judeans had lived by under Persians, Ptolemies, and until then under Seleucids too. And once political independence under the Hasmoneans had been achieved, it seems that this definition, perhaps never too firmly specified, took several concrete but deviating forms. Sadducees, Damascus Covenanters, Pharisees, Essenes, and who knows how many other groups each knew what "Judaism" was, and each accepted the authority of the scriptures. Each, of course, interpreted them in different ways. Perhaps once the Hasmoneans were in a position to (and obliged to?) clarify what "Judaism" meant, in terms of calendar, festivals, Temple cult, political appointments, and whatever else, conformity or dissent were the only options. Dissent clearly occurred, and with it a heightening of religious commitment to what was "right."

Of particular interest in this regard is the "Damascus" sect, who, on the evidence of their own laws, attempted to create a society based strictly on the "law of Moses" as they understood it. Their existence was based on the premise that Israel should obey that law, fully and entirely, and this was not being done, indeed, had not been done since the beginning of the Second Temple period. Hence the attempt to live, within a wicked Israel, as a true Israel, in secluded communities living according to the true law. The administration of justice in this sect is in the hands of a *mebaqqer* (CD 9.17ff.): although priests and Levites also play a role in interpreting the law (13.1-7), supremacy lies with the *mebaqqer* (13.5). (The priest and the chief *mebaqqer*, as indicated in CD 14.7-12, seem, incidentally, to prefigure or represent the "messiahship" of Israel and Aaron, the ideal leadership of the nation.)

But these "Damascus Covenanters" are not the sole example. The Pharisaic movement and its similar but more circumscribed attempt to integrate biblical holiness laws into the everyday lifestyle of even a non-priest is another example of the appropriation of originally non-legislative written laws into actual praxis. In the case of both these movements, we can finally see biblical law very decidedly in the arena of praxis.

But we are still dealing only with certain kinds of Judaisms, those that for whatever reasons chose to try and define themselves and regulate their daily life by means of scriptural laws. The home of biblical law even in late Second Temple times still for the most part remained, I suspect, the social space of the educated intellectual, the school, Temple (to a lesser extent the marketplace, where ideas as well as goods were bought and sold). Judaism as individual observance of *torah* may not have been universally recognized as the only orthodox kind until the formative and definitive work of the rabbis.

BIBLIOGRAPHY

Blenkinsopp, J., "The Mission of Udjahorresnet and Those of Ezra and Nehemiah," in *JBL* 106 (1987), pp. 409-421.

Blenkinsopp, J., "Temple and Society in Achaemenid Judah," in *Second Temple Studies* (1991), pp. 22-53.

Carmichael, C., *The Origins of Biblical Law. The Decalogues and the Book of the Covenant* (Ithaca, 1992).

Carter, C., "The Province of Yehud in the Post-Exilic Period," in Eskenazi, T.C., and K.H. Richards, eds., *Second Temple Studies 2. Temple and Community in the Persian Period* (Sheffield, 1994).

Davies, P.R., "Halakhah at Qumran," in Davies, P.R., and R.T. White, eds., *A Tribute to Geza Vermes. Essays on Jewish and Christian Literature and History* (Sheffield, 1990), pp. 37-50.

Davies, P.R., *In Search of Ancient Israel* (Sheffield, 1992).

Davies, P.R., "Scenes from Early Judaism," in Edelman, D.V., ed., *The Triumph of Elohim. From Yahwisms to Judaisms* (Kampen, 1995), pp. 145-184.

Davies, P.R., "Ezra and Nehemiah Revisited," unpublished paper read at the SBL International Meeting, Budapest, 1995.

Davies, P.R., *Sects and Scrolls. Essays on Qumran and Related Topics* (Atlanta, 1996).

Falk, Z.W, *Introduction to Jewish Law of the Second Commonwealth*, 2 vols. (Leiden, 1978).

Finkelstein, I., *The Archaeology of the Israelite Settlement* (Jerusalem, 1988).

Fishbane, M., *Biblical Interpretation in Ancient Israel* (Oxford, 1985).

Flesher, P.V.M., *Oxen, Women, or Citizens? Slaves in the System of the Mishnah* (Atlanta, 1988).

Jackson, B., "Biblical Laws of Slavery: A Comparative Approach," in Archer, L., ed., *Slavery and Other Forms of Unfree Labour* (London, 1988), pp. 86-101.

Jackson, B., "Ideas of Law and Legal Administration: A Semiotic Approach," in Clements, R.E., ed., *The World of Ancient Israel* (Cambridge, 1989), pp. 185-202.

Jolowitz, H.F., and B. Nicholas, *Historical Introduction to the Study of Roman Law* (Cambridge, 1972).

Krauss, F.R., "Ein zentrales Problem des altmesopotamischen Rechts: Was ist der Codex Hammurabi," in *Genava* 8:1960, pp. 283-296.

Marshall, J., *Israel and the Book of the Covenant. An Anthropological Approach to Biblical Law* (Atlanta, 1993).

Newman, K.S., *Law and Economic Organization* (Cambridge, 1983).

Niehr, H., *Rechtsprechung in Israel: Untersuchungen zur Geschichte der Gerichtsorganisation im Alten Testament* (Stuttgart, 1987).

Patrick, D., *Old Testament Law* (Louisville and London, 1985).

Paul, S., *Studies in the Book of the Covenant in the Light of Cuneiform and Biblical Law* (Leiden, 1970).

Phillips, A., *Ancient Israel's Criminal Law* (Oxford, 1985).

Sprinkle, J.M., *"The Book of the Covenant:" A Literary Approach* (Sheffield, 1994).

Watson, A., *Law Making in the Later Roman Republic* (Oxford, 1974).

Weinberg, J., *The Citizen-Temple Community* (Sheffield, 1993).

Weinfeld, M., *Deuteronomy and the Deuteronomic School* (Oxford, 1972).

Westbrook, R., *Studies in Biblical and Cuneiform Law* (Paris, 1988).

Westbrook, R., *Property and the Family in Biblical Law* (Sheffield, 1991).

Williams, R., "The Sage in Egyptian Literature," in Gammie, J.G., and L. Perdue, eds., *The Sage in Israel and the Ancient Near East* (Winona Lake, 1990), pp. 19-30.

Wilson, R., "The Role of Law in Early Israelite Society," in Halpern, B., and D.W. Hobson, eds., *Law, Politics and Society in the Ancient Mediterranean World* (Sheffield, 1993), pp. 90-99.

II. SADDUCEES AND PHARISEES

Lester L. Grabbe
University of Hull

Religion among the Jewish people in the late Second Temple period has often been seen in terms of the "sects," especially the Pharisees and Sadducees. Writers on the subject have tended to give a somewhat more nuanced picture in recent years, but the old emphasis on the Pharisees and Sadducees has by no means gone away. Although I feel that focusing on the sects is likely to distort our understanding of Second Temple Judaism(s), there is no question that these two groups are important. They are also extremely difficult to come to grips with, despite the frequent statements made with great confidence about them. One problem with a number of recent treatments is their concentration on the Pharisees rather than recognizing that the Sadducees are as prominent in the sources as the former. This leads to a skewed discussion because of concentrating on the Pharisees in isolation.

We cannot afford to take anything for granted. Any study of the Pharisees and Sadducees has to go back to the basics. This is what I propose to do here, looking first of all at the sources and the problems with using them with as few preconceptions as possible. Then I shall try to ask whether anything can be said with confidence about them, or at least said with some degree of probability. What I hope will be clear to all is the basis of any positivistic statement I make about the Pharisees and Sadducees. Any conclusions must come from the analysis.[1] The first part of my article is devoted to sources

---

[1] A detailed discussion of the Pharisees and Sadducees is in my *Judaism from Cyrus to Hadrian* (Minneapolis, 1992; London, 1994), pp. 467-487. Since the completion of the manuscript in 1990, a number of important studies and considerations have entered the debate. By 1990, statements were already being made about the importance of 4QMMT for the question, though the text was not made officially available until 1994. Also appearing after my manuscript was sent to the publisher was Steve Mason, *Flavius Josephus on the Pharisees: A Composition-Critical Study* (Leiden, 1991); on this, in addition to my comments below, see the reviews by Rebecca Gray (*JTS* 43 [1992], pp. 216-220), Seth Schwartz (*AJS Review* 19 [1994], pp. 83-88), and L.L. Grabbe (*JJS* 45 [1994], pp. 134-136). Another study is Günter Stemberger, *Pharisäer, Sadduzäer, Essener* (Stuttgart, 1991), translated as *Jewish Contemporaries of Jesus: Pharisees, Sadducees, Essenes* (Minneapolis, 1995). Most recently, see Jacob Neusner and Clemens

and is meant to be primarily descriptive: what do the sources actually say? The main analysis is postponed until the second part. in which the implications of the data in the sources are considered in the light of all information.

THE SOURCES

Even selecting which sources to use is not an easy task. One might think that at least the sources for the Pharisees and Sadducees were generally agreed on, but this is not the case, and choosing which sources to use already sets the agenda to some extent. Because of limits of space, I look only at the major sources that have been suggested as potentially important by recent studies and consider whether they seem to be relevant. However, I have not consciously rejected any without discussion. The sources are contained essentially in three collections: the writings of Josephus, the New Testament, and the Rabbinic literature. It has also recently been suggested that some Qumran writings represent Sadducean viewpoints and, by implication, give an insight into the development of the Pharisaic movement.

Josephus[2]

The writings on Josephus are extremely important because he lived at a time when the Pharisaic and Sadducean movements were active and he had personal knowledge of some prominent Pharisees and Sadducees.

Thoma, "Die Pharisäer vor und nach der Tempelzerstörung des Jahres 70 n. Chr.," in Simon Lauer and Hanspeter Ernst, eds., *Tempelkult und Tempelzerstörung (70 n. Chr.): Festschrift für Clemens Thoma zum 60. Geburtstag* (Judaica et Christiana 15; Bern, 1995), pp. 189-230.

[2] Quotations from Josephus in this section are from H. St. J. Thackeray, et al., *Josephus* (London and Cambridge, 1926-65). The detailed discussion of each passage by Mason, op. cit., has been a good deal of help in analyzing Josephus' statements. However, I often disagree with his interpretations, especially his tendency to read a negative attitude toward the Pharisees into Josephus' statements, though in a number of cases this is without warrant or evidence. See below at ns. 3-5, 7, 9, and 11-14.

War of the Jews

War 1.5.2-3 §§110-114:[3]

Beside Alexandra, and growing as she grew, arose the Pharisees, a body of Jews with the reputation of excelling the rest of their nation in the observances of religion, and as exact exponents of the laws. To them, being herself intensely religious, she listened with too great deference; while they, gradually taking advantage of an ingenuous woman, became at length the real administrators of the state, at liberty to banish and to recall, to loose and to bind, whom they would. In short, the enjoyments of royal authority were theirs; its expenses and burthens fell to Alexandra.... But if she ruled the nation, the Pharisees ruled her.... Thus they put to death Diogenes, a distinguished friend of Alexander, accusing him of having advised the king to crucify his eight hundred victims. They further urged Alexandra to make away with the others who had instigated Alexander to punish those men; and as she from superstitious motives always gave way, they proceeded to kill whomsoever they would.

War 1.29.2 §§571:

The king [Herod the Great] was furiously indignant.... He, accordingly, assembled a council of his friends and relations and accused the wretched woman [Pheroras' wife] of numerous misdeeds, among others of insulting his own daughters, of subsidizing the Pharisees to oppose him, and of alienating his brother, after bewitching him with drugs.

War 2.8.14 §§162-166:[4]

Of the two first-named schools, the Pharisees, who are considered the most accurate interpreters of the laws, and hold the position of the

---

[3] Mason (*Pharisees*, pp. 106-113) argues that when Josephus says the Pharisees "seem/have a reputation" (*dokeō*) of being accurate interpreters of the law, he means that they only "pretend" to be such. This is a possible reading, but his own discussion shows that it is only one alternative. Josephus is not necessarily negative in his statement. He could be neutral ("they have a reputation of being accurate interpreters," but I am not stating my own personal opinion) or even positive ("they have a reputation of being accurate interpreters," with which I agree). Mason's attempt to show that Josephus can use such a common term with only a single meaning is misguided—competent users of a language are quite capable of employing the same expression with different meanings, depending on the context. A common word such as *dokeo* is unlikely to be used consistently, with only a single unvarying meaning whatever the context, by a competent writer. Mason is simply determined to wring a negative connotation from even Josephus' general usage. And, having determined that this particular passage is negative toward the Pharisees, he proceeds to read a negative connotation into any passage where reference is made to the Pharisaic reputation for accurate interpretation, even if the passage as a whole shows no such negative tendencies.

[4] Mason sees this as a crucial passage (*Pharisees*, p. 120), yet he is hard put to find anything negative in it: his claim (p. 175) that a negative judgment is shown because

leading sect, attribute everything to Fate and to God; they hold that to act rightly or otherwise rests, indeed, for the most part with men, but that in each action Fate co-operates. Every soul, they maintain, is imperishable, but the soul of the good alone passes into another body, . while the souls of the wicked suffer eternal punishment.

The Sadducees, the second of the orders, do away with Fate altogether, and remove God beyond, not merely the commission, but the very sight, of evil. They maintain that man has the free choice of good or evil, and that it rests with each man's will whether he follows the one or the other. As for the persistence of the soul after death, penalties in the underworld, and rewards, they will have none of them.

The Pharisees are affectionate to each other and cultivate harmonious relations with the community. The Sadducees, on the contrary, are, even among themselves, rather boorish in their behavior, and in their intercourse with their peers are as rude as to aliens.

War 2.17.2-3 §§410-11:

> [At the beginning of the 66-70 revolt:] Thereupon the principal citizens assembled with the chief priests and the most notable Pharisees to deliberate on the position of affairs, now that they were faced with what seemed irreparable disaster.

Antiquities of the Jews

Ant. 13.5.9 §171-172:[5]

> Now at this time there were three schools of thought among the Jews, which held different opinions concerning human affairs; the first being that of the Pharisees, the second that of the Sadducees, and the third that of the Essenes. As for the Pharisees, they say that certain events are the work of Fate, but not all; as to other events, it depends upon ourselves whether they shall take place or not.... But the Sadducees do away with Fate, holding that there is no such thing and that human actions are not achieved in accordance with her decree, but that all things lie within our own power, so that we ourselves are responsible for

---

Josephus was already supposedly negative in *War* 1.5.2-3 §§110-114 is not very convincing (see n. 3, above), while his explanation of *apago* looks rather tendentious. That Josephus has "far from unrestrained enthusiasm for the group" (p. 175) is not the same as a negative portrait. It is notable that, by contrast, the Sadducees are presented in a derogatory manner as "rude" and "boorish."

[5] Mason (*Pharisees*, pp. 211-212) recognizes that this passage is positive toward the Pharisees. His explanation is that all three "schools" are presented in a favorable light here; that is true but irrelevant to his thesis. Why would gentile readers read only this passage and not the others about the Pharisees? If Josephus was as consistently negative toward the Pharisees as Mason is trying to prove, there is no reason for him to be more positive here than elsewhere. On the contrary, this passage simply illustrates that Josephus gives a variety of perspectives on the sect.

our well-being, while we suffer misfortune through our own thoughtlessness.

Ant. 13.10.5-7 §§288-99:[6]

As for Hyrcanus, the envy of the Jews was aroused against him by his own successes and those of his sons; particularly hostile to him were the Pharisees, who are one of the Jewish schools, as we have related above. And so great is their influence with the masses that even when they speak against a king or high priest, they immediately gain credence. Hyrcanus too was a disciple of theirs, and was greatly loved by them.

Josephus now tells the story of a feast given by John Hyrcanus in which the Pharisees were present. On asking them to speak frankly, one Eleazar[7] was critical of him. When Hyrcanus took counsel as to how he should punish Eleazar, Jonathan (a friend of Hyrcanus and belonging to the party of Sadducees) suggested that the king let the Pharisees sentence Eleazar:

And Jonathan in particular inflamed his anger, and so worked upon him that he brought him to join the Sadducaean party and desert the Pharisees, and to abrogate the regulations which they had established for the people, and punish those who observed them. Out of this, of course, grew the hatred of the masses for him and his sons.... [T]he Pharisees had passed on to the people certain regulations handed down by former generations and not recorded in the Laws of Moses, for which reason they are rejected by the Sadducaean group, who hold that only those regulations should be considered valid which were written down (in Scripture), and that those which had been handed down by former generations need not be observed. And concerning these matters the two parties came to have controversies and serious differences, the Sadducees having the confidence of the wealthy alone but no following among the populace, while the Pharisees have the support of the masses.

Hyrcanus was faced with a revolt caused, if the *Antiquities* is to be believed, by his breach with the Pharisees. The *War* says nothing

---

[6] Emmanuelle Main, "Les Sadducéens vus par Flavius Josèphe," in *RevB* 97 (1990), pp. 161-206, especially pp. 190-202, argues that this tradition should be associated with Alexander Janneus, as in B. Qid. 66a.

[7] Mason (*Pharisees*, pp. 229-230) argues that Eliezar was not a Pharisee. He is correct that the Eliezar is not explicitly said to be a Pharisee, but the context strongly implies this. Indeed, the banquet was specifically said to be for the Pharisees. Apart from Hyrcanus himself, the only individuals mentioned are Eliezar and Jonathan, and Jonathan is specifically said to be a Sadducee. If Eliezer was *not* a Pharisee, we would expect to be informed of this. Josephus thus means us to understand that Eliezar was a Pharisee. It is, of course, a problem for Mason if Eliezar is a Pharisee.

about the Pharisees but ascribes the revolt to the "successes" (*eupragia*) of Hyrcanus and his sons, which is also how the *Antiquities* actually begins the passage. Despite supposedly not having the people behind him, Hyrcanus put down the revolt, and the rest of his reign was peaceable (both the *War* and the *Antiquities* give the same picture). So much for the power of the Pharisees.

Ant. 13.15.5—16.1 §§401-408:

> And then, he [Alexander Janneus, on his deathbed] said [to his wife Alexandra], on her return to Jerusalem..., she should yield a certain amount of power to the Pharisees, for if they praised her in return for this sign of regard, they would dispose the nation favorably toward her. These men, he assured her, had so much influence with their fellow-Jews that they would injure those whom they hated and help those to whom they were friendly; for they had the complete confidence of the masses when they spoke harshly of any other person, even when they did so out of envy; and he himself, he added, had come into conflict with the nation because these men had been badly treated by him.... "Promise them also that you will not take any action, while you are on the throne, without their consent...."
>
> Thereupon Alexandra...conferred with the Pharisees as her husband had suggested, and by placing in their hands all that concerned his corpse and the royal power, stilled their anger against Alexander, and made them her well-wishers and friends....
>
> Alexander then appointed Hyrcanus as high priest...; and she permitted the Pharisees to do as they liked in all matters, and also commanded the people to obey them; and whatever regulations, introduced by the Pharisees in accordance with the tradition of their fathers, had been abolished by her father-in-law Hyrcanus, these she again restored. And so, while she had the title of sovereign, the Pharisees had the power. For example, they recalled exiles, and freed prisoners, and, in a word, in no way differed from absolute rulers.

Ant. 13.16.1-5 §§408-423:

> And throughout the entire country there was quiet except for the Pharisees; for they worked upon the feelings of the queen and tried to persuade her to kill those who had urged Alexander to put the eight hundred to death.... Some time after this the queen was stricken by a serious illness, whereupon Aristobulus decided to make an attempt to seize power.... [H]e was just then especially fearful that on her death their whole family might come under the rule of the Pharisees....

Ant. 15.1.1 §3:

> Especially honored by him [Herod the Great] were Pollion the Pharisee and his disciple Samais, for during the siege of Jerusalem these men had

advised the citizens to admit Herod, and for this they now received their reward. This same Pollion had once, when Herod was on trial for his life, reproachfully foretold to Hyrcanus and the judges that if Herod's life were spared, he would (one day) persecute them all. And in time this turned out to be so, for God fulfilled his words.

Ant. 15.10.4 368-371:

As for the rest of the populace, he [Herod] demanded that they submit to taking an oath of loyalty, and he compelled them to make a sworn declaration that they would maintain a friendly attitude to his rule.... He also tried to persuade Pollion the Pharisee and Samais and most of their disciples to take the oath, but they would not agree to this, and yet they were not punished as were the others who refused, for they were shown consideration on Pollion's account. And those who are called by us Essenes were also excused from this necessity.

Ant. 17.2.4—3.1 §§41-47:[8]

There was also a group of Jews priding itself on its adherence to ancestral custom and claiming to observe the laws of which the Deity approves, and by these men, called Pharisees, the women (of the court) were ruled. These men were able to help the king greatly because of their foresight, and yet they were obviously intent upon combating and injuring him. At least when the whole Jewish people affirmed by an oath that it would be loyal to Caesar and to the king's government, these men over six thousand in number, refused to take this oath, and when the king punished them with a fine, Pheroras' wife paid the fine for them. In return for her friendliness they foretold—for they were believed to have foreknowledge of things through God's appearances to them—that by God's decree Herod's throne would be taken from him, both from himself and his descendants, and the royal power would fall to her and Pheroras and to any children that they might have. These things...were reported to the king, as was the news that the Pharisees had corrupted some of the people at court. And the king put to death those of the Pharisees who were most to blame.... He also killed all those of the household who approved of what the Pharisee said....

After punishing the Pharisees who had been convicted of these charges, Herod held a council of his friends and made accusations against Pheroras' wife.... The fine that had been imposed by him (on the Pharisees) had been evaded, thanks to the payments that she had made, and nothing was now being done without her help.

---

[8] Albert I. Baumgartner ("Rivkin and Neusner on the Pharisees," in Peter Richardson and Stephen Westerholm, eds., *Law in Religious Communities in the Roman Period: The Debate over* Torah *and* Nomos *in Post-Biblical Judaism and Early Christianity* [Waterloo, 1991], pp. 109-226, esp. pp. 119-120) notes that this is a very hostile passage toward the Pharisees.

Antiquities 18.1.3 §§4-23:[9]

But a certain Judas, a Gaulanite from a city named Gamala, who had
enlisted the aid of Saddok, a Pharisee, threw himself into the cause of
rebellion....

The Pharisees simplify their standard of living, making no concession
to luxury. They follow the guidance of that which their doctrine has
selected and transmitted as good, attaching the chief importance to the
observance of those commandments which it has seen fit to dictate to
them. They show respect and deference to their elders, nor do they
rashly presume to contradict their proposals. Though they postulate
that everything is brought about by fate, still they do not deprive the
human will of the pursuit of what is in man's power, since it was God's
good pleasure that there should be a fusion and that the will of man
with his virtue and vice should be admitted to the council-chamber of
fate. They believe that souls have power to survive death and that there
are rewards and punishments under the earth for those who have led
lives of virtue or vice: eternal imprisonment is the lot of evil souls, while
the good souls receive an easy passage to a new life. Because of these
views they are, as a matter of fact, extremely influential among the
townsfolk; and all prayers and sacred rites of divine worship are performed according to their exposition. This is the great tribute that the
inhabitants of the cities, by practicing the highest ideals both in their
way of living and in their discourse, have paid to the excellence [*arete*] of
the Pharisees.

The Sadducees hold that the soul perishes along with the body. They
own no observance of any sort apart from the laws; in fact, they reckon
it a virtue to dispute with the teachers of the path of wisdom that they
pursue. There are but few men to whom this doctrine has been made
known, but these are men of the highest standing. They accomplish
practically nothing, however. For whenever they assume some office,
though they submit unwillingly and perforce, yet submit they do to the
formulas of the Pharisees, since otherwise the masses would not tolerate
them....

As for the fourth of the philosophies, Judas the Galilaean set himself
up as leader of it. This school agrees in all other respects with the
opinions of the Pharisees, except that they have a passion for liberty

---

[9] Contrary to the allegations of some writers on the subject, this passage makes
assertions about the power of the Pharisees found in no other of Josephus' writings.
It cannot be read and quoted as a "proof text" in isolation from Josephus' other
statements on the Pharisees and Sadducees. On this passage Mason admits that we
"have here unqualified, unrestrained praise on the part of Josephus" (*Pharisees*, p.
286). His only response is to say, "It is extremely doubtful, however, that this aristo-
crat shares the popular enthusiasm" (ibid.). He also tries to explain away Josephus'
use of *arete* (§15) in reference to the Pharisees. This passage is a good example of how
Mason simply refuses to take Josephus' statement in its most natural sense but must
read his thesis into it.

that is almost unconquerable, since they are convinced that God alone is their leader and master.

Ant. 20.9.1 §§199-200:[10]

The younger Ananus, who, as we have said, had been appointed to the high priesthood, was rash in his temper and unusually daring. He followed the school of the Sadducees, who are indeed more heartless than any of the other Jews, as I have already explained, when they sit in judgment.... And so he convened the judges of the Sanhedrin and brought before them a man named James, the brother of Jesus who was called the Christ, and certain others. He accused them of having transgressed the law and delivered them up to be stoned.

The Life

Life 2 §§10-12:[11]

At about the age of sixteen I determined to gain personal experience of the several sects into which our nation is divided. These...are three in number—the first that of the Pharisees, the second that of the Sadducees, and the third that of the Essenes. I thought that, after a thorough investigation, I should be in a position to select the best. So I submitted myself to hard training and laborious exercises and passed through [*diēlthon*] the three courses. Not content, however, with the experience thus gained, on hearing of one named Bannus.... With him I lived for three years and, having accomplished my purpose, returned to the city. Being now in my nineteenth year I began to govern my life [*politeuesthai*] by the rules of [*katakolouthōn*] the Pharisees, a sect having points of resemblance to that which the Greeks call the Stoic school.

---

[10] As pointed out by William Poehlmann ("The Sadducees as Josephus Presents Them, or The Curious Case of Ananus," in A.J. Hultgren, D.H. Juel, and J.D. Kingsbury, eds., *All Things New: Essays in Honor of Roy A. Harrisville* [St. Paul, 1992], pp. 87-100), the somewhat negative picture of Ananus here is exceptional. In the *War* and also in the *Life*, Ananus is presented in a very positive manner.

[11] Mason has written at length to argue that Josephus does not claim here to have joined the Pharisees at age nineteen: *Pharisees*, pp. 342-356 and "Was Josephus a Pharisee? A Re-Examination of *Life* 10-12," in *JJS* 40 (1989), pp. 31-45. He states that those who say Josephus became a Pharisee are dependent on the phrase *tē Pharisaiōn hairesei katakolouthōn*, but if so, "he has chosen an excruciatingly circuitous way of saying it" (*Pharisees*, pp. 355-356). Mason is right about the round about way of speaking, but Hellenistic historians were often more interested in rhetoric and literary style than in being straightforward and clear. In fact, the predominant judgment does not depend on just that phrase but also on the entire context, in which the most natural way of understanding Josephus' statement is that at age nineteen he became a Pharisee. Mason rightly points out that there is no evidence elsewhere that Josephus was a Pharisee, but that is beside the point—Josephus often makes claims according to the circumstances, not necessarily according to the truth.

Life 5 §§21:

> When Menahem and the chieftains of the band of brigands had been
> put to death I ventured out of the Temple and once more consorted
> with the chief priests and the leading Pharisees.

Life 38 §§191:

> This Simon was a native of Jerusalem, of a very illustrious family, and
> of the sect of the Pharisees, who have the reputation of being unrivaled
> experts in their country's laws [*ta patria nomima*].

Life 39 §§196-198:

> The scheme agreed upon was to send a deputation comprising persons
> of different classes of society but of equal standing in education. Two of
> them, Jonathan and Ananias, were from the lower ranks and adherents
> of the Pharisees; the third Jozar, also a Pharisee, came of a priestly
> family; the youngest, Simon, was descended from high priests. Their
> instructions were to approach the Galilaeans and ascertain the reason
> for their devotion to me. If they attributed it to my being a native of
> Jerusalem, they were to reply that so were all four of them; if to my
> expert knowledge of their laws, they should retort that neither were they
> ignorant of the customs of their fathers [*ethē ta patria*]; if, again, they
> asserted that their affection was due to my priestly office, they should
> answer that two of them were likewise priests.

Conclusions about Josephus

There are a number of points we can draw from the data just presented:

1. Josephus himself had personal acquaintance with the Pharisaic
and Sadducean movements and knew or had knowledge of prominent figures in the movements. However, there is no evidence that he
was himself ever a member of either movement.[12]

2. His attitude toward both movements is ambivalent. Toward the
Pharisees, he is sometimes favorable, sometimes neutral, and occasionally negative.[13] Toward the Sadducees, there are positive points

---

[12] Mason has rightly pointed this out, but he was not the first to do so. For
example, I had come to this conclusion long before seeing Mason's study (cf.,
Grabbe, *Judaism from Cyrus to Hadrian*, p. 5), but others were before me.

[13] Mason's thesis requires that Josephus be consistently negative toward the Pharisees. When, in my review, I pointed out that this was not the case, another scholar
suggested to me privately that Mason's argument has "cumulative" force. Such a
statement completely misses the essence of the argument. Josephus is consistently
negative only if he is consistently negative; if there is a passage—a single passage—
in which he is positive, the argument fails. Therefore, one must demonstrate this

in his descriptions, but he often has an edge to his presentation and never seems completely favorable or even neutral. To what extent he follows his sources in individual passages is debatable. Although in typical Hellenistic manner, he usually rewrote his sources, this does not mean that he imposed a consistent view on them and could have (or has) in some cases allowed the viewpoint of the original source to stand.[14]

3. In the later *Antiquities*, he has the Pharisees in some passages where they do not appear in the earlier *War*, especially with regard to John Hyrcanus and Alexander Janneus. Why this is so is not completely clear. It could be that he abbreviated his sources in the earlier work or perhaps used sources that did not have them. Equally, he could have had different sources in the later work or even have introduced them artificially or at least given them greater prominence than the sources did. Whether he might have been trying to curry favor with the Pharisees in some of the later passages is also debated, though it still seem to me that he *claims* (falsely) to have become an adherent of the Pharisees at an early age in *Life* 2 §§10-12.

4. According to his presentation, both the Pharisees and Sadducees have political aspirations much of the time. Although so little is said about the Sadducees that it is difficult to draw certain conclusions, one has the impression that the Sadducees—or at least certain individual Sadducees—were significantly involved in government. They include the wealthy and prominent among their number or their sympathizers. The Pharisees are often pictured as seeking political power, sometimes exercising it as a group (as under Alexandria Salome), and sometimes having individuals with a prominent position. The only time Josephus depicts them as actually in power, however, is under Alexandra Salome.

5. Both groups are portrayed as having religious beliefs, but very little is actually said regarding what these are. Apart from the somewhat irrelevant question of fate, the Pharisees are characterized as having "traditions from the fathers" (though what these were is never spelled out in detail) and respect the teachings of the elders. They also believe in reward and punishment after death. They have a

---

negative verdict in each passage in isolation—without interpreting by reference to Josephus' views in other passages, as Mason often does.

[14] Although Mason correctly argues that Josephus rewrote his sources, thus making them his own in one sense, this does not mean that Josephus necessarily imposed a particular or consistent point of view on them in every case.

reputation for accurate interpretation of Scripture and are influential among the common people The Sadducees do not accept anything not written in Scripture and allow younger members to argue with elders. They reject reward and punishment after death. In several passages the Pharisees have a reputation for being able to predict the future.

6. In one passage (*Ant.* 18.1.3 §§12-17), the Pharisees are alleged to be able to enforce their views on the Sadducees and cause public worship to be conducted according to their rites (whatever these are—we are never told). However, this passage is not supported by the rest of Josephus' statements on the two groups except in the nine-year reign of Alexandra. The Pharisees are kept under control by Alexander Janneus and by Herod and not even mentioned in conjunction with other rulers. The priests are in charge of the Temple.[15] The Hasmoneans, Romans, and Herodians rule the country; only under Alexandra do the Pharisees have sufficient influence to get their way. As far as we can tell, this influence came to an end when Alexandra died; there is no evidence that it continued after her. Some "notable Pharisees" (such as Simon b. Gamaliel) are involved in the leadership at the time of the revolt, but they are only a part of it and do not necessarily dominate (or at least do not do so because of their Pharisaic membership). After all, Simon was subordinate to the high priest Ananus who was a Sadducee (*Life* 38 §§189-194).

The New Testament

The Apostle Paul

Paul is the one individual claiming to be a Pharisee whose actual words we seem to have. Information about his Pharisaic background is given in two sources: the genuine letters of Paul and the Acts of the Apostles (on use of the latter source, see below.) Philippians 3:4-6 (NRSV):

> If anyone else has reason to be confident in the flesh, I have more: circumcised on the eighth day, a member of the people of Israel, of the tribe of Benjamin, a Hebrew born of Hebrews; as to the law, a Pharisee; as to zeal, a persecutor of the church; as to righteousness under the law, blameless.

---

[15] E.g., *Ag. Apion* 2.21 §184-187; 2.23 §§193-194. Cf., also Mason, "Priesthood in Josephus and the 'Pharisaic Revolution,'" in *JBL* 107 (1988), pp. 657-661.

The problem is that Paul's Christian teachings in some cases represent a reaction against his Jewish background. It is difficult, therefore, to determine which (if any) of Paul's views or beliefs or teachings show a Pharisaic influence. His being a Pharisee is associated with observance of the law. Beyond that it is difficult to go.

The Gospels

The following parallels in the Synoptic Gospels show the opponents of Jesus in the various pericopae:

Mark	Matthew	Luke
2:1-12: Jesus is brought a paralytic; the scribes criticize him	9:1-8: scribes	5:17-26: Pharisees and teachers; scribes
2:16-17: Scribes of Pharisees criticize him for eating with sinners/tax collectors	9:11-13: Pharisees	5:30-32: Pharisees and their scribes
2:18: John's disciples and Pharisees fast	9:14: disciples of John	5:33: disciples of John and disciples of Pharisees
2:23-24: Pharisees criticize Jesus for letting disciples pluck grain on Sabbath	12:1-2: Pharisees	6:1-2: Pharisees
3:1-6: Pharisees criticize Jesus for healing on Sabbath, then plot with Herodians	12:9-14: Pharisees	6:6-11: scribes and Pharisees
3:22: Scribes say Jesus possessed by Beelzebul	9:32-34: Pharisees say he casts out demons by Beelzebul/12:22-24: Pharisees	11:14-15: some
7:1-5: Pharisees and some of scribes criticize disciples for eating with unwashed hands	15:1-3: Pharisees and scribes	11:37-39: a Pharisee/the Pharisees
7:14-23: Disciples ask about saying on what defiles a person	15:12: Pharisees offended at his saying	—

Mark	Matthew	Luke
8:11: Pharisees seek a sign from Jesus to test him	6:1-4: Pharisees and Sadducees/12:38: some of the scribes and Pharisees	111:16: others
8:15: Jesus says beware the leaven of the Pharisees and the leaven of Herod	16:5-12: Pharisees and Sadducees	12:1: Pharisees
10:2: Pharisees ask Jesus about divorce to test him	19:3: Pharisees	16:14-18: Pharisees
11:27-33: Chief priests, scribes, and elders ask Jesus about his authority	21:23-27: chief priests and elders of the people	20:1-8: chief priests and scribes with elders
12:12: They tried to arrest him	1:45-46: chief priests and Pharisees	20:19: scribes and chief priests
12:13: Pharisees and some of the Herodians sent to entrap him	22:15-16: Pharisees and Herodians	20:20: they (scribes and chief priests?)
12:18-27: Sadducees ask him about resurrection	22:23-33: Sadducees	20:27-40: Sadducees
12:28: One of scribes asks about the first commandment	22:34-35: Pharisees, one of them a lawyer	10:25: lawyer
12:35: Scribes teach about the Christ	22:41-42: Pharisees	20:41: they
12:37-40: Jesus says, "Beware of the scribes"	23:1-12: scribes and Pharisees sit in Moses' seat	20:45-47: beware of scribes
14:3: Jesus eats at the house of Simon the leper	26:6: Simon the leper	7:36-39: Pharisee's house

Mark	Matthew	Luke	John
14:43-52: Judas comes from chief priests, scribes, and elders	26:47-56: chief priests and elders of the people	22:47-53: —	18:2-12: chief priests and the Pharisees

Q Document

Luke	*Matthew*
3:7-9: John excoriates multitudes when they come for baptism	3:7-10: Pharisees and Sadducees
7:30: Pharisees and lawyers rejected God's purpose	(11:7-19 is parallel to Luke 7:24-35, but no exact parallel to this verse)
—	23:15: scribes and Pharisees
11:39: Pharisees cleanse outside of cup	23:25 ,,
11:42: Pharisees tithe small herbs	23:23 ,,
11:43: Pharisees love best seats in synagogues and salutations	—
11:44: You are like graves	23:27 ,,
11:47: You build tombs of prophets	23:29 ,,
11:52: Lawyers (*nomikoi*) prevent entering kingdom	23:13 ,,

Matthew (No Parallels)

5:20: righteousness must exceed that of scribes and Pharisees
27:62: chief priests and Pharisees gather to ask for Jesus' tomb to be guarded

Luke (No Parallels)

13:31: Pharisees threaten Jesus with Herod
14:1-3: Jesus dines at house of Pharisee; speaks to lawyers and Pharisees
15:1-3: Scribes/Pharisees grumble because he eats with sinners (Mat. 18:12: teaching disciples)
17:20-21: Jesus asked by Pharisees about the kingdom of God
18:10-11: A Pharisee and a tax collector pray in the temple
19:39: Pharisees criticize Jesus for not rebuking disciples

Fourth Gospel

1:24: Jews send priests and Levites; sent by the Pharisees
3:1: A Pharisee named Nicodemus comes to Jesus secretly by night
4:1: Jesus knows that the Pharisees have heard he baptized more disciples than John
7:32-52: chief priests and Pharisees try to arrest Jesus; Nicodemus defends him
[8:3: Pharisees bring woman caught in adultery to Jesus]
·8:13: Pharisees debate with Jesus
9:1-41: Jesus heals blind beggar; Pharisees refuse to accept the miracle and cast the healed man out ("the Jews" had agreed that anyone professing Jesus would be put out of the synagogue)

11:46-47: chief priests and Pharisees plot against Jesus because of his raising of Lazarus from the dead

11:57: chief priests and Pharisees plotting to arrest Jesus

12:19: Pharisees astonished at the crowds who meet Jesus on his entry into Jerusalem

12:42: authorities who believed in Jesus do not confess him out of fear because the Pharisees would cast them out of the synagogue

(On 18:3, see above under Mark and parallels.)

Conclusions about the Gospels

1. The gospel traditions are difficult because of their tradition history and the question of their interrelationships. The two earliest sources of the gospel tradition are, by a strong consensus, Mark and Q. There is very little Q information on the question, the main parallel being Q 11:39-52.[16] The most valuable source of information is therefore Mark (usually considered the earliest gospel, written around 70 or not long afterward) with its synoptic parallels.

2. There is also the problem that certain groups and individuals seem only to be ciphers set up as Jesus' opponents simply for the sake of being knocked down. Despite this, some patterns emerge. The opponents of Jesus most frequently cited in Mark are the Pharisees, but they appear in only slightly more than half the pericopae; further, they often appear accompanied by others (scribes, Herodians, John's disciples), and there are quite a few others (e.g., scribes) cited alone. (Interestingly, the Herodians found three times in Mark disappear except for Matthew 22:15-16.)

3. There is a tendency to add the Pharisees or to change from another name to the Pharisees in the synoptic parallels where Mark does not have them.

4. The teachings of the Pharisees include agricultural law, the Sabbath, washing, and ritual purity in general. They also ask Jesus about the messiah and Roman rule.

5. The pericopae that imply special religious authority for the Pharisees are in the later sources (Mat. 23:2; John 9:22-35; 12:42).

---

[16] Q is conventionally cited according to Luke chapter and verse numbering.

Book of Acts

There is considerable disagreement among New Testament scholars on the extent to which Acts is a credible historical source.[17]

Acts 4:1-2:

> While Peter and John were speaking to the people, the priests, the captain of the temple, and the Sadducees came to them, much annoyed because they were teaching the people and proclaiming that in Jesus there is the resurrection of the dead.

Acts 5:17-39:

> Then the high priest took action; he and all who were with him (that is, the sect of the Sadducees), being filled with jealousy, arrested the apostles and put them in the public prison.... When the high priest and those with him arrived, they called together the council and the whole body of the elders of Israel, and sent to the prison to have them brought.... When they heard this, they were enraged and wanted to kill them. But a Pharisee in the council named Gamaliel, a teacher of the law, respected by all the people, stood up and ordered the men to be put outside for a short time....

Acts 22:3:

> "I am a Jew, born in Tarsus in Cilicia, but brought up in this city at the feet of Gamaliel, educated strictly according to our ancestral law, being zealous for God, just as all of you are today."

Acts 22:30—23:10:

> Since he wanted to find out what Paul was being accused of by the Jews, the next day he released him and ordered the chief priests and the entire council to meet.... When Paul noticed that some were Sadducees and others were Pharisees, he called out in the council, "Brothers, I am a Pharisee, a son of Pharisees. I am on trial concerning the hope of the resurrection of the dead." When he said this, a dissension began between the Pharisees and the Sadducees, and the assembly was divided. (The Sadducees say that there is no resurrection, or angel, or spirit; but the Pharisees acknowledge all three.)

The Sadducees are associated with the high priest. In addition they form an important part of the Sanhedrin. There are also Pharisees on the Sanhedrin, though the Sadducees are dominant even in the 60s.

---

[17] For a useful summary of the major positions, see A.J. Mattill, Jr., "The Value of Acts as a Source for the Study of Paul," in C.H. Talbert, ed., *Perspectives on Luke-Acts* (Edinburgh, 1978), pp. 76-98.

The Pharisee Gamaliel is usually identified with Gamaliel the Elder, and the portrayals of him in Acts and in Rabbinic literature are remarkably parallel.[18] The statement that Paul studied under Gamaliel has no confirmation in the genuine Pauline writings.

Rabbinic Literature

Zaddûqîm *and* Perûshîm *in Tannaitic Sources*[19]

A number of passages in Tannaitic literature that mention the *Zaddûqîm* and *Perûshîm* have been taken at one time or another to refer to the Sadducees and Pharisees of the Greek sources. Here is a brief list of the main ones:

M. Hag. 2:7: This compares the relative purity of the clothes of different groups: the *am haaretz*, the *Perûshîm*, those who eat heave offerings, those dealing with the water of the sin offering.

M. Sot. 3:4: a saying of various things that wear out the world, including a foolish saint, a clever fool, a hypocritical woman, and the wounds of the *Perûshîm*.

M. Mak. 1:6: differences between the *Zaddûqîm* and sages on the question of executing false witnesses.

M. Men. 10:3: the Boethusians and the wave-sheaf day.

M. Toh. 4:12: cleanness of the *perîshût*.

M. Par. 3:7 : the *Zaddûqîm* and the *Tevûl yôm*.

M. Nid. 4:2: daughters of *Zaddûqîm* are like the daughters of the Samaritans (with regard to menstrual impurity) unless they separate and follow the "Israelites."

M. Yad. 4:6-8: differences between the *Zaddûqîm* and *Perûshîm* on various matters of halakhah.

T. Ber. 3:25: the "blessing" of the Eighteen Benedictions about the *minim* includes that against the *Perûshîm*.

T. Shab. 1:15: a *zav* of the *Perûshîm* does not eat with a *zav* of the *am haaretz*.

T. R.H. 1:15: the Boethusians hire witnesses to mislead the sages about the new moon because of the counting of Pentecost.

---

[18] See Jacob Neusner, *The Rabbinic Traditions about the Pharisees* (Leiden, 1971), vol. 1, pp. 347, 373-376.

[19] The main relevant texts have been conveniently collected by E. Rivkin, "Defining the Pharisees: The Tannaitic Sources," in *HUCA* 43 (1972), pp. 205-240.

T. Yom. 1:8: a Boethusian (high priest) prepares the incense for the Holy of Holies contrary to the opinion of the sages and dies as result.

T. Suk. 3:1: the Boethusians attempt to prevent the beating of the willows on the Sabbath, contrary to the halakhah that permits it.

T. Hag. 3:35: the *Zaddûqîm* laugh at the *Perûshîm* for immersing the menorah after the festival.

T. San. 6:6: Judah b. Tabbai wants to root out the false notion of the Boethusians about the execution of false witnesses.

T. Sot. 15:11-12: the rabbis taught that the *Perûshîm* multiplied in Israel after the Temple was destroyed.

T. Par. 3:8: high priest of the *Zaddûqîm*, about to burn the red heifer, made unclean by Yohanan b. Zakkai.

T. Yad. 2:20: debates between the *Perûshîm* and the Boethusians.

Other Rabbinic Traditions[20]

The traditions about the named pre-70 sages and the houses of Hillel and Shammai have often been drawn on for evidence about the Pharisees. The problem is that these figures are not labeled Pharisees. The Tannaitic pericope that talk about the *Perûshîm* never associate them with the named sages or their schools. This might lead one to conclude that there was no connection. Yet this does not settle the matter, because we have the additional complication that two of the pre-70 sages *are* called Pharisees in other sources: Gamaliel the Elder looks very much like the individual called Gamaliel in Acts 5:34; similarly, Simeon b. Gamaliel of the Rabbinic traditions seems to be the Simon son of Gamaliel known from Josephus (*Life* 38 §§190-91).

Summary of Tannaitic Literature

1. The terminology of *Perûshîm* and *Zaddûqîm* is already problematic. *Perûshîm* could be used in the sense of "separatists" or "abstainers/ascetics" as well as Pharisees.[21] *Zaddûqîm* was sometimes inserted in manuscripts in place of an original *minîm* or similar expression.

---

[20] The relevant sources have been collected and analyzed in Neusner, op. cit.

[21] Compare the translation of Herbert Danby (*The Mishnah* [Oxford, 1933]), which generally renders by "Pharisee," with that of Jacob Neusner (*The Mishnah: A New Translation* [New Haven, 1988]), which often uses "abstainer" to interpret the Hebrew word.

2. It is difficult to take all references to the *Perûshîm* as referring to the same group (whether Pharisees or something else). Although the teachings of the *Perûshîm* seem to agree with those of the sages most of the time, it is interesting to see that none of the pre-70 figures is designated as one of the *Perûshîm*.[22]

3. The pericopae about the "debates" (it is not even clear that these were real debates) between the *Perûshîm* and *Zaddûqîm* are given with a bias toward the former. But what emerges is that the *Perûshîm* are interacting with equals or near equals. In other words, despite the pro-*Perûshîm* flavor of the pericopae's present form, the *Zaddûqîm* are able to hold their own or to be treated as serious rivals. There is no evidence that the views of the *Perûshîm* prevail without further ado. One does not get the impression that the *Perûshîm* are in charge of religious belief or practice or of societal norms.

4. There are several possibilities with regard to the historical reality about the debates between the *Perûshîm* and *Zaddûqîm*. They could be (1) a memory of actual pre-70 debates; (2) a memory of debates between post-70 groups; or perhaps (3) an artificial construct to reflect a contemporary debate by using old or traditional names. There may also be other possibilities, and determining which is the correct evaluation is not easy.

5. Dating the pericopae is very difficult. Only two of those with both the *Perûshîm* and *Zaddûqîm* concern matters relevant only to the pre-70 situation (T. Hag. 3:35, on the immersion of the menorah; cf., also M. Par. 3:7, on the *Zaddûqîm* and "the elders"). Another with the *Zaddûqîm* alone concerns matters that relate to a time when the Temple still stood (T. Par. 3:8); the same applies to the pericope about the Boethusians, who seem especially to be associated with the Temple. Most of the others give no indication that they are supposed to be related to Second Temple times.

6. Whether the Boethusians are to be equated with the *Zaddûqîm* is a moot point. No explicit equation is made in Rabbinic literature, yet there are indications that the Boethusians may be closely related to the *Zaddûqîm*. Neither seems to recognize the status of "*Tevûl yôm*," and the debates between the *Perûshîm* and *Zaddûqîm* in M. Yad. 4:6-8

---

[22] Günter Stemberger (*Jewish Contemporaries of Jesus*, p. 44) has asserted that none of the citations with *perush* in the singular is clearly a reference to a Pharisee. This may be true, but it seems to beg certain questions. His explanation of the "seven kinds of *Perûshîm*" pericope, which may in fact contradict this thesis, seems to make use of circular reasoning, if I understand him correctly.

are said, in T. Yad. 2:20, to be between the *Perûshîm* and the Boethusians. Sometimes the high priest is identified with the *Zaddûqîm* and sometimes with the Boethusians.

4QMMT and the Temple Scroll (11QT)

It has recently been argued that some of the regulations in 4QMMT and also the Temple Scroll represent Sadducean halakhah and specifically oppose Pharisaic rulings. I have dealt with the question in detail elsewhere.[23] Out of the seventeen separate rules in 4QMMT, only four have been suggested as agreeing with the Sadducees. Of these four, I argue that only two are possibilities. Even if one or two of these regulations in fact coincide with the views of the *Zaddûqîm* alleged by Rabbinic literature, this is a long way from saying that the author(s) of 4QMMT were Sadducees and opposed the Pharisees.

ANALYSIS IN THE CONTEXT OF RECENT STUDY

The most important fact to notice about the sources is that we have no statement from anyone who seems to be a Pharisee or Sadducee. The Christian Paul claims to have been a Pharisee, but this is also a part of his past. Although late in his life, Josephus seems to claim to have become a Pharisee at age nineteen, this is belied by his own account of his activities and his descriptions of the Pharisees. The Rabbinic sources refer to individuals who may have been Pharisees, but these are either in the past or, possibly, a contemporary but separate group. Thus, all our information is from external sources. Some of those mentioning the Pharisees appear to identify with them or at least to be friendly. With regard to the Sadducees, we have neutral sources at best, while in a number of cases the sources are plainly hostile. It is from the Greek sources that the name "Pharisees" and "Sadducees" are taken; we must therefore begin there.

---

[23] L. Grabbe, "4QMMT and Second Temple Judaism," in M. Bernstein, F. García Martínez, and J. Kampen, eds., *Legal Texts and Legal Issues: Proceedings of the Second Meeting of the International Organization for Qumran Studies, Cambridge 1995, Published in Honour of Joseph M. Baumgarten* (Leiden, 1997), pp. 89-108.

Josephus

Josephus is our best source because (a) he knew individual Pharisees (and possibly a Sadducee) and had the opportunity to know of the groups firsthand; (b) he has descriptions of the various Jewish "philosophies;" (c) his accounts claim to speak of the Pharisees and Sadducees before the 66-70 revolt. With regard to the Pharisees, his attitude seems to have varied (whether because of his own changing views or those of his sources), from very friendly to quite critical. Although he refers to Pharisees in a variety of passages, he makes two essential points: first, he states that they have traditions of the fathers not written in the Scripture; second, he presents them as a group trying to gain political power and advantage. Unfortunately, he gives very little information about the special Pharisee tradition (*paradosis*), confining his observations to the question of fate and what happens after death.

The main question is what place the Pharisees had in society. Few individual Pharisees are named, the main one being Simon son of Gamaliel who was a prominent individual at the time of the 66-70 revolt. Two other named Pharisees (Pollion and Samais) are not described in such a way as to suggest their social or economic background, except that Pollion was able to speak with Hyrcanus II and other prominent people. Pharisees also had access to the women of Herod's court. However, religious teachers may have an entrance into circles far above their socio-economic status. One individual Pharisee is identified as a priest. It has been suggested that the Pharisees belonged to the "retainer" class, meaning those "whose roles in society were military, governing, administrative, judicial and priestly...mostly townspeople who served the needs of the governing class as soldiers, educators, religious functionaries, entertainers and skilled artisans."[24] This has a prima facie cogency, but there is little evidence to resolve the question one way or the other. Their supposed popularity with the common people does not settle the question, either, since popular leaders may come from any class. The few data we have suggest Pharisees came from a variety of socio-economic strata.

---

[24] Anthony J. Saldarini, *Pharisees, Scribes and Sadducees in Palestinian Society: A Sociological Approach* (Wilmington, 1988), pp. 37-38; cf., also his article "Pharisees," in *Anchor Bible Dictionary* (New York, 1992), vol. 5, p. 302.

The power of the Pharisees has been a major area of debate. In one oft-cited passage, Josephus says that they are believed if they speak against a king or high priest (*Ant.* 13.10.5 §§288), and religious rituals are conducted according to their dictates even if the Sadducees are in office (*Ant.* 18.1.3 §§15-17). Although several episodes show the Pharisees in the process of seeking political power, the only time that the Pharisees are shown to operate as de facto head of state and supreme religious authority is under Alexandra Salome. In other passages, Josephus emphasizes the place of the priests in carrying out the cult and in teaching the people.[25]

He speaks of the Sadducees on three occasions: as a group in competition with the Pharisees in the time of John Hyrcanus, as one of the main "philosophies" with certain beliefs (on fate, dependence on the written word, and lack of an afterlife), and an individual high priest who was a Sadducee. Josephus says that although they are few in number, they include "men of the highest standing." This is the only indication he gives of the socio-economic identity of the Sadducees.

New Testament

The gospels are hostile to a variety of groups seen as opponents of Jesus. In many cases one suspects the various opponents are mere straw figures to be knocked down by Jesus, so that use of a particular name has no specific content or significance. This is certainly the impression one has with the synoptic parallels to Mark, where the groups named in Mark are often different in Matthew and Luke. Also, the Pharisees tend to appear in the two later gospels where they do not occur in Mark. In John "the Jews" have ceased to be the Jewish people and become simply an opponent of Jesus; that epithet seems to alternate with "Pharisee." In Mark and Q, the Pharisees are not said to have special religious authority; it is in Mat. 23:2 that they sit in Moses' seat (along with the scribes), and in John that they have authority to expel people from the synagogue (9:22-35; 12:42).

The one statement by Paul about his Pharisaic past does not give any real information on the group. Acts is especially difficult to evaluate, often being untrustworthy yet at times seeming to have some reliable information. It associates the Sadducees with the party of the

---

[25] See above, n. 15.

high priest and makes them dominant on the Sanhedrin. It also mentions Gamaliel, who has some remarkable parallels to Gamaliel the Elder in Rabbinic literature.[26] Its description of the Sadducees as not believing in angels or the resurrection also coincides with information in Josephus.

The beliefs of the Pharisees coincide in part with the interests of the Mishnah and Tosefta, especially on traditions not found directly in the written Scripture and its concern with details of tithing, ritual purity, and Sabbath observance. The Pharisees are also pictured as wanting to rid themselves of Jesus, seen as a rival and as being interested in the question of Roman and Herodian rule; Josephus has statements on the Pharisees that fit reasonably well with this. The one belief without parallel concerns the messiah.

Rabbinic Literature

The Rabbinic literature is the hardest to evaluate. The pericopae mentioning the *Perûshîm* and *Zaddûqîm* are taken by some as the key to the historical Pharisees and Sadducees, whereas others regard them as practically useless for the subject. Even if one regards them as reflecting actual pre-70 groups, few would see every reference to the *Perûshîm* as referring to Pharisees, or every reference to the *Zaddûqîm* as to the Sadducees. Some would find the decisive window on the historical sects of pre-70 times in those passages that mention a debate between the two groups, yet only two such passages have a definite pre-70 setting. Even if one assumes that we are dealing with actual historical debates between the Pharisees and Sadducees, could these be references to *post*-70 groups?

It is generally assumed that named figures such as Hillel, Shammai, Gamaliel, and Simon were Pharisees. One cannot help feeling that there must be a connection between Hillel, Shammai, and their houses with the Pharisees, but definite proof is lacking. After all, the Rabbinic tradition was quite capable of "rabbinizing" all sorts of historical figures. However, there is some evidence in other sources that Gamaliel I and his son Simeon were Pharisees, and it may be that the family of Gamaliel is an important link between the Pharisees and the later Rabbinic movement.[27]

---

[26] Cf., Neusner, op. cit., vol. 3, p. 291.
[27] Cf., Neusner/Thoma, "Die Pharisäer," pp. 198-199.

A significant connection may be found in the New Testament, which centers the interests of the Pharisees around such matters as Sabbath observance, tithing, ritual purity, and other halakhic matters. Although this is only a brief catalogue in comparison with the entire Mishnah/Tosefta, yet considering the brevity of the Gospel passages, there is an interesting coincidence between the Pharisaic concerns and those of the Mishnah. Sadly, Josephus, who mentions the importance of the "traditions of the fathers" on several occasions, in fact gives little information on the content of the Pharisaic tradition.

Summary and Conclusions

We have essentially three sources, each one with problems of dating, *Tendenz*, and reliability. In many cases, the sources are so problematic, one wonders whether we can know anything about the Pharisees and Sadducees. Yet the main sources all seem to be independent of each other, which makes coincidences between their different pictures of potential significance. Whatever our conclusions, though, they can only be tentative at best; we simply do not know a great deal about these groups.

Josephus is the most valuable source: he knew certain individual Pharisees and had access to information on the group before 70; he wrote while they were in existence or during the time that they were transforming themselves; his biases are probably the easiest to analyze and to take into account. The New Testament writings cover a considerable span of time and are characterized by a generally hostile attitude to the various Jewish groups. Although post-70, both Mark and Q seem to have had some pre-70 traditions and show a more nuanced description than the synoptic parallels and the Fourth Gospel. Acts is very difficult to evaluate. Rabbinic literature is the latest and most problematic to use. Even the Tannaitic writings were redacted long after 70 C.E., and the extent to which genuine pre-70 data is preserved is not easy to determine. References to the *Perûshîm* and *Zaddûqîm* may or may not have the historical pre-70 Pharisees and Sadducees in mind; on the other hand, those figures most often -designated as Pharisee in modern treatments are not so identified in Rabbinic literature. Keeping in mind these major difficulties with using and evaluating the sources, some tentative concluding observations can be made:

1. The Greek sources (and possibly Rabbinic literature) make both the Pharisees and the Sadducees important at least some of the time, beginning about the reign of John Hyrcanus (135-104 BCE). They also make the Sadducees and Pharisees rivals, both seeking political power at the expense of the other.

2. There may have been certain socio-economic differences between the groups in that the Sadducees are said to have the support of the wealthy and prominent persons, whereas the Pharisees have the support of the masses (Josephus); on the other hand, popular leaders do not necessarily come from the lower social strata, and some priests are said to be Pharisees.

3. The Sadducees and Pharisees are also alleged to differ on a number of religious beliefs. The Pharisees are especially characterized by the traditions of the fathers, whereas the Sadducees do not accept as authoritative anything not in the written Scripture (Josephus). The Pharisees believe in the survival of the soul and reward and punishment in the afterlife; the Sadducees reject this. (If the Boethusians are to be associated with the Sadducees, the two groups also differ on the counting of the wave-sheaf day and the celebration of Pentecost.) According to Josephus, the Pharisees (like the Essenes) have a reputation for knowing the future.

4. Two of our sources seem to make the Pharisees especially concerned about halakhic matters. The gospels have them particularly exercised about tithing, ritual purity (washings), Sabbath observance, and the like. According to Rabbinic literature, the *Perûshîm* and *Zaddûqîm* also have certain halakhic differences. The Pharisaic agenda according to the Gospels—as far as one can determine it from the few brief references—accords well with the contents of the Mishnah/Tosefta (with the exception of the Gospels' debates about the messiah and the question of the government of Judea).

5. The sources that depict the Pharisees' general dominance in religious belief and practice come later in relation to parallel sources. Thus, only two later passages in the *Antiquities* state that public worship is carried out according to Pharisaic regulations and that the Sadducees are required to follow them even when they hold office. This is not stated in the *War* and is not borne out in Josephus' other passages on the Pharisees. The one exception is the reign of Alexandra; indeed, the statement of Josephus about the Pharisees' controlling the king and high priest fits well with her reign. Similarly, although the Gospels give considerable prominence to the Pharisees as

opponents of Jesus, only the late Fourth Gospel suggests that they can cast people out of the synagogues. It is also the later passages in Acts that suggest that the Pharisees make up a significant part of the Sanhedrin (though they are still not dominant). The later, Ushan, stratum of Tannaitic literature begins to assert that Hillel controlled the Temple.[28]

6. An important question concerns whether the Boethusians of Rabbinic literature represent another group or are identical with (or a sub-division of) the Sadducees. There is no clear answer on this, but the Boethusians are associated with the priesthood, and their teachings seem to be closer to those of the Sadducees. The argument that the term is derived from the high priestly family of Boethus is plausible and seems more likely than the theory that they are the Essenes;[29] however, in the present state of knowledge, any discussions should not confuse or interchange them with one another.

Finally, I wish again to emphasize the tentativeness of our knowledge about the Pharisees and Sadducees. Despite the vast amount of literature written over the past couple of centuries, we have few data, and what data we do have are often contradictory or problematic. We know little about the structure, aims, or beliefs of these two groups and can only make intelligent guesses about their place in Judean society at the turn of the era. It is perfectly legitimate to attempt to make historical reconstructions involving them, but these must take account of all the data (unfortunately, those that do not fit are too often ignored) and can never be more than theories to be tested continually.

BIBLIOGRAPHY

Baumgartner, Albert I., "Rivkin and Neusner on the Pharisees," in Richardson, Peter, and Stephen Westerholm, eds., *Law in Religious Communities in the Roman Period: The Debate over* Torah *and* Nomos *in Post-Biblical Judaism and Early Christianity* (Waterloo, 1991), pp. 109-226.
Grabbe, Lester, *Judaism from Cyrus to Hadrian* (Minneapolis, 1992; London, 1994).

---

[28] See Neusner, *Rabbinic Traditions*, vol. 3, pp. 255-259.

[29] Cf. Y. Sussmann, "The History of *Halakha* and the Dead Sea Scrolls: A Preliminary to the Publication of 4QMMT," in *Tarbiz* 59 (1989-90), pp. 11-76, especially pp. 40-60. Appendix 1 of Qimron/Strugnell, *Discoveries in the Judaean Desert 10*, pp. 179-200, gives an English translation of the text but not all the notes of the preceding article; on the Essenes, see pp. 111-121.

Grabbe, Lester, "4QMMT and Second Temple Judaism," in Bernstein, M., F. García Martínez, and J. Kampen, eds., *Legal Texts and Legal Issues: Proceedings of the Second Meeting of the International Organization for Qumran Studies, Cambridge 1995, Published in Honour of Joseph M. Baumgarten* (Leiden, 1997), pp. 89-108.

Main, Emmanuelle, "Les Sadducéens vus par Flavius Josèphe," in *Revue Biblique* 97 (1990), pp. 161-206.

Mason, Steve, "Priesthood in Josephus and the 'Pharisaic Revolution,'" in *Journal of Biblical Literature* 107 (1988), pp. 657-661.

Mason, Steve, "Was Josephus a Pharisee? A Re-Examination of *Life* 10-12," in *Journal of Jewish Studies* 40 (1989), pp. 31-45.

Mason, Steve, *Flavius Josephus on the Pharisees: A Composition-Critical Study* (Leiden, 1991)

Mattill, A.J., Jr., "The Value of Acts as a Source for the Study of Paul," in Talbert, C.H., ed., *Perspectives on Luke-Acts* (Edinburgh, 1978), pp. 76-98.

Neusner, Jacob, and Clemens Thoma, "Die Pharisäer vor und nach der Tempelzerstörung des Jahres 70 n. Chr.," in Lauer, Simon, and Hanspeter Ernst, eds., *Tempelkult und Tempelzerstörung (70 n. Chr.): Festschrift für Clemens Thoma zum 60. Geburtstag* (Bern, 1995), pp. 189-230.

Neusner, Jacob, *The Rabbinic Traditions about the Pharisees* (3 vols., Leiden, 1971).

Poehlmann, William, "The Sadducees as Josephus Presents Them, or The Curious Case of Ananus," in Hultgren, A.J., D.H. Juel, and J.D. Kingsbury, eds., *All Things New: Essays in Honor of Roy A. Harrisville* (St. Paul, 1992), pp. 87-100.

Rivkin, E., "Defining the Pharisees: The Tannaitic Sources," in *Hebrew Union College Annual* 43 (1972), pp. 205-240.

Saldarini, Anthony J., *Pharisees, Scribes and Sadducees in Palestinian Society: A Sociological Approach* (Wilmington, 1988).

Stemberger, Günter, *Pharisäer, Sadduzäer, Essener* (Stuttgart, 1991), translated as: *Jewish Contemporaries of Jesus: Pharisees, Sadducees, Essenes* (Minneapolis, 1995).

Y. Sussmann, "The History of *Halakha* and the Dead Sea Scrolls: A Preliminary to the Publication of 4QMMT," in *Tarbiz* 59 (1989-90), pp. 11-76.

III. ISSUES IN SAMARITANISM

R.J. Coggins
Formerly of University of London

A curious ambiguity is reflected in recent studies in Samaritanism. On the one hand, there has been a remarkable flourishing of scholarly interest, which can be illustrated by two examples out of many possibilities: the establishment of the Société d'Études Samaritaines, which has borne fruit in the publication of a number of volumes of its proceedings; and the publication of a greatly enlarged bibliography, consisting of 3653 items, including books and articles in many journals and a variety of languages.[1] On the other hand, Samaritan studies remain somewhat marginal within the larger context of ancient Judaism. Many much acclaimed works have virtually nothing to say about the Samaritans; even when they are mentioned, there is a curious ambiguity relating to their position within the larger context of Judaism.

This dichotomy is regrettable, for it may introduce a tendency for Samaritan studies to go their own way, independent of the larger context of Jewish religion and history within which they must surely have a place. In particular, such an isolation has the unfortunate effect of causing some scholars to detect Samaritan influence and origin in all sorts of improbable contexts.[2]

In the present context, we may identify three relevant "issues" within that more general context that still seem far from any resolution: the question of Samaritan origins; the political, religious and social settings within which the Samaritans are properly to be placed; and their place within the larger spectrum of Judaism, or, to borrow a usage made familiar by Jacob Neusner, where Samaritanism should be placed among the "many Judaisms."

---

[1] A.D. Crown, *A Bibliography of the Samaritans* (2nd ed.: Metuchen and London, 1993)

[2] Pummer has rightly warned against this tendency, in his 1987 article and elsewhere.

SAMARITAN ORIGINS

There has been such a great upsurge of interest in Second Temple Judaism in recent years that it is salutary to remind ourselves of the limited nature of the ancient evidence concerning that period. Perhaps a helpful way of illustrating this may be by pursuing a parallel issue and considering what is known of the origin and establishment of synagogues. The New Testament, most of which we may assume to have been written in the last third of the first century C.E., takes the existence of synagogues in Palestine and elsewhere for granted, so that there is apparently no question of their being a novelty at the turn of the eras. Yet when we attempt to trace their earlier existence, the evidence is extremely sparse and its interpretation disputed. There is no clear, or even likely, reference within the Hebrew Bible itself. Some envisage the institution as emerging from the Babylonian Exile, perhaps as early as the sixth century B.C.E., but there is no secure basis on which to support this hypothesis. So one of the most recent surveys of the evidence suggests that while it is likely that synagogues existed in the diaspora from the mid-third century B.C.E., the data "suggest that the number of synagogues in Palestine before 70 (C.E.) was rather limited."[3]

The example of the origin of the synagogue has been chosen deliberately as an illustration of the problem relating to Samaritan origins. As with the synagogue, the New Testament (or at least some parts of it) takes the Samaritans for granted as part of the ecclesiastical landscape of Judaism. (It is of course disputed whether the Samaritans are properly to be regarded as being within that "landscape;" that is an issue to which we shall return later.) When, however, we look for earlier evidence, it becomes very elusive. Again it is unlikely that there is any clear reference within the Hebrew Bible itself.

It has commonly been assumed that the Samaritans existed as an identifiable group from a period long before the turn of the eras, and, at first glance, there appears to be some biblical support for this, in the form of a reference to them in 2 Kgs. 17:29. The Hebrew *hash-shomᵉronim* is rendered as "people of Samaria" by NRSV, but versions as recent as REB still use the term "Samaritans."

Many studies, including two the present writer published more

---

[3] L.L. Grabbe, *Judaism from Cyrus to Hadrian* (Minneapolis, 1992), p. 541.

than twenty years ago,[4] have attempted to show that the identification of the people of Samaria in 2 Kgs. 17 with the later Samaritans owed more to Jewish polemic than to historical plausibility, and the views there set out seem to have been generally accepted by those who have studied the matter. (The polemical, anti-Samaritan, reading of this chapter will concern us again later in this essay.) From time to time, however, one still encounters treatments that refer to "the Samaritans," as if they could be seen as an established group: occasionally as far back as the eighth century B.C.E., rather more often in the time of Haggai and Zechariah (sixth century B.C.E.), and quite frequently as opponents of Ezra and/or Nehemiah (fifth-fourth century B.C.E.). In fact, there is no unambiguous reference to the Samaritans as such before the second century B.C.E. From that period, the reference in Sirach 50:26 to "the foolish people that live in Shechem" seems to be a clear starting-point. Like the synagogues in the New Testament, only from that point can they be taken for granted as a group within the wider spectrum of Judaism; there is no indication how much further back they can be traced.

It is at this point in our search for Samaritan origins that continuing differences of opinion emerge. For some, the Samaritans are most appropriately seen as inheritors and continuators of long-established traditions originating in the one-time Northern kingdom of Israel. If that were so, it would be proper to consider the Samaritans as being essentially a political or ethnic group. Others, however, hold that their origin is to be traced to what we should regard as more directly "religious" causes, perhaps in a specific breach with the authorities of the Jerusalem Temple, as suggested long ago by Bowman.[5] This debate will form the background to much of this paper, and it is hoped at its end to make some more positive suggestions relating to this problem.

The standard work of reference most likely to be consulted on matters Samaritan is that edited by Crown.[6] It begins with two essays on "Samaritan History" by Menachem Mor. After rightly warning that many of the received views of Samaritan origins are based on

---

[4] R.J. Coggins, "The Old Testament and Samaritan Origins," ASTI 6, 1967/68, pp. 35-48, and *Samaritans and Jews: The Origins of the Samaritans Reconsidered* (Oxford, 1975).

[5] J. Bowman, "Ezekiel and the Zadokite Priesthood," in *TGUOS* 16, 1955-56, pp. 1-14.

[6] A.D. Crown, ed., *The Samaritans* (Tübingen, 1989).

religious polemic rather than historical evidence, he asserts that "our knowledge of the Samaritans begins at the time of Nehemiah's governorship in Jerusalem." Yet the reasons for this identification are nowhere set out; it is simply assumed that the opponents of Nehemiah must have been Samaritans. The chief of them, Sanballat, is described in the biblical text as "a Horonite." There is a dispute as to the implications of this description, but it nowhere has any links with the Samaritans; yet Mor states unequivocally that "Sanballat was a Samaritan."

In fact, the remainder of that sentence should be quoted, for it highlights the problem: "Sanballat was a Samaritan who served as the Persian governor of Samaria." Here two important points are being made that deserve scrutiny. First, this identification gives the Samaritans a political role. One of their number was, it is maintained, the leading imperial representative in Palestine. Second, his seat of office was located in Samaria.

There are difficulties with each of these points. There is no evidence, either in Samaritan tradition or elsewhere, that the Samaritans were in any sense to be regarded as linked with a ruling elite during the Persian period. There is of course danger in separating the religious and political domains too rigorously in the ancient world, but it seems clear that the differences between Samaritans and Judean Jews were essentially over religious observances, the proper understanding and interpretation of sacred traditions, rather than on political issues. And the city of Samaria was never a center of Samaritanism. Though there was a Samaritan diaspora, traces of which may be found at various points in the eastern Mediterranean world, their Palestinian base was clearly Shechem, and the holy mountain, Gerizim, rather than Samaria. For this reason, Mor's further discussion, claiming additional information about the Samaritans from the Elephantine papyri on the grounds that letters addressed to the sons of the governor of Samaria showed that the Elephantine Jews "considered the Samaritans to be their brethren," must also be regarded as suspect.

One other point relating to Sanballat should be borne in mind. It is striking that part of the attack on him in Nehemiah is based, not on any link with a sanctuary on Mount Gerizim, but on his association with the *Jerusalem* Temple. Neh. 13:28 implies that Sanballat's daughter had married a grandson of the Jerusalem high priest Eliashib: scarcely likely if Sanballat were a Samaritan, with their devotion to Mount Gerizim.

The whole issue of nomenclature has caused problems in Samaritan studies. It is well expressed by van den Horst:[7]

> Even though there is a growing awareness among scholars that the Greek terms *Samarites* and *Samareus* and the Latin term *Samaritanus* do not necessarily mean "Samaritan," it is by no means yet common knowledge.... The words concerned can also denote a "Samarian," which is the recently coined term for an inhabitant of Samaria who is not a member of that religious community.

As has been shown by, for example, Egger,[8] the recognition of such a distinction is also essential if we are to come to a right understanding of Josephus' usage with regard to the Samaritans and other groups.

On these and similar grounds, we should recognize that the various stories in Josephus and elsewhere about Samaritan dealings with Alexander the Great tell us little about real Samaritan history. We are still in the realm of Jewish anti-Samaritan polemic. This indeed may pervade much of Josephus' retelling of the people's history. Thornton[9] has argued that Josephus' retelling of events in Deuteronomy, Joshua, and Judges displays anti-Samaritan feeling. It is more difficult to decide whether this was Josephus' own contribution or whether it was already present in his sources; more difficult still to determine the underlying reasons for this hostility. In any case, to revert to the fourth century B.C.E., the article in the *Companion to Samaritan Studies* on "Alexander"[10] rightly ends by expressing a doubt "if there is any kernel of historical truth" in Josephus' description of events.

It has long been hoped that our ignorance concerning developments at the time of Alexander might be lessened through study of the papyri from Wadi Daliyeh, near the Jordan. These date from the fourth century B.C.E., and they have often been described as the "Samaria papyri," because it appears that those who were apparently killed there came from Samaria. But it will at once be seen that we face the same problem here as was noted earlier: reference to Samaria cannot be taken as an indicator of Samaritanism. There is an

---

[7] P.W. van den Horst, "Samaritans and Hellenism," in D.T. Runia, ed., *Studia Philonica Annual, VI: Studies in Hellenistic Judaism* (Atlanta, 1994), p. 33. I am grateful to Dr. Tessa Rajak for making this article available to me.

[8] R. Egger, *Josephus Flavius und die Samaritaner* (Freiburg and Göttingen, 1986).

[9] T.C.G. Thornton, "Anti-Samaritan Exegesis Reflected in Josephus' Retelling of Deuteronomy, Joshua and Judges," in *JTS NS* 47, i, 1996, pp. 125-130.

[10] A.D. Crown, R. Pummer, and A. Tal, eds. (Tübingen, 1993).

additional difficulty: though the papyri were discovered in 1963, and
it was claimed that they would throw dramatic new light on the
history of the period from which they date, very few of their contents
have been published, and those that have been made available have
little bearing on Samaritan origins. They are for the most part slave
conveyances, interesting for the light they shed on the social history
of the period but irrelevant for our understanding of the Samaritans.

At this point, another parallel with the Judaism of the turn of the
eras may be helpful. The time has passed when serious attempts were
made to trace back the origins of Pharisees and Sadducees into the
second century B.C.E. or earlier, for example, by speaking of Ben
Sira as a "proto-Sadducee" or the like. It is now generally recognized
that our knowledge of the Judaism of the last two centuries B.C.E. is
insufficient to enable us to engage in such reconstruction. So it is with
the Samaritans. As we have noted already, Ben Sira speaks slight-
ingly of a community at Shechem (but not at Samaria!), whom he
regards as failing to measure up to his standards of wisdom. They are
a "foolish people" (*goy nabal* in the Hebrew text at 50:26), who do not
even deserve the title of "people." Yet we do not know why he utters
this harsh comment. Perhaps some rift had recently taken place that
had aroused his contempt, but we have no means of knowing what
that may have been, and it is at least as likely that he is simply
expressing established hostility. It is striking and, it must be confessed, rather disappointing that, in their excellent commentary on
Sirach, Skehan and di Lella[11] simply rehearse the standard—and
surely unhistorical—polemic, tracing the Samaritans back to the account offered in 1 Kgs. 17.

The upshot of this somewhat negative discussion seems to be that
attempts to trace some specific historical context as leading to the
"origin" of the Samaritans should be abandoned. Older books used
to speak of "the Samaritan schism," as if there were some event, in
principle traceable, that could have led the Samaritans to break away
from "normative" Judaism. Such a manner of referring to the matter
has generally, and rightly, been abandoned, but its legacy is still with
us. The origin of the Samaritans should not be presented in those
terms. Schur[12] still engages in extensive discussion of the events we
have outlined, as if they had something to say about Samaritan ori-

---

[11] P.W. Skehan and A.A. di Lella, *The Wisdom of Ben Sira* (New York, 1987).
[12] N. Schur, *History of the Samaritans* (2nd ed., Frankfurt, 1992).

gins, but he rightly warns us that "there was no 'Samaritan schism,' the continuity of development was unbroken."[13]

There is a temptation to concentrate too exclusively on these negative aspects of the issue of Samaritan origins. We have seen that some alleged references to them, either as a community or as individuals, are likely either to be polemic or to refer to Samaria rather than Shechem. We have seen how elusive are any possible references earlier than the second century B.C.E. Yet the fact remains that the Samaritans were certainly present as a community at the turn of the eras. The assumption must surely be that, long before there were specific references to them in the surviving literature, there was a group centered on Shechem and Mount Gerizim, which venerated that as the true holy place, in opposition, open or implied, to the rival claims made on behalf of Jerusalem.

If we try to pursue this theme a little further, two broad possibilities present themselves. One is to see in Samaritanism essentially a continuation and development of the older traditions of the northern kingdom of Israel. The other is to envisage a more specifically "religious" cause underlying their emergence: differences with regard to some of the distinctive tenets of Judaism as they emerged during the last centuries B.C.E. Among such tenets one could at once consider as possibilities the place of the one true sanctuary; questions as to true priesthood; the nature of beliefs in a future life; and the extent of the emerging canon of Scripture. No doubt other possibilities could readily be brought to mind. In any case this is a natural transition to the second issue with which we are concerned.

Before we make that transition, it is important to notice that much of the material discussed in this first section apparently relates to a period long before the turn of the eras. But that impression can be somewhat misleading; in a number of instances, most notably with regard to 2 Kgs. 17, we are dealing with a later understanding or interpretation of this earlier material. Such re-interpretation cannot be precisely dated, but it contributes to the general impression of deepening hostility between Jerusalem Jews and Samaritans around the turn of the eras. The point could be further illustrated from references to Samaritans in Josephus, but that is a topic I have dis--cussed briefly elsewhere and it is fully treated by Egger.[14]

---

[13] Ibid., p. 32.

[14] R.J. Coggins, "The Samaritans in Josephus," in L.H. Feldman and G. Hata, eds., *Josephus, Judaism and Christianity* (Detroit, 1987), pp. 257-273.; Egger, op. cit.

The Setting of Samaritanism

It is natural that those treatments of early Samaritanism that either deliberately or unthinkingly identify Samaritans and Samarians should suppose that the Samaritans simply represent the continuation of older northern Israelite traditions, but positive evidence in support of this view is extremely elusive. It seems certain that the material in the Hebrew Bible has passed through a process of Jerusalemite editing, and the view there taken of northern practices is an extremely negative one. We thus have no sure means of knowing whether the Yahwism of the north differed in significant ways from that which came to be established as normative in and around Jerusalem.

Furthermore, after the fall of the Northern kingdom to the Assyrians in 722 B.C.E., our knowledge for all practical purposes ceases entirely. It is as if that whole area was written out of the script, and we can know very little of either political or religious developments. When occasional characters from the north are introduced, it is extremely difficult to decide how to understand their role. As we have already seen, Sanballat, apparently the governor of Samaria at the time of Nehemiah, offers a good example. At one level, it might appear as if he and his colleagues are presented as aliens. Sanballat is called a "Horonite" (exact meaning unknown), and his name, presumably a Hebraized version of "Sin-uballit," might suggest foreign origin, with its link to the moon-god Sin; Tobiah is called an Ammonite, traditionally an enemy of Israel (Neh. 2:10). But our suspicions are soon aroused; have we heard the whole story? The name Sanballat in itself is no more foreign than is that of, for example, Zerubbabel, who was the leader of the Jerusalem community c. 520 B.C.E. and is nowhere subject to criticism.[15] Again, Tobiah is a good Yahwistic name. Further, if the references in the Elephantine papyri are to the same Sanballat, as seems extremely likely and is assumed by most scholars, then his sons also bore good Yahwistic names: Delaiah and Shelemaiah. Perhaps we are dealing here not with foreigners but with those who took a different view of the proper way in which Yahweh should be served. It is then obviously possible that they represented one northern tradition, based as they seem to have been in Samaria.

---

[15] See H.G.M. Williamson, "Sanballat," in D.N. Freedman, ed., *Anchor Bible Dictionary* (New York, 1992), vol. 5, p. 973.

But we have seen that there is nothing whatsoever to link San-ballat with Samaritanism. We have already noted his family connection with the Jerusalem Temple hierarchy. If the Samaritans did indeed embody a northern tradition, there is nothing which would lead us to suppose that it was identical with, or close to, that represented by Sanballat. He, whatever his precise status, was in a position of some political prominence. There is no evidence to suggest a comparable role for the Samaritans or any of their representatives in the period with which we are concerned. Admittedly, it is slender evidence, but the condemnation in Sirach 50:25-6 gives no hint of false pretensions of this kind.

If we look for traces of Samaritan self-understanding in their own literature, the results are very meager indeed. Claims made by the editor of the *Samaritan Chronicle II* on behalf of its antiquity and reliability are now generally regarded with a good deal of skepticism, but it is striking that that Chronicle very consciously differentiates between the true "Samaritan Israelites," worshipping God on Mount Gerizim, and the "rebellious" group who followed Jeroboam at the time of the division of the kingdom.[16]

In practice, therefore, it is only the consistent claims made on behalf of Shechem and its holy mountain, Gerizim, that provide a link between the Samaritans and the territory and traditions of the former northern kingdom. It seems unlikely that that was a linkage of the kind we might describe as "political;" the skepticism I expressed in an earlier article[17] still seems to be justified. Rather it may well have been due to a conscious archaizing, harking back to the evidence set out in the Torah. There is in many strands of Samaritanism a conscious conservatism, a looking back to the supposedly ancient and reliable traditions, a suspicion of what are perceived as new religious developments. It is not difficult to envisage that the "northern" tradition is little more than a conscious seeking for the origins of the true community. Abraham's first resting-place upon his entry into the holy land had been at the place of Shechem (Gen. 12:6). We know that Abraham played a significant role in the thought of the Judaism of the last centuries B.C.E. Where more appropriate, then,

---

[16] J. MacDonald, *The Samaritan Chronicle II (or Sepher Ha-Yamim) from Joshua to Nebu-chadnezzar* (Berlin, 1969), pp. 157f.

[17] R.J. Coggins, "The Samaritans and Northern Israelite Tradition," in A. Tal and M. Florentin, eds., *Proceedings of the First International Congress of the Société d'Études Samaritaines* (Tel Aviv, 1991).

to maintain the ancient traditions than by conscious devotion to his first place of settlement? Van den Horst[18] draws attention to the prominence given to Abraham in two of the few fragments of Samaritan writing that may have survived from the Hellenistic period, Ps. Eupolemus and the "epic poet" Theodotus.

It is indeed striking that Samaritan origins have been proposed for a number of other fragmentary texts from Second Temple Judaism, mostly preserved for us in the Christian context of Eusebius' *Praeparatio Evangelica*. Two such texts have just been mentioned; another possibility is Cleodemus Malchus, whose date is uncertain but was probably prior to the first century B.C.E.[19] All of these texts share an interest in the patriarchs, Abraham in particular, and references to Shechem are frequent. Yet, as their modern editors have pointed out, they contain nothing that could plausibly be construed as a link with distinctive Samaritan beliefs, so that, for example, R. Doran, the editor of the alleged "Pseudo-Eupolemus," rejects the theory of such an additional author, sometimes known as "the anonymous Samaritan," and ascribes all the surviving material to Eupolemus.[20]

Such issues should remind us of the danger of supposing that there was, in the last centuries B.C.E., an identifiable "mainstream" Judaism by whose standards deviations could be measured. Such an idea comes from that type of Christian church history that thinks in terms of a "Catholic" norm and various heretical or schismatic departures from that norm. Rather, we should envisage that within the Judaism of that period numerous disputes occurred on what we should term "religious" issues: the status to be granted to Jerusalem, its cultic officials and practice; the amount of tolerance to be allowed to rival sanctuaries. It is widely maintained that one of the tensions between the Qumran community (whether or not it is properly to be described as "Essene") and the official hierarchy of the time turned on this issue: the wickedness of the "wicked priest" was to be found at least as much in the whole system he represented as in any personal failings he embodied.

Since reconstructions based simply on historical evidence are not viable, it seems appropriate to look for other means of coming to an understanding of early Samaritanism. What may prove to be a more

---

[18] Op. cit., pp. 30f.

[19] All are translated with introductions in J.H. Charlesworth, ed., *The Old Testament Pseudepigrapha* (London, 1985).

[20] Ibid., vol. II, pp. 874-876.

rewarding approach has been suggested by Geller in a work whose main concern lies quite elsewhere. In a study entitled "The Rape of Dinah," he explores the relation between the main stream of Judaism and various alien groups with which it came into contact. He shows how what he calls "the Canaanite slot" of biblical times came to be occupied by the *am haaretz* of a later period and goes on to comment that "Groups such as the Samaritans, supposedly ethnic hybrids, are entirely outside the sanctified pale; for nothing so irritates a world view than a category that crosses boundaries, like heretics and recusants."[21] As we have seen, we should be careful about the use of the term "heretics," but his main point is well taken; the fact that there was in fact no single identifiable mainstream in no way rules out bitter intra-religious disputes, with harsh accusations leveled against those whose view of particular issues differs from one's own.

At this point, one would like to reflect upon how the Samaritans were perceived by other voices within Judaism. Solid bases for such reflection are very few, but Sirach once again provides us with an appropriate starting-point. The NRSV translation of 50:25-26 records:

> Two nations my soul detests,
>   and the third is not even a people:
> Those who live in Seir, and the Philistines,
>   and the foolish people that live in Shechem.

This is based on the Hebrew text and is widely regarded as the most probable understanding. Where the Hebrew has *yosh'be s'ir* the Greek has *hoi kathemenoi en orei Samareias*. The AV/RV translations, completed before knowledge of the Hebrew text became available, followed the Greek here, but all modern translations—including the Jerusalem Bible, which often shows a preference for Greek readings—have accepted the Hebrew as original. Even when the Greek is given its own weight as an independent interpretation, it does not imply that those who dwelt on the mountain of Samaria should be identified as Samaritans. They are clearly distinguished, as a separate group, from *ho moros ho katoikon en Sikimois* in the following line.

More important for our immediate purpose than these textual details are the various descriptive terms used. In both Hebrew and Greek two terms are used: *goy* and *'am.* in the Hebrew, *ethnos* and *laos*

---

[21] S.A. Geller, *Sacred Enigmas: Literary Religion in the Hebrew Bible* (London, 1996), p. 155.

in the Greek. NRSV also uses two terms, as noted above ("nations" and "people"), but by a curious irony there is no consistency in usage between any of the versions. Hebrew has *goy* for the first and third use, *'am* for the second, Greek has *ethnos* for the first and second, *laos* for the second, while NRSV has "nations" for the first, and "people" for the second and third. In the face of such inconsistency, it would be unwise to build any elaborate theory.

There may nevertheless still be some significance in the usage. By the use of these terms, and still more by comparing them with the Edomites of Mount Seir and the traditional Philistine enemies, Sirach is putting forward a view of the Samaritans that regards them, not as one religious group within Judaism but as aliens. His viewpoint seems to be close to that of the final editor of 2 Kgs. 17, which also came to be read as implying that the Samaritans were the descendants of settlers brought in by the Assyrians. Josephus certainly propagated this view, which was also implicit in the description of the Samaritans as "Kuthim." He also describes the Samaritans as an *ethnos*.

This brings us to the important issue of how the Samaritans were to be "placed" within the larger framework of Judaism at the turn of the eras. Was a political description of the kind we have just noticed an appropriate one, so that the Samaritans really did represent a distinct ethnic group? Or was this no more than hostile propaganda, the alienation of any whose religious practices did not correspond to what was deemed appropriate? One is reminded of the speculation that there might be links between the Qumran community and the Samaritans,[22] a speculation based less on positive evidence than on the similar alienation from the Jerusalem authorities.

Evidence of a somewhat different kind may here be drawn from the New Testament and particularly from the Gospel of Luke and the Acts of the Apostles. The commissioning of the apostles at Acts 1:8 speaks of them as witnesses "in Jerusalem, in all Judea and Samaria, and to the ends of the earth." It is agreed that the author of Acts envisages a mission to both Jews and gentiles; much less obvious is whether Samaria here refers to the Samaritans, and, if so, whether they are to be considered as being among the gentiles or within Judaism. Scholars have disagreed sharply on this point, some claiming that for the author of Luke-Acts the Samaritans were gentiles,

---

[22] J. Massingberd Ford, "Can We Exclude Samaritan Influence from Qumran?," in *Revue de Qumran* 6, 1967, pp. 109-129.

others placing them firmly within the spectrum of Judaism. My own conclusion set out some years ago[23] is one that I should still wish to maintain, that "Just as it is clearly wrong to regard the Samaritans as Gentiles *tout court*, so it equally impossible to treat them as Jews *tout court*." They occupied an ambiguous position, not neatly classifiable for the author of Luke-Acts as either Jew or gentile. And that is precisely the kind of situation described by Geller that often leads to the bitterest tension.

SAMARITANISM WITHIN THE SPECTRUM OF JUDAISM

Much of this essay must have seemed excessively negative in its approach, focusing on the difficulties of knowing anything about the Samaritanism of the turn of the eras. I conclude with a proposal that will, I hope, be more positive. It is admittedly speculative, but often the rash speculations of one scholar can lead colleagues to more appropriately nuanced assessments of the evidence.

It is now widely recognized that the Judaism centered upon Jerusalem in the earlier part of the Second Temple period can be understood as a "Citizen-Temple Community." The phrase is taken from the work of J. Weinberg,[24] and while many details have been questioned and refined, the basic concept he proposed is now widely accepted. The group centered on Jerusalem and its immediate environs during the Persian and earlier Hellenistic periods owed its existence to the Temple and all that it meant in terms of economic and political, as well as religious, identity. Characteristic of the period from the foundation of the Second Temple right down to the second century B.C.E. was the influence of the high priest over the community centered on Jerusalem. During that time, we hear virtually nothing of any rival understandings of the people's traditions; they were, as we might say, written out of the script. But that is no reason for doubting that there *were* such rival understandings. It has often been supposed, for example, that the group known as the Tobiads was one such group.[25] Similarly, those whose loyalty was to the sacred site of

---

[23] R.J. Coggins, "The Samaritans and Acts," in *New Testament Studies* 28, 1982, pp. 423-34, p. 431.

[24] See especially, J. Weinberg, *The Citizen-Temple Community* (Sheffield, 1992).

[25] See the discussion of T. Eskenazi, "Tobiah," in Freedman, op. cit., vol. 6, pp. 584-585.

Mount Gerizim will have offered a rival understanding of the community's history. Archaeological evidence concerning the existence of a temple there remains ambiguous; the evidence presented by Wright[26] has been modified only in details. On this matter, we can only speculate, but it seems likely that, if pressed to describe themselves, they would have used the name "Israelites" rather than "Samaritans."

In the course of the second century, however, circumstances in Jerusalem changed dramatically. Whether the behavior of different members of the high priestly families was as deplorable as it is presented to us in the books of Maccabees need not here concern us; the upshot was that after half a century of turmoil, the Jerusalem community emerged with a very different structure. Now the Hasmonean family had taken control, reviving ancient claims of kingship and political ambitions of a kind of which we had heard little during the previous four centuries. To the best of our knowledge, nothing comparable took place with what we may from this period on call the Samaritan community. They continued, apparently under their own priestly hegemony. The conservatism, the readiness to stay with the old ways, which has characterized much of Samaritan history, would in this reading already have been characteristic. As we have noted already, the earlier silence with regard to the Samaritans now starts to give way to dismissive references to them as failing to understand their true destiny: Sirach 50:26 would be an obvious example, and 2 Macc. 6:2 might also be included here, though there is much in dispute about the proper interpretation of that passage.

There is, in short, no easy and generally acceptable answer to the question of where we place Samaritanism within the spectrum of Judaism. If it is indeed legitimate to speak of "many Judaisms" at the turn of the eras, then it is right that the role of Samaritans as embodying one understanding of the community's traditions should be recognized and accepted. If, on the other hand, one's definition of Judaism is bound up with a recognition of the claims of Jerusalem, its priesthood and its Temple, then the Samaritans were, as they have so often been since, excluded.

---

[26] G.E. Wright, *Shechem: the Biography of a Biblical City* (London, 1965).

BIBLIOGRAPHY

Bowman, J., "Ezekiel and the Zadokite Priesthood," in *TGUOS* 16, 1955-56, pp. 1-14.

Charlesworth, J.H., ed., *The Old Testament Pseudepigrapha* (London, 1985).

Coggins, R.J., "The Old Testament and Samaritan Origins," in *ASTI* 6, 1967/68, pp. 35-48.

Coggins, R.J., "The Samaritans and Acts," in *New Testament Studies* 28, 1982, pp. 423-34.

Coggins, R.J., "The Samaritans and Northern Israelite Tradition," in Tal, A., and M. Florentin, eds., *Proceedings of the First International Congress of the Société d'Études Samaritaines* (Tel Aviv, 1991).

Coggins, R.J., "The Samaritans in Josephus," in Feldman, L.H., and G. Hata, eds., *Josephus, Judaism and Christianity* (Detroit, 1987), pp. 257-273.

Coggins, R.J., *Samaritans and Jews: The Origins of the Samaritans Reconsidered* (Oxford, 1975).

Crown, A.D., *A Bibliography of the Samaritans* (2nd ed.: Metuchen and London, 1993).

Crown, A.D., ed., *The Samaritans* (Tübingen, 1989).

Crown, A.D., R. Pummer, and A. Tal, eds., *A Companion to Samaritan Studies* (Tübingen, 1993).

Egger, R., *Josephus Flavius und die Samaritaner* (Freiburg and Göttingen, 1986).

Eskenazi, T., "Tobiah," in Freedman, D.N., ed., *Anchor Bible Dictionary* (New York, 1992), vol. 6, pp. 584-585.

Ford, J. Massingberd, "Can We Exclude Samaritan Influence from Qumran?," in *Revue de Qumran* 6, 1967, pp. 109-129.

Geller, S.A., *Sacred Enigmas: Literary Religion in the Hebrew Bible* (London, 1996).

Grabbe, L.L., *Judaism from Cyrus to Hadrian* (2 vols., Minneapolis, 1992).

MacDonald, J., *The Samaritan Chronicle II (or Sepher Ha-Yamim) from Joshua to Nebuchadnezzar* (Berlin, 1969).

Pummer, R. "ARGARIZIN: A Criterion for Samaritan Provenance?," in *Journal for the Study of Judaism* 18, 1987, pp. 18-25.

Schur, N., *History of the Samaritans* (2nd ed., Frankfurt, 1992).

Skehan, P.W., and A.A. di Lella, *The Wisdom of Ben Sira* (New York, 1987).

Thornton, T.C.G., "Anti-Samaritan Exegesis Reflected in Josephus' Retelling of Deuteronomy, Joshua and Judges," in *JTS NS* 47, i, 1996, pp. 125-130.

van den Horst, P.W., "Samaritans and Hellenism," in D.T. Runia, ed., *Studia Philonica Annual, VI: Studies in Hellenistic Judaism* (Atlanta, 1994), pp. 28-36.

Weinberg, J., *The Citizen-Temple Community* (Sheffield, 1992).

Williamson, H.G.M., "Sanballat," in Freedman, D.N., ed., *Anchor Bible Dictionary* (New York, 1992), vol. 5, p. 973.

Wright, G.E., *Shechem: the Biography of a Biblical City* (London, 1965).

DEBATES ON THE DEAD SEA SCROLLS

IV. THEORIES OF QUMRAN

Johann Maier
University of Cologne

For a long time it has been taken for granted that a religious community existed at Khirbet Qumrân since as early as ca. 130 B.C.E. and that its members produced the major part of the scrolls remains of which have been found in the Caves 1-11 near the alleged "center," although no single fragment has been excavated in the ruins of the site itself.[1] It was also widely accepted that the supposed "Qumran community" formed the nucleus of at least a part of the "Essene" group described by Josephus (War II, 120-161) and that, in an early stage, they were in some way related to the "Hasideans" of 1-2 Maccabees.[2] Consequently, a widespread scholarly consensus concerning the history and character of the "Qumran community" emerged. It was and is still primarily based on the evidence of the relatively well preserved scrolls from cave 1Q. But in the light of new publications, some of these premises had to be revised.[3]

(a) 1QS has been conceived as the "Manual of Discipline" of the community at Qumran, with an impressive number of parallels to the description of the Essenes by Josephus. It is now, however, generally accepted and affirmed by fragments from 4Q that this copy (written at the beginning of the first century B.C.E.) presupposes a rather complicated pre-Qumranic history of traditions and of redactional phases during the second century B.C.E. We don't really know to what extent and at what time the regulations in 1QS really corresponded to practical life in a group before or during the period at Khirbet Qumrân.

---

[1] On this fact Norman Golb based his criticism of Qumran research. See his *Who Wrote the Dead Sea Scrolls?* (New York, 1994). He supposed that the scrolls might have been brought from outside into the caves. For the archaeological evidence, see now: R. DeVaux, B. Humbert, and A. Chambon, *Fouilles de Khirbet Qumrân et de Aïn Feshkha I* (Fribourg and Göttingen, 1994); R. DeVaux, F. Rohrhirsch, and B. Hofmeir, *Die Ausgrabungen von Qumran und En Feschcha* (Die Grabungstagebücher, 1996).

[2] J. Kampen, *The Hasideans and the Origin of Pharisaism. A Study in 1 and 2 Maccabees* (Atlanta, 1988).

[3] Cf., vol. I, pp. 84-108.

It is clear that it was a group dominated by priests who aligned themselves to the Sadoqite tradition, to the priestly elite. Thus their traditions and points of view cannot be derived and explained only as results of a "sectarian development," for they represented at least in part the heritage of Sadoqite priests who maintained older official positions. In that sense and to that extent, the group behind the Qumran texts represented a "conservative" wing of the priestly Sadoqite elite. Also the *yahad* as an organizational device seems to be pre-Qumranic, originally connected with the self-administration of the priests in service at the Temple and subsequently adapted and developed according to the requirements of the separated group.

The relationship between "old" and "new" (or "sectarian") is, consequently, more complicated than usually assumed, and its definition depends on the respective theories of the pre-history of the Qumranic evidence.

(b) The "Sadoqite Documents" (or CD: *Covenant of Damascus*), known from medieval manuscripts, have been associated with related communities outside of Khirbet Qumrân and were attributed by most scholars to the married branch of the Essenes, described by Josephus in War II, 160-161. After the publication of the fragments from 4Q, a similar situation emerged for CD as for the case of 1QS: even as we have more text and text forms and know more about their contents and tendencies, their historical and social function remains a riddle.

(c) The hymns in 1QH. Many scholars interpreted a number of them as expressions of the personal experiences and convictions of the "Teacher of Righteousness," in most cases doing so in order to find (or construct) parallels and contrasts to the historical Jesus.

(d) The description of the eschatological war in 1QM and the eschatological "Order of the community" in 1Q28a (1QSa) with liturgical benedictions for the installation of functionaries in 1Q28b (1QSb) revealed a priestly dominated constitutional device. Research concentrated, however, on the ("anointed") functionaries (High priest and ruler), interpreting them as "messiahs," more or less according to a christological "savior" figure.

e) The Pesher-commentaries, all of them relatively late, written after ca. 63 B.C.E. (in the Roman period), are the basis for the historical locating of the texts. For the reconstruction of the community's history, scholars used to combine hints at events and at persons in the Habakkuk Pesher (1QpHab), in the Pesher Nahum (4Q169) and in a Pesher to Psalms (4Q171) with dates reported in 1-2 Maccabees and in the works of Flavius Josephus concerning the history of the Maccabees and, particularly, Jonathan Maccabaeus. The documentary foundations for this construction are, however, rather feeble, its character being by far more hypothetical than usually assumed.[4]

Only in a few instances is it possible to identify some of the mentioned events or persons through reference to corresponding passages in non-Qumranic sources, and these passages concern Alexander Yannai (103-76 B.C.E.), the last prominent Hasmonean ruler. The passages about persons and events in connection with the "Teacher of Righteousness" and the decisive early phase of development of the group behind the texts, are, on the contrary, by far more enigmatic. Due to the authors' desire to stress the fundamental traits and essential issues of what they saw as a crucial period in the history of Israel, they omitted names and individual characteristics of persons as well as concrete dates that had only "historical" value. For they did not intend to write a documentary history but to describe the decisive processes of an eschatological drama. They focused, therefore, on the function of the "Teacher of Righteousness" and did not even mention his name. They described the disastrous consequences of the activities of his adversaries, naming them only with pejorative nicknames according to their negative role in this drama, for instance, "Man/Preacher of lies," "Scoffer," "Wicked priest" etc. The "scoffer" separated himself with his adherents from the "Teacher of Righteousness" on a not-specified date during the early phase of these developments (cf., CD I, 14); a "wicked priest" appeared at the place of the "Teacher of Righteousness" just on the Day of Atonement (according to the solar oriented calendar) in order to "swallow him" (1QpHab XI,4-8), etc. Such events were not conceived as mere "historical" occurrences but as decisive steps in the course of "the end of the days," partly prefigured by corresponding events in Israel's past. The events are evaluated as steps in a process that transcends the human realm, so that the historical and individual character of events and persons withdraws into the background. They appear on the stage only in their alleged eschatological role, accentuated by contrasting lighting techniques, suggesting at the same time corresponding and interfering actions that take place on a human, cosmological-angelological and demonological level of the stage.

---

[4] See the critical appraisal by P.R. Callaway, *The History of the Qumran Community* (Sheffield, 1988).

The reconstruction of the pre-history of the Qumran community on the basis of such dates and statements in the *Pesharim* is, consequently, a difficult task. In 1-2 Maccabees and in Josephus, the Hellenization of Jerusalem appears as the core of the conflict in the early second century B.C.E. The authors of the Qumran *Pesharim* evidently saw its essential causes in other issues that had already been disputed a long time before.

Theories about the pre-history of the Qumran community and its relationship to "Hasideans" and "Essenes" have emerged to bolster the larger consensus just described. Particularly prominent are the theories of Philip R. Davies[5] and the "Groningen hypothesis."[6] The latter is now of particular interest because of the assumption that the polemic designation "wicked priest" refers not to one Hasmonean high priest (Jonathan) alone but to any high priest regarded as illegitimate by the followers of the "Teacher of Righteousness." The wider chronological horizon of this hypothesis corresponds to the chronographic evidence implied in calendaric texts from cave 4.

New Evidence

Due to a re-examination of the archaeological evidence and the publication of new texts, particularly from 4Q and 11Q, the apparently firmly established picture of the "Qumran community" has changed in several respects.

(a) The assumption that the installations at Khirbet Qumrân had been founded in about 130 B.C.E. was based on the restricted and dubious numismatic evidence favored by R. DeVaux in order to arrive at a comparatively early date. More likely, construction of the installations began under Alexander Yannai (103-76), towards 100 B.C.E.

(b) The "Covenant in the Land of Damascus," mentioned in CD as a presupposition for the correct Torah practice as represented by the "Teacher of Righteousness" and his followers cannot refer to a community at Qumran but belongs to an earlier phase of history.

---

[5] See his contribution to this volume; his *Behind the Essenes. History and Ideology of the Dead Sea Scrolls* (Atlanta, 1987); and his "The Birthplace of the Essenes: Where Is 'Damascus'?," in *Revue de Qumran* 14/56 (1990), pp. 503-519.

[6] F. García Martínez and A.S. van der Woude, "A 'Groningen' Hypothesis of Qumran Origins and Early History," in *Revue de Qumran* 14/56 (1990), pp. 521-541.

This covenant predates the split that led to the isolation of the "Teacher of Righteousness" and his group, and the "Teacher" obviously died already some time before the founding of the Qumran installations.

(c) Texts with calendaric contents from 4Q provide the clue for a sophisticated Sadoqite chronographic system based on the priestly service cycles. It implies a world chronology calculated by periods of 294, 340, and, particularly, 490 years, a system presupposed also in the Book of Jubilees, in the apocalypses in 1 Enoch 80-90 and 93, and in parts of the Book of Daniel.[7] The system predates the "Damascus Covenant" and calculated periods of 490 years each for the times of the First and Second Temples.

(d) It was and is still common practice to presuppose in an anachronistic manner an essentially Christian or modern Jewish concept of the "Bible" (and the biblical "canon") for the alleged "Qumran sect" and to assume that the biblical texts (and laws) predate in any case and respect all texts from the Qumran caves. Accordingly, their relationship was conceived as one between given texts (with textual variants) and later interpretations, additions, omissions, expansions or reworking. A particularly crucial point is the Pentateuch. In Christian biblical scholarship, it is usually identified with "the Torah" in general. In the eyes of orthodox Jewish scholars, literary-historical investigation of the Pentateuch—"written Torah" from Sinai, a revealed law "from heaven"—is a kind of taboo. In addition, Jewish scholars like to presuppose a Torah administration that corresponds more or less to later Rabbinic practice.

For an appropriate understanding of the legal Qumran texts it is indispensable to consider a number of points.[8] The first is the common Jewish distinction between "Torah," in the sense of absolutely binding norms tied to a unique kind of "Torah prophecy" (Moses, eventually a "Prophet like Moses"), and normal "prophetic" revelations and other scriptures. The second is the claim to exclusive priestly Torah administration in legislative as well as in judicial respect, as expressed in biblical texts and in Qumran texts that vigorously defended against laicistic aspirations. The third concerns legal history. When the First as well as the Second Temples stood, of course, many regulations concerned cult and ritual. Only some of

---

[7] J. Maier, *Die Qumran-Essener* (Munich, 1996), vol. III, pp. 52-160.

[8] Cf., vol. I, pp. 92-97.

these are included in legal collections incorporated in the Pentateuch, and there they form part of a cultic order adapted to the situation of the "tent of meeting" (or "tabernacle") and re-projected into the far past of Israel's sojourn in the desert. This happened apparently according to a broad priestly consensus in matters of cultic practice. Readers of Qumran texts should keep in mind that the redaction of the Pentateuch took place at some time during the Persian period and that the re-projected cultic order of the "tabernacle" certainly did not replace its model, that is, the cultic order at the existing Second Temple.

It also is evident that the pentateuchal laws do not represent the whole system of law practiced during the various stages of the Second Temple period. There was, consequently, no need to deduce cultic regulations from that re-projected cult order for the tabernacle or to refer to it except in cases of disputes about differing opinions and practices. Even in such cases of dispute, the reference to the written tradition (*katûb*) is rather vague and not a decisive argument, as illustrated by 4QMMT.[9] Current research largely ignores these facts of legal history, thinking instead only in terms of a one-sided relationship between an authoritative "text" (the Torah) and its "interpretation."

(e) The dating of the texts was, from the beginning, intensely discussed. In retrospect, it seems admirable how experts in Hebrew/Aramaean paleography succeeded quickly in establishing the approximate dates of the copies, even as carbon-14 tests provided only rather vague support. Today, however, the technical methods for carbon-14 dating are so improved that their dating of the materials are almost totally congruent with the paleographical datings. The major part of the copies comes, consequently, from the first century B.C.E., a smaller part from the early first century C.E., while another small part was written earlier, in the second century B.C.E. There is, of course, a difference between copy, "Vorlage," and original text,

---

[9] E. Qimron and J. Strugnell, *Qumran Cave 4.V. Miqṣat Maʿase ha-Torah* (Oxford, 1994). Qimron stresses the dependence on scriptural proofs certainly too much; cf., M.J. Bernstein, "The Employment and Interpretation of Scripture in 4QMMT," in J. Kampen and M.J. Bernstein, eds., *Reading 4QMMT. New Perspectives on Qumran Law and History* (Atlanta, 1996), pp. 29-51. Bernstein himself tried for most cases to find a scriptural base but admitted that the text refers only vaguely to the scriptural passages that he and others imagine to have been intended. I suppose that at least some of these *katûb* passages refer to non-pentateuchal law books at that time still extant among priests.

the latter possibly being considerably older. Many Qumran texts are composite works, consisting of incorporated sources and transformed by redactional processes covering a span of time and a number of stages that cannot be exactly defined. They direct our attention, however, more and more to developments during the early Hellenistic and late Persian periods.

f) The description of a third Jewish party called "Essenes" by Flavius Josephus appears to be a an apologetic construction based on four different sources.[10]

THE HISTORICAL FRAME

The new evidence also demands a critical revision of the traditional picture of Jewish history as reconstructed on the basis of the first two Books of Maccabees and Josephus. These main extant sources for knowledge of Judaism during the Hellenistic-Roman periods represent the tendentious view of that priestly party that emerged victorious from the crisis of the second century B.C.E. They describe the events under Antiochus IV (175-164 B.C.E.) as a struggle of pious Jews for the traditional Torah order against the partisans of "Hellenization."

The simple alternatives—"Torah" or "Hellenization"—appear, however, as a propagandistic scheme, for the people behind the Qumran texts saw the primary issue of the conflict in concrete differences concerning Torah-practices within the priestly elite, as listed in 4QMMT. Members of a "conservative" wing strived for a reform according to their norms, and, according to CD I, a return to the correct norms and practices indeed took place 390 years after Nebucadnezzar's capture of Jerusalem. This is about 198 B.C.E., when Antiochus III took over control of Koile Syria. CD I indicates also that the reform culminated twenty years later (about 178 B.C.E.) in radical measures taken by a *môreh çedeq* (usually: "Teacher of Righteousness") but failed apparently already before Antiochus IV.

An agreement between various groups, in CD called the "covenant in the Land of Damascus," served as a basis for the reform. Its failure was partly due to the fact that this coalition split because of the extreme claims of the "Teacher of Righteousness" and probably

---

[10] See vol. I, pp. 85-86.

because of practical difficulties resulting from the rigid legal reform practices. It may also have failed for political reasons, for the practical problems may have affected the revenues due to the Seleucid ruler and given rise to suspicions concerning a pro-Ptolemaic attitude. Such suspicions were not without foundations, for the Tobiad family, the sons of Joseph, pursued not only its own material interests but was in any case involved in the Seleucid-Ptolemaic struggle, a consequence of its prominent role in the administration of Koile Syria and of the uncompromising pro-Ptolemaic attitude of Hyrcanus, the youngest of the brothers, who had his residence at Araq el-Emir near Jericho and still disposed of deposits at the Temple of Jerusalem. He certainly retained tight political relations with pro-Ptolemaic circles in Judea.

In any case, the officiating high priest, Onias III, got in serious trouble, tried in vain to explain the situation at the Seleucid court, and had to take refuge in an asylum near Antioch while, in Jerusalem, the counter reform ran out of control and led to extreme reactions, aimed at the abolition of the traditional hierocratic order, a tendency backed for some time by the new king, Antiochus IV Epiphanes. He is probably the king mentioned polemically in 4Q246 together with his son as pretending to be Highest God and Son of God. Since 4Q390 speaks of renewed apostasy of Israel during the seventh jubilee after the "desolation of the Land" and in the generation of return from exile, it is now certain that the figure "390 years" of CD I (taken from Ezek. 4:5-10) has to be taken literally and not approximately or symbolically and that it refers to events about and after 198 B.C.E. The figure of Ezek. 4:5-10 could be used and understood as a prophetic prediction of this date.

The extremist reformers at Jerusalem did not intend to abolish the Torah itself but only the traditional priestly dominated constitution of Judea.[11] It is, however, certainly not this extreme action alone that CD I and 4Q390 deems the renewed apostasy of Israel; it refers, more likely, to the subsequent rule of the Maccabees/Hasmoneans. Indeed, the Maccabees restored the priestly rule and traditional order, but not in the sense of that "conservative" Sadoqite reform, and they ignored the claims of the "Teacher of Righteousness" to be a Torah-prophet like Moses. In addition, they abolished the hereditary

---

[11] Which Josephus, however, regarded as the constitution in accordance with the Torah.

succession of the high priesthood traditionally held by the Oniad family, accepting this office for themselves as soon as the Seleucid throne offered it to Jonathan 152 B.C.E. And when Jonathan's successor Simon succeeded 141 B.C.E. to get rid of the Seleucid rule, he obtained from the people for himself and his heirs the privilege of dynastic succession, including the functions of a political leader and that of high priest. Hasmonean propaganda added for Simon's successor John Hyrcanus (134-104 B.C.E.) a third function, that of prophet, originally probably in the sense of a "prophet like Moses."[12] In this way they countered tendencies towards a complete restoration of the traditional constitution, including this kind of a "prophet like Moses.

The rift between the "Teacher" and his opponents and the presupposed "Covenant in the Land of Damascus" predate considerably the period of Jonathan and even that of Antiochus IV Epiphanes, as indicated clearly by CD I-II and 4Q390. The issue of the high priest's office was certainly an important point but evidently not the central subject of the controversies. Thus it is likely that the polemical designation "wicked priest" (*kohen ha-räsha`*) was used for each hostile high priest, as has been suggested already for a long time and is presupposed in the "Groningen hypothesis."[13]

During the government of John Hyrcanus (135-104 B.C.E.) and particularly under the reign of Alexander Yannai (103-76 B.C.E.), a remarkable change in the politics of the Hasmoneans took place. They owed their success primarily to laicisticly oriented groups with a corresponding support among the broader social layers of the Jewish society. The Hasmoneans, as members of a prominent priestly class, began after the consolidation of their power to favor again those with a proper priestly background, particularly the group later called "Sadducees" in Greek texts. Their elite members belonged, like the Qumran priests, to the Sadoqite lineage, but, contrary to the "Teacher of Righteousness" and his adherents, they collaborated with the Hasmoneans and strived continuously for political influence

---

[12] Josephus described it in Antiquities XIII, 299f., however, demonstrably as normal foretelling prophecy. He favored the traditional constitution, which provides three leading institutions: high priest, Gerusia, and the (Torah) prophet (Antiquities IV, 218).

[13] A.S. van der Woude, "Wicked Priest or Wicked Priests?," in *Journal of Jewish Studies* 33 (1982), pp. 349-359; Martínez and van der Woude, op. cit., pp. 521-541; A.S. van der Woude, "Once Again: The Wicked Priests in the *Habakkuk Pesher* from Cave I of Qumran," in *Revue de Qumran* 17/65-68 (1996), pp. 375-384.

at the expense of the laicistic oriented "Pharisees," an approach that was particularly successful under John Hyrcanus and Alexander Yannai.

John Hyrcanus had introduced a standing military force consisting if foreign mercenaries and was, therefore, not longer to the same extent dependent on the support of the people. Josephus reports about bitter conflicts and rebelliousness already under John Hyrcanus, whom the Pharisees demanded resign as high priest. Aristobulus I (104/103 B.C.E.) and his brother Alexander Yannai assumed the title "king" and accentuated this the conflict. Alexander Yannai was a rather incalculable politician and a military genius. While his wars sometimes had disastrous consequences with, they led, on the whole, to triumphant results. Notably, according the Sadoqite chronography, his military activities marked the beginning of a new period of 490 years, which 1 Enoch 93 characterizes as "period of the sword" and of campaigns of revenge against the enemies of Israel. The Qumran Sadoqites seem to have pinned their hope at least for a short time on this king and prayed, according to 4Q448, for his welfare. 4Q168 (4QpNah) reports a cruel measure taken by a ruler called "lion of wrath" against Jewish enemies who collaborated with the Seleucids: he ordered them hung alive "on the tree," a punishment that 11Q19 col. 64 prescribes in cases of treason against the people. This corresponds to Josephus (War I, 97-98/Antiquities XIII, 380-381), who reports that Alexander Yannai crucified hundreds of rebellious Pharisees.

"Teacher of Righteousness," Torah Enacting, Torah Directing, and Pesher Interpretation

"Teacher of Righteousness" and High Priest: It is a widespread assumption that the "Teacher of Righteousness" strived for the office of the high priest. Some scholars assume that he in fact officiated as high priest after the death of Alkimos (161/60 B.C.E.) and lost his post in consequence of the appointment of Jonathan Maccabaeus as high priest by the Seleucid king in 152 B.C.E. There is, however, no proof in the sources for such assumptions. The claims of the "Teacher" were, in fact, of a different nature and concerned a function that formed part of the traditional constitution of post-exilic Judaism, prefigured in the concept of functions and authority represented by Moses, Aaron, and

Joshua in the Pentateuch. Moses represents all three functions and in this sense the Moses-figure throughout Jewish history remained unique. Moses himself bestowed the priestly function on his brother Aaron, whose descendants accordingly formed a priestly clan with patrilinear successional claim to priestly office. Aaron, however, and, in the same way, all his successor priests and high priests, were not allowed to appear before YHWH except on the prescribed cultic-liturgical occasions (Lev. 16:2). After Moses' death, God directs his commands to Joshua, whose installation as successor of Moses is described in Num. 27:12-23. But there is a difference, for God admonishes Joshua explicitly to keep the extant Torah (Josh. 1:8-9) as in connection with the king's law. The formulations in Josh. 1:16-18 demonstrate, indeed, a certain affinity between the functions of a ruler obedient to the Torah and the function of the Torah prophet, an affinity found in the case of the high priest. The reason is at hand: the duties of the priest are meticulously regulated, while new problems and questions arise regularly in the political and social realms. Thus the relationship between the Torah authority of the "Prophet like Moses" and a ruler whose primary obligations consists in Torah obedience is in the frame of this constitutional device, from its beginnings a controversial and crucial one. The pentateuchal narratives about conflicts between Moses and the people or certain functionaries are probably echoes of frequent conflicts of this kind during the period of the kings in Judah.[14]

In understanding this concept, the philological and juridical significance of two *termini technici* connected with Torah authority and administration is of particular concern.

Hôrôt and d̂rôsh: The usual translation of the verbs *le-hôrôt* and *lidrôsh* is "to teach" and "to interpret" (or similar). While "to teach" correctly translates the general sense of *le-hôrôt*, in a legal context, the verb means a legislative act that implies an authoritative claim, that of a revelation of *tôrah* (a term derived from the verb *hôrôt*), of God's absolutely binding will concerning a concrete problem, either before the revelation at Sinai (Exod. 18) or thereafter (Num. 12:6-8; Deut. 1:17): "to direct a Torah to somebody"/"to enact or proclaim a Torah regulation."

More complicated are the semantics of the verb *lidrôsh*. Its general sense is "to keep close to"/"to look after"/"to seek"/"to demand." In

---

[14] Cf., concerning the description of Isaiah, P. Höffker, "Der Prophet Jesaja beim Chronisten," in *Biblische Notizen* 81 (1996), pp. 82-90.

forensic contexts, its sense is "to investigate." As a term of oracular practice, it denotes three acts: (a) the question for an oracle directed to a prophet or priest; (b) the prophet/priest demands from the deity an answer to the question; (c) the transmitting of the divine oracle by the prophet/priest to the person who had put the question to him. While they are polar opposites, directing the question (a) and transmitting the oracle/answer (c) could nevertheless be denoted by the same verb *dʳrôsh*: the prophet's/priest's proclaiming act of the divine answer presupposes his action of *derôsh* in front of the deity as a matter of course, and thus the proclaiming act could be named by the same verb. In such contexts, the verb *dʳrôsh* means "to put a question" by the pious as well as "to deliver an oracle (or binding advice)" by an officiating priest or prophet.

In most cases, of the biblical phrase "to seek God," the underlying sense concerns "asking God (practically a priest/prophet) for an answer to a question." This technical terminology remained intact as long as the priestly claim to Torah administration prevailed, notwithstanding a remarkable change. The (normal) expert directed the question put to him not to the deity for an oracular answer but to the authoritative tradition, written or not, and his answer—designated as an act of *dʳrôsh*—got the meaning of an official proclamation of a legal ruling based on extant authoritative sources, eventually but not necessarily including also interpreting steps. It is from this use of the term that the meaning of the noun *midrash* (usually translated as "interpretation") in old times is "booklet"/"official record" (*biblion; graphê*, cf., 2 Chron. 13:22; 24:27); in Qumran texts, *midrash* appears as a synonym of *serek*, "fixed order" (cf., 1QS V,1 par. 4Q256 Frg. 5). Contrary to the traditional lexicographic tradition where for *li-drôsh* and *midrash* the meanings "to interpret" and "interpretation" prevail, there is no evidence for this meaning in texts before 70 B.C.E. Even the early Rabbinic tradition (Mishnah, Tosefta, halakhic midrashim), in legal contexts, never denotes *dʳrôsh* primarily an interpretative act but always as an act by which a concrete regulation is proclaimed to be valid or to be applicable to some concrete case.

The difference in the Qumran employment of the term is not semantic but sociological: the people behind the Qumran texts defended rigorously the priestly claim to exclusive Torah authority, the rabbis claimed this authority for themselves. Even the different levels remained intact. While *dʳrôsh* regards the normal proclamation of regulations on the basis of extant authoritative sources, the verb *hôrôt* and the designation of the function of a *môreh* concern a higher authoritative level. The *môreh halakah* is a Rabbinic authority entitled to direct binding new regulations and decisions in cases in which a solution cannot be obtained by normal procedures. The Rabbinic *môreh* is, however, not a single functionary like the "prophet like Moses" of antiquity; he is, in this laicistic kind of Judaism, one among many who claim for themselves supreme Torah authority and who are, therefore, obliged to discuss every new decision of an individual authority in order to arrive at a consensus regarding the ruling's applicability.

The proper understanding of the semantics of terms as *l̂-hôrôt* and *tôrah*, *li-drôsh* and *midrash* connected with an adequate historical consideration of the concept of Torah in general and of the rival claims to Torah authority on the basis of the constitutional foundations in Jewish tradition are indispensable presuppositions for a proper understanding of the fundamental conflict during the last centuries of the Second Temple period.

Contrary to the usual ideas about "Bible" and "Bible interpretation," a surprising situation emerges. It is generally accepted that the Pentateuch as "Torah" formed the first corpus of the Jewish "canon" and that on that allegedly fixed scriptural basis its interpretation became the foremost task in Jewish tradition. But legal history followed different patterns, the scriptural basis being by far less decisive than imagined. Nothing in the scrolls points to a surpassing legal authority of the Pentateuch. The Pentateuch gained its prestige in legal matters during these centuries thanks to its character as a document of compromise between prevailing Jewish groups (including the Samaritans!) and due to its official role and apologetic quality in front of the foreign powers (Persia, Ptolemaic Egypt). The groups themselves probably never used the Pentateuch as a book of law; they had their own books of law, and they referred to the Pentateuch initially only as a document they had in common with their opponents.

Such Torah traditions and Torah enacting included, of course, interpretative acts as far as written Torah laws were involved. But the hermeneutics underlying these processes were totally different from that underlying the interpretation of non legal texts. The term Pesher (see below) never appears in connection with a Torah regulation and a non-legal text appears never as subject to a procedure called *hôrôt* or *d̂rôsh*.

Môreh çedeq: It is true that Jewish tradition regarded the Torah from Sinai as "perfect" (Ps. 19:8) and as including all necessary regulations for Israel. But this did not mean that all Torah regulations were in any case at hand. There existed, consequently, an institution for cases that could not be settled on the basis of the known Torah rules, an institution entitled to proclaim Torah and decide a lawsuit with the same supreme authority as attributed to Moses. Deut. 17: 8-13 presupposes an institution of this kind as supreme court but mentions there only the claim to absolute authority of this priestly controlled court without defining its membership in particular. In Deut. 18, its decisive function appears in the context of prophecy regarding insoluble legal cases. The passage rejects in a polemical style solutions obtained by (normal) prophetic divination, which it denounces as characteristic for gentiles. For Israel, God provided, on the contrary, an institution of its own, a "prophet like Moses," who is able to obtain the required Torah regulation directly from God and who has the authority to proclaim it as a sentence or to enact it as an absolutely binding law. Flavius Josephus defined the Supreme court of Deut. 17:8-12 in his *Antiquities* IV, 218 in this sense as consisting of the high priest, "the prophet," and the *gerousia*. It may be that 4Q375 contained a description of such a sort of revelatory priestly procedure. The known Jewish sources never attribute to a normal prophet a competence in Torah legislation. They retained in this respect a polemical attitude in the line with Deut. 18, precisely distinguishing between "prophecy" in general and "prophecy like Moses."

1 Mac. 4:46 contains traces of this Torah prophecy. According to it, a decision in a ritual matter (how to proceed with the stones of the defiled altar; cf., Num. 17: 1-5) had to be postponed until "a prophet" entered office; a second instance is recorded in 14:41, the introduction of the dynastic rule for the Hasmoneans under the same condition. The subjects in question are not those of prophecy but legal issues, the first a ritual, one the other a matter of constitutional law. The "prophet" who in 1QS IX,11 is mentioned together with the anointed ones (high priest and ruler) from Aaron and Israel in the frame of the restored constitution of Israel at the end of the days is probably also this "prophet like Moses."

Pesher interpretation: The running Pesher -interpretation of non-legal scriptures emerged as a consequence of a historical situation characterized by eschatological expectations and polemical controversies. The Pesher is a case of perfect harmony between genre and contents. The aim of a Pesher is the definition of a certain span of time or of specific events as part of an eschatological process. In the Qumran texts, the Pesher-method appears in close connection with the claims and activities of a certain *môreh çedeq* who, in addition to his Torah competence, pretended to dispose of the true meaning of prophetic texts. According to 1QpHab II, 7-10, God had foretold all events of the last days through the words of his prophets, but it was a certain priest—evidently the said *môreh çedeq*—to whom God revealed the true meaning and message of the prophetic texts. 1QpHab VII,2 expresses the same idea more precisely: God did not tell the prophet Habakkuk the real meaning and dates of the eschatological events; it was the "Teacher of Righteousness" to whom he revealed all mysteries of the prophetic words. The claims of this teacher concerned not Torah authority alone, which confronted normal men with the alternatives of obedience or disobedience. The claim to know the true meaning of the prophetic texts as regarding the events of the last days confronted the people with the alternative belief or disbelief. At this point the possibility of a sectarian development began to change into reality.

The followers of this *môreh çedeq* applied the Pesher method to prophetic texts (including the Psalms of David as inspired prophetic poetry) and this consequently in the frame of their eschatological interpretation of past and current events. The aim of a Pesher-procedure is, however, not exegesis of the text itself or an investigation of its original meaning but a pre-conceived pseudo-interpretative result obtained independent from text which in this case has only the task to transport the intended message.

Actualizing interpretations of scriptural passages seem to have been a common feature in eschatologically oriented groups and are also attested in later traditions. But in the form of a running commentary to a given text, as a literary genre, the Pesher seems to be a characteristic of the group that backed the position of that concrete *môreh çedeq*. The dates of the extant copies of Pesher-commentaries correspond to the described development: all the *Pesharim* belong to a period after the decisive split that led to the isolation of the "Teacher of Righteousness" and his group and are, therefore, indicators of the sectarian trend that consequently emerged.

SECTARIAN TRENDS

Sectarian trends are connected not only with the evolution of the Pesher-interpretation. Symptomatic of sectarian development is also the treatment of the "revealed" or actual valid law as a secret unknown to Israelites who were not members of the *yahad* (1QS VIII,16-18, 4Q258 Frg. 1 i:8-9), for 4QMMT (4Q394-399) depicts (at least in literary form) an attempt to convince a non-member, although a ruler, that the group's legal traditions should be observed officially. Arcane discipline also surrounded doctrinal contents, as indicated by 1QS X,25 and by the frequent use of *sôd* (secret) or *raz* (mystery) in theological ("sapiential") and poetical-liturgical texts. They refer to creation and cosmos as well as to salvific history, combined with the secrets of cultic calendar calculation and chronography.

It seems that, in the course of time, the treatment of originally arcane priestly professional traditions has been expanded to the specific secret heritage of the group behind the Qumran texts. The concept of election underwent a parallel development. This concept as a whole is, of course, well attested in the Qumran texts, but it is the election of Levi and his descendants, particularly the election of the sons of Aaron, which prevails in this priestly dominated tradition. As soon as the *yahad* community regarded itself as the true remnant of Israel and as the nucleus of the whole of Israel to be restored in the new era, the membership in the *yahad* was identied with the collective of the elected. So the rift within Israel developed into an antagonism between the adherents of the *yahad* and all other Israelites, whom the *yahad* regarded as traitors and as allies of the enemies of God, to be eliminated during the final wars of the "sons of light" against the "sons of darkness."

In this new context, dualistic images and metaphors, frequently used in poetic and prophetic texts, were subjects of a realistic theological, cosmological, and anthropological concern. The powers of light and darkness, opposed since their creation, are continuously striving for predominance in the world as a whole as well as in every single man. Only in a final stage of the eschatological drama shall this antagonism between good and evil find an end, the good ones shall be purified and the evildoers eliminated (cf., 1QS III,26 - IV,25). Some texts even mention a new creation. It is evident that all this transcends the realm of salvific history with the restoration of Israel as its final goal. In spite of such tendencies to systematization the texts contain no detailed plan for the final goals of redemption, nor for the whole of history and creation, nor for man's final destination. The concept of a resurrection of the body is in some instances attested, but this hope seems not to have been a central issue. Comparatively more frequent seems to have been the belief in a kind of spiritual survival after death, more or less akin to the concept of an immortal soul. Still more frequent are, however, statements concerning a kind of eternal existence in terms of the priestly communion with angelic beings.

Apparently it was this priestly view that dominated the self-consciousness of the group and its evaluation of man. For the specific view of the priests' nature and function appears so frequently in poetical-liturgical pieces and in didactic contexts that it determined the religious view of man (within the limits of the group, of course) in the DSS. Man is viewed as nothing before his creator, by his nature only a structure (*yeçer*) formed out of a mixture of dust and water, and, due to his sinful deeds, burdened with guilt and shame. By virtue of his election to function as a priest, however, man gains an exalted position among the angelic servants of the Lord. Unless all such statements were still meant to refer to priests alone, we have to assume that within the *yahad* this concept has been transformed and applied to all members of the group, even if the organizational and social distinction between priests, Levites, and laymen was not abolished.

The eschatology of the DSS is, consequently a complex one. The traditional expectation of a restoration of the whole of Israel and of a certain constitution (with an anointed high priest, an anointed ruler, a Torah prophet, etc.) is still accepted but obviously not connected with the final goal of redemption. 1 Enoch 93 speaks of three eschatological periods of 490 years. In the first one the pious receive a sword to wage wars of revenge and the restoration of Israel and the erection of a third temple shall take place; the next "week" concerns the general judgment of men and the last the judgment of the angels. But one element transcends the realm of history or "end of days," and its basic concept is priestly: in any period of salvific history, the priest belongs to a higher realm, corresponding more to the concepts of holy space than to that of holy times. It is in this—restricted—sense that the DSS at times present a kind of "realized eschatology."[15]

---

[15] In a more generalized manner described by H.W. Kuhn, *Enderwartung und gegenwärtiges Heil. Untersuchungen zu den Gemeindeliedern von Qumran* (Göttingen, 1966).

BIBLIOGRAPHY

Bernstein, M.J., "The Employment and Interpretation of Scripture in 4QMMT," in J. Kampen and M.J. Bernstein, eds., *Reading 4QMMT. New Perspectives on Qumran Law and History* (Atlanta, 1996), pp. 29-51.

Callaway, P.R., *The History of the Qumran Community* (Sheffield, 1988).

Davies, Philip, "The Birthplace of the Essenes: Where Is 'Damascus'?," in *Revue de Qumran* 14/56 (1990), pp. 503-519.

Davies, Philip, *Behind the Essenes. History and Ideology of the Dead Sea Scrolls* (Atlanta, 1987)

DeVaux, R., B. Humbert, and A. Chambon, *Fouilles de Khirbet Qumrân et de Aïn Feshkha I* (Fribourg and Göttingen, 1994)

DeVaux, R., F. Rohrhirsch, and B. Hofmeir, *Die Ausgrabungen von Qumran und En Feschcha* (Die Grabungstagebücher, 1996).

Golb, N., *Who Wrote the Dead Sea Scrolls?* (New York, 1994).

Höffker, P., "Der Prophet Jesaja beim Chronisten," in *Biblische Notizen* 81 (1996), pp. 82-90.

Kampen J., *The Hasideans and the Origin of Pharisaism. A Study in 1 and 2 Maccabees* (Atlanta 1988).

Kuhn, H.W., *Enderwartung und gegenwärtiges Heil. Untersuchungen zu den Gemeindeliedern von Qumran* (Göttingen 1966).

Maier, J., *Die Qumran-Essener* (Munich, 1996).

Martínez, F. García, and A.S. van der Woude, "A 'Groningen'-Hypothesis of Qumran Origins and Early History," in *Revue de Qumran* 14/56 (1990), pp. 521-541.

Qimron, E., and J. Strugnell, *Qumran Cave 4.V. Miqsat Ma'ase ha-Torah* (Oxford, 1994).

van der Woude, A.S., "Once Again: The Wicked Priests in the *Habakkuk Pesher* from Cave I of Qumran," in *Revue de Qumran* 17/65-68 (1996), pp. 375-384.

van der Woude, A.S., "Wicked Priest or Wicked Priests?," in *Journal of Jewish Studies* 33 (1982), pp. 349-359

V. THE CURRENT STATE OF QUMRAN STUDIES: CRISIS IN THE SCROLLERY A DYING CONSENSUS

Albert I. Baumgarten
Bar Ilan University

The importance of scholarly consensus as a means by which we orient ourselves in a realm of knowledge has been much emphasized in the past generation; recognition of its role in creating the framework that enables us to understand the world is now the prevailing view.[1] A challenge to an existing consensus, whether caused by new evidence or by new approaches to already available evidence, is therefore troubling and often heartily resisted. Some respond to that challenge by maintaining the old consensus unchanged, while others may react by making greater or lesser changes to take account of the new perspective. A third possibility also exists: the new circumstances may prompt some scholars to propose new ways of organizing knowledge on the subject, renouncing the old paradigm entirely in favor of some new one. Perhaps the best known of these paradigm shifts comes from the world of natural science, the challenge to Ptolemaic astronomy posed by the heliocentric theories of Copernicus.[2]

These considerations are important in understanding the current state of Dead Sea Scroll studies. The Second Temple period (beginning with the return from the Babylonian exile in the sixth century B.C.E. until the destruction of the Temple by the Romans in 70

---

[1] L. Fleck, *The Genesis and Development of a Scientific Fact* (Chicago, 1979); T. Kuhn, *The Structure of Scientific Revolutions* (Chicago, 1970); M. Douglas, *How Institutions Think* (London, 1987).

[2] As one example of a crisis caused by new evidence in the realm of ancient Jewish history, see the discussion that ensued as a result of the discovery of the archeological remains of ancient Jewry. The radical reinterpretation of E.R. Goodenough, summarized in his *Jewish Symbols in the Greco-Roman Period, vol. 12: Summary and Conclusions* (New York, 1965), should be compared with the minimalizing response of E.E. Urbach, "The Rabbinical Laws of Idolatry in the Second and Third Centuries in the Light of Archeological and Historical Facts," in *Israel Exploration Journal* 9 (1959), pp. 149-165, 229-245. In between these two extremes are the positions of M. Smith, "Goodenough's Jewish Symbols in Retrospect," in *Journal of Biblical Literature* 86 (1967), pp. 53-68, and E.J. Bickerman, "Sur la théologie de l'art figuratif," in *Studies in Jewish and Christian History* (Leiden, 1986), vol. III, pp. 245-269.

C.E.) was a determining era for Judaism. Crucial changes took place between the Maccabean revolution in the second century B.C.E. and the end of the first century C.E., notably the rise of Christianity and the emergence of the Pharisees as the dominant group in Jewish life. Yet our sources for these years are relatively few. Once we exhaust the events covered by the narrative of 1 and 2 Maccabees, we must rely on the historian Josephus. He tells us much of interest about this Jewish world of Palestine, about the Pharisees, Sadducees, and Essenes; he mentions John the Baptist and alludes to the early Christians. Still, his narrative is only at the level of a secondary source, and, for all his merits, Josephus cannot replace direct knowledge of these groups. The New Testament also fills in some details, but it consists of texts sacred to a group that ultimately parted from the Jewish people and was in conflict with much that was taking place in the Jewish world of its time.

Hence the significance of the scrolls of the Judean desert, discovered, beginning in 1947, in caves near the shore of the Dead Sea, in the vicinity of the place known by the modern name of Qumran, and therefore usually called the Dead Sea Scrolls or the Qumran texts. Apparently securely dated by the convergence of paleographic, archaeological, and radio carbon methods to the Second Temple period,[3] these texts, offer unparalleled insight into the Jewish world of that era. While widely viewed as the work of an extreme group or groups, the Dead Sea Scrolls nevertheless can teach us much about the mainstream institutions of their time and thus help elucidate the transformations that took place in those decisive years. For example, they may be able to enlighten us concerning the place of the Pharisees prior to their dominance. Such information is important, for victorious groups regularly rewrite their past, often claiming that they always occupied the place they only achieved later.[4] For this reason, the Dead Sea Scrolls are a subject of great popular interest, whether "at home" in the Shrine of the Book of the Israel Museum or in the

---

[3] See G. Bonani, et. al., "Radiocarbon Dating of the Dead Sea Scrolls," in *Atiqot* 20 (1991), pp. 27-32. On the significance of these results, see further H. Shanks, "Carbon 14 Tests Substantiate Scroll Dates," in *Biblical Archeology Reader* 17 (November/December, 1991), p. 72. These results were reconfirmed in a subsequent independent test, as reported by A.J.T. Jull, et. al., "Radiocarbon Dating of Scrolls and Linen Fragments from the Judean Desert," in *Atiqot* 28 (1996), pp. 85-93.

[4] The classic study remains W. Bauer, *Orthodoxy and Heresy in Earliest Christianity* (Philadelphia, 1971). The extent to which the Bauer thesis could or should be applied to the history of Judaism in antiquity has been the subject of much debate.

scrollery at the Rockefeller Museum in Jerusalem; "on the road," as in the recent exhibition at major museums and libraries in the U.S.A.; or "on location," so to speak at Qumran, a regular stop on the itinerary of tourist groups.

Popular curiosity aside, a scholarly consensus on how to view these documents is essential, for without it we are in intellectual chaos. Without a consensus we cannot situate the Dead Sea documents in their time and place and certainly cannot use them to provide a context within which to position other movements and their histories. A scholarly consensus on how to understand these documents is thus a crucial part of the intellectual framework in which to place definitive moments in the history of Judaism, as well as in the context in which Christianity was born.[5] Challenges to an existing consensus concerning the Dead Sea Scrolls therefore have implications far beyond the explicit confines of Qumran studies.

CONSENSUS FORMATION

The initial wave of publications of the Dead Sea Scrolls took place within a few years of the discovery. It included several works: the Manual of Discipline or Community Rule (1QS), a set of regulations for the life of the group; the Thanksgiving Hymns (1QH), a series of poems thanking God for the life of a sectarian; commentaries on biblical prophets, such as Pesher Habakkuk (1QpHab); as well as Biblical texts themselves, such as the Isaiah scrolls.[6] Analysis of these works led to the establishment of a consensus[7] that asserted three

---

[5] The implications of the Dead Sea Scrolls for the history of Christianity have remained a source of ongoing curiosity and an incentive to speculation. Thus one Greek fragment found at Qumran (7Q5) was proclaimed to be a version of the Gospel of Mark. See B. Mayer, *Christen und christliches in Qumran?* (Regensburg, 1992). Allusions to Jesus or to a crucified and/or resurrected messiah have been "discovered" with regularity in the Dead Sea Scrolls. See R. Eisenman and M. Wise, *The Dead Sea Scrolls Uncovered* (Rockport, 1992).

[6] Of the many English translations available, the most widely accessible remains G. Vermes, *The Dead Sea Scrolls in English* (Harmondsworth, 1990).

[7] The (unfair?) advantage enjoyed by the first texts that come to the knowledge of ·the scholarly community in establishing the initial consensus is obvious on reflection. For one example of the revisions necessary when scholars remember that first to be discovered is not necessarily primary in other senses, see M. Bernstein, "Introductory Formulas for Citation and Re-Citation of Biblical Verses in the Qumran Pesharim," in *Dead Sea Discoveries* 1 (1994), pp. 30-70.

conclusions: (1) that these were the writings of a single group; (2) that group was the Essenes, and (3) they arose in opposition to the Maccabees.

None of the scrolls were found at the site at Qumran proper, which was excavated by DeVaux from 1951-1956,[8] but only in nearby caves. Nevertheless Qumran—the site of a sectarian group with explicit communal food regulations, hence possessing only one dining hall and a single central kitchen (cf., the finds at Massada, at which there were many cooking sites and places where people ate)—was posited as the central locus of *the* group responsible for all the scrolls, though, from the earliest stages of the discussion, it was clear that not *all* the scrolls were sectarian: the first finds included biblical texts sacred to all Jews. Next, scholars concluded that the inhabitants of Qumran were the Essenes, known from Greek and Latin authors—both Jewish and non-Jewish, such as Philo, Josephus, and Pliny the Elder—who lived as celibate communities of males, with common meals and a common purse.[9] Furthermore, this group was believed to have important links to the Sadoqite priesthood, which had ruled in the Jerusalem Temple, supposedly from the days of King David onwards, until they had been displaced by the Maccabees in the middle of the second century B.C.E. This process was understood as having played an important role in the formation of the Qumran sect, where Sadoqite priests occupied a central role.[10] The principal cause of the emergence of the Dead Sea Scroll group was posited to be the dissatisfaction of these priests with their loss of power. This last conclusion was given definitive form by F.M. Cross, Jr., in a paper delivered at

---

[8] See R. DeVaux, *Archaeology and the Dead Sea Scrolls* (London, 1973). DeVaux never prepared a final formal report on his excavations. For the difficulties now complicating the preparation of a final report (made even more severe by the loss of finds in the interim), see R. Donceel, "Reprise des travaux de publication des fouilles au Khirbet Qumran," in *Revue Biblique* 99 (1992), pp. 557-573. For DeVaux's field notes, see J. B. Humbert and A. Chambon, *Fouilles de Khirbet Qumrân et de Aïn Feshkha. Volume I. Album de photographies, répertoire du fonds photographique, synthèse des notes de chantier du P. Roland de Vaux* (Freiburg, 1994). For one example of an important find overlooked by DeVaux, but now the focus of much attention, see M. Albani and U. Glessmer, "Un instrument de mesures astronomiques à Qumrân," in *Revue Biblique* 104 (1997), pp. 88-115.

[9] A convenient collection of these sources, with introductions and commentary, is G. Vermes and M. Goodman, *The Essenes According to the Classical Sources* (Sheffield, 1989). Josephus also knew of a marrying order of Essenes, ignored in the description above for the sake of simplicity.

[10] On the role of the Sadoqites at Qumran, see J. Liver, "The 'Sons of Zadok the Priests,'" in *Revue de Qumran* 6 (1967/70), pp. 1-30. See also the discussion below.

a symposium in March, 1966, and later published in the collection *New Directions in Biblical Archeology*, edited by D. Freedman and J. Greenfield. Cross celebrated the consolidation of "coherent patterns of fact and meaning"[11] in Qumran studies:

> the ancient Zadokite house gave way to the lusty, if illegitimate Hasmonean dynasty. Essene origins are to be discovered precisely in the struggle between those priestly houses and their adherents.[12]

In defeat, according to Cross, the Essenes withdrew, forming their own community in exile at Qumran, led by a counter-priesthood, opposed to all the evil ways of the usurpers.[13]

An important place in this scheme was filled by the role assigned to the "wicked priest." This figure, an enemy of the Qumran community, as is obvious from his name, played a significant part in the writings of the group, such as Pesher Habakkuk. While there was to be vigorous debate concerning his precise identity, the conclusion that he was one of the Hasmonean rulers was widely shared.[14] Consideration of the role of the "wicked priest" thus reinforced conclusions drawn on the basis of other evidence: the identity of the "wicked priest" proved that the community at Qumran was implacably opposed to the dynasty of the Maccabees; understanding their origins as a result of that hostility was thus further strengthened. While there were dissenters from this consensus, some of the latter

---

[11] F.M. Cross, Jr., "The Early History of the Qumran Community," in D. Freedman and J. Greenfield, eds., *New Directions in Biblical Archeology* (Garden City, 1971), p. 70.

[12] Ibid., p. 81. The views represented by Cross were not his lone creation. They represented the culmination of a long series of contributions, made by Sukenik, DeVaux, Dupont-Sommer, and Vermes (to mention but a few of the distinguished members of this chain of scholarly tradition). The notion that the rise of the Hasmoneans created a fundamental change in Jewish life, with the attendant demotion of the old Sadoqite families, is an old one. It goes back, in one form or another, at least as far as A. Geiger, *Urschrift und Übersetzungen der Bibel in ihrer Abhänglichkeit von der innern Entwicklung des Judentums* (Frankfurt, 1928), pp. 101-102; idem, *Judaism and Its History* (New York, 1952), pp. 102-103. Note also Cross's identification of the Qumran group with the Essenes, discussed by him at greater length, "Early History," pp. 75-77.

[13] Ibid., pp. 77-78.

[14] A.S. van der Woude, "Wicked Priest or Wicked Priests? Reflections on the Identification of the Wicked Priest in the Habakkuk Commentary," in *Journal of Jewish Studies* 33 (1982), pp. 349-359, was to despair of the possibility of suggesting a precise identification for the "wicked priest." He therefore suggested that "wicked priest" was a generic term for all rulers of the Hasmonean dynasty.

were dismissed as cranks,[15] while others were simply overlooked,[16] a usual fate awaiting those who do not accept the common view.

The wave of publication of texts that began with the Temple Scroll in 1977 and has continued (too slowly at times) into the present has brought new sources to the attention of the scholarly community. In the process, a significant challenge to the old consensus has emerged, producing a crisis in the scrollery. Each of the challenges has come independently. Each attacked some other aspect of the old consensus, and each weakened that consensus in some way. The cumulative effect has been devastating. As I have discussed the nature of the relationship between Qumran and the Essenes at length elsewhere,[17] I will focus here on the demise of the old consensus concerning the first and third points above—the unity of the Qumran library, its origin in the writings of a single group, and the nature of the relationship between the Qumran community and the Maccabees.

Doubts Accumulate and Multiply

The first significant doubts arose while the consensus that was to emerge was still not complete, as early as 1952, at the time of the discovery of the Copper Scroll, a list of treasures buried in the caves of the desert. That text seemed to come from Temple circles, a world very different from that of other Qumran sectarian documents such as the Manual of Discipline. What did that source therefore mean for the nature of the works discovered in the caves, as a whole? Could scholars continue to consider them as the products of *one* group that

---

[15] One of the most notable players of this part was S. Zeitlin, who in a long series of articles in *Jewish Quarterly Review* denounced the Dead Sea Scrolls as medieval forgeries. A vigorous consensus can be ruthless in branding those who refuse to accept its conclusions as deviants. By a process whose dynamics I leave to others to explain, those regarded as deviants begin to respond as deviants.

[16] This is especially true of Liver's comments on the role of the Sadoqites at Qumran. See further Liver, "Sons of Zadok," pp. 27-30, and the discussion of his views below.

[17] See A.I. Baumgarten, "The Rule of the Martian as Applied to Qumran," in *Israel Oriental Studies* 14 (1994), pp. 121-142; "The Temple Scroll, Toilet Practices, and the Essenes," in *Jewish History* 10 (1996), pp. 9-20. For a slightly different perspective on these issues, but reaching a conclusion I share wholeheartedly, see now M. Goodman, "A Note on the Qumran Sectarians, the Essenes and Josephus," in *Journal of Jewish Studies* 46 (1995), pp. 161-166.

lived at the site uncovered by the excavations? Was only one group burying works in caves, or might many different hands have secreted the texts discovered in modern times? The difficulty posed by the Copper Scroll was resolved to the satisfaction of most scholars of those days by the decision that the Copper Scroll was the product of sheer imagination, thus enabling the old conclusion that all the scrolls discovered were the works of one group to continue to dominate.[18]

Questions, however, intensified with publication of the Temple Scroll (in 1977), a first-person account dictated by God to Moses, containing a revision of biblical law, including a detailed description of the Temple to be built.[19] What did the Temple Scroll indicate concerning the nature of the Qumran library? Was that library a coherent and consistent whole, or a collection of writings of various origin and outlook? In particular, what was the relationship of the Temple Scroll to other works found in the caves surrounding the settlement? The opening salvo in this attack was fired by B. Levine, and he was soon joined by numerous others.[20] Scholars began to posit the existence of a periphery around the Qumran community consisting of groups prior to or contemporary with the settlement at Qumran. Some of our sources came not from Qumran proper, they argued, but from that periphery.

Eventually, the notion that not all the works were sectarian, in the strict sense of the word, became widely discussed and accepted. One of the first questions scholars now ask themselves in evaluating the place of a work from Qumran is whether that work was sectarian or

---

[18] For a recent attempt to assert the sectarian nature of the Copper Scroll, see S. Goranson, "Sectarianism, Geography and the Copper Scroll," in *Journal of Jewish Studies* 43 (1992), pp. 282-287.

[19] Initial publication in Y. Yadin, *The Temple Scroll* (Jerusalem, 1977).

[20] See B. Levine, "The Temple Scroll: Aspects of its Historical Provenance and Literary Character," in *Bulletin of the American School of Oriental Research* 232 (1978), pp. 5-23. See also L. Schiffman, "The Temple Scroll in Literary and Philological Perspective," in W.S. Green, ed., *Approaches to Ancient Judaism* II (Missoula, 1980), pp. 143-155. Many of the essays in G. Brooke, ed., *Temple Scroll Studies* (Sheffield, 1989) treat this issue. Other important contributions to the discussion include B.Z. Wacholder, *The Dawn of Qumran* (Cincinnati, 1983); D. Rokeah, "The Temple Scroll, Philo, Josephus and the Talmud," in *Journal of Theological Studies* 34 (1983), pp. 515-526; H. Stegemann, "The Origins of the Temple Scroll," in *Supplement to Vetus Testamentum* 40 (1988), pp. 235-256; idem, "The Institutions of Israel in the Temple Scroll," in D. Dimant and U. Rappaport, eds., *The Dead Sea Scrolls—Forty Years of Research* (Leiden and Jerusalem, 1992), pp. 156-185; D. Dimant, "The Qumran Manuscripts: Contents and Significance," in D. Dimant and L. Schiffman, eds., *Time to Prepare the Way in the Wilderness* (Leiden, 1995), pp. 23-58.

part of the periphery of texts (now known to have been quite wide) to be found there.[21] The idea that all the works found in the caves surrounding Qumran originated with *one* group was now effectively abandoned. These conceptions also enabled new theories concerning Qumran origins to arise. These theories were based on reconstructions of the relationship between Qumran and groups in its periphery, established as a result of the analysis of the connection between works in the Qumran periphery and sectarian Qumran sources in the strictest sense of the word. At least some of these theories of Qumran origins suggested trajectories in which disgruntled Sadoqite priests played no part.[22]

A substantial delay in publication of further texts ensued in the aftermath of the appearance of the Temple Scroll. A central part in that delay was played by the halakhic letter known as 4QMMT, which was supposed to have been published by 1985 but did not actually appear formally until 1994 (see below, n. 36). The reasons for that delay and the resultant public scandal are perhaps too well known to require comment, but we cannot overlook the role of H. Shanks and of his journal *Biblical Archaeology Review* as a gadfly in contributing to an environment in which delay was no longer possible. One explanation of that delay, however, has been suggested by Golb, and it deserves mention.[23] Perhaps scholars were reluctant to publish their texts because they were aware that these new sources posed a dilemma to the established consensus, to which they themselves were loyal. Not sure what to make of the new writings, realizing that they might overturn views they held themselves, scholars simply stalled, hoping that something would emerge that would

---

[21] See especially Dimant, "The Qumran Manuscripts," pp. 23-58, who develops a coherent pattern of correlation between cave find and sectarian character of the works. Even if some of the works, found in certain caves, have an intimate connection with a sect that inhabited the nearby site (thus, access to Cave Four is impossible other than through the site at Qumran), that is not true of all the caves and their works. There is thus much room for debate and disagreement concerning the manner in which these non-sectarian works reached those caves. For my views on these matters at an earlier stage of my research, see "Rule of the Martian," pp. 138-141.

[22] See for example F. García Martínez and A.S. van der Woude, "A Gronigen Hypothesis of Qumran Origins," in *Revue de Qumran* 14 (1990), p. 537. See also P.R. Davies, *Behind the Essenes* (Atlanta, 1987), pp. 35-36.

[23] N. Golb, *Who Wrote the Dead Sea Scrolls?* (New York, 1995), pp. 177-216. Note that Golb's interpretation of the reason for the delays in publication of Qumran texts, attractive as it may be, is less than perfect: it cannot explain why biblical texts, which posed no dilemma to the established consensus, were also slow to appear.

clarify the significance of these scrolls, while leaving the consensus intact.[24] Whether Golb's suggestion is correct or not, when the logjam of unpublished texts began to break, in the early 1990s, virtually every new source to appear posed a difficulty of one sort or other to the established consensus.

The first inkling of the new round of difficulties, even if not analyzed in any depth at the time, was an observation made by G. Vermes. The "sons of Sadoq the priests" occupy an important place in texts such as the Manual of Discipline and the Damascus Document (= CD; a work of the Qumran type known first from the Cairo Genizah and now from additional manuscripts from Cave Four at Qumran).[25] Their prominence in these sources would seem to confirm the hypothesis that priests belonging to (or at the very least loyal to) the Sadoqite line played a distinctive role in the formation of the Qumran community, as posited by the consensus view. That conclusion, however, was now called into question by the Cave Four fragments of the Manual of Discipline discussed by Vermes.[26] In the

---

[24] On the tendency of scholars faced with uncongenial data to respond with silence, see Kuhn, *Structure*, pp. 81-82, and Fleck, *Genesis and Development*, p. 30. Fleck cites the example of the orbital motion of Mercury as related to Newton's laws: "Experts in the field were aware of it, but it was concealed from the public because it contradicted prevailing views."

Scholars facing perplexing data that confutes strongly held judgments are like the subjects of an experiment reported by Kuhn, *Structure*, pp. 63-65, who were shown normal playing cards, then cards in which the categories were deliberately blurred and made anomalous (a red six of spades, for example). Subjects regularly experienced extreme discomfort as a result of the incongruity. One commented:

I can't make the suit out, whatever it is. It didn't even look like a card that time. I don't know what color it is now or whether it's a spade or a heart. I'm not even sure now what a spade looks like.

In an academic context, a first result of circumstances of this sort is silence. Those who doubt the lengths to which scholars go to save a paradigm should consult Fleck's selection of examples of pure creative fictions, magical realizations of ideas, in which individual interpretations and expectations are fulfilled, *Genesis and Development*, pp. 32-38.

[25] The Genizah manuscripts of the Damascus Document were discovered by S. Schechter and first published by him in 1910. See his *Documents of Jewish Sectaries* (New York, 1970). See now the new edition of these manuscripts, M. Broshi, *The Damascus Document Reconsidered* (Jerusalem, 1992). A pre-publication edition of the Cave Four fragments can be found in B.Z. Wacholder and M. Abegg, *A Preliminary Edition of the Unpublished Dead Sea Scrolls—The Hebrew and Aramaic Texts from Cave Four, Fascicle One* (Washington, 1991), pp. 1-59. See now J. Baumgarten, *Discoveries in the Judean Desert XVIII, Qumran Cave 4, XIII, The Damascus Document* (Oxford, 1997).

[26] G. Vermes, "Preliminary Remarks on Unpublished Fragments of the Community Rule from Qumran Cave Four," in *Journal of Jewish Studies* 42 (1991), pp. 254-255.

crucial places where one would expect to find mention of the "sons of Sadoq the priests," based upon our knowledge of the text from 1QS, they were missing in earlier versions of the source now becoming known from Cave Four.

An uncomfortable question thus had to be asked: if the "sons of Sadoq the priests" really occupied a crucial role in the origins of the sect as the old consensus asserted, how could they possibly not be present in the earliest versions of the Manual of Discipline? Doesn't their later insertion into the Manual of Discipline support the conclusion that Sadoqite lineage did *not* play a critical role in Qumran origins? Vermes' evidence would seem to support the conclusion, already suggested by some, that the Sadoqite phase at Qumran was an interlude, which took place *sometime after the formation* of the group, and was not foundational, as posited by the old consensus.[27] Perhaps the Sadoqite connection was nothing more than a fiction, congenial to be argued at some stage in the group's life, rather than history. If that were the case, it would not be the first example of a fiction created to fill a need at some moment in a group's experience.[28] These are but a few of the possibilities opened by the manuscripts analyzed by Vermes. When Vermes published his article, however, none of these possibilities was made explicit: he merely noted the readings of the Cave Four manuscripts of the Manual of Discipline, the differences between them and that of 1QS, without discussing any of the possible consequences of these facts for theories of Qumran origins.[29]

---

[27] See Davies, *Behind the Essenes*, pp. 51-72.

[28] See the collection of studies published by E. Hobsbawm and T. Ranger, *The Invention of Tradition* (Cambridge, 1983).

[29] Vermes's silence is puzzling, but he was not the only scholar strangely silent on the implications of the 4Q fragments. As Vermes, "Preliminary Remarks," p. 251, himself noted, his predecessor as editor of this fragment, T.J. Milik, reviewed P. Wernberg-Møller, *The Manual of Discipline Translated and Annotated* (Leiden, 1957) in *Revue Biblique* 67 (1960), pp. 410-416. In that review, Milik listed many variants to 1QS from Cave 4 MSS., commented on the distinctive virtues of the readings of those MSS. for column 5, but did not disclose any details of variants relating to 1QS 5, prior to line 26. See Milik, "Review of Wernberg-Møller," p. 412.

How might this reticence be explained? One can only speculate. Scholars often are struck with silence when dealing with material they find uncongenial, which does not agree with conclusions dear to their hearts and crucial to the ways they have proposed understanding the evidence. On this point, see n. 24 above.

Milik in his *Ten Years of Discovery in the Judean Wilderness* (London, 1959) played a key role in the crystallization of the consensus concerning the Sadoqite nature of Qumran origins (summarized above in the formulation of F.M. Cross, Jr.). Vermes too has consistently maintained the importance of the Sadoqite origins of the Qumran

The next problem to emerge was of a different sort, one that could not possibly be overlooked. With the publication of 4Q448,[30] the "Prayer for the Welfare of King Jonathan," the easy conclusion of Qumran opposition to the Maccabees was in serious difficulty. How was it conceivable that the members of this sect prayed for the welfare of King Jonathan the Maccabee? What was this scrap doing in the Qumran library? How could its being found there possibly be reconciled with the usual view of Qumran origins, particularly as King Jonathan was another name for Alexander Jannaeus, one of the leading candidates for the role of wicked priest? A number of answers to this question would be suggested, some of which have a desperate tone, with the insistence of their authors clearly audible: Please do not force us to change views we and many other scholars have held for years!

On the more credible level, several scholars suggested that this prayer was not really for Jonathan's welfare but a curse directed against his rule.[31] Others have proposed that the Jonathan in question was Judah Maccabee's younger brother, who ruled in the mid second century B.C.E., at the beginning of the house's rise to power. This conclusion must contend, however, with the widely accepted view that subsequent members of the dynasty were the first to call

---

group. See, e.g., Vermes, *Dead Sea Scrolls in English*, pp. 21-22, 32. On the role played by Milik and Vermes in formulating and propagating the notion of Sadoqite origins for the Qumran group, see Davies, *Behind the Essenes*, p. 15. Yet the 4Q fragments raise a serious difficulty against that conclusion, so dear to these scholars. Hence, I suggest, their silence. On the role of the Sadoqite priests at Qumran, see now A.I. Baumgarten, "The Zadokite Priests at Qumran: A Reconsideration," in *Dead Sea Discoveries* 4 (1997), pp. 137-156.

Of late, the relationship of the Cave Four fragments of the Manual of Discipline to 1QS has attracted much attention. In addition to my article cited above, see J. Charlesworth and B. Strawn, "Reflections on the Text of Serek Ha-Yahad Found in Cave IV," in *Revue de Qumran* 17 (1996), pp. 403-435; P. Alexander, "The Redaction History of Serekh Ha-Yahad: A Proposal," in *Revue de Qumran* 17 (1996), pp. 437-455; R. Kugler, "A Note on 1QS 9:14; the Sons of Righteousness or the Sons of Zadok?" in *Dead Sea Discoveries* 3 (1996), pp. 315-320; P. Rainbow, "The Last Oniad and the Teacher of Righteousness," in *Journal of Jewish Studies* 48 (1997), pp. 50-52.

[30] See E. and H. Eshel and A. Yardeni, "A Qumran Composition Containing Part of Ps. 154 and a Prayer for the Welfare of King Jonathan and his Kingdom," in *Israel Exploration Journal* 42 (1992), pp. 192-229.

[31] See D. Harrington and J. Strugnell, "Qumran Cave 4 Texts: A New Publication," in *Journal of Biblical Literature* 112 (1993), pp. 498-499. For a more fully developed version of this argument see E. Main, "For 'King Jonathan' or Against: The Use of the Bible in 4Q448," in Orion Center for the Study of the Dead Sea Scrolls and the Associated Literature, International Symposium, *Biblical Perspectives* (Leiden, 1998), pp. 113-135. Main bases her interpretation of 4Q448 on Zech. 2:10 and 2:17.

themselves kings, yet the Jonathan of 4Q448 is explicitly denoted as king.[32] On a less credible level, one scholar began by arguing (on the basis of other Qumran texts) that Jonathan, that is, Alexander Jannaeus (ruler from 103-76 B.C.E.) was not, in fact, a favorite of the Qumran group. Nevertheless, he proposed, the "Prayer for King Jonathan" did not require us to change our view of the place of Jonathan (= Alexander) Jannaeus in the eyes of the sect. The "Prayer for King Jonathan" also contained a section from the extra-canonical psalm 154, and such works, this scholar argued, were much beloved of Qumran members. Hence they preserved 4Q448, without really paying attention to its contents as a whole, disregarding the prayer for Jonathan's welfare (which would not have been to their liking).[33] To what lengths will lovers of literature not go![34] Even more extreme is the view reported to me orally by Dr. Hanan Eshel, as having been suggested to him. The "Prayer for King Jonathan" is admittedly difficult to read, its decipherment a triumph of skill and determination of the paleographers. Perhaps, it was indicated to Hanan Eshel, the Qumran sectarians found it equally difficult to read, hence they preserved it without quite realizing its contents and the difficulty it would pose to accepted theories thousands of years later.[35] If only the Qumran librarians had been better at reading poorly written texts, they might have discarded this scrap and thus saved scholars the need to reconsider long accepted conclusions.

All this might be overlooked as the difficulty posed by an isolated problematic text, perhaps best understood not as a prayer but as a curse, in any case, or perhaps requiring us to change our views of the history of the royal claims of the Hasmonean house. But reasons to doubt the conventional view continued to mount. To take one example, the halakhic letter known as 4QMMT, much discussed even

---

[32] See E. Puech, "Jonathan le prêtre impie et les débuts de la communauté de Qumrân," in *Revue de Qumran* 17 (1996), pp. 241-269, esp. 258-263.

[33] See D. Flusser, "Some Notes about the Prayer for King Jonathan," in *Tarbiz* 61 (1991/92), pp. 297-300 [in Hebrew].

[34] Patterns of tolerance and intolerance on the part of the Qumran covenanters, towards predecessors, rivals, renegades and the indifferent majority merit investigation, as they were neither as simple nor as obvious as might be expected, particularly when approached by means of our logic, based on our experience. Nevertheless, to assume a love for poetry that conquers all begs the question.

[35] In view of the implausibility of this interpretation, and the sheer stubborn refusal to change one's mind it exhibits, I consider it no accident that this view was suggested orally, and that no one has yet dared to propose it seriously in writing.

before its recent official publication,[36] was apparently a foundational document of the community, whose numerous copies indicate its status. Based on the existing consensus, we should expect the "priests sons of Sadoq" to play a dominant role there, and the Qumran sect's hatred of the Hasmoneans to be prominent. Neither is the case. The "priests sons of Sadoq" are never mentioned in 4QMMT, and the letter was apparently sent to a Hasmonean ruler, who was viewed with favor by its author. That ruler has the promise of justification in God's eyes, in anticipation of the end of days, held out before him, should he but choose to follow the advice of the author. All he need do is accept the sect's understanding of biblical law and act accordingly.[37] How can this favorable attitude towards a Hasmonean leader possibly fit with the consensus view that posits an unbreachable gap between the Qumran community and the national leadership?

These texts oblige us to return to a point made virtually thirty years ago by J. Liver. In an article assessing the place of Sadoqite priests at Qumran, Liver noted that the usual view of the role of the Sadoqites could not possibly be correct. The "wicked priest," Liver reminded us, was described as having been "called in the name of truth when he arose (Pesher Habakkuk viii, 9)." The wicked priest did not begin as an enemy of the truth: his origins and first actions were good.[38] This conclusion, which did not fit the consensus view of Qumran origins, was largely overlooked at the time (a usual fate awaiting authors who dare propose conclusions not in accord with

---

[36] See E. Qimron and J. Strugnell, "An Unpublished Halakhic Letter from Qumran," in *Israel Museum Journal* 2 (1984-85), pp. 9-12; idem, "An Unpublished Halakhic Letter from Qumran," in *Biblical Archeology Today: Proceedings of the International Conference on Biblical Archeology Jerusalem April 1984* (Jerusalem, 1985), pp. 400-408; See also L. Schiffman, "The New Halakhic Letter (4QMMT) and the Origins of the Dead Sea Sect," in *Biblical Archaeologist* 53 (1990), pp. 64-73; Y. Sussmann, "Research on the History of the Halacha and the Scrolls of the Judean Desert," in *Tarbiz* 59 (1989/90), pp. 11-76 [in Hebrew]. See also J.Z. Kapera, "An Anonymously Received Pre-Publication of the 4QMMT," in *The Qumran Chronicle* 2 (1990), pp. 1-12. The official publication was as E. Qimron and J. Strugnell, *Discoveries in the Judean Desert X, Qumran Cave 4, V, Miqsat Maase ha-Torah* (Oxford, 1994).

[37] These points are based on a summary of the hortatory epilogue of the halakhic letter, 4QMMT section C. The dilemma posed by this section to the old consensus is such that even when 4QMMT was finally formally published, after more than a -decade of delay (see the previous note, and Golb's analysis of the reasons for delay), there was no full-scale discussion of section C. As Strugnell concludes in his afterword, *Discoveries in the Judean Desert, X*, p. 205: "such an important study remains to be done."

[38] See above, n. 16.

the reigning thought collective of their day). Yet today, in the light of the new evidence from recently published texts, it seems clear that Liver was correct. If the "wicked priest" was some ruler of the Hasmonean dynasty, the members of the Qumran sect thought well of him at the outset. This favorable attitude towards the Hasmoneans displayed in Pesher Habakkuk is now confirmed by a number of other sources. How can we still accept a theory of Qumran origins that argues that lack of acceptance of the legitimacy of the Maccabees on the part of people who felt that they had been deposed by that family is at the foundations of the Qumran sect?

OTHER CHALLENGES

The cumulative effect of these independent challenges to the received wisdom is devastating. Simultaneously, another line of analysis of the Qumran texts was to combine with the considerations above so as to make the consensus view even less convincing. Based on the Jewish-Christian debate, in which the crucial issue was once perceived to be the difference in beliefs concerning the identity of the messiah, scholars assumed that to be the seedbed of sectarian self-definition. Hence they looked to diverging messianic scenarios as a primary cause for the emergence of groups. This situation prevailed until the late 1950s, when Morton Smith pointed out that Qumran and other bodies of evidence made it evident that a single group could hold a diversity of messianic beliefs without being troubled by that situation.[39] If one group could hold a number of views, differences in messianic expectation, Smith concluded, could not have been the seedbed of sectarian self-definition. That role, Smith argued, was to be reserved for the halakhah. Disagree over the law, he suggested, and one has the makings for the rise of a new group.[40]

Evidence published over the years made Smith's perspective seem particularly convincing. This was especially the case when word began to circulate concerning 4QMMT, the halakhic letter from Qumran discussed above, which explained the separation of the sect from other Jews as a consequence of disagreement over the calendar and

---

[39] M. Smith, "What is Implied by the Variety of Messianic Figures?" in *Journal of Biblical Literature* 78 (1959), pp. 66-72.

[40] M. Smith, "The Dead Sea Sect in Relation to Ancient Judaism," in *New Testament Studies* 7 (1960), p. 360.

twenty or so additional points of law. At the same time, the issue of
the identity of the Qumran sect became increasingly muddled. Some
points of Qumran halakhah, upon closer analysis, turned out to share
positions with the law attributed by the rabbis to the Sadducees.[41] Yet
Qumran Sabbath law, as had already been argued by L. Ginzberg at
the beginning of the century on the basis of the Damascus Document, was remarkably similar to that of the Rabbis.[42] Qumran
halakhic terminology and that of the rabbis had a number of crucial
items in common.[43] How were these overlaps to be explained, and
what did they teach us about the history of halakhah?

On the one hand, the potential importance of Qumran evidence
for writing the history of halakhah cannot be overstated. Prior to the
discovery of the Qumran texts our main sources for this endeavor
were Rabbinic. Within this mass of evidence, scholars could attempt
to identify earlier or later strata by means of literary analysis, always
a less than certain enterprise. Qumran sources prove that certain
halakhic positions were ancient, a conclusion we can then compare
with the evidence as seen through the eyes of the rabbis when subjected to literary analysis.

On the other hand, what did these analyses of Qumran halakhah
teach us concerning the identity of the Dead Sea sect? Could one
continue to discuss the group at Qumran as distinctive when their
law had much in common with that of other supposedly rival groups?
If law was so crucial, as argued by Smith and others, what was the
law that made a Qumran sectarian a member of his group and of no
other?[44] Where, in all this complex set of overlaps, was there any

---

[41] Sussmann, "Research," pp. 11-76.

[42] See Ginzberg's studies of the Damascus Document, which appeared long after
his death, in English, as L. Ginzberg, *An Unknown Jewish Sect* (New York, 1976).
Ginzberg's conclusions have been confirmed by the detailed research of L. Schiffman, *Law, Custom and Messianism in the Dead Sea Sect* (Jerusalem, 1993), pp. 90-135 [in
Hebrew].

[43] Sussmann, "Research," pp. 26, 37; E. Qimron, "Halakhic Terms in the Dead
Sea Scrolls and their Contribution to the History of the Early Halakha," in M.
Broshi, S. Japhet, D. Schwartz, and S. Talmon, eds., *The Scrolls of the Judean Desert—
Forty Years of Research* (Jerusalem, 1992), pp. 128-138 [in Hebrew].

[44] Cf., H. Stegemann, "The Qumran Essenes—Local Members of the Main Jew-
ish Union in Late Second Temple Times," in J. Barrera and L. Montaner, eds., *The
Madrid Qumran Congress: Proceedings of the International Congress on the Dead Sea Scrolls,
Madrid, 18-21 March 1991* (Leiden, 1992), vol. 1, pp. 106 -107, and J. Baumgarten,
"The Disqualification of Priests in 4Q Fragments of the 'Damascus Document,' A
Specimen of the Recovery of pre-Rabbinic Halakha," in ibid., vol. 2, pp. 510-513.

room for the explanation of Qumran origins as beginning in opposition to the Maccabees?[45]

COLLAPSE

One last symptom of the dying consensus deserves mention. When a consensus is reigning, its adherents advance knowledge by working on questions requiring clarification *within* the context it provides. The consensus itself is rarely challenged: as was discussed above, challenges, if any, are either resisted or overlooked. In some senses, the consensus matters more than any mere facts, as these facts only have meaning within a consensus. A dying consensus, however, attracts challengers like flies. As the realization spreads that the old intellectual thought patterns are no longer adequate to the job, many scholars try their hands at suggesting replacement systems.

Such has been the case in the past few years in Qumran studies, with articles and monographs all proposing new theories abounding.[46] In spite of Cross's almost triumphant proclamation of the emergence of coherent patterns of thought and meaning around the old consensus, Golb has declared that Qumran was a desert fortress and the scrolls had no connection to the site, having been placed in caves by Jews with a variety of affiliations as part of their effort to save examples of works significant in their world, prior to the destruction of Jerusalem by the Romans in 70 C.E.[47] The Donceels have proposed that Qumran was an agricultural villa of a rich Jerusalemite.[48] Humbert has suggested that Qumran was a Hasmonean

---

[45] This point was conceded by Cross in the concluding sentences of his "Some Notes on a Generation of Qumran Studies," in *Madrid Qumran Congress*, vol. 1, p. 14.

[46] In the discussion below, I summarize briefly different scholarly positions without attempting any evaluation and without commenting which proposal seems more or less convincing. I have adopted this approach because the existence of these different views is the crucial fact for my argument, much more important than what can be said for or against the plausibility of any individual interpretive scheme. Nevertheless, on the other side of the coin, I should note that the ostraca just now published by F.M. Cross and E. Eshel, "Ostraca from Khirbet Qumrân," in *Israel Exploration Journal* 14 (1997), pp. 17-28, are likely to serve as the basis for the argument that only minimal revision of the old consensus is necessary.

[47] Golb has argued this conclusion in a long series of articles written over the years, now summarized in his *Who Wrote the Dead Sea Scrolls?*

[48] For a first statement of this view, see P. Donceel-Voute, "Coenaculum—La salle à l'étage du locus 30 à Khirbet Qumran sur la Mer Morte," in *Banquets de l'Orient=Res Orientales* 4 (1992), pp. 61-84.

villa, at which the Essenes built a place of worship where they offered sacrifices.[49] Closer to the old consensus, but nevertheless modifying it significantly, Stegemann has argued that Qumran was a center of the Essenes, perhaps their workshop for producing scrolls. The Essenes needed many scrolls for the use of their members, because they were the main Jewish group of the Second Temple era. As appropriate to their role as the main Jewish group, Stegemann sees disagreement and mutual delegitimation between the Essenes and the Temple authorities as minimal.[50] Taking a different tack, Schiffman has emphasized the Sadducean nature of the Qumran group, insisting that its members were not different from the Sadducees as described by Josephus and the New Testament. One and the same reality, according to Schiffman, stood behind the Qumran covenanters and the Jerusalem Sadducees whom we know from Greek sources. Any apparent differences are merely those of the perspective of the writers of our sources.[51] Thus, at a later period, Josephus, according to Schiffman, knew a sub-group of the larger movement; hence his Sadducees differed from those at Qumran.[52]

In all these suggestion, what if anything is left of the old clarity of the Qumran group arising in protest against the usurpation of the priesthood by the Maccabees? Very little; in fact, next to nothing.

Which of these proposals, if any, will turn out to be the new consensus? That is too early to tell, but the existence of these numerous new theories, expounded in many monographs and articles, guarantees that intensive discussion will continue. Perhaps the old consensus will yet arise, Phoenix-like, from the ashes of its apparent demise, confirmed by explicit statements in some text as yet unpublished. While I consider this outcome unlikely (the nature of the unpublished material is known, and it has been assigned for editing;[53]

---

[49] J.B. Humbert, "L'Espace Sacré à Qumran," in *Revue Biblique* 101 (1994), pp. 161-214.

[50] Stegemann, "Qumran Essenes," pp. 82-166. Stegemann has expanded the treatment of these matters in his *Die Essener, Qumran, Johannes der Taufer und Jesus, ein Sachbuch* (Freiburg, 1994).

[51] Schiffman, "New Halakhic Letter," p. 72, n. 15.

[52] See L. Schiffman, "Pharisaic and Sadducean Halakhah in Light of the Dead Sea Scrolls," in *Dead Sea Discoveries* 1 (1994), pp. 289-299. Schiffman has recently expanded his thesis concerning the Sadducean nature of the Qumran community in a monograph length study, *Reclaiming the Dead Sea Scrolls: The History of Judaism, the Background of Christianity, the Lost Library of Qumran* (Philadelphia, 1994).

[53] See E. Tov, "The Unpublished Qumran Texts from Caves 4 and 11," in *Journal of Jewish Studies* 43 (1992), pp. 101-136.

if these sources contained information of this magnitude of importance, they would have already come to the attention of scholars), the Dead Sea Scrolls have been a source of unending surprise since the day the Bedouin shepherd entered Cave One. Hence, no possibility can be ruled out with certainty. As the Dead Sea is in an active seismic zone, along the Syro-African rift, the possibility that some future earthquake will uncover new caves containing new texts also exists.

Even events since work on this article was begun provide a perfect illustration of the fact that Qumran studies are an ongoing saga that will hold our attention for some time in the future. For almost fifty years, the area surrounding Qumran has been intensively searched for cave sites, and all existing caves were supposedly identified and explored. Hence, the possibility of new caves' being discovered was raised in the text above only as a possible result of some future earthquake. Nevertheless, the press of August 11, 1995, contained an announcement of the find by Dr. Hanan Eshel, of Bar Ilan University, of four previously unknown man-made caves near Qumran, since then excavated by an expedition led by Dr. Eshel and Mr. Magen Broshi of the Shrine of the Book, of the Israel Museum.

Man-made caves are very likely to contain human artifacts of one sort or other (indeed, six of the eleven known scroll caves were man-made). Finds in the four previously unknown caves, as revealed by the winter 1996 digs, meet these expectations. They elucidate patterns of settlement and living arrangements—indicating that Qumran members lived in caves and tents around the site, coming to the main center to study, purify themselves, and eat the communal meals.[54] The discovery of new caves and their excavation corroborate the sense that the story of Dead Sea Scroll studies may have many more breath-taking episodes before it reaches a new finale.

Whatever the reason, so long as the labor of publishing the full collection of texts is incomplete, no new consensus is likely to emerge. Having been proven wrong in a premature judgment based on partial evidence, the scholarly community is now virtually guaranteed to delay reaching a new common conclusion until all the data is known.

---

[54] See M. Broshi and H. Eshel, "How and Where Did the Qumranites Live," forthcoming in the Proceedings of the 1996 International Dead Sea Scrolls Conference, Provo, Utah, July, 1996, to be edited by E. Ulrich and D. Parry. I would like to thank the authors for discussing the results of their work with me prior to its appearing in print.

The crisis in the scrollery, with all its attendant discomfort, is therefore still far from being over.[55]

CONCLUSION

Perhaps the best summary of the situation one can offer is to return to Plato's Allegory of the Cave. It is unpleasant to be dragged out of the cave into the bright light of day. Those thought wise at identifying the shadows of copies on the wall of the cave may discover that much of their wisdom has been disproved; they may not find the new world of knowledge congenial. New skills are needed to see clearly in the new bright light. Convincing those remaining behind in the cave of the knowledge now available and deserving to be brought to bear on issues of great concern may not be easy: the philosopher forced to return to the cave and explain reality, as only he has come to know it, to the inhabitants may well be executed. Nevertheless, for all the unpleasantness, in spite of all the confusion engendered by wandering around without a reliable guide in a changed world, who would return to the previous conditions? The willingness to acknowledge uncongenial data and the attempt to understand sources that challenge accepted views are, after all, among the most significant marks of historical scholarship, distinguishing the latter from mere rhetoric or propagandizing. The fact that a new consensus will likely only become dominant when the full range of Qumran sources has been published is the chief reason, in my view, for encouraging those responsible to complete their labors as quickly as possible. We depend on their work to establish the conditions necessary for a new consensus and the intellectual order only it can provide. In the meantime, a drama of the highest intellectual order is being played out before our eyes. Even while we are waiting for its conclusion, while the tension of its uncertainty and open-endedness may sometimes seem unbearable, while the pain of abandoning old views can still be felt, there is, in fact, much to learn and even much to enjoy.

---

[55] According to the timetable of the official publication committee, all the unpublished texts *were* to be edited and submitted ready for publication by the end of 1996.

BIBLIOGRAPHY

Albani, M., and U. Glessmer, "Un instrument de mesures astronomiques à Qumrân," in *Revue Biblique* 104 (1997), pp. 88-115.

Alexander, P., "The Redaction History of Serekh Ha-Yahad: A Proposal," in *Revue de Qumran* 17 (1996), pp. 437-455

Baumgarten, A.I., "The Rule of the Martian as Applied to Qumran," in *Israel Oriental Studies* 14 (1994), pp. 121-142

Baumgarten, A.I., "The Temple Scroll, Toilet Practices, and the Essenes," in *Jewish History* 10 (1996), pp. 9-20.

Baumgarten, A.I., "The Zadokite Priests at Qumran: A Reconsideration," in *Dead Sea Discoveries* 4 (1997), pp. 137-156.

Baumgarten, J., *Discoveries in the Judean Desert XVIII, Qumran Cave 4, XIII, The Damascus Document* (Oxford, 1997).

Bernstein, M., "Introductory Formulas for Citation and Re-Citation of Biblical Verses in the Qumran Pesharim," in *Dead Sea Discoveries* 1 (1994), pp. 30-70.

Broshi, M., *The Damascus Document Reconsidered* (Jerusalem, 1992).

Cross, F.M., Jr., and E. Eshel, "Ostraca from Khirbet Qumrân," in *Israel Exploration Journal* 14 (1997), pp. 17-28.

Davies, P.R., *Behind the Essenes* (Atlanta, 1987).

Donceel, R., "Reprise des travaux de publication des fouilles au Khirbet Qumran," in *Revue Biblique* 99 (1992), pp. 557-573.

Eisenman, R., and M. Wise, *The Dead Sea Scrolls Uncovered* (Rockport, 1992).

Golb, N., *Who Wrote the Dead Sea Scrolls?* (New York, 1995)

Goodman, M., "A Note on the Qumran Sectarians, the Essenes and Josephus," in *Journal of Jewish Studies* 46 (1995), pp. 161-166.

Goranson, S., "Sectarianism, Geography and the Copper Scroll," in *Journal of Jewish Studies* 43 (1992), pp. 282-287.

Harrington, D., and J. Strugnell, "Qumran Cave 4 Texts: A New Publication," in *Journal of Biblical Literature* 112 (1993), pp. 491-499.

Kugler, R., "A Note on 1QS 9:14; the Sons of Righteousness or the Sons of Zadok?" in *Dead Sea Discoveries* 3 (1996), pp. 315-320

Martínez, F. García, and A.S. van der Woude, "A Gronigen Hypothesis of Qumran Origins," in *Revue de Qumran* 14 (1990), pp. 521-541.

Rainbow, P., "The Last Oniad and the Teacher of Righteousness," in *Journal of Jewish Studies* 48 (1997), pp. 30-52.

Schiffman, L., "Pharisaic and Sadducean Halakhah in Light of the Dead Sea Scrolls," in *Dead Sea Discoveries* 1 (1994).

Schiffman, L., "The Temple Scroll in Literary and Philological Perspective," in W.S. Green, ed., *Approaches to Ancient Judaism* II (Missoula, 1980).

Schiffman, L., *Reclaiming the Dead Sea Scrolls: The History of Judaism, the Background of Christianity, the Lost Library of Qumran* (Philadelphia, 1994).

Smith, M., "The Dead Sea Sect in Relation to Ancient Judaism," in *New Testament Studies* 7 (1960), pp. 347-360.

Smith, M., "What is Implied by the Variety of Messianic Figures?" in *Journal of Biblical Literature* 78 (1959), pp. 66-72.

Stegemann, H., "The Origins of the Temple Scroll," in *Supplement to Vetus Testamentum* 40 (1988), pp. 235-256.

Tov, E., "The Unpublished Qumran Texts from Caves 4 and 11," in *Journal of Jewish Studies* 43 (1992), pp. 101-136.

van der Woude, A.S., "Wicked Priest or Wicked Priests? Reflections on the Identification of the Wicked Priest in the Habakkuk Commentary," in *Journal of Jewish Studies* 33 (1982), pp. 349-359.

Vermes, G., "Preliminary Remarks on Unpublished Fragments of the Community Rule from Qumran Cave Four," in *Journal of Jewish Studies* 42 (1991), pp. 250-255.

Vermes, G., and M. Goodman, *The Essenes According to the Classical Sources* (Sheffield, 1989).

RABBINIC JUDAISM:
THE DEBATE ABOUT "TALMUDIC HISTORY"

VI. RABBINIC SOURCES FOR HISTORICAL STUDY: A DEBATE WITH ZE'EV SAFRAI

Jacob Neusner
University of South Florida and Bard College

Israeli scholarship in what is called there "the history of the Jewish people in the period of the Mishnah and the Talmud" defines a special chapter in the larger debate on critical utilization of Rabbinic sources for historical study. The reason is that an iron consensus operates, fully articulated, institutionally enforced, that, in general, all sources serve, except for the ones that do not serve. This is stated in so many words by Ze'ev Safrai, when he says, "Almost all Talmudic texts that meet the examination outlined in (a) should be accepted. However, each text should also be examined in the light of related historical sources to establish whether the picture portrayed makes sense according to all other available information."[1] He further alleges, "...we confidently follow a path that has been paved by many students of Jewish history, such as Büchler, Alon, Epstein, and others...." And, further, "With all due respect, this is just one of dozens of similar projects, and an extensive discussion of the issue of methodology is beyond our scope." So Safrai may serve as a reliable witness to the methods that dictate how historical study of Talmudic and Rabbinic writings is carried on in the State of Israel and its universities. It may be characterized very simple: it is simply intellectually primitive and historically uncritical. Its questions are trivial, and its results, incoherent. No important insight into the character of the Judaism of the age emerges, and compelling answers to urgent questions do not derive from work that believes whatever the sources allege but, out of that credulity, produces neither consequential facts nor provocative hypothesis. For, as we shall see in a moment, Safrai (confidently) utilizes "almost all" Rabbinic texts pertinent to his subject and deems everyone of them to present us with hard facts on economic life and behavior.

To show how accurately Safrai in his fundamental allegation concerning the historicity of "most" of what the Talmud and related

---

[1] Ze'ev Safrai, *The Economy of Roman Palestine* (London and New York, 1994), p. 4.

writings say represents the methods of Israeli university scholarship on Talmudic history, let me point to the journal *Zion*, published by the Israel Historical Society, and focus upon the character of the articles in the field that that journal has printed. When people practice Talmudic history in *Zion*, they limit their discussion to Talmudic history in particular. The field does not encompass its period, but only one set of sources emergent from its period. And this explains the triviality of the results: while many of the scholars represented in *Zion* draw upon *sources* outside the Talmud, none of the articles deals with a *problem* outside the Talmud. Accordingly, Talmudic history in this Israeli journal finds definition as the study of historical problems pertinent to a given *source* rather than to a chronological *period* to which that source attests.[2] It follows that Talmudic history severely limits itself, in *Zion*, to literary evidence. While, once again, we may find allusion to archaeological data, no article in the past half-century has entered the category of inquiry in which archeology, as much as literature, defines the problem or contributes to its solution.

The methodology of reading the literary sources, which are the only ones to define the problems and solutions of Talmudic history in *Zion*, begins in an assumption universally adopted by the scholars of the journal: whatever the Talmud says happened happened. If the Talmud attributes something to a rabbi, he really said it. If the Talmud maintains that a rabbi did something, he really did it. If the Talmud tells a story, it stands for an actual event, controlling only for implausible miracles. So, among the twenty-one articles under discussion, I find not a single one that asks the basic critical questions with which historical study normally commences: how does the writer of this source know what he tells me? How do I know that he is right?

On the contrary, the two Talmuds serve, as much in fifty years of the journal *Zion* as in Safrai's latter-day book, as encyclopedias of facts about rabbis and other Jews in the land of Israel and Babylonia. The task of the historian is to mine the encyclopedias and come up with important observations on the basis of the facts at hand. The work of the historian, then, is just what Safrai shows he thinks it is: solely the collection and arrangement of facts, the analysis of facts, the synthesis of facts. It is not in the inquiry into the source and character of the facts at hand. It does not require inquiry into penetrating questions concerning culture, ideas, or intellect. Just as, for

---

[2] I return to this matter below.

the literary scholar, the text constitutes the starting point of inquiry, so, for the historian, the text at hand defines the facts and dictates the character of inquiry upon them. This is the case, beginning and end, from Menachem Alon to Reuven Kimelman (an American, as a matter of fact). Whether it is Alon, telling us what Yohanan ben Zakkai meant in his conversation with Vespasian in August 70, on the assumption that Vespasian and Yohanan were attended by secretaries who wrote down their every word, or whether it is Kimelman, telling us about the politics of the priesthood and exilarchate as reported by a story in Yerushalmi Shabbat 12:3, the method is the same: believe it all, paraphrase it all, regurgitate it all, and call the result "history."

Safrai himself confirms my judgment that the fifty years of Talmudic history in *Zion* and his own method correspond exactly. That Safrai stands for the generality of mainstream Israeli scholarship, and that the same rules of evidence, which we shall examine, govern throughout, is indicated by Safrai's confident statement that, in general, Israeli work follows the lines he summarizes and that in no way does he innovate in the use of evidence. He points, in particular, to another contemporary, younger Israeli scholar, Y. Gafni, who has written a book in accord with the same rules; speaking of the use of the Babylonian Talmud as a historical source, Safrai says, "In this area we have also followed numerous scholars, and have not sought any methodological innovations. Our position on this subject is summarized by Gafni in his discussion of the Babylonian texts in general, and the Jewish community in Babylon in particular."[3] The community of scholarship in the State of Israel[4] has established a firm con-

---

[3] He refers to Y.M. Gafni, *The Jews of Babylonia in the Talmudic Era* (Jerusalem, 1991), in Hebrew. Gafni's work was supposed to have been published in English translation by Yale University Press, but, as of this writing, five years after the Israeli edition in Hebrew, no word on the date of publication in English has been received.

[4] Scholarship in Europe concerning the history of the Jews and Judaism in late antiquity ("the Talmudic period") responds to the critical agenda of biblical studies and attempts a more critical stance toward the sources. But the results prove only marginally less gullible than the Israeli ones. Rather facile solutions to complex problems produce a veneer of criticism covering a foundation of credulity, that is, pseudo-criticism; see for example Martin Goodman, *State and Society in Roman Galilee, AD 132-212* (Ottawa, 1983). Goodman's work is exemplary of what is not uncritical but pseudocritical. In the U.S.A., by contrast, only a few scholars manufacture facts by simply alluding to a page of the Talmud, though retrograde work does appear from time to time. Such scholars, in general, are employed in Jewish-sponsored centers of learning and not in secular universities. But retrograde work comes from the academy too, as in the deplorable book, *The Monarchic Principle. Studies in Jewish*

sensus on these matters, which, as we see, Safrai confidently claims to represent in his work. Hence, in the use of Rabbinic writings in the composition of Safrai's *Economy of Roman Palestine* we gain a reliable picture of the established methods there, and, because matters are thoroughly articulated, it follows, we may compose a systematic critique of that position as well.

Since publication of Safrai's *Economy of Roman Palestine* defines the occasion, a brief preliminary word about the quality of his book is appropriate. Safrai's discussion of the economy of Roman Palestine combines archaeological with Talmudic and some classical sources in a survey of various topics: settlement patterns (classification of settlements); modes of production (agriculture, crafts and industry, services); trade in the land of Israel in the Roman period; the organizational framework of farming; open or closed economy in the land of Israel during the Roman period (self-sufficiency vs. specialization); demographic multiplication and economic growth. Safrai does not set forth his goals or why he thinks an account of an "economy" is either possible or consequential in this context. What else we know, if we know, e.g., that people raised sheep, he does not suggest. The result is a huge compilation of what Safrai claims are facts, but a considerable failure of intellect: information without purpose. He provides no account of a working economy, only a repertoire of data, some plausible, some dubious, out of which such an account might be constructed by an economic historian of antiquity.

But—and here is the point of this debate—Safrai's completely uncritical reading of the Rabbinic writings casts doubt on the facticity of his alleged facts. Whether Safrai has intelligently and accurately utilized the archaeological reports in a critical and intelligent manner I cannot say. But his use of Rabbinic evidence is retrograde and ignorant. He allows Babylonian sources to tell us all about Palestine. Worse still, he quotes with equal confidence documents concluded in the third century and in the seventh century and in medieval times, all to tell us how things were long before the redaction of those documents, and he believes pretty much everything he reads in the Rabbinic literature. The result is a pastiche: a gullible reading of Talmudic texts covered by a veneer of pseudo-

---

Self-Government in Antiquity, by David Goodblatt (University of California at San Diego) (Tübingen, 1994). Goodblatt's entire program of questions rests on the premise that answers on what named persons really said and did are to be found in the Rabbinic documents; absent that premise, he could not have framed the issues as he did.

critical verbiage. Among five hundred pages of examples, the following gives the flavor of the whole:

> A number of other sources tell of the great number of sheep in Judaea. Thus, for example, the Tosefta states regarding the Temple that "calves were brought from the Sharon and sheep from the desert" (T. Menahot 9:13). BT Menahot 87a (= BT Sotah 34b) explains that the "calves came from the Sharon and the sheep from Hebron" and adds that Absalom, the son of David, had gone to Hebron in order to bring sheep from there. A midrash on the blessing of Jacob to Judah states in a similar vein that "all the valleys will turn white from the fields of wheat and the flocks of sheep" (Bereshit Rabbati 49:12) All this would seem to prove that the raising of sheep in the Hebron mountains was quite prevalent. Thus it appears that sheep gracing was rather limited in the Galilee and a rather widespread phenomenon in Judaea.... (p. 169).

Quite how the literary sources yield the economic facts that Safrai imputes is not clear. The Tosefta is a document that reached closure around two centuries after the destruction of the Temple; why, then, we should take as fact its information about prior practices (of limited pertinence to the larger question he proposes to answer!) Safrai does not tell us. The Talmud of Babylonia, redacted in ca. 600 C.E., then imputes to Absalom, son of Scripture's king David, in ca. 900 B.C.E., fifteen hundred years earlier [!], the intent of bringing sheep from Hebron. So sheep come from Hebron. By Bereshit Rabbati I am not sure whether Safrai refers to Bereshit Rabbah (Genesis Rabbah) of ca. 450 C.E., or to a much later, medieval compilation, but it makes little difference. Whatever Safrai finds in a Rabbinic document, he believes as fact, within the most trivial and lenient strictures of what he imagines is "criticism." But the pseudo-critical character of the whole cannot be missed, since all of this "evidence" proves nothing much, and "would seem to prove" cannot obscure Safrai's grossly uncritical use of literary sources in the reconstruction of economic facts.

Lest the cited passage that illustrates Safrai's method of finding his facts in the literary evidence be thought exceptional, let me cite one more. This should establish that characterizing Safrai's method as a simple opening of a document and believing pretty much everything he finds there is no caricature. The following is Safrai's account of Lod:

> Talmudic traditions from the Tannaitic period, and particularly from the end of the Second Temple and Javneh period, describe many rich landowners. R. Eliezer b. Hyrcanus was a resident of this city [Lod]. His family owned many lands as is clear from the Talmudic tradition

describing his early years (Genesis Rabbah 41...). His father, at the end
of the Second Temple period, had rather extensive holdings. R. Eliezer
himself had a field at Kefar Tov, a site as yet unidentified. A rich
landowner living in the city and owning lands in the hinterland was a
common phenomenon in the Roman world.

Another rich sage deriving from an important family and living in
Lod was R. Eleazar b. Azariah. R. Eleazar is basically associated with
the Javneh period, and, apparently, also with Lod. Talmudic traditions
do not mention his lands, but he must have had such possessions, since
that is what would have made him and his family wealthy. He did have
flocks of sheep, however (BT Shabbat 54b; PT Shabbat V, 7c, and
parallels). Another rich sage of the Javneh period in Lod was R. Tarfon.
R. Tarfon is described as a landowner (see for example PT Sheviit IV,
25b; BT Nedarim 62a...). One tradition relates that R. Tarfon gave R.
Akiva money in order to buy an estate for the two of them (Leviticus
Rabbah 34:16). These three sages were priests and came from important families. None of this is coincidence, but this is not the correct
forum in which to discuss the matter (Safrai, pp. 93-94).

Genesis Rabbah reached closure at ca. 450 C.E.; the story that Safrai
cites involves a long account of how some four hundred years earlier
Eliezer left his father's fields to go and study the Torah with Yohanan
ben Zakkai. How all this makes him a "rich landowner" is not clear;
I wonder how many rich landowners had their sons working in the
fields, as Eliezer is supposed to have been when he got the call to
study the Torah. The treatment of Eleazar is equally bizarre; surely
in Palestine at that time not everyone who was thought wealthy
invested in real estate, though the Roman aristocracy and the Judaic
sages alike deemed real estate the only form of worldly wealth.
Tarfon is described as wealthy in two fifth and one seventh century
documents—long after he lived; how these documents got the information they set forth Safrai does not say.

The story he cites in Leviticus Rabbah concerns the equation of
wealth and Torah-learning, the latter deemed superior to real estate,
an idea that otherwise does not occur in the mouths of first century
sages at all, let alone in documents redacted prior to the fifth century.[5] Nor were all priests wealthy, nor did all priests own real estate
of consequence, nor were all priests from important families, nor
were all important families wealthy in real estate. But why go on? For
none of these considerations affects Safrai's reading of the evidence

---

[5] I demonstrate that fact in my *The Transformation of Judaism. From Philosophy to
Religion* (Champaign, 1992), which Safrai does not cite, though the work contains two
chapters devoted to the economics of Rabbinic Judaism.

or his use thereof. It suffices to say that his work yields many hundreds of equally uncritical readings of the Rabbinic documents, which are taken at face value as sources of historical facts of the kind Safrai requires for his work.

To his credit, Safrai systematically sets forth his views on why it is proper to read the documents in the way that he does. I cite the entirety of his discussion and then comment on it, before setting forth in a more systematic way my own view of the problem at hand. This is what he says; note my italics at (b):

THE RABBINIC SOURCES

On the question of the reliability of the Talmudic texts as historical sources.

The Talmudic texts are the main basis of our study and the source of information for most of the questions, answers and hypotheses put forward. In terms of the utilization of such sources, we have added nothing new, and we confidently follow a path that has been paved by many students of Jewish history, such as Büchler, Alon, Epstein, and others. This approach can be summarized as follows:

(a) Every source must be thoroughly checked, examining the original version against manuscripts and quotations of the 'Rishonim' (interpreters of the early Middle Ages) as well as additional evidence. After this, parallel sources are used to determine that this is really the original version of the law. Is the text different or distorted? What can be learned from the differences between the sources and from the ensuing questions and investigations?

(b) *Almost all Talmudic texts that meet the examination outlined in (a) should be accepted.* However, each text should also be examined in the light of related historical sources to establish whether the picture portrayed makes sense according to all other available information.

(c) Naturally, one should suspect texts of exaggeration and excessiveness, and of changes made to correspond with the esthetic and theoretical framework of the story and anachronistic descriptions (mainly of the Biblical period). Such exaggeration is, of course, more common in legends than in halacha, and the latter can be expected to be much more accurate. The researcher must identify the historical core in the text; it is this information that can serve as a source of knowledge.

(d) After the authenticity of the source has been established, the researcher must study it and determine its significance and the conclusions that can be drawn. In this context, a number of questions will be asked, and related options will be examined. For example, does the text represent something customary or something exceptional: Is the story an exceptional example that tells us about a general occurrence, or does it refer to an isolated incident or episode? Was the decision of the beit midrash actually carried out?

What period does the source represent? What does it incorporate
from earlier times and what new elements did the rabbis of the
period add? The answers to such questions, in turn, lead to further
investigation.

(e) All these tests apply to the Palestinian texts. We treated the Babylonian texts differently, as discussed below.

(f) This method of study based on deduction and analogy serves as an
alternative to two other main methods. On the one hand, there is
the traditional method, which is based on absolute belief in every
source. Accordingly, the research focuses on application of the information. In addition, since all sources are considered indisputable
truth, it is necessary to explain the discrepancies between them.
These explanations generally ignore the constraints of reason and
logic and require a willingness to reject some other sources such as
manuscripts, texts from the Geniza..., some of the midrashim, and
the like.

In contrast, another method challenges the belief in the rabbinic literature and its use as a historical source. We discuss this below.

In the context of the present research, it is not necessary to discuss the
methodological assumptions presented. After all, this is not the first
study of the history of the people of Israel and of Palestine. With all due
respect, this is just one of dozens of similar projects, and an extensive
discussion of the issue of methodology is beyond our scope.

Nevertheless, this does not excuse us altogether from the need to
address the question of method. The main conclusion that arises from
this essay is likely (or liable) to seem utopian. The summary seems too
neat, and therefore it is not credible. Thus we must defend the way in
which we utilized the sources, in general and in principle.

For this purpose we consider an alternative method of studying ancient sources. Using this method, numerous respected researchers...have
presented arguments that question the validity of using rabbinic texts as
a source of social history. The major arguments are as follows.

(1) In the Mishnah and Talmud periods, the rabbis headed isolated
batei midrash. The laws that they developed emerged in these detached,
isolated 'islands' of study. Thus the rabbis neither understood nor knew
the reality of their times; it was not the background to their decisions,
their attitudes nor even the legends told in the batei midrash. Sometimes this argument is presented in an even more extreme manner. The
Talmudic literature is depicted not as a summary of opinions of a group
of rabbis, but as personal literary creations. Accordingly, the Mishnah is
not a public text, but the work of a single editor or group of editors.
Consequently, each book or part of a book has a different social background, which must be discussed separately. Obviously, this type of
research does not require the knowledge of all Talmudic texts, and such
study becomes simple, one-dimensional, and unequivocal.

Applying this theory to our study, the image that emerges of the
economy, the community and the settlement would not be true history
but 'literary history,' or 'economics of the beit midrash.'

(2) The public at large did not obey the rabbis. Among the Jews, only a minority followed the rabbis, obeyed their decisions and was influenced by their sermons and moral teachings. It was also this small group that influenced the outlook of the beit midrash; its customs and attitudes constitute the social and historical background for the decisions made in the beit midrash. According to this perspective, then, the texts do not provide a true image of the community, but that of a small group, a social stratum whose ties with the wider public were few and problematic...

As noted, although we will not discuss these broad methodological issues, brief discussion of those subjects directly related to our field of research seems warranted. Some of the following comments are restricted to this area, and some also have more general theoretical significance. Prior to the discussion, another aspect, more psychological than scientific, should be considered. The Talmudic texts pose an extremely difficult challenge to the scholar. The archaic Hebrew and Aramaic integrated with Hebrew are a primary hardship. Moreover, the texts are written in a sort of inner code, the code of the beit midrash (school). All the interpretive and traditional Mishnaic texts assume that this code is known to the reader, so instead of interpreting it they use it. Thus the first sentence in the Mishnah Brachot 1,1 would be translated literally as, 'From when they call: listen!' when it actually means, 'From when people have to pray the Prayer of Shema.' In addition, the corresponding scripture for many of the passages is not clear; sometimes the textual basis for whole chapters is not explicitly mentioned. The material is not organized by subjects and the same issue appears in numerous sources. Conflicts between the sources, errors in a version and later editing of some of the texts all create additional difficulties. Furthermore, until recently there was no lexicon...and most of the essays have not yet been published in scientific, or even semi-scientific, editions.

It is no wonder, then, that many scholars have erred in their understanding of the texts and made mistakes in using them. Someone who does not know the Talmudic texts intimately will have difficulty making full use of all the rabbinic literature.

Needless to say, in this respect, graduates of the Jewish religious institutions have a distinct advantage. In modern institutions of this type, two to five hours a day are devoted to studying the Talmud...

These 'technical' difficulties must not influence our position regarding the reliability of the rabbinic sources. After all, difficulty in reading an inscription does not dissuade researchers, but actually stimulates them to make greater efforts to utilize the hidden information and to determine its implications.

For our purposes, a distinction should be made between three types of conclusions that may arise from the study of rabbinic texts.

(a) Did the rabbis succeed in changing or influence the social environment through their teachings? For example, did the prohibition against charging interest have an impact on lenders and borrowers?

Did the rabbis' utopian position (and their opposition to trade and urban lifestyles) affect the public? Did their moralistic policy and their desire to help the poor and the weak influence the economic structure? ...These questions actually apply to only a small group of subjects, as the rabbis generally did not try to mold economic life or to pronounce utopian commands;[6] they did not consider it their role to decide what to grow, how to produce, how to sell or to interfere in other purely economic matters.

(b) In the course of their writings, the rabbis refer to a certain religious-social background as though it were real. Thus, for instance, the rabbis assume that the entire public observes kashrut, keeps the Sabbath and attends synagogue. These assumptions relate to matters that were important to the rabbis. They considered these aspects of life as their realm, and in this respect the distance between themselves, their students, and the general public was prominent. After all, the whole community could not be holy. Regarding these matters, the rabbis' writings reflect the customs only of those who were accepted in the stratum of rabbis. Accordingly, one might expect that the background described in the text applies to the society of the beit midrash (school) alone....

(c) In the course of their discussions, the rabbis relate *by the way* to the situation outside the beit midrash. Thus, for instance, when they discuss the obligation of tithing, they assume that in some places most of the produce is sent to market.... Perhaps the laws of tithing were theoretical, and most of the public paid no attention to them at all, but is there any reason to doubt that there were places where most of the harvest was sent to the market? In this case it might still be argued that the description is theoretical and is presented as a dialectic possibility alone. Even more notable an example is the rabbis' description of the sale of a house, in which they assume that it includes a cooker and stove.... We still do not know how common the sale of houses was, but there is no reason to doubt that the cooker and stove were an integral part of a residential dwelling, and it is also clear that they were considered the most characteristic components of such a house.

The decisive majority of subjects with which this work deals belong to the latter type and resemble the last example presented here. A small portion are similar to the previous example of tithing laws. In these cases we must

---

[6] Safrai's statements here are astonishing; it appears he has not opened the pages of Mishnah-tractate Shebiit, which legislates for the sabbatical year in a utopian spirit, among many tractates that deal with economic and political matters without attending to actualities. I challenge him, for instance, to demonstrate how Mishnah Sanhedrin is other than utopian, with its government in the hands of a king, high priest, and sages' court set forth in an age in which there was no king of Judea and no Temple high priesthood either. Much that follows in these paragraphs is pure gibberish. Perhaps in Hebrew the discussion in the next paragraph (b) is intelligible, but in English it is beyond deciphering.

clarify whether the background to the text is realistic, or whether it was presented for the purpose of a theoretical dialectic discussion.

Only very few of the references in this book belong to type (a) or (b) above. In general, the rabbis did not deal with formation of the economic structure but with personal behavior and lifestyle within the economic structure of their time.[7] The rabbis were interested in questions of ritual, ceremony, morals and social justice, and economic circumstances only served as a framework, a setting for them. It is actually because the economic, technological and agricultural subjects were not generally the focus of the rabbinic literature that it can be used as a source for the study of the economy (Safrai, pp. 3-8).

At this point Safrai wishes to explain why "the historical description that emerges from Rabbinic literature" is not "supported, echoed and confirmed by parallel external sources of information, such as Roman and Christian documents..." He points out that Roman literature represents "the imperial and urban establishment," and Christian literature for its part contains little information. He proceeds with statements that must astound scholars of Syriac literature, from Aphrahat forward, which assuredly represented no "establishment," whether Iranian or Roman, but a group as humble as the Judaic one:

> The rabbinic literature reflects a completely different social stratum... This is the only literature from that period that represents the native residents and not the establishment, which was saturated in Greek and Roman culture. The Talmudic literature emerged mostly in the rural community, out of a struggle against the imperial culture, literature, and religion. ...Nevertheless, in the course of this work we do occasionally refer to evidence derived from external sources. In general, the comparisons and parallels with non-Jewish evidence are extremely limited and cast no doubt on our conclusions... (Safrai, pp. 8-9).

But as to archaeological evidence:

> In general, the archaeological findings confirm and validate the rabbinic texts and the use of these sources in our work.

---

[7] A study of the cases reported in the pages of the Talmud of Babylonia will show that the rabbis of that satrapy most certainly did deal with conduct in the market place and claimed to decide cases about concrete matters of all kinds, fixing pricing, settling real estate disputes, imposing the law of the Mishnah on a variety of conflicts. This matter is discussed extensively in my *History of the Jews in Babylonia* (Leiden, 1965-1970), vols. I-V, which Safrai does not appear to know. Safrai's treatment of ˙the sages' range of interest as mainly personal, having to do with what he calls "lifestyle," contradicts virtually every page of both Talmuds, as well as every line of the Mishnah in every division. But these claims of his play so inconsequential a role in the hundreds of pages of dreary narrative that it hardly suffices to pursue the matter. We focus only on issues of historical epistemology.

We may leave it to archaeologists to judge whether Safrai's characterization of matters accurately portrays the facts, and to classicists
and historians of early Christianity to evaluate his reasons for excluding pertinent evidence in those bodies of writings.

He excludes, also, the whole of extra-Rabbinic Judaic literature,
on grounds that it is too early to attest to the period of which he
wishes to speak, but that clearly does not lead him to omit, also, the
documents of Rabbinic Judaism that come long after the times that
he claims to portray. So Philo and Josephus are too early, but medieval compilations of Rabbinic sayings (many of the Midrash-compilations he cites for facts) are not too late—not to mention the Talmud
of Babylonia, ca. 600, two hundred years after Safrai closes his gate.
Since his systematic account supposedly pertains to "Roman Palestine," I should not have thought he would wish to exclude pertinent
evidence concerning Greek- and Latin-speaking residents, on the one
side, or the Aramaic-speaking Christians, on the other. I should have
imagined that an account of an economy by definition must encompass all players in that economy, not only one group and the evidence of its activities. But in this debate we are not concerned with
issues of economic history; nor, for that matter, for most of his slog-
ging journey through nearly a hundred pages on grains, wine, pi-
geons, olives, is he; the realia of economic activity do not form an
account of an economy, they only contribute to such an account,
which, in the end, Safrai cannot be said to have set forth.

Safrai articulates a method. Let us now take him at his word and
address each of its components, then set forth in more general terms
what, in the framework of what he wishes to do, I propose is a valid
scholarly program. Let us work our way through his arguments point
by point, then generalize.

(a) All parties concur that every source must be thoroughly
checked. I cannot point to a single instance in his book in which the
procedure he prescribes has materially affected his presentation. This
point, on which no one differs, must form part of the background of
discourse. It supplies a veneer of pseudo-criticism alone. But the
premise contained within it that, if we have "the original version,"
then we have a reliable fact, is obviously fundamental to Safrai's view
of matters. We may call this "philological fundamentalism:" a reliable text-version, properly understood word for word, constitutes a
historical fact, not merely a textual one.

(b) Here is the crux of matters. What we have here is an argument from content, which is to say, if an ancient source makes an allegation, we must accept that allegation unless we find grounds on the basis of which to reject it. That same position was outlined to me in so many words in a conversation with the late E.E. Urbach in 1976, and I have heard the same apophthegm set forth time and again on those occasions, admittedly not very many, on which Israeli colleagues have engaged in discussion with me. Arguments from content rapidly deteriorate into allegations concerning [1] the ring of truth, [2] why our holy rabbis would not lie, and [3] the kernel of historical truth that is contained within the legend. On that basis, it goes without saying, a paraphrase of the biblical books from Genesis through Kings, with a few omissions of obviously implausible miracles ("related sources...makes sense..."), supplies us with a reliable, critical history of pre-exilic Israel: if it sounds true ("makes sense according to all other available information"), it is true.

Arguments from content such as these simply ignore the critical issues: how does a given fact reach written form (or other permanent formulation), and how does the written form of the fact then reach us? Without answers to those questions, we find ourselves in the position of believing everything (except what we choose not to believe) in documents that reached closure long after the period of which they speak. Such stout faith may afford access to Heaven, but it cannot today dictate the shape of critical, historical knowledge, any more than it has for academic learning in all other fields of history for two centuries and more. Why Safrai finds unnecessary an *Auseinandersetzung* with the entirety of biblical scholarship, on the one side, and the whole of critical historical literature, on the other, baffles me. Outside of the little world in which he works, scholars who deal with sources of comparable character treat as urgent questions that he regards as bearing no consequence whatsoever. He states with blithe innocence positions deemed uncritical, indeed credulous and gullible, in every other field of academic learning but his own, and in whole continents in which his own field of learning is carried on, except his own.

(c) No one will dispute this point, which is necessary, but not sufficient, for any critical method.

(d) Quite what Safrai intends in this rather lugubrious formulation eludes me. The reason is that Safrai does not spell out the alternatives or tell us the consequences that he draws from the theoretical answers to his theoretical questions. Customary or exceptional? Then what is at stake? Are we to believe in what is routine but not epi-

sodic? Then what has happened to point (b)? When Safrai introduces
the matter of "period," "what period does the source represent?," he
assumes an answer to that question. But throughout his book, all
facts are classified as to period by appeal to the authority to whom
sayings are attributed. Then periodization of sayings and the facts
they contain for him entirely depends upon the attribution of a saying to a sage. But these attributions are notoriously unreliable, for
everyone knows that what is assigned to one authority here is given to
someone else in another passage; sages themselves readily exchanged
names and opinions as logic required; an entire document, the Tosefta, systematically reconfigures what is assigned to a set of sages;
and the entire matter of attributions awaits systematic, critical investigation in its own terms. It is the simple fact that, at this time, we
have no universal method of falsifying attributions, therefore, also, no
method of validating them. Methods that may serve for some specific
documents (my own for the Mishnah and the Tosefta) prove suggestive but not probative, and no others have been proposed within the
framework of critical discourse.

(f) Safrai here proposes to distinguish himself from the yeshiva-
world on the far horizon of the integrationist-Orthodoxy of Bar Ilan
University, a world where everybody believes everything, not just
nearly everything. But this "traditional" method—yielding the task of
harmonizing what Safrai calls "discrepancies"—and Safrai's own gullible method only marginally differ, for the reasons already spelled out.

Now to the second part of his argument, alternative approaches. I
have reproduced Safrai's picture of contrary methods, but I find no
reason to debate with him about them. A few remarks serve.

(1) It suffices to say that Safrai simply does not show a grasp of the
methods he rejects, but only caricatures them. A single case suffices.
Safrai alludes, at this paragraph, to my *The Economics of the Mishnah*.[8]
That book addresses the questions, why does the Mishnah set forth
an economics, and what systemic message is conveyed through economics and only could have been conveyed through economics?
Safrai's account of the matter shows no comprehension of that simple fact. The larger problematics of the documentary hypothesis lies
beyond his horizon. The history of economic thought in antiquity
plays no role in his picture of the economy of Roman Palestine.

(2) Safrai's characterization of the results of scholarship produced

---

[8] Chicago, 1989. Safrai has the date wrong, but his gross inattention to detail
throughout proves disheartening.

by those who have not studied in yeshivas can only be dismissed as bizarre. His language, as readers will have observed, is characteristically murky, but his intention is obvious: people who have not studied in yeshivas cannot study Rabbinic literature, just as those who (like Safrai himself) have not abandoned the intellectual premises of the yeshivas about the inerrancy of the holy books also cannot study history. But his example proves little less than risible. I cannot point to any translation of the Mishnah-passage he cites, in any language, that makes the stupid mistake Safrai admonishes us not to make. And his translation is simply ludicrous, since it does not portray the Hebrew at all, which yields not his preferred, rather exotic, "From when people have to pray the Prayer of Shema," but "From what time may they recite the Shema in the evening? From the hour that the priests enter [their homes] to eat their heave offering...." One does not have to study in a yeshiva to master a line of the Rabbinic literature of late antiquity, and a strong case can be made against yeshiva-study for those who wish to focus upon that literature. But one does have to study in a yeshiva to master the entirety of the halakhah of Judaism, which is a different matter; indeed, yeshiva-learning neglects a great many of the texts that Safrai himself cites or studies those texts superficially and at odd intervals, not in a systematic and sustained way.

For all his insistence that yeshiva-training is necessary for an understanding of the Talmud in its own terms and the rest of the Rabbinic documents of ancient times in their own terms, Safrai's own grasp of the Talmudic literature proves impressionistic, alas, infirm at best. That is because in yeshivot, people study line-by-line but rarely aim at a grasp of the whole of a document. For example, his allegation that material is not organized by subjects is simply false for the Mishnah and mostly false for most of the rest of the Rabbinic literature organized around the Mishnah; and it is equally false for the Midrash-compilations, properly set forth.[9] He probably means, it is not organized by abstract principles, which is true. No one will argue with Safrai that someone who does not know the texts "intimately" will have difficulty using them; but nothing in his account of matters shows how that "intimate" knowledge, gained in yeshiva-learning and only there,

---

[9] See my *The Components of the Rabbinic Documents: From the Whole to the Parts* (Atlanta, 1996ff.), in twelve volumes. This work provides a complete outline of the twelve Midrash-compilations of late antiquity and shows that the documents are cogent and very carefully organized. Safrai seems to have formed the impression in his yeshiva-studies that the Rabbinic literature is simply chaotic, and that is the result of the exegetical studies that dominate in yeshivot.

has given him a deeper grasp of matters than the less "intimate" knowledge that is afforded to those who have studied only in seminaries and universities. What advantage alumni of the schools he favors enjoy hardly emerges in the pages of his book or in any others cited in his bibliography. In the end, this claim that only one approach to learning affords access to the documents emerges as self-serving, spurious, and ad hominem. It will persuade only the believers, but they are unlikely to read writings that rest on premises other than their own. It suffices to say that this entire mode of argument is contemptible. The rest of Safrai's discussion of method need not detain us, since involved are questions not of method but historical fact. I include the discussion because he presents it within the stated rubric.

Let me now generalize from the examples of Safrai.[10] I focus discussion on the concrete errors that render useless for historical purposes nearly all work on the Talmud as history carried on in the State of Israel, whether at the secular Hebrew University or at the Orthodox-Judaic Bar Ilan University. The articles in *Zion*, as well as elsewhere, like Safrai's book, take for granted that the numerous specific stories concerning what given rabbis and other Jews actually said and did under specific circumstances—on a given day, at a given place, in a given setting—tell us *exactly the way things were*. I speak, then, of a species of the genus, fundamentalism. Safrai has provided a solid example; now let us generalize on the basis of the example.

The philological fundamentalists have generally supposed that once we have established a correct text of a Rabbinic work and properly interpreted its language, we then know a set of historical facts. Safrai is explicit on this matter at his point (a). The facticity will be proportionately greater the earlier the manuscript and the better its condition. These suppositions are correct. But these facts will concern *only* what the compiler of the text wished to tell us. Whether or not the original text was veracious is to be settled neither by textual criticism nor by philological research, valuable though both of these ancillary sciences are for the historical inquiry.

---

[10] This part of my contribution to the debate derives from a revision of my lecture that was written for the Historical Society of Israel conference in celebration of its journal, *Zion*, on the occasion of its fiftieth volume, scheduled for July 2, 1984, in Jerusalem. The paper was mailed to Jerusalem on January 27, 1984, and the invitation to present it was withdrawn in a letter dated March 5, 1984. Israeli scholarship does not give a hearing to viewpoints contrary to those currently regnant there. That accounts for (among other failures of learning) Safrai's strikingly limited knowledge of the work of those he criticizes, as noted above.

The fundamentalists further suppose that any story, whether occurring early or late in the corpus of Rabbinic literature, may well contain valuable information, handed on orally from generation to generation, until it was finally written down. It is no caricature to impute to the Israelis the conviction that all Rabbinic material was somehow sent floating into the air, if not by Moses, then by someone in remote antiquity (the Men of the Great Assembly, the generation of Yavneh); it then remained universally available until some authority snatched it down from on high, placed his name on it, and so made it a named tradition and introduced it into the perilous processes of transmission. By this thesis, nothing is older than anything else: "there is neither earlier nor later in the Torah." But Safrai does not even enter into the question of how sayings reach their final resting place in documents, or how the framers of documents acquired the information concerning long-ago times that they purpose to transmit. His certainty that all attributions are reliable forms a corollary to that prior conviction.

That documents' framers make choices and revise received materials is an established fact. Let me give one example of work Safrai does not appear to have read, or, if he read it, understood. Synoptic studies of the traditions of Yohanan b. Zakkai and of the Pharisees before 70[11] indicate that versions of a story or saying appearing in later documents normally are demonstrably later than, and literally dependent upon, versions of the same story or saying appearing in earlier documents. This is important, for it shows that what comes late is apt to be late, and what comes in an early compilation is apt to be early. Admittedly, these are no more than probabilities—extrapolations from a small number of demonstrable cases to a large number in which no demonstration is possible. But at least there are grounds for such extrapolation.

By contrast, the primary conviction of Talmudic fundamentalism is that the story supplies an accurate account of what actually happened. It is difficult to argue with that conviction. A study of Rabbinic sources will provide little, if any, evidence that we have eyewitness accounts of great events or stenographic records of what people actually said. On the contrary, it is anachronistic to suppose the Talmudic rabbis cared to supply such information to begin with. Since they did not, and since they asserted that people had said

---

[11] *Development of a Legend. Studies on the Traditions concerning Yohanan ben Zakkai* (Leiden, 1970) and *The Rabbinic Traditions about the Pharisees before 70* (Leiden, 1971), 3 vols.

things of which they had no sure knowledge, we are led to wonder about the pseudepigraphic mentality. By the time we hear about a speech or an event, it has already been reshaped for the purpose of transmission in the traditions. It is rarely possible to know just what, if anything, originally was said or done. Sometimes we have an obvious gloss, which tells us the tradition originated before the time the glossator made his addition. But knowing that a tradition was shaped within half a century of the life of the man to whom it was attributed helps only a little bit. It is very difficult to build a bridge from the tradition to the event, still more difficult to cross that bridge. The fact is that the entire Rabbinic canon is a completely accurate record of the viewpoint of those who are responsible for it. But the specification of those people, the recognition of the viewpoint of a particular group, place, and time to which the Talmud's various facts pertain—these remain the fundamental task still facing us.

In all, as Safrai himself rightly emphasizes, Talmudic history cannot be said to deal with great affairs, vast territories, movements of men and nations, much that really mattered then. Even the bulk of Israel, the Jewish nation, in the time of the composition of the canonical writings at hand, by the testimony of the authors themselves, falls outside of the frame of reference. Most Jews appeared to the sages at hand to ignore—in the active sense of willfully *not knowing*—exactly those teachings that seemed to the authors critical. To use the mythic language, when God revealed the Torah to Moses at Mount Sinai, he wrote down one part, which we now have in the Hebrew Scripture ("the Old Testament"), and he repeated the other part in oral form, so that Moses memorized it and handed it on to Joshua, and then, generation by generation, to the contemporary sages. Now, to the point, the contemporaries of the sages at hand did not know this oral half of the Torah, only sages did, and that by definition. Only sages knew the whole of the Torah of Moses. So, it follows, the Talmudic corpus preserves the perspective of a rather modest component of the nation under discussion.

How could we define a subject less likely to attract broad interest than the opinions of a tiny minority of a nation about the affairs of an unimportant national group living in two frontier provinces on either side of a contested frontier? Apart from learning, from the modest folk at hand, some facts about life on the contested frontier of the ancient world—and that was only the one that separated Rome from Iran, the others being scarcely frontiers in any political sense—what is to be learned here that anyone would want to know must seem puzzling.

Self-evidently, no one can expect to find stories of great events, a continuous narrative of things that happened to a nation in war and in politics. The Jews, as it happens, both constituted a nation and sustained a vigorous political life. But the documents of the age under discussion treat these matters only tangentially and as part of the periphery of a vision of quite other things. But if manifest history scarcely passes before us, a rich and complex world of latent history—the long-term trends and issues of a society and its life in imagination and emotion—does lie ready at hand. For the Talmudic canon reports to us a great deal about what a distinctive group of people were thinking about issues that prove to be perennial and universal, and, still more inviting, the documents tell us not only what people thought but how they reasoned.

That is something to which few historians gain access, I mean, the philosophical processes behind political and social and religious policy, class struggle, and popular contention. For people do think things out and reach conclusions, and, for the most part, long after the fact, we know only the decisions they made. Here, by contrast, we hear extended discussions of a most rigorous and philosophical character on issues of theory and of thought. In these same discussions, at the end, we discover how people decided what to do and why. That sort of history—the history of how people made up their minds—proves particularly interesting, when we consider the substance of the story. The Jews in the provinces and age at hand adopted the policies put forward by the sages who wrote the sources we consider. The entire subsequent world history of the Jews—their politics, social and religious world, the character of the inner life and struggle of their community-nation—refers back to the decisions made at just this time and recorded in the Talmud. The stakes are very high. That explains why Safrai's (and other Israelis') failure exacts so heavy a cost on the common culture of their own country, which, after all, should find nourishment in exactly the documents under study here.[12]

A further aspect of the character of the principal sources for Talmudic history, moreover, will attract attention even among people

---

[12] On this point, see Ithamar Gruenwald, "Judaic Studies at a Crossroads: Cultural Substance or Academic Framework?," in *The Annual of Rabbinic Judaism: Ancient, Medieval and Modern* I (Leiden, 1998).

not especially concerned with how a weak and scattered nation explained how to endure its condition. The Talmudic canon bears the mark of no individual authorship. It is collective, official, authoritative. Now, were it to hand on decisions but no discussion, that collective character would not mark the literature as special. We have, from diverse places and times, extensive records of what legislative or ecclesiastical bodies decided. But if these same bodies had recorded in detail how they reached their decisions, including a rich portrait of their modes of thought, then we should have something like what the Talmud gives us.

But the points of interest scarcely end there. The Talmudic corpus stands in a long continuum of thought and culture, stretching back through the biblical literature for well over a thousand years. Seeing how a collegium of active intellectuals mediated between their own age and its problems and the authority and legacy of a vivid past teaches lessons about continuities of culture and society not readily available elsewhere. For their culture had endured, prior to their own day, for a longer span of time than separates us in the West from the Magna Carta, on the one side, and Beowulf, on the other. If these revered documents of our politics and culture enjoyed power to define politics and culture today, we should grasp the sort of problem confronting the Talmud's sages. For, after all, the Talmud imagined as normative a society having little in common with that confronting the sages—isolated, independent, free-standing, and not—as the sages' Israel was—assimilated in a vast world-empire, autonomous yet subordinate, and dependent upon others near and far.

The principal fault of Safrai's representation of matters is not its fundamentalism but its triviality. The work is simply dull, and even if he were right about every fact, he still has given us no plausible and consequential account of the economy of Roman Palestine, only a massive collection of bits and pieces of unintegrated information. If this is what one learns in those many years in yeshivot, then the world must conclude that those years are mostly wasted on unimportant matters. It is beyond the walls of the yeshivot, Rabbinical schools, and orthodox universities, U.S. and Israeli alike, that the Talmuds and other Rabbinic writings are read for reasons of intellectual and cultural consequence.

VII. RABBINIC SOURCES AS HISTORICAL: A RESPONSE TO PROFESSOR NEUSNER

Ze'ev Safrai
Bar Ilan University

Professor Neusner's review of my book *The Economy of Roman Palestine* provides an excellent opportunity for a methodological discussion of the use of the Rabbinic sources as a historical source. Prof. Neusner's criticism is composed of two intermingled sections. The main part of the review consists of a discussion of the ways in which the Rabbinic sources are to be used. The second, shorter part contains extremely general arguments relating to the structure and logic of the book itself. In the main section of the review, which is more important, Prof. Neusner does not attack the book but rather the research method, which he terms the "Jerusalem," "traditional," "fundamentalist," etc., method. Personally, I regard this criticism as highly flattering: my book is presented as an example of the "Jerusalem" method, while I cannot claim with any certainty that it indeed constitutes a model of this method.

A methodological discussion is the perfect forum for an objective examination of the research method. In an article or book the researcher utilizes sources, but he cannot always engage in a comprehensive discussion of the ways in which conclusions are drawn from these sources. If I had done so in my book, such a discussion would have encompassed thousands of pages. I therefore welcome the opportunity to reveal to the readers several of my behind-the-scenes considerations.

Before entering into the discussion itself, it should be noted that the stereotypical division of research into the "Jerusalem" and "enlightened" methods is schematic and general in nature and is not reflective of the reality. Thus, for instance, the statement that at Bar Ilan University "everyone believes in everything." This is an engaging formulation that attracts attention, but it is divorced from the .reality. I studied in Jerusalem, under teachers who employed different approaches. The teaching methods of some resembled the traditional approach, while others were more critical. I currently teach at Bar Ilan, and it seems that my attitude toward the sources is more critical than it was a decade ago. Bar Ilan boasts a diverse range of teachers. Some regard me as a "heretic," while others are convinced that I am a "fundamentalist." All these slogans are too general and the product of too fertile imaginations. As researchers, we should devote our energies to the subject under examination, not to stereotypes. If I use the term "the Jerusalem study method" in this response, this will be only as a matter of convenience, following Prof. Neusner's terminology. In a more positive vein, I will present the research method with which I agree, and which I attempt to apply, albeit with almost certain errors in details or methodology. My remarks therefore will bear a personal tint; nonetheless, I do not claim to blaze new methodological paths, but rather to explain the method of study used by some (the majority?) of the scholars in the various centers of scholarly research.

My critique of Neusner's criticism is composed of two principal arguments:

1. Neusner's criticism is not directed against the "Jerusalem" research method, with which he is unfamiliar, or, to be precise, that he does not criticize. His criticism would have been suitable for the traditional method of study, and I accept some of his arguments.

2. The method of study he proposes is excessively critical and does not put a cutting edge on research (which is a healthy and productive process), but rather leads to the degeneration and paralysis of academic inquiry, with the consequent only partial utilization of the sources.

First, to Prof. Neusner's main arguments:

1. The extant sources are not representative of the authentic teaching, since it developed in the batei midrash and was redacted in such a manner as to have lost its original content. Furthermore, he negates the use of a later source as testimony regarding an earlier period, and every source postdates the period it claims to describe.

The argument itself is not controversial; such a conception has been accepted in historical research beginning in the nineteenth century. Classical research also distinguished between the contemporary account of an event and a later description. Every novice researcher knows that the descriptions of Thucydides are not identical with those of Plutarch. The distinction between the source and the development of the tradition is a rudimentary component of any scholarly effort. Notwithstanding this, would anyone attempt to study the history of the Peleponnesian War without Plutarch?

THE DISTINCTION BETWEEN THE AMORAIC AND TANNAITIC TRADITIONS

The distinction between the Amoraic and Tannaitic traditions is known and accepted by "Jerusalem" researchers as well, and, indeed, it constitutes one of the cornerstones of modern research. In the final analysis, this claim is a non-issue. Thus, e.g., Gafni published an instructive study in which he argued that the perception of the land of Israel as the Holy Land began only in the Ushan generation,[1] and I published an article in which I claimed that all the sources discussing the Aramaic translation of the Torah in the synagogue are only from this period on.[2] My book on the economy of Palestine contains many such distinctions. Thus, e.g., the claim that all references to the growing of flax are limited to the second century (*Economy*, p. 156), or that the testimonies of the import of wheat to Palestine are all from the Amoraic period (idem., pp. 110-111), and many additional examples. Differentiating between early and later testimonies lies at the heart of modern research.

We may now concentrate on the methodological arguments raised by the reviewer.

TANNAITIC SOURCES

We may exemplify this argument with the Rabbinic testimony mentioning the normal possibility that caravans of donkey drivers traveled between settlements. For me as a historian, this constitutes an important proof of the method of rural commerce. Mishnayot on this subject are stated, inter alia, in the name of R. Judah, who was active ca. 140-160 (idem., pp. 234-237). According to Neusner's methodology, these halakhot are not historical and teach nothing, for the extant version is not reflective of the original dicta by R. Judah. For the sake of argument I am willing to—temporarily—accept this claim. The Mishnah was redacted ca. 200-220, and the Tosefta approximately ten to fifteen years afterwards. Even if we assume that the redactor does not transmit R. Judah's exact statement, he never-

---

[1] Y. Gafni, "Bringing Deceased from Abroad for Burial in Eretz Israel—On the Origin of the Custom and Its Development," in *Cathedra* 4 (1977), pp. 113-20 (in Hebrew).

[2] Z. Safrai, "The Origins of Reading the Aramaic Targum in Synagogue," in M. Lowe, ed., *The New Testament and Christian-Jewish Dialogue: Studies in Honor of David Flusser, Immanuel* 24-25 (1990), pp. 187-93

theless was familiar with the latter's period and is reflective of it. At this stage of the research, we cannot describe the specific reality of the years 146, 184, or 212, but we are capable of depicting in general terms economic life in the later Tannaitic period, or at the time of the redaction of the Mishnah. Mishnayot reflect the conclusions of laws and discussions conducted in the beit ha-midrash, and all those who studied the halakhah related to the contemporary reality. I referred to this situation in my introduction, by determining that every source is credible, unless there is a reason to believe otherwise. I assume that this was the reality, or at least one aspect of a diverse reality, during the time in which this tradition was formulated, even if such a reality cannot be dated to the exact decade. The "Jerusalem" method differs from Neusner's writing in that we seek proofs for distinguishing between periods, while Neusner's argument lacks a solid foundation.

AMORAIC SOURCES

The Jerusalem Talmud is home to many testimonies. The dictum is attributed to an earlier or later Amora, or is left without attribution. Once again, I assume the extant version is not identical with the original formulation as it was conceived by R. Yohanan or R. Haninah, but the redactor, who was active in the second half of the fourth century, was knowledgeable of the reality of his own time and reflects it. Again, the means at our disposal do not enable us to determine the conditions in Judea in a specific decade, but we may regard the dictum as a source reflective of the conditions and values generally prevalent in Judea in the time of the Amoraim or toward the end of this period.

Furthermore, the Amoraic midrash, e.g., depicts Jerusalem and Bethar as cities containing hundreds of synagogues. The narrative is patently exaggerated in the extreme and was intended merely to describe the size of the cities. For the author, a great number of synagogues is evidence of a large settlement, just as a modern writer would describe a developed urban settlement as one with expressways and public buildings. Obviously, we cannot learn from this source that Second Temple Jerusalem boasted a plethora of synagogues, but rather two simple conclusions: first, that Jerusalem and Bethar are recalled as large and vibrant settlements, i.e., this is how they were remembered in the fourth century. Second, that the synagogue was a common phenomenon in the fourth century, and a multiplicity of synagogues is evidence of a large settlement. These conclusions are corroborated by the archaeological finds. A regular Jewish settlement contained a single synagogue, and only large and exceptional settlements possessed more than one such institution. Consequently, the Amoraic teaching is credible and is to be regarded as reflective of a reality, but not the reality it presumes to describe, rather the actual and literary contemporary situation.

A description of the destruction of Migdal, Cabul, and Shihin, three Galilean towns, is provided by an anonymous Amora (Y. Ta. 4:69a). The description is embellished, but it is plain that memories of settlements that had been destroyed (almost certainly in the Great War) were widespread in the fourth century. These recollections, however faded, reflect the accepted historical memory at some point in the third and fourth centuries. The question arises whether events that had occurred two or three centuries previously were remembered in the fourth century. The reigning conditions at the time lead us to a positive answer. The memory was undoubtedly dimmed, exaggerated, and distorted, but why should it be doubted? The fact that two of these settlements suffered damage in the Great War, as is attested by Josephus, constitutes additional proof of the realistic roots of the Rabbinic tradition and may possibly also teach of the reliability of other testimonies that have no parallel in Josephus.

The Babylonian Talmud is different. Prof. Neusner forcefully contends that the Babylonian sources are unreliable in their descriptions of events in the land of Israel. Unfortunately, I do not argue this point, nor do the majority of scholars of the "Jerusalem" school. This distinction was the first subject I learned in my father's research seminars, and it is the first lesson that I teach my students; the reader is directed to pp. 14-15 of my book, where I state this explicitly. Perhaps I should have begun my book with this passage for additional clarity.

In the methodological discussion in the book, I cited the Babylonian Talmud as a test case, as a sort of "control group" for the land of Israel sources. The Babylonian Talmud makes use of the same materials as the Jerusalem Talmud but nevertheless cannot serve as a historical source for the land of Israel, and possibly not for Babylonia as well (p. 13). This distinction emphasizes the uniqueness and value of the Jerusalem Talmud.

The historical material in the Babylonian Talmud is problematic, because the *sugiyah* (Talmudic discussion) is composed of several strata:

—the land of Israel reality learned from land of Israel sources (Tannaim and Amoraim).
—the Babylonian reality.
—the method of study practiced in the Babylonian yeshivot—the dialectic of the Talmud.
—the different redactional strata.

It is difficult, and frequently impossible, to differentiate between these strata. Incidentally, in the same Talmud department in which I studied under the late "fundamentalist" Urbach (to use Neusner's terminology), I also learned from Prof. Sussmann that the redactional strata also corrupted and transformed the method of study and logic of the sugiyah, and not only the realistic background. Based on my personal knowledge, I have difficulty in accepting the stereotyping of the "Jerusalem school." However, any discussion of "schools" belongs to the realm of academic folklore and not to the academic disciplines themselves.

Should we then reject any attempt to use the Babylonian Talmud in land of Israel studies? It is quite tempting to respond in the affirmative. This sounds quite "scientific" and modern, not to mention convenient, since the Talmud itself is difficult, its study poses many obstacles, and textual and interpretive questions exhaust the researcher. The temptation is even greater since Jewish law, beginning in the medieval period, has sanctified the Babylonian tradition. The Babylonian Talmud has become the primary foundation of the halakhah and midrash. Consequently, undermining its authenticity is liable to serve argumentative ends. Such an answer, however, seems to be too easy, for several reasons:

a) as was noted above, the foundation of the sugiyah contains material that originated in the reality and/or in the land of Israel study hall.

b) the Babylonian Talmud at times parallels the land of Israel material. These instances may contain textual variants or changes of great value, and in such cases the Babylonian text may indeed be the original version.

c) the reality in Babylonia differed from that in the land of Israel. The two communities were situated in provinces of different empires; the land and climatic conditions were similarly disparate. Regarding everyday life, however, an examination of all the data from the nearby provinces is of great scholarly interest. The researcher examining the economy of the land of Israel, and especially its agriculture, is well advised to make the widest possible use of testimonies from the adjoining provinces (Egypt or Greece). The ethno-archaeological testimony from the traditional Arab village also is relevant. It is within this context that the Babylonian testimonies must be examined, albeit with care—but they certainly cannot be ignored.

A few brief examples will suffice. The land of Israel sources use the term "manah [appointed]" to describe the appointment of a sage as a member of the Sanhedrin or as a "Rabbi," while the Babylonian Talmud makes exclusive use of the verb "samakh." As Albeck has demonstrated, in early times, an appointment was made by the laying on (*semikhah*) of the hands on the head of the candidate. The form of the ceremony was later changed, apparently so as to prevent any similarity to Christian practices. The land of Israel sources "updated" the sources and their language and used the new term, while the Babylonian Talmud, which was unaware of the comparison with Christianity, preserved the previous formulation.[3]

The Babylonian Talmud declares that "any town whose roofs are higher than the synagogue will eventually be destroyed" (B. Shab. 11a). Obviously, this opinion is proof only that, according to the rabbis, the synagogue should be higher than the other buildings in the town. It is not even an operative guideline, but merely expresses the desire and preference of the rabbis. There is also a Tannaitic source for this opinion, with a different formulation (T. Meg. 3:23). (Incidentally, this guideline was followed in many, but not all, towns.) Babylonian synagogues were generally situated outside the city, while such public buildings in the land of Israel were located within the settlement itself. The dicta of the Babylonian Amoraim therefore reflect the reality of the land of Israel, but with Babylonian examples and in Babylonian formulation. In this instance, the study of synagogues in the land of Israel may ignore the Babylonian testimony, since a Tannaitic source is available to the researcher.

In another law, the Babylonian Amoraim disagree regarding the obligation to recite Havdalah (the prayer marking the end of the Sabbath) in the synagogue. The reason given by the proponents of its recitation is that guests sleep in the synagogue (B. Pes. 101a). Once again, this explanation is suitable only for the land of Israel, in which

---

[3] H. Albeck, "Semikha and Minnui and Beth Din," in *Zion* 8 (1943), pp. 85-93 (in Hebrew).

accommodations were provided in the synagogues (based on both Talmudic and archaeological proofs), but it is doubtful whether such a rationale was applicable to Babylonia, in which the synagogues were located outside the settlements. In such a case, the Babylonian source is importance for its description of synagogue life in the land of Israel. If this were an isolated source, nothing could be learned from it regarding the reality in the land of Israel; however, in conjunction with land of Israel sources, it enables the researcher to draw a less monochromatic and more profound picture.

The main drawback of my book is that it does not contain a discussion of each individual source. Consequently, I was forced to decide whether and how to use a specific source, but without explaining my reasoning. I used few sources from the Babylonian Talmud only in two instances:

1. if they refer to a phenomenon not present in Babylonia, and it was highly probable that the described reality existed only, or mainly, in the land of Israel;

2. if the Babylonian testimony is joined by proofs from the land of Israel. On the other hand, I examined whether the Babylonian testimony differs from that of the land of Israel and at times noted such instances; among the many examples of this, see, e.g., pp. 298, 383, 397, and many more. This seems to me to be a careful and balanced approach, and is not "fundamentalist," erring neither by noncritical acceptance nor by extreme and indiscriminate criticism.

THE MIDRASHIC LITERATURE

The midrashic literature was redacted after the completion of the Talmud, ca. the fifth-eighth centuries. It presumably could be argued that the testimony in this literature is reflective solely of the reality during this period. This claim requires an exhaustive examination; within the limited purview of this response, I will confine myself to noting that most of the midrashim contain only earlier material and do not reflect the reality from the time of their redaction or reflect it only in limited degree. Thus, e.g. the enemy is still pagan Rome, and Christianity is still not the enemy, generally speaking; Islam is hardly mentioned. There are a number of exceptions to this rule, such as Pirkei de-Rabbi Eliezer, but this not the forum for a proper discussion of this phenomenon.

THE BARAITOT INCORPORATED IN THE AMORAIC SOURCES

The Amoraic sources frequently incorporate Tannaitic teachings, which are introduced by a series of well known terms. In the Babylonian Talmud: "*tanu Rabbanan* [our masters taught]," "*tanya*," "*detanya*," etc., and in the land of Israel sources: "*it tani* [one Tanna...]," etc. These expressions presumably could constitute proof for the Tannaitic period, but, conversely, they raise the suspicion that the teachings of the Tannaim were altered: the chain of transmission was damaged, and the early testimony was "corrected" or "updated." The researchers of the period are undecided on this point. I changed my opinion on this issue following a study I concluded a few years ago. I learned from a precise examination that *sometimes* the dicta of the Tannaim were changed and "updated." This is discernible in a subject discussed in many sources, both Tannaitic and Amoraic, when all the testimonies in the Tannaitic literature present one approach, and all, or the majority, of the Amoraic sources (including baraitot and extra-Mishnaic citations of Tannaim) favor another view. This issue is deserving of a separate detailed methodological discussion; in this review, only a single example will suffice: the Rabbinic literature contains testimonies of the payment of wages and the giving of charity to the rabbis. Such testimonies are present only in the Amoraic literature (including baraitot), while the Tannaitic sources oppose, or ignore, such a possibility. This arouses our suspicion that the granting of payment to the rabbis was a purely Amoraic concept and practice. This conclusion is not mere supposition but is based on a meticulous comparison of the traditions appearing in the midrashei halakhah or in the Tosefta with their transmission in the Talmuds and on a compilation of a large number of sources.[4]

On the other hand, many baraitot were undoubtedly transmitted verbatim. This can easily be discerned in the many instances in which a baraita is present in both the Jerusalem Talmud and in the Tosefta. Moreover, some of the changes are legitimate, seem to be original, and are merely an opinion different from that in the Tannaitic source; in such instances, it cannot be determined that the Tannaitic teachings were "corrected" or "updated" in the Talmud.

The methodological conclusion is clear. If a baraita cited in the Talmud has a Tannaitic source, the two must be compared. If there

---

[4] A detailed discussion of the subject will appear in a book jointly authored by C. Safrai and myself (to appear shortly).

are differences, the Tannaitic source is slightly preferable, albeit subject to the judgment of the scholar and his understanding of the
conditions of the period. The researcher makes a breakthrough when
he can indicate a series of Tannaitic sources and an additional series ·
of testimonies in the Amoraic literature attributed to Tannaim, while
the Amoraic sources present a picture or approach different from
that in the parallels in the Tannaitic literature; this would constitute
a clear example of change and development. If, on the other hand,
the baraita in the Talmud has no earlier parallels, nor are there any
close Tannaitic testimonies, this may lead us to suspect that such
testimony was influenced by later positions and a later reality. In
such an instance, this dictum may attest to Amoraic teachings. No
testimony is to be rejected out of hand, but rather is to be first given
its day in court. It is to be accepted as testimony, while the researcher
must carefully consider whether to date it to the Amoraic period or to
the Tannaitic.

Rabbinic Narratives—Literature or Reality?

Another argument, which Prof. Neusner did not raise in the current
critique, is that Rabbinic narratives do not describe the reality.
Rather, they constitute a literary genre whose contents were dictated
by a literary model. They were not written to describe a reality but
rather to advance a religious idea or educational message, to which
the "realistic" description is wholly subservient. It is patently un-
feasible to examine each individual testimony, narrative, and legal or
social expression. Such a subservience of content to literary form
most likely occurred at times; this argument has not been proved, nor
has any rationale been advanced to support it. I further maintain that
a literary expression constitutes the realistic truth par excellence.

A single example will suffice for our purposes. It is related that a
load of beans from "abroad" arrived in Miron, and R. Aqiba ruled
(on a provisional basis) that all the beans in the marketplace were to
be regarded as originating outside the land of Israel, which was of
great halakhic significance (T. Dem. 4:13). It may be concluded from
this narrative that in the time of the Tannaim (the tradition regarding R. Aqiba's decision was transmitted by R. Yose) a cargo from
abroad was likely to come to Miron, with the possible conclusion that
this was an exceptional occurrence, and that Miron was a quite large

Jewish settlement with its own marketplace. R. Yose related this narrative in order to exemplify a legal principle.

Did the incident actually take place? Perhaps. But this is not the issue at hand. It may be assumed that R. Yose told his audience a logical story. If the narrative were schematic or fictional, he most likely would have spoken of wheat or olives instead of beans, and have set it in Jerusalem or Sephhoris, and not in Miron. Furthermore, even if the story did not actually take place, it had to sound logic to the audience; in the final analysis, a rabbi would not have illustrated a halakhic ruling with an imaginary story that would seem strange to his audience. Accordingly, the narrative presents a reasonable and normal reality. Moreover, if the incident actually occurred, it is to be regarded as episodic—not as a description of life in general, but as an isolated, random event that is hardly indicative of daily life, merely a single stone of the entire mosaic awaiting completion. If, on the other hand, this is a theoretical narrative, it is indicative of a conception of the reality, i.e., how the contemporary scholars viewed their life. For the historian, this is the highest level of reality, not a transient episode but summary, not a single stone of a mosaic, but rather the picture in its entirety. This is still not the reality but only its image in the eyes of the sage; the question of differentiating between the reality and its image is a separate issue (see below).

Every essay, even if it deals with a fictitious law, reflects the reality known to it. Take, for example, the well known imaginary story of Baron Munchausen, who participated in a winter hunt, and the trumpet blasts were frozen in his trumpet. It was only in the inn that the trumpet "thawed out" and the blast issued forth. Did this actually take place? It is doubtful. But does it reflect a reality? The depiction of the hunt and the inn is realistic, as is the winter, albeit with exaggerations, hyperbole, literary and tendentious motifs, and, needless to say, changes resulting from the development of the narrative and fading memory in later times. We see that the passing of time leads to a blurring of the clarity of the sources. Recent studies indicate the weakness of human memory. In these researches, events as remembered by the public a generation after they occurred are compared with the testimonies from the time of the occurrence itself—the memories of living people in comparison with contemporary archival sources. These studies teach how treacherous oral memory can be and to what degree it is "updated" under the influence of developments. No modern scholar, however, would refrain from using these testimonies and recollections, and the events of the past can be reconstructed on the basis of this foundation. This necessitates research and comprehension, carefulness, and sensitivity to the spirit of the period. Scholars of the "Jerusalem school" wrestle with such issues—not innocence, but rather critical and careful research.

An additional problem is whether the background for the dicta of the rabbis was the reality for the society as a whole or that of the subculture of their immediate environment. The question deserves extensive study but is of lesser significance for the economic realm, which is the subject of my book. For example, the midrash explains that when a righteous individual, such as Jacob, leaves a city, "its splendor and its glory depart." This description may have reflected only what was sensed by the members of the study hall society, while the repercussions of such an individual's departure would be much more limited within the public at large. Moreover, this description is not neutral, and the rabbis sought to make use of it for the education of the people. Consequently, the dictum does not reflect the reality within all strata of the society, but, rather, constitutes a demand of the public whose fulfillment is the subject of a struggle. The economic descriptions in the Rabbinic literature, on the other hand, usually do not bear an ideological message. Thus, e.g., the rabbis deliberate regarding the question of when tithes are to be set aside and distinguish between locations in which most of the crop is intended for storage in the house of the farmer and those places in which most of the crop is sent to the marketplace. It is possible that most of the public did not set aside tithes, but there is no reason to argue that the rabbis' dicta are not reflective of the market structure. Indeed, could they have related in such a concrete manner to an imaginary economic structure? Furthermore, the multistratified Rabbinic literature is so rich and complex that it contains not only an expression of the reality of the rabbis but also an echo of the public as a whole. This argument requires proofs and an additional discussion, which would exceed the scope of the present article.

Yet another question is whether all the halakhah established by the rabbis was in fact honored. It may safely be assumed that it was not. Even modern law is not implemented in its entirety; otherwise, police forces would have a surfeit of time on their hands. We can compose from within the Rabbinic literature a list of laws that did not enjoy full compliance and other areas in which the public did heed its sages. Once again, a much more comprehensive discussion of this issue is in order.

DATING TRADITIONS BY ATTRIBUTION AND THE RELIABILITY OF THE CHAIN OF TRANSMISSION

Some researchers date Rabbinic dicta on the basis of their attribution. Prof. Neusner opposes this for two reasons: 1) There is no certainty that the name of the author of the teaching has been accurately transmitted; and 2) the dictum may have been distorted, and the original teaching cannot be reconstructed on the basis of the extant text.

If such criticism had been directed against *The Economy of Roman Palestine*, I would not have felt the need to respond, since the overwhelming majority of the arguments in my book are not based on the attributed author of dicta; for my purposes, dating as Amoraic or Tannaitic suffices. I relied upon attribution only in a number of exceptional cases (see below). Even according to those who maintain that the attribution is reliable, this is the latest date, for at times a sage transmits the teaching of his teacher. With this proviso, Neusner's two assumptions are problematic, and citing them as axiomatic does not contribute to a proper discussion of the matter at hand.

The Reliability of Attribution: Scholars have mainly examined the chain of transmission in the Babylonian Talmud, which is not the subject of my study. The Tannaitic and land of Israel sources have been less thoroughly examined. The subject is a complex one and is worthy of a detailed discussion. In the current context, I will mention only a few contradictory propositions and data:

1. The ancient world was decidedly quite adept at preserving early traditions; nor can there be any doubt that the transmission process was accompanied by distortions and developments. Due, however, to the limited nature of orderly written transcription, the oral transmission was of paramount importance. Thus, e.g., the Muslim Hadith traditions preserve chains of transmission extending over more than ten generations. Such written records are an inexhaustible source of historical information, even though at times the same dictum may have been transmitted in a number of alternative chains. Why should such documents be more reliable than the transmission traditions in the Rabbinic sources? Merely because they are not written in Hebrew?

2. The Rabbis undoubtedly prided themselves on the accuracy of their transmission. The Rabbinic literature repeats the obligation to properly attribute the teachings one relates. A Tannaitic midrash

already presents this as part of the teacher-pupil relationship (Sifrei, Bamidbar 157, p. 213), and this thought is repeated dozens of times in the Palestinian midrashim and in both Talmuds. Sifrei asks: "From whence do we know that the one who exchanges the attribution of teachings by Rabbi Eliezer to Rabbi Joshua...and who declares the impure pure and the pure impure transgresses a negative commandment?..." (Sifrei, Devarim 188, p. 227; cf., Midrash Gadol, Deut. 19:14; Midrash Tannaim, ed. Hoffmann, p. 115). There are many additional proofs of this, which should be compiled in orderly fashion.

3. Nonetheless, the rabbis were aware of the possible confusion in the attribution of teachings. The Rabbinic literature contains a recurring model of the abandoning and forgetting of one's learning. There are three stages to this process of forgetting: in the first phase, "he declares the impure pure," in the second phase, "he exchanges the names of sages," and in the third and final phase, "he forgets chapter headings" (Avot de-Rabbi Nathan, ver. A, 24, p. 78; Tanna de-Vei Eliyahu Zuta 17, ed. Freidmann, p. 8). It is of interest that names are not the first detail to be forgotten and that in their estimation this was likely to be forgotten in a later stage of the process. The partial parallel in Sifrei Devarim 48 (pp. 108-109) mentions all types of corruptions but not the forgetting of names. In the second parallel (quoted above), the order of forgetting is reversed.

4. In practice, the names of the transmitters were corrupted at times. The same dictum is attributed to different sages, and contradictions appear in the words of the same Tanna. These are not necessarily corruptions but constitute sufficient reason to accept the possibility of corruptions. The phrase "one says...and the other says" appears more than three hundred times in the Jerusalem Talmud and the midrashim, and it is not clear which sage held which opinion. More than twenty times the Talmud adds, "and we do not know who stated one opinion and who stated the other," with an attempt to reconstruct the proper attribution. The term used by the Babylonian Talmud for such a clarification is "*tistayem* [will be named]," which begins a sugiyah attempting to determine the attribution. The phrase "*it tani* [there is one who teaches]..." appears in the Jerusalem Talmud, followed by a baraita slightly different from the preceding version. And similarly, "*it de-mahlifi* [there are those who exchange the attribution]."

This leads us to conclude that already in the beit midrash there was an awareness of problems in transmission and great care was taken in this matter. They did not seek to ignore such corruptions but rather regarded them as, at worst, an individual failing or attempted to resolve and bridge the gap between the different traditions. Their fundamental assumption was that the chain of transmission is reliable and that an attempt must be made to determine the source of the current corruption or transposition, without undermining the conventions of the system of transmission. Incidentally, the attempt to resolve traditions is more prevalent in the Babylonian Talmud. The Palestinian Talmud generally presents them as they are, without any additional explanation.

The picture that emerges from all this therefore is not simple. It is obvious, on the one hand, that the attributions are corrupted, while, on the other hand, that rabbis made efforts to prevent such distortions. The question is whether these corruptions were so numerous as to undermine any reliance upon the names. The sources themselves do not concur with such a bleak picture.

The names of hundreds of Tannaim and Amoraim appear in the sources. Despite all the corruptions and questions of formulation and reliability, a preponderance of such corruptions is not indicated. The inventory of the extant names enables us to prepare a satisfactory chronological chart of the teachers, their pupils, and their pupils' pupils. Kalmin has recently published a book on the Rabbis in Babylonia and the traditions regarding them. The style of the Babylonian Talmud draws a clear distinction between X's addressing his teacher, the teacher's addressing his pupil, and two rabbis of the same period and level speaking among themselves. There are thousands of extant narratives from which a chronology of the rabbis may be constructed with great certainty, including a division by academy: Nehardea, Pumbedita, and Sura. If the names of the transmitters were corrupted, how could a later redactor have succeeded in presenting such an elegant, consistent, and precise system? Is such a sophisticated fabrication likely? Boyarin correctly stated that these doubts are nothing more than a house of cards that collapsed.[5]

The Tannaitic sources present a similar picture. Thus, e.g., a rabbi addresses his fellow as "*ahi* [my brother];" there are no known instances in which a later rabbi addressed an earlier rabbi in such a

---

[5] R. Kalmin, *Stories, Authors, and Editors in Rabbinic Babylonia* (Atlanta, 1994); see also D. Boyarin, review in *Hebrew Studies* 36 (1995), pp. 218-220.

manner. Rabban Gamaliel, e.g., never met R. Meir; and the latter never transmitted a teaching from anyone other than his teacher. We may thus state with certainty that R. Judah studied under R. Aqiba and under R. Eliezer, but R. Meir studied only under R. Aqiba— once again: who could have invented such a consistent system comprising many dozens of rabbis and many hundreds of dicta?

For the sake of comparison: The Zohar also contains the name of rabbis, but we immediately sense that it does not represent a reliable tradition. Tannaim disagree with Amoraim, sages from different generations meet, and a second-generation sage, e.g., transmits a dictum from the pupil of his pupil. This is not the case in the Talmudic literature. Corruptions have crept in here and there, but on a localized basis, and there is no reason to assume that the entire transmission system is corrupted.

Conversely, what proof is there of general corruption in this system? Why should such a doubt-ridden argument be regarded as "scientific"? Can such a system-wide failure be proven?

Science must progress. The fears that have been raised of the corruption of the transmission systems are almost totally groundless. A careful examination reveals the existence of individual transmission corruptions, but the system as a whole was found to be reliable. It is high time for the facts to take the place of myths. These suspicions, even if they are presented in an assertive manner, do not have a sufficient basis in the reality.

Corruptions in the Content of Dicta: Life is not easy for the researcher in this realm as well. The situation may be summarized as follows:

1. The rabbis took great care in the transmission of teachings. Accordingly, they would not change the formulation of a dictum, even if its language was archaic. They explain the use of the archaic *hin* (a measure) by insisting that "a person must state [teachings] in the language of his teacher" (M. Ed. 1:3). The above dicta constitute only a small fraction of the Rabbinic teachings on this issue.

2. Rabbis present themselves as the transmitters of the correct tradition. This, by itself, does not obligate the modern scholar to accept this self-evaluation at face value.

3. Corruptions obviously occurred at times. Thus, e.g., close to fifty times some rabbi declares in the Tosefta that "X and Y disagreed only regarding..." (T. Ber. 5:1; T. Shev. 2:5, and many more). In other words, there was a lack of consensus regarding the content of the early disagreement. For example one passage relates that

Rabban Gamaliel banned R. Aqiba; R. Judah remarks on this that it
was not R. Aqiba who was banned but, rather, the head of a city (or
town) was deposed by this rabbi (Y. R.H. 1:57b). At times disagreements are presented as if historical data were in dispute. Thus, e.g.,
in the controversy regarding the sanctity of the Song of Songs, R.
Aqiba claims, "No man in Israel disputed regarding the Song of
Songs" (M. Yad. 3:5), while this very passage contains such a disagreement. R. Aqiba's statement is therefore not a historical evaluation but a religious edict: it is forbidden to dispute the sanctity of the
book, even though this point was disputed. Nonetheless, it is clear
that at times the reliability of the tradition was questioned.

4. Such questioning generally relates to the halakhah or to one of
its details, while the historical and social background is unchallenged.
Historical research is primarily interested in the historical, social,
geographical, technological, and economic background; such realms
are less subject to corruption. For example, the identity of the individual banned by Rabban Gamaliel has not been determined; he
might not have banned anyone. It is similarly doubtful if it can be
deduced from this narrative that the Nasi was formally authorized to
dismiss the Jewish head of a city or town. But is it possible that the
position "head of a town" did not exist? Or that the teller of this
narrative would relate a story that would seem unrealistic to his
listeners?

INTERIM CONCLUSION

While the historical reliability of the tradition, therefore, may be
suspect, it does reflect the world of values and the realistic background of the time of the transmitter of the dictum (with one reservation; see below). This problem is not limited to the Jewish sources but
is present also in Roman, Greek, and medieval sources, both Jewish
and non-Jewish. The researcher must be aware of the problem, but
the concept of dead-end criticism exists in no realm of academic
inquiry. The researcher must contend with the problem but cannot
refuse to make use of the material.

In *The Economy of Roman Palestine* and in other studies, I attempted
to refrain from dating a mishnah or dictum solely on the basis of the
attribution but rather also made use of corroborating data, such as:

1. a number of extant dicta all of which are no earlier than a
certain date. Thus, e.g., I wrote that flax was not common in the land

of Israel in the Yavneh generation, since it is mentioned, for the most part, only in later sources. In another article, I demonstrated that all the dicta relating to liturgical translation in the synagogue are before the Ushan generation.[6] All the sages bearing the title "Rabbi" are from the Yavneh generation or later, all the testimonies regarding burial in the land of Israel do not predate the Ushan generation,[7] and all the instances of banning are from the Ushan generation,[8] etc.

2. if the dictum possesses inner historical logic. Thus, e.g., the testimonies regarding the sages of Usha are compatible with the Bar Kokhba rebellion.

CASE STUDY

From throughout my lengthy book and in a review extending over close to twenty pages, Prof. Neusner patently chose outstanding examples of methodical shortcomings, which should be examined as case studies:

1. *The proofs for the raising of flocks in Hebron.* Neusner asks how I could learn about the Second Temple period from the Tosefta, and about the time of David's son Absalom from the Babylonian Talmud. Such questions seem to be impressive, until we recall the subject of the book: *Roman Palestine*—after the destruction of the Temple. I was not concerned with the economic situation in the Second Temple period and certainly not with that during the First Temple period. To the contrary, the sources are indicative of the time of their redaction, namely, the Roman period, and not of earlier periods.

Can we learn from the midrash regarding the time of Absalom? Certainly not; at any rate, this is not the subject of my book. If the midrash had sources so early it would be irrelevant to the study of the Rabbinic period. To the contrary: the midrash lacks early sources. If so, then why did the exegete add that Absalom went to "the wilderness" to bring sheep? He added this detail because this was the *reality known to him from his own time.* Consequently, the biblical exegesis of the Babylonian Talmud is conducted on the background of the land of

---

[6] Note 2, above.

[7] Note 1, above.

[8] G. Leibson, "Determining Factors in Herem and Nidui (Ban and Excommunication) during the Tannaitic and Amoraic Periods," in *Annual of the Institute for Research in Jewish Law* 2 (1971), pp. 292-342 (in Hebrew).

Israel reality in the time of the specific Amoraic author of the dictum.

If the Babylonian Talmud were an isolated source, we might well suspect that it is unrealistic; however, it is joined by a series of land of Israel sources. As for the Tosefta: can we learn from it regarding the Second Temple period? Possibly, but that is not the subject of my book. The exegete evidently thought that sheep were raised in Hebron, apparently because this was the reality with which he was familiar. This is the subject of the book, and this is the conclusion indicated by the sources.

This is not the complete picture. The three pages discussing the issue cite additional Talmudic proofs for the raising of flocks in "the wilderness" as well as archaeological proofs. Thus, e.g., the sketch of an estate house with a residential structure and six ship or goat pens. Furthermore, it is difficult to discuss the economy or a region without knowledge of the area.

The Hebron region is located in the desert fringe, and the raising of flocks is the main economy in the desert, almost universally throughout the world, both in the past and at present. Consequently, the sources that were regarded with suspicion do in fact indicate an actual, proven, and reasonable reality.

The fear was raised that the Talmudic sources, and especially the Babylonian Talmud, are unreflective of the historical reality. No proof has been offered for such a claim, and it serves only to sow doubt. In this case, at least, such a fear is groundless, and even the Babylonian Talmud reflects an early reality. The methodological conclusion to be drawn from this is that, at least in this instance, *the method of disputing the sources has collapsed, regardless of the aggressive formulation of the charges, and no matter how many times they are repeated.*

2. *R. Tarfon's wealth*: In support of this thesis, I cited the narrative regarding R. Tarfon's contribution to R. Aqiba (Lev. Rabbah 34:16, p. 812). I would not quote this narrative today, because I have since learned that all the narratives regarding gifts to rabbis appear only in the Amoraic sources (above).[9] Nonetheless, R. Tarfon is recalled in the historical memory of generations as a rich man, in a series of sources. Do these sources reflect a true memory?

---

[9] On the other hand, the parallel in Pesiqta Rabbati 25, 126a-127b states that R. Aqiba used the money for "mitzvot," i.e., charity, and it does not state that the money was given to rabbis. The mss. of Lev. Rabbah also make no mention of the giving of money to rabbis.

The answer is positive, with proof provided by testimonies that already appear in the Tannaitic literature. Thus, e.g., it is related that he married three hundred women in a drought year in order to feed them from terumah (T. Ket. 5:1). The story is undoubtedly aggadic in nature, and it is doubtful whether it actually took place, but, once again, why is this related specifically about R. Tarfon? The answer is that, seventy years after his death, he was still remembered as a rich man. There is no reason to doubt such a tradition.

Moreover, there is an extant series of Amoraic narratives regarding R. Tarfon's wealth (some of which are cited in my book). Consequently, this is a popular, widespread, and accepted memory, which had its beginnings at least two generations after the sage in question. It patently is exaggerated, but is there a tangible basis for doubting it? Do scholars consider and evaluate Hellenistic, Roman, or Byzantine traditions in a similar manner?

3. *The wealth of R. Eliezer b. Hyrcanus.* The beginning of R. Eliezer's scholarly career is described in four Amoraic traditions.[10] The traditions differ in formulation and content, but they share a common nucleus that describes R. Eliezer as the son of wealthy parents in the late Second Temple period and says that he began to study at an early age, against the wishes of his affluent father. In other words, R. Eliezer is remembered in the collective memory of the people, or at least in the memory of those frequenting the study halls, as the son of wealthy parents. One source, Avot de-Rabbi Nathan, is, at the latest, from the early Amoraic period, slightly more than a century after the incident it describes. Is there any reason to assume that the narrative is corrupted? Moreover, an allusion to R. Eliezer's belonging to the affluent classes appears in the Mishnah, which describes him as the owner of a vineyard in Kfar Tabbi, near Lydda (T. M.S. 5:16). The area of the vineyard is not specified. The usual arrangement in the Roman Empire, however, was that the wealthy individual lived in a central settlement and his distant land holding in the village was worked by sharecroppers, hired laborers, or slaves. Such an arrangement is reflected in the tradition regarding R. Eliezer, thus corroborating the report of his wealth.

The purpose of our discussion of R. Tarfon's and R. Eliezer's wealth was to demonstrate the existence of a series of testimonies

---

[10] Gen. Rabbah 41 (42)a, p. 398; Avot de-Rabbi Nathan, ver. A, chap. 6; ver. B, chap. 13, pp. 30-31; and additional sources.

relating to wealthy residents of Lydda in the Yavneh generation. These traditions list, in addition to these two, R. Eleazar b. Azariah, Baitos b. Zonin, and others. Was the preservation of a quite exceptional series of narratives of the wealthy from Lydda in the Yavneh generation merely coincidental? As was noted, the series substantiates the single testimony; in such a case, the testimony is seen to be reliable and may be dated in accordance with the entire series.

As chance would have it, two years after the publication of my book, a magnificent mosaic pavement, apparently the finest such pavement in the land of Israel from the Roman period, most probably from a private house, was excavated in the ancient Lydda. The finds are fragmentary and have not been published. Nonetheless, we cannot ignore their suitability to the conclusion that a special group of the wealthy lived in Roman Lydda.

PROGRESS OR STAGNATION

Science must advance. A generation ago, following a number of earlier works, Prof. Neusner advanced the *hypothesis* that the Rabbinic sources could not be used as a historical source because of distortions in transmission and because of the isolation of the rabbis from the public. He argued that the traditions may have been corrupted or that this was highly likely. This argument, albeit without proof, was justified, raised doubts, and also undermined the conventional wisdom. Some researchers accepted the new methodology he proposed, while others opposed it. My book was not written as a methodological treatise. Its methodological contribution is minor, and it focuses on two issues:

A. The collection of Talmudic testimonies together forms a consistent, continuous, and logical description of an open market economy.

B. The series of archaeological proofs constitutes a proof parallel and independent to the Rabbinic sources. The archaeological testimony supports both certain details and the comprehensive picture. The list of parallels is extremely long, and, in another essay, I enumerated several dozen such testimonies. Five such testimonies that I cited in my book will suffice:

1. The Rabbinic sources describe a regional center of potters in Kfar Hananiyyah. Excavations at the site uncovered a kiln, and a

detailed archaeometric study showed that all the vessels in Galilee were made from the clay in the vicinity of the village.[11]

2. The Rabbinic literature discusses the building of rural roads, which were found throughout the land of Israel.[12] The large number of roads corresponds to the literary testimonies regarding donkey caravans going from one village to the next, which provided the primary means of marketing between the city and the village.

3. The Rabbis tell of towers that had been built in the past in vineyards, and such towers from the Hellenistic period have been found, mainly throughout Samaria and northern Judea.[13]

4. The many literary testimonies concerning the use of cash and the high level of commerce are confirmed by the rich numismatic finds in the villages and by synagogue inscriptions mentioning monetary contributions (*Economy*, p. 428).

5. The rabbis' description of a "fair" corresponds to the Roman fair and its many special practices (*Economy*, pp. 243-62).

Mention should also be made of an additional example not mentioned in the book. The Rabbinic literature contains testimonies regarding the priestly families that functioned in the Temple in the late Second Temple period and that were later (after the Bar Kokhba rebellion?) concentrated in the villages of Galilee. This would seem to be a literary construction based on Biblical verses. To our surprise, however, testimonies regarding such families are to be found in Josephus, the New Testament, inscriptions, and a document from the Dead Sea finds. We learn of the families in the Galilean villages also from synagogue inscriptions in Israel. The realistic background of their activity is debatable, but the Rabbinic literature indisputably depicts the thoughts and opinions prevalent at the time. A synagogue in Rehob contains a lengthy inscription that copied the laws of the Palestinian Talmud. The differences between the inscription and the extant text of the Palestinian Talmud provided material for several studies. It is clear, however, that the Palestinian Talmud constituted the basis for the inscription, and it was an important document for contemporary Jews, far in excess of the significance assigned it by Prof. Neusner.

---

[11] *Economy*, p. 205; D. Adan-Bayewitz, *Common Pottery in Roman Galilee* (Ramat Gan, 1993).

[12] *Economy*, pp. 269-287; S. Dar, *Landscape and Pattern* (Oxford, 1986), pp. 126-146.

[13] Dar, pp. 88-125; *Economy*, pp. 133-134.

These and other arguments pose a serious challenge to those questioning the value of the Rabbinic literature as a historical source. The question arises, how could "questionable", "late," and "confused" sources have produced a consistent picture, and how could they correspond to the archaeological testimonies? It is hardly conceivable that all this is mere coincidence.

The correspondence between the archaeological finds and the Rabbinic testimonies is not total, nor is that between the archaeological finds and the Roman literary sources. The modern researcher is aware that the literary sources, like the archaeological finds, illuminate the ancient reality in a partial manner, each from its own frame of reference. They do not furnish contradictory pictures but, rather, different strata of the same reality. Furthermore, the authors of antiquity did not depict the reality as it was, but its image—the world as they knew and evaluated it. Even today, despite the plethora of available information, the same reality is subject to differing interpretations and evaluations. It accordingly is only natural that an early author (the Roman writer or the Jewish sage) would depict his assessment as the reality, despite the misleading details inherent in the former.

Thus, e.g., the Tannaitic sources frequently mention the synagogue as a prevalent reality as early as the second century. According, however, to the archaeological finds, synagogues were constructed only in the first and third centuries, and we possess no evidence of synagogues in the Yavneh and Usha generations. The degree of correspondence between the Dead Sea documents and the Rabbinic halakhot also requires study.

The situation at present is that doubts have been raised regarding the reliability of the Rabbinic literature as a historical source. The picture that emerges from a careful study, however, is more complex. In most instances in which we possess parallel testimonies, they correspond or are close to the reality indicated by the Rabbinic literature. The differences are significant, and require clarification. This is the direction that further study must take, and I hope to continue to participate in this effort.

The modest methodological contribution made by my book lies in the presentation of these two arguments, to be precise, of the data from the economic sphere, since I did not discuss information pertaining to other realms. Further research, as well as the methodological critique, therefore, must focus upon these arguments, which break new ground. I see no reason to repeat the old arguments that have already been expressed so cogently in print so many times.

The author of a book is usually not given the opportunity to respond to criticism of his work. Within this forum, I will raise only a number of points, in place of a response to the arguments directly pertaining to my book.

1) I did not argue that anyone who did not study in a yeshivah is not qualified to engage in the Rabbinic sources (incidentally, I did not study in a yeshivah either). I merely sought to explain the difficulties entailed in gaining accessibility to these sources.

2) I provided an example of the linguistic difficulty of studying the Rabbinic literature for those fluent in modern Hebrew. Unfortunately, Prof. Neusner took this personally. The truth is that when I wrote these lines I had in mind my Israeli colleagues who have difficulty in understanding these sources.

3) I did not argue that the Rabbis have no utopian vision. To the contrary, I devoted a short chapter to the economic Utopia of the Rabbis (pp. 304-314). Notwithstanding this, I claimed that they did not attempt to change the economic reality but rather to adapt their demands accordingly. They did not determine how to sow or reap, which fruit to pick, but rather the method of setting aside tithes and when the fruit acquires impurity according to the existing practices. On second thought, I should have added a reservation that this was the general rule. On occasion, however, they sought to change the economic reality; regarding interest, e.g., the sages attempted to uproot this economic structure (without much success, according to their testimony). They also sought to curb commerce within the context of the Roman fair; here, too, they were forced to surrender to the prevailing reality.

4) I am accused of accumulating unimportant facts. Chapters 2 and 3 describe the productive and commercial branches; in my estimation, the economy is fueled mainly by the productive branches. The other chapters discuss the usual economic topics discussed in studies of ancient economies. I know of no other way in which to engage in research of the subject. Obviously, I did not deal with every economic issue, such as, e.g., monetary matters.

5) I made minimal use of Josephus and the New Testament because the book deals with the period after the destruction of the Second Temple, and these sources are irrelevant to the period under study.

This does not put an end to the methodological discussion, which is at the heart of Neusner's critique and my response. I am not certain that my book is an example of the proper utilization of the sources, but I hope that it may have shed light on several methodological questions. The study of the sources must be careful and critical, but excessive critical inquiry is to be discouraged. A critical approach must lead to careful research and not to an excuse in futility—dead-end criticism. Most importantly, fundamentalism, which accepts the sources uncritically, is to be opposed—along with the scholar who is fundamentally critical and believes in criticism for its own sake.

VIII. RABBINIC SOURCES FOR HISTORICAL STUDY

Günter Stemberger
University of Vienna

The use of Rabbinic literature for historical study has a long tradition. Already in the early Middle Ages, the author of the *Seder Tannaim we-Amoraim* and Sherira Gaon, followed by many others, like Abraham ibn Daud and Maimonides, based themselves on Rabbinic sources in order to reconstruct chains of tradition that were to guarantee the reliability of doctrines, the legitimacy of later institutions, and the like. They thus continued the reasoning of tractate Abot, which sought to derive the doctrinal authority of the rabbis directly from the revelation at Sinai. These early texts already consider Jewish history as a history of scholars and their institutions, interrupted time and again by periods of persecution. Classical Jewish historiography since the nineteenth century continued this tradition: Heinrich Graetz, Isaac H. Weiss, Isaac Halevy and others were bound to this strongly biographical orientation of Jewish history in the Talmudic period. Their uncritical approach affects mainly their reconstruction of the interior history of Judaism, but to a more limited extent also general history where it intersects with that of the Jewish people. The Rabbinic texts are taken at face value (unless what they say seems too miraculous, exaggerated, or for other reasons incredible); they are read from the point of view of a much later situation; and the agenda is completely dictated by what the Rabbinic sources want to tell us, without any real control from outside.

A New Critical Consciousness

There have, of course, always been isolated cases of a more critical approach, but only in the last decades has criticism become more systematic, reasoned, and pervasive. If one were to name a single work most typical for this change of paradigm, I should point to Jacob Neusner's *Development of a Legend*.[1] Here, Neusner demonstrated

---

[1] Jacob Neusner, *Development of a Legend. Studies on the Traditions Concerning Yohanan ben Zakkai* (Leiden, 1970).

that, contrary to his earlier attempt to write a biography of Yohanan ben Zakkai,[2] one could not legitimately piece together every bit of information to be found in the Rabbinic sources and fit it into a chronological sequence. The first task, rather, is to study the texts in the documents in which they appear and to analyze the development of traditions from one document to another. The outcome is a history of tradition that only indirectly may lead to the reconstruction of a factual history.

What followed was the demise of Rabbinic biography. Not just the dearth of information about most rabbis—in most cases, just a legal or doctrinal opinion or some interaction with another rabbi is mentioned—that makes it impossible to write biography; an additional problem is that, where real stories are told, they generally depict typical situations and not unique events in the personal life of a certain rabbi: *De rebus agitur, de personis indicatur*. There is no possibility to check information about rabbis in non-Jewish sources.

But it is not just a question of biography. What Rabbinic sources may tell us about institutions of the world of the rabbis—Rabbinic schools, Sanhedrin, and patriarchate—is equally problematic. Other currents of contemporary Judaism are completely neglected; historical developments of a later period are frequently projected back into the beginnings of the Rabbinic movement, and it is hardly possible to recognize historical developments. If we were to take Rabbinic sources at face-value, already a century before the destruction of the Temple, the predecessors of the rabbis, led by the family of Hillel, were the dominant force in the Sanhedrin and powerful enough to tell even the high priests how they had to conduct the cult. After 70, they would have been the sole leaders of the Jewish people in Palestine.

Rabbinic sources, of course, never put forward such claims explicitly. It is, rather, a reconstruction based on unconnected pieces of information found here and there. It does not take into account that the Rabbinic literature is not a uniform corpus but a collection from different periods, with different intentions, and practically all works of propaganda in one way or another. But even most recent attempts to reconstruct a history of the patriarchate on the basis of a critical reading of all the sources arrive at results widely differing one from another.[3] With regard to other institutions like the Sanhedrin, Rab-

---

[2] Jacob Neusner, *A Life of Rabban Yohanan ben Zakkai* (Leiden, 1962).

[3] Cf., David Goodblatt, *The Monarchic Principle. Studies in Jewish Self-Government in Antiquity* (Tübingen, 1994); Martin Jacobs, *Die Institution des jüdischen Patriarchen. Eine*

binic schools, or ordination, there is even less agreement among scholars.

Not only inner-Rabbinic history poses nearly insoluble problems. Similar difficulties arise with regard to general history where we do have the possibility to control Rabbinic data by non-Jewish texts and archaeological evidence. A good example is the Bar Kokhba revolt. For the reconstruction of the factual history, Rabbinic sources are used mainly to supplement external evidence; without such evidence, they are hardly ever considered to be reliable (here again, scholars diverge widely from each other). Their main value seems to be that they witness the long-term impact of these events on Jewish consciousness, the subjective Jewish experience and memory of these events.[4]

It is certainly important to learn about the subjective historical experience of a people, and here the Rabbinic sources are certainly of the greatest value. But, as scholars still wish to look to these sources for factual history, some have turned to them in particular for areas in which no special interests of the Rabbinic redactors are involved, mainly in the fields of administration and economic history, where Rabbinic sources seem to promise better results. But here again, one soon encounters problems. How, for instance, are we to evaluate the frequent complaints about a bad economic situation, rising prices, high taxes, draughts, and failing crops, etc.? Do laments about the unjustness of Roman courts, the pressure of the demands of the Roman army, really reflect reality or does this again just reflect a subjective discontent with foreign rule? Apart from that, one is again confronted with the problems of how to use specific texts for a particular historical period, how to reconstruct an economic *history* in the true sense of the word. The critical acceptance of *per se* important studies by Daniel Sperber and Ze'ev Safrai point to important methodological problems.[5]

---

quellen- und traditionskritische Studie zur Geschichte der Juden in der Spätantike (Tübingen, 1995); L.I. Levine, "The Status of the Patriarch in the Third and Fourth Centuries: Sources and Methodology," in *JJS* 48 (1996), pp. 1-32.

[4] See Peter Schäfer, *Der Bar Kokhba-Aufstand* (Tübingen, 1981). For the more general impact of Roman rule on Jewish historical consciousness, cf., Günter Stemberger, *Die römische Herrschaft im Urteil der Juden* (Darmstadt, 1983); Mireille Hadas-Lebel, *Jérusalem contre Rome* (Paris, 1990).

[5] Daniel Sperber, *Roman Palestine 200-400. Money and Prices* (Ramat Gan, 1991); cf., Karl Strobel, "Inflation und monetäre Wirtschaftstrukturen im 3.Jh. n.Chr. Zu Daniel Sperbers Bild der wirtschafts- und währungsgeschichtlichen Krise," in *Münstersche Beiträge zur Antiken Handelsgeschichte* 8,2 (1989), pp. 10-31; Ze'ev Safrai, *The Economy of Roman Palestine* (London, 1994); cf., Jacob Neusner in this volume.

The Scholarly Response

The new awareness of these many and seemingly insurmountable problems has led to different reactions. Some just despair of the situation and think that we have to give up completely a historical reading of Rabbinic texts. This would be an easy way out but certainly an overreaction and a great loss to scholarship. Others think that all this new criticism is too iconoclastic to be accepted, a historical nihilism. They just ignore the new developments and go on as if nothing had happened. A long tradition of reading the texts seems to justify their earlier understanding.

Most of us try to steer a sound middle course of moderate skepticism. We have to ask ourselves how to justify this position—is it just common sense or are there real criteria?

Are we to accept everything that is not intrinsically unbelievable? But what is believable, what not?

Are we to accept what is not contradicted by other texts and by what is known about the period from non-Jewish sources or from archaeology? This criterion would leave very many details without a possibility of control, because there is no independent attestation.

Are we to accept Rabbinic texts as speaking only for the generation of their redaction? But how can we date the final redaction, how can we be certain that texts have not been changed in the course of transmission? And is this point of view not a minimalism that ought to be overcome by closer study of the texts?

One could continue enumerating similar positions. Whatever position one adopts, a certain measure of arbitrariness remains (not quite unlike the situation in general historiography). It is probably a waste of energy to look for a general set of criteria to be applied in all cases alike. Every case is different and has to be analyzed following a mixture of controls and criteria available in each separate case. And however critical the approach may be, there will always remain a certain amount of common sense and personal judgment.

Test-cases

Absent general criteria to be enumerated, we can best make our point by presenting a few cases that demonstrate what can be done. In a first part, we shall discuss examples illustrating how archaeological discoveries may provide ways of controlling the data of Rabbinic texts; a second part is devoted to examples within Rabbinic literature itself or in which Rabbinic texts may be compared with newly discovered literary material.

For Jewish history in Babylonia, we still have to rely almost exclusively on literary sources. In Palestine, on the other side, extensive archaeological excavations teach us to correct the picture offered by the Rabbinic sources, or—more correctly—to revise our traditional reading of these sources. An particularly striking example is the synagogues with their figurative art that nobody would have expected on the basis of the written sources. Another example, not so easily correlated with the textual evidence, is the excavation of whole cities important in the Rabbinic world. A few short remarks on both types of new evidence will have to suffice in this context.

Synagogue excavations: Systematic surveys of ancient synagogues started about a century ago. Scientific excavations began much later; really sophisticated and comprehensive methods have been applied only in recent decades. After the excavation of dozens of late antique synagogues in Palestine, one negative result is striking: There are only a few traces of synagogues before 70; synagogues identifiable as such became a common phenomenon only in the third century and later.

In Jerusalem, the Theodotos-inscription remains the only archaeological evidence of a synagogue. This synagogue (its date before 70 is controversial) is clearly an institution of Jews returning from the diaspora and serving all visitors from the diaspora. The centrality of the Temple in Jerusalem (and for Judea) seems to have rendered an institution like the synagogue unnecessary, perhaps even an unwanted competitor. Rabbinic texts speaking of hundreds of synagogues in Jerusalem (Y. Ket. 13,35c; Y. Meg. 3,73d; B. Git. 58a; B. Ket. 105a, etc.) have generally been considered to be exaggerated but basically reliable. New Testament texts (mainly Acts 6:9) seemed to support them. Rereading the texts in the light of archaeological discoveries, one sees that the New Testament references to synagogues may be understood as congregations or associations of Cyrenians, Alexandrians, etc., and not of synagogue buildings. This is also the correct understanding of *k̆nesset* in M. Yom. 7:1 (= M. Sot. 7:7f.), which frequently has been understood to refer to a synagogue on the Temple Mount. There is only one early Rabbinic text that clearly speaks of a synagogue building in Jerusalem: Eleazar b. R. Zadoq buys the synagogue of the Alexandrians in Jerusalem (T. Meg. 2:17;

MS. Erfurt 3:6). One might think of identifying this synagogue with the synagogue of the Alexandrians (or freedmen) mentioned in Acts 6:9 and also with the Theodotos-synagogue (Theodotos was perhaps a freedman), thus reducing the whole evidence to just one synagogue for diaspora Jews in Jerusalem.[6] The Talmudic texts speaking of many synagogues in Jerusalem are thus clearly a late ideal picture as the rabbis would have liked it—central is not the Temple and its sacrificial cult but the synagogue and the school connected with it.

The lack of archaeological evidence for synagogues in the time of the Mishnah and the Tosefta also calls for a rereading of what these Rabbinic documents have to say about the synagogue, without reading between the lines what we know about the later situation (mainly since the Middle Ages). There is very little material to be found in the Mishnah, a little more in the Tosefta, and even more in the Yerushalmi, witnessing a growing awareness of the importance of the synagogue on the side of the rabbis. But even at the end of the development, Tzvee Zahavy states: "The limited scope of the sources taken as a whole suggests in my opinion the limitation of Rabbinic control and interest in synagogue administration even down to the fifth century."[7]

David Amit has tried to explain the architectural layout of four synagogues in the Southern Judean Hills—entrance in the east although the wall facing Jerusalem was in the north—with the halakhah (T. Meg. 4[3]:22).[8] If one may speak of "halakhic" reasons, it should be pointed out that this halakhah may have been a pre-Rabbinic custom, recorded in just one Rabbinic text and disregarded in most synagogues, even synagogues much more likely to be under Rabbinic influence (e.g., Hammat Tiberias). One should be very cautious when explaining phenomena of the material culture of this period by halakhah, especially if the term is to demonstrate Rabbinic influence. Many halakhic rules laid down by the rabbis may just follow and register the status quo and not innovate rules the people were supposed to obey.

---

[6] See Günter Stemberger, "The Pre-Christian Paul: Reflections on Recent Publications," in Aharon Oppenheimer and Menahem Mor, eds., *The Beginnings of Christianity* (Jerusalem, forthcoming).

[7] Tzvee Zahavy, *Studies in Jewish Prayer* (Lanham, 1990), p. 86.

[8] David Amit, "Architectural Plans of Synagogues in the Southern Judean Hills and the 'Halakah'," in Dan Urman and Paul V.M. Flesher, eds., *Ancient Synagogues. Historical Analysis and Archaeological Discovery*, 2 vols., (Leiden, 1995), vol. I, pp. 129-156 (first published in Hebrew: *Cathedra* 68, 1993, pp. 6-35).

That the rabbis in general did not determine what was to be done in the synagogue is especially clear from the synagogues' figurative art, found mainly on mosaic floors. When the synagogues of Bet Alfa and Dura Europos were discovered, one still had enormous difficulties reconciling this evidence with the prohibition of images. Only in light of these finds did full attention need to be paid to what is reported in Y. A.Z. 3:3, 42d, that in the days of Yohanan they began to paint on the walls and (as a Genizah fragment adds) in the days of Abun they began to lay mosaics with pictures on them, and they (that is, the rabbis) did non stop them. Many of the developments in the synagogue did not come about on the initiative of the rabbis; they only had to accept what the people did (and this certainly not only in the field of architecture and decoration).

The lack of influence of the rabbis in the synagogue, clearly to be seen also in many Rabbinic sayings, is well illustrated by another fact. About fifty rabbis are mentioned in Palestinian *inscriptions* from the Rabbinic period; the greater part are funerary inscriptions, but a number of synagogue inscriptions also mention rabbis as donors. Shaye Cohen may be too skeptical when he states: "We cannot securely identify any of our epigraphical rabbis with figures known to us from Talmudic texts;"[9] some names mentioned in the catacombs of Beth Shearim are at least very likely to be the names of Talmudic rabbis. But he is absolutely right when he sums up: "the synagogue is not the primary locus of our epigraphical rabbis" (p. 14). Many people were called rabbi without forming part of the Rabbinic establishment; their honorary title was in no way connected with a certain function in the synagogue. Most of them were just local dignitaries.

Dan Urman has tried to identify two rabbis mentioned on inscriptions from the Golan with well-known Rabbinic scholars. One stone from Qisrin bears the Hebrew inscription: "Rabbi Abun, may his resting place be in honor." Urman identifies him with the elder of two Abuns mentioned in the Yerushalmi (early fourth century) and takes a Zoharic statement (Midrash ha-Ne'elam to Ruth, 29a) that "Rabbi Bun spent his whole life in Qisrin" as an authentic tradition referring to Qisrin in the Golan (and not to Caesarea Maritima).[10]

---

[9] Shaye J.D. Cohen, "Epigraphical Rabbis," in *JQR* 72 (1981), pp. 1-17 and especially p. 12. One item has to be added to his repertory: Rabbi Tanhum, mentioned on a lintel in Qisrin; Dan Urman, "Additional Jewish Inscriptions from Dabûra and Qîsrîn in the Golan" (Hebrew), in *Tarbiz* 65 (1995), pp. 515-521.

[10] Dan Urman, "Public Structures and Jewish Communities in the Golan Heights," in Urman and Flesher, op. cit., vol. II, pp. 373-617, 478-481.

The identification is certainly not impossible but highly doubtful, since no Rabbinic source connects Abun with the Golan. Even more problematic is Urman's attempt to rewrite at least a small part of Rabbinic history on the basis of a lintel from Dabûra in the Golan with the Hebrew inscription: "This is the beit midrash of Rabbi Eliezer ha-Qappar." This famous contemporary of Judah ha-Nasi, whom Saul Lieberman tried to identify as the redactor of Sifre Zutta and in whose name a collection of *mishnayyot gedolot* is frequently quoted, is usually thought to have lived and taught in the south, most probably at Lydda; his most important disciple, Hoshaya the Great, founded the school at Caesarea. On the basis of this inscription, Urman transfers both to the Golan.[11] The inscription seems to be secondary, poorly added to the well-sculpted lintel only afterwards and not to be dated precisely. There is always the possibility of homonymy (although ha-Qappar is rare) or that a beit midrash has been named much later in honor of a famed rabbi. Whatever the correct interpretation of the inscription, it is certainly rash on its foundation to make of the Golan a major Rabbinic center and to transfer to it traditions connected with the far more important Jewish center Caesarea, the administrative capital of Palestine. This example clearly demonstrates the dangers inherent in a too direct a combination of archaeological materials and Rabbinic texts.

A last example from the world of the synagogue is the famous halakhic inscription in the synagogue of Rehob in the Beth Shean valley.[12] This inscription of the late sixth century to a large extent reproduces, albeit with small variants, texts known to us from the Yerushalmi concerning the laws of the sabbatical year. Additional halakhic and liturgical texts were written on the plaster covering the columns of the synagogue but have not yet been published, apparently due to the difficulty of reading and combining the many small fragments of plaster. This inscription not only is the earliest copy extant of a Rabbinic text (although redacted in order to fit the context); it gives us valuable insights into the knowledge of Rabbinic halakhah among certain segments of the Jewish population (Rehob

---

[11] Urman, ibid., pp. 432f. For a full discussion, see Dan Urman, "Regarding the Location of the Batei-Midrash of Bar Kappara and Rabbi Hoshaya Rabbah," in *8th World Congress of Jewish Studies* II, Jerusalem 1982, Hebrew Part 8-16; idem, "Rabbi Eliezer ha-Qappar and Bar Qappara—Father and Son?" (Hebrew), in *Beer-Sheva* 2 (1985), pp. 7-25.

[12] Yaacov Sussmann, "A Halakhic Inscription from the Beth-Shean Valley," (Hebrew) in *Tarbiz* 43 (1973), pp. 88-158.

was just a small village, not a Rabbinic center!) and, we may also suppose, of the growing influence of the rabbis among the people. It also allows us to draw certain conclusions regarding the practical impact of halakhic decisions of the rabbis. It would be premature to generalize on the basis of this inscription, but it will certainly influence our reading of other Rabbinic texts as well.

Larger archaeological contexts: Important as isolated finds—synagogues, tombs, inscriptions—are for reshaping our approach to Rabbinic texts as historical sources, still more promising are the excavations of entire cities of the Talmudic period. Tiberias as the center of the patriarchate and rabbinate for a long period would be of the utmost interest; but the presence of the modern city does not allow systematic excavation. In Caesarea, the Jewish presence was not important enough to have a real impact on the shape of the capital and its material remains. More promising are the large-scale excavations at Scythopolis—Beth Shean—although most of the finds postdate the redaction of the Yerushalmi. For Gideon Fuks, Byzantine Scythopolis was just an epilogue in his history of the city;[13] now this later period would certainly be an important chapter of the book.

Much is to be expected of the still ongoing excavations at Sepphoris.[14] When Stuart Miller wrote his history of Sepphoris, he still had to rely mainly on literary sources, above all the rich Talmudic and midrashic material referring to the city.[15] Yehuda Ne'eman could already take into account several seasons of the new excavations;[16] but the chapters on the archaeological remains and those based on literary sources are still largely juxtaposed and not really integrated into one coherent whole. At any rate, the book came too early—the synagogue was discovered only when it was already in print, and the excavations are still going on.

There are, of course, many elements in the Rabbinic sources that by their nature cannot find expression in material remains. But much can be related to the results of the excavations, as, e.g., the general character of the city (the statements of Eusebius and Epiphanius that Sepphoris was a completely Jewish city seem to be thoroughly con-

---

[13] Gideon Fuks, *Scythopolis — A Greek City in Eretz-Israel* (Hebrew) (Jerusalem, 1983).

[14] For a recent survey of the results, see Zeev Weiss and Ehud Netzer, "The Hebrew University Excavations at Sepphoris," (Hebrew) in *Qadmoniot* 30,1 (1997), pp. 2-21.

[15] Stuart S. Miller, *Studies in the History and Traditions of Sepphoris* (Leiden, 1984).

[16] Yehuda Ne'eman, *Sepphoris in the Period of the Second Temple, The Mishnah and the Talmud* (Hebrew) (Jerusalem, 1993).

tradicted by the monumental pagan remains), the relative importance of the different segments of the population, their relative
wealth, the mixture or segregation of the different groups, etc. (It is,
of course, too early to draw far-reaching conclusions from the situation of the synagogue away from the center). Many statements of the
Rabbinic sources referring to Avodah Zarah and how to avoid con-
tacts with pagans on their festivals may find their illustration by the
results of archaeology. The remains of churches and monasteries and
their dates of construction may also teach us how to interpret the
silence of Rabbinic sources regarding the advance of Christianity.
Did the Christians arrive too late to make a real impact on the mind
of the rabbis, could they still be mixed up with pagans, or did the
rabbis just prefer to ignore the changes?

One special point deserves note: On the basis of some non-Jewish
texts, historians postulated a revolt of the Jews of Sepphoris against
the Caesar Gallus in 351 or 352; when the revolt was crushed, the
whole city is said to have been razed to the ground. A number of
Rabbinic sources were found to reflect these disastrous events (mainly
Pesiqta Rabbati 8) and were used for a detailed reconstruction of the
revolt.[17] Already before the excavations, there had been a growing
skepticism against the amalgamation of several incoherent Rabbinic
texts into a full picture of a Jewish revolution and its being crushed.[18]
The excavations seem to confirm this skepticism. Whereas the
American archaeologists at Sepphoris think that at least one building
destroyed by fire may be related to the "Gallus-revolt," the Israeli
team is convinced that up to now there is no level of destruction that
can be clearly related to these events; whatever destruction there was
in the middle of the fourth century may better be explained as the
result of the earthquake of 363.[19]

What do we learn from the excavation of whole cities like Scythopolis and Sepphoris? How can we relate texts (not only Rabbinic
texts) and material remains? There is a certain danger of harmoniza-
tion, of reading the archaeological results selectively in order to confirm the Rabbinic sources; also to be avoided is the use of archaeological materials as mere illustration without real integration of the

---

[17] See Michael Avi-Yonah, *The Jews under Roman and Byzantine Rule* (Jerusalem,
1984), pp. 176-181.

[18] See Günter Stemberger, *Juden und Christen im Heiligen Land. Palästina unter Konstan-
tin und Theodosius* (Munich, 1987), pp. 132-150.

[19] Weiss and Netzer, op. cit., p.10.

different sets of evidence. We still have to work out methods to make
the most of all the evidence; but the newly discovered material will
certainly contribute to our way of reading Rabbinic texts as historical
sources. The thereby sharpened awareness of how the redactors of
these sources perceive reality, what they choose to see or to ignore,
will teach us also how to read texts that cannot be related to material
remains. We have here, then, far more than the mere possibility of
verifying certain isolated texts.

Literary problems: We now briefly examine some problems of using
Rabbinic texts for historical study where no archaeological controls
are available but where a literary analysis can help us decide whether
the text is historically useful or not. It is comparatively easy to eliminate texts from historical consideration; but a positive decision must
always remain tentative, since no real proofs are available. The following examples are all concerned with the question of whether Rabbinic texts contain reliable traditions going back before 70.

The reliability of baraitot: Tannaitic traditions outside of the Mishnah,
marked by quotation formulas like *tannu rabbanan, tanya,* and the like
and written in Tannaitic Hebrew, are still frequently considered reliable witnesses to the beginnings of the Rabbinic movement and even
to an earlier period. This assumption of historicity often is made
without consideration of where the baraita is recorded, in an early
Palestinian writing, in the Babylonian Talmud, or in a late midrashic
compilation. The remark that a tradition is a baraita decides for
many the historical usefulness of the text without further questions.
The awareness that not every baraita is equally trustworthy is not
new; some geonim already saw the problem. But this has had little
impact on the historical use of such texts. Only in recent decades has
a careful linguistic analysis of Babylonian baraitot shown that their
language does not reflect the earliest level of Tannaitic Hebrew and
that, consequently, they may not be used to create a historical grammar and dictionary of Mishnaic Hebrew.[20] To a more limited extent,
the problem also exists in Palestinian baraitot and even in the Tosefta. It is possible, of course, that the language of a tradition has
been somewhat modernized in the course of transmission without

---

[20] Menahem Moreshet, "The Language of the Baraytot in the T.B. is not Mhel"
(Hebrew), in *H. Yalon Memorial Volume* (Ramat Gan, 1974), pp. 275-314; idem, "New
and Revived Verbs in the Baraytot of the Babylonian Talmud," (Hebrew) in *Archive
of the New Dictionary of Rabbinical Literature* I (Ramat Gan, 1972), pp. 113-162.

affecting the contents. But such changes suggest that one has to use such texts very cautiously.

A good test case is the baraita on the eighteen decrees decided according to the teaching of the school of Shammai in the upper room of Hananiah ben Hizkiyya (Y. Shab. 1:6, 3c-d). This text has frequently been used by historians for the reconstruction of the events leading up to the Jewish revolt against Rome in 66.[21] On the basis of it, it has been concluded that, probably in 66 C.E., after a bloody clash, the radical Shammaites outnumbered the more compromising Hillelites and decreed a number of measures: no longer to accept sacrifices from gentiles and to draw a strict line of demarcation between Jews and non-Jews. This led to the outbreak of the Great War.

A closer analysis of the baraita reveals that it is based on a text in M. Shab. 1:4 that hints to eighteen halakhot that have been decided in the upper room of Hananiah ben Hizkiyya on a single day when the Shammaites had the majority over the Hillelites. The text does not specify which halakhot were decided that day; the context suggests that they had to do with the law of the Sabbath. In T. Shab. 1:16, the passage is quoted with the added comment: "and that day was as harsh for Israel as the day when the golden calf was made." As the continuation in T. Shab. 1:17 makes clear ("On that day they overfilled the *seah* measure.... For so long as the measure is full and one puts more into it, in the end it will give up part of what [already] is in it"), this comment is based on the fear that exaggerated halakhic rigor will endanger the observance even of the most essential halakhot (at Soferim 1:7, the same phrase describes the day the Torah was translated into Greek; according to the redactors of Soferim, the translation endangered the true Torah).

The baraitot in the Yerushalmi try to solve two questions: what were the eighteen decrees and what is the meaning of the Tosefta's comparison of this day with that of the golden calf? As to the eighteen decrees, following a hint in the Tosefta, which included in this context two laws regarding purity, Y. completed the list by adding purity laws of the Mishnah where the Shammaites outvoted the Hillelites (M. Miq. 4:1; M. Oh. 18:1). Several different lists were proposed, all on the

---

[21] See, e.g., Martin Hengel, *Die Zeloten* (Leiden, 1961), pp. 204-211; Israel Ben-Shalom, *The School of Shammai and the Zealots' Struggle against Rome* (Hebrew) (Jerusalem, 1993), pp. 252-272.

basis of the Mishnah, but clearly as a result of a careful reading of the Mishnah and not on the basis of already available lists.

The comparison with the day of the golden calf led the attention of the authors of the baraita to Exod. 32. The commentator in the Tosefta may have thought of the fact that this day the tables of the law were broken (32:19); the baraita is rather based on 32:17, 27: "a noise of war in the camp.... Put every man his sword by his side...and slay every man his brother, and every man his companion...and there fell of the people that day about three thousand men"—exactly the number of victims as in the fight between Shammaites and Hillelites according to a medieval chronicle! It seems that the bloody fight between the two schools has been deduced from the Bible. Another baraita in the Yerushalmi that immediately follows upon the first one says there was no real fight; supporters of the school of Shammai armed with swords and spears only prevented the Hillelites from entering the hall and thus guaranteed that the Shammaites could outvote the Hillelites. This second line is followed in B. Shab. 17a, where Hillel and Shammai personally, and not only their schools, discuss the halakhot until Hillel gives in to Shammai; swords are not here for fighting but are planted in the floor at the entrance of the hall in order to prevent the students from leaving before a decision is reached. It would go to far to develop in detail the literary background of the Babylonian version. The only result that matters in this context is the fact that these baraitot are not based on tradition but on exegesis of a number of texts; they are of no value in reconstructing historical events.[22]

This example shows how careful one has to be before exploiting baraitot for historical purposes. But there are certainly cases in which baraitot do transmit historical knowledge. A number of baraitot in the Yerushalmi contain information that seem to be based on (literary) sources of the late Second Temple period, mainly genealogical lists and priestly traditions. This is confirmed above all by parallels with Josephus that certainly are not derived from Josephus' text. Many similar details that cannot be checked in Josephus or other sources are likely to be equally trustworthy. On the other hand, it is clear that the Yerushalmi does not just transcribe its sources but

---

[22] For a fuller analysis of these traditions, see Günter Stemberger, "Il contributo delle baraitot babilonesi alla conoscenza storica della Palestina prima del 70 d.C.," in Paolo Sacchi, ed., *Il Giudaismo palestinese dal I secolo a.C. al I secolo d.C.* (Bologna, 1993), pp. 213-229.

reformulates them freely; this can be demonstrated by a comparison between baraitot in the Yerushalmi and parallels in the Tosefta and in halakhic midrashim.[23]

One thing is clear: The baraitot are not a uniform corpus of traditions; there are no general criteria regarding their historical value. Some certainly contain valuable traditions; others are based on traditions but expanded and transformed in the process of transmission; others are purely literary creations. Every case has to be treated separately.

Parallels between Rabbinic texts and Josephus: In the preceding paragraph, we mentioned parallels with Josephus as a possible criterion of a genuine historical tradition. Many authors use such parallels in order to justify their claim that there was an independent and reliable oral tradition within Rabbinic Judaism; otherwise, one could not explain such parallels frequently to be found only in late Rabbinic sources and certainly not dependent on Josephus whom the rabbis did not read.

One has to be very careful to interpret such parallels correctly. In the case of names of high priests mentioned by Josephus and also to be found in the Yerushalmi, but without the narrative context of Josephus, and in similar cases it is most unlikely that the rabbis depended on Josephus—they had access to genealogical lists and similar texts. In such cases Josephus may be used as an independent confirmation of what is told in Rabbinic texts. But there are many other cases where the general outline of whole stories with many common details is to be found in Rabbinic texts and also in Josephus or other sources of the Second Temple period (the books of the Maccabees, Judith, etc.). Most of these Rabbinic stories seem to be completely unknown to earlier rabbis but become important later on (e.g., the Megillat Antiokhos and other texts to be read at the feast of Hanukah).[24] The later such parallels turn up and the more elaborate they are, the more likely is some direct contact between Rabbinic texts and Josephus.

---

[23] For more details, see Günter Stemberger, "Narrative Baraitot in the Yerushalmi," in Peter Schäfer, ed., *The Yerushalmi in its Greco-Roman Context* (Tübingen, forthcoming).

[24] See Günter Stemberger, "The Maccabees in Rabbinic Tradition," in Florentino García Martínez, et al., eds., *The Scriptures and the Scrolls. Studies in Honour of A.S. van der Woude* (Leiden, 1992), pp. 193-203; idem, "La festa di Hanukkah, il libro di Giuditta e midrashim connessi," in Giulio Busi, ed., *WE-ZO'T LE-ANGELO. Raccolta di studi giudaici in memoria di Angelo Vivian* (Bologna, 1993), pp. 527-545.

In most such cases, it seems likely that knowledge of texts found in Josephus' writings is based neither on independent Rabbinic tradition that just by accident had never before been recorded nor on a personal reading of Josephan texts by the rabbis (some even postulated that the Aramaic version of Josephus' Bellum Judaicum was still available at that time). It most probably derives from discussions with Christians who quoted Josephus and other early Jewish texts that had disappeared from Jewish tradition after 70. Such oral transmission (based on the written text of Josephus) may explain the popular form of such Rabbinic parallels and also why such parallels become more and more frequent the later the Rabbinic texts are. This kind of contact and exchange between Christians and Jews may have become more frequent in Palestine with the victory of Christianity after Constantine; but much of this material may also have re-entered Jewish tradition at a much later period, in the liberal climate of Baghdad in the eighth and ninth centuries or even later on in Southern Europe.

Thus, here again, no general judgment is possible. Some parallels may confirm independent Rabbinic traditions and thus offer criteria for which kind of Rabbinic material is likely to be historically useful; many other parallels do not confirm the high reliability of Rabbinic oral tradition but are secondary and depend on an (indirect) knowledge of the texts of Josephus.

Parallels with Qumran: A last point briefly to be discussed is the evidence to be derived from the texts of Qumran and other texts that have been found in the region of the Dead Sea. There has been a growing consciousness that Rabbinic texts are not reliable witnesses for the period before 70. In recent years, however, the debate has been reopened by scholars in favor of a more traditional approach to Rabbinic sources and much more confidence that Rabbinic texts truly reflect the reality not only of their own time but also of an earlier period for which they had reliable traditions. The manuscript discoveries around the Dead Sea seem to provide them with good arguments.

An important case in point is what the rabbis have to tell us about the Sadducees. The Rabbinic stories about the Sadducees and their disputes with the sages are viewed rather critically and are not much trusted.[25] But the Dead Sea Scrolls have revealed an enormous wealth

---

[25] See Günter Stemberger, *Pharisäer, Sadduzäer, Essener* (Stuttgart, 1991). The American version, *Jewish Contemporaries of Jesus* (Minneapolis, 1995), is unreliable.

of halakhic detail that agrees with Rabbinic halakhah and thus confirms that many halakhic decisions recorded in the Mishnah and in later sources are based on a much older tradition. Even more noteworthy in our context is that many of the halakhic opinions ascribed in Rabbinic sources to the Sadducees or Boethusians are defended in *4QMiqtsat Ma'aseh haTorah* as the positions of the priestly group of the Essenes (or a closely related group), whereas the attacked positions that are generally attributed to the Pharisees (or proto-Pharisees) correspond to Rabbinic halakhah.[26]

The publication of this text has led to considerable discussion of the relationship between Sadducees and Essenes. This is not the place to enter into this discussion. The aspect important in our context is the fact that the Rabbinic sources have been confirmed regarding several halakhot, however imaginary the narrative context may be. This cannot be generalized but certainly tends to corroborate the historical value of halakhic traditions in Rabbinic sources, especially where priestly interests are concerned. The importance of priestly traditions in early Rabbinism is not to be underestimated. Jacob Neusner rightly emphasized the great amount of material in the Mishnah that is rooted in priestly concerns (purity laws, among others). Other priestly traditions (lists of high priests, priestly genealogies) have already been pointed out in this paper. It would be very important to restudy systematically the Mishnaic tractates dealing with the Temple and its cult in order to sort out what is based on Rabbinic exegesis and system-building and what may really go back to priestly traditions. One should, however, be very careful not to transfer results regarding halakhic materials to narrative material, wisdom sayings, etc. A paradigmatic case is tractate Abot, which frequently is considered to represent true Pharisaic tradition. Much of the contents and the literary expression of this tractate are late and not attested in early Rabbinic literature; the confirmation of halakhic traditions should not lead to a wholesale rehabilitation of Abot or other materials.

A case closely related to that of the texts from Qumran is that of slightly later legal documents found in the Judean desert. Marriage

---

[26] See Yaacov Sussmann, "The History of the Halakha and the Dead Sea Scrolls," in Elisha Qimron and John Strugnell, eds., *Qumran Cave 4. V: Miqsat Ma'ase ha-Torah* (Oxford, 1994), pp. 179-200 (a more fully documented Hebrew version appeared in *Tarbiz* 59 (1989f), pp. 11-76. For a more general presentation see Lawrence H. Schiffman, *Reclaiming the Dead Sea Scrolls* (Philadelphia, 1994).

contracts and documents dealing with the transfer of property are rather close to what is known from Rabbinic halakhah. Some have been inclined to insist on the similarities; they see in these documents a clear confirmation that Rabbinic halakhah was accepted almost immediately after 70. A closer comparison, however, shows fundamental differences between Rabbinic law and the legal traditions represented by these legal deeds. They are very important in order to see how much Rabbinic halakhah is not an independent creation of the rabbis but rather rooted in a larger context of a legal tradition in which the halakhic process took place. The texts from Qumran as well as the newly published legal documents will help us better to understand the Rabbinic movement and how the rabbis harmonized older legal traditions, including non-Jewish ones with the results of their study of the Torah. But one should be very careful not to take these texts as a basis for a return to a pre-critical historicism.[27]

CONCLUSIONS

In this discussion, the Babylonian Talmud has been left aside, mainly because there is nearly no possibility of outside control. But the methods learned in comparing Babylonian texts with those coming from Palestine, and even more so from studying Palestinian Rabbinic texts in comparison with Christian texts and archaeology, may be of use here as well.

At the present state, we may accept what can be confirmed by outside materials. This does not enlarge our factual knowledge but teaches us how Rabbinic sources treat historical facts. The question we have to ask is whether we may transfer these criteria to the inte-

---

[27] See Naphtali Lewis, *The Documents from the Bar Kokhba Period in the Cave of Letters. Greek Papyri* (Jerusalem, 1989); the second volume (*Hebrew, Aramaic and Nabatean Documents*, Yigal Yadin, Jonas C. Greenfield, et al., eds.) is forthcoming; Hannah M. Cotton, Ada Yardeni, *Aramaic, Hebrew and Greek Documentary Texts from Nahal Hever and Other Sites* (DJD 27, Oxford, 1997). For a list of all the material see Hannah M. Cotton, W.E.H. Cockle, Fergus G.B. Millar, "The Papyrology of the Roman Near East: A Survey," *JRS* 85 (1995), pp. 214-235. For a comparison of the marriage contracts and Rabbinic law, see Michael Satlow, "Reconsidering the Rabbinic *ketubah* Payment," in Shaye J.D. Cohen, ed., *The Jewish Family in Antiquity* (Atlanta, 1993), pp. 133-151: "None of the extant Jewish marriage contracts from the rabbinic period show any familiarity with the rabbinic ketubah payment" (p. 141). Cf., also Hayim Lapin, "Early Rabbinic Civil Law and the Literature of the Second Temple Period," in *JSQ* 2 (1995), pp. 149-183.

rior history of the Rabbinic movement where we have no external control (but where so many interested parties have access to the texts that a complete invention of history is unlikely). There is no general procedure advisable: a certain measure of personal judgment remains in every historical reconstruction. But although it is no longer possible to use Rabbinic sources in a naive way for reconstructing history, it is still extremely useful for historical questions. It would be the greatest damage to the history of Judaism if the Rabbinic texts were neglected altogether in the historical enterprise.

IX. RABBINIC LITERATURE OF LATE ANTIQUITY AS A SOURCE FOR HISTORICAL STUDY

Richard Kalmin
Jewish Theological Seminary of America

Few scholars in the field today claim that Rabbinic literature of late antiquity should be accepted at face value as historical evidence. It is axiomatic that statements and stories have often been molded, distorted, or invented to reflect the desires and fantasies of the Rabbinic authors and their audience. There is no such consensus, however, about the extent to which Rabbinic sources provide useful historical information. When is it possible to separate reality from distortion in Rabbinic traditions? Under what circumstances are these materials susceptible to historical inquiry? What methodological obstacles must be overcome and what kinds of history do the sources permit us to write? The Babylonian Talmud, for example, purports to contain sources centuries older than the document's final editing in the sixth or seventh centuries C.E. and to contain Palestinian sources despite its final redaction in Persia. Is the Talmud primarily a late Babylonian pseudepigraph, or are its claims regarding the date and provenance of its sources often trustworthy?

To address such questions, this essay describes several methodologies useful in separating fact from fiction in the Rabbinic sources. These methodologies take account of the rabbis' tendency to use literature as a vehicle for the expression of moral and theological truths rather than as a context for verbatim quotations and historically accurate descriptions of personalities and events. Thus, we examine a partly didactic, partly polemical tale and attempt to show that Talmudic narratives whose concerns are fundamentally non-historical are often susceptible to analysis in historical terms. The essay also describes several phenomena that reveal the Talmud's composite character, a necessary first step in evaluating the historicity of its source material. These phenomena enable us to decide in many cases whether the Talmud supplies evidence of the development of Rabbinic institutions or roles in society, or records instead the fantasies and desires of late Babylonian authors.

GRECO-ROMAN AND PERSIAN SOURCES IN THE STUDY OF RABBINIC HISTORY

Greco-Roman and Persian sources of late antiquity can be helpful in evaluating the historicity of the Rabbinic traditions. According to Rabbinic sources, for example, Babylonian rabbis tend to (1) publicize the identity of families they claim to be of inferior or tainted genealogy and (2) use genealogy as a weapon against prominent non-rabbis. In contrast, Palestinian rabbis (1) tend to emphasize the importance of discretion in matters of genealogy and (2) do not depict competition between rabbis and prominent non-rabbis.[1]

Rabbinic accounts of differing Palestinian and Babylonian attitudes toward genealogy correspond to distinctions between the Persian and Greco-Roman host cultures within which the rabbis flourished and are most likely accurate historically (but see below).[2] Persian society throughout the Sasanian period is rigidly hierarchical, and movement between the various classes is extremely difficult.[3] As Isaiah Gafni observes, "a small number of well-born families" stood at the apex of Persian society.[4]

While differences between Persia and Rome should not be over-emphasized,[5] Roman society beginning in the third century C.E. is less rigidly hierarchical, and boundaries separating classes are more permeable in Rome than in contemporary Persia. The most striking illustration of this claim is the imperial decree of 212 C.E. conferring citizenship on all free inhabitants of the Roman empire. The structure of Persian society, the strength and prestige of the hereditary Iranian aristocracy, very likely contributed to the Babylonian Rabbinic emphasis on proper birth.

---

[1] For further discussion of the importance of genealogy in Rabbinic society, see, for example, Rafael Yankelevitch, "*Mishkalo Shel ha-Yihus ha-Mishpahti ba-Hevrah ha-Yehudit be-Erez-Yisrael bi-Tekufat ha-Mishnah ve-ha-Talmud*," in Menahem Stern, ed., *Uma ve-Toldoteha* (Jerusalem, 1983), vol. 1, pp. 151-162, and the literature cited there.

[2] For documentation of these claims, see Richard Kalmin, "Genealogy and Polemics in Rabbinic Literature of Late Antiquity," in *Hebrew Union College Annual* 67 (1996), pp. 77-94.

[3] The following discussion owes much to that of Isaiah Gafni, *Yehudei Bavel bi-Tekufat ha-Talmud* (Jerusalem, 1991), pp. 126-29, although Gafni does not connect the differing Palestinian and Babylonian attitudes toward genealogy with social differences between the Roman and Persian empires. See also Salo Baron, *A Social and Religious History of the Jews* (Philadelphia, 1952), 2nd edition, vol. 2, p. 234; and Richard N. Frye, *The History of Ancient Iran* (Munich, 1984), pp. 218-221, 315-316, 329, and 334.

[4] Gafni, *Yehudei Bavel*, pp. 127-128.

[5] See ibid., p. 126.

Perhaps the position of Babylonian Jews as a tiny minority in a foreign land was also a contributing factor. Their status as exiles among the nations may have fostered a desire to bolster their Jewish identity by constructing elaborate genealogical barriers against the outside world. Even Palestinian Jewry had to contend with the encroachment of foreign elements, of course. With much justification even Palestine can be described as "exilic" throughout this period, but perhaps the exile was experienced less acutely in Palestine than in Babylonia, which might help explain the more relaxed Palestinian attitude.

Isaiah Gafni's claim regarding non-Rabbinic leadership in the two Rabbinic centers may explain the Babylonians' greater willingness to challenge powerful non-Rabbinic adversaries. Gafni claims that Babylonian Talmudic sources depict rabbis and exilarchic officials as leaders of the Babylonian Jewish community. Palestinian sources, however, also assign leadership roles to non-rabbis drawn from the ranks of local municipalities.[6] Perhaps in Babylonia, the rabbis are strong enough to challenge their relatively weak and unimportant non-Rabbinic competitors. In Palestine, non-Rabbinic competition is perhaps much stronger, and aggressive confrontations by Palestinian rabbis are riskier and therefore comparatively rare.

On the other hand, the portrayals of Babylonian rabbis as *effective* opponents of prominent non-rabbis are perhaps not accurate historically. They may indicate merely that a propaganda technique used by Babylonian authors was not used in Palestine. Perhaps to promote themselves as capable leaders, Babylonian rabbis picture themselves subduing powerful opponents by exposing their lowly ancestry.

Reality, however, might have been quite different. Babylonian rabbis were perhaps unable to turn public opinion against their powerful opponents by unmasking them as bastards and slaves. The sources perhaps attest to Babylonian wishful thinking rather than to the rabbis' powerful impact on non-Rabbinic Jewish society in Babylonia.[7]

---

[6] Ibid., pp. 104-109.

[7] See B. Qid. 72b for statements attributed to or involving Babylonian rabbis that criticize or run counter to the dominant Babylonian attitude and criticize the Babylonian obsession with genealogy.

The Talmud's Diversity of Source Material

Historical conclusions are much more difficult when non-Jewish sources are unavailable to corroborate Talmudic portrayals. Usually we have only the Talmud's word on a particular issue; how can we establish whether the text before us is a Rabbinic fantasy or a description of reality?

One way to tackle this question is to examine large numbers of traditions in an effort to determine whether patterns emerge that change according to the chronology or geography of the sources. Using chronological and geographical data supplied by the Rabbinic documents, it is often possible to determine whether portrayals of institutions, Rabbinic functions, or personalities change over time or differ from one Rabbinic center to another.

The Talmud's chronological and geographical data, while largely unverifiable from external sources, is strikingly consistent throughout Rabbinic documents and from one Rabbinic document to another. There is little basis for denying the accuracy of this information, and it is a useful tool for describing particular rabbis, generations, or periods, or for describing later Rabbinic conceptions about earlier rabbis, generations, or periods.[8]

In other words, it is often possible to determine whether the Talmud is the work of late pseudepigraphers or is divisible into diverse sources, some early and others later, some Palestinian and others Babylonian. The two issues: the Talmud's composite character and the historicity of its sources are closely related, since it is necessary to determine the former before fully evaluating the latter. Phrased differently, the history we derive from Talmudic sources depends heavily on decisions we make regarding the geography and chronology of these sources.

Numerous factors establish the Babylonian Talmud's composite character. Not only do isolated and scattered traditions derive from diverse times and places, but also distinct layers and clusters of traditions often possess objectively definable characteristics that set them apart from other layers. These characteristics often correspond to and confirm the Talmud's claim that its component parts are (1) early or later, (2) Palestinian or Babylonian, (3) anonymous or attrib-

---

[8] See also Isaiah Gafni, "*Le-Heker ha-Khronologiah be-Igeret Rav Sherira Gaon*," in *Zion* 52 (1987), pp. 1-24; and *Yehudei Bavel*, pp. 239-265.

uted, and (4) citations from Rabbinic documents or from dream manuals or medical textbooks deriving from non-Rabbinic circles.

For example, early layers of the Talmud are sympathetic to professional dream interpreters but later layers are hostile. Early rabbis are portrayed interpreting the symbolic dreams of non-rabbis, even non-Jews, and one story justifies a rabbi's demand to receive payment for his services. Later rabbis are portrayed interpreting only the message dreams of rabbis. In other words, early rabbis are shown translating dream symbols into coherent thoughts and speech, and later rabbis are shown explaining the significance of statements, usually quotations of scripture, read to their students in dreams. Later rabbis are pictured equipping people to handle the disturbing and potentially inimical power of dreams on their own, eliminating the need to resort to professional interpreters, and polemicizing against a professional interpreter who gives favorable interpretations to those who pay for his services and negative interpretations to those who do not pay. The Talmud's claim to be divisible into early and later sources is confirmed by the differing characteristics of early and later rabbis.[9]

In addition, Rabbinic narratives sometimes contain contradictions that indicate the Talmud's character as a composite. The Talmud contains a rich supply of polemics and hagiography, of sources designed to enhance or damage the reputations of competing sages and schools.

This claim is not based solely on the presence of contradictions between narratives nor on the depiction of behavior that strikes a modern audience as reprehensible but that is perfectly acceptable to the rabbis themselves. Rather, it is based on narratives that portray an individual as fundamentally flawed or saintly from the perspective of the ancients themselves, provided that the portrayals of personalities are not totally subservient to the story's intended message.

These points bear restating. Numerous accounts in the Bavli describe Yohanan, for example, as pious, learned, and saintly, and these most likely derive from sources sympathetic to him or to Palestinian learning in general.[10] Other accounts portray him as wicked, and in the following pages we analyze one such source and attempt to show its character as a polemic either against Yohanan or against Palestinian learning in general. At the same time, we shall demon-

---

[9] See also Richard Kalmin, *Sages, Stories, Authors, and Editors in Rabbinic Babylonia* (Atlanta, 1994), pp. 61-80.

[10] See, for example, B. Yom. 82b, B. Pes. 3b, and B. Ta. 21a.

strate the independence of its polemical features from its intended
message, to show that the unsympathetic portrayals of personalities
are not simply vehicles serving the story's moral or theological concerns. The story is as follows:

> One day R. Yohanan was bathing in the Jordan. Resh Laqish saw
> him.
> He thought he was a woman. He stuck his lance into the Jordan and
> jumped after him into the Jordan.[11]
> He said to him, "Your strength for Torah."
> He said to him, "Your beauty for women."
> He said to him, "If you change your ways, I will give you my sister
> who is more beautiful than I am."
> He agreed. He wanted to return to bring his clothes, but could not
> return.
> He taught him Bible and Mishnah and made him a great man. One
> day they were disputing in the study house: A sword, a knife, a dagger,
> a lance, a hand saw, and a scythe, when do they become impure? When
> they are complete. And when are they complete?
> R. Yohanan said, "After he smelted them in the furnace."
> Resh Laqish said, "After he polished them in water."
> He said to him, "The brigand knows his trade."
> He said to him, "What good have you done me? There they called
> me Rabbi, and here they call me Rabbi."[12]
> R. Yohanan got upset. Resh Laqish got ill. His sister came crying.
> She said to him, "Do it for my children."
> He said to her, "'Leave me your orphans, I will rear them'" (Jer.
> 49:11).
> "Do it for my widowhood."
> He said to her, "'Let your widows rely on me'" (Jer. 49:11).
> R. Simeon ben Laqish died, and R. Yohanan pined after him.
> The rabbis said, "Who will go and settle his mind? Let R. Eleazar
> ben Pedat go, for his traditions are sharp."
> He went and sat before him. Concerning everything that R. Yohanan
> said, he said to him, "There is a Baraita supporting you."
> He said, "You are like Bar Lakisha? Bar Lakisha, when I would say
> something, he would raise twenty-four objections against me, and I
> would respond to him with twenty-four resolutions, and the tradition
> would be clarified. And you say, 'There is a Baraita which supports
> you.' Don't I know that I speak well?"
> He tore his clothes as he walked, crying, "Where are you Bar
> Lakisha, where are you Bar Lakisha?"
> And he shouted until he lost his mind. The rabbis prayed for him and
> he died.

---

[11] See *Dikdukei Soferim*, ed. Rafael Rabbinovicz, n. lamed.

[12] See *Dikdukei Soferim*, n. nun.

What is this story's message?[13] Absolute certainty on this question is impossible due to the cultural divide separating us from ancient Rabbinic authors. Very likely, however, the story is in part a Babylonian critique of the actions of Palestinian rabbis. It disapproves either of specific individuals (Yohanan, Resh Laqish, and Eleazar ben Pedat) or of Palestinian Amoraim in general, choosing as protagonists a few prominent sages who stand for the collective.[14]

The story very likely criticizes (1) Yohanan for using unworthy methods to convince Resh Laqish to pursue a life of Torah study and (2) Resh Laqish for pursuing a scholarly career for ulterior motives rather than for its own sake. Yohanan entices Resh Laqish to study by promising him his beautiful sister in marriage, and Resh Laqish declares that his career change has profited him nothing: "There they called me Rabbi and here they call me Rabbi."

The story apparently criticizes ongoing attempts to win disciples from among the non-Rabbinic population. It protests against the inferior product produced by this outreach effort and warns that the search for disciples needs to be carried out with discretion and restraint. The speed with which Resh Laqish despairs of the importance of Torah study demonstrates the shallowness of his "conversion."

The story most likely does not criticize Yohanan's refusal to allow his student to break out of the rigid master-disciple framework and confront his teacher as a near-equal. I say this because the Bavli depicts Babylonian rabbis either as students or colleagues, but never as students who go on to become colleagues. In other words, Babylonian teachers demand of their students what Yohanan demands of Resh Laqish according to this story, and it makes little sense to suggest that they criticize him for doing so.

The Bavli depicts Palestinian students, however, confronting their teachers as near-equals. Unlike Babylonians, Palestinian students are

---

[13] For earlier discussion of this story, see Yonah Fraenkel, *Iyunim ba-Olamo ha-Ruhani Shel Sipur ha-Agadah* (Tel Aviv, 1981), pp. 73-77; Eliezer Segal, "Law as Allegory? An Unnoticed Literary Device in Talmudic Narratives," in *Prooftexts* 8, no. 2 (1988), pp. 250-251; and Daniel Boyarin, *Carnal Israel*, (Berkeley, 1993), pp. 212-219. The following discussion incorporates sevaral of their insights.

[14] In the discussion below I maintain the viability of both possibilities, namely that the story is either a polemic against specific Palestinian rabbis or against Palestinian rabbis in general. I refer throughout, however, to the story as a polemic against specific Palestinian rabbis. To consistently state both possibilities would require a great deal of clumsy repetition. The gain in ease of expression, I believe, more than compensates for the loss of precision.

depicted expressing halakhic opinions contrary to those of their teachers, in their teachers' presence. Evidently the Babylonian authors of this story criticize a Palestinian relationship that in their opinion leads to psychological stresses and inevitably breaks out into bitter conflict.

Resh Laqish begins his career as Yohanan's clear inferior, claims the story. As Yohanan fondly remembers their relationship, he has the first and last word whenever they speak together, and Resh Laqish's role is confined to that of posing objections against his teacher's opinions. Trouble begins and their relationship breaks down when Resh Laqish claims a measure of equality with his teacher and expresses a contradictory opinion in Yohanan's presence.[15] The story, in other words, criticizes Resh Laqish's attempt to achieve near-equality with his teacher, which leads to the story's tragic conclusion.

Very likely, the narrative also disapproves of Yohanan's reaction to Resh Laqish's attempt to achieve near-equality. "The brigand knows his trade," he says angrily, violating the Rabbinic prohibition against publicly humiliating one's fellow by reminding him of his sordid past.[16] In response to Yohanan's insult, Resh Laqish declares that his present life is no better than his former life, as if the only benefit of Torah study is the esteemed title it confers. Yohanan gets upset (literally, his mind weakens), and Resh Laqish falls sick, and apparently Yohanan himself causes Resh Laqish's illness and determines its severity.

Yohanan's sister, Resh Laqish's wife, tries to convince her brother to intercede on her husband's behalf. Yohanan, in what the story views as false piety, cloaks himself behind biblical verses and leaves Resh Laqish's fate to God. The rabbis' ability to heal, or to pray for the heavenly powers to heal, is the subject of many Rabbinic narratives,[17] and it is no piety on Yohanan's part to refrain from action and allow Resh Laqish to die. Yohanan's false piety is particularly contemptible because he uses scripture to mask the real motive behind his decision not to act: the strength of his anger toward Resh Laqish. Yohanan causes pain to a widow and orphans, further decreasing his stature in our eyes since the Torah repeatedly mandates compassion for these poor and defenseless members of society.

---

[15] See also Kalmin, *Sages, Stories, Authors, and Editors*, pp. 97-109.

[16] See Segal, "Law as Allegory?," p. 255, n. 41, and the references cited there.

[17] See, for example, B. Ber. 5b, for stories involving Yohanan.

The circumstances of Yohanan's death further support our evaluation of his character. Typically, Rabbinic stories devise divine punishments that fit the crime. Yohanan's death is no exception. Yohanan dies when the rabbis mercifully pray for his death, a punishment that fits his crime of cruelly refusing to pray for Resh Laqish's life.

The story is also preoccupied with sublimation and its role in the life of the scholar. As Daniel Boyarin observes, Resh Laqish is sexually attracted to the effeminate Yohanan, whom he sees bathing in the Jordan River and mistakes for a woman. He vaults after him on his lance, phallic imagery symbolic of Resh Laqish's unbridled virility. He takes on a life of scholarship, losing his strength in the process, and marries Yohanan's sister. His raw physical strength and sexual virility are diverted into rabbinically acceptable channels: a heterosexual relationship, a passion for Torah study, and devoted discipleship to his teacher.[18]

Upon becoming a scholar, Resh Laqish does not lose his passion but submerges and redirects it, as shown by the vehemence of his halakhic dispute with Yohanan. The passion that makes one a great brigand, the story teaches, also makes one a great Torah scholar. The study house and the battlefield are similar arenas. Debates in the study house are a matter of life and death, every bit as dangerous as a fight to the death between brigands. Rabbis discuss knives and daggers and don't use them, yet their words can kill no less effectively than can actual weapons.

The opinions of the two scholars very likely constitute more than a "simple" halakhic debate. Rather, they express the importance of sublimation as a key to understanding the story. Talmudic narratives often center around arcane issues of ritual purity, making the point that even ostensibly inoperative areas of Jewish law are crucially important, so much so that even God is a vitally interested participant in the discussion.[19]

In the present instance, the halakhic debate is analogous to the human conflict between Yohanan and Resh Laqish. Yohanan thinks Resh Laqish is "complete" when he has become "forged in the fire," i.e., red hot and passionate, on the edge of but not yet having achieved consummation. Resh Laqish wants more. He wants to cool

---

[18] Boyarin, op. cit., pp. 215-216.
[19] See, for example, B. B.M. 86a.

the fire in water, to achieve consummation by uniting with Yohanan, by attaining near-equality with him and coming as close as possible to full identification with his teacher. Homoerotic sexual attraction fuels this desire, although my claim is not that Resh Laqish consciously wants to have sex with his teacher. Resh Laqish reveals through his halakhic opinion that he is as hungry for consummation now as when he first encountered Yohanan in the river and is unable to endure the life of continual sublimation demanded by his teacher. Resh Laqish's opinion is symptomatic of dissatisfaction with the role assigned to him by Yohanan, a fact that Yohanan perceives and that accounts in part for the intensity of his reaction to Resh Laqish's halakhic opinion.

Very likely, it is no accident that Resh Laqish pursues Yohanan into a river, and Yohanan sees to it that Resh Laqish leaves the river. Yohanan is fully complete; he has cooled himself in water. Resh Laqish is not, but passionately wants to be, just like his teacher.

To sum up, the Yohanan-Resh Laqish story does not portray events as they actually happened. The story is historical in the sense that it attests to (1) Babylonian polemics against Palestinian rabbis or schools; (2) efforts by rabbis to win converts from among the non-Rabbinic population and unease over the superficial nature of some of these conversions; and (3) Babylonian discomfort with a unique form of Palestinian relationship.

The story also attests to the Talmud's composite character, since, as noted above, other traditions describe Yohanan as a saint. These traditions derive from different circles than do the authors of the story of Yohanan's tragic demise.

Other proofs of the Talmud's composite character include the presence of diverse quotation forms in early, middle, and later Amoraic literature. The term "quotation forms" refers to technical terms that do not form part of a statement but that introduce the statement and indicate that a particular rabbi is its author and other rabbis serve as tradents. One term introduces statements by early rabbis in the Bavli, a different term introduces statements by later rabbis, and statements by middle-generation rabbis are sometimes introduced by the "early" term and other times by the "later" term. As I argue elsewhere, this evidence is difficult to explain as the work of later editors, since no correlation exists between the content of the statements and the quotation form used to introduce the statements. According to the theory that these forms identify distinct layers of

Talmudic discourse, however, the evidence is easily explicable. The various forms were added to the Talmud at different times, with the middle-Amoraic period a transitional era separating the early from the later periods.[20]

THE HISTORICITY OF THE TALMUD'S DIVERSE SOURCE MATERIAL

It would be a simple matter to multiply examples of the Talmud's diversity of source material. It is far more difficult, however, to determine the historical accuracy or inaccuracy of these sources. We find, for example, that early Babylonian sources depict distinct judicial and academic hierarchies, i.e., one hierarchy based on judicial expertise and another hierarchy based on halakhic knowledge and dialectical skill. Later Babylonian sources, in contrast, depict only a single hierarchy. Do these diverse sources provide an accurate picture of changing conditions in Babylonia, or do they reflect deliberate falsification by later Babylonian storytellers, whose motive, perhaps, was to minimize the role of the exilarch in the judicial hierarchy? We find echoes of the exilarch's importance in the judiciary in early Babylonian sources, as well as evidence that these sources deliberately minimized his role. Perhaps we find a continuation of this process in the later depiction of a judiciary completely controlled by rabbis and devoid of exilarchic influence.[21]

Similarly, as noted above, Talmudic sources depict early Palestinian rabbis as professional dream interpreters without the slightest hint of criticism, but favorably depict later Babylonian rabbis interpreting only the message dreams of their students. Only one story depicts a later Babylonian rabbi as a professional interpreter and does so in harshly critical terms. Does this Talmudic picture of later Babylonian Rabbinic insularity and disconnectedness from society[22] correspond to reality? Or are we witness instead to a polemic against a common Babylonian Rabbinic practice, a polemic that takes the form of an attempt by Talmudic storytellers virtually to deny the existence of professional Rabbinic interpreters in Babylonia? In other words, perhaps later Babylonian storytellers disapprove of profes-

---

[20] See Kalmin, *Sages, Stories, Authors, and Editors*, pp. 127-140.
[21] See ibid., pp. 81-85.
[22] At least with respect to dream interpretation.

sional interpretation and mention it only to criticize it even though
the phenomenon was quite common.

CONCLUSION

Despite these difficulties, inquiry into the composite nature of the
Talmud permits some reasonably firm historical conclusions. The
discovery of diverse sources in the Talmud, for example, supports the
historicity of the Talmud's portrayal of a Rabbinic "movement"
characterized by disunity and minimal contact between each generation's most important leaders. In addition, the Talmud's portrayal of
minimal contact between Rabbinic leaders confirms the above conclusions regarding diverse sources, since the Talmud portrays a Rabbinic movement likely to have produced and transmitted the diverse
sources described above.

These points bear elaboration. According to Talmudic portrayals,
the dominant rabbis in every generation have little face-to-face contact, even when they live in close proximity. Rabbis of widely different status, however, interact with much greater frequency. Very
likely, the intensity of competition induced Rabbinic leaders to avoid
one another, and/or societal norms called for leading rabbis to strike
out on their own and found their own schools. These motives are
inapplicable in the case of rabbis of widely different status, which
explains their far more frequent interaction.[23]

The historicity of this portrayal of a fragmented Rabbinic movement receives support from the discovery of diverse Talmudic
sources. A unified Rabbinic movement would be unlikely to produce
and transmit the contradictory polemical narratives described above.
A unified Rabbinic movement would be unlikely to use different
quotation forms to introduce statements deriving from the same time
period. A unified Rabbinic movement would be unlikely to Baby-
lonianize most, but not all, Palestinian sources.[24]

Phrased differently, diverse, even totally unrelated sources repeatedly yield the same conclusion. Analysis of (1) relationships between
the most prominent rabbis, (2) of rabbis of widely different status, (3)

---

[23] For more on the structure of the Rabbinic movement in Babylonia, see Kalmin,
op. cit., pp. 175-212.

[24] See ibid., pp. 87-110.

of the polemical intent of stories, and (4) of quotation forms show the diversity of the Rabbinic movement and the corresponding diversity of the literature produced by this movement.

I am well aware that an objection can be raised against this argument. Later editors might have created these and numerous other features of Talmudic discourse. The "unrelated sources" referred to above might have been composed, shaped, or placed in their present contexts by later editors, in which case the above arguments for the historicity of these sources disappear.[25]

Virtually anything is possible when speculating about the activity of ancient editors, and mathematical certainty on this issue is beyond our grasp. The best one can achieve is a convincing demonstration of a theory's usefulness, or lack thereof, in accounting for the extant data, and the above-mentioned findings show the problematic nature of the theory that views the Talmud as primarily the work of later editors. This theory requires us to posit editors of unbelievable sophistication and thoroughness. In the absence of ancient models for such editors, I prefer to view the above phenomena as the product of genuine historical processes rather than the work of outstanding geniuses centuries ahead of their time.

---

[25] See the voluminous writings of Jacob Neusner on this subject, for example, *Making the Classics in Judaism* (Atlanta, 1989), pp. 1-13 and 19-44; and *Sources and Traditions: Types of Composition in the Talmud of Babylonia* (Atlanta, 1992).

X. RABBINIC SOURCES FOR HISTORICAL STUDY

David Kraemer
Jewish Theological Seminary of America

Scholars, mostly Jewish but also non-Jewish, have been using Rabbinic sources for historical study for well over a century. These studies—one "History of the Jews in the Talmudic Period" or another—have been, almost without exception, what Jacob Neusner terms "gullible." They have assumed, in other words, that the Rabbinic record can, more or less, be taken at its word and that, once one has determined the "original version" of a teaching and discounted obviously fabulous material, one may accept that teaching as historically reliable.

By this stage in the development of Judaic scholarship, the folly of these earlier habits is broadly recognized. Neusner and others have pointed to a variety of crucial and even fatal flaws in the approach just described, and there is hardly a scholar writing today about the history of Jews in late antiquity who does not at least pay lip service (though often no more than lip service!) to the much repeated critique. But even the critical questions that have been articulated—Can we believe Rabbinic attributions for purposes of dating a tradition? Why should we believe what any given tradition reports? and so forth—do not capture the full scope of the problem of using such records for writing history. In the following pages, I will describe the obstacles that would have to be overcome before we could be sure that a Rabbinic record contains historically reliable evidence. I will conclude that these obstacles are effectively insurmountable and that most sorts of political, social, or religious histories cannot be constructed on the basis of Rabbinic testimony.

Let us begin with the nature of Rabbinic teachings themselves. Rabbinic tradition claims of itself that it was an oral tradition, passed from master to disciple by word of mouth. If we accept this claim,[1]

---

[1] Even if we do not accept the "Oral Torah" claim in its extreme form, admitting instead, with Lieberman and others, that Rabbinic sages and their disciples sometimes kept personal written notes, we still have to assume a basically oral context. Because of the difficulty of producing books and widespread illiteracy (education was not necessarily synonymous with actual reading), memorization and oral repetition were the most common forms of "textuality" in the ancient world. Thus, even if

then we shall have to ask about the reliability of transmission in oral cultures. Those who have studied oral cultures notice a great degree of fluidity and change in the repetition of traditions. This is true even of recitations of the same person from one repetition to the next, even when the speaker claims that he has repeated the tradition or story in a form that is identical—word for word—with the previous recitation. Walter Ong reports that even in oral societies where verbatim repetition is a goal, success is quite limited.[2] Where training (memorization) begins early and traditions are chanted or sung, success is greater, but even such repeaters "make changes...of which they are unaware."[3] The most successful instances of verbatim repetition are found in the context of ritual performance, but even here changes are regular. The many differences in formulation in the prayers and blessings of Jewish liturgy will attest to this reality.

If Rabbinic teachings were originally transmitted orally, then the many variations in traditions from one record to another are evidence of the reality just described. It is in the nature of an oral tradition that teachings change from one recitation to the next, mostly unnoticed. If we could capture and compare snapshots of these recitations, as we often can in the Rabbinic case, we would be able to demonstrate the ubiquity of such changes, large and small. Compare any chapter of the Tosefta with the record of related baraitot in the Yerushalmi and the Bavli and you will have no question of the consequences of oral transmission. Compare the attributions and details of "the same" teaching in different Rabbinic documents or in different contexts in the same document and you will be unable to avoid the same conclusion. It is unnecessary to demonstrate or "prove" this claim; examples are found literally on every page of the classical Rabbinic corpus.

The unsensed changes that typify all oral traditions are often a function of the habits, assumptions, beliefs, and prejudices of the context in which any given tradition is repeated. Again, examples in the Rabbinic corpus are abundant. I offer just one example: When we compare the responses of Yohanan and his colleagues to suffering

---

canonical texts were sometimes written—even if they were first composed in writing—their authoritative versions (plural) were surely those spoken by recognized authorities.

[2] Walter J. Ong, *Orality and Literacy: The Technologizing of the Word* (London and New York, 1982), pp. 62.

[3] Ibid., p. 63.

as recorded in the Bavli (B. Ber. 5a) to those preserved in Song of Songs Rabbah (2, 35), we find that in the former version sufferings are rejected ("[I want] neither them nor their reward!") whereas, in the latter, acceptance is recommended ("Don't say this but, rather, say 'The trustworthy God!'"). These and other differences in the respective formulation of the traditions are significant, and they conform completely to approaches to suffering that widely and unmistakably typify the Babylonian and Palestinian Rabbinic traditions respectively.[4] The Rabbinic repeaters may not have been aware of the changes they were introducing into their teachings, but change them they did, under the inexorable pressures of the settings in which they were living.

The next problem with the Rabbinic evidence, as we preserve it, lies in the simple fact that teachings that were originally given oral expression, by and before living, authoritative masters of the tradition, are now (more or less) "frozen" in writing. Oral and written expressions differ in significant ways, and if "the medium is the message," then the reduction of oral Rabbinic teachings to the written form will have changed them radically. I cannot improve on Martin Jaffee's articulation of the consequences of this step:

> ...the passage of a literary work from exclusively oral to written/oral transmission is profoundly transformative. What was once present as direct address and shaped inevitably to suit the needs of the moment as these took shape in the interaction of speaker and audience is now deprived of the fluid form which constitutes its social reality. A tradition, once reformulated and changed with each performance, is now stabilized and objectified in a form which exerts a powerful control over future performances or readings. What was formerly "authored" at each recitation must now be reproduced "as it is written."[5]

To this description, Walter Ong adds several important observations. "Written words," he writes, "are isolated from the fuller context in which spoken words come into being." What difference does this make? "Spoken words are always modifications of a total situation

---

[4] See my lengthy discussion in *Responses to Suffering in Classical Rabbinic Literature* (New York, 1995).

[5] Martin S. Jaffee, "How Much 'Orality' in Oral Torah? New Perspectives on the Composition and Transmission of Early Rabbinic Tradition," in *Shofar* v. 10, n. 2 (Winter, 1992), p. 66. Reuven Firestone offers a magnificent case study of an oral tradition and its written records in *Journeys in Holy Lands: The Evolution of the Abraham-Ishmael Legends in Islamic Exegesis* (Albany, 1990). See particularly pp. 15-18 and 153-155.

which is more than verbal.... In oral speech, a word must have one or another intonation or tone of voice—lively, excited, quiet, incensed, resigned, or whatever." Context, tone, audience, and the like all affect the meaning of a communication. Written communication, in contrast, will always "lack a verifiable context." When words are written, removing the eyes, the brow, the hand movement, the tone of voice, then the force of the words will be thrown into doubt, their meaning subject to differing interpretation. As Ong points out, one need only consider the hours an actor spends determining how best to utter the written words of a script (and the drastically different interpretations of how to utter and perform the same words) to appreciate how radically a transformation of medium affects the message.[6]

The writing down of originally oral teachings shifts context in more than one way. In whatever document Rabbinic traditions find their written home, the choice of a precise context for quotation is rarely that of the "original" speaker or later repeater. It is, instead, ultimately the decision of the "author" or "redactor" of the document. This fact is particularly evident in the Bavli, where traditions are constantly quoted in "new" contexts—interpretations of texts from *Toharot* find themselves in discussions of teachings from *Nashim*, statements that "originally" pertained to one Mishnaic pericope are quoted over and over again in connection with others, and so forth. If we admit that all meaning is contextual (and I, following many others, insist that this is true) then the choice of a context for written record transforms earlier meanings perhaps significantly. And once a teaching has found a written home, its earlier oral context—and therefore meaning—can never be fully recovered.

Of course, written records, too, are subject to the manipulations of copying and transmission. Only mechanical printing can reproduce a text with (almost) complete accuracy. Manual copying is, by its nature, fraught with problems and imperfections. Eyes skip, hands slip, short-term memories fail. One sees on the page what one has been prejudiced to see, and one copies the version of one's memory, not the version on the page. Moreover, Rabbinic teachers and copyists often doubted the accuracy of the written word before them. They didn't understand a particular step or conceived a different interpretation. If the interpretation demanded a different wording, they often

---

[6] Ong, pp. 101-102.

did not hesitate to change the reading in front of them. Naturally, what they found in front of them was already transformed by earlier interpretations, so they could find precedent for the steps they were now taking. And why not? In the end it would be impossible to recover the "original" version in any case.

So, to use the evidence of a Rabbinic text for history, one would have to correct for errors and changes and recover the "original" written record. One would then have to correct for changes in context and meaning that accompanied the reduction of the evidence to writing; one would have to reconstruct the pre-written oral version. One would then have to correct for all of the (often) many changes that transformed the evidence from the time of its first articulation to its last oral repetition. If one could recover that "original," one could then commence with the act of interpretation.

It is safe to say that such a recovery is virtually impossible. This is not to say it could never be done. It is only to admit that one could never be sure when one had actually captured the "original" teaching, if there ever was an original to begin with. (It is equally possible that a teacher articulated a teaching with slight modifications from one repetition to the next, in which case we cannot speak of an original). It is for these reasons that the method demonstrated by Halivni's *Meqorot Umesorot* is perceived as so subjective and has been followed by so few. Halivni is properly sensitive to the storms of oral transmission. But he imagines that he has the information he would need to reconstruct the original, and it is here that his confidence does not persuade others. Oral studies suggest that we do not have the information we would need to know when any given reconstruction has hit the mark. We therefore cannot rely on such reconstructions even if, on unknown occasions, they are correct.

Where does this analysis leave us? Are there other approaches or other kinds of information that might lead us to conclusions about which we could be more confident?

Students of the Rabbinic period have long recognized the potential contributions of archeology to our understanding of the world in which the rabbis lived and taught. Some have even argued that the archaeological record might be used to confirm or challenge the reliability of the Rabbinic evidence. In a balanced discussion of the potential contributions of archaeology to Rabbinic history, Eric Meyers enumerates the following: First, he observes, archeology can help "set the lives and teachings of men in their true contexts," adding, crucially, that it can "tell us a great deal about the impact [or lack of impact! -DK] of men on their fellowmen."[7] This is undoubtedly correct, and it is clearly necessary to reconstruct as much as we can of the historical setting before we can interpret the teachings of any given period. Next, Meyers observes, archaeology can supplement the ancient record or bring greater clarity to obscure texts. It can also offer correctives to the textual record, contradicting, as it sometimes does, the written tradition.

But it is precisely the contradictions that render this whole direction so problematic. When the picture suggested by the material record contradicts the picture of the Rabbinic literary record—as is not infrequently the case—then it is the Rabbinic record we must call into question. In such circumstances, the rabbis may be speaking for a small elite, or they may be speaking theoretically, but they are surely not preserving history. From such examples, we learn to doubt the Rabbinic evidence. But from cases in which the material remains support the Rabbinic record we do not learn to trust that same record, for we could not have known whether or not to rely on the rabbis' testimony without the material proof. In reality, it is archaeological inquiry that genuinely serves as the foundation for history, for even the mute testimony of material remains obviously reflects *some* reality. The Rabbinic record, in contrast, may well reflect the reality of the mind and have no direct connection to any lived reality. At best, the Rabbinic texts can be relied upon to contribute only slight details.

Perhaps the most important potential contribution of archeology, as Meyers understands it, is to help date Rabbinic texts—a matter of central concern in this discussion. To illustrate this possibility, Meyers observes that the practice of ossilegium—secondary burial—discussed in detail in the minor tractate *Semahot*, is shown by archaeology to have been common in the first four centuries of the common era but not later. This fact, he argues, disproves the common opinion that sees this minor tractate, as other minor tractates, as a geonic work, and broadly supports the earlier dating proposed by Zlotnick. The problems with this suggestion are, however, manifold. To begin with, the tractate claims for itself a Tannaitic origin, that is, second century and not later. But the archaeological remains at best give us a *terminus ante quem* of the mid-fourth century—hardly a proof of the

[7] "The Use of Archaeology in Understanding Rabbinic Materials," in *Texts and Responses: Studies Presented to Nahum N. Glatzer...* (Leiden, 1975), p. 31.

text's claims for itself! Furthermore, this entire method presupposes that Rabbinic writers have no particular motivation to anachronize or idealize (= preserve earlier authoritative teachings as valid for all times). But the same method, applied to Maimonides' *Mishneh Torah*, would demand a dating of the early first century for that work: How else to explain the extensive treatment of the laws of the Temple in a language resembling one used in the first century? Archeological evidence dates the attested practices, not the literary record which might, even many centuries later, preserve descriptions of the same practice.

But if it is risky using archaeological evidence to date documents, perhaps we can be more secure using it to date isolated traditions, as the example just considered seems to suggest. Indeed, in recent research I have come upon an example which strikes me as just such a case. In the largest of the burial caves at Beth Shearim (cave 20), archaeologists have found more than one-hundred and fifty burials in large stone sarcophagi. A striking feature of these sarcophagi—mentioned in reports but barely commented upon—is their lids: all are covered by immense stone lids with gabled "roofs" and blunt, uncarved "acroteria" at each of the four corners. These acroteria resemble nothing so much as the "horns" of ancient altars, Jewish and pagan, found by archaeologists in Israel. What makes this resemblance so interesting is a teaching first found in the Tosefta, dated by many scholars to the mid-to-late third century, which declares "anyone who is buried in the land of Israel is as though buried under the altar" (T. A.Z. 4:3). Is this resemblance of design and teaching a mere coincidence, or does this passage shed light on the mute burial phenomenon and the phenomenon provide a date for this teaching of the Tosefta?

The major problem with seeing here more than mere coincidence is the fact that the altars that the lids most resemble date to centuries long before the burials at Beth Shearim. It is obviously unlikely that the community of Jews associated with Beth Shearim were familiar with the ancient form. It is not impossible, of course, that these Jews uncannily captured the form of the ancient altar by means of interpretation of the scriptural commandment describing altars, but this conclusion, too, would require a leap of faith. It is far more likely that, like their pagan neighbors, these Jews sought to borrow architectural forms that characterized Hellenistic and Roman Temples. But, far from disproving the relationship speculated above, this very borrowing suggestively supports it. With all of the acculturation of Jews residing in the Roman Empire during this period, it is still noteworthy that they would employ pagan symbolism in their burials. If the gabled roofs with acroteria symbolically communicate "Temple," we have to assume that, to Jewish eyes, this Temple was the Jewish Temple. In other words, in the absence of a visual witness to the Jerusalem Temple, destroyed several generations before these burials, these Jews would have envisioned their Temple according to models with which they were familiar in their environment. Therefore, burying their deceased beneath these powerful "Temple" symbols, they may well have been expressing their belief that, here in the most important Jewish burial ground in Palestine, they were in effect burying them beneath the altar.

I am, as I said, tempted by this interpretation, but it remains, in the end, only an interpretation. Possibly the Rabbinic text has contributed to our understanding of the burial practice at Beth Shearim, but only possibly. And this lack of clear conclusion should serve as a cautionary tale to those who would use these bodies of evidence to illumine one another. Undoubtedly, there are occasions when this approach genuinely provides us a window to ancient realities. But the temptation to over-interpret or make assumptions too quickly is ever present. Just because a Rabbinic text *might* explain a material discovery doesn't mean we should assume it does. We must press ourselves to consider alternatives, because they, too, may provide the correct explanation.

In an earlier article, "On the Reliability of Attributions in the Babylonian Talmud,"[8] I examined at length the question articulated in the title, a question central to the present deliberation. I argued at that time that there are two methods available for verifying attributions with at least moderate confidence. In retrospect, it seems to me that even those relatively moderate claims are probably too ambitious.

In discussions of the problems of verifying attributions (in the Bavli and, by extension, in other Rabbinic documents), Neusner observed that if a tradition were cited in a source "entirely external to Rabbinic tradition" this could be considered valid verification of that source and its attribution.[9] I then suggested that it is unnecessary that

---

[8] *HUCA* 60 (1989), pp. 175-190. Reprinted in Michael Chernick, ed., *Essential Papers on the Talmud* (New York, 1994), pp. 276-292.

[9] See *The Pharisees: Rabbinic Perspectives* (Hoboken, 1973), p. 233.

the source be entirely external to the tradition; what is necessary is that the source be independent of the traditions being evaluated.[10] Thus, if we agree with the common scholarly opinion that the Bavli, as a completed document, is independent of the final Yerushalmi— that it does not know the earlier completed document and therefore cannot borrow from it or otherwise be dependent on it—then parallel teachings that appear in both documents can be considered "verified" and we may rely upon them to do traditions-history. By "verification," I argued, we must mean that the parallel teachings in fact derive from the "circle" of the named sage.

But there are two problems: first, even if this conclusion is accepted, we have in fact gained relatively little and, second, it now seems to me likely that I went beyond what the evidence would allow. In my analysis of traditions attributed to Yohanan in Bavli Shabbat, I found that only thirty-eight of one hundred-thirteen have any parallel in the Yerushalmi. Of those thirty-eight , nine give the same opinion in the name of a different authority and three give different rulings. Only twenty-six are closely parallel—less than a quarter of the sample. Three-quarters of the sample, in other words, admit to no verification whatsoever. If this sample is representative,[11] a large majority of attributed Rabbinic teachings may not be used for purposes of writing history.

It seems to me now that I probably went too far in arguing that such verification brings us back to "the circle" of the identified teacher. All we really know, based upon this sort of evidence, is that two different Rabbinic documents (say, the Bavli and the Yerushalmi) preserve traditions that derive from a common source. This source might be the circle of the named sage, but it could just as easily be the circle of a later repeater, separated by generations from the "original" teacher. We can be sure that there was once a common tradition; we can be sure that the tradition split and came to be recorded in different documents. When this split occurred and how far removed it was from the first articulation of the teaching we can never know.

---

[10] "On the Reliability...," *HUCA*, p. 179.

[11] It seems to me that, if anything, this sample probably overstates the frequency of possible "verifications" by this method. To test this method, I chose to focus on traditions attributed to Yohanan, one of the most frequently mentioned sages in both the Yerushalmi and Bavli. Other important sages, such as Abbaye and Rava, are frequent spokesmen in one Talmud (the Bavli) but not the other. The thousands of teachings attributed to these sages, among many others, cannot, therefore, be verified in this way.

A second method for verifying attributions that may be defensible is described by Neusner in the following words: "If...we knew that there was a characteristic mode of formulating ideas, always particular to one authority or school, and never utilized by some other authority or school, we should have a solid, because superficial, criterion for sorting out valid from invalid attributions."[12] It seems to me that Neusner errs in insisting that the "modes of formulation" be unique to one party and never be utilized by another; such purity could easily be the product of stereotyped, artificial formulation. But the rest of Neusner's proposal captures an important truth. If we could discover some superficial criterion of formulation that is not rhetorically obvious, and therefore could not be the result of artifice, then we will have a means of verifying that certain teachings indeed were formulated at one time and not another.

In earlier research,[13] I discovered that Amoraic teachings in the Bavli are in fact characterized by such stylistic criteria, criteria that change from one period to another and allow us, therefore, to identify certain modes of formulation with different periods. In one period, brief teachings of law predominate; in a later period, interpretive elaborations or argumentational exchanges become much more common. I see no way to explain such characteristics—detectable only through a detailed accounting of large numbers of traditions attributed to teachers of a given period—as fiction. I therefore argued then—and continue to believe now—that a sort of traditions-history, yielding a history of religious ideas, can be constructed on the foundation of these many teachings.[14]

But, even after such painstaking analysis, the value of this evidence for history remains quite limited. What we may verify by such an approach is the relative dating of large numbers of attributed teachings. Nothing in this method will allow us to verify a particular teaching, no matter how characteristic its form. We may therefore interpret the meaning of the form of teachings characteristic to a given period, to the extent that form has meaning, but we may never know whether Rabbi so-and-so said this or that, nor whether he did this or that. In *The Mind of the Talmud*,[15] I offered the sort of history (a history

---

[12] *Judaism in Society* (Chicago, 1983), p. 31.

[13] *Stylistic Characteristics of Amoraic Literature*, Ph.D. dissertation, Jewish Theological Seminary of America, 1984.

[14] For a fuller discussion of this approach, see "On the Reliability...," pp. 183-187.

[15] New York, 1990.

of religious ideas) that I think such evidence justifies.[16] I see no way of going beyond what I did there.

Where does this leave us? As Neusner has repeatedly argued, the only dating we may be relatively sure of is the date of the final formulation of a document. (I say "relatively," because there is ample room to debate the date of redaction of all classical Rabbinic documents except the Mishnah.) We may say with confidence that teachings preserved in the Mishnah represent the canonical Rabbinic tradition of the late second-to-early third century. Teachings preserved in the Yerushalmi represent the canonical Rabbinic tradition in Palestine in the mid-fifth century. Many of the preserved traditions may have originated at an earlier time, but we can never be sure when this is so, nor can we ascertain how later repetitions of a tradition relate to earlier ones. We only know for sure how it was received in the final, redactional stage. So we may analyze and interpret the canonical record of the Yerushalmi and Genesis and Leviticus Rabbah and compare that record to the earlier record of the Mishnah. In his writings, Neusner has shown the value of such an approach (even if we may dispute his particular interpretations). Such a history of religious ideas we may indeed write.

We may also, in at least some cases, do a history of large bodies of traditions and interpret their literary forms. I am confident that the Bavli will allow such an approach; the work has yet to be done to ascertain whether other Rabbinic documents preserve the same sort of evidence.

But beyond this, the literary records of the rabbis allow very little. We may seek to write religious and social histories of the Jews in late antiquity, but, on the basis of the literature, we may never be sure of precise datings. So, for example, B. Shab. 151b-152a reveals much about attitudes toward aging among rabbis in Babylonia in late antiquity. But from what period precisely? Did attitudes change from one period to the next? Do attitudes reflect social realities? How do Rabbinic attitudes compare with those of other Jews? Such questions, unfortunately, can never be answered with confidence, at least not on the basis of the Talmudic record.

To say more, we have to turn to other kinds of evidence, that is, to extra-Rabbinic sources and archaeological remains. These too will

---

[16] One may surely disagree with my particular interpretation of the literary phenomena. Here I am arguing only on behalf of the method.

have to be read with a skeptical eye, ever-aware of the limits of any evidence and the difficulty of any interpretation. But from these sources, we may actually learn something about the world in which the rabbis lived. Moreover, given the nature of the evidence (the archeological record can usually be dated with some confidence; most non-Rabbinic documents do not present the same difficulties of dating as the Rabbinic composites), we may be more precise in dating what we discover.

As I said at the beginning of this essay, the obstacles are immense, mostly insurmountable. Rabbinic sources for historical study? Barely.

XI. RABBINIC SOURCES FOR HISTORICAL STUDY

Louis H. Feldman
Yeshiva University

With What Assumption Does One Start? In a recent letter (December, 20, 1995) to the present writer, Fergus Millar remarks:

> I suppose that the truth is that I become more and more skeptical as to whether *any* use can be made of Rabbinic sources for the period before the fall of the Temple. I would certainly rule out absolutely any use of either the Jerusalem or the Babylonian Talmud, given the length of time which had elapsed and the profoundly changed circumstances under which both were written.... So, although there is a vast bibliography, in my present view it is pretty well all systematically misleading. One must start from the genuine contemporary documents (and of course contemporary literary texts, like Josephus).

Indeed, in his recent monumental survey, *The Roman Near East 31 BC-AD 337*, one will note Professor Millar's deliberate and almost total disregard of Rabbinic evidence, and this despite the fact that the rabbis have so much to say about the period that he covers. Similarly, in another recent book, Price[1] baldly states that any Rabbinic story unconfirmed by outside sources is to be treated as fiction.

Methodologically, should one start with the assumption that the Rabbinic literature is not trustworthy in historical matters unless proven otherwise, in view of the fact that the earliest of the midrashim dates from no earlier than 400 C.E. and the codification of the Jerusalem Talmud dates from about the same time and the codification of the Babylonian Talmud dates from about a century later, and in view of the fact that the Rabbinic documents are concerned with history in only the most incidental way, and in view of the fact that we do not know how broad were the circles they reflect; or should one start with the opposite assumption? There are at least six reasons why one should start with the premise that statements by the rabbis in historical matters are deserving of some consideration:

1) It is much more difficult to tell a lie, especially systematically, than to tell the truth. Human beings may well be defined as "truth-

---

[1] Jonathan J. Price, *Jerusalem under Siege: The Collapse of the Jewish State 66-70 C.E.* (Leiden, 1992), p. 264.

speaking animals." We shall do well to be guided by this principle, which is really based upon an understanding of human nature. Examples in Rabbinic literature abound. Thus, says Hamnuna (B. Ket. 22b, B. Ned. 91a), if a woman says to her husband, "You have divorced me," she is believed even when there is no further evidence, the presumption being that a woman would not be so insolent as to lie in his presence, though the Talmud (B. Ket. 22b) is quick to add that this is the case only when there are no witnesses who support her, but that when there are witnesses who support her, she may be brazen enough to lie. Likewise, we have a right to presume (B. B.M. 3a) that a debtor would not be so impertinent toward his creditor as to give a complete denial to the latter's claim. Furthermore, we may assume that an employer, even in the absence of witnesses, is believed when he says that he paid his employee at the end of the day's labor, since we presume that he would not transgress the biblical law that requires him to do so (Lev. 19:13); and, in any case, we have a right to assume that the employee would not permit delay of his payment. We may counter by saying that in our day people are brazen enough to make such denials; but the point to be emphasized is that the rabbis, in their era, felt secure in making such an assumption.

2) The rabbis were well aware of the biblical commandment to keep far from falsehood (Exod. 23:7). God's very seal is truth; and the rabbis deduce from the fact that the Hebrew word for truth, *emet*, has the first, middle, and last letters of the Hebrew alphabet that God is the first, middle, and last in time (Gen. Rab. 81.2). The world itself is said to be preserved by three things, the first of which is truth (M. Ab. 1:18).

3) The Talmud is a sacred book, and it is hard to imagine that in such a work the authors would be deliberately negligent of the truth. In particular, as we can see from the statement (B. Meg. 15a) of the third-century Eleazar ben Pedath in the name of Hanina, "Whoever reports a saying in the name of its originator brings deliverance to the world," how important it was to acknowledge accurately one's indebtedness to a predecessor.

4) The Talmud is a book of debate, with rabbis constantly challenging one another. The rabbis are not afraid to admit that they do not know, and, indeed, in no fewer than three hundred nineteen instances, the Talmud, after recording a disputed point, uses the word *teku* to admit that the matter remains undecided. In particular,

the rabbis were sharply divided in their attitude toward the Romans.[2] It is almost as if the motto of the work is "Dubito ergo sum." B. Meg. 9a records the miracle that the seventy (or seventy-two) translators of the Torah into Greek agreed in their versions, though they were in separate cubicles; we may suggest that it would have been a greater miracle if they had agreed after being in the same room. In such a setting that encourages critical method, the participants would have been constantly alert to avoid falsehood lest their credibility be impugned.

5) It is precisely because the Talmud is not a history book that the remarks of rabbis concerning historical details should be of particular value, inasmuch as they are usually said incidentally, casually, and in passing. In this respect, as Lieberman has remarked, Rabbinic literature has much in common with the non-literary papyri and inscriptions.[3]

6) As for the gap in time between the events and the rabbis who report them, we must realize how carefully they cultivated their memories, as even Jerome, who is often hostile to Judaism, acknowledged (Epistle to Titus 3:9). Let it be stated here emphatically, however, that, like Azariah dei Rossi in his *Meor Eynayim*, we do not ascribe Rabbinic recollection of historical details in the Rabbinic corpus to the oral tradition emanating from Sinai, since this corpus includes personal opinions that are subject to contradiction and error. Moreover, one must draw a sharp line of distinction between Halakhah, which is religious law and which is traditionally regarded as binding, and Aggada—and this includes scientific information, as well as the historical data comprising the present essay, which is lore and which the rabbis themselves treated with considerable freedom.[4] In particular, we may call attention to Azariah's view that round hyperbolic numbers in Rabbinic literature are to be understood not literally but rather as stereotypical qualitative statements; and this will explain discrepancies in such matters between the Babylonian and Jerusalemite Aggadot. Likewise we may explain Rabbinic identification of distinct historical personalities and discrepancies between

---

[2] Ibid., pp. 39-81.

[3] Saul Lieberman, "The Martyrs of Caesarea," in *Annuaire de l'Institut de Philologie et d'Histoire Orientales et Slaves* 7 (1939-44), p. 395.

[4] See Salo W. Baron, "Azariah de' Rossi's Historical Method," in Salo W. Baron, *History and Jewish Historians: Essays and Addresses* (Philadelphia, 1964), p. 221.

Rabbinic passages as due to Rabbinic aims to teach and moralize.[5] The errors of the rabbis in matters of science and history are due to the era in which they lived and to the fact that in such matters they were subject to human error. Finally, matters of chronology, as Azariah notes, are of no practical halakhic concern, and hence we may explain the rabbis' error in indicating that the Persian period lasted thirty-four years and that the First Temple was destroyed in 421 B.C.E., when biblical and both Jewish and non-Jewish historical writing assert that it lasted much longer and that the First Temple was destroyed in 587 B.C.E.[6]

We may suggest that a somewhat similar problem arises in what use, if any, is to be made of the so-called *Scriptores Historiae Augustae*. This is a collection of thirty biographies, for the most part of individual Roman emperors of the second and third centuries, attributed to six different authors and addressed to Diocletian, Constantine, and others. On the surface this would seem to be a work similar to the biographies by Cornelius Nepos, Plutarch, and Suetonius, which contain numerous anecdotes of the sort found in the Rabbinic literature. What makes the *Scriptores Historiae Augustae* particularly similar to the historical data found in Rabbinic literature is that the work seems to have been edited by a single author, since the separate authors of the biographies show great similarity and construction and language; moreover, as in Rabbinic literature, there is a considerable amount of repetition from one biography to another and numerous inconsistencies and anachronisms. Just as the Rabbinic literature presents data from several centuries earlier though it was not codified until the fourth century at the earliest, so the *Scriptores Historiae Augustae* is generally thought to be the product of a single writer or editor at the end of the fourth or the early fifth century. The work has been termed historical romance;[7] yet, as even the ultra-critical Syme admits, a

---

[5] Azariah dei Rossi, *Me'or 'Eynayim* (reprinted: Jerusalem, 1970), pp. 227-228, 235-239. The most famous example of Azariah's readiness to concede that the Rabbinic aggadah need not be taken literally is his understanding (p. 217) of the Rabbinic statement (Pirqe de-R. Eliezer 49, B. Git. 56b) that God sent a gnat that entered into the nostril of Titus, that it made its may into his brain, and that it became like a young pigeon weighing two pounds. To Azariah, convinced that such a creature could not have survived thus and that the non-Jewish sources of Titus' death make no mention of this, the passage is to be understood as a pedagogical device of the rabbis to illustrate the consequences of sinfulness.

[6] See dei Rossi, ibid., pp. 310-325.

[7] Ronald Syme, *Ammianus and the Historia Augusta* (Oxford, 1968), pp. 205, 219.

wealth of valuable details can be disengaged from it.[8] We may cite as an example its statement (*Life of Hadrian* 14.2) that the cause of the Bar Kokhba rebellion was Hadrian's decree forbidding circumcision. In contrast, Dio Cassius (69.12.1-2) gives the cause as Hadrian's decision to establish a city of his own on the site of the ruined Jerusalem, as well as a temple dedicated to Zeus on the site of the Jewish Temple. The Vermes-Millar revision of Schürer,[9] realizing that it must choose between the two reasons, prefers to accept the *Historia Augusta*'s explanation, since there is direct evidence for the universality of the ban on circumcision in regard to the Arabs, Samaritans, and Egyptians, and not merely in regard to the Jews.

Parallels between Rabbinic Literature and Josephus—Agrippa I: Shaye Cohen[10] concludes that the Rabbinic tradition in historiography must be tested by comparing it with parallels in Josephus or other sources. Josephus is, moreover, at least a century older than the recording of the earliest Rabbinic source. Does this, however, mean that the Rabbinic sources should be disregarded? Let us look at some examples.

The potential importance of Rabbinic literature as a source for the history of the Second Temple period is particularly great because our chief source for the period, Josephus, is so suspect, especially for those events in which he personally was involved. A case in point is the portrayal of Agrippa I. As Schwartz[11] has noted, neither Philo nor Josephus seems to have any sources antagonistic to Agrippa I, even though we may well suspect that he was less than admirable, to judge from his luxurious living and the large payments he made to the Emperor Tiberius' freedmen in the hope of securing their cooperation (Josephus, *Ant.* 18.145), as well as from the fact that he seems to have enjoyed being flattered and did not rebuke his flatterers even when they referred to him as more than mortal (*Ant.* 19.345-346). Moreover, we may well be suspicious that the conclave in Tiberias to which Agrippa I invited five kings (*Ant.* 19.338-342) and which Marsus, the Roman governor of Syria, ordered to be broken up, was

---

[8] Ibid., p. 177.

[9] Emil Schürer, *The History of the Jewish People in the Age of Jesus Christ (175 B.C.-A.D. 135)*, eds. Geza Vermes and Fergus Millar (Edinburgh, 1973), vol. 1, pp. 537-540.

[10] Shaye J.D. Cohen, "Parallel Historical Tradition in Josephus and Rabbinic Literature," in *Proceedings of the Ninth World Congress of Jewish Studies*, 1985, Division B, vol. 1 (Jerusalem, 1986), pp. 7-14.

[11] Daniel R. Schwartz, *Agrippa I: The Last King of Judaea* (Tübingen, 1990), pp. 157-171.

an instance of Agrippa's ambition for greater power.[12] The fact that Josephus (*Ant.* 19.328-331) goes out of his way to present an encomium for Agrippa, comparable to the encomia that he writes for a number of biblical figures, notably Moses (*Ant.* 4.328-331), Samuel (*Ant.* 6.292-294), Saul (*Ant.* 6.343-350), and David (*Ant.* 7.390-391), and such as he presents for no other post-biblical figure, and in particular to contrast him, in the most glowing terms, with Herod is a clue to the tremendous admiration he wishes his readers to conceive for Agrippa. We may well wonder whether Agrippa played the key role in getting Claudius to be emperor in succession to Caligula (*Ant.* 19.236-245), whereas Dio Cassius (60.8.2) simply asserts that Agrippa cooperated with Claudius in seeking the rule, since he then happened to be in Rome.

It is precisely in such a situation, where the contemporary sources seem to be biased, that we may find the Rabbinic sources of some value, if read carefully. We may, of course, express skepticism as to whether the rabbis are objective when it comes to relations with Rome, in view of the terrible destruction Rome wrought in the Great War of 66-74 in which the Temple, the central feature of Jewish religious life, was destroyed by the Romans, as well as in view of the terrible losses suffered by the Jews at the hands of the Romans in the uprisings led by Lukuas-Andreas in 115-117 and by Bar Kokhba in 132-135. One might have expected the rabbis to speak about Agrippa in the most bitter terms, inasmuch as he was the man who represented Rome's most serious attempt to establish a *modus vivendi* with Judea.[13] But the rabbis by no means speak with one voice; and hence it should come as no surprise that even as there are rabbis who condemn the Romans, still, such an influential figure as the third-century Palestinian Resh Laqish (Gen. Rab. 9.13), commenting on the verse (Gen. 1:31), "And behold it was very good," says that this refers to the earthly kingdom, that is Rome; and, in particular, he compliments the Romans for their administration of justice. His contemporary, Rabbi Levi, is especially impressed with the security that the Empire had brought its inhabitants against robbers (Lev. Rab.

---

[12] Schwartz, pp. 138-139, suggests that the conference was simply a friendly meeting, a kind of class reunion. But Marsus may well have had grounds for being suspicious of Agrippa's ambition in view of the elaborate entertainment that Agrippa gave to these kings (*Ant.* 19.339) and in view of the appreciation Agrippa showed for the honor given him by these kings.

[13] See Schwartz, p. 158.

35.5). His contemporary, the Palestinian Yose bar Hanina, although well aware of the oppression by the empire and its rapacity toward its subjects, regards its success and prosperity as evidence of God's justice (Eccl. Rab. 5.7.1).

What complicates the use of Rabbinic sources for Agrippa I, however, is that the rabbis speak merely of "King Agrippa," without specifying whether Agrippa I or II is meant. But, as Schwartz[14] has suggested, it seems reasonable to conclude that the rabbis did not see much difference in their attitude toward Agrippa I and Agrippa II, since otherwise they would have distinguished between the two. They (M. Sot. 7:8), like Josephus (*Ant.* 19.331), note Agrippa's scrupulous observance of the Jewish tradition, adding that when he read the Torah at the septennial ceremony (Deut. 31:10-13), he read from it standing, whereupon he was praised by the sages.

M. Sot. 7:8 may even help us to establish the Greek text of Josephus. Thus we read (*Ant.* 19.332) that a certain Jew named Simon denounced Agrippa on the grounds that the right of entrance to the Temple should be restricted to those who were ἐγγενέσιν, that is, those who are of native Jewish stock. Niese, in his edition of Josephus, emends this to εὐαγέσιν, that is, those who are ritually clean, since, in the previous sentence in Josephus, we read that Simon had denounced Agrippa as "unholy." But the Mishnah here notes that when Agrippa read from the Torah and came to the passage, "You may not set over you [as king] a foreigner" (Deut. 17:15), he burst into tears, presumably because he was of part Edomite descent.

A key point in Josephus' portrayal of Agrippa I is, as we have noted, that he did not reject the extreme flattery uttered by his followers (*Ant.* 19.345). Here the evidence of the rabbis (B. Sot. 41b, T. Sot. 7:16), though, to be sure, they do not indicate which Agrippa is meant, is in accord with Josephus, for we read: "It was said in Rabbi Nathan's [second century, Babylonian and Palestinian] name: Israel was doomed to destruction because they flattered King Agrippa." What is striking here is that we have a tradition that is highly critical of Agrippa and that may correct the undue favoritism shown by Philo and Josephus.[15]

---

[14] Ibid., p. 162.

[15] Though it is tempting to think that Agrippa II, a contemporary of the destruction of the Temple, is meant here, a tradition that attempts to explain the destruction of the Temple might well view a generation as a brief period, as we find, for example, in the case of the Christian tradition that viewed the destruction of the Temple as divine punishment for the death of Jesus. So Schwartz, ibid., p. 161.

The Conversion of the Adiabenians: The account of the conversion of the Adiabenians exemplifies how information from Rabbinic literature may be useful in confirming and supplementing data from other sources.

Our major source for this episode is Josephus (*Ant.* 20.17-96). It seems likely, in view of the fact that Josephus begins the passage with a standard phrase indicating that he is moving from one source to another,[16] that he is dependent upon a new and special source detailing this episode. That, indeed, he is dependent upon a special source would seem to be indicated by the fact that in three instances (*Ant.* 20.48, 53, 96) within this pericope he promises the reader that he will later provide certain information that he actually fails to supply. The fact that Josephus did not delete the cross-references would indicate that he here did little, if anything, to check his data. Hence, information from other sources, particularly for these unfulfilled promises, is especially welcome.

There are at least seven details where the Rabbinic sources confirm or supplement what we find in Josephus: 1) Josephus (*Ant.* 20.49-53) tells us that Helena, the mother of the king of Adiabene, seeing that peace prevailed in the kingdom, visited Jerusalem in order to make a thanksgiving offering in the Temple and that she and King Izates supplied with food the inhabitants there, who were hard pressed by famine. The reader would like to know more about what preceded the peace that prevailed in the kingdom and precisely why she made the trip to Jerusalem at this particular time. Josephus (*Ant.* 20.48), immediately after his account of Izates' conversion, declares that he will report later how God rewarded Izates and his children for their piety, but we do not hear of the miraculous escape from the dangers that confronted Izates' children. Nor do we hear of God's aid to Izates during the period that elapsed between Izates' conversion and Helena's journey to Jerusalem. Josephus (*Ant.* 20.53) tells us that he will "leave to a later time the further tale of good deeds performed for our city by this royal pair." M. Naz. 3:6 likewise tells of Helena's journey to Jerusalem but, additionally, explains to us why she made the trip at that particular time. Whereas Josephus (*Ant.* 20.49) states merely that peace prevailed in the kingdom of Adiabene and that Helena conceived a desire to go to Jerusalem to worship in

---

[16] Daniel R. Schwartz, "Κατὰ τοῦτον τὸν καιρόν: Josephus' Source on Agrippa II," in *JQR* 72, 1981-82, pp. 241-268.

the Temple and to make thank-offerings there, the Mishnah supplements this account by telling us that her son had gone off to war and
that she had vowed that if he returned safely she would become a
Nazirite for seven years. It adds that when, indeed, he did return
safely she fulfilled her vow and that thereafter she went to the land of
Israel, whereupon, in accordance with the view of the House of
Hillel, she became a Nazirite for another seven years, at the end of
which time she was made unclean, so that she became a Nazirite for
still another seven years.[17]

Josephus (*Ant.* 20.52) tells us that because of her benefactions to
the Jews of Jerusalem at the time of the famine, Queen Helena "left
a very great name that will be famous forever." The rabbis (T. Suk.
1:1) give us further insight into the reason for her fame, namely, that
she was so observant of the commandments that she built a huge
sukkah even though she, being a woman, was not required to fulfill
the commandment of dwelling in the booth and that, indeed (B. Suk.
2b), she acted in all matters in accordance with the sages. Moreover,
according to Josephus (*Ant.* 20.71), Izates sent five sons of tender age
to Jerusalem to get a thorough knowledge of the Hebrew language
and culture at the same time that his mother Helena had gone to
worship in the Temple. This does not, to be sure, accord completely
with the Rabbinic tradition (T. Suk. 1:1), which speaks of seven
rather than five sons and refers to them as Helena's rather than
Izates'; but it speaks of them as *talmide hakhamim*, and the main point
is the same, namely, that the royal family of Adiabene educated its
children in Jerusalem to be learned in Jewish lore.[18] Moreover, in the
Rabbinic tradition, the injunction "And thou shalt make them
known unto thy sons and they sons' sons" is said to mean that to him
who teaches his son Torah, the Torah ascribes merit as though he

---

[17] Lawrence H. Schiffman, "The Conversion of the Royal House of Adiabene in
Josephus and Rabbinic Sources," in Louis H. Feldman and Gohei Hata, eds., *Josephus, Judaism, and Christianity* (Detroit, 1987), p. 298, concludes that the account of
Josephus and that of the rabbis are completely at variance regarding the issue of the
timing of Helena's trip to Jerusalem, inasmuch as the Mishnah assumes that Helena
left Adiabene after the battles in which her son Izates was involved, whereas Josephus relates that she left Adiabene before those battles. However, previous to his
account of Helena's trip, Josephus (*Ant.* 20.48) asserts that Izates and his children
were often threatened with destruction and were preserved through divine interven-
tion. There is no reason why we have to assume that all the battles occurred after she
left.

[18] There is not necessarily a contradiction here, inasmuch as Josephus (*Ant.* 20.71)
does not speak of *the* five sons of Izates but rather of five sons.

had taught him, his son, and his son's son until the end of all time. Moreover, whereas Josephus (*Ant.* 20.53) fails to fulfill his promise that he will at a later time tell us of the good deeds performed for Jerusalem by the royal family, M. Yom. 3:10 supplies us with the detail that Queen Helena set a golden candlestick over the door of the sanctuary of the Temple and also made a golden tablet, on which was written the pericope concerning the wife accused of infidelity. Furthermore, there is an allusion to the charitable deeds of the royal family in the Rabbinic passage (T. Pe. 4:18) in which Izates' brother and successor, Monobazus, when accused of squandering his treasury, replies, "My brothers stored up below [that is, on earth], but I have stored up above [that is, in heaven]." Here we may note that there is no necessary contradiction between what Josephus and the rabbis say, inasmuch as the former speaks of the good deeds performed by the royal family (βασιλεῦσιν, literally kings), without specifying which members of the family, whereas the Tosefta specifies that it was Monobazus, Izates' brother and successor.

As to the central feature of the narrative, namely the actual conversion of Izates, there are, to be sure, a number of differences between Josephus' account and that of the rabbis (Gen. Rab. 46:11). In the first place, Josephus focuses at length on the conversion of Izates (*Ant.* 20.34-48) and does not mention the conversion of Monobazus until later (*Ant.* 20.75) and then only briefly, whereas the Rabbinic account has them convert at the same time. Second, the Rabbinic account speaks of Izates and Monobazus as the sons of King Ptolemy, whereas Josephus (*Ant.* 20.18) gives the name of their father as Monobazus. Third, according to the Rabbinic account, the conversion took place while Izates' father was still alive, whereas, according to Josephus, it occurred after the death of the father (*Ant.* 20.24). Fourth, Josephus (*Ant.* 20.34) mentions the role of a Jewish merchant named Ananias in influencing the king's wives as well as Izates to convert to Judaism, but there is no mention of such a role in the midrash. Fifth, according to Josephus (*Ant.* 20.39), Izates' mother tried to stop him from being circumcised because she regarded it as dangerous if his subjects should discover that he had taken such strange rites upon himself. Sixth, Josephus (*Ant.* 20.43) mentions the role of another Jew, named Eleazar, who urged Izates to undergo circumcision, whereas Ananias had urged him not to do so since it would antagonize his subjects; the rabbis, on the other hand, mention no such role. Seventh, it is the father of Izates and Monobazus who is rewarded for agreeing to the circumcision of his sons, whereas in Josephus (*Ant.* 20.48), it is Izates who is rewarded. There can, indeed, be no denying that there are differences in details; but the Rabbinic account is in accord with that of Josephus in the most important points, namely that those converted included Helena, Izates, and Monobazus; that Izates did at first hesitate to be circumcised; that, in fact, the immediate occasion for the decision to be circumcised was that he was reading from the Pentateuch (*Ant.* 20.44), and that he realized it was necessary not merely to read from it but also to do what it commanded. Moreover, in Josephus, as in the midrash, the conversion is followed by Izates' victories over the Arabs (*Ant.* 20.77-80) and the vaunted Parthians (*Ant.* 20.81-91), due to the providence of God. As to the midrash's identification of Izates' father as Ptolemy, this may be, in the eyes of the rabbis, a general name for kings during the period, just as Pharaoh was in an earlier period.

Finally, Josephus (*Ant.* 20.96) promises the reader that he will later narrate the acts of Izates' brother and successor, King Monobazus; but he never fulfills this promise. The Talmud (B. Men. 32b), however, supplements Josephus' account by relating that the members of the house of Monobazus were so pious that they carried a mezuzah with them and set it up in the inns where they stayed, even though a mezuzah is not required for such temporary dwelling-places.

The Jewish War against the Romans (66-74)—The Siege of Jerusalem: When it comes to the Jewish War against the Romans, there can be no doubt that Josephus has much more information than what we find in the Rabbinic literature. Josephus (*War* 2.409) states that the immediate cause of the war against the Romans in 66 was the failure of those who officiated in the Temple to accept sacrifices on behalf of the Roman Empire and its emperor. Eleazar son of Ananias the high priest, who then held the position of captain of the Temple, is named by Josephus as the one who persuaded those in charge of the Temple services to reject such gifts. B. Git. 56a likewise ascribes the outbreak of the war to the refusal of those in charge of the Temple sacrifices to accept an offering submitted by the Roman emperor. Here, however, Zechariah b. Abkulas is named as the one responsible for persuading the people not to accept the sacrifice. What is to be emphasized is that the Talmudic version is corroborated in its main point, namely, that the immediate cause of the war was the failure to accept a sacrifice on behalf of the Roman emperor. Moreover, Josephus (*War*

6.94) and M. Ta. 4:6 are in accord in noting that the daily sacrifice ceased to be offered on the seventeenth of Tammuz. As to the discrepancy between the two accounts of the name of the one responsible for persuading the people, there is not necessarily a discrepancy at all. In Josephus (*War* 4.225-226), we read that Zacharias the son of Amphicalleus (presumably Abkulas), a priest, was one of the leaders of the Zealots. The fact that both Eleazar and Zacharias are priests must have established a kinship between them. One may suggest that Zacharias turned to a fellow priest who had more influence than he, namely, the son of the high priest, and that it was the latter who succeeded.

B. Git. 55b-56a has an account, unparalleled as such in Josephus, that ascribes the destruction of Jerusalem to an event involving a certain Kamtza and Bar Kamtza. According to this narrative, by mistake a certain man's servant, sent to invite Kamtza, invited Bar Kamtza, his master's enemy, instead. When the master refused to admit Bar Kamtza, even when the latter offered to pay for the cost of the entire party and when, despite this, the rabbis, who were present, remained silent, Bar Kamtza, in revenge, informed the emperor that the Jews were rebelling against him. When the emperor asked for evidence, he was told to test their loyalty by sending them an offering so see whether they would offer it. We may well ask what connection there was between the insult offered to Bar Kamtza and the accusation of a rebellion by the Jews against Rome. However, by putting the two accounts, those of the rabbis and of Josephus, together we may shed light on the stance of the rabbis toward revolution against Rome. The Talmudic version declares that the rabbis were inclined to continue the offerings in order not to offend the Roman government. Likewise, Josephus (*War* 2.410) states that the chief priests and the notables (γνωρίμων) besought those who officiated in the Temple not to abandon the customary offering for their rulers. It would appear reasonable to suggest that the rabbis were among those notables. We may wonder why the revolutionaries were able to hold out so long against the mighty Roman army and why they seemed to command considerable support among the populace. The fact that at least one of them, Zacharias, was a Zealot and the fact that he was able to convince the other rabbis is an indication that the Zealots found some support among the rabbis themselves.

Here the Rabbinic account would appear to supplement and correct that of Josephus. According to the latter (*War* 2.410), the chief priests and the notables earnestly but unsuccessfully besought the priests who officiated in the Temple services not to abandon the customary offering for the Roman emperor. According to the Talmud (B. Git. 56a), the rabbis, who, as we have suggested above, were presumably among the notables, were divided in their opinions, most of them being inclined, in the name of peace, not to offend the Roman government, but were eventually convinced by Zechariah. Whether or not, therefore, we accept the historicity of the account of Kamtza and Bar Kamtza, the Rabbinic account not only corroborates Josephus' version of the immediate cause of the rebellion but also sheds important light on the Rabbinic attitude toward the rebellion. Furthermore, the Rabbinic account serves as an important corrective to that of the *Sibylline Oracles* (5.28-29), which attributes to Nero the entire responsibility for the war.

Where we are on the safest ground is where we find agreement of Josephus, Tacitus, and the rabbis. Such an instance is found in the tradition that during the siege of Jerusalem vast quantities of grain were burnt. Tacitus (*Histories* 5.12) very briefly states that there were continual incendiary fires, and that a vast quantity of grain was burnt. The most famous incident in Rabbinic literature connected with the siege of Jerusalem is Yohanan b. Zakkai's escape and his encounter with Vespasian.[19] This has been the subject of a vast literature,[20] most of which has been critical of its historicity. And yet, even those who cast doubt on the account will have to admit that the circumstances of the escape are in accord with the information that we have from Josephus, namely, the tremendous shortage of food. The Rabbinic account (B. Git. 56a) tells how the servant of Martha, one of the richest women in Jerusalem, sought and failed to find some fine flour, then white flour, then dark flour, then barley flour. Then she herself went out to see if she could find anything at all to eat, but she found nothing. Finally, some dung stuck to her foot and she died.

The shortage of grain and its consequent, high price and the implied search finally for dung, are both corroborated in Josephus

---

[19] There are four major versions of the story: B. Git. 56a-b, Lam. Rab. 1.31, Abot de-Rabbi Nathan, version A, chapter 4; and Abot de-Rabbi Nathan, version B, chapter 6.

[20] See the bibliography in Peter Schäfer, "Die Flucht Johanan b. Zakkais aus Jerusalem und die Gründung des 'Lehrhauses' in Jabne," in *ANRW* 2.19.2 (1979), pp. 43-101; and most recently, Price, ibid., pp. 264-270.

(*War* 5.571): "A measure of corn had been sold for a talent, and...
later when it was no longer possible to gather herbs, the city being all
walled it, some were reduced to such straits that they searched the
sewers for old cow dung and ate the offal therefrom, and what once ·
would have disgusted them to look at had now become food." The
Rabbinic literature, like satire, is particularly useful in evoking the
mood of the time, even if, as in satire, it may resort to exaggeration.
Thus the rabbis (Lam. Rab. 4.12) recall that so great was the hunger
at the time of the destruction that there were not even thistles to eat,
whereupon the Romans roasted kids adjacent to the city of Jerusalem, which so aroused the appetite of the Jews that they died. This is
very similar to what we find in Josephus (*War* 5.521), namely, that
the Romans displayed masses of food so as to inflame the pangs of
the Jews' hunger.

Moreover, that the revolutionaries refused to permit any to leave
the besieged city is clear not only in the Rabbinic version (B. Git.
56a) but also in Josephus (*War* 5.30), who states that "watch was kept
everywhere, and the brigand chiefs, divided on all else, put to death
as their common enemies any in favor of peace with the Romans or
suspected of an intention to desert."

The Jewish War against the Romans—Masada: Many have wondered
why so striking an event as the mass mutual suicide at Masada is
mentioned only in Josephus. Here, too, the rabbis may cast some
light. We read in Cant. Zuta (end), as Lieberman[21] has noted, that, as
a result of the dissension between a certain Menahem and a certain
Hillel, Menahem left with eight hundred students. This may very
well be consonant with Josephus' statement (*War* 2.433) that Menahem took some intimate friends off with him to Masada, where he
took some weapons, and then returned to Jerusalem, where he was
murdered (*War* 2.448). According to Josephus (*War* 2.447), Eleazar
ben Yair, a relative of Menahem, together with some others, managed to escape to Masada. According to the midrashic text, Menahem's students were dressed in golden scale armor; but one of the
manuscripts reads that they were dressed in *seriqonin*, that is, silk
dresses. We may here suggest, however, that the word should be
emended to *siqariin*, that is, daggers, whence the name Sicarii. Indeed, Josephus (*War* 7.253) tells us that it was the Sicarii who had
occupied Masada under the leadership of Eleazar b. Yair. The

---

[21] Saul Lieberman, *Greek in Jewish Palestine* (New York, 1942), pp. 179-184.

number eight hundred is close to the total number of 967 at Masada (*War* 7.400), which included women and children. To be sure, the midrash does not mention the murder of Menahem, but it does mention the murders of Hanin b. Matron and Judah the brother of Menahem; and Hanin may perhaps be identified with the high priest Ananias, who is mentioned by Josephus (*War* 2.442) as having been murdered by the revolutionaries.

The Story of Abba Kolon and the Founding of Rome: An example, admittedly speculative, of light that may be cast by a midrashic story upon historical events may be seen in a passage (Cant. Rab. 1.6.4) in which the third-century Palestinian authority Levi notes that at the founding of Rome each time two huts were built they collapsed, until an old man named Abba Kolon told the Romans that unless water from the Euphrates were mixed with mortar, the buildings would not stand. He volunteered to get the water and, disguised as a wine carrier, journeyed to the Euphrates, where he obtained some water, returned, and mixed it with the mortar. The huts then remained standing. The city thus built was called Rome-Babylon.[22]

This enigmatic story may be understood against the background of the third century, when Levi flourished. At that time, there were sharp fluctuations in the fortunes of the two great powers, Rome and Persia. In the year 258, Gaul and Spain were invaded by the Franks, the Goths ravaged Greece and Asia Minor, and King Shapur I of Persia seized the important city of Nisibis in Mesopotamia. The nadir in Roman fortunes occurred in 259, when, after a reverse at the hands of the Persians near Edessa in northwestern Mesopotamia, the emperor Valerian was forced to make peace with the Persians. Then came the height of ignominious disgrace, when Valerian was abducted by Shapur and indeed ended his life in captivity in that year. In 260, with the collapse of the Roman army, Shapur managed to occupy Antioch and most of Asia Minor, as far north as the Sea of Marmora. Such staunch Persian patriots as Samuel, who was apparently a close friend of Shapur, would seem to have rejoiced in these victories; and his sentiments would appear to have been shared by the Jewish inhabitants of Palestine, who were exploited by exorbitant taxes and now saw the Roman Empire disintegrating.

But then, with Persia at the height of its success, came an utterly

---

[22] See Louis H. Feldman, "Abba Kolon and the Founding of Rome," in *JQR* 81 (1990-91), pp. 239-266.

unexpected challenge from Palmyra, which was the principal station on the caravan route from Damascus to Seleucia and which had previously paid homage to Persia. A succession of Roman emperors had given special privileges to the city, notably permitting it to levy tolls upon all goods passing through it. Most significantly for the understanding of our passage, Palmyra had been raised to the status of a Roman colony early in the third century and was exempted from the land tax, probably by Caracalla or Septimius Severus (see Ulpian, *Digest* 50.15.1.5). The very word *Kolon*, a pseudo-Greek word, appears in both Greek and Palmyrene in a bilingual inscription dating from the very century in which a nobleman named Odaenathus lived, on a Palmyrene bust of a certain Marcus Julius Maximus Aristeides, a *kolon* (colonist) of Berytus.[23]

Palmyra, under the command of Odaenathus and at the very height of Persian success in 260, made a counter-raid into Mesopotamia, and, to the amazement of all, defeated Shapur on the western bank of the Euphrates and in a series of other engagements. Indeed, in 262, because of his fidelity to the emperor Gallienus when two leading generals of the Roman Empire, Cyriades and Macrianus (*Scriptores Historiae Augustae, Tyranni Triginta* 2.1-2, 15.4), had renounced their allegiance, he was appointed *dux Orientis*, a kind of associate emperor for the East. There would seem to be an allusion to this event in the midrash (Gen. Rab. 76.6), which states: "'And behold, there came up among them another horn, a little one'—this refers to Ben Natzor—'before which three of the first were uprooted' —this refers to Macr[ian]us, Carus [?], and Cyriades." This midrashic passage then proceeds to refer to Ben Natzor as "my brother who advances upon me on behalf of Esau [i.e., Rome]." There would appear to be good reason to identify this Ben Natzor with Odaenathus.[24]

Thus, when R. Levi declares that the huts in Rome collapsed until Abba Kolon brought water from the Euphrates and mixed it with mortar, he may well be referring to the dependence of the Roman Empire upon the natural resources of the East and, in particular, upon the colony of Palmyra. The fact that Palmyra, the most important trading post between the Roman and Persian states, was an oasis in the desert will explain the significance of bringing water from the

---

[23] Ibid., p. 259, n. 51.
[24] Ibid., p. 260, n. 54.

East.[25] The equation of Rome and Babylon (so in pseudepigraphic, Rabbinic, and Christian sources)[26] may reflect the fact that the two Temples had been destroyed respectively by the Babylonians and the Romans, as well as the fact that an ally in the East, Palmyra, had now saved the West. Thus the Rabbinic passage may shed some light on an otherwise relatively obscure historical event in the third century.

Conclusion: Admittedly, though the first work in the canon of Jewish writings, namely the Bible, is, to a great degree, a history, the Rabbinic writings are not history books; and there is not a single Rabbinic work, with the exception of the *Seder Olam*, that may be classed as a history. But the rabbis are keen observers of events; and, what is more, they glory in independence of judgment—precisely the crucial characteristics of good historians. While it is true that many of the events they mention in passing occurred hundreds of years before the codification of the Rabbinic writings, the rabbis place a great premium upon truth and, in their reverence for the past, take pains not to forget it. Of course, this does *not* mean that they cannot err in details. But their *general* impressions of events ring true; and where we can compare them with other sources, as, for example, Josephus, their descriptions are often corroborated. And where they are not, there is often reason to dispute the versions of writers such as Josephus, who are no better than their sources and who are frequently less than impartial.

Bibliography

Baron, Salo W., "Azariah de' Rossi's Historical Method," in Baron, Salo W., *History and Jewish Historians: Essays and Addresses* (Philadelphia, 1964), pp. 205-239, 422-442.

---

[25] The connection with water may perhaps explain the name Kolon, inasmuch as the Greek word that occurs at M. M.Q. 1:1 (the letter *waw* in Kolon and the letter *yod* as in a Greek transcription are often indistinguishable) refers to a mechanical contrivance for raising water by a waterwheel or bucket from a deep well. We may also suggest that there may be a play on the name Kolon, since the associated Greek word in the plural is used in the Septuagint (Num. 14:29, Is. 66:24) in the sense of "corpses;" hence Abba Kolon would be the father of corpses—an indication of the decrepit state of the Roman Empire. On the other hand, a similar Greek word means glue (as it is also found in M. Pes. 3:1); and perhaps the indication would be that to glue the disintegrating Roman Empire together requires an accommodation with Persia.

[26] See Feldman, ibid., pp. 245-246, ns. 15-17.

Cohen, Shaye J.D., "Parallel Historical Tradition in Josephus and Rabbinic Literature," in *Proceedings of the Ninth World Congress of Jewish Studies*, 1985, Division B, vol. 1 (Jerusalem, 1986), pp. 7-14.

Feldman, Louis H., "Abba Kolon and the Founding of Rome," in *JQR* 81 (1990-91), pp. 239-266.

Feldman, Louis H., "Some Observations on Rabbinic Reaction to Roman Rule in Third Century Palestine," in *HUCA* 63 (1992), pp. 39-81.

Lieberman, Saul, *Greek in Jewish Palestine* (New York, 1942).

Lieberman, Saul, "The Martyrs of Caesarea," in *Annuaire de l'Institut de Philologie et d'Histoire Orientales et Slaves* 7 (1939-44), p. 395-446.

Millar, Fergus, *The Roman Near East 31 BC-AD 337* (Cambridge, 1993).

Price, Jonathan J., *Jerusalem under Siege: The Collapse of the Jewish State 66-70 C.E.* (Leiden, 1992).

dei Rossi, Azariah, *Me'or 'Eynayim* (reprinted, Jerusalem, 1970).

Safran, Bezalel, "Azariah de Rossi's Meor Eynaim" (diss., Ph.D., Harvard University, 1979).

Schäfer, Peter, "Die Flucht Johanan b. Zakkais aus Jerusalem und die Gründung des 'Lehrhauses' in Jabne," in *ANRW* 2.19.2 (1979), pp. 43-101.

Schiffman, Lawrence H., "The Conversion of the Royal House of Adiabene in Josephus and Rabbinic Sources," in Feldman, Louis H., and Hata, Gohei, eds., *Josephus, Judaism, and Christianity* (Detroit, 1987), pp. 293-312.

Schürer, Emil, *The History of the Jewish People in the Age of Jesus Christ (175 B.C.-A.D. 135)*, eds., Geza Vermes and Fergus Millar, vol. 1 (Edinburgh, 1973).

Schwartz, Daniel R., "Κατὰ τοῦτον τὸν καιρόν: Josephus' Source on Agrippa II," *JQR* 72, 1981-1982, pp. 241-268.

Schwartz, Daniel R., *Agrippa I: The Last King of Judaea* (Tübingen, 1990).

Syme, Ronald, *Ammianus and the Historia Augusta* (Oxford, 1968).

RABBINIC JUDAISM: LITERATURE

XII. THE BUTCHERING OF JEWISH TEXTS TO FEED THE MASSES

Herbert W. Basser
Queens University

As the ghetto walls began to disappear, many Jews, more wrongly than correctly, imagined the possibility of gaining acceptance in the world of enlightened gentiles. It was not uncommon for Jews to begin to imitate the fads and styles current in the larger gentile world and to disparage their age old traditions and patterns of behavior. Many led dual lives, acting as Jews at home and as gentiles out of the house. A small segment of intellectuals, accepting the age-old condemnation of the Church and embarrassed by what they mistook as the trivial, old-fashioned, risible, and embarrassing ways of their ancestors tried to forge their ancient traditions into new forms that they claimed were in tune with the sentiments and spirit of modern, Christian Europe. They were mainly unsuccessful, and the more they seemed to be like Christians, the more the Christians scoffed at them. In the end, their misguided efforts brought them no acceptance and no relief from persecution.

Today, we find a parallel situation in academia. In order to gain respect and admittance into the university halls of scholarship, Jewish academics more and more are turning to the models of study that are in fad in Christian study. I am speaking of the methods of selecting themes and theories that are *au courant* in the non-Jewish world and that are counterproductive in Jewish Studies. Claiming ancient Jewish texts are best analyzed using modern literary theories, when there exists a perfectly fine consistent tradition of reading these texts, does not enhance any historical understanding of texts, even as it destroys the possibility of reading the texts as they have been read and were meant to be since they were produced. Furthermore, the assumptions of Protestant and Catholic categories are of no use to a literature that came out of a non-Christian milieu.[1]

---

[1] I am not referring to legitimate methods of inquiry that might have borne fruit. If Christian studies had found some worthwhile tool, certainly so-called "scholars of Jewish Studies" might productively have applied it. For instance when a method called "form-criticism" was hailed as a method of study of the New Testament,

In the attempts to date materials and form chronologies, the modern so-called "scholars of Judaism" have not paid attention to the vast evidence that show many of these materials to be much more ancient than ever imagined, or simply undatable. What appears to be medieval today surfaces tomorrow with a new archaeological find as being antique. It simply is impossible to date most materials found in Rabbinic literature. Yet, wild and self serving claims abound in modern books and journals pretending to show how the latest historical and anthropological theories fit Jewish texts perfectly.

As for feminist issues, the people involved in doing these studies often form their theories of "patriarchy" first and then forge texts to claim these theories are now verified. Indeed, much of the anthropological study of Judaism is that way. So scads of putative Jewish scholars now write about the human body (in line with the fad current in general academic religious studies) and its significance in the Jewish tradition, without much basis for their claims. Most disturbing is the demonstrable fact that almost all of these smug people, holding prestigious positions, are incapable of dealing with the sources as they present themselves. Those who claim to be working scientifically from manuscripts have not the slightest idea how to evaluate proper or spurious readings, and those claiming expertise in Jewish ritual, more often than not, have not the foggiest notion of what Jewish ritual is. The chance of picking up a book or an article and finding it something of real value is very, very slim. Most of what is written is utter rot. It is so because the people doing the work feel bound to use methods ill suited for their work and simply wish to impress the world that Judaism is a worthwhile study in the academy. In their haste to justify their enterprise in universities, they have carved Rabbinic literature to shapes it cannot take. While the academic study of Rabbinic literature has much to offer linguists and historians and students of religions, the enterprise will not be used within its own legitimate sphere so long as it is abused in other spheres.

One could even say the motivations of the typical professor of Jewish studies are praiseworthy. In the desire to protect the ancient

---

Jewish texts were typed according to certain forms which were said to come from some various school or other. When it was discovered that such methods were not useful in New Testament studies, the method was abandoned in Jewish studies as well. That is all to the good. Many good tools and observations utilized by scholars of Classical Literature are very helpful in making sense of Jewish texts but these are hardly the kinds of rages that are swamping modern academia and in the end may threaten the existence of the humanities.

literature against the age-old harangues that it is "drivel and tall tales," the modern scholar of Rabbinic literature will portray the latest fads in scholarship as "Talmudic;" false claims that cannot hold and in the end only reinforce the impression that the rabbis indeed wrote "drivel and tall tales."

Now it so happens that Judaism is indeed a worthwhile study and the study of the Talmud undoubtedly the most important of all subjects and might very well be the only subject worthy of being called Jewish Studies, since all Jewish Studies relate to it. It is the great repository of a system of Judaism by which to understand other systems that in truth were never really very distant from Talmudic Judaism. Philo and Josephus, when read against the back drop of the Talmud, become works of vast importance, whose import can be gauged from our knowledge of the Talmud. The late Professor Harry Wolfson demonstrated this many times over.

Indeed, Christian Studies could well be enhanced by Jewish Studies. An understanding of the New Testament is much illumined by understanding the language, metaphor, folklore, and law of the Talmud. The time spans separating the documents are no so great when one discovers it is possible to find very early materials within the Talmudic texts, and the NT itself often shows the elementary fact of early traditions lying embedded in the Talmud. All of this is today overlooked because Jewish scholars are in the main fixated on rigid ideas, current in academia: that no ancient text tells truths, that late texts never contain earlier materials, that whatever sounds most academically acceptable is unquestionably true. This latter point often comes to mean that any claim made by a practitioner is automatically false while any claim that denies the traditional understanding of a ritual or passage is almost certainly true.

But of course all this simply is besides the point. There are good ways of doing work in Jewish Studies. They are not easy to acquire and that is another reason many scholars in Judaic Studies today are frauds. It takes at least ten years of solid study, day and night, to begin to understand the Talmud. While two or three scholars in the field have done this kind of work, the vast majority have not. I personally know two people, and doubtless they are typical of the many, who have doctorates in Jewish Studies, indeed, degrees in Talmud. Both are incapable of reading a single line of the Talmud or even of Rashi's commentary to the Bible. Yet they hold prestigious positions, teach courses in Talmud, and supervise theses in it. Again, the political agenda of academia allowed them to get degrees and to pass on their ignorance to a receptive student body. Anyone can master Talmud with enough sweat and tears and tenacity. But few in academia do. Instead, political crazes rule the day to the ultimate detriment of the university and its legitimate mandate to search for understanding with honest and informed arguments.

The proper study of Talmud involves the line-by-line and word-by-word analysis of texts, the mastery of all secondary literatures pertinent to the topic, including the traditional commentaries. And a good critical mind that can deal with the issues that are in the Talmud and can be studied rather than issues that the Talmud does not reflect upon. I examine seven works representing works of American, Israeli, and British scholarship. Tens of examples could have been cited, and more samples of the works mentioned could have been presented.[2] However, the cumulative affect of these seven should signal the need to examine how or even whether to engage the modern trends in academia to attempt to open the treasures of the Rabbis.

---

[2] Here is a list of my reviews that deal with agenda-oriented studies. Those marked with an * are pertinent to the present work: *"The Status of the Mishnah in Women Studies: Judith Romney Wegner's Dismissal of my 'Picayune' Critique of her Book," in *Approaches to Ancient Judaism*, New Series, vol. 12; *"'Feminism' and Mishnaic Law: A Response to Judith Romney Wegner," in *Approaches to Ancient Judaism*, New Series, vol. 11, 1997, pp. 3-15; *"Is Midrash to be Sterilized?," in *Approaches to Ancient Judaism*, New Series, vol. 5, 1993, pp. 97-106; *"A Thorn Among the Lillies," in *Approaches to Ancient Judaism*, New Series, vol. 2, 1991; "This Passage Refutes Their Claim," in *Tarbiz* 59, 1989-1990, pp. 233 ff.; *Jeffrey L. Rubenstein, *The History of Sukkot In The Second Temple and Rabbinic Periods* (Scholars Press, Atlanta, 1995), in *Ioudaios Reviews*; Kenneth E. Pomykala, *The Davidic Dynasty Tradition in Early Judaism: Its History and Significance for Messianism* (SBL Early Judaism and Its Literature 7; Atlanta: Scholars, 1995) in *Catholic Biblical Quarterly* (1996); Michael Chernick, *Gezerah Shavah: Its Various Forms in Midrashic and Talmudic Sources* (Haberman Institute for Literary Research, Lod, 1994), in *AJS Review* (1996); Deborah F. Sawyer, *Midrash Aleph Bet* (South Florida Studies in the History of Judaism, Atlanta, Scholars Press 1993), in *Critical Review of Books in Religion*, 1995 (issued 1996), pp. 437-439; Avigdor Shinan, *The Embroidered Targum* (Jerusalem: Magnes Press, 1992). in *Ioudaios Reviews*, 1994; *Fraade, Steven, *From Tradition to Commentary: Torah and Its Interpretation in the Midrash Sifre to Deuteronomy* (Albany: SUNY 1991), in *Jewish Quarterly Review* 1993, pp. 82-90; *Stern, David, *Parables in Midrash: Narrative and Exegesis in Rabbinic Literature* (Cambridge, London, 1991), *Ioudaios Review*, June, 1992 (reprinted: *Approaches to Ancient Judaism*, New Series, vol. VIII); Boyarin, Daniel, *Intertextuality and the Reading of Midrash* (Bloomington and Indianapolis, 1990), in *Jewish Quarterly Review*, 1991, pp. 427-434; *Newton, Michael, *The Concept of Purity at Qumran and in the Letters of Paul* (Cambridge: Cambridge University Press, 1985), in *Studies in Religion* 15 (1986), pp. 401-402.

Judith Wegner's *Chattel or Person? The Status of Women in the Mishnah* (New York, London: Oxford University Press, 1988) is an agenda-oriented attempt to read Mishnaic texts without reference to the primary texts of Rabbinic literature but to ideas of cultural anthropology alone, so as to "reveal" that the Mishnah wants to oppress women in certain ways by assigning their sexual functions to husbands and fathers. This book neither renders the text of the Mishnah accurately nor interprets it plausibly. We can learn nothing at all from it about what the rabbis of the Mishnah thought of women. Her readings fail everywhere because they are biased by an agenda other than the plain sense of matters. Not only is there no documentation for her assertions in all pertinent instances, there is substantial testimony that the rabbis legislated the opposite to what she claims. The book's only value, in my opinion, is to show that extreme care must be exercised when assessing the usefulness of feminist theories of patriarchy to a document as knotty as the Mishnah. Wegner may or may not be an authority on some subjects, but on the matter of the status of women in the Mishnah she decidedly is not.

Now I am not saying or making any claims here about the status of women in the Mishnah (except to note they were never ever treated as sexual chattel as she claims). I am simply saying that Wegner has not shown her major points in regards to the Mishnah and woman. Instead, she shows herself unschooled in dealing with the complex of materials she engages. If she wants to interpret a legal system she had better learn it first.

If Wegner errs repeatedly, it is because she is repeatedly driven by an agenda other than the material at hand. Where scholars do not do this throughout their work, some pieces hang together well. In general those who play the role of literary critic do somewhat better but may still fall prey to their needs to sound *au courant* with the latest academic fads. David Stern in *Parables in Midrash: Narrative and Exegesis in Rabbinic Literature* (Cambridge, London: Harvard University Press, 1991) tells us, in broad terms, that the parable by itself cannot be decoded by the reader sufficiently as clear exegesis because the preacher provides more information than is required in the *mashal* parable in order to suit the audience's security needs at the time. Stern's claims here of reversals, etc., etc., are literary extremisms that have no virtue as they are not true to the text.

One can see that the need to incorporate modern literary notions can lead one to ignore the obvious. The student of Midrash does not require them and they can greatly mislead. In passing, we should note that Stern does not err to the extent that Wegner does nor even to the extent that Daniel Boyarin does in his *Intertextuality and the Reading of Midrash* (Bloomington and Indianapolis, 1990). For one example, Boyarin informs us that in Jer. 2:6, the "Where is the Lord..." passage means the Israelites should have said but did not say it, while in the midrash it is to their credit that they did not say it. How does Boyarin know this? He does not. The midrash in fact follows Jeremiah's view of Israel's ancestors. So not only Wegner but also Boyarin and Stern want to defend their areas as worthy of study in the university and to do so must create it in the image of the latest fads.

Sometimes, otherwise careful scholars can miss the boat in the zeal to show the advantage of modern scholarship over the "dark ages" of the past. In *Gezerah Shavah: Its Various Forms in Midrashic and Talmudic Sources* (Lod: Haberman Institute for Literary Research, 1994), Michael Chernick tells us his work is an advance over previous scholarship on his topic of Rabbinic hermeneutics because he, unlike his predecessors, will utilize the scholarly consensus that Rabbi Ishmael and Rabbi Aqiba had different schools and utilized different terminologies and different techniques of exegesis. In the end Chernick's work will falter when he attempts to apply these pseudo-academic methods.

Apart from dysfunctional agendas of structural and literary claims, we find an undue emphasis on historical speculation can mar proper perspectives of midrashim. Some think that such speculation can make their work appear "sophisticated." An example is Avigdor Shinan's *The Embroidered Targum* (Jerusalem: Magnes Press, 1992). Shinan cites selectively both his primary and secondary sources. Indeed, I found it hard to grasp that Shinan believed his own textual-historical arguments for his scenarios. For instance, I found no evidence for his claim that some targumic passages had to be post-Islamic (and so the whole work too, although I grant there is some later obvious interpolation). There is nothing post-Islamic about these renditions. There is a needless attempt to impress by recourse to historical references and a fad to date materials as late as possible.

Steven Fraade's *From Tradition to Commentary: Torah and its Interpretation in the Midrash Sifre to Deuteronomy* (Albany: SUNY, 1991) tries to combine literary and historical approaches to study midrash. The result is a disaster. He misinterprets because he relies on findings of modern critical scholars without any understanding of his own. He is able to proclaim passages illustrate a sophisticated literary slippage; in fact, his convoluted interpretation illustrates his own slip. Professor Harry Fox has confirmed that Fraade's misuse of manuscripts shows him entirely unsuited to make the kinds of claims he does, while confirming my criticisms are entirely justified.[3]

We now turn to Jeffrey L. Rubenstein's *The History of Sukkot in the Second Temple and Rabbinic Periods* (Atlanta: Scholars Press, 1995). Rubenstein gives us his anthropological approach to sukkah roofing. He delineates this in structuralist terms as *skhakh* mediating between the polarities of life/death, nature/culture, and outside/inside. He bases his worthless claims upon rules that are not even intrinsic to the sukkah and that the rabbis would not insist upon in certain circumstances. One could go on at great lengths about Rubenstein's abuse of Rabbinic legal sources to push some theory or other.

It is time to try to place Rabbinic literature within the frames of language and modes of thought of Rabbinic Judaism and nowhere else. Students of Rabbinical literature at the end of the 1990s will be well advised to heed Professor L. Silberman's advice of the 1980s, "to hearken to the redactors text and thus to seek to understand his hearkening to the traditional material he had at hand and behind that to understand the hearkening to Scripture of those whose interpretations are woven together by the redactor into his own statement of the faith of Israel."[4] The results of ignoring this program have proven unfruitful.[5]

Professor Jacob Neusner, an editor of this volume, has been so convinced by my criticisms (not only of some of his student's works but also of his own early works) that he decided in mid-course of

---

[3] "One readily sees that it is Basser who is the more astute and careful text critic. It is his judgment that should be trusted as it is generally based on superior methodology regarding primary text witnesses." See H. Fox, "From Simplicity to Complexity: A Response to a Response," in *Approaches to Ancient Judaism* 10, 1997, pp. 17-20.

[4] L.H. Silberman, "A Theological Treaty on Forgiveness: Chapter Twenty-Three of Pesiqta deRab Kahana," in *Studies in Aggadah, Targum, Jewish Liturgy in Memory of Joseph Heinemann* (Jerusalem, 1981), p. 96.

[5] I have not at all dealt here with matters of general incompetency to read Rabbinic texts and understand matters cogently. That problem is not as severe and could be corrected if instead of concentrating on being accepted in the academy we concentrated on more basic issues of reading properly and knowing the material on its own terms. The excessive amount of ignorance of even those who hold important positions will have to be addressed soon if we are to have anything worthwhile to offer.

some projects to consult me and follow my methods, based on word-by-word readings of texts in context. He abandoned some of his own agenda-based ideas of chronology and development, of logic and exegesis, so that today his work is focused on careful detailed word-by-word translations and commentaries. He even provided me forums to protest the abuses of theory at the expense of deep textual knowledge and, through his own experience, has accepted my judgments of what is acceptable or unacceptable scholarship as decisive. His own honesty and integrity have allowed him to move forward in his studies while others not only refuse to heed proper criticism, they are too dim-witted and ignorant to even understand it. On the other hand there are some very fine, cultivated, scholars[6] as well but they are too often over-run by the noxious weeds in the field.

Good scholarship is a product of intense learning and acumen to argue points cogently based on pertinent texts. When patterns emerge that allow theories to be formed these theories must be tested against the texts, not the texts against the theories. Professor Jacob Neusner articulates this principle, mostly neglected in contemporary academic Judaic research:

So in this exercise we undertake first description, that is, the text, then analysis, that is, the context, and finally interpretation, that is, the matrix, in which a system has its being. When this order of procedure becomes reversed the results are untrustworthy and solely ideologically motivated. Now it is certainly possible that agenda-oriented studies might be cogent, just as it is possible that paranoids have real enemies. Such studies must be based on unbiased readings and solid scholarship. Dr. Allan Nadler is right on target when he reviews Naomi Seidman, *A Marriage Made in Heaven: The Sexual Politics of Hebrew and Yiddish* (Berkeley: University of California Press, 1997): "However a critical examination of her work only highlights the pitfalls, rather than the glorious possibilities, of ideologically motivated scholarship."[7] There are very few, if any, examples of contemporary studies based on ideological motivations that have succeeded. Abysmal failure is generally the case. Yet, one need not be Jewish, religious or non-religious, to succeed in Jewish Studies, and some fine scholars in the past have been of non-Jewish faiths. Good scholarship

---

[6] Other names that come to mind are Professors Daniel Sperber, Sid Leiman, and Ben-Zion Wacholder and perhaps a dozen more. But there are literally hordes who are disgraces to the enterprise of serious Judaic Studies.

[7] *Forward*, June 27, 1997, p. 12.

is independent of one's personal belief system. Too often, the weak student of the literature will feel there is no need to listen to a critic who holds some belief system other than his or her own. All that matters is the argument and its faithfulness to the evidence.

It is time to recognize the errors of our ways and correct them. It is time universities cared enough about their own programs to place knowledgeable people on their hiring and evaluating committees. I was much impressed by the Province of Quebec's initiative to convene an evaluating process inviting authentic scholars in Jewish Studies to evaluate the integrity of a proposed program in Jewish theology. It was a process entirely free of any political meddling, if they carry out the recommendations of the evaluating committee. I believe they will. If such policies are not followed universally, we will not have and we will not deserve to have Jewish study programs in universities. In the meantime we continue to suffer the many unlettered teachers and writers of widely popular appeal who are nothing more than cheap charlatans. They themselves pollute the precious treasures of Judaism by praising each other's stylish ideas as they imagine them to be in their fantasies, while cursing the careful work of those few who endeavor to represent the texts and traditions as in fact they are.

GENERAL INDEX

INDEX OF ANCIENT SOURCES

JUDAISM IN LATE ANTIQUITY

PART THREE

SECTION TWO

TABLE OF CONTENTS

PREFACE

This second collection of state of the question papers, shading over into systematic scholarly debate on current issues in the study of Judaism in late antiquity, carries forward the project of nurturing *Auseinandersetzungen* among the active scholars of the present day. The editors mean to hold up a mirror for the field by affording a hearing to argument and contention: here is where we differ and why. Only by pursuing issues in this manner are people going to carry out their responsibility not only to say what they think but also to explain themselves and spell out the choices they make, the alternative views they reject, and the reasons therefor.

Why devote so much effort, within the exposition of the state of scholarship, to contemporary debates? It is because the editors place the highest priority upon affording a platform for public discussion of controverted points of learning: facts, methods, interpretations alike. Learning progresses through contentious pursuit of controversy, as hypotheses are put forth, tested against evidence, advocated, and criticized. Then public discourse, dense and rich in rigorous argument and explicit discussion, stimulates. Choices present themselves, what is at stake is clarified, knowledge deepens. Those who serve as gate-keepers in scholarship—editors of journals and monograph series, for example—therefore find a place for everything and its opposite. That is their task. They value what is best expressed in the German word, *Auseinandersetzungen*.

What the editors by creating this book and its companions mean to oppose also comes to expression in a German word uniquely serviceable to scholarship, *Todschweigen*, meaning, to murder through silence (ostracism, suppression, above all, active, ostentatious acts of ignoring views one does not hold). What costs do we aim to avoid? Learning atrophies when political consensus substitutes for criticism and when other than broadly-accepted viewpoints, approaches, and readings find a hearing only with difficulty if at all.

Having presented in Volumes I and II of this series some of the main results of contemporary learning on Judaism in late antiquity,[1]

---

[1] *Handbuch der Orientalistik. Judaism in Late Antiquity.* Volume One. *Literary and Archaeological Sources* (Leiden, 1995: E.J. Brill); Volume Two. *Historical Syntheses* (Leiden, 1995: E.J. Brill).

in the several parts of Volume III we proceed to portray issues and
debates that animate the field. Such an account of contemporary
debates, along with a picture of the state of knowledge, is necessary.
That is because any responsible account for colleagues of the shape
and standing of learning in a given subject must outline not only the
present state of pertinent questions but also the contemporary character of debate and discussion. That is especially the case here, for the
study of ancient Judaism forms one of the most contentious subjects
in the contemporary humanities. And it is also driven as much by
politics and personalities as it is guided by rationality and civil discourse. When people disagree, they simply refuse to read the books
and articles of those with whom they differ. Were such conduct to go
unchallenged, the study of ancient Judaism would lose all academic
plausibility—and should.

What accounts for the highly controverted character of this aspect
of the study of ancient religion, culture, history, and literature? It is
not only for the obvious, theological reason, that Judaism and Christianity today have a heavy stake in the results of academic learning
about olden times. Many debates come about because of contemporary political or theological considerations, not by reason of issues
intrinsic in the sources themselves. But a second fact precipitates quite
strong difference of opinion. It is because long-established approaches
have been called into question as new methods and new definitions of
critical learning take center-stage. There is a third factor as well:
much new information emerges of both a literary and an archaeological character, and, it goes without saying, reasonable people may
form different opinions in describing, analyzing, and interpreting in
context the meaning of facts simply unknown to prior generations of
scholars. Not only so, but the state of the contemporary humanities
and social sciences brings to the forefront issues hitherto not considered at all. Altogether new perspectives now emerge, new questions
deriving from other areas of the humanities than the study of religion,
such as women's studies and studies of render and the social construction of sexuality, emerge, to which even a generation ago no one gave
thought. It goes without saying that, in the study of ancient Judaism,
all four sources of contention contribute to contemporary debate.
Armed with a range of new interests, people turn to that diverse set of
kindred religious systems we call "Judaism," rightly anticipating fresh
and suggestive answers.

But the nature of the evidence itself—literary and archaeological—makes its own contribution as well. Read even in their own

framework, the principal literary sources as well as the main archaeological remains contain many ambiguities. They leave ample
space for diverse viewpoints to take shape. Read in one way for
nearly half-a-century, now, the Dead Sea Scrolls, fully available after
such a long wait, require fresh approaches and receive them. An
established consensus gives way. Questions not asked at all demand
attention, even as diverse answers to long-settled questions are put
forth.[2] Not only so, but another principal component of the documentary legacy of ancient Judaism, the Rabbinic literature, forms the
focus of most vigorous debates. And these represent only two among
many of the sub-fields of ancient Judaism that today provoke contentious discussion.

But these debates seldom take the form of a public *Auseinandersetzung*, an exchange of opposed views among persons of shared rationality, mutual respect, and good will, an exchange to the point, on a
single issue, within a shared consensus of pertinent sources, considerations, and rationalities. Scholarly media print book reviews but
most forbid the right of response, as though scholarly argument were
disruptable, rather than the necessity of all reasoned discourse. Journals automatically reject work that does not conform to the regnant
viewpoint of a given set of editors (not seldom appointed for other
than scholarly achievement), and university presses and monograph
series practice censorship of an other-than-academic character as
well. Conferences on a given problem commonly exclude viewpoints
not shared by the organizers, and university faculties rarely make
certain that their students hear views not shared by the professors of
those faculties. Indeed, it is only a small exaggeration to say that,
given a list of the conferences a person has attended or the universities at which he or she has lectured, we may easily construct the
opinion of that person on the entire agenda of learning in his or her
field of specialization.

But debate, discussion, on-going exchanges of views, systematic
and sustained criticism—these impart to all fields of academic learn-

---

[2] In *Judaism in Late Antiquity*. Volume Five. *Judaism at Qumran*, we plan to ask
hitherto unasked questions of system and structure of the Judaic religious system
adumbrated by the Dead Sea library: what kind of Judaism can have produced this
writing? Until now, problems of historical, philological, and archaeological character
have predominated, and the religious reading of the writings has been subordinated.
Happily, we have been able to enlist in the project an ample number of colleagues
who specialize in research in that subject and who are willing to address the questions we have formulated for them.

ing such dynamics as will sustain them over time. Repeating oneself and the views of one's friends and ignoring other positions, not even alluding to them in footnotes or in bibliographies, as though *Todschweigen* accomplished its goal—these modes of dealing with dif- · ference serve no one. And in this book and its companions, the editors mean to show a better way of doing the work of learning in the study of ancient Judaism.

Here, therefore, the editors have invited colleagues systematically to outline their views in an *Auseinandersetzung* with contrary ones. We asked them to tell us how, in broad and sweeping terms, they see the state of learning in their areas of special interest. We wanted sharply-etched state of the question studies, systematic presentations of a distinctive viewpoint and very particular results, and other evidence of how scholarly debate goes forward. We hoped to portray some of the principal issues, to set forth a few of the alternative positions presently maintained about fundamental questions of method and substance. We invited the leading players in the U.S.A., Europe, and the State of Israel, in the study of ancient Judaism, both in Second Temple Times and after 70 C.E. The responses proved so many and, as this second part of the project shows, so intellectually ambitious, that several sizable books are required to set forth the representative sample of debate on a few large questions that we wished to present here. Not only so, but we have systematically invited those whose views are criticized to respond to their critics, and we anticipate that, in the third and last part of the project, positions outlined in parts one and two will come under further discussion and debate.

Some may wonder why the vehement espousal of the value of *Auseinandersetzungen* and the equally strong denunciation of *Todschweigen* that this book and its companions means to embody. The reason is that when it comes to the study of ancient Judaism, the scholarly interchange is rare, the academic excommunication is commonplace. It is a matter of common knowledge that in the scholarly communities in which ancient Judaism comes under academic study, people will not engage with critics. It is the fact characteristic of universities, university presses, and journals that those who control the media of public discourse close the door on views they do not like. They print violent and *ad hominem* advocacy of one viewpoint but do not permit replies; as with the *Journal of the American Oriental Society*, they publish intemperate reviews aimed at nothing short of character-assassination but suppress answers thereto. Many scholarly journals, university presses, and monograph series take an essentially political position on scholarship, closing off debate and imposing a rigid orthodoxy upon such learning as they disseminate. They will not even consider articles that bear the wrong names or books or monographs from the camp with which they do not identify.

It remains to express our gratitude to those who have made this project a success. For on-going support of their joint and separate scholarly enterprises, the two editors express thanks to our respective universities and colleges, the University of South Florida and Bard College, for Jacob Neusner, and the College of the Holy Cross, for Alan J. Avery-Peck.

We further thank E.J. Brill and its editors, in particular Drs. Elisabeth Venekamp, for guidance and commitment to this project. We remember with special appreciation Dr. Elisabeth Erdman-Visser, Brill's editor when the project got under way. We call attention to the fact that, of all the scholarly publishers in the U.S.A., Europe, and the State of Israel, none has devoted more effort to opening doors and windows than has E.J. Brill, with whom we are proud to be associated. The senior editor published his first book with Brill in 1962, when Dr. F.C. Wieder, Jr., was the director, and remembers with thanks many editors and directors over the past decades. Brill in this generation has carried forward a great tradition of scholarship, one that has sustained us all.

And, finally, we thank the contributors to this part of *Judaism in Late Antiquity* Volume III for their prompt and conscientious work. We are proud that so many distinguished scholars have joined in this effort publicly to show where we stand in contemporary issues and debates on ancient Judaism.

Jacob Neusner
Distinguished Research Professor of Religious Studies
University of South Florida, Tampa, Florida
and
Professor of Religion
Bard College, Annandale-on-Hudson, New York

Alan J. Avery-Peck
Kraft-Hiatt Professor of Judaic Studies
College of the Holy Cross, Worcester, Massachusetts

I. THE HISTORICAL-CRITICAL METHOD AND LATE SECOND TEMPLE JUDAIC WRITINGS

Jonathan G. Campbell
University of Bristol

In his book *Reading the Old Testament,* J. Barton tells the story of Biblical Studies in relation to the Hebrew Scriptures.[1] His aims are two-fold: first, to explain the chief manifestations of academic Biblical Studies; second, to consider the meta-critical question of method in Biblical Studies. It is my conviction that there is a need for scholars of Second Temple Judaic literature to engage more fully with the issues highlighted by Barton and others. Before trying to unpack this in connection with one particular Second Temple writing, it is worth setting out in a little detail the Biblical Studies story as Barton describes it.

Barton employs two important ideas throughout his book: "literary competence" and "genre-recognition." Although not the sort of technical vocabulary in use among students of the Bible until recently, these terms nevertheless represent what Barton considers the driving-force of all academic Biblical Studies over the past 150 years or so: the need to find recognizable genres in biblical texts so that they might be read competently in terms of the literary conventions appropriate to them. In the first half of his book, Barton seeks to demonstrate this in respect of historical-critical Biblical Studies, tracing a logical and more-or-less chronological development from nineteenth-century Source Criticism through Form Criticism to the Redaction Criticism of the mid-twentieth century. All three, he argues, essentially have to do with the desire to attain literary competence through an appropriate recognition of genre.

Source or "Literary" Criticism arose first, of course, as scholars chose to leave aside the interpretative paradigms provided by Synagogue and Church. Viewed solely as texts from the ancient past, however, they discovered that many biblical books seemed to make

---

[1] J. Barton, *Reading the Old Testament* (2nd ed., London, 1996). What follows in this introductory section, as will be obvious, is much dependent on Barton.

little sense in view of their inconsistent and repetitious nature. On the one hand, the old ecclesiastical harmonizations no longer seemed convincing; on the other, it proved difficult to read many a scriptural book on its own terms as a meaningful whole. Consequently, the constituent parts believed to make up the documents became the focus for attention—most famously, in Wellhausen's documentary hypothesis on the Pentateuch.[2] In other cases, the proposed original form of the text could be separated from later supplements. Source critics found that it was only at the level of these earlier forms of the text, which presumably once had an independent life of their own, that scriptural works could be read meaningfully. The competence of scholars improved accordingly: biblical books like the Pentateuch might be unreadable as they now stand, but the shape of the original sources from which they were made could be recognized and read more-or-less successfully in their own right.

Form Criticism took forward this interest in the smaller components underlying the biblical text. Not only was it possible to work out the literary sources employed by biblical writers, including their original genre and setting, but form critics also suspected that some of the units traced by source critics, and much more besides, had actually been employed orally in ancient Israel. These once oral units could be ascribed a *Gattung* and *Sitz im Leben* within the life and institutions of Israel, thereby transforming the conventions for reading them. The result was a further improvement in scholars' ability to recognize genre and handle the scriptures competently. Mowinkel's work on the Psalms exemplifies the insights that result from this kind of form-critical analysis.[3] In particular, once texts are deemed to have functioned orally, the meanings they can bear have clear parameters, so that certain observations, pertinent perhaps in relation to essentially literary pieces, are rendered obsolete. Thus, if a Psalm is an anonymous liturgical text for public usage, a concern for the intentions of an individual author becomes meaningless.

Both source and form critics have been concerned with the layers of Old Testament tradition behind the biblical text. Although that text is frequently problematic in its present state, by appealing to earlier—and, by implication, purer and more original—literary and

---

[2] J. Wellhausen, *Prolegomena to the History of Israel* (Edinburgh, 1885).
[3] Mowinkel, *Psalmenstudien I-IV* (Oslo, 1921-1924).

oral strata, those problems can often be by-passed. As a result, scholars ended up with scriptural components the original genre or *Gattung* of which could be recognized and whose true historical meaning could be worked out accordingly: whether a literary piece such as the "J" source in the Pentateuch or an oral unit like an individual Psalm. Through Traditio-historical Criticism, moreover, the results of Source and Form Criticism on particular passages and books could be combined, helping scholars reconstruct the broader picture of Israel's history and religion in hitherto undreamed of complexity and detail.[4]

By the mid-twentieth century, some turned their attention to the final editors held responsible for collating the disparate literary and oral traditions into the biblical books we now have. Previously assumed to be mere compilers, it now occurred to scholars that new insights might be gained from an analysis of their work. Redaction Criticism, therefore, is concerned with entering the mind of the final editor, understanding how he arranged the pre-existing traditions isolated by source or form critics, and how he may have altered or added to them in order to convey his own message. The answers to such questions are likely to be different from the answers given to the same questions posed by source and form critics in relation to the earlier layers, inasmuch as the redaction critic's concern is to reconstruct the identity of the final editor and his audience, his aims in writing, and his place within the world of Israelite or Judaic tradition in the late biblical period. Redaction Criticism has been applied successfully to Old Testament material, as in the case of the so-called Deuteronomic History.[5] But any biblical book in which the traces of editorial work can be found might be subjected to this approach. Thus, the final editor of Amos, despite his preservation of the eighth-century prophet's critical words interspersed with various negative Deuteronomic additions, collated his material with encouragement in mind, as is demonstrated by the positive message placed at Amos 9:11-15. These words of restoration, which sit rather uncomfortably with the preceding gloom, must have been aimed at the returned

---

[4] See the myriad of volumes outlining the history or religion of Israel produced over the past century. Recent examples include J.A. Soggin, *An Introduction to the History of Israel and Judah* (London, 1993), and R. Albertz, *A History of Israelite Religion in the Old Testament Period* (London, 1994), 2 vols.

[5] See M. Noth, *The Deuteronomistic History* (Sheffield, 1981).

exiles who needed to understand not only that Israel and Judah had been punished for their sins but also that a hopeful future lay ahead for their descendants.

This simplified overview has surveyed three mainstays of Old Testament Studies over the past century and more. They have been and still are essentially concerned with retrieving historical facts about the dates, authors, events, theological currents, and literary evolution behind biblical writings. It is not difficult to see how each progresses logically from the insights of the previous method. Nor can it be denied that the application of Source, Form, and Redaction Criticism has led to great strides in our ability to read the Old Testament—or, at least, its constituent parts—competently, even if the latest generation of historical-critical scholars, experiencing the gradual breakdown of consensus and disagreeing on an increasing number of points of detail, has become more diffident in its claims.

However, there are tensions between the respective insights of Source, Form, and Redaction Criticism. Most serious are those between Source and Form Criticism, on the one hand, and Redaction Criticism, on the other. Essentially, it is inconsistent to argue on the basis of internal details alone that a work is made up of sources or has been interpolated, as evidenced by the apparent contradictions left within it, and claim that the final edition is also the relatively unified result of conscious literary activity by an editor. Redaction Criticism requires a successful distinction between the early traditions at the disposal of the final editor and the final editor's own additions to and arrangement of that traditional material. The more it can be shown that a final redactor has shaped his text into a unified piece that makes sense, however, the less the modern scholar ought to be able to make that distinction in the first place. Viewed in this way, Redaction Criticism, as well as its source- and form-critical underpinnings, self-destructs. If ancient authors were content to issue biblical books in their present form, source- and form-critical observations are perhaps less perceptive than we are apt to think, while more often than not the redaction critic fails to explain satisfactorily how the final text worked from the viewpoint of the ancient author and his audience. The danger is that, rather than uncovering historical realia, source, form, and redaction critics have, more often than not, indulged in a flight of fancy. It is not surprising, therefore, that some scholars have argued that all we have in the last resort is the final form of the text and, given the severe limitations of the historical quest, Redaction

Criticism should now give way to the kind of "literary criticism" familiar to students of English literature.

Indeed, in the second half of his study, Barton turns his attention to those within Biblical Studies who in the last thirty years or so have taken this route. The methodological confusion just described and a decreasing confidence in the ability of historical-critical methods to solve the problems that led to their employment in the first place have given rise to three main types of radical alternative. These are Biblical Structuralism, Poststructuralism, and so-called Canon Criticism. They center more on what the text means than on what it meant, inasmuch as the latter, unlike the former, is deemed to be either uninteresting or irrecoverable. However, although representing a paradigmatic shift away from the historical-critical approach to what might be called text-immanent concerns, the interests of Canon Criticism and Biblical Structuralism or Poststructuralism can still be seen in terms of genre-recognition and literary competence.

Canon Criticism emphasizes the fact that words, sentences, chapters, and whole books of the Bible take their meaning primarily from the other words, sentences, chapters, and books alongside which they are placed in the canon, even though that meaning might be different from that intended by the original authors, if and where such historical matters can be determined. This approach is particularly associated with Childs, and Barton shows that it is close to the New Criticism of English Studies, popular during the first half of this century, with its emphasis on the text as an artifact within a canon.[6] As far as Biblical Studies are concerned, Canon Criticism is attractive to those who feel that traditional historical-critical work seems increasingly fruitless: not only may its results be less certain than was once supposed, but even Redaction Criticism, as glimpsed above in relation to Amos, fails to provide us with the skills necessary to read the final form of biblical books competently in that it requires a clear disjunction between pre-existing material and signs of the redactor's hand.

The canonical approach also appeals to those who wish to re-unite academic study of the Bible with their faith community, given the gulf that has developed between ordinary believers and biblical scholars of a historical-critical orientation. The main difficulty with this ap-

---

[6] See B.S. Childs, *Introduction to the Old Testament as Scripture* (Philadelphia, 1979).

proach, however, is that the importance of the canon for the determination of meaning renders the issue of which canon to adopt a vital but, without appealing to some criterion external to the text, essentially unanswerable question. Nevertheless, taking a particular canon as a given, Canon Criticism certainly allows us to see how that canon can be read competently, on the assumption that meaning functions at the level of the text itself in the setting within which it is placed. The canon can be treated as if it had a single author, without for a moment implying it did so historically, each of its parts constrained in their meaning by their juxtaposition alongside all the other parts making up the whole.

Similar to the canonical approach, but without the theological baggage of Childs and his followers, is Biblical Structuralism. In a more thorough-going literary way, its proponents draw on the application of Structuralism to literature by holding that meaning always functions at the level of the detail of a particular text within a given culture's literary conventions. Biblical books, like all works of literature, operate at the level of the rules that govern them: just as we know how to read a novel or poem, so a scriptural book is constrained to be read in a particular way by virtue of the fact that its contents are what they are.[7] The structuralist critic is concerned with how we are constrained to read the text now, not with what ancient readers made of it, let alone what the ancient author meant. Most recently, Structuralism has spawned several approaches to the Bible that are usually dubbed poststructuralist or postmodern in orientation. Aimed at providing a critique from various overlapping standpoints outside the ideology of the scriptural text, these approaches include Feminist Criticism and Reader-response Criticism.[8] In the case of the latter, a concern for the text itself is combined with the realization that the reader plays an important role in the creation of meaning. Such an interest does not imply that a text can be made to mean whatever the reader wishes but, rather, that there are always "gaps" in a text, however subtle, that can only be filled by the reader.

Many traditionally-minded biblical scholars feel appalled by this kind of text-immanent approach, although they might take comfort

---

[7] See, Barton, op. cit., pp. 138-139, for bibliographical details.
[8] A useful selection of poststructuralist studies can be found in J.C. Exum and D.J.A. Clines, *The New Literary Criticism and the Hebrew Bible* (Sheffield, 1993).

from the fact that the number of committed biblical structuralists and poststructuralists is small. Thus, much that has gone under the name of Biblical Structuralism constitutes an attempt to get a different angle on reading works historically, without seriously grappling with structuralist ideas. That there are difficulties with the latter has been amply demonstrated by Barton. For instance, the successful application of structuralist theory to western literature (e.g., poems or novels) does not mean it is relevant for other types of modern writing (shopping lists!) or can be applied without difficulty to works from a distant time and place.[9] Nevertheless, there are important insights to be gleaned from Structuralism. In particular, it is important to acknowledge that genre-recognition and literary expectation are central for the formation of meaning in all literary cultures; we should not assume that these remain unchanged from century to century or location to location simply because we normally read successfully without being consciously aware of their importance. More generally, that the text as we have it should be the main focus of attention makes good sense in the case of Old Testament books that, despite clues that appear promising at first sight, rarely provide sufficient data to render theories of authorship, date, setting, or redaction anything other than highly speculative.

If this introductory outline is accurate, it will be clear that the Biblical Studies story has been at once logical in its evolution and varied in its concrete manifestations. It is not surprising that a battle still rages between factions of the academic community representing historical-critical approaches over against text-immanent ones. Barton's main meta-critical conclusion, however, is that no method should be heralded as the key to all biblical study, since scriptural reading, like reading in general, is ultimately intuitive and circular. Hence, all the methods surveyed have something to offer, as long as they are not overplayed, while genre-recognition and literary competence should always be kept at the forefront of our minds. Only time will tell whether Barton's eclecticism prevails within the realm of Biblical Studies.

Meanwhile, there is no reason why scholars of Second Temple Judaism should shy away from looking at their own discipline in the light of the story of Biblical Studies. After all, the barriers between

---

[9] Barton, op. cit., pp. 185-190.

subjects in the humanities—especially Biblical Studies, Jewish Studies, Ancient History—are increasingly blurred, so that many university teachers and students find themselves straddling two or more such areas. An engagement with the Biblical Studies story, therefore, may have a positive impact on the study of Judaic literature from the Second Temple period. In what follows, I hope to demonstrate in a preliminary way that the study of Second Temple texts has already preceded a long way down the path of Biblical Studies and scholars need to consider some of the issues raised above.

The Damascus Document from Qumran

The study of texts from the Second Temple period tends to lag behind developments in work on the Old and New Testaments by anything from fifty to one hundred years, depending on how terms are defined. This is partly due to the fact that much relevant Second Temple material has been subjected to systematic study only during the last five decades. The Dead Sea Scrolls from Qumran, discovered in caves on the shore of the Dead Sea between 1947 and 1956, are the obvious example. Largely as a result of the effort put into their analysis, there has been an awakening of interest in the literature of the Second Temple period as a whole: books from the Apocrypha and Pseudepigrapha, the Dead Sea Scrolls, and the writings of Philo and Josephus.[10] Scholars now recognize that, despite intersections with biblical material, Second Temple Judaic writings have their own character and history. It is no longer acceptable to project forwards from Old Testament texts, as if Judaism remained unchanged from early post-exilic times, or backwards from the New Testament, as if Second Temple religion were a mere preamble to the rise of Christianity.[11]

Because of this recent flourishing of Second Temple Studies, it comes as a surprise to be reminded that some texts from the period have a history of analysis as old as that pertaining to biblical books. Works from the Apocrypha were subjected by late nineteenth- and

---

[10] See, e.g., L.L. Grabbe, *Judaism from Cyrus to Hadrian* (London, 1992) and the bibliographical details contained therein.

[11] Neither is it right, of course, at least from a historical perspective, to read Rabbinic Judaism back into the biblical or Second Temple records.

early twentieth-century scholars to Source Criticism, for example, as were the Pentateuch and Gospels. Thus, Kabisch was the first to work source-critically on 2 Esdras, followed by Box.[12] The latter argued that the disjointed nature of the work's core allowed the tracing of five pre-existing sources (S: the bulk of 3-10; E: 4:52-5:13a, 6:13-29, 7:26-44, 8:63-9:12; A: most of 11-12; M: the bulk of 13; E2: most of 14). The source closest to the views of the final editor, according to Box, was S (so called after "Salathiel" in 3:1), while other material was added to assuage objections from traditionalist circles. As this summary demonstrates, Box's work, whatever its detailed merits, clearly belongs to the world of the Biblical Studies of his day and beyond.

Yet, the fact that, before the discovery of the Dead Sea Scrolls, Second Temple study was often treated as an adjunct to work on ancient Israel or early Christianity meant that, until recent times, the application of historical-critical methods to Second Temple texts was intermittent and haphazard. And, given that work on the Dead Sea Scrolls has a history of only fifty years, it is unsurprising that those handling this material have generally not progressed as far as their contemporaries in Biblical Studies. We should not, of course, assume that the path of the Second Temple specialist will prove to be the same as that of the biblical scholar. But I would argue that discussion of the methodological questions raised in the previous section as they might pertain to Second Temple literature—especially in relation to the contradictory insights of Source, Form, and Redaction Criticism—will be one of the most challenging issues facing students of Second Temple Judaism in the twenty-first century.

One text from among the so-called sectarian Dead Sea Scrolls that may illustrate that such questions need to be raised is the Damascus Document (CD, 4QD[a-h], 5QD, 6QD), so named because of its references to "Damascus." Discovered in a Cairo synagogue in 1897 (CD: C = Cairo, D = Damascus), fifty years before being retrieved from Caves 4, 5, and 6 at Qumran (4QD[a-h], 5QD, 6QD), it was subjected to critical analysis in the early twentieth century before subsequently featuring prominently in all attempts to understand the group behind

---

[12] See R. Kabisch, *Das vierte Buch Esra auf seine Quellen untersucht* (Göttingen, 1889); G.H. Box, *The Ezra-Apocalypse* (London, 1912). A more recent introduction is B.W. Longenecker, *2 Esdras* (Sheffield, 1995).

the Dead Sea Scrolls.[13] The Cairo witnesses consist of two partly overlapping medieval manuscripts (Ms. A and Ms. B), one made up of sixteen columns (Ms. A: CD 1-16) and the other of two (Ms. B: CD 19-20, where CD 19:1-34 = 7:6-8:21 with important divergences). In terms of content, the material divides naturally into two types: CD 1-8, 19-20 contain admonitory paraenesis ("the Admonition"), while CD 9-16 comprise biblical and sectarian laws ("the Laws").

Much of this material, both the admonitory and legal, is contained in the Qumran copies of the work, although these documents became fully available only upon the release of outstanding Dead Sea Scrolls in 1991.[14] Before then, most had to depend on the Cairo manuscripts that, it transpires, reliably preserve the older text. However, the Qumran witnesses include additional passages at the beginning and end of the document, as well as extra legal material scattered in between. It is the Damascus Document in this fuller form that must now be combined with other Qumran documents to reconstruct the identity of the Second Temple group behind the collection. Although revision of older theories is necessary, there is thus far no reason to abandon the hypothesis that that group is to be linked primarily with the Essenes described by Philo, Josephus, and Pliny.[15] It is not my intention in this essay to justify this particular statement. Rather, inasmuch as the Damascus Document has featured prominently in such debates, a brief consideration of its subjection to historical-critical methods will serve to demonstrate that a measure of methodological reflection among Second Temple scholars is required.

In the earliest days after its discovery, scholars noticed features within the Damascus Document that implied that the work had a complicated history. Thus, there are similar formulae repeated at 1:1, 2:2 and 2:14, as well as marked variations in content (e.g., between

---

[13] For the text of CD and 4QD , respectively, see M. Broshi, ed., *The Damascus Document Reconsidered* (Jerusalem, 1992), and J.M. Baumgarten, *Qumran Cave 4, XIII: The Damascus Document (4Q266-273)* (Oxford, 1996). The small fragments from Caves 5 and 6 appeared in M. Baillet, J.T. Milik, and R. de Vaux, *Les 'Petites' Grottes de Qumrân* (Oxford, 1962), pp. 128-131, 181.

[14] The corpus is now available on microfiche in E. Tov, ed., *The Dead Sea Scrolls on Microfiche* (Leiden, 1992), while publication of the official series *Discoveries in the Judaean Desert* (Oxford, 1955-) now proceeds apace.

[15] For Philo, Josephus, and Pliny on the Essenes, see G. Vermes and M. Goodman, *The Essenes according to the Classical Sources* (Sheffield, 1989). Further summary arguments in favor of an Essene connection can be found in J.G. Campbell, *Deciphering the Dead Sea Scrolls* (London, 1996), pp. 57-104.

the admonitory and legal sections) and style (compare the historical language of 1:1-2:1 with the midrashic in 4:12b-5:15a). There are also more serious historical and theological contradictions. The freely-chosen wickedness recounted in 2:14-3:12a, for instance, sits uncomfortably with the theological predeterminism of 2:2-13, while it is difficult to reconcile the community's origins narrated in 1:1-2:1 with what is found in either 3:12b-4:12a or 5:15b-6:11a. In light of some of these markers, Schechter, the first to publish the Hebrew text of the Damascus Document, felt the work was badly arranged:[16]

> ...[The Damascus Document's] whole contents, at least as they are represented by Text A, are in a very fragmentary state, leaving the impression that we are dealing with extracts from a larger work, put together, however, in a haphazard way, with little regard to completeness or order.

More recently, Wise, Abegg, and Cook have observed that various "passages seem to have been added after the original Exhortation was composed, as they sometimes interrupt the train of thought."[17] As this citation shows, scholars today find the Damascus Document as problematic as their academic forebears. One might easily conclude, therefore, that the work's awkward features reflect earlier forms of the document, sources incorporated into it, or oral units originally employed liturgically. Previous resistance to speculation along these lines, at least as long as the Cave 4 manuscripts remained unpublished, clearly no longer holds force, because 4QD, although supplying important additions, especially in the legal portions of the work, essentially represents the same composition as the Cairo text.[18]

Nevertheless, despite the common recognition that there are difficulties in the Damascus Document, the detailed historical-critical theories proposed to explain them over the decades have been many and varied.[19] It is not possible to conduct an exhaustive survey, but one important solution is to posit the existence of an original poetic core behind parts of the Admonition. Charles' early influential com-

---

[16] See S. Schechter, *Documents of Jewish Sectaries* (Cambridge, 1910), p. x.

[17] M. Wise, M. Abegg, and E. Cook, *The Dead Sea Scrolls: A New Translation* (London, 1996), p. 50.

[18] Reluctance to engage in source-critical speculation is reflected in E. Schürer and G. Vermes, *The History of the Jewish People in the Age of Jesus Christ* (Edinburgh, 1987), vol. III.1, pp. 394-395.

[19] P.R. Davies, *The Damascus Covenant* (Sheffield, 1982), pp. 1-47, provides an excellent overview of such theses.

mentary, for instance, relegates parts of the text to the status of secondary addition largely on this basis.[20] In a recent doctoral thesis, Boyce extended this hypothesis to the whole of CD 1-8, 19-20. The following layout of CD 1:1-2:1 illustrates his approach:[21]

> [1]And now, listen, all who know righteousness,
>> and consider the dealings of [2]God,
> for he has a dispute with all flesh
>> and works judgment against all who despise him.

> [3]For, when they were unfaithful and forsook him,
>> he hid his face from Israel <and from his sanctuary>
>>> [4]and gave them to the sword.

> But, when he remembered the covenant of the first ones,
>> he left a remnant [5]to Israel
>>> and did not give them to destruction.
> And in the age of wrath, <three hundred and [6]ninety years after giving them into the hand of Nebuchadnezzar, king of Babylon>, [7]he visited them
>> and made sprout from Israel <and Aaron> a root of
>> planting, to inherit [8]his land
>> and to grow fat on the goodness of his soil.

> And they understood their iniquity
> and knew [9]they were guilty <men>;
> but they were like the blind
> and like those who grope for the way [10]<for twenty years>.
> Then God considered their deeds,
> for they sought him with a whole heart,
> [11]and he raised for them a Teacher of Righteousness
> to lead them in the way of his heart.

> And he made known [12]to the final generations
>> what he had done to the final generation, <the congregation of traitors. [13]They are the turners from the way. This is the time about which it is written "Like a stubborn heifer, [14]thus was Israel stubborn">,
> when the scoffer arose

---

[20] See R.H. Charles, *Apocrypha and Pseudepigrapha of the Old Testament* (Oxford, 1913), vol. II, pp. 785-834. Note also G. Jeremias, *Der Lehrer der Gerechtigkeit* (Göttingen, 1963), pp. 151-152; M. Knibb, *The Qumran Community* (Cambridge, 1987), pp. 17-18.

[21] The arrangement is taken from Boyce's presentation of the Hebrew text in his summary article, "The Poetry of the *Damascus Document* and its Bearing on the Origin of the Qumran Sect," in *Revue de Qumrân* 14 (1989), pp. 617ff., while the translation is based on J.G. Campbell, "Scripture in the Damascus Document 1:1-2:1," in *Journal of Jewish Studies* 44 (1993), pp. 90ff.

who preached to Israel 15waters of deceit
and led them astray in a trackless waste,
    so as to bring down the eternal pride,
    turn aside 16from the paths of righteousness
    and remove the boundary <which the first ones laid> in their inheritance,
    in order to 17make the curses of his covenant cling to them,
    so as to deliver them to the sword wreaking the vengeance of 18the covenant.

Inasmuch as
    they sought smooth things and chose delusions,
    and watched for 19breaches and chose the fair neck,
    and justified the wicked and condemned the righteous,
    20and transgressed the covenant and broke the statute
    and banded together against the soul of the righteous,
    and all who walked 21perfectly their soul abhorred
    and they pursued them with the sword,
    and exulted in the dispute of the people.

And there was kindled the anger 1of God against their congregation,
    so as to ravage all their multitude,
    and their deeds were as impurity before him.

This poem, comprising four stanzas with an introduction and conclusion, can be reconstructed by bracketing secondary words or phrases interrupting the original meter.[22] The same process applied elsewhere, argues Boyce, shows that the Damascus Document once consisted of numerous poems used annually at a Renewal of the Covenant ceremony: 1:1-2:1; 2:2-13; 2:14-3:20; 5:11-6:3; 8:4-9/19:16-21; 20:27-34. An editor subsequently added the chronological references (e.g., 1:5-6, 10) and laws (CD 9-16), while a later redactor inserted portions interpreting Scripture (1:12b-14a; 3:20-4:6; 4:12-5:11; 6:3-11; 7:14-21; 19:7-13; 8:9-12/19:21-24). Both supplementary layers stand out either as glosses spoiling the poems or as prosaic additions of a legal or midrashic nature. Boyce's line of argument, or

---

[22] Boyce's reasons for designating as secondary additions to the Hebrew text those words and phrases placed in brackets (<...>) are: better parallelism is achieved by removing "and from his sanctuary" (1:3); "three hundred and ninety...king of Babylon" (1:5-6) is a fictitious gloss disrupting the meter; "from Aaron" (1:7) likewise spoils the meter; removing "for twenty years" (1:10) as another disruptive gloss renders "guilty men" (1:9) too long, so that "men" is also to be omitted; the whole of "the congregation of traitors...thus was Israel stubborn" (1:12-14) is secondary, like all biblical interpretation in the Admonition, and breaks the meter; "which the first ones laid" (1:16) is to be removed in light of Josh. 16:5 and 19:10, 41.

something like it, certainly seems appealing to those—myself included—trained in traditional critical scholarship, given the Damascus Document's obvious internal tensions.

However, it is important to ask how his position can be maintained, since many ancient texts could be transcribed as theoretical poems in this way. It is certainly possible that such an arrangement represents an earlier form of the composition, but there is no way of being sure without extant manuscript support. This response might seem overly skeptical. After all, much fruitful historical-critical work on many biblical and some Second Temple works has entailed hypothesizing along these lines. Yet, caution is in order in view of the fact that several other equally plausible but contrary theses have been put forward to explain how the Damascus Document reached its current state. In this regard, it is worth mentioning in outline the theories of Murphy-O'Connor and Davies, for their observations have been as perceptive as those of any biblical scholar. Both note the document's changes in style and content, as well as its historical and theological tensions; both propose explanations as to the origins and growth of the Damascus Document and the community behind it.[23]

Central for Murphy-O'Connor is the thesis that CD 2:14-6:1 forms an Essene Missionary Document, demarcated by the introductory formula clearly addressed to outsiders in 2:14 ("And now, children, listen...") and by a new section interpreting the Bible that begins in 6:2ff.[24] Originating with a group of Essenes returning from Babylon, as implied by the narrative in 3:12ff, the document's authors sought to reverse the laxity they found in Palestine by drawing others to their interpretation of the Law; at this stage, probably the mid-second century B.C.E., there was no Teacher of Righteousness or Qumran community. The message of the Essene Missionary Document was rejected by the populace, however, and onto the

---

[23] For similar studies of the Community Rule and War Rule, respectively, see J. Murphy-O'Connor, "La genèse littéraire de la règle de Qumrân," in *RB* 76 (1969), pp. 528-549, and P.R. Davies, *The War Scroll from Qumran. Its Structure and History* (Rome, 1977). A redactional study of 4QMMT by M. Pérez Fernández is due to appear in a forthcoming issue of *Revue de Qumrân*.

[24] See J. Murphy-O'Connor, "An Essene Missionary Document? CD II,14-VI,1," in *RB* 77 (1970), pp. 201-229; "A Literary Analysis of Damascus Document VI,2-VIII,3," *RB* 78 (1971), pp. 210-232; "The Critique of the Princes of Judah (CD VIII,3-19)," in *RB* 79 (1972), pp. 200-216; "A Literary Analysis of Damascus Document XIX,33-XX,34," in *RB* 79 (1972), pp. 544-564. Murphy-O'Connor, it should be pointed out, has refined his earlier views somewhat in "The *Damascus Document* Revisited," in *RB* 92 (1985), pp. 223-246.

scene at this difficult point entered the Teacher of Righteousness. He caused a split within the movement, and so the rest of the Admonition comprises additions aimed at those insiders who accepted him and eventually went to Qumran. Thus, for example, we now find a historical and theological preface (1:1-2:1 and 2:2-13) added for internal consumption, as demonstrated by the formulae in 1:1 ("you who know righteousness") and 2:2 ("members of the covenant"). Its tone is different from that of the Missionary Document, for those in error are no longer potential converts but former co-religionists who are bitterly criticized as "turners from the way" (1:13ff). These opponents, unable to cope with the people's rejection, had either deserted the Essene movement altogether or, by not accepting the Teacher of Righteousness as God's envoy in the resulting crisis of confidence (1:9ff), formed a rival Essene group. Various permutations of this *Sitz im Leben* underlie the remaining sections of the Admonition, while the laws of CD 9-16 confirm that the group's earliest experience, before its return to Palestine, was in a gentile environment. As can be seen from this summary, Murphy-O'Connor's skills as a biblical scholar, whatever is to be made of the detail of his argument on this or that point, have enabled him to make some sense of the Damascus Document, confident that it is rendered "more intelligible by separating source from redaction."[25] Whether such confidence is in fact justified is a question to which we shall be forced to return below.

Similar in outline but different in detail, Davies has argued that the first three sections of the Damascus Document—dealing with history (1:1-4:12a), laws (4:12b-7:9), and warnings (7:9-8:19)—are pre-Teacher of Righteousness and pre-Qumranic in origin.[26] Along with Jubilees and the Temple Scroll, this material is nevertheless Essene and reflects a Palestinian religious tradition whose adherents believed they could trace their roots to the Babylonian exile, as recounted in CD 2:14-3:12a, 5:15b-6:11a and, in an earlier version, 1:1-2:1. To this Essene core have been added various interpolations, as well as a whole new section on the New Covenant (19:33b-20:34), by a splinter group that, once the Teacher of Righteousness had provoked schism within the Essene movement, settled with him at

---

[25] "An Essene Missionary Document?," p. 202.

[26] See P.R. Davies, *The Damascus Covenant: An Interpretation of the "Damascus Document,"* (Sheffield, 1982); *Behind the Essenes: History and Ideology in the Dead Sea Scrolls* (Atlanta, 1987). It is only fair to say that the outlook of Davies, like that of Murphy-O'Connor, has evolved between the publication of these works and others since.

Qumran. It so happens that some of these additions are the same as those noted by Boyce on poetic grounds, but Davies envisages quite a different setting for the earlier version of the document reconstructed by their removal. Indeed, the *Sitz im Leben* represented by the original form of the Damascus Document was that of a relatively mainstream Essene parent group, whereas it is the Essene splinter faction at Qumran that is reflected in the secondary additions and in other sectarian Dead Sea Scrolls.

This distinction, Davies has maintained, explains many of the difficult features of the Admonition we have already mentioned. A central example is the apparent contradiction between the exilic foundation of the group described at CD 1:4-5a, 3:10ff and 6:1ff, on the one hand, and the more recent events narrated in CD 1:5b-6, 11a, on the other. With the removal of the latter as an awkward interpolation, we end up with three narratives agreeing on the Babylonian origins of the parent group that, according to the third passage, looked forward to the arrival of a messianic figure who would "teach righteousness at the end of days" (6:11a). As for the additions to the composition, however, we can also see that the Qumran schismatics, unlike the Essenes who refused to join them, believed that this future figure had now arrived in the form of the Teacher of Righteousness during the second century B.C.E.[27] Mention of him as a recent hero raised up by God, as interpolated at CD 1:11a, is intended to show that the splinter faction under the Teacher of Righteousness alone represents and continues the Essene traditions inherited from the parent group.

The work of Davies, as summarily discussed here, is certainly as impressive as that of Murphy-O'Connor, upon whom he has drawn in some measure. The traditional biblical scholar in me is carried along by his argument, not least in light of the example just given, which so neatly resolves the apparent contradiction between an exilic and a second-century origin and, more particularly, between a future teacher of righteousness in CD 6:11a and the past Teacher of Righteousness in 1:11a. There is no doubt in my view that few scholars have been more fine-tuned to the Damascus Document in all its detail than Davies and Murphy-O'Connor, while aspects of their wider traditio-historical reconstructions of the group(s) behind the

---

[27] See further Davies, *The Damascus Covenant*, pp. 68f, 125, 198-201.

composition, based on data supplied by source- and form-critical analyses of the Damascus Document and other Dead Sea Scrolls, are attractive.

Nevertheless, the same basic problem affects their work as afflicts Boyce's theory. In other words, how can we be sure that such proposals, however well formulated, reflect historical realia rather than a vivid imagination? The hypotheses of these scholars are certainly plausible, but there can be no proof without some kind of external support. Moreover, given that they do not agree with each other in either broad outline or detail, on what basis could one decide between them—not to mention the other theories that we have not had time to survey? One response to this question is to reaffirm the efficacy of historical-critical methods and to argue that we simply have to exercise our own skills in judging between contrary hypotheses. On this view, many of the features noticed by these scholars are indeed the tell-tale signs of multiple authorship over a period of time, and it is our duty to decide which theory best matches the raw data or else to come up with a better hypothesis of our own. However, this rather unselfconscious advocacy of the historical-critical method ignores a more serious contradiction between the source-critical and, to a lesser extent, form-critical work of these scholars, on the one side, and the contrary assumptions of redaction criticism, on the other.[28] Indeed, it is at the redaction-critical level that the work of Boyce, Murphy-O'Connor, Davies, and others is at its weakest.

Thus, while all try to distill through painstaking analysis what can be discovered about the original Damascus Document and each subsequent redactional layer, they have not sought to grapple seriously with the final form of the composition. Despite some overtures in this direction, the assumption that the work lacks an essential unity as it stands is as pervasive as the resultant conviction that it is at the level of its earlier forms that its significance is to be found. Thus, Murphy-O'Connor's summation of the results of his literary analysis of the whole Admonition and Davies' brief summary chapter entitled "The Redaction of the Admonition" are concerned in the main with the

---

[28] For the specific suggestion that parts of the Admonition functioned orally in a liturgical setting, see in the first instance G. Vermes, *The Complete Dead Sea Scrolls in English* (London, 1997), pp. 127, 150. Although drawing on Form Criticism in other respects, Murphy-O'Connor and Davies are less keen to envisage a specifically oral or liturgical setting; see P.R. Davies, *The Damascus Covenant*, p. 53, and J. Murphy-O'Connor, "A Literary Analysis," p. 563.

parts rather than with the whole.[29] As with much work in Biblical Studies until recently, they have tended to assume that the hypothetical tracing of original sources and their settings, as well as the identification of additional layers and the circumstances that produced them, gives an understanding of the text as it is now found.

But this is surely not the case, in that the meaning of any work is more than the mere sum of its sources. Hence, Murphy-O'Connor's view that the Damascus Document is rendered more intelligible by separating source from redaction is untrue, for, even if his hypothesis were proven correct by a manuscript discovery testifying to the once separate existence of, say, an Essene Missionary Document (CD 2:14-6:1), the final form of the Damascus Document, whether the Qumran edition or the somewhat shorter Cairo version, would still be a mystery. Seen in this light, we are no nearer being able to recognize the genre of the work than Schechter nearly a century ago; nor have we discovered the literary conventions within which it was written and which would enable us to read the piece as a meaningful whole. Since the work's ancient readers presumably had no such problem, the source-, form-, and redaction-critical efforts of the scholars we have discussed ultimately fail to explicate the historical meaning of the finished text.

Here, we can see that students of the Damascus Document are in danger of finding themselves in the same sort of methodological dilemma as that in which some biblical scholars recently felt they had become trapped. In other words, how can it be, on the one hand, that an individual or group was happy to propagate the Damascus Document in its extant form and, on the other, that we apparently can detect all kinds of vestiges of earlier editions that undermine its status as a unified piece? As noted above in connection with Biblical Studies, Redaction Criticism, which is the closest the historical-critical method gets to grasping the final form of a work, trips up on the source- and form-critical underpinnings at its base. To my knowledge, there has been little discussion to date about such issues among scholars concerned with Second Temple Judaic literature.

---

[29] See J. Murphy-O'Connor, ibid., pp. 562-564; P.R. Davies, *The Damascus Covenant*, p. 198-201.

Conclusion

Indeed, there will doubtless be those who, like their equivalents within Biblical Studies, argue that there is no methodological crisis here and we should carry on as normal. But perhaps the very starting-point from which the sort of historical-critical work surveyed above begins is flawed. It may be that Schechter was wrong to describe the Damascus Document as haphazard and that, instead of fleeing from the text as it now stands, we should look for a satisfactory way of reading the finished work, even if it means going against the grain of an initial negative intuitive response. This kind of approach has certainly produced some interesting readings of biblical books.[30]

In a recent study of the Admonition, I also sought to work along these lines.[31] My argument was that a select body of biblical contexts is regularly employed in CD 1-8, 19-20, not only by way of quotation but also through numerous allusions to Scripture. Both overt and subtle references to the Bible seem to form a single phenomenon, for most citations are taken from biblical passages that reappear as the source of allusions or other quotations elsewhere. Such literary complexity, contrary to the judgment of Schechter and most others, implies that the Admonition is in fact a well-constructed text. For instance, there are at least two echoes from Is. 30 in CD 1:1-2:1, one in 1:11 ("Teacher;" cf., Is. 30:20, "your teachers") and another in 1:18 ("they sought smooth things and chose delusions;" cf., Is. 30:10, "Speak to us smooth things and prophesy delusions").[32]

Now, according to Davies, as we saw above, mention of the Teacher of Righteousness in CD 1:11 is a secondary addition, while the phrase in 1:18 belongs to the original version of the Damascus Document. But, inasmuch as it is possible to see unity in the way the document operates at the level of its employment of scripture, there is perhaps, after all, no need to go down the interpolatory route, for which some kind of awkwardness in the text is a prerequisite. If the most important feature of the Admonition, from the perspective of its Second Temple readers, was its prominent use of certain scriptural passages, then the difficulties noted by twentieth-century scholars

---

[30] See, e.g., D.J.A. Clines, *The Theme of the Pentateuch* (Sheffield, 1978).

[31] J.G. Campbell, *The Use of Scripture in the Damascus Document 1-8, 19-20* (Berlin, 1995).

[32] For further illustrations, see my summary article, "Scripture in the Damascus Document 1:1-2:1," in *Journal of Jewish Studies* 44 (1993), pp. 83-99.

miss the point and possibly derive from the fact that the modern measure of coherent literature is simply different from that assumed by ancients. By persevering with the final form of the work, in contrast, the Admonition, in view of the fact that its contents are what they are, is constrained to be read in terms of its intricate usage of scripture. Theories about alleged sources or redaction, of course, could still conceivably represent the work's historical evolution accurately. But, if the text's supposed awkwardnesses can be estimated otherwise, the foundations for such hypotheses crumble, so that the theories concerned could equally be misreadings arising from the fact that literary expectations fluctuate across time, place and culture. As long as the text can be read as a piece, then without external evidence of some kind, there is no way of deciding between these two options.[33] Even if manuscripts were discovered that confirmed one of the source-critical theories discussed above, it would be those manuscripts—not the supposed problems in the text we already possess— that proved the work had been expanded in the process of transmission, for the final redactor's handiwork would still require an adequate explanation as to its shape and meaning.

The approach to the Admonition being commended here bears a resemblance to that adopted by some biblical scholars who, without committing themselves wholeheartedly to Structuralism, find that some structuralist insights can be added to the "historical-critical toolbox."[34] Barton himself borrowed ideas about genre-recognition and literary competence from Structuralism, as he freely admits, and it may be worth considering other late Second Temple texts often regarded as problematic in the light of these notions.[35] Similar benefits might accrue from investigating further some of the strategies for reading that lie behind Canon Criticism, thereby providing historians with another angle on Judaic texts from the Second Temple period. In particular, a canon-critical approach might help us understand how the Dead Sea Scrolls from Qumran worked as a "canon" for their readers, assuming they constituted some kind of library for a group with links to the Essenes.

---

[33] In a recent review, D.K. Falk, in *Journal of Theological Studies* 48 (1970), pp. 587-589, makes several constructive criticisms of my study of the Admonition, but appears to have passed over this vital point by mistaking my argument for unity as an attempt to prove no interpolations were ever added.

[34] Barton, ibid., p. 131.

[35] Barton, ibid., p. 134.

Yet, the embryonic reader-response critic within me suspects that the borrowing of ideas from these text-immanent approaches necessarily raises the question of where these forms of engagement with the text properly belong. In other words, are they concerned with what the work meant in ancient times or with what it means now? Here, it is worth remembering that it was frustration with the decreasing returns of the historical-critical method that encouraged some biblical scholars to consider alternative approaches—whether the canon-critical, structuralist, poststructuralist, or a more general appreciation for the Bible's literary artistry. But it is clear that that same frustration inevitably pushes us towards the here-and-now, as any fully-fledged canon critic, structuralist, or poststructuralist will insist. Thus, it is not obvious that the reading of the Admonition suggested above is anything other than a contemporary one, despite the veneer of historicity given to it.

The same goes for the suggestion that Canon Criticism might help us grasp how the Dead Sea Scrolls were read by their Second Temple owners, for it would be impossible to be sure whether such a reading derived from anything other than our own encounter with the Dead Sea Scrolls canon today. There are those within Biblical Studies who have been happy to accept this ambiguity, since the tacit assumption is usually that, whatever their historical value, scriptural books are still worth reading given their inherent religious authority or literary merit. A few have even embraced wholeheartedly the view that reading is always and only conducted in terms of the contemporary culture of the reader. Second Temple scholars, however, may find this more difficult, because Second Temple documents—apart from some works from the Apocrypha and, of course, the New Testament—have generally been studied solely for the historical data they provide rather than for their permanent spiritual or literary value. This underlying factor is probably worthy of further investigation, as may be indicated, for example, by the simple fact that—in contrast to recent Bible translations such as the NRSV or REB—no-one has yet produced an English version of the sectarian Dead Sea Scrolls employing inclusive language!

Indeed, an engagement with these and other questions may, as I hope I have begun to demonstrate in this essay, provide genuine insight into the nature and purpose of the academic enterprise in relation to the texts of Second Temple Judaism. If this proves to be the case, Second Temple scholars of the twenty-first century may then be in a position to feed back into Biblical Studies some of the fruits of their labor.

Bibliography

Albertz, R., *A History of Israelite Religion in the Old Testament Period* (London, 1994), 2 vols.

Barton, J., *Reading the Old Testament* (London, 1996).

Box, G.H., *The Ezra-Apocalypse* (London, 1912).

Boyce, "The Poetry of the *Damascus Document* and its Bearing on the Origin of the Qumran Sect," in *Revue de Qumrân* 14 (1989).

Campbell, J.G., *Deciphering the Dead Sea Scrolls* (London, 1996).

Campbell, J.G., "Scripture in the Damascus Document 1:1-2:1," in *Journal of Jewish Studies* 44 (1993).

Campbell, J.G., *The Use of Scripture in the Damascus Document 1-8, 19-20* (Berlin, 1995).

Childs, B.S., *Introduction to the Old Testament as Scripture* (Philadelphia, 1979).

Clines, D.J.A., *The Theme of the Pentateuch* (Sheffield, 1978).

Davies, P.R., *Behind the Essenes: History and Ideology in the Dead Sea Scrolls* (Atlanta, 1987).

Davies, P.R., *The Damascus Covenant: An Interpretation of the "Damascus Document"* (Sheffield, 1982).

Davies, P.R., *The War Scroll from Qumran. Its Structure and History* (Rome, 1977).

Grabbe, L.L., *Judaism from Cyrus to Hadrian* (London, 1992).

Kabisch, R., *Das vierte Buch Esra auf seine Quellen untersucht* (Göttingen, 1889).

Longenecker, B.W., *2 Esdras* (Sheffield, 1995).

Murphy-O'Connor, J., "The *Damascus Document* Revisited," in *RB* 92 (1985), pp. 223-246.

Murphy-O'Connor, J., "An Essene Missionary Document? CD II,14-VI,1," in *RB* 77 (1970), pp. 201-229.

Murphy-O'Connor, J., "La genèse littéraire de la règle de Qumrân," in *RB* 76 (1969), pp. 528-549.

Murphy-O'Connor, J., "A Literary Analysis of Damascus Document XIX,33-XX,34," in *RB* 79 (1972), pp. 544-564.

Schechter, S., *Documents of Jewish Sectaries* (Cambridge, 1910).

Vermes, G., and M. Goodman, *The Essenes according to the Classical Sources* (Sheffield, 1989).

Wise, M., M. Abegg, and E. Cook, *The Dead Sea Scrolls: A New Translation* (London, 1996).

II. REVISITING JOSEPHUS'S PHARISEES

Steve Mason
York University

About ten years ago I submitted a manuscript on Josephus's Pharisees to E.J. Brill.[1] That study was one small current in a river of revitalized interest in the Pharisees, which had been created when Jacob Neusner[2] and Ellis Rivkin[3] opened up the two thousand year old dams of historical and literary method. My study was one of several that attempted to harness the new river's energy by posing new methodological questions to one segment of the evidence for the Pharisees. My own goal was to establish a prolegomenon to historical study by interpreting Josephus's narratives concerning this group.[4]

Since my book went to press in 1988, at least three major works—by Anthony J. Saldarini,[5] Lester L. Grabbe,[6] and E.P. Sanders[7]—have undertaken the much larger task of trying to explain all of the relevant evidence by situating the Pharisees and other groups historically in pre-70 Judean society. In this paper I should like to contribute to the question "Where have we come in the study of the Pharisees?" by first restating my own results, then discussing ways in which my more recent work on Josephus develops or modifies those results, and then assessing the three works mentioned above against the criteria that I have offered.

Flavius Josephus on the Pharisees

The goal of my dissertation, revised substantially for the monograph, was simple enough. Faced with a dispiriting cacophony of claims about the Pharisees, Neusner and Rivkin had independently arrived at the insight that it was necessary to control the evidence one used

---

[1] *Flavius Josephus on the Pharisees: A Composition-Critical Study* (Leiden, 1991).

[2] *The Rabbinic Traditions about the Pharisees before 70* (Leiden, 1971).

[3] *A Hidden Revolution* (Nashville, 1978).

[4] See *Flavius Josephus on the Pharisees*, pp. 10-17 and 40-44.

[5] *Pharisees, Scribes and Sadducees in Palestinian Society: A Sociological Approach* (Wilmington, 1988).

[6] *Judaism from Cyrus to Hadrian* (Minneapolis, 1992).

[7] *Judaism: Practice and Belief, 63 BCE–66 CE* (London and Philadelphia, 1992).

for describing them. They agreed that the only admissible sources for the first round of such analysis were those that mentioned the Pharisees by name *and* had some promise of access to pre-70 realities in Judea. These collections were the writings of Josephus, the New Testament, and the early Rabbinic literature. They also agreed, in principle at least, that each source group had to be understood in its own terms before one could propose a comprehensive account of the Pharisees. Although Rabbinic literature was the professional focus of both scholars, Neusner and Rivkin were compelled by their method to attempt preliminary interpretations of the Pharisees in Josephus and the gospels before drawing their larger conclusions. My study began with a deep appreciation of their work, but from the premise that their interpretations of Josephus's Pharisees were not yet convincing. I wanted to contribute to the quest they had initiated by offering a more adequate reading of Josephus. First, I attempted to develop the general method that Neusner (in particular) had worked out most fully for the Rabbinic literature and applied cursorily to the gospels and Josephus.[8] Since I understood this methodological point to be one of my main contributions, and since I shall use it in the critique below, I briefly elaborate here.

Neusner insisted upon reading each source within its own context before proceeding to historical analysis. For the Rabbinic literature, this meant understanding the aims, shape, composition history, and rhetorical features of that literature. My task was to apply Neusner's model to the rather different case of Josephus's extensive narratives. With particular debt to R.G. Collingwood,[9] I argued that a historical narrative is an entire world of discourse, an author's interpretation of the past that is both conscious and unconscious, and marked by various levels of themes and characteristic language. We only know anything about the Pharisees from Josephus because he had stories to tell, and the Pharisees contributed in some way to those stories. Therefore, his Pharisee passages are imbued with the language and emphases of his larger stories. His "information" about the Pharisees is in the first instance his own construction, and it has no independent meaning outside of his stories. What can it mean that the Pharisees "*seem* to be most accurate in their exegesis of the laws" (*War* 1.110) if

---

[8] *From Politics to Piety: The Emergence of Pharisaic Judaism* (Englewood Cliffs, 1973).
[9] *The Idea of History* (Oxford, 1948).

we disregard the fact that this is Josephus's own formulation, used to compare the Pharisees with others in his stories who "seem to be accurate"? It is not a datum, a disembodied *fact*, that the Pharisees have this appearance; it is *Josephus's* artful construction, a part of his appropriation of the Platonic dualism: seeming and being.[10] There is no alchemy that can turn such a formulation into *raw data* about the real Pharisees.

The task of the interpreter, then, is to expose the contours of the narrative and the function of particular episodes within it. In historical reconstruction, by contrast (so Collingwood), the investigator changes modes and, like Sherlock Holmes, begins to build another reality that nevertheless explains how the various stories of the witnesses came into being. But before we can argue anything about the historical Pharisees, we need an adequate understanding of why Josephus wrote what he wrote and of precisely how the Pharisees served his literary interests—indeed, of what Josephus actually says.

This distinction between literary interpretation and historical reconstruction is critical to our common enterprise. It is familiar in both Classics and New Testament Studies: The historical Domitian or Jesus was obviously not the figure presented in Suetonius or Tacitus or any one of the Gospels.[11] But in using Josephus for the history of ancient Judaism, we tend to minimize or even ignore the problem, to shade "Josephus says"—albeit with dutiful caveats or even the occasional harsh disclaimer—into "It happened thus." As we shall see, this demon is insidious; it does not flee at the sound of scholars' charms or imprecations against "Josephus's biases."

I do not mean to suggest that a fixed chasm separates literary and historical processes, for the germ of the one is always latent in the other, yin-yang-like. Nevertheless, the two processes cannot be confused without serious consequences. So, without pretending to be ignorant of historical questions about the Pharisees, I wanted to jump into Josephus's world of ideas and language, to understand how the Pharisees function *in his stories*.

For the *Judean War*, I argued that our priest-aristocrat strives to defend the Jews who survived 70 from post-war animosity. To do that, he must present the Jewish ideal of harmony and good citizen-

---

[10] Mason, *Flavius Josephus on the Pharisees*, pp. 106-113.

[11] Brian W. Jones, *The Emperor Domitian* (London, 1992); Pat Southern, *Domitian: Tragic Tyrant* (Bloomington and Indianapolis, 1997).

ship alongside some persuasive explanation of the revolt's causes. In this scenario, the Pharisees do not figure significantly: they are absent from vols. 3 to 7, the heart of the book. But where they do appear, in the earlier background sections, Josephus is rather cool towards them. Their public influence and reputation allowed them to be a contributing factor in the downfall of the glorious Hasmonean house, which had marked the apogee of the once independent Judean state (*War* 1.110-14). And they were on the wrong side of the renowned King Herod, the most famous Judean ally of the Romans (*War* 1.571). When Josephus describes the Judean ideal, he is at pains to distinguish the rebel philosophy from the main-stream philosophy, which includes that of the Pharisees, but even here his Essenes appear as the most exemplary Jews (*War* 2.118-66). A later notice (*War* 2.411) acknowledges that Pharisaic leaders were among those who opposed the war, but this is quite incidental to his main portrayal that *all* right-thinking people opposed the war.

In the *Antiquities*, I argued at that time, Josephus wished to defend his people against common accusations that their national origins were mean and their customs base. Once again, he had to chart the Jewish ideal alongside some more realistic explanation of the ways in which the Judeans had come to lose their city and Temple. He did this by invoking the Deuteronomistic (and classically Greek) scheme of reward and punishment: the Judean laws are universally and inevitably effective. The possession of these laws is itself what makes Judean culture uniquely admirable. But it also explains Jewish suffering and occasional catastrophe, which result from violations of the laws.

In the *Antiquities*, then, as in the *War*, Josephus presents the Pharisees in two ways. On the ideal side, he mentions them as one of the three historical philosophical schools, the various modern expressions of the ancient national philosophy that began with Abraham (cf., *Ant.* 1.25, 154-57, 161), which correspond roughly to the Stoic, Epicurean, and Pythagorean schools among the Greeks (*Ant.* 13.171-73; 18.12-15; *Life* 12). He once again drives a wedge between these recognized schools and the aberrant philosophy of the militant rebels (*Ant.* 18.9-11). But as we see also in the case of the Sadducees (cf., *War* 2.164; *Ant.* 20.199), mere recognition *as* a philosophical school does not imply Josephus's favor. Whenever our priest describes the Pharisees' actions in the *Antiquities*, almost without exception, he excoriates them. It was the Pharisees who led the popular opposition to his hero

John Hyrcanus (*Ant.* 13.188-98); they who recklessly drove the government of Queen Alexandra to disaster (13.400-32); they who unjustly manipulated the opposition to King Herod (17.41-45); and, in the appended booklet on his life, they caused him no end of trouble in Galilee (*Life* 189-98 *et passim*).

The common thread in all of this destructive activity is the Pharisees' enormous influence with the people, which the aristocratic priest Josephus resents. Although he makes special mention of their "tradition of the fathers" (*Ant.* 13.297-98; 18.12), his own expert priestly analysis of Judean law and custom (e.g., *Ant.* 1-11; *Apion* 2.146-295) implies that he did not embrace the Pharisaic tradition, but found the law of Moses entirely sufficient. Finally, I argued that the admittedly puzzling sentence in *Life* 12 about his "following the Pharisees" is best interpreted, in its immediate and larger contexts, as an allusion to what *he has recently said* about the pragmatic constraints facing anyone who assumes public office: they must defer to the Pharisees' program (*Ant.* 18.17).

Because my book was merely a prolegomenon to historical study of the Pharisees, I did not yet attempt to answer the many historical questions that surround the group. I did, however, indicate in my conclusions where current historical hypotheses foundered on misreadings of Josephus. The chief casualty—"chief" in proportion to its growing popularity at the time—was the notion that Josephus wrote the *Antiquities/Life* in order to present himself as a Pharisee and to support the nascent Pharisaic-Rabbinic movement at Yavneh. An adequate interpretation of Josephus would show that he did not promote the Pharisees.

Implications for Josephus's Pharisees of My Recent Work

Since that book appeared, I have not thought a great deal about the Pharisees in Josephus *per se*. My work has moved in two main directions. First, I have begun to investigate the whole complex of problems, hardly dealt with before in a methodical way, of Josephus's situation in Rome, his social standing, his first readers, his friends or patrons. Although some of these questions are new for me, they are continuous with my ongoing concern to interpret Josephus's narratives as his first readers might have heard them. For example, if he wrote for gentiles, which gentiles exactly would have endured his complicated narratives, and why? Second, giving due attention to the

prominence of rhetorical training in his day,[12] I have tried to be
increasingly attentive to the likely effects and resonances of his persuasive techniques within his Roman context. These new directions
have turned up some significant though preliminary results, which
have a further bearing on the Pharisee passages in Josephus. Unfortunately, I cannot repeat the detailed arguments in this space; interested readers are referred to the articles in question.[13]

1. Far from serving as the Flavians' lackey, Josephus remained a
peripheral figure in Roman society. Although Vespasian and his sons
amply rewarded and promoted Eastern nobility who had assisted
them in achieving power, including the Judeans Agrippa II and
Berenike as well as members of Philo's family, Josephus was apparently not among their circles of friends. The honors he celebrates in
Life 414-29 are not, after all, very special.

2. It is not even clear that Josephus enjoyed direct Flavian patronage for his first work, the *Judean War*. More likely, Agrippa II and
Berenike were his immediate patrons. Writing a book in Josephus's
day was usually a social affair that required a group of friends who
might serve as a core audience and broker a larger readership. Perhaps Agrippa and Berenike arranged for Josephus's audiences. Who
were these first readers? Vespasian and Titus appear to have seen the
book when most of it was already completed (*Life* 361-63).

3. Josephus wrote all of his works in Rome and mainly for gentiles
(e.g., *War* 1.3, 6, 9-12; *Ant.* 1.5, 9; 20.262; cf. 1.128-29; 3.317; 14.1-3,
186-87; 16.175; 17.200, 213; 20.106, 216, 262; *Life* 1, 12). But these
gentiles must have been somewhat sympathetic to Judaism in order to
tolerate such lengthy expositions of the glories of the Judean God and
culture. We have, as it happens, abundant evidence of interest in
Judean culture, especially among the educated class, in post-war
Rome.

4. Josephus writes the *War* in order to combat post-war slander of
the Judeans. We can discern from comments by later Greek and
Roman authors, from earlier tendencies among observers of Judaism,
and from what Josephus actually says, that the slander comprised two

---

[12] E.g., George Kennedy, *A New History of Classical Rhetoric* (Princeton, 1993).

[13] Steve Mason, "An Essay in Character: The Aim and Audience of Josephus's
Life," in Folker Siegert and Jürgen Kalms, eds., *Internationales Josephus-Kolloquium
Münster 1997* (Münster, 1997), pp. 31-77. Steve Mason, "'Should Anyone Wish to
Enquire Further' (*Ant.* 1.25): The Aim and Audience of Josephus's *Judean Antiquities*,"
in Steve Mason, ed., *Understanding Josephus: Seven Perspectives* (Sheffield, 1998, pp. 64-
103).

main charges, viz.: the revolt was an expression of the Judeans' mis-
anthropic national character; and the Roman victory represented the
triumph of the Roman gods and the defeat of the Judean God, who
had schooled his followers in hatred of all other cults. These charges
were only sharpened forms of older perceptions: Judeans were routinely accused of atheism and hatred of humanity. Josephus, concerned about post-war reprisals among other things, responds that
the Judeans have always been exemplary world citizens, and that is
precisely because they repose in the knowledge that their God controls the rise and fall of empires.[14] Their fundamental values, *eusebeia*
and *dikaiosynē*, are those recognized by the whole world. Even the
destruction of the Temple was only the Judean God's way of purging
his home, by means of Roman instruments, of the pollution caused
by the rebels. This is a thoroughly Judean argument (hardly Roman
propaganda), meant to challenge the chauvinistic Roman accounts of
the revolt already in circulation. But *War* was not likely aimed immediately at the authors of anti-Judean literature themselves (see 3
above) so much as those sympathetic gentiles who needed to have
answers for the slanderers.

   5. The *Antiquities* is not, as most of us have thought, a defensive or
(in that sense) apologetic work. Rather, the prologue announces two
major themes, which also define the content of the book as a whole,
namely: the Judean constitution and Judaism as philosophy. Josephus
writes, he says, because certain gentiles who "love to learn" have long
been pressing him to give them an account in Greek of the Judean
political constitution (*Ant.* 1.5, 10). Wishing, in accord with Judean
tradition, to share good and beautiful things with others, and not
wanting to hoard these benefits (*Ant.* 1.11-12), he obliges. This constitution, the finest the world has known, rejects all forms of autocracy
in favor of an ancient aristocracy (*Ant.* 4.223; 5.135; 6.36; 11.111).
The hereditary priestly elite, which also constitutes the nation's senate
(e.g., *Ant.* 5.15, 43, 55, 135; 12.138, 142; 13.166, 169), has properly
governed the people since its foundation long ago. Kings were temporary aberrations, and they brought disaster (e.g., *Ant.* 17.168-81;
19.343-59). In the second part of the prologue, Josephus develops the
philosophical character of this constitution: it accords perfectly with

---

[14] Steve Mason, "Josephus, Daniel, and the Flavian House," in Fausto Parente
and Joseph Sievers, eds., *Josephus and the History of the Greco-Roman Period: Essays in
Memory of Morton Smith* (Leiden, 1994), pp. 161-191.

the laws of nature; it holds out the divine as a model of emulation; it always rewards virtue and punishes vice; and it is universally effective (*Ant.* 1.18-26). Throughout the narrative of *Antiquities*, Josephus celebrates the constitution and the philosophy behind it. Champions of the Judean constitution were also great philosophers, from Abraham, Moses, David, Solomon, and Daniel to the current schools.

Constitution and philosophy were live issues for Josephus's readers in Rome. Old Greek debates about the best constitution (e.g., Plato, *Republic*; Aristotle, *Politics*) had become life-and-death matters in Rome with the brothers Gracchi, the various dictatorships, the civil wars, and ultimately the breakdown of the city-state republican system in the mid-first century B.C.E.[15] More recently, the outrageous year of the four emperors (68-69 C.E.), the accession of the Flavians, and Domitian's overt monarchic style had exacerbated the tensions.[16] Republican agitation (the "Stoic opposition") had—or claimed— deep philosophical roots, and many philosophers faced exile or death under the Flavians.[17]

Therefore, when Josephus presents the Judean constitution as the basis of an ancient and ideal priestly aristocracy that opposes monarchy, when he praises this as the finest constitution in existence, and when he links this constitution with basic philosophical principles, he is painting a picture that would resonate with an upper-class Roman audience already interested in Judean culture. This connection becomes particularly obvious in his extended treatment of the negotiations between the Roman senate and Claudius after the murder of Gaius (*Ant.* 19.221-71),[18] an episode that highlights the strains under which the Roman constitution was laboring in the face of demands by senate, *princeps*, and *plebs*.

Throughout the *Antiquities* (as also the *War*) a kind of counterpoint is provided by the mob, the always potentially threatening majority of the populace: "the general mass, with its innate delight in decrying those in authority and its opinion swayed by what anyone said" (*Ant.* 4.37). The masses need direction, and this is properly given by the

---

[15] Ronald Syme, *The Roman Revolution* (Oxford, 1939); Erich S. Gruen, *The Last Generation of the Roman Republic* (Berkeley, 1974).

[16] Brian W. Jones, *The Emperor Domitian* (London, 1992), pp. 23-30.

[17] Ramsay MacMullen, *Enemies of the Roman Order: Treason, Unrest, and Alienation in the Empire* (New York, 1992), pp. 46-94.

[18] My student, Claire Shoreman, drew my attention to the significance of this passage.

priestly aristocracy. Things can go terribly wrong, however, when the mob is allowed to bring its power to bear and so to indulge its blind, ephemeral desires: to oppose Moses and Aaron, to demand a king, to challenge John Hyrcanus, and so on.

Korah appears as the archetypal demagogue. He was a Catiline-like member of the nobility who, becoming jealous of Moses's honor, used his rhetorical ability to curry favor with the people, denouncing Moses and Aaron as despots (*Ant.* 4.14-19); he used the *appearance* of concern for the people to further his naked ambition (4.20). In more recent times, the Pharisees—a sort of Judean *populares*—by assuming the mantle of "the people" have wielded considerable influence for ill (*Ant.* 13.288, 401; 17.41-45; 18.9-17).

This problem, too, would have been well understood by an aristocratic Roman audience. The senatorial aristocracy and the *princeps* in particular faced the constant problem of appeasing the masses,[19] even though the latter had little access to formal instruments of power. As Sallust had long before observed with respect to the *Catilinarian Conspiracy* (37.3): "In every community those who have no means envy the good, exalt the base, hate what is old and established, long for something new, and from disgust with their own lot desire a general upheaval." Josephus agreed.

In short, the *Antiquities* responds to the need and request for a Greek manual of Judean culture, a primer or handbook for interested outsiders with an aristocratic perspective. Although it rambles in places, the book also shows many signs of consistent attention to its major themes: the origin, philosophical nature, and impact of the Judean constitution. Even the much criticized final volumes are not extraneous material but further examples, drawn from every corner of the world, of the Judean code's effectiveness. Those who adopt these laws as their own, even if they seem to have a great deal to lose by doing so, are invariably protected and rewarded by God (*Ant.* 20.17-96). At the end of the work, Josephus lists the high priests who have guaranteed the constitution from its inception under Moses in remotest antiquity until the return to aristocracy after the monarchical experiments (*Ant.* 20.224-51).

6. The *Life* is a true appendix to the *Antiquities*, not an extraneous work responding to the threat posed by Justus of Tiberias. Josephus

---

[19] Zvi Yavetz, *Plebs and Princeps* (Oxford, 1969).

writes this to support his claims about the Judean constitution by reference to his own character. He wants to assure his friends and hearers that he is a living representative of this glorious tradition, a highly honored member of the Judean aristocracy he has been promoting so vigorously. He focuses on the six-month period of his command in Galilee mainly because one needed to demonstrate one's character by one's public life, and that was the only period in which he was much involved in public affairs. His responses to his opponents, whether John of Gischala, the delegates from Jerusalem, or Justus of Tiberias, are not really defensive, in the sense that he faced any ongoing threat from them. Rather, he uses them as foils for throwing his own character into sharper relief. Again, his sarcastic and dismissive tone shows that he expects an uncritically friendly audience.

7. The same sort of audience is expected for the *Against Apion*. There, Josephus does tackle common slanders about Judean origins head-on, but he is still having fun with the Judeans' detractors from a position of strength. His arguments and cavalier jibes would not convince the skeptical. In the final quarter of this book (2.14-295), Josephus reaches his most sublime rhetorical heights, as he praises his nation's unique and ancient aristocratic government. Again, he incidentally celebrates his nation's openness to foreigners and recommends full conversion.

8. Finally, Josephan scholarship has underestimated the importance of rhetoric. Assuming an Enlightenment sense of factual truth and falsity, we have tended to find great significance in every small difference between *War* and *Antiquities/Life*, supposing that Josephus has hidden or suppressed information in one work and that he is making truthful admissions in the other. The truth must lie in one of these texts. But of course, in the first century, rhetorical training required speakers and writers to be able to make very different cases from the same evidence. This ability, featured in the recreational exercise of declamation, was celebrated. Therefore, when Josephus makes different cases from the same evidence, we should not assume that he has let his guard down, that he has changed his views, or that he has a guilty conscience. Since he deliberately refers readers back to his own conflicting accounts, we should assume that he is not embarrassed about the changes in his narratives. This observation does not preclude historical analysis "between the lines," but it should prevent us from hoping to expose Josephus in any simple way.

I do not offer this summary, of course, with any implicit complaint that the books I am about to discuss did not deal with these same points. I simply want to indicate that there is much to be done in the investigation of Josephus's literary aims, themes, and contexts. The problem is that each of the following studies of the Pharisees downplays or overlooks altogether *the basic methodological problem* of understanding Josephus's narratives, which are arguably our main avenue to a reconstruction of the Pharisees.

Three Comprehensive Studies of the Pharisees

Anthony Saldarini: About the time my 1991 book went to press, Anthony Saldarini's *Pharisees, Scribes and Sadducees: A Sociological Approach* appeared in print (1988)—too late for me to discuss it then. This investigation took its departure from roughly the same place as mine: the disarray in scholarship on the Pharisees, the new controls of evidence proposed by Rivkin and Neusner, and the need to treat each source collection in its particularity before proposing historical hypotheses. In the second of his three main sections, accordingly, Saldarini works though Josephus, the New Testament, and the rabbis in turn. Yet his goals were much more ambitious than mine, not only in the scope of texts considered but also in his ultimate aim. He wanted to assess the sources in dialogue with sociological models and so to produce a truly adequate reconstruction of the place of the Pharisees, scribes, and Sadducees "within the whole of society."[20]

Using a duly qualified functionalist approach indebted to Gerhard Lenski and S.N. Eisenstadt, Saldarini concludes early that the Pharisees matched Lenski's "retainer" class. "These retainers," he writes, "were mostly townspeople who served the needs of the governing class as soldiers, educators, religious functionaries, entertainers and skilled artisans..." (pp. 37-38). And again, "Their offices could become hereditary, but more often they were bureaucratic and so subject to the appointment of the ruler" (p. 41).

Because Saldarini is so careful to identify some limitations of sociological theory, to warn against the importation of modern assumptions, to qualify simple models with reference to other theories, to insist on a dialectic between model and literary evidence, and to call attention to the particulars of changing situations in the ancient

---

[20] Saldarini, op. cit., p. 10. Page references in the following are to this work.

world, it seems *almost* impossible for a reasonable person to disagree with him. Nevertheless, I would challenge his decision to place the sociological analysis first, as the ground and framework for his study. That is because sociological analysis requires usable *data*, and we do not have data on the Pharisees but only literary accounts in the context of certain authors' agendas.

In my view, sociological models ought only to be invoked when one has already done the fine literary work and wishes to proceed to historical reconstruction, the second phase described above. Such models can be extremely helpful in suggesting critical questions to pose of authors and in assisting with reconstruction. But they cannot deal effectively with a particular author's creative world of language and thought. To be sure, structuralists might argue that certain sociological or anthropological codes are already embedded in the deep structure of texts, irrespective of an author's aims. But efforts to isolate these codes have not impressed many scholars in the field and, in any case, that is not Saldarini's aim. To make sociology a "guide," as he says (pp. 14, 48, 54), to reading the ancient texts is to gloss over the fundamental difference between a literary statement and datum. Neusner speaks somewhere of "asking the historical question too quickly," and it seems to me that this is what Saldarini has done.

This theoretical quibble is not without substantive consequences, the most important of which I adduce here. They all stem from using sociological theory as more of a guide to reading Josephus than his own literary cues.

First, in order to make the sociological approach plausible for dealing with the Pharisees, Saldarini must qualify it beyond obvious usefulness. He continually emphasizes exceptions to norms and the need for flexibility of models. Although he asserts, for example, that the emergence of the Pharisees and other groups "can be effectively explained by the sociological process of group formation" (p. 59), he is not able to show that explanation in practice. He relies mainly on ordinary historical conditions. And after having given a fairly detailed itemization of group types, he must conclude: "the boundaries of groups and people's identification with groups is [sic] often less definitive and significant for life than they appear to be when formally listed" (pp. 280-281). So he must turn in the end to the particular evidence for the Pharisees.

Second, Saldarini shares a tendency common among sociologists of antiquity to idealize the values and motives of those who lived around the ancient Mediterranean. This is clearest when he speaks of honor and shame as basic categories. "Most people in a peasant society...engage in constant challenge and riposte in a quest for more honor among their fellow citizens" (p. 55). This idealization extends to his reading of Josephus's Pharisees: "Thus, the conflicts for influence and power evident in Josephus's treatment of the Pharisees...are all contests for honor in the community" (p. 55). This is, however, not part of Josephus's treatment of the Pharisees; it comes from somewhere else.

Third, Saldarini's opening list of Lenski's nine social classes does not sit well with Josephus's own categories. For example, it distinguishes the ruler (such as an emperor), a governing class, and a priesthood. Yet we have already seen that Josephus presents the priesthood *as* the governing class and rejects the notion of an individual ruler in favor of aristocracy. Moreover, we know that Roman aristocrats were deeply suspicious of monarchy, which is why they preserved the forms of the republic, and that ancient authors often debated the optimal form of government: aristocracy, democracy, and monarchy were the main options. It simply does not match the wealth of ancient literary evidence to assume that there was a single class structure for "agrarian societies."

Fourth, having listed Lenski's classes, Saldarini seems obliged to locate the Pharisees among them. His choice of the retainers as defined above, however, hardly matches Josephus's or anyone else's portrayal of the Pharisees. Since Josephus, posturing as a spokesman for the aristocracy, complains about this populist group, one would not surmise from his narratives that the Pharisees were "religious functionaries," akin to soldiers, educators, and bureaucrats, serving in some way the needs of the governing class.

Most important, fifth: without offering any systematic analysis of Josephus's own themes or language on this central point, Saldarini identifies the historian's main concern as *order*. He repeatedly asserts that as a member of the governing class, Josephus will support *strong* leaders who maintain stability, but that he rejects weak rulers (pp. 84-85, 90-92, 97, 105, 115, 128-129, 131): Josephus "favored a strong, stable ruling force" (p. 84). Yet this language comes not from Josephus but from the sociological model to which he has been accommodated. It leads Saldarini to misrepresent, for example, Josephus's portrait of Herod, whom *Antiquities* decries in blistering terms for his violation of the constitution (pp. 84, 97). Saldarini thinks that the portrayal is mainly positive because Herod is a strong ruler. Even more to the point, this construction leads him to portray the Pharisees as approved of by Josephus when they are a force for order, but criticized when they contribute to disorder (p. 131). Yet this characterization, too, ignores Josephus's narrative. When he has Alexander Janneus advise his wife to give the Pharisees some power, this is not approval, as Saldarini thinks (p. 90), but the opening premise of a story that will pointedly disparage the group (*Ant.* 13.409-411, 426, 430-432). The issue is not order and disorder but the efficacy of the Judean constitution.

Sixth, in spite of Saldarini's good intention to deal with each source in turn, his main analysis of Josephus's Pharisees (chapter 5) does not even distinguish consistently between *War* and *Antiquities*. He does not discuss their prologues or main literary themes, and he opts to lump the parallel material of the two works together. This suggests a preference for sociological system over the particularity of Josephus's individually crafted literary worlds (pp. 79-106).

Finally, one of the most debated issues surrounding the Pharisees concerns the degree and quality of their public influence. This is also an issue to which Saldarini pays considerable attention. The problem is that his many statements about Josephus's portrayals of the Pharisees' influence do not seem to agree with each other: p. 91, they held substantial but not unlimited power under Alexandra; p. 103, "important, influential and powerful enough to be heard through [their] leaders;" p. 121, "the leading and most influential school of thought;" p. 157, a religious interest group with political goals, but not a dominant group; p. 181, "an active political force in Jewish society with influence and control among the people;" p. 211, "Josephus keeps them within more probable historical bounds as a small group of limited influence;" p. 229, "Josephus says that the Pharisees were very influential with the people;" p. 277, "they were one small group among many;" p. 283, "they were established and influential in Jewish society and were looked on favorably by at least some of the population."

Having made these criticisms, I must hasten to concede that Saldarini has given us an important study. Over against much scholarship on the Pharisees, he insists on the inextricability of religion and culture (p. 5). He challenges other scholars by showing the coherence of Josephus's various statements on the Pharisees, even between Josephus's summary statements and narratives; he also rejects improbably radical source theories (pp. 99-101, 121, 129). While allowing that Josephus claims to have chosen Pharisaism, he astutely observes, and repeatedly, that Josephus does not write as a Pharisee (pp. 81, 93, 111, 118-119) and that his use of the verb *dokeiō* distances Josephus from the group. Although he follows Neusner's methodological lead, he vehemently rejects the Smith/Neusner hypothesis that Josephus wrote to promote the Pharisaic/Rabbinic movement at Yavneh (pp. 83, 128-132). All of this, not to mention Saldarini's examination of the New Testament and Rabbinic literature, makes the book a most valuable contribution.

The difficulties would have been avoided, I have suggested, if he had distinguished clearly between interpreting the relevant texts and reconstructing the historical Pharisees, using sociological models only in the latter phase. By contrast, Lester Grabbe's 1992 survey of *Judaism from Cyrus to Hadrian* does make such a clear distinction in *principle*. Its weakness is in the execution.

Lester Grabbe:[21] Grabbe sets out to provide "a handbook for students studying the history and religion of the Judean state during the Second Temple period" and a "two-volume reference for scholars" (p. xxv). Like Schürer and the producers of the other great manuals, he examines much more than the Pharisees: in this case, he provides an even-handed treatment of the seven centuries from the Exile to the aftermath of the Bar Kokhba revolt.

Unlike the other manuals, however, Grabbe sets a high standard for public historical argumentation. For every question he touches, he intends to delineate the sources and the ways in which the "major interpretations" make use of them (p. xxvi). This procedure ought to obviate any naive quest for pure historical "facts." Most chapters, accordingly, follow the same plan: bibliographical guide, primary sources, historical studies and issues, followed by Grabbe's attempt at synthesis. Presumably, it is this ordered layout that will preserve Grabbe's book from the fate of earlier specialized reference tools ("such works can quickly become out-of-date in some respects," p. xxv), for if one understands the basic material and the historical *method*, one can intelligently assimilate new data as they emerge.

---

[21] This section borrows extensively from my review article, "Method in the Study of Early Judaism: A Dialogue with Lester Grabbe," in *Journal of the American Oriental Society* 115, 1995, pp. 463–472. It is reprised with permission. Page references in the following are to Grabbe's *Judaism from Cyrus to Hadrian*.

In addition to surveying the particular primary sources for each topic, Grabbe acknowledges at the outset that Josephus has a special importance as his major source, and so he offers an opening account of Josephus's life and writings. This is brief, however, and mainly reflects old scholarship: the *War* was written to show that Rome was invincible, to glorify the Flavians, and to show the causes of the revolt (Roman governors' incompetence and a small minority of Jewish agitators); the *Antiquities* was an apology for Judaism, defending it against common slander; and the *Life* was in the main a response to Justus of Tiberias's attack. Oddly, Grabbe describes the famously misnamed *Against Apion* as if it were indeed simply a reply to Apion (p. 10). Most interesting is his observation that "the Jewish historian's works have often been misused and cited without actually being read" (p. 10). This raises the reader's hopes that Grabbe will attempt to discuss Josephus's narratives before using his statements in historical reconstruction. At this point, he offers five general considerations for *using* Josephus, viz.: his aims and biases must be carefully examined; his sources must always be carefully considered; one must allow for the constraints of ancient historiography; one must take special care with passages that are obviously apologetic; and all other relevant sources must be used as checks and balances.

Because this is an introduction and reference work, one cannot easily summarize Grabbe's many conclusions. Indeed, the strongest impression left by the book is that a great deal remains unknown. After locating each kind of evidence *in situ*, discussing its biases and limitations, and weighing the plausibility of various hypotheses, Grabbe often refreshingly concludes that we simply lack sufficient material to decide the matter with any probability (pp. 93, 98, 111, 268, 281).

Although he deals with the Pharisees only in his lengthy eighth chapter, on "religious pluralism from the Maccabees to Yavneh," which also considers hasidim, Sadducees and Boethusians, Scribes, Essenes, Therapeutae, Zealots, Fourth Philosophy and Sicarii, Herodians, Samaritans, baptismal sects, "revolutionaries and other popular movements," gnostic tendencies, "charismatics, preachers, and miracle workers," *ammei ha-aretz* and *haverim*, the Pharisees are more important than any of these other groups for his study. We know that because on the very last page of the work, Grabbe states as one of his major conclusions: "Whatever the precise beliefs of the Pharisees, the long-prevalent view that they dominated the society and religion of first-century Judaism can no longer be maintained, whether this view comes from Josephus, the New Testament, or the earlier traditions of rabbinic literature" (p. 616). As we have seen, the three source collections named here are also the only first-order witnesses to the Pharisees (p. 468), and they independently agree that the Pharisees exercised the dominant influence in first-century Jewish society—whether Jesus's Galilee or Josephus's Jerusalem. How, then, does Grabbe explain the evidence? The Pharisees are the clearest case in which he departs from his customary method of surveying and then explaining the sources by public historical reasoning; this departure is all the more glaring because of his firm commitment to the principle elsewhere.

First, he atomizes Josephus's narrative, plucking out two passages that allegedly describe the Pharisees in the abstract (*War* 2.162-164; *Ant.* 18.12-15). He claims that these do not actually say much about the Pharisees and that only the *Antiquities*, written twenty years later than the *War*, credits the Pharisees with social dominance. He does not explain, however, what he has just quoted from *War* 2.162: the Pharisees "hold the position of the leading sect."

Then, over against these abstract statements, Grabbe cites "actual historical incidents" (p. 470) related by Josephus, in which the Pharisees figure and finds these clustered "around two periods of time" (p. 470). It is not immediately clear which two periods he means, for he cites passages from the reigns of John Hyrcanus, Alexandra Salome, and Herod the Great, and from the outbreak of the war in the 60s C.E. In fact, these are *all* of the major periods covered by Josephus's post-biblical narratives. As Grabbe observes elsewhere (p. 371), neither the *War* nor the *Antiquities* has much to say about Judea in the period from 6 to 66 C.E. But, strangely, this gap does not prevent him from arguing that "the actual influence of the Pharisaic movement tended to be concentrated in particular periods, especially the latter part of the Hasmonean kingdom, after which their actual impact...does not appear to have been great" (p. 476). He seems to be expecting from Josephus a kind of day-by-day video coverage of Judean antiquity; only so can he infer that the Pharisees' absence as *literary characters* from a particular period *in Josephus's story* means that the *historical Pharisees* were then inactive. But this kind of assumption vitiates Grabbe's whole project, which is grounded in the limitations and perspectives of the sources. (And, we may note for the record, about one-third of all of Josephus's references to the Pharisees actually fall in the period between Herod's rule and the war: *War* 2.161-166, 411; *Ant.* 18.12-15; *Life* 10-12, 21, 188-198.)

According to Grabbe, then, Josephus's isolated *claims* about the Pharisees' great influence, which allegedly occur only in the *Antiquities*, are not supported by his *narratives* concerning their actions—even in the Hasmonean period, but especially thereafter (pp. 470-471). Why, then, did Josephus make such artificial claims? Grabbe follows Morton Smith[22] in suggesting that the Josephus of the 90s wished to "throw in his lot with the Pharisees" (p. 474), who had become the dominant group in the post-70 Rabbinic coalition at Yavneh. Josephus wrote the *Antiquities* in part to promote the Pharisees/rabbis before the Roman authorities as the appropriate ruling party in Judea.

All of this argumentation fails, however, to deal straightforwardly with the phenomena that require explanation: Josephus's narratives. First, one cannot excerpt Josephus's "claims" about the Pharisees' influence from the "narrative," for they are part and parcel of the narrative. As a good Hellenistic historian, Josephus frequently includes editorial asides to move the story forward. His claims about Pharisaic influence occur not only in the places Grabbe has identified but consistently from the first appearance of the Pharisees in the *War:* they managed to ruin Alexandra's otherwise promising reign through their influence (*War* 1.110-114); Herod the Great was deeply concerned about their intrigues (*War* 1.571); and in the first century they continued to "hold the position of the leading school" (*War* 2.162), their representatives joining with the chief priests and other eminent citizens to try to avert war (*War* 2.411).

That Josephus's statements about the Pharisees' influence should become more numerous in *Antiquities/Life* is not surprising, since the amount of space devoted to the post-biblical and pre-war period (*Ant.* 12-20) increases more than five-fold over the *War* parallel (*War* 1.31-2.270). But there too, those claims are an integral part of the narrative. Josephus's story of John Hyrcanus's break with the Pharisees in *Ant.* 13.289-296, for example, plainly supports his *claim* at the close of that section about their great popular appeal (13.297-298), which in turn explains why his favorite Hasmonean should have faced such massive domestic upheaval (13.288). The sequel shows that the

---

[22] "Palestinian Judaism in the First Century," in Moshe Davis, ed., *Israel: Its Role in Civilization* (New York, 1956), pp. 68-71.

Hasmoneans could not avoid major civil war as long as they continued to alienate the Pharisees (13.401), a state of affairs Josephus deplores in further editorial comments (13.430-32).

If one simply reads the narrative as a coherent story, Alexandra's reinstatement of the Pharisaic ordinances (13.408) abrogated by Hyrcanus earlier in the same volume explains why the Pharisees continue to be so influential in Herod's court (17.41-45), at the time of Quirinius's census (6 C.E.; 18.4), and in Josephus's own experience of Judean life before the war (18.15, 17; *Life* 189-198). Surely Josephus does not need to interrupt his narrative of Gaius's assassination in Rome (*Ant.* 19. 15-114) or affairs in Babylonia (18.310-379) to say: "by the way, back in Judea the Pharisees were still dominant at this point." His stories are not about the Pharisees per se, but what he does say about them is, as Saldarini has pointed out, broadly consistent. His claims are part of his narrative.

Josephus's evident hostility toward the Pharisees throughout almost all of the stories in which they appear (cited above) plainly contradicts Grabbe's claim that the story "is fairly neutral toward the Pharisees, showing neither hostility nor particular favor" (p. 475). This hostility was noted long ago by the greatest of the source critics, G. Hölscher,[23] and on the strength of it Hölscher attributed most of the Pharisee material to Josephus's sources, supposing that Josephus-the-Pharisee (*Life* 12) could not have written so negatively.

But even if Grabbe were right that Josephus was "neutral" toward the group, it would then be unclear how a few *neutral* references to the Pharisees, sprinkled sparsely through the later volumes of the mammoth *Antiquities*, could have been intended as Josephus's "clever" effort to promote the Yavnean coalition and so to help himself (Grabbe: 480).

It is a legitimate and basic principle of historical analysis that one seek out incidental or unintentional evidence in texts, to circumvent an author's bias. But in order to read between the lines, one must know where the lines are. It is not enough to say, with Grabbe, that Josephus's intention is to put the Pharisees in control of society; therefore, passages that show the priests in control, or that describe events with no reference to the Pharisees, *contradict* Josephus's agenda. Grabbe avers, for example, that "despite Josephus's claim, the Pharisees had not taken away the prerogatives of the priesthood" (p. 476).

---

[23] "Josephus," in *PWRE*, 1916, 18, col. 1936.

He argues that since John Hyrcanus was able to break away from the Pharisees with impunity, Alexander Janneus did not find them a serious threat, Herod largely ignored them in his rule, and they do not appear much in the narrative after Alexandra Salome's time, they could not really have controlled society (pp. 472-473).

This analysis, however, rests on a false appraisal of Josephus's claims, for he nowhere suggests that the Pharisees exercised formal control, much less that they had taken away the prerogatives of the priesthood. He always and everywhere sees his fellow priests, under the headship of the high priest, as the sole legitimate leaders of Judean society. When he mentions the Pharisees it is usually to complain about their influence. For Josephus, the Pharisees' influence arises not from controlling institutions but from popular appeal: their views endear them to the masses (*Ant.* 18.15), and rulers cannot ignore them for that reason. That is apparently a major point of the whole John Hyrcanus/Alexander Janneus/Alexandra Salome narrative complex in *Ant.* 13: civil war ended in Judea only when the Pharisees were appeased (*Ant.* 13.401-408)—even though Josephus resents this state of affairs.

If Grabbe deals recklessly with Josephus on this issue, his virtual dismissal of "the New Testament" evidence about the Pharisees in a single page (pp. 476-477)—as if the New Testament were but one text—is very odd. He seems to portray Matthew and Luke here as merely secondary elaborations of Mark (p. 476), although in another context he will allow that "Luke sometimes has independent information about pre-70 Judaism," which should be taken seriously (p. 489). The anachronism "New Testament" allows Grabbe to dispense too easily with several partly independent accounts that also give the Pharisees a prominent role in Jesus's world.

His claim that the portrayals of the Pharisees in Josephus and in the gospels result from post-70 realities—i.e., from developments at Yavneh, which should then have been clear to Josephus and the gospel writers—is inherently improbable according to *Grabbe's own analysis elsewhere.* For in the section on Yavneh, he notes: that "events may have gone largely unnoticed by many Jews at the time" (p. 593); that the Yavnean pioneer Yohanan ben Zakkai may not even have been a Pharisee (p. 594); that Yavneh involved a "synthesis" of many Jewish groups, perhaps five different factions (pp. 482, 594); and that even this coalition "seems to have been quite small at first"—it took "well over a century" for the new kind of Judaism to become dominant (p. 593). Yet Grabbe has no difficulty crediting even the gentile Christian gospel authors, who wrote between 65 and 100 or so, with a brilliant revision of their narratives so as to read Pharisaic dominance back into the pre-70 situation in the light of Yavneh. This is surely a case for the veracity of Christian prophecy! His analysis of the Yavneh traditions also undermines his argument about *Josephus* as champion of the Pharisees/Yavnean rabbis in the 90s.

In the end, Grabbe's reconstruction of the Pharisees relies most heavily on Neusner's analysis of early Rabbinic traditions about them.[24] Grabbe concludes that, since the pre-70 traditions of the Mishnah (allegedly) concern internal Pharisaic issues such as table fellowship and contain no agenda for civil governance, the pre-70 Pharisees were a small group of limited influence: "the sources do not preserve discussions about matters outside the sect" (p. 547; cf., p. 478). "The sources" must mean here the Rabbinic literature as analyzed by Neusner, for Josephus certainly does speak of Pharisaic regulations for all of society (abrogated by John Hyrcanus and restored by Alexandra; *Ant.* 13.296, 408) and of their agenda for the nation's religious life (*Ant.* 18.15); Luke-Acts portrays their meddling quite aggressively in the non-Pharisee Jesus's career (Luke 5:17; 7:36) and presents the Pharisee Gamaliel's advising the Sanhedrin about the Christians as a matter of public policy (Acts 5:34-39).

Grabbe must also be preoccupied with the Rabbinic literature when he states: "The Pharisees discussed many points of law, but one subject not aired *in the extant literature* is Torah study. There is no reference to getting together to study Torah, which was so characteristic of rabbinic Judaism" (p. 480; emphasis added). Again, "Torah-centredness and the religious efficacy of study" were important new themes developed at Yavneh (p. 594). This is perplexing, however, because Josephus often claims that, in a society uniquely devoted to the study of the laws (*Ant.* 20.264; *Against Apion* 2.173-178), the Pharisees were commonly reputed to interpret the laws with the greatest precision (*War* 1.110; 2.162; *Ant.* 17.41; *Life* 191). Acts describes the Pharisee Gamaliel, at least, as a revered "teacher of the law" (Acts 5:34). Indeed, Grabbe himself later concludes that for both Israelite and early Jewish religion, "Observance of the law—obedience to the law in all its forms—counted as a religious service to God" (p. 608).

---

[24] *The Rabbinic Traditions about the Pharisees before 70* (3 vols.; Leiden, 1971).

But how did people observe the Torah so scrupulously and become renowned experts in it if they did not, as Josephus says, encourage the study of it? Grabbe's argument is unclear.

He is, of course, free to reject the non-Rabbinic evidence with cogent arguments. But these do not appear, and so it is improper to say that "the sources" restrict the Pharisees' vision as he would wish. Even if we limited our focus to Neusner's isolation of the earliest Rabbinic traditions, the problem is Grabbe's own admission that (a) not all pre-70 Rabbinic tradition is Pharisaic; and (b) the pre-70 figures who stand at the base of the Rabbinic tradition might have thought and done much more than was preserved in this later legal literature (p. 479). These two concessions completely undercut his deductions, from putative early strata of Rabbinic literature, that pre-70 Pharisees had little influence. It is remarkable that he should give these hypothetically distilled early traditions from third-century literature, of admittedly uncertain origin (Pharisaic? scribal? other?), decisive weight against the claims and assumptions of several independent first-century sources (Josephus and the gospels).

In Grabbe's magnificent study of seven centuries, then, we have an analysis of Josephus and the Pharisees that simply does not match up to his overall project, which is indeed successful in other cases. Because his introduction stresses the importance of knowing Josephus's narrative aims (pp. 4-5), the reader expects that he will first examine each piece of evidence in its native environment, then propose a hypothesis concerning what really happened, then finally put all the pieces back together again, showing how this hypothesis explains the narrative evidence. Yet in the sequel, while making extensive use of Josephus, he hardly refers to those narrative aims again. He thus implies that it is permissible, after all, to ignore the context in which some of our most valuable material appears.

E.P. Sanders: In the same year that Grabbe's handbook appeared, E.P. Sanders published his monograph, *Judaism, Practice and Belief, 63 BCE – 66 CE*. This study, which had been taking shape in Sanders's workshop for many years, was motivated primarily by the constructive goal of describing Judean life in a comprehensive and realistic way, emphasizing social-historical questions rather than reducing Judaism to its thought. He wanted to paint a picture of the common Judaism experienced by most people, who were unaffiliated with the small parties or sects, a Judaism based in the Temple and the priesthood. The central issue for Sanders is: Who controlled the national institutions and, therefore, society? Sanders's new building project required him also to remove the rubble generated by previous scholarship, in particular that of Schürer and Jeremias, who had propagated a pan-Pharisaic model of ancient Judaism. They had assumed that Rabbinic literature was both Pharisaic and descriptive of first-century realities; they had proposed on this basis that Pharisees effectively ran society, both directly through the Sanhedrin, school, and synagogue, and, indirectly, by exerting pressure on Temple functionaries. Sanders's thesis is that the Pharisees had considerable popular *influence*, but no real control after the reign of Queen Alexandra.

One of the distinctive features of his study, Sanders hopes, will be his transparent historical reasoning. Rather than merely listing scholarly conclusions, he will try to show in each case how his hypotheses explain what is in the primary sources. Like Grabbe, he acknowledges at the outset the singular importance of Josephus, and so gives an account of Josephus's life and writings (Sanders, pp. 5-7). Strangely, however, in view of his determination to provide an original analysis, that account is very brief and wholly conventional.

Also like Grabbe, he offers at this early stage a methodological key for using Josephus. Namely: "It is helpful to compare Josephus's generalizations with his accounts of individual events. We shall see below, for example, that he says that the Pharisees were so popular that they always got their way. Yet it is extremely hard to find any specific incidents in which this is true. Generalizations are easier to write and more likely to reflect an author's bias than his report of individual events" (p. 7).

After sketching a historical context for first-century Judaism in Part I, Sanders devotes the heart of the book, Part II, to charting the contours of "common Judaism." I hardly need to say that this is a major contribution. Sanders relentlessly pursues real-life questions about what it felt like to walk through Herod's Temple, to see the priests at work preparing sacrifices, to pay taxes and tithes, and to observe the purity laws.

In this central section, Sanders does not appeal to a consistent method for using Josephus, and yet the priest Josephus is a crucial ally for his presentation of a Temple-centered Judaism. He makes much of Josephus's expert knowledge, which he thinks was assisted by documents and assistants. In some places he marvels at Josephus's precision (pp. 60, 64, 95); in others he opts to believe Josephus where there might be room for dispute (p. 79). In this section he rightly sees

Josephus as a strong advocate of the priestly prerogative in adminis-
tering the laws (pp. 171-173).

But some methodological problems come to the surface already
here, and they will become especially severe in the third section,
which tries to put the various "groups and parties" in their proper
place within a Temple-based system. There, Sanders tackles most
directly the older view that the Pharisees controlled things, a view he
traces in large measure to Josephus's generalizations. So, picking up
the point made in his introduction, he must show that the general
statements are not supported by Josephus's historical narrative.

As I broach the difficulties with Sanders's analysis, I should make
clear that I find his general thesis of priestly *control* and Pharisaic
influence fairly close to Josephus's own view of the matter, although the
language is different. The problem is that Sanders appears to think
that Josephus says something else entirely and then resorts to improbable strategies to get past this artificial Josephus.

Here are the problems. First, Sanders often fails to distinguish
clearly between Josephus's narrative and history. For example, he
cites *War*'s notice about the priests' continuation of their sacrificial
duties, oblivious to the invading army of Pompey (*War* 1.48-49),
which is laden with Josephus's narrative themes and language, as
proof of the priests' historical character: "They did not grab the day's
profits and run" (p. 92). Of course, we have no idea what they really
did or what their motives were. Again, he cites the seventh of
Josephus's portents of doom before the Temple's fall—the one about
Jesus son of Ananias crying out in Jeremianic lamentations for seven
years, night and day without a break, his voice never flagging because
of divine inspiration (*War* 6.300-9)—as a historical event, even
though he would presumably not put much stock in the preceding six
omens (e.g., cows giving birth to lambs, massive gates opening of their
own accord; *War* 6.288-99), and even though the strong evocation of
Jeremiah fits precisely with Josephus's literary aims in this section (pp.
140-141).

This confusion between Josephus's story and historical reality becomes more significant in the chapters on the Pharisees. Sanders
begins the first of those chapters with the sentences: "The
Pharisees...*are mentioned* at the time of Jonathan. The *earliest event in
which Pharisees figure* comes a few decades later, early in the reign of
Hyrcanus I" (p. 380; emphasis added). There is no awareness expressed here that we are dealing with one of Josephus's stories. Even

though Sanders mentions an occasional phrase of Josephus's in what follows, he slides back and forth between the rather different stories of the *War* and the *Antiquities* without alerting the reader that he is doing so, as if this was all material of a single piece (pp. 381-382). While discussing Josephus on Queen Alexandra, conflating the stories of *War* and *Antiquities*, he pauses to say, "At this stage of *history* it is clear, within broad terms, who the Pharisees were" (p. 383). But there has been no historical analysis yet. And consider this: After saying that he is going to deal with "the few remaining stories [about the Pharisees] in *Josephus*" (p. 384), Sanders then discusses the incident of the teachers who had their students pull down Herod's eagle from the Temple, concluding that these men "were, in all probability, Pharisees" (p. 385). Then he is able to use this incident as part of *Josephus's account* of the Pharisees, even though Josephus nowhere makes this identification and we have no basis for assuming that his first readers were expected to understand it. We have slid from narrative to history and back again. In the same section, Sanders rather violently—but without explaining his analysis to the reader—separates Josephus's story of the Pharisees under Herod (*Ant.* 17.41-45) into two separate incidents (p. 384 and n. 5), the former of which (concerning the oath to Herod) he sees as a doublet of another story that Josephus had put much earlier in Herod's reign (*Ant.* 15.2-3). Yet he treats all of this as if it were *in Josephus*.

Although Sanders aspires to explain what is in the primary sources, then, with this procedure, the reader cannot possibly maintain a picture of *Josephus's* Pharisees, of how they function in his narratives.

This problem of confusing ancient story with historical analysis becomes most obvious when Sanders, like Grabbe, tries to make direct historical deductions from the narrative. We pick up his account at p. 386 (emphasis added):

> Pharisees do not appear again [after 6 C.E.] in Josephus' history for sixty years.... They seem to have *been* completely outside the counsels of the Jewish leaders until a very late date, when the strife between Roman soldiers and the Jerusalem populace had gone too far to be checked.

This is a very peculiar way to read Josephus's narratives, for the reasons already given: (a) Josephus constructs the *Antiquities* in such a way as to establish the Pharisees' popular influence from the Hasmonean period to his own time without a break (above); (b) for the period 6-66 C.E. *in Judea*, his narrative in both *War* and *Antiquities* is exceedingly thin. In the *War* it is a few pages (*War* 2.117-279), mostly taken up with the lengthy description of the Jewish schools, including the Pharisees (*War* 2.118-66). In the *Antiquities*, he reaches the deposition of Archelaus only at the beginning of vol. 18. He devotes most of the remainder of vols. 18-20 to events in Rome (Gaius's death, Claudius's accession, the Agrippa family) and Mesopotamia (the great massacre and the house of Adiabene). To make deductions about the absence of Pharisees from this narrative as if that implied anything about their absence from Judean *history* is futile. (c) When Josephus does return to Judea, he simply assumes what he has already established about the Pharisees' continuing popular influence (*Ant.* 18.12-17; *Life* 10-12, 21, 189-97). I do not understand how scholars can talk about the disappearance of the Pharisees from *history* in the early first century, when we have only the stories of one man who chose not to tell us much about this period, but who nevertheless insisted that the Pharisees retained popular influence throughout.

This brings us to the heart of Sanders's announced method: his use of Josephus's narrative against Josephus's general statements. This is extremely problematic in both theory and in execution. The theory would only work if one had a model of Josephus's method as follows: he took over large amounts of source material in a lazy frame of mind, determined to alter it as little as possible. If he operated that way, it might indeed be easy to spot his light editorial remarks because of their contrast with his narrative. But, in fact, he did not operate that way. No one doubts that the *War* is a carefully composed *tour de force*.[25] Similarly with *Ant.* 1-13, at least, numerous studies have shown Josephus's determination to craft the narrative details (*not* merely editorial additions) so as to convey his themes.[26] Thousands of individual narrative examples could be adduced. Nor does anyone

---

[25] E.g., Henry St. John Thackeray, *Josephus: The Man and the Historian* (New York, 1929 [repr. 1967]), pp. 23-50; Helgo Lindner, *Die Geschichtsauffassung des Flavius Josephus im Bellum Judaicum* (Leiden, 1972); Tessa Rajak, *Josephus: The Historian and His Society* (London, 1983), pp. 185-222.

[26] E.g., André Pelletier, *Flavius Josèphe, adapteur de lat lettre d'Aristée* (Paris, 1962), pp. 252-255; Harold W. Attridge, *The Interpretation of Biblical History in the Antiquitates Judaicae of Flavius Josephus* (Cambridge, 1976), p. 17; Thomas W. Franxman, *Genesis and the 'Jewish Antiquities' of Flavius Josephus* (Rome, 1979), pp. 288-290; Louis H. Feldman, *Studies in Josephus' Rewritten Bible* (Leiden, 1998), *passim*, and the many articles cited in his *Jew and Gentile in Antiquity: Attitudes and Interactions from Alexander to Justinian* (Princeton, 1993), pp. 594-596.

doubt that the *Against Apion,* even though it makes liberal use of sources, was carefully tailored to make Josephus's points.[27]

In short, we now have overwhelming evidence—admittedly overturning the suppositions of much scholarship from the period prior to 1920—for the common-sense presumption that Josephus's works are his and convey his themes.[28] It happens not infrequently that a given passage retains a feature of its source, a word or phrase, that stands in some tension with Josephus's larger narrative aims or typical usage, but that needs to be shown in any given case. It is a demonstrably invalid *basic premise* that Josephus's general statements are at variance with his narrative. He wrote both his narratives and his summaries even though he made extensive use of sources.

In any case, when Sanders comes to implement his leading principle, the situation becomes very confusing. For when he discusses the Pharisees of *Ant.* 13-20, it is precisely Josephus's *general statements* that he now wishes to attribute to non-Josephan sources, ignoring his basic premise. For example, *Ant.* 13.288-298 tells the story of John Hyrcanus's break with the Pharisees. Josephus has just recounted at some length the brilliant successes of Hyrcanus and his sons in capturing Idumea, destroying the old enemy Samaria (13.275-83), and winning a good deal of respect from the faltering Seleucid government. All of this lengthy narrative is Josephus's own: he cites Nicolaus of Damascus and other sources such as Strabo and Jewish oral tradition with approval (13.282-3, 286-7, 250-51), but he controls the narrative, introducing his characteristic themes of Hyrcanus's piety (13.230, 234, 242-45, 251) and desire to reinstate the traditional *politeia* (13.245), the prince's consequent favor with the deity (13.282-3), and the flourishing of the Judeans when they followed the constitution.

Now comes the story of the banquet, at which Hyrcanus is denounced, and this is framed by editorial comments. At the beginning, the author links this episode with his preceding account of the success of Hyrcanus and his sons (13.288). He says that their success aroused

---

[27] E.g., Louis H. Feldman and John R. Levison, eds., *Josephus' Contra Apionem: Studies in its Character and Context with a Latin Concordance to the Portion Missing in Greek.* (Leiden, 1996).

[28] Further: Horst Moehring, "Novelistic Elements in the Writings of Flavius Josephus" (Dissertation: University of Chicago, 1957), p. 145; Heinz Schreckenberg, *Rezeptionsgeschichtliche und Textkritische Untersuchungen zu Flavius Josephus* (Leiden, 1977), p. 173.

the envy of the Judeans and especially of the Pharisees, who are one of the Judean schools, concerning which he has already spoken. This is evidently a reference to *Ant.* 13.171-173, the only prior reference to the Pharisees in *Antiquities*, though Josephus may also have *War* 2.119-66 in mind. At the end of the banquet story, which has an angry Hyrcanus finally abrogating the Pharisees' ordinances (*nomima*, 13.296), the author hastens to explain that the Pharisees had special extra-biblical *nomima*, which were not accepted by the Sadducees (13.297-98). But, he says, the Sadducees have the respect only of a wealthy elite, whereas the Pharisees have the support of the masses. Then he refers the reader back to his *Judean War* for details about these groups and the Essenes. This is the final episode of Hyrcanus's life that Josephus recounts: after it comes a eulogy on this prince, including the note that he lived happily after putting down the revolt, and the story of the tragic downfall suffered by his sons, who did not share their fathers' good fortune (*Ant.* 13.299-300).

Sanders's treatment of this important story is baffling. First, against all of these narrative indicators, he places the story near the *beginning* of Hyrcanus's reign, so that he can argue thus: "This was an early uprising, but *then* Hyrcanus allied himself with the Sadducees and governed excellently and in tranquillity for thirty-one years.... The long and peaceful reign of a Sadducean adherent, who explicitly rejected the Pharisees, does not agree with the summary that he had to follow them" (Sanders, p. 390, emphasis added). But of course, Josephus puts this rupture near the end of Hyrcanus's brilliant thirty-one year reign. And once he had abrogated the Pharisaic ordinances, John allegedly incurred the extreme hostility of the masses, which continued through the reign of his son Alexander Janneus, until Alexander's widow reinstated these ordinances (*Ant.* 13.400-432).

A related puzzle is Sanders's insistence that Josephus's allusion to the success of Hyrcanus's sons (*Ant.* 13.288) looks *forward* to the subsequent narrative of Aristobulus and Alexander Janneus. Accusing me of "seriously misconstruing" 13.288, he claims again that it is but the opening of the story concerning Hyrcanus's sons (p. 534, n. 22). But this remarkable assertion entirely ignores the narrative context, which I have described above: Hyrcanus and his sons are brilliantly successful (*Ant.* 13.275-83, etc.), and that *eupragia* is what arouses the envy of the Judeans in 13.288. This cannot refer to the following narrative because: (a) the reader could not then be expected to make sense of it (not yet having read what is to come), and (b) the narrator says plainly that Hyrcanus's sons forthwith *lost* their father's *eutuchia* (13.300) and he will now relate the story of their *downfall* (*katastrophē*). To take Josephus's remark about the success of Hyrcanus and his sons as looking ahead to their disastrous reigns would make nonsense of Josephus's entire narrative. It is true that 13.296 re-animates the hatred of the people toward Hyrcanus and his sons with a new motive—his abrogation of the Pharisaic ordinances. But that is a new development over the jealousy described in 13.288, not a simple restatement of the topic sentence.

Now Sanders asserts (p. 390; emphasis added):

> Josephus probably took both *Antiq.* 13.288 and 298 [i.e., Josephus's editorial comments framing the banquet story] from the history written by Nicolaus of Damascus, Herod's courtier, spokesman and historian, and thus these two paragraphs may throw light *on the period of Herod's reign* [a century later].

It is not easy to imagine why one would attribute Josephus's editorial remarks, which bridge this story with the Josephan material that precedes and explicitly refer to Josephus's own work in other places (13.298), to someone other than Josephus. Although Sanders has already asserted that such editorial remarks are relatively easy to make, he abandons that principle here for no compelling reason.

In support, while ignoring Josephus's narrative context, he cites an old argument from the days of radical source criticism. In 13.288, namely, the writer says that the Pharisees have such great influence with the masses that, even when they speak against a king and against a high priest they are trusted. Some source critics of a bygone day proposed that the alleged distinction here between the offices of king and high priest did not match the reign of Hyrcanus, who was a high priest but not a king; they argued as Sanders does that only in Herod's time was there such a *distinction* of offices in Judea, and so this sentence must come from Nicolaus in Herod's day!

But this argument has no merit and it should be abandoned forthwith. Josephus does not suggest here that kings and high priests must be different people simultaneously governing at the time of his writing. His general statement is a reflection on the Pharisees in the present tense; these remarks are not tied to any particular historical context. Aside from the general implausibility of the notion that Josephus would have needed to consult Nicolaus for such an introductory sentence, which runs counter to everything we know of our author's general practice, and aside from the prominent cross-refer-

ence to Josephus's own works in 13.298, we have the compelling
evidence of the concordance, which I have treated in detail elsewhere.[29] Everything here, from the pro-Hasmonean and pro-
Hyrcanus posture, to the theme of troublesome Pharisaic influence,
to the particular choice of word and phrase—success (*eupragia*) breeds
envy (*phthonos*), the coupling of *phthonon* and *misos*, and the phrase
phthonon ekinēse—all of this points to Josephus, the proud Hasmonean
descendant who named his first son Hyrcanus (*Life* 5).

This somewhat detailed critique of Sanders on *Ant.* 13.288-298 has
been necessary because his treatment of this passage lays the ground
for his handling of other Pharisee passages in *Ant.* 13-20. By the time
he gets to Josephus's criticism of the Pharisees in *Ant.* 17.41-45, during Herod's reign, he declares it "almost certain" that this passage
comes from Nicolaus. Sanders's reasons here are: (a) the similarity of
language with *Ant.* 13.288, which, as we have seen, he attributed to
Nicolaus, (b) this passage's anti-Pharisaic stance, and (c) the general
observations that Nicolaus wrote in detail about Herod's reign and
Josephus is known to have used Nicolaus extensively (p. 392).

But these observations provide no support for the argument that
Josephus took over *Ant.* 17.41-45 unedited from any other source, let
alone Nicolaus. Note that the most famous Josephan source critic had
attributed this passage to a biography of Herod by Ptolemaeus of
Ashkelon,[30] not to Nicolaus! No one doubts that Josephus used
Nicolaus extensively for the Herodian period, any more than they
doubt that he used the Bible for *Ant.* 1-11. Yet, as we have seen,
Josephus typically shapes his source material to serve his narrative
ends. In this particular case, the anti-Pharisaic stance is consistent
with his general posture. Moreover, the passage fully reflects the awkward "Thucydideanesque" style adopted by Josephus throughout the
whole of *Ant.* 17-19,[31] and it includes a peculiar turn of phrase ("what
the Pharisee says") that connects it squarely with *Ant.* 18.17—though
no one could extend Nicolaus's influence to *Ant.* 18 or 19. Both of
these passages reflect the fairly uniform narrative style of *Ant.* 17-19,
where many sources are used and which is rather different from that
of *Ant.* 13-16, where Nicolaus was also a major source. So they cannot, on such grounds as Sanders offers, be excised bodily and credited

---

[29] Mason, *Flavius Josephus on the Pharisees*, pp. 224-227.
[30] Hölscher, op. cit., pp. 1977, 1979, 1981.
[31] Thackeray, op. cit., pp. 108-120.

to another author. Someone other than Nicolaus has tailored these episodes to their present narrative contexts, and the only plausible candidate for that someone is Josephus.

There is yet a further turn in Sanders's argument. In his discussion of Josephus's Pharisees, he proposes that Josephus has two related biases: one is to suppress any information about the Pharisees' participation in rebellion, and the other is "possibly...to bolster their standing" after 70 because they "held the future of Israel in their hands" (pp. 409-410). Later, Sanders declares that Josephus "wrote that the Pharisees ran everything because he had become a Pharisee and a backer of the house of Gamaliel" (p. 489)—another reference to Yavneh. In discussing Grabbe's proposals, we have already seen the problems with the Yavneh hypothesis. Without responding to Sanders's propositions in further detail, we may simply reassert that there are too many incongruities in his claiming simultaneously: that Josephus wished to support the Pharisees; that summary statements are very easy to create; that nevertheless he both carelessly copied and chronologically misplaced even Nicolaus's hostile summaries on the Pharisees.

Once again, it is impossible to get around Josephus's biases if one does not have an assessment of those biases that is broadly adequate to the evidence of the entire text. Sanders writes, for example: "Against his [Josephus's] own view that the chief priests were perfectly reliable leaders and rulers of the nation, he tells stories that discredit some of them" (pp. 187-188). But this assessment rests on a demonstrable misunderstanding of Josephus, who quite deliberately bends his tales of priestly misdeeds *to his goal* of showing the efficacy of the Judean laws, for the priests' crimes brought severe divine punishment (*Ant.* 20.179, 181, 218). This *is* Josephus's "own view," not a contradiction of it.

A basic question, of course, for determining Josephus's biases in his accounts of the Pharisees is whether or not he was a Pharisee himself. Usually, Sanders writes as if Josephus was not a Pharisee. For example, he traces the Mishnah's system of twelve tithes in every fourteen-year cycle to the Pharisees but, while doing so, repeatedly contrasts Josephus's fourteen-tithe system (pp. 149-152). He says that there is no known Sadducean literature and that Pharisaic views must be "painstakingly extracted from later rabbinic literature" (p. 378), implying again that Josephus's writings are not those of a Pharisee. He even says that Josephus's portrait of the Pharisees is not that of an insider (p. 387). Yet in a few other places, when talking about Josephus's views of Judaism, Sanders allows without qualification that he writes as a Pharisee ("a priest, a Pharisee, and a convinced Jew"— pp. 246, 277; cf., p. 333). Even this elementary feature of Josephus's bias is not broached as a problem.

If Josephus's basic perspectives are so unclear, it will be impossible to use his narratives (by circumventing their biases) for historical reconstruction of the Pharisees. We cannot boil down the criteria for using Josephus, as Grabbe and Sanders do, to a simple principle that narratives should be preferred over generalizations. The only really useful criterion for historical reconstruction lies in a question similar to the one that text critics ask: "What is the historical hypothesis that will best explain how all of the relevant sources, with their different perspectives, came into being?" Working out the consequences of that question will be a very complex business.

Conclusion

In these major studies by Saldarini, Grabbe, and Sanders, we have a welcome new beginning after the methodological breakthroughs made by Neusner and Rivkin. Each one attempts a more adequate reconstruction of the Pharisees' place in society on the basis of a fresh examination of the primary sources. Grabbe and Sanders in particular single out Josephus and promise to make their use of his narratives transparent to the reader. Without question, there is much that is new and provocative in each book.

But precisely at the critical juncture, these works fail: They do not yet distinguish consistently between Josephus's narratives and history, nor do they devote much effort to understanding their main source of information. My critique is not that they have a comprehensive view of Josephus's narratives that happens to differ from mine. Rather, it is that they do not even try to interpret each of Josephus's relevant works in a comprehensive way, in terms of his own narrative aims and strategies, and therefore they see no need to explain how their several reconstructions, if correct, produced his impressions. In the process, they make assumptions and claims about Josephus's aims and biases that cannot bear scrutiny.

Lest any doubt remain: I am not here advocating any particular historical reconstruction, least of all the old view that the Pharisees "ran society" through the Sanhedrin, school, and synagogue. My point is that the careful building of alternative scenarios requires an adequate explanation of Josephus, which we do not see in such efforts. No one in this post-Neusner era has yet crafted, from the ground up, a historical picture of the Pharisees that explains Josephus in a plausible way. Attempts thus far have underestimated both the sophistication and consistency of his work.

Bibliography

Attridge, Harold W., *The Interpretation of Biblical History in the Antiquitates Judaicae of Flavius Josephus* (Cambridge, 1976).

Cohen, Shaye J.D., "The Significance of Yavneh: Pharisees, Rabbis, and the End of Jewish Sectarianism," in *Hebrew Union College Annual* 55, 1984, pp. 27-53.

Collingwood, R.G., *The Idea of History* (Oxford, 1948).

Feldman, Louis H., *Jew and Gentile in Antiquity: Attitudes and Interactions from Alexander to Justinian* (Princeton, 1993).

Feldman, Louis H., *Studies in Josephus' Rewritten Bible* (Leiden, 1998).

Feldman, Louis H., and John R. Levison, eds., *Josephus' Contra Apionem: Studies in its Character and Context with a Latin Concordance to the Portion Missing in Greek.*(Leiden, 1996).

Franxman, Thomas W., *Genesis and the 'Jewish Antiquities' of Flavius Josephus* (Rome, 1979).

Grabbe, Lester L., *Judaism from Cyrus to Hadrian* (Minneapolis, 1992).

Gruen, Erich S., *The Last Generation of the Roman Republic* (Berkeley, 1974).

Hölscher, Gustav, "Josephus," in *PWRE*, 1916, 18, pp. 1934-2000.

Jones, Brian W., *The Emperor Domitian* (London, 1992).

Kennedy, George, *The Art of Persuasion in Greece* (Princeton, 1963).

Kennedy, George, *The Art of Rhetoric in the Roman World* (Princeton, 1972).

Kennedy, George, *A New History of Classical Rhetoric* (Princeton, 1993).

Kennedy, George, *Quintilian* (New York, 1969).

Levine, Lee, "Judaism from the Destruction of Jerusalem to the End of the Second Jewish Revolt: 70-135 C.E.," in Shanks, Hershel, ed., *Christianity and Rabbinic Judaism: A Parallel History of their Origins and Early Development* (Washington, 1992), pp. 125-149.

Lindner, Helgo, *Die Geschichtsauffassung des Flavius Josephus im Bellum Judaicum* (Leiden, 1972).

MacMullen, Ramsay, *Enemies of the Roman Order: Treason, Unrest, and Alienation in the Empire* (New York, 1992).

Mason, Steve, "An Essay in Character: The Aim and Audience of Josephus's *Life*," in Siegert, Folker, and Jürgen U. Kalms, eds., *Internationales Josephus-Kolloquium Münster 1997* (Münsteraner Judäistische Studien 2; Münster, 1997), pp. 31-77.

Mason, Steve, *Flavius Josephus on the Pharisees: A Composition-Critical Study* (Leiden, 1991).

Mason, Steve, "Josephus, Daniel, and the Flavian House," in Parente, Fausto, and Joseph Sievers, eds., *Josephus and the History of the Greco-Roman Period: Essays in Memory of Morton Smith* (Leiden, 1994), pp. 161-191.

Mason, Steve, "Method in the Study of Early Judaism: A Dialogue with Lester Grabbe," in *Journal of the American Oriental Society* 115, 1995, pp. 463-472.

Mason, Steve, "'Should Anyone Wish to Enquire Further' (*Ant.* 1.25): The Aim and Audience of Josephus's *Judean Antiquities*," in Mason, Steve, ed., *Understanding Josephus: Seven Perspectives* (Sheffield, 1998), pp. 64-103.

Moehring, Horst, "Novelistic Elements in the Writings of Flavius Josephus" (Dissertation: University of Chicago, 1957).

Neusner, Jacob, "The Formation of Rabbinic Judaism: Yavneh (Jamnia) from A.D. 70 to 100," in *ANRW*, 1979, 2.19.2, pp. 3-42.

Neusner, Jacob, *From Politics to Piety: the Emergence of Pharisaic Judaism* (Englewood Cliffs, 1973).

Neusner, Jacob, *The Rabbinic Traditions about the Pharisees before 70* (Leiden, 1971).

Pelletier, André, *Flavius Josèphe, adapteur de lat lettre d'Aristée* (Paris, 1962).

Rajak, Tessa, *Josephus: The Historian and His Society* (London, 1983).

Rivkin, Ellis, *A Hidden Revolution* (Nashville, 1978).

Saldarini, Anthony J., *Pharisees, Scribes and Sadducees in Palestinian Society: A Sociological Approach* (Wilmington, 1988).

Sanders, E.P., *Judaism: Practice and Belief, 63 BCE—66 CE* (London and Philadelphia, 1992).

Schreckenberg, Heinz, *Rezeptionsgeschichtliche und Textkritische Untersuchungen zu Flavius Josephus* (Leiden, 1977).

Schürer, Emil, *The History of the Jewish People in the Age of Jesus Christ*, ed. Vermes, Geza, Fergus Millar, and Matthew Black (Edinburgh, 1987).

Smith, Morton, "Palestinian Judaism in the First Century," in Davis, Moshe, ed., *Israel: Its Role in Civilization* (New York, 1956), pp. 68-71.

Southern, Pat, *Domitian: Tragic Tyrant* (Bloomington and Indianapolis, 1997).

Syme, Ronald, *The Roman Revolution* (Oxford, 1939).

Thackeray, Henry St. John, *Josephus: The Man and the Historian* (New York, 1929 [repr. 1967]).

Yavetz, Zvi, *Plebs and Princeps* (Oxford, 1969).

III. WAS JUDAISM PARTICULARIST OR UNIVERSALIST?

James D.G. Dunn
University of Durham

All questions need to have their terms clarified before they can become either meaningful or useful as questions. In this case, that preliminary task is particularly important. Why? Because the question itself arises out of a long established Christian opinion that the two adjectives in the question summarize the (or at least a) historic and clearly distinguishing difference between Judaism and Christianity. That is to say, the terms begin not as descriptive but as prejudicial: it is a *Christian* perspective that sees *Judaism* as "particularist" and that, by way of contrast, defines *Christianity* as "universalist." As such, the two terms are part of and express the deeply rooted Christian claim that the breadth of Christian universalism superseded or left behind or rose above or broke free from the narrowness of Jewish particularism.

In the modern period, the claim was posed most explicitly by F.C. Baur, and the effects of his exposition have lingered through most of the twentieth century. Already in his *Paul* book,[1] Baur sets out his program for a history of earliest Christianity, when he claims that

> the idea (of Christianity) found in the bounds of the national Judaism the chief obstacle to its universal historical realization. How these bounds were broken through, how Christianity, instead of remaining a mere form of Judaism, although a progressive one, asserted itself as a separate, independent principle, broke loose from it, and took its stand as a new enfranchised form of religious thought and life, essentially differing from all the national peculiarities of Judaism is the ultimate, most important point of the primitive history of Christianity.

When Baur turned to his own history of Christian beginnings, he expressed himself even more explicitly.[2] The universal tendency of the Roman Empire was a fitting context for

---

[1] F.C. Baur, *Paul: the Apostle of Jesus Christ* (1845; 2 vols.; London, 1873, 1875), p. 3.

[2] F.C. Baur, *The Church History of the First Three Centuries* (1854; 2 vols.; London, 1878), pp. 4-6, 33, 43, 47.

the beginning of the religion in which all religious particularism disappeared and gave way to universalism.... The universalism of Christianity is essentially nothing but that universal form of consciousness at which the development of mankind had arrived at the time when Christianity appeared.... What is it in Christianity that gives it its absolute character? The first and obvious answer to this question is that Christianity is elevated above the defects and limitations, the one-sidedness and finiteness, which constitute the particularism of other forms of religion.

Here then we meet again the characteristic feature of the Christian principle. It looks beyond the outward, the accidental, the particular, and rises to the universal, the unconditioned, the essential.... the all-commanding universalism of its spirit and aims... (Paul was) the first to lay down expressly and distinctly the principle of Christian universalism as a thing essentially opposed to Jewish particularism.

The force of the contrast/antithesis (particularism/universalism) is clear. In Baur's terms, "Jewish particularism" denotes also "defects and limitations," "one-sidedness and finiteness," "the outward, the accidental," to all of which "Christian universalism" is "a thing essentially opposed." And although Baur's language is itself dated, reflecting the prevailing philosophy of the time (idealism), and although his own distinctive working out of his vision has been left behind long ago in the history of histories of Christianity's beginnings, the echoes and overtones of Baur's formulations still cling to the use of these words today, not least in the title for this chapter.

I

That early formulation of the contrast (particularist/universalist), however, could never be sustained so simply or crudely. The term "particularist," as a way of contrasting or denigrating Judaism by comparison with Christianity, was first to come under criticism. It could be sustained only so long as Liberal Protestantism was willing to define Christianity in terms of non-historical essences and timeless moral principles (hence, universal).[3] But as soon as History of Religions research began to view earliest Christianity as just one mystery-like cult among the religions of the eastern Mediterranean basin,[4] it became impossible to treat Christianity as "universal" in the same way.

---

[3] The classic statement is A. Harnack, *Das Wesen des Christentums* = *What is Christianity?* (London, 1901).

[4] E.g., W. Bousset, *Kyrios Christos* (1921; Nashville, 1970).

And even if the subsequent emergence of Christianity as the dominant religion of the Roman Empire continued to feed the idea of Christian "universalism," how could an equivalent "particularism" be denied to Christianity? For, on the one hand, a Christianity that sets boundaries of baptism and eucharist on membership is as particularist (or as non-particularist) as any other boundary-setting group. A religion that came to cherish missionary ambitions within the historical territory (e.g., India) of another (universal) religion, can hardly function as other than particularist in its appeal. And, on the other, a Christianity that became a state religion (as in Scandinavia) is hardly different in national character from an ethnic religion like Judaism.

The issue was cloaked during the heyday of Christian existentialism, since, at this point, twentieth century Christian existentialism played the same role as nineteenth century Christian idealism. Baur's talk of "finiteness" and "the accidental" was simply replaced by Bultmann's talk of primitive and pre-scientific myth.[5] The universal ideal and the timeless moral principle was replaced by the kerygma and the summons to authentic being, which, for Bultmann, still spoke through the mythical forms of the New Testament. But, in post-Holocaust Europe, the denigratory antithesis has had to be confronted and exposed, as at best an echo of a time when the superiority of Christianity to Judaism was simply taken for granted.

At the same time, as part of the agonized self-reappraisal of post-Holocaust Christianity, the falseness and injustice of denying a term like "universalism" to Judaism has become steadily clearer. Special credit should be given here to a pivotal but too little appreciated article by Nils Dahl,[6] in which he makes the obvious, but again too little appreciated, observation that Israel's monotheistic claims were/ are inevitably universalistic. To say that the God of Israel is also the God of the gentile nations is to be both particularist and universalist.[7] Dahl concludes by criticizing Ernst Käsemann for failing

to break radically with the common but simplistic notion of a contrast between Christian universalism and Jewish particularism. Jewish monotheism at the time of Paul was universalistic in its own way, and Christian

---

[5] R. Bultmann, "New Testament and Mythology," in W.H. Bartsch, ed., *Kerygma and Myth* (London, 1953), pp. 1-44.

[6] N.A. Dahl, "The One God of Jews and Gentiles (Romans 3.29-30)," in *Studies in Paul* (Minneapolis, 1977), pp. 178-191.

[7] See now and further J.D. Levenson, "The Universal Horizon of Biblical Particularism," in M.G. Brett, ed., *Ethnicity and the Bible* (Leiden, 1996), pp. 143-169.

monotheism remained exclusive. The condemnation of idolatry is an evidence of that (see, e.g., Rom. 1:18ff). We would come closer to the truth by saying that both Jewish and Christian monotheism are particular as well as universal, specific as well as general.... The universal law and. order, embodied in the Torah, has been replaced (*sic*) by the universality of God's judgment, grace, and righteousness, revealed in the gospel....

Dahl's observation places in serious question whether there is anything still of value in retaining these terms as a way of contrasting or comparing Judaism and Christianity. Apart from anything else, "universalist" has itself become too elusive in its reference. The concept of principles or ideals or values of universal validity is too dependent on a Platonic-type philosophical world view, itself too much disputed to claim universal validity. If such language is still to be used, better to build on the theological axioms, common to Judaism and Christianity, of the one God as creator of all. Beyond that, "universalism" can hardly amount to much if it simply asserts a religion's right to present its message universally. *Any* claim to the universal validity of specific beliefs is itself a form of particularism (our belief and not yours). And *any* notion of special revelation, quite apart from the idea of special election (of a people or group), likewise cannot avoid being particularist.[8] The more logical solution would be to limit the term to the claim that not one human being will be excluded from salvation ("universalism"), with "particularism" as its contrast (not every human being, only an elect will be saved). But here again Judaism and Christianity are equally uncertain or equally divided, each particularist in principle (M. San. 10:1; John 14:6; Acts 4:12), each wrestling with qualifications in practice (the righteous gentile, the "anonymous Christian"). These are matters to which we will have to return.

II

If, then, the contrast, "particularist"/"universalist," is inappropriate and misleading in describing a key difference between Judaism and Christianity, even though that was the context where the contrast arose, do the terms have any value in a description of Judaism itself? Once we cut through the ideology and prejudice of the older charac-

---

[8] Cf., again Levenson, "Universal Horizon," pp. 143-145, 166-167; e.g., the Torah is not to be simply equated with some universal moral law (pp. 157-158).

terization, do either or both of the terms highlight features of or tensions within Judaism that are still worthy of attention? And are there contrasts between Judaism and Christianity that these terms obscured more than illuminated but that can be expressed more accurately?

These questions open too long an agenda for present purposes. But two aspects can be explored sufficiently at least for us to offer an answer to the question that forms the title.

The first aspect picks up the other key term in the title, "Judaism." In other circumstances it might be assumed that the descriptor "Judaism" does not require any discussion; it obviously refers to "the religion of the Jews." But in this case some analysis is necessary.

The relevance of the term to the issue of "particularism/universalism" becomes obvious when it is recalled that the term "Jew" (*Yehudi*, *Ioudaios*) emerged from the term "Judea" (*Yehudah*, *Ioudaia*).[9] In broad terms of English usage we can say that the Greek term *Ioudaios* denoted "Judean" before the more general "Jew" became appropriate for members of a people no longer so closely identified with that land as such.[10] "Judaism" in turn emerged from "Jew," that is, as a Greek term (*Ioudaismos*) from *Ioudaios*. As is well known, *Ioudaismos* was in fact initially coined to describe the religion of the Judeans (2 Macc. 2:21; 8:1; 14:38) in their opposition to the Hellenizing policies of their Syrian overlords.[11]

The significance of this basic observation is that "Judaism" in its beginnings is a term closely linked to a particular territory. In that sense we would have to say that Judaism was particularist: it identi-

---

[9] It could be said, of course, that both "Jew" and "Judea" are derived from the son of Jacob (Judah). But the significant feature is that the use of "Jew" first emerges in 2 Kgs. 16:6 and 25:25, several times in Jeremiah (between 32:12 and 52:30), and thereafter in Ezra-Nehemiah and Esther (also Zech. 8:23 and 2 Chron. 32:18), and always with reference to the southern kingdom Judah, then Judea. In *Ant.* 11.173, Josephus observes that "the Jews" was "the name by which they (the returnees from Babylon) have been called from the time they went up from Babylon;" that is, they were identified by reference to the land (Judea) from which they had been deported, and to which they returned.

[10] Hence the possibility of translating *Ioudaios* as "Judean" in John's Gospel, particularly John 7:1 and 11:7; M. Lowe, "Who were the *Ioudaioi*?," in *Novum Testamentum* 18 (1976), pp. 101-130, attempts to push the argument further.

[11] See also S.J.D. Cohen, "Ioudaios: 'Judean' and 'Jew' in Susanna, First Maccabees, and Second Maccabees," in H. Cancik, et al., eds., *Geschichte—Tradition—Reflexion*, M. Hengel FS, *Band I, Judentum* (ed. P. Schäfer) (Tübingen, 1996), pp. 211-220 (here, p. 219); G. Harvey, *The True Israel: Uses of the Names Jew, Hebrew and Israel in Ancient Jewish and Early Christian Literature* (Leiden, 1996), pp. 11-20.

fied with a particular land. Nor is it any accident that the term
emerged in opposition to a policy intended to obliterate national and
religious distinctiveness. It should be no surprise, in other words, that
the term emerged in Greek, precisely as a way of marking out the
Judeans' distinctiveness within a wider Hellenism that valued
commonality more than distinctiveness. In that sense Judaism was
resistant to a certain kind of "universalism," one that attempted to
absorb and eliminate Judaism's particularism.

Given this early history of the terms it should occasion no surprise
if "Jew" and "Judaism" continued to retain an unavoidably ethnic
association with a particular land (Judea). Hence the division of all
nations and races into the two categories of "Jews" and "gentiles/
(other) nations"—"Jews" as those who belong to a nation/people
distinct from all other nations/peoples.[12] Even in the diaspora, "Jews"
were by definition those whose identity was determined by their ethnic origin and continuing loyalty to the Temple cult (of Jerusalem),
whose maintenance had been the *raison d'etre* for Judea's existence as
a political entity since the Persian and Hellenistic periods.[13] Hence
the ambiguity of the terms "Jew" and "Judaism:" do they describe an
ethnic or a religious identity? The answer was, at that time, Both,
since the two went so closely together.[14] In other words, the original
overtone of "particularism" continued to cling to these terms through
their early usage, simply because the definition they provided was
unavoidably particularist.

I need hardly elaborate the point much further. In one measure or
another, the same particularist reference to Judea/Jerusalem remained a feature throughout the centuries of the Jewish dispersion
("Next year in Jerusalem"). And the same reference to the land as

---

[12] To draw in the other relevant *ioudai-* term, Jews, of course, did not "Judaize"
(*ioudaizein*); only gentiles could "Judaize," because the term denoted a non-Jew/gen-
tile's acting or living like a Jew, that is, following practices that distinguished and
identified Jews ethnically and religiously (see also below n. 30).

[13] Most notably signaled by the strongly continued and (within the Roman empire) highly unusual tradition of the temple tax—taxation money flowing across the
empire to somewhere other than Rome itself! "Jerusalem was the religious focus for
all Jews, wherever they lived" (M. Smallwood, *The Jews under Roman Rule from Pompey
to Diocletian* [Leiden, 1981], p. 124; see further, pp. 120-143). Note also the conclusion of J.M.G. Barclay, *Jews in the Mediterranean Diaspora from Alexander to Trajan (323
BCE - 117 CE)* (Edinburgh, 1996): "it was ethnicity—precisely the *combination* of ancestry and custom—which was the core of Jewish identity in the Diaspora" (p. 404).

[14] Cf., particularly, L.H. Schiffman, *Who Was a Jew? Rabbinic and Halakhic Perspectives on the Jewish-Christian Schism* (Hoboken, 1985).

fundamental to Jewish identity remains at the heart of the modern state of Israel's present political crisis. The emergence of a strong tradition of secular Jewishness has certainly heightened the tension marked by the divisive question, "Who is a Jew?" But the tension is so fierce precisely because it is so difficult to hold apart ethnic and religious identity. That is to say, the question is so difficult precisely because of the particularism implicit in the basic term itself from the first.

In view of recent discussion, two points of clarification are perhaps called for. In the first place, it should be noted that I am speaking exclusively here of the terms "Jew" and "Judaism," not of the further term "Israel." Indeed in my earlier writing in this area I have been careful to distinguish the last mentioned from the others. I have pointed out that characteristically "Israel" denotes an insider's perspective, a term of self-definition, identity determined by relation to God (Gen. 32:28); whereas "Jew" denotes an outsider's perspective, a term of description, identity determined by distinction from other peoples.[15] It is precisely because of that distinguishing function of the terms "Jew" and "Judaism" that the adjectives "ethnic" and "particularist" are appropriately attached to them. And, for the same reason precisely, I have avoided using the term "ethnic," or now "particularist," in relation to "Israel." Unfortunately Jack Neusner has missed this point in his criticism of my earlier work.[16] He ignores the distinction I made and criticizes me for defining *Israel* as having both an "ethnic" and religious identity. And he responds by referring solely to the writings of Rabbinic Judaism: "there is no ethnic Israel that is distinct from a religious Israel at all, not in the sources that attest the Judaism of which Dunn speaks."[17] Here he ignores the fact

---

[15] Citing K.G. Kuhn, *TDNT* 3, pp. 359-365; see further P. Tomson, "The Names Israel and Jew in Ancient Judaism and in the New Testament," in *Bijdragen* 47 (1986), pp. 120-140, 266-289; and the conclusions of Harvey on Philo and Josephus (*True Israel*, pp. 46, 61). E.g., in John's Gospel, the title "king of the Jews" is used of Jesus by outsiders (18:33, 39; 19:3, 19), but insiders speak of "the king of Israel" (1:49; 12:13). See also my "The Question of Anti-semitism in the New Testament," in J.D.G. Dunn, ed., *Jews and Christians: The Parting of the Ways AD 70 to 135* (Tübingen, 1992), pp. 177-211 (here, pp. 186-187); also my *The Theology of Paul the Apostle* (Grand Rapids, 1998), pp. 505-506.

[16] J. Neusner, "Explaining the Great Schism: History Versus Theology," in *Religion* (1998) 28, pp. 139-153, referring to my *The Partings of the Ways between Christianity and Judaism* (London and Philadelphia, 1991), p. 230, but ignoring the earlier statements on pp. 144-146.

[17] Neusner, "Explaining the Great Schism," p. 144.

that the sources from which I drew my observations were the biblical and more immediately post-biblical Jewish documents, not the Rabbinic traditions.[18] He also seems to have missed the observation I drew from Solomon Zeitlin in my contribution to a previous volume in this series, that "in the Rabbinic writings 'Israel' and not 'Jews' is the almost universal self-designation."[19] Perhaps it will suffice to reiterate here, therefore, that the present discussion relates only to "Judaism" as used by and in reference to early Judaism (hence the past tense of the question).

The other point of clarification perhaps necessary is that the "Judaism" spoken of here is not to be confused with the modern tendency to recognize many kinds of Judaism, indeed many Judaisms, in the late Second Temple Judaism period. This is also a point made earlier, but it is probably worth reiterating here, that the talk of "many Judaisms" is only possible from a modern sociological perspective. For non-Jews "looking in" there would have been only one "Judaism," just as there was only one nation of "the Jews;" however strange and diverse these Jews were, their distinctive *ethnos* and traditions marked them out as one. And for insiders, there would also be only one Judaism, Judaism as practiced by themselves—whether the "common Judaism" of the general populace of the land of Israel or Judaism as practiced by their own particular sect or faction.[20] The only difficulty with the latter formulation, however, is that, as already noted, the insiders' preferred self-reference would have been "Israel" rather than the outsiders' referent "Judaism."

The only directly relevant text within the New Testament on this precise issue provides an interesting confirmation and at the same time suggests the one point at which emerging Christianity can properly be said to have reacted against Jewish "particularism" of the time. The text is Gal. 1:13-14:

---

[18] Neusner is justified in his comment, however, in that what I said in *Partings*, p. 230, refers to the period of formative Judaism running through the second century. Here we meet the problem (also taken up in the next paragraph) that *Rabbinic Judaism* is a later description and in fact continues the outsider perspective on that religion that the earlier "Judaism" also denoted (in contrast, in both cases, to the "insider's" *Israel*); in each case it is the outsider's perspective, distinguishing the referent from other religions, that carries the nationalist and ethnic overtone.

[19] "Judaism in the Land of Israel in the First Century," in J. Neusner, ed., *Judaism in Late Antiquity: Part Two: Historical Syntheses* (Leiden, 1995), pp. 229-261 (here, p. 235), citing S. Zeitlin, *The Jews: Race, Nation, or Religion?* (Philadelphia, 1936), pp. 31-32.

[20] I deal with these issues at some length in my "Judaism in the Land of Israel."

> For you have heard of my way of life previously in Judaism, that in excessive measure I persecuted the church of God and tried to destroy it; and that I progressed in Judaism beyond many of my contemporaries among my people, being exceedingly zealous for my ancestral traditions.

Although Galatians was written more than a hundred years after 2 Maccabees, the Gal. 1:13-14 reference is still among the earliest extant occurrences of the term "Judaism." Of interest, then, is the fact that the usage is similar to that of 2 Maccabees. Paul's "life in Judaism" was marked by two features: fervent hostility to a threat by the Nazarenes against the distinctiveness of that Judaism—whether in terms of the Temple (according to Acts 6-8), or in terms of set-apartness from the other nations; and an almost competitive zeal to maintain loyalty to covenant and Torah.[21] This was Paul's Judaism— Judaism as he believed it should be and as he tried to live it. We today would call it Pharisaic Judaism and recognize other "Judaisms." But for Paul, his Judaism was Judaism.

More to the point here, his Damascus road experience caused him to abandon this Judaism, Judaism as so characterized. Why? The implication is clear: he reacted against this Judaism, that is, against these two features: he turned to the gentiles from whom he had been trying to keep separate ("it pleased God...to reveal his Son in me, in order that I might preach him among the gentiles"); and he turned away from the competitive zeal he had displayed as a Pharisee ("Whatever gains I had, these I have come to regard as loss because of Christ," Phil. 3:7).[22]

If this is a correct analysis of Paul's conversion, as Paul himself saw and remembered it, then it could be said that Paul's conversion was a reaction against Jewish particularism as he himself had maintained it as a Pharisee. That is, he reacted against the particularism that emphasized Israel's set-apartness from other nations as integral to Israel's election and the particularism that interpreted Israel's status and Torah obligation in terms of the elaborated halakhah of the Pharisees.

It could also be said that his reaction was towards universalism, in that he wanted thereafter to break down the barriers (of Torah, not least) between Jews and gentiles and to open the gospel and the

---

[21] I have elaborated these points more than once; see most recently my *Theology of Paul*, pp. 347-353.

[22] See again my *Theology of Paul*, p. 353.

inheritance of Abraham to other nations. Yet the reality was that he sought to break down barriers only between Jewish and gentile *believers*. That is, on the one hand, he maintained the boundaries between Jew and gentile marked out by monotheistic belief and unyielding opposition to idolatry and *porneia*.[23] And, on the other, he replaced the particularism of Jewish election with the particularism of faith in Jesus the Christ, of circumcision in the flesh by baptism in the name of Jesus. So if "universalism" is a term appropriate to describe Paul's reaction against his former Judaism, it was in effect only an expansion or redefinition of Judaism's particularism.

III

So far we have focused on the particularism that seems to be integral to the very term "Judaism" and on the earliest Christian reaction to that particularism. But what about the other side of the picture— Jewish universalism? What about the way and degree to which Second Temple Judaism integrated its universalist aspirations with its particularism, without and prior to such Christian reaction? Was Paul's reaction to (his) Judaism a reaction of incipient Christianity to a different religious system or simply part of the ongoing tension within Judaism, the reaction of Jewish universalism to Jewish particularism?

Two lines of inquiry and reflection open up at this point. One is well covered in a recent article by Terence Donaldson in which he has attempted to identify what he calls "three broad 'patterns of universalism'" within Jewish thinking about the gentiles in Second Temple Judaism, that is, "three distinct ways in which hope for the 'salvation' of the Gentiles was entertained."[24]

The first was, of course, proselytism. This should not be confused with missionary-minded evangelism. There would, after all, be something odd about an ethnic religion going out of its way to seek converts;[25] Judaism was hardly to be confused with a mystery religion or

---

[23] For the relevant data, I may simply refer once again to my *Theology of Paul*, pp. 31-33, 689-692, 701-706.

[24] T.L. Donaldson, "Proselytes or 'Righteous Gentiles'? The Status of Gentiles in Eschatological Pilgrimage Patterns of Thought," in *JSP* 7 (1990), pp. 3-27 (here, p. 3).

[25] Cf., Smallwood, *Jews*, pp. 129-130: "The national basis of Judaism precluded large-scale missionary activity."

cult, like that of Isis. And recent studies do in fact confirm that Second Temple Judaism was not in fact evangelistic.[26] Nevertheless, there is plenty of evidence that Judaism did prove to be attractive to many gentiles and that Judaism was generally very hospitable to gentile "God-fearers" and welcoming of those who went the whole way to become proselytes.[27]

Second, there was the righteous gentile. Whether the explicit category was in circulation in the first century is doubtful.[28] And whether for our period the category can be regarded as more or less equivalent to the "God-fearer" is unclear.[29] But presumably Jewish synagogue acceptance of gentile adherents or sympathizers included in some cases at least a willingness to recognize that such gentiles *per se* might also have a place in the world to come.[30]

---

[26] S. McKnight, *A Light among the Gentiles: Jewish Missionary Activity in the Second Temple Period* (Minneapolis, 1991); M. Goodman, *Mission and Conversion: Proselytizing in the Religious History of the Roman Empire* (Oxford, 1994), chap. 4. The issue is not to be confused with Jewish *apologetic* that aimed not so much to convert gentiles as to enable diaspora Jews to hold up their heads in diaspora contexts; contrast the general thesis of L.H. Feldman, *Jew and Gentile in the Ancient World* (Princeton, 1993); see further the discussion by J.J. Collins, *Between Athens and Jerusalem: Jewish Identity in the Hellenistic Diaspora* (New York, 1983).

[27] See, e.g., the data in P.F. Stuehrenberg, *Anchor Bible Dictionary*, vol. 5, pp. 503-505.

[28] Problematic here is whether the tradition of "the apostolic decree" in Acts 15:20 and 21:25 provides any evidence for an early version of the Noahide commandments. On the latter, see particularly D. Novak, *The Image of the Non-Jew in Judaism* (New York, 1983). See also A.F. Segal, "Universalism in Judaism and Christianity," in T. Engberg-Pedersen, ed., *Paul in His Hellenistic Context* (Minneapolis, 1995), pp. 1-29 (here, pp. 13-27). Cf., Levenson, "Universal Horizon," p. 149: "The Noahide and the God-fearer, like the *ger toshav* of rabbinic literature (with whom they may be identical), testify to a theology that holds that the true religion is larger than the religion of the core of insiders, which it includes. The convenient dichotomy of insider-outsider is too crude to accommodate the Jewish conception of the divine-human relationship." Levenson notes also, p. 159, the traditional Israelite solicitude for the "stranger" and "resident alien."

[29] Within scriptural tradition one might consider, for example, Jethro (Exod. 18), Rahab (Josh. 2), Naaman (2 Kgs. 5), and the repentant Ninevites of Jonah. Levenson cites Gen. 20:11, Ps. 145:18, and the international character of much of the wisdom tradition ("Universal Horizon," pp. 149-151). In Christian writing, Paul's description of judgment on gentiles in Rom. 2:6-16 leaves open the question whether he identified the gentiles who "do by nature what the law requires" (2:14) solely with the Christian gentiles, or whether he (as Jew and/or Christian) recognized the possibility of gentiles whose righteousness would be acknowledged by God in the final judgment quite apart from their knowledge (or otherwise) of Judaism or Christianity. See also Segal, "Universalism," pp. 20-21.

[30] Note, not least the tradition of gentiles "Judaizing"—Esther 8:17 (LXX); Theodotus in Eusebius, *Praep. Evang.* 9.22.5; Plutarch, *Cicero* 7.6.5; Josephus, *War* 2.454, 462-3; Ignatius, *Magn.* 10.3.

Third, Donaldson points to and focuses on that strand of Jewish eschatological expectation that saw gentiles as full participants in eschatological salvation (particularly in terms of their pilgrimage to Zion) as a by-product of the end-time restoration of Israel.[31] His principal thesis is that "there is no explicit indication in any of these texts that 'eschatological pilgrimage Gentiles' were expected to become full proselytes," that "no clear and unambiguous picture emerges from these texts concerning the religious status of eschatological pilgrimage Gentiles," and that "proselytism cannot be read into these texts as something simply taken for granted by their authors and intended readers."[32] His conclusion is that "this strand of Jewish eschatological tradition tended to anticipate the inclusion of the gentiles *as gentiles*. Those gentiles...would have a share in the blessings of the age to come, but without being fully incorporated into the covenant community of Israel."[33]

Whatever the precise taxonomy of texts here, and whether or not the Jewish attitudes to gentiles expressed by these texts should be described as a form of "universalism," there can be little doubt that there was within Jewish thought and practice of the period an alternative to or qualification of the sort of particularism that Saul the Pharisee had espoused and defended—an openness to gentiles in principle and practice that ran ultimately counter to the separatism instinctive to so many (other) Jews.[34]

The second line of inquiry and reflection focuses on the presence within Jewish scripture and tradition from very early days of a recognition that Israel's calling was not simply for its own benefit. This can be rooted in the founding promises given to Abraham and the patriarchs. For as well as the promise of seed and land, there was also the promise of blessing to the nations in or by or through Abraham and

---

[31] Donaldson, "Proselytes" 8, citing, inter alia, Is. 2:2-4//Mic. 4:1-3; Is. 56:6-8; 66:21; Amos 9:12; Zech. 2:11; Tob. 13:11; 14:6-7; 1 Enoch 10:21; 90:30-33; 91:14; Sib. Or. 3:564-570, 715-723, 757-775; Philo, *Mos.* 2.43-44.

[32] Donaldson, "Proselytes," pp. 12-25, citing 12, 25, and 27.

[33] Donaldson, "Proselytes," p. 27. See also particularly P. Fredriksen, *From Jesus to Christ* (New Haven, 1988), p. 150; and cf., Levenson, "Universal Horizon," pp. 162-164.

[34] See also S.J.D. Cohen, "Crossing the Boundary and Becoming a Jew," in *Harvard Theological Review* 82 (1989), pp. 13-33; also "'Those Who Say They Are Jews and Are Not:' How Do You Know a Jew in Antiquity When You See One?," in S.J.D. Cohen and E.S. Frerichs, eds., *Diasporas in Antiquity* (Atlanta, 1993), pp. 1-45; and the discussion of levels of assimilation among diaspora Jews by Barclay, *Jews in the Mediterranean Diaspora*.

his seed (Gen. 12:3; 18:18; 22:17-18; 26:4; 28:14). This can properly be described as a major root of Jewish universalism: the promise consistently takes the form that "all the families/nations of the earth" will experience this blessing. That, of course, does not necessarily indicate Israel's responsibility to provide that blessing in a missionary or evangelistic way; it could simply imply that Israel's success would spill over to other nations or that the other nations by acknowledging Israel's success and becoming subservient to Israel would thereby share in its blessed state.[35] In other words, we are back into the question whether the eschatological pilgrimage of the gentiles is to serve Israel or to share with Israel.

It is also to the point to note that, whereas all three strands of the promise to Abraham (seed, land, blessing to nations) are given more or less equal emphasis in Genesis itself, the third strand receives much less prominence subsequently. Indeed, the only passages within the Hebrew Bible in which we can recognize a clear allusion to the promise of blessing for the gentiles are Ps. 72:17 and Jer. 4:1-2. Of course, we could recognize something at least of the influence of that third strand in the prophetic commission "to the nations" (Jer. 1:5) and the commission of Israel itself to be "a light to the nations that my (the Lord's) salvation may reach to the end of the earth" (Is. 49:6): But here again the ambiguity emerges: is the prophet's commission like that of Amos 1:2-2.5 (judgment), or like that of Jonah (deliverance from catastrophe through repentance)? Does Israel's light simply reveal the privileged position of Israel and the darkness of the other nations (as Rom. 2.17-20 implies), or is it intended to shine with saving power (as at Acts 13:47, citing Is. 49:6)?

Interestingly enough, it is precisely at this point that we can once again locate both Paul's own position and his contribution to the discussion. For in describing his conversion, he clearly characterizes it as a prophetic calling, and precisely in the terms used by both Jer. 1:5 and Is. 49:1-6—set apart from his mother's womb...to the gentiles (Gal. 1:15-16). And subsequently in Gal. 3:8 he cites the third strand of the Abrahamic promise as the gospel preached beforehand to Abraham: "in you shall all the nations be blessed" (citing Gen. 12:3 and 18:18). In other words, in order to justify his own sense of com-

---

[35] Cf., e.g., G.J. Wenham, *Genesis 1-15* (Waco, 1987): "The subsequent stories in Genesis illustrate these principles in action. Groups well disposed to Abram and his descendants prosper: those that oppose them do not" (p. 278).

mission to the gentiles, Paul cited the universalistic strand of Israel's
own self-understanding ("all the nations"). Which is also to say, that if
Paul's apostleship was at least in some sense a reaction to what he
now perceived as Judaism's particularism, it was also in response to
Judaism's own universalist impulse. Alternatively, we could say that
Paul was the first Jew of whom we have clear evidence who took
Israel's commission to be a light to the nations as a call to mission and
evangelism.[36]

At the same time, however, we should also recall our opening
observations and recognize that Paul's gospel was thoroughly rooted
in Israel's own sense of election and claims to special revelation.
Indeed, we should further note the possibility of integrating the first
line of inquiry and reflection at this point. For it is possible that the
collection to which Paul devoted so much of his energies latterly, as
part of his missionary outreach to the gentiles, was intended in some
measure to fulfill the hope of the eschatological gentile pilgrimage to
Zion (Rom. 15:27).[37] In this case, we note too the same ambiguity as
before as to whether such pilgrimage is primarily to pay tribute or
also to share in Israel's worship and blessings (cf., Is. 45:14; 60:5-17;
61:6; Mic. 4:13; Tob. 13:11; 1QM 12:13-15). Did Paul play on that
ambiguity in order to defend and commend Judaism's universalist
strand to Judaism's particularist strand? That is an imponderable
question. But at least it adds further plausibility to the argument that
Paul saw his missionary calling not so much as a renunciation of his
previous religious obligation, but precisely as a recognition of it and
as an attempt to be true to it.

IV

We find ourselves, then, caught in a tension between two equally
clear strands within Second Temple Judaism, two strands for which
we can use the catchwords "particularism" and "universalism" without too much danger of misdirecting the discussion. And we find too,

---

[36] Cf., F. Rosenzweig's conception of "Christianity as the rays that shoot out into
the dark night of 'paganism' from the fiery star that is Judaism: Christianity is
Judaism for the gentiles" (*The Star of Redemption* [New York, 1970], pp. 336-379), cited
by Levenson, who adds appositely that "Judaism itself can also be Judaism for the
gentiles," ("Universal Horizon," p. 165).
[37] See particularly R.D. Aus, "Paul's Travel Plans to Spain and the 'Full Number
of the Gentiles' of Rom. 11.25," in *Novum Testamentum* 21 (1979), pp. 232-262.

rather intriguingly, that Saul the Pharisee become Paul the apostle is caught right at the heart of the tension. How to do justice to both strands?

Is this the point at which the distinction between "Judaism" and "Israel" might be re-introduced to help us? For the tension, we could say, is actually between Judaism and Israel, that is, between the identities denoted by the two terms. If I am right, there was something unavoidably particularist in the term "Judaism" when it came into currency towards the end of the previous era (B.C.E.) and into the common era. But "Israel" was not so bound up with overtones of nationalism and ethnicity (as Neusner has also observed).[38] Might we say, then, that "Judaism" represents the "particularist" strand within Israel, while "Israel" represents the "universalist" strand within Judaism? If so, then it may be appropriate to note again that Saul/ Paul was an important voice in that *intra muros* dialogue within Judaism/Israel, who still deserves a hearing, not as an apostate or heretical voice, but as one who wrestled with the tension of Israel's heritage and covenant obligation from within.

One final problem that such an analysis leaves should not be ignored. For the usage on which much of the above reflections is based has, of course, changed since the period under review. Whereas "Judaism" gained its particularist tinge from the territory named Judea and "Israel" had ceased to be a territorial name, today the territorial designation is linked to "Israel" whereas "Judaism" is now, to use common parlance, one of the world (universal?) religions. On the other hand, to bring the issue into the present is simply to remind us that the *intra muros* debate on "Who is a Jew?" is still as lively as ever, and though the political issues have changed and become ever more complex, the theological issue is the same—Judaism's particularism (not least in terms of land)[39] and universalism (recognition of the "divine rights" of gentiles as gentiles) still in unresolved tension.

---

[38] "Israel is a supernatural entity for the Judaism (*sic*) of the dual Torah...a supernatural entity, not an ethnic one.... This "Israel" forms the counterpart to Church or Nation of Islam, not to the Albanians or the Italians or the Algerians or the Swedes" (Neusner, "Explaining the Great Schism," p. 144).

[39] Cf., Levenson's characterization of "nationalism" as "the Judaism of the secularized" ("Universal Horizon," p. 169).

Bibliography

Aus, R.D., "Paul's Travel Plans to Spain and the 'Full Number of the Gentiles' of Rom. 11.25," in *Novum Testamentum* 21 (1979), pp. 232-262.

Barclay, J.M.G., *Jews in the Mediterranean Diaspora from Alexander to Trajan (323 BCE - 117 CE)* (Edinburgh, 1996).

Baur, F.C., *Paul: the Apostle of Jesus Christ* (London, 1873, 1875).

Baur, F.C., *The Church History of the First Three Centuries* (London, 1878).

Bousset, W., *Kyrios Christos* (1921; Nashville, 1970).

Bultmann, R., "New Testament and Mythology," in Bartsch, W.H., ed., *Kerygma and Myth* (London, 1953).

Cohen, S.J.D., "Crossing the Boundary and Becoming a Jew," in *Harvard Theological Review* 82 (1989), pp. 13-33.

Cohen, S.J.D., "Ioudaios: 'Judean' and 'Jew' in Susanna, First Maccabees, and Second Maccabees," in Cancik, H., et al., eds., *Geschichte—Tradition—Reflexion*, M. Hengel FS, *Band I, Judentum* (ed. P. Schäfer) (Tübingen, 1996), pp. 211-220.

Cohen, S.J.D., "'Those Who Say They Are Jews and Are Not:' How Do You Know a Jew in Antiquity When You See One?," in Cohen, S.J.D., and E.S. Frerichs, eds., *Diasporas in Antiquity* (Atlanta, 1993), pp. 1-45.

Collins, J.J., *Between Athens and Jerusalem: Jewish Identity in the Hellenistic Diaspora* (New York, 1983).

Dahl, N.A., "The One God of Jews and Gentiles (Romans 3:29-30)," in *Studies in Paul* (Minneapolis, 1977), pp. 178-191.

Donaldson, T.L., "Proselytes or 'Righteous Gentiles'? The Status of Gentiles in Eschatological Pilgrimage Patterns of Thought," in *JSP* 7 (1990), pp. 3-27.

Dunn, J.D.G., "Judaism in the Land of Israel in the First Century," in Neusner, J., ed., *Judaism in Late Antiquity: Part Two: Historical Syntheses* (Leiden, 1995), pp. 229-261.

Dunn, J.D.G., *The Partings of the Ways between Christianity and Judaism* (London and Philadelphia, 1991).

Dunn, J.D.G., "The Question of Anti-semitism in the New Testament," in Dunn, J.D.G., ed., *Jews and Christians: The Parting of the Ways AD 70 to 135* (Tübingen, 1992), pp. 177-211.

Dunn, J.D.G., *The Theology of Paul the Apostle* (Grand Rapids, 1998).

Feldman, L.H., *Jew and Gentile in the Ancient World* (Princeton, 1993).

Harnack, A., *What is Christianity?* (London, 1901).

Harvey, G., *The True Israel: Uses of the Names Jew, Hebrew and Israel in Ancient Jewish and Early Christian Literature* (Leiden, 1996).

Levenson, J.D., "The Universal Horizon of Biblical Particularism," in Brett, M.G., ed., *Ethnicity and the Bible* (Leiden, 1996), pp. 143-169.

Lowe, M., "Who were the *Ioudaioi*?," in *Novum Testamentum* 18 (1976), pp. 101-130.

M. Goodman, *Mission and Conversion: Proselytizing in the Religious History of the Roman Empire* (Oxford, 1994).

McKnight, S., *A Light among the Gentiles: Jewish Missionary Activity in the Second Temple Period* (Minneapolis, 1991).

Neusner, J., "Explaining the Great Schism: History Versus Theology," in *Religion* (1998) 28, pp. 139-153.

Novak, D., *The Image of the Non-Jew in Judaism* (New York, 1983).

Schiffman, L.H., *Who Was a Jew? Rabbinic and Halakhic Perspectives on the Jewish-Christian Schism* (Hoboken, 1985).

Segal, A.F., "Universalism in Judaism and Christianity," in Engberg-Pedersen, T., ed., *Paul in His Hellenistic Context* (Minneapolis, 1995).

Smallwood, M., *The Jews under Roman Rule from Pompey to Diocletian* (Leiden, 1981).

Tomson, P., "The Names Israel and Jew in Ancient Judaism and in the New Testament," in *Bijdragen* 47 (1986).

Zeitlin, S., *The Jews: Race, Nation, or Religion?* (Philadelphia, 1936).

IV. RABBINIC JUDAISM IN NIHILISTIC PERSPECTIVE: THE GOLDBERG-SCHÄFER SCHOOL AND THE THEORY OF THE EMPTY TEXT

Jacob Neusner
University of South Florida and Bard College

A school of Rabbinic Judaism, the Goldberg-Schäfer School, together with its Dutch offshoot, nihilistically treats Rabbinic Judaism as a set of textual problems, a dead religion, lacking all contents that require attention.[1] For tragic reasons, which require no exposition, scholars of Judaism in Middle Europe do not commonly encounter Judaism as a living religion, and it is easy for them to reduce that religion to a set of textual problems and variant readings, on the one side, and to a theory for computer analysis, out of all phase with the substance of matters, on the other. What I shall show is how nihilistic scholarship denies the very integrity of the texts of Judaism, their textuality, and how the accompanying Computer scholarship dismisses the contents of the texts in favor of their formal characteristics, classifying instead of analyzing the components of the documents. Then Judaism persists as a set of empty formalities, just as theologian-scholars of religion have always made it out to be: a dead religion.

I. *The Goldberg-Schäfer School*

The school founded by Arnold Maria Goldberg, a German Jewish convert to Catholic Christianity, and Peter Schäfer, his student and heir, finds itself fixated on the problem of manuscript variants. The Goldberg-Schäfer school insists that, by reason of the broad variation in readings of this or that manuscript or passage, no substantive historical work can be carried on in the study of Rabbinic Judaism. We have variant readings but no text to study for context and analyze for

---

[1] See *The Place of the Tosefta in the Halakhah of Formative Judaism. What Alberdina Houtman Didn't Notice* (Atlanta, 1998: Scholars Press for South Florida Studies in the History of Judaism). The argument of that book is summarized below.

matrix in a religious system of a given time and place—only an accumulation of diverse wordings of we-know-not-what. In the context of the profoundly historicistic Germany academy in which that judgment is set forth, such a position removes from the realm of active culture and contemporary discourse the entire presence of Judaism, embodied as it is in its classical, Rabbinic documents. It is, therefore, a nihilistic position, which reduces scholarship to computerization of manuscript variations and the consequent reproduction thereof— without judgment, indeed, without palpable purpose. In the Goldberg-Schäfer school, no historical work, no history of ideas, no investigation of the context for the text, can take place, for we have no text. My own work explicitly dismissed because, in Schäfer's view, I posit a text that can be studied historically, I found it necessary to take an interest in his criticism, to see what is to be learned from it.

The one thing no one had to learn from Schäfer was that the various documents come to us in diverse versions. Along with everybody else, I was taught to take account of variants, large and small. That is why, from the very beginning of the documentary method,[2] I took account of the problem of determining that on which I was working, taking full account of the uncertainty of the text tradition for any given passage or even for documents as a whole. Indeed, the uncertainty of readings in any one passage provoked the search for recurrent and large-scale formal uniformities. For the case of the Mishnah, for example, the method focused upon the characteristics that recur throughout a document, not on the details that appear only here or there. Not episodic but fixed traits of form therefore dictated the analytical procedures: recurrent patterns in rhetoric, definitive traits in the principles of logical coherence in holding together compositions in composites, composites in a whole and complete statement.

At no point does my description of a document rest upon a specific reading or unique traits that occur in some one place. On the con-

---

[2] Spelled out in *Introduction to Rabbinic Literature* (New York, 1994: Doubleday. The Doubleday Anchor Reference Library), and see also *The Documentary Foundation of Rabbinic Culture. Mopping Up after Debates with Gerald L. Bruns, S.J.D. Cohen, Arnold Maria Goldberg, Susan Handelman, Christine Hayes, James Kugel, Peter Schäfer, Eliezer Segal, E.P. Sanders, and Lawrence H. Schiffman* (Atlanta, 1995: Scholars Press for South Florida Studies in the History of Judaism).

trary, the very essence of the documentary method is to describe the whole, and that means, traits that are uniform throughout. By definition, these traits of the document as a whole also will characterize the diverse manuscript evidence of the bits and pieces of the part, and no one who has examined the problem of the text of the Mishnah can fail to recognize that simple fact! That focus on the permanent, the recurrent, and the characteristic and definitive takes full account of variations of detail. It goes without saying that no thesis on the history of the religion set forth in a given document can rest securely on the foundations of one reading as against some other, any more than we can rely for facts on attributions of sayings to specific named sages, on the one side, or narratives of events involving them, on the other. Other data have to be identified, described, analyzed, and interpreted, for the study of history and of the history of the religion, Judaism.

Now, when we ask which text tradition, or which version, of a document we subject to documentary description, analysis, and interpretation, we therefore take up a question that by definition simply does not apply. For, as a matter of fact, every Rabbinic document we possess from the formative age, however diverse or fluid the text tradition on which we work, exhibits throughout its textual testimonies precisely those uniformities of rhetorical, topical, and logical traits that come under description in the documentary method. I cannot point to a single judgment of a documentary character set forth in any of my accounts that relies upon one reading rather than another. Where we have critical editions, it goes without saying I translate and analyze those versions, e.g., Theodor-Albeck for Genesis Rabbah, Finkelstein for Sifra and Sifre to Deuteronomy; where we do not, I work on the standard printed edition.

II. *The Theory of the Vacant Text [I]*

Goldberg and his student Schäfer have found themselves so impressed by the obstacles put forth by a fluid and sparse text tradition as to claim we have no documents at all, only variant readings. That nihilistic position—the theory of the vacant text—then defines the task of learning as the assembly of variant readings and the publication, with virtually no critical judgment, of a mass of this and that. Work of a historical and cultural character simply loses its bearings if we have no documents at all. Take for example Arnold Maria Goldberg, "Der Diskurs im babylonischen Talmud. Anregungen für eine Diskursanalyse," in *Frankfurter Judaistische Beiträge* 1983, 11, pp. 1-45: "Once it has been written, every text is exclusively synchronic, all the textual units exist simultaneously, and the only diachronic relation consists in the reception of the text as a sequence of textual units whose 'first' and 'then' become 'beforehand' and 'afterwards' in the reception of the text.... The synchronicity of a text is...the simultaneous juxtaposition of various units, independent of when the units originated."[3]

Schäfer proceeds, "This emphasis on a fundamental synchronicity of the texts of rabbinic literature is completely consistent with Goldberg's methodological approach. The text as it stands is exclusively synchronic and, since we cannot go back beyond this state, there remains only the classifying description of that which is there.... A historical differentiation is deliberately excluded, because in effect the texts do not permit it. Whilst analysis of the forms and functions of a text makes its system of rules transparent, 'the comprehension of rabbinic texts through habituation and insight could be superseded by a comprehension of the rules of this discourse as competence....'"[4]

Goldberg's dogmatic definition of matters notwithstanding, a sustained examination of the various documents leaves no doubt whatsoever that we can identify not only "beforehand" but "first," showing that the formation of composites out of fully-articulated compositions took place prior to the definition of a document's distinctive traits. Had Goldberg read my *The Formation of the Jewish Intellect. Making Connections and Drawing Conclusions in the Traditional System of Judaism*,[5] he would have found ample grounds, based on the logics of coherent discourse alone, to reconsider his position.

But now data that prove the exact opposite of Goldberg's premised position emerge fully and completely, for the Talmud, in my *The Talmud of Babylonia. An Academic Commentary*. Atlanta, 1994-1995: Scholars Press for *USF Academic Commentary Series*, and in its compan-

---

[3] Cited in Peter Schäfer, "Research into Rabbinic Literature," in *Journal of Jewish Studies* 1986, 37, p. 145.

[4] ibid., ad loc.

[5] Atlanta, 1988: Scholars Press for Brown Judaic Studies.

ion, *The Talmud of Babylonia. A Complete Outline.*[6] Not only so, but I have devoted *Initial Phases* to just this problem. [7] Why Goldberg takes the position that he does I cannot say, since it contradicts the facts of the characteristics of the documents he purportedly discusses. The facts that are set forth in *Academic Commentary, Complete Outline,* and *Initial Phases*, indicate that Goldberg certainly cannot have known through his own, first-hand analysis, a great deal about the literary traits of the Rabbinic literature as exemplified by the Bavli. For he seems to have confused a kind of abstract philosophizing with the concrete acts of detailed learning that scholarship requires. That explains why he left no imposing legacy of scholarship to sustain his opinion, which is at once doctrinaire and eccentric. Goldberg's nihilism has no continuators, except for his student, Peter Schäfer, and I do not see much basis on which to contend with his obscure and solipsistic legacy. We shall deal with Schäfer's own, equally nihilistic, position in due course.

I do not share Goldberg's position, because I have shown, on the exactly same basis of phenomenology on which he lays out his view, that the contrary is the fact. Having completed the work on the Talmud of Babylonia, the Talmud of the Land of Israel, a systematic comparison of the two, and then counterpart work on all of the Midrash-compilations of late antiquity,[8] I can state very simply: Goldberg is wrong. His position will not find in the other documents any support at all. The documents as we know them certainly encompass not only materials that serve the clearly-manifest program of the

---

[6] Atlanta, 1994-1995: Scholars Press for *USF Academic Commentary Series.*

[7] *The Initial Phases of the Talmud's Judaism* (Atlanta, 1995: Scholars Press for South Florida Studies in the History of Judaism): I. *Exegesis of Scripture.* II. *Exemplary Virtue.* III. *Social Ethics.* IV. *Theology.*

[8] *The Talmud of Babylonia. An Academic Commentary* (Atlanta, 1994-1996: Scholars Press for USF Academic Commentary Series); *The Talmud of Babylonia. A Complete Outline* (Atlanta, 1995-1996: Scholars Press for USF Academic Commentary Series); *The Talmud of the Land of Israel. An Academic Commentary to the Second, Third, and Fourth Divisions* (Atlanta, 1998-1999: Scholars Press for USF Academic Commentary Series); *The Talmud of The Land of Israel.. An Outline of the Second, Third, and Fourth Divisions* (Atlanta, 1995-1996: Scholars Press for USF Academic Commentary Series); *The Two Talmuds Compared* (Atlanta, 1995-1996: Scholars Press for USF Academic Commentary Series); *The Components of the Rabbinic Documents: From the Whole to the Parts* (Atlanta, 1997: Scholars Press for USF Academic Commentary Series); and *The Documentary Form-History of Rabbinic Literature. I. The Documentary Forms of the Mishnah* (Atlanta, 1998: Scholars Press for USF Academic Commentary Series).

framers or compilers of the documents, but also the self-evident interests of authors of compositions and framers of composites who had other plans than those realized in the documents as we have them. But the question is, how do we identify components of a composition, or of a composite, that took shape outside of the documentary framework and prior to the definition of the documentary traits of a given compilation? Unless we take at face value the attributions of sayings to specific, named authorities at determinate times and places, we must work by paying close attention to the material traits of the compositions and composites. That requires moving from the end-product backward and inward—and in no other way. Two intellectually lazy ways have led nowhere, Goldberg's denial that it is a question, and the Israelis' insistence that attributions *eo ipse* equal facts. Finding no promise in such labor-saving devices—settling questions by decree—I have resorted to sifting the facts, and that is what I have done and now do.

III. *Schäfer's Own Anti-Textualism*

This brings us to the explicit statement of Schäfer that we have no documents, just variant readings.[9] Schäfer's statement of matters proves murky and obscure, so exact citation of his language is required, lest I be thought to caricature or exaggerate the full confusion that envelopes his position. For the purpose of a proper *Auseinandersetzung*, let me cite his exact language, beginning with his critique of Goldberg and pronouncement of a still more extreme position; I number those paragraphs that I shall discuss below.

> 1. The question that arises here is obviously what is meant by "texts."
> What is the text "once it has been written"—the Babylonian Talmud, the Midrash, a definite Midrash, all Midrashim, or even the whole of rabbinic literature as a synchronic textual continuum whose inherent system of rules it is necessary to describe? Indeed, in such a description, neither the concrete text concerned, nor the form a particular textual tradition takes, needs to be important. Every text is as good—or rather as bad—as every other, the "best" being presumably the one representing the latest redactional stage.

---

[9] "Research into Rabbinic Literature," in *Journal of Jewish Studies* 1986, 37, pp. 145ff.

2. But this is precisely where the problem begins. Goldberg himself must finally decide on one text, and, in doing so...must decide against or for several other texts. Whether he wants to or not, he inevitably faces historical questions. This problem can be elucidated by the second line of research within the "literary" approach.

3. This second line of research...is that of the interpretation immanent in the work. Complete literary works are analyzed as a whole, as literary systems so to speak, and are examined for their characteristic arguments.... Neusner has ...sent to press such analyses.... The plane on which this research approach moves...is the final redaction of the respective work.... Two closely related problems arise from this.

4. The approach inevitably disregards the manuscript traditions of the work in question. But especially in the case of rabbinic literature, this is essential. Thus, to give an example, both Vatican manuscripts of the Bereshit Rabba...represent texts which are quite different from that of the London manuscript...The variations are sometimes so great that the redactional identity of the work is debatable. Is it meaningful to speak of one work at all, or rather of various recensions of a work? But then how do these recensions relate to one another? Are they different versions of one and the same text...or are they autonomous to a certain extent, and is Bereshit Rabba merely an ideal or a fictitious entity? What then constitutes the identity of the work "Bereshit Rabbah"? Any preserved manuscript or the modern "critical" edition by Theodor-Albeck....

5. The problem becomes more acute when the question of the boundaries of works is taken into consideration. To remain with the example of Bereshit Rabba, the problem of what relation Bereshit Rabba and the Yerushalmi bear to one another has been discussed since the time of Frankel.... How are Bereshit Rabba and Yerushalmi related to one another...? Does Bereshit Rabba quote Yerushalmi, i.e., can we regard Bereshit Rabba and Yerushalmi at the time of the redaction of Bereshit Rabba as two clearly distinguishable works, one of which being completed? Did the redactor of Bereshit Rabbah therefore "know" with what he was dealing and from what he was "quoting"? With regard to the Yerushalmi, this conclusion is obviously unreasonable, for we immediately have to ask how the Yerushalmi of the Bereshit Rabba is related to the Yerushalmi existent today. The Yerushalmi cannot have been "complete" at the time of the redaction of Bereshit Rabba since it is not identical to the one we use today.[10]

---

[10] Schäfer, pp. 146-147.

6. A brief reference to Hekhalot literature will constitute a last example. This is without doubt the prototype of a literature where the boundaries between the works are fluid. Every "work" in this literary genre that I have investigated more closely proves to be astonishingly unstable, falls into smaller and smaller editorial units, and cannot be precisely defined and delimited, either as it is or with reference to related literature. This finding is of course valid with regard to the works of Hekhalot literature to a varying degree, but can be generalized as a striking characteristic feature of the whole literary genre....[11]

7. The questioning of the redactional identity of the individual works of rabbinic literature inevitably also disavows the research approach to the work at the level of the final redaction. The terms with which we usually work—text, "Urtext," recension, tradition, citation, redaction, final redaction, work—prove to be fragile and hasty definitions that must be subsequently questioned. What is a "text" in rabbinic literature? Are there texts that can be defined and clearly delimited, or are there only basically "open" texts which elude temporal and redactional fixation? Have there ever been "Urtexte" of certain works with a development that could be traced and described? How do different recension of a "text" relate to one another with respect to the redactional identity of the text? How should the individual tradition, the smallest literary unit, be assessed in relation to the macroform of the "work" in which it appears? What is the meaning of the presence of parts of one "work" in another more or less delimitable "work"? Is this then a quotation in work X from work Y?

8. And finally what is redaction or final redaction? Are there several redactions of a "work"—in chronological order—but only one final redaction? What distinguishes redaction from final redaction? What lends authority to the redaction? Or is the final redaction merely the more or less incidental discontinuation of the manuscript tradition?[12]

Enough of Schäfer's presentation has now been quoted to permit a simple statement in response.

The definition of a text is simply put forth: the "text" loses its quotation-marks when we describe, analyze, and interpret recurrent formal properties that occur in one document but not in some other, or, in the particular congeries at hand, not in any other. To state matters as required in the present context, we simply reverse the predicate and the subject, thus: a writing that exhibits definitive traits

---

[11] Ibid., p. 149.
[12] Ibid., pp. 149-150

of rhetoric, logic, and topic that occur in no other writing constitutes a text.

That simple definition permits us to respond to the long list of questions and to sort out the confusion that characterizes Schäfer's conception of matters. Let me systematically respond to his unsystematic formulation of his position, which, as we see at the end, rests heavily on his observations of an odd and unrepresentative writing, which may or may not originate in the Rabbinic canon at all.

[1] I shall stipulate that my "document" corresponds to Schäfer's "text." The rest of this paragraph is unintelligible to me. I do not grasp the distinctions that Schäfer thinks make a difference, e.g., between "a definite Midrash, all Midrashim, or even the whole of rabbinic literature...." Here he seems to me to shade over into sheer chaos. How the several following sentences relate to one another I cannot discern. I am baffled by the sense of his allegation, "Every text is as good—or rather as bad—as every other, the 'best' being presumably the one representing the latest redactional stage." It is not clear to me whether this is his view or one he imputes to someone else, and, as is clear, apart from Goldberg, I know no one to whom these words even pertain.

[2] Goldberg's comments leave no doubt on his meaning; he denies all possibility of historical or cultural research. This he says in so many words. As I said, in the context of German academic culture, such a result condemns the Rabbinic classics to the dustbin.

[3] Schäfer's characterization of my description ("for their characteristic arguments") proves uncomprehending. I define a document by appeal to the standard indicative traits of classic literary analysis: rhetoric, logic, topic. Rhetoric covers the forms of expression; logic the principles of coherent discourse; topic pertains to the prevailing program, hermeneutics, or even proposition of a given piece of writing. (Not all compilations can sustain such documentary analysis, Mekhilta—dubiously assigned to late antiquity to begin with—standing apart from all the other items in the Rabbinic canon, for instance.) Still, Schäfer is correct in his main point: I do focus on what in his terms is "the final redaction of the work," and, in my terms, the definitive congeries of traits distinctive to this complex of composites and no other.

[4] Here Schäfer spells out what he means by disregarding manuscript traditions, and he gives as his example the diverse versions of

Genesis Rabbah. But he would do well to address more directly the question of the occurrence of a single pericope in two or more documents. When we find such a case, are we able to identify the document to the definitive traits of which the pericope conforms? If we are, then we can safely describe the pericope within the framework of one document and not the other(s) in which it appears.

When Schäfer made these statements, they formed a set of fair and pertinent questions. But they have been answered, and whether or not Schäfer has found the answers persuasive (or has even understood them) I cannot say, since so far as I know, he has not followed up on this point at all. Indeed, his astonishing silence on this matter since he printed the paper at hand suggests that Schäfer is quite oblivious to work that raised precisely the question he asks—and answered it. I refer in particular to *From Tradition to Imitation. The Plan and Program of Pesiqta deRab Kahana and Pesiqta Rabbati*.[13] I raised that question when I reflected on Schäfer's problem and systematically addressed the challenge he set forth; that is why it is so disappointing to seek evidence of his serious response to the answer. There I am able to show that pericope common to both compilations conform to the definitive traits that characterize Pesiqta deRab Kahana and do not conform to those that characterize those pericopes of Pesiqta Rabbati that do not occur, also, in Pesiqta deRab Kahana.

[5] Here Schäfer wanders a bit, and his problem with "boundaries of works" suggests he cannot hold to a single subject. For the problem of the peripatetic pericope has nothing to do with that of the shared pericope. The entire range of questions he raises here reveals an underlying confusion, which can be overcome by detailed work, an examination of the specifics of matters; this Schäfer has never done for the matter at hand. But, at any rate, for reasons already stated, his questions have nothing to do with the documentary method.

[6] Schäfer here talks about that on which he is expert. His allegation about generalizing from the document he knows to those on which he has not worked therefore hardly demands serious consideration. He can be shown to be wrong in treating the one as in any way analogous, or even comparable, to the other. What he does not

---

[13] Atlanta, 1987: Scholars Press for Brown Judaic Studies.

know and cannot show, he here simply assumes as fact.

[7] This is the most egregious break in the strain of coherent argument, for here Schäfer confuses the pre-history of documents with the documents as we now know them. What I have said about the phenomenological inquiry into the pre-history of documents suffices to answer the questions that he raises. His questions are probably meant, in his mind, to form arguments in behalf of his fundamental proposition. In fact they are susceptible to clear answers; his labor-saving device of sending up obscure clouds of rhetorical questions accomplishes no good purpose. But for his instruction, let me take up his questions and address those that pertain to the documentary method.

[A] What is a "text" in Rabbinic literature? A text (= document) in Rabbinic literature is a writing that conforms to a distinctive set of definitive traits of rhetoric, topic, and logic.

[B] Are there texts that can be defined and clearly delimited, or are there only basically "open" texts which elude temporal and redactional fixation? The Rabbinic canon (with only a few exceptions) contains texts that can be defined and clearly delimited (from one another) by reference to the distinctive congeries of rhetoric, topic, and logic, characteristic of one but not the other, or characteristic solely of the one. We can establish sequence and order among these documents, determining what is primary to a given document because it conforms to the unique, definitive traits of that document. What Schäfer means by "open" texts I cannot say, so I do not know the answer to his "or"-question, but what I do grasp suggests he is reworking Goldberg's position.

[C] Have there ever been "Urtexte" of certain works with a development that could be traced and described? The answer to this question remains to be investigated, text by text (in my language: document by document).

I do not know the answer for most of the documents. I have done the work to state the answer for some of them. The Mishnah, it is clear, proves uniform through all but two of its tractates, Eduyyot and Abot. All the others conform to the single program of formulary traits, logical characteristics, modes of exposition and argument. That does not suggest that within the Mishnah are not already-completed compositions, utilized without much change; the contrary can be demonstrated on formal grounds alone. Forming compositions by appeal to the name of a single authority, as in Mishnah-tractate Kelim Chapter Twenty-Four, or by utilization of a single formulary pattern, as in Mishnah-tractates Arakhin and Megillah, or by illustration through diverse topics of a single abstract principle—all these other-than-standard modes of composition and composite-making do occur. But these ready-made items take up a tiny proportion of the whole and do not suggest the characteristics of an Urtext that would have held together numerous compositions and even composites of such an order. We may then posit (and many have posited) the existence of documents like the Mishnah but in competition with it, formed on other rhetorical, logical, and even topical bases than the Mishnah. But these do not stand in historical relationship with the Mishnah, e.g., forming a continuous, incremental tradition from some remote starting point onward to the Mishnah as we know it.

[D] How do different recensions of a "text" relate to one another with respect to the redactional identity of the text? This repeats Schäfer's earlier question, e.g., concerning Yerushalmi and Genesis Rabbah. Here by text he seems to mean a given saying or story that circulates from one document to another. Part of Schäfer's problem is imprecision in the use of terms, e.g., employing the same word when he means different things.

[E] How should the individual tradition, the smallest literary unit, be assessed in relation to the macroform of the "work" in which it appears? The answer to this question is both clear and not yet fully investigated. It is obvious that we move from the whole to the parts, so the individual composition (Schäfer's "tradition," whatever he can mean by that word) finds its place within the framework of the document's definitive characteristics. But the investigation of the traits of compositions and composites that stand autonomous of the documents in which they occur has only just begin, and only with the continuation and completion of my *Academic Commentary* will the data have been collected that permit us to deal with this question document by document. For the Bavli we have a set of viable answers; for no other document do I claim to know the answer. For the Mishnah I do not think that this is an urgent question, though it is a marginally relevant one.

[F] What is the meaning of the presence of parts of one "work" in another more or less delimitable "work"? Is this then a quotation in work X from work Y? The question of the composition or even composite that moves hither and yon is a variation of the question just now considered. My preliminary probe is in *The Peripatetic Saying: The Problem of the Thrice-Told Tale in Talmudic Literature* (Chico, 1985: Scholars Press for Brown Judaic Studies. Reprise and reworking of materials in *Development of a Legend; Rabbinic Traditions about the Pharisees before 70*, vols. I-III). Schäfer does not appear to know that work, which appeared long before the article under discussion here.

[G] And finally what is redaction or final redaction? Are there several redactions of a "work"—in chronological order—but only one final redaction? What distinguishes redaction from final redaction? What lends authority to the redaction? Or is the final redaction merely the more or less incidental discontinuation of the manuscript tradition? These questions suggest only more confusion in Schäfer's mind, and since I cannot fathom what he wants to know, or why he frames matters as he does, I also cannot presume to respond. If Schäfer spelled out with patience and care precisely what he wishes to know, others could follow his line of thought, e.g., what he means by "authority...redaction?" Schäfer makes such remarkable statements as the following: *And finally what is redaction or final redaction? What distinguishes redaction from final redaction?* What can he possibly mean by this set of questions? When we look at such unintelligible sentences as this, we wonder, indeed, whether Schäfer is not simply saying the same thing over and over again.

My best sense is that Schäfer has not reflected very deeply on the premises and arguments of the work he wishes to criticize; if he had, he would have grasped the monumental irrelevance of his critique. The formulation of his thought suggests to me not so much confusion as disengagement; the wordiness conceals imprecision, for we naturally assumed that each sentence bears its own thought and are not disposed to conclude that he is simply repeating himself. But one judgment surely pertains: in the end, Schäfer simply has not understood that, in taking account of precisely the considerations he raises, I formulated the form-analytical problem in such a way as to address the issue of the definition of a text. As I reflect his machine-gun bursts of questions and slowly examine each in turn, I find not so much a close engagement with issues as utter disengagement, an offhand contentiousness rather than a considered critique—in all, more silliness than sense. But Schäfer's inattention to how others have responded to precisely the problems he highlights finds its match in the case that comes next, which draws our attention to a failure even to grasp the sorts of data that yield the results of form-analysis.

IV. *The Empty Text [II]:*
What Happens When Texts Bear No Contents

An ambitious and deeply flawed dissertation presented at Utrecht University but explicitly situated by the author within the Goldberg-Schäfer school shows the results of the nihilism that characterizes that school's reading of Rabbinic Judaism.[14] The nihilism consists in two convictions. First, we may posit a condition contrary to fact and ignore the facts. Second, we may simply ignore the contents of documents in assessing their relationship, limiting our consideration to the formal traits of said documents. Both of these convictions stand for know-nothing-ism in the academy, hence, nihilism.

The first, and basic flaw in Dr. Houtman's monograph is simple. She has the odd notion that we may invent a condition contrary to fact and then conduct research to prove that that condition describes the fact. She wishes to show that we may read the Tosefta as a free-standing document, as though there were no Mishnah. (She does not doubt that the contrary also is the case.) Since she wants to know whether she may read the Tosefta as if the Mishnah did not exist, she does just that. She finds the Tosefta mostly intelligible, and she is happy with the arrangement of the Tosefta, which she sees as well ordered in its own terms. So if there were no Mishnah, the Tosefta would serve for the same purpose, the presentation of the law.

As to the "hypothesis" that the Tosefta is to be read as though the Mishnah did not exist, what is to be said? In fact we do have the Mishnah, and no plausible theory of the Tosefta can be formulated in contradiction to that fact. Not only so, but Houtman as much as admits that fact. Much of the evidence by her own analysis indicates

---

[14] Alberdina Houtman, *Mishnah and Tosefta. A Synoptic Comparison of the Tractates Berakhot and Shebiit* (Tübingen, 1996: J.C.B. Mohr [Paul Siebeck]), 225 pp.; Alberdina Houtman, *Mishnah and Tosefta. A Synoptic Comparison of the Tractates Berakhot and Shebiit. Appendix Volume. Synopsis of Tosefta and Mishnah Berakhot and Shebiit* (Tübingen, 1996: J.C.B. Mohr [Paul Siebeck]), 92 pp.

that the Tosefta must be read in relationship to the Mishnah. That is because, she admits, the Tosefta is comprised by various types of material, some of it free-standing, some not but dependent on the Mishnah, and some of it citing the Mishnah in so many words. Further, some of it is arranged in intelligible composites, some of it set forth in composites that derive cogency only from their relationship to the Mishnah (but that is something Houtman does not notice). In producing these results of hers, moreover, she recapitulates work complete and in print twenty years ago, part of which she knows but has not understood, part of which she does not appear even to have examined at all.

The second and devastating flaw is that she does not take account of the contents of the Mishnah or of the Tosefta and substitutes classification of formal traits for analysis of substantive statements in the two documents. Houtman wishes to ignore the substance of the documents and concentrate on the form. That explains why at no point does she ask about the relationship, as to logic and premise, between the law set forth in the Mishnah and the law set forth in the Tosefta. To do so, she would have had to study the halakhah of the documents—pay attention to matters of substance. She would, in other words, have had to enter into, to master the interiorities of the halakhah. Apart from her power to paraphrase what is clear in the text itself, however, she shows no halakhic acumen or perspicacity. That is why she can treat the Mishnah and the Tosefta as simply co-equal statements.

But had she looked at the sequence of statements of a halakhic character on a given topic (from the Mishnah to the Tosefta to the Yerushalmi to the Bavli, or, if she liked, from the Tosefta to the Mishnah and so on), she would have noticed that the Mishnah consistently sets forth what is logically, halakhically primary and fundamental, the Tosefta consistently amplifies, instantiates, and extends the Mishnah's generative halakhah, the Yerushalmi adds only little halakhah but much analysis, and the Bavli, less halakhah but still more analysis. For the Tosefta, Yerushalmi, and Bavli set forth only new details about the halakhic topic with its interior logic that the Mishnah has defined in its basic characteristics. The subsequent documents carry forward the exposition. As a matter of fact, the halakhic structure—topics, problematics—emerges nearly whole and complete in the Mishnah, to be refined and amplified and complemented later on, but never to be vastly reconstructed as to its generative categories. Reading the Tosefta outside out of relationship with the Mishnah—as if we had no Mishnah—as Houtman does proves possible only if we ignore all questions of content, as Houtman, alas, has done. Like others of the Goldberg-Schäfer School, Houtman treats nihilistically the religion, Judaism, that values the contents, the substance of these documents, not only the formal problems they manifest.

A single, brief instance, shows how the Mishnah declares the law, the Tosefta gives the reasons, clarifies the details, and otherwise complements and supplements the Mishnah's statements. In the present case the two Talmuds add no halakhah whatsoever, though their analysis of the Tosefta's clarification of the Mishnah proves compelling. We deal with Mishnah-tractate Berakhot 8:1ff., given in italic type, and the Tosefta's complement, in regular type:

M. 8:1   *In reciting the sequence of blessings for wine and the Sabbath, one blesses over the wine, and afterward one blesses over the day.*

T. 5:25   The reason is that it is [the presence of the cup of] wine [at the table] that provides the occasion for the Sanctification of the Day to be recited. The benediction over the wine is usual, while the benediction for the day is not usual [and that which is usual takes precedence over that which is infrequent].

M. 8:2-4   *In preparing to recite the Grace after the Meal, they mix the cup and afterward wash the hands. He dries his hands on the cloth and lays it on the pillow. They wash the hands, and afterward they clean the house.*

M. 8:5   *The sequence of blessings at the end of the Sabbath is: Light, and spices, and food, and Habdalah.*

T. 5:29   One who enters his house after the end of the Sabbath recites the benediction over the wine, the light, the spices and [then] recites [the] *Habdalah* [benediction]. And if he has but one cup [of wine], he sets it aside until after the meal and strings together all [these benedictions] after it [i.e., after the benediction for the meal]. One recites *Habdalah* at the end of the Sabbath, and at the end of festivals, and at the end of the Day of Atonement, and at the end of the Sabbath [which immediately precedes] a festival, and at the end of a festival [preceding] the intermediate days of the festival. One who is fluent [or, accustomed to doing so] recites many *Habdalot* [i.e., enumerates many kinds of separations in his *Habdalah* benediction, e.g., "Praised be Thou, O Lord...(1) who separates the holy from the profane, (2) who separates Israel from the nations, (3) who separates light from darkness...,"] and one who is not fluent recites one or two.

If we read the Tosefta as though there were no Mishnah, we should have no formidable problems in understanding the Tosefta. But, as we see, that begs the question. We do have the Mishnah, and we do have ample evidence that the framers of compositions located in the Tosefta responded to the contents of the Mishnah. Contrary to Dr. Houtman's preference, we really do have to pay attention to the contents of the texts, not only to their formal traits.

V. The Problem of Mishnah-Tosefta Relationships

Let us consider the state of the question before Dr. Houtman began her work. In completed research of my own,[15] I maintained that the Tosefta forms a problem in the unfolding of the writings of Judaism, since its importance lies in its relationship to three other documents, the Mishnah, which came earlier, and the Talmud of the Land of Israel and the Talmud of Babylonia, which were completed later on. The Tosefta does not present a system of its own, as does the Mishnah, nor does it present both an inherited system and one of its own, as do both Talmuds. Rather, like a vine on a trellis, the Tosefta rests upon the Mishnah, having no structure of its own; but it also bears fruit nourished by its own roots. A small fraction of the Tosefta's contents can have reached final formulation prior to the closure of the Mishnah, but most of the document either cites the Mishnah verbatim and comments upon it, or can be fully and completely understood only in light of the Mishnah even though the Mishnah is not cited verbatim. The Tosefta's materials, some formed

---

[15] *A History of the Mishnaic Law of Purities* (Leiden, 1974-1977: Brill), vols. I-XXII; *A History of the Mishnaic Law of Holy Things* (Leiden, 1979: Brill), vols. I-VI; *A History of the Mishnaic Law of Women* (Leiden, 1979-1980: Brill), vols. I-V; *A History of the Mishnaic Law of Appointed Times* (Leiden, 1981-1983: Brill), vols. I-V; *A History of the Mishnaic Law of Damages* (Leiden, 1983-1985: Brill), vols. I-V. My graduate students of that period did the work on the Mishnaic Law of Agriculture. The detailed analysis of Mishnah-Tosefta relationships for the whole of the Mishnah and the Tosefta therefore has been in print from 1974. Houtman not once refers to any of these forty-three volumes, not even *A History of the Mishnaic Law of Purities* (Leiden, 1977: Brill), vol. XXI. *The Redaction and Formulation of the Order of Purities in the Mishnah and Tosefta.* I should have thought that a computer-search would have lead her to a work on Mishnah-Tosefta relations that speaks of "redaction and formulation." That is why I have to dismiss her scholarship as incompetent.

into cogent composites, most incoherent and cogent not among themselves but only in relationship to the Mishnah, serve as the Mishnah's first commentary, first amplification, and first extension—that is, the initial Talmud, prior to the one done in the Land of Israel · by ca. 400 and the one completed in Babylonia by ca. 600.

The Tosefta, defined in relationship to the Mishnah—a process Houtman undertakes, as we shall see—contains three types of materials, two of them secondary to, therefore assuredly later than, the Mishnah's materials, the third autonomous of the Mishnah and therefore possibly deriving from the same period as the sayings compiled in the Mishnah.

The first type of materials contains a direct citation of the Mishnah followed by secondary discussion of the cited passage. That type of discourse certainly is post-Mishnaic, hence by definition Amoraic, as much as sayings of Samuel, Rab, Judah, and Yohanan, are Amoraic.

The second sort of materials depends for full and exhaustive meaning upon a passage of the Mishnah, although the corresponding statements of the Mishnah are not cited verbatim. That sort of discussion probably is post-Mishnaic, but much depends upon our exegesis. Accordingly, we may be less certain of the matter.

The third type of passage in the Tosefta stands completely independent of any corresponding passage of the Mishnah. This is in one of two ways. First, a fully-articulated pericope in the Tosefta may simply treat materials not discussed in a systematic way, or not discussed at all, in the Mishnah. That kind of pericope can as well reach us in the Mishnah as in the Tosefta, so far as the criterion of literary and redactional theory may come to apply. Second, a well-constructed passage of the Tosefta may cover a topic treated in the Mishnah but follow a program of inquiry not dealt with at all in the Mishnah. What the statements of the Tosefta treat, therefore, may prove relevant to the thematic program of the Mishnah but not to the analytical inquiry of the framers of the Mishnah. Such a passage, like the former sort, also may fit comfortably into the Mishnah. If any components of the received Tosefta derive from the second century, that is, the time of the framing of the Mishnah, it would be those of the third type.

In proportion, a rough guess would place less than a fifth of the Tosefta into this third type, well over a third of the whole into the first. In all, therefore, the Tosefta serves precisely as its name suggests, as a corpus of supplements—but of various kinds—to the Mishnah.

The Tosefta depends upon the Mishnah in yet another way. Its whole redactional framework, tractates and subdivisions alike, depends upon the Mishnah's. The Mishnah provides the lattice, the Tosefta, the vines. The rule (though with many exceptions) is that the Tosefta's discussion will follow the themes and problems of the Mishnah's program, much as the two Talmuds' treatments of the passage of the Mishnah are laid out along essentially the same lines as those of the Mishnah. The editorial work accordingly highlights the exegetical purpose of the framers of both the two Talmuds and the Tosefta. The whole serves as a massive and magnificent amplification of the Mishnah. In this regard, of course, the framers of the Tosefta may claim considerably greater success than those of the two Talmuds, since the Tosefta covers nearly all the tractates of the Mishnah, while neither Talmud treats more than two-thirds of them (and then not the same two-thirds).

But the Tosefta's redactors or arrangers tend to organize materials, within a given tractate, in line with two intersecting principles of arrangement. First, they follow the general outline of the Mishnah's treatment of a topic. Accordingly, if we set up a block of materials in the Tosefta side-by-side with a corresponding block of those of the Mishnah, we should discern roughly the same order of discourse. But, second, the Tosefta's arrangers also lay out their materials in accord with their own types. That is to say, they will tend:

(1) to keep as a group passages that cite and then comment upon the actual words of the Mishnah's base-passage, then
(2) to present passages that amplify in the Tosefta's own words opinions fully spelled out only in response to the Mishnah's statements, and, finally,
(3) to give at the end, and as a group, wholly independent and autonomous sayings and constructions of such sayings.

I stress that this redactional pattern may be shown only to be a tendency, a set of not-uncommon policies and preferences, not a fixed rule. But when we ask how the Tosefta's editors arranged their materials, it is not wholly accurate to answer that they follow the plan of the Mishnah's counterparts. There will be some attention, also, to the taxonomic traits of the units of discourse of which the Tosefta itself is constructed. That is why two distinct editorial principles come into play in explaining the arrangement of the whole.

When we turn from the definition of the Tosefta and of its editorial and redactional character to the contents of the document as a whole, the Mishnah once more governs the framework of description. For the Tosefta, as is already clear, stands nearly entirely within the circle of the Mishnah's interests, rarely asking questions about topics omitted altogether by the Mishnah's authors, always following the topical decisions on what to discuss as laid down by the founders of the whole. For our part, therefore, we cannot write about the Tosefta's theology or law, as though these constituted a system susceptible of description and interpretation independent of the Mishnah's system. At the same time, we must recognize that the exegetes of the Mishnah, in the Tosefta, and in the two Talmuds, stand apart from, and later than, the authors of the Mishnah itself.

Accordingly, the exegetes systematically say whatever they wish to say by attaching their ideas to a document earlier than their own and by making the principal document say what they wish to contribute. The system of expressing ideas through re-framing those of predecessors preserves the continuity of tradition and establishes a deep stability and order upon the culture framed by that tradition.

VI. *Houtman's Dissertation*

Alberdina Houtman's monograph claims to set forth "a new way of dealing with the problematic relationship between the Mishnah and the Tosefta." In prior work she finds the faults that the Mishnah is given "higher religious status," research has focused "on a single relationship in terms of unidirectional dependence," and "most of the comparative research was done on the textus receptus of the texts." That prior research identified multiple relationships she does not concede; had she done so, she would have had no dissertation, no "new methodology." But Houtman insists that she has worked out what she proclaims to be "a new methodology:"

> a computer-assisted analysis of the texts on the basis of the most important manuscript material, and a computer program was made for the compilation of different synopses. The program can take the Mishnah as a running text to which the Toseftan material is synoptically arranged, but it can also reverse the procedure. This enables an unbiased comparison of the two texts.

She then applies this methodology to Mishnah- and Tosefta-tractates

Berakhot and Shebiit. Her thesis is "the texts are interwoven so closely that it is almost possible to consider them as a single literary work." That statement will have pleased our sages of blessed memory, who, after all, did set forth the Mishnah, the Tosefta, and the Yerushalmi, or the Mishnah, the Tosefta, and the Bavli, as single literary works; that is how they wanted us to see the halakhah, and they were absolutely right. But Houtman has not set forth to prove our sages to have been right about what they created, namely, the halakhic corpus. She wants the computer to settle some scores of her own, to do so without reference to the contents of the documents. That is something that our sages cannot have approved, because in their view, the halakhah, not the media of the halakhah, is what mattered.

She begins with what she claims to be "a history of research." But her history (12 pp. in all!) shows she has read rather selectively. She assumes that before her, no one raised the question of complex relationships between materials in the Mishnah and those in the Tosefta. But, as I have just shown, in the decades before Houtman did her work, a systematic study of the entirety of the Mishnah and the Tosefta by myself and my students has shown in detail three relationships now indicated above: the Tosefta cites and glosses the Mishnah and makes no sense except in relationship to the Mishnah; the Tosefta amplifies materials in the Mishnah but can be understood on its own; and the Tosefta makes statements that stand entirely on their own and do not intersect in any way with the Mishnah's. Not only so, but the same study has shown the tendency, within the Tosefta, to arrange materials of these three types in distinct groups, first compositions in which Tosefta cites and glosses the Mishnah, then dependent, and finally autonomous compositions, all in a composite situated to match the Mishnah's. Houtman does not seem to grasp that that study has produced, without computers, a much more systematic and complete analysis of the two documents—not two tractates but all tractates!—than her work on two tractates has yielded, and her results (though not her claims for her results, let alone her interpretation) replicate existing work. Nor does she grasp that others, before her, have concluded that if the Mishnah is a highly crafted document, the Tosefta by the same criteria is not. In her own right, then, she presents the diverse relationships between statements in the two documents, some are called "parallel," some "supplementary," some "additional." But as is obvious, all she is doing is recapitulating long-available work, which she clearly has not dealt with in a scholarly manner. That is why what is important in the dissertation is not new, and what is new is trivial and mechanical—and, in the end, chimerical, for she wants us to pretend we do not have the Mishnah, but we do.

The reason that she has not benefited from prior research is that she has not paid much attention to it. Her summary is superficial and slipshod. She thinks hers is the first synoptic study, ignoring both prior episodic ones and also the complete one in the *History of the Mishnaic Law* series—forty-three volumes!—in print for nearly two decades now, but (predictably) not utilized by her. She knows my summaries (*The Tosefta: Its Structure and Its Sources* [Atlanta, 1986] and *Introduction to Rabbinic Literature* [N.Y., 1994]) but not the systematic and complete study. No wonder that she assigns to me a view I find incomplete: "the authors of the Tosefta cited or glossed the halakhot of the Mishnah or they simply alluded to them. However, Tosefta sometimes reproduced autonomous, obviously older material." That is her rather clumsy formulation of the results summarized above. The "summary" simply is fabricated to suit her purpose, which is to claim to innovate—with a computer, no less—when in fact she replicates results already systematically achieved for the entire Tosefta. The tripartite division of the materials, the systematic ordering of the several types—these she does not set forth in her account of my results. That is why she can praise Peter Schäfer's formulation of matters without recognizing that in 1986[16] he repeated my conclusions, in print for a decade by then: "Even on the level of the individual tractate, one constant factor determining the relation will not always emerge, but the individual tractate...will contain different material which, within the same tractate, requires different models of the relation between Mishnah and Tosefta." As readers will note, that is precisely the result I set forth from 1974 onward. By identifying the tripartite relationship between pericopes of the Mishnah and the

---

[16] "Research into Rabbinic Literature: An Attempt to Define the *Status Quaestionis*," in *Journal of Jewish Studies* 1986, 37, pp. 139-152.

Tosefta, I systematically proved exactly the point Schäfer takes as his own.[17]

Clearly, Houtman writes in haste, wishing to establish that she has something new to say, even at the cost of an incomplete reading of the prior literature—not the mark of mature scholarship. Now to what Houtman wishes to do on her own. She wishes to attempt a "two-way intertextual comparison." All she means by that mantric word, "intertextual," is "comparison between two text corpora." She wants to prepare two sets of textual comparisons ("synopses"), one with the Mishnah as running text and one with the Tosefta:

> For the one the arrangement of the Mishnah was accepted and the Tosefta material was arranged to it; for the other, the Tosefta was the point of departure and the Mishnah material was synoptically arranged to it. Only after studying both synopses could it be decided which synopsis illustrated the relationship in the best possible way.

I simply cannot understand what she means by the language, "which synopsis illustrated the relationship in the best possible way." What "relationship" does she have in mind, that of the discrete pericopes, that of the whole two documents, or that of something in between? And how are we going to know what is "the best possible way," unless she spells out all of the ways she has in mind and further explains what would indicate "the best"—the clearest, the most economical, or whatever. But, predictably, Houtman never spells out all of the "possible ways" of which the chosen one is the "best." This language is so imprecise as to be unintelligible; we simply cannot know what she means.

Here her ignorance of published scholarship shows. She notes that the Tosefta is four times larger than the Mishnah. She jumps to the conclusion, "So, even in the hypothetical case that each mishnah [she means, Mishnah-paragraph] had a complete parallel in the Tosefta, three quarters of the Tosefta had no complete parallel in the

---

[17] Still, by showing the tendency to order materials in a consistent manner, I also found reason to reach a conclusion, as to the documentary character of the Tosefta, different from his. In my view, the implication is that the Tosefta is a different sort of compilation from the Mishnah; if the latter is a document, the former is to be classified elsewhere.

Mishnah." Here again I find her language incomprehensible. What can she possibly mean by "parallel" or "complete parallel"? It is the fact that the Tosefta will present a systematic illustration of a principle stated by the Mishnah, or will instantiate and amplify the implications of a case in the Mishnah. Is this what she means by "a parallel"? But the words are not the same, or not the same throughout. So in such instances the Tosefta clarifies in many words what the Mishnah has stated in a few words. Then when the Tosefta proceeds, it will commonly restate what the Mishnah has said, now through a variety of instances; it may well introduce complications and distinctions, new cases, and the like. This material does not cite the Mishnah, and it can be comprehended in its own terms, but with the Mishnah in hand, we are able to make best sense of it. By "best sense," I mean, we are able to place the Tosefta's statements into the context of the halakhic principles that the Mishnah—and the Mishnah alone—has laid out in a generative formulation.

But to locate those instances of systematic clarification, the Tosefta by the Mishnah, formalities such as are identified by a computer hardly suffice. Rather, one has to pay attention to the contents of the Mishnah and to the substantive, not merely formal, relationship of what the Mishnah says to what the Tosefta says. This Houtman does not do, and her monograph never suggests that she could have conducted halakhic analysis had she recognized the need to do so. Her grasp of the halakhah is superficial, seldom transcending the capacity merely to paraphrase the words that are before us and perfectly clear on their own. When, then, I characterize the Tosefta as the Mishnah's first talmud, what I mean is that the Tosefta stands in relationship to the Mishnah as the two Talmuds (sometimes) stand in relationship to the Tosefta. None of this makes an impact on Houtman's formulation of matters, because, so far as I can see, she has a very limited understanding of the documents she claims to study, being able at best to paraphrase what they say, but not to analyze their contents, the logic of what is said, and how the logic of one document's statement relates to that of the other document's statement. I do not see how one can claim to analyze the relationship between two halakhic documents if one knows so little of the halakhah. Only if she reduces the whole to a matter of formalities can the computer do any work at all for her, but only if to begin with she brings to the halakhah an infirm grasp of matters could she conceive of doing what she has done, which is simply to ignore the substance of matters and to let the computer dispose of formalities.

She undertakes, then, to compose a hierarchy: parallels, supplementary, then additional material. Forthwith the computer program emerges:

> The material can be treated according to this inherent hierarchy: for a given sentence in the basis [sic] corpus, the reference corpus can be searched for a complete parallel. If there is a complete parallel, it is placed in a parallel column at the same level as the sentence of comparison. If there is no complete parallel, the reference corpus is searched for supplementary material. If there is, it is placed in the parallel column one level lower than the sentence of comparison. Subsequently, the reference corpus is searched for additional material. If there is any, it is placed one level below the supplementary material. If there is no supplementary material, the reference corpus is still searched for additional material. If there is additional material, it is placed one level below the sentence of comparison. The same procedure is followed if there is indeed parallel material.

There follows "a decision tree," leading to this conclusion: "if there is both supplementary and additional material, the supplementary material is given first and then the additional material. If there is only supplementary material, or only additional material, then it is reproduced one level below the sentence of comparison." And so on and so forth.

The computer enters in once she has tagged the materials:

> First, the tractates of the two corpora were studied on their own merits in a traditional literary manner. What are the topics of the tractate? Are these topics clustered? If so, how are they clustered? And how are the clusters for their part arranged? Did the compilers use literary means to embellish the texts or to emphasize the structures? If so, what are those means?

Then the computer accomplishes a quantitative analysis, involving word frequencies and indices "to establish which content words were highly frequent and where they occurred." Then she proceeded to the small units of the tractates:

> The nature of the halakhic tannaitic material, as found in both Mishnah and Tosefta, meant that these units could be classified as thematic, literary-thematic, or literary. A theme may be discussed without recognizable recurring literary traits, the binding element being purely thematic. Such a unit may be delimited by an inclusion or simply by its contrast with the

preceding and following subject matter. The collection of sentences may then be marked as a thematic unit.

And so on and so forth.

All of this work was to make possible tests of the arrangement of the material: "the Tosefta text could be used as a basis for comparison, to which the Mishnah material was attached synoptically, the Mishnah text could be used as a basis for comparison, to which the Tosefta material was attached synoptically; material could be selected from both corpora according to thematic or literary criteria, ignoring the original arrangement within the corpora." Why the computer was needed to deal with a mere two tractates I do not grasp; Zahavy and Newman, both of them highly computer literate, never imagined that they would find insight in a computer analysis of what they preferred to take up item by item, in rich, substantive detail. How then does Houtman interpret the synopsis?

> The synopsis enabled us to see at a glance where the texts agreed, and where and how they differed. Both aspects were relevant to the question of the relationship between the corpora...If the Tosefta were composed as a commentary on the Mishnah, one would expect that either every sentence it explained or commented upon would be repeated or none of them. To clarify possible reasons for parallelism, the literal rendering of the texts must be scrutinized and compared with variant readings in a search for minor difference that may throw light upon the question whether perhaps there was disagreement about the wording of the sentences.

As I said, for the paltry sample at hand, she has gone to a great deal of trouble to ask machines to do work that can take on weight and meaning only when issues of substance are addressed. She would have done better to spend her intellectual energy on the halakhah, not on epiphenomena of "Are these topics clustered?" and the like. The characteristics of her reading of prior scholarship extends, alas, to her program of research and its methodology.

When she reaches the tractates themselves, she wants to know whether the Tosefta tractate "proves readable and intelligible as it is, without falling back on the Mishnah." Had she asked me, I would have answered, some of it is, some isn't, some may be. Others who have worked on the problem have produced the same results, though worded differently. Consulting completed research would have told her that some passages are readable and intelligible as is, some are not, and some are intelligible as is but still more consequential in dialogue with the Mishnah. She does not pay attention to content and therefore she cannot deal with that third possibility at all, even though, I have shown, fully half of the Tosefta falls into that interstitial category of rhetorical independence, but substantive dependence. In other words, Houtman wants to pretend that the Mishnah does not exist, except when she concedes that it does.

Her discussion from this point deals with the Tosefta. Only in her appendix does she give (in Hebrew) the texts that she discusses. As a result, we have to refer back and forth, and the whole is exceedingly difficult to follow. As to the substance of her presentation of the Tosefta, unit by unit, I state very flatly, there is much less here than meets the eye. The theses announced at the outset are forgotten more often than not. Houtman talks about what she wants to talk about, and there is no predicting what, at any point, that might be. She seems to intend a commentary to the language of the Tosefta, but the program of the commentary is so diffuse and confused that little comes of it all. Then there is a good deal of sheer paraphrase, the necessity of which a translation would have obviated. So we are left with a great deal of "X says this...Y says that...," which is to say, she tells us what the text says, as though we do not know the text. But an absence of intellectual energy leaves her satisfied with quite paltry results. She concludes, "Tosefta Berakhot is for the most part readable without other material. The tractate is well arranged. The sequence of topics is logical...."

But these conclusions, which are incontestable, also beg the question. She wants to know about the relationship between the Mishnah and the Tosefta. No one questions that the Tosefta is for the most part "readable without other material." But by "readable" she seems to mean, simply, a statement that is comprehensible in its own terms. As I said at the outset, I estimate that a sixth of the Tosefta cites and glosses the Mishnah, so, by that estimate, five sixths conform to her conclusion, and I should guess that part of that last sixth could be understood as well (e.g., the Tosefta's citations and glosses of Mishnah-tractate Berakhot Chapter Eight are so fully spelled out that on their own they make perfect sense). In other words, Houtman has proven that the wheel is round. But she has not shown how to use it for transportation.

She has no difficulty in proving that the Mishnah-tractate (in context: Berakhot) also is an "autonomous literary production." I cannot think of anyone who has thought otherwise, not now, and not for the last fifteen centuries, nor does she name her imagined opponent. So here she wants to reinvent the same wheel everyone has been using all along. Once more, the "commentary" is prolix and diffuse, commenting on this, that, and the other thing. One main conclusion is, "There are no instances in Mishnah Berakhot where the formulation of the text suggests that it comments on other texts or refers to them. Nevertheless, there are a few instances where the text is hardly comprehensible without some extra information." Indeed so, as the earliest Amoraim noticed a long time ago.

Houtman's "synoptic reading of Tosefta and Mishnah Berakhot," consequent upon her reading of each as autonomous literary productions, concludes:

> Both works were indeed independent in that each work could be read and understood without the help of the other. At the same time, however, each work presented some literary difficulties. They were comprehensible at a halakhic level, though there were some scars and irregularities at a literary level.

Now comes the issue of relationship: "By considering the synopsis as if the two columns form one compound work—note: consisting of either a basic text with explanatory additions and supplements or of two parts of an originally larger corpus—we will try to establish whether this premise [that the two works have relations with each other] is tenable."

The synopsis treats "the Mishnah as the running text, with toseftan material arranged to it," then "the Tosefta as running text and the mishnaic material arranged to it." In doing so, Houtman found that it was not necessary to do so:

> "first, the arrangement of the topics in Tosefta and Mishnah Berakhot was similar. But besides this similarity, each corpus had also its own preferences and peculiarities, the one stressing a certain aspect more than the other. There were also topics discussed in only one of the two corpora. Therefore it was considered prudent occasionally to combine some slightly different units into a larger unit of a more general nature in order to show how the two corpora relate to each other. The original arrangement could be maintained anyway. So a preference for the one or the other was not necessary.

What I take this rather obscure language to mean is more or less the same thing just now set forth, that is, we can indeed read the two documents each on its own. If she wanted to compare the Mishnah and the Tosefta as programmatic statements, all she had to do was outline them—in full, not just in key-words as she does—and set up the outlines side by side, as I did for the two Talmuds (in fourteen volumes in *The Two Talmuds Compared*).[18]

Her other conclusion is more important:

> It turned out to be undesirable to choose for one or the other of the synopses. Under the procedure of compiling a synopsis..., taking one of the texts as a starting point automatically causes that text to take the lead in the discourse on a certain topic. If the collation of material within a unit is studied closely in the two synopses, it turns out that the discourse sometimes has a better inner logic with the Tosefta as a starting point and sometimes with the Mishnah. I therefore decided to rearrange the material within the units in a way that renders the most logical discourse. So in some units, the Tosefta takes the lead in the discussion and in other units the Mishnah. This presentation reflects my conclusion that it is not systematically one of the two texts that opens the discussion on a certain topic and the other that always supplements it or comments upon it.

This is the heart of her monograph.

Much depends, then on which comes first, the Mishnah or the Tosefta, as Houtman's "logic" dictates. So far as the monograph ever undertakes to meet an intellectual and substantive challenge, not just to compare matters of formality, this is the point at which the challenge arises. Here, therefore, I looked with special care to identify a passage in which Houtman's own logic dictates that the Tosefta's version "renders the most logical discourse." Her reading of the Tosefta as the baseline, the Mishnah as secondary, yields not a single case. What she alleges she never demonstrates, in so many words, in a coherent argument, start to finish. Not once. She apparently thinks that if she says something, it is so. The upshot is disheartening. Houtman promises an exercise in "logic," which will explain why she thinks she will demonstrate that Tosefta takes the lead here, the Mishnah there. I find myself unable to point to the passages in which

---

[18] Atlanta, 1995-6: Scholars Press for USF Academic Commentary Series.

she does so. Or perhaps she means by the language she uses something other than what she leads us to anticipate.

Still, our sages will have taken pleasure in her results, though not for her reasons. She concludes:

> The texts of Mishnah and Tosefta Berakhot are closely interwoven, even to the extent that they might almost be considered one literary work. This close connection reveals itself among other things in the parallel arrangement of the material. Moreover most of the passages marked as problematic in the independent reading of Tosefta and Mishnah Berakhot are elucidated when the two texts are read synoptically [all she means is: side by side].

I wonder whether the framers of any tractate of either Talmud will want to differ, since that is precisely how they represent matters, citing the Mishnah and the Tosefta out of all documentary context and treating their formulations of a given halakhah, along side formulations not situated in either document ("beraitot"), as part of a single, seamless fabric of halakhah. But that has no bearing upon the question at hand, which—by her own word—concerns not how the documents might be read, but how they have been represented, as autonomous and free-standing statements (in the case of the Mishnah) or as partly autonomous, partly contingent and dependent, statements (in the case of the Tosefta). So too, they come to us, each with its own distinctive documentary traits. But Houtman's computer was not programmed to pick up these traits.

If her results produce a rather dubious picture, her conclusion also yields one incontrovertible result. She finds that the Mishnah-Tosefta relationships are complex, yielding these results: the Tosefta agrees verbatim with the Mishnah or varies only slightly; the Tosefta augments the Mishnah with glosses and discussions; the Tosefta functions like a commentary on unquoted Mishnah material; the Tosefta offers additional substance without direct reference to material in common with the Mishnah; the Tosefta discusses topics that do not occur in the Mishnah; the Tosefta opens a discussion with a general rule after which both the Mishnah and the Tosefta treat the subject in more detail, and so on and so forth. As I said, here she assembles much detail that replicates exactly the results I set forth in my *History of the Mishnaic Law*.

The book is a good bit longer than it has to be, because Houtman addresses problems of text-tradition that have no bearing upon her thesis; the chapter on Berakhot (so too the one on Shebiit) is then padded with a sizable portion of irrelevant charts and pointless calculations.

It remains to observe that Houtman simply ignores all problems of textual formulation. Treating the Tosefta's materials as free-standing certainly saved her much work and made it easy to prove the point she wished to demonstrate. But then she asks us to accept a thesis that dismisses a vast amount of relevant evidence. Formulations of rules that occur in the Tosefta find counterparts in other documents, however, and reading the Tosefta out of all relationship with corresponding citations of the same sayings produces no viable thesis at all, but only an empty exercise in vacuous verbiage. Take for instance the fine statement of the facts of the matter by M.D. Herr, whose *Encyclopaedia Judaica* entries are the starting point for research on these matters:

> Very often a baraita quoted in the Talmud in a corrupt form is found in the Tosefta in its original coherent form. Furthermore, very often there is a discussion in the Talmud about the exact meaning of the words of a certain tanna (either in the Mishnah or in the baraita), while the parallel statement as found in the Tosefta is manifestly clear. It would therefore seem obvious that the Tosefta in its present form was not edited before the end of the fourth century c.e. and cannot therefore be identified with any of the...earlier collections of beraitot. It is certain that the Tosefta was composed in Erez Israel, since the beraitot which it contains resemble more those of the Jerusalem Talmud than those of the Babylonian Talmud.[19]

At no point does Houtman address the question of the relationship between formulations of rules set forth by the Tosefta and the corresponding formulations in cognate documents. None of this matters to her. It would have taken a lot of bother to compare formulations in not only the Mishnah and the Tosefta but the Tannaite Midrash-compilations, the baraitot of the two Talmuds, and the numerous other formulations of halakhah on the same issue or principle that the Mishnah and the Tosefta set forth. I can state, as a matter of theory, what she will have found for them all: "The texts [supply:] of the

---

[19] *Encyclopaedia Judaica*, vol. 15, cols. 1283-1285. In the nearly three decades since the publication of that article, I have seen no other than has superseded it when it comes to the dating of the documents and the positioning of the contents in relationship to one another.

halakhah bearing Tannaite *sigla* are closely interwoven, even to the extent that they might almost be considered one literary work." All depends then upon the "almost." That is where rigorous scholarship begins.

This brings us to the appendix volume, *Synopsis of Tosefta and Mishnah.* By "synoptic," all Houtman means is, "a research tool that affords a broad view of the parallel and non-parallel material of different texts" (p. 4). But why call it "parallel...non-parallel" synoptic, when all she means is a side by side comparison of documents? When she gives her "synoptic comparison," she does just that. Houtman's *Synoptic Comparison,* circulated as an appendix, presents the Hebrew texts, the two documents being laid out in relationship with one another. She found "the number and character of variant readings did not justify an extended synopsis." She uses Kaufman for the Mishnah, Vienna for the Tosefta. She gives the Mishnah at the right, the Tosefta at the left: "As the discussion on a certain topic is usually started by the Mishnah, the Mishnah text was printed in the column on the right side, and the Tosefta text on the left side."

Houtman cannot be accused of an excess of humility when she (predictably) rejects out of hand *all* emendations of Saul Lieberman, saying, "My reason was that 'apparent' is not the same as 'obvious.' The emendations suggested by Lieberman are not always irrefutable. Therefore I have chosen to leave the assessment of the text to the reader." This is pure fakery—an excuse and not a reason. For she has not done the work of explaining why she deems Lieberman's hundreds, even thousands, of proposals to be "refutable." Granted that Saul Lieberman exhibited in his work striking intellectual flaws and limitations—and who does not?—I find it simply appalling that his monumental *oeuvre* should be dismissed so casually, so irresponsibly.[20]

---

[20] Lieberman's exegetical genius in Tosefta studies is evident to all who have undertaken such studies. In connection with my *History of the Mishnaic Law,* I worked through every line of Tosefet Rishonim and Tosefta Kipshutah's long commentary, and that is the basis for my judgment. I do not know the basis for Houtman's judgment. Lieberman's problem was that he could not think coherently or cogently, so his strength—episodic exegesis, based on free-association and huge erudition— also defines his weakness. His uncritical and often intellectually incompetent work in historical and literary problems is set forth in my *Why There Never Was a "Talmud of Caesarea." Saul Lieberman's Mistakes* (Atlanta, 1994: Scholars Press for South Florida Studies in the History of Judaism). The compelling quality of his exegetical work is acknowledged throughout my *History of the Mishnaic Law.*

Houtman marks herself as a person unable to pay respect to other scholars.

The appendix dismisses not only Lieberman but others who have done precisely the work at hand on exactly the same documents. Specifically, while citing their work, she does not give a hint that T. Zahavy, *The Mishnaic Law of Blessings and Prayers: Tractate Berakhot*[21] and L. Newman, *The Sanctity of the Seventh Year: A Study of Mishnah-tractate Shebiit*[22] have already done systematic and detailed comparison of the Mishnah and the Tosefta, unit by unit. The only difference is that they commented upon and explained the relationships between the corresponding statements in the one and the other, and Houtman says absolutely nothing in the context of the presentation of the texts. She discusses the texts in the main book, presents them in her appendix. She should have discussed the texts where she presented them. The upshot is a complete waste: a "comparison" where nothing is said about similarity and difference.

A huge amount of collecting and arranging has gone into a work that stands or falls not on the information that is gathered but on the analysis thereof. But of analysis there is precious little. What Houtman has produced is a work of enormous confusion. Part of the problem is that she writes in a foreign language, with a devastating consequence for precision and clarity. She would have done better to write in Dutch and have the work translated into English, so that, in her own language, she could have attained that level of grace and effect that in English she is unable to reach. As it is, I find myself unable to understand much of the theoretical intent of the book.

The upshot is that she has promised a great deal more than she has delivered, and I think the principal reason is her failure to master the scholarship prior to her own. She has not paid attention to work that addressed the same question and produced results that, to say the least, are competitive with the ones that she wished to set forth. The second reason is her halakhic incapacity. Reducing the work to a set of formal relationships solves all problems but the consequential ones.

---

[21] Atlanta, 1987: Scholars Press for Brown Judaic Studies.
[22] Chico, 1983: Scholars Press for Brown Judaic Studies.

As a result, she misses most of the interesting questions that still require systematic work, as her failure to carry out her promise to show how logic produces one arrangement, rather than another, of parallel pericopes in the two documents.

That explains why the work is prolix, disorganized, and full of empty information. Houtman simply does not advance the study of its problem. She would have done well to pursue her research on the Tosefta with specialists in the subject, perhaps in Jerusalem or Tel Aviv for example (Professor Ithamar Gruenwald at Tel Aviv University even now gives a seminar on this very subject!). But she ought at least to have mastered the scholarly literature and done her homework. That is why, if Dr. Houtman were to ask me what I consider to be the fundamental cause of her utter failure in this monograph, I should have to say, it is not intellectual sloth but her failure to read the work of others with care and in a systematic way and to try to cover the entire scholarly literature pertinent to her work. Her casual, unreasoned dismissal of Saul Lieberman tells the whole story. Her superficial and slipshod reading of the prior literature has lead her to believe that she could learn only by looking into the mirror and has persuaded her to suppose that scholarship consists in obscurely, verbosely, and promiscuously alleging what others have said clearly and economically—and the opposite thereof. In this exercise in scholarly solecism, Houtman has taken the easy way. But that is the nihilistic way taken by Middle European scholarship on Rabbinic Judaism. Schäfer wants us to believe we have no texts, just variant readings. Houtman then wishes to add that even if we had texts, they would have no contents, just formal traits awaiting classification.

VII. *Texts Do Bear Contents, which Make a Difference*

Houtman ignores that documents not only exhibit interesting formal traits but also make statements. And these statements bear meaning, so that we may ask which of them presupposes another of them, or where among the documents we find the most basic, the most consequential statements, and where we find only the results of principles set forth in some other writing. Consequently, if we wish to examine the relationships between kindred writings, we have to pay attention not only to style but substance. We have also to address the logic that governs the law, identifying statements that take priority, those that come later, in the unfolding of the sense of the halakhah.

Let me spell out how these obvious truths pertain to Houtman's problem: Mishnah-Tosefta, and Tosefta-Mishnah relationships. We have to ask whether the law of the Tosefta rests upon the logic set forth in the Mishnah or vice versa. Along these same lines, we have to identify the generative problematics of the halakhah and determine where the governing conceptions of what precipitates the exegesis of the law first surface, the Mishnah, the Tosefta, the Yerushalmi, or the Bavli. When we do, we may compare not only the forms of documents—the superficial traits of program and the like—but the interior construction of the halakhah. Then we may identify where, within that construction, the contribution of the several documents finds its place.

I regret to report that to none of these questions of a halakhic character does Houtman pay attention. She decided to make her mark by utilizing the computer in her research. She thought that computer research was required to permit reading the Mishnah against the base-line of the Tosefta as much as the Tosefta against the base-line of the Mishnah. But when it comes to matters of the halakhah and its logic and animating principles, computers cannot replace intellect, but acumen and perspicacity govern and shape taste and judgment. Neglecting that fact yields a genuinely unconvincing monograph.

When I read her dissertation on the relationship of the Tosefta and the Mishnah, I was in the midst of work of my own in which I was interested in setting forth a systematic statement of the repertoire of the halakhah of formative Judaism, the Mishnah, the Tosefta, the Yerushalmi, and the Bavli.[23] The halakhah was to be viewed as a single seamless statement. In other words, I had in mind a meta-documentary inquiry into the unfolding of the halakhah from its basic principles to its secondary and tertiary levels of development, the whole viewed as a logical, not a formal problem. This corpus of writings I examined not as a set of discrete literary entities but as a

---

[23] *The Halakhah of the Oral Torah. A Religious Commentary* (Atlanta, 1999-2000: Scholars Press for South Florida Studies in the History of Judaism), 24 vols.

continuous exposition of the law of a given topic. Accordingly, I determined to set aside the issues of documentary relationships and focus only on the presentation, by the documents read in sequence, of topical disquisitions of halakhah. What I noticed was two facts.

First, the Mishnah's statement of the halakhah always is fundamental to the exposition of the halakhah seen as a seamless system, the Tosefta's merely illuminating. The one pronounces the foundations of the halakhah, not just the topics but the principles that govern, the other clarifies the pronouncement. The Tosefta then amplifies and extends the Mishnah's halakhah and richly instantiates it, but rarely offers a halakhic principle at the fundamental character of the Mishnah's statement of the halakhah. Now that is a trait of the two documents that emerges only when we focus upon the substance of the halakhah, its logic and problematic. Treating the halakhic discourse as unitary and not fragmented into documents, I found that I could identify the Mishnah's contribution to the halakhah, viewed systematically, by its characteristics of logic and intellect, that is, by the basic and generative character of its statements. The Tosefta's contribution to the halakhah was equally susceptible of characterization. Viewed in the context of the topic of the halakhah and its systematic (not documentary) exposition, the Tosefta's statements did not precipitate inquiry but only amplified it, responding to a program of logical exposition of topics not present but presupposed in its own halakhic program.

Second, it turns out, by an examination of not the point of origin of a statement but of the content of the halakhic statements, seen side by side, but in any sequence (the Tosefta first, then the Mishnah, or even the Bavli first, then the Tosefta, then the Mishnah), by appeal to the characteristics of thought that register in what is said, we can readily place the several statements into the documents that follow the sequence, [1] the Mishnah, then [2] the Tosefta. What the Tosefta says often presupposes the principles set forth in the Mishnah, but what the Mishnah says rarely, if ever, presupposes principles (hermeneutics, exegetics) set forth in the Tosefta; that statement of logical relationships of the substance of the law can be evaluated only in a close reading of the details of the law in the seamless manner just now indicated. When we patiently review the halakhic pronouncements of the Mishnah, Tosefta, Yerushalmi, and Bavli, we consistently see the conceptual priority of the Mishnah in the halakhic process. The Tosefta commonly formulates large aggregates of facts in a cogent and felicitous construction; the Mishnah has its own work to do.

A specific test repeatedly yields that result. In those tractates that expound the law in response to a set of questions of a fundamental character that I call the generative problematics, where do we find the statement of that generative problematics? It is in the Mishnah, and so far as I have found to date, only in the Mishnah's statement of the halakhah. And, that fact established, we dismiss as silly the exercise of reading the Tosefta on its own, not in relationship to the Mishnah. That exercise requires that we pretend we have no Mishnah, but we do, and the rest follows.

Houtman's monograph thus illustrates what happens when people do not really grasp the halakhah but work on halakhic documents anyhow. They remark on unremarkable things and miss the important issues altogether. The result is a vast collection of useless and meaningless information. What is crucial is whether we are able to assess the relationships between documents solely on the basis of formal traits, or whether we must pay close attention to the substantive characteristics of those documents: what they say and what they mean. I do not exaggerate the consequence of what Houtman did not notice. She made the choice of resorting to computer analysis of two rather modest pieces of writing, which means she supposed that all she had to do was classify data, not think about them. Houtman seems to imagine that by a computer analysis, which by definition ignores all considerations of the contents of the writings, she can solve any problems at all. She is wrong, and her results leave no doubt that she is wrong. Computer research has merit in collating variant readings and other mechanical tasks. Computers cannot assess on the basis of the classification of formal evidence the logical relationships of documents and their substantive contents.

These are matters of broader erudition and more mature judgment and reflection than Houtman seems to me to possess. She knows a little bit about two modest and easy tractates. That explains why what she did not notice is that the Tosefta and the Mishnah make a great many substantive halakhic statements and set forth a halakhic topic through response to a system therewith that generates the details of the laws. Her computer work did not help her to identify what matters and what does not, with the result that she based her entire project on facts wildly irrelevant to her question concerning documentary autonomy. She shows that the documents are formally autonomous; each *can* be read in its own terms. She admits that is not wholly true for the Tosefta but it is entirely so for the Mishnah. I cannot point to a single scholar in the past hundred and fifty years who has reached any other conclusion. Can she?

What are the traits of the corpus of halakhah expounded by each compilation? That is to say, what would Houtman have noticed had she paid attention to the substance of the document and not only to its superficial, formal traits? Simply stated, the halakhic exposition of the Mishnah ordinarily finds in a topic a particular point of special interest; sages come with a set of governing principles, which they wish to lay out through the medium of halakhic discourse. The Mishnah is where these governing principles are laid out and exposed in full clarity. The Tosefta takes over the results—the halakhah that has been laid out—and gives numerous instances of the same few principles, or finds secondary and derivative points of clarification to contribute. If we read the Tosefta without the Mishnah, we receive information out of context. Houtman did not notice that, because her computer program paid no attention to the substance of the halakhah, its logic and its problematic.

It is the fact that most, though not all, Mishnah-tractates work out the implications of a generative problematic deemed to inhere in a given topic, a set of problems or questions that sages designate as what matter in the exposition of that topic. And, for the tractates for which we may identify a generative problematic that animates the exposition of the topic, that problematic comes to full exposure in the Mishnah, always in the Mishnah, and only in the Mishnah. The Tosefta for the tractates I have examined simply amplifies what the Mishnah says, and, in its free-standing compositions never contributes a statement that embodies a generative problematic of any sort: information without analysis or the stimulus of analysis. Seeing everything but the main thing, Houtman knows nothing of all this, because her examination of the tractates Berakhot and Shebiit does not extend to a penetrating account of what imparts to the law its dynamic. Admittedly, tractate Berakhot would not have signaled to her that the law unfolds in response to a generative problematic, but Shebiit certainly does. So she has indeed paid attention to the form but not the substance of the document.

But that is for a good reason. In its entirety, her claim that we may read the Tosefta without the Mishnah by its nature requires us to pay no attention to the character of the halakhah that the Mishnah and the Tosefta set forth. When we do, we may consistently characterize the halakhah of the Mishnah for the large-scale topics as primary and generative and that of the Tosefta as secondary and derivative. She says that we may read the Mishnah without the Tosefta and the Tosefta without the Mishnah. Indeed so. But what is proved by pretending that we have no Mishnah when we do? So hers is not a comparison, so much as an evasion. And the fact is, we can understand the Mishnah without the Tosefta, meaning, we can identify the generative problematic that defines sages' exposition of a given topic, the problems they find worthy of close attention, the hermeneutics that defines their exegetical program. But we cannot understand the Tosefta without the Mishnah, meaning not simply make sense of its sentences but rather account for the character of its halakhah.

So while it is the fact that much of the Tosefta can be read on its own, not in relationship to the Mishnah, and all of the Mishnah can be read on its own, not in relationship to the Tosefta, it is also the fact that we do not have the occasion to read the one without the other. That is because we do have both, and gain nothing by pretending we do not. And when we read the two in relationship with one another, we deal with matters of substance, not form alone. And then we see that the Mishnah is primary and generative, the Tosefta secondary and derivative. It suffices to state that the problematics of the halakhah emerges wholly in the formulation of the Mishnah and not a single component makes its initial appearance in the Tosefta. To read the Tosefta out of phase with the Mishnah is indeed quite feasible, as Houtman alleges. But it is to miss the point of the halakhah— and to misconstrue the character of the Tosefta. When nihilistic scholarship on Rabbinic Judaism begins with the premise of the empty text, it ends with the hopeless results that Houtman has published.

V. THE TARGUMIM AND JUDAISM OF
THE FIRST CENTURY

Bruce Chilton
Bard College

The term "targum" simply means "translation" in Aramaic, but the type and purpose of the rendering involved differs enormously within the available corpus. The general phenomenon of targum needs to be appreciated, and the specific documents involved (Targumim) need to be described, before the question of targumic development within the first century may be taken up.

Aramaic survived the demise of the Persian Empire as a *lingua franca* in the Near East. It had been embraced enthusiastically by Jews (as by other peoples, such as Nabateans and Palmyrenes), and the Aramaic portions of the Hebrew Bible (in Ezra and Daniel) testify to a significant change in the linguistic constitution of Judaism. Abraham himself, of course, had been an Aramaean, although the variants of the Aramaic language during its history are stunning. Conceivably, one reason for Jewish enthusiasm in embracing Aramaic was a distant memory of its affiliation with Hebrew, but it should always be borne in mind that Hebrew is quite a different language. By the time of Jesus, Aramaic appears to have been the common language of Judea, Samaria, and Galilee (although distinctive dialects were spoken); Hebrew was understood by an educated (and perhaps nationalistic) stratum of the population, and some familiarity with Greek (and even Latin) was a cultural—and especially a commercial and bureaucratic—necessity. As the principal language of Jewish, agricultural Galilee, however, the place of Aramaic has been well established.

The linguistic situation in Judea and Galilee demanded that translation be effected for the purpose of popular study and worship. Although, in that they are translations, fragments of Leviticus and Job in Aramaic discovered at Qumran are technically targumim, the fact is that they are unrepresentative of the genre "targum" in literary terms. They are reasonably "literal" renderings; that is, there is some attempt at formal correspondence between the Hebrew rendered and the Aramaic that is presented. The Targumim that are extant as documents deliberately guarded within Rabbinic Judaism are of an altogether different character.

In that the aim of targumic production was to give the sense of the Hebrew Scriptures, paraphrase is characteristic of the Targumim. Theoretically, a passage of Scripture was to be rendered orally by an interpreter (*meturgeman*) after the reading in Hebrew; the *meturgeman* was not to be confused with the reader, lest the congregation mistake the interpretation with the original text (cf., M. Meg. 4:4-10 and B. Meg. 23b-25b). (Regulations specifying the number of verses that may be read prior to the delivery of a targum probably date from the Talmudic period.) Although the renderings so delivered were oral in principle, over the course of time, traditions in important centers of learning became fixed, and coalescence became possible. Moreover, the emergence of the rabbis as the dominant leaders within Judaism after 70 C.E. provided a centralizing tendency without which literary Targumim would never have been produced. The Targums preserved by the rabbis are notoriously difficult to characterize. They are paraphrases, but the theological programs conveyed are not always consistent, even within a given Targum.

Although the rabbis attempted to control targumic activity, the extant Targumim themselves sometimes contradict Rabbinic proscriptions. For example, M. Meg. 4:9 insists that Lev. 18:21 ("You must not give of your seed, to deliver it to Moloch") should not be interpreted in respect of sexual intercourse with gentiles; the Targum Pseudo-Jonathan—a late work, produced long after Rabbinic authority had been established—takes just that line. The Targumim evince such oddities because to a significant extent they are the products of a dialectical interaction between folk practice and Rabbinic supervision—sometimes mediated through a love for dramatic speculation, a dynamic tension that continued over centuries. All of the extant Targumim crystallize that relationship at the moments their constituent traditions were formed.

The Targumim may conveniently be divided among those of the Torah (the Pentateuch), those of the Prophets (both "Former Prophets," or the so-called historical works, and the "Latter Prophets," or the Prophets as commonly designated in English), and those of the Writings (or Hagiographa), following the conventional designations of the Hebrew Bible in Judaism. The fact needs to be stressed at the outset, however, that although the Hebrew Bible is almost entirely rendered by the Targumim in aggregate, there was no single moment, and no particular movement, that produced a comprehensive Bible in Aramaic. The Targumim are essentially complex in proveniences, purposes, and dialects of Aramaic.

Pentateuchal Targumim

Among the Targumim to the Pentateuch, Targum Onqelos is a suitable point of departure. Onqelos appears to correspond best of all the Targumim to Rabbinic ideals of translation. Although paraphrase is evident, especially in order to describe God and revelation in suitably reverent terms, the high degree of correspondence with the Hebrew of the Masoretic Text (and, in all probability, with the Hebrew text current in antiquity) is striking. The dialect of Onqelos represents a literary transition between biblical Aramaic and Talmudic Aramaic. For that reason, it has been called "Middle Aramaic,"[1] but in view of

---

[1] For an approach that has become standard, see J.A. Fitzmyer, *Essays on the Semitic Background of the New Testament* (Missoula, 1974); *A Wandering Aramean. Collected Aramaic Essays* (Missoula, 1979). My own outline of the development of the language departs from his, in placing Judaic dialects within a more comprehensive context:

Ancient Aramaic (1100-500 B.C.E) is in fact attested over a wider period than Fitzmyer suggests and had become a *lingua franca* (and was certainly "official") prior to the period of the Persians.

Imperial Aramaic (500-200 B.C.E.) shows the very clear influence of Babylonian forms, introduced and made remarkably standard by Darius's decision to use Aramaic as the language of the Achaemenid administration. The biblical Aramaic of Ezra and Daniel reflects both Imperial Aramaic and its modulation into what followed.

Transitional Aramaic (200 B.C.E.-200 C.E.) embraces the various dialects (Hasmonean, Nabatean, Palmyrene, Arsacid, Essene, as well as Targumic) that came to be used during the period.

In *Regional Aramaic* (200 C.E.-700 C.E.) "Eastern" and "Western" emerge as the principal way of categorizing dialects once the dialects are freed from the standards of Imperial Aramaic. This is most obvious with the emergence of Syriac in Osrhoene during the second century as a principal form of Eastern Aramaic, but also of Samaritan Aramaic and Galilean as examples of Western Aramaic. The typology only becomes stronger with the later development in the east of a Christian literature in Syriac, and of Talmudic Aramaic and Mandean. In the west, Samaritans and Christians continued to develop their own dialects, and Galilean Aramaic emerges in Judaism.

Academic Aramaic (700 C.E.-1500 C.E.) is a category that has not been considered, but the fact is that Rabbinic scribal and liturgical activity was significant during the Middle Ages and came to dominate the form of the language then current in academic circles. After the period of the Muslim conquests in the seventh century and later, Arabic supplanted Aramaic as the *lingua franca* of the Near East, and Aramaic became a more academic language within Judaism.

its literary persistence (attested by its usage), I think it is better described as Transitional Aramaic. Under either designation, a current understanding of the linguistic evidence would place the Targum between the first century B.C.E. and the third century C.E. It should be dated towards the end of that period, in the wake of similar efforts to produce a literal Greek rendering during the second century and well after any strict construal of the principle that targumim were to be oral. By contrast with the Rabbinic ethos that permitted the creation and preservation of Onqelos, one might recall the story of Gamaliel, who is said during the first century to have immured a Targum of Job in a wall of the Temple (B. Shab. 115a).

The Targum Neophyti I was discovered in 1949 by Alejandro Díez Macho in what was called the Library of the Neophytes in Rome. The paraphrases of Neophyti are substantially different from those of Onqelos. Entire paragraphs are added, as when Cain and Abel argue in the field prior to the first case of murder (Gen. 4:8);[2] the rendering is looser overall, and it is impossible to predict when remarkable freedom is to be indulged. The dialect of Neophyti is conventionally known as "Palestinian Aramaic," to distinguish it from the "Babylonian Aramaic" of Onqelos. But the chronology of the two Targums is about the same; the differences between them are a function more of program than dating. Given the center of gravity of Rabbinic activity from the second century and later, it is better to distinguish "Tiberian" Aramaic from "Babylonian" Aramaic, since the adjective "Palestinian" has been used in a now discredited attempt to argue that all Targums of this type represent a pre-Christian and coherent tradition of Targum. In fact, the diversity, as well as the lateness of the Tiberian Targums is what distinguishes them, and it

---

That rich contribution, in turn, was taken up in the great projects of printing during the sixteenth century and is the basis of most knowledge of Aramaic in Europe and America today.

Modern Aramaic (1500-the present day) enjoys a dwindling number of speakers today in Azerbaijan, Iran, Iraq, Israel, Kurdistan, Lebanon, Syria, and Turkey. The Gulf War and the subsequent campaigns involving the Curds in Iraq and Turkey must have had a disastrous impact, in human and cultural terms, on the population of Aramaic speakers.

[2] See Bruce Chilton, "A Comparative Study of Synoptic Development: The Dispute between Cain and Abel in the Palestinian Targums and the Beelzebul Controversy in the Gospels," in *Journal of Biblical Literature* 101 (1982), pp. 553-562, and *Targumic Approaches to the Gospels. Essays in the Mutual Definition of Judaism and Christianity* (Lanham and London, 1986), pp. 137-149.

appears likely they reflect academic speculation as well as local idiosyncrasies. The rabbis of Babylonia, who called Onqelos "our Targum," exerted greater influence there than did their colleagues in the west, and they seem to have kept the exigencies of public worship more clearly in view. However the dialects are distinguished, it is crucial to be aware that regionalization was a typical feature of Aramaic dialects from around the year 200 C.E., so that the emergence of linguistically distinct Aramaic traditions within Judaism followed as a matter of course.

The latest representative of the type of expansive rendering found in Neophyti is Targum Pseudo-Jonathan. Its reference to the names of Mohammed's wife and daughter in Gen. 21:21 put its final composition sometime after the seventh century C.E. (This oddly designated Targum is so called in that the name "Jonathan" was attributed to it during the Middle Ages, because its name was abbreviated with a *yod*. But the letter probably stood for "Jerusalem," although that designation is also not established critically. "Pseudo-Jonathan" is therefore an admission of uncertainty.) Neophyti and Pseudo-Jonathan are together known as "Palestinian Targums," to distinguish their dialects and their style of interpretation from those of Onqelos. For the reasons already stated, the designation "Tiberian Targums" is better, and in no case should the once fashionable usage of the singular, "Palestinian Targum," be accepted.

Neophyti and Pseudo-Jonathan are to be associated with two other Targums, or, to be more precise, groups of Targums. The first group, in chronological order, consists of the fragments of the Cairo Geniza. They were originally part of more complete works, dating between the seventh and the eleventh centuries, which were deposited in the geniza of the Old Synagogue in Cairo. In the type and substance of its interpretation, these fragments are comparable to the other Targums of the Tiberian type. The same may be said of the Fragments Targum, which was collected as a miscellany of targumic readings during the Middle Ages. An interesting feature of the Targumim of the Tiberian type is that their relationship might be described as a synoptic one, in some ways comparable to the relationship among the Gospels. All four of the Tiberian Targumim, for example, convey a debate between Cain and Abel, and they do so with those variations of order and wording well known to students of the Synoptic Gospels.

Although the analogy of a synoptic relation among Targumim is rightly of interest to students of the Synoptic Gospels, it is to be stressed that it is only an analogy. No responsible dating in the current literature would place any Targum to the Pentateuch within the first century.[3] The extant, literary Targumim date from the third century (in the case of Onqelos and, perhaps, Neophyti) and the seventh or eighth centuries (in the case of Pseudo-Jonathan), and there is ample evidence of a more speculative turn in Targumic activity during the Byzantine and Medieval periods (attested, respectively, by the fragments from the Cairo Geniza and the Fragments Targum). That consensus by no means rules out the reflection of earlier traditions within Pentateuchal Targumim, but neither may it be assumed by default that Targumic traditions are to be dated within the first century.

Targum Jonathan to the Prophets

Both the Former and the Latter Prophets are extant in Aramaic in a single collection, although the date and character of each Targum within the collection needs to be studied individually. The entire corpus, however, is ascribed by Rabbinic tradition (B Meg. 3a) to Jonathan ben Uzziel, a disciple of Hillel, the famous contemporary of Jesus. On the other hand, there are passages of the Prophets' Targum that accord precisely with renderings given in the name of Joseph bar Hiyya, a rabbi of the fourth century (cf., Isaiah Targum 5:17b and B. Pes. 68a). The Isaiah Targum has been subjected to more study than any of the Targumim to the Prophets (both Former and Latter); it shows signs of a nationalistic eschatology that was current just after the destruction of the Temple in 70 C.E. and of the more settled perspective of the rabbis in Babylonia some three centuries later. That finding of critical exegesis comports well with periods of the two rabbis identified in Talmud, Jonathan ben Uzziel from the period of the Tannaim (tradents of mishnaic tradition who lived prior to the publication of the Mishnah in 200 C.E.), and Joseph bar Hiyya from the period of the Amoraim (commentators on the Mishnah after 200 C.E. and before the publication of the Babylonian Talmud, c. 600 C.E.).

It appears that Targum Jonathan as a whole is the result of these two major periods of collecting and editing Rabbinic traditions of

---

[3] For a good recent survey of the field, see Uwe Glessmer, *Einleitung in die Targume zum Pentateuch* (Tübingen, 1995).

rendering the Prophets, the first period being Tannaitic and the second Amoraic. Long after Targum Jonathan was composed, probably near the same time the Fragments Targum to the Pentateuch was assembled, targumic addenda were appended in certain of its manuscripts; they are represented in the Codex Reuchlinianus from the twelfth century and in a manuscript from the Bibliothèque Nationale (numbered 75 in the current catalog) from the fourteenth century. The topic of the Targumic addenda will not immediately occupy us in the present essay, because they assume the existence of an established Targumic tradition, to which the medieval additions amount to creative extensions. But they are witnesses of the continuing consciousness that the production of Targumim was not simply a matter of translating but of conveying the sense of Scripture in its theological fullness. Although Reuchlinianus and Bibliothèque Nationale 75 do not represent the development of Targum Jonathan in its formative period, they do reflect the kind of interpretative enterprise that went into the development of the Targumim.

The Prophets' Targum, both to the Former and the Latter Prophets, has received renewed attention as the best source for the explication of Scripture in synagogues during periods of early Judaism and Rabbinic Judaism. The current phase of discussion is predicated upon the fundamental work of Pinkhos Churgin, who located Targum Jonathan in the intersection between worship in synagogues and Rabbinic discussion.[4] Today, it may seem obvious that the principal Targumim are the result of the dynamics between synagogues and schools,[5] but there have been times when an almost entirely folk origin has been proposed.[6] Churgin held that Targum Jonathan emerged during the formative period of Rabbinic influence, between the second century B.C.E. and the seventh century C.E. Linguistic discussion, primarily the work of A. Tal, E.Y. Kutscher, and M.

---

[4] Cf., *Targum Jonathan to the Prophets* (New Haven, 1927).

[5] Cf., A.D. York, "The Dating of Targumic Literature," in *Journal for the Study of Judaism* 5 (1974), pp. 49-62; "The Targum in the Synagogue and the School," in *Journal for the Study of Judaism* 10 (1979), pp. 74-86; Chilton, *The Isaiah Targum. Introduction, Translation, Apparatus, and Notes* (Wilmington and Edinburgh, 1987), pp. xxv-xxviii.

[6] Cf., R. Le Déaut, *Introduction à la littérature targumique* (Rome, 1966); J. Bowker, *The Targums and Rabbinic Literature. An Introduction to Jewish Interpretation of Scripture* (Cambridge, 1969); Martin McNamara, *Targum and Testament. Aramaic Paraphrases of the Hebrew Bible: A Light on the New Testament* (Shannon, 1972).

Goshen-Gottstein,[7] focused attention particularly on the second century C.E., that is, just subsequent to the Aramaic of Qumran and
transitional to the language of the Amoraim, as the likely period of
formation. But one of the features noted has been the stable, one
might say standard, quality of the Aramaic employed in Targum
Jonathan, which makes an assessment of date predicated upon linguistic considerations alone appear inadequate.

Twenty years ago, I took up a method of comparative analysis
designed to substantiate or to qualify the work of linguists.[8] The exegeses incorporated in the Isaiah Targum were compared systematically with departures from the Hebrew text evidenced in the
Septuagint, the Apocrypha and Pseudepigrapha, the scrolls of
Qumran, the New Testament, the Mishnah, the two Mekhiltas, Sifra,
Sifre, the two Talmuds, Midrash Rabbah, the two Pesiqtas, the Pirqe
de R. Eliezer, and the Yalkut Shimoni. The conclusion was that
targumic traditions were incorporated within an exegetical framework, a version—perhaps incomplete—of Isaiah in Aramaic composed by a *meturgeman* (identified in the Talmud as Jonathan ben
Uzziel) who flourished between 70 C.E. and 135.[9] That work was
completed by another *meturgeman*, identified in the Talmud as Joseph
bar Hiyya of Pumbeditha, who died in 333.[10] Throughout the process, the communal nature of the interpretative work of the *metur-*

---

[7] Cf., A. Tal, *The Language of the Targum of the Former Prophets and Its Position within the
Aramaic Dialects* (Tel Aviv, 1975 [Hebrew]); Kutscher, "Das zur Zeit Jesu gesprochene
Aramäische," in *Zeitschrift für die neutestamentliche Wissenschaft* 51 (1960), pp. 46-54; (tr.
M. Sokoloff), *Studies in Galilean Aramaic* (Ramat Gan, 1976); Goshen-Gottstein, "The
Language of Targum Onqelos and the Model of Literary Diglossia in Aramaic," in
Journal of Near Eastern Studies 37 (1978), pp. 169-179. Although the discussion cannot
now detain us, mention should also be made here of Fitzmyer's contributions, al-
ready cited in note 1, and to two articles that appeared in 1973, M. Delcor, "Le
Targum de Job et l'araméen du temps de Jésus," in J.-E. Ménard, ed., *Exégèse biblique
et judaïsme* (Strasbourg, 1973), pp. 78-107; S. Kaufman, "The Job Targum from
Qumran," in *Journal of the American Oriental Society* 93 (1973), pp. 317-327.

[8] Cf., *The Glory of Israel. The Theology and Provenience of the Isaiah Targum* (Sheffield,
1982), pp. xi. Since the time I wrote those pages, however, discussion of the development of the Aramaic language has tended to offer further support of the position that
I developed upon an exegetical basis, as remarks below will indicate; cf., *The Isaiah
Targum*, p. xxi.

[9] Within that early framework, materials were incorporated that appear to reflect
the interpretations of earlier periods, including the period of Jesus. Cf., Chilton, *A
Galilean Rabbi and His Bible. Jesus' Use of the Interpreted Scripture of His Time* (Wilmington,
1984; also published with the subtitle, *Jesus' Own Interpretation of Isaiah*; London, 1984).

[10] *The Glory of Israel*, pp. 2, 3; *The Isaiah Targum*, p. xxi. For the sections of the
Targum most representative of each *meturgeman*, cf., *The Isaiah Targum*, p. xxiv.

gemanin was acknowledged; insofar as individuals were involved, they spoke with the voice of synagogues and of schools. The production of the Isaiah Targum through the stages of two exegetical frameworks, one Tannaitic and one Amoraic, has been widely accepted and applied to the understanding of Targum Jonathan as a whole.

Within both exegetical frameworks, *meturgemanin* preface some of their most innovative renderings with the innovative introduction, "The prophet said...."[11] In aggregate, the Aramaic interpreters implicitly claim to speak with quasi-prophetic authority, in the wake of the departed Shekhinah. Two such cases in the Isaiah Targum permit us to see the work of the *meturgemanin* of the two frameworks, virtually side by side, in chapters 21 and 22.

Chapter 21 is redolent of the military power of the Sassanids and the nascent threat of Arabians[12] and indulges in proleptic glee at "Babylon's" demise. As the *meturgemanin* state in 21:9, "Fallen, *and also about to fall*, is Babylon."[13] The Amoraic setting of the *meturgemanin* is also reflected in a particularly revealing theological statement (21:12):

> *The prophet* said, *"There is reward for the righteous* and *retribution for the wicked. If you are penitent, repent while you are able to repent."*

The meturgemanin here address those individuals who are prepared to listen (cf., 33:13; 57:19), while the usual assumption of this Targum is that Israel is obdurate.[14]

---

[11] *The Glory of Israel*, pp. 52-53, 55; *The Isaiah Targum*, pp. xiii, xiv. The observation is confirmed in respect of Targum Jonathan more generally in R. (Robert [or C.T.R.]) Hayward, *The Targum of Jeremiah* (Wilmington and Edinburgh, 1987), p. 32. Kevin J. Cathcart and Robert P. Gordon, *The Targum of the Minor Prophets* (Wilmington and Edinburgh, 1989), themselves translate an instance in which the Targumic *incipit* prefaces an expansive rendering at Habakkuk 2:1f.; yet for some reason they then attempt to explain away their own observation.

[12] *The Isaiah Targum*, pp. 40-43. In his recent monograph, *Studies in the Targum to the Twelve Prophets, from Nahum to Malachi* (Leiden, 1994), pp. 142-146, Gordon has made additional arguments in the same direction.

[13] The significance of this interpretation was brilliantly explained by Churgin, pp. 28-29, and further pursued in *The Isaiah Targum*, pp. 41-43 (see also *The Glory of Israel*, pp. 5, 3, 45, 121). Gordon has tried to dispute the finding on the grounds that the phrase "and is about to fall" is—in his words—"as much an exegetical matter as an expression of a particular historical perspective" (*Studies*, p. 140). That, of course, may be said of any targumic rendering. But even exegetes say things when they decide to employ "exegetical matter," and in the present case a *meturgeman* is speaking of the future demise of Babylon. Gordon himself concludes than he can offer no "decisive argument against Churgin's Sassanid explanation," although he also cautions that it is not "demanded by the evidence."

[14] *The Glory of Israel*, pp. 37-46.

A more typical complaint within the earlier framework (28:10a) takes up a theme also expressed within the close of the biblical canon (cf., Mal. 2:10-11):

> *They were commanded to perform the law, and what they were commanded they did not wish to do. The prophets prophesied concerning them, that if they repented...and they did not listen to the sayings of the prophets.*

In theological terms, a shift from the claim that repentance has been globally rejected to one in which individuals might be found who are penitent is considerable. Just that shift is involved as one moves from the Tannaitic framework to the Amoraic framework.

Repentance in 21:12 is also associated more with the eschatological judgment of individuals than with the restoration of the Temple and the people, Israel's intended end in the earlier framework. The usage of the phrase "The prophet said" here is Amoraic, as it is at 21:8, 9, where reference is innovatively made to the imminent fall of Babylon, the ruling force with which the Amoraim in Babylon needed to reckon. Perhaps the closest approximation to the reading is to be found in Numbers Rabbah 16.23, which cites Is. 21:12 and observes (with particular reference to the term "morning" in the Hebrew), "when the time of the world to come arrives, which is called morning, we shall know in whom he delights."[15]

The emphasis is quite different in chapter 22 of the Isaiah Targum, which focuses on the depredations of Jerusalem, the victories of the Romans, and the fate of the sanctuary,[16] characteristic interests of the Tannaitic *meturgemanin*. A particular threat is directed against those who feast in a time when the prophet calls for fasting (22:12, 13), and the threat, articulated at 22:14, is couched in language also found in the Revelation of John:

> *The prophet said,* With my ears *I was hearing when this was decreed before* the Lord God of hosts: "Surely this *sin* will not be forgiven until you *die the second death,*" says the Lord God of hosts.

---

[15] The passage also connects Mal. 3:18 with Is. 21:12, which is reminiscent of the Isaian passage in Targum Jonathan. For a further discussion, including references to other analogies, cf., *The Glory of Israel*, pp. 43, 44.

[16] Cf., *The Isaiah Targum*, pp. 42-45, and Chilton, "Shebna, Eliakim, and the Promise to Peter," in J. Neusner, P. Borgen, E.S. Frerichs, R. Horsley, eds., *The Social World of Formative Christianity and Judaism* (Philadelphia, 1989), pp. 311-326, also available in *Targumic Approaches to the Gospels. Essays in the Mutual Definition of Judaism and Christianity* (Lanham and London, 1986), pp. 63-80.

The fact that the same theologoumenon appears in Rev. 2:11, 20:6, 14, and 21:8 does not alone settle the questions of the chronology and meaning of the phrase. Charles Perrot and Pierre-Maurice Bogaert cite the usage in various Targumim and in *the Pirqe de R. Eliezer* (34).[17] But at Is. 22:14 in particular, the rabbis from the second century onward regularly refer to death in the straightforward sense (cf., Mekhilta Bahodesh 7.24-25; cf., B. Yom. 86a),[18] so that the communal eschatology of the Tannaitic *meturgemanin* appears to be reflected here.

The idea of a phasal development within Targum Jonathan, resulting in two exegetical frameworks, the one developed prior to 135 C.E. and the other of Amoraic provenience, has been generalized from the Isaiah Targum to other documents within Jonathan in a way that could only be intimated twenty years ago.[19] In his commentary on the Jeremiah Targum, Robert Hayward advances an argument based upon the treatment of prophecy to suggest that an earlier, Tannaitic framework was especially influential in the text as it can be read today. He observes that the "translation of 'prophet' in certain cases as 'scribe' produces the association of priests with scribes" in the Jeremiah Targum, an association also made in Josephus and the New Testament.[20]

Scribes, on this reading, are "*a powerful and influential group*" during the time of the Targum's composition.[21] Care should be taken, however, not to apply Hayward's suggestion globally. There are instances

---

[17] *Les Antiquités bibliques II*: Sources Chrétiennes 230 (Paris: Les éditions du Cerf, 1976), p. 56, n. 3.

[18] Cf., *The Glory of Israel*, p. 56.

[19] *The Glory of Israel*, p. 117. The same paradigm is applied in Daniel J. Harrington and Anthony J. Saldarini, *Targum Jonathan of the Former Prophets* (Wilmington and Edinburgh, 1987), p. 3; Hayward, *The Targum of Jeremiah:*, p. 38; Samson H. Levey, *The Targum of Ezekiel* (Wilmington and Edinburgh, 1987), pp. 3, 4; Cathcart and Gordon, pp. 12-14. Levey's acceptance of the paradigm is especially noteworthy, in that he had earlier argued that Targum Jonathan (especially Isaiah) should be placed within the period of the ascendancy of Islam, cf., "The Date of Targum Jonathan to the Prophets," in *Vetus Testamentum* 21 (1971), pp. 186-196. Although the model has been applied, the editions cited do not, in fact, test it by consistent comparative reference to Rabbinic and early Christian literature, which is the method recommended in *The Glory of Israel*.

[20] Hayward, op. cit., pp. 36, 37. He cites the Jeremiah Targum 8:10; 14:18; 23:11, 33, 34; 26:7, 8, 11, 16; 29:11 and *Antiquities* 12.3.3 §142; Mark 11:27; Matthew 2:4; 16:21:20:18; Acts 4:5, 6.

[21] Hayward, op. cit., p. 33. His argument was earlier developed in "Some Notes on Scribes and Priests in the Targum of the Prophets," in *Journal of Jewish Studies* 36 (1985), pp. 210-221.

in which the association is not operative in the Jeremiah Targum,[22] and the "prophets" of the Masoretic Text often become "prophets of falsehood" as well as "scribes" in the Targum.[23] *Meturgemanin* of Jeremiah, as those of Isaiah,[24] evidently wished to insulate the unqualified usage of "prophet" as such from any charge of deception. That results in referring to prophets who lie,[25] and in the grouping of other classes of leaders in criticisms from which prophets are protected. That is quite a different matter from the presentation of the Gospels, in which priestly and scribal leaders are particularly in view as a result of their alleged responsibility in the execution of Jesus.[26]

Hayward's comparison of the Jeremiah Targum with the Gospels illustrates a difficulty in the assessment of the Targumim in respect of more ancient documents. Words and phrases are more easily shared than are meanings, especially among speakers who commonly—and independently—refer to an authoritative collection of Scriptures. The *meturgemanin* of Jeremiah sometimes referred to "scribes" in order to protect "prophets" from criticism; the Gospels' framers attack "scribes" in order to discredit an alternative view of religion. Unless the sense of references is evaluated, observations of brute similarities of usage are pointless and may prove misleading.[27]

Hayward also notes a tendency to introduce the term "prophet" in the Targum Jeremiah, as at 35:4 (in reference to Hanan, the son of Yigdaliah). He does not observe, however, that the usage cited is part of a pattern within Jonathan generally, in which prophecy is associated with the Temple (cf., also the Isaiah Targum 8:2, in respect of Uriah the priest); that positive assessment of a priestly charism emerges only sporadically and likely rests upon an ancient claim, much in the manner of Josephus.[28] Generally speaking, the whole of Jonathan represents a tendency to portray "prophecy as a unified

---

[22] Cf., 6:13; 18:18, from Hayward's own lists (pp. 32, 36, 37).

[23] Hayward, op. cit., p. 32; as he notes, and as is the case elsewhere in Targum Jonathan, "teacher" is a possible surrogate for "prophet" in the Masoretic Text.

[24] Cf., *The Glory of Israel*, p. 54, citing 9:14; 28:7.

[25] Hayward, op. cit., p. 33, helpfully corrects the surmise of Churgin that idolatrous prophets are particularly in view when the phrase "prophets of falsehood" appears.

[26] Cf., Michael J. Cook, *Mark's Treatment of the Jewish Leaders* (Leiden, 1978).

[27] Cf., the method of exegetical comparison recommended in *Targumic Approaches to the Gospels*, cited above.

[28] Cf., Joseph Blenkinsopp, "Prophecy and Priesthood in Josephus," in *Journal of Jewish Studies* 25 (1974), pp. 239-262.

phenomenon which is understood as true contact with God involving revelatory significance," and to introduce characterizations designed to protect the perceived integrity of prophecy.[29] That is the conclusion of Harrington and Saldarini in respect of the Targum of the Former Prophets, and it is sufficiently unexceptionable to be applied to the corpus as a whole.

From the second century, the rabbis taught that prophecy was a phenomenon proper to the land promised by God to his people (cf., Mekhilta Pisha 1.42-44). Such an understanding was at apparent odds with the experience of Ezekiel, which is explicitly set in Babylon (see Ezek. 1:1-3), and was a problem that needed to be confronted in the Aramaic rendering of the book. As Samson H. Levey points out, the *meturgemanin* resolved the difficulty by having Ezekiel's revelation in 1:3 begin in Jerusalem and be renewed in the land of the Chaldeans.[30]

Cathcart and Gordon similarly associate the presentation of the prophets within the Targum of the Minor Prophets with the theology of the Amoraim. Unlike Hayward, they locate the usage of "scribe" in that latter phase of the Targum's development, on the theological grounds that the rabbis held that prophecy had passed from the prophets to the sages.[31] Obviously, that analysis fails to take account of the negative sense that sometimes accompanies use of the term "scribe" in Jonathan; if they are more correct than Hayward in their chronology, they are equally approximate in their exegesis.

Moreover, they do not call attention to the connection of priesthood and prophecy at Hosea 4:4,[32] nor to the repeated theme of Israel's rejection of the prophetic message (cf., Hos. 6:5; 9:7; Zeph. 3:2); both of those features are important links to the Tannaitic phase of Targum Jonathan. Finally, they do not observe the vital link be-

---

[29] So Harrington and Saldarini, op. cit., pp. 11, 12. Cf., also Saldarini, "'Is Saul Also among the Scribes?' Scribes and Prophets in Targum Jonathan," in *Essays on Aggadah and Judaica for Rabbi William G. Braude* (New York, 1986).

[30] Levey, op. cit., p. 13.

[31] Cathcart and Gordon, op. cit., pp. 3, 199, n. 5, citing B. B.B. 12a. Cf., also Gordon, "Targum as Midrash: Contemporizing in the Targum to the Prophets," in M. Goshen-Gottstein, ed., *Proceedings of the Ninth World Congress of Jewish Studies* (Jerusalem, 1988), pp. 61-73.

[32] A reference to priesthood at the close of the verse in the Masoretic Text occasions the statement, "*For they say, 'The scribe shall not teach, and the prophet shall not admonish.' So your people argue with their teachers.*" See also the link between false prophets and priests in Zeph. 3:4.

tween their Targum and the rest of Jonathan in its received form: the
tendency to present the message of all the prophets as consonant.
That is particularly accomplished by identifying the biblical prophets
as such, despite the impression of redundancy which sometimes results (cf., Nah. 1:1; Hab. 1:1; Hag. 2:1; Zech. 1:1). Their distinction
from the false prophets, cf., Hos. 4:5; Mic. 3:5; Zeph. 3:4; Zech. 13:2,
4 is another link to the normal pattern of Jonathan.

After the theory of two exegetical frameworks was developed for
the Isaiah Targum, it was applied (as we have seen) to the Targum of
the Former Prophets, the Targums of Jeremiah and Ezekiel, and the
Targum of the Minor Prophets. Today, then, the phasal development
of Targum Jonathan as a whole appears to be a matter of consensus.
Even claims to offer radical departures from the consensus wind up
confirming it. For example, it has recently been asserted that the
Targum Jonathan was not intended for popular usage in synagogues
but for academic reflection.[33] In fact, the original theory of two
frameworks called attention to the disparity between the Rabbinic
experts who produced the Targumim and the synagogues that were
the targets of the operation. Moreover, the difference between the
interpretation of the first framework and the interpretation of the
second framework is manifest. Propaganda for revolt and homilies for
settled accommodation to the Sassanids are obviously not the same
thing.

The consensus, then, is faring well in its second decade, although
continuing historical work will no doubt be welcomed. The challenge
that most pressingly remains to be faced, however, is of a different
order. While the differences in the interpretative strategies of the
distinct frameworks within Targum Jonathan have been widely recognized, little analysis of the particular characteristics of the frameworks as readings of Isaiah has been offered.

To some extent, no doubt, that has been a consequence of the
conventional attitudes among Targumists. For much of the time since
1949, interest in the Targumim has been greatest among those concerned with the New Testament and Christian origins. Such scholars
will be concerned with issues of dating and historical development
first of all. But even Targumists who claim that no such application is
in their minds often display the traits of historicists of the old style.
They proceed as if questions of the purpose and theme and character

---

[33] See Willem F. Smelik, *The Targum of Judges* (Leiden, 1995).

of a Targum will take care of themselves, if only the Targumist will focus exclusively with how individual passages are to be dated.[34] Since historical allusions must always involve a strong element of inference, the circularity of the old historicism of some Targumists is evident.

The analysis of exegetical frameworks was intended as a defense against circularity. The focus was not merely on this or that particular passage (which might be older or younger than the substantial inter- pretation that produced a Targum), but on characteristic terms and phrases that link a framework within a coherent, interpretative project. Characteristic interpretations within the framework were then compared with those presented within Rabbinic literature. The resolution of my analysis into two frameworks, one Tannaitic and one Amoraic, emerged out of that extended work of comparison. Obvi- ously, inference remains a vital part of such an approach, but the inference proceeds on the basis of elements within each framework that are shown to be central, not on the problematic supposition that references to events from the past directly tell us the date of the Targum.

While the theory of two frameworks has done its work within the study of the literary history of Targum Jonathan, in another respect analysis has not been pursued. Globally, the differences of interpreta- tive strategy from exegetical framework to exegetical framework are evident to Targumists, which is why the theory of frameworks has been well accepted in the first place. The next step, engaging the deeper literary issue, addresses the question, "What is the purpose and procedure of interpretation, such that a distinctive reading of the book of Isaiah (or of whatever book is at issue) results?"

Modern Targumists are well aware that Targums are translations, but they sometimes do not reflect that every translation involves, together with a text to be rendered, the purpose and theory of the translator. That is the object of our larger inquiry: the purpose and theory of the *meturgemanin* of the Tannaitic framework and of the *meturgemanin* of the Amoraic framework. The Aramaic term *metur- gemanin* ("interpreters" or "translators") is here used collectively, of all those who were involved in the interpretative process of producing a given exegetical framework. The fact that we have access to two such

---

[34] Gordon concludes his monograph with a statement of that now antiquated program, p. 153.

frameworks, each evolved in association with the same base text (Isaiah in Hebrew), is a great help, since comparative characterization will become possible.

The Messiah in the Two Frameworks of the Isaiah Targum

The messianic perspective of the Tannaitic *meturgemanin* comes to expression early in the Isaiah Targum (4:2-3):

> In that *time the Messiah* of the Lord shall be for *joy* and for glory, and *those who perform the law* for pride and for praise to the survivors of Israel. And it shall come to pass that he who is left *will return* to Zion and he who *has performed the law will be established* in Jerusalem; he will be called holy. Every one who has been recorded for *eternal* life *will see the consolations of Jerusalem.*

From the point of view of its content, the rendering is straightforward. The messiah is associated with the performance of the law (and therefore its correct interpretation), and those who actually do perform it anticipate eternal life in a consoled Jerusalem.

The likely social context of that anticipation, and its development, is not our particular concern here.[35] We wish rather to focus on how the *meturgemanin* arrived at their rendering from the Hebrew text then available in order to appreciate the interpretative method involved. The term "branch" in Hebrew has a richly messianic association within the biblical tradition (cf., Jer. 23:5; 33:15; Zech. 3:8; 6:12), and the *meturgemanin* simply read the association as the text. That is: what is there in Hebrew is replaced by what it is held to mean in Aramaic. Although that method is straightforward, it is also daring.

The dominance of the association is such that further transformations of the Hebrew text occur. "Fruit of the land" in 4:2b of the Masoretic Text becomes "those who perform the law" in the Targum, because the messiah is to be productive of that fruitful performance. That is what is to enable him to realize the promise of Israel in Israel's land. The eschatological perspective of this hope is articulated in the expressions "eternal life" and "consolations of Jerusalem," both of which recur in the Targum.

The idea of the messiah then, invoked by the term "branch" in Hebrew, is what the text conveys in the rendering of the *meturgemanin*. That meaning occasions not only additions to the text but also sub-

---

[35] That work is available in *The Glory of Israel*, pp. 86-96.

tractions: "branch" and "fruit of the land" simply disappear, or at least seem to. We may contrast the technique involved with the interpretation by pesher at Qumran, where the Hebrew text is preserved in actual quotations (sometimes with variants),[36] and then interpreted. That permits close fidelity to the Hebrew original (and certain variant readings), while also indulging some famously speculative developments of meaning.

The Tannaitic *meturgemanin* take the occasion of a principal trigger in the Hebrew text ("branch") to develop a messianic transformation of the whole by addition and subtraction. The transformation that is the agency of the interpretation, once it begins, affects the whole of the text. But because a verbal trigger is involved, the transformation is of a literal nature. "Branch" becomes "messiah;" "fruit" becomes the "law" performed; "life" becomes "eternal." Interpreting the text by literal transformation, the *meturgemanin* underscore their rendering by what is omitted as well as by what is added. That is, the Targum is better understood if one knows that "branch" is now messiah and that "fruit" is now law. Those promises are still present and vivified by the eschatological dimension of messianic meaning.

The literal transformation of the Tannaitic *meturgemanin* may be compared and contrasted with the transformations typical of the Synoptic Gospels. There, transformation can occur on the basis not of text but of the supposed meaning of a passage. For example, the parable of the man, the seed, and the earth in Mark 4:26-29 does not appear in the Gospel according to Matthew, but Matthew does present a fuller parable of a man who planted seed only to have his enemy introduce weeds (Mat. 13:24-30). The Matthean commitment to the fuller parable as the meaning of the image is represented by the detailed interpretation attributed to Jesus in Mat. 13:36-43.

Matthew actually instances two sorts of interpretation here. The easier sort is the careful explanation in 13:36-43. No transformation is involved, only a point by point explication (of what is already rather obvious). Even here, however, it is notable that the explanation proceeds more on the basis of the meaning of each image than with a view to literal interpretation. For that reason, there is no precise

---

[36] See Chilton, "Commenting on the Old Testament (with particular reference to the pesharim, Philo, and the Mekhilta)," in D.A. Carson and H.G.M. Williamson, eds., *It Is Written: Scripture Citing Scripture, Essays in Honour of Barnabas Lindars* (Cambridge, 1988), pp. 122-140.

analogy to the technique of pesher. Rather, the approach better corresponds to the apocalyptic interpretation that influenced the Synoptic Gospels quite deeply. Within Mat. 13 itself, the interpretation of the parable of the sower presents another example of the same technique (see 13:18-23). Matthew's version is of a more explicitly apocalyptic cast than its Synoptic counterparts (see Mark 4:13-20 and Luke 8:11-15), but in each case the method of deciphering images in view of their meaning for the end of the world is evident. Ultimately derived from the sort of apocalyptic explanation instanced in Daniel 7, although far less elaborate (and therefore probably not originally literary), Synoptic interpretations of this type present a consistent character. Matthew extends the technique somewhat in the present case.

The other type of Synoptic interpretation Matthew instances here (that is, in 13:24-30) is of greater interest from the point of view of the Tannaitic *meturgemanin*. The parable of the man who had to deal with his enemy's weeds is only distantly similar to the parable of the man, the seed, and the earth in Mark 4:26-29. Scholars have been divided over the issue of whether they are in fact related.[37] But whether Matthew represents a version of the Markan parable itself, or a cognate use of imagery, there is consensus that the Matthean form is *Matthean*, a characteristic development of an earlier usage. The transformation Matthew's parable represents, then, is so dramatic that the issue of its antecedents is problematic.

Matthew's transformation here is conceptual rather than verbal (as in the Targumic example we have considered). In describing the technique of the Tannaitic *meturgemanin* of Isaiah as transformative, therefore, no implication of disregard for the Hebrew text should be taken to be implied. Indeed, the fact is that knowing what is not included from the Hebrew text actually enhances one's appreciation of the Targumic rendering. That suggests that, although targeted for usage in synagogues, the Targum was best enjoyed where it was produced: in academies. That insight will prove to be important for an assessment of the character of Targum Jonathan generally.

The technique of literal transformation is easily instanced in other

---

[37] But see the bold analysis of Robert H. Gundry, *Matthew. A Commentary on His Handbook for a Mixed Church under Persecution* (Grand Rapids, 1994), pp. 261-265, which seems to me to resolve the issue in favor of Matthean reference to the Markan parable. Compare W.D. Davies and Dale C. Allison, *A Critical and Exegetical Commentary on the Gospel according to Saint Matthew* (Edinburgh, 1991), pp. 406-415, 426-432, for a more cautious assessment that nonetheless moves in the same direction.

examples of the messianic interpretation of the *meturgemanin*. The theological problem posed by the Hebrew text of Is. 9:5 (9:6 in English versions) is neatly sorted out. How can the "son" who is referred to be called "wonderful, counselor, mighty God, everlasting father, prince of peace"? The *meturgemanin* solve the difficulty by having the son called "*the messiah in whose days* peace *will increase upon us*." He is so named "*before the* wonderful counselor, *the* mighty God." An extra phrase and a preposition clarify the situation, and the assumption is that the "son" is the messiah, who is to be distinguished from God himself.

That assumption is explicitly flagged by the innovative introduction in the Targum, "*The prophet said to the house of David....*" With this preface, the *meturgemanin* assert that the true meaning of the prophet, whatever his words, was messianic, and messianic in a manner that did not compromise monotheism. Everything is dependent, then, on knowing whose "son" is at issue: David's progeny is the topic, specified so as to avoid the difficulty that the general imagery of the Masoretic Text might occasion. Once the precise topic is established, the other changes already mentioned become explicable: the messiah is there so that "peace *will increase upon us*," and he is named "*before the* wonderful counselor, *the* mighty God." Similarly, the "dominion" that rests on his shoulder in the Hebrew text becomes, in the Targum, his agreement to accept and keep the law. Anyone who knew that would know that the secret of the Davidic messiah's rule was fidelity to the law.

The messianic interpretation of Is. 11:1 comes as no surprise in the context of what we have already seen and calls for little comment here. It simply pursues the interpretation of the "branch" referred to in the Masoretic Text (*neṣer*, in the second half of the verse, where "*messiah* " appears in the Targum) in messianic terms:

> And a *king* shall come forth from the *sons* of Jesse, and *the messiah* shall *be exalted* from *the sons of* his *sons*.

Just as "branch" in Hebrew occasions reference to the messiah in the second part of the verse, so the "stump" (*geza'*) of Jesse becomes the "*sons* of Jesse" in the first part of the verse. In contrast, the rendering involved in 14:29 is striking:

> Rejoice not, all you Philisti*nes*, because *the ruler* who was *subjugating* you is broken, for *from the sons of the sons of Jesse the messiah* will come forth, and his *deeds* will be *among you* as a *wounding* serpent.

Because the imagery of the Hebrew text speaks of a viper coming from a snake and of a flying serpent, the transformation of meaning involved here seems more extreme than what he have considered so far.

But the precise phrasing of the *meturgemanin's* Hebrew text explains the innovative rendering: "from the root (*mishoresh*) of the snake the viper came forth...." The "root" is taken by the *meturgemanin* to be akin to Jesse's "stump" in Is. 11:1, which is already (and straightforwardly) taken to be messianic. Once that has occurred, it is a simple and consistent transformation—again, along literal lines—to make the "rod" of Philistia into the ruler of the Philistines, set in antithesis to the victorious messiah.

The messiah, then, is to supplant every ruler. So the "ruler of the earth" in the Hebrew of Is. 16:1 (set out here) must be the messiah:

Send a lamb to the ruler of the earth,
from Sela, by the wilderness,
to the mount of the daughter of Zion.

That initial change is straightforward, but what follows demands some explanation:

They will offer tribute to the Messiah of Israel,
who prevailed over the one as the wilderness,
to the mount of the *congregation* of Zion.

The phrase "from Sela (*misela'*) by the wilderness" becomes a reference to the messiah "*who prevailed (detaqyph) over the one as* the wilderness." The verb *taqeyph* occurs frequently in the Targum and is the preferred usage for the exertion of strength.

It is occasioned here by taking *misela'* as if it were a participle, preformative *m* with *sela'*, taking the latter root in its etymological meaning of "split." (Because the messiah has displayed such strength, he is to receive "*tribute*," not just the "lamb" of the Masoretic Text.) Once again, the *meturgemanin's* playfulness involves a literal transformation, and one's enjoyment is enriched by recollecting the Hebrew counterpart of his rendering.

By comparison, the associations of messiah with the "throne" in Is. 16:5 and with the "crown" in 28:5 are quite easily explained along the lines of the literal transformation that is the model proposed here:

Tg: *then the* throne *of the Messiah of Israel* will be established....
MT: and a throne will be established....

Tg: In that *time the Messiah of* the Lord will be a *diadem* of *joy* and a *crown* of praise...

MT: In that day the Lord of hosts will be a crown of beauty and a diadem of praise...

Both those references have been identified as the work of the Tannaitic *meturgemanin*, in view of their clear preoccupation with the theme of the imminent vindication of Israel over its enemies.

That motif, in turn, becomes the principle underlying the famous rendering of Is. 52:13-53:12. The issue that has consumed the secondary literature has been whether that interpretation is pre-Christian and whether it might have influenced the tradents of the New Testament. In view of the statement of 53:12, that the messiah *"handed over* his soul to death," it seems unlikely that this passage of the Targum was composed with a view to the challenges of Christian theology. On the other hand, the assumption that Jerusalem and the sanctuary have been desolated is evident throughout, so that a dating prior to 70 C.E. seems implausible. The rendering of 53:5 is telling:

Tg: And he *will build the sanctuary which was profaned for our sins, handed over* for our iniquities; *and by his teaching his* peace *will increase* upon *us*, and in *that we attach ourselves to his words our sins will be forgiven us.*

MT: And he was wounded for our transgressions, bruised for our iniquities; the chastisement that makes us whole was upon him, and by his wounds we are healed.

Attribution to the Tannaitic *meturgemanin(in)* between 70 and 132 commends itself, because vindication is eagerly and pragmatically awaited. The messiah might well risk his life ("hand over his soul to death," 53:12), but the aim of that heroism is triumph on behalf of Israel.[38]

But if the dating of the passage is not a complicated matter, an innovation in the interpretative technique it manifests must be observed. The term "servant" is enough to invoke the messianic theme in 52:13, but in 53:10 the development of the theme is a little more complicated:

---

[38] For a full discussion, see Jostein Ådna, "Der Gottesknecht als triumphierender und interzessorischer Messias. Die Rezeption von Jes 53 im Targum Jonathan untersucht mit besonderer Berücksichtigung des Messiasbildes," in B. Janowski and Peter Stuhlmacher, eds., *Der leidende Gottesknecht. Jesaja 53 und seine Wirkungsgeschichte* (Tübingen, 1996), pp. 129-158.

MT: he will see his seed
Tg: *they* will see *the kingdom of their Messiah.*

"Seed," by the sort of literal transformation we have already observed, is rendered in terms of the seed of David, and in that vein the
messiah discovered.

But on what basis do "they" see, instead of the "he" of the Hebrew
text? In addition to the principle of literal transformation, another
transformation is at work here. It was first (although incompletely)
identified by R.A. Aytoun. Over seventy years ago, he commented
that "the exaltation of the Servant is applied to the Messiah, but his
sufferings fall in part upon Israel, in part upon the Gentiles."[39] The
present case shows that "exaltation" can fall to Israel, as well as to the
messiah, because the passage continues in the Targum, "*they shall
increase sons and daughters, they* shall prolong days; *those who perform the law*
of the Lord shall prosper in his *pleasure.*" Their prosperity is all the
more marked in that, as we have already seen, in the Targum the
messiah, too, can become vulnerable to death. The gentiles, Israel,
and the messiah indeed constitute three distinct foci within the interpretation, but their relationship to one another is spelled out dynami-
cally, within the eschatological vindication that is anticipated.

In the end, therefore, the literal transformation at the base of the
meturgemanin's technique within the Tannaitic framework is supplemented. Once the messianic rendering is achieved by literal means,
there is a cumulative effect, so that the entire theme may be invoked
by a single, verbal trigger within the Hebrew text. In addition, the
theme of the messiah itself carries with it the distinction between
those to whom messiah is a promise and those to whom messiah is a
threat. And that conceptual transformation—applied to the messianic
motif and whatever triggers it in the Hebrew text—is also a principle
of interpretation that emerges in the Tannaitic framework. The limitation of that more global transformation to whatever occasions reference to the messiah makes the principle more predictable than the
sorts of transformation we find among the Synoptic Gospels. That
limitation justifies the characterization of "literal transformation"
overall as the hermeneutic of the Tannaitic framework. But that sort

---

[39] "The Servant of the Lord in the Targum," in *Journal of Theological Studies* 23
(1921-1922), p. 178. He also observed "that though it seems to have departed far
from the original Hebrew, yet actually the Targum has stuck remarkably close to the
letter of the Hebrew." The present discussion will fill out his insight.

of transformation is pointing ahead to another kind, more clearly evidenced within the Amoraic framework.

The messiah is not absent from the Amoraic framework of the Isaiah Targum: the hope of messianic vindication continued to be a governing concern at that later stage. But the hope is expressed in a different key. The reference to "my servant" in the Hebrew text of Is. 43:10 is enough to occasion mention of "my messiah in whom I am well pleased" in the Targum:

> MT: "You are my witnesses," says the Lord, "and my servant whom I have chosen..."
>
> Tg: "You are witnesses *before me*," says the Lord, "and my servant *the Messiah with* whom I *am pleased*..."

The point of that rendering in its present setting is that the messiah is an eternal witness before God, testifying to God's power in creation, his revelation to Abraham, his salvation at the Exodus, and his giving of the law at Sinai, all of which feature explicitly within the surrounding context in the Targum. As the Targum innovatively has God say within the same verse, "*I am he that was from the beginning, even the ages of the ages are mine...:*" God's eternity and the eternal witness of his messiah go hand in hand. The situation addressed by that witnessing is one of exile:

> "For your *sins'* sake *you were exiled* to Babylon..." (Targum Isaiah 43:14).

The circumstances of the Babylonian Amoraim come to expression here, and the modulation of their theology, from the direct eschatology of the earlier period to an emphasis upon eternity and transcendence, becomes apparent. Part of that modulation is an interpretative matter. Literal transformation (from "servant" in Hebrew to "messiah" in Aramaic, as the example below will show) is still the occasion of the rendering, but it assumes that the reference to the servant of the Lord is alone enough to justify messianic reference. That is, the Amoraic *meturgemanin* are more programmatic than the Tannaitic *meturgemanin*.

The contrast becomes plain in a comparison of chapter 42 and chapter 43 in the Isaiah Targum. Chapter 42, where the concerns of the Tannaitic *meturgemanin* are evident, refers simply to the "servant" (42:1) without explicitly messianic specification. Nonetheless, immediate vindication is in view, when the purpose of that servant's commission is portrayed (42:7):

Tg: to open the eyes of *the house of Israel who are as* blind *to the law*, to
     bring out *their exiles, who resemble* prisoners, from *among the gentiles*, to
     deliver *from the slavery of the kingdoms those who are jailed as prisoners of*
     darkness.
MT: to open the eyes of the blind, to bring out the prisoner from the
     dungeon, from jail those who dwell in darkness.

The connection between the servant and the messiah was not made
within the Tannaitic framework until chapter 52, as we have already
seen. Here, in chapter 42, the identification of the "servant" is different: the place of Israel as such is in view. In 42:8, God does not only
say "my glory I will not give," but: "my glory—*that I am revealed upon
you*—I will not give to another *people*." The "servant" in the Tannaitic
framework may refer to Israel, as in 49:3 (which remains unchanged
in the Targum): "You are my servant, Israel, in whom I will be
glorified." But chapter 43—as we have already seen—assumes a global transformation of "servant" into "messiah," and on that basis the
messiah becomes an eternal witness of divine power and vindication
in 43:10.

The two renderings of Isaiah we have considered as examples of
the interpretations of the Tannaitic and Amoraic *meturgemanin* permit
us insight into the development of distinct methods of transformation
of meaning from the Hebrew text into the Aramaic Targum. In both
cases, transformation is the appropriate category, because there is no
question of simple translation. The Tannaitic *meturgemanin* transform
the Hebrew of Isaiah literally into a messianic theology of the
eschatological vindication of Israel. The Amoraic *meturgemanin* transform both the work of their predecessor and those parts of the Hebrew text that had not already been rendered into Aramaic by means
of systematic indications of God's messianic transcendence.

The Messiah in other Tannaitic and Amoraic Frameworks

Targum Jonathan to the Former Prophets is famously conservative
(or "literal") in its rendering, and yet it develops a characteristic
policy of messianic expectation. David has a particular place in the
theology of Targum Jonathan, because he is the object of prophetic
prediction. What is said by the prophet Nathan in 2 Sam. 7, commonly known as the Davidic covenant, is not simply a promise of
enduring prosperity, but *"for the age that is coming,"* a *"vision for the sons
of men"* (2 Sam. 7:19). Because the Davidic house is the object of that

vision, David himself emerges as an instrument of prophecy (2 Sam. 22:1), and he announces the salvation of the house of Israel, despite their apparently poor fortunes *"in this world "* (22:28).

At the close of 2 Samuel, David expatiates on Israel's salvation with particular reference to the vindication to come (22:32):

> *Therefore on account of the sign and the redemption that you do for your Messiah and for the remnant of your people who are left, all the nations, peoples, and languages will give thanks and say, "There is no God except the Lord..."*

The Targumic David invokes an insistence dear to the Targum Jonathan, that there is no God but the Lord.[40] At the same time, the theme of the universal recognition of messianic vindication comes to open expression. David's *"words of prophecy"* are said to be *"for the end of the world, for the days of consolation that are to come,"* days that will see *"the messiah to come who will arise and* rule" (1 Samuel 23:1, 3).

Targum Jonathan of the Former Prophets presents a full, well articulated hope of messianic vindication, involving the messiah in the destruction of Rome, renewed dedication to the service of the Lord in his Temple, and faithfulness to the Torah. Any number of handbooks and articles refer to this Targum as being a literal translation, and to some extent that reputation is justified. It is remarkably economical compared to the Targums to the Latter Prophets. But the innovative matter included, of which I have given only one example,[41] makes it clear beyond any reasonable contradiction that the Targum is a literary translation of the corpus as a whole, targeted on the issue of messianic vindication as attested by the prophets and warranted by the authority of Rabbinic teachers in synagogues and schools.

The emphasis on the condition of exile is a programmatic feature of Targum Jonathan to the Former Prophets, as may be seen within the song of Deborah.[42] The target of her prophecy, in a setting of hardship, is specified in the Targum (Judg. 5:9):

> *I was sent to give praise to the scribes of Israel who, when that affliction happened, did not cease from studying the Law; and who, whenever it was proper for them, were*

---

[40] See *The Glory of Israel*, 6-7.

[41] In a more comprehensive work, an introduction to the Targumim I am writing with Paul Flesher, more such material is treated.

[42] Cf., Daniel J. Harrington, "The Prophecy of Deborah: Interpretative Homiletics in Targum Jonathan of Judges 5," in *Catholic Biblical Quarterly* 48 (1986), pp. 432-442.

sitting in the synagogues at the head of the exiles and were teaching the people the words of the Law and blessing and giving thanks before God.

The social map implied within the Targum suggests that the framework of Targum Jonathan to the Former Prophets was essentially Amoraic. Unlike the Isaiah Targum, the immediate hope of a rebuilt Temple and a return from exile is not a programmatic feature. Even the messiah is present more as a symbol and seal of ultimate triumph than as an instrument of victory. These indications, together with the probable allusion to the tradition of the Isaiah Targum at 1 Sam. 2:5, suggest that Targum Jonathan to the Former Prophets emerged during the third century in Babylonia. It no doubt was composed on the basis of earlier materials, and the reference to prophets and teachers and scribes is comparable with both the Isaiah Targum and the Jeremiah Targum (which manifest a Tannaitic phase of development), but it is the economy of the Targum to the Former Prophets that is most striking and which probably reflects the influence of the Amoraic *meturgemanin*.

Following my analysis of the Isaiah Targum, Robert Hayward has suggested that the Jeremiah Targum evolved in two stages, principally during the first and the fourth centuries.[43] The messiah is characterized as "messiah of righteousness" in a way consistent with the Scrolls of Qumran;[44] such links confirm Hayward's finding that, "The general tone of the Messianic hope in this Tg. is simple, straightforward, and uncomplicated; and there is the likelihood that it is of very ancient lineage."[45]

Hayward did not have access to Harrington and Saldarini's volume, which was published in the same year as Hayward's. So he was not in a position to see that the messiah in the Jeremiah Targum aligns himself more with the providential figure of the Former Prophets Targum than with the triumphant rebuilder of the Temple anticipated in the earliest stages of the Isaiah Targum. As son of David, he is keenly anticipated because his revelation among the people means their redemption, safety, and their recognition of the source of their vindication (23:5-6; 30:9, 21; 33:13, 15-17, 26), not because he trium-

---

[43] *The Targum of Jeremiah* (Wilmington and Edinburgh, 1987), p. 38. His observations of coherence with the biblical interpretation of Jerome (340-420 C.E.; p. 35, as well as the index, p. 203) are especially interesting.

[44] Cf., Jeremiah Targum 23:5 with 4QPatr 3-4; see also the reference to prophecy in Jeremiah Targum 1:2 with 11QPs DavComp 27.1; Hayward, p. 27.

[45] Hayward, p. 33.

phantly rebuilds the Temple. This messiah, as in the Amoraic phase (rather than the Tannaitic phase) of the Isaiah Targum, is a teacher in the manner of the rabbis: "the *people* shall yet *eagerly pursue the words of the messiah* " (Jeremiah Targum 33:13).

There is no question, however, of the messiah within the Jeremiah Targum simply reflecting the more settled expectation of the Amoraic period. He is also, as in the Isaiah Targum's early phase, associated quite closely with the priesthood (33:20-22) and with worship in the Temple (30:9, 21). The rebuilding of the sanctuary is in fact an object of faith in this Targum (31:12); it is just that the messianic means of its rebuilding are not articulated as in the Isaiah Targum. By comparison, then, a certain attenuation of a vigorous hope of restoration seems apparent.

It therefore comes as no surprise that, in Jeremiah Targum 2:21, the phrase *"as a plant of a choice vine"* is imported from Isaiah Targum 5:2 and applied to the people of Jerusalem. The point in the Isaiah Targum is to speak of Israel's identity as centered in the sanctuary,[46] but by the time of the Jeremiah Targum the phrase is more like a slogan and is applied in a less specific way. It speaks of Israel without specifying the need to rebuild the Temple. Likewise, in Jeremiah Targum 8:16 the theme of a rejection of the cult in the sanctuary is present, but entirely historicized:

> *Because they worshipped the calves which were in* Dan, *a king with his troops shall go up against them and shall take them into exile...*

Where it is more typical of the Isaiah Targum to speak in terms of the contemporary defect of worship in the Temple, the Jeremiah Targum is inclined to speak of the punishment of idolatry by means of the destruction of the Temple as occurring in the distant past.

Still, the threat of idolatry is ever present, especially within the Sassanid regime in Babylon, which proffered an astral aspect.[47] The worship of Venus was an especial concern. The planet is specifically mentioned in Jeremiah Targum 7:18 as "the star of heaven" in the

---

[46] Hayward cites the *Liber Antiquitatum Biblicarum* 23:12; 28:4; 39:7 by way of comparison. But he follows an uncritical school of British research in dating the *LAB* exclusively with the first century.

[47] See the imagery of the eagle in 18:1 and the discussion of both the eagle and the winged solar disk in Chilton, *The Isaiah Targum*, p. 37; Edith Porada, *Iran ancien. L'art à l'époque préislamique*:(Paris, 1963), p. 226, and pp. 139-154. In Isaiah Targum 44:13, the innovative reference to a woman in a house fits the Sassanid period quite well; see Chilton, pp. 87-89, and Porada, p. 62.

context of idolatry, where the Masoretic Text reads "the queen of heaven." A return from that Babylon, from a region that might eventually lead to a loss of Israel's identity, is therefore a paradigmatic concern, and Jeremiah is just the prophet to give occasion to emphasize that concern (see Jeremiah Targum 16:14, 15, and the Masoretic Text). Yet although the concern for an end of exile is paradigmatic, it is not immediate. The *meturgeman* must look to the ministry of teachers to follow in the testimony of the prophets, much as in the Former Prophets Targum. But the Jeremiah Targum was an especially good occasion (given the themes of the biblical book) to dilate on the disastrous consequences of the failure to listen to such teachers (see 6:29):[48]

> *Behold, like* bellows *which blow what is burnt in the midst of the fire, so the voice of their prophets is silent, who prophesy to them: Return to the Law! But they have not returned. And like* lead *which is melted in the smelting pot, so the words of the prophets who prophesy to them are void in their eyes. Their teachers have taught them* without profit, and they have not *forsaken their evil deeds.*

In a condition of persistent exile, attention to the echo of the prophetic voice under the authority of the rabbis becomes a matter of survival. But the fact that obedience is vital is no guarantee that it will be achieved.

It has been argued that the absence of the term "messiah" from the Ezekiel Targum attests that it is a first-century composition.[49] In fact, the restraint of the *meturgemanin* of Ezekiel only extends to explicit use of the noun "messiah." The figure of the messiah is keenly anticipated (Ezekiel Targum 17:22-23):

> ...I myself will bring near *from the kingdom of the house of David which is likened to* the lofty cedar, *and I will establish him, a child among his sons' sons; I will anoint and establish him by my Memra...and he shall gather together armies and build fortresses and become a mighty king; and all the righteous shall rely on him, and all the humble* shall dwell in the shade *of his kingdom...*

Given that the verb "anoint" is used here, and used innovatively in respect of the Hebrew text, it seems pedantic to deny that this is an explicitly messianic expectation. Similarly, "son of David" is not used word for word here; but to deny that the interpretation serves the Rabbinic expectation of such a figure would be silly. The Davidic

---

[48] The passage is especially innovative in comparison to the Masoretic Text. Hayward, p. 69, explains the logic of the rendering very well.

[49] See Levey, p. 33.

messiah is to be king, and the righteous are therefore to be vindicated, just as in the Isaiah Targum 16.[50]

Once it has been appreciated that the Ezekiel Targum does in fact reflect the theology of messianic vindication that is more evident in the Isaiah Targum, its relative reserve is more easily explained as a result of a more recent date, nearer to the time of composition to the Targum of the Former Prophets than to the Tannaitic framework of the Isaiah Targum. Such an explanation would also correspond to a fact which Levey's theory does not accommodate: the greater stringency of the translation in the Ezekiel Targum, which is comparable to the "literal" character of Targum Jonathan of the Former Prophets.

Finally, the themes of both Tannaitic and Amoraic *meturgemanin* are more in evidence within the Zechariah Targum, which Rabbi Joseph cited as an already extant source (see B. Meg. 3a; B. M.Q. 28b). At 3:8, the identification of the "branch" with the messiah is made explicit, as at Isaiah Targum 4:2, and the messiah is also portrayed as being "revealed," a locution reminiscent of 4 Ezra 7:28. Martin McNamara has argued that this usage is characteristic of the first century,[51] and it is repeated in 6:12-13 of the Zechariah Targum, where the messiah (for "branch" in the Masoretic Text) is to build the Temple and be at peace with a *"high"* priest." By comparison, the precise designation of the messiah as him whose *"name is told from of old"* seems to be an Amoraic motif (cf., Micah Targum 5:1; Psalms Targum 72:17; the Pirqe of Rabbi Eliezer 3; Pesahim 54a).[52]

Targum Jonathan to the Prophets grew up in stages that may be characterized by means of the types and styles of interpretation utilized. The earliest stage, associated with synagogal practice until the time of the revolt of Simeon bar Kosiba, is reflected in the incomplete exegetical frameworks of the Isaiah and Zechariah Targums. They center on the immediate restoration of worship in the Temple as the

---

[50] In an earlier work, Levey himself remarked, "Everything points to a Targumic Messiah innuendo, but the Messiah's designation as such is absent;" in *The Messiah: An Aramaic Interpretation. The Messianic Exegesis of the Targum* (Cincinnati, 1974), p. 79. (Here, the alleged connection is to Hillel [cf., B. San. 99a], rather than Yohanan.) The interpretation strikes me as being quite straightforward and most unlike an "innuendo."

[51] *The New Testament and the Palestinian Targum to the Pentateuch* (Rome, 1966/1978), p. 249.

[52] So Cathcart and Gordon, pp. 122, 194, and their citation of G.F. Moore's reading and Chilton, *The Glory of Israel*, p. 114.

kingdom of God and the messiah are revealed. During the late third
and fourth centuries these frameworks were filled out in the interests
of a messianic theme of a return from exile within the entire program
of the salvation of Israel. The result was the production of Targum
Jonathan of the Former Prophets, as well as the Isaiah, Jeremiah,
Ezekiel, and Zechariah Targums. The fifth century (too late for our
consideration here[53]) saw the completion of the work, with Hosea,
Amos, Nahum, Obadiah, Micah, and Zephaniah in Targum
Jonathan representing a development of the exilic theology, and then
Joel, Jonah, and Habakkuk in Targum Jonathan moving that theol-
ogy in an individualistic direction.

Targumim of the Writings

Of the three categories of Targumim, that of the Writings is without
question the most diverse. Although the Targum to Psalms is formally
a translation, substantially it is better described as a midrash, while
the Targum to Proverbs appears to be a fairly straightforward rendition of the Peshitta, and the Targum to Esther seems designed for use
within a celebration of the liturgy of Purim. The Targums to the
Writings are the most problematic within modern study, but they are
also of the least interest of the three general categories of Targumim
from the present point of view of owing to their late (in most cases,
medieval) date.

Although caution is even more emphatically recommended here
than in the study of the Targumim generally, there appear to be three
distinct types of interpretative activity that produced the Targumim
of the Writings. The first is exegetical interpretation, such as produced the Prophets Targum. It is evidenced in the Job Targum (fifth
century, and unrelated to the so-called Targum of Job from
Qumran), and in the earliest phases of the Qohelet and the Chronicles Targums.

Next is a type of midrashic intercalation, represented by the two
Esther Targums, the Ruth Targum, and the Qohelet Targum in its
present form. They are joined by the Lamentations Targum and the
Song of Songs Targum. Taken together, these five constitute the
Megillot, assigned for specific, liturgical occasions: Canticles for
Passover, Ruth for Pentecost, Ecclesiastes for Tabernacles, Esther for

---

[53] Again, see my forthcoming book with Professor Flesher.

Purim, and Lamentations for the ninth of Av.[54] These Targumim, all composed from the seventh century and later,[55] seem to have been composed for such a rendering, and to have served homiletic needs within that setting.

Finally, a more restrained policy is evident in the Proverbs and Chronicles Targum, and the latter also represents the second type. The decision to render the Peshitta in the Proverbs Targum probably represents the drive to counter Christian Syriac claims of charismatic utterance in Solomon's name. That is a reminder that apparently literal rendering is no less a culturally contexted act than other forms of interpretation.

Conclusion

The significance of the Targumim for appreciating Jesus and the Gospels follows naturally from assessing their purpose and provenience within early Judaism and in comparison with the literature of the New Testament. The relationship between the New Testament and the Targumim, in turn, permits of assessment of the value of the Targumim for the study of Judaism in the first century. Fundamentally, the Targumim constitute evidence of the first class for the way in which the Hebrew Scriptures were understood, not simply among rabbis but more commonly by the congregations for whom the Targumim were intended. Insofar as what is reflected in a Targum is representative of the reception of Scripture in the first century, that Targumic material is of crucial importance for any student of the New Testament. But care must also be taken, lest the perspective of later materials be accepted uncritically as representative of an earlier period: that would result in anachronistic exegeses. There are clearly readings in the Targumim that presuppose events long after the death of Jesus. One example of such a reading is Targum Isaiah 53:4, 5, 10-11a, which clearly anticipates that the reader takes the destruction of the Temple as given.

A particular problem is posed for modern study by the persistent notion that there is somewhere extant today a "Palestinian Targum,"

---

[54] See Albert van der Heide, *The Yemenite Tradition of the Targum of Lamentations. Critical Text and Analysis of Variant Readings* (Leiden, 1981), pp. 15-21.

[55] The method of midrashic intercalation continued much later, for example in the Codex Reuchlinianus and Codex Vaticanus Urbaniti 1; see Pierre Grelot, "Deux Tosephtas targoumiques inédites sur Isaïe," in *Revue Biblique* (1972), pp. 511-543.

which substantially represents the understanding of the Hebrew Bible
in the time of Jesus. There was a time when that was a comprehensible position, because it was taken that "Palestinian Aramaic" was
more ancient than "Babylonian Aramaic." Today, however, the discoveries at Qumran have cast a dazzling new light on Onqelos and
Jonathan, which makes them appear more ancient than was supposed some sixty years ago, and more similar to Aramaic as spoken in
Palestine. Pseudo-Jonathan appears to represent a more recent tendency, not only in language, but also in its historical allusions and its
form. Moreover, the present understanding of early Judaism is that it
was too variegated to allow of the formation of a single, authoritative
tradition of rendering, such as the designation "Palestinian Targum"
would suggest.

The difficulty of assessing the precise form of targumic tradition(s)
within the first century should also make us wary of any claim that we
know the dialect(s) of Aramaic that were current in that period. The
literary remains of the language are sporadic, dialectical variation was
great, and there sometimes appears to have been a significant difference between the language as spoken and the language as written.
For all those reasons, attempts to "retranslate" the Greek Gospels
into Jesus' own language are extremely speculative; when the
Targumim are appealed to by way of antecedent, speculation is piled
upon speculation. For the purposes of linguistic retroversion, it is
obvious that the Aramaic of Qumran is a more reliable index of how
Aramaic was spoken in the first century. Even then, however, the
mixture of forms evidenced in the Dead Sea Scrolls should be taken
as a warning against any claim that the Aramaic of Jesus and his
followers can be specified.

The composite nature of the Targumim is nonetheless such that
upon occasion one may discern in them the survival of materials that
did circulate in the time of Jesus and that therefore influenced his
teaching and/or the memory of that teaching among those disciples
who were familiar with such traditions. An example of such a survival
might be Lev. 22:28 in Pseudo-Jonathan, "My people, children of
Israel, since our father is merciful in heaven, so should you be merciful upon the earth." The expansion in the Targum is unquestionably
innovative, as compared to what may be read in the Masoretic Text,
so that the possible echo in Luke 6:36, within the address known
conventionally as "the sermon on the plain," is with the Targum, or
with nothing at all. It is, of course, theoretically possible that the

saying originated with Jesus and was then anonymously taken up within the Targum. Without doubt, the statement is rhetorically more at home within Luke than in Pseudo-Jonathan, where it appears unmotivated. But it seems inherently unlikely that Pseudo-Jonathan, which of all the Pentateuchal Targumim is perhaps the most influenced by a concern to guard and articulate Judaic integrity, would inadvertently convey a saying of Jesus. More probably, both Pseudo-Jonathan and Luke's Jesus are here independently passing on the wisdom of a proverbial statement. The Targumic echo is therefore most certainly not the source of Jesus' statement, but it may help us to describe the nature of Jesus' statement.

Examples such as this demonstrate that the Targumim might have a heuristic value in illustrating the sort of Judaism Jesus and his followers took for granted. Recent study has greatly increased the catalog of such instances. But there are also cases in which Jesus appears to have cited a form of the book of Isaiah that is closer to the Targum than to any other extant source; in such cases, an awareness of the fact helps us better to understand his preaching. Targum Isaiah 6:9, 10 is an especially famous example, and it helps to explain Mark 4:12. The statement in Mark could be taken to mean that Jesus told parables with the purpose that (*hina*) people might see and not perceive, hear and not understand, lest they turn and be forgiven. But the Targum also (unlike the Masoretic Text and the Septuagint) refers to people's not being forgiven (rather than not being healed), and that suggests that the Targum may give the key to the meaning supposed in Mark. The relevant clause in the Targum refers to people who behave in such a way so that (*d*) they see and do not perceive, hear and do not understand, lest they repent and they be forgiven. It appears that Jesus was characterizing people in the Targumic manner, as he characterizes the son of man similarly in Mark with a clause employing *hina* (cf., 9:12), not acting in order to be misunderstood.

Time and again, the Targumim present a synoptic relationship among their materials, be it in the instance of the dispute between Cain and Abel (as already mentioned), the Aqedah (Gen. 22 in the Tiberian Targumim and Is. 33:7 in the margin of Reuchlinianus), or the Poem of the Four Nights (Exod. 12:32 in the Tiberian Targums). In that the synopticity of the Targumim is evinced among four documents, not three (as in the case of the relationship among the Gospels), it is even more complicated to trace a purely documentary, rigidly literary relationship among the texts. The study of the synoptic aspect of the Targumim remains in its infancy, but it appears possible that, once it is better understood, we will find that we also conceive of the literary relationship among the Gospels in a different way.

The Targums are a rich source of that form of early Judaism and Rabbinic Judaism where the folk and the expert aspects of the religion met. For that reason, serious students of the New Testament might well read them as helping them to comprehend the context within which Jesus taught and his movement first developed, before the transition to a Hellenistic compass and to the Greek language. In particular cases, the Targums uniquely present material that helps illuminate Jesus' teaching. (In other instances, they may support what we know from other sources.) It might be that a Targum just happens to preserve proverbial material that Jesus cites or alludes to. But there are also cases in which Jesus seems to have been influenced by a specifically Targumic understanding of the Bible. Finally, quite apart from what they may tell us of particular passages in the Gospels, the Targums give us an example of how composite documents evolved within Judaism, and to that extent they may provide an analogy for understanding the Gospels themselves. Within the study of early Judaism, the emphatic and messianic eschatology of the Targums provides us with an element that is otherwise notable largely for its absence in the teaching of the rabbis who attempted to make sense of what went on before.

Bibliography

Ådna, Jostein, "Der Gottesknecht als triumphierender und interzessorischer Messias. Die Rezeption von Jes 53 im Targum Jonathan untersucht mit besonderer Berücksichtigung des Messiasbildes," in Janowski, B., and Peter Stuhlmacher, eds., *Der leidende Gottesknecht. Jesaja 53 und seine Wirkungsgeschichte* (Tübingen, 1996), pp. 129-158.

Aytoun, R.A., "The Servant of the Lord in the Targum," in *Journal of Theological Studies* 23 (1921-1922).

Blenkinsopp, Joseph, "Prophecy and Priesthood in Josephus," in *Journal of Jewish Studies* 25 (1974), pp. 239-262.

Bowker, J., *The Targums and Rabbinic Literature. An Introduction to Jewish Interpretation of Scripture* (Cambridge, 1969).

Cathcart, Kevin J., and Robert P. Gordon, *The Targum of the Minor Prophets* (Wilmington and Edinburgh, 1989).

Chilton, Bruce, "Commenting on the Old Testament (with particular reference to the pesharim, Philo, and the Mekhilta)," in Carson, D.A., and

H.G.M. Williamson, eds., *It Is Written: Scripture Citing Scripture, Essays in Honour of Barnabas Lindars* (Cambridge, 1988), pp. 122-140.

Chilton, Bruce, "A Comparative Study of Synoptic Development: The Dispute between Cain and Abel in the Palestinian Targums and the Beelzebul Controversy in the Gospels," in *Journal of Biblical Literature* 101 (1982), pp. 553-562.

Chilton, Bruce, *A Galilean Rabbi and His Bible. Jesus' Use of the Interpreted Scripture of His Time* (Wilmington, 1984).

Chilton, Bruce, *The Glory of Israel. The Theology and Provenience of the Isaiah Targum* (Sheffield, 1982).

Chilton, Bruce, *The Isaiah Targum. Introduction, Translation, Apparatus, and Notes* (Wilmington and Edinburgh, 1987).

Chilton, Bruce, "Shebna, Eliakim, and the Promise to Peter," in Neusner, J., P. Borgen, E.S. Frerichs, R. Horsley, eds., *The Social World of Formative Christianity and Judaism* (Philadelphia, 1989), pp. 311-326.

Chilton, Bruce, *Targumic Approaches to the Gospels. Essays in the Mutual Definition of Judaism and Christianity* (Lanham and London, 1986).

Cook, Michael J., *Mark's Treatment of the Jewish Leaders* (Leiden, 1978).

Davies, W.D., and Dale C. Allison, *A Critical and Exegetical Commentary on the Gospel according to Saint Matthew* (Edinburgh, 1991).

Delcor, M., "Le Targum de Job et l'araméen du temps de Jésus," in Ménard, J.-E., ed., *Exégèse biblique et judaïsme* (Strasbourg, 1973), pp. 78-107.

Fitzmyer, J.A., *Essays on the Semitic Background of the New Testament* (Missoula, 1974).

Fitzmyer, J.A., *A Wandering Aramean. Collected Aramaic Essays* (Missoula, 1979).

Glessmer, Uwe, *Einleitung in die Targume zum Pentateuch* (Tübingen, 1995).

Gordon, Robert P., "Targum as Midrash: Contemporizing in the Targum to the Prophets," in Goshen-Gottstein, M., ed., *Proceedings of the Ninth World Congress of Jewish Studies* (Jerusalem, 1988), pp. 61-73.

Goshen-Gottstein, M., "The Language of Targum Onqelos and the Model of Literary Diglossia in Aramaic," in *Journal of Near Eastern Studies* 37 (1978), pp. 169-179.

Grelot, Pierre, "Deux Tosephtas targoumiques inédites sur Isaïe," in *Revue Biblique* (1972), pp. 511-543.

Gundry, Robert H., *Matthew. A Commentary on His Handbook for a Mixed Church under Persecution* (Grand Rapids, 1994).

Harrington, Daniel J., "The Prophecy of Deborah: Interpretative Homiletics in Targum Jonathan of Judges 5," in *Catholic Biblical Quarterly* 48 (1986), pp. 432-442.

Harrington, Daniel J., and Anthony J. Saldarini, *Targum Jonathan of the Former Prophets* (Wilmington and Edinburgh, 1987).

Hayward, C.T.R., "Some Notes on Scribes and Priests in the Targum of the Prophets," in *Journal of Jewish Studies* 36 (1985), pp. 210-221.

Hayward, C.T.R., *The Targum of Jeremiah* (Wilmington and Edinburgh, 1987).

Kaufman, S., "The Job Targum from Qumran," in *Journal of the American Oriental Society* 93 (1973), pp. 317-327.

Kutscher, E.Y., "Das zur Zeit Jesu gesprochene Aramäische," in *Zeitschrift für die neutestamentliche Wissenschaft* 51 (1960), pp. 46-54.

Kutscher, E.Y., *Studies in Galilean Aramaic* (Ramat Gan, 1976).

Le Déaut, R., *Introduction à la littérature targumique* (Rome, 1966).

Levey, Samson H., *The Messiah: An Aramaic Interpretation. The Messianic Exegesis of the Targum* (Cincinnati, 1974).

Levey, Samson H., *The Targum of Ezekiel* (Wilmington and Edinburgh, 1987).

McNamara, Martin, *The New Testament and the Palestinian Targum to the Pentateuch* (Rome, 1966/1978).

McNamara, Martin, *Targum and Testament. Aramaic Paraphrases of the Hebrew Bible: A Light on the New Testament* (Shannon, 1972).

Saldarini, Anthony, "'Is Saul Also among the Scribes?' Scribes and Prophets in Targum Jonathan," in *Essays on Aggadah and Judaica for Rabbi William G. Braude* (New York, 1986).

Smelik, Willem F., *The Targum of Judges* (Leiden, 1995).

Tal, A, *The Language of the Targum of the Former Prophets and Its Position within the Aramaic Dialects* (Tel Aviv, 1975 [Hebrew]).

van der Heide, Albert, *The Yemenite Tradition of the Targum of Lamentations. Critical Text and Analysis of Variant Readings* (Leiden, 1981).

York, A.D., "The Dating of Targumic Literature," in *Journal for the Study of Judaism* 5 (1974), pp. 49-62.

York, A.D., "The Targum in the Synagogue and the School," in *Journal for the Study of Judaism* 10 (1979), pp. 74-86.

VI. THE STATUS OF WOMEN IN ANCIENT JUDAISM

Mayer I. Gruber
Ben-Gurion University

In my earlier study, "Women in the Cult according to the Priestly Code,"[1] I succeeded, I believe, in debunking the thesis widely held in Christian confessional Old Testament scholarship according to which the role of Israelite and Jewish women in public life progressively deteriorated from the late Bronze Age until it reached its nadir in the late Second Temple period when Jesus of Nazareth came to the rescue.

In fact, Hebrew Scripture, which is still widely perceived as giving divine sanction to the treatment of women as second-class citizens with no role in public life, takes for granted that women did and should serve, *inter alia*, as judges (Judg. 4:4-5), officiating clergy at funerals (Jer. 9:16-19), slaughterers of animals for both human and divine consumption,[2] sages (2 Sam. 14; 20:16-22) and prophetesses,[3] and that provision was made for women to combine child-rearing with participation in the divine service of periodic public reading of Scripture.[4]

As I already showed in "Women in the Cult," one can point out many specific areas of private and public life with respect to which Rabbinic Judaism extended woman power.[5] At the same time, it should be acknowledged, there were many specific areas with respect

---

[1] Mayer I. Gruber, "Women in the Cult according to the Priestly Code," in Jacob Neusner, Baruch A. Levine, and Ernest S. Frerichs, eds., *Judaic Perspectives on Ancient Israel* (Philadelphia, 1987), pp. 35-48; this study was republished in Mayer I. Gruber, *The Motherhood of God and Other Studies* (Atlanta, 1992), pp. 49-68. Hereinafter all pages references to this article refer to the latter volume. For the view attacked therein, see, e.g., Clarence J. Vos, *Women in Old Testament Worship* (Delft, 1968); Susan T. Foh, *Women and the Word of God* (Grand Rapids, 1979); Samuel Terrien, "The Omphalos Myth and Hebrew Religion," in *VT* 20 (1970), pp. 315-338.

[2] Gruber, "Women in the Cult," pp. 64-65.

[3] S.D. Goitein, "Women as Creators of Biblical Genres," in *Prooftexts* 8 (1988), pp. 1-33.

[4] Mayer I. Gruber, "Breast-Feeding Practices in Biblical Israel and in Old Babylonian Mesopotamia," in *The Motherhood of God*, p. 77.

[5] Gruber, "Women in the Cult," p. 59, n. 22; pp. 64-65.

to which Rabbinic Judaism took away from women power they previously held according to the testimony of the Hebrew Scriptures.[6]

Elsewhere I have shown that women in the Levant in the Late Bronze Age (1550-1200 B.C.E.) through the period of Persian hegemony (ending 330 B.C.E.), the eras portrayed in the Hebrew Scripture, were employed outside of the home and farm as priestesses and para-cultic functionaries (Exod. 38:8; 1 Sam. 2:22); prophetesses; sages (2 Sam. 14; 20); poetesses (Exod. 15:21; Judg. 5:1-31; Prov. 31:1-9); keening women (Jer. 9), which is to say clergy who officiated at funerals; musicians (Ps. 68:26); queens; midwives, wet-nurses; baby-sitters; business persons; scribes, cooks, bakers and producers of cosmetics (1 Sam. 8:13), as well as innkeepers and prostitutes (Josh. 2).[7] In her brilliant and incisive *Mine and Yours are Hers*, Tal Ilan has shown that in the Mishnah, women's public roles have been reduced from these eighteen to the following four: keening women,[8] midwives, hairdressers, and innkeepers.[9]

It has been pointed out that of the 1,426 named persons in the Hebrew Scripture, only 111 are women,[10] that is, only 7.78% of the persons identified by name. In fact, numerous prominent women are identified in Hebrew Scripture only as "the wife of" or "the daughter of." In this connection, Ilan writes:

---

[6] To Deborah's functioning as judge (Judg. 4:4-5), we may contrast Rabbinic Judaism's taking it for granted that women *qua* women are disqualified from serving as judges. Rabbinic Judaism's exegetical tradition engages in verbal acrobatics in order to show that the facts of Scripture do not undermine what the rabbis take for granted; see, e.g., Tosafot at B. B.Q. 15a, s.v. "which you place." While Rabbinic Judaism treats both biblical Queen Esther and first century C.E. Queen Helene of Adiabene as culture heroines, this religion declares unequivocally that when and if Israelites choose for *themselves* a sovereign in accord with Deut. 17:15, the sovereign must be a man and not a woman; see Sifre Deuteronomy, ed. Finkelstein, p. 208, line 13.

[7] Mayer I. Gruber, "Women's Roles in the Ancient Levant," in Bella Zweig, ed., *Women's Roles in Ancient Civilizations* (Westport, in press), Chapter 5.

[8] In antiquity, keening women composed and sang poetic eulogies; see Jer. 9 and 2 Chron. 35:25. In modern times, some trends in Orthodox Judaism, especially in the State of Israel, prevent women's very attendance at funerals. This is the background to the Conservative Rabbinical Assembly of Israel's dignifying with a *responsum* the question of whether indeed women should be allowed to attend funerals. See Rabbi Professor David Golinkin, "The Participation of Women in Funerals," in *The Rabbinical Assembly of Israel Law Committee Responsa 5747* (Jerusalem, 1997), pp. 31-42 (in Hebrew); English summary, pp. v-vii.

[9] Tal Ilan, *Mine and Yours Are Hers* (Leiden, 1997), pp. 230-231.

[10] Cullen Murphy, "Women and the Bible," in *Atlantic Monthly*, August 1993, p. 42.

the question why women more often than not were left unnamed is interesting but the answer is fairly straightforward, as demonstrated by much feminist research into the marginality of women in androcentric societies and their literature.[11]

Indeed, the rabbis of the Talmud were so embarrassed by this that they endeavored to supply names for some of these prominent but unnamed biblical women.[12]

Nevertheless, Ilan shows just how marginalized women have become in Rabbinic Judaism vis-a-vis the respective worlds of both the Hebrew Scripture and Hellenistic period Judaism, noting that, "In the entire Rabbinic corpus only 52 [non-biblical] women are mentioned by name (as opposed to about 1000 men)."[13] These figures mean that in the Rabbinic corpus women constitute 4.94% of the named persons, such that the status of women, as measured by their mention in the historical record, has decreased by 2.84%. The concomitant tendency into the twentieth century of male historians of Judaism to write women out of history has recently been demonstrated most poignantly by Leah Shakdiel in her recent review article concerning three important books about Jewish clergywomen of the nineteenth and twentieth centuries.[14] With respect to at least one female sage of the Tannaitic era, the rabbis bequeathed a papyrus trail, which shows how they wrote her out of the official record of "our Mishnah." In T. Kel. B.M. 1:6, Beruriah is quoted by name,

---

[11] Ilan, *Mine and Yours Are Hers*, p. 279.

[12] Ibid., p. 278, n. 4; see, e.g., B. B.B. 91a; on the latter text see Tal Ilan, "Biblical Women's Names in the Apocryphal Traditions," in *Journal for the Study of the Pseudepigrapha* 11 (1993), p. 12.

[13] Ilan, *Mine and Yours Are Hers*, p. 279.

[14] Leah Shakdiel, "The Straightforward, the Comfortable and the Conflicted," in *Nashim: A Journal of Jewish Women's Studies and Gender Issues* 1, no. 1 (1988), pp. 154-161; especially poignant is the following note (p. 157) concerning Fraulein Rabbiner Regina Jonas, who perished in Auschwitz in 1944: "It was discomforting to read how even my hero Victor Frankl, her colleague in pastoral work in Theresienstadt, never mentioned her in his many writings, recalling her only when he was reminded recently by her researcher." With respect to Lily Montagu, founder of Britain's liberal movement in Judaism and for many years president of the World Union for Progressive Judaism who has, as it were, been restored to history by Ellen Umansky, *Lily Montagu and the Advancement of Liberal Judaism* (New York, 1983), Judith Romney Wegner, *Chattel or Person: The Status of Women in the Mishnah* (New York, 1988), pp. 187-188, writes as follows: "Despite the many people (including the present writer [i.e., Wegner]) who were privileged to hear her preach during her lifetime, Lily Montagu, after her death, 'wasn't there' until Umansky resurrected her." On the continued omission of women from the writing of Jewish history from antiquity to the present day, see Sondra Henry and Emily Taitz, *Written Out of History* (New York, 1978).

while in M. Kel. 11:4 the dictum is taken away from Beruriah and assigned to R. Joshua![15]

Before examining three areas—prayer, study of Torah, and divorce—in which over the course of time Rabbinic Judaism disempowered women, let us look at two worthy examples of the rabbis' yeoman attempt to give women more power than they are given in Hebrew Scripture. The first of these pertains to a woman suspected by her husband of adultery. Num. 5 seems to suggest that when a woman is suspected by her husband of adultery and there are no witnesses, she can be convicted or exonerated by what seems to be an ordeal.[16] The obvious objection raised by feminist biblical scholars and most people with open minds and common sense is the question, Where is the comparable rite that would acquit or convict a husband suspected of adultery?[17] One may reply with M. Sot. 5:1, which seem to answer the challenge, stating: "Just as the bitter potion tests her innocence or guilt so does the bitter potion test his innocence or guilt." Moreover, B. Sot. 28a corroborates and exegetes this assertion where it well could have ignored or eisegeted this amazing passage out of existence:

> ...how does Rabbi [Judah the Patriarch] know that "Just as the bitter waters test her innocence or guilt so do the bitter waters test his innocence or guilt"? He derives that idea from what is stated in a *baraita:* "'Make the belly to swell and the thigh to fall away' (Num. 5:22) refers to the belly and thigh of the man who penetrates. You say that [Num. 5:22 refers to] the belly and thigh of the man who penetrates, but is it not [a reference to] the belly and thigh of the woman who is penetrated? When

---

[15] Ilan, *Mine and Yours Are Hers*, pp. 57-58; cf., Boyarin, p. 182; see also Ann Goldfeld, "Women as Sources of Torah in the Rabbinic Tradition," in Elizabeth Koltun, ed., *The Jewish Woman: New Perspectives* (New York, 1976), pp. 257-271. In *Mine and Yours Are Hers*, pp. 297-310, Tal Ilan proposed the daring hypothesis that Matrona, who asks Yose b. Halafta questions concerning biblical exegesis in Genesis Rabbah and elsewhere, is, in fact, the personal name of a female Jewish Torah scholar of the Tannaitic period.

[16] For the interpretation of Num. 5:11-31 as an ordeal, see Tikva S. Frymer, "Ordeal, Judicial," in Keith Crim, ed., *The Interpreter's Dictionary of the Bible, Supplementary Volume* (Nashville, 1976), pp. 638-640. For a most convincing dissenting view, see Herbert Chanan Brichto, "The Case of the *Sotah* and a Reconsideration of Biblical Law," in *HUCA* 64 (1973), pp. 55-70. Brichto argues that the purpose of the so-called ordeal is to vindicate the wife of a husband who is jealous without cause. See also Mayer I. Gruber, "Marital Fidelity and Intimacy: A View from Hosea 4," in Athalya Brenner, ed., *A Feminist Companion to the Latter Prophets* (Sheffield, 1995), p. 171.

[17] See, e.g., Dennis T. Olson, *Numbers, Interpretation: A Bible Commentary for Teaching and Preaching* (Louisville, 1996), p. 36; cf., Judith Hauptman, *Rereading the Rabbis: A Woman's View* (Boulder, 1998), p. 16.

it [Scripture] says, 'her belly will swell and her thigh will fall away' (Num. 5: 27), look! It [Scripture] refers to the belly and the thigh of the woman who is penetrated. Say [therefore]: How do I interpret [the obviously not redundant but similar expression in Num. 5:22], '*the* belly will swell and *the* thigh will fall away'? [The answer is, of course]: his belly and his thigh, belonging to the man who penetrated."[18]

Unfortunately, the Babylonian Talmud does not spell out in detail how the bitter waters might be administered to a man. The reason may be simply that following M. Sot. 9:9, B. assumes that under legislative authority granted by God to the rabbis in Deut. 17:11,[19] Yohanan b. Zakkai abolished the administration of bitter waters:

> When adulterers [note the masculine form!] became numerous the rite of the bitter waters ceased, and Rabban Yohanan b. Zakkai abolished it for it is written in Scripture, "I will not punish your daughters when they are unfaithful nor your daughters-in-law when they commit adultery, for they themselves [the Israelite fathers and fathers-in-law] have sex with whores" (Hos. 4:14).[20]

In my "Women in the Cult according to the Priestly Code," I showed how the Mishnah and later Rabbinic exegesis of both the Bible and Mishnah affirmed the right and duty of women as well as men to engage in the ritual slaughter of animals for both sacrifice and for secular purposes.[21] In fact, the rabbis contend that the distinction between the lay function of slaughtering animals for sacrifice and the purely priestly function of pouring the blood on the altar, at the base thereof, or elsewhere depending on the nature of the sacrifice[22] derives from Lev. 1:5, which employs the impersonal third person masculine "he/she (i.e., the neutral *adam*, "person," mentioned in Lev. 1:2) shall slaughter" followed by the declaration "the sons of Aaron shall present the blood."[23]

Strange to relate, the Mishnah, that very document of Rabbinic Judaism that seems to apply the rite of the bitter potion to adulterous

---

[18] Two shorter recensions of the *baraita* here quoted are found in *Siphre d'Be Rab*, ed. H.S. Horovitz (Leipzig, 1917; repr., Jerusalem, 1966), p. 20, lines 1-7, and p. 236, lines 15-16.

[19] See, e.g., Kahana in B. Ber. 19b; Awia in B. Shab. 23a; see also B. Suk. 46a.

[20] I.e., they are unfaithful to their wives. Hosea, speaking in the name of God, argues, exactly as in B. Sot. 28a, to quote a non-Talmudic proverb: "What is good for the goose is good for the gander."

[21] Gruber, "Women in the Cult," pp. 64-65.

[22] See M. Zeb. Chapter 5.

[23] See Sifra Lev. at Lev. 1:5.

men as well as to adulterous women seems also, for a brief moment, to follow the lead of numerous other cultures of ancient Western Asia and include women among the persons who may perform the exclusively priestly function of pouring sacrificial blood in its appropriate place so that atonement may be effected. The crucial passage, M. Qid. 1:8, reads:

> Laying one's hands on the sacrificial animal, waving [the meal offering], bringing it close to the altar, taking the handful [of the meal offering] and burning it, wringing the necks of bird offerings, sprinkling the blood and receiving the blood are customarily performed by men but not by women except for the meal offering of the suspected adulteress [sotah] and the naziritess, for which they themselves perform the waiving.

Against the possibility that this passage suggests that by God's law women are entitled to engage in all of the above cultic activities and that it is custom established by Jewish men that has excluded women of Aaronide descent from the priestly function of pouring and receiving blood, Judith Hauptman argues that elsewhere in the Mishnah and Tosefta the verbs nohagim and nohagot, literally, "they [masculine] are accustomed and they [feminine] are accustomed," mean not "they are accustomed to" but "they may."[24] This may be so. It must, however, be observed that in B. Hag. 16b we read, "R. Yose and R. Simeon say: 'The women of Israel may perform the laying of hands on a sacrifice voluntarily,'" a text Hauptman quotes just a few pages after her discussion of M. Qid. 1:8.[25] If Hauptman's translation of the Mishnah is correct and ours is wrong, it is rather strange that none of the sages quoted in B. Hag. cites that passage to prove, in Hauptman's words, that, in fact, "women may not," which is the opposite of what R. Yose says that R. Simeon says. What we have here in M. Qiddushin is what we have so often in the Mishnah's and Tosefta's discussion of women's empowerment: a clause that giveth followed by a clause that taketh away. Two classic examples are T. Meg. 3:11 and T. Meg. 2:7. The first reads:

> All are included in the number of seven [called to read from the Torah at the public service on Sabbath morning] even a woman and a minor. One does not bring a woman to read for the multitude.

The version of this text quoted as a baraita in B. Meg. 23a reads:

---

[24] Hauptman, Rereading the Rabbis, p. 227.
[25] Ibid., p. 234.

> All are included in the number of seven even a minor and even a woman. However, sages legislated [*ameru*]: a woman shall not read from the Torah because of the honor of the congregation.

In light of my demonstration elsewhere that the expression "sages legislated" refers to man-made legislation,[26] it is clear that what we have through a glass darkly in T. Meg. 3:11 and as clear as the light of day in B. Meg. 23a is another example of how later sages cancel out empowerment of women, which had been acknowledged by earlier sages. Similarly, M. Meg. 2:4 declares:

> All are qualified to read the Scroll of Esther [to fulfill their own and other persons' religious obligation on the festival of Purim] except for a deaf-mute, an imbecile, and a minor.

Obviously, women are not excluded. In fact, the Palestinian Amora Joshua b. Levi (fl. 240 C.E.) says, rather patronizingly, in B. Meg. 4a, "*Women* [my italics; his word] are obligated with respect to the reading of the Megillah because they *too* [my italics; his word] were part of that miracle." To the same Joshua b. Levi is attributed the similarly patronizing remark at B. Shab. 23a: "Women are obligated with respect to the Hanukkah light because they *too* were part of that miracle." Nevertheless, what the Tosefta manages to do to the implicit meaning of M. Meg. 3:4, namely, to cancel its egalitarian (with respect to women) tendency should no longer surprise us. Here is the relevant section of T. Meg. 2:7:

> Women, slaves, and minors are exempt [from hearing the chanting of the Scroll of Esther on Purim], and they may not fulfill the obligation on behalf of the public [by chanting from the Scroll of Esther].[27]

Interestingly enough, Rashi (1040-1105) and Maimonides (1135-1204) both accept as legally normative the view implicit in the Mishnah that women are obligated to hear the chanting of the Scroll of Esther on Purim and that they may chant it on behalf of men and on behalf of mixed congregations. Other authorities quoted by Joseph Caro (1488-1575) in his Beit Yosef take the Tosefta very seri-

---

[26] Mayer I. Gruber, "The Mishnah as Oral Torah: A Reconsideration," in Gruber, *The Motherhood of God and Other Studies*, pp. 259-260.

[27] As for the relative positions of the Mishnah and Tosefta *vis-a-vis* the empowerment of women, contrast Hauptman, *Rereading the Rabbis*, p. 8; Tal Ilan, "Patriarchy, the Land of Israel and the Legal Position of Jewish Women in Rabbinic Literature," in *Nashim* 1 (1998), p. 47.

ously and suggest that women should not read the Scroll of Esther even for themselves but have it read to them by a man! By the time we get to Caro's Shulhan Aruk (1564), the author of that highly influential compendium inclines not to encourage the liberal view implied in the Mishnah and fleshed out by Joshua b. Levi, Rashi, and Maimonides.

A similar fate befalls the assertion in M. Ber. 3:3 that while women, slaves, and minors are exempt from reciting the Shema and tefillin, they are obligated with respect to "the prayer," *mezuzah*, and the grace after meals. Unquestionably, here as in M. Ber. 3:1-2 and 3:5 "the prayer" refers to the prescribed liturgical prayer commonly called "Eighteen Benedictions."[28] Now it is explained in B. Ber. 20b that it was necessary for the Mishnah explicitly to mention that women are obligated with respect to "the prayer" because it might otherwise be assumed that women are exempt insofar as prayer is a positive time-bound precept. B. followed by Rashi and Tosafot explain that "the prayer" is one of many exceptions to the generalization in M. Qid. 1:7 that women are exempt from time-bound positive precepts. Rashi, followed by Tosafot, rejects as spurious the reading in the standard text of B., according to which "the prayer" is a man-made obligation, which would mean that the entire subject is less weighty than both the reading of the Shema and tefillin, from which God, according to the Mishnah, exempted women! Now in light of M. R.H. 3:8, which declares that a person can perform on behalf of others any precept for which that person is obligated, it would appear that while women would be disqualified from leading mixed congregations in the singing of the Shaharit service, which includes the reading of the Shema, they should certainly be encouraged to lead mixed congregations in the singing of the Musaf, Minhah, and Neilah services, all of which contain only "the prayer." As we might expect, the exegetical tradition culminating in Maimonides Mishneh Torah, Laws of Prayer 1:1ff. came up with the amazing idea that 1) when God invented prayer God meant for women to pray; 2) when God allowed the rabbis (all of them men!) by means of Rabbinic eisegesis of Deut. 17: 9-11[29] to create legislation to implement God's constitu-

---

[28] For the text of this prayer, see Philip Birnbaum, *Daily Prayer Book* (New York, 1977), pp. 81-96.

[29] See above, n. 19.

tion, the written and oral Torah,[30] God invested the rabbis with authority to exclude women from the obligation to recite the prescribed "Eighteen Benedictions."[31] This assertion for which, as Rashi and Tosafot attested, there is no basis in either M. or B., coupled with M. R.H. 3:8, effectively reduces women from the active participants they were in the Temple cult[32] to passive listeners to the chanting of a priesthood open to the 49% of post-pubertal persons assumed to have a penis!

Tragically, the very same Tractate Sotah that seems to extend the bitter waters ordeal to both sexes and to reinforce Hosea's view of open marriage also aided and abetted the disempowerment of women by recording a seemingly innocent debate on the brownie points that one can accumulate to be called in on one's day in court by engaging in that most quintessential Rabbinic act of piety, study of Torah. M. Sot. 3:4 contains the following discussion:

> [If the bitter potion is administered and nothing happens to the woman suspected of adultery who knows that she is, in fact, guilty][33] and she has[34] merit, she attributes [her being acquitted by the bitter potion] to it

---

[30] See Martin S. Jaffee, "The Taqqanah in Tannaitic Literature: Jurisprudence and the Construction of Rabbinic Memory," in *JJS* 41 (1990), pp. 204-225; Gruber, *The Motherhood of God and Other Studies*, pp. 249-62.

[31] Maimonides' views and their antecedents are thoroughly explicated in Gerald J. Blidstein, *Prayer in Maimonidean Halakha* (Jerusalem, 1994), pp. 23-68 (in Hebrew). Once it is understood that the Maimonidean view that recital of the Eighteen Benedictions is human rather than God-made has important antecedents, we can better understand that Rashi is fighting a very important battle when he tells some of these earlier authorities, "You are working from a bad manuscript." Like the very best of modern *Wissenschaft*, Rashi is utilizing lower criticism to fight battles that have to do with the real world of men and women and empowerment, not some petty squabble in academia. Without Blidstein's brilliant demonstration of the pre-Maimonidean roots of the Maimonidean view of the authority for reciting the Eighteen Benedictions, one might never understand just what is at stake in Rashi's bringing into the discussion the issue of textual criticism!

[32] In addition to my "Women in the Cult According to the Priestly Code," cited above, see Susan Grossman, "Women and the Jerusalem Temple," in Susan Grossman and Rivkah Haut, eds., *Daughters of the King: Woman and the Synagogue* (Philadelphia, 1992), pp. 15-37; Tal Ilan, *Jewish Women in Greco-Roman Palestine* (Tübingen, 1995), pp. 176-84; contrast Hauptman, *Rereading the Rabbis*, p. 228.

[33] Cf., Jacob Neusner, *The Talmud of Babylonia: An American Translation XVII. Tractate Sotah* (Chico, 1984), p. 131.

[34] This is the accepted reading in Y. and in the authoritative medieval MSS. of the Mishnah, such as Ms. Kaufmann A 50. It is well known that the vulgar texts of M. and B. frequently turn the Mishnah's present-tense descriptions of what is, that is to say, what should be when the Temple is restored, into past-tense narration of what supposedly took place in Second Temple times.

[her merit]. There is merit that suspends [her being condemned by the bitter potion] for one year, and there is merit that suspends [her being condemned by the bitter potion] for two years, and there is merit that suspends [her being condemned by the bitter potion] for three years. On the basis of this [commonly held conviction that the woman's meritoriousness in other areas of life can result in the bitter potion's producing a false verdict of innocence] Ben Azzai opines, "A person[35] is obligated to teach one's daughter Torah so that if she should have to drink [the bitter potion] she should know that merit suspends on her behalf [the condemnation by the bitter potion]." R. Eliezer opines, "Whoever teaches one's daughter Torah teaches her lasciviousness."[36]

It might seem that Ben Azzai suggests that by teaching women Torah they may learn, among other things, that the merit earned either through dedication to the study of Torah or to other precepts can obviate a guilty verdict and make it possible for them to be pious in other areas of life while being unfaithful to their husbands. In the same vein it might seem that Eliezer is suggesting that for women to know Torah is harmful because it will lead to the very same kind of lasciviousness that Ben Azzai seems to encourage. Most plausibly, however, Marc D. Angel argues that Ben Azzai wants women to be taught Torah so that they will fully understand that the merit of Torah study and other pious deeds does not yield an acquittal but a suspension of the guilty verdict for a maximum of three years. Likewise, Angel argues, Eliezer's typically hyperbolic statement means only that Ben Azzai's strategy of going out of one's way to teach women precisely the law that merit suspends the verdict of the bitter potion for as long as three years may result in the woman's incorrect conclusion that "she can escape altogether."[37]

Even Angel admits that the exegetical traditions of Rabbinic Judaism culminating in Maimonides Mishneh Torah, Laws of Study of Torah 1:13 canonized not Angel's reading of what Ben Azzai and

---

[35] Heb.: *adam*; since, as we shall see, Ben Azzai does believe that study of Torah in its fullest sense should be a shared activity of females and males there is no reason not to assume that in this context *adam* refers to a person of either sex or the humanity collectively as in Biblical Hebrew. On *adam* in Biblical Hebrew, see Gruber, "Women in the Cult," p. 63, and the literature cited there. Since, however, in the eighth cent. B.C.E. Phoenician royal inscription of Azitawadda *'dm* is the opposite of *'št* (= Heb.: *ishah*, woman), it would probably be a very good idea for some scholar to undertake a systematic investigation of the nuances of *adam* in Rabbinic Hebrew.

[36] Daniel J. Boyarin, *Carnal Israel* (Berkeley, 1993), p. 171, points out that the Hebrew term *tiflut* means literally "'childish things' or 'foolishness'...however, it is a frequent euphemism for lasciviousness;" hence our rendering here.

[37] Marc D. Angel, "Understanding and Misunderstanding Talmudic Sources," in *Judaism* 26 (1977), p. 441.

Eliezer may have *meant in context* but rather what Eliezer, according to M. Sotah, actually said. Moreover, in B.'s exegesis of M. Sot. 3:4 at B. Sot. 21a it is made explicit 1) that women are excluded from the obligation of Israelites to study Torah; 2) that women, as a class, have less chance to earn merit, since the single precept that confers the most merit is obligatory study of Torah; and 3) that whatever merit women might acquire through performance of precepts to which they are subject is not enough to save them, in the long run, from the guilty verdict rendered by the bitter potion.

Demonstrating that the Jerusalem Talmud took for granted that the punishment mitigating merit referred to in M. Sot. 3:4 is, in fact, the merit earned from studying Torah, Boyarin writes:

> According to the Palestinian reading, the knowledge that the daughter should have of Torah is in no way restricted to issues having to do with the ritual of the errant wife, and it is the very merit of having studied Torah that stands in her favor. This view would lead to a practice in which women would have studied Torah no less than men, for in a situation in which merit is required, the more the better. Since the rabbinic discourse had enormous normative force in Jewish culture, such an interpretation would have had quite radical implications for the status of women in a society in which the study of Torah was the most valued of all practices. It leads to a construction of gender in which the roles of the sexes in symbolic life are not as differentiated as they have been in all traditional West Asian societies, including Judaism.[38]

The most insidious way in which Rabbinic Judaism disempowered women was in its law of divorce, which it sought to read back into Deut. 24:1-4. In fact, Deut. 24:1-4, as has long been noted,[39] closes an important loophole to what is today often called "swinging" and which in plain language may be called spouse swapping. Since Hebrew and other ancient Near Eastern law prohibited a married woman from having sex with any man other than her husband, the only way that women and men who took seriously the prohibition against adultery, which is called throughout the ancient Near East "the great sin,"[40] could engage in swinging was for the wife of A to be legally divorced from A before having sex with B and then to be

---

[38] Boyarin, p. 172; to Boyarin's suggestion that women were excluded from the public life of letters and liturgy in all traditional West Asian Societies, contrast Tikva Frymer-Kensky, *In the Wake of the Goddesses* (New York, 1992) and the series of studies on women in various cultures of ancient Western Asia in Bella Zweig, ed., *Women's Roles in Ancient Civilizations* (Westport, in press).

[39] See, e.g., the Pentateuch commentaries of Moses Nahmanides (1194-1270) and Don Isaac Abrabanel (1437-1508), ad loc.

divorced from B before returning to A at the end of the evening of swinging. Deut. 24 closes this loophole by prohibiting Mrs. A from returning to A after having been the legal wife of B. Deut. 24 mentions in passing that it was the habit of men to write and hand over to their erstwhile wives a bill of divorce. Deut. 24 does not say that only a man can initiate a divorce, nor does it prohibit a woman from initiating a divorce.[41]

In fact, there is significant evidence that in ancient Western Asia from the time of Hammurapi (1792-1750 B.C.E.) onward provision was made for women both 1) to initiate a divorce[42] and 2) to guarantee for themselves in a pre-nuptial agreement their right to initiate a divorce.[43] Moreover, there is significant testimony that in both Second Temple times and in the Tannaitic era Jewish women still had the right to initiate divorce.[44] In fact, as demonstrated by Mordecai

---

[40] See, e.g., William L. Moran, "The Scandal of the 'Great Sin' at Ugarit," in *JNES* 18 (1959), pp. 280-281.

[41] Hauptman actually alludes to the literature on this subject in *Rereading the Rabbis*, p. 126, n. 3; see the various commentaries on Exod. 21:10-11, which is widely regarded as granting the wife the right to initiate divorce.

[42] Yair Zakovitch, "The Woman's Right in the Law of Divorce," in *Jewish Law Annual* 4 (1981), pp. 28-46. Strengthening the case presented by Zakovitch that the ill-fated Levite's wife had divorced her husband is Codex Alexandrinus of the Septuagint, which translates the verb *wattizneh* in Judg. 19:2 by *orgisthe auto*, "she became angry at him.' The tradition preserved in this recension of the Septuagint assumes that the Heb. *wattizneh* is here a cognate of Akkadian *zenû*, "hate," a semantic equivalent of the verb *zêru* employed in Code of Hammurabi #142 with reference to a woman's divorcing her husband (see next note) and the semantic equivalent of *sn'*, primary meaning "hate," with the legal, technical sense of "divorce" in the fifth century B.C.E. Elephantine papyri and in Prov. 30:23.

[43] E. Lipiński, "The Wife's Right to Divorce in the Light of an Ancient Near Eastern Tradition," in *Jewish Law Annual* 4 (1981), pp. 9-27.

[44] Jesus, who utterly opposes divorce and who considers remarriage after divorce by *man* or woman to be adultery takes it for granted that among the Jews of the early first century C.E. it was customary for either wife or husband to terminate a marriage by sending the spouse a writ of divorce. So Mark 10:11-12: "Who divorces his wife and marries another commits adultery against her; and if she divorces her husband and marries another, she commits adultery." Likewise, Josephus, *Antiquities* XV, vii, 10, states, "When Salome quarreled with Costobarus, she sent him a bill of divorce and terminated her marriage with him although this was not according to the Jewish laws." Again in *Antiquities* XVIII, v, 4, Josephus writes, "...Herodias took upon herself to confound the laws of our country and divorced herself from her husband while he was alive, and she married Herod [Antipas]." Josephus testifies that in the Second Temple era Jewish women did, indeed, divorce their husbands, but he states that for a woman to do so is "against the Jewish laws." However, in the Aramaic papyrus from Nahal Hever dated 134 or 135 C.E., in the very heart of the Tannaitic era, we read: "I, Shlamzion daughter of Yehosef Qbšn from Ein-Gedi, have no claim against you, Eleazar son of Hananiah, who previously were my husband and who had (have) from me a document of divorce and expulsion." (Transla-

Friedman, for a millennium after the dawn of the Rabbinic period, Jewish women throughout the Middle East continued to take advantage of the age-old pre-nuptial guarantee of their rights as persons.[45]

---

tion: Hannah M. Cotton and Elisha Qimron, "XHev/Se ar 13 of 134 or 135 C.E.: A Wife's Renunciation of Claims," in *JJS* 49 (1998), p. 115.) Reflecting the view adumbrated by Josephus, Adiel Schremer, "Divorce in Papyrus Se'elim 13 Once Again: A Reply to Tal Ilan," in *HTR* 91 (1998), pp. 193-202, argues that the words "who had from me a bill of divorce" must be a quotation from the words of the erstwhile husband to Shlamzion rather than the words of Shlamzion herself to Yehosef, because, after all, "there is not the slightest hint in all the Talmudic corpus which would indicate...a different system of the laws of divorce" than the one under which husband can divorce wife but wife cannot divorce husband. Clearly, just as Josephus, adumbrating the view set forth in M. Yeb. 14:1, accuses women who divorce husbands of not being good Jews, so does Schremer argue that Shlamzion, presumed to have been a good Jewess, could not possibly have observed a system of Torah law different from the one canonized in the Rabbinic corpus. Cotton and Qimron, p. 116, suggest, "Either these Jews [Shlamzion and Yehosef] went against Halakha or the Halakhah had not yet become normative." Demonstrating again how delightfully confessional is our generation of Judaic scholars, Cotton and Qimron conclude their article with the following *proof* that, in fact, Shlamzion and Yehosef were good Jews and that they simply followed a different tradition of God's law: the dating of the document "on the twentieth of Sivan, year three of the liberation of Israel in the name of Shimeon son of Kosiba, President of Israel" (Cotton and Qimron, p. 118). Perhaps, Cotton and Qimron may be reading into a two thousand year old papyrus the situation in the State of Israel two millennia later in which extreme nationalism and careful adherence to halakhah as defined by an Orthodox religious establishment frequently go hand in hand. In fact, the very same dating invoked by Cotton and Qimron could just as well be used to support this writer's hypothesis (below) that, so long (until the defeat of Bar Kosiba/Kokhba) as Jewish men could achieve their sense of manliness by attempting to shape history, they were less inclined to stake out for themselves (to the exclusion of womankind) total control in the spheres of Torah study, synagogue worship, and family law! Taken together, the papyrus, Josephus, and Mark suggest that in the Second Temple and Tannaitic periods there were at least three views: 1) only husband can initiate divorce; 2) divorce itself by either party is contrary to God's design (Mal. 2:16; Mat. 19:3-9); 3) divorce can by initiated by either party. Why did the "husband only" party win out in Judaism? The answer is hinted at in the prologue to the Laws of Hammurabi, which states that the purpose of laws is to prevent the strong from oppressing the weak. History, told as *his* story, is, all too often, the narrative of how, in fact, the strong, including men, oppress the weak, including women.

[45] Mordechai Akiva Friedman, *Jewish Marriage in Palestine* (Tel Aviv and New York, 1980), vol. 1, p. 19: "Most conspicuous in the Palestinian tradition is the provision which entitled both parties to initiate divorce proceedings." He shows also (pp. 316-322) that this proviso is endorsed in Y. Ket. 5:10. The latter proviso shares with the Elephantine documents of the fifth century B.C.E. 1) guaranteeing both parties equally the right to initiate divorce and 2) the use of the verb *sn'* in the technical sense "divorce." In light of Lipínski's study (see above, n. 43), it should be clear that guaranteeing the wife the right to initiate divorce is part of the common legacy of ancient Western Asian societies going back at least to the fifth year of the reign of King Shu-Sin of Ur (2037-2029 B.C.E.). The eisegesis of Deut. 24 reflected in Sifre Deut. and canonized in the Mishnah and in Orthodox and Conservative Judaism today is, therefore, historically speaking, an aberration, for which Jewish women have paid dearly over almost two millennia!

Notwithstanding the various precedents for women being able to initiate divorce both in the ancient Near East and among rabbanite Jews, M. Yeb. 14:1 ("A woman may be divorced willingly or unwillingly but a man divorces only willingly") and ultimately all the surviving Judaisms based on the Mishnah granted this right only to men and thereby reduced Jewish women to chattels.

Mirabile dictu, the "Conclusion" to Judith Hauptman *Rereading the Rabbis: A Woman's Voice* includes the following triumphalist observation:

> It is therefore remarkable that in virtually every major area, as we have noted, the law was moving in the direction of extending to women more rights. Why did the rabbis make these changes? They were not feminist or proto-feminist. I can only speculate that a growing self-awareness on their part, a growing discomfort with patriarchal privilege, a deepening moral critique of society drawn from the words of Torah themselves, greater familiarity with surrounding cultures, and even pressure brought by the people themselves, such as by women seeking divorce relief from gentile courts[46]—all of this led to change.[47]

We have seen that, like the Hebrew Scripture, the Rabbinic corpora contain pronouncements that could lead to the empowerment of women, but we have also seen how over the course of time Rabbinic Judaism almost totally succeeded in shutting women off from the study of Torah, from participation as more than spectators in synagogue liturgy, and took away from them the right to initiate divorce.

These facts about Rabbinic Judaism bring us back to the question formulated by Jacob Neusner over twenty years ago:

> When we reflect upon the important social, political, and religious role open to women in the times of ancient Israel, with its women-prophets, queens, and other kinds of religious and political figures who were women, the significant role open to women later on, for instance, in the Hasmonean court, and the prominence of women in the art of synagogues of this very period, we must find it anomalous that only three groups of this period are unable to provide for women an equivalently distinguished role. These are, first the Essenes of Qumran, who have no place for women in the leadership of the commune;[48] second, the priests of the Temple, who keep women outside of the main sanctuary and allow them no role whatsoever in the conduct of the cult, and finally the rabbis

---

[46] Hauptman, *Rereading the Rabbis*, pp. 117-118; p. 129, n. 34.

[47] Ibid., pp. 245-246.

[48] I shall take up the issue of the status of women at Qumran in a forthcoming study.

of Mishnah-Tosefta, who carry forward the legacy of the Pharisees, scribes, and priests of the period before A.D. 70.[49]

Neusner himself suggested the following answer to the question of why Rabbinic Judaism systematically disempowered womankind:

> ...the attitudes toward women which lie at the foundations of Mishnah-Tosefta and which form the fundamental traits of the system of Rabbinic Judaism from its beginnings, in the late first and second century, to the present day, are likely to originate in priestly circles. These will long antedate the period before 70. They must go back to the time of Ezra, when the Priestly Code was given its ultimate structure and shape.[50]

Starting with what was in 1979 the state of the art in the study of Hebrew Scripture, namely, the conviction that the post-586 B.C.E. Priestly Code took away from women the power and status they had achieved in the Iron Age,[51] Neusner concluded that Rabbinic Judaism's disempowerment of women represents that Judaism's faithfulness to its priestly legacy. However, I demonstrated that the priestly strata of the Pentateuch do in fact give women greater power in the cult than they seem to have been granted by earlier biblical codes.[52] Moreover, I demonstrated that the extension of women's power is reflected also in Ezra-Nehemiah and Chronicles.[53] Hence, the source of Mishnah-Tosefta's disempowerment of women must be sought elsewhere than the legacy of the sixth century B.C.E. priestly schools believed to be responsible for much of the Pentateuch.

Twenty years ago Neusner accounted for the disempowerment of women in Ancient Judaism primarily on the basis of the male fear of menstrual blood: "The framers of Mishnah viewed women as abnormal, anomalous, dangerous, dirty and polluting."[54] A decade later Judith Romney Wegner tried to show the following:

> Whenever some man has a proprietary interest in the sexual function of a specified girl or woman, the Mishnah's framers treat the woman as that man's chattel in all matters that affect his ownership of her sexuality; in all other contexts, the dependent woman is treated as a person. When, by

---

[49] Jacob Neusner, *The Tosefta Translated from the Hebrew, Third Division: Nashim (The Order of Women)* (New York, 1979), p. x.

[50] Ibid., p. xi.

[51] This view is still reflected in Carol Meyers, "The Roots of Restriction: Women in Early Israel," in *BA* 41 (1978), pp. 91-103.

[52] Gruber, "Women in the Cult;" see above, n. 1.

[53] Ibid., p. 66

[54] Jacob Neusner, *Method and Meaning in Ancient Judaism* (Missoula, 1979), p. 97.

contrast, no man has a legal claim on the woman's sexuality, the system always treats her as a person, both in sex-related and other matters.[55]

This thesis is, indeed supported, inter alia, by 1) the delineation in the Mishnah and subsequent Rabbinic halakhah of the status of bogeret—"the adult single woman"—who simply does not exist in the system of Num. 30, where females who are competent to vow are treated as subject to the authority of either their fathers or their husbands;[56] 2) the total autonomy of the divorcée; and 3) the autonomy of the widow.[57] However, Wegner's thesis that the adult single woman, the divorcée, and the widow are persons and not chattels in Mishnaic Judaism does not account for the systematic exclusion of all females from an active role in synagogue worship and from study of Torah. Here Wegner, like previous scholars, invokes "the danger of pollution by contact with a menstruant.[58] Wisely, however, Wegner suggests also the following, much more cogent explanation of why the men (i.e., males) who framed the Mishnah, Tosefta, and the Talmuds succeeded, in the long run, in excluding all females including the prepubertal, the pregnant, and the postmenopausal from the public domain: "The self-identification of an in-group ('us') automatically places all others in an out-group ('them')."[59]

What Rabbinic Judaism actually has to say about males and females as sources of pollution with reference to the Rabbinic cultus of synagogue and house of study is contained in T. Ber. 2:12:

> Men who have experienced an abnormal genital discharge and women who have experienced an abnormal genital discharge (see Lev. 15:1-15) as well as menstruating women and women who have recently given birth (see Lev. 12:1-8) are permitted to chant Torah, Prophets, and Hagiographa out of a scroll and to chant from memory Mishnah, midrash, *halakhot*, and *aggadot*. Men who have experienced an emission of semen are barred from all of these activities.

The very same view that men's semen is an impediment to participation in divine service but uterine blood is not is expressed even more strongly in the *baraita* quoted in B. Ber. 22a:

> Men who have experienced an abnormal genital discharge and lepers

---

[55] Wegner, p. 19 and passim.

[56] Hauptman, p. 88; contrast Wegner, p. 14.

[57] Wegner, pp. 137-138, 196.

[58] Ibid., p. 18.

[59] Ibid., p. 177.

and men who have had intercourse with menstruating women are permitted to chant Torah, Prophets, and Hagiographa out of a scroll and to chant from memory Mishnah, Talmud midrash, *halakhot*, and *aggadot*. However, men who have experienced an emission of semen are forbidden.

Boyarin[60] and Lieberman[61] have both pointed out that while the Tosefta takes for granted the participation of women in the aforementioned acts of worship, the baraita quoted in the Babylonian Talmud takes for granted that those acts of worship are exclusively male prerogatives. It is equally important to note that the following religious beliefs are common to both T. Ber. 2:12 and the baraita : 1) menstrual blood does not disqualify persons from participating in the divine service of singing Scripture and Rabbinic traditions, and 2) contact with wet semen does disqualify persons from the divine services of singing Scripture and Rabbinic traditions. Clearly, the reason for the exclusion of women from that prerogative is to be found elsewhere than in biblical and Rabbinic conceptions of pure and impure!

Not unrelated to the issues of empowerment and disempowerment played out in the realm of Torah is the assertion by the anonymous Talmud in B. Ber. 22b that the common view of Lev., Deut., the Tosefta, and baraita that a man who has emitted semen is barred from participation in public divine service is not applicable to the divine service of Rabbinic Judaism that consists of singing words of Torah. According to B. Ber. 22b, the rationale for this *innovation* is the authoritative rule attributed to the Tanna, Judah b. Bathyra: "Words of Torah cannot be defiled."

The very same Jewish men who were ready to exclude more than half of the Jewish community—all those who were born female—

---

[60] Boyarin, pp. 180-81; Boyarin, there, suggests that the *baraita* makes no sense because it assumes that a man could engage in sexual intercourse and not become defiled by his own semen. It is reasonable to suggest, however, that the *baraita* takes for granted that Talmudic sages and their disciples who wanted 1) to enjoy sex frequently; 2) properly to pleasure their women (on this aspect of the mentality of Talmudic men, see B. Nid. 31a-b; see now the discussion of this text in Hauptman, *Rereading the Rabbis:*, p. 162); and 3) to avoid becoming disqualified by ejaculation from participating in the sacred rites of Torah study and prayer would have learned ·to both delay and avoid ejaculation. On the physiological aspects, which seem to have escaped Boyarin, see Alfred Kinsey, Wardell B. Pomery, and Clyde E. Martin, *Sexual Behavior in the Human Male* (Philadelphia and London, 1948), pp. 580-581; cf., James Leslie McCary, *Human Sexuality* (New York, 1967), pp. 200-201.

[61] Saul Lieberman, *Tosefta Ki-Fshutah, Order Zeraim, Part I* (New York, 1955), p. 20.

from study of Torah and who to this very day have kept them in ignorance and let them believe that it is because they just might be suffering from uncleanness generated by uterine blood[62]—were not ready to surrender the most important empowerment they had, namely study of Torah. Tragically, they abused their power by denying women the right to study Torah. By so doing, generations upon generations of Jewish women were denied access to the very corpora of what their religious community believed to be a divine constitution and a body of man-made laws legislated on the basis of God-given power to legislate.

I suggest that the correct answer to the question of why Rabbinic Judaism systematically disempowered women is found in the following observations written more than a quarter of a century ago by Jacob Neusner about the nature of Rabbinic Judaism from its beginnings:

> After 70, with the destruction of Jerusalem, the whole people faced the situation of the earlier Pharisees, who had been few in number, unable to control the course of events, and forced to accommodate themselves to a situation they could not control and probably did not like. In turning the nation into a religious community, in eschewing force, which they did not have, in favor of faith, which they might nurture, and in lending matters of faith—even humble details of keeping the law—a cosmic, transcendent importance, the Pharisees succeeded in reshaping the life of Jewry in a way appropriate to its new situation. Their success in the next four centuries in Pharisaizing, or rabbinizing, the Jewish people assured that the Jews might flourish in an age in which they would be unable to make important decisions, but could very well control homely matters.

---

[62] Shaye J.D. Cohen, "Purity and Piety: The Separation of Menstruants from the Sancta," in Susan Grossman and Rivkah Haut, eds., *Daughters of the King: Women and the Synagogue* (Philadelphia, 1992), pp. 103-115, calls attention to the seventh cent. C.E. *Baraitha de Niddah*, i.e., "Apocryphal Tannaitic teaching concerning the menstruant," that prohibits a woman from lighting the Sabbath candles during her period and forbids a man from reciting a benediction in the presence of a menstruant, lest her responding "Amen" desecrate God's name! Cohen emphasizes that normative halakhic sources never accepted these views. Nevertheless, in light of the text discussed by Cohen, it would seem fair to suggest that the popular view that women must be barred from cultic activities because of the menstrual taboo cannot be dismissed as "an old wives' tale," which term is both misogynic and misoanilitic (from Lat. *anilis* 'old womanish' from Lat. *anus* 'an old woman'). On the contrary, it turns out, the popular view, rejected by normative halakhah and aggadah, to which Jewish women had very little access, may be seen as a counter-tradition, albeit from my point of view and, from the point of view adopted in Ilana Pardes' famous "countertraditions" (see Ilana Pardes, *Countertraditions in the Bible: A Feminist Approach* [Cambridge and London, 1992]), a sexist and politically incorrect countertradition!

The Pharisees helped the Jews to reconcile themselves to their new situation, to accept what could not be changed, and to see significance in what could yet be decided. They invested powerlessness with such meaning that ordinary folk, living everyday lives might still regard themselves as a kingdom of priests and a holy people. The ideals of Hillel and Yohanan ben Zakkai for twenty centuries illuminated the humble and, from a worldly viewpoint, unimportant affairs of a homeless, often persecuted, despised, and alien nation, dwelling alone among other nations.[63]

The same idyllic picture of the world of Rabbinic Judaism is painted also in Neusner's *Androgynous Judaism*, a poignant description of the self-perception of Jewish manhood in Rabbinic midrash. There Neusner writes:

God wants holy Israel now to embody traits defined as feminine, women to the nations' ravishing man, so that, in the world that is coming, Israel may find itself transformed into man—but man still with woman's virtues.[64]

Feminine Israel in the here and now, we shall see, makes itself worthy of the coming of the Messiah at the end of days, at which point Israel assumes its masculine identity (once again).[65]

Placed in dialogue with feminist theory applied to machismo among oppressed minorities in North America and among colonial and post-colonial peoples throughout the world, Neusner's description of Roman-Byzantine period Jewish manhood drawn from the Rabbinic midrash cannot help but remind us of the following:

...nationalism typically has sprung from masculinized memory, masculinized humiliation and masculine hope. Anger at being "emasculated"—or turned into a nation of "bushboys"—has been presumed to be the natural fuel for igniting a nationalist movement.[66]

The significance of the community's women being raped...by foreign men is that the honor of the community's men has been assaulted.[67]

---

[63] Jacob Neusner, *From Politics to Piety: The Emergence of Pharisaic Judaism* (Englewood Cliffs, 1973), pp. 153-154.

[64] Jacob Neusner, *Androgynous Judaism: Masculine and Feminine in the Dual Torah* (Macon, 1993), p. vii.

[65] Ibid., p. ix.

[66] Cynthia Enloe, *Bananas, Beaches and Bases: Making Feminist Sense of International Politics* (Berkeley and Los Angeles, 1990), p. 44.

[67] Ibid., p. 62; cf., Sheila Rowbotham, *Women, Resistance and Revolution* (New York, 1974), p. 205: "The white imperialists did not only colonize economically but psychologically. They usurped the men from their manhood, they took over from the colonized men control of their women." See also, *inter alia*, Michelle Wallace, *Black Macho and the Myth of the Superwoman* (London and New York, 1990), pp. 1-85.

The Jews in the Rabbinic era had ceased to be a sovereign people. Jewish men were carried away as slaves, conscripted against their will into gentile armies to fight other peoples' wars. In order to prevent their wives' falling afoul of the levirate law in Deut. 25, many of these men would issue a conditional bill of divorce upon leaving home. The divorce would take effect if, after the elapse of a certain amount of time, the husband had not returned. Much of the discussion in the Mishnah and Talmuds revolves around the dire consequences of the woman's decision to remarry after the elapsed time only to find out that her husband, learning of his imminent return from captivity or military service, secured a court order for the cancellation of the divorce document. The consequences, often tragic, were especially tragic as viewed from the perspective of biblical and Rabbinic law, with their concepts of adultery and bastardy.[68]

Another issue that comes up more than once in the Mishnah is the sexual molestation of little girls. In M. Ket. 1:2 we read:

> As for the female proselyte, the free female who was taken captive and the slave woman who were respectively converted to Judaism, redeemed from captivity or freed from slavery prior to the age of three years and one day, their bride-price [Heb.: *ketubah*][69] is two hundred [dinars].

Similarly, we read in M. Ket. 3:2:

> These are woman [for the seduction of whom the perpetrator] has not to pay monetary compensation [for the loss of their virginity]: he who has sex with a female proselyte, a free female who was taken captive, or a slave woman, who were respectively converted to Judaism, redeemed from captivity or freed from slavery after the age of three years and one day.

The issue of sexual abuse of girls under the age of three comes up again in M. Nid. 5:4: "If she is younger than this [three years and one day], it is as though one puts a finger in the eye." Moreover, according to B. Nid. 43a, the rule that a girl who had sex prior to the age of three is legally speaking considered a virgin is a law given to Moses at Sinai, which is to say a God-given law known by tradition rather than from Scripture or by logical deduction from Scripture.

---

[68] See Hauptman, *Rereading the Rabbis*, pp. 109-110, and the sources cited there.

[69] The use of *ketubah* in this context seems to rule out the contention that the rabbis had completely moved beyond the biblical bride-price; contrast Hauptman, *Rereading the Rabbis*, p. 63.

Each of these four texts takes for granted both 1) that the virginity spoken of in Exod. 22:15-16, Deut. 22:28-29, and elsewhere in Scripture and tradition is virginity as determined by an apparently intact hymen; 2) that the hymens of girls who are violated prior to the age of three years and one day grow back;[70] and 3) that, in Roman Palestine, girls below the age of three years and one day are routinely violated. Strangely, at least four scholars who dealt with these texts failed to pursue the question, "What is the scientific basis for the assertion that the hymen of a girl violated prior to the age of three years and one day will grow back?"[71] I, on the other hand, searched some of what is a vast medical literature on the subject, and the following is just a little of what I found:

> Acute tears or bruising are rare because force is seldom a part of the sexual acts committed against a child. A vaginal opening of greater than 5 mm is not common and may indicate vaginal penetration with a finger, object or penis. An "intact" hymen does not necessarily preclude vaginal penetration. Lack of physical evidence never rules out abuse because many sexual acts leave no physical findings.[72]

Members of the medical and legal professions now acknowledge the following: 1) hymens of girls and women who have not given birth vaginally do heal so that inexperienced professionals might not be aware that the hymen had, in fact, been ruptured as a result of sexual abuse; 2) physical evidence is important in order to convict the abuser and put him away so that he can no longer abuse; and 3) rampant sexual abuse of little girls is a fact. Consequently, a number of medical professionals, prominent among them Prof. Abbey Berenson of the University of Texas Medical Center at Galveston, have compiled

---

[70] Wegner, p. 23, writes most eloquently, "They perceive the girl not as a human being...but as a chattel whose owner pays bride-price for an intact hymen...its chief significance is the perception of the female as mere sex object."

[71] Julius Preuss, *Biblical and Talmudic Medicine*, trans. Fred Rosner (New York, 1978), p. 479; Rachel Adler, "I've Had Nothing Yet So I Can't Take More," in *Moment* 8 (September, 1983), p. 25, quoted in Judith Plaskow, *Standing Again at Sinai* (San Francisco, 1990), p. 63; Wegner, pp. 22-23; Hauptman, *Rereading the Rabbis*, p. 100, n. 31.

[72] M.E. Herman-Giddens and T.E. Frothingham, "Prepubertal Female Genitalia: Examination for Evidence of Sexual Abuse," in *Pediatrics* 80 (1987), p. 203; Carolyn J. Levitt, "Medical Evaluation of the Sexually Abused Child," in *Primary Care* 20, no. 2 (1993), pp. 343-354, stresses the rapid healing of the hymen in sexually abused little girls, precisely the frightening human reality behind those passages in the Mishnah and Talmud!

data bases consisting of a) photographs of the genitalia of very young girls whose attackers confessed to having penetrated; and b) a control group of photographs of the genitalia of very young girls who had not been abused. The photographs of girls from the latter group are generally obtained by parental consent when the children are admitted to a hospital for minor surgery.[73]

What the Mishnah alludes to again and again is a very ugly and brutal world in which Jewish men, the erstwhile warriors who were defeated by the Romans in 70 C.E. and again in 135 C.E., have been psychologically emasculated. They cannot protect their daughters from being violated nor guarantee that they will be home to protect and provide for their wives. Like men in many societies around the world in the twentieth century, the Jewish men of the Talmudic era had been psychologically castrated. It is this psychological emasculation that is probably reflected in the rabbis' depiction of the nation of Israel as a dependent woman so eloquently described in Neusner's *Androgynous Judaism.*[74] It is this same successful, from the point of view of the outsiders, emasculation of the Old Israel by the self-styled New Israel of Christendom that is expressed in the medieval Christian conviction that Jewish men menstruate.[75] Why should they not? They are not really men!

This, I submit, is the single most cogent explanation of what went wrong from a feminist point of view in much of Rabbinic Judaism from antiquity to the present. The Jewish men sought and found in the study of Torah, the Rabbinic courts of law, which had jurisdiction

---

[73] Abbey B. Berenson, et al., "Appearance of the Hymen in Prepubertal Girls," in *Pediatrics* 89 (1992), pp. 387-394; Abbey B. Berenson, "The Appearance of the Hymen at Birth and One Year of Age: A Longitudinal Study," in *Pediatrics* 91 (1993), pp. 820-825; id., "A Longitudinal Study of Hymenal Morphology in the First Three Years of Life," in *Pediatrics* 95 (1995), pp. 490-496; J. McCann, J. Voris, and M. Simon, "Genital Injuries Resulting from Sexual Abuse: A Longitudinal Study," in *Pediatrics* 89 (1992), pp. 307-317; R.A. Underhill and J. Dewhurst, "The Doctor Cannot Always Tell: Medical Examination of the 'Intact' Hymen," in *The Lancet* 1978, vol. 1, pp. 375-376; A.H. Heger and S.J. Emans, *Evaluation of the Sexually Abused Child: A Medical Textbook and Photographic Atlas* (New York, 1992).

[74] See above, n. 64.

[75] See now Irven Resnick, "On Roots of the Myth of Jewish Male Menses in Jacques de Vitry's 'History of Jerusalem,'" in *International Rennert Guest Lecture Series* 2 (1998) [in press]. I am most grateful to Prof. Resnick and to my colleague Prof. Daniel J. Lasker for having provided me with this reference; on the belief among Christians that Jewish men menstruate, see also David Katz, "Shylock's Gender: Jewish Male Menstruation in Early Modern England," in *Review of English Studies* (in press).

over marriage and divorce and petty economic transactions, a new arena to assert their manliness, which is to say their power to influence the world. Feminist theory most cogently suggests that it is no wonder that they sought to banish women from these few areas in which, under the Roman-Byzantine and Parthian and Sassanian yoke, they could feel like powerful men rather than powerless little boys.[76]

What, then, is the common basis of the attempts of confessional Jewish scholars of Rabbinic literature, especially Neusner, Wegner, Boyarin, Hauptman, Ilan—and the list keeps growing, and it is already difficult to keep up with the worthwhile literature—to figure out both what went right and what went wrong with Rabbinic Judaism with respect to women, who played many and important roles in other ancient societies? The often unarticulated goal of these researchers is to find out how the system believed to contain Torah, the word of God, can be made to work for the liberation and spiritual advancement of both women and men. Seeing how and why women were systematically excluded from the study of Torah, public worship, and ultimately personhood enables those who are so inclined, I among them, to ally themselves with modern Jewish religious movements that seek to preserve the dual Torah of Moses our Rabbi without the tragic machismo born of psychological emasculation. Jewish scholarship on Rabbinic literature, especially with respect to the role of women in the religion(s) represented by and expounded in that literature, is clearly confessional. It seeks to understand, to deconstruct, and ultimately to reconstruct a living religious tradition, in which not a few Jewish women and men show that they have a very clear stake.[77]

---

[76] Rabbi Gilah Dror of Congregation Eshel Avraham of Beersheva informs me (oral communication) that she has arrived at similar conclusions independently. To the suggestion of a colleague that I have been anticipated by Daniel Boyarin, *Unheroic Conduct: The Rise of Heterosexuality and the Invention of the Jewish Man* (Berkeley, 1997), I hasten to quote from a personal communication (June 1, 1998) from Prof. Boyarin to the effect the only way that I could have derived my thesis from his would be by a process that he calls "a weird distortion of my [i.e., Boyarin's] thesis." For another view, see Michael L. Satlow, "'Try to Be a Man:' The Rabbinic Construction of Masculinity," in *HTR* 89 (1996), pp. 19-40. For still another related approach, much more optimistic than mine, see Aviva Cantor, *Jewish Women/Jewish Men* (San Francisco, 1995), pp. 79-98.

[77] Cf., Rachel Biale, *Women and Jewish Law* (New York, 1984), pp. 265-266.

Bibliography

Adler, Rachel, "I've Had Nothing Yet So I Can't Take More," in *Moment* 8 (September, 1983), pp. 22-26.

Angel, Marc D., "Understanding and Misunderstanding Talmudic Sources," in *Judaism* 26 (1977), pp. 436-442.

Biale, Rachel, *Women and Jewish Law* (New York, 1984).

Boyarin, Daniel J., *Carnal Israel* (Berkeley, 1993).

Boyarin, Daniel J., *Unheroic Conduct: The Rise of Heterosexuality and the Invention of the Jewish Man* (Berkeley, 1997).

Brichto, Herbert Chanan, "The Case of the *Sotah* and a Reconsideration of Biblical Law," in *Hebrew Union College Annual* 64 (1973), pp. 55-70.

Cantor, Aviva, *Jewish Women/Jewish Men* (San Francisco, 1995).

Cohen, Shaye J.D., "Purity and Piety: The Separation of Menstruants from the Sancta," in Grossman, Susan, and Rivkah Haut, eds., *Daughters of the King: Women and the Synagogue* (Philadelphia, 1992), pp. 103-115.

Enloe, Cynthia, *Bananas, Beaches and Bases: Making Feminist Sense of International Politics* (Berkeley and Los Angeles, 1990).

Foh, Susan T., *Women and the Word of God* (Grand Rapids, 1979).

Friedman, Mordecai Akiva, *Jewish Marriage in Palestine* (Tel Aviv and New York, 1980).

Frymer, Tikva S., "Ordeal, Judicial," in Crim, Keith, ed., *The Interpreter's Dictionary of the Bible, Supplementary Volume* (Nashville, 1976), pp. 638-640.

Frymer-Kensky, Tikva, *In the Wake of the Goddesses* (New York, 1992).

Goitein, S.D., "Women as Creators of Biblical Genres," in *Prooftexts* 18 (1988), pp. 1-33.

Goldfeld, Ann, "Women as Sources of Torah in the Rabbinic Tradition," in Koltun, Elizabeth, ed., *The Jewish Woman: New Perspectives* (New York, 1976), pp. 257-271.

Golinkin, David, "The Participation of Women in Funerals," in *The Rabbinical Assembly of Israel Law Committee Responsa 5747* (Jerusalem, 1997), pp. 31-42 (in Hebrew; English summary, pp. v-vii).

Grossman, Susan, "Women and the Jerusalem Temple," in Grossman, Susan, and Rivkah Haut, eds., *Daughters of the King: Woman and the Synagogue* (Philadelphia, 1992), pp. 15-37.

Gruber, Mayer I., "Marital Fidelity and Intimacy: A View from Hosea 4," in Brenner, Athalya, ed., *A Feminist Companion to the Latter Prophets* (Sheffield, 1995).

Gruber, Mayer I., *The Motherhood of God and Other Studies* (Atlanta, 1992).

Gruber, Mayer I., "Women in the Cult according to the Priestly Code," in Neusner, Jacob, Baruch A. Levine, and Ernest S. Frerichs, eds., *Judaic Perspectives on Ancient Israel* (Philadelphia, 1987), pp. 35-48.

Gruber, Mayer I., "Women's Roles in the Ancient Levant," in Zweig, Bella, ed., *Women's Roles in Ancient Civilizations* (Westport, in press).

Hauptman, Judith, *Rereading the Rabbis: A Woman's Voice* (Boulder, 1998).

Henry, Sondra, and Emily Taitz, *Written Out of History* (New York, 1978).

Ilan, Tal, "Biblical Women's Names in the Apocryphal Traditions," in *Journal for the Study of the Pseudepigrapha* 11 (1993), pp. 3-67.

Ilan, Tal, "Patriarchy, the Land of Israel and the Legal Position of Jewish Women in Rabbinic Literature," in *Nashim* 1 (1998), pp. 42-50.

Ilan, Tal, *Jewish Women in Greco-Roman Palestine* (Tübingen, 1995).

Ilan, Tal, *Mine and Yours Are Hers* (Leiden, 1997).

Jaffee, Martin S., "The Taqqanah in Tannaitic Literature: Jurisprudence and the Construction of Rabbinic Memory," in *Journal of Jewish Studies* 41 (1990), pp. 204-225.

Katz, David, "Shylock's Gender: Jewish Male Menstruation in Early Modern England," in *Review of English Studies* (in press).

Kinsey, Alfred, Wardell B. Pomery, and Clyde E. Martin, *Sexual Behavior in the Human Male* (Philadelphia and London, 1948).

Lipínski, E., "The Wife's Right to Divorce in the Light of an Ancient Near Eastern Tradition," in *Jewish Law Annual* 4 (1981), pp. 9-27.

McCary, James Leslie, *Human Sexuality* (New York, 1967).

Meyers, Carol, "The Roots of Restriction: Women in Early Israel," in *Biblical Archaeologist* 41 (1978), pp. 91-103.

Moran, William L., "The Scandal of the 'Great Sin' at Ugarit," in *JNES* 18 (1959) pp. 280-281.

Murphy, Cullen, "Women and the Bible," in *Atlantic Monthly*, August, 1993, p. 42.

Neusner, Jacob, *Androgynous Judaism: Masculine and Feminine in the Dual Torah* (Macon, 1993).

Neusner, Jacob, *From Politics to Piety: The Emergence of Pharisaic Judaism* (Englewood Cliffs, 1973).

Pardes, Ilana, *Countertraditions in the Bible: A Feminist Approach* (Cambridge and London, 1992).

Plaskow, Judith, *Standing Again at Sinai* (San Francisco, 1990).

Preuss, Julius, *Biblical and Talmudic Medicine* (New York, 1978).

Resnick, Irven, "On Roots of the Myth of Jewish Male Menses in Jacques de Vitry's 'History of Jerusalem,'" in *International Rennert Guest Lecture Series* 2(1998) [in press].

Rowbotham, Sheila, *Women, Resistance and Revolution* (New York, 1974).

Satlow, Michael L., "'Try to Be a Man:' The Rabbinic Construction of Masculinity," in *Harvard Theological Review* 89 (1996), pp. 19-40.

Schremer, Adiel, "Divorce in Papyrus Ṣe'elim 13 Once Again: A Reply to Tal Ilan," in *Harvard Theological Review* 91 (1998), pp. 193-202.

Shakdiel, Leah, "The Straightforward, the Comfortable and the Conflicted," in *Nashim: A Journal of Jewish Women's Studies and Gender Issues* 1, no. 1 (1998), pp. 154-161.

Terrien, Samuel, "The Omphalos Myth and Hebrew Religion," in *Vetus Testamentum* 20 (1970), pp. 315-338.

Umansky, Ellen, *Lily Montagu and the Advancement of Liberal Judaism* (New York, 1983).

Vos, Clarence J., *Women in Old Testament Worship* (Delft, 1968).

Wallace, Michelle, *Black Macho and the Myth of the Superwoman* (London and New York, 1990).

Wegner, Judith Romney, *Chattel or Person: The Status of Women in the Mishnah* (New York, 1988).

Zakovitch, Yair, "The Woman's Rights in the Law of Divorce," in *Jewish Law Annual* 4 (1981), pp. 28-46.

VII. WOMAN AS OTHER IN RABBINIC LITERATURE

Judith R. Baskin
State University of New York, Albany

The literary documents of Rabbinic Judaism are complex multi-stranded texts that interweave traditions, motifs, and influences from a variety of sources, time periods, and diverse environments, reflective of the extended duration of their composition and redaction. Far from monolithic in the views and attitudes expressed within its canon, Rabbinic discourse incorporates a variety of competing interpretations and opinions, generally privileging majority views but preserving minority opinions as well. Given this multivocal literary structure it is not surprising to find that a diversity of outlooks are expressed concerning women and their activities. What unites these views, however, whether expressed as legal ordinance, anecdote, folklore, or midrashic expansion of a biblical text, and whether reflecting biblical, Greco-Roman, or Persian influences and milieus, is the conviction that "women are a separate people" (B. Shab. 62a), a created human entity essentially different in physical characteristics, innate capacities, and social function from men. This essay explores the ways in which this certainty of woman's profound alterity from man in body, in moral and intellectual endowments, in social roles and legal responsibility, and in relationship to the divine, is manifested and justified in Rabbinic literature.

The interpreters and expositors of Rabbinic Judaism were men, and the ideal society they imagined was decidedly oriented towards the centrality of their own sex. With few exceptions, female voices are not heard in Rabbinic literature, and when they are they are mediated through male assumptions about women's nature and their intellectual, spiritual, and social status. Indeed, the Rabbinic written tradition believes that male Judaism is Judaism. Women did not play an active part in its development, nor were they granted a significant role in any aspect of Rabbinic Judaism's communal life of leadership, study, and worship. Neither women's religious rituals, which undoubtedly existed, nor female understandings of their lives, experiences, or spirituality, are retrievable in any significant way from Rabbinic Judaism's corpus of writings. Moreover, it is important to remember that Rabbinic texts tell us very little about the actualities of women's lives in any particular era or locale. The ideal visions of Jewish practice represented in Rabbinic texts were frequently at odds with the everyday lives of the Jewish cultures that existed in the different times and places during which the literature of Rabbinic Judaism was produced and edited.[1] What is unquestionable, however, is that this androcentric Judaism, constructed by a small group of sages in the first five or six centuries C.E., ultimately became the central authority and patternbook for almost a millennia and a half of Jewish existence.

To say that "women are a separate people" expresses the basic Rabbinic conviction that females occupy a subordinate place in a cosmos in which only free unblemished Jewish males participate fully in Israel's covenant with God. Despite the egalitarian vision of human creation found in the first chapter of Genesis, in which both male and female appear to share equally in the divine image, there is little doubt that Rabbinic Judaism is far more comfortable with the view of Gen. 2:4ff., that women are a secondary conception, unalterably different from men, and at a further remove from the divine.[2] This certainty of woman's ancillary place in the scheme of things permeates Rabbinic thinking. Thus, B. Nid. 31b states that the preferred position for sexual intercourse is that in which the man, on top, looks towards his origins in the earth (i.e., to the cosmic substance from which God created him), while the woman, facing upward, looks toward the man from whose body she was created. As Judith Romney Wegner has pointed out, the symbolism here is transparent: the male communicates directly with God and the cosmos; the woman experiences that relationship only indirectly, if at all—through her subordinate relationship to the man.[3]

Indeed, Gen. Rab. 17:8, in an extended midrashic excursus on this second version of creation, meditates on the enduring negative consequences for women's lives of female creation from the rib of the male. So central is this midrash to Rabbinic Judaism's discourse on women

---

[1] E.g., Ross S. Kraemer, *Her Share of the Blessings: Women's Religions Among Pagans, Jews, and Christians in the Greco-Roman World* (New York, 1992), pp. 93-94, 99, 102; Tal Ilan, *Mine and Yours are Hers: Retrieving Women's History from Rabbinic Literature* (Leiden, 1997).

[2] Judith R. Baskin, "Rabbinic Judaism and the Creation of Woman," in Miriam Peskowitz and Laura Levitt, eds., *Judaism Since Gender* (New York, 1997), pp. 125-130.

[3] Judith Romney Wegner, "Women in Classical Rabbinic Judaism," in Judith R. Baskin, ed., *Jewish Women in Historical Perspective* (Detroit, 1991), p. 78.

that I cite it in full since many of its themes will be addressed throughout this essay:

> R. Joshua was asked: "Why does a man come forth [at birth] with his face downward, while a woman comes forth with her face turned upwards?" "The man looks towards the place of his creation [the earth], while the woman looks towards the place of her creation [the rib]." "And why must a woman use perfume, while a man does not need perfume?" "Man was created from earth," he answered, "and earth never putrefies, but Eve was created from a bone. For example: if you leave meat three days unsalted, it immediately goes putrid." "And why has a woman a penetrating voice, but not a man?" "I will give you an illustration," he replied. "If you fill a pot with meat it does not make any sound, but when you put a bone into it, the sound [of sizzling] spreads immediately." "And why is a man easily appeased, but not a woman?" "Man was created from the earth," he answered, "and when you pour a drop of water on it, it immediately absorbs it; but Eve was created from a bone, which even if you soak it many days in water does not become saturated." "And why does the man make [sexual] demands upon the woman, whereas the woman does not make demands upon the man?" "This may be compared to a man who loses something," he replied; "he seeks what he lost, but the lost article does not seek him." "And why does a man deposit sperm within a woman while a woman does not deposit sperm within a man?" "It is like a man who has an article in his hand and seeks a trustworthy person with whom he may deposit it" [a woman can be assumed to be trustworthy since she has only one husband, but not a man since he may have several wives]. "Why does a man go out bareheaded while a woman goes out with her head covered?" "She is like one who has done wrong and is ashamed of people; therefore she goes out with her head covered." "Why do [women] walk in front of the corpse [at a funeral]?" "Because they brought death into the world, they therefore walk in front of the corpse, [as it is written], "**For he is borne to the grave...and all _men_ draw _after_ him, as there were innumerable** [women] **_before_ him**" (Job 21:32f.). "And why was the precept of menstruation given to her?" "Because she shed the blood of Adam [by causing death], therefore was the precept of menstruation given to her." "And why was the precept of dough (_hallah_) given to her?" "Because she corrupted Adam, who was the dough of the world, therefore was the precept of dough given to her." "And why was the precept of the Sabbath lights given to her?" "Because she extinguished the soul of Adam, therefore was the precept of the Sabbath lights given to her."

According to this passage, woman is essentially other than man because of the nature of her creation, and the inalterable effects of her origination account for many of her innate shortcomings and social disadvantages. Moreover, the text establishes that it was woman who brought death into the world. By linking the inferior nature of female creation with woman's responsibility for human mortality, Gen. Rab. 17:8 defends Rabbinic sexual politics and the male/female status quo by portraying woman's numerous faults and disadvantages both as divinely ordained and as deserved.

Woman's inferior body also accounts for her lack of standing in Jewish public and ritual life. Circumcision, *b'rit milah*, is the prerequisite for full entry into the *b'rit*, the covenant between God and Israel, whose primary obligation is obedience to the legal code revealed at Sinai. In this covenantal alliance marked on the flesh, women, for lack of the organ with which they were not created, are excluded *de facto* from complete participation in worship and religious service. As Howard Eilberg-Schwartz has noted, "Since circumcision binds together men within and across generations, it also establishes an opposition between men and women." Moreover, he argues, since circumcision was a symbol of potential fertility, the priestly writers of the Hebrew Bible portrayed it as the decisive confirmation of genealogical membership within the community of men descended from Abraham.[4] This preeminent emphasis on male generation, which traces descent from father to son and mandates male procreation as a legal obligation, also devalued and minimized women's roles in reproduction. And one must go further and say that if what makes men like God is their ability to create offspring, then women, viewed solely as vessels, passive bearers of male generated life, are secondary not only in relation to men but in their resemblance to the divine.

This conviction of the secondary status of women is evident in virtually every aspect of Rabbinic social legislation. The male sages who produced Rabbinic texts apportioned separate spheres and responsibilities to women and men, making every effort in their blueprint for an ideal society to confine women and their activities to the private realms of the family and its concerns, including economic activities that would benefit the household. Although wives had distinct personal and property rights, Rabbinic social policy primarily considered a married woman in her relationship to her husband, as she fell under his control, contributed to his comfort and to the bearing and nurturing of his children. When no man had a legal claim on a woman, however, as in the cases of an adult daughter, a widow, or

---

[4] Howard Eilberg-Schwartz, *The Savage in Judaism: An Anthropology of Israelite Religion and Ancient Judaism* (Bloomington, 1990), pp. 171, 176. On the following, see p. 233.

a divorcée, women had significant autonomy in the private domain of relationships between individuals, were legally liable for any vows they might make, and could litigate in court. Although such female independence was theoretically possible, in practice Rabbinic society was profoundly uncomfortable with unmarried women and the ambiguities they represented. While marriage and procreation were considered legal obligations only for men, being married was deemed such an absolute social necessity for women that girls were usually betrothed while still minors and communities would supply dowries for the indigent to enable them to find a spouse.[5]

As long as women satisfied their essential domestic expectations, they were revered and honored for enhancing the lives of their families, and, particularly, for enabling their male relatives to fulfill their religious obligations. As B. Ber. 17a relates, women earn merit "by sending their children to learn [Torah] in the synagogue, and their husbands to study in the schools of the rabbis, and by waiting for their husbands until they return from the schools of the rabbis." While texts such as Gen. Rab. 18:2 condemn gadabout and light-minded women who do not conform to patriarchal expectations, Rabbinic literature is not lacking in words of praise for the supportive, resourceful, and self-sacrificing wife, nor is there a lack of consideration for her physical and emotional needs and welfare.[6] Indeed, as Hauptman has demonstrated, Rabbinic jurisprudence goes beyond biblical precedents in its efforts to ameliorate some of the disadvantages and hardships women faced as a consequence of biblical legislation, and often devotes particular attention to extending protection to women in such areas as the formulation of betrothal, marriage, and divorce documents.[7] Moreover, many halakhic authorities have his-

---

[5] On the preceding, see Judith R. Baskin, "The Separation of Women in Rabbinic Judaism," in Y.Y. Haddad and E.B. Findly, eds., *Women, Religion and Social Change* (Albany, 1985), pp. 3-18; Jacob Neusner, *Method and Meaning in Ancient Judaism* (Missoula, 1979), p. 95; Judith Hauptman, *Rereading the Rabbis: A Woman's Voice* (Boulder 1998); Judith Romney Wegner, *Chattel or Person? The Status of Women in the Mishnah* (New York, 1988), pp. 143-145; Judith R. Baskin, "Rabbinic Reflections on the Barren Wife," in *Harvard Theological Review* 82 (1989), pp. 103-104; and Judith R. Baskin, "Silent Partners: Women as Wives in Rabbinic Literature," in Maurie Sachs, ed., *Active Voices: Women in Jewish Culture* (Urbana and Chicago, 1995), pp. 23, 26-28. See also B. Ta. 24a.

[6] Baskin, "Silent Partners," pp. 26-32.

[7] Judith Hauptman, "Feminist Perspectives on Jewish Studies: Rabbinics," in Shelly Tenenbaum and Lynn Davidman, eds., *Feminist Perspectives on Jewish Studies* (New Haven, 1994), p. 54.

torically sought to be flexible in easing difficulties individual women might encounter because of their disadvantaged position in Rabbinic legislation of personal status issues, including complications resulting from levirate marriage, desertion, the inability to divorce a husband, or to contest an undesired divorce.[8] Still, despite some willingness to consider an individual woman's personal situation sympathetically, the purport of Rabbinic opinion is that a woman best contributes to a smoothly functioning society when she is submissive to and supportive of male authority.

This commitment to women's primary domestic role is also reflected in Rabbinic Judaism's subordination of women's spiritual activities in the public domain. For one thing, Rabbinic Judaism generally understood women to be exempt from most regular religious communal obligations, especially those bound to be performed in the synagogue at specified times (M. Qid. 1:7; B. Ket. 29a). As a consequence, women were excluded from full inclusion in many religious activities that took place in the communal sphere, and from those endeavors, particularly intellectual pursuits, that conferred social and religious status. This is not to say that women were granted no spiritual status: women, like men, were not only responsible for obeying all of Judaism's negative commandments but also for observing the Sabbath and all of the festivals and holidays of the Jewish calendar, although male and female obligations on these days often differed. Moreover, according to B. Ber. 20a-20b, although women are exempt from participation in communal prayers that must be recited at specific times, women are not released from the obligation to pray. Later Jewish tradition understood that women were to make a personal address to God as they started their day and that the content of women's prayers might be spontaneous rather than according to an established liturgy.[9] We do not find extant versions of specific prayers for women, however, until the end of the medieval period.[10]

---

[8] See Hauptman, *Rereading the Rabbis*.

[9] Rachel Biale, *Women and Jewish Law* (New York, 1984), p. 20. Judith Hauptman, "Women and Prayer: An Attempt to Dispel Some Fallacies," in *Judaism* 42:1 (Winter, 1993), pp. 94-103, and "Some Thoughts on the Nature of Halakhic Adjudication: Women and *Minyan*," in *Judaism* 42:4 (Fall, 1993), offers a close re-examination of the issues involved in Rabbinic sources concerned with women and prayer. She concludes that women, like men, have always been obligated to pray several times a day according to a fixed liturgy.

[10] It seems likely that prayers specifically for women, centered particularly around rituals central to their private and domestic lives and in vernacular languages, have existed for many centuries. Extant versions of such prayers, however, date only from

It is often suggested that women were exempted from time-bound commandments because of their family responsibilities and obligations that might prevent their regularly fulfilling them. Saul Berman, for example, has suggested that many of the social and legal disabilities women suffer in Rabbinic Judaism are accidental by-products of the system's insistence on her confinement to the duties of the domestic sphere, noting that, "The exemption from communal presence seems to be a central element of women's status in Jewish law, necessary to ensure that no mandated or preferred act conflict with the selection of the protected role."[11] However, women's exclusion from communal worship and related activities cannot be explained away solely on the grounds of women's domestic duties, for women are not required to participate in communal worship even at those times in their lives when they are independent of the authority or demands of others, as childless adults, for instance, or as widows with grown children.

Judith Hauptman has suggested that woman's exemption from performing ritual acts at specific times is emblematic not only of her household responsibilities but of her subordinate social position, because were she to be so obligated this "would lessen her husband's dominance over her because she would have to cease temporarily from serving him and instead serve God."[12] Similarly, Wegner has written that Rabbinic Judaism is based on "a legal presumption that men, as heads of households, perform cultic precepts on behalf of wives, children, slaves, and all within their jurisdiction."[13] Moreover, while male children and slaves have the potential to join the covenant community as spiritual equals when their circumstances change, a woman is always a woman, and therefore is condemned by the essential biological qualities and deficiencies specific to her gender to permanent restriction from fully sharing in the privileges and

---

the late Middle Ages in manuscript and from the sixteenth century in printed form. On such religious literature for women, see Chava Weissler, "The Religious World of Ashkenazic Women," in Judith R. Baskin, ed., *Jewish Women in Historical Perspective* (Detroit, 1991), pp. 159-181; for examples of such literature, see Ellen M. Umansky and Dianne Ashton, eds., *Four Centuries of Jewish Women's Spirituality: A Sourcebook* (Boston, 1992).

[11] Saul Berman, "The Status of Women in Halakhic Judaism," in Elizabeth Koltun, ed., *The Jewish Woman* (New York, 1976), p. 123; cf., Biale, op. cit., pp. 10-17.

[12] Judith Hauptman, "Women and the Conservative Synagogue," in Susan Grossman and Rivka Haut, eds., *Daughters of the King: Women and the Synagogue* (Philadelphia, 1992), p. 169.

[13] Wegner, *Chattel or Person?*, pp. 147-148.

responsibilities of male-defined covenantal Judaism. Her presence is inappropriate in the central communal domains of prayer and study, regardless of whether or not her attendance would interfere with her domestic functions.

Although the details are mostly lost, women did participate in their own religious observances in the private domain, including abstention from work on *Rosh Hodesh*, the new moon (Y. Ta. 1:6, 64c). Women also were expected to obey a number of ritual regulations within the domestic sphere. These included preparation and serving of food according to Rabbinic dietary laws (*kashrut*), observance of limitations on marital contact during the wife's menstruation, and ritual immersion a prescribed period thereafter, indicating that marital relations might resume (*niddah*). Similarly, women were expected to separate and burn a piece of the dough used in making Sabbath bread (*hallah*), a reminder of Temple sacrifice, and to kindle Sabbath lights (*hadlaqah*). Doubtless, these rituals provided satisfying spiritual avenues for sanctification of aspects of daily life for many women. Yet, as indicated in the passage from Gen. Rab. 17:8 quoted above, at least some strands of Rabbinic tradition do not regard women's performance of these ordinances as *mitzvot*, that is, as divine commandments whose observance enhances the religious life of the observer and assures divine favor, but rather as eternal punishments brought upon woman to remind her of Eve's responsibility in the death of Adam and, therefore, in all human mortality.

In Gen. Rab. 17:8, this interpretation follows an enumeration of the disadvantages to which a woman is prone, including being subject to male demands; being limited, unlike men, to one spouse at a time; and having to be veiled like someone who has done wrong whenever she leaves the house.[14] The text then explains that women walk in front of a corpse during a funeral procession "Because they brought death into the world." A parallel remark in B. Ber. 51a goes even further in linking women with death:

> R. Joshua b. Levi said: The angel of death told me...'Do not stand before women when they return from a funeral procession, because I

---

[14] On veiling, see Leah Bronner, "From Veil to Wig: Jewish Women's Hair Covering," in *Judaism* 42:4 (Fall, 1993), who notes that it was customary for most women in the ancient Near East and in the Greco-Roman world to cover their hair when they went outside and suggests, p. 468, that for married Jewish women, "hair covering was a sign not only of rabbinically enjoined modesty, but of a wife belonging to a particular man, and the veil had to be worn whenever she was in mixed company or went out in public."

dance in front of them. My sword is in my hand and I have the power to smite."[15]

These themes of the female as deservedly disadvantaged, at fault in human mortality, and, indeed, as in some ways threatening to men, are now linked with the three commandments particularly incumbent on women, all of which are said to be permanent chastisements, following directly from the first woman's sin.

According to M. Shab. 2:6, disregard of these three commandments brings dire results: "For these transgressions do women die in childbirth: for heedlessness of the laws concerning their menstruation, the dough offering, and the lighting of the Sabbath lamp." In the adumbration of this passage at Y. Shab. 2:6, 8b, virtually the same midrash about Eve's responsibility for human mortality is repeated as justification for women's having to fulfill these precepts. Women's risk for death if they fail in these three specific areas is also reiterated several times in B. Shab. 31b-34a, which goes on to speculate about the causes of various human misfortunes for both women and men in general, with virtually every ill and catastrophe justified as the consequences of a specific human disobedience. Indeed, the major issue of discussion on the punishment women receive for transgressing the commandments of *niddah*, *hallah*, and *hadlaqah* is whether women's disobedience of these commandments leads to death in childbirth specifically (the opinion of the rabbis) or may be the reason for any premature death (the opinion of Eleazar cited at B. Shab. 32a). That dire consequences will follow on their neglect is not disputed.[16]

It is difficult to fathom what lies behind this formulation connecting these commandments for women with Eve's supposed responsibil-

---

[15] Similar notions are found as well in Jewish Hellenistic literature, as in Wisdom of Ben Sira 25:24: "The beginning of sin is from woman and because of her we all die." Mordechai Friedman, "Tamar, a Symbol of Life: The 'Killer Wife' Superstition in the Bible and Jewish Tradition," in *Association for Jewish Studies Review* 15:1 (Spring, 1990), has traced recurring superstitions associating particular women with "life-endangering demonic forces" through biblical, Rabbinic, and medieval sources. While such views, he argues, were never mainstream and were generally rejected by authoritative voices, the fact that they keep reappearing in various Rabbinic associations of women and death indicates the deep resonance they found within Rabbinic culture.

[16] Other explanations for women's premature deaths in this passage include washing diapers on the Sabbath. In addition, this text also appears to imply that premature deaths of wives (and children) may not always be due to their own faults but might occur as punishment for their husbands' sins.

ity for human mortality. Certainly it is repeated often enough to merit description as a mainstream Rabbinic view. Ross S. Kraemer writes that this passage may exemplify "the phenomenon that intensification of prescriptions against women is often a response to the increased autonomy and authority of women," and suggests that these passages may reflect some "Rabbinic opposition to the power and prestige of women in Jewish communities" which were just beginning to come under the influence and authority of Rabbinic traditions. Kraemer also suggests that the severity of these statements may reveal a Rabbinic effort to remove external non-Jewish associations from female rituals which had parallels in the "religious observances of women in the various forms of paganism with which Jewish women were likely to come into contact."[17]

A complementary explanation may be that such dire pronouncements are part of a Rabbinic polemic against widespread non-compliance with these precepts, perhaps particularly in regard to non-observance of *niddah* regulations. As Kraemer has pointed out, "except for the prescriptions of the rabbis themselves, we have no evidence for women separating dough, baking Sabbath bread, lighting Sabbath candles, or observing kashrut or Niddah, the laws of menstrual purity."[18] Significant evidence suggests that observance of ritual prohibitions outside of Rabbinic circles was often weak, both in the Rabbinic period and later in Jewish history.[19] Threats of early death may have been one Rabbinic stratagem to ensure higher degrees of compliance to what were seen as defining rituals for women. Certainly the anxiety one can discern in Rabbinic literature in regard to controlling women's activities may reflect the dissonance between what many women actually did and what the Rabbinic sages preferred that they would do.

A closer look at these texts also makes clear that they belong to a larger body of Rabbinic theological speculation that attempts to demonstrate that divine justice is fully operative in the world. All misfortunes and human suffering have a cause and often, if not always, this cause can be identified and waylaid by changes in human behavior.

---

[17] Ross S. Kraemer, *Her Share of the Blessings: Women's Religions Among Pagans, Jews, and Christians in the Greco-Roman World* (New York, 1992), p. 100.

[18] Ibid., p. 107.

[19] Ibid., p. 99, and Ephraim Kanarfogel, "Rabbinic Attitudes toward Nonobservance in the Medieval Period," in Jacob J. Schacter, ed., *Jewish Tradition and the Nontraditional Jew* (Northvale, 1992), pp. 3-35.

Women were demonstrably at great risk of death in childbirth, a tragedy unique to their gender. It is not surprising that Rabbinic expositors found a explanation for this frequent misfortune in the disobedience of these uniquely female observances. And at the same time, causes were found for calamities affecting men. B. Shab. 32a teaches that women's righteousness is examined at childbirth, a liminal moment of crisis, but then goes on to discuss extensively the parallel moments at which men are examined. Similarly, Boyarin points out that in Eccl. Rab. 3:3, a document that was probably redacted in the land of Israel, the text, "For three things women die in childbirth," is accompanied by the parallel construction, "and for three things men die."[20] Rabbinic theodicy may eschew ultimate certainty on all of the causes of specific human misfortunes, but that there were causes could not be denied without calling into question the reality of divine justice.

But finally, one must ask: Did the Rabbis believe that women were blessed with three empowering commandments or cursed with three eternal punishments? Did women view these obligations as special opportunities for sanctity or as deserved punishments for Eve's sin? These questions cannot be answered. The polyphonic complexity of Rabbinic literature renders its formulations as irreducible as they are ultimately mysterious; meanwhile, women's voices are absent entirely. Although one may agree with Boyarin that "these [commandments] are particularly given to women because they belong particularly to woman's sphere as understood by Rabbinic culture, to her body, cooking, and the comfort of the house, just as other commandments, which belong to the 'male' spheres of public life and worship are restricted to men,"[21] it is also the case that we do not see a similar construction of male obligations as punishments rather than as avenues to righteousness. Rather, it seems no accident that all three of these commandments/punishments specifically directed at women have to do with separation. All three may be read as symbolizing the chasm between the sacred and the profane, the holy and the secular, the pure and the impure, the realm of men who obey commandments and that of women who suffer disabilities, and ultimately between the realms of life and death themselves. As such, they epito-

---

[20] Daniel Boyarin, *Carnal Israel: Reading Sex in Talmudic Culture* (Berkeley, 1993), p. 94.

[21] Ibid., p. 92.

mize the profound disparity significant voices within Rabbinic Judaism recognized and wished to maintain between the lives and experiences of men and women.

Male speculation about the precise disadvantages women suffer as compared to men, and the reasons for these handicaps, a major theme of Gen. Rab. 17:8, is also pursued in B. Erub. 100b, which relates that Eve, as all women after her, was cursed with ten curses. The first six curses, based on a sequential exegesis of Gen. 3:16, are the blood shed at menstruation, the blood shed at the loss of virginity, the pain of bringing up children, the pain suffered during pregnancy, the pain of childbirth, and a woman's desire for her husband when he is away on a journey. The seventh, based on the end of the same biblical verse, "and he shall rule over you" is said to mean that a woman may not address her husband sexually with words but must ingratiate herself with him by her actions when she is desirous of sexual attention. Having to express her needs covertly is indicative of the sexual passivity imposed on women, certainly an undesirable condition from the male vantage point, and hence one of Eve's curses.

At this point, the discussion turns to the three remaining burdens that make women's lot so much less appealing than that apportioned to men. According to Dimi, the final three curses are, "She is wrapped up like a mourner, banished from the company of all men, and confined within a prison." Here is a strong descriptive statement, indeed, of the consequences for women of their separation from participation in the major activities of Jewish communal life, as well as evidence that men were quite aware of the consequences of that deprivation. "Wrapped up like a mourner" cannot but evoke the connections drawn between women and death in parallel texts such as Gen. Rab. 17:8 and B. Ber. 51a. Even if it is understood as a straightforward reference to women's having to veil themselves when they appear in public, the comparison of woman's ordinary public state to that of a mourner is a telling and disturbing remark. B. Erub. 100b then goes on to debate the meaning of "banished from the company of all men," since it seems so similar to "confined within a prison," the disability that immediately follows. What ultimately distinguishes these two conditions is that while "confined within a prison" means that a woman is best kept occupied at home, "banished from the company of all men" is said to refer to the fact that a woman is forbidden to be married to two men at the same time. Again, we see an appreciation here, as in Gen. Rab. 17:8, of the male's relative sexual freedom, which allows him access to more than one woman at a time, while patriarchal norms demand that a wife's fidelity be assured; it is interesting that this lack of sexual variety is seen as a disadvantage for women that must be justified.[22]

Virtually all of women's perceived disadvantages in this passage result from their physical differences from men. Indeed, B. Erub. 100b concludes its discussion of women's disagreeable lot with three alternate curses derived from a *baraita*, two of which also stress aspects of woman's physical otherness as undesirable, while the third is simply a bald acknowledgment of the distasteful nature, from a male perspective, of woman's supportive role: "She grows long hair like Lilith, sits when making water like a beast, and serves as a bolster for her husband." These, and similar remarks, add strong support to the contention that the roots of the exclusion of women from communal participation and literary culture and their relegation to domestic, enabling roles are deeply embedded in Rabbinic Judaism's profound consciousness of corporeality and its consequences.

Rabbinic Judaism is not unique in division of gender roles or in the reasoning behind it. Anthropologists have noted that in many cultures females are seen as closer to nature because of the "natural procreative functions specific to women alone," such as fertility, maternity, and menstrual blood. Although this perception is more a human construct than a fact of nature, it is often "embodied in institutional forms that reproduce her [perceived] situation."[23] Thus, a number of societies define women almost exclusively in terms of their sexual functions, many of which may be frightening or threatening to men.[24] Significant strands within Rabbinic Judaism, too, are most anxious to circumscribe, defuse, and control the biological/sexual

---

[22] Polygyny and concubinage have been little explored in Rabbinic literature; they appear to have been commoner than apologists have maintained. Isaiah M. Gafni, "The Institution of Marriage in Rabbinic Times," in David Kraemer, ed., *The Jewish Family: Metaphor and Memory* (New York, 1989), pp. 21-25, suggests that the sources indicate that polygyny was far more typical of Jewish life in the Babylonian milieu than in the land of Israel. All of these curses, including the last three here attributed to Dimi, are also found in Avot de-Rabbi Nathan A, chap. 1, and Avot de-Rabbi Nathan B, p. 117. The same chapter in ARNA relates that three decrees were decreed against Adam on the day of his disobedience and three were also decreed against Eve.

[23] Sherry Ortner, "Is Female to Male as Nature is to Culture?," in Michelle Zimbalist Rosaldo and Louise Lamphere, eds., *Women, Culture and Society* (Stanford, 1971), pp. 73-74, 87.

[24] Michelle Zimbalist Rosaldo, "Woman, Culture, and Society: A Theoretical Overview," in Rosaldo and Lamphere, op. cit., pp. 31-32.

attributes of the female as both polluter and temptress. For one thing, as has been noted above, women lack the organ of generation that defines both masculine virility and symbolizes man's likeness to God. Moreover, in some traditions within Rabbinic Judaism, as Eilberg-Schwartz has noted, study and the transmission of learning themselves became a form of generation when reproduction was redefined away from biological fatherhood and projected onto the educational relationship. For adherents of this view, the insemination of Torah knowledge and the production of disciples is said to take precedence over the legal obligation to beget biological offspring.[25] In this Rabbinic model of cultural generativity, women could become altogether dispensable, coming to represent "the very antithesis of Torah and Torah study."[26]

Moreover, it is not only what the female body lacks that marks its difference; the fact of female menstruation is central to the Rabbinic construction of women.[27] Since the menstruating or postpartum woman is a potential source of danger to male ritual purity,[28] the strictures that limit contact with a *niddah* are fundamental to the Rabbinic separation of women. While men are also subject to discharges and states of ritual impurity, in the case of males such physical ailments are unusual and sporadic. But for women, such discharges are characteristic; they are normal and expected, and, as Eilberg-Schwartz has pointed out, the blood of menstruation is linked with defilement, estrangement from God, and death.[29]

Women are also problematic because they are sexually attractive to men.[30] Jacob Neusner has discussed the part played by Rabbinic

---

[25] Eilberg-Schwartz, *Savage*, p. 230-231.

[26] Ibid., p. 233. On attitudes towards celibacy in Rabbinic Judaism, see Boyarin, op. cit., pp. 47, 134-136, 139-141, 163-165. He notes, p. 136, that "Rabbinic culture...is beleaguered with a constant unresolved tension—almost an antimony—between the obligation to marry and the equal obligation to devote oneself entirely to the life of Torah-study." For similar conclusions, see Eliezer Diamond, "Hunger Artists and Householders: The Tension between Asceticism and Family Responsibility among Jewish Pietists in Late Antiquity," in *Union Seminary Quarterly Review* 48 (1996), pp. 28-47.

[27] Baskin, "Separation of Women," pp. 12-13; Biale, op. cit., pp. 147-174.

[28] Shaye J.D. Cohen, "Purity and Piety: The Separation of Menstruants from the Sancta," in Susan Grossman and Rivka Haut, eds., *Daughters of the King: Women and the Synagogue* (Philadelphia, 1992), pp. 108-109.

[29] Eilberg-Schwartz, *Savage*, pp. 184-85.

[30] The dangers to men of contact with attractive women who are not their wives are well documented in Rabbinic literature; see B. Ber. 24a; B. Ned. 20a, B. Shab. 64b; and B. Meg. 15a.

Judaism's heightened consciousness of sexuality and its potential consequences in his analysis of Mishnaic texts concerned with the contracting and dissolving of marriages, arguing that, in the patriarchal world of Rabbinic Judaism, man is normal and woman is abnormal—she is always capable of upsetting the rabbis' ordered program for reality. He suggests that Rabbinic Judaism is especially anxious to keep women subject to men and to establish rules that regulate the transfer of a woman from one man to another at liminal moments when her situation is likely to be most disturbing and disruptive.[31] Certainly a preponderance of voices within Rabbinic Judaism advise extremely limited contact between unrelated men and women in all circumstances to prevent the possibility of sexual contact between inappropriate partners, both in order to avert adulterous or incestuous relationships, and to prevent the conception and birth of illegitimate children (*mamzerim*).

Thus, while individual women, with their potential for reproduction and their ability to provide essential family support services, are valuable and often cherished beings who must be safeguarded by specific men, Rabbinic opinion overwhelmingly regards women in general as potential sources of enticement, societal disorder, and pollution, which are best kept separate from centers of communal governance, scholarship, and holiness. One halakhic justification for the exemption of women from the obligation of synagogue attendance rests on the Talmudic statement, "The voice of woman is indecent" (B. Ber. 24a), based on a ruling a man may not recite the *Shema* if he hears a woman singing, since her voice might divert his concentration from the prayer.[32] Extrapolating from hearing to seeing, Rabbinic prohibitions on male/female contact in worship eventually led to a physical barrier (*mehitzah*) between men and women in the synagogue to preserve men from sexual distraction during prayer.[33] The similar

---

[31] Neusner, op. cit., p. 97.

[32] Emily Taitz, in Susan Grossman and Rivka Haut, eds., *Daughters of the King: Women and the Synagogue* (Philadelphia, 1992), p. 61.

[33] Biale, op. cit., p. 167; Cohen, op. cit., pp. 108-109. It became common in medieval times for women to express piety by not attending synagogue and other public places during their period of *niddut*, even though the Rabbinic laws of *niddah* proper do not exclude a woman from such activities (Biale, p. 167). Cohen, p. 108, writes, that "in the conception of the Mishnah and the Talmuds the menstruant is impure and transmits impurity to persons and objects, but she is not a source of danger." He points to a sixth or seventh century text, *Baraita de Niddah*, probably written in the land of Israel, as responsible for a major and negative shift in popular attitudes towards the dangerous influence of the menstruant who, according to this

concern, rooted in popular piety, that a menstruating woman should not enter the synagogue, may also have contributed to the insistence that the non-menstruant, too, must sit separately and out of sight and sound.[34] Since Rabbinic Judaism was solely concerned with the quality of male worship in the communal sphere, the deleterious effects on female spirituality as a consequence of this isolation were rarely considered.[35]

Women's physical differences from men are also seen as accounting for their intellectual and moral otherness. While women are credited with more compassion and concern for the unfortunate than men, perhaps as a result of their nurturing roles (B. Ta. 23b; B. Ket. 67b and 104a), they are also linked with witchcraft (M. Ab. 2:7; Y. Qid. 4, 66b), and wantonness, licentiousness, and sexual abandon (M. Sot. 3:4; B. Ket. 65a). One tradition teaches that women possess four traits: they are greedy, eavesdroppers, slothful, and envious (Gen. Rab. 45:5); according to some accounts, they are prone to steal and to be frivolous (B. Shab. 33b; Gen. Rab. 18:2). B. Qid. 49b relates that "ten measures of speech descended to the world and women took nine of them." Often these moral flaws are also seen as consequences

---

tract, must be distanced not only from her husband but is also forbidden to enter a synagogue, to come into contact with sacred books, to pray, or to recite God's name. He indicates, pp. 112-113, that while these widespread and popular practices reflected popular folk religion, not halakhic norms, their separation of the menstruant from public sacred space confirms "the marginality of all women, menstruating or not, in the organized, public expressions of Jewish piety."

[34] On the issue of when separate seating for men and women was institutionalized in the synagogue, see articles by Hannah Safrai, Emily Taitz, and Norma Baumel Joseph in Grossman and Haut, op. cit.; all agree that separation of the sexes does not appear to become a hard-and-fast ruling until the late twelfth or early thirteenth centuries.

[35] As evidence that attitudes towards women and worship have not changed very much in some traditional Jewish circles, I include the following excerpts from a letter written by Rabbi Pinchas Stolper, Executive Vice President, Union of Orthodox Jewish Congregations of America, which appeared in *Moment Magazine* 19:3 (June 1994), p. 13, addressing an earlier article on the possibility of women being ordained as rabbis in Orthodox Judaism: "...There are two overwhelming, powerful, magnetic forces in life: the attraction between a man and a woman and the attraction of people to God. The synagogue is the place where the man-God attraction must be exclusive and supreme. It can tolerate neither competition nor distraction of any kind. The distracting quality of women, no matter how much Orthodox Jews have grown accustomed to a degree of the mixing of the sexes, is not a matter of dispute. To place a woman on the pulpit, in front of the *aron kodesh*, is to defeat the very purpose of the synagogue. It is bad enough that some men are unable to control sexual thoughts, especially here in America where sex is all-pervasive, but to place sex in front of our eyes in the very holy of holies is dangerous and self-defeating."

of woman's secondary and inferior mode of creation. (Gen. Rab. 18:2). In fact, such characterizations betray extreme Rabbinic anxiety to designate women as different from men and as deficient in what are seen as men's admirable qualities, particularly wisdom, stored up knowledge, and analytical abilities.

Rabbinic aggadic traditions frequently diminish women's abilities and qualities in biblical exegeses, general comments, and personal anecdotes. Women do utter wise words in a few Rabbinic stories, but generally such tales are related in a tone of surprise. Often, the woman's sagacity serves either to confirm a Rabbinic belief about women's character, such as women's higher degree of compassion for others, or it delivers a rebuke to someone in need of chastisement; to be bested by a woman is humiliation indeed.[36] Stories about Meir's learned wife Beruriah, for example, demonstrate her knowledge of Rabbinic biblical exegesis, a sophisticated ability to manipulate traditional texts, and her quick wit (B. Pes. 62b; B. Erub. 53b-54a). Yet, her reputed scholarship was a problem for Rabbinic culture, and in later Rabbinic tradition she is shown to reap the tragic consequences of the "lightmindedness" inherent in woman's makeup: the eleventh century commentator Shlomo ben Isaac (Rashi) relates a tradition in his commentary on B. A.Z. 18b that Beruriah was seduced by one of her husband's students and subsequently committed suicide. While contemporary scholars have shown that the scholarly Beruriah is a literary construct with little historical reality,[37] they agree that the traditions about her articulate profound disquiet about the role of women in the Rabbinic enterprise. Rachel Adler suggests that Beruriah's story expresses Rabbinic ambivalence about the possible place of a woman in their wholly male scholarly world of "teachers and students and study partners," in which her sexuality was bound to be a source of havoc,[38] while Boyarin writes that for the Amoraic sages of the Babylonian Talmud Beruriah serves as proof of "R. Eliezer's statement that 'anyone who teaches his daughter Torah, teaches her lasciviousness'(M. Sot. 3:4)."[39] In Rabbinic culture, he writes, "The

---

[36] Judith R. Baskin, "The Separation of Women in Rabbinic Judaism," in Haddad and Findly, op. cit., pp. 6-7; Judith Hauptman, "Images of Women," pp. 201-204.

[37] Tal Ilan, "The Quest for the Historical Beruriah, Rachel, and Imma Shalom," in *AJS Review* 22:1(1997), pp. 1-17.

[38] Rachel Adler, "The Virgin in the Brothel and Other Anomalies: Character and Context in the Legend of Beruriah," in *Tikkun* 3/6 (1988), p. 32.

[39] Boyarin, op. cit., pp. 188-189.

Torah and the wife are structural allomorphs and separated realms...
both normatively to be highly valued but also to be kept separate."[40]

Recently, some scholars have shown that not all Rabbinic authorities agreed on the isolation of women from learning and communal
prayer, demonstrating that some minority strands more supportive of
women's intellectual and spiritual abilities and needs also weave
through the tradition, particularly from sources in the land of Israel.
Boyarin suggests that while the dominant discourse in both the Babylonian and Palestinian Talmuds suppresses women's participation in
study and communal worship, in Palestine a dissenting voice was
tolerated while in Babylonia "this issue seems to have been so threatening that even a minority voice had to be entirely expunged."[41] As
he notes, however, "The historical effect of the Babylonian text...
which was hegemonic for later European Jewish culture, was to suppress quite thoroughly the possibilities for women to study Torah
until modern times."[42]

The Rabbinic construction of women is a highly complex and
many-layered phenomenon. Yet it can be said that in the Rabbinic
taxonomy of human beings, women are other than men in a number
of ways. As a secondary creation, physically incapable of virility and
generation, they are excluded from the responsibilities, privileges, and
power conferred by full partnership in the divine covenant. Sexually
attractive to men, they represent a potential source of enticement and
societal disorder that must be maintained under male control, while
at the same time their periodic uncleanness presents recurrent threats
to the ritual purity of their husbands' persons. But different as they
are imagined to be, women are also acknowledged as essential to
men, for it is they who constitute the indispensable social mortar that
sustains Rabbinic society. As wives, mothers, and economic contributors, women were indeed indispensable "bolsters to their husbands"
(B. Erub. 100b).[43] Nevertheless, women's spiritual and intellectual
needs are seen as subordinate to men's, and most voices within Rabbinic Judaism agree that women are best kept separate from centers
of communal governance, holiness, and learning.

---

[40] Ibid., p. 196.
[41] Ibid., p. 169.
[42] Ibid., pp. 169-70.
[43] Judith R. Baskin, "Silent Partners," pp. 26-28.

Bibliography

Adler, Rachel, "The Virgin in the Brothel and Other Anomalies: Character and Context in the Legend of Beruriah," in *Tikkun* 3/6 (1988), pp. 28-32, 102-105.

Baskin, Judith R., "The Separation of Women in Rabbinic Judaism," in Haddad, Y.Y., and E.B. Findly, eds., *Women, Religion and Social Change* (Albany, 1985), pp. 3-18.

Baskin, Judith R., "Rabbinic Reflections on the Barren Wife," in *Harvard Theological Review* 82 (1989), pp. 1-14.

Baskin, Judith R., "Silent Partners: Women as Wives in Rabbinic Literature," in Sachs, Maurie, ed., *Active Voices: Women in Jewish Culture* (Urbana and Chicago, 1995), pp. 19-37.

Baskin, Judith R., "Rabbinic Judaism and the Creation of Woman," in Peskowitz, Miriam, and Laura Levitt, eds., *Judaism Since Gender* (New York, 1997), pp. 125-130.

Berman, Saul, "The Status of Women in Halakhic Judaism," in Koltun, Elizabeth, ed., *The Jewish Woman* (New York, 1976), pp. 114-128.

Biale, Rachel, *Women and Jewish Law* (New York, 1984).

Boyarin, Daniel, *Carnal Israel: Reading Sex in Talmudic Culture* (Berkeley, 1993).

Bronner, Leah, "From Veil to Wig: Jewish Women's Hair Covering," in *Judaism* 42:4 (Fall, 1993), pp. 465-477.

Cohen, Shaye J.D., "Menstruants and the Sacred in Judaism and Christianity," in Sarah B. Pomeroy, ed., *Women's History and Ancient History* (Chapel Hill, 1991), pp. 273-99.

Cohen, Shaye J.D., "Purity and Piety: The Separation of Menstruants from the Sancta," in Grossman, Susan, and Rivka Haut, eds., *Daughters of the King: Women and the Synagogue* (Philadelphia, 1992), pp. 103-116.

Diamond, Eliezer, "Hunger Artists and Householders: The Tension between Asceticism and Family Responsibility among Jewish Pietists in Late Antiquity," in *Union Seminary Quarterly Review* 48 (1996), pp. 28-47.

Eilberg-Schwartz, Howard, *The Savage in Judaism: An Anthropology of Israelite Religion and Ancient Judaism* (Bloomington, 1990).

Friedman, Mordechai A., "Tamar, a Symbol of Life: The 'Killer Wife' Superstition in the Bible and Jewish Tradition," in *Association for Jewish Studies Review* 15:1 (Spring, 1990), pp. 23-61.

Gafni, Isaiah M., "The Institution of Marriage in Rabbinic Times," in Kraemer, David, ed., *The Jewish Family: Metaphor and Memory* (New York, 1989), pp. 13-30.

Grossman, Susan and Rivka Haut, eds., *Daughters of the King: Women and the Synagogue* (Philadelphia, 1992).

Hauptman, Judith, "Images of Women in the Talmud," in Ruether, Rosemary Radford, ed., *Religion and Sexism: Images of Women in Jewish and Christian Traditions* (New York, 1974), pp. 184-212.

Hauptman, Judith, "Women and Prayer: An Attempt to Dispel Some Fallacies," in *Judaism* 42:1 (Winter, 1993), pp. 94-103.

Hauptman, Judith, "Some Thoughts on the Nature of Halakhic Adjudication: Women and *Minyan*," in *Judaism* 42:4 (Fall, 1993), pp. 396-413.

Hauptman, Judith, "Feminist Perspectives on Jewish Studies: Rabbinics," in Tenenbaum, Shelly, and Lynn Davidman, eds., *Feminist Perspectives on Jewish Studies* (New Haven, 1994), pp. 40-61.

Hauptman, Judith, *Rereading the Rabbis: A Woman's Voice* (Boulder, 1998).

Ilan, Tal, "The Quest for the Historical Beruriah, Rachel, and Imma Shalom," in *Association for Jewish Studies Review* 22:1(1997), pp. 1-17.

Ilan, Tal, *Mine and Yours are Hers: Retrieving Women's History from Rabbinic Literature* (Leiden, 1997).

Kanarfogel, Ephraim, "Rabbinic Attitudes toward Nonobservance in the Medieval Period," in Schacter, Jacob J., ed., *Jewish Tradition and the Nontraditional Jew* (Northvale, 1992), pp. 3-35.

Kraemer, Ross S., *Her Share of the Blessings: Women's Religions Among Pagans, Jews, and Christians in the Greco-Roman World* (New York, 1992).

Neusner, Jacob, *Method and Meaning in Ancient Judaism* (Missoula, 1979).

Ortner, Sherry, "Is Female to Male as Nature is to Culture?" in Rosaldo, Michelle Zimbalist, and Louise Lamphere, eds., *Women, Culture and Society* (Stanford, 1971), pp. 67-87.

Wegner, Judith Romney, *Chattel or Person? The Status of Women in the Mishnah* (New York, 1988).

Wegner, Judith Romney, "Women in Classical Rabbinic Judaism," in Baskin, Judith R., ed., *Jewish Women in Historical Perspective* (Detroit, 1991), pp. 68-93.

VIII. WHO WAS A JEW?

Gary G. Porton
University of Illinois

Defining a Jew at any point in history is a difficult task. At any specific moment in history there have been a variety of different groups or individuals who call themselves Jews or who are described by others as Jews. There are always competing sets of criteria for being classified as a Jew, some of which may even be mutually exclusive.[1] For example, in late antiquity, the Covenantors at Qumran had a vastly different image of a legitimate Jew from Jews who lived in Jerusalem, worshipped at the Temple, and regularly employed the priesthood resident there.[2] Similarly, Rabbinic attempts to equate Samaritans with other Palestinian Jews met with varying degrees of success during late antiquity.[3] Furthermore, in the first centuries C.E., those who accepted Jesus as the messiah and those who rejected that messianic claim both called themselves "Israel."[4] The definition of a Jew often depends upon whom one asks.

Generations of scholars and non-scholars have been interested in the nature of Jews and Judaism in late antiquity and have either directly or indirectly answered the question, "Who was a Jew?" Recently, students of Judaism in late antiquity have investigated the nature of Jews and Judaism in terms of ethnicity, religion, or even

---

[1] On the variety of Jews in late antiquity, see Gary G. Porton, "Diversity in Postbiblical Judaism," in Robert A. Kraft and George W.E. Nickelsburg, *Early Judaism and Its Modern Interpreters* (Atlanta, 1986), pp. 57-80.

[2] In my opinion, the best single volume on the Dead Sea sect and scrolls is Frank Moore Cross, *The Ancient Library of Qumran* (Minneapolis, 1995). The best English version of the scrolls is Geza Vermes, *The Dead Sea Scrolls in English* (London, 1995).

[3] James D. Purvis, "The Samaritans and Judaism," in Kraft and Nickelsburg, pp. 81-98. Ferdinand Dexinger, "Limits of Tolerance in Judaism: The Samaritan Example," in E.P. Sanders, A.I. Baumgarten, Alan Mendelson, eds., *Jewish and Christian Self-Definition Volume Two: Aspects of Judaism in the Graeco-Roman Period* (Philadelphia, 1981), pp. 88-114. John Bowman, *The Samaritan Problem: Studies in the Relationships of Samaritanism, Judaism, and Early Christianity* (Pittsburgh, 1975).

[4] Marcel Simon, *Verus Israel: A Study of the Relations Between Christians and Jews in the Roman Empire (135-425)* (Oxford, 1986). Rosemary R. Reuther, *Faith and Fratricide: The Theological Roots of Anti-Semitism* (New York, 1974). Jack T. Sanders, *Schismatics, Sectarians, Dissidents, Deviants: The First One Hundred Years of Jewish-Christian Relations* (Valley Forge, 1993).

nationality, and, as Jacob Neusner has noted, one reason for employing this terminology is the desire to differentiate Christianity from Judaism. It is commonly assumed that Judaism's ethnicity stands in sharp contrast to Christianity's universalism.[5] This essay enters into the discussion of the appropriateness of labeling Judaism in late antiquity as an ethnic group and/or a religious community.[6] To state our conclusion at the outset: We will argue that Judaism in late antiquity was an ethnic group based on a religious event. For this reason, those two categories, the religious and the ethnic, are always present and intertwined. Because the two are in some ways essentially incompatible, they may exist in tension with each other, and one may even perceive a change in emphasis through time or among different groups or documents.

Before we move into our analysis, however, we need to be aware of two major problems inherent in this discussion. Religion and ethnicity are modern classifications that were unknown in the period with which we are concerned. Current scholars have employed these labels to enable us to understand the Jews of late antiquity *in our terms*; they are not categories those Jews would have understood or employed. Also, the terms religion and ethnicity carry a variety of meanings, even among scholars who regularly apply them to groups of people. For this reason, we must be clear on what the terms mean and how they are being used.

II

Our first task is to clarify the nature of the material upon which we shall base our definition of a Jew and the significance of the labels we shall employ, so that we know from whose perspective we are answering our question. We will limit our investigation to the Rabbinic texts of late antiquity and to the definitions of a Jew created by those rabbis who appear in and produced those documents. These data are 1) our largest unambiguously identifiable Jewish source of informa-

---

[5] Jacob Neusner, "Was Rabbinic Judaism Really 'Ethnic'?," in *Catholic Biblical Quarterly* LVII, 2 (April, 1995), p. 281.

[6] We will not discuss the label "nation," because many political theorists have argued that nations in any meaningful sense are modern phenomena. For a brief discussion of this debate, see Gary G. Porton, *Goyim: Gentiles and Israelites in Mishnah-Tosefta* (Atlanta, 1988), pp. 296-297, n. 48.

tion about Jews in late antiquity, and 2) they provide the bases upon which all subsequent Jewish discussions of "who is a Jew" take place. To define a Jew in terms of the Rabbinic documents supplies us with information relevant to late antiquity and to all subsequent periods of Jewish history.

The nature of the Rabbinic documents, however, makes it virtually impossible to discover one simple answer to our question of "Who was a Jew?" The Rabbinic texts—the Mishnah, Tosefta, the Midrashim, the Babylonian and Palestinian Talmuds—are collections. They are compilations of diverse, discrete units constructed in a limited number of literary forms. None reflect the work of one author; none were written at one time; none follow an easily identifiable agenda. Some of their elements are fairly simple, while others are rather complex.[7] Each document has undergone a protracted editorial process during which the nature and contents of its constituent units have been altered. It is doubtful that we have the *ipssima verba* of any of the sages quoted in these texts or that we would be able to distinguishes a rabbi's actual sayings from those that are merely attributed to him or that have been altered over time. We cannot ascertain with certainty how Rabbi X would have defined a Jew or how the rabbis of the fourth, or any other, century would have answered our question. The most we can uncover is what a particular document tells us Rabbi X and his contemporaries said.[8]

The Rabbinic collections do not offer us a set of seamless, unchanging Rabbinic ideas. Each document must be read in its own terms and not only as part of a larger mythological Rabbinic whole. Reading each text in this manner permits us to recognize change and development within Rabbinic thought. This method of reading the Rabbinic corpus is in sharp contrast to those who approach these texts through the eyes of the Rabbinic myth of the "Dual Torah." This latter approach accepts the Rabbinic idea that everything contained in Rabbinic literature was actually revealed to Moses on

---

[7] Jacob Neusner is the pioneer in the literary study of the Rabbinic documents. The work began with *Development of a Legend: Studies in the Traditions Concerning Yohanan Ben Zakkai* (Leiden, 1970) and *The Rabbinic Traditions About the Pharisees Before 70* (Leiden, 1971), 3 vols. See most recently, *Introduction to Rabbinic Literature, The Anchor Bible Reference Library* (New York, London, Toronto, Sydney, Auckland, 1994) and *Rabbinic Judaism: Structure and System* (Minneapolis, 1995).

[8] William S. Green, "What's in a Name?—The Problematic of Rabbinic 'Biography,'" in William S. Green, ed., *Approaches to Ancient Judaism: Theory and Practice* (Missoula, 1978), pp. 77-96.

Mount Sinai, so that it is all interconnected and interrelated. According to this view, a fourth century Babylonian rabbi's explanation of a first century Palestinian document is *by definition* an accurate account of what the text meant in the first century. Nothing changes, and nothing develops, because it was all revealed to Moses, and the rabbi of late antiquity actively participates in that revelation which occurred on Mount Sinai.[9] We, on the other hand, will find change and will encounter development in the ideas expressed in the Rabbinic collections, because we will not accept the validity of the Rabbinic myth of the "Dual Torah." A fourth century explanation of a first century saying probably tells us more about Rabbinic thought of the fourth century than it does of Rabbinic ideas of the first century.

Despite the variety among and within the documents, they all reflect the ideas of a single class of Jews, the rabbis of late antiquity. The rabbis composed the elite intellectual class of the Jewish communities of Palestine and Babylonia. As a group, they created the form of Judaism that survived the destruction of the Temple and the end of the sacrificial cult. The religion of the Bible and the Second Temple period centered on the sacrificial cult, the priests who approached the altar, and the purity concerns that affected the Israelites' ability to bring sacrifices to the altar and the priests' capacity to make the offerings. The rabbis transformed that Israelite religion into Judaism, a system centered on the written Torah and the oral Torah as the complete, accurate record of YHWH's revelation and on the human body as the medium through which Jews could put into practice YHWH's commands recorded in the Dual Torah. While one became a priest by means of descent from a member of the priestly class, one became a rabbi through acquiring knowledge of the Dual Torah. A rabbi was a person who had studied with a rabbi, who had himself studied with a rabbi, who could therefore trace his teachers back through the line of rabbis, to "the pairs," to the men of the Great Assembly, to the prophets, to the elders, to Joshua, to Moses, and finally to YHWH on Mount Sinai (M. Ab. 1:1). The rabbis func-

---

[9] Neusner, *Introduction*, pp. 3-7. For an excellent example of this approach with reference to our topic, see Lawrence H. Schiffman, *Who Was a Jew? Rabbinic and Halakhic Perspectives on the Jewish-Christian Schism* (Hoboken, 1985). See also Sacha Stern, *Jewish Identity in Early Rabbinic Writings* (Leiden, 1994). This is a careful and sophisticated analysis of Rabbinic literature, focused, however, on the latter documents. Stern assumes the interrelatedness of the Rabbinic collections; therefore, what he demonstrates to be true within the later texts he claims was also true in the earlier strata.

tioned primarily in their schoolhouses, the Jewish market places, and other local community arenas. They exercised their limited public authority by the grace of the Roman and Sassanian governments and their Jewish political allies. They did not have widespread authority over those Jews who chose not to follow them, and they could affect the Jews' private lives only through the force of their personalities and whatever power the average Jews willingly relegated and ascribed to them.[10]

Because virtually all we know about the world in which the rabbis lived comes from their documents, we do not know if the rabbis' ideas in the literature found widespread expression or implementation in the world outside of the literary texts. We often find a variety of opinions on any topic, some of them contradictory, even if attributed to a single sage, and we do not know which, if any, he might have applied to life situations. We do not know which of the myriad of sayings assigned to any master were the most important to him, nor can we ascertain on which ones he was willing to compromise. We have little narrative information about the contexts in which the Rabbinic comments were uttered, so that we do not know when most of them were said or what occasioned their being spoken. We have access only to the documents available to us, and we know only what they chose to tell us. From them, we can discover what the editors of those collections chose to transmit about the Rabbinic definition of a Jew. It is the definition created by a few members of a small, intellectual class of Jews. We cannot firmly establish that it had a life outside of the texts in the same form that it appears in those documents.

III

Having begun with the nature of the relevant documents and their authors, we must now unpack the meaning of "religion" and "ethnicity." A definition of "religion" is not self-evident. In the words of Jonathan Z. Smith:

> ...[W]hile there is a staggering amount of data, of phenomena, of human experiences and expressions that might be characterized in one culture or another, by one criterion or another, as religious—*there is no data for reli-*

---

[10] My views of the rabbis have been shaped by the work of Jacob Neusner. See especially *A History of the Jews in Babylonia* (Leiden, 1965-1970), 5 vols.

gion. Religion is solely the creation of the scholar's study. It is created for the scholar's analytic purposes by his imaginative acts of comparison and generalization. Religion has no independent existence apart from the academy.[11]

Classical Greek, early Latin, and Hebrew do not have words for "religion." Arthur Darby Nock suggests that *eusebeia* may be the closest word, but it means the "regular performance of due worship in the proper spirit."[12] Thomas Finn agrees that the closest ancient word to religion was

> "piety" or "dutiful reverence" (*eusebia*, Greek; *pietas*, Latin) or the "observance of Torah (*dat*, Hebrew).... Late Latin acquired a term for religion—*religio*, a word of uncertain derivation—and Augustine attempted a definition: "Religion offers concern and veneration to a certain higher nature, which people call divine." .... [R]eligion is the traditional way of offering dutiful reverence to the divinity. The heart of the matter was ritual....[13]

As Smith notes, there are innumerable acts we may classify as religious in late antiquity, and non-Jewish and non-Christian Romans and Sassanians engaged in much the same religious activities as did Jews and Christians.[14] In addition, it is often difficult to differentiate a specific set of religious activities from non-religious behaviors. Melford E. Spiro has written an insightful essay on scholarly attempts to define religion,[15] and his definition will serve our purposes well. He defines religion as "an institution consisting of culturally patterned interaction with culturally postulated superhuman beings."[16] From this point of view, Judaism in late antiquity was a religion, and a Jew, as defined in the Rabbinic texts, was a religious being. But that is not all a Jew was.

It is virtually impossible to set forth a universally accepted defini-

---

[11] Jonathan Z. Smith, *Imagining Religion: From Babylon to Jonestown* (Chicago and London, 1982), p. xi.

[12] Arthur D. Nock, *Conversion: The Old and the New in Religion from Alexander the Great to Augustine of Hippo* (Oxford, 1933), p. 10.

[13] Thomas M. Finn, *From Death to Rebirth: Ritual and Conversion in Antiquity* (New York and Mahway, 1997), p. 8.

[14] Finn and Nock make this point. See also Ramsay MacMullen, *Paganism in the Roman Empire* (New Haven and London, 1981).

[15] Melford E. Spiro, "Religion: Problems of Definition and Explanation," in Benjamin Kilborne and L.L. Langness, eds., *Culture and Human Nature: Theoretical Papers of Melford E. Spiro* (Chicago and London, 1987), pp. 187-222.

[16] Spiro, p. 197. At pp. 197-198, he carefully explains each term in his definition, but a discussion of them is unnecessary for our purposes.

tion of ethnicity or to compile a list of the essential characteristics of an ethnic group. George Devereux describes ethnicity as "a sorting device" that develops "only out of a confrontation with and differentiation from 'others' to whom a different identity is ascribed."[17] An important element of ethnicity is the group's sense of itself as a unified set of individuals or subgroups that shares characteristics not possessed by other human aggregates. Fredrik Barth writes that an ethnic group "has a membership which identifies itself and is identified by others as constituting a category distinguishable from other categories of the same order."[18] Frank D. Bessac defines an ethnic group as "a group of people who...have a sense of common identity."[19] In a like manner, Cynthia H. Enloe writes that ethnicity "refers to a peculiar bond among persons that causes them to consider themselves as a group distinguishable from others."[20] We must realize, however, that ethnicity is not static; it is a dynamic phenomenon. As Michael M.J. Fischer notes, "ethnicity is something reinvented and reinterpreted in each generation.... Ethnicity is not something that is simply passed on from generation to generation, taught and learned...."[21]

While scholars agree that ethnic groups perceive themselves as a connected entity that is different from other human collectives, we find less agreement over exactly what actually binds the group together. Several researchers have placed culture at the center. Enloe writes that "the content of the bond [that unites an ethnic group] is shared culture..."[22] Similarly, Peter I. Rose writes:

> Groups whose members share a unique social and cultural heritage passed on from one generation to the next are known as *ethnic groups*. Ethnic groups are frequently identified by distinctive patterns of family life, language, recreation, religion, and other customs that cause them to be differentiated from others.[23]

---

[17] George Devereux, "Ethnic Identity: Its Logical Foundations and its Dysfunctions," in George De Vos and Lola Romanucci-Ross, eds., *Ethnic Identity: Cultural Continuities and Change* (Palo Alto, 1975), p. 48.

[18] Fredrik Barth, *Ethnic Groups and Boundaries: The Social Organization of Cultural Difference* (Bergen-Oslo, 1969), p. 14.

[19] Frank D. Bessac, *Current Anthropology* V 4 (October, 1964), p. 293.

[20] Cynthia H. Enloe, *Ethnic Conflict and Political Development* (Boston, 1973), p. 15.

[21] Michael M.J. Fischer, "Ethnicity and the Post-Modern Arts of Memory," in James Clifford and George E. Marcus, *Writing Culture* (Berkeley and Los Angeles, 1986), p. 195.

[22] Enloe, p. 15.

[23] Peter I. Rose, *They and We: Racial and Ethnic Relations in the United States* (New York, 1981), p. 7.

Norman Yetman argues that an ethnic group is socially defined on the basis of cultural characteristics:

> Ethnicity, or the sense of belonging to a particular ethnic group... implies- the existence of a distinct culture or subculture in which group members feel themselves bound together by common history, values, attitudes, and behaviors—in its broadest sense, a sense of peoplehood— and are so regarded by other members of society.[24]

Barth, however, argues that the shared culture is a *result*, rather than a "definitional characteristic," of the ethnic group's organization.[25]

Such discussions of ethnicity lead to even more complex attempts to define culture. William A. Haviland writes that

> [c]ulture consists of the abstract values, beliefs, and perceptions of the world that lie behind a people's behavior, and which that behavior reflects. These are shared by the members of a society, and when acted upon they produce behavior considered acceptable within that society. Cultures are learned, through the medium of language, rather than inherited biologically, and the parts of a culture function as an integrated whole.[26]

Similarly, Richard A. Barrett emphasizes that cultures are learned: "[culture is] the body of learned beliefs, traditions, and guides for behavior that are shared among members of any human society. The key word is *learned*."[27]

Another mode of analyzing culture views it as a symbol system. However, exactly how one should interpret the symbols is open to disagreement. Leslie A. White writes that "culture ... is a class of things and events, dependent upon symboling considered in an extra-somatic context."[28] One should study the symbolates only in relationship to one another and not in relationship to the human beings. The study of culture permits one to explain why people do particular things, while the study of human behavior, which is the subject matter of psychology, examines how people act.[29] Spiro, on the other hand, argues that "cultural doctrines, ideas, values, and the like exist

---

[24] Norman R. Yetman, *Majority and Minority: The Dynamics of Race and Ethnicity in American Life* (Boston, 1985), p. 6.

[25] Barth, p. 1.

[26] William A. Haviland, *Cultural Anthropology* (New York, 1983), p. 29.

[27] Richard A. Barrett, *Culture and Conduct: An Excursion in Anthropology* (Belmont, 1984), p. 54.

[28] Leslie A. White, "The Concept of Culture," in M.F. Ashley Montagu, ed., *Culture and the Evolution of Man* (New York, reprint, 1972), p. 46.

[29] White, pp. 44, 57.

in the minds of social actors.... [S]ince [cultural symbols] neither possess nor announce their meanings, they must be found in the minds of the social actors."[30]

The connection between ethnicity and culture is murky, for it is impossible to determine the cause-and-effect relationship between the two, even if one were able to define culture. And, there is disagreement over the location of the meanings of a culture's symbols. Therefore, we will do well to identify another factor that binds the members of an ethnic group together.

Several scholars have argued that shared ancestry is the central feature of an ethnic group. Chester Hunt and Lewis Walker have written that "an ethnic group is a collection of people whose membership is largely determined by ancestry...."[31] Gerald D. Berreman quotes approvingly H.S. Morris's statement that an "ethnic group consists of people who conceive of themselves as being alike by virtue of a common ancestry, real or fictitious...."[32] George De Vos also points to the importance of a common ancestry for an ethnic group's sense of itself, listing "common ancestry" as one among the "set of traditions" an ethnic group holds in common.[33] Elsewhere he writes that ethnicity is "primarily a sense of belonging to a particular ancestry or origin and of sharing a specific language or religion."[34] In a like manner, Charles F. Keyes has written that "ethnicity...derives from a cultural interpretation of descent." Descent does not need to be biological; rather, "descent presupposes socially validated parent/child connection."[35] For Keyes, "kin selection provides the underlying motivation that leads human beings to seek solidarity with those whom they recognize 'as being of the same people,' or 'sharing descent.'" According to Keyes, descent "is predicated upon the cultural construal of what characteristics indicate that others do or do not belong to the same people as oneself."[36] Finally, Pierre L. van den

---

[30] Melford E. Spiro, "Collective Representations and Mental Representations in Religious Symbol Systems," in Kilborne and Langness, pp. 161-162.

[31] Chester L. Hunt and Lewis Walker, *Ethnic Dynamics: Patterns of Intergroup Relations in Various Societies* (Homewood, 1974), p. 3.

[32] Gerald D. Berreman, "Race, Caste, and Other Invidious Distinctions in Social Stratification," in Yetman, p. 23.

[33] George De Vos, "Ethnic Pluralism: Conflict and Accommodation," in De Vos and Romanucci-Ross, p. 9.

[34] De Vos, p. 19.

[35] Charles F. Keyes, *Ethnic Change* (Seattle and London, 1981), p. 5.

[36] Keyes, p. 6.

Berghe argues that ethnicity, like race, is an extension of the idiom of kinship and that it is in reality an "attenuated form" of kin selection.[37]

Following those who have argued that descent and kinship are definitional elements of an ethnic group, we shall argue that the Rabbinic texts define a Jew as a member of an ethnic group, as someone who belongs to a particular descent group, "the children of Israel/Jacob." We shall further suggest that the descent group was created through a religious experience. These two definitional traits, ethnic and religious, are not always compatible. One is born into an ethnic group; one may change a religious community. Therefore, there is an inherent tension in the Rabbinic documents in defining a Jew precisely because these two categories are not always totally compatible. However, Judaism brings them together in a way that allows them to co-exist and to be mutually important in defining who was a Jew in late antiquity.

IV

The terminology in the Rabbinic documents points to the importance of the Jews' ethnicity. Following the Bible's lead, the Rabbinic texts speak of "the children of Israel," not of Jews. The designation "children of Israel," first appears in Gen. 32:33, immediately after a divine being wrenched Jacob's hip out of place. From then on, it appears over eight hundred times in the Hebrew Scripture. The Bible clearly prefers this term to "Hebrew," *'brym*, which appears approximately eighteen times.[38]

The Mishnah and Tosefta share the Bible's preference for "children of Israel;" the term appears approximately one hundred thirteen times in these collections as the preferred designation for Jews. "He-

---

[37] Pierre L. van den Berghe, "Race and Ethnicity: A Sociological Perspective," in Yetman, p. 56.

[38] In Gen. 40:15, Joseph reports to Pharaoh that he had been kidnapped from "the land of the Hebrews" (*m'rs h'brym*), and in Gen. 43:32 we are told that the Egyptians cannot dine with the Hebrews. In Exod. 2:6, Pharaoh's daughter identifies the child she withdraws from the rivers as "a Hebrew child," and in Exod. 2:13, Moses encounters two Hebrew men, *'nšym 'brym*, fighting. Exod. 5:3, 7:16, 9:1, 9:13, and 10:3 speak of "the God of the Hebrews." The term identifies a people in the following verses from 1 Sam, especially in contrast to the Philistines: 4:6, 4:9, 13:3, 13:7, 13:19, 14:11, 14:21, 29:3.

brew" most often appears as a modifier of "servant," distinguishing a
Hebrew slave from a Canaanite one, thus pointing to biblical, not
Rabbinic, times.[39]

Tracing the people's origins to Jacob instead of to Abraham or to
Isaac is significant, for Jacob was the only patriarch all of whose
progeny worshipped YHWH. Abraham was the father of Ishmael,
whom the Bible clearly indicates will become the father of a great
nation different from the Israelites (Gen. 21:13). Similarly, the Torah
pictures Esau, Jacob's brother, as the head of an independent people.
Unlike Jacob, whose wives came from the proper family line, Esau
had a Canaanite and an Ishmaelite wife (Gen. 28:6).[40] He did not
marry into the proper ethnic group.

The different religions of the patriarchs' children appear also in
the Rabbinic documents. The Ishmaelites are the Muslims, and Esau
becomes the father of the Romans and the Christians.[41] Jacob's children's fidelity to YHWH is clearly spelled out in a discussion of the
Shema in Sifre Deuteronomy 31. *Hear O Israel, YHWH is our God,
YHWH is One* (Deut. 6:4) are the words of Jacob's children to their
father, Israel:

> *Listen, Israel,* our father, just as there is no division in your heart [concern-
> ing your devotion to YHWH], so there is no division in our hearts con-
> cerning the One Who Spoke and the World Was [Created], for *YHWH
> is our God, YHWH is One.*

From the perspectives of both the Bible and the Rabbinic documents,
Jews are most often labeled a descent group, individuals who trace
their ancestry back to Jacob. Furthermore, as Naomi Steinberg has
shown, the authors of Genesis were concerned with showing that
the Patriarchs married wives with the proper family lineage. Because
they are Jacob's children, the Rabbinic texts also strictly regulate
whom Jews may marry. But we must keep in mind that while this is
clearly a major factor in defining an ethnic group, this particular
ethnic group was established through a religious encounter, for

---

[39] See the following texts in the Mishnah and Tosefta: M. M.S. 4:4, M. Erub. 7:6,
M. B.M. 1:5, M. Arak. 8:5, T. M.S. 4:2, T. Erub. 6:7, T. Pis. 7:4, T. B.Q. 9:3, T.
B.Q. 9:8, T. B.Q. 10:10, T. Toh. 6:9. In M. Git. 9:6 the term modifies the noun
"witness."

[40] On the importance of the family lines of the patriarchs' wives, see Naomi
Steinberg, *Kinship and Marriage in Genesis: A Household Economics Perspective* (Minneapolis,
1993).

[41] J. Neusner, *Judaism and Its Social Metaphors: Israel in the History of Jewish Thought*
(Cambridge, 1989).

Jacob's name became Israel only after he had wrestled with a divine being.[42]

As we saw above, ethnicity is a means of group-formation and group-differentiation, and the Mishnah and Tosefta depict Israel as a religious ethnicity through the ways it compares and contrasts Israelites and non-Israelites.[43] The earliest documents of Rabbinic culture assume and regulate the daily, continuous interaction of gentiles and Israelites. The Mishnah and Tosefta assume that gentiles and Israelites live in close proximity to one another, even in the same apartment complexes and courtyards. These texts take for granted that Israelites and gentiles will buy and sell land from one another or rent property to and from one another. They will also engage in joint farming ventures.[44] The Mishnah and Tosefta further set forth rules that govern the interactions of Israelites and gentiles in the Israelite court system, discussing matters of testimony and carefully describing the protocols that regulate damage claims between Israelites and gentiles. We also encounter rules governing the slaughter of animals and eating of meat prepared by Israelites and gentiles. The financial dealings between gentiles and Israelites are carefully outlined; even the etiquette required in social situations is the subject of some discussion. In addition, limitations on the business transactions between the two groups are also discussed, especially with regard to the gentiles' religious practices. Finally, the Mishnah and Tosefta assume that gentiles will wish to offer sacrifices to YHWH, so that they discuss the interaction of gentiles with the Temple cult and the application of Israelite purity rules to non-Israelites. All of the passages emphasize that Israelites and gentiles are different, and because they may constantly interact, their relationships with each other must be carefully regulated. This is in line with Barth's claim that the formation of an ethnic group leads to

> a systematic set of rules governing inter-ethnic social encounters, a structuring of interactions, a set of prescriptions governing situations of contact and allowing for an articulation in some sectors or domains of activity and a set of proscriptions on social situations preventing inter-ethnic interaction....[45]

---

[42] Gen. 32:23-33. In Gen. 35, God again declares Jacob's name to be Israel. In both cases, the name change results from Jacob's encounter with a divine being.

[43] The following discussion summarizes the investigation in Porton, *Goyim*.

[44] Porton, *Goyim*, pp. 173-203, 217-218. On the following, see pp. 221-229, 241-255, and 257-283.

[45] Barth, pp. 15-16.

The Mishnah and Tosefta assume and regulate the interaction of gentiles and Israelites in virtually every sphere of normal daily activity. However, there is one form of interaction that is absolutely forbidden. Israelites cannot engage in sexual activity with gentiles. The texts consistently forbid sexual intercourse between the two groups. Such intercourse produces non-Israelite children; the marriage is neither recognized nor acknowledged. Intercourse between an Israelite woman and a gentile male produces *mamzerim*, defective Israelites who suffer ritual and social limitations. The marriage is not recognized, but the children of an Israelite female cannot be ignored.[46] Because of the importance of kin-selection and descent as ethnic markers, after the first century C.E., these children of an Israelite mother cannot be excluded from the group.[47] Again, this concern with whom one may marry is typical of ethnic groups.

Even the negative stereotypes applied to gentiles are typical of ethnic groups and do not reflect a uniquely Jewish anti-gentile sentiment. At times the Mishnah and Tosefta describe gentiles as less civilized than Jews, as unable to curb their sexual urges, even engaging in sexual acts with babies, children, and animals. Some assumed that any gentile who is in a position to harm an Israelite would probably do so. Gentiles could not always be trusted, and under certain conditions it was permissible to lie to a gentile.[48]

As we said above, these statements are typical of ethnic descriptions of "the other;" they are not the result of Jewish particularity or misanthropy. Rodney Needham has written:

> It is a frequent report from different parts of the world that tribes call themselves alone by the arrogant title 'man.' And that they refer to neighboring peoples as monkeys or crocodiles or malign spirits. When European voyagers explored the world, they often enough had a clear eye for physique, dress, habitations, but they more often had a distorted or derogatory view of the moral aspects of exotic peoples. Typically, these strange societies had no religion, or no law, or no idea of the family or not even a true form of language to qualify them as truly human.[49]

---

[46] Porton, *Goyim*, pp. 222-223.

[47] Shaye J.D. Cohen, "From the Bible to the Talmud: The Prohibition of Intermarriage," in Reuben Ahroni, ed., *Hebrew Annual Review: Biblical and Other Studies in Honor of Robert Gordis* 7 (1983), pp. 23-39.

[48] Porton, *Goyim*, pp. 236-237.

[49] Rodney Needham, *Primordial Characters* (Charlottesville, 1978), p. 5.

Barbara A. Babcock has noted that ethnic groups often describe members of other groups as mirror-opposites, even picturing "the other" as walking on their hands or unable to stand upright.[50]

Although the Mishnah and Tosefta describe the Jews and their relationship with gentiles in a manner common among ethic groups, they underscore the religious basis of Israel's ethnicity by carefully regulating the ways in which non-Israelites can relate to Israel's major religious symbols: YHWH, the land of Israel, sacred time, the People Israel, and the Temple and its cult. The Mishnah and Tosefta are part of the Dual Torah, religious texts, so that they cannot and do not separate Israel's ethnicity from Israel's relationship to YHWH. The Mishnah and Tosefta clearly demonstrate that a Jew is a member of an ethnic group that is defined in terms of its religion.

The Mishnah and Tosefta are intent upon making YHWH the exclusive object of worship of the People Israel, so that they stress over and over again that Israelites should not worship foreign deities. On the other hand, the Rabbinic documents assume that gentiles will worship idols, and they do not attempt to prevent this, except perhaps within the land of Israel. YHWH is a major symbol around which Israelites and gentiles are differentiated.[51] There is little, if any, Jewish evidence that the rabbis sent missionaries to the gentiles to bring them to the worship of YHWH.[52] The Rabbinic corpus seems to assume that gentiles will naturally worship their own deities; the only important thing is that Jews do not worship these foreign deities or aid the gentiles in their religious acts.[53]

The Torah records that YHWH gave the land of Israel to the Israelites, and their residence on the land is dependent upon their following YHWH's mandates.[54] Within the context of the Bible and the Rabbinic documents, the land of Israel was meant to be an exclusive Israelite possession, but this never was the case. By the time of the Mishnah and Tosefta, the Land held hundreds of thousands of gentiles, and several passages attempt to regulate gentile ownership of portions of the Land. The Land and her produce belong to YHWH;

---

[50] Barbara A. Babcock, *The Reversible World: Symbolic Inversion in Art and Society* (Ithaca, 1978).

[51] David Novak, *The Image of the Non-Jew in Judaism* (New York, 1983).

[52] Gary G. Porton, *The Stranger Within Your Gates: Converts and Conversion in Rabbinic Literature* (Chicago and London, 1994), p. 9.

[53] Porton, *Goyim*, pp. 241-258.

[54] W.D. Davies, *The Territorial Dimension of Judaism* (Minneapolis, 1991), pp. 1-30.

therefore, they are holy. Israelites must continually recognize and respond to the Land's sacred nature; however, the sages cannot agree about the gentiles' obligations in this regard. Some state that gentiles may, if they wish, acknowledge YHWH's stewardship of the Land by separating heave-offering and the tithes. Others did not allow this. All of the rabbis agree, however, that gentiles cannot separate the ethnic agricultural gifts that are given to the Israelite poor. Similarly, Israelites may give money to the poor among the gentiles, but they may not give them the agricultural gifts that they give to the needy within their own community.[55] In sum, while gentiles *may*, Israelites *must* acknowledge the holiness of the land of Israel.

From the perspective of the Mishnah and Tosefta, the Sabbath is an exclusively Israelite sacred period, and the Sabbath becomes an important ethnic identifier.[56] Passover, which marks the creation of the People Israel, is obviously important only to Israelites. In the Mishnah and Tosefta, the gentiles have no responsibility on their own for observing Passover and the Sabbath. The rites, rituals, and alternations of normal activity that are incumbent upon Israelites do not apply to gentiles. However, if gentiles come into contact with an Israelite, especially on the Sabbath, the former must alter their actions, so that the Israelites' observance of the Sabbath may affect the gentiles' ability to pursue their normal activities. These restrictions are applied only from the Israelite point of view and only when the activity impinges, or might impinge, upon the Israelites. This means that the concerns with gentiles' working on the Sabbath focus on the relationship of ideas of work and rest to the Israelites.[57]

In the Rabbinic period, the observance of Passover revolves around the possessing and eating of leaven. An Israelite is a person who does not possess leaven during Passover, while a gentile is one who does. In fact, the gentile is pictured as the mirror-image of the

---

[55] Porton, *Goyim*, pp. 173-203.

[56] We should note that the Bible gives two reasons for celebrating the Sabbath. Gen. 2:1-4, Exod. 20:8-12, Exod. 31:14-17, and Exod. 34:17 connect the Sabbath to God's creation of the world. In this sense, it is cosmic and should be acknowledged by all human beings. The other reason, noted in Deut. 5:12-15, connects the Sabbath to the Exodus from Egypt, so that it is a specifically Israelite sacred moment. On the Sabbath as a Jewish marker, see Robert Goldenberg, "The Jewish Sabbath in the Roman World up to the Time of Constantine the Great," in Hildegard Temporini and Wolfgang Haase, eds., *Aufsteig und Nidergang der römischen Welt* (Berlin and New York, 1979), vol. II.19.1, pp. 414-444.

[57] Porton, *Goyim*, pp. 206-211. On the following, see pp. 211-213 and 259-268.

Israelite, with the possession of leaven being the crucial element that distinguishes the two people.

The Mishnah and Tosefta see the Temple as 1) Israel's ethnic shrine and 2) as YHWH's residence. When viewed in the former sense, the gentiles had limited access to its precincts; they could not contribute to its upkeep by dedicating items for its repair or by paying the half-*sheqel* tax. On the other hand, gentiles could bring freewill-offerings. If the gentiles had not provided the drink-offerings with their freewill gifts, the Israelite community could provide them. Even so, the complex rules that applied to Israelites' offerings did not apply to those of gentiles: when gentiles presented offerings to YHWH, they did so differently from the way in which Israelites would have made those same sacrifices.

Disagreements over the causes, effects, and nature of ritual purity and impurity divided Jewish groups in late antiquity.[58] The application to gentiles of the rules of ritual purity is complex. On the one hand, the vast majority of purity issues does not apply to gentiles. Gentiles *qua* gentiles do not necessarily convey uncleanness. The laws of skin-disease and mildew do not apply to gentiles or their possessions. Neither gentiles' semen nor their blood pollutes. And a gentile's corpse does not convey uncleanness by carrying.[59]

On the other hand, several passages assume that gentiles are ritually impure and that they convey these impurities. Because gentile women do not follow the Rabbinic rules concerning vaginal flows, all spittle found in a town in which there was a gentile woman is unclean. Because gentiles were assumed to bury their aborted children near their homes, their domiciles were often considered to be unclean, so that in some contexts they are pictured as sources of various levels of ritual impurity.[60] Again, we discover that gentiles are different from Israelites, and the Israelites' concerns do not apply to them in the same way that they apply to Israelites.

In the Mishnah and Tosefta, the earliest Rabbinic compilations, Jews are members of a specific kin-group; they are *bny yśr'l*, children of Israel. Because of this, they may marry only other members of the same group. In addition, they are very much concerned with distin-

---

[58] Morton Smith, "The Dead Sea Sect in Relation to Ancient Judaism," in *New Testament Studies* VII (1960), pp. 347-360. Jacob Neusner, *The Idea of Purity in Ancient Judaism* (Leiden, 1973).

[59] Porton, *Goyim*, pp. 272-273.

[60] Porton, *Goyim*, pp. 273-276.

guishing themselves from the non-Israelites among whom they live and who live among them. They regulate their interaction with gentiles in accordance with patterns scholars have discerned among contemporary ethnic groups. However, this ethnic group came into being through a religious event, and it formulates its distinctiveness in terms of its religious symbols. If Jews in late antiquity were members of an ethnic group, that group was decidedly religious in nature. In fact, the Rabbinic documents do not separate ethnicity from religiosity.

V

The religious nature of the Jewish ethnic group is illustrated in the Rabbinic discussions of the convert and conversion.[61] Ethnicity relates to descent; conversion implies a spiritual reorientation and change.[62] Conversion to Judaism is a post-biblical concept that came into vogue in the last centuries B.C.E. and the first centuries C.E.[63] The conversion ritual has not been clearly agreed upon by the sages who appear in the Babylonian *gemara*, so that conversion to Judaism does not appear to have been a clearly defined and uniform phenomenon in the Rabbinic period.[64] However, examining the rabbis' discussions of the convert and conversion does shed light on the Rabbinic definitions of a Jew and the nature of the Jewish community.

Because ethnic descent lines are culturally determined and need not reflect biological reality, the rabbis were able to assimilate the converts into the People Israel. However, the Rabbinic discussions of the convert reflect the complex nature of the People Israel. A major marker of the converts' new status is their changed relationship to their birth-family. The Rabbinic texts assume that converts have broken their relationship to their natural family. In fact, converts are the

---

[61] This section summarizes the work in Porton, *Stranger*.

[62] Porton, *Stranger*, pp. 193-220. Finn, pp. 17-44. Shaye J.D. Cohen, "Conversion to Judaism in Historical Perspective: From Biblical Israel to Postbiblical Judaism," in *Conservative Judaism* XXXVI, 4 (Summer, 1983), p. 31. Arthur L. Griel, "Previous Dispositions and Conversion to Perspectives of Social and Religious Movements," in *Sociological Analysis* XXXVIII, 2 (1977), pp. 115-125.

[63] Cohen, "Conversion," pp. 33-35. Morton Smith, *Palestinian Parties and Politics that Shaped the Old Testament* (New York and London, 1971), pp. 178-182.

[64] Porton, *Stranger*, pp. 132-154. On the following, see pp. 166-176, 181-183, and 186-187

only members of the People Israel about whom it is assumed that they could die without leaving any heirs.

We saw above that gentiles and Israelites do not relate in the same way to the major religious symbols of Judaism. In almost all cases, converts relate to those symbols as Israelites, so that the actions incumbent upon the converts clearly mark them as members of the Jewish religious community. For example, converts and Israelites, but not gentiles, separate the agricultural gifts for the poor. Similarly, all of the Israelite purity rules apply to the converts. Converts are obligated to follow all of the Sabbath-regulations, even though it may take them some time to learn them, and they must fully observe Passover, even though they may not be trusted to do everything on their own. The earliest midrashic collections never miss the opportunity to remind us that there should be one law for converts and the native-born.[65] As early as the Tosefta we are told that the souls of converts witnessed the revelation at Sinai (T. Sot. 7:5). If converts reject their Judaism, they are classified as apostate *Israelites* (T. Dem. 2:4).

On the other hand, although converts become Israelites, in the ideal world in which the Temple exists and Israelites, and Israelites alone, all live in the Holy Land, converts are not totally equated to native-born unimpaired Israelite males. Many sages held that converts could not recite the Avowal connected with the offering of the First Fruits that includes Deut. 26:3-10, which refers to YHWH's promise of the Land to Abraham and his descendants. One passage holds that converts cannot own a portion of the Land, because they were not included among the tribes when the Land was originally apportioned among the Israelites. Finally, unlike unimpaired male native-born Israelites, converts suffer under some restrictions concerning whom they may marry within the Israelite community.[66]

The fact that converts do not enjoy total equality with unimpaired Israelite males does not mean that they have not been totally assimilated into the ethnic Israelite community. Several different classes of persons made up that community: priests, Levites, Israelites, converts, *mamzerim*, *netinim*, *shetuqim*, and *asufim*. One's line of descent and/or one's parentage determined into which category one fit. One's classification determined which other Israelites one could marry and ex-

---

[65] Porton, *Stranger*, pp. 53-56, 57-58, 61-62, 66-67.
[66] Porton, *Stranger*, 179-186. On the following, see pp. 18-21, 35, 57, 75-76, 102-103.

actly which ritual acts one could perform. However, these were all types of Israelites. Thus, converts who were once gentiles but who now accepted YHWH as their deity and agreed to live according to YHWH's revelation were now Israelites and would be classified as Israelites for the rest of their lives.[67]

On virtually every level, converts are equated with native-born Israelites. Gentiles can become members of the People Israel and function almost totally as every other Jew in the social and religious worlds of Israel. They can do this because the rabbis treat the People Israel and the individual Jews as religious entities. Even the rare contexts in which, the documents note, converts would be differentiated from native-born Jews do not pertain at the present time, because the Temple does not stand and all of the People Israel do not live in and do not control the Land. Even in these instances, moreover, converts are seen as part of the People Israel and as Jews.

VI

If one defines religion only from the perspective of Christianity, Judaism's ethnic dimension presents a difficulty. However, from its inception, Judaism has not distinguished between its ethnic and religious components. The Bible's first eleven chapters depict YHWH as the deity of all humankind. Israel is not the only people with whom YHWH is concerned. However, this ethnic group does enter into a unique relationship with YHWH through the covenants with Abraham, Isaac, and Jacob. That relationship is more sharply defined through the covenant at Sinai, the event that according to the Rabbinic tradition defines Israel. In the Rabbinic imagination, the souls of Jews, native-born and converts, stood at Sinai and freely signed the covenant. Thus, the event that created the Jews created all Jews, religious Jews and native-born Jews. This means that the scholarly dichotomy between religious and ethnic Jews is just that, a creation of the modern scholar.

---

[67] Adults who freely converted could not change their minds; others had a small window of opportunity to reject their conversion; Porton, *Stranger*, p. 102.

Bibliography

Babcock, Barbara A., *The Reversible World: Symbolic Inversion in Art and Society* (Ithaca, 1978).

Barrett, Richard A., *Culture and Conduct: An Excursion in Anthropology* (Belmont, 1984).

Barth, Fredrik, *Ethnic Groups and Boundaries: The Social Organization of Cultural Difference* (Bergen-Oslo, 1969).

Bowman, John, *The Samaritan Problem: Studies in the Relationships of Samaritanism, Judaism, and Early Christianity* (Pittsburgh, 1975).

Cohen, Shaye J.D., "Conversion to Judaism in Historical Perspective: From Biblical Israel to Postbiblical Judaism," in *Conservative Judaism* XXXVI,4. Summer, 1983, pp. 31-45.

Cohen, Shaye J.D., "From the Bible to the Talmud: The Prohibition of Intermarriage," in Reuben Ahroni, ed., *Hebrew Annual Review: Biblical and Other Studies in Honor of Robert Gordis* 7, 1983, pp. 23-39.

Cross, Frank Moore, *The Ancient Library of Qumran* (Minneapolis, 1995).

Davies, W.D., *The Territorial Dimension of Judaism* (Minneapolis, 1991).

De Vos, George, and Lola Romanucci-Ross, eds., *Ethnic Identity: Cultural Continuities and Change* (Palo Alto, 1975).

Dexinger, Ferdinand, "Limits of Tolerance in Judaism: The Samaritan Example," in Sanders, E.P., A.I. Baumgarten, and Alan Mendelson, eds., *Jewish and Christian Self-Definition Volume Two: Aspects of Judaism in the Graeco-Roman Period* (Philadelphia, 1981), pp. 88-114.

Enloe, Cynthia H., *Ethnic Conflict and Political Development* (Boston, 1973).

Finn, Thomas M., *From Death to Rebirth: Ritual and Conversion in Antiquity* (New York and Mahway, 1997).

Fischer, Michael M.J., "Ethnicity and the Post-Modern Arts of Memory," in Clifford, James, and George E. Marcus, *Writing Culture* (Berkeley and Los Angeles, 1986), pp. 194-233.

Goldenberg, Robert, "The Jewish Sabbath in the Roman World up to the Time of Constantine the Great," in Temporini, Hildegard, and Wolfgang Haase, eds., *Aufstieg und Nidergang der römischen Welt* (Berlin and New York, 1979), vol. II.19.1, pp. 414-444.

Green, William S., "What's in a Name?—The Problematic of Rabbinic 'Biography,'" in Green, William S., ed., *Approaches to Ancient Judaism: Theory and Practice* (Missoula, 1978), pp. 77-96.

Griel, Arthur L., "Previous Dispositions and Conversion to Perspectives of Social and Religious Movements," in *Sociological Analysis* XXXVIII,2, 1977, pp. 115-125.

Haviland, William A., *Cultural Anthropology* (New York, 1983).

Hunt, Chester L., and Lewis Walker, *Ethnic Dynamics: Patterns of Intergroup Relations in Various Societies* (Homewood, 1974).

Keyes, Charles F., *Ethnic Change* (Seattle and London, 1981).

Kilborne, Benjamin, and L.L. Langness, eds., *Culture and Human Nature: Theoretical Papers of Melford E. Spiro* (Chicago and London, 1987).

Kraft, Robert A., and George W.E. Nickelsburg, eds., *Early Judaism and Its Modern Interpreters* (Atlanta, 1986).

MacMullen, Ramsay, *Paganism in the Roman Empire* (New Haven and London, 1981).

Needham, Rodney, *Primordial Characters* (Charlottesville, 1978).

Neusner, Jacob, *A History of the Jews of Babylonia* (Leiden, 1965-1970), 5 vols.

Neusner, Jacob, *Development of a Legend: Studies in the Traditions Concerning Yohanan Ben Zakkai* (Leiden, 1970).

Neusner, Jacob, *Introduction to Rabbinic Literature, The Anchor Bible Reference Library* (New York, London, Toronto, Sydney, Auckland, 1994).

Neusner, Jacob, *Judaism and Its Social Metaphors: Israel in the History of Jewish Thought* (Cambridge, 1989).

Neusner, Jacob, *Rabbinic Judaism: Structure and System* (Minneapolis, 1995).

Neusner, Jacob, *The Idea of Purity in Ancient Judaism: The Haskell Lectures, 1972-1973* (Leiden, 1973).

Neusner, Jacob, *The Rabbinic Traditions About the Pharisees Before 70* (Leiden, 1971), 3 vols.

Neusner, Jacob, "Was Rabbinic Judaism Really 'Ethnic'?," in *Catholic Biblical Quarterly* LVII.2, April, 1995, pp. 281-305.

Nock, Arthur D., *Conversion: The Old and the New in Religion from Alexander the Great to Augustine of Hippo* (Oxford, 1933).

Novak, David, *The Image of the Non-Jew in Judaism* (New York, 1983).

Porton, Gary G., *Goyim: Gentiles and Israelites in Mishnah-Tosefta* (Atlanta, 1988).

Porton, Gary G., *The Stranger Within Your Gates: Converts and Conversion in Rabbinic Literature* (Chicago and London, 1994).

Reuther, Rosemary R., *Faith and Fratricide: The Theological Roots of Anti-Semitism* (New York, 1974).

Rose, Peter I., *They and We: Racial and Ethnic Relations in the United States* (New York, 1981).

Sanders, Jack T., *Schismatics, Sectarians, Dissidents, Deviants: The First One Hundred Years of Jewish-Christian Relations* (Valley Forge, 1993).

Schiffman, Lawrence H., *Who Was a Jew? Rabbinic and Halakhic Perspectives on the Jewish-Christian Schism* (Hoboken, 1985).

Simon, Marcel, *Verus Israel: A Study of the Relations Between Christians and Jews in the Roman Empire (135-425)* (Oxford, 1986).

Smith, Jonathan Z., *Imagining Religion: From Babylon to Jonestown* (Chicago and London, 1982).

Smith, Morton, *Palestinian Parties and Politics that Shaped the Old Testament* (New York and London, 1971).

Smith, Morton, "The Dead Sea Sect in Relation to Ancient Judaism," in *New Testament Studies* VII. 1960, pp. 347-360.

Steinberg, Naomi, *Kinship and Marriage in Genesis: A Household Economics Perspective* (Minneapolis, 1993).

Stern, Sacha, *Jewish Identity in Early Rabbinic Writings* (Leiden, 1994).

White, Leslie A., "The Concept of Culture," in Montagu, M.F. Ashley, ed.,

Culture and the Evolution of Man (New York), pp. 38-64.

Yetman, Norman R., ed., *Majority and Minority: The Dynamics of Race and Ethnicity in American Life* (Boston, 1985).

INDICES

GENERAL INDEX

INDEX OF BIBLICAL, TALMUDIC AND
ANCIENT REFERENCES

JUDAISM IN LATE ANTIQUITY

PART THREE

SECTION THREE

TABLE OF CONTENTS

PREFACE

This third collection of state of the question papers carries forward the project of nurturing *Auseinandersetzungen* among the active scholars of the present day. The editors mean to hold up a mirror for the field by affording a hearing to argument and contention: here is where we differ and why. Only by pursuing issues in this manner are people going to carry out their responsibility not only to say what they think but also to explain themselves and spell out the choices they make, the alternative views they reject, and the reasons therefor.

Why devote so much effort, within the exposition of the state of scholarship, to contemporary debates? It is because the editors place the highest priority upon affording a platform for public discussion of controverted points of learning: facts, methods, interpretations alike. Learning progresses through contentious pursuit of controversy, as hypotheses are put forth, tested against evidence, advocated, and criticized. Then public discourse, dense and rich in rigorous argument and explicit discussion, stimulates. Choices present themselves, what is at stake is clarified, knowledge deepens. Those who serve as gate-keepers in scholarship—editors of journals and monograph series, for example—therefore find a place for everything and its opposite. That is their task. They value what is best expressed in the German word, *Auseinandersetzungen*.

What the editors by creating this book and its companions mean to oppose also comes to expression in a German word uniquely serviceable to scholarship, *Todschweigen*, meaning, to murder through silence (ostracism, suppression, above all, active, ostentatious acts of ignoring views one does not hold). What costs do we aim to avoid? Learning atrophies when political consensus substitutes for criticism and when other than broadly-accepted viewpoints, approaches, and readings find a hearing only with difficulty if at all.

Having presented in Volumes I and II of this series some of the main results of contemporary learning on Judaism in late antiquity,[1] in the several parts of Volume III we proceed to portray issues and

---

[1] *Handbuch der Orientalistik. Judaism in Late Antiquity.* Volume One. *Literary and Archaeological Sources* (Leiden, 1995: E.J. Brill); Volume Two. *Historical Syntheses* (Leiden, 1995: E.J. Brill).

debates that animate the field. Such an account of contemporary debates, along with a picture of the state of knowledge, is necessary. That is because any responsible account for colleagues of the shape and standing of learning in a given subject must outline not only the present state of pertinent questions but also the contemporary character of debate and discussion. That is especially the case here, for the study of ancient Judaism forms one of the most contentious subjects in the contemporary humanities. And it is also driven as much by politics and personalities as it is guided by rationality and civil discourse. When people disagree, they simply refuse to read the books and articles of those with whom they differ. Were such conduct to go unchallenged, the study of ancient Judaism would lose all academic plausibility—and should.

What accounts for the highly controverted character of this aspect of the study of ancient religion, culture, history, and literature? It is not only for the obvious, theological reason, that Judaism and Christianity today have a heavy stake in the results of academic learning about olden times. Many debates come about because of contemporary political or theological considerations, not by reason of issues intrinsic in the sources themselves. But a second fact precipitates quite strong difference of opinion. It is because long-established approaches have been called into question as new methods and new definitions of critical learning take center-stage. There is a third factor as well: much new information emerges of both a literary and an archaeological character, and, it goes without saying, reasonable people may form different opinions in describing, analyzing, and interpreting in context the meaning of facts simply unknown to prior generations of scholars. Not only so, but the state of the contemporary humanities and social sciences bring to the forefront issues hitherto not considered at all. Altogether new perspectives now emerge, new questions deriving from other areas of the humanities than the study of religion, such as women's studies and studies of render and the social construction of sexuality, emerge, to which even a generation ago no one gave thought. It goes without saying that, in the study of ancient Judaism, all four sources of contention contribute to contemporary debate. Armed with a range of new interests, people turn to that diverse set of kindred religious systems we call "Judaism," rightly anticipating fresh and suggestive answers.

But the nature of the evidence itself—literary and archaeological—makes its own contribution as well. Read even in their own

framework, the principal literary sources as well as the main archaeological remains contain many ambiguities. They leave ample space
for diverse viewpoints to take shape. Read in one way for nearly half-
a-century, now, the Dead Sea Scrolls, fully available after such a long
wait, require fresh approaches and receive them. An established consensus gives way. Questions not asked at all demand attention, even
as diverse answers to long-settled questions are put forth.[2] Not only
so, but another principal component of the documentary legacy of
ancient Judaism, the Rabbinic literature, forms the focus of most
vigorous debates. And these represent only two among many of the
sub-fields of ancient Judaism that today provoke contentious discussion.

But these debates seldom take the form of a public *Auseinandersetzung*, an exchange of opposed views among persons of shared rationality, mutual respect, and good will, an exchange to the point, on
a single issue, within a shared consensus of pertinent sources, considerations, and rationalities. Scholarly media print book reviews but
most forbid the right of response, as though scholarly argument were
disruptable, rather than the necessity of all reasoned discourse. Journals automatically reject work that does not conform to the regnant
viewpoint of a given set of editors (not seldom appointed for other
than scholarly achievement), and university presses and monograph
series practice censorship of an other-than-academic character as
well. Conferences on a given problem commonly exclude viewpoints
not shared by the organizers, and university faculties rarely make
certain that their students hear views not shared by the professors of
those faculties. Indeed, it is only a small exaggeration to say that,
given a list of the conferences a person has attended or the universities at which he or she has lectured, we may easily construct the
opinion of that person on the entire agenda of learning in his or her
field of specialization.

---

[2] In *Judaism in Late Antiquity*. Volume Five. *Judaism at Qumran*, we plan to ask
hitherto unasked questions of system and structure of the Judaic religious system
adumbrated by the Dead Sea library: what kind of Judaism can have produced this
writing? Until now, problems of historical, philological, and archaeological character
have predominated, and the religious reading of the writings has been subordinated.
Happily, we have been able to enlist in the project an ample number of colleagues
who specialize in research in that subject and who are willing to address the questions we have formulated for them.

But debate, discussion, on-going exchanges of views, systematic
and sustained criticism—these impart to all fields of academic learning such dynamics as will sustain them over time. Repeating oneself
and the views of one's friends and ignoring other positions, not even
alluding to them in footnotes or in bibliographies, as though *Todschweigen* accomplished its goal—these modes of dealing with difference serve no one. And in this book and its companions, the editors
mean to show a better way of doing the work of learning in the study
of ancient Judaism.

Here, therefore, the editors have invited colleagues systematically
to outline their views in an *Auseinandersetzung* with contrary ones. We
asked them to tell us how, in broad and sweeping terms, they see the
state of learning in their areas of special interest. We wanted sharply-
etched state of the question studies, systematic presentations of a
distinctive viewpoint and very particular results, and other evidence
of how scholarly debate goes forward. We hoped to portray some of
the principal issues, to set forth a few of the alternative positions
presently maintained about fundamental questions of method and
substance. We invited the leading players in the U.S.A., Europe, and
the State of Israel, in the study of ancient Judaism, both in Second
Temple Times and after 70 C.E. The responses proved so many and,
as this fourth part of the project shows, so intellectually ambitious,
that several sizable books have been required to set forth the representative sample of debate on a few large questions that we wished to
present.

Some may wonder why the vehement espousal of the value of
Auseinandersetzungen and the equally strong denunciation of *Todschweigen* that this book and its companions mean to embody. The
reason is that when it comes to the study of ancient Judaism, the
scholarly interchange is rare, the academic excommunication is commonplace. It is a matter of common knowledge that in the scholarly
communities in which ancient Judaism comes under academic study,
people will not engage with critics. It is the fact characteristic of
universities, university presses, and journals that those who control
the media of public discourse close the door on views they do not
like. They print violent and *ad hominem* advocacy of one viewpoint but
do not permit replies; as with the *Journal of the American Oriental Society*,
they publish intemperate reviews aimed at nothing short of character-assassination but suppress answers thereto. Many scholarly journals, university presses, and monograph series take an essentially po-

litical position on scholarship, closing off debate and imposing a rigid orthodoxy upon such learning as they disseminate. They will not even consider articles that bear the wrong names or books or monographs from the camp with which they do not identify.

It remains to express our gratitude to those who have made this project a success. For on-going support of their joint and separate scholarly enterprises, the two editors express thanks to our respective colleges, Bard College, for Jacob Neusner, and the College of the Holy Cross, for Alan J. Avery-Peck.

We further thank E.J. Brill and its editors for guidance and commitment to this project. We call attention to the fact that, of all the scholarly publishers in the U.S.A., Europe, and the State of Israel, none has devoted more effort to opening doors and windows than has E.J. Brill, with whom we are proud to be associated. The senior editor published his first book with Brill in 1962, when Dr. F.C. Wieder, Jr., was the director, and remembers with thanks many editors and directors over the past decades. Brill in this generation has carried forward a great tradition of scholarship, one that has sustained us all.

And, finally, we thank the contributors to this part of *Judaism in Late Antiquity* Volume III for their prompt and conscientious work. We are proud that so many distinguished scholars have joined in this effort publicly to show where we stand in contemporary issues and debates on ancient Judaism.

Jacob Neusner
Research Professor of Religion and Theology
Bard College, Annandale-on-Hudson, New York

Alan J. Avery-Peck
Kraft-Hiatt Professor of Judaic Studies
College of the Holy Cross, Worcester, Massachusetts

1. WHO WERE THE PHARISEES?

Ellis Rivkin

Hebrew Union College—Jewish Institute of Religion

Since the question "Who were the Pharisees?" is still being posed, it bears witness enough to how difficult it is to come up with a definitive answer. This difficulty stems from the fact that the Pharisees could not have been both the authoritative teachers of the two fold Law (the Written and the Oral), teachers who sat on Moses's seat and whose *halakhot, takkanot,* and *gezerot* governed the lives of the majority of the Jewish people from the time of the Hasmonean Revolt through the destruction of the Second Temple in 70 C.E. and beyond, and, at the same time, been a sect, an organization or confraternity or table fellowship of those who were to be distinguished from the *am ha-aretz,* the masses, by their meticulous observance of the laws of ritual purity. And since it is evident that the Pharisees could not have been both an authoritative scholar class and a sect, the question of "Who were the Pharisees?"—mainstream or sect, scholars (*Soferim, Hakhamim*) or a table fellowship of ritual purists—is still very much with us. And what is haunting and daunting is that on the answer to this question hangs the structural and institutional history of the Jewish people during the intertestamental period. Until a definitive answer, not a consensus, is forthcoming—after all there is no consensus as to whether there was or was not a Roman Senate but absolute agreement—the history of one of the most creative epochs in history must remain a medley of fragments, a chaos of facts without structure, a congerie of speculations without grounding.

In many articles[1]—not to speak of my book *A Hidden Revolution*—I have sought to move from consensus to certainty by analyzing from many different angles all the relevant sources—Josephus, the New

---

[1] "The Internal City," in *Journal of Scientific Study of Religion* 5 (1966), pp. 225-240; "The Pharisaic Revolution," in *Perspectives in Jewish Learning*, vol. 2 (Chicago, 1966), pp. 26-51; "Prolegomenon" in N.O.E. Oesterly ed., *Judaism and Christianity* (1937-1938; reprint: New York, 1969); "Pharisaism and the Crisis of the Individual in the Greaeco-Roman World," in *Jewish Quarterly Review* 61 (July, 1970), pp. 27-52; "Defining the Pharisees: The Tannaitic Sources," in *Hebrew Union College Annual* 40-41 (1962-1970), pp. 205-249; "Pharisees" in *Interpreters Dictionary of the Bible* (Nashville, 1976) Supplementary Volume; "Pharisees" in *Encyclopedia of Religion*.

Testament, and the Tannaitic literature, by means of an objective methodology, a methodology that yields a definition beyond critical challenge. This definition rests on the fact that the term *Perushim* when it truly means Pharisees is absolutely synonymous with *Soferim* and *Hakhamim*. As such, the Pharisees must have been the authoritative teachers of the two-fold Law, the written and the unwritten, which governed the overwhelming majority of the Jews from the time of the Hasmonean Revolt through the destruction of the Second Temple in 70 C.E. and beyond. Although my hopes of moving scholars from consensus to certainty fell short of realization, my conviction is that the definition I elicited from all the sources is objective and beyond critical challenge. This conviction has not been diluted by any evidence that has been marshaled since I first spelled out my methodology and its implication in a paper entitled "The Pharisaic Revolution," presented at the College of Jewish Studies in Chicago (now Spertus College) in 1966 and published in volume II of *Perspective in Jewish Learning*, edited by M.A. Shulvass, pp. 26-51. This being so, I came to the conclusion that the better part of wisdom would be to republish that paper with some non-substantive additions since, in the absence of space, it stands on the sources as firmly now as it did then and thereby demonstrates that the solution of the problem as to who the Pharisees were had been solved more than three decades ago.

1.

Few problems in historiography are as tantalizing as those that surround the Pharisees. For here is a historical phenomenon whose significance is readily recognized by Jewish and Christian scholar alike, and whose contemporary relevance is sustained by the sacred texts of both Judaism and Christianity. Yet this phenomenon is still undefined. Not that definitions have been lacking. There are any number that sport respectable scholarly credentials. But they all suffer from a sort of congenital uncertainty stemming from the ambiguous quality of the sources. The scholar simply cannot find a clear-cut definition, for the data available are either obscure or contradictory. How, for example, is one to frame a definition of the Pharisees that will be simultaneously confirmed by Josephus, the New Testament, and the Tannaitic literature—without, mind you, selecting only those elements that happen to jibe and rejecting those that would prove embarrassing? And how is one to reconstruct a history of so vital and long-lived a historical phenomenon when no source whatsoever, not even Josephus, pinpoints its emergence into history, and when no source whatsoever, not even Josephus, gives us a connected account of its vicissitudes even after it had unquestionably emerged? And if Josephus fails us, can such sources as the New Testament and the Tannaitic literature come to our rescue—the former interested only in the relationship of the Pharisees to Jesus, and the latter unconcerned with historical reconstruction and narrative?

Since in this essay I will concentrate on techniques for solving a stubborn historical problem, I shall not begin with a history of the Pharisees but with the construction of an objective definition. But since this definition is derivable only from sources that came into existence after—and for the most part only long after—the Pharisees had a history, it is necessary to begin with the known before venturing on the elucidation of the unknown. Indeed, the construction of an objective definition is necessarily the first task; for should this prove impossible, then the unknown may prove to be unknowable. But if possible, such a definition sets severe limits to possible historical reconstructions. The defined object could only have had a history that had as its outcome the object that has been objectively defined.

2.

Although in the vast secondary literature devoted to the Pharisees any number of definitions may be found,[2] the one that has won the widest scholarly consensus is, with unessential variations, that put forward by E. Schürer at the turn of the century. With definitiveness, underpinned by his impressive scholarship, Schürer affirmed that since the term Pharisees is derived from the Hebrew *perushim*, and

---

[2] See A. Michel and J. LeMoyne, "Pharisees" in *Supplement on Dictionnaire de la Bible* (Paris, 1964); Louis Finkelstein, *The Pharisees* (Philadelphia, 1962), vol. II, pp. 903-945; and most notably Jacob Neusner, "Bibliographical Reflections" in his *The Rabbinic Traditions about the Pharisees Before 70* (Leiden, 1971) vol. III, pp. 20-68; Ralph Marcus, "The Pharisees in the Light of Modern Scholarship," in *Journal of Religion* XXXII (1952), pp. 153-164; Anthony J. Saldarini, *Pharisees, Scribes and Sadducees in Palestinian Society* (Wilmington, 1988); Günter Stemberger, *Jewish Contemporaries of Jesus: Pharisees, Sadducees, Essenes* (Minneapolis, 1995), pp. 150-156

since this conveys the meaning of "separatists," the Pharisees must have been those who underwent a separation that the rest of the people did not undergo, namely from the *am ha-aretz*, the masses, and from the gentile nations, because of a greater scrupulousness with respect to the laws of ritual purity. Schürer believed that this separation had taken place in the time of Ezra and represented the onset of that process of ossification that turned the religion of Israel into the legalistic, spirit-drained Judaism of the Rabbis.[3] For this hostile definition, Schürer not only drew on the New Testament but on the Tannaitic literature as well; for he called upon a seemingly irrefutable proof-text from M. Hag. 2:7: "The garments of the *am ha-aretz* are a source of *midras* uncleanness to the *perushim*, 'the Pharisees.'" Clearly then the separation that gave the Pharisees their name related to a rigorous concern for the laws of ritual purity.

Now it is indeed true that scholars, Jewish and non-Jewish, have had their differences with Schürer, concerning when the Pharisees emerged and even with respect to how they got their name. And, needless to say, Jewish scholars such as Finkelstein, and liberal Christian scholars, such as Herford, took issue with the *negative* implications of Schürer's definition. Nevertheless, the Hagigah passage seemed to be overriding as a proof text and hence supportive of Schürer's claim that the Pharisees were a sect differentiated from the masses by virtue of their scrupulous observance of the laws of ritual purity.[4]

Indeed, even Jacob Neusner, in his *From Politics to Piety: The Emergence of Pharisaic Judaism* (Englewood Cliffs, 1973) pictures the Pharisees as a sect that (1) "laid great stress on eating with the right people, specifically those who obeyed the purity laws..." (2) "held 'a tradition of the Elders' about this matter which required that one wash hands before eating and performing other ritual ablutions... (3) laid stress on eating the right kinds of food... (4) tithed with great care." For Neusner, the Pharisees were the Jews who believed

> one must keep the purity laws outside the Temple...namely, at the table. Therefore, one must eat secular food (ordinary everyday meals) in a state of ritual purity as if one were a Temple priest. The Pharisees

---

[3] Emil Schürer, *History of the Jewish People in the Time of Jesus Christ* (New York, (1902), Second Division, vol. II, pp. 10-28.

[4] Cf., Louis Finkelstein, *The Pharisees* (Philadelphia, 1962), vol. I, pp. 75-78; vol. II, pp. 606-607; George F. Moore, *Judaism* (Cambridge, 1927), vol. 1, pp. 56-71; A. Finkel, *The Pharisees and the Teacher of Nazareth* (Leiden, 1964), pp. 42-57.

arrogated to themselves—and to all Jews equally—the status of Temple priests on account of that status. The table of every Jew in his home was seen as being like the table of the Lord in the Jerusalem Temple. The commandment "You shall be a kingdom of priests and a holy people" was taken literally: Everyone is a priest, everyone stands in the same relationship to God, and everyone must keep the priestly laws. At this time [prior to 70], only the Pharisees held such a viewpoint, and eating unconsecrated food as if one were a Temple priest at the Lord's table was one of the significations that a Jew was a Pharisee and a sectarian."

Subsequently, in his three-volume study, *The Rabbinic Traditions About the Pharisees before 70*, Neusner asserts that before 70, "the Pharisees were (whatever else they were) primarily a society for table fellowship, the high point of their life as a group."

The prevailing conception, then, among most scholars, be they Christian or Jewish, is that the Pharisees were a *sect* bound together by some set of regulations setting them apart from the rest of Jewry— most scholars assume that *perushim* and Haberim are synonymous terms—and that this sect adhered to the two-fold law, the Written and the Oral. For support of this definition appeal is made to Josephus, the New Testament, and the Tannaitic literature.[5]

This definition, however, is highly suspect, despite its apparent grounding in the conflicting sources. *It is suspect because of the method utilized to construct the definition.* Scholars, it would seem, began with the word *perushim* and then sought to explain the phenomenon by conjuring up what the name must imply. They did not recognize at the outset that the very name might be the most stubborn stumbling block in the way of a definition; for by its very nature as derivative from a common root—*parosh*, "to separate"—and not from a proper noun, as in the case of the Sadducees—it falls into a class of words that (1) have an origin and meaning prior to and distinct from the highly differentiated and specific phenomenon to which, at some historical moment, it becomes attached, (2) have a continued independent existence alongside the highly specific and highly differentiated usage, (3) outlive the specific and highly differentiated usage.

---

[5] Only Prof. Solomon Zeitlin has consistently (cf., especially his *"Ha-Zedukim we-ha-Perushim"* in *Horeb*, *II* (1936), pp. 56-89, and *The Rise and Fall of the Judean State*, vol. I, pp. 176-187) argued that the Pharisees were not a sect and that the Hagigah passage does not refer to them at all. Though very close to Zeitlin in definition and certain aspects of interpretation, I radically differ with him on the historical circumstances of their emergence. See E. Rivkin, "Solomon Zeitlin's Contribution to the Historiography of the Intertestamental Period," in *Judaism* (XIV 1965), pp. 354-367.

Words of this type are not only numerous but are to be found universally in societies that have had any kind of complex historical development. Citing merely a few examples is sufficient to underwrite how common the category is: democrat and Democrat, republican and Republican, whig and Whig, dissenter and Dissenter, socialist and Socialist, communist and Communist, protestant and Protestant, catholic and Catholic, church and Church, liberal and Liberal, etc.

And Judaism, precisely because of its complex history, abounds in instances: consider the historical vicissitudes of the word *hasid* which began so simply as a designation of an attribute applicable to any individual and was called upon to name a movement that arose on the eve of the Hasmonean revolt. Although these Hasidim subsequently disappeared, the word did not. It was available for naming two distinctly different movements separated by centuries: the *Hasidim* of twelfth-thirteenth century Germany and the *Hasidim* of the eighteenth century. Yet the word itself could be used and was so used and is even now used to designate a pious person who has no connection with the Hasidic movement at all. Indeed the term *hasid* was applied to the Vilna Gaon, who was a deadly enemy of the *Hasidim*, he, of course, being the true *hasid* in the eyes of the *mitnagdim*. Similarly, one has only to mention such terms as *zaddik*, *rav*, *rabbi*, *sofer*, *nasi*, *gaon*, to evoke a checkered history of multiple and at times even contradictory usage.

Since the term *perushim* bears all the marks of belonging to such a class of words, the scholar needs to check out, before drawing any conclusions, the possibility that the term may have had a history analogous to that of numberless such words and hence studded not only with possible ambiguity but contradictions as well. Especially would one be constrained to rigorous procedures when dealing with a language that has no capital letters to differentiate between a common and a proper noun. One would therefore be *obligated* to set up some *objective* methodological procedure for differentiation, a procedure that would afford every scholar the opportunity to test the claims made for the definition. One cannot use indiscriminately any or every text in which *perushim* occurs as though the term means "Pharisees." But since this is no mean task, it is methodologically sounder to abandon, for the time being, the term itself and its specific meaning and concentrate on extracting from the sources what *they* reveal the Pharisees to have been.

But such an extraction itself is fraught with difficulties, since the sources seem to be irreconcilable. The scholar would seem to be obliged to formulate a definition in order to determine which data should be deemed reliable in the sources. Thus if one has already concluded that the Pharisees were a sect, one would translate the term *haeresis* in Josephus as "sect," with all of its connotations of "deviation from an established religious system" and of "limited number" and of "organizational structure," even though the Greek merely means "school of thought" without regard to deviation, number, or structure. An *haeresis* in no way precludes a following embracing the overwhelming majority of the people, indeed, its being the Establishment—though it by no means necessitates that it so be. Such a scholar would tend to accommodate all the specific information about the Pharisees given by Josephus to his or her own notion of a sect and thus foreclose other possibilities, even though Josephus himself uses philosophy, *and philosophy only*, as a synonym for *haeresis*.

Such a procedure is scarcely likely to yield an objective definition. Nor is this goal attainable by intermixing sources, i.e., freely calling upon all sources to support a statement, as though the sources were corroborative throughout. Thus one might draw on some text in the New Testament and some text in the Tannaitic literature that seems supportive of something in Josephus, even though equally pertinent texts might not jibe at all. And certainly an objective definition cannot be hammered out of sources that either do not mention the Pharisees by name at all—e.g., the apocalyptic literature, the Dead Sea Scrolls—or are post-Tannaitic—e.g., the Babylonian and Palestinian Talmuds, the scholion to *Megillat Taanit*, or the *Abot deRabbi Nathan*—and hence dependent themselves on their comprehension of Josephus, the New Testament, or the Tannaitic literature for their conception of the Pharisees.

However, the method I have applied and defend avoids all these pitfalls by advocating the following procedures: (1) Openness to a definition elicited from the sources; i.e., no *a priori* definition nor one derivable only from a single source. (2) An analysis of each type of source separately and without recourse to any other type. In this way a definition would be elicited separately from each source, Josephus, the New Testament, and the Tannaitic literature. These definitions derived independently of each other would then be compared for congruence. Should the definitions prove to be identical, then an objective definition would necessarily follow. Should the definitions be incongruent and mutually exclusive of each other, e.g., a sect *and* a scholar class during the same time period, then some other methodology would have to be designed, or, this failing, the problem would have to be viewed as contingently insoluble. (3) No document would be utilized as a source that does not give internal evidence of its right to be heard, i.e., it must mention the Pharisees by name and it must belong to a body of literature some segment of which belongs to a time when the Pharisees flourished and the Sadducees were contending with them.

3.

Only three sources meet the rigorous criteria of self-authentication: Josephus, the New Testament, and the Tannaitic literature. However much their focus may vary, they all are reacting to an entity that they experienced or observed or had some knowledge of. And, as such, they are reacting, whether with favor or disfavor, to a functioning reality. If with favor then surely the object stripped of the plaudits is bound to be substantive. If with disfavor, then surely stripped of the venom is bound to be substantive, since nothing can generate more intense hostility than the reality of an object. After all, it is the reality, the substance of the object, that triggers the hostility. Luther denounced papal authority; he did not fabricate it.

Although all three sources, Josephus, the New Testament and the Tannaitic literature, knew the object, the Pharisees, their knowledge was communicated for radically different reasons. Josephus knew the Pharisees (1) as an object of choice, i.e., he decided to follow the system of law of the Pharisees after weighing the alternative possibilities of becoming a Sadducee or an Essene; (2) as a Judean phenomenon that needed to be explained to a Graeco-Roman readership; (3) as significant participants in the tumultuous events that Josephus personally had witnessed; (4) and as an entity that had played a very crucial role in the more distant past, especially during the High Priesthood of John Hyrcanus (134-104 B.C.E.), and the reigns of Alexander Janneus (103-76 B.C.E.) and Salome Alexandra (76-67 B.C.E.); (5) as a self-conscious historian writing with Thucydides as his model.

The New Testament writers, on the other hand, either knew or had access to the communications of those who had known the Pharisees, but had only a single interest in them: their relationship, predominantly hostile, to Jesus. At no time do they feel called upon to define the Pharisees explicitly or to delve into their prior history. For the purposes of rigorous analysis, however, a distinction must be made between the testimony of Paul who had been a Pharisee, the Synoptic Gospels and Acts that draw upon sources, oral or written, of actual involvements, and the Gospel of John which gives considerable internal evidence that the writer had no knowledge of the Pharisees other than what was inferred from whatever sources he drew upon.

As for the Tannaitic literature, it stands in sharp contrast to both Josephus and the New Testament. It neither defines them nor chronicles their history; it merely takes them for granted, i.e., assumes that the listener or reader is fully aware of who they are. Yet all scholars agree that the Tannaitic literature is in some way or other interconnected with the Pharisees, however beclouded this relationship in the light of some of the identifications that have currency. But precisely because ambiguity was impossible for those who knew the Pharisees as a matter of course, the term *perushim* could be used without qualification; i.e., no one could possibly mistake *Perushim*, i.e., Pharisees, a proper noun, with *perushim*, i.e., separatists, a common noun.

4.

Let us turn to building up a definition of the Pharisees from Josephus without recourse to any other sources. In doing so, we must distinguish the core definition from a subsidiary one. The former would be the definition that differentiates the Pharisees from all other groupings; the latter, specific doctrines of the Pharisees that might or might not be held by others. Thus, the Pharisees may have shared with the Essenes some belief in immortality, and with the Sadducees a belief in the divine revelation of the Pentateuch, in the binding character of this revelation, and a high evaluation of righteousness. Josephus, because of his presumed readership, tended to expatiate on specific doctrines rather than on the core, especially in those passages in which he turns aside from his narrative to explain to his readers the three schools of thought among the Jews. However, when he has to make comprehensible to the reader how a break between the Pharisees and John Hyrcanus could have had such dire consequences—

more than a generation of civil war—he concentrates on the core definition. Here are Josephus' exact words (*Ant.* XIII:408):

> ...the Pharisees had passed on to the people certain laws handed down by former generations and not recorded in the laws of Moses [*hoti nomima tina paredosan to demo hoc Pharisaioi ek pateron diadoxes*], for which reasons they are rejected by the Sadducean group, who hold that only those laws should be considered valid which were written down (in Scripture), and that those which had been handed down by former generations should not be observed [*lego ekeina dein hegisthai nomima ta gegraximena, ta d'ek paradoseos ton pateron me terein*].

Josephus thus stresses that it was the issue of the authority of the *paradosis*, the unwritten laws, that generated the hostility between the Pharisees and the Sadducees. This he confirms when he tells us that Salome Alexandra, heeding the death-bed advice of her husband Alexander Janneus, brought the Pharisees back to power and "commanded the people to obey them and whatever laws were introduced by the Pharisees in accordance with the Tradition (*paradosis*) of their Fathers and had been abolished by her father-in-law Hyrcanus, these she again restored. And so, while she had the title of sovereign, the Pharisees had the power" (*War* II:166, *Ant.* XVIII:15).

Nothing Josephus says elsewhere is in any way incongruous with this core definition; for the specific doctrines and the teachings of this scholar class were not only followed by a majority of the Jews but evoked such strong loyalties that the masses were ready to lay down their lives for the *paradosis*, unwritten laws, and the sages who transmitted these laws. Josephus leaves no doubt that the Pharisees were anything but aloof from the people, for he describes them as friendly to each other, dedicated to the welfare of the community at large, models of the virtuous life (*Ant.* XVIII:15, 17). He bears witness to their control over the cult, prayer, and worship, and to the fear that the Sadducees had of them because of their power over the masses (*War* II:163, III:374, *Ant.* XVIII:14). And though Josephus makes mention of their belief in immortality and the resurrection of the dead (*War* II:163), and of their reputation for expertness in the laws (*War* II:163, *Ant.* XIII:172, XVIII:13), and of their balancing the individual between Fate and Providence (*Life* 12), he neither alludes to a meticulous concern for laws of ritual purity, nor to a sectarian organizational structure, nor to an antipathy to the masses. Indeed, when he refers to his own decision to follow the Pharisees, he uses the Greek term *politeusthai* (*Ant.* XIII:296-298), "to adopt a constitution or a system of laws." He does not say that he became a member of some sect or confraternity. What in fact Josephus was saying was that, "Henceforth I will follow the twofold Law of the Pharisees, a system of Law not only available to all but prescribed for all." And of course there is the fact that in Josephus's day *haeresis* meant "school of thought" and not "sect." This is confirmed by his use of "philosophy" as the only synonym for *haeresis* that was fitting.

Not only does Josephus reveal that the Pharisees were a scholar class bespeaking the two-fold Law, but also as a class that was deeply involved in the complex power struggles of the Hasmonean, and post-Hasmonean periods. They were not simply scholars, but audacious and realistic champions of two-fold Law Judaism—ready, willing and able to marshal whatever pressure or coercive power might be necessary to secure the triumph of their system of law. When their laws were abrogated by John Hyrcanus, insurrection followed (ibid. 408-411). And though successfully put down by him, it was followed by decades of civil war under Alexander Janneus. Only when Salome Alexandra re-introduced the *paradosis*, the unwritten laws, did the Pharisees acquiesce to Hasmonean rule, and they consolidated their power by physically liquidating the opposition (*Ant.* XIV:172-176, XV:3, 370). Josephus thus reveals to us a scholar class that was simultaneously a revolutionary class, capable of resorting to whatever violence might be necessary to secure their ends.

This image of the Pharisee as scholar-leader-statesman is reinforced by Josephus's description of outstanding Pharisees who lived long after the civil war. Samaes and Pollio were very much alive to the realities of power politics, as Herod's careful treatment of them amply proves.[6] And surely Josephus's evaluation of Simeon ben Gamaliel in the following passage is marked by a deep appreciation of his political shrewdness:

> "This Simeon was a native of Jerusalem, of a very illustrious family, and of the *haeresis* (school of thought) of the Pharisees, who have the reputation of being unrivaled experts in their country's laws. A man highly gifted with intelligence and judgment, he could by sheer genius retrieve an unfortunate experience in affairs of state."[7]

---

[6] *Life* 191-2. Except for *"haeresis* [school of thought]" the translation is H. St. J. Thackeray's in *Josephus I, The Life* (Cambridge, 1956), p. 7.

[7] *War* IV:158-159. The translation is likewise Thackeray's *Josephus, III, The Jewish War* (Cambridge 1957), p. 49.

Nor does Simeon shrink from decisive action when the radical revolutionary elements elevated a simple villager to the High Priesthood
(*Ant.* XVIII:4-11, 23-25; cf. *War* II:118):

> This latest outrage was more than the people could stand, and as if for
> the overthrow of a despotism one and all were now aroused. For their
> leaders of outstanding reputation, such as Gorion, son of Joseph, and
> Simon son of Gamaliel, by public addresses to the whole assembly and
> by private visits to individuals urged them to delay no longer to punish
> these wreckers of liberty and purge the sanctuary of its bloodstained
> polluters.

Thus, according to Josephus, the Pharisees played shifting roles with
respect to the state, at times—during the early years of John
Hyrcanus and throughout the reign of Salome Alexandra enjoying
decisive power, and at times, detached from direct involvement. Such
fluctuations, however, in and of themselves do not spell out passivity,
but only a pragmatic assessment of political realities. So long as the
state—be it Hasmonean, Herodian, or Roman—did not interfere
with the *operation* of the two-fold Law, the Pharisees could, and, according to Josephus, did, rule the issue of state sovereignty as out of
bounds. Long before Jesus, the phrase "render unto Caesar what is
Caesar's and to God what is God's" was the watchword of the Pharisees. Thus the Pharisees refused to give sanction to Judas of Galilee's
call for resistance against Rome, not because the Pharisees were qui-
etists but because the authority of the two-fold Law was not at issue.
Indeed, they clearly took so firm a stand against Judas of Galilee that
he and his followers came to be viewed as forming a separate and
distinct *haeresis*, a Fourth Philosophy, even though the question of the
state was the only issue dividing them. The Pharisees thus did not
stand idly by but threw their weight about so effectively that only a
minority were drawn after Judas (Phil. 4:4b-6).

If, then, we seek to formulate a definition of the Pharisees from
Josephus, it would read: *The Pharisees were an aggressive scholar class that
championed the authority of the two-fold Law—the Pentateuch and the paradosis
—earned and held the respect and support of the masses, and advocated loyalty to
any state that recognized the authority of the two-fold Law.*[8]

---

[8] See Appendix A.

5.

When we turn to the New Testament to pry loose a definition of the Pharisees, we are faced not only with the problem of hostility but also with the complexity of the sources. Unlike Josephus, the New Testament writers are, with the exception of Paul, shrouded in anonymity and separated from each other in time and place and perspective. Although authentic traditions reaching back to Jesus' day are preserved in the Gospels, scholars are at a loss to devise an objective method that will permit an absolute differentiation between the historical and the fictive. Fully alive to the hazards, we must proceed gingerly.

Fortunately, Paul was, by his own admission, a Pharisee, and therefore in a position to know who they were. We must therefore scrutinize every iota of information he reveals. In Epistle to the Philippians 3:4-6, he writes:

> If any other man thinks he has reason for confidence in the flesh, I have more: circumcised on the eighth day, of the people of Israel, of the tribe of Benjamin, a Hebrew born of Hebrews; as to the Law a Pharisee, as to zeal a persecutor of the church, as to righteousness under the law blameless....

The meticulous ticking off of all the elements that would authenticate Paul's confidence in the flesh guarantees that he is pinpointing the hallmark of the Pharisees, and this hallmark is their position on the Law. A Pharisee was differentiated by his concept of the Law. Now it is true that Paul does not specifically say here in Philippians that the Pharisee championed the two-fold Law, but he does make this explicit in Galatians 1:13-14, where he speaks as follows of his early life in Judaism:

> For you have heard of my former life in Judaism, how I persecuted the Church of God violently and tried to destroy it; and I advanced in Judaism beyond many of my own age, so extremely zealous was I for the traditions (the *paradosis*) of my fathers.

"The traditions of my fathers" (*Ton patrikon mou paradoseon*) can only mean the Oral Law. "As to the Law a Pharisee" in Philippians thus could only have meant the two-fold Law.

If then we move from Paul to the Gospels and Acts with this definition of the Pharisees, we have a control from within the New Testament itself over data emanating from the Gospels bereft of any certainty as to authorship. But so long as the Gospels and Acts communicate data that are either derivative from or compatible with the definition derived from Paul, such data may be freely used to undergird that definition. If, however, data emerges which are either incompatible with or contradictory to the definition of the Pharisees drawn from Paul, such data would be most suspect. This methodological principle when applied yields striking results, for it frees the scholar of a dependence on a prior determination of date, authorship, or place of origin of the Gospels or Acts. One can as readily begin with Matthew as with Mark; with John as with Luke.

Since space is at such a premium, I shall make no attempt to analyze each and every text in which Pharisees are found. I shall confine myself to the definition that such an analysis reveals: that the Pharisees were a scholar class that championed the two-fold Law and aggressively countered any challenge to its authority. This definition is underwritten even by the most hostile anti-Pharisaic texts in Matthew, texts that are nonetheless prefaced by an acknowledgment that: "The scribes and Pharisees sit on Moses's seat; so practice and observe whatever they tell you, but not what they do; for they preach, but do not practice" (Mat. 23:1-3)· But since Matthew and Mark make it evident that the Pharisees were champions of the paradosis— that *very term that Josephus used to designate the unwritten Laws—then* to sit on Moses' seat was to wield the two-fold Law.

It should further be noted that one fails to find in the New Testament any data that would support the notion that the Pharisees were hostile to the masses or that they were primarily concerned with rigorous adherence to the laws of ritual purity. As for the former, the Pharisees turn their back only on association with inveterate sinners and tax collectors, and, as for the latter, the very "tradition" prescribing the washing of the hands is evidence of an amelioration of the very strict Pentateuchal rules requiring bodily immersion and the setting of the sun for removal of ritual uncleanness (M. Yad. 4:6-7, T. Yad. 2.2).[9]

6.

However paradoxical, it is the Tannaitic literature, and not the New Testament, that has undergirded a definition of the Pharisees as a

---

[9] Cf., M. Par. 3:7.

sect separated organizationally from the masses because of their scrupulous concern with the laws of ritual impurity. As previously indicated, this definition is mandatory in the face of the proof text from Hagigah where it is flatly affirmed that the garments of an *am ha-aretz* are a source of *midras* uncleanness for *perushim*. Assuming that *perushim* must mean Pharisees, and noting that the *perushim* in the Hagigah text seem to be identical with the Haberim of tractate Demai, scholars concluded that the organizational form of the Haberim was the same as that of the *perushim* in Hagigah.

Such an identity, however, was established without taking into account the possibility that not all *perushim* were *Perushim*, i.e., that the term *perushim* in a Tannaitic text need not mean Pharisees at all, since *perushim* belongs to a category of words that are by their nature suspect, and hence imposes on the scholar the burden of proving when the term is or is not designating a movement of some kind. To establish such proof, however, one must set up rigorous controls that will preclude a subjective decision as to when the word does or does not mean Pharisees.

Such a system of controls can be devised. *We can affirm with certainty that only those texts that juxtapose the perushim to the Zedukkim, the Sadducees, give absolute internal evidence that the Pharisees must be meant.* The control on this meaning is *Zedukkim*, for unlike *perushim* it is not derivative from a verb but from a name *and hence its counterpart perushim must be, in these texts, those who are fittingly juxtaposed to the Sadducees.* A text where *perushim* is used but not *Zedukkim* has no legitimate claim for the framing of a definition of the Pharisees, since the Hebrew term *perushim* when not juxtaposed to *Zedukkim* need not mean Pharisees but "separatists" of one sort or another.

A systematic analysis of all the texts in which the *perushim* are juxtaposed to *Zedukkim*, whether they be those with the formula "The Sadducees say...the *Perushim* say..." (B. Yom. 19, B. Nid. 33b, T. Yom. 1:8), or those that merely indicate some controversy or event (T. Suk. 3:1), reveals the following definition: The Pharisees are the champions of the halakhah, i.e., the Oral Law, and vigorously support its authority against the counter claims of the Sadducees. *And what is of especial significance is that in each and every one of these texts the Pharisees are the source of the halakhah, never its object, and that they are never juxtaposed to the am haaretz either as opponents or as bound by a different set of laws*—the one instance in which they are involved with the *am ha-aretz*, the latter go to heroic efforts to carry out the Pharisaic *halakhah* to beat the willows on Hoshanah Rabbah when the festival falls on the Sabbath, in opposition to the Boethusians-Sadducees (M. Par. 3:7). So too they champion legislation ameliorating the laws of ritual purity—as witness their insistence that when the ritual of the burning of the red heifer has to be carried out by a priest who has been *deliberately* made ritually unclean and has immersed in water while the sun is still high in the sky to demonstrate that immersion alone was sufficient for cleansing as the Pharisees claimed. Or consider that the Bet Din compelled the High Priest (M. Yom. 1:1) to swear that he will not deviate from the procedures as set forth in the *halakhah* for the ritual of Yom Kippur; and that they insisted that the cutting of the sheath take place on the second day of Passover, even if it was the Sabbath, and not as the Sadducees claimed on the morrow of the Sabbath after the first ripening of barley on a Sunday (B. Nid. 33b). These texts make clear enough that the Pharisees not only held power but did not hesitate to use it, going so far as to regulate the ritual calendar and the mode of the High Priest's entry into the Holy of Holies, his exclusive turf, on Yom Kippur.

These juxtapositional texts are to be insulated from all other texts in which the term *perushim* occurs, but not *Zedukkim*. The meaning Pharisees for *perushim* in these texts alone is self-validating. *Hence whatever definition is constructed from these texts may be used to determine the possible meaning of perushim in other texts, but it cannot be modified or altered by texts that are not self-validating. Since the* Hagigah *passage does not juxtapose perushim to Zedukkim, the term perushim could be translated Pharisees only if the context would reveal a definition identical to that of the self-validating texts.* But such congruence is not forthcoming. Indeed the fact that the *perushim* in the Hagigah text and in those other texts where the *perushim* are not juxtaposed to *Zedukkim* are the *object* of the *halakhah* and not its *source* is in and of itself proof positive that the term *perushim* in these texts cannot mean Pharisees. And as for utilizing Tannaitic texts as sources for evidence of the operation of the *halakhah* prior to the destruction of the Temple, it should be stressed that since the unwritten laws, the *halakhot*, the *paradosis*, were transmitted orally, they cannot be expected to show up in written form. If they did, they would undercut the claim that they were orally transmitted until they were written down in part in the Mishnah. Nonetheless the fact that they were transmitted orally would mean that some of these unwritten laws would necessarily have been preserved and included in the Mishnah, Tosefta, and Beraitot and hence retrievable if methodological safeguards are vigorously enforced.

Once the cornerstone Hagigah text collapses, the entire structure built upon this text shares the same fate. The Haberim cannot be synonymous with the Pharisees, for the latter are not the *Perushim* of the Hagigah passage and consequently are not differentiated in status from the *am ha-aretz*. Nor are the Haberim ever the source of the *halakhah*, but their object. And, whereas no Pharisee is ever recorded as being simultaneously a Sadducee, a *Haber* Sadducee is attested to (B. B.B. 60b).

And along with the Hagigah passage go all the other Tannaitic texts where *perushim* is used without Sadducees. In not a single instance, does any such text reveal affinities to those that are self-validating. In not a single instance do these *perushim*, unhinged from Sadducees, legislate, or debate over the law. They are not a legislating scholar class but sectarians of one sort or another. All texts that do not belong to the self-validating corpus use the term *perushim* to mean something other than Pharisees. And this can be demonstrated by an appeal to strictly objective criteria, established by a procedure that can be tested and re-tested by any scholar working with these sources. The disqualification of the Hagigah and other similar texts is thus grounded in an objective method and can lay down just claim to being definitive.

Although no other proof of such disqualification may be necessary, other proof is forthcoming, proof that affords us an additional control. Scholars have always recognized that there were a few Tannaitic texts in which the term *perushim* could not mean Pharisees, the very scholars who do not hesitate to translate *perushim* as Pharisees in the Hagigah text. One of these *perushim* texts reads:

> Our Rabbis taught: "When the Temple was destroyed for the second time, *perushim* multiplied in Israel, who took it upon themselves not to eat meat or drink wine... The *Hahamim* have therefore ordained thus: 'A man may stucco his house, but leave a little bare...'"[10]

The term *perushim* is translated here by Soncino "ascetics,"[11] by Jastrow, "abstemious,"[12] by Goldschmidt, "Enthaltsame."[13] Further it should be underscored that the *perushim* in this passage are at odds with the *Hahamim* and the *halakhah!* Another text is to be found in B. Pes. 70b:

---

[10] *The Babylonian Talmud, Baba Bathra*, trans. I. Epstein (London, 1935), p. 245.

[11] *Dictionary of Talmud and Midrash*, p. 1223.

[12] *Der Babylonische Talmud*, Baba Bathra, trans. Lazarus Goldschmidt, p. 1101.

[13] *Babylonian Talmud*, trans. H. B. Freedman (London, 1938), p. 361.

> It was taught: "Judah son of Durtai separated himself (*piresh haveh*) from
> the Hahamim, the Sages, both he and his son Durtai... Rav said: 'What
> is the reason of the son of Durtai?' ... Said Rav Ashi: 'And are we to
> arise and explain the reasons of *perushim?*'"

The Soncino renders *perushim* "Schismatics,"[14] Jastrow, "Seceders,"[15]
Goldschmidt, *"die sich sondern."*[16] Again note that these *perushim* take a
stand against the *Hahamim* and the *halakhah*; indeed, they are called
perushim for this very reason!

And a third text, T. Ber. 3:25:

> The eighteen benedictions referred to by the Hahamim correspond to
> the eighteen memorials (*azkarot*) of the Psalm that begins, "Give unto
> the Lord, 0 ye sons of might."
> The blessing which pertains to the *minim* (heretics) includes that against
> the *perushim*; that of the proselytes includes the *zekenim* ... If one said
> these separately and the others separately, he has fulfilled his obliga-
> tion.

Perushim is here a synonym for *minim*, "heretics;" the text affirms this
explicitly and the scholars echo this affirmation: Jastrow, "Renegades,"[17] Saul Lieberman, "People who are accustomed to separate
from the ways of the collective group" (B. Sot. 22b). Again note that
these *perushim* are not only the object of the *halakhah*, but execrated by
the *Hahamim*!

Once one recognizes that the term *perushim* can mean not only
something other than Pharisees but also a grouping highly disap-
proved of and legislated against in Tannaitic texts, one can ask on
what grounds scholars assume that in other texts *perushim* must mean
Pharisees? What controls have scholars set up to distinguish one usage of *perushim* from another? Why, for example, should not the term
perushim in the Hagigah text be translated "ascetics" when there is no
hesitation to so translate it when it appears in B. B.B. 60b? And why,
for example, should scholars insist on translating *isha perusha* of M.
Sot. 3:4 as "Pharisaic woman," or *makkot perushim* as "the plague of
Pharisees," when "ascetic woman" and the "flagellations of ascetics"
are not only fully justifiable on the basis of the Baba Batra passage
but demanded by the context. And how long will scholars reiterate

---

[14] Op. cit., p. 33.
[15] *Der Babylonische Talmud, Pesahim*, p. 572.
[16] Op. cit.
[17] *Tosefta ke-Peshuta* (New York, 1955), vol. 1, p. 54.

that there were seven types of Pharisees when seven types of ascetics are meant (M. Yad. 3:2)?

All non-self-validating Tannaitic texts thus fall away on two grounds: (1) they are inassimilable with the structure and content of the self-validating texts, and (2) they are absolutely assimilable with those texts where *perushim* is recognized by all scholars to mean something other than Pharisees.

Now that all irrelevant texts have been swept away, we are in a position not only to construct a definition of the Pharisees drawn from the Tannaitic literature but to explain why so few texts mention them. The *Perushim*-Pharisees are identical with the *Soferim* and the *Hahamim*. They are the promulgators and the teachers of the *halakhah*. They are to be found everywhere in the Tannaitic literature as *Hahamim* and *Soferim* but only rarely as *Perushim*. And for a good reason indeed! *They never called themselves Perushim except when juxtaposed to Zedukkim.*

This fact is strikingly evident in the Mishnaic treatment of the Holy Scripture's rendering the hands unclean. In M. Yad. 6:3, we read: "The *Zedukkim* say, 'We complain against you *Perushim*, for you say that Holy Scriptures render the hands unclean....'" Yet several passages earlier, M. Yad. 3:2, the principle "Holy Scriptures render the hands unclean" is cited first as the prevailing *halakhah* and then as the *"dibre Soferim,"* the words of the Scribes." The term *Perushim*, however, does not appear at all! Without the *Zeddukim*, we have not *Perushim* but *Soferim!* The very *Soferim* whose authority is not challengeable from Scripture: "We do not deduce the words of the Torah from the words of the *Soferim*; nor the words of the *Soferim* from the words of the Torah; nor the words of the *Soferim* from the words of the *Soferim*". Their teachings need not be logically justified, nor need they have any logical connection. The words of the *Soferim* are Law!

The Pharisees of the Tannaitic literature thus turn out to be that scholar class that promulgated and championed the two-fold Law. And it is no rash speculation to suspect that they *deliberately* avoided the name *Perushim*, except when engaged in controversy with the Sadducees who must have first hurled the term *Perushim* at them with contempt, denying their right to the honored name of *Soferim*, a name reserved for *Soferim* like Ben Sira who were champions of the Aaronides and the written Law literally read. To the Sadducees, these self-proclaimed *Soferim* were "separatists," "heretics," for in proclaiming the authority of the *paradosis*, two-fold Law, they were deemed to be undermining God's immutable written revelation to which neither jot nor title was to be added or subtracted!

7.

Josephus, the New Testament, and the Tannaitic literature have now, each independently, yielded a definition of the Pharisees, which is identical: the Pharisees were the authoritative teachers and exponents of the twofold Law. They were *not* a sect, they were *not* organized in a confraternity dedicated to a rigorous observance of the laws of ritual purity, and they were *not* merely scholars. They were leaders and legislators who acted firmly and decisively when their authority and the twofold Law were at stake. The sources are not at odds at all as to who the Pharisees were irrespective of how much they may have loved them or hated them.

Now, with an objectively constructed definition of the Pharisees at hand, we can begin to grapple with the more difficult problem of historical reconstruction. Here some of the obstacles are insurmountable: we have no source that specifically informs us of Pharisaic origins, and we have no source that gives us a continuous interconnected history of this scholar class. And since this history, however short it may have been, spans no less than two hundred years, years witnessing tumultuous events and torturous change, we can never hope to devise a method that will be able to trace this history with detailed precision. Nonetheless we can design procedures that will (1) preserve all the specific history that is recoverable, (2) reduce distortion to a minimum, (3) and set secure limits to possible origins and possible reconstructions.

First, the definition itself severely limits the range of historical experience possible. Since this definition was constructed objectively, the Pharisees could have had only that kind of a history that would yield the Pharisees as objectively defined. The Pharisees thus could not have had a history yielding a sect separated from the masses. They necessarily would have had a history that yielded a revolutionary scholar class sitting on Moses's seat whose twofold law governed the overwhelming majority of the Jewish people.

Second, rigorous controls can be set up to determine the approximate time of emergence. Optimally, there should be at least one set of sources that leave no doubt whatsoever that at a specific point in

time the Pharisees did indeed emerge as a differentiated entity, balanced by a set of sources that testify to their non-existence at some
earlier point in time. Fortunately, Josephus is a source of the first
type, while the Wisdom of Ben Sira is a source of the second.

Josephus makes no mention of the Pharisees prior to the time of
Jonathan the Hasmonean. His first full-bodied treatment of the
Pharisees is reserved for the account of John Hyrcanus's break with
the Pharisees. Significant here are the following facts: (1) John
Hyrcanus is at first pictured as a disciple of the Pharisees; i.e., they
and not the Sadducees have his ear (*Ant.* XIII:296). (2) When John
Hyrcanus breaks with the Pharisees, he abrogates their *paradosis*, the
laws not written down by Moses (*Ant.* XIII:297-298). *Hence their paradosis must have been operative prior to its abrogation* (*Ant.* XIII:299). (3) An
insurrection follows the abrogation of the laws but is put down (*Ant.*
XIII:372-376, 379-83, 398-404). (4) A new uprising occurs during the
reign of Alexander Janneus, which is not effectively crushed (*Ant.*
XIII:405-409). (5) Salome Alexandra restores the Pharisees to favor
and reintroduces the *paradosis* of the Pharisees, and the civil war
comes to an end (*Ant.* XIII:410-411). (6) The Pharisees liquidate
much of the Sadducean leadership.

The question that Josephus leaves unanswered however is not only
how the Pharisees came to be so influential with John Hyrcanus but
how their laws came to be operative in the first place. He likewise
fails to explain how the masses of people became so attached to the
Pharisees and their laws that they were willing to rise up against the
Hasmonean family, a family that had so recently gained for them
independence. Since Josephus makes no mention of the Pharisees
prior to Jonathan, we must conclude that the Pharisees, sometime
during the Hasmonean revolt, must have gained such popularity with
the masses that they were able to invest Simon through *a non-
Pentateuchal body*, the *Keneset ha-gedolah*, with the High Priesthood, on
the grounds of an authority that they claimed as the transmitters of
the *paradosis*. Owing their very legitimacy as High Priest to the Pharisees and their *paradosis*, first Simon and then John Hyrcanus considered themselves disciples of the Pharisees and confirmed the *paradosis*,
the unwritten laws, as binding.

Although Josephus does not reveal when the Pharisaic two-fold
Law first became operative, he leaves no room for doubt that the *legal
system* for governing the Jews was the crucial issue operative in the
early years of John Hyrcanus's rule. But since the legal system is the

very foundation of any complex functioning society, the displacement of one legal system by another is never an academic matter. It shakes a society at its very roots. And Josephus makes it very evident that Judean society was no exception. The disagreement was not over a legal decision but over the fundamental principle of whether Moses was given a onefold or twofold Law.

If then the abrogation of the two-fold Law unleashed insurrection and civil war, would not the original introduction of the two-fold Law as an operative system presuppose some revolutionary upheaval? If as late as the time of John Hyrcanus and Alexander Janneus a system of law based on a literal rendering of the Pentateuch was operable, surely it must have been viable and operable in the pre-Hasmonean period. And since Josephus knows nothing of the Pharisees or the twofold Law prior to the Hasmonean revolt and since the pre-Hasmonean society that he describes is one in which the Aaronide-Zadokite High Priest holds ultimate authority, we must posit that sometime during the convulsions that rocked Judean society during the Hasmonean revolt the Pharisaic Revolution occurred, and the two-fold Law displaced the one-fold Law as the legally operative system of law in Judean society. And among their first revolutionary acts must have been the legitimization of Simon as High Priest in the face of the Pentateuchal command that only the descendents of Phineas were to hold this office. Little wonder then that John Hyrcanus first appears in Josephus as a disciple of the Pharisees and as the supporter of the two-fold Law! Little wonder then that the masses were enraged when John Hyrcanus broke with the Pharisees and abrogated the two-fold Law; for the Pharisees had carried through a revolution, the Hasmoneans a revolt!

Josephus is one source that points to the revolutionary origins of Pharisaism; Ben Sira another. For in Ecclesiasticus we have spread before us a detailed description of Judean society as it functioned sometime prior to the Hasmonean revolt, written not only by a native of Jerusalem, but by a *Sofer*, a Scribe. And what we see is triumphant Aaronidism! The society is ruled by the Aaronide priests under the direction of a High Priest descended from Phineas and Zadok (Ecclesiasticus 45:17). The authority over the Law is securely vested in the Aaronides and in no other class (Ecclesiasticus 39:1-11). The *Soferim* of Ben Sira's day are hierocratic intellectuals who sing the praises of the Aaronides and underwrite their God-given supremacy

(Ecclesiasticus 45:18-22).[18] They applaud God's destruction of Korah for his rebellion against Aaronide hegemony.[19] They have no independent legal authority; indeed, their metier is Wisdom and obedience to the Law, not authority over it. Ben Sira knows nothing of a two-fold Law, nothing of a *Bet Din Ha-Gadol*, nothing of synagogues. His legal vocabulary is limited to the terms of the written law: *halakhah, gezerah, takkanah* are unknown to him. His names for God are biblical—never does he use *Shekhinah, Makom, ha-Kadosh Barukh Hu.* Ben Sira is a *Sofer* of the one-fold law; for no other kind of *Sofer* existed in his day.[20]

If then, using Ben Sira as our control we analyze all pre-Hasmonean sources, we discover that not a single one knows of the two-fold Law, or of the Pharisees, or the *Bet Din ha-Gadol*, or of synagogues, or of *Shekhinah, ha-Kadosh Barukh Hu, Makom* as names for God. Indeed, one searches in vain throughout the entire Psalter for such names or legal terminology. Even Psalm 119 knows only the written Torah! And with good reason. Aaronide hegemony was unchallenged. And since the source of this hegemony was to be found in the literal reading of the Pentateuch, the Pentateuch was so read.

Is one to suppose that so powerful a hierocracy as appears in Ben Sira abdicated without a struggle? That armed as it was with God-given power spelled out explicitly in any number of Pentateuchal verses, it passively moved aside to allow a new scholar class trumpeting a novel idea of a two-fold Law to take over control of the Pentateuch? To raise these questions is to answer them. Only a crisis of confidence in Aaronide leadership could undercut its popular support, and only a revolution could replace one ruling class by another. The buying and the selling of the High Priesthood in the reign of Antiochus discredited the Aaronide leadership; the problems unleashed by the Hasmonean revolt stirred up a new class of leaders with novel answers; the support of an enraged people in arms made

---

[18] Ecclesiasticus 45:23-24. It is to be noted that Aaron is accorded many more verses (45:6-22) than Moses (45:1-5).

[19] For the significance of Ben Sira as a source for pre-two-fold Law Aaronidism ·and the hierocratic *Sofer*, see E. Rivkin, "Ben Sira and the Non-Existence of the Synagogue" in Silver, ed., *In The Time of Harvest* (New York, 1963), pp. 321-354.

[20] For the extent of the transformation, see Victor Tcherikover, *Hellenistic Civilization and the Jews* (Philadelphia, 1959), pp. 1-174; cf., also Solomon Zeitlin, *The Rise and Fall of the Judean State* (Philadelphia, 1962), vol. I, pp. 1-93.

available the coercive means for putting the new scholar class of the two-fold Law in power.

And there is a third line of reasoning that likewise points to a major revolutionary upheaval. A radical economic and social and cultural transformation had steadily undermined the society based on literal Pentateuchalism and Aaronide hegemony. The basically simple class structure of a society of peasants and priests had steadily become more complex, as agricultural surpluses enriched the Temple establishment, created a city dwelling leisure class, and laid the foundation for cultural sophistication. One need but compare Judean society on the eve of the canonization of the Pentateuch as it is refracted through the memoirs of Nehemiah with that in which Ben Sira lived to realize how vast the gulf is between the two worlds.

The process of transformation had begun under Persian rule, was considerably speeded up under the Ptolemies, and precipitated the need for radical decisions on the eve of the Hasmonean revolt. The penetration of the *polis* form into the Near East had set in motion economic, social, political, and cultural forces that radically altered the structural configuration of Judean society, even though the Aaronide hierocracy was left untouched. The emergence of the Tobiads, however, as a powerful new Hellenistic element in Judea is conclusive evidence that, even under the Ptolemies, the impact of *polisification* was having more than a negligible impact on Judea. And the rapidity with which Hellenistically oriented Jews clamored for *polis* rights following the Seleucid takeover in 197 B.C.E. testifies to deep structural re-arrangements that had been taking place. Whatever the ultimate solution, it was clearly evident that the old Aaronide hierocratic system was inadequate to cope with the needs of a society so radically altered from that presupposed by the literal Pentateuch, and with such questions as to "Why die for the Law?" in the face of Antiochus's decrees promising death for those who remained loyal to the Law that promised them neither eternal life for the soul or resurrection for the body.

The solution offered by the Hellenistic factions under the leadership of Jason and Meneleus is well-known and need concern us only insofar as it discredited hierocratic leadership and displayed its spiritual bankruptcy. Of far greater significance is the solution that has gone relatively unnoticed because attention was diverted to the role of the Hasmonean family in challenging the Hellenizing efforts of Antiochus and his Jewish collaborationists. Both 1 and 2 Maccabees make it appear that Mattathias and his sons led a rebellion *to restore* the hierocratic system, not a *revolution* to replace it. Yet a *revolution* it must have been, for according to 1 Maccabees itself a *synagoge megalé* (*kenesset ha-gedolah*) invested Simon with the dual authority of High Priest and ruler. The authority for Simon's power was thus not the Pentateuch where no such institution is mentioned. And this *synagoge megalé* that installed a High Priest who was not in a direct line from Aaron-Eleazer-Phineas-Zadok, whence was its authority derived? Surely not from the Pentateuch, which gave Phineas and his descendants the High Priesthood forever! Surely not from the Pentateuch, for it contains no provision for any assembly of any kind to tamper with high priestly succession. The one assembly—not called a *kenesset*—that had made such an effort under Korah's leadership ended up in *sheol*. Only a direct revelation from God through Moses or Aaron or Eleazer could have authority, and surely such a direct revelation had not been vouchsafed the *synagoge megalé*. If then the *synagoge megalé* exercised a power that overrode the literal Pentateuch, and if it exercised a power that is not spelled out *literally* in the Pentateuch, then must we not conclude that the source of its authority was the Pharisees who affirmed the concept of the two-fold Law and who were the *living* spokesmen for Moses? The authority over the two-fold Law had been transmitted by Moses to Joshua, to the elders, to the prophets, to the men of the *kenesset ha-gedolah*, the *synagoge megalé*.[21] The authority over the Law had never been invested in the Aaronides! They were cultic functionaries, under the authority of the Law, not over it. As such, the Aaronides are totally excluded from the chain of legitimate authority reaching back to Moses on Sinai, and

---

[21] M. Ab. 1:1. The contradictions in the Pentateuch enabled the Pharisees to justify their overthrow of the Aaronides, for they could point to the Pentateuchal text that explicitly transmits authority from Moses, a non-Aaronide, to Joshua, likewise a non-Aaronide. They could also draw on the contradictions as evidence of the existence of an oral Law to adjudicate and harmonize the contradictions. Furthermore, the Pharisees could utilize the historical and prophetic books as evidence that not only were those in authority non-Aaronides, but, as in the case of Elijah, could nullify the Pentateuch to deal with the religious crisis of baalism; i.e., authority was vested in the prophetic class as the transmitters of the two-fold Law and hence they had the right to determine the Law in the light of the circumstances provided that it was not written down. The process by which the Pharisees overthrew the Aaronides is spelled out in my *A Hidden Revolution: The Pharisees' Search for the Kingdom Within* (Nashville, 1978).

hence guilty of falsifying the true nature of God's Law when they claimed that God had revealed the Written Law only.

The Pharisees thus offered a revolutionary solution to the problems unleashed by *polisification*. Without abandoning either the one God or his revelation to Moses, this new class of leaders forged highly original concepts for mastering the perplexing challenges of the Hellenistic world. They drew on its most powerful elements and rearranged them within a monotheistic framework, and stamped them with the template of Judaism. But in doing so they so completely transmuted these elements that only the most refined analysis can expose them.

This mode of analysis can be briefly sketched. The Pharisees affirmed that the Pentateuch had been given by God to Moses. They did not raise the issue of whether there had been a revelation, *only whether authority to legislate unwritten laws had been revealed simultaneously with the written laws*. The Pharisees also affirmed that the prophetic and historical books had been divinely inspired.

Now what is truly astonishing is that the Pharisees did not follow biblical models but struck out along novel lines: (1) They posited an oral Law, though no such Law is explicitly referred to in the Pentateuch or the prophets. (2) They vested authority over the revealed two-fold Law in a scholar class that had no such authority in either the Pentateuch or Prophets. Law had always been directly revealed to a prophetlike individual, never to a scholar class. Indeed the Pharisaic term for teacher, *rav*, is not so used in the Bible, nor is *talmid haham*, designating that unique master-disciple relationship of Pharisaism, a biblical concept. Even the terms *haham and sofer*, though biblical, never conveyed the notion of law-determining authority. (3) They created an institution with ultimate responsibility for the law that is nowhere to be found in the Bible: the *Bet Din ha-Gadol*, "the Grand Legislature" or "Senate." The Pentateuch knows of a *kahal*, of an *edah*, but nothing of a *Bet din*. This *Bet Din ha-Gadol* promulgated oral laws under such rubrics as *halakhah, takkanah, gezerah*, terminology nowhere to be found in biblical legal terminology. (4) They coined new names and concepts for God: *Makom, shekhinah, ha-Kadosh Barukh Hu, Abinu Shebashemayim*. (5) They forged the doctrines of *Olam ha-ba* and *tehiat hametim*, which for the first time assured the *individual* immortality. (6) They introduced mandatory prayer and a cluster of blessings along with the synagogue for communal prayer—an institution that did not exist before the Hasmonean Revolt.

So too the Pharisees, though committed to the divinely revealed status of the Pentateuch, clearly did not feel bound to biblical models or biblical concepts. Indeed, what is perhaps most strikingly novel is their notion of a non-writing scholar class that venerated divinely revealed books! Whereas the great religious leaders of the Bible either write themselves or have others write for them or about them, the Pharisees put nothing in writing. How unlike the *Soferim*, the hierocratic intellectuals of Ben Sira's day! And in their withdrawal from writing, they abandoned the narrative and poetic mode of communication! The Pharisees were the progenitors in Judaism of the individual law severed from historical or narratival involvement, the *halakhah* or *mishnah* form, the *midrash* form with its proof-texting, and of the isolated episode, and the moral paradigm with no narratival or historical or poetic framework—the *aggadah* form. The Pharisees communicated via separate and distinct items. They may have quoted biblical narratives, read continuous passages from prophets and Wisdom literature, recited the Psalms, and explicated verses, but they never formulated either orally or in writing down any of *their* laws, doctrines, teachings, prayers, etc., in any biblical type framework.

And just as they turned away from biblical models for their *form* of teaching, so did they abandon biblical models for their *mode* of teaching. Instead they adopted logical deductive methods and abstract legal concepts. Whereas the Pentateuch envelops contradictory legislation and doctrine without resolution, the Pharisees are keenly aware of the law of non-contradiction.[22] Whereas the Pentateuch sets forth law casuistically, the Pharisees sought to ground individual laws in general principles.

Even the most superficial glance at the Mishnah, the Tosefta, and the Tannaitic Midrash reveals a non-biblical orientation. The Mishnah and Tosefta have a logical arrangement and are almost exclusively limited to legal materials. The Bible clearly was not their

---

[22] This is evident from the *prosboul(e)* enacted by Hillel, which is a Greek rendering of *lifne bet din*. Sanhedrin was not used for *Bet din* before 70 C.E. The Gospels are thus accurate in their insistence that Jesus was brought before a sanhedrin; he was not tried by the *boulé*, i.e., the *bet din*. During Jesus's lifetime, no one in Judea would have called the *bet din* in Greek anything but a *boulé*, or a diakasterion. The *bet din* was strictly a Pharisaic institution as was the synagogue. The Sanhedrin problem is far too complex to discuss here but is fully explored in my "Bet Din, Boulé, Sanhedrin— A Tragedy of Errors," in *Hebrew Union College Annual* 46.

model. As for the Tannaitic Midrash, it may be attached to the biblical order, but nowhere in the Bible is the exegetical, commentative mode to be found. And of no little significance, the entire book of Genesis and the first eleven chapters of Exodus are excluded from Tannaitic midrashic concern. The narratival, historical framework of the Pentateuch found no imitative response.

The Tannaitic literature likewise abounds in legal terminology that reveals a reaching out for abstract concepts and principles of systematization. Thus we meet up with such non-biblical terminology as "this is the general rule," "there are principle categories (*abot*)," "proprietary right (*reshut*)," "*shetar* (deed)," *hayyab* and *patur*" (obligated and free of obligation), "*kellal u-prat*" (general and particular), "*kal we-homer*" (a fortiori argument)—but why continue. Any student of this literature knows that its distinctive terminology is non-biblical.

If the Pharisees did not follow biblical models, what models, if any, did they follow? To answer this question we must look to the source of the problem for which the Pharisees sought a solution. And this, briefly put, was the restructurization of the Near East along Hellenistic lines. The spread of the *polis* and *polis* culture awakened new needs and interests even among those Jews who vigorously resisted outright Hellenization. They may have rejected the polytheistic suppositions of the *polis* world, even as they were impressed with its law-making institutions, the *boulé*; with the logical-deductive mode of thinking that it encouraged; with the emphasis that it placed on individuality; with the teaching role of the scholar-sage-philosopher; with the elevated status of lawgivers and lawmakers. The Pharisees drew upon all these elements within the Hellenistic world and transmuted them through their commitment to monotheism and to a divine revelation by Moses. Thus the *Bet Din ha-Gadol* was patterned after the *boulé*—indeed this was its original Greek rendition, not *sanhedrin*—*individual* immortality, from the high value placed on the individual by the *polis* culture; logical deductive, categorical, and abstract thinking from the Hellenistic preoccupation with such modes of thought. But the essential genius of the Pharisees is to be found in their highly original utilization of these Hellenistic elements and in their own unique contributions. For though they may have gotten their idea of unwritten laws from the Hellenistic world and though they may have had the *boulé* as the model for the *Bet Din ha-Gadol*, the affirmation that the unwritten laws ultimately determine the meaning of the written laws, that all new legislation must be *unrecorded*, that the *boulé* be restricted to a scholar class, that all laws, be they seemingly secular or religious, were underwritten by a divinely mandated authority revealed to Moses on Sinai and ultimately transmitted to the men of the *Kenesset ha-gedolah* and the *Soferim/Hakhamin/Perushim.*[23]

But if one were to attempt to pinpoint the most highly original and lasting achievement of the Pharisees, it would be their linking up the individual and not just prophets, for the first time, to a single, cosmic Father God who offered the individual personal immortality in the world to come and ultimately the resurrection of one's body as a reward for one's loyalty to the internalized two-fold Law. The internalization of a legal system, i.e., the impressing of the two-fold Law on the individual's conscience, created a direct relationship between the individual and the single cosmic law-giving Father God. Each individual for the first time confronted a single omnipotent, omnipresent God without any intermediation. One's individuality was thus given cosmic status and the potential for eternal individuation. The consequences of this achievement were momentous, for not only did it guarantee the survival and development of Judaism under the most stressful strains of its subsequent history, but it set the stage for the advent of Christianity. Not only was the belief in a resurrected Jesus made possible by the Pharisaic doctrine of the resurrection of the dead, but Paul's rebellion against the *internalized* two-fold Law of the one Father God drove him to the *internalization* of Christ. Individual immortality was now assured by the Father God's grace and not by obedience to His two-fold Law.

Here then are the Pharisees: a revolutionary scholar class who originated and championed the concept of the two-fold Law, who shaped a highly original form of Judaism out of Pentateuchal and Hellenistic elements, who resorted to whatever means were necessary to affirm their authority, and who stirred the overwhelming majority of the Jews to lay down their lives, if necessary, for the preservation of the two-fold Law and its promise of eternal individuation.[24]

How, short of a quantum leap, could such radical a break-through

---

[23] The only Greek rendition possible for the chain transmission in M. Ab. 1:1, the masora would be *paradosis*, a usage confirmed by both Paul and Josephus.

[24] For a fuller exposition of the role of internalization in Pharisaism, see E. Rivkin, "The Internal City," in *Journal for the Scientific Study of Religion*, V (1966), pp. 225-240, and in "Pharisaism and the Crisis of the Individual," in *Jewish Quarterly Review*.

as *halakhic* Judaism have become the dominant form of Judaism following on the Hasmonean Revolt, a form of Judaism still so vibrant in our own day that millions still voluntarily observe not the Written Law alone but the twofold Law? The *paradosis*, the *halakhah* of the Pharisees, has triumphed over time, tide, and circumstance and lives on.

APPENDIX
A Hidden Revolution, pp. 321-324

There is indeed a text—*Ant.* XVII:41-45—that uses the term *pharisaoi* in connection with a clique of religious fanatics who were very much involved with the palace intrigues going on behind Herod's back. Most scholars have simply taken for granted that these *pharisaoi* are the Pharisees even though they are incongruent with the picture of the Pharisees as drawn by Josephus in all other passages in which the word *pharisaoi* is used. It is for this reason that I have not included this passage in the body of the text.

Nonetheless since scholars have written using this passage as though the term *pharisaoi* were a sufficient guarantee that the Pharisees are meant, it is vital that this text be set down in full and critically analyzed.[25]

The text in question occurs in connection with the alleged anti-Herodian activities of Pheroras and his wife. The passage reads as follows:

> For there was also a clique *[morion]* of Jews priding itself on its adherence to ancestral custom and claiming to observe the laws which the Deity approves, and by these men, called Pharisees, the women [of the court] were ruled. These men were able to help the king greatly because of their foresight, and yet they were obviously intent upon combating and injuring him. At least when the whole Jewish people affirmed by oath that it would be loyal to Caesar and to the king's government, these men, over six thousand in number, refused to take this oath, and when the king punished them with a fine, Pheroras' wife paid the fine

---

[25] See especially Steve Mason, *Flavius Josephus on the Pharisees*, pp. 274-278. It seems that Mason overlooked the definition of the Pharisees elicited in *A Hidden Revolution* from all the other passages in Josephus, the New Testament, and the Tannaitic literature which picture them as the authoritative teachers of the twofold Law and not sectarians.

for them. In return for her friendliness they foretold—for they were believed to have foreknowledge of things through God's appearance to them—that by God's decree Herod's throne would be taken from him, both from himself and his descendants, and that the royal power would fall to her and Pheroras and to any children they might have.[26]

These things, which did not remain unknown to Salome, were reported to the king, as was the news that the Pharisees had corrupted some people at court. And the king put to death those of the Pharisees who were most to blame, and the eunuch Bagoas, and a certain Caras, who was outstanding among his contemporaries for his surpassing beauty. He killed also those of his own household who approved of what the Pharisees said. Now Bagoas had been carried away by their assurances that he would be called the father and the benefactor of him who would some day be set over the people with the title of king, for all the power would belong to him and he would give Bagoas the ability to marry and to beget children of his own. (*Ant.* XVII:41-45)

This passage bristles with difficulties. *Pharisaoi* are explicitly mentioned. They are linked to the exact observance of the Law and to religious concerns. They refuse to take the oath of loyalty to Herod. Hence they seem at first glance to have some points in common with the Pharisees described elsewhere in Josephus's writings. Yet on closer scrutiny, one discovers that there is no congruence whatsoever.

In the first place, these *pharisaoi* are not called a *haeresis*, a school of thought, but rather a *morion*—a faction, a sect—of Jews. The term *morion* definitely connotes a comparatively small number, and this notion is confirmed when the *pharisaoi* who refused to take the oath

---

[26] Once it is recognized that the term Pharisoi when juxtaposed to Sadducees as a school of thought or a philosophy is synonymous with *Soferim/Hakhamin*, it becomes evident that they could not have numbered six thousand. One has only to recall how few are the number of Tannaim recorded in the Mishnah and Tosefta and to reflect on the implications the following passage from *Ant.* XX:262-265:

"And now I take heart from the consummation of my proposed work to assert that no one else, either Jew or Gentile, would have been equal to the task, however willing to undertake it, of issuing so accurate a treatise as this for the Greek world. For my compatriots admit that in our Jewish learning I far excel them. I have also laboured strenuously to partake of the realm of Greek prose and poetry, and after having gained a knowledge of Greek grammar, although the habitual use of my native tongue has prevented my attaining precision in the pronunciation. For our people do not favour those persons who have mastered the speech of many nations, or who adorn their style with smoothness or diction, because they consider that not only is such skill common to ordinary freemen but that even slaves who so choose may acquire it. *But they give credit for wisdom to those alone who have an exact knowledge of the Law and who are capable of interpreting the meaning of the Holy Scripture. Consequently, though many have laboriously undertaken this training, scarcely two or three have succeeded, and have forthwith reaped the fruit of their labours.*" (Emphasis added)

are said to have numbered six thousand. If these *pharisaoi* are identical with the Pharisees, then why did Josephus use the term *morion* rather than *haeresis*?

Second, these *pharisaoi* are described as laying claim to being exact observers of the country's laws and not expounders or interpreters of the laws. This is in contrast with Josephus's reiterations that the Pharisees were the most accurate expounders of the laws.

Third, among the distinguishing characteristics of these *pharisaoi* are their influence with women and their foreknowledge of things to come. The Pharisees elsewhere in Josephus do not share these characteristics.

Fourth, the *pharisaoi* are pictured as meddlers in palace intrigue and as persistent opponents of Herod's rule. This contrasts sharply with Pollion and Samaias's positive relationship with Herod.

Fifth, the *pharisaoi* who refused to take the oath of allegiance to Caesar and Herod were punished with a fine, whereas Pollion, Samaias, and their disciples were not punished at all.

Sixth, these *pharisaoi* are not juxtaposed to the Sadducees or Essenes.

At the heart of the dilemma is thus a stark contradiction. If Josephus is rendering an accurate account of the relationship between Pollion and Samaias and Herod, then the Pharisees were honored and respected by Herod and they, in turn, did not oppose his rule. What, then, are we to do with the *pharisaoi*, if they are the Pharisees, in view of the fact that they were active in attempting to overthrow Herod? The contradiction is heightened when the oath of loyalty is taken into account. Here was a demand that took place at a specific time. Pollion, Samaias, and their disciples refused to take the oath. The *pharisaoi* refused to take the oath. Pollion and Samaias and their disciples are exempted and are not punished; the *pharisaoi* are fined. If the *pharisaoi* are the Pharisees, then how does Herod at one and the same time treat the *pharisaoi* punitively and the Pharisees benignly? It therefore appears the *pharisaoi* in this text cannot be the Pharisees whom Josephus has been portraying consistently throughout his writings.

How, then, are we to account for the fact that the Greek word *pharisaoi* is one and the same? The answer is to be found in the fact that the Greek word is a modified transliteration of the Hebrew *perushim*, with a Greek plural ending attached, *pharisai-oi*. If, then, it can be demonstrated that the Hebrew *perushim* can mean either

Pharisees, i.e., with a capital "P," or separatists of one sort or another, the *pharisaoi* in this passage need not be the Pharisees. The criteria for determining when the term *pharisaoi* means Pharisees and when it meant separatists, dissenter, fanatics, etc., would be dependent on the *context* and not in the spelling of the word itself. Since the *pharisaoi* of the Pheroras-Herod episode are so unlike the *pharisaoi* of the rest of Josephus, the one precludes the other. Herod's dual treatment of the *Pharisaoi*, "Pharisees," and the *pharisaoi*, "fanatics," is conclusive: The Pharisees Pollion and Samaias *and* their disciples were so respected by him that he exempted them from a loyalty oath, since their loyalty could be taken for granted; the *pharisaoi*, on the other hand, were engaged in Rasputin-like palace intrigue to unseat him and were fined when they refused to take the oath of loyalty.

It would seem that Josephus simply would not tamper with his source, which had transliterated the Hebrew *perushim*, meaning separatists, fanatics and not the Hebrew *Perushim* meaning Pharisees.

2. THE PHARISEES: A RESPONSE TO STEVE MASON

Lester L. Grabbe
University of Hull

The manuscript of my book, *Judaism from Cyrus to Hadrian*,[1] went to press in 1990. Although I added some references to my own forthcoming publications during the editorial process, it was not possible to take much account of further secondary literature. For this reason, I did not have the opportunity to digest Steve Mason's work[2] until quite some time later.[3] If I had read Mason's book before publication, I would have changed a number of points in my argument, though not my ultimate conclusions. However, the field of Second Temple studies is changing so rapidly that dozens of books and countless articles would already need to be taken into account in any update of my history. These days it seems that one cannot finish a manuscript without finding that something very important appears not long afterward.

Professor Mason's critique of my treatment of the Pharisees[4] is a slightly shortened version of his published review[5] and does not add anything to it. His review of my book overall was generous and positive, indeed quite complimentary. He had several criticisms, but the one on which he devoted most space concerned the Pharisees.[6] It

---

[1] *Judaism from Cyrus to Hadrian: Vol. I: Persian and Greek Periods; Vol. II: Roman Period* (Minneapolis: Fortress Press, 1992; British edition in one-volume, London: SCM, 1994).

[2] *Flavius Josephus on the Pharisees: A Composition-Critical Study* (SPB 39; Leiden: Brill, 1991).

[3] See my review in *JJS* 45 (1994), pp. 134-136.

[4] "Revisiting Josephus's Pharisees," in Jacob Neusner and Alan J. Avery-Peck, eds., *Judaism in Late Antiquity: Volume Three. Where We Stand: Issues and Debates in Ancient Judaism* (Leiden, 1999), vol. 2, pp. 23-56.

[5] "Method in the Study of Early Judaism: A Dialogue with Lester Grabbe," *JAOS* 115 (1995), pp. 463-472, especially 468-471. Cited below as Mason, 1995.

[6] The main ones were the following:

1. Relationship of Qumran and the Essenes (1995, p. 466). Contrary to the impression left by Mason's remarks, I do not assume the "Qumran-Essene hypothesis." I treat Qumran and the Scrolls in ch. 5 and do not deal with the Essenes until ch. 8. When discussing the Essenes I naturally address the question of their relationship to Qumran. At the time, I concluded that the evidence indicated some sort of connection, though I was very cautious about saying precisely what it might be. Things

is unfortunate that Mason has not seen my most recent discussion of the Pharisees.[7] This supersedes the section in my 1992 book and would have met a number of his criticisms. However, at this point I shall briefly respond to what seem to be Mason's main points.

As might be expected from one who has made Josephus the focus of his work, Mason's main objections relate to my use of Josephus. This is a substantial criticism since to my mind Josephus is our most important source for the Pharisees. However, I think Mason has not fairly conveyed the amount of time and energy I devote to analyzing Josephus in the book.[8] My study was based on a systematic reading of

---

have moved on since then, with publication of many more documents and further factors in the debate. For more recent comments, which continue to stress caution about the Essene-Qumran connection, see my article, "The Current State of the Dead Sea Scrolls: Are There More Answers than Questions?" in S.E. Porter and C.A. Evans, eds., *The Scrolls and the Scriptures: Qumran Fifty Years After* (Roehampton Institute London Papers 3 = Journal for the Study of the Pseudepigrapha Supplement 26; Sheffield Academic Press, 1997), pp. 54-67, and my review of Norman Golb, *Who Wrote the Dead Sea Scrolls?*, in *Dead Sea Discoveries* 4 (1997), pp. 124-28.

2. The competence of the Sanhedrin to try capital cases (1995, p. 467). I find Mason's comments peculiar here and fail to see anything but nitpicking. I had to discuss a great many complex issues in a compressed amount of space, and Mason's remarks at this point seem to have nothing to do with the real issue, which is whether any Jewish (or other native) institution could condemn and then execute without Roman permission. I do not even know whether he actually disagrees with my conclusions. The whole issue of the Sanhedrin needs a full study, but I could hardly give it in the space available at this point.

3. The evaluation of the last Roman governors before the 66-70 revolt (1995, p. 467). My discussion here needs rethinking not only in the light of Mason's remarks but also the more detailed critique of James S. McClaren, *Turbulent Times? Josephus and Scholarship on Judaea in the First Century CE* (JSPSup 29; Sheffield Academic Press, 1998).

4. The synagogue in pre-70 Palestine (1995, p. 468). Here he criticizes my necessarily brief remarks without apparently having read my cited study, "Synagogues in Pre-70 Palestine: A Re-assessment" in *JTS* 39 (1988), pp. 401-410, which actually addressed most of his concerns. All I can add at this point is that studies appearing since my article have tended to confirm my position, e.g., D. Urman and P.V.M. Flesher, eds., *Ancient Synagogues: Historical Analysis and Archaeological Discovery* (2 vols.; Leiden, 1995); Howard Clark Kee, "The Transformation of the Synagogue after 70 C.E.: Its Import for Early Christianity" in *NTS* 36 (1990), pp. 1-24; Heather A. McKay, *Sabbath and Synagogue: The Question of Sabbath Worship in Ancient Judaism* (Leiden, 1994).

[7] "Sadducees and Pharisees," in Jacob Neusner and Alan J. Avery-Peck, eds., *Judaism in Late Antiquity: Volume 3. Where We Stand: Issues and Debates in Ancient Judaism* (Leiden, 1999), pp. 35-62.

[8] See especially 1995, pp. 481-482. Here and there he acknowledges the amount of space that I devote to Josephus, but someone reading only the section on the Pharisees would be left with a rather different impression.

Josephus as a major source for much Second Temple Jewish history. In addition to a general section in the introductory chapter, I devote a section in each chapter to Josephus. Above all, I constantly interact with Josephus where he is an important witness, so that a considerable portion of my overall text is a dialogue with Josephus. Mason may disagree with my treatment of Josephus, but anyone reading my book would know that I always take account of what Josephus says even if I end up querying his account.

Mason first argues that I atomize Josephus's accounts of the Pharisees and do not read them in context. In some cases, the Pharisees are an integral part of the narrative, in which case I usually dealt with them not only in my chapter on sects but also at the appropriate place in the historical survey (e.g., the Pharisees and Alexandra Salome were discussed in the chapter on the Hasmoneans).[9] In the chapter on the various sects, I naturally treat only the relevant passages, but I do list and consider every passage that mentions the Pharisees. Because of the limitations of space, I do not quote the passages at length nor spend a lot of time on each passage (unlike my more recent article), but every reference to the Pharisees was taken into account. On the other hand, it must be noted that some main passages are insertions into the narrative flow and have little or no direct connection with the context, including the oft-cited passages in *War* 2.8.14 §§162-66 and *Ant.* 13.5.9 §§171-72. I therefore reject completely Mason's statement that I have not considered the contexts of the Pharisee passages.

On the contrary, Mason here violates his own principle of respecting the integrity of the texts, because he assimilates the statements of the various writings in his argument instead of respecting the individuality of the separate works. He has not recognized that there are important differences between the *War* and the *Antiquities*, however one explains those differences.[10] Notice some of these:

---

[9] Mason strangely states that Grabbe "deals with the Pharisees only in his lengthy eighth chapter." On the contrary, they are mentioned a good deal in the narrative sections of my history; a glance at my index shows that the Pharisees are mentioned on twenty-seven separate pages outside chapter 8.

[10] Mason criticizes Saldarini and Sanders for not noting the differences between the *War* and the *Antiquities*, but it seems to me that he makes the same error.

War	*Antiquities*
Nothing about the Pharisees under John Hyrcanus.	13.10.5-7 §§288-299: Pharisees oppose Hyrcanus; they are so influential that they are believed even when they speak against a king or high priest. Hyrcanus I was their disciple but fell out with them.
Nothing about the Pharisees under Alexander Janneus.	13.15.5 §§401-4: on his death bed Alexander Janneus advises his wife to make up with the Pharisees.
1.5.2-3 §§110-114: Pharisees arise under Alexandra Salome and take advantage of her.	13.16.1-6 §§405-32: power of the Pharisees over Alexandra Salome.
1.29.2 §§571: Herod accuses Pheroras's wife of instigating the Pharisees against him.	17.2.4-3.1 §§41-47: Pharisees allegedly corrupt some people in Herod's court, and he punishes them.
No claim that the Pharisees in any way controlled worship or religion or other aspects of society in the country.	18.1.3 §§4-23: because of their influence with the common people, all prayers and divine worship are carried out according to their views. Although the Sadducees include men of the highest standing, they accomplish nothing but must submit to the regulations of the Pharisees.

This table clearly contradicts Mason's statement that the only difference between the *War* and the *Antiquities* is the greater amount of space in the latter, which means that the Pharisees inevitably get greater prominence. On the contrary, Josephus inserts Pharisees into episodes in the later work where they were absent in the earlier, and he makes claims in the latter that are out of character with the former. As anyone who reads my book will know, although I use all of Josephus's works, I always compare them and note any differences that seem significant to me. This is a very basic principle of historical work.

In arguing that in the *War* Josephus gives a similar picture of the Pharisees to that of the *Antiquities*, Mason states:

> His [Josephus's] claims about Pharisaic influence occur not only in the places Grabbe has identified but consistently from the first appearance of the Pharisees in the *War*: they managed to ruin Alexandra's otherwise promising reign through their influence (*War* 1.110-114); Herod the Great was deeply concerned about their intrigues (*War* 1.571); and in the first century they continued to "hold the position of the leading school" (*War* 2.162), their representatives joining with the chief priests and other eminent citizens to try to avert war (*War* 2.411).

Not at all. The only period in which Josephus presents the Pharisees as having significant influence is under Alexandra. Their "first appearance" in the *War* is in Alexandra's reign (the *Antiquities* makes them appear much earlier); they then disappear for about half a century until some of them *attempt* to gain influence in Herod's household *but fail*; they then disappear for another half century[11] until 66 C.E. when some prominent Pharisees (not the Pharisees as a group) happen to be one of a number of groups who discuss what to do about the situation.[12] It is true that in the *War* 2.8.14 §162 the Pharisees are designated "the leading sect," according to Mason's translation.[13] But what are the implications, if we take his preferred meaning? Josephus himself does not really tell us, but he does not indicate that it means very much in practical terms. Some of the sects are important to Josephus in a few passages, but they are only now and then given significance even when mentioned.[14] Being the "leading

---

[11] Mason tries to connect the treatment of the three sects in *War* 2.8.2-14 §§117-66 specifically with the first century, but this section is clearly an insertion into the context because the "Fourth Philosophy" is mentioned. It is an opportunity to discuss all three groups, as Josephus could have done at a number of points in his narrative, with the same information. There is nothing to associate his description with a particular chronological period.

[12] Jonathan J. Price, *Jerusalem Under Siege: The Collapse of the Jewish State 66-70 CE* (Leiden, 1992) has demonstrated that Josephus's own text shows that the leadership during the war was that which we would have expected because they formed the leadership before the war: the leading priests, the aristocrats, and the Herodian family. There was the odd Pharisee, just as there was an Essene who became a general, but there is no indication in *any* of Josephus's narratives that the Pharisees led the revolt. Although some sects were important, these were not the three main "philosophies" but such groups as the Sicarii and the Zealots.

[13] Mason is well aware that the exact meaning of the phrase has long been disputed. He himself has discussed the matter at length and concluded it means the "chief" or "most important" sect rather than "oldest" or "first to develop" (*Josephus on the Pharisees*, pp. 125-132). This is a legitimate conclusion, though I doubt that he has settled the debate once and for all.

[14] The assumption often seems to be that the sects somehow dominated the religious scene of the time. I dispute this. The information we have on numbers gives no reason to think so. Long ago I argued that they were only a small portion of society ("Orthodoxy in First Century Judaism: What Are the Issues?" in *JSJ* 8 [1977], pp. 149-153); more recently a similar argument has been used by Albert I. Baumgarten (*The Flourishing of Jewish Sects in the Maccabean Era: An Interpretation* [JSJSup 55; Leiden, 1997], pp. 7-9, 42-48). One can chose to disbelieve the numbers, but they are, as Mason so often reminds us, a part of the narrative. Baumgarten's recent study confirms their relatively marginal status, even if their impact was greater than their small size might suggest. That the Pharisees figure prominently in the Gospels is hardly surprising, since one small sect (the Jesus movement) is likely to make an issue of its interactions with other sects. That does not mean that either was important in society at the time.

sect" does not seem to have counted for very much in most of his narrative.

In discussing these gaps in the narrative, Mason dismisses any significance in them, pointing to Josephus's purpose or aim in his narrative as a given and then criticizing others for not paying attention to it. He seems not to recognize that this is a begging of the question. What Josephus is trying to say in a narrative is not a "fact" but an interpretation. It is an inference from Josephus's own statements, the shape of his narratives, significant themes, and many narrative details, but ultimately it is a scholarly construct. When he states that Josephus "insisted that the Pharisees retained popular influence throughout," even when they disappear from the narrative, he is not dealing in fact but interpretation. My interpretation—as will be clear—is different from his. I see the absence of the Pharisees as potentially crucial, not because I ignore the thrust of Josephus's narrative but because I see it differently from Mason.

To surmise a narrative aim from the text and then to turn around and say that a particular interpretation is incorrect because it does not fit that purpose is circular reasoning. Circular reasoning of various sorts is inevitable in historical study, but arguing from overall purpose is no more justified from a methodological point of view than to compare all accounts of a particular episode and then to make a judgment on what Josephus is doing. Both approaches involve interpretation; one is not necessarily "purer" than the other, but each must be judged on how well it explains the data.

Part of Mason's critique here is of the "Smith-Neusner" hypothesis that whereas Josephus was not particularly favorable toward the Pharisees in the *War*, he actively promotes them in the *Antiquities* and *Life*, perhaps because he wants to throw his lot in with a group he sees as gaining power. I accept that there are some problems with the thesis and that a number of the passages are more complicated than the hypothesis allows. Whether it will stand up in revised form, I shall not predict at this point.[15] However, the thesis had the merit of pointing out some significant differences in the portrayal of the Pharisees between the earlier and later works. The differences between Josephus's representation of a particular episode in one work

---

[15] I understand that Neusner may have now abandoned it.

as compared with another can be very great, as a comparison between the *War* and the *Life* shows.[16]

Furthermore, the statements in the *Antiquities* about the power of the Pharisees do not match the historian's own statements elsewhere. For example, he says that the Sadducees contain men of the highest standing, yet they accomplish nothing but must follow the Pharisees (*Ant.* 18.1.4 §17). If they accomplish nothing, how can they be "men of high standing"? How can they "gain office" if they can do nothing without Pharisaic say-so? Strangely, Josephus mentions Sadducees who accomplish a good deal without Pharisaic approval (John Hyrcanus, the high priest Ananus). He also states that the religious rites follow the Pharisaic regulations, yet he continually emphasizes the leadership of the priests in the Temple and worship. He states that if they speak against a king, ruler, or high priest, they are listened to, but when did they get their way with any king or high priest in his narrative except under Alexandra? According to *Ant.* 13.10.5-7 §§288-99, the people revolted against John Hyrcanus, led by the Pharisees.[17] But John put down the revolt and lived the rest of his reign in peace. So much for the power of the Pharisees, even in Josephus's own terms.

But then I find myself puzzled, because Mason says that the Pharisees did not exercise formal control but only had "influence." I am not sure I know what he means us to understand by this. In my studies I have not made any distinction between formal control and control through other channels. If the Pharisees had power, they had power, regardless of whether it was formalized or not. Some of Josephus's statements imply that they controlled the Temple cult and society at large. Others of his statements only suggest that they have a reputation for interpreting the law. There is a big difference. You can have a reputation but exert no real influence in society.[18]

---

[16] The most detailed comparison of the relevant passages is found in S.J.D. Cohen, *Josephus in Galilee and Rome: His Vita and Development as a Historian* (Leiden, 1979).

[17] The *War* says nothing about the Pharisees but ascribes the revolt to the "successes" (*eupragia*) of Hyrcanus and his sons, which is also how the *Antiquities* actually begins the passage—an example of how the *War* and *Antiquities* give quite different pictures.

[18] Baumgarten (*Flourishing of Jewish Sects*, pp. 56, 133) points out that the claim to be accurate interpreters of the law was a common sectarian claim. Similarly, we do not generally have the reactions of ordinary people to them (Baumgarten, pp. 60-62). The common people may have given them some respect, but they would also have resented their exclusivist attitudes (Baumgarten, p. 62).

This is important when it comes to the New Testament, which Mason accuses me of having treated simplistically. Considering our differences of opinion and the inevitable compression in a review, Mason has generally treated my position with reasonable fairness, but here I must complain of completely misleading—even distorting— remarks. My discussion of the NT is short, but it is detailed and much more nuanced and complex than he recognizes; indeed, it is his own statements that look simplistic. I certainly do not treat the NT as an undifferentiated whole as he alleges. First of all, I address the relation- ships between the synoptic gospels (which he does not even acknowl- edge) and the fact that parallel passages often do not even have the same names.[19] Secondly, I point out the widely recognized fact that the opponents of Jesus are there not primarily as part of a historical record but as straw-men to be slaughtered by the hero of the narrative. Thirdly, at various points I deal with Luke's problematic accounts (not just on the Pharisees), which in some cases show rather interesting information but at other times show gross ignorance.[20]

Mason's assertion that my "reconstruction of the Pharisees relies most heavily on Neusner's analysis of early Rabbinic traditions about them" is incorrect. The Rabbinic tradition is to me the most prob- lematic to deal with. I was cautious about it in my book, noting that the traditions used by Neusner do not explicitly mention the Phari- sees, though I still believe that the bulk of the figures treated by Jacob Neusner[21] were likely to have been Pharisees.[22] Nevertheless, today I would be more cautious about emphasizing too much the pre-70 Rabbinic figures because of this problem, which is why I am even more circumspect in my most recent discussion.[23] Rabbinic literature has to be dealt with on this issue, and I have found Neusner's analysis very helpful, but ultimately any reconstruction has to take account of all sources.

---

[19] Mason misses the fact that I discuss the relationships between the gospels also under other groups, such as on pp. 488-491.

[20] See pp. 384-385, 428, 485, 489-490. I have continued to study the question and have presented a conference paper, "What Did the Author of Acts Know about Pre- 70 Judaism?" It has not yet been published, and Mason would not know of it, of course, but my more recent study confirms that one must deal carefully with Luke's narrative. Mason's brief remarks on Luke appear rather uncritical.

[21] Primarily his *Rabbinic Traditions about the Pharisees Before 70* (3 vols.; Leiden, 1971).

[22] Cf., also S.J.D. Cohen, "The Significance of Yavneh: Pharisees, Rabbis, and the End of Jewish Sectarianism" in *HUCA* 55 (1984), pp. 27-53.

[23] See n. 6 above.

With regard to my statement that the Pharisees did not make Torah study a central religious act, my discussion at this point was dependent on the studies of Neusner. On the other hand, I think Mason has missed Neusner's argument on this issue; he has certainly missed mine. The point is not that the Pharisees were not interested in the law nor that Josephus is wrong about their reputation as interpreters of the law. Many of the traditions discussed in Neusner's work relate to halakhah, after all. The point is, rather, that the traditions about pre-70 figures do not suggest Torah-study as a religious act. To study the law in order to gain knowledge so that one tithes correctly or does not violate purity rules is one thing, and this is what we find in the pre-70 traditions. To study the Torah because study in and of itself is efficacious and a means of worshipping God is a different conceptualization of Torah study, one we certainly find in later layers (according to Neusner's analysis) but not in the pre-70 ones. The emphasis of Josephus on the Pharisees' devotion to interpretation of the law and the general importance of the law at that time is a separate matter and not one that I questioned.

Much of Josephus's comments about the Pharisees would fit very well a modern analogy, that of the Freemasons.[24] Perhaps the term "sect" might not fit so well, but we could refer to the Masons as a "leading group" or organization. There are influential people who admit to being Masons or who are known historically to have been Masons (e.g., Mozart). One can also find all sorts of claims that the Masons control society; others avoid such exaggerated claims but still believe that the Masons have too much influence. That individual Masons may be in high positions or that they are "influential" does not put the Masons as such in control of the society's institutions. Their actual influence will be differently evaluated by different writers. A historian coming across such statements must use every means of evaluating them.

Many of Josephus's statements about the power and influence of the Pharisees are capable of more than one evaluation. Therefore, we have to ask what other evidence there is to back up these statements. In his narratives in context—to which Mason asks us to pay special attention—he does not show the Pharisees actually controlling the

---

[24] Lest someone think I am being facetious, I had thought of the analogy and was already working it out before it occurred to me that someone might think it is a deliberate play on Steve Mason's name.

society or the religion, except for during the reign of Alexandra Salome.[25] He shows some unsuccessful attempts at gaining power, including under Herod. He occasionally shows individual Pharisees in positions of responsibility, just as he shows individual Essenes. The Essenes were not in control of society any more than the Pharisees, according to Josephus's narrative. Josephus does not show that the Pharisees as a group took over leadership of the war effort in 66-70, despite Mason's claims, though one of the leaders at one time happened to be a Pharisee.[26]

In his book, Mason concentrates on literary analysis, which is one of its strengths. I thoroughly agree that literary analysis is a step in the process of evaluating Josephus. Mason's aptitude is in this area, and his more recent attempts to determine Josephus's aims in his various writings[27] are welcome, even if some are more convincing than others.[28] However, literary analysis alone does not determine whether Josephus is right or not; one must go on to ask *historical* questions. Mason himself makes this point,[29] yet this is also where he

---

[25] Mason seems to feel that it is important to me "that the Pharisees exercised formal control" (1995, p. 469), but he does not say why he thinks this. On the contrary, I do not care how the control is expressed; I only want to know whether it is real.

[26] On leadership during the revolt, see n. 11 above.

[27] See the items cited in Mason's article.

[28] For example, I fail to understand his denial that the *Antiquities* is apologetic. He argues that it was meant to explain Judaism to a sympathetic gentile audience, and this may be correct, but this need not exclude an apologetic intent as well. Then why does he say, "In the *Antiquities*, I argued at that time, Josephus wished to defend his people against common accusations that their national origins were mean and their customs base"? If that is not an apologetic intent, what is? Or are we to understand that Mason is now rejecting that interpretation? If he is, he has not clearly said so. Further, Mason's denial that Justus of Tiberias is at least in part the cause of writing the *Life* is also peculiar. Why then are Justus and his brother, who were not even mentioned in the *War*, said to be the main cause of the war with Rome in the *Life* (9 §41). Josephus is doing more than just writing "to support his claims about the Judean constitution by reference to his own character."

[29] He points out the gap between literature and history, and he is quite correct. This is not a new concept to me since I have been arguing it for years. See, e.g., my *Priests, Prophets, Diviners, Sages: A Socio-historical Study of Religious Specialists in Ancient Israel* (Valley Forge, 1995), pp. 2-12, and the various contributions in Lester L. Grabbe, ed., *Can a "History of Israel" Be Written?* (JSOTSup 245 = European Seminar in Historical Methodology 1; Sheffield Academic Press, 1997), including my own (pp. 19-36). But here I think he misconstrues the historical task. Of course, what is in the literature is merely raw data (though he strangely rejects the term "data" for it); history is what we reconstruct from it, but that does not make the literature any less important a source than artifacts or inscriptions.

falls down in his analysis. In fact, in all of Mason's writings known to me, including his criticisms of my book, he nowhere discusses how we go about evaluating Josephus from a historical point of view. He admits that in his book he "did not yet attempt to answer the many historical questions that surround the group" and indicates that his more recent work has not been of a historical nature. He even makes the statement,

> Lest any doubt remains: I am not here advocating any particular historical reconstruction, least of all the old view that the Pharisees "ran society" through the Sanhedrin, school, and synagogue.

I suspect I am not the only one rather astonished by this statement, because in his book, in his review of my book, and in his most recent article, he sounds remarkably like someone advocating a particular historical reconstruction. Although he never suggests that we should accept Josephus uncritically, he seems to do precisely that much too often. If there are specific historical principles he applies, he does not make them explicit. Mason is quite correct that we should not ask the historical question too quickly, but by not asking it all, the result is to answer it by default—by naively taking Josephus's statements at face value.

I think Josephus has a variety of purposes, some explicit and probably a lot subconscious. In individual episodes he seems to have aims that override any overall intent of his narrative. I think that, like all of us, he is inconsistent and contradicts himself some of the time. He aims to give us a picture of his own making. I do not think Josephus lies all the time, only when it is convenient, useful, advantageous, or his source has given him the wrong information. It would be easier if he were more consistent. There are times when I accept his story whereas, if the truth be known, he has deceived us dreadfully. On the other hand, I may suspect his story completely unfairly. My evaluation today may be different from that yesterday or tomorrow. Unfortunately, that is the nature of the historical task.

Mason is quite right to emphasize the importance of rhetoric in Josephan studies, but that should not make us overestimate Josephus's ability as a composer of narrative. By all means let us analyze his narrative, but let's read it for what it says, not some artificial, completely consistent, mechanically constructed work above normal human fallibility. I have many times witnessed well-educated and knowledgeable people present arguments that are convincing to no one but themselves. On the other hand, I have never known anyone to concede more than necessary to one's opponents. That one's enemies are so strong that they force you to do what you do not want to do may be true, and you may admit it in private, but you are not likely to say that publicly. Yet we supposedly have Josephus saying (*Life* 2 §12), "I don't like the Pharisees. In fact, I hate their guts. But of course when I decided to go into public life, I followed the Pharisees because they controlled it. I didn't want to but I had to." It sounds almost like a Monty Python sketch.

What Mason presents us with is an author who has a clear purpose that he always fulfills, who never contradicts himself, who never gets sidetracked, who never gets lost in other purposes, and who never has motives for some of the individual episodes completely at odds with his main overall purpose.[30] Why do I evaluate Josephus differently than Mason does? Perhaps my experience of life is different from his; perhaps Hull University in England is quite different from York University in Canada, though my wide experience of academic life and politics in both Europe and North America only confirms that my present university is not unusual. In my world I find highly intelligent people using unpersuasive arguments, being grossly inconsistent, taking self-serving positions that are then justified on high moral grounds, and contradicting themselves dreadfully. Mason is quite happy to say that some of the rest of us do not accomplish our stated aims, so why not Josephus!

Once again, I appreciate Mason's contributions on the literary side of Josephus, and I hope he will continue his work here. Literary analysis is one of the steps toward asking historical questions, and I am ready to learn from him as from the many other soldiers, past and present, in the fray of Josephan combat. But my ultimate concerns are historical, and history has to be read and reconstructed in all its complexity from the multi-voiced cacophony of the survivals from the past. I cannot just sit on the fence and discuss Josephus's aims and narrative construction. I have to take the sources and try to make sense of them—all of them, not just Josephus. My recent article has once again emphasized the paucity of information available on the Sadducees and Pharisees. Nevertheless, when I look at the *langue*

---

[30] I find very credulous, even bordering on the naive, Mason's defense of Josephus's seriously divergent accounts of the same events in separate writings as merely rhetorical.

dureé of Second Temple Jewish history, I see the place of the Pharisees rather differently from some passages in Josephus, but this is partly because Josephus's own data elsewhere do not support some of his individual claims. For a full treatment of my latest thinking on the Pharisees, readers should see my most recent study which, unfortunately, was not available to Mason.[31]

---

[31] See n. 6 above.

3. PHILO AND PHILOSOPHY

Robert M. Berchman
Dowling College

Traduttore, traditore

- Nietzsche -

Studies in Philo have a checkered history. Philo himself was a Protean figure and the study of his writings has attracted more than its fair share of scholars. On the whole, Philo has been well served by modern scholarship, but perhaps never more so than in the last twenty years, where it has been fashionable to deny one of the more obvious and distinctive features of his thought. Recently a number of scholars have reminded us about the marginal (and problematic) role of philosophy in Philo's writings. I say "reminded us" because the denial of this reading of Philo appears driven by a late-modern (postmodern) concern for the problematic role of narratives for historical and philosophical inquiry.

This claim may strike many as ironical or metaphorical given the stolidly "historicist" agenda of contemporary Philo studies. Nonetheless, the consequences of the judgment of an absence of philosophical narrative in Philo has led contemporary scholars to abandon the notion that Philo was a philosopher *tout court*. His writings are only philosophically valuable as background material for reconstructing the origins and sources of Middle Platonism, Pythagoreanism, and the Middle Stoa.[1] His philosophical ideas are only valuable as background material to his "exegetical intention," which is not philosophical in content. In *nuce*, Philo is judged to stand outside the "totalizing" agenda of philosophical narrative and discourse.[2]

---

[1] This view was initially proposed by E.R. Dodds, "The *Parmenides* of Plato and the Origins of the Neoplatonic One" in *CQ* 22 [1928], p. 132, n. 1; W. Theiler, *Die Vorbereitung des Neuplatonismus* (Berlin, 1930), p. 30; and A.J. Festugiere, *La Revelation d'Hermes Trismegiste* (Paris, 1945-1954), vol. 2, p. 534. Its most recent proponent is J. Dillon, *The Middleplatonists* (Ithaca, 1977), pp. 135-183, esp. pp. 182-183.

[2] This view was initially proposed by D.T. Runia and his school. See *Exegesis and Philosophy* (Aldershot, 1990).

Narrative has always been important for scholars. Students of
Philo generally situate their work by telling a story of what happened
before they came along—a story that has its own heroes and villains.
This is the way in which scholars are always creating and recreating
their own traditions and canons. The stories they tell are systematically interwoven with what they think are their distinctive contributions. Consider Wolfson's studies about the insights of his predecessors in grasping the multidimensional character of Philo's religious
philosophy.[3] Or—to leap to the contemporary scene—think of the
story that Runia tells us about the confusions and blunders of many
of his predecessors. Each had a few bright moments that anticipate
his own interpretation of Philo.[4]

In brief, scholars tells stories of anticipations, setbacks, and trials
that culminate in the progressive realization of truth and reason,
which is identified with what these scholars now see clearly—a
"truth" that their predecessors saw only through a glass darkly. It is
not my intention to develop a typology of narrative patterns in Philo
studies although it would be extremely illuminating. Rather a context
needs to be set for what is attempted in this essay. I want to outline
a narrative—or, more accurately and modestly, a narrative sketch.

Although schematic, this sketch is complex for several reasons:
First, it is a narrative about narratives, specifically about recent developments in Philo studies, which itself relates judgments about Philo's
thought, or what thinkers such as Weber and Habermas call "rationalization" processes.[5] Second, it is a narrative that isolates a specific
story line. Third, it is not one of those narratives in which all the
loose threads are neatly tied together at the end in a grand *Aufhebung*.
The reason is that this is essentially an unfinished story.

My aim is to confront some deeply troubling contemporary questions in Philo studies. Why today are there so many voices against
Philo and "philosophia"? Why is it when philosophy is mentioned
with Philo the association is summarily dismissed? These questions
are especially poignant and perplexing when we realize that not so

---

[3] H.A. Wolfson, *Philo, Foundations of Religious Philosophy in Judaism, Christianity, and Islam* (Cambridge, 1947, 1968[4]).

[4] Runia, op. cit., vol. II, pp. 185-198.

[5] The term "rationalization" is misleading, because in the Anglo-American context it suggests a false, misleading, and distortive justification. The expression influenced by this German sociological tradition does not have such associations. It refers
to a process by which a type of rationality increases over time.

long ago such linkage elicited a renaissance in Philo studies to which we all are heirs and whose closure may well signal its closure. It is important not only to understand what is happening but also what ought to be a critical response to this unfortunate situation.

Philo and Philosophy

Wolfson, Malingrey, Nikiprowetsky, Winston, Reale, Runia, Radice, and Tobin have brought to the philosophical study of Philo the clarity and learning for which they are justly known. These thinkers possess two virtues. They write clearly and comprehensively, if not always succinctly. Moreover, Malingrey, Nikiprowetsky, Reale, and Winston have the additional sense to have taught us that the current fad for denying the possibility of Philo's doing philosophy is just that—a fad and no more, and one that should already have had its day.

Ever since H.A. Wolfson, scholars have recognized the need to speak of *philosophia* in Philo with some caution. A.M. Malingrey argues there are various meanings of the term philosophy in Philo.[6] The first is the understanding of philosophy as the preparatory science for *sophia*; the second is the contemplation of the cosmos; and the third is regarded as God's theoretical and moral revelation to Israel.

V. Nikiprowetsky extends this argument further by arguing that the core of Philo's thought contains an "exegetical intention" that reveals itself in the *Allegorical Commentary*. He proposes that the philosophical foundation of Philo's exegesis lies in divine wisdom as revelation and natural law. Philo's purpose is to interpret the hidden meaning of God and scripture. The instrument of this interpretation is exegesis that he uses to illustrate the philosophical coherence of the *LXX*.[7] Moreover, Nikiprowetsky argues, Philo's modes of exegesis require study if the intention of his writings are to be disclosed. For example, in the *De gigantibus* and *Quod Deus immutablis sit*, Philo comments on Gen. 6:1-4 and 4b12 via a *questio* followed by a *solutio*. The

[6] A.M. Malingrey, *'Philosophia': etude d'un groupe de mots dans la litterature grecque des Presocratiques au IVe siecle apres J.-C.* (Paris, 1961), pp. 77-91.

[7] V. Nikiprowetsky, *Le commentaire de l'Ecriture chez Philon d'Alexandre: son caractere et sa portee; observations philologiques*, ALGHJ 11 (Leiden, 1977).

development of exegesis lies in the progression from one question and answer to the next based on the biblical text under discussion.[8] Nikiprowetsky's studies are significant because they highlighted the need to define the 'exegetical intention" of Philo's writings. Moreover, they reveal that Philo's writings are structured. This allows for further studies in the aesthetic dimensions of Philonic exegesis.

Other contributors to the study of Philo and philosophy merit attention as well. G. Reale argues that Philo represents a turning point in the philosophy of the imperial age. His writings point to a fundamental convergence in which Philo, as Middleplatonist, releases classical philosophy from the limits of Stoic materialism. As a Jew, he also introduced a monotheistic and creationist concept of God unknown to the Greeks. As a pious man, he raised for the first time the problem of the relationship of faith and reason and argued for a moral intellectualism based on a divine wisdom grounded in scripture.[9]

D. Winston also offers the portrait of a Philo who draws his deepest inspiration from philosophy, especially Platonic philosophy. This is most clear in his doctrines of the Logos, soul and cosmos, and creation. In his cosmology, Philo evinces a mystical monotheism that anticipates Plotinus in that inner experience grasps the whole of reality in a variety of forms.[10] Here Winston proposes a series of Philonic starting points for further studies in the history of philosophy, particularly Plotinian Platonism.

In a more specific sense, little concern has been directed in Philo studies to what today would be said to belong to aesthetics. The reasons for this are puzzling given the central role of exegesis, or "exegetical play" in Philo's writings. J. Cazeaux,[11] J. Leopold,[12] and

---

[8] See V. Nikiprowetsky, "L'Exegese de Philon d'Alexandrie dans le De Gigantibus et le Quod deus " in D. Winston and J. Dillon, eds., *Two Treatises of Philo of Alexandria* (Chico, 1983), pp. 5-76.

[9] G. Reale, "Filone di Alessandria et la 'filosofia mosaica'" in *Storia della filosofia antica*, vol. 4, *Le scuole dell'eta imperiale* (Milan, 1978, 1987[5]).

[10] D. Winston, *Logos and Mystical Theology in Philo of Alexandria* (Cincinnati, 1985).

[11] J. Cazeaux, *La trame et la chaine: structures litteraires et exegese dans cinq traites de Philon d'Alexandrie*, ALGHU 15 (Leiden, 1983); *L'epee du Logos et le soleil de midi*, Collection de la maison de l'Orient Mediterraneen 13, Serie Litteraire et Philosophique 2 (Lyon, 1983). Cazeaux argues that the nature and methods of Philo's exegesis are revealed in the literary structure of his allegorical writings. Influenced by structuralist views on discourse he argues that Philo's treatises are tightly woven masterpieces, a kind of tapestry, an interplay between "substitution" [*suppleance*] and "redundancy" [*redondance*]. Through such symmetry and movement, Philo organizes the texts and exegetical figures which he places into chapters. Such units or basic structures appear

T. Conley[13] are notable exceptions.

Although controversial, Cazeaux's "structuralist" reading of the nature and methods of Philo's exegesis is an important contribution to Philo studies. It strongly suggests that through the art of exegesis Philo embraces the proposition that language (*logos*) embraces the whole of reality.[14] If Cazeaux is correct, Philo can be viewed as an "aestheticist"—that is, one who sees "art," "language," "discourse," or "text" as constituting the primary realm of human experience.[15] This is significant because it allows for a complementary approach to the art of Philonic exegesis proposed by Nikiprowetsky. We not only have to determine the "exegetical intention" of Philo's writings but also interpret Philonic exegesis within the context of what today we call philosophical aesthetics.

This "aestheticist turn" extends our conversation into Leopold's studies on the relation of rhetoric and allegory in Philo's writings. He has shown that Philo stands close to the Platonic/Pythagorean tradition found in Plutarch.[16] As a complement to this, Conley has demonstrated that Philo uses rhetorical *topoi* extensively to argue philosophical ideas.[17] These studies are important for they open up the possibility of comparative studies in Philonic and Middle Platonic uses of rhetorical, allegorical, and stylistic devices in doing philosophy through the art of exegesis.

If Malingrey, Nikiprowetsky, Reale, and Winston are right, there is an enormity of the net cast by Philo's use of the term "philosophia." If Cazeaux, Leopold, and Conley are correct, then there is an *aestheticism* inherent in Philo's practice of "philosophia."

---

in the form of "cradles" or "curves" throughout the five allegorical treatises. As such four basic rules explain Philonic exegesis: 1] the pre-eminence of the biblical text; 2] the biblical text has a life in that it partly repeats itself as exegesis unfolds; 3] each allegorical development can be read psychologically and ethically; and 4] these moral journeys have a symmetrical or curved line.

[12] J. Leopold, "Philo's Style and Diction" in Winston and Dillon, op. cit., pp. 129-170.

[13] See T. Conley in Winston and Dillon, op. cit., pp. 171-180.

[14] See J. Cazeaux, *La trame et la chaine* (Leiden: 1983), cf., e.g., *Sacr.* 83, where he illustrates his thesis. Also see J. Cazeuux, *Philon d'Alexandrie: de la grammaire a la mystique*, Supplement au Cahier Evangelie 44 (Paris: 1983), pp. 77ff.

[15] This appears so regardless whether one accepts Cazeaux's "structuralist" reading of Philonic exegesis or not. On this work of Cazeaux, see R.M. Berchman in *Religious Studies Review* 15.2 January (1990), p. 127.

[16] See Winston and Dillon, op. cit., pp. 129-170.

[17] Ibid., pp. 171-180.

The New Orthodoxy

It is just on these points that opponents of these readings of Philo take issue. As D. Runia sees it, while Philo's writings give valuable evidence for the *Umwelt* of Middle Platonism, there is no *textual* evidence to suggest he was a Middleplatonist.[18] It is on this fulcrum that a "new orthodoxy" turns. It is precisely such "reductionism" that requires further comment.

Runia is not as dismissive of Philo and "philosophia" as E.R. Dodds, W. Theiler, A.J. Festugiere, or even J. Dillon.[19] He merely proposes that since: 1) Philo did not know the writings of contemporary Platonists such as Thrasyllus, the *Anonymous Theaetetus Commentary*, and the works of Eudorus of Alexandria; 2) did not exegete philosophical texts; and 3) did not use philosophical methods of commentary when he exegeted scripture,[20] it follows that, while he was aware of philosophical ideas, his "exegetical intention" evinces little or no philosophy.[21]

This view is complemented by T. Tobin, who claims that Philo's interpretations of the story of creation in Gen. 1-3 cannot be resolved in terms of philosophical interpretation but owe their existence to the composite nature of Philo's work and his reliance on Jewish traditions established by his exegetical predecessors. Although Philo is aware of contemporary philosophical developments, his exegesis is not philosophical in character.[22] R. Radice continues this trend in Philo studies by arguing that the structure of the *De opificio mundi*, and especially its presentation of the cosmological week, rules out the possibility of an interpretation of creation in a single philosophical and exegetical category.[23]

---

[18] Again this is most evident in Runia's collection of essays, *Exegesis and Philosophy Studies in Philo of Alexandria* (Aldershot, 1990), esp. II, IV, V, VI, VIII, IX.

[19] See E.R. Dodds, "The *Parmenides* of Plato and the Origins of the Neoplatonic One" in *CQ* 22 [1928], p. 132, n. 1; W. Theiler, *Die Vorbereitung des Neuplatonismus* (Berlin: 1930), p. 30; A.J. Festugiere, *La Revelation d'Hermes Trismegiste* (Paris: 1945-1954), vol. 2, p. 534; J. Dillon, *The Middle Platonists*, pp. 182-183.

[20] D.T. Runia, "Redrawing the Map of Early Middle Platonism: Some Comments on the Philonic Evidence" in *Hellenica et Judaica*, pp. 85-104.

[21] D.T. Runia, "How to Read Philo" in *NTT* 40 [1986], pp. 185-198.

[22] T.H. Tobin, *The Creation of Man: Philo and the History of Interpretation*, CBQ.MS (Washington, 1983).

[23] R. Radice, "Ipotesti per una interpretazione della struttura della kosmopoiia nel De opificio mundi di Filone di Alessandria" in *Hellenica et Judaica* [1986], pp. 69-87.

Much of the case for this understanding of Philo is built around two extended arguments. The first focuses on his apparent ignorance of contemporary philosophical texts, and the methods of philosophical commentary used by philosophers on their own canon. The second deals with the status of philosophical ideas called on by Philo when he engages in his special exegetical task that is the interpretation of the *LXX*. In brief, there is little of what could be called "philosophia" in Philo, because he does not exegete scripture the way philosophers who wrote commentaries on the writings of Plato, Aristotle, or the Stoa did philosophy.

One of the main goals of this trend in scholarship is to locate Philo's attitude toward texts and exegesis outside the traditions of Greek philosophy. It appears that Runia, Tobin, and Radice sometimes reject, largely on the basis of *a priori* considerations, what are correctly philosophical issues in Philo. Perhaps, they have fallen into the kind of trap Runia accuses E.R. Goodenough and H.A. Wolfson of, but with a twist. They offer "a reconstruction of what he would have said if he had articulated what he had really meant to say...."[24] The point is the least transparent of esotericisms Philo practices is philosophy. The problem is that he does not practice philosophy in the way philosophy should be practiced.

In sketching out this story they omit what is surely an important part of the tradition of Greek philosophy that Philo draws upon. This is its connection to allegory and rhetoric.[25] The philosophical dimension of Philo's allegorical exegesis is subtly rhetorical. If, as Leopold and Conley suggest, Philo consciously connected philosophy and rhetoric in exegesis so as to continue scriptural inquiry, then "philosophia" may well be central to Philo's "exegetical intention."

My second observation is that opponents of Philo and "philosophia" probably place too much emphasis on Philo's supposed goal of preserving the distinctiveness of *LXX* exegesis and the Judaism it symbolizes. In speaking this way, they obscure the connection Philo wants to make between Jewish and Greek wisdom. This is paralleled by a similar overemphasis on the exclusively Pentateuchal character of Philo's exegesis, an emphasis that threatens to collapse philosophy

---

[24] D.T. Runia, *Exegesis and Philosophy*, p. 226.
[25] See J. Leopold's analysis in Winston and Dillon, op. cit., pp. 151, esp. 163-170

into exegesis.[26] Although such scholars note that subdivisions must be made in this exclusive notion, they also argue that text and exegesis are a unified notion rather than an equivocal one in Philo. This appears to be based on the claim that Philo is a member of what contemporary philosophers would call a distinct linguistic community that practices a special "language game."

Here it is apposite to remind ourselves of Wittgenstein, who argued against the possibility of private language games.[27] His insights have value for Philo studies.[28] By private language, Wittgenstein means one that is logically impossible for anyone but the speaker or a private community to understand. This notion, connected to the issue of Philo and philosophy, makes it logically impossible for anyone to dispute the claim that Philo was speaking a "private language" that only Alexandrian-Jewish exegetes of the Septuagint could understand.[29]

The argument that such projects are incommensurable with other language games—specifically those offered by Greco-Roman philosophers—that Philo's references are to the private language of his community, requires critical reflection. Moreover, if the signs in which Philo's concepts were supposed to be embodied constituted a "private language," then they would not have had any meaning for those who later read and interpreted him. That is to say, Philo would not have had a criterion that not only included the "language games" of ancient Platonists, Pythagoreans, Stoics, and Christians, but also those who do history of philosophy and religions today.[30]

In brief, the private language game hypothesis is open to challenge. First, we should recall that Nikiprowetsky found evidence for

---

[26] Cf., e.g., Tobin, op. cit.; D.T. Runia, "Mosaic and Platonist Exegesis: Philo on 'Finding and Refinding'" in *VC* 40 [1986], pp. 105-138.

[27] L. Wittgenstein, *Philosophical Investigations* (Cambridge, 1953), pars. 258, 293.

[28] There are heated contemporary discussions in philosophy of mind about the efficacy of Wittgenstein's theory. For one account, see A.J. Ayer, *Wittgenstein* (Chicago, 1985), pp. 67-86. Contemporary disputes with Wittgenstein's thesis have no bearing on this debate. My point of departure is not epistemological or linguistic but historically grounded.

[29] Again see the many examples offered in Tobin, *The Creation of Man*, and Runia, *Exegesis and Philosophy*, and "How to Read Philo," pp. 185-192.

[30] This would include figures such as H.A. Wolfson, D. Winston, and G. Reale who see in Philo's work a series of problematics that engaged philosophers and theologians from the Church Fathers to Spinoza. Philo also engages those who might want to bring him into contemporary debate.

"philosophia" primarily in Philo's association of divine wisdom as revelation and natural law. Second, while Runia recognizes this, he rejects a philosophical reading of this association by claiming that Philo's "exegetical intention" stands outside a philosophical agenda. To prove this, he makes a crucial move by arguing that if Philo's philosophical ideas are identified and then related to exegetical *loci* under discussion,[31] one would be convinced that there are not any philosophical conclusions connected to his exegesis of scripture.[32]

This leads to another possible objection. Throughout their presentation of Philo's exegetical position, those opposed to the association of Philo and "philosophia" consistently circumscribe the words of Philo's text. That is to say, the language that does not make Philo sound like a philosopher does not come from Philo. Rather it comes from conclusions reached independently of Philo that are based on conclusions they introduce into his exegesis of the *LXX*.

Here it must be emphasized how far they depart from Philo's texts to build their case. They realize that Philo does not speak as they interpret him. But their way of accounting for this amounts to an ingenious argument from silence. Why doesn't Philo describe directly the boundaries of his philosophical thought and language? Why doesn't he speak clearly of his philosophical intent? They answer these questions by turning to an analysis of Philo's role as a Jewish exegetical expert. On the basis of this alone it can be shown what Philo's "exegetical intention" was.

Since Philo limits his speculation to a community-based tradition of text and exegesis, his exegetical position can be distanced from the strong but ambiguous claim that he is "doing philosophy." In brief, Philo is able to put the often obscure and conflicting theories of Greek philosophy into rigorous exegetical order, but does so without appealing to Greek philosophical conclusions. That is to say, Philo charts the limits of Greek philosophical language, but he never becomes a philosopher himself.

The question is whether Philo's silence signifies a refusal to do philosophy or whether it is perhaps a sign that Philo was simply a more careful "internalist" than philosophers like Plato or Plotinus.

---

[31] Runia, "How to Read Philo," pp. 185-192.

[32] Passages on epistemology, cf., Runia, "Redrawing the Map of early Middle Platonism," pp. 85-104. The divine epithet *huphistos* furnishes some striking support for Runia's claims. Cf. "How to Read Philo," pp. 185-192.

Philo usually maintains his internality more consistently than Plato and Plotinus, refusing, most of the time, in a technical philosophical sense, to articulate his philosophy directly. He does his philosophy internally or textually through the arts of exegesis and rhetoric.

Taken in isolation my remarks may seem dogmatic. But the intelligible force of Scripture was not mere dogma for Philo. By being properly receptive to Scripture, one is brought to know what is true about divine wisdom. Knowledge is not qualified by the externality of the Septuagint text. It is guided by the internal forms of the Logos impressing themselves upon the receptive soul through the internality of the *LXX*, which reveals itself through exegesis.

Those who deny the philosophical intent of Philonic exegesis are perhaps blinded by it. We may pretend not to see. But if Malingrey is right, Philo's "philosopia" displays a profound sensitivity. It is a matter of being open to Philo's notion that philosophy is the preparatory science for *sophia*, which includes the contemplation of the cosmos and God's theoretical and moral revelation to Israel. It also involves the ability to grasp that Philo's philosophy is the art of exegesis itself.

Like the proverbial door, no one can entirely miss philosophy and exegesis in Philo. To the extent that we do miss it, the cause of the difficulty is not in Philo's "exegetical intention" but in us. As the eyes of bats are to the blaze of day, so is the reason in our soul to the things that are by nature most evident. There is a divine wisdom Philo is trying to understand. Indeed, he is inviting us to understand it as he exegetes the *LXX*.

The New Constellation

This narrative is not yet finished because the story told is still unfolding. It is not one of those where all loose ends are neatly tied up at the "end." We should recall Benjamin's and Adorno's metaphor of a "constellation" and suggest with Bernstein that we find ourselves in a "new constellation."[33] In this "post-narrative philosophical era" of Philo studies, some say that the very idea of Philo and philosophy belong to the dustbin of a now-discredited history of Philonic studies.

---

[33] R.J. Bernstein, *The New Constellation The Ethical-Political Horizons of Modernity/Postmodernity* (Cambridge, 1993), esp. pp. 33-56.

There are others, as well, who argue that philosophy stands at the center of Philo's exegetical effort.

Are there any truths to be appropriated from this debate? Isaiah Berlin once commented that "the history of thought and culture is, as Hegel showed with great brilliance, a changing pattern of great liberating ideas, which turn into suffocating straitjackets, and so stimulate their own destruction by new emancipating, and at the same time, enslaving conceptions."[34]

Berlin's insight is anticipated in Runia's, Tobin's, and Radice's deep suspicion of what narratives, particularly philosophical narratives, have become in Philo studies. Malingrey, Nikiprowetsky, Reale, and Winston have also shown us that suspicions quickly become trends and fads or "suffocating straightjackets" and "enslaving conceptions" themselves. But there are even more subtle, unobtrusive, and even more pernicious dangers that need to be unmasked and revealed.

There can be no dialogue unless values and commitments, and even emotions and passions, are shared in common. It is almost difficult to resist the conclusion that we are—as Gadamer says of Heidegger—living in "the 'cosmic night' of the forgetfulness of being,' the nihilism that Nietzsche prophesied."[35] Rarely before has a claim that Philo studies constitutes communicative reason been so threatened from so many different directions. But as Habermas suggests, the claim to reason has a stubbornly transcending power, because it is renewed with each act of unconstrained understanding.[36]

Sometimes what is required to communicate, to establish a reciprocal "we," is rupture and break—a refusal to accept arguments proposed by the "other." Hence, when we think through what the opponents of "Philo and philosophy" are saying, we must resist arguments of textual *necessity* spoken in terms of the exclusive nature of Jewish scripture and Philonic exegesis. Narratives of exegesis and philosophy that see "philosophia" only ending in false understandings of Philo's "exegetical intention" must be challenged. If not we shall surely be enclosed in a conversation of darkness, forgetfulness, and betrayal wherein Philo studies is reduced to just another research program.

---

[34] I. Berlin, "Does Political Theory Still Exist?" in P. Laslett and W.C. Runciman, eds., *Philosophy, Politics, and Society* [2nd Series] (Oxford, 1962), p. 17.

[35] H.-G. Gadamer, *Truth and Method* (New York: 1989[3]), p. xxxvii.

[36] See J. Habermas, "A Reply to my Critics" in J.B. Thompson and D. Held, eds., *Habermas: Critical Debates* (London, 1982), p. 227.

Philo scholars should aim at continuing a conversation rather than at discovering "truth." This is not a claim to "relativism," a subordination of truth to edification in Philo studies. As Bernstein notes the difference between conversation and inquiry turned into a research program parallels Sartre's distinction between thinking of oneself as *pour-soi* and as *en-soi*.[37] Thus the cultural role of scholarship is to help us avoid the self-deception that comes from believing that we know Philo by knowing a set of objective exegetical facts.

Sartre helps explain why this confusion is so frequent and why its results are purveyed with so much moral earnestness.[38] The notion of "one right way" of describing and explaining Philo contained in the study of his texts is a way of Philonic description and explanation imposed on us in the way in which Sartre says stones impinge on our feet, or to switch metaphors, in the notion of having facts unveiled to us, not as in a glass darkly, but with a concrete immediacy that makes all other discourse and description superfluous.

The need to see "one right way" of describing and interpreting Philo and to view this pursuit as a matter of *necessity* is the urge to be rid of the freedom to erect yet another alternative theory or vocabulary. As Bernstein argues to look for commensuration rather than continued conversation, to look for a way of making further redescription unnecessary by finding a way of reducing all possible descriptions to one, is to attempt to escape from humanity.

This attempt to slough off dialogical responsibility is what Sartre calls the attempt to turn oneself, or in this case Philo, into a thing—into an *etre-en-soi*.[39] That is to say, if knowledge about Philo can be converted from something discursive, something attained by continual adjustments of ideas or theories, into something as ineluctable, then we no longer have the responsibility for choice among competing ideas, theories, and vocabularies.

Yet, despite all the consequential differences among students of Philo, most of us share a common perspective. We agree not only that a Philo project is viable but that critique itself can be properly grounded. Malingrey, Nikiprowetsky, Reale, and Winston never seriously doubt that reason can self-reflexively examine itself and that we can determine the conditions for the possibility of philosophical con-

---

[37] J.-P. Sartre, *Being and Nothingness* (New York, 1956), pp. 79-101.
[38] Ibid., pp. 47-72.
[39] Ibid., pp. 617-628.

clusions in the works of Philo. Runia, Radice, and Tobin do not doubt that the *telos* of critique is *Wissenschaft*—a system of text-analysis that internally "justifies" its own standards of critique.

But it is precisely confidence in approaching Philo from various perspectives that has been shaken for some of us. If a suspicion of narrative plays a decisive role in calling into question the philosophical foundations of Philo's thought, then we are faced with only one way of reading Philo. If we pursue such a reductionist approach, we court disaster. That is to say, a suspicion of philosophical narrative eventually consumes the critical impulse itself.

If Philo's writings are no longer permitted to operate in an open realm, then much of the analysis and critique of his texts lose their meaning. Moreover, for those who engage in a rejection of this prospect, critique turns upon and undermines itself. They are caught in a "performative contradiction" where they at once practice critique and undermine the very possibility of critique. As a result, they consume the philosophic impulse that consumed Philonic exegesis.

Such a development in Philo studies would have brought an admonition from Arnaldo Momigliano who taught us that history is not about the sources. History is an interpretation of that reality of which the sources are "segni indicativi o frammenti." We study by examining texts, but inevitably we must look through them to the realities they propose, represent, fail to suppose, even at times conceal. Excellent advise when we reflect, as in a mirror, on Philo and philosophy.

In The Mirror of Medusa

At Lycosura in Arcadia the most honored divinity was called Despoina. She was represented sitting in her temple alongside her mother, Demeter. On either side of them framing their double thrones stood Artemis and the Titan, Anytos. Toward the exit out of the sanctuary, there was a mirror on the right wall. Pausanius says that whoever looks at it either only sees himself as an obscure reflection, faint and indistinct (*amudros*) or sees nothing at all. The figures of the goddesses and the throne that supports them show up clearly in the mirror. One can see them clearly (*enargos*).[40]

---

[40] Pausanius 8.37.7.

In the sacred place where it hangs, the mirror inverts its natural properties and shifts from its normal role to another, opposite function. Instead of reflecting appearances and returning the image of visible objects before it, the mirror opens a gap in the backdrop of "phenomena," displays the invisible, reveals the divine, allowing it to be seen in the brilliance of divine epiphany.

This story emphasizes the ambiguous nature of an image reflected in a mirror. The image oscillates between two contrary poles. At one time it is an empty shadow, an illusion; at other times reality appears on its surface as in the transparency of spring waters. Remote, alien to this world, this other reality is fuller and stronger than what the world offers to the eyes of mortals.

Plato adds to our understanding of the visual imagery that besets us by helping us see why imagery is always trying to transcend itself.[41] The notion of an unclouded mirror is the notion of a mirror that would be indistinguishable from what is mirrored and thus would not be a mirror at all. The notion of a human being whose mind is such an unclouded mirror, and who knows this, is the image of God. He would have no need and no ability to choose actions or descriptions.

These stories are told so that we come to abandon the notion that historical and philosophical research must show all possible discourse converging to a consensus, just as normal inquiry does. Acceptance of this proposition would be to abandon the hope of being anything more than merely human. It would be to abandon Platonic and Philonic notions of Truth, Reality, and Goodness as entities that may not be directly seen but only dimly mirrored as through a glass darkly.

Dialogical Rationality and Exegetical Intention

Here it may be helpful to pursue another line of inquiry that takes us in a very different direction—Philo's link to Gadamer and the tradition of hermeneutics and practical philosophy that Gadamer helped to revitalize.[42] There are consequential differences between the two in their understandings of the character and preconditions required for dialogic rationality. The clash is between their ontological concerns. Their common ground Gadamer would call *die Sache*.

---

[41] Plato, *Tim.* 45b-46b.
[42] See Gadamer, op. cit.

Gadamer's critical appropriation of themes in Heraclitus, Plato, Aristotle, (Hegel, and Heidegger) can be applied to Philo. In his ontological version of hermeneutics, Gadamer has been arguing that our being-in-the-world is to be dialogical beings. We also find in Philo one of the subtlest and most sensitive analyses of the interplay and essential openness of dialogue. His practice of philosophy as exegesis shows us what authentic dialogue involves. Philo's understanding of *logos* is one of the oldest and most persistent themes in Western philosophy.

Richard Rorty has argued that in every sufficiently reflective culture, there are those who single out one area, one set of practices, and see it as the paradigm of human activity.[43] They then try to show how the rest of culture can profit from this example. In the mainstream of the Greek philosophical tradition, this paradigm has been *knowing*—possessing justified true beliefs or beliefs so intrinsically persuasive as to make justification unnecessary.

Successive philosophical revolutions were produced by philosophers excited by new cognitive feats. Among these revolutions in the first century was the rediscovery of Plato and Philo's use of philosophical and rhetorical ideas to exegete scripture. Even when he integrates the Peripatos and Stoa in his narrative of Mosaic rationality, he highlights its communicative aspects.

Philo's entire corpus can be read as an invitation to join him in the rediscovery and redemption of the richness and concreteness of the dialogical presence of the Logos's being-in-the-world. Philo was motivated by the inclusive, not exclusive, character of Mosaic philosophy. He wanted to reveal its truths in the tradition of a philosophy that allows us to understand and critically evaluate a wide range of philosophical problematics inherent in Mosaic wisdom as revelation and natural law.

In brief, much of what Philo explored can be understood as a commentary on the claim that philosophical thinking is possible. He is concerned with exegetically probing the conditions required to cultivate exegesis as communicative reason in the revelation of Moses. The first can be traced back to his use of the metaphysical construction of the metaphysical Plato, with his two-world theory, his denigration of corporeality, and his celebration of eternal immutable forms that are the *telos* of *dianoia* and *noesis*. The second can be traced

---

[43] R. Rorty, *Philosophy and the Mirror of Nature* (Princeton, 1979), p. 366.

back to the "other" Plato Philo engages. This is the Plato who is the defender of "a philosophic art of writing" and exegesis that are always open to novel turns and that knows no finality.[44]

There are some who think that posing these issues as I have done invites the notion that there is or can be more than one answer to Philo's "exegetical intention." My answer is that while all effective critique of Philo's work is local, specific, and dependent on exegetical context, a focus on context, specificity, and locality does not preclude facing up to the possibility that Philo in his time "did philosophy" in a new way that baffles some of his modern interpreters.

At the same time, we must honestly confront the instability of any project of critique. We must recognize there cannot be any critique without affirmation and that we must be prepared to defend our affirmations and standards of critique when they are challenged. Moreover, we cannot fully anticipate those contingencies that will rupture our affirmations. We have to maintain a vigilant double attitude by which we are aware of the need for affirmation, and we must accept that such affirmation can be called into question. Since defense can never be conclusive, a variety of strategies—argumentation, narrative, and tracing new possibilities must be undertaken— hence this essay.

As Philonic participants, our critiques and affirmations are always tentative, fallible, open to further questioning. Such a bricolage will not satisfy those who want something more solid and secure, something with a more conclusive grounding for Philo studies. This is the space, the *topos*, in which critique thrives. Indeed, a practical commitment to the avenging *energia* of *logos* is the basis, perhaps the only academic basis, for preserving communicative reason within Philo studies.

Philo and "Philosophia" Reconsidered

We should heed Nietzsche and avoid the "hypertrophy of the historical sense" that afflicts much scholarship, including Philo studies to-

---

[44] For an interpretation of Plato's *Phaedrus* and his defense of "a philosophic art of writing," see R. Burger, *Plato's Phaedrus. A Defense of the Philosophic Art of Writing* (Huntsville, 1980); and on Philo's "exegetical intent," see Nikiprowetsky in Winston and Dillon, op. cit., pp. 5-76.

day.[45] When discussing Philo and philosophy, those who are sympathetic to the view that Philo is a philosopher deal primarily with a "problematic elucidation" of his work,[46] while opponents focus on the form and structure of Philo's exegesis.[47] The difference here goes much deeper than mere style. It is about how Philo should be read.

Two equally extreme generalizations about how to read Philo should be disowned. One sees Philo as a philosopher in the image of a first century Platonist like Antiochus of Ascalon or Thrasyllus, commenting upon and exegeting philosophical texts.[48] The other views Philo as an exegete whose sole purpose is bereft of anything remotely philosophical because he does not write commentaries on philosophical texts or offer conclusions to philosophical problematics.[49] Both views approximate the truth about how to read Philo. The first, though partially wrong, is much more nearly right. The second, while technically correct, is certainly incomplete.

Philo practiced a curiously partial approach to philosophy. The limitations of his use of philosophy can be summed up in three words: atomism, fundamentalism, and criticism. First, Philo never considers a single philosophical work as a whole. He uses philosophical ideas, but he never wrote a commentary or even exegeted one work of Plato, Aristotle, or the Stoa. He quotes snippets, he generalizes, but he does not ask how passages he cites might function in their original philosophical context, much less what a Platonic or an Aristotelian work is all about, or what Stoics and Pythagorians were up to.

Second, he pursued a non-doxagraphical approach to philosophical ideas. His quotations of philosophical ideas are ripped from their original context and stripped of much of their technical philosophical value. But to say that his readings of the philosophers are non-contextual would be a grossly misleading understatement. However, the point is worth stressing because in all these respects he was imitated first by Clement and Origen of Alexandria, then by later allegorists

---

[45] F. Nietzsche, *On the Use and Abuse of History for Life* (Indianapolis and New York, 1957), pp. 10-11.

[46] See J. Passmore, "The Idea of a History of Philosophy" in *History and Theory* Supplement 5 [1965], pp. 1-32.

[47] For a critique of this method, see Runia, *Philo of Alexandria*, p. 46.

[48] See H. Tarrant, *Thrasyllan Platonism* (Ithaca and London, 1993), pp. 113-116.

[49] In Philo studies D.T. Runia is sympathetic to this view. See, e.g., "How to Read Philo," pp. 185-198. Also see D.T. Runia, "Redrawing the Map of Early Middle Platonism, pp. 85-104.

such as Didymus the Blind, and finally by philosophical theologians such as the Cappadocian Fathers.

Third, Philo's criticism does not consist merely in his general readiness to pass judgments on the meaning of philosophical ideas, which he does in an atomistic and fundamentalist way. It is that he considers the overall meaning of philosophical ideas only within the context of exegesis.

The concern of Philo with exegesis begins with his interest in the problem of knowledge. In terms of the subject-object relation, it is fair to say that Philo stressed, with Parmenides, Heraclitus, Plato, Aristotle, and Plotinus, the objective aspects of this relation. Being, Logos, the Ideas, Substance, and Nous satisfied a normative requirement for an invariant object understood as a necessary condition of knowledge, the object that is known, and the subject that knows.

Philo pushed this proposition two steps further. First, he understood that the normative requirement of an invariant object of knowledge presented itself in the Septuagint. Moreover, the necessary condition of knowledge, the object that is known, and the subject that knows merges in the very play of scriptural exegesis. That is to say, through exegesis of the Septuagint the normative and necessary conditions of knowledge are set and met. Second, he set this interplay of language, text, and reality aesthetically within the context of the macrocosmic role the *Logos* plays in creation and the microcosm of a person's own reasoning power that is a *logos* in the sense of the operations of definitional and demonstrational reasoning.[50]

In brief, Philo can be viewed as an "aestheticist"—one who sees "art" or "language" or "discourse" or "text" as constituting the primary realm of human experience.[51] That is to say, through the art of exegesis, Philo can embrace the proposition that language (*logos*) embraces the whole of reality. Usually employed, the word *aestheticism* denotes an enclosure within a self-contained realm of aesthetic objects and sensations that suggests a separation from the "real world" of nonaesthetic objects. A different meaning of the term is suggested here. It does not refer to the condition of being enclosed within the

---

[50] This association in Philo has been noted by D.T. Runia, *Philo of Alexandria and the Timaeus of Plato* (Leiden, 1986), pp. 447, 449, and Tarrant, op. cit., pp. 113-116.

[51] As Heidegger puts it, language becomes "onto-genetic." See M. Heidegger, *Holzwege* (New York, 1950), ch. 1.

limited territory of the aesthetic but rather to an attempt to expand the aesthetic to the whole of reality.[52] In Philo, the ontologically creative potential of the "art" of exegesis becomes absolutely decisive. In this sense, "text" and "language" embrace the whole of reality and reality itself is revealed through the "art" of exegetical "discourse," which is a "language" disclosed in scripture.[53]

The point is that Philo worked within an "aestheticist" perspective, even as he paradistically tried to reduce this to a vantage-point emanating from the Logos alone. It seems to me that the emergence of the style of philosophy represented by Philo, while not identical, is consistent with that offered by Clement, Origen, and Plotinus. Looking at these thinkers together, one is struck by how they all are "aestheticist," in their sensibility.

A consideration of Philo's atomism, fundamentalism, criticism, and aestheticism should make one skeptical of those who want to distance Philo from philosophy. It should also make one wary of the concept of a philosophical tradition used to criticize those who link Philo and philosophy.

The idea of a philosophical tradition, as now understood, is relatively recent and was introduced by Hegel.[54] He was the first to regard the history of philosophy as a kind of Platonic dialogue extending through time, in which later thinkers build, or attempt to improve, on earlier theories. His understanding of the way that philosophical theories are taken up in the philosophical tradition presupposes an exclusive, not inclusive, definition of philosophy.

This means that Platonism, Pythagoreanism, or Stoicism are viewed as fixed, or stable entities. Philosophical theories are viewed as always and necessarily there in the tradition as a precondition for philosophical discussion. Moreover, concepts are also tradition-bound, which means they can only be read within a specific philosophical tradition and not across different philosophical and religious traditions.

Hegel's underlying historical assumption of a single philosophical tradition is insightful, interesting, but finally mistaken. Although we

---

[52] See Allan Megill on aestheticism in *Prophets of Extremity* (Berkeley, Los Angeles, and London, 1987), pp. 2-5.

[53] The aesthetic dimension of Philonic exegesis has been structurally assessed by J. Cazeaux, op. cit..

[54] There are many references to this idea. See esp. Hegel's *Lectures on the Philosophy of World History* (Cambridge, 1973), Introduction: Reason in History.

can read a philosophical tradition historically, by identifying a specific body of texts and distinct types of commentary, other perspectives are possible. Writings that compose philosophical traditions, and even a tradition, are variables. Texts change and are added to. Consequently, interpretations of philosophical theories also change. As such, philosophical traditions are not frozen but are mutable and take on an amorphous quality. Furthermore, different views of a philosophical tradition lead to vastly different readings of the history of philosophy and exegesis and point to vastly different ideas of what constitutes a philosophical tradition.

The problem remains that those who separate Philo from philosophy follow in the shadow of Hegel's definition of what "philosophia" constitutes. First, Dodds, Theiler, and Festugiere argued for an exclusive notion of ancient philosophical traditions. Next, Runia, Tobin, and Reale make this idea one of the foundations for incommensurability, for a separation of Philo's "exegetical intention" from his use of philosophical ideas.

The principle of unity appropriate to Philo and "philosophia" is not Hegel's paradigm of history and tradition. Rather it is Wittgenstein's image of a rope of many strands and family resemblance.[55] The application of Philo's use of philosophical ideas to a number of exegetical *foci* does not depend on their having a single "exegetical intention" or even a set of intentions in common but rather in their possession of a variety of philosophical features that constitute family resemblance.[56]

Unfortunately, Hegel's assumption of a single philosophical tradition and Wittgenstein's warning against private language games are respectively shared and ignored by the "new orthodoxy." They presuppose a traditions approach to the history of philosophy that excludes Philo from "philosophia." They also propose a "private language game" for Philonic exegesis and philosophy that again excludes Philo from philosophy.

Philo's "language game" was public and his philosophical attitude "aperspectival." He avoided the appearance of favoring a particular philosophical perspective by favoring them all. His philosophical vocabulary and exegetical grammar were commensurable (but not

---

[55] L. Wittgenstein, *The Blue and Brown Books* (Cambridge, 1958).
[56] This would include philosophical ideas such as Plato's *logos* and Philo's appropriation of such ideas for exegesis.

identical) with other contemporary "language games." Again this is evident when one reflects on those who read and understood him from Clement of Alexandria onwards.

Alas, there is no royal road to entering into Philo studies, but, difficult though it may be, it is a road along which we must be encouraged to stumble. The debate going on conjures up the watchful eye of the owl of Minerva. Reflection, perhaps even some learning, is going on. We may have reached the time when midnight windows are opened and fireworks light up the sky. Like Janus, the two faced God, and Silvester, to whom the last days of the year are dedicated, we should look not only backward but forward. It is time to sweep the floor of dust, to break with the past, not only by throwing out old anachronisms, but by dismissing new prejudices as well. While we sweep we should also remember that:

> When we try to examine the mirror
> in itself, we discover in the end
> nothing but things upon it. If we
> want to grasp the things, we finally
> get hold of nothing but the mirror.
> This in the most general terms is
> the history of knowledge.[57]

BIBLIOGRAPHY

Ayer, A.J., *Wittgenstein* (Chicago, 1985).

Berlin, I., "Does Political Theory Still Exist?" in Laslett, P., and W.C. Runciman, eds., *Philosophy, Politics, and Society* (Oxford, 1962), pp. 1-36.

Bernstein, R.J., *The New Constellation: The Ethical-Political Horizons of Modernity/Postmodernity* (Cambridge, 1993).

Burger, R., *Plato's Phaedrus. A Defense of the Philosophic Art of Writing* (Huntsville, 1983).

Cazeaux, J., *La trame et la chaine: structures litteraires et exegese dans cinq traites de Philon d'Alexandrie*, ALGHU 15 (Leiden, 1983).

Cazeaux, J., *L'epee du Logos et le soleil de midi*, Collection de la maison de l'Orient Medoiterraneen 13, Serie Litteraire et Philosophique 2 (Lyon, 1983).

---

[57] F. Nietzsche, *Daybreak: Thoughts on the Prejudices of Morality* (Cambridge, 1982), #243.

Cazeaux, J., *Philon d'Alexandrie: de la grammaire a la mystique*, Supplement au Cahier Evangelie 44 (Paris, 1983).

Conley, T., "Philo's Use of Topoi" in Winston, D., and J. Dillon, eds., *Two Treatises of Philo of Alexandria* (Chico, 1983), pp. 171-180.

Dillon, J., *The Middle Platonists* (Ithaca, 1977).

Dodds, E.R., "The Parmenides of Plato and the Origins of the Neoplatonic One," in CQ 22 [1928], pp. 129-142.

Festugiere, A.J., *La Revelation d'Hermes Trismegiste* (Paris, 1945-1954).

Gadamer, H.-G., *Truth and Method* (New York, 1989[3]).

Habermas, J., "A Reply to My Critics," in Thompson, J.B., and D. Held, eds., *Habermas: Critical Debates* (London, 1982).

Hegel, G.F.W., *Lectures on the Philosophy of World History: Reason in History* (Cambridge, 1973).

Leopold, J., "Philo's Style and Diction" in Winston, D., and J. Dillon, eds., *Two Treatises of Philo of Alexandria* (Chico, 1983), pp. 129-170.

Malingrey, A.M., *'Philosophia' etude d'un groupe de mots dans la litterature grecque des Presocratiques au IVe siecle apres J.-C.* (Paris, 1961).

Nietzsche, F., *On the Use and Abuse of History for Life* (Indianapolis and New York, 1957).

Nietzsche, F., *Daybreak: Thoughts on the Prejudices of Morality* (Cambridge, 1982).

Nikiprowetsky, V., "L'Exegese de Philon d'Alexandrie dans le De Gigantibus et le Quod Deus," in Winston, D., and J. Dillon, eds., *Two Treatises of Philo of Alexandria* (Chico, 1983).

Nikiprowetsky, V., *Le commentaire de l'Ecriture chez Philon d'Alexandrie: son caractere et sa portee; observations philologiques*, ALGHJ 11 (Leiden, 1977).

Passmore, J., "The Idea of a History of Philosophy," in *History and Theory* Supplement 5 [1965], pp. 1-32.

Radice, R., "Ipotesi per una interpretazione della struttura della kosmopoiia nel De opificio mundi di Filone di Alessandria," in *Hellenica et Judaica* [1986], pp. 69-87.

Reale, G., "Filone di Alessandria et la 'filosofia mosaica,'" in *Storia della filosofia antica*, vol. 4, *Le scuole dell'eta imperiale* (Milan, 1978 [1987/5]).

Rorty, R., *Philosophy and the Mirror of Nature* (Princeton, 1979).

Runia, D.T., *Exegesis and Philosophy* (Aldershot, 1990).

Sartre, J.-P., *Being and Nothingness* (New York, 1956).

Tarrant, H., *Thrasyllan Platonism* (Ithaca and London, 1993).

Theiler, W., *Die Vorbereitung des Neuplatonismus* (Berlin, 1930).

Tobin, T.H., *The Creation of Man: Philo and the History of Interpretation*, CBQ.NS (Washington, 1983).

Winston, D., and J. Dillon, eds., *Two Treatises of Philo of Alexandria* (Chico, 1983).

Winston, D., *Logos and Mystical Theology in Philo of Alexandria* (Cincinnati, 1985).

Wittgenstein, L., *The Brown and Blue Books* (Cambridge, 1958).

Wittgenstein, L., *Philosophical Investigations* (Cambridge, 1953).

Wolfson, H.A., *Philo, Foundations of Religious Philosophy in Judaism, Christianity, and Islam* (Cambridge, 1947 [1968/4]).

4. JUDAISM AND PARTICULARISM:
A REPLY TO JAMES DUNN

William Scott Green
University of Rochester

"Particularism" is a bane in the study of Judaism. It has long been applied as a defining trait of Jewish religion, as a term that captures and reveals something essential about Judaism's nature, values, and commitments. James Dunn[1] shows that "particularism" is used in two basic ways, one polemical, the other analytical.

In religious polemic, "particularism" is supposed to mark a systemic weakness or failure in Judaism, a flaw that both necessitates and justifies Christianity as its successor religion. The work of Nils Dahl and others amply demonstrates that this usage is theologically and religiously groundless. As Dunn states, "Any claim to the universal validity of specific beliefs is itself a form of particularism (our belief and not yours). And any notion of special revelation, quite apart from the idea of special election (of a people or a group), likewise cannot avoid being particularist" (p. 60).

But if "particularism" is worthless polemic, can it have analytical value? Dunn cautiously suggests that a focus on the Greek term *Ioudaismos* ("Judaism;" "Jewish religion") may allow the category "particularism" still to help elucidate ancient Judaism. He claims that "the Greek term *Ioudaismos* denoted 'Judean' before the more general 'Jew' became appropriate for members of a people no longer so closely identified with that land as such" (p. 61). And he notes that "...*Ioudaismos* was in fact initially coined to describe the religion of the Judeans (2 Macc. 2.21; 8.1; 14.38) in their opposition to the Hellenizing policies of their Syrian overlords" (P. 61). On this basis, he argues that the terms "Judaism" and "Jew" have ineluctably "particularist" overtones. His argument runs as follows:

> The significance of this basic observation is that "Judaism" in its beginnings is a term closely linked to a particular territory. In that sense we

---

[1] "Was Judaism Particularist or Universalist?," in Jacob Neusner and Alan J. Avery-Peck, eds., Where We Stand: Issues and Debates in Ancient Judaism (Leiden, 1999), vol. 2, pp. 57-73. Pages references within the text are to this work.

would have to say that Judaism was particularist: it identified with a particular land. Nor is it any accident that the term emerged in opposition to a policy intended to obliterate national and religious distinctiveness. It should be no surprise, in other words, that the term emerged in Greek, precisely as a way of marking out the Judeans' distinctiveness within a wider Hellenism which valued commonality more than distinctiveness. In that sense Judaism was resistant to a certain kind of "universalism," one that attempted to absorb and eliminate Judaism's particularism.

Given this early history of the terms it should occasion no surprise if "Jew" and "Judaism" continued to retain an unavoidably ethnic association with a particular land (Judea). Hence the division of all nations and races into the two categories of "Jews" and "gentiles/(other) nations"—"Jews" as those who belong to a nation/people distinct from all other nations/peoples. Even in the diaspora, "Jews" were by definition those whose identity was determined by their ethnic origin and continuing loyalty to the Temple cult (of Jerusalem), whose maintenance had been the *raison d'etre* for Judea's existence as a political entity since the Persian and Hellenistic periods. Hence the ambiguity of the terms "Jew" and "Judaism:" do they describe an ethnic or a religious identity? The answer was, at that time, Both, since the two went so closely together. In other words, the original overtone of "particularism" continued to cling to these terms through their early usage, simply because the definition they provided was unavoidably particularist (pp. 61-62).

This thesis supposes that "Hellenism" and "Judaism" historically were contrary cultural categories; it also requires precision about the meaning of "particularist." If "Judaism" did not (inherently) oppose "Hellenism," and if the nature of "particularism" is unclear, the thesis cannot be persuasive. On these points, Dunn's article needs better evidence and more clarity to make its case.

Consider first the notion of "Hellenism" and "Judaism." There seems to be little textual basis for the idea that these terms constitute opposing categories. The terms first appear in 2 Maccabees—"Hellenism" five times and "Judaism" three times—and Erich Gruen's careful analysis shows that "nowhere does II Maccabees juxtapose them as rival or competing concepts.... None of the references to Judaism singles out Hellenism or Hellenizers as the targets of Jewish wrath."[2] Second, it is unlikely that the motivation of Antiochus Epiphanes was to "obliterate national and religions distinctiveness" or to advocate a "wider Hellenism which valued commonality more than

---

[2] Erich Gruen, *Heritage and Hellenism: The Reinvention of Jewish Tradition* (Berkeley, 1998), pp. 3-4.

distinctiveness." Rather, the complexities surrounding the Maccabean revolt make Antiochus's policies exceptional, if not anomalous,
within the general practices of his regime in particular and Hellenism
in general. As Gruen notes, "The Maccabean rebellion exploded
against implementation of the king's policies, not against Hellenism
as such."[3] Moreover, Antiochus clearly was getting advice from other
Jews, some of whom were part of the Temple establishment, and all
Jews in this period were to some extent Hellenized. Gruen's trench-
ant summary judgment makes the point:

> The construct of a clash between Greek and Jew during the
> Hasmonean period is a red herring, even on the political and military
> front.... Greek historians of the Hellenistic period rarely have an unkind
> word to say for the Hasmoneans, and nowhere regard their expansion-
> ism as directed against Greek cities or Hellenic civilization.... The
> Maccabean movement arose in response to the aberrant and abhorrent
> policies of Antiochus Epiphanes. It soon became embroiled, however,
> in conflicts with other Jewish groups and directed much of its energies
> against Gentiles in Palestine who could be portrayed as heirs of biblical
> enemies rather than against the purveyors of Hellenism.[4]

Dunn suggests that in 2 Maccabees, the term *Ioudaismos* means "the
religion of the Judeans." But against the reality that the Hasmoneans
had Jewish as well as gentile enemies, perhaps a more nuanced rendering is justified, such as "the religion of *some* Judeans" (i.e., those
who followed or were represented by the Maccabees). Indeed, it is
plausible to think that in 2 Maccabees *Ioudaismos* is a term that establishes religious boundaries or points of identity *within* Jewish culture
rather in opposition to a non-Jewish Hellenistic one. On this basis,
the claim that "Judaism" signaled a particularist hostility to a
universalist Hellenism requires reassessment.

It may be, as Dunn proposes, that "'Judaism' continued to retain
an unavoidably ethnic association with a particular land (Judea)" (p.
62), but for this claim to be analytically useful, we would need to
know why having a homeland reveals something particular about
Judaism. Most religions of the ancient Mediterranean had native and
diaspora forms, so the association of a religion with a particular location is not especially noteworthy. We need more information than
Dunn provides. Moreover, Dunn's criteria for association with the

---

[3] Ibid.
[4] Ibid., p. 28

land of Israel obscure the meaning of "particularism." The article collapses "ethnic origin" and "loyalty to the Temple cult (of Jerusalem)" into one another, so that they appear as variations of the same phenomenon. But geographic derivation (if that is what is meant by "ethnic origin") and commitment to a native cult seem on the face of it to represent different and inherently separable kinds of identification and attachment. Was it impossible to come from Judea and not support the Temple's religion? Were there no Temple loyalists from outside Judea? It is not clear which distinctive traits of Judaism the label "unavoidably particularist" reveals.

The article's perspective on the nature of ancient Judaism also makes it difficult to discern what is at stake in the claim of Judaism's "particularism." Dunn suggests that,

> For non-Jews "looking in" there would have been only one "Judaism," just as there was only one nation of "the Jews;" however strange and diverse Jews were, their distinctive *ethnos* and traditions marked them out as one. For insiders, there would also be only one Judaism, Judaism as practiced by themselves—whether the "common Judaism" of the general populace in the land of Israel, or Judaism as practiced by their own particular sect or faction (p. 64).

This suggests that the religion outsiders perceived as monolithic, insiders knew to be fractious and variegated. This suggestion confuses rather than clarifies the meaning of "particularism." Does it mean one thing ("ethnic distinction") for non-Jews and something else ("doctrinal error") for Jews? Which distinctive traits of ancient Judaism is "particularism" supposed to display?

The article's treatment of Paul raises similar questions. Dunn claims that Paul's use of the term *Ioudaismos* in Gal. 1:13-14 resembles that in 2 Maccabees, such that

> Paul's "life in Judaism" was marked by two features: fervent hostility to a threat by the Nazarenes against the distinctiveness of that Judaism—whether in terms of the Temple (according to Acts 6-8), or in terms of set-apartness from the other nations; and an almost competitive zeal to maintain loyalty to covenant and Torah (p. 65).

There are two difficulties here. First, it is not clear that the Nazarenes' problem with Judaism was about Judaism's "distinctiveness," and Dunn does not supply a textual basis for this claim. Rather, the fundamental viability of some Judaic teachings seemed to be at issue between the two groups. Second, the article again blurs the distinction between loyalty to the Temple cult and group identity.

Dunn's discussion of "particularism" seems shaped by issues in Paul's teachings. He suggests that Paul

> ...reacted against the particularism that emphasized Israel's set-apartness from other nations as integral to Israel's election, and the particularism that interpreted Israel's status and Torah obligation in terms of the elaborated halakhah of the Pharisees. It could also be said that his reaction was towards universalism, in that he wanted thereafter to break down the barriers (of Torah, not least) between Jews and gentiles (p. 65).

But even this discussion leaves critical aspects of "particularism" unclear. What does "set-apartness" mean? Is it a trait distinctive to Judaism? In every religion, are not the recipients and practitioners of its teachings distinguished from those who are not recipients of those teachings? What, in principle, makes being a Pharisee more "particularist" than being a Cynic or a follower of Isis? The correlative claim that Paul was needed to "break down the barriers (of Torah...) between Jews and gentiles" also needs clarification. Gentiles had been joining Judaism at least since the time of the book of Judith. According to Josephus, the Hasmoneans even gave some gentiles a forced welcome into Judaism. As Dunn himself mentions, there is consistent evidence down at least to John Chrysostom that non-Jews found synagogues welcome religious environments and contributed to their welfare. From this perspective, Paul did not "break down barriers...of Torah," nor solve a problem within Judaism, nor bring Torah to the gentiles. Rather, he replaced Torah and its commandments with an alternate revelation and thereby fabricated a new religion.

Two factors inhibit the use of "particularism" as a lens for the study of ancient Judaism. First, it is helpful to distinguish "particularism" from exclusivism. All religions are by nature particular. They affirm some defined set of beliefs and practices and reject others. Hence all religions have insiders and outsiders. How a religion regards its outsiders is a function of varied forces, including its doctrine, its ritual, and its politics. As a monotheistic religion, Judaism—in all its forms—tends towards exclusivism, the view that if its teachings are right, those of the outsiders must be wrong. That tendency encourages and also is generated by competition among Jewish groups in antiquity. The various divisions—"sects"—that flourished beginning with the late Persian period were more interested in differentiating themselves from one another than in marking their differences from non-Jews. The response of the Dead Sea Scrolls to the "defiled" priests of the Jerusalem Temple and the utterly gratuitous scorn the Gospel of Matthew heaps on its hated "scribes and Pharisees" are two of the most obvious examples. But, as Dunn notes, the boundaries between Jews and non-Jews—or Israel and the Nations—were not porous. Even Paul, the apostle to the gentiles, exhibits undisguised contempt for pagan culture as against belief in the one God. On this analysis, particularism is not an especially revealing category for studying ancient Judaism.

The second factor complicating a discussion of "particularism" is the pluralism within ancient Judaism. Dunn's article acknowledges this pluralism but tends to discuss ancient Judaism as if it were a monolith. This makes it difficult to be precise about the meaning of "particularism."

In the end, the attempt to preserve some analytical value for the term "particularist" falls short of success. It is, as Dunn suggests at the outset of his piece, a term of religion polemic that is especially relevant in a highly particular setting. As a term of analysis or description, however, there seems little to recommend it.

5. DAVID WEISS HALIVNI'S
SOURCES AND TRADITIONS REVISITED

Jacob Neusner
Bard College

In his commentary to selected passages of the Talmud of Babylonia, David Weiss Halivni has given us a complete theory of the history of the formation of the Bavli. This he has worked out in not merely episodic and *ad hoc* remarks about diverse passages but in a sustained hermeneutics, in which a theory of the whole has guided him in his identification of problems demanding solution. In *Sources and Traditions*[1] he sets forth the theory that the Bavli is made up of sources, "those sayings which have come down to us in their original form, as they were uttered by their author," and traditions, "those which were changed in the course of transmission." Changing these "traditions" required later generations to deal with the remains of earlier statements, and they did so by a "forced interpretation" (in Halivni's language). The importance of Halivni's work is simple. He has made a serious effort to confront the problem of finding out how, in the Bavli, we may identify passages that were written prior to the closure of the document as a whole. He has taken as his focus not the document as we have it, peeling back its layers in a patient way, but rather individual items: this saying, that composition, the other composite. But Halivni builds on a shaky premise, for he believes that if a saying is attributed to a given name, that sage certainly said that saying. His entire hermeneutics rests upon that undemonstrated, and surely uncritical, premise. The reliability of attributions is the only justification for that approach, and as we shall presently see, if Halivni did not believe in the attributions as valid, he would have slight reason to claim that he knows anything at all about the condition of materials in the Bavli prior to the Talmud's redaction.

Now let us turn to the source. Halivni knows how to deal with the

---

[1] *Meqorot umesorot* (Tel Aviv, 1968 et. seq.).

problem of the "forced interpretation," distinguishing it from the simple one as follows, in the account of Robert Goldenberg:[2]

> The simple interpretation of a text is defined as "the interpretation which arises from the text itself, without either adding to it or subtracting from it." "Sometimes a simple comparison with parallel sources is sufficient to show that a forced explanation has its origin in an incorrect text.... In most cases, however, it is necessary to study the sugya in depth, to break it into its parts before the motivation for the forced explanation becomes clear."

Halivni's sense for the self-evidence of his position is expressed as follows: "Any divergence from the simple interpretation is a divergence from the truth."[3] The work is entirely exegetical; there is no historical inquiry whatever. He takes for granted the reliability of all attributions, the historicity of all stories.[4] Literary criticism plays no role in his identification of exegetical problems or in their solution, and everything is either a source or a tradition. As Goldenberg puts it, "The reliability of the tradition and the manner of its formation are to a great extent simply assumed, despite the mass of evidence of a more complicated situation that Weiss's own book reveals."[5]

Part of the problem of studying Halivni's *oeuvre* is his failure to deal with competing theories of the literature, on the one side, and his incapacity to compose a null hypothesis for the testing of his hermeneutic, on the other. His unwillingness to read other scholars' treatment of the same literature and problems has now become so notorious as to elicit the comments of book-reviewers.[6] We really do not know, therefore, how Halivni has taken into account other approaches to the same literature, competing theories of its character, origins, and, consequently, correct hermeneutics. That fact, his failure to read and comment on the work of others and its implications for his own work, renders the critical reading of Halivni's *oeuvre* exceedingly parlous.

The omission of a null hypothesis can be demonstrated to form a fatal flaw in his entire hermeneutical fabrication. I shall show how

---

[2] Robert Goldenberg, "David Weiss Halivni, Meqorot umesorot: Ketuvot," in J. Neusner, ed., *The Formation of the Babylonian Talmud* (Leiden, 1970), p. 136.

[3] Cited by Goldenberg, p. 137.

[4] See Goldenberg, p. 146.

[5] Goldenberg, p. 147.

[6] Cf., for example, David Singer in *Commentary*, April, 1988, on Halivni's remarkable disinterest in views other than his own. He apparently does not even read and take account of competing readings of the same documents.

one might compose and test a null hypothesis as to the character of the sources subjected to exegesis. On that basis we shall see that Halivni's premise of a composite text, in which materials that preserve original versions are mixed together with materials that exhibit deformations of those original versions, contradicts the character of the Talmud of the Land of Israel or Yerushalmi. Indeed, any exegesis that rests upon Halivni's premises will violate the fundamental literary traits of the Yerushalmi, and, everyone must then recognize, the Bavli as well, which in these traits does not differ in any material way.

Having devoted considerable effort to study of Halivni's work,[7] I am prepared to address its principal positions and to demonstrate that they contradict the evidence, read from an analytical and critical perspective. They form merely another chapter in the dreary story of fundamentalist exegesis of a text not studied but merely recited. Absent a null hypothesis presented and analyzed by Halivni himself, we have no alternative but to judge as a missed opportunity his entire exegetical *oeuvre* and the hermeneutical theory on which it rests.

Here is the null hypothesis: If Halivni is right, then we should identify in the Talmuds a multiplicity of voices. But, as we shall see, the opposite characterizes the Yerushalmi.[8] The Talmud Yerushalmi

---

[7] See the articles by Goldenberg and Shamai Kanter, "David Weiss Halivni, *Meqorot uMesorot. Qiddushin*" in *Formation of the Babylonian Talmud*, pp. 148-156, and David Goodblatt, "David Weiss Halivni, *Meqorot uMesorot. Gittin*" in *Formation of the Babylonian Talmud*, pp. 164-173; also Jacob Neusner, ed., *The Modern Study of the Mishnah* (Leiden, 1973), in particular Joel Gereboff, "David Weiss Halivni on the Mishnah," pp. 180-196; and William Scott Green, ed., *Law as Literature = Semeia. An Experimental Journal for Biblical Criticism* 27 (Chico, 1983), pp. 37-116. Note in particular Louis Newman, "The Work of David Weiss Halivni: A Source Critical Commentary to b. Yebamot 87b," in which Newman compares Halivni's exegetical approach to that of Shamma Friedman, treated at length in the same collection of papers. All of these papers were prepared in my graduate seminar. For fifteen years, from 1968 through 1983, I regularly devoted semesters to the comparative study and history of the exegesis of the Rabbinic literature and paid close attention to Halivni's work in the context of the modern hermeneutics of the Talmud, broadly construed. In the context of Singer's devastating comments on Halivni, the three monographs that I have brought into being, whole or in part, should be called to mind. My impression is that Halivni has so persuaded himself of the correctness of his views that he has found it unnecessary to read competing approaches just as he clearly has found it unproductive to compose a null hypothesis and to test it. In his defense, however, it should be said that what outsiders might deem to be intellectual sloth or mere self-absorption is in fact an established convention in the field of rabbinics, one that Halivni merely replicates.

[8] I deal with the Bavli in *The Bavli's One Voice: Types and Forms of Analytical Discourse and Their Fixed Order of Appearance* (Atlanta, 1991).

utilizes a single, rather limited repertoire of exegetical initiatives and rhetorical choices for whatever discourse about the Mishnah the framers of the Talmud Yerushalmi propose to undertake. The Yerushalmi identifies no author or collegium of authors. When I say that the Talmud Yerushalmi speaks in a single voice, I mean to say it everywhere speaks uniformly, consistently, and predictably. The voice is the voice of a book.

The ubiquitous character of this single and continuous voice of the Talmud Yerushalmi argues for one of two points of origin. First, powerful and prevailing conventions may have been formed in the earliest stages of the reception and study of the Mishnah, then carried on thereafter without variation or revision. Or, second, the framing of sayings into uniform constructions of discourse may have been accomplished only toward the end of the period marked by the formation of the Talmud Yerushalmi's units of discourse and their conglomeration into the Talmud of the Land of Israel as we know it. This latter possibility is pertinent to Halivni's claim that the Talmud (he speaks of the Bavli, but the Yerushalmi provides a perfectly adequate extension to his position) rests upon prior writings or traditions and that these writings or traditions are preserved in the document as we have it. Let us examine the two possibilities for explaining the Yerushalmi's authorship's uniformity of discourse.

In the former case, we posit that the mode of reasoned analysis of the Mishnah and the repertoire of issues to be addressed to any passage of the Mishnah were defined early on, then persisted for two hundred years. The consequent, conventional mode of speech yielded that nearly total uniformity of discourse characteristic of numerous units of discourse of the Yerushalmi in which a law of the Mishnah is subject to discussion. In the latter case, we surmise that a vast corpus of sayings, some by themselves, some parts of larger conglomerates, was inherited at some point toward the end of the two hundred years under discussion. This corpus of miscellanies was then subjected to intense consideration as a whole, shaped and reworded into the single, cogent and rhetorically consistent Talmud Yerushalmi discourse before us. That would seem to me to contradict the position outlined by Halivni in his exegetical work on the Bavli. Indeed, if we see this Talmud (and the other) as a work accomplished essentially in the ultimate phase of its redaction, then there can be no strong case for the authorship's extensively using and preserving prior "traditions" and "sources," in the language of Halivni. In that case, his entire exegetical program rests upon false premises. Seeing the document whole argues strongly in favor of the second of the two possibilities and hence against Halivni's fundamental hermeneutics.

As between these two possibilities, the latter seems by far the more likely. The reason is simple. I cannot find among the Yerushalmi's units of discourse concerning the Mishnah evidence of differentiation among the generations of names or schools. But a null hypothesis, that is, evidence against my position and in favor of Halivni's, would dictate that such differentiation among the putative "sources and traditions" should be much in evidence. To the contrary, there is no interest, for instance, in the chronological sequence in which sayings took shape and in which discussions may be supposed to have been carried on. That is to say, the Talmud Yerushalmi approaches the explanation of a passage of the Mishnah without systematic attention to the layers in which ideas were set forth, the schools among which discussion must have been divided, the sequence in which statements about a Mishnah-law were made. That fact points to formation at the end, like igneous rock, and assuredly not agglutination in successive layers of intellectual sediment, such as Halivni's "sources and traditions" leads us to anticipate.

Once the elemental literary facts make their full impression on our understanding, everything else falls into place as well. Arguments such as the ones we shall now review did not unfold over a long period of time, as one generation made its points, to be followed by the additions and revisions of another generation, in a process of gradual increment and agglutination running on for two hundred years. That theory of the formation of literature cannot account for the unity, stunning force, and dynamism of the Talmud Yerushalmi's dialectical arguments. To the contrary, someone (or small group) at the end determined to reconstruct, so as to expose, the naked logic of a problem. For this purpose, oftentimes it was found useful to cite sayings or positions in hand from earlier times. But these inherited materials underwent a process of reshaping, and, more aptly, refocusing. Whatever the original words—and we need not doubt that at times we have them—the point of everything in hand was defined and determined by the people who made it all up at the end. The whole shows a plan and program. Theirs are the minds behind the whole. In the nature of things, they did their work at the end, not at the outset. To be sure, the numerous examples we shall now inspect may, as I just said, yield one of two conclusions. We may see them as either the gradual and "natural" increment of a sedimentary process or as the creation of single-minded geniuses of applied logic and sustained analytical inquiry. But there is no intermediate possibility.

One qualification is required. I do not mean to say the principles of chronology were wholly ignored. Rather, they were not determinative of the structure of argument. So I do not suggest that the framers of the Talmud Yerushalmi would likely have an early authority argue with a later one about what is assigned only to the later one. That I cannot and do not expect to instantiate. I do not think we shall find such slovenly work in either Talmud. Our sages were painstaking and sensible. The point is that no attention ever is devoted in particular to the sequence in which various things are said. Everything is worked together into a single, temporally-seamless discourse. Thus if a unit of discourse draws upon ideas of authorities of the first half of the third century, such as Simeon b. Laqish and Yohanan, as well as those of figures of the second half of the fourth century, such as Yose, Jonah, Huna, Zeira, and Yudan, while discourse will be continuous, discussion will always focus upon the logical point at hand.

If Halivni were right, then principles of composition and conglomeration would prove contradictory, so that a discourse or sustained discussion of a problem would appear jerry-built and ad hoc. But any analysis of whole units of discourse, as distinct from the sentences that define the arena for Halivni's analysis, shows the opposite. Analysis of any passage beginning to end demonstrates that the whole is the work of the one who decided to make up the discussion on the atemporal logic of the point at issue. Otherwise—again the null-hypothesis that would favor Halivni's position—the discussion would be not the way it is: continuous. Rather, discourse would prove disjointed, full of seams and margins, marks of the existence of prior conglomerations of materials that have now been sewn together. What we have are not patchwork quilts, but woven fabric. Along these same lines, we may find discussions in which opinions of Palestinians, such as Yohanan and Simon b. Laqish, will be joined together side by side with opinions of Babylonians, such as Rab and Samuel. The whole, once again, will unfold in a smooth way, so that the issues at hand define the sole focus of discourse. The logic of those issues will be fully exposed. Considerations of the origin of a saying in one country or the other will play no role whatsoever in the rhetoric or literary forms of argument. There will be no possibility of differentiation among opinions on the basis of where, when, by whom, or how they are formulated, only on the basis of what, in fact, is said.

In my view it follows that the whole—the unit of discourse as we know it—was put together at the end. At that point everything was in hand, so available for arrangement in accordance with a principle other than chronology and in a rhetoric common to all sayings. That other principle will then have determined the arrangement, drawing in its wake resort to a single monotonous voice: "the Talmud Yerushalmi." The principle is logical exposition, that is to say, the analysis and dissection of a problem into its conceptual components. The dialectic of argument is framed not by considerations of the chronological sequence in which sayings were said but by attention to the requirements of reasonable exposition of the problem. That is what governs.

The upshot is simple. In these two traits the Yerushalmi's character utterly refutes the hermeneutical premises of Halivni's reading of the Talmud. First, the Yerushalmi speaks with a single, fixedly-modulated voice. Second, the Yerushalmi exposes the logic of ideas in a dialectical argument framed without regard to the time and place of the participants. In fact, the Yerushalmi (not to mention the Bavli) is like the Mishnah in its fundamental literary traits, therefore also in its history. Both documents were made up at the end, and whatever materials are used are used to achieve the purposes of ultimate redaction. Any theory of "sources" as against "traditions" will have to explain why some things were changed and some things were not changed. But all Halivni explains is that where he finds "forced interpretations," that imputed trait, which he himself fabricates or posits, identifies the "tradition" as distinct from the "source." And then the exegesis takes on its own momentum.

But, to the contrary, the literary history of the Mishnah, and, by analogy, of the Yerushalmi and the Bavli, begins on the day it concludes. Therefore there can be no distinguishing "sources" from "traditions" on the foundation of the evidence of the document, and that is the only evidence (as distinct from premise or postulate or first principles, to which, these days, intellectual discourse rarely appeals!) that we have. Accordingly, Halivni's basic mode of thought is, in a precise sense, a recrudescence of medieval philosophy, which begins not with data and inductive analysis thereof but from postulates, premises, and first principles. In the case at hand, we know that the Mishnah was formulated in its rigid, patterned language and carefully organized and enumerated groups of formal-substantive cognitive units, in the very processes in which it also was redacted. Otherwise the correspondences between redactional program and formal and patterned mode of articulation of ideas cannot be explained, short of invoking the notion of a literary miracle. Then on what basis shall we know the difference between "sources" and "traditions," unless we know without evidence that the work is composed, indifferently, of sources and traditions.

The same argument pertains to the Talmuds. The Yerushalmi evidently underwent a process of redaction, in which fixed and final units of discourse (whether as I have delineated them or in some other division) were organized and put together. The probably-antecedent work of framing and formulating these units of discourse appears to have gone on at a single period. By this I mean, among a relatively small number of sages working within a uniform set of literary conventions, at roughly the same time, and in approximately the same way. These framers of the various units of tradition may or may not have participated in the work of closure and redaction of the whole. We do not know the answer. But among themselves they cannot have differed very much about the way in which the work was to be carried on. For the end-product, the Talmud Yerushalmi, like the Mishnah, is uniform and stylistically coherent, generally consistent in modes of thought and speech, wherever we turn. That accounts for the single voice that leads us through the dialectical and argumentative analysis of the Talmud Yerushalmi.

Now let us move on to evidence. We begin with a set of instances that illustrate the fundamental traits of discourse. What we see is that the discussion is coherent and harmonious, moving from beginning to what was, in fact, a predetermined end. The voice, "the Talmud Yerushalmi," speaks to us throughout, not the diverse voices of real people engaged in a concrete and therefore chaotic argument. As in Plato's dialogues, question and answer—the dialectical argument—constitute conventions through which logic is exposed and tested, not the reports of things people said spontaneously or even after the fact. The controlling voice is monotonous, lacking all points of differentiation of viewpoint, tone, mode of inquiry and thought. That is what I mean to illustrate here. To prove this same proposition incontrovertibly, I should have to cite a vast proportion of the Yerushalmi as a whole. A few instances must suffice.

Y. Hor. 2:1

Here is a sustained discussion on the exegetical foundations of a law of the Mishnah. The voice of the Talmud Yerushalmi is undifferentiated; the entire passage concentrates on the substance of matters. A single hand surely stands behind it all, for there is not a single seam or margin. So to give an account of the matter, we must speak in the name of "the Talmud Yerushalmi." That is, "the Talmud Yerushalmi" wants to know the relationship of an anointed priest to a court, the reciprocal authority of autonomous institutions. Scripture has specified several autonomous persons and institutions or groups that atone with a bullock for erroneous actions committed inadvertently. So the Talmud Yerushalmi now raises the interesting question of the rule that applies when one of these autonomous bodies follows instructions given by another. The unit explores this question, first establishing that the anointed priest is equivalent to the community, just as Scripture states, and drawing the consequence of that fact. Then comes the important point that the anointed priest is autonomous of the community. He atones for what he does, but is not subject to atonement by, or in behalf of, others.

A. [If] an anointed [high] priest made a decision for himself [in violation of any of the commandments of the Torah] doing so inadvertently, and carrying out [his decision] inadvertently,

B. he brings a bullock [Lev. 4:3].

C. [If] he [made an erroneous decision] inadvertently, and deliberately carried it out.

D. deliberately [made an erroneous decision] and inadvertently carried it out,

E. he is exempt.

F. For [as to A-B] an [erroneous] decision of an anointed [high priest] for himself is tantamount to an [erroneous] decision of a court for the entire community.

I.A. ["If any one sins unwittingly in any of the things which the Lord has commanded not to be done and does any one of them, if it is the anointed priest who sins, thus bringing guilt on the people, then let him offer for the sin which he has committed a young bull" (Lev. 4:23-30.] "Anyone...," "If it is the high priest...,"—lo, [the Scripture would seem to imply that] the high priest is tantamount to an individual [and not, vs. M. Hor. 2:1F, to an embodiment of the community and thus not subject to a bullock-offering.]

B. [In this case, Scripture's purpose is to say:] Just as an individual, if he ate [something prohibited] at the instruction of a court is exempt, so this one [subject to court authority], if he ate something at the instruction of the court, is exempt.

C. Just as an individual, if he ate [something prohibited] without the instruction of a court is liable, so this one, if he ate something not at the instruction of a court, is liable.

D. [To encounter that possible interpretation] Scripture states, "Thus bringing guilt on the people" [meaning], lo, [the high anointed priest's] guilt is tantamount to the guilt of the entire people [just as M. Hor. 2:1F states].

E. Just as the people are not guilty unless they gave instruction [Lev. 4:13], so this one is not guilty unless he gave instruction.

F. There is a Tannaitic tradition that interprets [the matter with reference to] the people [and] the court:

G. Just as [if] the people gave instruction and other people did [what the people] said, [the people] are liable, so this one, [if] he gave [erroneous] instruction and others did [what he said], should be liable.

H. [It is to counter that possible interpretation that] Scripture states, "[If it is the high priest] who sins," [meaning] for the sin that this one himself committed he brings [a bullock], but he does not have to bring a bullock on account of what other people do [inadvertently sinning because of his instruction].

I. There is a Tannaitic tradition that interprets the [matter with reference to] the people [and] the community:

J. Just as, in the case of the people, if others gave erroneous instruction and they [inadvertently] committed a sin, they are liable, so in the case of this one, [if] others gave erroneous instruction and he carried it out [and so sinned], he should be liable.

K. [To counter that possible, wrong interpretation,] Scripture states, "[If it is the high priest] who sins," [meaning] for the sin that this one committed, he brings [a bullock], but he does not have to bring a bullock on account of what other people do [inadvertently sinning because of their instruction].

Y. San. 4:9

We find here a further instance in which the argument is so constructed as to speak to an issue without regard to the source of sayings or the definition of the voices in conversation. A question is asked, then answered, because the rhetoric creates dialectic, movement from point to point. It is not because an individual speaks with, and interrogates, yet another party. The uniform voice of the Talmud Yerushalmi is before us, lacking all distinguishing traits, following a single, rather simple program of rhetorical conventions.

II.A.   And perhaps you might want to claim, "What business is it of ours to convict this man of a capital crime?"[M. San. 4:9].

B.   It is written, "And about sunset a cry went through the army" (I Kings 22:36).

C.   What is this cry?

D.   Lo, it a song, as it is said, "When the wicked perish, there is a song" (Prov. 11:10).

E.   But, on the contrary, it also is said, "[That they should praise] as they went out before the army [and say, 'Give thanks unto the Lord, for his mercy endures for ever']" (2 Chr. 20:21).

F.   [Omitting the words, 'for he is good,'] is to teach you that even the downfall of the wicked is no joy before the Omnipresent.

Y. Mak. 1:5

Here is yet another example in which a sustained conversation on a passage of Scripture, unfolding through questions and answers, conforms to a simple rhetorical program. The voice of the interlocutor is not differentiated from the source of the respondent, for the whole is a single discourse: not a "real" conversation but, rather, an effective presentation of a simple idea is at hand.

I.A.   [Scripture refers to the requirement of two or three witnesses to impose the death penalty, Deut. 17:6. Scripture further states, "Only on the evidence of two witnesses or of three witnesses shall a charge be sustained" (Deut. 19.15). The former deals with capital cases, the latter with property cases. Since both refer to two or three witnesses, the duplication is now explained:] Scripture is required to refer to property cases and also to capital cases.

B.   For if it had referred to property cases and not to capital cases, I might have said, In the case of property cases, which are of lesser weight, three witnesses have the power to prove two to be perjurers, but two may not prove three to be perjurers.

C.   How do I know that that is so even of a hundred?
D.   Scripture states, "Witnesses."
E.   Now if reference had been made to capital cases, and not to property cases, I might have said, In capital cases, which are weightier, two witnesses have the power to prove that three are perjurers but three do not have the power to prove that two are perjurers.
F.   How do I know that that applies even to a hundred?
G.   Scripture says, "Witnesses." [It follows then the Scripture must refer to "two or three" in the context of each matter, since one could not have derived the one from the other.]

All of the units of discourse before us exhibit the same traits. In each instance we see that the conversation is artificial. What is portrayed is not real people but a kind of rhetoric. The presence of questions and answers is a literary convention, not a (pretended) transcription of a conversation. So we may well speak of "the Talmud Yerushalmi" and its voice: that is all we have. The absence of differentiation is not the sole striking trait. We observe, also, a well-planned and pointed program of inquiry, however brief, leading to a single purpose for each unit of discourse. While the various units in theme are completely unrelated to one another, in rhetoric and mode of analysis they are essentially uniform: simple questions, simple answers, uncomplex propositions, worked out through reference to authoritative sources of law, essentially an unfolding of information.

Up to this point, we have seen only that the Talmud Yerushalmi takes on a persona, becomes a kind of voice. The voice is timeless. On the face of it, the units we have reviewed can have been made up at any time in the period in which the Talmud Yerushalmi was taking shape, from 200 to 400 C.E. The uniformity of style and cogency of mode of discourse can have served as powerful scholastic-literary conventions, established early, followed slavishly thereafter. The bulk of the units of discourse, however, are not anonymous. They constitute compilations of statements assigned to named authorities. These on the surface testify to specific periods in the two centuries at hand, since the authorities mentioned lived at specific times and places. If, now, we observe the same uniformity of tone and dialectic, we shall address a somewhat more refined problem: discourse involving named authorities

The important point in the examples that follow is that while named authorities and sayings assigned to them do occur, the dialectic of argument is conducted outside the contributions of the specified sages. Sages' statements serve the purposes of the anonymous voice rather than defining and governing the flow of argument. So the anonymous voice, "the Talmud Yerushalmi," predominates even when individuals' sayings are utilized. Selecting and arranging whatever was in hand is the work of one hand, one voice.

Y. A.Z. 1:5

What is interesting in this account of the language of the Mishnah is that the framer of the entire discussion takes over and uses what is attributed to Hiyya. The passage requires Hiyya's version of the Mishnah-rule. But Hiyya is not responsible for the formation of the passage. It is "the Talmud Yerushalmi" that speaks, drawing upon the information, including the name, of Hiyya. Only the secondary comment in the name of Bun bar Hiyya violates the monotone established by "the Talmud Yerushalmi." And at the end, that same voice takes over and draws matters to their conclusion, a phenomenon we shall shortly see again. It is not uncommon for later fourth-century names to occur in such a setting.

A.   These are things [which it is] forbidden to sell to gentiles:

B.   (1) fir cones, (2) white figs, (3) and their stalks, (4) frankincense, and (5) a white cock.

A.   We repeat in the Mishnah-pericope [the version]: A white cock.

B.   R. Hiyya repeated [for his version of] the Mishnah-pericope: "A cock of any sort."

C.   The present version of the Mishnah [specifying a white cock] requires also the version of R. Hiyya, and the version of R. Hiyya requires also the [present] version of the Mishnah.

D.   [Why both?] If we repeated [the present version of the Mishnah], and we did not repeat the version of R. Hiyya, we should have reached the conclusion that the sages state the rule only in regard to a white cock, but as to any sort of cock other than that, even if this was all by itself [M. A.Z. 1:5D], it is permitted. Thus there was need for the Mishnah-version of R. Hiyya.

E.   Now if one repeated the version of R. Hiyya, and we did not repeat the version before us in the Mishnah, we should have ruled that the rule applies only in the case of an unspecified cock [requested by the purchaser], but [if the purchaser requested] a white cock, then even if this was all by itself, it would be prohibited [to sell such a cock].

F.   Thus there was need for the Mishnah-version as it is repeated before us, and there also was need for the Mishnah-version as it is repeated by R. Hiyya.

G.   Said R. Bun bar Hiyya, "[In Hiyya's view, if a gentile said, 'Who has] a cock to sell?' one may sell him a white cock, [so Hiyya differs from, and does not merely complement, the version of the Mishnah-pericope]."

H.   [Now if the gentile should say, "Who has] a white cock to sell," we then rule that if the white cock is by itself, it is forbidden, but if it is part of a flock of cocks, it is permitted to sell it to him. [This clearly is the position of the Mishnah-pericope, so there is no dispute at all, merely complementary traditions, as argued at D-E.]

Y. Sheb. 3:7

Here is yet another instance, but a more complex and better articulated one, in which topically-interesting sayings attributed to two principal authorities, Yohanan and Simeon b. Laqish, provide a pretext for a rather elaborate discussion. The discussion is conducted about what Yohanan and Simeon are supposed to have said. But the rhetoric is such that they are not presented as the active voices. Their views are described. But they, personally and individually, do not express views. Predictably, the language in no way differentiates between Yohanan's and Simeon b. Laqish's manner of speech. Only the substance of what is said tells us how and about what they differ. The reason is obvious. The focus of discourse is the principle at hand, the logic to be analyzed and fully spelled out. The uniform voice of "the Talmud Yerushalmi" speaks throughout.

A.   "I swear that I won't eat this loaf of bread," "I swear that I won't eat it," "I swear that I won't eat it"—

B.   and he ate it—

C.   he is liable on only one count.

D.   This is a "rash oath" (Lev. 5:4).

E.   On account of deliberately [taking a rash oath] one is liable to flogging, and on account of inadvertently [taking a rash oath] he is liable to an offering of variable value.

I.A.   [If someone said], "I swear that I shall eat this loaf of bread today," and the day passed, but then he ate it—

B.   R. Yohanan and R. Simeon b. Laqish—both of them say, "He is exempt [from flogging for deliberate failure]."

C.   The reason for the position of one authority is not the same as the reason for the ruling of the other.

D.   The reason for the ruling of R. Yohanan is on the grounds that the case is one in which there can be no appropriate warning [that what the man is about to do will violate the law, because the warning can come only too late, when the day has already passed].

E.   The reason for the ruling, in R. Simeon b. Laqish's view, is that [by not eating] the man is thereby violating a negative rule which does not involve an actual, concrete deed.

F.   What is the practical difference between the positions of the two authorities?

G.   A case in which he burned the bread and threw it into the sea.

H.   If you say that the reason is on the count that the man is not in a position to receive a warning, the man will be exempt [on the same grounds in the present case].

I.   But if you say that the reason is that the matter involves a negative commandment in which there is no concrete deed, here we do have a concrete deed [namely, throwing the bread into the sea].

Y. Sheb. 3:9

Here we have a still more striking instance in which the entire focus of discourse is the logic. No rhetorical devices distinguish one party to the argument from the other one. The two speak in rigidly patterned language, so that what is assigned to the one always constitutes a mirror image of what is assigned to the other. That the whole, in fact, merely refers to positions taken by each is clear in the resort to third person and descriptive language, in place of the attributive, "said."

A.   "I swear that I shall eat this loaf of bread," "I swear that I shall not eat it"—the first statement is a rash oath, and the second is a vain oath [M. Sheb. 3:9A-B].

B.   How do they treat such a case [in which a man has taken these contradictory oaths, one of which he must violate]?

C.   They instruct him to eat [the loaf].

D. It is better to transgress a vain oath and not to transgress a rash oath.

E. "I swear that I shall not eat this loaf of bread," "I swear that I shall eat it"—the first is rash oath, the second a vain oath.

F. How do they treat such a case?

G. They instruct him not to eat it.

H. It is better to transgress a vain oath by itself, and not to transgress both a vain oath and a rash oath.

I. "I swear that I shall eat this loaf of bread today," "I swear that I shall not eat it today," and he ate it—

J. R. Yohanan said, "He has carried out the first oath and nullified the second."

K. R. Simeon b. Laqish said, "He has nullified the first and not carried out the second."

L. "I swear that I shall not eat this loaf of bread today," "I swear that I shall eat it today," and he ate it—

M. R. Yohanan said, "He has nullified the first oath and carried out the second."

N. R. Simeon b. Laqish said, "He has nullified the first oath and as to the second, they instruct him to carry it out with another loaf of bread."

O. "I swear that I shall eat this loaf today," "I swear that I shall eat it today," and he ate it—

P. R. Yohanan said, "He has carried out both oaths."

Q. And R. Simeon b. Laqish said, "He has carried out the first, and as to the second, they instruct him to carry it out with another loaf of bread."

R. "I swear that I shall not eat this loaf of bread," "I swear that I shall not eat it today," and he ate it—

S. in the view of R. Yohanan, he is liable on only one count.

T. In the view of R. Simeon b. Laqish, is he liable on two counts?

U. [No.] Even R. Simeon b. Laqish will concede that he [has repeated himself] because he merely [wishes to] keep himself away from prohibited matters [and that is why he repeated the oath, but only one count is at hand].

Y. San. 5:2

The final example does utilize the attributive, with the implication that we have an effort to represent not merely the gist of an authority's opinion but his exact words. Even if we assume that before us are *ipsissima verba* of Rab and Yohanan, however, we have still to concede the paramount role of "the Talmud Yerushalmi" in the formation and unpacking of the argument. For, as we notice, as soon as Rab and Yohanan have spoken, curiously mirroring one another's phrasing and wording, the monotonous voice takes over. At that point, the argument unfolds in a set of questions and answers, the standard dialectic thus predominating once again. The secondary expansion of the matter, beginning at O, then adduces a piece of evidence, followed by an anonymous discourse in which that evidence is absorbed into, and made to serve, the purposes of the analysis as a whole. Once more the fact that each item is balanced by the next is not the important point, though it is striking. What is important is that movement of the argument is defined by "the Talmud Yerushalmi" and not by the constituents of discourse given in the names of specific authorities. The mind and voice behind the whole are not Rab's and Yohanan's, or, so far as we can see, their immediate disciples'. The voice is "the Talmud's." "The Talmud Yerushalmi" does not tire, as its tertiary explication, testing the views of each and showing the full extent of the position taken by both principal parties, runs on and on. Only at the end, with Mana and Abin, fourth-century figures, do named authorities intervene in such a way as to break the uniform rhetorical pattern established by "the Talmud Yerushalmi."

A. There we learned:
B. He concerning whom two groups of witnesses gave testimony—
C. these testify that he took a vow to be a Nazir for two spells,
D. and those testify that he took a vow to be Nazir for five spells—
E. The House of Shammai say, "The testimony is at variance, and no Naziriteship applies here at all."
F. And the House of Hillel say, "In the sum of five are two spells, so let him serve out two spells of Naziriteship" [M. Naz. 3:7].
G. Rab said, "As to a general number [the Houses] are in disagreement [that is, as to whether he has taken the Nazirite vow at all]. But as to a specific number, all parties agree that [the testimony is at variance]. [Following the versions of Y. Yeb. 15:5, Naz. 3:7: the sum of five includes two, as at M. 5:2F.]"
H. R. Yohanan said, "As to spelling out the number of vows there is a difference of opinion, but as to a general number, all parties concur that [within the general principle of five spells of

Naziriteship there are two upon which all parties concur]. [The testimony is at variance.]"

I. What is meant by the "general number," and what is meant by "counting out the number of specific vows" [the man is supposed to have taken]? [Examples of each are as follows:]

J. The general number—one party has said, "Two," and one party has said, "Five."

K. Counting out the number of vows one by one is when one said "One, two," and the other said, "Three, four."

L. Rab said, "If the essence of the testimony is contradicted, the testimony is not null."

M. And R. Yohanan said, "If the essence of the testimony is contradicted, the testimony is null."

N. All parties concede, however, [that] if testimony has been contradicted in its nonessentials, the testimony [of the first set of witnesses] is not nullified.

O. The full extent of the position taken by R. Yohanan is seen in the following case:

P. For Ba bar Hiyya in the name of R. Yohanan: "The assumption [that a loan has taken place is] confirmed [by testimony] that one has counted out [coins].

Q. "If this witness says, 'From his pocket did he count out the money,' and that one says, 'From his pouch did he count out the money,'

R. "we have a case in which a testimony is contradicted in its essentials [within the same pair of witnesses, who thus do not agree]. [This testimony is null.]"

S. Here even Rab concedes that the testimony is null.

T. Concerning what do they differ?

U. Concerning a case in which there were two groups of witnesses.

V. One states, "From the pocket did he count out the money," and the other says, "From the pouch did he count out the money."

W. Here we have a case in which testimony is contradicted in its essentials. The effect of the testimony [in Yohanan's view] is null.

X. But in the view of Rab, the effect of the testimony is not null.

Y. If one witness says, "Into his vest did he count out the money," and the other says, "Into his wallet,"

Z. in the opinion of all parties, the testimony is contradicted in its nonessentials and therefore the testimony is not nullified. [This testimony is not about the essence of the case.]

AA. If one party says, "With a sword did he kill him," and the other party says, "With a staff did he kill him," we have a case in which testimony has been contradicted in its essentials [just as in a property case, so in a capital one].

BB. Even Rab concedes that the effect of the entire testimony is null.

CC. In what regard did they differ?

DD. In a case in which there were two sets of two witnesses:

EE. One group says, "With a sword...," and the other says, "With a staff..."

FF. Here we have a case in which the testimony has been contradicted in its essentials, and the effect of the testimony is null.

GG. But in the view of Rab, the effect of the testimony is not null.

HH. One witness says, "[The murderer] turned toward the north [to flee]," and the other witness says, "He turned toward the south," in the opinion of all parties, the testimony [of one group] has been contradicted in its nonessentials, and the testimony has not been nullified.

II. The full force of Rab's opinion is indicated in the following, which we have learned there:

JJ. [If one woman says, "He died," and one says, "He was killed," R. Meir says, "Since they contradict one another in details of their testimony, lo, these women may not remarry."] R. Judah and R. Simeon say, "Since this one and that one are in agreement that he is not alive, they may remarry" [M. Yeb. 15:5B-D].

KK. Now did he not hear that which R. Eleazar said, "R. Judah and R. Simeon concur in the matter of witnesses [that where they contradict one another in essentials, their testimony is null]?"

LL. If so, what is the difference between such contradiction when it comes from witnesses and the same when it comes from co-wives?

MM. They did not treat the statement of a co-wife concerning her fellow-wife as of any consequence whatsoever.

NN. Said R. Yohanan, "If R. Eleazar made such a statement, he heard it from me and said it."

OO. The Mishnah-pericope is at variance with the position of Rab. All the same are interrogation and examination in the following regard: When the witnesses contradict one another, their testimony is null [M. San. 5:2F]. [Rab does not deem it invariably null, as we have seen.]

QQ. Said R. Mana, "Rab interprets the Mishnah-rule to speak of a case in which one witness contradicts another [but not in which a set of witnesses contradicts another such set in some minor detail]."

RR. Said R. Abin, "Even if you interpret the passage to speak of contradictions between one set of witnesses and another, still Rab will be able to deal with the matter. For a capital case is subject to a different rule, since it is said, 'Justice, [and only] justice, will you pursue'" (Deut. 16:20). [Thus capital trials are subject to a different set of rules of evidence from those applicable in property cases, of which Rab spoke above at L.]

Since this final example is somewhat protracted, we had best review the point of citing it before we proceed. The issue of the interpretation of the passage of the Mishnah, A-F, is phrased at G-H, the conflict between Rab and Yohanan. We note that the former spent most of his mature years in Babylonia, the latter, in the Land of Israel. Accordingly, considerations of geographical or institutional relationship play no role whatsoever. The language of the one is a mirror image of what is given to the other. Then the Talmud Yerushalmi takes over, by providing an exegesis of the cited dispute, I-K. This yields a secondary phrasing of the opinions of the two authorities, L, M, with a conclusion at N. Then the position of Yohanan is provided yet a further amplification, O-R. But what results, S, is a revision of our view of Rab's opinion. Consequently, a further exegesis of the dispute is supplied, T-U, spelled out at W-X, then with further amplification still, now at Y-BB. Once more we attempt a further account of the fundamental point at issue between the two masters, CC-HH, and, in the model of the foregoing exercise with Yohanan, Rab's view is carried to its logical extreme, II-JJ. The final part of the passage, tacked on and essentially secondary, allows for some further discussion of Rab's view, with a late authority, Mana, and his contemporary, Abin, QQ-RR, writing a conclusion to the whole. Up to that point, it seems to me clear, what we have is a rather elegant, cogent, highly stylized mode of exposition through argument, with a single form of logic applied time and again.

So much for probes to test Halivni's thesis against the character of the evidence at hand. When I claim that the Talmud's focus of interest is in the logical exposition of the law, here is a good instance of what I mean. The materials are organized so as to facilitate explanations of the law's inner structure and potentiality, not to present a mere repertoire of ideas and opinions of interest for their own sake. The upshot is a sustained argument, not an anthology of relevant sayings. But Halivni's theory requires the opposite, that is, an anthology of diverse materials, some changed, some not changed, from their "original" formulation. A null hypothesis offered by Halivni should turn up precisely the document as we now have it. A null hypothesis offered by me should turn up the opposite of what the Yerushalmi gives us.

Such a cogent and ongoing argument as we find characteristic of both Talmuds is more likely the work of a single mind than of a committee, let alone of writers who lived over a period of ten or fifteen decades. The role of individuals in the passages we have reviewed is unimportant. The paramount voice is that of "the Talmud Yerushalmi." The rhetoric of the Talmud Yerushalmi may be described very simply: a preference for questions and answers, a willingness then to test the answers and to expand through secondary and tertiary amplification, achieved through further questions and answers. The whole gives the appearance of the script for a conversation to be reconstructed, or an argument of logical possibilities to be reenacted, in one's own mind. In this setting we of course shall be struck by the uniformity of the rhetoric, even though we need not make much of the close patterning of language, e.g., Rab's and Yohanan's, where it occurs.

The voice of "the Talmud Yerushalmi," moreover, authoritatively defines the mode of analysis. The inquiry is consistent and predictable; one argument differs from another not in supposition but only in detail. When individuals' positions occur, it is because what they have to say serves the purposes of "the Talmud Yerushalmi" and its uniform inquiry. The inquiry is into the logic and the rational potentialities of a passage. To these dimensions of thought, the details of place, time, and even of an individual's philosophy, are secondary. All details are turned toward a common core of discourse. This, I maintain, is possible only because the document as a whole takes shape in accord with an overriding program of inquiry and comes to expression in conformity with a single plan of rhetorical expression. To state the proposition simply: it did not just grow, but, rather, someone made it up.

This view is reinforced by the innumerable instances of the predominance of logic over chronology. The Talmudic argument is not indifferent to the chronology of authorities. But the sequence in which things may be supposed to have been said—an early third century figure's saying before a later fourth century figure's saying—in no way explains the construction of protracted dialectical arguments. The argument as a whole, its direction and purpose, always governs the selection, formation, and ordering of the parts of the argument and their relationships to one another. The dialectic is determinative. Chronology, if never violated, is always subordinated. Once that fact is clear, it will become further apparent that "arguments"—analytical units of discourse—took shape at the end, with the whole in mind, as part of a plan and a program. That is to say, the components of the argument, even when associated with the names of specific authorities who lived at different times, were not added piece by piece, in order of historical appearance. They were put together whole and complete, all at one time, when the dialectical discourse was made up. By examining a few units of discourse, we shall clearly see the unimportance of the sequence in which people lived, hence of the order in which sayings (presumably) became available.

The upshot is that chronological sequence, while not likely to be ignored, never determines the layout of a unit of discourse. We can never definitively settle the issue of whether a unit of discourse came into being through a long process of accumulation and agglutination, or was shaped at one point—then, at the end of the time in which named authorities flourished—with everything in hand and a particular purpose in mind. But the more likely of the two possibilities is clearly the latter.

Let me first review a passage already set forth. It is at Y. San. 5:2. Here Rab and Yohanan both are assumed to have flourished in the middle of the third century. Placing their opinions in conflict does not violate chronology. There is a Mana who was a contemporary of Yohanan. The first Abin, a Babylonian, is supposed to have flourished about a half-century later. Perhaps Mana's saying at QQ stood by itself for a while, and Abin's at RR was added later on. But it is also possible that QQ and RR were shaped in response to one another—that is, at the same time, as yet another layer of argument. The flow of argument from Yohanan and Rab to Mana and Abin is smooth and uninterrupted. The addition at PP-RR seems to me a colloquy to be read as a single statement. If that is the case, then the whole is a unity, formed no earlier than its final element. This seems confirmed by the fact that the set at PP-RR is made necessary by the question at OO, and that question is integral to the exposition of Rab's position in toto.

Accordingly, it would appear that what we have in the names of the latest authorities is an integral part of the secondary expansion of the primary dispute. In that case, part of the plan of the whole, at the very outset, was the inclusion of these final sayings as elements of the amplification of the dispute. If so, the construction will have come into being as a whole not much earlier than the early or mid-fourth century. At the same time, we notice that the glosses of the positions of Rab and Yohanan do not reach us in the name of authorities who are assumed to have flourished prior to the times of the principal authorities. The main point must not be missed: The needs of the analysis of the positions of Rab and Yohanan, with attention, in particular, to the logic behind the view of each and the unfolding of the argument to expose that logic, explain the composition of the whole. So a clear conception of the direction and purpose of inquiry existed prior to the assembly of the parts and governed the layout of arguments and the dialectic of discourse. Let us now consider from the present perspective further instances in which the names of diverse authorities figure. What then dictates the composition of a passage? It is logic that forms the governing principle of construction, and that logic is prior to the construction and controls all components thereof.

I take as my example, among innumerable possibilities, Y. B.Q. 2:13. In this protracted discussion, we see how one authority cites another, earlier figure, with the result that the question of consistency of the view of the first authority comes under discussion. Simeon b. Laqish's interpretation of the Mishnah-passage is compared with a view of Hoshaiah, yet earlier by a generation and so cited by Simeon b. Laqish. A further discussion has Ami, slightly later than Simeon b. Laqish, interpret Simeon's view. Then an opinion of Hoshaiah— hence prior to both Ami and Simeon b. Laqish—comes under discussion. The reason is not that Hoshaiah is represented as conducting a face-to-face argument with Simeon or Ami. Hoshaiah's position is formulated quite separately from theirs. But it intersects in topic and logic. Therefore the framer of the whole found it quite natural to cite Hoshaiah's views. The context is the main thing. Ilfai-Hilfa was a contemporary of Yohanan. His position in the construction hardly has been dictated by that fact. Rather, what he has to say forms a final topic of discussion, in sequence after the view of Rab, who surely came earlier in the third century than Ilfai.

The main point bears repeating. We do not find that the chronology of authorities bears any important relationship to the arrangement of opinions. We also do not find violation of the order in which authorities flourished. The long argument has been laid out in accord with the principles of logical exposition at hand. For that purpose no attention needs to be paid to the sequence in which people may have expressed their views. But people of different centuries are not made to talk to one another.

A. "How is the tooth deemed an attested danger in regard to eating what is suitable for [eating]" [M. 1:4C]?

B. An ox is an attested danger to eat fruit and vegetables.

C. [If, however] it ate [a piece of] clothing or utensils, [the owner] pays half the value of the damage it has caused.

D. Under what circumstances?

E. [When this takes place] in the domain of the injured party.

F. But [if it takes place] in the public domain, he is exempt.

G. But if it [the ox] derived benefit [from damage done in public domain], the owner pays for the value of what [his ox] has enjoyed.

I.A. [To what does the statement, M. 2:3D-G, "Under what circumstances?" apply?] R. Simeon b. Laqish said, "It applies to the first clause. [If, in the public domain, a beast ate what it usually eats, the owner pays nothing. But if, even in the public domain, it ate clothing or utensils, the owner is liable because people commonly leave things in public domain, and the owner of the beast has the responsibility to watch out for such unusual events.]"

B. R. Yohanan said, "It applies to the entire pericope [including the consumption of unusual items, such as clothing or utensils]. [If someone left clothing or utensils in the public domain, the owner of the beast is exempt, because it is not common to leave such things in public domain.]"

C. The opinions imputed to R. Simeon b. Laqish are in conflict.

D. There R. Simeon b. Laqish has said in the name of R. Hoshaiah, "[If] an ox stood still and ate produce which was stacked in piles, [the owner] is liable." [Hence the owner of the beast is liable if the beast eats what it usually eats in the public domain. M. makes no distinction between the beast's doing so while walking along and while standing still.]

E. And here he has said that [the owner is exempt if the beast eats produce in the public domain, on the grounds that that is common.]

F. They said, "There he spoke in the name of R. Hoshaiah while here he speaks in his own name."

II.A. A statement which R. Simeon b. Laqish said: "[If there were two beasts in the public domain, one walking, one crouched and] the one which was walking along butted the one which was crouching, [the owner] is exempt [because the one which was crouching bore responsibility for changing the normal procedure, and it is not normal for a beast to crouch in public domain]."

B. A statement which R. Yohanan said: "[If] the one which was walking along butted the one which was crouching, [the owner] is liable." [The owner of the crouching beast still may ask, "Who gave your beast the right to butt mine?"]

C. [And, Yohanan further will maintain,] it is not the end of the matter that if the one which was walking along butts the one which was crouching, or the one which was crouching butts the one which was walking along, [the owner of the aggressor is liable].

D. But even if the two of them were walking along, and one of those which was walking along butted the other which was walking along, [the owner] is liable [on the same grounds, namely, while both beasts had every right to be where they were, there is no right for one beast to butt the other].

E. [Dealing with these same matters in behalf of Simeon b. Laqish,] R. Ami said, "R. Simeon b. Laqish's position applies only to a case in which a beast which was walking along butted a beast which was crouching, in which case [the owner] is exempt.

F. "But if a beast which was crouching butted one which was walking along, or one which was walking along butted another which was walking along, [the owner in either case] will be liable."

G. R. Hoshaiah taught, "In all cases, [the owner] is exempt."

H. The basis for R. Hoshaiah's position is that liability for injury done by an ox's horn does not apply in public domain anyhow. [Pené Moshe prefers to read: "This is not a case of damages done by an ox's horn in the public domain."]

I. Rab said, "If the beast stood still [in public domain] and ate up produce which was lying in piles—

J. "now they have made a lenient rule in the case of tooth, in which case an ox walking along consumed produce lying in piles [and so] standing [still],

K. "while they have made a more stringent rule in the case of damages done by the horn,

L. "in which a beast which was walking along has butted a beast which was standing still. [That is, the beast which was walking along does not impose liability on its owner for produce eaten by the way. In this regard a more stringent rule applies to damages done by the beast's horn than those done by the beast's tooth, since if the beast walking along butted one lying down, the owner is liable, while, as we saw, in the case of tooth, the owner is exempt. If, to be sure, the beast had stood still and eaten produce, also in the case of damages done by tooth, the owner is liable.]"

M. Ilfai remarked, "If the beast had stood still and eaten the produce which was lying in piles, [the owner] would be liable.

N. "Now they have made a lenient rule in the case of tooth, in that if the beast which was walking along and ate produce which was lying around, the owner is exempt from paying damages.

O. "But a more stringent rule applies in the case of damages done by the horn when a beast which was walking along butted another beast which was walking along, [and the owner in this case would be liable to damages]."

The upshot is that we may speak about "the Talmud Yerushalmi," its voice, its purposes, its mode of constructing a view of the Israelite world. The reason is that, when we claim "the Talmud Yerushalmi" speaks, we replicate both the main lines of chronology and the literary character of the document. These point toward the formation of the bulk of materials—its units of discourse—in a process lasting (to take a guess) about half a century, prior to the ultimate arrangement of these units of discourse around passages of the Mishnah and the closure and redaction of the whole into the document we now know.

Now, admittedly, the arguments that constitute the exegetical and amplificatory work of the Talmud Yerushalmi often contain names of specific authorities. These figures are assumed to have lived not only at the end of the process of the formation of the document, but at the beginning and middle as well. If we could demonstrate that these authorities really said what was attributed to them, we should be able to compose a history of the exegetical process, not merely an account of its end-product. And that is what Halivni claims in his *Sources and Traditions* to have accomplished. But as soon as we recognize the simple fact that attributions are just that—not facts but merely allegations as to facts—we realize the remarkably shallow foundations that underlie his towering construction.

We have very good reason to suppose that the text as we have it speaks within the limited context of the period of the actual framing of the its principal building blocks. As I have already pointed out, the evidence points to these traits of the writings:

(1) The building blocks—units of discourse—give evidence of having been put together in a moment of sustained deliberation, in accordance with a plan of exposition, and in response to a finite problem of logical analysis.

(2) To state matters negatively, the units of discourse in no way appear to have taken shape slowly, over a long period of time, in a process governed by the order in which sayings were framed, now and here, then and there, later and anywhere else (so to speak). Before us is the result of considered redaction, not protracted accretion, mindful construction, not sedimentary accretion, such as Halivni's theory of matters requires.

As I said at the outset, the traits of the bulk of the Talmud Yerushalmi may be explained in one of only two ways. One way is this: the very heirs of the Mishnah, in the opening generation, ca. 200-225 C.E., agreed upon conventions not merely of speech and rhetorical formulation, but also of thought and modes of analysis. They further imposed these conventions on all subsequent generations, wherever they lived, whenever they did their work. Accordingly, at the outset the decision was made to do the work precisely in the way in which, two hundred years later, the work turns out to have been done. The alternative view is that, some time late in the formation of diverse materials in response to the Mishnah (and to various other considerations), some people got together and made a decision to rework whatever was in hand into a single, stunningly cogent document, the Talmud Yerushalmi as we know it in the bulk of its units of discourse. Whether this work took a day or a half-century, it was the work of sages who knew precisely what they wished to do and who did it over and over again. This second view is the one I take. The consequence is that the Talmud Yerushalmi exhibits a viewpoint, portrayed in what I have called "the Talmud's one voice."

In claiming that we deal not only with uniform rhetoric but with a single cogent viewpoint, we must take full account of the contrary claim of the Talmud's framers themselves. This claim they lay down through the constant citations of sayings in the names of specific authorities. It must follow that differentiation by chronology—the periods in which the several sages cited actually flourished—is possible. To be sure, the original purpose of citing named authorities was not to set forth chronological lines but to establish the authority behind a given view of the law. But the history of viewpoints should be possible. As I argued earlier, it would be possible if we could show, on the basis of evidence external to the Talmud Yerushalmi itself, that the Talmud's own claim in attributing statements to specific people is subject to verification or falsification. But all that I can show is a general respect for chronology, not only authority, in the unfolding of discussion. That is, we are not likely to find in the Talmud Yerushalmi that an authority of the early third century is made to comment on a statement in the name of a sage of the later fourth century.

But the organizing principle of discourse (even in anthologies) never derives from the order in which authorities lived. And that is the main point. The logical requirements of the analysis at hand determine the limits of applied and practical reason framed by the sustained discourses of which the Talmud Yerushalmi is composed. Now it may well be that sayings not reworked into the structure of a larger argument really do derive from the authority to whom they are ascribed. But if the discrete opinions at hand then do not provide us with a logical and analytical proposition, they also do not give us much else that is very interesting. They constitute isolated data, lacking all pattern, making no clear point. The fact that Rabbi X held opinion A, while Rabbi Y maintained position Q, is without sense, unless A and Q together say more than they tell us separately.

To conclude: in a given unit of discourse, the focus, the organizing principle, the generative interest—these are defined solely by the issue at hand. The argument moves from point to point, directed by the inner logic of argument itself. A single plane of discourse is established. All things are leveled out, so that the line of logic runs straight and true. Accordingly, a single conception of the framing and formation of the unit of discourse stands prior to the spelling out of issues. More fundamental still, what people in general wanted was not to create topical anthologies—to put together instances of what this one said about that issue—but to exhibit the logic of that issue, viewed under the aspect of eternity. Under sustained inquiry we always find a theoretical issue, freed of all temporal considerations and the contingencies of politics and circumstance.

None of these traits exhibited by the literature Halivni purports to correct and explain favors his theory that the document took shape out of prior documents, some changed in the process of later (re)formulation and redaction, some not changed at all ("sources and traditions" once more), which the authorship preserved in such a way that we may identify them. Any claim, such as forms the basis for Halivni's massive exegetical exercise, that we deal with differentiable sources and traditions, contradicts the elementary facts of the Yerushalmi, and, obviously, the Bavli as well. What has gone wrong for Halivni is the simple fact that he never composed a null-hypothesis and told us what sort of evidence would prove the proposition contrary to his own. Having failed to do that, he has built the entire edifice on nothing more than the presupposition that attributions of sayings to named authorities are—must be—valid. Absent that premise, his whole hermeneutics proves hopeless because it contradicts the generative and indicative traits of the text he claims to expound. To dismiss the entire structure Halivni has erected as mere *pilpul* of the old yeshiva-type seems to me the only reasonable conclusion, and it is one that, after many years of careful study of his writings, I find myself constrained to adopt.

In responding to Halivni's claim to know the difference between sources and traditions as he defines them, let me close with my own view of how we should define, then distinguish between, sources and traditions, which forms the principal inquiry of Halivni's exegetical *oeuvre*. The Talmud of Babylonia, or Bavli, draws upon prior materials. The document was not made up out of whole cloth by its penultimate and ultimate authorship, the generations that drew the whole together and placed it into the form in which it has come down from the seventh century to the present day. The Bavli's authorship both received out of the past a corpus of *sources* and also stood in a line of *traditions* of sayings and stories, that is, fixed wordings of thought the formulation and transmission of which took place not in completed documents but in ad hoc and brief sentences or little narratives. These materials, deriving from an indeterminate past through a now-inaccessible process of literary history, constitute traditions in the sense of an incremental and linear process that step by step transmits out of the past an essential and unchanging fundament of truth and writing.

Traditions: some of these prior materials never reached redaction in a distinct document and come down as sherds and remnants within the Bavli itself. These are the ones that may be called traditions, in the sense of materials formulated and transmitted from one generation to the next, but not given a place in a document of their own.

Sources: others had themselves reached closure prior to the work on the Bavli and are readily identified as autonomous writings. Scripture, to take an obvious example, the Mishnah, tractate Abot (the Fathers), the Tosefta (so we commonly suppose), Sifra, Sifre to Numbers, Sifre to Deuteronomy, Genesis Rabbah, Leviticus Rabbah, the Fathers according to Rabbi Nathan, Pesiqta deRab Kahana, Pesiqta Rabbati, possibly Lamentations Rabbah, not to mention the Siddur and Mahzor (order of daily and holy day prayer, respectively), and various other writings had assuredly concluded their processes of formation before the Bavli's authorship accomplished their work. These we call *sources*—more or less completed writings. On that basis, what I believe to be a more critical, nuanced, and altogether productive exegetical task finds definition, one that Halivni may well wish to consider as well.

6. THREE OF ADIN STEINSALTZ'S MISCONSTRUCTIONS OF THE TALMUD

Jacob Neusner
Bard College

When Rabbi Adin Steinsaltz introduced his "Steinsaltz Talmud," he set forth a variety of points on which he misconstrues the character of the document. Here we address three of his most egregious misrepresentations in *The Talmud. The Steinsaltz Edition. A Reference Guide* (N. Y., 1989: Random House). In that book he purported to portray the document as a whole. But Steinsaltz puzzled other scholars of the same subject by his apparent ignorance of a hundred years of scholarship on the Bavli and by his claim to be the first to "discover" and present it. When various critics took issue with statements in that *Reference Guide*, to my knowledge, Steinsaltz has not taken notice of their criticism, nor has he as yet addressed the contrary propositions and the evidence adduced in behalf of those views. In a sequence of essays devoted to scholarly debate on ancient Judaism, this absence of debate is noteworthy. To advance the discussion of the issues of the characterization of the Bavli, I review three principal positions that Steinsaltz takes in his "Steinsaltz Talmud" and lay out a portion of the evidence that in those positions he drastically misrepresents the character of the Talmud. These three positions of his, stated in his own words, are contradicted by contrary propositions of mine, in the successive segments of this essay.

1. "THE TALMUD HAS NO FORMAL, EXTERNAL ORDER" VS. THE TALMUD IS CAREFULLY AND SYSTEMATICALLY ORDERED

Steinsaltz maintains that no coherent plan everywhere instructs the compilers or authors of the Bavli how to order their materials. I shall show that a strict protocol governs throughout, which Steinsaltz has not grasped. While he is unable to see the redactional considerations that account for the Bavli's inclusion of massive miscellanies—sometimes impeding systematic exposition of a given problem—we shall see that, even if the Bavli exhibits a certain miscellaneous character, in fact it follows a careful program.

2. "The Talmud Deals with All Possible Subjects in the World" vs. The Talmud Takes Up a Cogent Program

Steinsaltz alleges that the Talmud conducts a "search for truth with regard to the entire Torah—in other words, with regard to all possible subjects in the world, both physical and spiritual." That is a manifest exaggeration. But it also misrepresents matters, for I shall show that in definitive structure, in its shank, which is to say, approximately 90% of the whole, the Talmud limits its systematic exegetical work to a commentary to thirty-seven of the sixty-three tractates of the Mishnah, encompassing a broad range of data, to be sure, pertinent to that commentary. Not only does the Bavli not deal with "all possible subjects in the world," but it does not even cover all the subjects set forth by the Mishnah, the Tosefta, and the corpus of the Halakhah embodied in legal formulations associated therewith. And, as a matter of simple fact, the subjects that the Talmud takes up in a more than episodic or casual manner are dictated by the Mishnah and the Halakhah more generally.

3. "The Structure of the Talmud Is Associative" vs. The Talmud Is Carefully Structured according to a Coherent Plan

The same issue resurfaces in different ways, Steinsaltz having a problem in cogently and lucidly expressing his ideas. Now he explains the character of the document by appeal to the mnemonics: "The structure of the Talmud is associative. The material of the Talmud was memorized and transmitted orally for centuries, its ideas are joined to each other by inner links, and the order often reflects the needs of memorization. Talmudic discourse shifts from one subject to a related subject, or to a second that brings the first to mind in an associative way." He does not know what he is talking about. A manifest and coherent plan governs the unfolding of every Talmud-tractate, and it does not focus upon mnemonic but substantive considerations. In fact we can outline every one of the Bavli's thirty-seven tractates, and, when we do, we see that all of them follow a rational and coherent program, one that does not admit free-association but everywhere dictates thoughtful selection and ordering of materials.

My response to Steinsaltz's propositions therefore consists of a systematic presentation of the contrary views, with brief reprises of texts,[1] so that readers can judge whether his or my description better fits the character of the writing under discussion. In each case a far more substantial presentation of the same matter is set forth in one or another monographs of mine, and these are cited in each case. Overall, I will show that the Talmud is not merely a compilation of miscellaneous sayings and discussions. It is, rather, systematic and orderly. It is, indeed, so well crafted, with so many signals of intent and the character of the construction at hand, that we ought always to know precisely where we are in the unfolding of an exposition of a topic and the successive components of an argument.

That thesis bears the burden of proof over the contrary proposition, which is that the Talmud contains everything and its opposite and exhibits no principles of organization and order. For if so experienced a Talmud-student as Steinsaltz can make the statements that he does, we must assume he has seen only chaos, where I have discerned order. For example, Steinsaltz says, "One of the principal difficulties in studying the Talmud is that it is not written in a systematic fashion; it does not move from simple to weighty material, from the definition of terms to their use. In almost every passage of the Talmud, discussion is based on ideas that have been discussed elsewhere, and on terms that are not necessarily defined on the page where they appear."[2] He further states, "Viewed superficially, the

---

[1] Full versions are given in my *How Adin Steinsaltz Misrepresents the Talmud. Four False Propositions from his "Reference Guide"* (Atlanta: Scholars Press for South Florida Studies in the History of Judaism, 1998), part of which I reprise in this essay.

[2] Adin Steinsaltz, *The Talmud. The Steinsaltz Edition. A Reference Guide* (N. Y.: Random House, 1989), p. vii. The more I study Steinsaltz's conception of the Talmud as set forth in his general introductions to his "edition," the more I am persuaded that he does not have a clear grasp of the character of the document at all, though his representation of matters, in the tradition of the Romm edition of the Bavli, certainly has much to recommend it. But his strength lies in the explanation of words and phrases, not in the characterization of the document or in the grasp of its structure and coherence. Whether his explanation of words and phrases bears the marks of more than periphrastic erudition is for specialists in philology and exegesis to indicate; my impression is that it does not.

Talmud seems to lack inner order.... The arrangement of the Talmud is not systematic, nor does it follow familiar didactic principles. It does not proceed from the simple to the complex, or from the general to the particular.... It has no formal external order, but is bound by a strong inner connection between its many diverse subjects. The structure of the Talmud is associative. The material of the Talmud was memorized and transmitted orally for centuries, its ideas are joined to each other by inner links, and the order often reflects the needs of memorization. Talmudic discourse shifts from one subject to a related subject, or to a second that brings the first to mind in an associative way."[3] We must concur with him in his choice of adjectives, for he is right—that is the result of a very, very superficial view.

I. *"The Talmud has No Formal, External Order"*
vs.
The Talmud is Carefully and Systematically Ordered

"The Talmud...deals with an overwhelmingly broad subject—the nature of all things according to the Torah. Therefore its contours are a reflection of life itself. It has no formal external order, but is bound by a strong inner connection between [sic] its many diverse subjects."[4]

Steinsaltz's Talmud exhibits no "formal external order." Mine does, because I have outlined the entire document and every one of its building blocks and shown where each belongs and why, and he has not done so. But that does not mean Steinsaltz has no basis for his impression. On the contrary, the Bavli exhibits a certain miscellaneous quality, shows in passages no "formal, external order." And in my outline of the Talmud, I have identified those miscellanies that run-on, moving this way and that, and denying the document that clear structure that it in fact possesses. So let us begin with Steinsaltz's strongest point: the absence of a sensible, careful, systematic order.

The Talmud of Babylonia makes use of two distinct principles for the formation of large-scale composites of distinct compositions, and the framers of the document very rarely set forth a composition on its

---

[3] Ibid., p. 7.
[4] *The Talmud*, p. 7.

own, standing without clear ties to a larger context. Ordinarily, they brought together distinct and free-standing compositions in the service of Mishnah-exegesis and amplification of law originating in a Mishnah-paragraph under analysis. For that purpose they would then draw upon already-written compositions, which would be adduced as cases, statements of principles, fully-exposed analyses, inclusive of debate and argument, in the service of that analysis. So all of the compositions in a given composite would serve the governing analytical or propositional purpose of the framer of the composite. Where a composition appears to shade over into a direction of its own, that very quickly is seen to serve as a footnote or even an appendix to the composite at hand.

Let us now concentrate upon the agglutinative composites that do not conform to the norms of rhetorical form and logical cogency that impart to the Bavli its wonderful cogency. What are traits that we may discern in this kind of compilation? How are we to establish some sort of hypothesis concerning the rules, if any, that govern and so make the miscellany accessible and purposeful, within the framework of the Bavli? To answer these questions, let us turn to a sample of what I characterize as a miscellany. It is given in Bavli Baba Batra Chapter Five, starting at 72B, with the further page numbers signified in the text. I abbreviate by giving only the opening statements of each pericope of which the composite is made up.

2.A. *Our rabbis have taught on Tannaite authority:*

B. **He who sells a ship has sold the wooden implements and the water tank on it.**

C. **R. Nathan says, "He who sells a ship has sold its rowboat."**

D. **Sumkhos says, "He who has sold a ship has sold its lighter" [T. B.B. 4:1A-C].**

3.A. *Said Raba, "The rowboat and the lighter are pretty much the same thing. But R. Nathan, who was a Babylonian, uses the word familiar to him, as people use that word in Babylonia when referring to the rowboat that is used at the shallows, and Sumkhos, who was from the Land of Israel, used the word that is familiar to him, as people say in the verse, 'And your residue shall be taken away in lighters' (Amos 4:2)."*

4.A. *Said Rabbah, "Sailors told me, 'The wave that sinks a ship appears with a white froth of fire at the crest, and when stricken with clubs on which is incised,* "I am that I am, Yah, the Lord of Hosts, Amen, Amen, Selah," *it will subside [and not sink the ship].'"*

5.A. *Said Rabbah, "Sailors told me, 'Between one wave and another there is a distance of three hundred parasangs, and the height of the wave is the same three hundred parasangs. Once, when we were on a voyage, a wave lifted us up so high that we could see the resting place of the smallest star, and there was a flash, as if one shot forty arrows of iron; and if it had lifted us up any higher, we would have been burned by the heat. And one wave called to the next, "Friend, have you left anything in the world that you did not wash away? I'll go and wipe it out." And the other said, "Go see the power of the master, by whose command I must not pass the sand of the shore by even so much as the breadth of a thread:* 'Fear you not me? says the Lord? Will you not tremble at my presence, who have placed the sand for the bound of the sea, an everlasting ordinance, which it cannot pass' (Jer. 5:22).'"*

6.A. *Said Rabbah, "I personally saw Hormin, son of Lilith, running on the parapet of the wall of Mahoza, and a rider, galloping below on horseback, could not catch up with him. Once they put a saddle for him two mules, which* **[73B]** *stood on two bridges of the Rognag, and he jumped from one to the other, backward and forward, holding two cups of wine in his hands, pouring from one to the other without spilling a drop on the ground. It was a stormy day:* 'they that go down to the sea in ships mounted up to he heaven, they went down to the deeps' (Ps. 107:27). *Now when the state heard about this, they killed him."*

7.A. *Said Rabbah bar bar Hannah, "I personally saw a day-old antelope as big as Mount Tabor. How big is Mount Tabor? Four parasangs. Its neck was three parasangs long, and his head rested on a spot a parasang and a half. Its ball of shit blocked up the Jordan River."*

8.A. *And said Rabbah bar bar Hannah, "I personally saw a frog as big as the Fort of Hagronia—how big is that? sixty houses!—and a snake came along and swallowed the frog; a raven came along and swallowed the snake; and perched on a tree. So you can just imagine how strong was the tree."*

B. *Said R. Pappa bar Samuel "If I weren't there on the spot, I would never have believed it!"*

9.A. *And said Rabbah bar bar Hannah, "Once we were traveling on a ship, and we saw a fish [whale] in the nostrils of which a mud-eater had entered. The water cast up the fish and threw it on the shore. Sixty towns were destroyed by it, sixty towns got their food from it, and sixty towns salted the remnants, and from one of its eyeballs three hundred kegs of oil were filled. Coming back twelve months later, we saw that they were cutting rafters from the skeleton and rebuilding the towns."*

10.A. *And said Rabbah bar bar Hannah, "Once we were traveling on a ship, and we saw a fish the back of which was covered with sand out of which grass was growing. We thought it was dry land so we went up and baked and cooked on the back of the fish. When the back got hut, it rolled over, and if the ship hadn't been nearby, we would have drowned."*

11.A. *And said Rabbah bar bar Hannah, "Once we were travelling on a ship, and the ship sailed between one fin of a fish and the other for three days and three nights; the fish was swimming upwards and we were floating downwards [with the wind]."*

12.A. *And said Rabbah bar bar Hannah, "Once we were travelling on a ship, and we saw a bird standing in the water only up to its ankles, with its head touching the sky. So we thought the water wasn't very deep, and we thought of going down to cool ourselves, but an echo called out, 'Don't go down into the water here, for a carpenter's axe dropped into this water seven years ago, and it hasn't yet reached the bottom.' And it was not only deep but also rapidly flowing."*

13.A. *And said Rabbah bar bar Hannah, "Once we were travelling in the desert, and we saw geese whose feathers fell out because they were so fat, and streams of fat flowed under them. I said to them, 'May we have a share of your meat in the world to come?' One of them lifted a wing, the other a leg [showing me what my portion would be]. When I came before R. Eleazar, he said to me, 'Israel will be called to account on account of these geese.'"* [Slotki: the protracted suffering of the geese caused by their growing fatness is due to Israel's sins, which delay the coming of the Messiah.]

14.A. *And said Rabbah bar bar Hannah, "Once we were travelling in the desert, and a Tai-Arab joined us, who could pick up sand and smell it and tell us which was the road to one place and which to another. We said to him, 'How far are we from water?' He said to us, 'Give me sand.' We gave him some, and he said to us, 'Eight parasangs.' When we gave him some sand later, he told us that we were three parasangs off.' I had changed the sand, but I was not able to confuse him.*

B.   *"He said to me, 'Come on, and I'll show you the dead of the wilderness [Num. 14:32ff.]. I went with him and saw them. They looked as though they were exhilarated.* **[74A]** *They slept on their backs and the knee of one of them was raised. The Arab merchant passed under the knee, riding on a camel with a spear on high and did not touch it. I cut off one corner of the purpose blue cloak of one of them, but we could not move away. He said to me, 'If you've taken something from them, return it, for we have a tradition that if anybody takes something from them, he cannot move away.' I went and returned it and then we could move away.*

15.A. *R. Yohanan told this story: "Once we were traveling along on a ship, and we saw a fish that raised its head from the sea. Its eyes were like two moons, and water streamed from its nostrils like the two rivers of Sura."*

16.A. *R. Safra told this story: "Once we were traveling along on a ship, and we saw a fish that raised its head from the sea. It had horns on which was engraved: 'I am a lesser creature of the sea. I am three hundred parasangs long, and I am going into the mouth of Leviathan.'"*

B. *Said R. Ashi, "That was a sea goat that searches for food, and has horns."*

17.A. *R. Yohanan told this story: "Once we were traveling along on a ship, and we saw a chest in which were set jewels and peals, surrounded by a kind of fish called a Karisa-fish. A diver went down* **[74B]** *to bring up the chest, but the wished realized it and was about to wrench his thigh. He poured on it a bottle of vinegar, and it sank. An echo came forth, saying to us, 'What in the world have you got to do with the best of the wife of R. Hanina, b. Dosa, who is going to store in it the purple-blue for the righteous in the world to come.'"*

18.A. *R. Judah the Hindu told this story: "Once we were traveling along on a ship, and we saw a jewel with a snake wrapped around it. A diver went down to bring up the jewel. The snake drew near, to swallow the ship. A raven came and bit off its head. The waters turned to blood. Another snake and took the head of the snake and attached it to the body again, and it revived. The snake again came to swallow the ship. A bird again came and cut off its head. The diver seized the jewel and threw it into the ship. We had salted birds. We put the stone on them, and they took it up and flew away with it."*

19.A. *Our rabbis have taught on Tannaite authority:*

B. There was the case involving R. Eliezer and R. Joshua, who were travelling on a ship. R. Eliezer was sleeping, and R. Joshua was awake. R. Joshua shuddered and R. Eliezer woke up. He said to him, "What's wrong, Joshua? How come you trembled?"

C. He said to him, "I saw a great light on the sea."

20.A. *Said R. Ashi, "Said to me Huna bar Nathan, 'Once we were traveling in the desert, and we had taken with us a leg of meat. We cut it open, picked out [what we are not allowed to eat] and put it on the grass. While we were going to get some wood, the leg returned to its original form, and we roasted it. When we came back after twelve months, we saw the coals still glowing. When I presented the matter to Amemar, he said to me, 'The grass was an herb that can unite severed parts, and the coals were broom [which burns a long time inside, while the surface is extinguished].'"*

21.A. "And God created the great sea monsters" (Gen. 1:21):

B.   *Here this is interpreted, "the sea gazelles."*

22.A. Said R. Judah said Rab, "Whatever the Holy One, blessed be he, created in his world did he create male and female, and so too, the Leviathan the slant serpent and Leviathan the tortuous serpent he created male and female, and if they had mated with one another, they would have destroyed the whole world.

B.   "What did the Holy One, blessed be he, do? He castrated the male and killed the female and salted it for the righteous in the world to come: 'And he will slay the dragon that is in the sea' (Is. 27:1).

23.A. And said R. Judah said Rab, "When the Holy One, blessed be he, proposed to create the world, he said to the prince of the sea, 'Open your mouth, and swallow all the water in the world.'

B.   "He said to him, 'Lord of the world, it is enough that I stay in my own territory.'

24.A. And said R. Judah said Rab, "The Jordan issues from the cave of Paneas."

B.   *So too it has been taught on Tannaite authority:*

C.   The Jordan issues from the cave of Paneas.

25.A. *When R. Dimi came, he said R. Yohanan said, "What is the meaning of the verse, 'For he has founded it upon the seas and established it upon the floods' (Ps. 24:2)? This refers to the seven seas and four rivers that surround the land of Israel. And what are the seven seas? The sea of Tiberias, the sea of Sodom, the sea of Helath, the sea of Hiltha, the sea of Sibkay, the sea of Aspamia, and the Great sea. And what are the four rivers? The Jordan, the Yarmuk, the Keramyhon, and the Pigah."*

26.A. *When R. Dimi came, he said R. Yohanan said, "Gabriel is destined to organize a hunt [75A] for Leviathan: 'Can you draw out Leviathan with a fish hook, or press down his tongue with a cord' (Job 40:25). And if the Holy One, blessed be he, does not help him, he will never be able to prevail over him: 'He only that made him can make his sword approach him' (Job 40:19)."*

27.A. *When R. Dimi came, he said R. Yohanan said, "When Leviathan is hungry, he sends out fiery breath from his mouth and boils all the waters of the deep: 'He makes the deep to boil like a pot' (Job 41:23). And if he did not put his head into the Garden of Eden, no creature could endure his stench: 'he makes the sea like a spiced broth' (Job 41:23). And when he is thirsty, he* makes the sea into furrows: 'He makes a path to shine after him' (Job 41:24)."

28.A. Rabbah said R. Yohanan said, "The Holy One, blessed be he, is destined to make a banquet for the righteous out of the meat of Leviathan: 'Companions will make a banquet of it' (Job 40:30). The meaning of 'banquet' derives from the usage of the same word in the verse, 'And he prepared for them a great banquet and they ate and drank' (2 Kgs. 6:23).

29.A. Rabbah said R. Yohanan said, "The Holy One, blessed be he, is destined to make a tabernacle for the righteous out of the hide of Leviathan: 'Can you fill tabernacles with his skin' (Job 40:31). If someone has sufficient merit, a tabernacle is made for him; if he does not have sufficient merit, a mere shade is made for him: 'And his head with a fish covering' (Job 40:31). If someone has sufficient merit, a shade is made for him, if not, then a mere necklace is made for him: 'And necklaces about your neck' (Prov. 1:9). If someone has sufficient merit, a necklace is made for him; if not, then an amulet: 'And you will bind him for your maidens' (Job 40:29).

30.A. "And I will make your pinnacles of rubies" (Is. 54:12):

B. *Said R. Samuel bar Nahmani, "There is a dispute between two angels in the firmament, Gabriel and Michael, and some say, two Amoraim in the West, and who might they be? Judah and Hezekiah, sons of R. Hiyya.*

C. *"One said, 'The word translated rubies means onyx...'*

D. *"The other said, 'It means jasper.'*

E. *"Said to them the Holy One, blessed be he, 'Let it be in accord with both this opinion and that opinion.'"*

31.A. "And your gates of carbuncles" (Is. 60:3):

B. *That is in line with what said when R. Yohanan went into session and expounded as follows:* "The Holy One, blessed be he, is destined to bring jewels and pearls that are thirty cubits by thirty and will cut out openings from them ten cubits by twenty, setting them up at the gates of Jerusalem."

C. A certain disciple ridiculed him, *"Well, jewels even the size of the egg of a dove are not available, so will jewels of such dimensions be found?"*

D. *After a while his ship went out to sea. He saw ministering angels engaged in cutting up jewels and pearls thirty cubits by thirty, on which were engravings ten by twenty. He said to him, "He said to him, "For whom are these?"*

32.A. *An objection was raised:*

B.   "And I will lead you upright" (Lev. 26:13) —

C.   [Since the word for "upright" can be read to mean, at twice the normal height], R. Meir says, "That means, two hundred cubits, twice the height of the First Man."

33.A. And said Rabbah said R. Yohanan, "The Holy One, blessed be he, is destined to make seven canopies for every righteous person: 'And the Lord will create over the whole habitation of Mount Zion and over her assemblies a cloud of smoke by day and the shining of a flaming fire by night, for over all the glory shall be a canopy' (Is. 4:5). This teaches that for every one will the Holy One create a canopy in accord with the honor that is due him."

B.   Why is smoke needed for the canopy?

34.A. Along these same lines you may say: "And you shall put some of your honor upon him" (Num. 27:20)—but not of your honor.

B.   The elders of that generation said, "The face of Moses glows like the face of the sun, the face of Joshua like the face of the moon.

C.   "Woe for the shame, woe for the reproach!"

35.A. Said R. Hama bar Hanina, "Ten canopies did the Holy One, blessed be he, make for the First Man in the garden of Eden: 'You were in Eden, the garden of God; every precious stone was your covering, the cornelian, the topaz, the emerald, the beryl, the onyx, the jasper, the sapphire, the carbuncle, and the emerald and gold' (Ezek. 28:13)."

36.A. *What is the meaning of* "by the work of your timbrels and holes" (Ezek. 28:13)?

B.   Said R. Judah said Rab, "Said the Holy One, blessed be he, to Hiram, king of Tyre, 'I looked at you [for your arrogance] when I created the excretory holes of human beings."

37.A. *What is the meaning of* "and over her assemblies" (Is. 4:5)?

38.A. And said Rabbah said R. Yohanan, "The righteous are destined to be called by the name of the Holy One, blessed be he: 'Every one that is called by my name, and whom I have created for my glory, I have formed him, yes, I have made him' (Is. 43:7)."

39.A. Said R. Samuel bar Nahmani said R. Yohanan, "There are three who are called by the name of the Holy One, blessed be he, and these are they: the righteous, the Messiah, and Jerusalem.

B.   "The righteous, as we have just said.

40.A. Said R. Eleazar, "The time will come when 'holy' will be said
      before the name of the righteous as it is said before the name of
      the Holy One, blessed be he: 'And it shall come to pass that he
      that is left in Zion and he that remains in Jerusalem shall be
      called holy' (Is. 4:3)."

41.A. And said Rabbah said R. Yohanan, "The Holy One, blessed be
      he, is destined to lift up Jerusalem to a height of three
      parasangs: 'And she shall be lifted up and be settled in her
      place' (Is. 4:3). '...in her place' means 'like her place' [Slotki:
      Jerusalem will be lifted up to a height equal to the extent of the
      space it occupies]."

42.A. *So how do we know that the place that Jerusalem occupied was three
      parasangs?*

43.A. And lest you suppose that there will be pain in the ascension,
      Scripture states, "Who are these that fly as a cloud and as the
      doves to their cotes" (Is. 60:8).

44.A. Said R. Hanina bar Pappa, "The Holy One blessed be he
      wanted to give Jerusalem a fixed size: 'Then said I, Whither do
      you go? And he said to me, To measure Jerusalem, to see what
      is its breadth and what is its length' (Zech. 2:6).

B.   "Said the ministering angels before the Holy One, blessed be
      he, 'Lord of the world, you have created in your world any
      number of cities for the nations of the earth, and you did not fix
      the measurements of their length or breadth. So are you going
      to fix measurements for Jerusalem, in the midst of which are
      your name, sanctuary, and the righteous?'

45.A. Said R. Simeon b. Laqish, "The Holy One, blessed be he, is
      destined to add to Jerusalem [Slotki:] a thousand gardens, a
      thousand towers, a thousand palaces, a thousand mansions.
      And each one of these will be as vast as Sepphoris in its hour of
      prosperity."

46.A. *It has been taught on Tannaite authority:*

B.   Said R. Yosé, "I saw Sepphoris in its hour of prosperity, and in
      it were one hundred and eighty thousand markets for those
      who sold pudding [alone]."

47.A. "And the side chambers were one over another, three and
      thirty times" (Ezek. 41:6):

B.   *What is the meaning of three and thirty times?*

I have collected all of the miscellanies of the Bavli, and before us is only one of a fair number. Here surely is no formal order but only an inner connection, such as Steinsaltz claims to discern throughout. From the viewpoint of the Bavli overall, the anomalous traits of the conglomerate are clear: once we have left behind us the Tannaite complement to the Mishnah, there is no clear purpose or point established in what follows; No. 3 provides a talmud to No. 2, that is to say, a well-crafted expansion, in this instance explaining the word-choices of the prior item. But then we have a sequence of units that have only the most tenuous connection to the foregoing. No. 2-3 have spoken of ships, and No. 4 speaks of a ship. No. 4 does not continue No. 3 (nor does any following unit); it is parachuted down because of a shared subject, that alone. But even the subject is not a substantial point in common, since No. 4 wants to talk about ships that sink and how God participates in the matter, and nothing could be further from the frame of reference of No. 3.

What, then, are the units that do coalesce in the conglomerate that follows? Clearly, Nos. 4, 5 talk about the supernatural in connection with ships that founder at sea. No. 6 runs along the same lines, but its connection to No. 5 is not much tighter than that of No. 4 to No. 3. No. 7, however, is another matter; it shares the "I personally saw"-formula, and not only so, but what the master personally saw is a quite extraordinary thing. So we can see how the compositions at Nos. 6, 7, 8 were formed into a piece; obviously, there is no explanation for why one is prior, another later, in the sequence; but there is a tight connection among the three items. Another such set begins at No. 9: "once we were travelling and...," which is the recurrent formula through Nos. 10-18+19. Now why have Nos. 9-18+19 been linked to Nos. 6-8? No. 8 speaks of "I personally saw a frog as big as...," and the next, "Once we were travelling and we saw a fish...as big as...." So the shift is from one rhetorical formula to another, but the subject matter remains the same. That strikes me as rather deft composite-making indeed. The following items, Nos. 10-12, conform to the same pattern, talking about wonders of nature that a sage saw. No. 13 then marks another shift, however, since while the wonders of nature go forward, the fat geese are not really of the same order as the amazingly huge fish; and the lesson is a different once, namely, "Israel will be called to account...."

That this is the commencement of a new topic, joined with the prior form, is shown at No. 14. Here we retain the "once we were

traveling"-formula; but we drop the sustaining theme, big fish and
the like, and instead, we pick up the new motif, God's judgment of
Israel, now: the dead raised by Ezekiel, No. 14; and the same story
repeats the new motif, now the theme of God's judgment of Israel in
connection with the oath of Sinai. What follows at No. 15 is yet
another formula: "X told this story; once we were traveling...," and
now we revert to the theme of the wonders of nature. Have we really
lost the immediately-prior theme? Not at all, for now our natural
wonders turn out to concern Leviathan, and, later on, that theme is
explicitly joined to the judgment of Israel: the righteous will get invited to the banquet at which Leviathan will form the main course.
So Nos. 15-17 (and much that follows) turn out to link the two
distinct themes that have been joined, and, we see, the movement is
quite deft. We have a rhetorical device to link a variety of compositions on a given subject, we retain that rhetorical device but shift the
subject, then we shift the rhetorical device but retain the same subject, and, finally, we join the two distinct subjects. The theme of
Leviathan holds together Nos. 21-22+23. No. 24 is tacked on because Leviathan plays a role, and the same is to be said for Nos. 30.
The general interest in the restoration of Israel moves from the
messianic meal to Jerusalem, Nos. 31-45+46, 47. So there is a clear
topical program, and while we have a variety of subunits, these are
put together in a way that we can explain without stretching.

Had Steinsaltz outlined the composite and identified the compositions of which it is constructed, what would he have seen? To restate
this analysis in outline form, let me reproduce the outline of the
entire composite, which shows still more clearly how matters fit together:

XL. Mishnah-Tractate Baba Batra 5:1A-D

A.   He who sells a ship has sold the mast:

   1. I:1: this refers to the mast, and so Scripture says, "They have
   taken cedars from Lebanon to make masts for you" (Ezek.
   27:5).

B.   sail:

   1. II:1: bears that meaning in line with this verse: "Of fine
   linen with richly woven work from Egypt was your sail, that
   it might to for you for an ensign" (Ezek. 27:7).

C.   and anchor:

   1. III:1: Repeated R. Hiyya as a Tannaite statement: "This

refers to the anchors, in line with this verse: 'Would you tarry for them until they were grown? Would you shut yourselves off for them and have no husbands' (Ruth 1:13)."

D.   And whatever steers it:

1. IV:1: What is the source in Scripture for that statement? Said R. Abba, "This speaks of the oars: 'Of the oaks of Bashan have they made your oars' (Ezek. 27:6)."

2. IV:2: He who sells a ship has sold the wooden implements and the water tank on it. R. Nathan says, "He who sells a ship has sold its rowboat." Sumkhos says, "He who has sold a ship has sold its lighter" (T. B.B. 4:1A-C).

3. IV:3: Gloss of foregoing. Said Raba, "The rowboat and the lighter are pretty much the same thing. But R. Nathan, who was a Babylonian, uses the word familiar to him, as people use that word in Babylonia when referring to the rowboat that is used at the shallows, and Sumkhos, who was from the Land of Israel, used the word that is familiar to him, as people say in the verse, 'And your residue shall be taken away in lighters' (Amos 4:2).

E.   COMPOSITE OF SEA-STORIES OF RABBAH BAR BAR HANNAH

1. IV:4: Said Rabbah, "Sailors told me, 'The wave that sinks a ship appears with a white froth of fire at the crest, and when stricken with clubs on which is incised, "I am that I am, Yah, the Lord of Hosts, Amen, Amen, Selah," it will subside and not sink the ship.'"

2. IV:5: Said Rabbah, "Sailors told me, 'Between one wave and another there is a distance of three hundred parasangs, and the height of the wave is the same three hundred parasangs...'"

3. IV:6: Said Rabbah, "I personally saw Hormin, son of Lilith, running on the parapet of the wall of Mahoza, and a rider, galloping below on horseback, could not catch up with him..."

   a.   IV:7: Said Rabbah bar bar Hannah, "I personally saw a day-old antelope as big as Mount Tabor..."

   b.   IV:8: And said Rabbah bar bar Hannah, "I personally saw a frog as big as the Fort of Hagronia..."

4. IV:9: And said Rabbah bar bar Hannah, "Once we were traveling on a ship, and we saw a fish whale in the nostrils of which a mud eater had entered. The water cast up the fish and threw it on the shore..."

5. IV:10: And said Rabbah bar bar Hannah, "Once we were traveling on a ship, and we saw a fish the back of which was covered with sand out of which grass was growing..."

6. IV:11: And said Rabbah bar bar Hannah, "Once we were traveling on a ship, and the ship sailed between one fin of a fish and the other for three days and three nights; the fish was swimming upwards and we were floating downwards with the wind."

7. IV:12: And said Rabbah bar bar Hannah, "Once we were traveling on a ship, and we saw a bird standing in the water only up to its ankles, with its head touching the sky."

   a. IV:13: And said Rabbah bar bar Hannah, "Once we were traveling in the desert, and we saw geese whose feathers fell out because they were so fat, and streams of fat flowed under them."

   b. IV:14: And said Rabbah bar bar Hannah, "Once we were traveling in the desert, and a Tai-Arab joined us, who could pick up sand and smell it and tell us which was the road to one place and which to another."

F.   OTHER TRAVELERS' TALES

1. IV:15: R. Yohanan told this story: "Once we were traveling along on a ship, and we saw a fish that raised its head from the sea. Its eyes were like two moons, and water streamed from its nostrils like the two rivers of Sura."

2. IV:16: R. Safra told this story: "Once we were traveling along on a ship, and we saw a fish that raised its head from the sea. It had horns on which was engraved: 'I am a lesser creature of the sea. I am three hundred parasangs long, and I am going into the mouth of Leviathan.'"

3. IV:17: R. Yohanan told this story: "Once we were traveling along on a ship, and we saw a chest in which were set jewels and pearls, surrounded by a kind of fish called a Karisa-fish. A diver went down to bring up the chest, but the fish realized it and was about to wrench his thigh. He poured on it a bottle of vinegar, and it sank. An echo came forth, saying to us, 'What in the world have you got to do with the chest of the wife of R. Hanina b. Dosa, who is going to store in it the purple-blue for the righteous in the world to come.'

4. IV:18: R. Judah the Hindu told this story: "Once we were traveling along on a ship, and we saw a jewel with a snake

wrapped around it. A diver went down to bring up the jewel. The snake drew near, to swallow the ship. A raven came and bit off its head. The waters turned to blood. Another snake and took the head of the snake and attached it to the body again, and it revived. The snake again came to swallow the ship. A bird again came and cut off its head. The diver seized the jewel and threw it into the ship. We had salted birds. We put the stone on them, and they took it up and flew away with it."

5. IV:19: There was the case involving R. Eliezer and R. Joshua, who were traveling on a ship. R. Eliezer was sleeping, and R. Joshua was awake. R. Joshua shuddered and R. Eliezer woke up. He said to him, "What's wrong, Joshua? How come you trembled?"

6. IV:20: Said R. Ashi, "Said to me Huna bar Nathan, 'Once we were traveling in the desert, and we had taken with us a leg of meat. We cut it open, picked out what we are not allowed to eat and put it on the grass. While we were going to get some wood, the leg returned to its original form, and we roasted it. When we came back after twelve months, we saw the coals still glowing. When I presented the matter to Amemar, he said to me, "The grass was an herb that can unite severed parts, and the coals were broom which burns a long time inside, while the surface is extinguished.'"

G. LEVIATHAN

1. IV:21: "And God created the great sea monsters" (Gen. 1:21): Here this is interpreted, "the sea gazelles."

2. IV:22: Said R. Judah said Rab, "Whatever the Holy One, blessed be He, created in his world did he create male and female, and so, too, Leviathan the slant serpent and Leviathan the tortuous serpent he created male and female, and if they had mated with one another, they would have destroyed the whole world...."

H. WATER: CHARACTER AND SOURCES

1. IV:23: And said R. Judah said Rab, "When the Holy One, blessed be He, proposed to create the world, he said to the prince of the sea, 'Open your mouth, and swallow all the water in the world.'"

2. IV:24: And said R. Judah said Rab, "The Jordan issues from the cave of Paneas....And it goes through the Lake of Sibkay

and the Lake of Tiberias and rolls down into the great sea, and from there it rolls onward until it rushes into the mouth of Leviathan: 'He is confident because the Jordan rushes forth to his mouth' (Job 40:23)." Objected Raba bar Ulla, "This verse speaks of Behemoth on a thousand hills."

    a. IV:25: When R. Dimi came, he said R. Yohanan said, "What is the meaning of the verse, 'For he has founded it upon the seas and established it upon the floods' (Ps. 24:2)? This refers to the seven seas and four rivers that surround the land of Israel. And what are the seven seas? The sea of Tiberias, the sea of Sodom, the sea of Helath, the sea of Hiltha, the sea of Sibkay, the sea of Aspamia, and the Great sea. And what are the four rivers? The Jordan, the Yarmuk, the Keramyhon, and the Pigah."

I. LEVIATHAN AGAIN

  1. IV:26: When R. Dimi came, he said R. Yohanan said, "Gabriel is destined to organize a hunt for Leviathan: 'Can you draw out Leviathan with a fish hook, or press down his tongue with a cord' (Job 40:25). And if the Holy One, blessed be He, does not help him, he will never be able to prevail over him: 'He only that made him can make his sword approach him' (Job 40:19)."

  2. IV:27: When R. Dimi came, he said R. Yohanan said, "When Leviathan is hungry, he sends out fiery breath from his mouth and boils all the waters of the deep: 'He makes the deep to boil like a pot' (Job 41:23). And if he did not put his head into the Garden of Eden, no creature could endure his stench: 'He makes the sea like a spiced broth' (Job 41:23). And when he is thirsty, he makes the sea into furrows: 'He makes a path to shine after him' (Job 41:24)."

  3. IV:28: Rabbah said R. Yohanan said, "The Holy One, blessed be He, is destined to make a banquet for the righteous out of the meat of Leviathan: 'Companions will make a banquet of it' (Job 40:30). The meaning of 'banquet' derives from the usage of the same word in the verse, 'And he prepared for them a great banquet and they ate and drank' (2 Kgs. 6:23)."

  4. IV:29: Rabbah said R. Yohanan said, "The Holy One, blessed be He, is destined to make a tabernacle for the righteous out of the hide of Leviathan: 'Can you fill tabernacles

with his skin' (Job 40:31). If someone has sufficient merit, a tabernacle is made for him; if he does not have sufficient merit, a mere shade is made for him: 'And his head with a fish covering' (Job 40:31). If someone has sufficient merit, a shade is made for him, if not, then a mere necklace is made for him: 'And necklaces about your neck' (Prov. 1:9). If someone has sufficient merit, a necklace is made for him; if not, then an amulet: 'And you will bind him for your maidens' (Job 40:29).

J. OTHER STATEMENTS CONCERNING THE TIME OF THE MESSIAH

1. IV:30: "And I will make your pinnacles of rubies" (Is. 54:12).
2. IV:31: "And your gates of carbuncles" (Is. 60:3).
3. IV:32: Continuation of the foregoing.
4. IV:33: And said Rabbah said R. Yohanan, "The Holy One, blessed be He, is destined to make seven canopies for every righteous person: 'And the Lord will create over the whole habitation of Mount Zion and over her assemblies a cloud of smoke by day and the shining of a flaming fire by night, for over all the glory shall be a canopy' (Is. 4:5). This teaches that for every one will the Holy One create a canopy in accord with the honor that is due him."
   a. IV:34: Supplement to the foregoing.
5. IV:35: Said R. Hama bar Hanina, "Ten canopies did the Holy One, blessed be He, make for the First Man in the garden of Eden: 'You were in Eden, the garden of God; every precious stone was your covering, the cornelian, the topaz, the emerald, the beryl, the onyx, the jasper, the sapphire, the carbuncle, and the emerald and gold' (Ezek. 28:13)."
   a. IV:36: Exegesis of proof-text used in the foregoing.
6. IV:37: Said Rabbah said R. Yohanan, "Jerusalem in the age to come will not be like Jerusalem in this age. To Jerusalem in this age anyone who wants to go up may go up. But to Jerusalem in the age to come only those who are deemed worthy of coming will go up."
7. IV:38: And said Rabbah said R. Yohanan, "The righteous are destined to be called by the name of the Holy One, blessed be He: 'Every one that is called by my name, and whom I have created for my glory, I have formed him, yes, I have made him' (Is. 43:7)."

8. IV:39: Said R. Samuel bar Nahmani said R. Yohanan, "There are three who are called by the name of the Holy One, blessed be He, and these are they: the righteous, the Messiah, and Jerusalem."

9. IV:40: Said R. Eleazar, "The time will come when 'holy' will be said before the name of the righteous as it is said before the name of the Holy One, blessed be He: 'And it shall come to pass that he that is left in Zion and he that remains in Jerusalem shall be called holy' (Is. 4:3)."

10. IV:41: And said Rabbah said R. Yohanan, "The Holy One, blessed be He, is destined to lift up Jerusalem to a height of three parasangs: 'And she shall be lifted up and be settled in her place' (Is. 4:3). '...In her place' means 'like her place' Jerusalem will be lifted up to a height equal to the extent of the space it occupies."

   a. IV:42: Further as to Jerusalem in time to come.
   b. IV:43: As above.
   c. IV:44: As above.
   d. IV:45: As above.
      I. IV:46: Footnote to foregoing.
   e. IV:47: As above.

K. PURCHASE OF A SHIP: TRANSFER OF TITLE

1. IV:48: As to the transfer of title to a ship—Rab said, "Once the purchaser has dragged it any distance at all, he has acquired title of possession to the ship."

   a. IV:49: Said R. Pappa, "One who sells a bond to someone else has to give him the following document in writing in addition: 'Acquire it and everything that is indentured within its terms.'"

   b. IV:50: Said Amemar, "The decided law is that letters are acquired by an act of delivery and there is no need to write a bill of sale as well, in accord therefore with the position of Rabbi."

What we see is how the massive miscellany has been parachuted down, whole, into the systematic exegesis of the Mishnah and the Halakhah—and we also can see why, as a topical appendix, the compiler found the composite pertinent. Readers already understand that, in our setting, we should place this information in footnotes or in an appendix at the end of the book, alternatives that were not technically available to the compilers of the Talmud, or, indeed, until the invention of printing.

II. *"The Talmud Deals with All Possible Subjects in the World"*
vs.
The Talmud Takes Up a Cogent Program

"The authority of the Talmud lies in its use of this rigorous method in its search for truth with regard to the entire Torah—in other words, with regard to all possible subjects in the world, both physical and spiritual."[5]

Since Steinsaltz is an Orthodox rabbi and can be assumed to believe that "the entire Torah" encompasses the Oral as much as the Written part, in this formulation he manifestly does not write carefully. For, as a matter of fact, the Talmud does not deal with all possible subjects in the world of the entire Torah, oral and written—let alone "all possible subjects in the world, both physical and spiritual." What can he possibly mean? Let us take him seriously and assume that he wishes to make a point, which is, the Talmud talks about everything, or at least, about "the entire Torah." A glance at the volumes of A. Hyman, *Torah hakketubah vehammesurah* for the Prophets and the Writings yields the fact that Steinsaltz is wrong regarding the Written Torah, every passage of which the Talmud does not discuss. Beyond this, one moment of reflection will have told Steinsaltz that the Bavli does not pay attention to every passage of "the entire Torah," meaning the Oral as much as the written, since, of the sixty-three topical-tractates of the Mishnah, the first document of the oral part of the Torah, the Talmud deals with only thirty-seven. So what he means is not self-evident, since Steinsaltz obviously knows that the Talmud does not deal with "the entire Torah."

To deal with this misrepresentation, let us ask, does the Talmud deal with one subject? And here I shall prove that it does, which is, the subject of the Mishnah. The Mishnah dictates nearly the entirety of the Talmud's topical program. The Bavli in form and substance presents a commentary to the Mishnah (inclusive of the components of its Halakhah that the Talmud's framers choose for analysis), and, to markedly lesser degree, Scripture as well. From 80% to 99% of the

---

[5] *The Talmud*, p. 3.

composites of the tractates of the Bavli—depending on the tractate—focus upon Mishnah-exegesis. Exegesis stands for many kinds of inquiry, as many as the hermeneutics that animate the exegesis. Therefore, to form a general theory of what the Talmud says, we classify the types of exegetical compositions and composites that accomplish the paramount goal of explaining the sense and meaning of the Mishnah.

To make my point I treat in particular the manner in which the Talmud of Babylonia proposes, in Bavli-tractate Moed Qatan, to read Mishnah-tractate Moed Qatan. Defining in detail what the sages of the Bavli did, and how they did it, imparts immediacy and concreteness to the general description of their writing as "a commentary to the Mishnah." Not only so, but by showing how most of the Bavli's composites, as well as the larger part of the compositions formed into those composites, form a commentary to the Mishnah or a secondary expansion of commentary to the Mishnah, I provide in highly graphic form a clear picture of the structure of the document as a commentary, covering also secondary elaboration of its own commentaries. At the end I shall identify the principal parts of the Bavli's exegetical program for the Mishnah and specify what I conceive to be the theological propositions set forth through the exposition of details in the same way again and again.

For the most part, the Talmud of Babylonia is a commentary to the Mishnah. Let me start by giving a simple example of what characterizes the initial phase of nearly every sustained composite of the Bavli: a commentary to the Mishnah. This is what I mean by Mishnah-commentary: I mark Mishnah-citation in bold face type, Aramaic in italics, Hebrew in regular type.

MISHNAH-TRACTATE BABA QAMMA 3:1

A. **He who leaves a jug in the public domain,**

B. **and someone else came along and stumbled on it and broke it—**

C. **[the one who broke it] is exempt.**

D. **And if [the one who broke it] was injured by it, the owner of the barrel is liable [to pay damages for] his injury.**

I.1A. *How come the framer of the passage refers to begin with to a* **jug** *but then concludes with reference to a* **barrel***? And so too we have learned in another passage in the Mishnah:* **This one comes along with his**

barrel , and that one comes along with his beam—[if] the jar of this one was broken by the beam of that one, [the owner of the beam] is exempt. *How come the framer of the passage refers to begin with to a* **barrel** *but then concludes with reference to a* **jug***? And so too we have learned in the Mishnah:* **This one is coming along with his barrel of wine, and that one is coming along with his jug of honey—the jug of honey cracked, and this one poured out his wine and saved the honey in his jar—he has a claim only for his wages [M. B.Q. 10:4A-E].** *How come the framer of the passage refers to begin with to a* **barrel** *but then concludes with reference to a* **jug***?*

B. Said R. Hisda, "Well, as a matter of fact, there really is no difference between a jar and a barrel."

C. *So what is the practical difference between the usages?*

D. It has to do with buying and selling.

E. *How can we imagine such a case? If it is in a place in which a jug is not called a barrel, nor a barrel a jug, for in such a case, the two terms are kept distinct!*

F. *The distinction is required for a place in which most of the people call a jug a jug and a barrel a barrel, but some call a barrel and jug and some call a jug a barrel. What might you then have supposed? That we follow the majority usage?* **[27B]** *So we are informed that that is not the case, for in disputes over monetary transactions, we do not follow the majority usage.*

All that we have here is an investigation of the linguistic properties of the cited Mishnah-paragraph. The framer of the anonymous writing notes that a variety of other passages seem to vary word choices in a somewhat odd way. The point of insistence—the document is carefully drafted, the writers do not forget what they were talking about, so when they change words in the middle of a stream of thought, it is purposeful—constitutes an exegetical point, pure and simple.

The foregoing exemplifies Mishnah-commentary as a process of clarification. But commentators in the Bavli stand not only within the framework of the Mishnah, aiming at the explanation of what it says. They also take a stance outside of that framework, and propose to challenge its statements or their implications. To understand precisely what the Bavli means by a commentary to the Mishnah, we have therefore begun with the clear picture that the Bavli asks the questions of not only the teacher, standing inside of the document and looking outward, but also of the reader, located outside of the document and looking inward. In what follows, the stance of the commentator is external to the text, and the commentator wants to know why the Mishnah finds self-evident what is not necessarily obvious to all parties:

1:7-8/I.1A. *So if it's* **an occasion of rejoicing for the groom**, *what's so bad about that?*

B. Said R. Judah said Samuel, and so said R. Eleazar said R. Oshaia, and some say, said R. Eleazar said R. Hanina, "The consideration is that one occasion of rejoicing should not be joined with another such occasion."

C. Rabbah bar R. Huna said, "It is because he neglects the rejoicing of the festival to engage in rejoicing over his wife."

D. Said Abbayye to R. Joseph, "This statement that has been said by Rabbah bar R. Huna belongs to Rab, for said R. Daniel bar Qattina said Rab, 'How on the basis of Scripture do we know that people may not take wives on the intermediate days of the festival? As it is said, "You shall rejoice in your feast" (Dt. 16:14), meaning, in your feast—not in your new wife.'"

E. Ulla said, "It is because it is excess trouble."

F. R. Isaac Nappaha said, "It is because one will neglect the requirement of being fruitful and multiplying" [if people postponed weddings until festivals, they might somehow diminish the occasion for procreation, which is the first obligation]."

G. *An objection was raised:* All those of whom they have said that they are forbidden to wed on the festival **[9A]** are permitted to wed on the eve of the festival. *Now this poses a problem to the explanations of all the cited authorities!*

H. *There is no problem from the perspective of him who has said,* "The consideration is that one occasion of rejoicing should not be joined with another such occasion," *for the main rejoicing of the wedding is only a single day.*

I. *And from the perspective of him who has said,* "It is because it is excess trouble," *the principal bother lasts only one day.*

J. *And from the perspective of him who has said,* "It is because one will neglect the requirement of being fruitful and multiplying," *for merely one day someone will not postpone the obligation for any considerable length of time.*

What is important in understanding the nature of commentary in the Bavli is the dual stance of the commentator: inside and outside.

To generalize on the basis of the cases before us: what I mean by a commentary is a piece of writing that depends for its program—topics to be treated, coherence and cogency, alike—upon some other writing. We know the difference between a base-text and a commentary because the base-text will be cogent in its own terms, and the commentary will make sense only in relationship to the base-text. And we know the difference between the one and the other because a commentary's author will always signal the text, e.g., by citing a phrase or by a clear allusion, and will further identify what he then proposes to contribute. Commentaries in this context may take a variety of forms, but the mark of them all will be the same: they make sense only by appeal to, in the context of, some piece of writing outside of themselves. But that common trait among them all scarcely exhausts the program that a commentary will undertake—or even defines it. One type of commentary will follow a quite well-defined program of questions, another will promiscuously comment on this, that, and the other thing, without ever suggesting that the commentator has a systematic inquiry in mind. And, it goes without saying, the range of issues subject to comment—philological, historical, aesthetic, not to mention theological—can be limited only by the number of texts deemed by an author or compiler to deserve a commentary.

Nothing so establishes orderliness as order. When the Bavli's authorship, having cited a passage of the Mishnah, begins its statement, it *always* begins with attention to the cited passage. When further materials, not those of Mishnah-commentary follow, these *always* relate to the initial discussion. So while many compositions, and even some very large composites, take shape in their own terms and stand independent of the Mishnah, when they find a place in the Bavli, it is ordinarily in the framework of Mishnah-commentary, very often as a secondary expansion of what is set forth to begin with for the exegesis of what is in the Mishnah. The part of the tractate that we have examined leaves no doubt about the coherence, with a cited passage of the Mishnah, of nearly everything in the Bavli. Materials that do not cohere either with Mishnah-exegesis, or with secondary amplification of that exegesis, prove sparse indeed. When we recall that sizable components of the Bavli—numerous compositions—stand on their own and not as Mishnah-commentary, we realize how much the authorship of the Bavli has done in reframing matters to serve its distinctive purpose: nearly everything that they utilized, they presented in the framework of Mishnah-commentary and amplification. Let us now review the types of Mishnah-commentary that, over all, forms the Bavli's primary discourse. We follow the order of types of exegeses that prevails throughout the Bavli. That is, where there is analysis of the Scriptural foundations of the Mishnah's laws, that analysis will *always* take first place in the Talmud's sequence of discussions, and so on throughout.

I. *Its Rhetorical Paradigms*

1. SCRIPTURAL FOUNDATIONS OF THE LAWS OF THE MISHNAH

The single most commonplace and characteristic inquiry of the Bavli is framed in the question: what is the source of the rule of the Mishnah? Conventionally, this inquiry occurs in simple language, e.g., "What is the source of this rule," always with the implication, "in Scripture"?

2. AUTHORITIES BEHIND THE LAWS OF THE MISHNAH

A primary exegetical question concerns whether or not a law stands for an individual's opinion or a consensus of sages. The inquiry takes a variety of forms. The simplest is, "Who is the authority behind the Mishnah's [anonymous] rule?" This allows us to find out whether we have a schismatic (individual) or normative (consensual) opinion; we may further ask whether the cited authority is consistent, testing the principle behind the rule at hand against the evidence of his rulings in other cases in which the same principle determines matters.

3. MEANINGS OF WORDS AND PHRASES

We come to Mishnah-commentary of the most conventional kind: explanation of the meanings of words and phrases of the Mishnah, appealing for scriptural parallels to set forth lexical evidence, on the one side, inquiry into the sense and meaning of sentences of the Mishnah, on the other.

4. TEXT-CRITICISM. THE ISSUE OF REPETITION

The matter of text-criticism covers a variety of distinct inquiries. In the first sort, we want to know why the Mishnah frames matters as it does, with the generative issue being whether or not the document repeats itself. The type of Mishnah-commentary is signaled by a single word, "it is necessary," and what will follow is an implicit justification of presenting more than a single rule or case. This form is not limited to Mishnah-criticism; on the contrary, it is commonly used for any formulation—Tannaite or other—of a variety of cases that illustrate the same principle, and the form, brief though it is, suitably sets forth the exegetical problem to be solved.

5. CONFLICT OF PRINCIPLES IMPLICIT IN THE MISHNAH'S RULES

One important issue in the Bavli's Mishnah-commentary is whether or not two rules, intersecting in detail or in fundamental principle, cohere. A sustained effort characterizes the Bavli's inquiry into the harmony of the law of the Mishnah, the object of which invariably is to demonstrate that the Mishnah's law form a single, wholly cogent law, perfect in their harmony.

6. EXECUTION OF THE LAW OF THE MISHNAH

Here is an example of how the Bavli will ask about the way in which the law is realized, here meaning, the conditions under which the Mishnah's statement applies:

1:3/I.1A. [on condition that one not water the entire field:] said R. Judah, "If the field's soil is clay, he may water it."

B. *So too it has been taught on Tannaite authority:*

C. When they made the rule that it is forbidden to irrigate on the intermediate days of a festival, they made that statement only concerning seed that had not drunk before the festival; but as to seed that had been watered before the festival, they may be watered during the intermediate days of the festival; and if the soil of the field was clay, it is permitted to water it. And a bare field [without a crop at that time] is not watered during the festival week. But sages permit doing so in both cases [where seeds were not watered, watering a bare field].

D. *Said Rabina, "That statement leads to the inference that it is permitted to hand-sprinkle a vegetable patch during the intermediate days of a festival. For in the case of a bare field, why is it permitted to do so? It is because that renders the soil fit to be sown or planted, and here too, that is permitted."*

At stake is where and how the simple rule of the Mishnah pertains; a Tannaite formulation of the same conclusion then reinforces the proposed reading of the Mishnah's rule.

7. THE OPERATIVE CONSIDERATION BEHIND THE LAW OF THE MISHNAH

The more penetrating and abstract compositions *always* follow the Mishnah-exegetical ones, such as those just now catalogued. In my

reference system, proof is readily apparent to the naked eye: the
"operative-consideration"-compositions will *always* bear a high Roman numeral, the Mishnah-exegetical ones a low number. One of
the exegetically-productive initiatives of the Bavli will raise the question of the operative consideration that has led to a given rule in the
Mishnah. That inquiry will lead us deep into the principles that are
given expression in concrete rules, and we often see how entirely
abstract conceptions are conceived to stand behind rather commonplace laws.

8. THE IMPLICATIONS, FOR THE LAW IN GENERAL, OF THE MISHNAH'S
PARTICULAR FORMULATION

9. SETTLING THE POINT SUBJECT TO DISPUTE IN THE MISHNAH

While not a principal focus of exegetical interest, some attention is
given to settling the dispute presented in the Mishnah by a statement
of the decided law.

II. *Theological Implications*

Not only is Steinsaltz wrong, he is also misleading. For the Talmud
does not treat "everything about anything" when it comes to the
Mishnah. It follows a very economical analytical program, which we
may readily describe in a few lines. The Talmud's exegetical program when it takes up any Mishnah-tractate or paragraph therein
may be summed up in the following way. Not only so, but the exegetical program bespeaks a theological hermeneutics that animate
these specific questions. A purposive program guides the articulation
of the Talmud's entire exegesis of the Mishnah: following a prescribed order of inquiry, as set forth above, in a severely truncated
repertoire of rhetorical paradigms, the sages of the Talmud systematically investigate an economical and focused set of questions to
prove a single theological proposition. What emerges from the Bavli's
reading of the Mishnah is a statement on the character of the
Mishnah, which is presented as a supernatural writing. So the point
of the Talmud is to demonstrate the perfection of the Mishnah. A
brief statement of the upshot of each of our repeated initiatives in
Mishnah-exegesis provides the outline of an answer, though a complete answer obviously will emerge only from a survey of not a single
tractate but all thirty-seven tractates. What follows, therefore, must
be regarded as only a preliminary hypothesis of the theological implications of the Bavli's exegetical program. The sole unproved premise

in what follows is that people do not ask questions unless they know in advance they will produce not merely answers but answers that conform to a larger systemic program.

1. SCRIPTURAL FOUNDATIONS OF THE LAWS OF THE MISHNAH

The premise of this question is that every statement of the Mishnah (to which the question is addressed) can indeed be shown to rest on scriptural foundations. Hence, it must follow, the Mishnah overall states what Scripture has already said, spelling out in its details principles or conceptions that the written Torah has laid forth.

2. AUTHORITIES BEHIND THE LAWS OF THE MISHNAH

The intent of the question, "this passage is/is not in accord with Rabbi. X," ordinarily is to demonstrate that the consensus of the sages, not a private individual, stands behind an anonymous statement of the Mishnah. Where an individual is identified, a further issue will be whether his rule here is consistent in its underlying principle with a rule elsewhere that rests on exactly the same principle or its opposite. The intent is to show that sages are consistent in their rulings.

3. MEANINGS OF WORDS AND PHRASES

Scripture or common speech ordinarily provides the meaning of otherwise unfamiliar words and phrases.

4. TEXT-CRITICISM

The purpose of text-criticism is to identify flaws in the formulation of the Mishnah and generally to show that the wording of the document is flawless. This will cover proofs that the framers of the document do not repeat themselves and demonstrations that, where the Mishnah seems to say something obvious, it is indeed necessary to make that point, since, if not made explicit, the purpose of the Mishnah's statement will otherwise be lost.

5. CONFLICT OF PRINCIPLES IMPLICIT IN THE MISHNAH'S RULES

The Mishnah's rules give expression, in concrete and exemplary form, to underlying principles. A few weighty principles underlie, and come to realization, in numerous rules. Can we show that the various cases' implicit principles are uniform and harmonious? Always.

6. EXECUTION OF THE LAW OF THE MISHNAH

I see no theological issue inherent in this approach to the explanation of the Mishnah.

7. THE OPERATIVE CONSIDERATION BEHIND THE LAW OF THE MISHNAH

The Mishnah's rules, when understood in the setting of the considerations at stake in making them up, prove weighty and consequential; the stakes are always high; the operative considerations are always entirely rational and accessible, also, to our reason.

8. THE IMPLICATIONS, FOR THE LAW IN GENERAL, OF THE MISHNAH'S PARTICULAR FORMULATION

When we understand what is at issue in the Mishnah's exemplary case, we are able to settle a great many more, and larger, questions than those at hand in that case in particular. So the Mishnah addresses weightier questions than its concrete cases apparently suggest, and when we have mastered its law, we may use what we know in a broad exploration of rules not at all set forth in the Mishnah in particular.

9. SETTLING THE POINT SUBJECT TO DISPUTE IN THE MISHNAH

Where the Mishnah contains disputes, the sages of the Torah can settle those disputes; the purpose of disputes is not process but proposition, and a decision can always be made upon the conflicted proposition of the Mishnah.

If, therefore, we had to state in a single sentence the exegetical proposition, indeed the hermeneutical principle, that animates the Bavli's reading of the Mishnah, it may be stated very simply:

> the Mishnah is a supernatural writing, because it can be shown to be flawless in its language and formulation, never repetitious, never slovenly in any detail, always and everywhere the model of perfection in word and thought; the Mishnah is moreover utterly rational in its principles; and of course, the Mishnah is wholly formed upon the solid foundations of the written Torah of Sinai.

No merely human being can have achieved such perfection of language and of thought in conformity with the Torah. That is the point made, over and over again, in the Bavli's primary discourse. I cannot explain why Steinsaltz has missed the point that on many things ("all possible subjects") the Talmud says one thing, and it has to do with the perfection of the Oral, as much as of the Written, Torah at that!

III. *"The Structure of the Talmud Is Associative"*
vs.
The Talmud Is Carefully Structured
According to a Coherent Plan

"Viewed superficially, the Talmud seems to lack inner order.... The arrangement of the Talmud is not systematic, nor does it follow familiar didactic principles. It does not proceed from the simple to the complex, or from the general to the particular... It has no formal external order, but is bound by a strong inner connection between its many diverse subjects. The structure of the Talmud is associative. The material of the Talmud was memorized and transmitted orally for centuries, its ideas are joined to each other by inner links, and the order often reflects the needs of memorization. Talmudic discourse shifts from one subject to a related subject, or to a second that brings the first to mind in an associative way."[6]

So Steinsaltz, in summary, thinks that the Talmud is the product of free-association, and he says so in so many words. Until now the Talmud's exegetes could debate the simple question of whether the Bavli followed a plan of organization for its materials, and, if it did, what that plan might be. Once I undertook an outline of the Bavli, start to finish, all thirty-seven tractates, I settled that question. The Bavli is exquisitely organized, once one discerns the principles of order and recognizes the problems the sages solved in adopting those principles. Just as the Bavli as a whole is cogent, doing some few things over and over again, so it follows a simple program, start to finish. Also, just as the Talmud conforms to a few simple rules of rhetoric, including choice of languages for discrete purposes, and that fact attests to the coherent viewpoint of the authorship at the end— the people who put it all together as we have it—because it speaks, over all, in a single way, in a uniform voice, so it exhibits traits of uniformity in program and exposition.

The Talmud is not merely an encyclopaedia of information, but a sustained, remarkably protracted, uniform inquiry into the logical traits of passages of the Mishnah or of Scripture. Most of the Talmud deals with the exegesis and amplification of the Mishnah's rules or of passages of Scripture. Wherever we turn, that labor of exegesis and amplification, without differentiation in topics or tractates, conforms to a few simple rules in inquiry, repeatedly phrased, implicitly or explicitly, in a few simple rhetorical forms or patterns. A tractate of the Bavli follows a simple and lucid outline, with nearly every composition and every composite given its place for a solid, considered reason. This demonstrates beyond any reasonable doubt that, viewed whole, the Talmud is carefully and reasonably organized, and we are able to identify the principles of systematic arrangement that govern,

---

[6] Ibid., p. 7.

once we decode the system and understand the redactional problems that faced the compilers of the documents. I have completed outlines for all thirty-seven Bavli tractates and for the Yerushalmi-tractates that correspond, and then compared the outlines of the Bavli- and Yerushalmi-tractates, showing where they intersect and where each goes its own way. This work has been done. Nothing that Steinsaltz has published suggests he knows it exists. So his opinion rests on ignorance of the field in which he works: his own impressions, not other peoples' investigations, of which he is oblivious.

I maintain that through the normal procedures of reasoned analysis we may discern in each tractate a well-crafted structure. I hold that the structure made manifest, we may further identify the purpose and perspective, the governing system of thought and argument, of those who collected and arranged each tractate's composites and put them together in the way in which we now have them. By "structure" I mean, how is a document organized? and by "system," what do the compilers of the document propose to accomplish in producing this complete, organized piece of writing? The answers to both questions derive from a simple outline of the tractate as a whole, underscoring the types of compositions and composites of which it is comprised. Such an outline tells us what is principal and what subordinate, and how each unit—composition formed into composites, composites formed into a complete statement—holds together and also fits with other units, fore and aft. The purpose of the outline then is to identify the character of each component of the whole, and to specify its purpose or statement. The former information permits us to describe the document's structure, the latter, its system.

The character of the outline dictates all further analytical initiatives. Specifically, when we follow the layout of the whole, with its indentations successively indicating the secondary and tertiary amplification of a primary point, we readily see the principles of organization that govern. These same guidelines on organizing discourse point also to the character of what is organized: complete units of thought, with a beginning, middle, and end, often made up of smaller, equally complete units of thought. The former we know as composites, the latter as compositions. Identifying and classifying the components of the tractate—the composites, the compositions of which they are made up—we see clearly how the document coheres: the plan and program worked out from beginning to end. When we define that plan and program, we identify the facts of a pattern that permit us to say in a specific and concrete way precisely what the compilers of the tractate intended to accomplish. The structure realizes the system, the program of analysis and thought that takes the form of the presentation we have before us. From what people do, meaning, the way in which they formulate their ideas and organized them into cogent statements, we discern what they proposed to do, meaning, the intellectual goals that they set for themselves.

These goals—the received document they wished to examine, the questions that they systematically and in an orderly manner brought to that document—realized in the layout and construction of their writing, dictate the points of uniformity and persistence that throughout come to the surface. How people lay out their ideas guides us into what they wished to find out and set forth in their writing, and that constitutes the system that defined the work they set out to accomplish. We move from how people speak to the system that the mode of discourse means to express, in the theory that modes of speech or writing convey modes of thought and inquiry. We move from the act of thought and its written result backward to the theory of thinking, which is, by definition, an act of social consequence. We therefore turn to the matter of intention that provokes reflection and produces a system of inquiry. That statement does not mean to imply I begin with the premise of order, which sustains the thesis of a prior system that defines the order. To the contrary, the possibility of forming a coherent outline out of the data we have examined defines the first test of whether or not the document exhibits a structure and realizes a system. So everything depends upon the possibility of outlining the writing, from which all else flows. If we can see the order and demonstrate that the allegation of order rests on ample evidence, then we may proceed to describe the structure that gives expression to the order, and the system that the structure sustains.

The experience of analyzing the document with the question of cogency and coherence in mind therefore yields a simple recognition. Viewed whole, any given tractate contains no gibberish but only completed units of thought, sentences formed into intelligible thought and self-contained in that we require no further information to understand those sentences, beginning to end. The tractate organizes these statements as commentary to the Mishnah. But large tracts of the writing do not comment on the Mishnah in the way in which other, still larger tracts do. Then how the former fit together with the latter frames the single most urgent question of structure and system I can identify.

What justifies my insistence that an outline of the document, resting on the premise that we deal with a Mishnah-commentary, governs all further description? To begin with, the very possibility of
outlining Babylonian Talmud tractates derives from the simple fact
that the framers have given to their document the form of a commentary to the Mishnah. It is in the structure of the Mishnah-tractate
that they locate everything together that they wished to compile. We
know that is the fact because the Mishnah-tractate defines the order
of topics and the sequence of problems. Relationships to the Mishnah
are readily discerned; a paragraph stands at the head of a unit of
thought; even without the full citation of the paragraph, we should
find our way back to the Mishnah because at the head of numerous
compositions, laid out in sequence one to the next, clauses of the
Mishnah-paragraph are cited in so many words or alluded to in an
unmistakable way. So without printing the entire Mishnah-paragraph at the head, we should know that the received code formed the
fundamental structure because so many compositions cite and gloss
sentences of the Mishnah-paragraph and are set forth in sequence
dictated by the order of sentences of said Mishnah-paragraph. Internal evidence alone suffices, then, to demonstrate that the structure of
the tractate rests upon the Mishnah-tractate. Not only so, but the
sentences of the Mishnah-paragraphs are discussed in no other place
in the entire Talmud of Babylonia in the sequence and systematic
exegetical framework in which they are set forth here; elsewhere we
may find bits or pieces, but only here, the entirety of the tractate.

That statement requires one qualification, and that further leads
us to the analytical task of our outline. While the entire Mishnah-
tractate in any given instance is cited in the Talmud, the framers of
the Talmud by no means find themselves required to say something
about every word, every sentence, every paragraph. On the contrary,
they discuss only what they choose to discuss, and glide without
comment by large stretches of the tractate. A process of selectivity,
which requires description and analysis, has told the compilers of the
Talmud's composites and the authors of its compositions[7] what de-

---

[7] This statement requires refinement. I do not know that all available compositions have been reproduced, and that the work of authors of compositions of
Mishnah-exegesis intended for a talmud is fully exposed in the document as we have
it. That is not only something we cannot demonstrate—we do not have compositions
that were not used, only the ones that were—but something that we must regard as
unlikely on the face of matters. All we may say is positive: the character of the

mands attention and what does not. Our outline has therefore to signal not only what passage of the Mishnah-tractate is discussed but also what is not discussed, and we require a general theory to explain the principles of selection ("making connections, drawing conclusions" meaning, to begin with, making selections).

It follows that the same evidence that justifies identifying the Mishnah-tractate as the structure (therefore also the foundation of the system) of the Talmud-tractate before us also presents puzzles for considerable reflection. The exegesis of Mishnah-exegesis is only one of these. Another concerns the purpose of introducing into the document enormous compositions and composites that clearly hold together around a shared topic or proposition, e.g., my appendix on one theme or another, my elaborate footnote providing information that is not required but merely useful, and the like. My characterization of composites as appendices and footnotes signals the fact that the framers of the document chose a not-entirely satisfactory way of setting out the materials they wished to include here, for large components of the tractate do not contribute to Mishnah-exegesis in any way at all. If these intrusions of other-than-exegetical compositions were proportionately modest, or of topical composites negligible in size, we might dismiss them as appendages, not structural components that bear much of the weight of the edifice as a whole. Indeed, the language that I chose for identifying and defining these composites—footnotes, appendices, and the like—bear the implication that what is not Mishnah-commentary also is extrinsic to the Talmud's structure and system.

But that language serves only for the occasion. In fact, the outline before us shows that the compositions are large and ambitious, the

---

compositions that address Mishnah-exegesis tells us about the concerns of the writers of those compositions, but we cannot claim to outline all of their concerns, on the one side, or to explain why they chose not to work on other Mishnah-sentences besides the ones treated here. But as to the program of the compositors, that is another matter: from the choices that they made (out of a corpus we cannot begin to imagine or invent for ourselves) we may describe with great accuracy the kinds of materials they wished to include and the shape and structure they set forth out of those materials. We know what they did, and that permits us to investigate why they did what they did. What we cannot know is what they did not do, or why they chose not to do what they did not do. People familiar with the character of speculation and criticism in Talmudic studies will understand why I have to spell out these rather commonplace observations. I lay out an argument based on evidence, not on the silences of evidence, or on the absence of evidence—that alone.

composites formidable and defining. Any description of the tractate's structure that dismisses as mere accretions or intrusions so large a proportion of the whole misleads. Any notion that "footnotes" and "appendices" impede exposition and disrupt thought, contribute extraneous information or form tacked-on appendages—any such notion begs the question: then why fill up so much space with such purposeless information? The right way is to ask whether the document's topical composites play a role in the re-presentation of the Mishnah-tractate by the compilers of the Talmud. We have therefore to test two hypotheses:

> 1. the topical composites ("appendices," "footnotes") do belong and serve the compilers' purpose, or
> 2. the topical composites do not participate in the re-presentation of the Mishnah-tractate by the Talmud and do not belong because they add nothing and change nothing.

The two hypotheses may be tested against the evidence framed in response to a single question: is this topical composite necessary? The answer to that question lies in our asking, what happens to the reading of the Mishnah-tractate in light of the topical composites that would not happen were we to read the same tractate without them? The outline that follows systematically raises that question, with results specified in due course. It suffices here to state the simple result of our reading of the tractate, start to finish: the question of structure, therefore also that of system, rests upon the position we identify for that massive component of the tractate that comprises not Mishnah-commentary but free-standing compositions and composites of compositions formed for a purpose other than Mishnah-commentary.

The principal rubrics are given in small caps. The outline takes as its principal rubrics two large-scale organizing principles. The first is the divisions of the Mishnah-tractate to which the Talmud-tractate serves as a commentary. That simple fact validates the claim that the tractate exhibits a fully-articulated structure. But the outline must also underscore that the Mishnah-tractate provides both more and less than the paramount outline of the Talmud-tractate. It is more because sentences in the Mishnah-tractate are not analyzed at all. These untreated Mishnah-sentences are given in bold face lower case caps, like the rest of the Mishnah, but then are specified by underlining and enclosure in square brackets.

Second, it is less because the structure of the tractate accommodates large composites that address topics not defined by the

Mishnah-tractate. That brings us to the second of the two large-scale modes of holding together both sustained analytical exercises and also large sets of compositions formed into cogent composites. These are treated also as major units and are indicated by Roman numerals, alongside the Mishnah-paragraphs themselves; they are also signified in small caps. But the principal rubrics that do not focus on Mishnah-commentary but on free-standing topics or propositions or problems are not given in boldface type. Consequently, for the purposes of a coherent outline we have to identify as autonomous entries in our outline those important composites that treat themes or topics not contributed by the Mishnah-tractate.

Accordingly, we are able for the first time to follow how the compilers of the document put things together. We can see what program of inquiry guided their work, how they decided what comes first and what takes second place, what types of materials they utilized, and, it must follow, what types of materials they did not introduce at all. In this way a variety of long-standing questions concerning the character of the Bavli are definitively settled. Not only so, but we are now able to identify the types of compositions and large-scale composites of which the Bavli's framers made use, and that permits us systematically to study the classifications of those types, e.g., Mishnah-commentary, other-than-Mishnah-commentary, to take the two most obvious classifications of all. Not by a repertoire of examples but by a complete catalogue of all items, therefore, we can now say precisely what types of materials are used, in what proportions, in what contexts, for what purposes, and the like. Before the presentation of this outline, we did not know how many is "many," or how much is "occasionally." From now on generalizations, accompanied by reasonably accurate statements of the numbers and proportions of exemplary data, take a probative role in all study of the character and definition of the Bavli.

I have chosen as my exemplary case Bavli Horayot, because it is a brief tractate but bears within itself a fair component of composites, to be seen in context and explained there. I give the entire Mishnah-tractate and then summarize the character of the Talmud's treatment of the Mishnah-paragraphs, even isolated sentences, as we proceed.

I. MISHNAH-TRACTATE HORAYOT 1:1

A.   [IF] THE COURT GAVE A DECISION TO TRANSGRESS ANY OR ALL OF THE COMMANDMENTS WHICH ARE STATED IN THE TORAH:

1. I:1: The Talmud raises the question omitted by the Mishnah, which is, the liability of the court in such a situation.

2. I:2: Reprise of the foregoing.

B. AND AN INDIVIDUAL WENT AND ACTED IN ACCORD WITH THEIR INSTRUCTIONS, [SO TRANSGRESSING] INADVERTENTLY:

1. II:1: Why not formulate the Tannaite rule as, and an individual went and acted in accord with their instructions? What need do I have for the emphatic addition, inadvertently?

C. WHETHER THEY CARRIED OUT WHAT THEY SAID AND HE CARRIED OUT WHAT THEY SAID RIGHT ALONG WITH THEM, (2) OR WHETHER THEY CARRIED OUT WHAT THEY SAID AND HE CARRIED OUT WHAT THEY SAID AFTER THEY DID, (3) WHETHER THEY DID NOT CARRY OUT WHAT THEY SAID, BUT HE CARRIED OUT WHAT THEY SAID— HE IS EXEMPT, SINCE HE RELIED ON THE COURT:

1. III:1: What need is there to cover in the Tannaite formulation all of these several cases?

D. [IF] THE COURT GAVE A DECISION, AND ONE OF THEM KNEW THAT THEY HAD ERRED, OR A DISCIPLE WHO IS WORTHY TO GIVE INSTRUCTION:

1. IV:1: What need do I have for both categories?

E. OR A DISCIPLE WHO IS WORTHY TO GIVE INSTRUCTION: AND HE [WHO KNEW OF THE ERROR] WENT AND CARRIED OUT WHAT THEY SAID, WHETHER THEY CARRIED OUT WHAT THEY SAID AND HE CARRIED OUT WHAT THEY SAID RIGHT ALONG WITH THEM, WHETHER THEY CARRIED OUT WHAT THEY SAID AND HE CARRIED OUT WHAT THEY SAID AFTER THEY DID, WHETHER THEY DID NOT CARRY OUT WHAT THEY SAID, BUT HE CARRIED OUT WHAT THEY SAID—LO, THIS ONE IS LIABLE, SINCE HE [WHO KNEW THE LAW] DID NOT IN POINT OF FACT RELY UPON THE COURT:

1. V:1: Like whom? Simeon b. Azzai and Simeon b. Zoma.

F. THIS IS THE GOVERNING PRINCIPLE: HE WHO RELIES ON HIMSELF IS LIABLE:

1. VI:1: What case is encompassed by the governing principle beyond those already specified?

G. AND HE WHO RELIES ON THE COURT IS EXEMPT:

1. VII:1: What case is encompassed by the governing principle beyond those already specified?

2. VII:2: The governing principle represents the position of R.

Judah, but sages say, "A private party who acted in accord with the instructions of a court [and inadvertently violated the law] is liable to present an offering."

3. VII:3: The governing principle represents the position of R. Meir, but sages said, "An individual who committed a transgression by following the instructions of the court is liable."

   a. VII:4: When reckoning what forms a majority, in the case of an erroneous decision by a court, the operative criterion is the greater part of the population of the entire land of Israel.

4. VII:5: With reference **THE GOVERNING PRINCIPLE: HE WHO RELIES ON HIMSELF IS LIABLE, AND HE WHO RELIES ON THE COURT IS EXEMPT,** we now turn to the dispute concerning the kind of offering required in various situations of public inadvertent sin involving court instruction, at M. 1:5, so that, when a majority violates the law by reason of the court's ruling, they make atonement through a communal offering of a bull, but if a minority does so, it is exempt since it relied upon the court, but what about a case in which before the offering is presented, the community's numbers diminish so that the ratio of transgressors to non-transgressors has changed? If the number of transgressors was a minority but through deaths in the interim became a majority of the community, what is the law?

5. VII:6: If the court gave the decision that suet is permitted , and a minority of the community went and acted in accord with that decision, and then the court retracted and gave correct instructions, and the court once more gave the decision that suet is permitted, but now a different minority of the community acted, what is the law?

6. VII:7: If the court gave instructions that suet is permitted, and a minority of the community went and acted in accord with that instruction, and then that court died, but another court was appointed and they retracted, but then they issued a new instruction to the same effect, and another minority acted in accord with the new instruction of this new court, what is the law?

7. VII:8: In a case in which a hundred who went into session to give instruction, liability for judicial error is incurred only if all of them will give that instruction, as it is said, "And if all

of the assembly shall err" (Lev. 4:13)—the court is exempt
unless everyone of them errs, meaning, unless their instruction has permeated throughout the community of Israel.

   a. VII:9: When ten sit in judgment, the chain of responsibil-
     ity is suspended on the necks of all of them.

      I. VII:10: R Huna: when he would go to court, he would
        bring with him from the school house ten Tannaite-
        tradition-memorizers, "so that each one of us may
        carry a chip of the beam."

      II. VII:11: R. Ashi: same saying based on a different
        story.

II. MISHNAH-TRACTATE HORAYOT 1:2-3

A.   [IF] THE COURT GAVE A DECISION AND REALIZED THAT IT HAD
ERRED AND RETRACTED, WHETHER THEY BROUGHT THEIR ATONE-
MENT OFFERING OR DID NOT BRING THEIR ATONEMENT OFFERING,
AND AN INDIVIDUAL DID IN ACCORD WITH THEIR INSTRUCTION—
R. SIMEON DECLARES HIM EXEMPT. AND R. ELIEZER SAYS, "IT IS
SUBJECT TO DOUBT."

   1. I:1: What is the operative consideration behind the ruling of
     R. Simeon?

   2. I:2: Tannaite version of the dispute and various opinions on
     the same matter as is treated in the Mishnah.

B.   WHAT IS THE DOUBT? [IF] THE PERSON HAD STAYED HOME, HE IS
LIABLE. [IF] HE HAD GONE OVERSEAS, HE IS EXEMPT. SAID R.
AQIBA, "I CONCEDE IN THIS CASE THAT HE IS NIGH UNTO BEING
EXEMPT FROM LIABILITY" SAID TO HIM BEN AZZAI, "WHAT IS
THE DIFFERENCE BETWEEN THIS ONE AND ONE WHO STAYS
HOME?" FOR THE ONE WHO STAYS HOME HAD THE POSSIBILITY
OF HEARING [THAT THE COURT HAD ERRED AND RETRACTED],
BUT THIS ONE DID NOT HAVE THE POSSIBILITY OF HEARING [WHAT
HAD HAPPENED]:"

   1. II:1: Did R. Aqiba make a valid statement to Ben Azzai?

C.   [IF] A COURT GAVE A DECISION TO UPROOT THE WHOLE PRINCI-
PLE [OF THE TORAH],
(1) [IF] THEY SAID, "[THE PROHIBITION AGAINST HAVING INTER-
COURSE WITH] A MENSTRUATING WOMAN IS NOT IN THE TORAH
[LEV. 15:19]." (2) "[THE PROHIBITION OF LABOR ON] THE SAB-
BATH IS NOT IN THE TORAH." (3) "[THE PROHIBITION AGAINST]
IDOLATRY IS NOT IN THE TORAH." LO, THESE ARE EXEMPT
[FROM THE REQUIREMENT OF LEV. 4:14].

      1. III:1: Tannaite proof of the proposition on the basis of
         Scripture.
         a. III:2: development of foregoing.
            i. III:3: as above.

D.   [IF] THEY GAVE INSTRUCTION TO NULLIFY PART AND TO CARRY OUT PART [OF A RULE OF THE TORAH], LO, THEY ARE LIABLE. HOW SO? [IF] THEY SAID, 'THE PRINCIPLE OF PROHIBITION OF SEXUAL RELATIONSHIPS WITH A MENSTRUATING WOMAN INDEED IS IN THE TORAH, BUT HE WHO HAS SEXUAL RELATIONS WITH A WOMAN AWAITING DAY AGAINST DAY IS EXEMPT." (2) "THE PRINCIPLE OF NOT WORKING ON THE SABBATH IS IN THE TORAH, BUT HE WHO TAKES OUT SOMETHING FROM PRIVATE DOMAIN TO PUBLIC DOMAIN IS EXEMPT." (3) "THE PRINCIPLE OF NOT WORSHIPPING IDOLS IS IN THE TORAH BUT HE WHO BOWS DOWN [TO AN IDOL] IS EXEMPT."—LO, THESE ARE LIABLE, SINCE IT IS SAID, "IF SOMETHING BE HIDDEN" (LEV. 4:13)—SOMETHING, AND NOT EVERYTHING:

      1. IV:1: The court is liable only if it gives wrong instruction in
         a matter that the Sadducees do not accept as a matter of
         revelation [that is, the oral Torah]. But in a matter that the
         Sadducees too concede, the court is exempt.
      2. IV:2: If the court announced that there is no prohibition
         against plowing on the Sabbath [vs. Ex. 34:21], what is the
         law?
      3. IV:3: If the court announced that there is no prohibition in
         the Torah against working on the Sabbath during the Sabbatical Year, what is the law?

III. MISHNAH-TRACTATE HORAYOT 1:4A-G

A.   (1) [IF] THE COURT GAVE A DECISION, AND ONE OF THE MEMBERS OF THE COURT REALIZED THAT THEY HAD ERRED AND SAID TO THEM, "YOU ARE IN ERROR,"

    OR (2) IF THE HEAD OF THE COURT WAS NOT THERE,

    OR (3) IF ONE OF THEM WAS A PROSELYTE, A MAMZER, A NETIN, OR AN ELDER WHO DID NOT HAVE CHILDREN—LO, THESE ARE EXEMPT [FROM A PUBLIC OFFERING UNDER THE PROVISIONS OF LEV. 4:14],

      1. I:1: how on the basis of Scripture do we know this fact?

B.   SINCE "CONGREGATION" IS SAID HERE [LEV. 4:13], AND "CONGREGATION" IS SAID LATER ON [NUM. 15:24]. JUST AS "CONGREGATION" LATER ON APPLIES ONLY IN THE CASE IN WHICH ALL

OF THEM ARE SUITABLE FOR MAKING A DECISION, SO "CONGREGA-
TION" STATED HERE REFERS TO A CASE IN WHICH ALL OF THEM
ARE SUITABLE FOR MAKING A DECISION:

1. II:1: As to the locus classicus of the proof, how do we know
   that fact to begin with?

IV. MISHNAH-TRACTATE HORAYOT 1:4H-L

A. [IF] THE COURT GAVE AN INCORRECT DECISION INADVERTENTLY,
    AND THE ENTIRE COMMUNITY FOLLOWED THEIR INSTRUCTION
    [AND DID THE THING IN ERROR] INADVERTENTLY, THEY BRING A
    BULLOCK. [IF THE COURT GAVE AN INCORRECT DECISION] DELIB-
    ERATELY, BUT THE COMMUNITY, FOLLOWING THEIR INSTRUCTION,
    DID THE THING IN ERROR] INADVERTENTLY, THEY BRING A LAMB
    OR A GOAT (LEV. 4:32, 27).

    [IF THE COURT GAVE INCORRECT INSTRUCTION] INADVERTENTLY,
    AND [THE COMMUNITY FOLLOWED THEIR INSTRUCTION AND DID
    THE THING IN ERROR] DELIBERATELY, LO, THESE ARE EXEMPT
    [UNDER THE PROVISIONS OF LEV. 4:4].

1. I:1: the one who inadvertently violated the law who is liable
   is equivalent to the one who intentionally violated the law in
   that both know the court to be in error yet only the latter
   does not present an atonement offering.

V. MISHNAH-TRACTATE HORAYOT 1:4

A. "[IF] THE COURT MADE AN [ERRONEOUS] DECISION, AND THE
    ENTIRE COMMUNITY, OR THE GREATER PART OF THE COMMUNITY,
    CARRIED OUT THEIR DECISION, THEY BRING A BULLOCK. IN THE
    CASE OF IDOLATRY, THEY BRING A BULLOCK AND A GOAT," THE
    WORDS OF R. MEIR. R. JUDAH SAYS, "TWELVE TRIBES BRING
    TWELVE BULLOCKS. AND IN THE CASE OF IDOLATRY, THEY BRING
    TWELVE BULLOCKS AND TWELVE GOATS." R. SIMEON SAYS,
    "THIRTEEN BULLOCKS, AND IN THE CASE OF IDOLATRY, THIRTEEN
    BULLOCKS AND THIRTEEN GOATS: A BULLOCK AND A GOAT FOR
    EACH AND EVERY TRIBE, AND [IN ADDITION] A BULLOCK AND A
    GOAT FOR THE COURT." "[IF] THE COURT GAVE AN [ERRONE-
    OUS] DECISION, AND SEVEN TRIBES, OR THE GREATER PART OF
    SEVEN TRIBES, CARRIED OUT THEIR DECISION, THEY BRING A BUL-
    LOCK. IN THE CASE OF IDOLATRY, THEY BRING A BULLOCK AND A
    GOAT," THE WORDS OF R. MEIR. R. JUDAH SAYS, "SEVEN TRIBES
    WHICH COMMITTED A SIN BRING SEVEN BULLOCKS. AND THE
    OTHER TRIBES, WHO COMMITTED NO SIN, BRING A BULLOCK IN
    THEIR BEHALF, FOR EVEN THOSE WHO DID NOT SIN BRING AN

OFFERING ON ACCOUNT OF THE SINNERS." R. SIMEON SAYS,
"EIGHT BULLOCKS, AND IN THE CASE OF IDOLATRY, EIGHT BUL-
LOCKS AND EIGHT GOATS: A BULLOCK AND A GOAT FOR EACH AND
EVERY TRIBE, AND A BULLOCK AND A GOAT FOR THE COURT."

1. I:1: Tannaite formulation of the matter.
   a. I:2: Who is the Tannaite authority who holds the posi-
      tion, Scripture says, "when the sin through which they
      incurred guilt becomes known,—not that the sinners
      should be made known?
   b. I:3: What is the scriptural basis for the positions of Judah,
      Simeon, and Meir of I:1?

B. "[IF] THE COURT OF ONE OF THE TRIBES GAVE AN [ERRONEOUS]
    DECISION, AND THAT TRIBE [ONLY] CARRIED OUT THEIR DECI-
    SION, THAT TRIBE IS LIABLE, AND ALL THE OTHER TRIBES ARE
    EXEMPT," THE WORDS OF R. JUDAH. AND SAGES SAY, "THEY ARE
    LIABLE ONLY BY REASON OF AN [ERRONEOUS] DECISION MADE BY
    THE HIGH COURT ALONE, AS IT IS SAID, 'AND IF THE WHOLE
    CONGREGATION OF ISRAEL SHALL ERR (LEV. 4:13)—AND NOT
    THE CONGREGATION OF THAT TRIBE [ALONE].'"

1. II:1: The question was raised: in R. Judah's opinion, if a
   single tribe commits a transgression on account of the instruction of the high court, do the rest of the tribes have to
   present offerings as well, or do they not have to do so?
2. II:2: The question was raised: in R. Simeon's opinion, if the
   law violation is done on the instructions of the high court, do
   they present an offering or not?
3. II:3: As to R. Judah and R. Simeon, who maintain that a
   single tribe may be classified as "the community," where in
   Scripture do they find proof for their position?
4. II:4: "They that had come from the captives of the exile
   offered up whole-offerings to the God of Israel, twelve bullocks for all Israel, ninety-nine rams, seventy-seven lambs,
   and, as a purification-offering, twelve he goats, all this as a
   burnt-offering for the Lord" (Ezra 8:35). In line with the
   Judah's, Simeon's, and Meir's positions at hand, how would
   we explain the requirement of these twelve bullocks?
5. II:5: If the court gave instructions in error but the members
   knew that they had erred and they retracted the ruling after
   the community had transgressed, but if one of the public has
   died before the offering was made, they are required to

present it in any event. If one of the court died, they are exempt. Who is the Tannaite authority behind this ruling?

VI. MISHNAH-TRACTATE HORAYOT 2:1

A. [IF] AN ANOINTED [HIGH] PRIEST MADE A DECISION FOR HIMSELF [IN VIOLATION OF ANY OF THE COMMANDMENTS OF THE TORAH], DOING SO INADVERTENTLY, AND CARRYING OUT [HIS DECISION] INADVERTENTLY, HE BRINGS A BULLOCK (LEV. 4:3).

   1. I:1:With what case do we deal? It is a case in which he gave instruction and forgot on what grounds he had given the instruction, and at the moment at which he erred, he said, 'Lo, I act on the basis of my instruction.' Now what might you have supposed? Since, if he realized the facts of the situation, he might have retracted, he is in the situation of one who acts deliberately and should not therefore be obligated under the present count. So we are informed that that is not the case.

B. [IF] HE [MADE AN ERRONEOUS DECISION] INADVERTENTLY, AND DELIBERATELY CARRIED IT OUT, DELIBERATELY [MADE AN ERRONEOUS DECISION] AND INADVERTENTLY CARRIED IT OUT, HE IS EXEMPT. FOR AN [ERRONEOUS] DECISION OF AN ANOINTED [HIGH] PRIEST FOR HIMSELF IS TANTAMOUNT TO AN [ERRONEOUS] DECISION OF A COURT FOR THE ENTIRE COMMUNITY.

   1. II:1: What is the source in Scripture for this ruling?
   a. II:2: Amplification of the foregoing.

VII. MISHNAH-TRACTATE HORAYOT 2:2

A. [IF] HE MADE AN [ERRONEOUS] DECISION BY HIMSELF AND CARRIED IT OUT BY HIMSELF, HE EFFECTS ATONEMENT FOR HIMSELF BY HIMSELF.

   1. I:1: What is the source of this ruling [that the anointed priest's atonement procedure is determined by the context of his error]?
   2. I:2: How can we imagine a case of his doing so?
   3. I:3: theoretical problem based on foregoing.

B. [IF] HE MADE [AN ERRONEOUS] DECISION WITH THE COMMUNITY AND CARRIED IT OUT WITH THE COMMUNITY, HE EFFECTS ATONEMENT FOR HIMSELF WITH THE COMMUNITY. FOR A COURT IS NOT LIABLE UNTIL IT WILL GIVE AN ERRONEOUS DECISION TO NULLIFY PART AND TO CARRY OUT PART [OF THE TEACHINGS OF THE TORAH]:

   1. II:1: How on the basis of Scripture do we know it is the fact

that a court is not liable until it will give an erroneous decision to nullify part and to carry out part [of the teachings of the Torah],

C. **AND SO IS THE RULE FOR AN ANOINTED [HIGH PRIEST]:**
1. III:1: How on the basis of Scripture do we know this fact?

D. **AND [THEY] ARE NOT [LIABLE] IN THE CASE OF IDOLATRY [SUBJECT TO AN ERRONEOUS DECISION] UNLESS THEY GIVE A DECISION TO NULLIFY IN PART AND TO SUSTAIN IN PART [THE REQUIREMENTS OF THE TORAH] [M. 1:3].**
1. IV:1: How on the basis of Scripture do we know this fact?

VIII. MISHNAH-TRACTATE HORAYOT 2:3A-C

A. **THEY ARE LIABLE ONLY ON ACCOUNT OF SOMETHING'S BEING HIDDEN (LEV. 4:13) ALONG WITH AN ACT [OF TRANSGRESSION] WHICH IS PERFORMED INADVERTENTLY:**
1. I:1: What is the scriptural source of this rule?

B. **AND SO IN THE CASE OF THE ANOINTED [HIGH PRIEST]**
1. II:1: as above.

C. **AND [THEY ARE] NOT [LIABLE] IN THE CASE OF IDOLATRY EXCEPT IN THE CASE OF SOMETHING'S BEING HIDDEN ALONG WITH AN ACT [OF TRANSGRESSION] WHICH IS PERFORMED INADVERTENTLY:**
1. III:1: as above.
2. III:2: But the Tannaite formulation of the Mishnah-rule has omitted reference to the rule governing the anointed priest when it comes to idolatry. Who is the authority behind the Mishnah-rule? It is Rabbi.
   a. III:3: What is the scriptural basis for the position of Rabbi?
   b. III:4: continuation of foregoing.
   c. III:5: as above.

IX. MISHNAH-TRACTATE HORAYOT 2:3D-F

A. **THE COURT IS LIABLE ONLY IF THEY WILL GIVE AN ERRONEOUS DECISION IN A MATTER, THE DELIBERATE COMMISSION OF WHICH IS PUNISHABLE BY EXTIRPATION, AND THE INADVERTENT COMMISSION OF WHICH IS PUNISHABLE BY A SIN OFFERING, AND SO IN THE CASE OF THE ANOINTED [HIGH PRIEST],**
1. I:1: how on the basis of Scripture do we know this fact?

B. **AND [THEY ARE] NOT [LIABLE] IN THE CASE OF IDOLATRY, EXCEPT IN THE CASE IN WHICH THEY GAVE INSTRUCTION IN A MATTER THE DELIBERATE COMMISSION OF WHICH IS PUNISHABLE BY EXTIRPATION, AND THE INADVERTENT COMMISSION OF WHICH IS PUNISHABLE BY A SIN OFFERING.**

1. II:1: How on the basis of Scripture do we know this fact concerning a case of idolatry?
2. II:2: Continuation of foregoing.
3. II:3: Continuation of foregoing.

X. MISHNAH-TRACTATE HORAYOT 2:4

A. THEY ARE NOT LIABLE ON ACCOUNT OF [A DECISION INADVERTENTLY VIOLATING] A POSITIVE COMMANDMENT OR A NEGATIVE COMMANDMENT CONCERNING THE SANCTUARY, AND THEY DO NOT BRING A SUSPENSIVE GUILT OFFERING ON ACCOUNT OF [VIOLATION OF] A POSITIVE COMMANDMENT OR A NEGATIVE COMMANDMENT CONCERNING THE SANCTUARY.

BUT THEY ARE LIABLE FOR [VIOLATING] A POSITIVE COMMANDMENT OR A NEGATIVE COMMANDMENT INVOLVING A MENSTRUATING WOMAN. AND THEY DO BRING A SUSPENSIVE GUILT OFFERING ON ACCOUNT OF [VIOLATION OF] A POSITIVE COMMANDMENT OR A NEGATIVE COMMANDMENT CONCERNING A MENSTRUATING WOMAN. WHAT IS A POSITIVE COMMANDMENT CONCERNING A MENSTRUATING WOMAN? TO KEEP SEPARATE FROM A MENSTRUATING WOMAN. AND WHAT IS A NEGATIVE COMMANDMENT? NOT TO HAVE SEXUAL RELATIONS WITH A MENSTRUATING WOMAN.

1. I:1: how on the basis of Scripture do we know that fact, that the community is not obligated to an offering in general, nor is the individual liable to a suspended built offering when it comes to imparting uncleanness to the Temple?

XI. MISHNAH-TRACTATE HORAYOT 2:5

A. THEY ARE NOT LIABLE [BECAUSE OF INADVERTENT VIOLATION OF THE LAW] (1) CONCERNING HEARING THE VOICE OF ADJURATION [LEV. 5:11, (2) A RASH OATH [LEV. 5:4], (3) OR IMPARTING UNCLEANNESS TO THE SANCTUARY AND TO ITS HOLY THINGS [LEV. 5:3]—" AND THE RULER FOLLOWS SUIT," THE WORDS OF R. YOSÉ THE GALILEAN.

1. I:1: What is the Scripture basis for the position of R. Yosé the Galilean?
   a. I:2: theoretical problem flowing from the facts of the foregoing. A ruler who was afflicted with the skin-ailment—what is the law that applies to him? The purification offering involves an offering of variable value, so Lev. 14:10, 21, but as we see, he is not liable to present such an offering.

B. R. AQIBA SAYS, "THE RULER IS LIABLE IN THE CASE OF ALL OF

THEM, EXCEPT IN THE CASE OF HEARING THE VOICE OF ADJURA-
TION. FOR THE KING DOES NOT JUDGE AND OTHERS DO NOT
JUDGE HIM, DOES NOT GIVE TESTIMONY, AND OTHERS DO NOT
GIVE TESTIMONY CONCERNING HIM:"

   1. I:1: What is the Scriptural foundation for the ruling of R.
     Aqiba?

XII. MISHNAH-TRACTATE HORAYOT 2:6-7

A.   IN THE CASE OF ALL THE COMMANDMENTS IN THE TORAH, ON
ACCOUNT OF WHICH THEY ARE LIABLE FOR DELIBERATE VIOLA-
TION TO EXTIRPATION, AND ON ACCOUNT OF INADVERTENT VIO-
LATION TO A SIN OFFERING, AN INDIVIDUAL BRINGS A FEMALE
LAMB OR A FEMALE GOAT [LEV. 4:28, 32]. A RULER BRINGS A
MALE GOAT [LEV. 4:23], AND AN ANOINTED [HIGH PRIEST] AND A
COURT BRING A BULLOCK [M. 1:5, 2:1]. BUT IN THE CASE OF
IDOLATRY, THE INDIVIDUAL, RULER, AND ANOINTED [HIGH
PRIEST] BRING A FEMALE GOAT [NUM. 15:27]. AND THE COURT
BRINGS A BULLOCK AND A GOAT [M. 1:5], A BULLOCK FOR A
WHOLE OFFERING AND A GOAT FOR A SIN OFFERING. AS TO A
SUSPENSIVE GUILT OFFERING, AN INDIVIDUAL AND A RULER MAY
BECOME LIABLE. BUT THE ANOINTED [HIGH PRIEST] AND COURT
DO NOT BECOME LIABLE. AS TO AN UNCONDITIONAL GUILT OFFER-
ING, AN INDIVIDUAL, A RULER, AND AN ANOINTED [HIGH PRIEST]
MAY BECOME LIABLE, BUT A COURT IS EXEMPT. ON ACCOUNT OF
HEARING THE VOICE OF ADJURATION, A RASH OATH, AND IMPART-
ING UNCLEANNESS TO THE SANCTUARY AND ITS HOLY THINGS, A
COURT IS EXEMPT, BUT AN INDIVIDUAL, A RULER, AND AN
ANOINTED [HIGH PRIEST] ARE LIABLE.

   1. I:1: In any case in which the individual is liable for a
     suspensive guilt offering, the ruler is in the same category,
     the anointed priest and the court are exempt. And in any
     case in which he is subject to an unconditional guilt offering,
     the ruler and the anointed priest are in the same category,
     and the court is exempt. As for violations involving not
     heeding the call to testify, uttering a vain oath, and contami-
     nation of the Temple and its Holy Things, the members of
     the court are exempt from the offering of variable value, but
     the ruler and the anointed priest are liable. Nonetheless, the
     ruler is not liable for failure to heed the call nor is the
     anointed priest for imparting uncleanness to the Temple and
     its Holy Things. Whenever the individual presents an offer-

ing of variable value, the rule is in his category, and the anointed priest and the court are exempt.

B. **"BUT A HIGH PRIEST IS NOT LIABLE FOR IMPARTING UNCLEANNESS TO THE SANCTUARY AND ITS HOLY THINGS," THE WORDS OF R. SIMEON.**

    1. II:1: What are the scriptural grounds for the position of R. Simeon?

C. **AND WHAT DO THEY BRING? AN OFFERING OF VARIABLE VALUE. R. ELIEZER SAYS, "THE RULER BRINGS A GOAT OFFERING."**

    1. III:1: R. Eliezer made this statement only in connection with imparting uncleanness to the sanctuary and its Holy Things, since reference is made in that regard to extirpation at Num. 19:20 just as is the case for violations that require an offering of fixed value.

    2. III:2: R. Eliezer concurs that the ruler need not present a suspended guilt offering if he only suspects he has violated the prohibition against imparting uncleanness to the Temple.

XIII. MISHNAH-TRACTATE HORAYOT 3:1-2

A. **AN ANOINTED [HIGH] PRIEST WHO SINNED AND AFTERWARD PASSED FROM HIS OFFICE AS ANOINTED HIGH PRIEST, AND SO A RULER WHO SINNED AND AFTERWARD PASSED FROM HIS POSITION OF GREATNESS—THE ANOINTED [HIGH] PRIEST BRINGS A BULLOCK, AND THE PATRIARCH BRINGS A GOAT [M. 2:6].**

    1. I:1: Now there is good reason to specify An anointed [high] priest who sinned and afterward passed from his office as anointed high priest and sinned...brings a bullock, for it is necessary to make explicit that the prior status governs his liability for transgression after he leaves office. But why does the Mishnah have to specify the case of an anointed high priest who passed from his office as anointed high priest and then sinned?

B. **AN ANOINTED [HIGH] PRIEST WHO PASSED FROM HIS OFFICE AS ANOINTED HIGH PRIEST AND THEN SINNED, AND SO A RULER WHO PASSED FROM HIS POSITION OF GREATNESS AND THEN SINNED—A HIGH PRIEST BRINGS A BULLOCK. BUT A RULER IS LIKE ANY ORDINARY PERSON.**

    1. II:1: What is the source in Scripture for this distinction?

XIV. MISHNAH-TRACTATE HORAYOT 3:3

A. **[IF] THEY SINNED BEFORE THEY WERE APPOINTED, AND THEN**

THEY WERE APPOINTED, LO, THEY ARE IN THE STATUS OF ANY ORDINARY PERSON.

1. I:1: How on the basis of Scripture do we know that if the anointed priest sinned prior to appointment to office, he presents the offering of an ordinary person?

2. I:2: Further exegesis of the same verses.

    a. I:3: Amplification of foregoing.

B. TO BE A RULER IS TO BE A SLAVE. THE RULER WHO SINS. "IN CASE IT IS A CHIEFTAIN WHO INCURS GUILT BY DOING UNWITTINGLY ANY OF THE THINGS WHICH BY THE COMMANDMENT OF THE LORD HIS GOD OUGHT NOT TO BE DONE" (LEV. 4:22)

1. I:4: "In case it is a chieftain who incurs guilt by doing unwittingly any of the things which by the commandment of the Lord his God ought not to be done" (Lev. 4:22)—excluding the one who is ill.

2. I:5: Happy is the generation, the ruler of which brings an offering for sinning inadvertently. If the ruler brings an offering, do you have to ask about ordinary folk? And if he brings an offering for an inadvertent sin, do you have to ask what he will do in the case of one that he does deliberately?

C. REWARD AND PUNISHMENT IN THIS WORLD AND IN THE NEXT. THE RIGHTEOUS AND THE WICKED

1. I:6: Happy are the righteous, for in this world they undergo what in the world to come is assigned as recompense for the deeds of the wicked, and woe is the wicked, for in this world they enjoy the fruits of what is assigned in the world to come to the deeds of the righteous.

D. THE CASE OF LOT AND ABRAHAM

1. I:7: What is the meaning of the verse of Scripture, "For the paths of the Lord are straight, that the righteous shall pass along them, but the transgressors will stumble in them" (Hos. 14:10)? The matter may be compared to the case of two men who roasted their Passover offerings. One of them ate it for the sake of performing the religious duty, and the other one ate it to stuff himself with a big meal. Lot becomes the focus.

2. I:8: "'A brother offended the mighty city:' this refers to Lot, who took his leave from Abraham in order to sin with his daughters. 'and contention is like the bars of a castle:' by siring Moab and Ben Ammi with his daughters, Lot made

contention between Israel and Amon, 'Neither an Amonite nor a Moabite shall come into the community of the Lord' (Dt. 23:4)."

3. I:9: "'To lust is a separatist drawn, and of any wisdom will be contemptuous' (Prov. 18:1): 'To lust is a separatist drawn:' this refers to Lot, who took his leave from Abraham."

E.   THE CASE OF TAMAR AND ZIMRI

1. I:10: Tamar committed an act of prostitution, and Zimri committed an act of prostitution. Tamar committed an act of prostitution, and there went forth from her kings and prophets. Zimri committed an act of prostitution, and how many myriads of Israel fell in consequence.

F.   THE IMPORTANCE OF THE RIGHT ATTITUDE

1. I:11: A transgression committed for its own sake, in a sincere spirit, is greater in value that a religious duty carried out not for its own sake, but in a spirit of insincerity.

2. I:12: A person should always be occupied in study of the Torah and in practice of the commandments, even if this is not for its own sake [but in a spirit of insincerity], for out of doing these things not for their own sake, a proper spirit of doing them for their own sake will emerge.

G.   R. SIMEON SAYS, "IF THEIR SIN BECAME KNOWN TO THEM BEFORE THEY WERE APPOINTED, THEY ARE LIABLE. BUT IF IT WAS AFTER THEY WERE APPOINTED, THEY ARE EXEMPT:"

1. II:1: "...from among the populace:" excluding the chieftain. "...from among the populace:" excluding the anointed priest.

2. II:2: What is the law on the office of ruler's interrupting one's continuity of status, so that when he rises to office, he is no longer culpable for transgression?

3. II:3: If when he was an ordinary person, he ate something that may or may not have been suet, and then he was appointed, and then the matter in doubt was discovered, what is the law?

4. II:4: What is the sense of the clause of Scripture, 'unwittingly incurs guilt by doing any of the things which by the Lord's commandments ought not to be done'? This refers to one who were he informed would simply refrain from carrying out the transgression, thus excluding an apostate, who were

he informed would not refrain from carrying out the transgression. There can be no issue that such a one violating the law does not do so either unwittingly or by reason of the inappropriate instruction of the court.

    a. II:5: What is the definition of an apostate.

        I. II:6: Clarification of foregoing.

        II. II:7: Clarification of foregoing.

        III. II:8: Clarification of foregoing.

H.   **AND WHO IS A RULER? THIS IS THE KING, AS IT IS SAID, "AND DOES ANY ONE OF ALL THE THINGS WHICH THE LORD HIS GOD HAS COMMANDED NOT TO BE DONE" (LEV. 4:22)—A RULER WHO HAS NONE ABOVE HIM EXCEPT THE LORD HIS GOD:**

    1. III:1: Scriptural proof for the proposition of the Mishnah: "Let it remain with him and let him read in it all his life, so that he may learn to revere the Lord his God, to observe faithfully every word of this Torah as well as these laws" (Dt. 17:19). Just as "his God' stated in that passage refers to a chieftain above whom is the authority only of the Lord his God, so "his God" stated here refers to a chieftain above whom is the authority only of the Lord his God

    2. III:2: Rabbi asked R. Hiyya, "What about me? Do I present a he-goat [as undisputed ruler]?"

XV. MISHNAH-TRACTATE HORAYOT 3:4

A.   **WHO IS THE ANOINTED [HIGH PRIEST]? IT IS THE ONE WHO IS ANOINTED WITH THE ANOINTING OIL, NOT THE ONE WHO IS DEDICATED BY MANY GARMENTS:**

    1. I:1: In the anointing oil that Moses made in the wilderness they would boil aromatic roots.

      a. I:2: secondary expansion of the foregoing.

      b. I:3: secondary expansion of the foregoing.

      c. I:4: secondary expansion of the foregoing.

      d. I:5: secondary expansion of the foregoing.

      e. I:6: secondary expansion of the foregoing.

        I. I:7: secondary expansion of the foregoing.

      f. I:8: secondary expansion of the foregoing.

        I. I:9: amplification of the foregoing.

        II. I:10: as above.

      g. I:11: secondary amplification of foregoing.

B.   ANOINTING KINGS

    1. I:12: The way in which the oil is applied to a king for the purpose of anointment.

    a. I:13: gloss on foregoing.

  2. I:14: Further Tannaite statements on the same topic.

    a. I:15: gloss of foregoing.

  3. I:16: Further Tannaite statements on the same topic.

    a. I:17: gloss of foregoing.

      ı. I:18: More good advice in line with the foregoing.

  4. I:19: Conclusion of I:17.

C. IT IS THE ONE WHO IS ANOINTED WITH THE ANOINTING OIL, NOT THE ONE WHO IS DEDICATED BY MANY GARMENTS:

  1. II:1: Tannaite proof from Scripture of the Mishnah's allegation.

    a. II:2: Secondary amplification of the foregoing.

D. THERE IS NO DIFFERENCE BETWEEN THE HIGH PRIEST WHO IS ANOINTED WITH ANOINTING OIL, AND THE ONE WHO IS DEDICATED WITH MANY GARMENTS, EXCEPT FOR [THE LATTER'S OBLIGATION TO BRING] THE BULLOCK WHICH IS BROUGHT BECAUSE OF THE [VIOLATION] OF ANY OF THE COMMANDMENTS. THERE IS NO DIFFERENCE BETWEEN A [HIGH] PRIEST PRESENTLY IN SERVICE AND A PRIEST [WHO SERVED] IN THE PAST EXCEPT FOR THE [BRINGING OF] THE BULLOCK OF THE DAY OF ATONEMENT AND THE TENTH OF AN EPHAH. (1) THIS ONE AND THAT ONE ARE EQUIVALENT IN REGARD TO THE SERVICE ON THE DAY OF ATONEMENT. (2) AND THEY ARE COMMANDED CONCERNING [MARRYING] A VIRGIN. AND THEY ARE FORBIDDEN TO [MARRY] A WIDOW. (3) AND THEY ARE NOT TO CONTRACT CORPSE UNCLEANNESS ON ACCOUNT OF THE DEATH OF THEIR CLOSE RELATIVES. (4) NOR DO THEY MESS UP THEIR HAIR. (5) NOR DO THEY TEAR THEIR CLOTHES [ON THE OCCASION OF A DEATH IN THE FAMILY]. (6) AND [ON ACCOUNT OF THEIR DEATH] THEY BRING BACK A MANSLAYER.

  1. III:1: Identifying the named authority behind the anonymous statement of the Mishnah.

  2. III:2: What is the Scriptural basis for the position of R. Meir?

    a. III:3: Secondary analysis of the key citation of the foregoing passage.

      ı. III:4: Gloss of the foregoing.

XVI. MISHNAH-TRACTATE HORAYOT 3:5

A. A HIGH PRIEST [ON THE DEATH OF A CLOSE RELATIVE] TEARS HIS GARMENT BELOW, AND AN ORDINARY ONE, ABOVE.

A HIGH PRIEST MAKES AN OFFERING WHILE HE IS IN THE STATUS OF ONE WHO HAS YET TO BURY HIS DEAD, BUT HE MAY NOT EAT [THE PRIESTLY PORTION]. AND AN ORDINARY PRIEST NEITHER MAKES THE OFFERING NOR EATS [THE PRIESTLY PORTION].

   1. I:1: "The word 'below' is meant literally, and the word 'above' is meant literally."

XVII. MISHNAH-TRACTATE HORAYOT 3:6

A.   [WHEN THE PRIEST FACES A CHOICE ON TENDING TO TWO OR MORE ANIMALS THAT HAVE BEEN DESIGNATED AS OFFERINGS, THEN:] WHATEVER IS OFFERED MORE REGULARLY THAN ITS FELLOW TAKES PRECEDENCE OVER ITS FELLOW:

   1. I:1: What is the source in Scripture for this rule?

B.   AND WHATEVER IS MORE HOLY THAN ITS FELLOW TAKES PRECEDENCE OVER ITS FELLOW.

   1. II:1: How do we know this?

C.   [IF] A BULLOCK OF AN ANOINTED PRIEST AND A BULLOCK OF THE CONGREGATION [M. 1:5] ARE STANDING [AWAITING SACRIFICE] —THE BULLOCK OF THE ANOINTED [HIGH PRIEST] TAKES PRECEDENCE OVER THE BULLOCK OF THE CONGREGATION IN ALL RITES PERTAINING TO IT.

   1. III:1: How do we know this?

   2. III:2: Tannaite formulation of the same rule on the strength of scriptural support.

   3. III:3: Continuation of foregoing.

XVIII. MISHNAH-TRACTATE HORAYOT 3:7

A.   THE MAN TAKES PRECEDENCE OVER THE WOMAN IN THE MATTER OF THE SAVING OF LIFE AND IN THE MATTER OF RETURNING LOST PROPERTY BUT A WOMAN TAKES PRECEDENCE OVER A MAN IN THE MATTER OF [PROVIDING] CLOTHING AND REDEMPTION FROM CAPTIVITY. WHEN BOTH OF THEM ARE STANDING IN DANGER OF DEFILEMENT, THE MAN TAKES PRECEDENCE OVER THE WOMAN.

   1. I:1: Tannaite statement of the same matter.

   2. I:2: In matters of uncleanness, with respect to the prefect of the priests and the priest anointed for battle, which takes precedence?

XIX. MISHNAH-TRACTATE HORAYOT 3:8

A.   A PRIEST TAKES PRECEDENCE OVER A LEVITE"

   1. I:1:Scriptural proof for that proposition.

B.   A LEVITE OVER AN ISRAELITE:

   1. II:1: Scriptural proof for that proposition.

C.   AN ISRAELITE OVER A MAMZER:
   1. III:1: The reason for that proposition.
D.   A MAMZER OVER A NETIN:
   1. IV:1: The reason for that proposition.
E.   A NETIN OVER A PROSELYTE:
   1. V:1: The reason for that proposition.
F.   A PROSELYTE OVER A FREED SLAVE"
   1. VI:1: The reason for that proposition.
G.   UNDER WHAT CIRCUMSTANCES? WHEN ALL OF THEM ARE
   EQUIVALENT. BUT IF THE MAMZER WAS A DISCIPLE OF A SAGE AND
   A HIGH PRIEST WAS AN AM HAARES, THE MAMZER WHO IS A DISCI-
   PLE OF A SAGE TAKES PRECEDENCE OVER A HIGH PRIEST WHO IS
   AN AM HAARES:
   1. VII:1: What is the source in Scripture for the proposition
      that learning in the Torah takes precedence over all else?
   2. VII:2: Secondary consideration of the proposition that a
      proselyte takes precedence over a freed slave.
   3. VII:3: Continuation of foregoing. Tangential reference to
      forgetfulness accounts for the continuation at No. 4.
      a. VII:4: Secondary expansion on a topic of the foregoing:
         forgetfulness. Five things cause what one has learned to
         be forgotten.
H.   THE HONOR THAT IS PAID TO A SAGE; THE TRAITS OF THE SAGE
   1. VII:5: Correct conduct when a sage enters the room.
      a. VII:6: Gloss of foregoing.
      b. VII:7: as above.
      c. VII:8: as above.
         I. VII:9: gloss of the foregoing.
   2. VII:10: The intellectual gifts. Erudition versus analytical
      skills.
   3. VII:11: Continuation of foregoing: story.
   4. VII:12: As above.
   5. VII:13: As above.

We find ourselves able to outline most of the tractate simply by
referring to the Mishnah-tractate's principal statements. The larger
composites that do not define their purpose within Mishnah-commentary take up themes called for by the contents of the Mishnah. I
find nothing in the tractate that cannot be situated in relationship to
the program of the Mishnah.

As we review the outline of the tractate, we note that one way or the other every principal allegation of Mishnah-tractate Horayot is subjected to discussion, though at many points a process of selection has guided the framers of this tractate to one set of problems rather than to some other. The main traits of mind that defined the choices are readily inferred from the pattern of results consistently attained. In general three sets of issues predominate: [1] the wording and sense of sentences in the Mishnah; [2] the foundations in the written part of the Torah, or Scripture, and [3] implications of the Mishnah's rule, which may lead to investigating questions provoked but not addressed by the Mishnah, secondary theoretical issues, and other modes of extension and augmentation. The intellectual quest therefore finds its definition in Mishnah-exegesis.

The greater part of the Talmud's system comes to expression in the questions the framers of the Talmud's Mishnah-exegesis address to the Mishnah; what they wished to say, they stated, for the most part, through the questions they brought to a prior document. Since so much of their commentary appears to adhere closely to the main lines of the Mishnah's own statements, it is easy to conclude that the Talmud's system replicated the Mishnah's. But that is deceiving. Not only do the questions of the Talmud—which clarify what the Mishnah's authors must have assumed was already clear, identify authority for the Mishnah that the Mishnah's authors did not find need to expose, say more than the Mishnah's authors found sufficient—subvert the Mishnah. Other than Mishnah-exegetical compositions and composites impart to the topic treated by the Mishnah a very different character altogether. The notion that, in the Talmud, we find pretty much what the Mishnah's statements mean but little else—the "plain meaning" in modern parlance, or the historically-determinate meaning initially intended by the Mishnah's writers—proves not only anachronistic but naive, even bordering on the disingenuous. Nothing in the writings before us compels us to imagine that the Talmud's compositions' and composites' writers conceived any meaning to inhere in the words before them except for the meaning they brought to those words—whatever it was.

The upshot is simply put: to the framers of the Talmud, a reasoned reading of the Mishnah defended the logical coherence of the document they proposed to compile. But then, the rationality proves formal, not substantive. But even at the level at which we work—large-scale aggregates and their formal testimonies—we may identify

points of violence to the rationality of order and form, and, violating
the structure established for the whole, these plunge us into issues of
system. When large-scale composites take shape around topics or
propositions not formed in response to statements in the Mishnah,
the structure defined by the character of the document overall bears
the weight of anomalies. I find these at XIV.B, C, D, E, F; XV.B,
and XIX.H.

Now we return to our starting point, the massive miscellanies of
Chapter One. Most of the paragraphs of the Mishnah are taken up
in one way or another. I noted only a few that were not fully
analyzed, and most of these turn out to be secondary expansions of
the Mishnah's own generalizations. But we should not fail to note
that even when the Talmud devotes itself to an analysis of the
Mishnah's statements, it may well go its own way, beyond the limits
of what Mishnah-exegesis requires, though still well within the limits
of the Mishnah's topical program. This observation directs our attention to a gray area, between Mishnah-exegesis and the presentation
of essentially autonomous discourse, such as is taken up in the next
rubric. Here, where Mishnah-commentary spells over into free-rang-
ing exploration of problems precipitated by the Mishnah's concerns
but far transcending the Mishnah's own program, we enter the
framework of independent thought given the form of subordinated
commentary. A survey of the entirety of the document will allow a
clearer focus upon this gray area. For the moment it suffices to note
that in the Bavli's Mishnah-commentary are embedded the marks of
much independent reflection.

Then we must ask, How do the topical composites fit into the
Talmud-tractate Horayot and what do they contribute that the
Mishnah-tractate of the same name would lack without them? Here
is the critical test of whether a system of thought has guided the
composition of the Bavli-tractate. Let us take the identified cases one
by one.

The composite in Unit XIV is provoked by the allusion at XIV.A
to the transformation of a common person into a ruler or high priest.
The change in status is marked—it is, after all, the critical focus of
our tractate as a whole!—and it is at that point that the condition of
the ruler enters in.

XIV.B: the first point remarks upon the enviable society, the ruler of
       which acknowledges even inadvertent transgression. That is

the mark of good government, accounting also for how rare good government is.

XIV.C: At the head of the next sequence is the contrast between the righteous and the wicked, with the certainty of reward and punishment in the world to come underscoring the justice of God in all things.

XIV.D: The first contrast between the good ruler and the bad one is Lot and Abraham, and the point is, the attitude of the ruler makes all the difference. People may do the same thing, but only if the motive is honorable is that deed consequential; if the motive is dishonorable, then the good that one does turns out to yield nothing. The same actions, e.g., Lot and his daughters, can be both good and bad, and the point of differentiation is the attitude of the ones who do said actions.

XIV.E: The same point, contrasting the good and the evil, emerges in the next example. Tamar and Zimri did the same thing, with very different results.

XIV.F: The key point of differentiation therefore is not the action but the attitude that infuses the action. And the right attitude is one of sincerity; this is stated in an extreme way, better the transgression done sincerely ("for its own sake") than the religious duty done insincerely ("not for its own sake"). But this same point is forthwith modulated: doing commandments and study of Torah in an insincere spirit (e.g., for personal gain) gives way to doing them in a sincere spirit.

XV.B: The composite on anointing kings does not vastly change the face of the unit in which it occurs; the Mishnah has dealt with anointing priests, and what the Talmud here contributes is simply a complement to the Mishnah's topic.

XIX.H: The point of the Mishnah, that the sagacity takes priority over hierarchical status, is not vastly transformed by the Talmud. The composite itself appears somewhat unfocused and diffuse; the unit on correct conduct when a sage enters the room and the secondary expansions and glosses thereof bears no proposition I can identify. The contrast between analytical skills and erudition, while interesting, really does not affect the main point, which is the hierarchical point that the Mishnah has stated in so many words. And yet, a second look suggests otherwise. Now we find ourselves deep

within the concerns of the Talmud's sages with analytical
capacities, not merely knowledge but the power to use
knowledge to form fresh knowledge, and that lies beyond the
imagination of the hierarchical program of the Mishnah's
framers. By introducing the considerations of hierarchization where they do not pertain—learning vs. analytical abilities indeed!—the framers of the Talmud's concluding units
place in a different light the very allegations about the status
accorded to the sage; that status, while a given, proves only
instrumental. It is what one can do with what one learns that
makes the difference, and that is not a matter of status at all.
In that same context the stories about Simeon b. Gamaliel
and Judah the Patriarch and their invocation of their political status in the setting of the superior learning of the sages
(also portrayed in an unflattering light, to be sure), form a
wry comment on the sages' hierarchical superiority. That
sages take precedence in the Talmud proves less weighty
than that, among sages, competition for power takes the
diverse form of politics, personalities, and preferment.

Can we state what the compilers of this document propose to accomplish in producing this complete, organized piece of writing? The key
to Mishnah-tractate Horayot lies in its location, which is in the Division of Damages, rather than in the Division of Holy Things. Since
the bulk of the problems finds resolution in whether a given party is
obligated to present an offering, and, if so, which offering said party
is required to present, the surface of the tractate is studded with issues
typical of the fifth division but rare in the fourth. But the organizer of
the Mishnah, laying out the divisions and assigning to them the
tractates and therefore the topical expositions they were to receive,
had his reasons. The fourth division concerns itself in significant part
with the civil administration of the Jews in the land of Israel. Tractate
Sanhedrin, with its account of the tripartite regime of high priest and
Temple, king and army, sages and court, set alongside the great
pinnacle of the Mishnah, the thirty chapters of Baba Qamma, Baba
Mesia, and Baba Batra, with their movement from the abnormal to
the normal, form a sustained account of the life of government and
secular relationships within the politics of holy Israel. What we learn
in Horayot concerns the errors of the civil authorities, apportioning
responsibility for the consequences of error, underscoring the obliga-

tion of the individual to face the results of his own actions. The real problem of the tractate as the Mishnah presents matters of government proves remarkably contemporary: what does the private person do when the community's officials err.

Faced with an error on the part of the government, what can a person do? If he knows the government errs, he may not find exculpation in the plea that he has merely carried out orders. If the government errs and the individual does not know better and therefore inadvertently has violated the law, then, but only then, the possibility of atoning is raised. So we require, for the process of remission to get underway, both political error and personal inadvertence. Since the issues derive from the right reading of the Torah, right instruction and right action are contrasted with wrong instruction and inadvertent error. That is why the key language throughout invokes the twin criteria, [1] They are liable only on account of something's being hidden (Lev. 4:13) along with [2] an act [of transgression] which is performed inadvertently. The former concerns a misinterpretation or exegetical error in the law, and the latter involves the mitigating circumstance of a deed in violation of the law done without intent to break the law.

So the principal point of concern of the tractate is that the law be properly known and intentionally observed; if the law is set forth in error by the responsible authorities, the remissive provisions of the law take over. No wonder the tractate reaches its conclusion where it does, with its meditation on the hierarchical inversion accomplished by the sage. For everything in the end depends upon informed government over responsible, critical citizens (to use an anachronistic term). Israel may have its high priest and king, its castes from times of old. But Israel in the end depends upon the sage, whatever his caste, he who can be relied upon not to commit an error of misinterpretation, and who provides the model for those who would avoid inadvertent sin. That explains the order of the exposition of the topic.

The Mishnah's version of the Halakhah of Horayot reaches its conclusion when it emerges from the complexities of responsibility for the public interest, the public's stake in the correct administration of law, and the subtle transformation that takes a private person and endows him with the status of embodiment of the community (what happens when one sins and then becomes high priest or ruler being one formulation of matters). Then, laying down the fundamental conviction that hierarchy in this world contrasts with the hierarchy established by the Torah, the Mishnah-tractate makes its final statement on issues of status and responsibility. That is specifically where we confront the Talmud's two striking additional points. Together they accomplish a surprise no less remarkable than the Mishnah-tractate's meditation on hierarchy.

The first treats as altogether null all questions of hierarchy, beginning to end, making the point that it is not the position one holds that matters, or even the acts that one performs in office, but the attitude that characterizes the office holder. This point is hammered home in the contrasts between Lot and Abraham, the two daughters of Noah, Zimri and Tamar, and in the elaborate essay on the centrality of right attitude. When all is said and done, then, we step aside from the Mishnah-tractate altogether, with its concern for error committed inadvertently, with oversight and misinterpretation of the law, by stating that what matters in the end is not what one does but the attitude that one brings to one's action. True, the Mishnah has invited that very point, by its insistence upon the criterion of inadvertence (inadvertently committing an act that is based upon an erroneous reading of the Torah). But inadvertence forms an invitation to the profound thinking on intentionality that the sizable composite the Talmud introduces places on display. The main point of the Mishnah concerns the consequences of inadvertent action, based upon the wrong decision of public authorities. The main point of the Talmud, where it speaks for itself and not in exegesis of the Mishnah, differentiates not actions at all, whether based upon improper government or uninformed sagacity, but rather attitudes by which one and the same action is carried out.

The second treats as null the datum of the tractate, that the sage forms a single and undifferentiated caste in the hierarchy of ruler and ruled, priests, Levites, Israelites, and on down. The sage stands at the apex by reason of learning; the caste of the sages requires no more sustained a process of differentiation than any other, than the priests (but for the high priest), than the Levites, than the Israelites. The main point of the Mishnah is that the sage disrupts all other established modes of hierarchization. The Talmud's treatment of that point subverts that celebration of the sage within the caste system by introducing those tensions of learning versus intellect, mastery of traditions versus power of logic and reason, that impose upon the status of sagacity those variables that the life of intellect generates. The status of "being a sage" no longer carries weight; various modes of sagacity impart complexity and subtle to the simplicities of the Mishnah's uncomplicated conception of hierarchization. Since no one can ultimately determine whether Sinai takes precedence over the one who can pierce mountains, the indeterminacy of intellect upsets all conceptions of hierarchization, and the sages move on into an altogether new and unpredictable plane of being. It would be difficult to point to a more complete, if subtle, subversion of a Mishnah-tractate than the one accomplished by the framers of the Bavli, who here present us with one of their (very many) intellectual masterpieces.

What have I shown? First, because of the character of the outline, we see that we may speak of a composition, not merely a compilation. That is because, first, the Talmud's authors or authorship follow a few rules, which we can easily discern, in order to say everything they wish. So the document is uniform and rhetorically cogent. The highly orderly and systematic character of the Talmud emerges, first of all, in the regularities of language. Second, the outline shows in enormous detail how the Talmud speaks through one voice, that voice of logic that with vast assurance reaches into our own minds and by asking the logical and urgent next question tells us what we should be thinking. So the Talmud's rhetoric seduces us into joining its analytical inquiry, always raising precisely the question that should trouble us (and that would trouble us if we knew all of the pertinent details as well as the Talmud does). The Talmud speaks about the Mishnah in essentially a single voice, about fundamentally few things. Its mode of speech as much as of thought is uniform throughout. Diverse topics produce slight differentiation in modes of analysis. The same sorts of questions phrased in the same rhetoric—a moving, or dialectical, argument, composed of questions and answers—turn out to pertain equally well to every subject and problem. The Talmud's discourse forms a closed system, in which people say the same thing about everything. The fact that the Talmud speaks in a single voice supplies striking evidence (1) that the Talmud does speak in particular for the age in which its units of discourse took shape, and (2) that that work was done toward the end of that long period of Mishnah-reception that began at the end of the second century and came to an end at the conclusion of the sixth century.

The outline shows in vast detail a single governing fact. It is that in a given unit of discourse, the focus, the organizing principle, the generative interest—these are defined solely by the issue at hand.

The argument moves from point to point, directed by the inner logic of argument itself. A single plane of discourse is established. All things are leveled out, so that the line of logic runs straight and true. Accordingly, a single conception of the framing and formation of the unit of discourse stands prior to the spelling out of issues. More fundamental still, what people in general wanted was not to create topical anthologies—to put together instances of what this one said about that issue—but to exhibit the logic of that issue, viewed under the aspect of eternity. Under sustained inquiry we always find a theoretical issue, freed of all temporal considerations and the contingencies of politics and circumstance.

Once these elemental literary and structural facts make their full impression, everything else falls into place as well. Arguments such as the one we followed just now did not unfold over a long period of time, as one generation made its points, to be followed by the additions and revisions of another generation, in a process of gradual increment and agglutination running on for two hundred years. That theory of the formation of literature cannot account for the unity, stunning force and dynamism, of the Talmud's dialectical arguments. To the contrary, someone (or small group) at the end determined to reconstruct, so as to expose, the naked logic of a problem. For this purpose, oftentimes, it was found useful to cite sayings or positions in hand from earlier times. But these inherited materials underwent a process of reshaping, and, more aptly, refocusing. Whatever the original words—and we need not doubt that at times we have them—the point of everything in hand was defined and determined by the people who made it all up at the end. The whole shows a plan and program. Theirs are the minds behind the whole. In the nature of things, they did their work at the end, not at the outset. There are two possibilities. The first is that our document emerges out of a gradual increment of a sedimentary process. Or it emerges as the creation of single minded geniuses of applied logic and sustained analytical inquiry. But there is no intermediate possibility.

IV. CONCLUSION

Why has Steinsaltz so misconstrued matters as to represent as chaotic so orderly and disciplined a piece of writing as this one? By reason of not its volume but its distinctive character, perhaps even its uniqueness, the Talmud defies easy description; it is not like any other writing or easily compared either. But because the document is so orderly and purposive, if we look at it whole, not only in bits and pieces, we are able to discern its definitive traits and so undertake to describe it and explain how it works. Steinsaltz has failed to address to the Talmud a variety of questions of purpose, system, and order. In identifying many of the document's uniformities and governing rules of thought and expression, I have decoded the writing and deciphered the intellectual glyphs of which it is comprised. If readers concur, then they will share my view that Steinsaltz does not represent the Talmud accurately but in fact misrepresents some of its critical characteristics of cogency and coherence. Now we shall wait for Steinsaltz's view of matters.

What is at stake in highlighting Steinsaltz's misconstruction and consequent misrepresentation of the character of the Talmud? What is to be deplored is not only loss of access to the intellect of the Talmud's own framers, who wrote this way, not that, and with brilliant success, in order to invite future generations to participate in the on-going discourse of logic and reason and tradition. It is also the misrepresentation of the authentic character of one of the greatest achievements of humanity's intellect, which is what the Talmud is. The atomistic presentation of the Talmud, Steinsaltz's approach, like the topical study of the Talmud, in dismissing the continuity of exposition and argument treats the document as a compilation of information, not as a sustained and coherent statement, one that is capable indeed of shaping our minds and changing us through its compelling and forceful logic. If the Talmud is as chaotic and confused and pointless as Steinsaltz says it is, then that judgment deprives Judaism's greatest writing of its authority and power. By showing that the Talmud is not disorganized, not confused, not haphazard, but exquisitely composed and crafted, lucid and nearly always clear as to its purpose, above all, consistent, orderly, and systematic, I may strengthen the received and authentic way: the way of the great masters of Talmud-study. Obviously, in showing some of the components of my theory on how I believe I have decoded principal messages that embody the Talmud and impart to it its character, I have not solved all critical problems. But I think I have answered questions of system, purpose, and method that require attention if we are to learn how to hear the Talmud's serene voice. The stakes are very high: the intellectual vitality of Judaism is at issue, and if Steinsaltz prevails, Judaism will lose access to its most valuable resource, the Talmud as embodiment of intellect, not merely as a source of exotic information, which is all he has given in his "Steinsaltz Talmud," that is to say, in the Talmud he has named for himself.

GENERAL INDEX

INDEX OF BIBLICAL, TALMUDIC, AND
ANCIENT REFERENCES

JUDAISM IN LATE ANTIQUITY

PART THREE

SECTION FOUR

THE SPECIAL PROBLEM OF THE SYNAGOGUE

TABLE OF CONTENTS

PREFACE

This fourth collection of state of the question papers, on the ancient synagogue, carries forward the project of nurturing *Auseinandersetzungen* among the active scholars of the present day. The editors mean to hold up a mirror for the field by affording a hearing to argument and contention: here is where we differ and why. Only by pursuing issues in this manner are people going to carry out their responsibility not only to say what they think but also to explain themselves and spell out the choices they make, the alternative views they reject, and the reasons therefor.

Why devote so much effort, within the exposition of the state of scholarship, to contemporary debates? It is because the editors place the highest priority upon affording a platform for public discussion of controverted points of learning: facts, methods, interpretations alike. Learning progresses through contentious pursuit of controversy, as hypotheses are put forth, tested against evidence, advocated, and criticized. Then public discourse, dense and rich in rigorous argument and explicit discussion, stimulates. Choices present themselves, what is at stake is clarified, knowledge deepens. Those who serve as gate-keepers in scholarship—editors of journals and monograph series, for example—therefore find a place for everything and its opposite. That is their task. They value what is best expressed in the German word, *Auseinandersetzungen*.

What the editors by creating this book and its companions mean to oppose also comes to expression in a German word uniquely serviceable to scholarship, *Todschweigen*, meaning, to murder through silence (ostracism, suppression, above all, active, ostentatious acts of ignoring views one does not hold). What costs do we aim to avoid? Learning atrophies when political consensus substitutes for criticism and when other than broadly-accepted viewpoints, approaches, and readings find a hearing only with difficulty if at all.

Having presented in Volumes I and II of this series some of the main results of contemporary learning on Judaism in late antiquity,[1]

---

[1] *Handbuch der Orientalistik. Judaism in Late Antiquity.* Volume One. *Literary and Archaeological Sources* (Leiden, 1995: E.J. Brill); Volume Two. *Historical Syntheses* (Leiden, 1995: E.J. Brill).

in the several parts of Volume III we proceed to portray issues and debates that animate the field. Such an account of contemporary debates, along with a picture of the state of knowledge, is necessary. That is because any responsible account for colleagues of the shape and standing of learning in a given subject must outline not only the present state of pertinent questions but also the contemporary character of debate and discussion. That is especially the case here, for the study of ancient Judaism forms one of the most contentious subjects in the contemporary humanities. And it is also driven as much by politics and personalities as it is guided by rationality and civil discourse. When people disagree, they simply refuse to read the books and articles of those with whom they differ. Were such conduct to go unchallenged, the study of ancient Judaism would lose all academic plausibility—and should.

What accounts for the highly controverted character of this aspect of the study of ancient religion, culture, history, and literature? It is not only for the obvious, theological reason, that Judaism and Christianity today have a heavy stake in the results of academic learning about olden times. Many debates come about because of contemporary political or theological considerations, not by reason of issues intrinsic in the sources themselves. But a second fact precipitates quite strong difference of opinion. It is because long-established approaches have been called into question as new methods and new definitions of critical learning take center-stage. There is a third factor as well: much new information emerges of both a literary and an archaeological character, and, it goes without saying, reasonable people may form different opinions in describing, analyzing, and interpreting in context the meaning of facts simply unknown to prior generations of scholars. Not only so, but the state of the contemporary humanities and social sciences bring to the forefront issues hitherto not considered at all. Altogether new perspectives now emerge, new questions deriving from other areas of the humanities than the study of religion, such as women's studies and studies of render and the social construction of sexuality, emerge, to which even a generation ago no one gave thought. It goes without saying that, in the study of ancient Judaism, all four sources of contention contribute to contemporary debate. Armed with a range of new interests, people turn to that diverse set of kindred religious systems we call "Judaism," rightly anticipating fresh and suggestive answers.

But the nature of the evidence itself—literary and archaeological—makes its own contribution as well. Read even in their own framework, the principal literary sources as well as the main archaeological remains contain many ambiguities. They leave ample space for diverse viewpoints to take shape. Read in one way for nearly half-a-century, now, the Dead Sea Scrolls, fully available after such a long wait, require fresh approaches and receive them. An established consensus gives way. Questions not asked at all demand attention, even as diverse answers to long-settled questions are put forth.[2] Not only so, but another principal component of the documentary legacy of ancient Judaism, the Rabbinic literature, forms the focus of most vigorous debates. And these represent only two among many of the sub-fields of ancient Judaism that today provoke contentious discussion.

But these debates seldom take the form of a public *Auseinandersetzung*, an exchange of opposed views among persons of shared rationality, mutual respect, and good will, an exchange to the point, on a single issue, within a shared consensus of pertinent sources, considerations, and rationalities. Scholarly media print book reviews but most forbid the right of response, as though scholarly argument were disruptable, rather than the necessity of all reasoned discourse. Journals automatically reject work that does not conform to the regnant viewpoint of a given set of editors (not seldom appointed for other than scholarly achievement), and university presses and monograph series practice censorship of an other-than-academic character as well. Conferences on a given problem commonly exclude viewpoints not shared by the organizers, and university faculties rarely make certain that their students hear views not shared by the professors of those faculties. Indeed, it is only a small exaggeration to say that, given a list of the conferences a person has attended or the universities at which he or she has lectured, we may easily construct the opinion of that person on the entire agenda of learning in his or her field of specialization.

---

[2] In *Judaism in Late Antiquity.* Volume Five. *Judaism at Qumran*, we ask hitherto unasked questions of system and structure of the Judaic religious system adumbrated by the Dead Sea library: what kind of Judaism can have produced this writing? Until now, problems of historical, philological, and archaeological character have predominated, and the religious reading of the writings has been subordinated. Happily, we have been able to enlist in the project an ample number of colleagues who specialize in research in that subject and who are willing to address the questions we have formulated for them.

But debate, discussion, on-going exchanges of views, systematic and sustained criticism—these impart to all fields of academic learning such dynamics as will sustain them over time. Repeating oneself and the views of one's friends and ignoring other positions, not even alluding to them in footnotes or in bibliographies, as though *Todschweigen* accomplished its goal—these modes of dealing with difference serve no one. And in this book and its companions, the editors mean to show a better way of doing the work of learning in the study of ancient Judaism.

Here, therefore, the editors have invited colleagues systematically to outline their views in an *Auseinandersetzung* with contrary ones. We asked them to tell us how, in broad and sweeping terms, they see the state of learning in their areas of special interest. We wanted sharply-etched state of the question studies, systematic presentations of a distinctive viewpoint and very particular results, and other evidence of how scholarly debate goes forward. We hoped to portray some of the principal issues, to set forth a few of the alternative positions presently maintained about fundamental questions of method and substance. We invited the leading players in the U.S.A., Europe, and the State of Israel, in the study of ancient Judaism, both in Second Temple Times and after 70 C.E. The responses proved so many and, as this fourth part of the project shows, so intellectually ambitious, that several sizable books have been required to set forth the representative sample of debate on a few large questions that we wished to present.

Some may wonder why the vehement espousal of the value of *Auseinandersetzungen* and the equally strong denunciation of *Todschweigen* that this book and its companions mean to embody. The reason is that when it comes to the study of ancient Judaism, the scholarly interchange is rare, the academic excommunication is commonplace. It is a matter of common knowledge that in the scholarly communities in which ancient Judaism comes under academic study, people will not engage with critics. It is the fact characteristic of universities, university presses, and journals that those who control the media of public discourse close the door on views they do not like. They print violent and *ad hominem* advocacy of one viewpoint but do not permit replies; as with the *Journal of the American Oriental Society*, they publish intemperate reviews aimed at nothing short of character-assassination but suppress answers thereto. Many scholarly journals, university presses, and monograph series take an essentially political position on scholarship, closing off debate and imposing a rigid orthodoxy upon such learning as they disseminate. They will not even consider articles that bear the wrong names or books or monographs from the camp with which they do not identify.

It remains to express our gratitude to those who have made this project a success. For on-going support of their joint and separate scholarly enterprises, the two editors express thanks to our respective colleges, Bard College, for Jacob Neusner, and the College of the Holy Cross, for Alan J. Avery-Peck.

We further thank E.J. Brill and its editors for guidance and commitment to this project. We call attention to the fact that, of all the scholarly publishers in the U.S.A., Europe, and the State of Israel, none has devoted more effort to opening doors and windows than has E.J. Brill, with whom we are proud to be associated. The senior editor published his first book with Brill in 1962, when Dr. F.C. Wieder, Jr., was the director, and remembers with thanks many editors and directors over the past decades. Brill in this generation has carried forward a great tradition of scholarship, one that has sustained us all.

And, finally, we thank the contributors to this part of *Judaism in Late Antiquity* Volume III for their prompt and conscientious work. We are proud that so many distinguished scholars have joined in this effort publicly to show where we stand in contemporary issues and debates on ancient Judaism.

Jacob Neusner
Research Professor of Religion and Theology
Bard College, Annandale-on-Hudson, New York

Alan J. Avery-Peck
Kraft-Hiatt Professor of Judaic Studies
College of the Holy Cross, Worcester, Massachusetts

1. THE QUESTION OF THE SYNAGOGUE: THE PROBLEM OF TYPOLOGY[1]

Jodi Magness
Tufts University

As an undergraduate majoring in archaeology at the Hebrew University of Jerusalem in the mid-1970s, I was taught that the ancient synagogues of Palestine (or, rather, the land of Israel) could be neatly divided into a tripartite typology. This typology was passed down from E.L. Sukenik, who established it, to successive generations of archaeology students at the Hebrew University; Sukenik's son, Y. Yadin, was one of my professors at the Institute of Archaeology.[2] This typology divides the synagogues of Palestine dating from the second or third to sixth centuries[3] into three successive architectural groups or types. The earliest group, described as "Galilean" and dated to the second-third centuries, is characterized by the following features: a basilical plan; a large, decorated facade (usually with three doors, but sometimes with only one) in the wall facing Jerusalem; richly carved stone reliefs; a flagstone floor; and no set place for the Torah ark or shrine. The synagogues at Capernaum, Chorazin, and Kfar Baram are examples of the "Galilean" type. The second group, described as "transitional," is dated to the fourth century and is characterized by a broadhouse plan, with the doorways in one of the narrow walls and a fixed place for the Torah ark in the Jerusalem-oriented wall; a decline in carved stone relief decoration; the appear-

---

[1] I am grateful to Andrea M. Berlin, Kenneth G. Holum, Lee I. Levine, and David Adan-Bayewitz for their comments on this essay. I assume full responsibility for its contents. I would also like to thank Eisenbrauns for their permission to reproduce E.M. Meyers, C.L. Meyers, and J.F. Strange, *Excavations at the Ancient Synagogue of Gush Halav* (Winona Lake, 1990), Figs. 4-6, 9, and the Studium Biblicum Franciscanum for their permission to reproduce V.C. Corbo, *Cafarnao I. Gli edifici della città* (Jerusalem, 1975), Figs. 11-12 and Pl. XI. During the writing of the essay, I was supported by a fellowship from the American Council of Learned Societies and a fellowship in Byzantine Studies at Dumbarton Oaks in Washington, D.C.

[2] See E.L. Sukenik, *Ancient Synagogues in Palestine and Greece* (London, 1934); also see M. Avi-Yonah, "Synagogue: Architecture," in *Encyclopedia Judaica* (Jerusalem, 1971), vol. 15, cols. 595-600; D. Urman and P.V.M. Flesher, eds., *Ancient Synagogues, Historical Analysis and Archaeological Discovery* (Leiden, 1995), pp. xxvi-xxvii.

[3] All dates are C.E. unless otherwise noted.

ance (in some) of floor mosaics; and (sometimes) no columns in the hall. The synagogues at Hammath Tiberias, Eshtamoa, and Khirbet Susiya are examples of the "transitional" type. The third group, described as "Byzantine," is dated to the fifth and sixth centuries. These synagogues are characterized by a basilical plan with an apse for the Torah ark in the Jerusalem-oriented wall, rubble construction, and interiors covered with floor mosaics. The synagogue at Beth Alpha is an example of the "Byzantine" type.

Within the last thirty years, this typology has been called into question. A number of scholars have pointed out that many of the differences in synagogue types are regional rather than chronological and that the synagogues do not fit into a neat typology. Accordingly, the broadhouse synagogues at Eshtamoa and Khirbet Susiya are now recognized as belonging to a group characteristic of southern Judea.[4] The broadhouse synagogue at Khirbet Shema' in Galilee appears to have been constructed in the late fourth to early fifth century instead of in the third century as the excavators claimed.[5] A late fourth to fifth century date has been proposed for "Galilean" type synagogues in the eastern lower Galilee, while those of the Golan have been dated to the fifth and sixth centuries.[6] Much of the controversy about the validity of the traditional typology has centered on the synagogue at Capernaum, which was always cited as the best example of the "Galilean" type but has been redated to the fifth century on the basis of renewed excavations. In this essay I examine the archaeological evidence for the dating of the "Galilean" type synagogues at Gush Halav and Capernaum. I conclude that the former was constructed no earlier than the second half of the fifth century, while the latter was constructed no earlier than the first half of the sixth century. This conclusion invalidates the traditional typology and, as will be seen, has a number of other far-reaching implications. I begin with Gush Halav, as it provides one of the most fully published examples of an excavated synagogue of the "Galilean" type.

---

[4] D. Amit, "Architectural Plans of Synagogues in the Southern Judean Hills and the 'Halakah,'" in Urman and Flesher, op. cit., vol. 1, pp. 129-156.

[5] J. Magness, "Synagogue Typology and Earthquake Chronology at Khirbet Shema' in Israel," in *Journal of Field Archaeology* 24, 1997, pp. 211-220.

[6] Z. Gal, "Ancient Synagogues in the Eastern Lower Galilee," in Urman and Flesher, op. cit., vol. 1, pp. 166-173; Z.U. Ma'oz, "The Art and Architecture of the Synagogues of the Golan," in L.I. Levine, ed., *Ancient Synagogues Revealed* (Jerusalem, 1982), pp. 98-115.

Gush Halav

Gush Halav (Greek: Gischala; Arabic: el-Jish) is located about eight kilometers (five miles) northwest of Safed, in Israel's Upper Galilee. A synagogue was surveyed in 1905 by H. Kohl and C. Watzinger and excavated in 1977-1978 by E.M. Meyers, C.L. Meyers, and J.F. Strange, under the auspices of the American Schools of Oriental Research.[7] The excavators distinguished four main phases in the synagogue's history:

Period I: 250-306	Middle-Late Roman
Period II: 306-363	Late Roman
Period III: 363-460	Byzantine I
Period IV: 460-551	Byzantine IIA

The synagogue was built over earlier levels dating from the Iron Age through Early Roman periods. Late Byzantine (IIB) and Early and Late Arab period remains were also represented in the post-synagogue levels.[8] The following review of the published architectural, stratigraphic, ceramic, and numismatic evidence indicates that there is only one synagogue building at Gush Halav, which was constructed no earlier than the second half of the fifth century, and one major phase of occupation, which lasted until the late seventh or early eighth century.[9]

Architecture: The synagogue at Gush Halav is a rectangular basilical structure consisting of a single hall (13.75 x 10.6-11 meters), whose main facade is oriented south towards Jerusalem (p. 74). The southern facade is constructed of nicely cut ashlars, while the other walls

---

[7] H. Kohl and C. Watzinger, *Antike Synagogen in Galilaea* (Leipzig, 1916), pp. 107-111; Meyers, Meyers, and Strange, op. cit. The ancient synagogue, which was associated with a village, apparently lies in a tel with remains from various periods; see Meyers, Meyers, and Strange, ibid., pp. 2, 10, 14.

[8] Meyers, Meyers, and Strange, ibid., pp. 7-13. Page and figure references in the following are to this work.

[9] After I wrote this essay, D. Adan-Bayewitz called my attention to E. Netzer, "Review of the Synagogues at Gush Halav and Khirbet Shema'," in *Eretz-Israel* 25 (1996), pp. 450-455 (in Hebrew, with English summary on p. 106*). Based on his analysis of the published excavation report, Netzer concluded, as I did, that there was only one synagogue building at Gush Halav, and that it was constructed during the excavators' Period II. He also does not believe that the synagogue was destroyed by the earthquake of 363. However, Netzer differs from me in accepting the excavators' chronology, placing the construction of the synagogue in the first half of the fourth century, and its destruction in 551.

are of more roughly cut stones (pp. 82, 112-113). The underside of the lintel of the only doorway in the south facade was decorated with a finely carved eagle with garlands (pp. 89-90). A secondary entrance through a passage with a stairway was located at the northwest corner of the synagogue (pp. 90-93). Walls outside of and parallel with the western, northern, and eastern walls of the synagogue's halls created narrow rooms or corridors surrounding it on those three sides, whose function and chronology are unclear (pp. 65, 69, 93-97). The western corridor, which according to the excavators existed from the earliest phase, was apparently used for storage, while the northern corridor may have served as a mezzanine in the later phases (pp. 70, 93-97, 105-112). The numerous fragments of roof tiles recovered in the excavations indicate that the building had a low-pitched, tiled roof, perhaps with a clerestorey (p. 115).

The interior was divided into a nave and two aisles by two rows of four columns each. The columns stood on stylobates of dressed ashlars which are parallel to the two north-south walls. Though the pedestals for the columns are virtually identical in form, their dimensions vary (p. 75). Similarly, the column fragments recovered in the excavations vary in dimension, and the seven capitals recovered differ in style (p. 100). There are also fragments of two heart-shaped columns with two matching capitals, whose placement within and association with the synagogue is uncertain (pp. 103-106). Other architectural features discovered inside the synagogue include field-stone benches along the western and northern walls, and a *bema* (or, according to the excavators, two consecutive *bemas*), against the south wall to the west of the doorway (pp. 77-79). The small number of tesserae found in the fills of the synagogue suggests that the floor was not tessellated (p. 79; but see p. 68 for the suggestion that they derive from a poor mosaic floor in the Period II synagogue). Rough stone pavers found *in situ* just inside the southern doorway were probably covered with plaster, and some plaster layers were found elsewhere in the hall (pp. 67-68, 79).

The Excavators' Chronology: According to the excavators, the synagogue was first constructed in the second half of the third century (pp. 65-66, Figs. 14-15). Extensive renovations and changes were carried out after the earthquake of 306. These included the outer walls (of the corridors) in the northeast, which may have been added at this time (but which may have already been in existence); extensive cuttings of stone *in situ* within the building, which suggest that the stylobate and other members were recut and reset; the erection of a column dedicated by Yose bar Nahum; and the repair of the roof. The mezzanine and the heart-shaped columns are assigned to this phase, or to after 363. The scattered tesserae found in the synagogue fills may come from a simple white mosaic floor in this phase (pp. 63-68). After the earthquake of 363, more major repairs and renovations were carried out on the synagogue. In fact, all of the resetting and repair operations associated with the earthquake of 306 may have taken place at this time. This is also the period in which many of the materials in the western corridor of the synagogue accumulated. The renovation of the *bema*, which involved raising it about one step and reducing its size, also probably took place at this time. No changes occurred in the synagogue's ground plan during the final phase of occupation (450-551). A pot containing a coin hoard, together with many other objects, were stored in the western corridor (see below). This phase ended when the earthquake of 551 destroyed the synagogue and the surrounding village. During the succeeding Byzantine IIb period, there was little activity at Gush Halav (p. 68). Pottery and oil lamps from the early Arabic (A1) period are apparently associated with temporary encampments. An oil lamp inscribed in Arabic was found near the *bema* (p. 72).

A Revised Phasing Sequence: The excavators' phasing sequence and chronology was created by associating a series of assumed destructions with historically attested earthquakes. As the case of the synagogue at Khirbet Shema‘ has illustrated, claimed evidence for earthquake destruction at archaeological sites is often problematic and needs to be carefully evaluated.[10] This holds true for Gush Halav, where the architectural, stratigraphic, ceramic, and numismatic evidence, when considered independently of any assumed earthquake destructions, yields a much different phasing sequence and chronology from those published by the excavators. To demonstrate this, it is first necessary to review the stratigraphic and architectural evidence for the construction and initial phase of occupation of the synagogue at Gush Halav.

As can be seen from the excavators' section drawings (Figs. 5, 6, 8), the original floor level of the synagogue lay at an approximate elevation of 704.5 meters (also see the threshold in Fig. 4, whose elevation is marked 704.565). Compacted fills and traces of rough plaster or

---

[10] Magness, op. cit.

lime surfaces that apparently represent the floor's bedding can be seen in the sections (Figs. 5, 6; L3012, L3022). These must have originally covered the rough flagstone pavement just inside the south doorway (Fig. 5). There are also at least two successive plaster surfaces at about 704.6/704.5 meters in the western corridor (Fig. 9; L4080, L4010, L1058; L4082, L4020, L1060). Other evidence confirms that the original floor level lay at approximately 704.5 meters. This includes the fact that 704.5 meters is the level of the top of the ashlar stylobates (L4036=L1011; L3005=L2005) and of the top of the threshold of the doorway in the inner west wall of the synagogue, which provided access into the western corridor. The top of the threshold of the doorway in the northwest corner of the synagogue lies at 704.316 meters. The tops of the benches lining the western and northern walls lie at a height of 704.64 meters (Fig. 4).[11] Most of the walls visible in the section drawings lie either partly or entirely below the original floor level of the synagogue (Fig. 5, L1045, L1017/ L2035; Fig. 6, L1002, L1004, L5002/L3002, L5030). They therefore represent the foundations of the synagogue or buildings that antedate it. Some of the earlier walls may have been rebuilt or incorporated into the synagogue (for apparent examples of this, see Fig. 5, L1045 [and Photo 7], and Fig. 6, L1002). As can be seen in the section drawings, the synagogue walls and even the stylobates have deep foundations (Figs. 5-8). Foundation trenches are clearly visible in the section drawings on the south side of L1017/L2035 (Fig. 5; L2042, L2041) and on the west side of L1002 (L1033). The latter is associated with the rebuilding of L1002. The relatively high level of this foundation trench, the top of which lies at about 704.8 meters, is apparently due to the fact that the outside of L1002 served as a retaining wall. The bottom of the foundation trench of L1017/L2035 (L2041/L2042) lies at about 702.4 meters, while its top is at ca. 703.2 meters. The foundations of the stylobates lie between about 703 and 704 meters (see L3014 in Fig. 6; and L2034 and L2044 in Fig. 8).

The depth of most of the fills around and between these walls indicates that they antedate the synagogue. They represent deposits associated with earlier, pre-synagogue structures in this area or ear-

---

[11] 704.643 is the only height indicated for a bench (L1030) on Fig. 4 in Meyers, Meyers, and Strange, op. cit. This is inconsistent with the excavators' statement on p. 77 that the benches are all about 40 centimeters above the synagogue's (latest) floor level.

lier accumulations through which the foundations of the synagogue were cut. Plaster pieces, including some painted fragments, indicate that the fills contained material from earlier buildings (p. 29; see for example L2042, which is the foundation trench on the south side of L1017/L2035, visible in Fig. 5; L2009 and L2016 next to L2002, in Fig. 8; and Photo 29). Except on the north side of the synagogue building, where late (postdestruction) debris reached as deep as 702 meters (see for example L1082, L1083), the loci identified by the excavators as representing Period I (the original construction of the synagogue) clearly lie below the level of the top of the synagogue's foundations and foundation trenches (see for example Fig. 5, L4054; Fig. 6, L1068, L1057, L3033, L3032, L3037, L5019, L5024, L5025, L5035).

This means that most of the excavators' Period I fills and occupation deposits antedate the synagogue (with a few exceptions, such as L5014, the stone cuttings visible in Fig. 7, and L3014, L3015, L3033, L2044, which are the bedding for stylobate L3005/L2005; see below). Instead, the loci identified by the excavators as belonging to Period II, which lie at the level of the foundation trenches of the walls and stylobates of the synagogue should be associated with its construction (see for example Fig. 5, L2003, L2037, L2042, L3029, L3030; Fig. 6, L1014, L1015, L1018, L1019, L1021, L1033 [this is the foundation trench for W1002, which according to the excavators was rebuilt in Period II], L1070, L3029, L3030 [these are associated by the excavators with repairs to the stylobate after the earthquake of 306], L5010, L5012, L5015, L5018, L5019; Fig. 8, L2009, L2013, L2015, L2018). The consistency of the foundation and floor levels, and the lack of evidence for the repeated major reconstructions posited by the excavators, indicate that there was only one major phase of construction. All of the remains cited by the excavators as evidence for later (post-Period I) renovations can be associated with this single, original phase of construction. These include the bedding for the stylobates, the *bemas*, and the benches. The presence of two successive plaster floors in the western corridor may reflect different, minor occupation phases during the lifetime of the building.

The Stylobates, Bema, Benches, and Architectural Fragments: According to the excavators, the "remains of extensive cuttings of stone in situ within the building suggest that the stylobate and other members were recut and reset" after the earthquake of 306, though some of these repairs could also have taken place after the earthquake of 363

(p. 68). However, the stone cuttings and buttressing of the stylobates associated with these rebuildings clearly belong to the original construction of the synagogue. In fact, the following description suggests that the excavators themselves could not distinguish between the original construction and supposed later repairs (p. 36):

> Locus 3032 appears in the section drawing as a layer of stone chips recovered near the base of the stylobate shoring. Its pottery may clearly be dated to Period I. Underneath L3032 is L3037, a corresponding layer from Period I; it represents Period I accumulations associated with the original laying of the stylobate. However, the most obvious point documented by the section drawing here is the Period II repair, not the founding. The only alternative to establish the date of founding was to fully dismantle the stylobate and the imposing bedding on either side. In the interest of preservation, we decided to do so at the more convenient points along the stylobate, points not on balk lines. The fact that L3014, the stylobate bedding, is laid down in Period I at this point along the stylobate is nonetheless helpful in understanding the overall stratigraphic picture. However, the stylobate is preserved predominantly in its Period II context. Lifting pavers here and there, though helpful, did not provide sufficient ceramic evidence for concluding which sections survived the 306 catastrophe and which ones were fully repaired.

L3014 is visible as a layer of stones, about half a meter wide and half a meter deep, on the eastern side of the foundations of stylobate L3005 (Fig. 6). The same kind of bedding was found at various points along both sides of the foundations of stylobate L3005/L2005 (L3015, L3033; see p. 35, and Photo 9; and L2034, L2044; 29, 74, and Photo 8, and Fig. 8). L3014, L3015, L3033, and L2044 were attributed by the excavators to Period I, while L2034 was attributed to their Period II. However, the published descriptions and section drawings indicate that all of the stylobate bedding belongs to one original phase of construction. While the deep foundations of the synagogue walls and the buttressed bedding for the stylobate foundations may reflect an awareness on the part of the builders of seismic activity in the area, as the excavators suggested (p. 41), surely their primary purpose was to support the weight of the thick walls and heavy tiled roof of the superstructure. The deep foundations were necessary because instead of resting on bedrock, they were sunk into a thick layer of soft and potentially unstable fills and accumulations.

According to the excavators, there were two successive stone platforms, which they identified as "*bemas*," just inside and to the west of the doorway in the south wall of the synagogue. The foundations were all that remained of the excavators' Period I *bema*, consisting of a rectangular frame of nicely-cut ashlars filled with earth and rubble, with preserved dimensions of ca. 2.00 x 1.75 meters. It abutted the eastern side of stylobate L4036, but because of the remains of the later *bema*, it is not clear how far to the west it extended (p. 79; see Photos 33, 37). The excavators' Period II *bema* (L4015) is a small structure (1.46 x 1.17 x 0.30 meters) made of less carefully dressed stones, which rested partly on the western half of stylobate L4036 and continued westward from there into the western aisle. It had traces of plaster on its north face (p. 79; see Photos 31, 32, 37). It is not clear why the excavators interpreted these remains as representing two different *bemas*. They can just as easily be understood as belonging to a single structure, with the excavators' Period I *bema* representing the foundations, and their Period II *bema* representing the remains of the superstructure. This is supported by the presence of another five blocks preserved on top of their Period I *bema*, which appear to be identical in size and quality with the stones of their Period II *bema*, on the other side of the stylobate (compare Photos 32 and 33). In fact, in the caption to Photo 33, these five blocks are identified as either the second course of the [Period I] *bema* or a remnant of a flagstone floor (p. 73, though on p. 79 they are identified as L4045, "the surviving pavers of Periods III and IV"). All of these remains should be identified as belonging to a single structure or *bema*. Its placement in relation to the main doorway of the south facade corresponds exactly with that of "Platform M" in the synagogue at Capernaum (though the latter appears to be made of unhewn blocks of stone).[12]

The attribution of all of these remains to a single structure is further supported by the associated levels of the floor and stylobate. According to the excavators, the stone pavers just inside the doorway of the south wall (L4051) were contemporary with their Period I *bema*. As they noted, however, their irregular nature suggests that they were originally covered with plaster. The upper surface of the five stone blocks on their Period I *bema* (L4046, described above) lies 0.40-0.45 meters above the level of the stone pavers inside the door (L4051) and is nearly even with the top of the adjacent stylobate (Photo 33). This means that there is nearly a half meter discrepancy

---

[12] Compare Photo 33 with Corbo, *Cafarnao*, Photo 52, upper right.

between the top of the stylobate and the excavators' Period I floor level and *bema*. Their suggestion that this was a deliberate device to solve drainage problems inside the building is awkward and unconvincing, since it means that the top of the stylobate would have been considerably higher than the floor (p. 79). Placing the excavators' Period I *bema* and the flagstone pavers inside the doorway (L4051) below the floor level solves this problem. The manner in which the five stones (L4045) above their Period I *bema* abut the stylobate suggests that they too were covered by the floor. In fact, what appears to be the original plaster and dirt floor (L4015; or the bedding for a floor) is visible to the west of the excavators' Period II *bema* (Photos 31, 32). Though this plaster and dirt floor was sectioned, the photographs indicate that it was at the same level as the top of the stylobate. As the caption to Photo 32 notes, this surface was associated with the [Period II] *bema* (p. 72). Thus, the excavators' Period II *bema* is actually the superstructure of a single *bema*, lying on top of the stylobate and associated with surface L4015. This plaster and dirt floor covered the pavers just inside the doorway (L4051) and the foundations of the *bema* (that is, the excavators' Period I *bema*), and covered or ran up to the top of the stylobate. Another plaster surface (L4018), which was revealed in a section just below L4015, can be understood as representing an earlier (minor) occupation phase, or part of the make-up of L4015, or together with L4015 part of the bedding for a floor that is not preserved.

Benches (L4019, L1030, L1072, L1073) lined the western and northern sides of the synagogue's interior. The bench on the north extends from the northwest corner eastwards, only as far as the eastern stylobate. The benches protrude 0.40-0.45 meters from the inner walls and are about 0.40 meters high. They are built of two rows of stones that were originally plastered over, as indicated by traces of plaster. Because the benches are not deeply founded but instead rest at or slightly below the latest floor level, and because one of them (L1072) partially obscures a design incised into plaster adhering to the inner face of wall L1017, the excavators assigned them to Period II or later. They noted that the various segments of the benches could have been added at different times. "Byzantine 1" pottery is mentioned as having been found inside bench 4019, though none is illustrated (pp. 77-78; Photos 36, 37). The photographs and descriptions suggest instead that all of the benches were constructed at the same time. No rebuilt or added segments are visible in the photographs, and the width and height of the benches is consistent, if slightly irregular. The top of bench L1030 appears to lie at a level of 704.6-704.7 meters (Fig. 6). The synagogue floor would have abutted the bench about halfway up its outer face. In fact, this is exactly what Photos 31, 36, and 37 show, with the dirt and plaster floor (L4015) abutting the base of the superstructure of the *bema* (the excavators' Period II *bema*) on the left and the middle of the outer face of the bench on the right (pp. 71, 78, 80). The "design" scratched into the plaster of the wall behind the benches, which is described as "stylized trees-of-life," is incisions made to roughen the face of the base coat, to hold a finer overlying layer (p. 67, caption to Photo 30).[13] Thus, the benches, stylobate bedding, and the excavators' Period I and II *bemas* belong to a single, original construction phase. The presence of at least two successive layers of dirt and plaster floors inside the hall and western corridor may reflect different, minor occupation phases during the building's lifetime, but not the series of violent destructions and major reconstructions posited by the excavators.

A Revised Chronology: When was the synagogue built? The excavators based their chronology on the numismatic and ceramic evidence and arrived at precise dates by bracketing the various phases or periods with historically attested earthquakes. The ceramic and numismatic evidence must be used with caution, since the presence of deep layers of earlier remains and fills beneath and around the synagogue means that there is a great deal of residual material. Thus, in many cases the pottery and coins provide a broad *terminus post quem* instead of the actual date of the associated phase or remains. This is especially true when only a few diagnostic sherds were recovered, as in the fills of the benches and *bema* and the bedding under stylobate L2005 (Pottery Plates BB; X:11-14).

As has been seen, most of the loci identified by the excavators as Period II (together with a few of the Period I loci) are associated with the foundation level of the synagogue. These include L1089, L1070, L4020, L4066, L4071, L4082, L1060, and L1080, which represent the bottom layer in the western corridor. This plaster and dirt level contained many lamps, lamp fragments, coins, iron nails, and frag-

---

[13] For a similar treatment of plaster see A. Negev, *The Architecture of Mampsis, Final Report. Volume I: The Middle and Late Nabatean Periods (Qedem 26)* (Jerusalem, 1988), p. 132: "All walls were plastered in two layers. The lower layer was a thick muddy plaster mixed with straw. Before this dried incisions were made in a herringbone pattern to ensure better adherence of the second layer of thinner plaster."

ments of glass vessels. Because, according to the excavators, the pottery and coins date to the Late Roman period, they assigned these loci to Period II, or the first use of the synagogue in the fourth century (306-363) (L1089, at the northern end of the corridor, is assigned to Periods I-II, but was contaminated by a Byzantine 1 pit; see pp. 51-52, 268). Three more loci identified by the excavators as Late Roman, L4033, L4035, and L4060, were excavated beneath these at the south end of the corridor (p. 52; see Fig. 9). The latest coins from these loci date to 364-367 (p. 281, R78265, C-137 from L4066; there is another unidentified Late Roman coin from this locus) and 383-392 (p. 282, R78271, C-144 from L4071). Their presence means that the associated level (the excavators' Period II) could not have been destroyed in the earthquake of 363. Instead, these coins provide a late fourth century *terminus post quem* for the construction of the synagogue.

The ceramic material, however, points to an even later date. Among the pottery illustrated from these loci is the rim of a Late Roman "C" (Phocean Red Slip) Ware Form 3 bowl, dated mainly from the second half of the fifth to first half of the sixth century (Pottery Plate EE:10).[14] It provides the first indication that the synagogue was constructed no earlier than the second half of the fifth century. More dating evidence comes from two large lamp fragments and one complete oil lamp from L1089 (Lamp Plate B:13-15). They represent a northern type related to those illustrated in Lamp Plates B:16, D:1-3, but differ in having incised rather than impressed decoration and flat instead of low ring bases. The cross on the nozzle of the example in Lamp Plate B:15 provides a Constantinian *terminus post quem*, while the oval form of the body, small filling hole, and pointed handle suggest a fourth to fifth century (or later) date. The lamp in Lamp Plate D:2, which represents a northern type with impressed decoration, also comes from L1089. The largest number of lamps of this type comes from the catacombs at Beth She'arim.[15] Since the excavators of Beth She'arim assumed that the cemetery there went out of use after the mid-fourth century, these lamps have

---

[14] Also see J.W. Hayes, *Late Roman Pottery* (London, 1972), pp. 329-338.

[15] R. Rosenthal and R. Sivan, *Ancient Lamps in the Schloessinger Collection (Qedem 8)* (Jerusalem, 1978), pp. 110-111; see B. Mazar (Maisler), *Beth She'arim, Report on the Excavations During 1936-1940. Volume I: Catacombs 1-4* (Jerusalem, 1973), Figs. 22:2; 24; N. Avigad, *Beth She'arim, Report on the Excavations During 1953-1958. Volume III: Catacombs 12-23* (Jerusalem, 1976), Pl. 70:12-26.

traditionally been dated from the third to mid-fourth century.[16] However, as F. Vitto recently demonstrated, the occupation of the site
and use of the cemetery at Beth She'arim continued through the
Byzantine period and probably into the early Islamic period.[17] The
morphology of these impressed lamps and their place in the sequence
at Gush Halav point to a fifth to sixth century date for the type.

The level above this, identified by the excavators as representing
Period III or Byzantine 1 (363-460), consists of L4021, L4010 (and
L4010.1), L4048 (and L4048.1), and L1058 (and L1058.1; ".1" appended to a locus number indicates the make-up of a surface; p. 6).
This surface consisted of mixed lime and soil rather than finished
plaster (p. 48). Like the layer below, this surface and its make-up
contained numerous artifacts, including many round, wheel-turned,
hanging lamps, oil lamp fragments, iron implements, bronze, glass,
and dozens of coins (p. 51). The latest coins from these loci provide a
fifth century *terminus post quem* for the make-up and floor of the synagogue (from L4010.1: R771285, C-27 dated to the fifth century;
R771320, C-38, dated 450-457; R771321, C-39, dated 425-450;
R771368, C-44, dated 425-450; R771329, C-50, dated 425-461;
R771372, C-58, dated 425-450; from L4048.1: R78042, C-67, dated
402-450; R78204, C-112, dated 450-457; R78202, C-115, dated
421-476; and from L1058.1: R771398, C-22, dated to the fifth century; there are also a number of unidentified Late Roman coins from
these loci; see pp. 266, 273-274, 278-279). A few of these coins could
be even later; G. Bijovsky has recently suggested that some of the
minimi from Gush Halav identified by J. Raynor as fifth century
instead date to the fifth to sixth centuries.[18] As in the case of the layer
below, the latest datable ceramic types from this level point to a date
no earlier than the second half of the fifth century for the construction and initial phase of occupation of the synagogue. These include
another example of Late Roman "C" (Phocean Red Slip) Ware
Form 3 (Pottery Plate EE:1) and numerous oil lamps and lamp fragments. Several oil lamp types are represented. Those illustrated in
Lamp Plate C:1-15, which come from the make-up of the floor

[16] Rosenthal and Sivan, ibid.

[17] F. Vitto, "Byzantine Mosaics at Bet She'arim: New Evidence for the History of
the Site," in 'Atiqot 28, 1996, pp. 138-141; many of the oil lamps illustrated from Beth
She'arim date to the Byzantine and early Islamic periods.

[18] J. Raynor, "Numismatics," in Meyers, Meyers, Strange, op. cit., pp. 230-245;
G. Bijovsky, "The Gush Halav Hoard Reconsidered," in 'Atiqot 35, 1998, pp. 81-83.

(L4048.1), have ovoid bodies and square handles and are made of thin, red-slipped ware, with geometric decoration in low relief (p. 128). At least some have multiple wick-holes. Molds for this type of lamp, which is common in the northern part of Israel, were found in the excavations at Caesarea. The suggested dates for this type range from the second half of the third century to the seventh century.[19] More examples of the type of northern oil lamp with impressed decoration found in the previous level are represented here as well (Lamp Plates B:16; D:1, 3).

The ceramic and numismatic evidence thus provides a *terminus post quem* in the second half of the fifth century for the construction and initial occupation of the synagogue. In other words, the synagogue was constructed no earlier than the second half of the fifth century. However, the presence of possible sixth century minimi and Late Roman "C" (Phocean Red Slip) Ware Form 3 bowls means that it could have been constructed as late as the first half of the sixth century (see the discussion of the Late Roman "C" Ware Form 3 bowls in relation to the synagogue at Capernaum, below). The pottery and coins found among the debris on top of the floors indicate when the occupation ended. This phase is referred to as Period IV by the excavators. Some of the best dating evidence for this phase again comes from the western corridor. A number of artifacts associated with the final occupation of the building lay buried beneath a layer of architectural fragments from its final collapse. These included an intact oil lamp and lamp fragments, bronze pieces, iron nails, parts of a bronze chandelier, roof tiles, and a few coins. In addition, a hoard of 1,953 coins was discovered in a cooking pot at the northern end of the corridor, which rested upon the plastered surface of the previous phase (L4010=L4048=L1058). The Period IV loci from the western corridor are L4009.1=L4044=L1046 (pp. 47-48). The hoard consists of coins of the lowest possible value, and all are badly worn from use. Most of the coins date from the mid-fourth to mid-sixth centuries, with 60% falling between the years 425 and 498 (Theodosius II to

---

[19] Rosenthal and Sivan, op. cit., pp. 124-125, nos. 513-514; V. Sussman, "Moulds for Lamps and Figurines from a Caesarea Workshop," in *'Atiqot* 14, 1980, pp. 76-79; Y. Israeli and U. Avida, *Oil Lamps from Eretz Israel, The Louis and Carmen Warschaw Collection at the Israel Museum, Jerusalem* (Jerusalem, 1988), p. 112; K.G. Holum, et al., *King Herod's Dream, Caesarea on the Sea* (New York, 1988), Fig. 140; A. Siegelmann, "Roman and Byzantine Remains in the Northern Coastal Plain," in *'Atiqot* 21, 1992, Fig. 4.

Anastasius I). According to Raynor, the contents and context of the hoard indicate that it was not a one-time deposit and that the fact that the cooking pot was set on top of the corridor's floor instead of being concealed in a pit suggests that it served as a depository for charity or operating moneys.[20]

According to the excavators, the hoard was deposited shortly before the destruction of the synagogue by the earthquake of 551. Other evidence, however, points to a later date for the end of the synagogue's occupation. The rim of a bowl of Cypriot Red Slip Ware Form 9 from L4044 dates from ca. 550 to the end of the seventh century (Pottery Plate FF:29).[21] The intact oil lamp from L4044 (Lamp Plate D:6) represents a later variant of the northern oil lamps with impressed and incised decoration found in the previous phases. R. Rosenthal and R. Sivan's late sixth to mid-seventh century date for this type is supported by the existence of one specimen decorated with the impressions of coins minted in the first half of the seventh century.[22] Another intact oil lamp from the last phase of the synagogue's occupation comes from L3012 (Lamp Plate D:7). L3012 is described as a compact fill buried beneath the collapse of the synagogue (L3008; see Fig. 6; see p. 271 for the assignment of L3012 to Periods II-III). It was located on the eastern side of the main hall of the synagogue, on the western side of stylobate L3005. The oil lamp from this locus represents a type dating from the seventh to early eighth century, though its pointed nozzle and relatively high tongue handle indicate that it lies at the later end of that range.[23] Another lamp comes from L4015 (Lamp Plate D:4), which is the dirt and plaster surface under L4007, west of L4008. This surface was associated by the excavators with their later *bema* (L4017) and with bench L4019 (which is assigned to Period IV; see p. 274). The shape of the lamp's body is similar to the previous example, but its low knob handle points to a seventh century date. This lamp appears to be associated with the latest occupation of the synagogue rather than

---

[20] J. Raynor, op. cit., pp. 243-245; Bijovsky, op. cit., has revised Raynor's identifications of some of the coins; and see the discussion of coin hoards in synagogues below.

[21] Hayes, op. cit., pp. 379-382.

[22] Rosenthal and Sivan, op. cit., pp. 123-124; A. Kindler, "A Seventh Century Lamp with Coin Decoration," in *Israel Exploration Journal* 8, 1958, pp. 106-109.

[23] J. Magness, *Jerusalem Ceramic Chronology circa 200-800 C.E.* (Sheffield, 1993), pp. 255-258, Oil Lamps Form 4C.

coming from beneath or within the floor. The ceramic and numismatic evidence from these loci, which by the excavators' definition antedate the collapse of the building, indicates that the synagogue's occupation ended in the late seventh to early eighth century.

This chronology is supported by the evidence from other loci that were associated by the excavators with later phases. L4039 represents a compact fill, which, like L3012, should be assigned to the final occupation phase of the synagogue (though it was assigned by the excavators to their B2b-A1, or postsynagogue, destruction period; see pp. 276-277). It was located to the east of stylobate L4036, buried beneath the surface debris L4038. The finds from this locus included a fragment of a Late Roman "C" (Phocean Red Slip) Ware Form 3 bowl and a coin dated to 565-568 (p. 277; Pottery Plate EE:2). The debris above (L4038) contained more fragments of Late Roman "C" (Phocean Red Slip) Ware Form 3 bowls (Pottery Plate EE:4, 7, 8, 12, 15) and its later variant, Late Roman "C" (Phocean Red Slip) Ware Form 10 (Pottery Plate EE:19-22), dated from the late sixth to mid-seventh century.[24] There were also fragments of Cypriot Red Slip Ware Form 9, dated from ca. 550 to the end of the seventh century (Pottery Plate FF:27)[25] and Cypriot Red Slip Ware Form 7, dated mainly from the second half of the sixth to early seventh century (Pottery Plate FF:30).[26]

Conclusion: All of the available evidence suggests that the synagogue at Gush Halav was constructed no earlier than the second half of the fifth century and perhaps as late as the first half of the sixth century. There were no major earthquake destructions followed by reconstructions as envisioned by the excavators. Instead, occupation continued until the late seventh or early eighth century. The possible presence of two successive floor levels in the western corridor and near the *bema* in the main hall may reflect minor occupation phases during the synagogue's lifetime. According to the excavators, the northwest entrance was blocked by broken architectural fragments after the earthquake of 363, with only the south doorway providing access into the main hall during Periods III-IV. They describe the debris that accumulated over the stairs (L1034, L1048, L1050, L1055) as containing material no later than Byzantine 1 (pp. 92-93).

---

[24] Hayes, op. cit., pp. 329-338, 343-346.
[25] Ibid., pp. 378-382.
[26] Ibid., pp. 378-379.

This includes the rim of a Late Roman "C" (Phocean Red Slip) Ware Form 3 bowl from L1048 (Pottery Plate EE:3). However, in the locus list, L1034 is defined as Period B2b, and it contained a coin dating to 575-576 (p. 265). The late date of the material from the debris over the stairs, together with the use of broken architectural fragments such as part of a column drum and a gable fragment indicate that the northwest entrance was blocked after the final abandonment and collapse of the synagogue.

The coin record at Gush Halav is consistent with that at other Galilean synagogue sites (see below). Late Roman coins of the fourth to fifth centuries are relatively plentiful. The century-long hiatus between the coins of Marcian (450-457) and Justin II (565-578) noted by Raynor is filled by the coins from the hoard, the latest of which date to the first half of the sixth century. The latest coin from the excavations dates to the reign of Maurice (582-602).[27] The almost complete absence of restorable vessels (except for a few oil lamps) from the final occupation level of the synagogue (Pottery Plate DD) suggests that the synagogue was abandoned before it was brought down by an earthquake. This is supported by the excavators' statement that, "The artifacts left for the expedition to recover do not reveal a building abandoned in haste with all its furnishings left behind after the great earthquake of 551" (p. 129). At the time of the abandonment, the coin hoard, which had lost its monetary value long before the seventh century, was left in its pot at the end of the northern corridor (see below). This proposed sequence is supported by the absence of evidence for burning in association with the destruction (p. 48), since oil lamps would presumably have been kept lit in an occupied building. It is also supported by the fact that the roof tiles lay beneath the collapse of the architectural fragments belonging to the upper part of the building, suggesting that the roof had caved in before the walls and columns were brought down (pp. 47-48). Though the excavators' description of the architectural fragments as lying more or less in a line and in the same layer is consistent with destruction by earthquake (p. 48), it is only possible at present to date this event after the abandonment of the building in the late seventh to early eighth century. The references to early Arab pottery (including glazed wares, no examples of which are published; see p. 13), in association with a squatters' occupation among the ruins, suggest that

---

[27] Raynor, op. cit., pp. 234, 243; Bijovsky, op. cit.

the earthquake may have occurred some time during the eighth century.

We now turn to the synagogue at Capernaum, which shares many points of similarity with the one at Gush Halav and appears to have been constructed at about the same time.

The synagogue at Capernaum

The white limestone synagogue at Capernaum was the cornerstone of the tripartite typology of ancient Palestinian synagogues, representing the "Galilean" type. Cleared early in this century by H. Kohl and C. Watzinger, it was dated on the basis of its architectural style to the second to third century.[28] However, the discoveries made by V.C. Corbo and S. Loffreda, who began conducting excavations beneath the synagogue in 1968 on behalf of the Studium Biblicum Franciscanum, have indicated a much later date for its construction. This later date has caused a great deal of ongoing controversy.[29] As I hope to demonstrate here, the architectural, stratigraphic, ceramic, and numismatic evidence points to a date no earlier than the first half of the sixth century for the construction of this synagogue.

The Synagogue Building: The synagogue consists of a basilical prayer hall (20.4 x 18.65 meters), with a courtyard to the east (11.25 meters wide at the front, referred to as a "Beth Midrash" by the excavators) and a narrow porch along the front (south) facade. A small room or annex, the original function of which is unclear, is appended to the northwest corner of the building. The entire structure, which is constructed of white limestone imported from elsewhere in Galilee, sits atop a raised platform of local black basalt. The structure is entirely paved with flagstones. The interior of the prayer hall is divided by three rows of Corinthian columns along the east, west, and north sides into a central nave and three aisles. The columns sit on raised pedestals on a stylobate. The courtyard is also surrounded on three sides (north, east, and south) by pedestaled Corinthian columns on a stylobate, which created roofed porticoes. The synagogue was decorated with richly carved reliefs, some of which were figured (and most

---

[28] Kohl and Watzinger, op. cit., pp. 4-40.

[29] See the studies of Corbo, Loffreda, Avi-Yonah, Foerster, and Tsafrir listed in the bibliography.

of which were later obliterated). The lintel of the central entrance to the prayer hall was carved with the Roman imperial eagle. There are also Jewish motifs such as a seven-branched menorah and what appears to be a Torah shrine. One column in the nave bears a Greek inscription reading, "Herod, son of Mo[ni]mos, and Justus, his son, together with [his] children, erected this column." On the shaft of another column, which apparently stood in the court of the synagogue, is an Aramaic inscription: "Halfu, the son of Zebidah, the son of Yohanan, made this column. May he be blessed." Two platforms (designated "M" and "N") flanked the inner side of the main entrance in the south facade. The presence of these platforms flanking the main doorway in the Jerusalem-oriented wall here and at Gush Halav disproves the traditional notion that there was no set place for the Torah shrine in "Galilean" type synagogues.[30] Though the synagogue at Capernaum is larger and more elaborate than the one at Gush Halav (presumably reflecting a more affluent community), both share this and other features, including a rectangular basilical prayer hall with interior columns resting on stylobates; the orientation of the main facade south towards Jerusalem (at Capernaum, with three doorways; at Gush Halav, with one); carved stone decoration including an eagle on the lintel of the central entrance to the prayer hall; columns bearing dedicatory inscriptions; stone benches lining some of the walls inside the prayer hall; and tiled roofs. Capernaum was paved with a flagstone floor; at Gush Halav the floor was apparently paved with stone or plastered. In addition, the architectural, stratigraphic, ceramic, and numismatic evidence suggests that both synagogues were constructed at about the same time.

Stratigraphy: The fact that the white limestone walls of the synagogue are not perfectly aligned with the top of the black basalt platform has led the excavators to suggest that the latter represents the remains of an earlier synagogue from the time of Jesus.[31] However, the homogeneous nature of the fill inside the platform and the fact that it was built over sloping ground support their original suggestion

---

[30] Corbo, *Cafarnao*, p. 120; J.F. Strange, "Review Article: The Capernaum and Herodium Publications," in *Bulletin of the American Schools of Oriental Research* 226, 1977, p. 70.

[31] S. Loffreda, *Recovering Capharnaum* (Jerusalem, 1985), pp. 46-49; the excavators also noted that the walls of the basalt platform do not run continuously beneath the stylobate. Also see Y. Tsafrir, "The Synagogues at Capernaum and Meroth and the Dating of the Galilean Synagogue," in J.H. Humphrey, ed., *The Roman and Byzantine Near East: Some Recent Archaeological Research* (Ann Arbor, 1995), p. 155.

that it was first constructed as the foundation for the limestone synagogue.[32] The platform was constructed over the remains of late Hellenistic and early Roman houses, which were apparently occupied at
least until the third to fourth century.[33] The houses were buried in a
layer of fill (designated Stratum B) that was up to four meters deep.
The remains of earlier structures that were destroyed when the platform and synagogue were constructed are represented by fragmentary walls and pavements of basalt stones and earth ("massicciata").[34]
The fill of Stratum B was, according to the excavators, "hermetically
sealed" by a thirty centimeter thick layer of white mortar (designated
Stratum C) on which the stone pavement of the building was laid.
This mortar was made of crushed limestone chips from the white
limestone of the synagogue, and more chips were found in spots
beneath the layer of mortar. Though in most places the limestone
pavement was not preserved, the impressions of the pavers were still
visible in the mortar.[35]

The fact that this same stratigraphic sequence has been revealed in
the twenty-five trenches excavated in the synagogue and its courtyard
contradicts the continuing claim of some archaeologists that Strata B
and C belong to a later reconstruction of a second to third century
synagogue building.[36] As J.F. Strange has pointed out, the fact that
the same fill has been found beneath the stylobates also argues
against a later rebuilding, since "the removal of the stylobate implies
removal of the entire upper structure of the building."[37] The excava-

---

[32] S. Loffreda, "Coins from the Synagogue of Capharnaum," in *Liber Annuus* 47,
1997, p. 225; S. Loffreda, "The Synagogue of Capharnaum. Archaeological Evidence for Its Late Chronology," in *Liber Annuus* 22, 1972, p. 11; Tsafrir, ibid.

[33] This level is designated Stratum A by the excavators; S. Loffreda, "The Late
Chronology of the Synagogue of Capernaum," in Levine, op. cit., pp. 54-55.

[34] See n. 31 above. The question of whether these fragmentary remains and the
platform belong to an earlier synagogue that stood on this spot lies beyond the scope
of this discussion.

[35] See for example Loffreda, "The Synagogue of Capharnaum," pp. 11-12, and
"Late Chronology," p. 54. To preserve what remained of the original stone pavement, the trenches in the prayer hall were opened in spots where it was not preserved (though the mortar bedding was intact). Some of the trenches in the courtyard
were cut through the original stone pavement; see Loffreda, "Coins from the Synagogue of Capharnaum," p. 227.

[36] See for example Tsafrir, op. cit., pp. 156-157; G. Foerster, "Notes on Recent
Excavations at Capernaum," in Levine, op cit., p. 59.

[37] Strange, op. cit., p. 70. Also see Loffreda, "Coins from the Synagogue at Capharnaum," p. 229: "in Trench 14 (the southern portion of the western aisle) more
than one hundred late Roman coins were found in the foundation of the stylobate."

tors have distinguished the following construction stages in the synagogue. The prayer hall was built independently, while the courtyard, porch, and northwest annex were added later. There is no architectural connection between the prayer hall and the other structures, including the foundations. In the prayer hall, the inner walls were plastered before the construction of the side benches. The benches and their foundations were built up against the plaster. The stone pavement of the prayer hall and the mortar underlying it were put in place before the construction of the stone benches, which partly overlap the stone pavement. On the other hand, the pavement and layer of mortar are later than the foundations of the two rectangular structures (M and N) located on both sides of the main entrance, since the mortar stops against their foundations.[38]

Chronology: It is clear from the above that the white limestone synagogue represents a single building with no evidence of major reconstructions. On the basis of the coins and pottery found beneath the pavement, mainly in Strata B and C, the excavators have suggested that construction was carried out over the course of a century, from the second half of the fourth century to the third quarter of the fifth, beginning with the prayer hall and ending with the courtyard.[39] As they have pointed out, this date accords well with the Aramaic dedicatory inscription on the column from the synagogue, which Sukenik assigned to the Byzantine period.[40]

Unfortunately, the excavators have published only a fraction of the potsherds and the approximately 25,000 coins they have found beneath the pavement of the synagogue.[41] Since the exact prove-

---

[38] Loffreda, "The Synagogue of Capharnaum," p. 26.

[39] Ibid., pp. 26-27; Corbo, *Cafarnao*, p. 168; Loffreda, "Late Chronology," p. 52. In his most recent article, "Coins from the Synagogue at Capharnaum," Loffreda proposed a slightly later date for the beginning of construction: "it seems that the initial date of the entire synagogue building (prayer hall, eastern courtyard and balcony) was not before the beginning of the 5th century, while the final date of the project is still kept at the last quarter of the fifth century" (p. 233).

[40] Sukenik, op. cit., p. 72; Loffreda, "Late Chronology," p. 52.

[41] S. Loffreda, "Potsherds from a Sealed Level of the Synagogue of the Synagogue at Capharnaum," in *Liber Annuus* 29, 1979, p. 218; Loffreda, "Late Chronology;" A. Spijkerman, "Monete della sinagoga di Cafarnao," in *La Sinagoga di Cafarnao* (Jerusalem, 1970), pp. 125-139; E.A. Arslan, "Monete axumite di imitazione nel deposito del cortile della Sinagoga di Cafarnao," in *Liber Annuus* 46, 1996, pp. 307-316; Loffreda, "Coins from the Synagogue at Capharnaum;" E.A. Arslan, "Il deposito monetale della Trincea XII nel cortile della sinagoga di Cafarnao," in *Liber Annuus* 47, 1997, pp. 245-328. Loffreda ("Coins from the Synagogue at Capharnaum," p. 230), lists a total of 24,575 coins found in all of the trenches and strata (A-C) beneath

nience of the pottery (and of many of the coins) is not provided, it is difficult to evaluate the building's chronology. However, a review of the numismatic and ceramic evidence suggests it was constructed in the sixth century, instead of by the third quarter of the fifth century as the excavators have proposed. Most of the coins found beneath the pavement of the synagogue date to the fourth and fifth centuries, with a few earlier specimens present. The pre-fourth century coins noted by Tsafrir in the lower layers of Stratum B are apparently associated with the Hellenistic and early Roman houses beneath the synagogue, which, according to the excavators, were occupied at least until the fourth century.[42] Fourth to early fifth century coins were the most numerous in the fills beneath the synagogue's floor, with the latest specimens reported until recently dating to the reign of Leo I, ca. 474.[43] Though the excavators have interpreted this evidence as meaning that the synagogue's construction was completed by the third quarter of the fifth century, it actually means that it was constructed no earlier than the third quarter of the fifth century. In other words, the coins found under the floor of the synagogue provide a *terminus post quem*, not a *terminus ante quem*, for its construction.

Other published numismatic evidence points to a construction date in the sixth century. This includes Loffreda's reference to a "very few Byzantine coins" from the hoard of 2,920 coins found on the south side of the western aisle of the prayer hall.[44] Unfortunately, because they have not been published, the number, identification, and date of these "Byzantine" coins are unknown. Most of the rest of the coins from this hoard date to the late fourth and early fifth centuries. The excavators seem to have disregarded the Byzantine coins because they did not accord with their proposed *terminus ante quem* in the third quarter of the fifth century.[45] Another hoard discov-

the floor of the synagogue, with a chart of their numbers according to trench and stratum.

[42] Tsafrir, op. cit., p. 156; also see Loffreda, "Coins from the Synagogue at Capharnaum," pp. 230, 240-241; Loffreda, "Late Chronology," pp. 54-55; Loffreda, "The Synagogue of Capharnaum," p. 14, for third and fourth century coins from Stratum A.

[43] Loffreda, "Potsherds," p. 218; see below for coins dating to the reign of Zeno.

[44] Loffreda, "The Synagogue of Capharnaum," p. 15.

[45] Though in many other places the original stone pavement was no longer in place, only here did the excavators use this as a reason for disregarding the numismatic evidence: "Since the stone pavement had been removed in ancient times, the presence of very few Byzantine coins can be disregarded for our purpose," Loffreda, "The Synagogue of Capharnaum," p. 15.

ered in Trench XII in the synagogue's courtyard contained 20,323
fractional bronze coins, coin fragments, and counterfeits embedded
in the mortar layer underlying the stone pavement. Specimens dating
to Zeno's second reign (476-491) are among the latest of the fifteen
percent of the coins from this hoard that have been analyzed and
published so far.[46] Instead of indicating that the synagogue was completed shortly after 476, as E.A. Arslan concluded, these coins provide a *terminus post quem* of 491 for its construction.[47] The hoard also
includes a number of imitation Axumite coins, which according to
Arslan were in circulation from the third quarter of the fifth century
to the third quarter of the sixth century. The lower end of this range
seems to be based largely on the assumption that the synagogue's
construction was completed no later than the beginning of Zeno's
second reign (476): "Se a Cafarnao l'accumulo... sembra chiudersi
poco dopo l'inizio del secondo regno di Zeno."[48] However, Arlan
noted that Axumite coins have been found elsewhere in contexts
dating to the sixth century: "...in altri luoghi la presenza della moneta
axumita appare prolungarsi notevolmente. A Baalbek viene ricono-
sciuta in un contesto chiuso con Giustino II (565-578)."[49] According
to Bijovsky, "these [imitation Axumite] coins circulated in the area
during the sixth century, as part of the repertory of Byzantine nummi."[50] The coins thus indicate a sixth century date for the construction of the synagogue at Capernaum.

The pottery found beneath the synagogue is consistent with the
coin evidence. The most closely dated pieces belong to imported Late
Roman Red Ware bowls. Though the illustrated sherds are not accompanied by descriptions of the fabric or identifications according
to J.W. Hayes' typology, most can be identified on the basis of the
line-drawings.[51] The following types are represented beneath the
pavement:

---

[46] Arslan, "Il deposito monetale della Trincea XII;" for the coins of Zeno see p.
322, nos. 1911-1913.

[47] Ibid., p. 247, "Il complesso venne quindi sigillato non molto tempo dopo 476
d.C."

[48] Arslan, "Monete axumite," p. 313.

[49] Ibid., pp. 313-314.

[50] Bijovsky, op. cit., p. 83.

[51] Hayes, op. cit. The pottery from the synagogue is not published in Loffreda,
Cafarnao II. La Ceramica (Jerusalem, 1974), though it is possible to correlate some of
the pottery types published elsewhere from the synagogue with those illustrated in
that volume.

1) African Red Slip Ware Form 59, dated ca. 320-420.[52]

2) Late Roman "C" (Phocean Red Slip) Ware Form 1, dated from the late fourth century to third quarter of the fifth century.[53]

3) Cypriot Red Slip Ware Form 1, dated from the late fourth century to about the third quarter of the fifth century.[54]

4) Late Roman "C" (Phocean Red Slip) Ware Form 5, dated around 460 through the first half of the sixth century.[55]

5) Cypriot Red Slip Ware Form 2, dated mainly to the late fifth and early sixth century.[56]

6) Late Roman "C" (Phocean Red Slip) Ware Form 3, dated mainly to the second half of the fifth and first half of the sixth centuries.[57]

The pottery and coins found beneath the synagogue thus provide an early sixth century *terminus post quem* for its construction, instead of a

---

[52] Hayes, ibid., pp. 96-100; for illustrated examples, see S. Loffreda, "La Ceramica della sinagoga di Cafarnao," in *La Sinagoga di Cafarnao* (Jerusalem, 1970), p. 78, Fig. 3:13; S. Loffreda, "Ceramica ellenistico-romana nel sottosuolo della sinagoga di Cafarnao," in Bottini, G.C., ed., *Studia Hierosolymitana III, Nell'Ottavo Centenario Francescano* (Jerusalem, 1982), p. 21, no. 10.

[53] Hayes, ibid., pp. 325-327; for illustrated examples, see Loffreda, "La Ceramica," p. 78, Fig. 3:1.

[54] Hayes, ibid., pp. 372-374; for illustrated examples see Loffreda, ibid., p. 78, Fig. 3:2-3.

[55] Hayes, ibid., pp. 339-340; for illustrated examples, see Loffreda, "Potsherds," p. 19, no. 21; Loffreda, "Ceramica ellenistico-romana," p. 21, no. 41.

[56] Hayes, ibid., pp. 374-376; for illustrated examples, see Loffreda, "Potsherds," p. 19, nos. 15-20; Loffreda, "Ceramica ellenistico-romana," p. 21, no. 15.

[57] Hayes, ibid., pp. 329-338; for illustrated examples see Loffreda, "La Ceramica," p. 78, Fig. 3:5, 8; Loffreda, "Potsherds," p. 19, nos. 1-14; Loffreda, "Ceramica ellenistico-romana," p. 21, nos. 21-34. The following later types appear to be represented as well:

1) Late Roman "C" (Phocean Red Slip) Ware Form 10, dated from the late sixth to mid-seventh centuries (Hayes, pp. 343-346; for an illustrated example see Loffreda, "La Ceramica," p. 78, Fig. 3:11).

2) Cypriot Red Slip Ware Form 7, dated mainly to the second half of the sixth to early seventh centuries (Hayes, pp. 377-379; for illustrated examples see Loffreda, "La Ceramica," p. 78, Fig. 3:9, 12).

3) Possibly Cypriot Red Slip Ware Form 9, dated from ca. 550 to the end of the seventh century (Hayes, pp. 378-382; for what may be illustrated examples of this type see Loffreda, "La Ceramica," p. 78, Fig. 3:7; Loffreda, "Ceramica ellenistico-romana," p. 21, nos. 12-13).

Since these pieces are so much later than the others, and their identification and provenience are uncertain, they are not included in this discussion. However, their presence means there is a possibility that the synagogue could postdate the mid-sixth century.

terminus ante quem in the third quarter of the fifth century as suggested by the excavators.

Other considerations support the assignment of the synagogue's construction to the first half of the sixth century or later. As Loffreda himself acknowledged, the variants of Late Roman "C" (Phocean Red Slip) Ware Form 3 bowls represented under the synagogue date to the first half of the sixth century: "I do agree with Dr. Hayes in recognizing this new feature as quite common in the first half of the sixth century A.D. However, on the evidence of coins, its appearance in Capharnaum must be set in the third quarter of the fifth century, during the reign of Leo I."[58] Second, since there appears to be a fairly large number of sherds representing this form and Cypriot Red Slip Ware Form 2 (as well as smaller amounts of Late Roman "C" Form 5) under the synagogue, time must be allowed for these types to have appeared, been in use, been broken and discarded, and then imported with the fills deposited beneath the synagogue. A date in the first half of the sixth century or later is also supported by the evidence of local ceramic types. Pieces of metallic storage jars with white-painted decoration on a dark background were found in the fill of the courtyard and porch and were embedded in the stucco fragments that decorated the synagogue's interior.[59] Evidence from Jerusalem suggests that the white-painted decoration first appeared on these northern Palestinian bag-shaped jars during the sixth century.[60] Other types described (but not illustrated) as embedded in the stucco fragments include a casserole with bevelled rim and large horizontal handles and an oil lamp decorated with a cross in relief.[61]

It is apparent from the excavators' publication of the synagogue excavations that they have progressively raised the construction date of the synagogue from the late fourth and early fifth century to the mid-fifth century and finally to the third quarter of the fifth century, as later and later coins were discovered beneath the floor. This has also led them to stretch the duration of construction over the course of about seventy-five years or more, beginning in the late fourth or early fifth century.[62] When Loffreda first prepared the publication of

---

[58] Loffreda, "Potsherds," p. 218.

[59] Corbo, *Cafarnao*, pp. 149, 165.

[60] Magness, *Jerusalem Ceramic Chronology*, p. 32.

[61] Corbo, *Cafarnao*, p. 149.

[62] Compare the dates in the following: Loffreda, "The Synagogue of Capharnaum," p. 26: "In conclusion the Synagogue of Capharnaum was built not earlier

the pottery from the excavations at Capernaum in the late 1960s and
early 1970s, he and Corbo proposed a late fourth to early fifth century date for the synagogue (which was, of course, much later than
the previously accepted date).[63] Loffreda based much of his chronology and typology of the local pottery on its association with coins of
the third to fifth centuries.[64] However, the numismatic evidence can
be misleading and provides only a very rough *terminus post quem*. In
addition, Loffreda's earliest publications of the pottery from the synagogue appeared in print before Hayes' typology of imported Late
Roman Red Wares.[65] By the time Hayes' volume was published,
indicating a range from the second half of the fifth through first half
of the sixth century for some of the types represented beneath the
synagogue, a *terminus ante quem* in the third quarter of the fifth century
had already been established by the excavators. It is now necessary to
examine the nature of the numismatic evidence, which is crucial to
the dating of the "Galilean" type synagogues.

---

than the second half of the fourth century A.D. and completed at the beginning of
the fifth century." Corbo, *Cafarnao*, p. 168: "In base alle numerosissime monete ed
all'abbondante ceramica, provenienti da contesti stratigrafici diversi e nondimeno in
constante armonia fra di loro, siamo pienamente convinti che gli edifici della sinagoga furono iniziati, come minimo, verso seconda meta del quarto secolo dopo
Christo e che il lavoro fu portato a termine, con la posa dei pavimenti, *verso gli inizi
della seconda meta del quinto secolo dopo Christo*" (my emphasis). Loffreda, "Potsherds," p.
220: "The latest pieces...suggest that the pavement of the courtyard of the synagogue
cannot be earlier than the mid-fifth century A.D., while the latest coins of Leo I
bring us to a date around 474 A.D." Arlsan, "Monete axumite," p. 308: "L'ipotesi
piu probabile...appare quella del deposito votivo di offerte...formatosi progressiva-
mente a partire da una data forse da collocare in eta teodosiana (dopo la demonetiz-
zazione dell *maiorina*) e conclusasi con la costruzione della pavimentazione della
Sinagoga in un anno di non molto successivo *all'inizio del secondo regno di Zenone (476
d.C.)*" (my emphasis). In his most recent article, Loffreda has suggested that construction began in the early fifth century; see "Coins from the Synagogue of Capharnaum," pp. 332-333: "After the recent identification of many other coins, it seems
that the initial date of the entire synagogue building (prayer room, eastern courtyard
and balcony) was not before the beginning of the 5th century, while the final date of
the project is still kept at the last quarter of the 5th century."
   [63] V.C. Corbo, "Nuovi scavi nella sinagoga di Cafarnao," in *La Sinagoga di Cafarnao, dopo gli scavi del 1969* (Jerusalem, 1970), p. 60; Loffreda, "La Ceramica."
   [64] Loffreda, *Cafarnao II*.
   [65] Hayes, op. cit.; see Loffreda, "La Ceramica," and "The Synagogue of Capharnaum."

Synagogues and coins

Deposits of hundreds and sometimes thousands of coins beneath the floors and foundations of ancient Palestinian synagogues are now a well-known though poorly understood phenomenon. The sites where this is attested include Capernaum, Chorazin, Gush Halav, Meroth (Khirbet Marus), Rehov (all in Galilee), Qazrin, Ein Neshut, Dabiyye, Horvat Kanaf (all in the Golan), and Horvat Rimmon (in Judea).[66] The coins are almost always small bronze denominations, the overwhelming majority of which date to the fourth and fifth centuries. As D.T. Ariel has noted, "this ubiquity is related to the inflationary economic character of that period, which rendered most of the coins...almost valueless."[67] These coins have been understood as providing evidence that the synagogues were built, occupied, or restored during the fourth to early fifth centuries, though at Horvat Kanaf, Ariel noted that "no coins representing the occupational period of the synagogue have yet been found."[68] As has been seen, at Gush Halav the ceramic evidence indicates that the synagogue was constructed no earlier than the second half of the fifth century, while at Capernaum it indicates a construction date no earlier than the first half of the sixth century. The similar pattern of coin finds from the foundations and beneath the floors at other synagogue sites suggests that they too may date to the late fifth or sixth century. The latest published coins from some of these sites are:

1) Ein Neshut: 193 coins (115 of which were identified) from two deposits under the foundations or thresholds of the synagogue. The latest are of Theodosius II or Valentinian III (425-450), with perhaps one coin of Zeno (474-491).[69]
2) Dabiyye: The latest coin from a deposit of 336 coins sealed by the flagstone floor dates to 408.[70]

---

[66] D.T. Ariel, "Coins from the Synagogue at 'En Nashut," in *Israel Exploration Journal* 37, 1987, pp. 148-149; also see Arslan, "Il deposito monetale della Trincea XII."

[67] Ariel, ibid, p. 148.

[68] Ibid.; D.T. Ariel, "Coins from the Synagogue at Horvat Kanef, Preliminary Report," in *Israel Numismatic Journal* 4, 1980, p. 60; D.T. Ariel, "Coins from the Synagogue at Dabiyye," in *'Atiqot* 20, 1991, p. 78.

[69] Ariel, "Coins from the Synagogue at 'En Nashut."

[70] Ariel, "Coins from the Synagogue at Dabiyye."

3) Meroth: The latest out of 520 coins found under the stone floor date to the late fifth century.[71]

4) Horvat Kanaf: The latest two out of 563 coins from the foundations and fill beneath the floors are of Anastasius I (498-518).[72]

5) Qazrin: 180 coins (64 of which could be identified) came from the rubble fill behind the added benches along the interior face of the northern wall. The latest date to the reign of Anastasius I (491-518).[73]

Ma'oz has discussed this phenomenon in relation to the Golan synagogues as follows (my translation from the Hebrew):[74]

> It is worth emphasizing that the two latest coins—which provide the Post quam [sic!] of the building are from the foundations and they indicate that the synagogue [at Horvat Kanaf] was constructed no earlier than the beginning of the sixth century. The rarity of fifth century coins in relation to the corpus (the majority as mentioned are from the late fourth century) is characteristic of the monetary policy of the pe-

[71] Z. Ilan, "The Synagogue and *Beth Midrash* of Meroth," in R. Hachlili, ed., *Ancient Synagogues in Israel, Third-Seventh Century C.E.* (Oxford, 1989), pp. 21-42.

[72] Ariel, "Coins from the Synagogue at Horvat Kanef;" Z.U. Ma'oz, *Ancient Synagogues in the Golan, Art and Architecture, Volumes I-II.* (Qazrin, 1995), p. 133.

[73] Z.U. Ma'oz and A. Killebrew, "Qasrin, 1983-1984," in *Israel Exploration Journal* 35, 1985, pp. 289-293, and D.T. Ariel, "A Hoard of Byzantine Folles from Qasrin," in *'Atiqot* 29, pp. 69-76. For Chorazin, see Z. Yeivin, "Excavations at Khorazin," in *Eretz-Israel* 11, 1973, pp. 144-157; Y. Meshorer, "Coins from the Excavations at Khorazin," in *Eretz-Israel* 11, 1973, pp. 158-162; Ariel, "Coins from the Synagogue at Horvat Kanef," p. 148, note 11. Ariel notes that at Chorazin, Z. Yeivin (the excavator) used deposits of fourth to fifth century coins to determine the date of abandonment of the synagogue. However, the similarities with coins from the other synagogue sites suggests that they instead provide a *terminus post quem* for the construction of the synagogue (Yeivin, p. 153). This is supported by the ceramic evidence. Though the provenience of the pottery published by Yeivin is not described (there are locus numbers, but no descriptions of the loci), it includes the same types of imported Late Roman Red Ware bowls found in the fills beneath the floors of the synagogue at Capernaum (for example, Late Roman "C" or Phocean Red Slip Ware Form 3 [Yeivin, p. 152, nos. 8-9]; Cypriot Red Slip Ware Forms 1 and 2 [p. 152, nos. 7 and 11, respectively]. Some later types are also illustrated, such as Cypriot Red Slip Ware Form 7 [p. 152, no. 1], and Egyptian Red Slip "A" Ware [p. 152, no. 2, and perhaps no. 4]). A sixth century date for the synagogue would account for Eusebius' description of the village as lying in ruins in his day (*Onomasticon* 174:23). It would also accord with the account of Petrus Diaconicus, who quoted an apparently sixth century source that referred to repeated attempts by the Jews of Chorazin to build their synagogue (Yeivin, p. 27).

[74] Ma'oz, *Ancient Synagogues*, p. 133.

riod, as is expressed also in the assemblages of coins from other sites.[75] I would like to say that in a corpus of over five hundred coins [from Kanaf], only twenty of the fifth century were found—only about 3.5%. If the number of coins recovered was much smaller, the chances of finding fifth century coins would diminish to almost zero. In such a case, the determination of the construction date of the building could be off by a century. It is also worth emphasizing that the distribution of coins in different pits in the hall indicates that these are not ordinary hoards, such as those someone would hide and with the purpose of recovering it in times of trouble. For it is not logical that someone would dismantle the floor of the synagogue in several spots in order to recover some poor pieces of copper. These are hoards of the type characteristic of synagogues—which were deposited at the time of construction.

Ma'oz makes two important points here: first, that these coins were never meant to be retrieved, since they had little or no monetary value, and, second, that these deposits date no earlier than the beginning of the sixth century. These points have also been made by Ariel, who noted that at Horvat Kanaf, the highest concentration of dated coins is found in the period between 383-395. After 408, and until the latest dated coin, the concentration of dated coins drops drastically. Ariel attributed both phenomena to the different quantities of coins minted at the time, instead of to any growth or decline in wealth at Horvat Kanaf.[76]

---

[75] Ariel, "Coins from the Synagogue at Horvat Kanef," p. 60.

[76] Ibid. For a recent suggestion that the paucity of fifth century coins reflects a dramatic decline in the size, number, and prosperity of contemporary settlements in Palestine, see Z. Safrai, *The Missing Century* (Leuven, 1998). Although a comprehensive review of this work lies outside the scope of this discussion, I would like to address a few specific points raised by Safrai. 1) Because few fifth century coins have been found in Jerusalem, Safrai concluded that "the economic activity in the city was in reality more limited than the representation of such activity in the contemporaneous literature and in the religious and possibly also the political sphere" (p. 22; also see p. 147). However, I have noted elsewhere that the paucity of fifth century coins and the fact that fifth century ceramic types are basically the same as fourth century types has made it difficult to identify fifth century levels at sites in Jerusalem. In other words, in the case of Jerusalem, the numismatic evidence led to the misdating of the associated ceramic types, and creates the false impression of a decline in prosperity during this period; see Magness, *Jerusalem Ceramic Chronology*, pp. 164-165. The possibility that a similar problem affects the Galilee is suggested by Safrai's statement that, "in most sites in which the numismatic data could be verified, a decrease in the quantity of coins was matched by a corresponding drop in the ceramic finds" (p. 22). In the conclusion to this paper, I note that the fact that the pottery types of the Galilee have been dated largely on the basis of the associated coins indicates that the local ceramic chronology may need to be revised. 2) The ceramic evidence contradicts the conclusion of the excavators (repeated by Safrai, p. 134), that the settlement

This conclusion is supported by similarities with the other synagogue sites mentioned here. The deposition of these small bronze
coins thus seems to postdate the reforms of Anastasius I (491-518),
who replaced the tiny bronze nummi, which had been almost the
only bronze coins of his predecessors, with larger pieces.[77] At Horvat
Kanaf, one small-module follis of Anastasius I is the latest coin represented, to the exclusion of the much more common large-module
follis.[78] This means that almost none of the coins represented in the
synagogue deposits had any legal monetary value when they were
deposited, though they appear to have remained in circulation in the
sixth century.[79] It also means that almost all, if not all, of the small
bronze coins from these synagogues antedate their construction. To
account for this phenomenon at Horvat Kanaf, Ariel suggested that
either the town did not survive long after the completion of the
monumental synagogue or that no recently-minted coins were lost at
the site after its occupation.[80] The latter appears to be the case. To
understand why so many small bronze coins were deposited in these
synagogues, it is first necessary to distinguish between different kinds
of hoards or deposits. As Ariel has noted, many of the coins appear to
have been deliberately deposited, individually or in large numbers,
during the construction of the synagogues. Such deposits cannot

---

at Khirbet Shemaʿ was abandoned after the earthquake of 419, and was renewed on
a limited scale only in the sixth century. In fact, the synagogue at Khirbet Shemaʿ
was apparently constructed in the late fourth or early fifth century, when Safrai
posits a large-scale decline; see Magness, "Synagogue Typology and Earthquake
Chronology at Khirbet Shemaʿ." 3) The case of the forts at Ein Boqeq and Upper
Zohar demonstrates the potentially misleading nature of the numismatic evidence.
All of the hundreds of small bronze coins (which could be identified) recovered from
these two forts antedate their occupation; see J. Magness, "Redating the forts at Ein
Boqeq, Upper Zohar, and other sites in SE Judaea, and the implications for the
nature of the *Limes Palaestinae*," in J.H. Humphrey, ed., *The Roman and Byzantine Near
East Volume 2, Some Recent Archaeological Research* (Portsmouth, RI, 1999), pp. 191-199.
Similarly, Abbasid coins are rare or unattested at many sites in Palestine with
Abbasid occupation. Because they are often found in association with the more
common Umayyad coins, many Abbasid ceramic types have been misdated to the
Umayyad period; see J. Magness, "The Chronology of Capernaum in the Early
Islamic Period," in *Journal of the American Oriental Society* 117.3, 1997, pp. 482-483.

[77] A.R. Bellinger, *Catalogue of the Byzantine Coins in the Dumbarton Oaks Collection and in
the Whittemore Collection. Volume One, Anastasius I to Maurice, 491-602* (Washington, D.C.,
1966), p. 2; Bijovsky, op. cit., pp. 84-85.

[78] Ariel, "Coins from the Synagogue at Horvat Kanef," p. 60.

[79] Bijovsky, op. cit., pp. 84-85.

[80] Ariel, ibid.

properly be considered hoards.[81] They may represent a type of "foundation deposit," though this phenomenon is still unexplained.[82]

For the purposes of this discussion, I suggest distinguishing between these groups of coins as follows:

1) Coins that were mixed with the earth or fills imported during the synagogue's construction. These are usually individual coins, though they can add up, as at Capernaum. These can be understood as incidental deposits, as it is not clear that the builders of the synagogues were aware of the presence of these coins mixed in with the earth.

2) Coins that were deliberately deposited, individually or in groups, during the construction of the synagogue. These were placed in or next to the foundations, or under the floors.

3) "Hoards" of small bronze coins such as those from Gush Halav and Horvat Rimmon. These were found stored together (usually in ceramic vessels) in a room in the synagogue, above the floor level (that is, they postdate the synagogue's construction). It is worth noting that these coins were placed in hidden places inside the synagogue, such as at the end of the western corridor at Gush Halav or in a small hole between two stones at Horvat Rimmon.

4) True hoards of coins of precious metals, such as the gold hoard from Horvat Rimmon and the gold coins found beneath the benches at Capernaum (see below).

True hoards of precious coins are relatively rare and are not included in this discussion. Since it is not known whether the builders were aware of the presence of the coins brought in with the fills, the first group of coins are not considered deliberate deposits either. This leaves the second and third groups, which I believe represent a similar phenomenon, as they were deliberately stored or deposited in or under synagogues and consist entirely or almost entirely of small bronze coins dating to the fourth and fifth centuries. In other words, Jews in sixth century Palestine deposited hundreds, thousands, and even tens of thousands of legally if not effectively worthless bronze

---

[81] Ariel, "Coins from the Synagogue at 'En Nashut," p. 148; Ma'oz, *Ancient Synagogues*, p. 133.

[82] Bijovsky, op. cit., p. 83; Ariel, ibid.; Arslan, "Monete axumite," p. 308; Arslan, "Il deposito monetale della Trincea XII," pp. 290-293.

coins in their synagogues, either in the foundations and below the floors, or in hidden places inside the building. The cooking pot containing 1,953 coins found at the end of the western corridor in the synagogue at Gush Halav represents such a deposit. The fact that the coins had no legal and little real monetary value by the time they were placed in the pot invalidates Raynor's suggestion that it served as a petty cash box or depository for charity or operating moneys.[83] According to Bijovsky's estimate, the purchasing power of the Gush Halav hoard in the mid-sixth century was only about 25 loaves of bread.[84] It has also been suggested that the coins were intended to bring the building and its congregants blessings and good fortune.[85] Z. Ilan has quoted a proposal by Y. Kentman:[86]

> [T]hese were coins used to redeem *ma'aser sheni* (the second tithe). Jewish law requires that *ma'aser sheni*, approximately 9% of certain crops, be eaten in Jerusalem. It is permissible to transfer (redeem) the value of the crops to a coin, carry that coin to Jerusalem, and purchase food and drink for consumption in the Holy City. In either case, *ma'aser sheni* could only be eaten in Jerusalem while the Temple stood. After the destruction of the Temple in 74 C.E. [sic!], crops still had to be redeemed before they could be eaten. Jewish law at this time allowed for the symbolic redemption of large amounts of crops with coins of little value. While it was impossible to redeem those coins since the Temple no longer existed, the coins retained a holy status and could not be used for any purpose. Jewish law therefore required that they be destroyed. In practice, since ruling authorities forbade the destruction of coins, other methods of disposing of the coins had to be found. Perhaps the coins underneath Meroth's floor were *ma'aser sheni* coins which were forbidden for use. They may have been collected elsewhere, over many years, and when the synagogue was built they were brought there.

While I do not necessarily accept Kentman's proposal, I believe it

---

[83] Raynor, op. cit., p. 245; Bijovsky, ibid. Bijovsky, p. 83, classifies this as a genuine hoard, despite the fact that it consists of tiny, ill-struck nummi instead of the usual gold and large bronze coins.

[84] Bijovsky, ibid.

[85] Ilan, op. cit., p. 28.

[86] Ibid. Without suggesting a direct connection between the practices, it is interesting to note the parallels between the coin deposits under synagogues and foundation deposits in the ancient Near East. The deposits described by R.S. Ellis in ancient Mesopotamia were usually placed under the floors or in the foundations of walls of temples and sacred precincts. Small pieces of copper were sometimes included, which are also mentioned in some of the building inscriptions. The latest examples of such practices mentioned by Ellis occurred under the Parthians. See R.S. Ellis, *Foundation Deposits in Ancient Mesopotamia* (New Haven, 1968), pp. 132, 134, 161.

reflects the kind of ritual considerations that lay behind the deposition of these large numbers of small bronze coins in and under synagogues.

Architectural style

"Galilean" type synagogues, especially the one at Capernaum, were originally dated to the second to third centuries on the basis of their architectural style.[87] As G. Foerster stated, "The late second or third century C.E. dating is founded on architectural and stylistic parallels in contemporary Roman art and architecture in Syria and Asia Minor."[88] Although these synagogues resemble Syrian temples of the second to third centuries, this architectural style continued in use for hundreds of years. It can be seen, for example, in the villages of northern Syria, which experienced a period of great expansion during the period from about 330-550 C.E.[89] The only excavations conducted to date in these villages (at Dehes), have indicated that at least some of the houses were constructed in the sixth century.[90] The continued use of this architectural style can also be seen in the fifth and sixth century churches of this region.[91] The Golan synagogues, which share many stylistic similarities with the "Galilean" type synagogues, have been dated by Ma'oz to the fifth to sixth centuries.[92] A

---

[87] Kohl and Watzinger, op. cit., pp. 147-173.

[88] Foerster, op. cit., p. 57.

[89] For example, compare the acanthus rinceaux motif on the buildings at Deir Sunbul and Mugleyya (G. Tate, Les campagnes de la Syrie du nord du IIe au VIIe siècle, Tome 1 [Paris, 1992], p.156, Figs. 221-223) with the same motif at Capernaum (Kohl and Watzinger, op. cit., p. 31, Abb. 61), and the grapevine (rinceaux) motif at Jebel Zawiye (Tate, p. 153, Fig. 216) with the same motif at Capernaum (Kohl and Watzinger, p. 12, Abb. 15; p. 13, Abb. 19).

[90] See J.-P. Sodini et al., "Déhès (Syrie du nord), Campagnes I-III (1976-1978), Recherches sur l'habitat rural," in Syria 57, 1980, pp. 1-303.

[91] See for example G. Tchalenko, Villages antiques de la Syrie du nord, le massif du Bélus a l'époque romaine, II (Paris, 1953), Pls. 156:1 (east church at Baqirha), 159-160, 202 (church at Qalbloze), 200 (east church at Behyo). Though most of these churches differ from the "Galilean" type synagogues in having a built (internal) apse, it is interesting to note the frequent presence of a colonnaded courtyard on one of the long sides of the prayer hall, and the narrow porch along the front of the building, like at Capernaum; see for example Tchalenko, ibid., Pl. 111 (the west basilica at Behyo).

[92] Z.U. Ma'oz, "Golan, Byzantine Period," in E. Stern, ed., The New Encyclopedia of Archaeological Excavations in the Holy Land (New York, 1990), p. 539.

late fourth to fifth century date has been proposed for the "Galilean" type synagogues of eastern lower Galilee.[93] Thus, a late fifth to sixth century date cannot be ruled out for the synagogues at Capernaum, Gush Halav, and others of "Galilean" type strictly on the basis of architectural style.[94] A sixth century date would also account for the much-debated inscription on the lintel of the "Galilean" type synagogue at Nabratein, which states that the building was constructed in 564.[95] Advocates of the traditional typology have attempted to account for this late date by claiming that the inscription was added to the lintel of an already standing building.[96]

Some scholars have objected to a late fourth to fifth century date for the synagogue at Capernaum because its architecture and decoration are so different from others in the vicinity, such as the fourth century synagogue at Hammath Tiberias, and the late fifth to sixth century synagogue at Beth Alpha. As Avi-Yonah stated, "If we consider all we know of the development of architectural styles, we would probably find this to be the only case of such astounding architectural diversity within so small an area."[97] These differences, however, seem to be regional rather than chronological. The "Galilean" type synagogues belong to a Roman architectural tradition in Syria that flourished into the sixth century. Synagogues like the one at Beth Alpha—constructed of unworked field stones, having a niche or apse built into the Jerusalem-oriented wall, and with decoration focused on mosaic floors—are related instead to churches of the late fifth to eighth centuries. Though basilical churches with a

---

[93] Gal, op. cit., pp. 166-173.

[94] As Loffreda ("Coins from the Synagogue of Capharnaum," p. 238) has noted, long before the current controversy began, Avi-Yonah suggested that the capitals of the synagogue at Capernaum appear to belong stylistically to the Byzantine period: "The capitals are mostly of Corinthian type, but they deviate strongly from the classical type...in their sharply-cut edges and geometrical interstices, they antedate by at least two centuries the typical Byzantine capital; in fact, if we did not know the approximate date of these synagogues, we would assign them, on the basis of their architectural decoration, to the Byzantine period." See M. Avi-Yonah, "Synagogue Architecture in the Classical Period," in C. Roth, ed., *Jewish Art, An Illustrated History* (New York, 1961), p. 166.

[95] E.M. Meyers, "Nabratein (Kefar Neburaya)," in Stern, op cit., p. 1077.

[96] M. Avi-Yonah, "Some Comments on the Capernaum Excavations," in Levine, op. cit., p. 60.

[97] Ibid., p. 61. In this passage, Avi-Yonah objected to a fourth century date for the synagogue at Capernaum because that would mean it was contemporary with the nearby (and quite different) synagogue at Hammath Tiberias.

semi-circular apse in the east wall and richly decorated mosaic floors are widespread, it is interesting to note the large number (apparently reflecting a concentration of mosaic workshops) in the territories of Madaba and Gerasa (Jerash).[98] Stylistically, synagogues like the one at Beth Alpha seem to belong to this architectural group and tradition.

Another argument that has been advanced against a fourth century or later date for the synagogue at Capernaum is historical, that the Jews could not possibly have constructed such a lavish structure during a period of oppressive Christian rule. To quote Avi-Yonah again, "Such a state of affairs might be conceivable in our ecumenical age, but it seems almost impossible to imagine that it would have been allowed by the Byzantine authorities of the fourth century."[99] However, as J.E. Taylor has pointed out:[100]

> The contemporaneity of the two buildings [synagogue and octagonal church at Capernaum] is only a problem if we insist that the Christian authorities exercised an effective absolute rule over Capernaum. There is no real evidence to show that they did. The situation may well have been quite the reverse; only this would account for the archaeological evidence.

Taylor makes the important point that the archaeological evidence should first be interpreted without preconceived notions and biases. Only after the chronology of each ancient synagogue has been established on the basis of the archaeological evidence will it be possible accurately to reconstruct the contemporary historical setting in which Jews lived and interacted with others.

Synagogues after the Muslim conquest

As has been seen, the archaeological evidence suggests that the synagogue at Gush Halav remained in use until the late seventh to early eighth century. An intact oil lamp with a molded Kufic Arabic inscription on the shoulder was found in the upper layer of debris in the western corridor of the synagogue. Only the beginning of the

---

[98] See M. Piccirillo, *The Mosaics of Jordan* (Amman, 1993).

[99] Avi-Yonah, "Some Comments on the Capernaum Excavations," p. 62.

[100] J.E. Taylor, *Christians and the Holy Places, The Myth of Jewish-Christian Origins* (Oxford, 1993), p. 293.

inscription, which reads, "In the name of Allah," can be made out.[101] Since this lamp can be dated on the basis of its morphology to the seventh to eighth centuries, it suggests Muslim presence at Gush Halav by that time.[102] Hoards of coins found at other synagogues indicate that occupation continued elsewhere after the Muslim conquest. At Meroth, for example, the latest of 485 coins (245 of which were gold and the rest bronze) from a hoard or "treasury" under the floor of the storeroom dates to 1193.[103] At Nabratein, the depiction of what may be a Torah shrine on a type of early Islamic bowl could point to Jewish presence at least into the eighth to ninth centuries.[104] At Capernaum, a small hoard of gold coins, the latest of which date to the third quarter of the seventh century, was found beneath the eastern benches of the prayer hall.[105] This discovery contradicts the excavators' conclusion that the synagogue was destroyed at the beginning of the early Islamic period.[106] In fact, the possible presence of "Mefjer" (buff) ware from the fill of Trench 11 and the foundations of the staircase near the northeast corner of the courtyard suggests that the building may have undergone some repairs in the second half of the eighth century or later.[107] The possibility that the synagogue remained in use well into the early Islamic period is supported by a bronze Tulunid coin dating to the second half of the ninth century found between the paving stones of the balcony.[108]

---

[101] Meyers, Meyers, and Strange, op. cit., p. 129; Lamp Plate D:8.

[102] See Rosenthal and Sivan, op. cit., p. 133, ns. 542-543; Magness, *Jerusalem Ceramic Chronology*, pp. 255-257, Oil Lamps Form 4.

[103] Ilan, op. cit., p. 30.

[104] J. Magness, "The Dating of the Black Ceramic Bowl with a Depiction of the Torah Shrine from Nabratein, in *Levant* 26, 1994, pp. 199-206.

[105] Loffreda, "The Synagogue of Capharnaum," p. 16; B. Callegher, "Un ripostiglio di monete d'oro bizantine dalla sinagoga di Cafarnao," in *Liber Annuus* 47, 1997, pp. 329-338.

[106] Corbo, *Cafarnao*, pp. 151, 169; Loffreda, *Recovering Capharnaum*, p. 31.

[107] See Corbo, ibid., p. 165, for a reference to jar fragments of a light yellow ware; Loffreda, *Cafarnao II*, pp. 61-63, Class E. According to Loffreda, *Recovering Capharnaum*, p. 40, "games" were inscribed on the paving stones of the synagogue after it went out of use in the Islamic period.

[108] Spijkerman, op. cit., p. 43, no. 346.

Conclusion

This essay has a number of implications:

1) The "Galilean" type synagogues at Gush Halav and Capernaum represent single, original (not reconstructed) buildings established no earlier than the second half of the fifth and first half of the sixth century, respectively, in an architectural style that had a long tradition in Roman Syria. Contemporary synagogues like the one at Beth Alpha were constructed in an architectural style that was commonly used for churches of the late fifth to eighth centuries and enjoyed great popularity in the territories of Madaba and Gerasa on the east side of the Jordan River.

2) The assignment of the "Galilean" type synagogue at Gush Halav to the second half of the fifth century or later, and the one at Capernaum to no earlier than the first half of the sixth century, invalidates the traditional typology and leaves a void in terms of archaeologically identifiable remains of second to third century synagogues in Palestine. It also means that we need to reevaluate our assumptions regarding the relations between the Jews and Christians of Palestine during the fifth, sixth, and seventh centuries.

3) The fact that so many of the coins found in the synagogues at Capernaum and Gush Halav antedate their construction and occupation suggests the need to reexamine the chronology of other synagogues. In the broadest sense, the coin problem affects the chronology of the entire Galilee during the late Roman and Byzantine periods. This is because the sites and the local pottery types have been dated largely on the basis of the associated coins. The fact that coins of fourth to fifth century date are found in sixth century contexts suggests that the local pottery chronology may need to be revised.[109]

4) The chronology of ancient synagogues must be established on the basis of carefully excavated and thoroughly published archaeological evidence. The synagogue at Gush Halav was chosen as the starting point for this discussion because it provides one of the few

---

[109] I suspect it is not a coincidence that the end of the manufacture of such common local types as "Galilean bowls" is dated to the first half of the fifth century. As a reading of D. Adan-Bayewitz, *Common Pottery in Roman Galilee, A Study of Local Trade* (Ramat-Gan, 1973), indicates, the chronological framework for the local pottery is based mainly on the evidence from Galilean synagogue sites, including and perhaps especially Capernaum.

examples of such a site. It remains to be seen whether the future publication of other excavated "Galilean" type synagogues will accord with the chronology proposed here.

Bibliography

Adan-Bayewitz, D., *Common Pottery in Roman Galilee, A Study of Local Trade* (Ramat-Gan, 1973).

Amit, D., "Architectural Plans of Synagogues in the Southern Judean Hills and the 'Halakah'," in Urman, D., and P.V.M. Flesher, eds., *Ancient Synagogues, Historical Analysis and Archaeological Discovery* (Leiden, 1995), vol. 1, pp. 129-156.

Ariel, D.T., "Coins from the Synagogue at Horvat Kanef, Preliminary Report," in *Israel Numismatic Journal* 4, 1980, pp. 59-62.

Ariel, D.T., "Coins from the Synagogue at 'En Nashut," in *Israel Exploration Journal* 37, 1987, pp. 147-157.

Ariel, D.T., "Coins from the Synagogue at Dabiyye," in *'Atiqot* 20, 1991, pp. 74-80.

Ariel, D.T., "A Hoard of Byzantine Folles from Qasrin," in *'Atiqot* 29, 1996, pp. 69-76.

Arslan, E.A., "Monete axumite di imitazione nel deposito del cortile della Sinagoga di Cafarnao," in *Liber Annuus* 46, 1996, pp. 307-316.

Arslan, E.A., "Il deposito monetale della Trincea XII nel cortile della sinagoga di Cafarnao," in *Liber Annuus* 47, 1997, pp. 245-328.

Avigad, N., *Beth She'arim, Report on the Excavations During 1953-1958. Volume III: Catacombs 12-23* (Jerusalem, 1976).

Avi-Yonah, M., "Synagogue Architecture of the Classical Period," in Roth, C., ed., *Jewish Art, An Illustrated History* (New York, 1961), pp. 157-190.

Avi-Yonah, M., "Synagogue: Architecture," in *Encyclopedia Judaica* (Jerusalem, 1971), vol. 15, cols. 595-600.

Avi-Yonah, M., "Some Comments on the Capernaum Excavations," in Levine, L.I., ed., *Ancient Synagogues Revealed* (Jerusalem, 1981), pp. 60-62.

Bellinger, A.R., *Catalogue of the Byzantine Coins in the Dumbarton Oaks Collection and in the Whittemore Collection. Volume One, Anastasius I to Maurice, 491-602* (Washington, D.C., 1966).

Bijovsky, G., "The Gush Halav Hoard Reconsidered," in *'Atiqot* 35, 1998, pp. 77-106.

Callegher, B., "Un ripostiglio di monete d'oro bizantine dalla sinagoga di Cafarnao," in *Liber Annuus* 47, 1997, pp. 329-338.

Corbo, V.C., "Nuovi scavi nella sinagoga di Cafarnao," in *La Sinagoga di Cafarnao, dopo gli scavi del 1969* (Jerusalem, 1970), pp. 11-60.

Corbo, V.C., "La sinagoga di Cafarnao dopo gli scavi del 1972," in *Liber Annuus* 22, 1972, pp. 204-235.

Corbo, V.C., *Cafarnao I. Gli edifici della città* (Jerusalem, 1975).

Ellis, R.S., *Foundation Deposits in Ancient Mesopotamia* (New Haven, 1968).

Foerster, G., "Notes on Recent Excavations at Capernaum," in Levine, L.I., ed., *Ancient Synagogues Revealed* (Jerusalem, 1981), pp. 57-59.

Gal, Z., "Ancient Synagogues in the Eastern Lower Galilee," in Urman, D., and P.V.M. Flesher, eds., *Ancient Synagogues, Historical Analysis and Archaeological Discovery* (Leiden, 1995), vol. 1, pp. 166-173.

Hayes, J.W., *Late Roman Pottery* (London, 1972).

Hayes, J.W., *A Supplement to Late Roman Pottery* (London, 1980).

Holum, K.G., R.L. Hohlfelder, R.J. Bull, and A. Raban, *King Herod's Dream, Caesarea on the Sea* (New York, 1988).

Ilan, Z., "The Synagogue and *Beth Midrash* of Meroth," in Hachlili, R., ed., *Ancient Synagogues in Israel, Third-Seventh Century C.E.* (Oxford, 1989), pp. 21-42.

Israeli, Y., and U. Avida, *Oil Lamps from Eretz Israel, The Louis and Carmen Warschaw Collection at the Israel Museum, Jerusalem* (Jerusalem, 1988).

Kindler, A., "A Seventh Century Lamp with Coin Decoration," in *Israel Exploration Journal* 8, 1958, pp. 106-109.

Kloetzi, G., "Coins from Chorazin," in *Liber Annuus* 20, 1970, pp. 359-369.

Kloner, A., "The Synagogues of Horvat Rimmon," in Hachlili, R., ed., *Ancient Synagogues in Israel, Third-Seventh Century C.E.* (Oxford, 1989), pp. 43-47.

Kohl, H., and C. Watzinger, *Antike Synagogen in Galilaea* (Leipzig, 1916).

Loffreda, S., "La Ceramica della sinagoga di Cafarnao," in *La Sinagoga di Cafarnao* (Jerusalem, 1970), pp. 61-123.

Loffreda, S., "The Synagogue of Capharnaum. Archaeological Evidence for Its Late Chronology," in *Liber Annuus* 22, 1972, pp. 5-29.

Loffreda, S., *Cafarnao II. La Ceramica* (Jerusalem, 1974).

Loffreda, S., "Potsherds from a Sealed Level of the Synagogue of the Synagogue at Capharnaum," in *Liber Annuus* 29, 1979, pp. 215-220.

Loffreda, S., "Review of *Ancient Synagogue Excavations at Khirbet Shema', Upper Galilee, Israel, 1970-1972*, by E.M. Meyers, A.T. Kraabel, and J.F. Strange (Durham, 1976)," in *Bulletin of the American Schools of Oriental Research* 244, 1981, pp. 75-79.

Loffreda, S., "Ceramica ellenistico-romana nel sottosuolo della sinagoga di Cafarnao," in Bottini, G.C., ed., *Studia Hierosolymitana III, Nell'Ottavo Centenario Francescano* (Jerusalem, 1982), pp. 273-312.

Loffreda, S., "The Late Chronology of the Synagogue of Capernaum," in Levine, L.I., ed., *Ancient Synagogues Revealed* (Jerusalem, 1981), pp. 52-56.

Loffreda, S., *Recovering Capharnaum* (Jerusalem, 1985).

Loffreda, S., "Capernaum," in Stern, E., ed., *The New Encyclopedia of Archaeological Excavations in the Holy Land* (New York, 1993), pp. 291-295.

Loffreda, S., "Coins from the Synagogue of Capharnaum," in *Liber Annuus* 47, 1997, pp. 223-244.

Magness, J., *Jerusalem Ceramic Chronology circa 200-800 C.E.* (Sheffield, 1993).

Magness, J., "The Dating of the Black Ceramic Bowl with a Depiction of the Torah Shrine from Nabratein," in *Levant* 26, 1994, pp. 199-206.

Magness, J., "The Chronology of Capernaum in the Early Islamic Period," in *Journal of the American Oriental Society* 117.3, 1997, pp. 481-486.

Magness, J., "Synagogue Typology and Earthquake Chronology at Khirbet Shema' in Israel," in *Journal of Field Archaeology* 24, 1997, pp. 211-220.

Magness, J., "Redating the Forts at Ein Boqeq, Upper Zohar, and Other Sites in SE Judaea, and the Implications for the Nature of the *Limes Palaestinae*," in Humphrey, J.H., ed., *The Roman and Byzantine Near East, Volume 2, Some Recent Archaeological Research* (Portsmouth, RI, 1999), pp. 188-206.

Ma'oz, Z.U., "The Art and Architecture of the Synagogues of the Golan," in Levine, L.I., ed., *Ancient Synagogues Revealed* (Jerusalem, 1981), pp. 98-115.

Ma'oz, Z.U., "Golan, Byzantine Period," in Stern, E., ed., *The New Encyclopedia of Archaeological Excavations in the Holy Land* (New York, 1993), pp. 538-545.

Ma'oz, Z.U., *Ancient Synagogues in the Golan, Art and Architecture, Volumes I-II.* (Qazrin, 1995).

Ma'oz, Z.U., and A. Killebrew, "Qasrin, 1983-1984," in *Israel Exploration Journal* 35, 1985, pp. 289-293.

Mazar (Maisler), B., *Beth She'arim, Report on the Excavations During 1936-1940. Volume I: Catacombs 1-4* (Jerusalem, 1973).

Meshorer, Y., "Coins from the Excavations at Khorazin," in *Eretz-Israel* 11, 1973, pp. 158-162.

Meyers, E.M., "Nabratein (Kefar Neburaya)," in Stern, E., ed., *The New Encyclopedia of Archaeological Excavations in the Holy Land* (New York, 1993), pp. 1077-1079.

Meyers, E.M., A.T. Kraabel, and J.F. Strange, *Ancient Synagogue Excavations at Khirbet Shema', Upper Galilee, Israel, 1970-1972. Annual of the American Schools of Oriental Research XLII* (Durham, 1976).

Meyers, E.M., C.L. Meyers, and J.F. Strange, *Excavations at the Ancient Synagogue of Gush Halav* (Winona Lake, 1990).

Negev, A., *The Architecture of Mampsis, Final Report. Volume I: The Middle and Late Nabatean Periods (Qedem 26)* (Jerusalem, 1988).

Netzer, E., "Review of the Synagogues at Gush Halav and Khirbet Shema'," in *Eretz-Israel* 25, 1996, pp. 450-455 (in Hebrew, with English summary on p. 106*).

Piccirillo, M., *The Mosaics of Jordan* (Amman, 1993).

Raynor, J., "Numismatics," in Meyers, E.M., C.L. Meyers, and J.F. Strange, *Excavations at the Ancient Synagogue of Gush Halav* (Winona Lake, 1990), pp. 230-245.

Rosenthal, R., and R. Sivan, *Ancient Lamps in the Schloessinger Collection (Qedem 8)* (Jerusalem, 1978).

Safrai, Z., *The Missing Century* (Leuven, 1998).

Siegelmann, A., "Roman and Byzantine Remains in the Northern Coastal Plain," in *'Atiqot* 21, 1992, pp. 63-67*.

Sodini, J.-P., et al., "Déhès (Syrie du nord), Campagnes I-III (1976-1978), Recherches sur l'habitat rural," in *Syria* 57, 1980, pp. 1-303.

Spijkerman, A., "Monete della sinagoga di Cafarnao," in *La Sinagoga di Cafarnao* (Jerusalem, 1970), pp. 125-139.

Spijkerman, A., *Cafarnao III. Le Monete della Città* (Jerusalem, 1975).

Strange, J.F., "Review Article: The Capernaum and Herodium Publications," in *Bulletin of the American Schools of Oriental Research* 226, 1977, pp. 65-73.

Sukenik, E.L., *Ancient Synagogues in Palestine and Greece* (London, 1934).

Sussman, V., "Moulds for Lamps and Figurines from a Caesarea Workshop," in *'Atiqot* 14, 1980, pp. 76-79.

Taylor, J.E., *Christians and the Holy Places, The Myth of Jewish-Christian Origins* (Oxford, 1993).

Tate, G., *Les campagnes de la Syrie du nord du IIe au VIIe siècle, Tome 1* (Paris, 1992).

Tchalenko, G., *Villages antiques de la Syrie du nord, le massif du Bèlus a l'époque romaine I-III* (Paris, 1953).

Tsafrir, Y., "The Synagogues at Capernaum and Meroth and the Dating of the Galilean Synagogue," in Humphrey, J.H., ed., *The Roman and Byzantine Near East: Some Recent Archaeological Research* (Ann Arbor, 1995), pp. 151-161.

Urman, D., and P.V.M. Flesher, eds., *Ancient Synagogues, Historical Analysis and Archaeological Discovery* (Leiden, 1995).

Vitto, F., "Byzantine Mosaics at Bet She'arim: New Evidence for the History of the Site," in *'Atiqot* 28, 1996, pp. 115-146.

Yeivin, Z., "Excavations at Khorazin," in *Eretz-Israel* 11, 1973, pp. 144-157.

Yeivin, Z., "Chorazin," in Stern, E., ed., *The New Encyclopedia of Archaeological Excavations in the Holy Land* (New York, 1993), pp. 301-304.

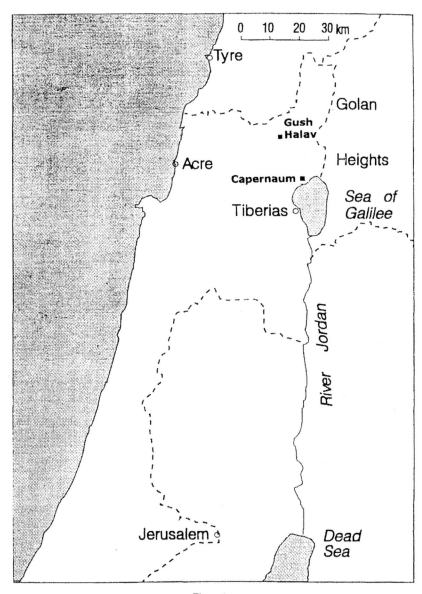

Figure 1.
Map of Galilee showing the location of Capernaum and Gush Halav.

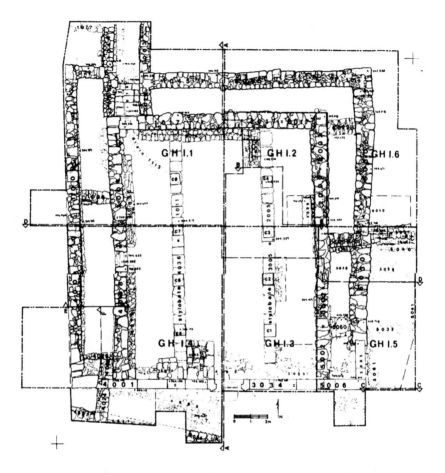

Figure 2.
Annotated stone-for-stone plan of the synagogue at Gush Halav, showing areas of excavation,
architectural loci, elevations, and the location of published sections.
Reproduced with permission from Meyers, Meyers, and Strange 1990: Fig. 4.

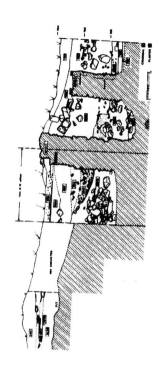

Figure 3.
Section A-A, the main north-south balk through the synagogue at Gush Halav, looking west.
Reproduced with permission from Meyers, Meyers, and Strange 1990: Fig. 5.

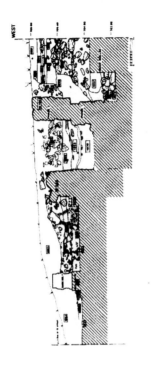

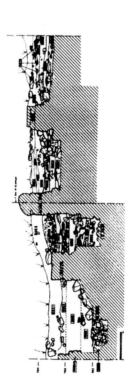

Figure 4.

Section D-D, the main east-west balk through the synagogue at Gush Halav, looking south.
Reproduced with permission from Meyers, Meyers, and Strange 1990: Fig. 6.

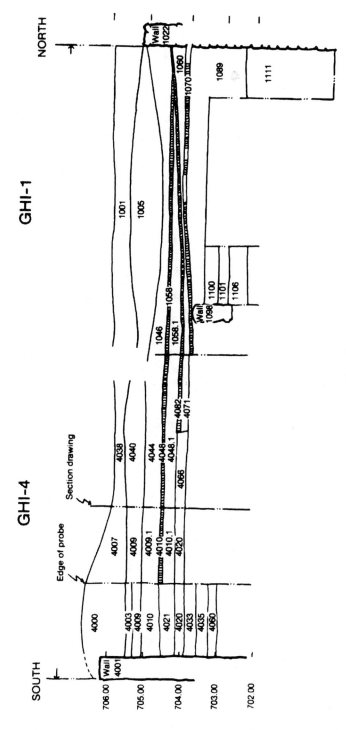

Figure 5.

Schematic section, north-south, through the "western corridor" of the synagogue at Gush Halav, looking west.
Reproduced with permission from Meyers, Meyers, and Strange 1990: Fig. 9.

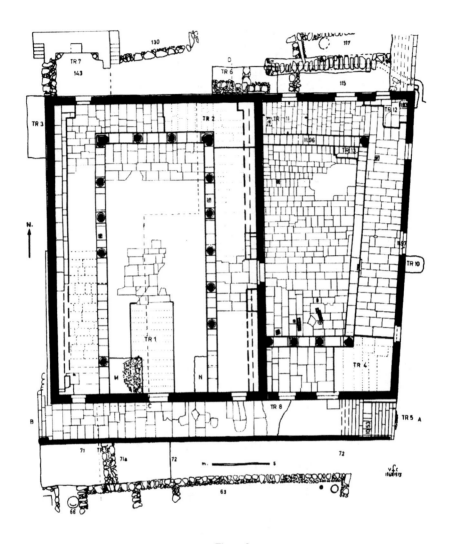

Figure 6.
Plan of the synagogue at Capernaum.
Reproduced with permssion from Corbo 1975: Pl. 11.

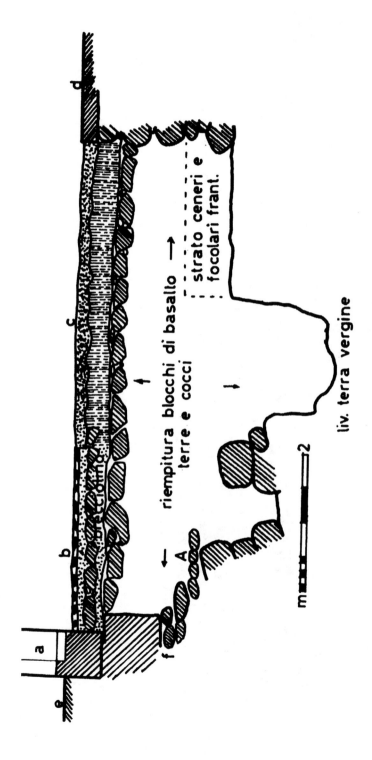

Figure 7.

North-south section in trench 1 in the synagogue at Capernaum, looking west.
Reproduced with permission from Corbo 1975: Fig. 11.

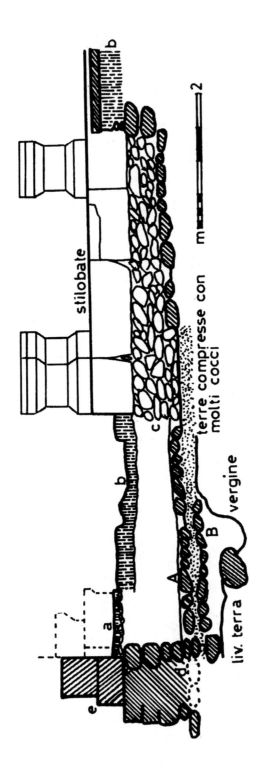

Figure 8.
East-west section in trench 2 in the synagogue at Capernaum, looking south.
Reproduced with permission from Corbo 1975: Fig. 12.

2. THE DATING OF THE GUSH HALAV SYNAGOGUE: A RESPONSE TO JODI MAGNESS

Eric M. Meyers
Duke University

Jodi Magness' article subtitled "The Problem of Typology" has a ring of anachronism about it. The "typology" to which she refers is an allusion to the older, largely Israeli scholarly view, which in truth has been inoperational since the early 1970s. The most articulate spokesman for that view was also the most articulate spokesman for its demise, Michael Avi-Yonah:

> Formerly regarded as the earliest of existing Galilean synagogues, the building [Capernaum] was now dated some two hundred years later on account of the fourth and fifth centuries found buried under the pavements or near the walls.... Other scholars have so far been skeptical of this opinion, which indeed leaves a great deal to be explained.[1]

Avi-Yonah was absolutely clear about the passing of the older chronology but expressed lingering doubts about why there would be a plurality of synagogue forms so close to one another in a single period.[2] But even the most ardent supporters of the older typology recognized that only new archaeological data could substantiate claims for dating. Though Magness claims that this is all she wants to do, namely, create new data from the reports, the fact is that in regard to Gush Halav she has misconstrued key data in the reports, which in turn has led her to new conclusions about chronology that must be rejected out of hand.

Before explaining how I believe Magness has gone wrong in her reading of the data and hence her conclusions, I would like to say something about common sense and the historical method. By suggesting that the Gush Halav and Capernaum synagogues are constructed in the fifth and sixth centuries respectively, Magness not only throws out the older typology but, indirectly as a result of her sugges-

---

[1] Avi-Yonah, "Ancient Synagogues," in *Ariel* 32 (1973), p. 38. See also R. Hachlili, "The Art and Architecture of Late Antique Synagogues," in S. Fine, ed., *Sacred Realm: The Emergence of the Synagogue in the Ancient World* (New York, 1996), p. 101.

[2] Hachlili, ibid.

tions, would question the very nature of Jewish life in Byzantine Palestine. To be sure, such a case has been made for a more vibrant and active Jewish community at that time, and even I have said this.[3] But both synagogues in question would have to have been constructed in an era when Christianity also flourished in the community, both possibly as communities in which Christian pilgrimage seem to have flourished.[4] At the least, Professor Magness might have offered an explanation about why the Jewish community would have undertaken such huge building campaigns at these times. But, no, she is content to stay with archaeological minutiae, and I only would say that the situation of the Jewish community in Christian, Byzantine Palestine was less than sanguine at the time and that the building restrictions on synagogues imposed by Theodosius II in 439 C.E. are surely relevant.[5] Similarly, many archaeologists and art historians still maintain that they can distinguish between a Roman-period and Byzantine-period building:

> Christianity was the leading power in the Byzantine Empire, and Christian architects determined the prevalent architectural styles. It was in a Christian-Byzantine cultural setting that the Jews originated a dialogue of adoption and adaptation. They could assimilate to or struggle against the environment, but they could not remove themselves from it.
>
> The answer to our initial question is yes. We can date a synagogue to the Roman or Byzantine period by its architecture, even when there are no clear archaeological data.[6]

Although I would not go so far as Tsafrir, his point is well taken.

---

[3] See for example my essays, "Ancient Synagogues: An Archaeological Introduction," in *Sacred Realm*, op. cit., pp. 14-20, and "The Current State of Galilean Synagogue Studies," in L.I. Levine, ed., *The Synagogue in Late Antiquity* (Philadelphia, 1987), pp. 127-139.

[4] See J. Wilkinson, *Jerusalem Pilgrims before the Crusades* (Warminster, 1977). It should be noted in regard to Gush Halav that by the fourth century C.E. there was a Christian community in Gush Halav in the upper city where a Christian tomb was excavated; so N. Makhouly, "Roch-Cut Tombs at El Jish," in *Quarterly of the Department of Antiquities of Palestine 8* (1939), pp. 45-50. It is not impossible that some of the coins in the Gush Halav hoard were actually tokens intended to be used by pilgrims to the Holy Land. Among the artifacts found in the tomb were amulets that might be considered "Jewish-Christian."

[5] For text and brief commentary see J.R. Marcus, *The Jew in the Medieval World* (Philadelphia, 1961), pp. 5-6.

[6] Y. Tsafrir, "The Byzantine Setting and Its Influence on Ancient Synagogues," in Levine, op. cit., p. 153; see especially n. 10.

Evidence of Earthquakes

Magness has attempted in another article to deny the relevance of earthquakes in establishing a chronology for the nearby site of Khirbet Shema'.[7] Since this subject is also relevant to the Gush Halav discussion, I will make a small excursus on Khirbet Shema' below and hopefully demonstrate the relevance of earthquakes in establishing chronology there, at Gush Halav, and at other sites.[8] I should state early on that in both excavations, geologists specializing in earthquakes visited the sites and suggested that Gush Halav and Khirbet Shema' lay in the Tzefat epicenter. Frequent earthquakes in this region of Upper Galilee—on the average of two per century— serve as a contemporary reminder of the geological instability of this area. Historical sources mention the years 1739, 1812, and 1837 as having especially strong earthquakes, and that the 1837 quake destroyed the medieval fort in nearby Tzefat down to its foundations.[9] Traces of the 1837 earthquake were also found in excavations at ancient Meiron, just 600 meters distant from Khirbet Shema'.[10] To dismiss earthquakes as not relevant to establishing the chronology of the Gush Halav synagogue is to ignore the obvious. Magness even admits that the nineteen meters of *cyma recta* molding that lay face down in debris of the western corridor "is consistent with destruction by earthquake," yet she refuses to attribute its collapse to earthquake due to the fact that there was some seventh and eighth century

---

[7] "Synagogue Typology and Earthquake Chronology at Khirbet Shema' in Israel," in *Journal of Field Archaeology* 24 (1997), pp. 211-220.

[8] The standard references on earthquakes in Israel are D.H. Kallner-Amiran, "A Revised Earthquake Catalogue of Palestine," in *Israel Exploration Journal* 1 (1950-1951), pp. 223-246; K.W. Russell, "The Earthquake of May 19, A.D. 363," in *Bulletin of the American Schools of Oriental Research* 238 (1980), pp. 47-64; and "The Earthquake Chronology of Palestine and Northwest Arabia for the 2nd through the Mid-8th Century A.D.," in *Bulletin of the American Schools of Oriental Research* 260 (1985), pp. 37-59.

[9] "Tzefat," in I. Press, *A Topographical-Historical Encyclopedia of Palestine* (Jerusalem, 1955), vol. 4, p. 803 (Hebrew).

[10] Remains of prayerbooks, newspapers, and other religious artifacts including scrolls from magical amulets were found in the course of excavating the Meiron tomb complex. The artifacts, along with some human remains, were given to the inspector of antiquities there at the time, Nathaniel Tefilinski, who identified them as coming form the time of the great earthquake in 1837. Parts of the ancient tomb had been used for local burials associated with the catastrophe of 1837.

material associated with the uppermost debris.[11] A careful observer can see how close to the modern surface the *cyma recta* molding of the latest building was (Photo 18, p. 50) and that the locus is not sealed from above. The later ceramic materials represent the accumulation of post-synagogue debris; the floor levels below represent the latest use-phase of the western corridor, not its construction phase as Magness alleges. In fact, the recent re-examination and re-publication of the synagogue hoard beneath this collapse shows that the hoard has coins that actually go right up to the date of the 551 earthquake.[12] Bijovsky, on the basis of her new dating of coins nos. 370 and 367, concludes that the entire hoard of coins "provide striking evidence that the accumulation of coins in the vessel continued through Period IV until the last days of the synagogue in 551 C.E."[13]

In noting the collapse of molding onto other architectural fragments and onto stones from the inner and outer walls of the western corridor, I would like to stress that while the area is not a sealed locus the pottery tended to become less and less disturbed by what both Magness and I would call "early Arabic" ceramics, and more late Roman and Early Byzantine in character, as we excavated the debris. This is apparent from both the Critical Locus List and the latest coins in the hoard, the Baduila coin (no. 370) and the "Christogram" minima of Justinian I (no. 367), neither of which must date later than 551 C.E.,[14] which were contained in a cooking pot set into the floor. It is impossible to consider that the material here is consistent with dating the period of the first construction of the building to the fifth century, or even later. All of the material of that period lies underneath the *cyma recta* molding which while unsealed from above seals

---

[11] See Gush Halav report, p. 11 and Photo 18 on p. 50. It is possible to see how the molding rests on fallen stones from the inner (4008=1004) and outer (4005= 1002) walls.

[12] G. Bijovsky, "The Gush Halav Hoard Reconsidered," in *'Atiqot* 35 (1998), pp. 77-106, and E.M. Meyers, "Postscript to the Gush Halav Hoard," in ibid., pp. 107-108. Bijovsky identifies coins No. 368-369 (pp. 82-83) as Egyptian imitations of coins brought by Christian pilgrims. Dating to the fifth century and circulating into the sixth century as part of the repertoire of Byzantine nummi these and other coins from the hoard raise the possibility that Christians or Jewish-Christians visited Gush Halav, and possibly the wadi synagogue.

[13] Bijovsky, ibid., p. 80.

[14] See Bijovsky's tabular presentation of coin data on p. 98 where she notes that in the case of the two latest coins the regnal dates extend beyond 551. In view of her comments on p. 80, however, it is clear that she considers that the coins were in good enough shape to have been issued and deposited by 551 C.E.

material beneath it; and that material is sixth century C.E. or earlier, the sixth century hoard providing a *terminus ad quem* for the synagogue building and other debris levels providing data for earlier phases.

The Fills

Magness alleges on the basis of the two main section drawings (Figs. 5 and 6) that the portions of walls visible in them and which may be associated with floor levels and the threshold in the southern facade, represent either the founding of the synagogue or portions of building that antedate it. In following her instincts, Magness points out the main anomaly of the excavation at Gush Halav, namely, that the synagogue rests upon an ancient *tel* that is not visible at ground level. The debris accumulation, although self-contained somewhat, did not result in the usual sort of buildup characteristic of Palestinian mounds. Because the site is situated in a wadi or canyon, the debris accumulated along the steep incline of the west-east slope. The architect of the expedition, Larry Belkin, took great pains to produce drawings that illustrated this.[15] Since the synagogue makes extensive use of pre-existing walls in its construction, the reader of the report must always be aware of how deep the courses are and how, for example, the two northern corners were originally founded in the Late Bronze or Iron Age and yet their uppermost courses were utilized in all the synagogue phases. Due to the fact that the southern facade wall and main entryway in it remained in use for all phases of the synagogue, using the elevations of the southern threshold or stylobate that is associated with it to establish founding dates for the associated walls that are so deeply founded is therefore a fruitless and meaningless exercise. Eyeballing the levels on the main sections and associating them with those elevations has led Magness erroneously to conclude that the four bearing walls of the synagogue were founded in the Byzantine period.

---

[15] To conceptualize and present this material, Belkin produced Figures 20, 21, 41, 43, 44, and 45, though other drawings may be helpful. Figures 20 and 21 in E.M. Meyers and C.L. Meyers with J.F. Strange, *Excavations at the Ancient Synagogue of Gush Halav* (Winona Lake, 1990) (hereafter referred to as *G*), pp. 82-83, give the most vivid impression of the most unusual setting for the synagogue site in a wadi on top of an artificial *tel* that is not visible from ground level.

The inappropriateness of establishing chronology on section drawings mainly may be appreciated in looking at Fig. 6 where Byzantine
material is found so high up in the west, roughly at floor level, while
nothing at all is found at the east at the same level. But in comparing
the material in the southeast corner with the material in the southwest corner note the following: phase 1 of the exterior western wall
(1002) may go back at least to the Persian period (L.1071) and possibly to the Iron Age, but excavation along its inner face produced
early remains of Period II or the Late Roman period (L.1070). The
material above it is associated with subsequent phases. Moving to the
east in Section D-D, L.3037, which is the earliest sealed material
associated with the inner wall (L.3002), we find either Middle Roman
material, or Period I data. On the exterior face of the eastern exterior
wall in the southeast corner material associated with the founding is
uniformly Middle Roman (L.5029 and 5035). These readings in my
opinion establish quite readily the fact that there could not possibly
be a Byzantine-period founding for the synagogue. Hopefully the
explanation of the western corridor hoard shows why that material
represents the latest use-phase and not a founding phase of the synagogue.

Magness fully recognizes that some of the walls of the synagogue
are left over from earlier, pre-existing structures. I also believe that
many parts of them predate the synagogues. The point to remember
is that significant sections of those walls were incorporated into and
used in association with *all* phases of the synagogue. In addition,
because of the downward slope of the wadi to the east, many important debris levels have been eroded. So, for example, Magness appears to be bothered by the foundation trench in fig. 6 (L.1033),
which the excavators assigned to Period II on the basis of nine homogeneous buckets of pottery dated to the fourth century, and with just
a little Middle Roman pottery in them. Because L.1033 appears to go
to the lowermost courses of what the balk drawing calls "Phase 1" of
the wall she misses the point that beneath it, L.1068, read homogeneous Middle Roman, and therefore dates both Period 1 and Period 2
uses of Wall 1002. Those fills are to be associated with renovations
and not founding. Judging from L.1071 Wall 1002 goes back to at
least the Persian period. Looking at the debris levels on the south face
of the wall–its inner face yields the same results: L.1070 may be
dated to Period II and above it L.1058 may be dated to a Period III
renovation. As it turns out we did not recover Period I founding

material there nor Period IV undisturbed debris because they were too close to modern surface. In looking at the east-west balk one can see that in elevation these loci are very close to the floor level.

Perhaps I should reiterate now what I wrote in the introduction to the final report regarding the manner in which we excavated. Why didn't we have wider trenches around the exterior walls of the synagogue? Why were our probes so small? The truth is that the expedition and the Israel Department of Antiquities could not successfully negotiate with the owners of the land around the site. Israel antiquities law is such that, when no agreement between the government and the owners of the land on which a ruin sits can be achieved, the government is only permitted to license excavation a very small distance from the outermost points of the visible ruins. Hence, we could excavate only two meters outside the exterior walls, a restriction that made digging there almost impossible. We were simply not able to extend outwards in any direction. Had we done so we surely would have been able to clarify the situation of the exterior walls much better, especially in the west. Nonetheless, such restrictions forced us to excavate more deeply on the inside of the building.

Figure 5, the north-south balk, illustrates this point very well. Where we could penetrate deeply we did, as in area 2. From the deep cut against the inner face of Wall 1017, the inner north wall of the synagogue, L.2037 provides ample data to date the Period II renovation, while L.2042 and 2043 provide genuine Period I material, which may be associated with the earliest use of this pre-existing wall as part of the synagogue. All of these chronological inferences may easily be drawn by consulting the pottery readings on the Critical Locus List. It should be noted, however, that not all loci appear on a section drawing because a balk represents only those debris levels encountered at the balk line itself. We also decided to publish pottery that was recovered from loci that appear in the main sections. This meant of course that important loci would not be published. The decision to do this was influenced by the unique circumstance of the slope and *tel*.

Magness avers that in reading Section D-D, the main east-west balk (Fig. 5), it is clear that all of the stylobate bedding and associated debris may be related to one construction phase, which in her view is fifth century. But the ceramics and coins associated with most of those fills may be dated to the Middle Roman or Late Roman periods, third and fourth centuries C.E. None of the deep fills can be dated to a fifth century founding, let alone a building that she says possibly stood for ca. 300 years, till the middle of the eighth century. Merely reading the loci from the Critical Locus List on the north-south balk in relation to the two stylobates, one is struck with the absence of any Byzantine-period ceramics in L.3022 (with one possible exception in bucket 54), 3032, 3037 on the eastern face of the eastern stylobate and L.3022, 3029, and 3033 on the western face. All of the readings were Period I or II. Unfortunately the debris east of the western stylobate was uniformly disturbed since it was exposed roughly at floor level since antiquity, as was the material in L.1006 and 1029, just below the modern debris level, L. 1003. The character of the steep slope in relation to the excavation may be seen in the architect's diagrams, Figures 20 and 21, pp. 82-83. A clearer picture with clean material emerges in Section B-B, an east-west balk between the east wall (2002) and the eastern stylobate (2005). All the loci here point to a founding phase in Period I, and a repair phase in Period II (see Critical Locus List: L.2013, 2018, 2037 and 2043). The excavators explained the stone fills up against the stylobates (see Photo 9, p. 35) as firstly original to Period I, and subsequently as a technique for stabilizing them in Period II, in the beginning of the fourth century. Since both fills have only third and fourth century pottery in them it is impossible to see how the synagogue could have been built in the fifth century. It is also impossible for me to conceptualize how all of these building activities occurred at one time. To be sure the original builders of Synagogue I must have had an awareness that the spot chosen for the synagogue had deep fills with numerous "ancient" walls protruding here and there. Some areas of founding needed more shoring up than others; and where you had massive walls that were standing some of the digging must have been of an investigative sort, the builders wanting to establish the stability of the "footers" or deepest courses.

The Bema(s)

Magness makes the claim that there is evidence of only one *bema* in the synagogue. Since her main argument is based on visual data, especially Photos 32 and 33, Magness contends that the five small blocks visible at right in Photo 33 and resting on the putative founding course of the *bema* from Period I survive from the only *bema*, namely the fifth-eighth century one she believes existed.[16] Because the field-stone character of the Period III-IV *bema* identified by the expedition resembles the five stones in front of a small depression in Photo 33, Magness has jumped to the erroneous conclusion that all of those field stones were part of a single, Byzantine-period (fifth century) construction. But the excavators recognized that the stones visible in Photo 33 had nothing to do with the *bema* pictured in Photo 32. Magness may be confused here since the ones in Photo 33 lie east of the stylobate and do not articulate in any way with the Byzantine-period *bema*, L.4017. Those stones might have been interior, filling stones of the earlier *bema* or remnants of a later flagstone surface but not a *bema*.[17] As in most cases the expedition relied on a series of earthen and plastered surfaces to date elements of the synagogue. The relevant fill is L.4015 and 4015.1. The debris is consistently Byzantine, the later clearly sixth century judging from the lamps and pottery.[18] These data lead to the conclusion that the smaller *bema* with plastered field stones was Byzantine in date. The earlier *bema* of ashlar construction (L.4050) lay on an earlier surface, which is definitely associated with L.4050.1 and which dates probably to Period II or earlier. The field readings were third or early fourth century C.E. These small earthen fills beneath surfaces at the very least suggest a late Roman-period *bema* and a Byzantine-period *bema*. Taking into account architectural considerations, drainage in the building, and the condition of the "early" and "late" buildings it is an inescapable conclusion that the ashlar construction is Roman-period and the field-stone *bema* Byzantine. A similar chronology may be established for the benches, preserved mainly in their later phases.

In regard to the *bemas* I should also mention the unique character of the southern facade wall, which is the only ashlar exterior wall, though a finished, ashlar corner may be observed in the southeast. The location of the *bema* on the interior face of the southern wall underscores the principle of sacred orientation whereby the wall facing Jerusalem receives special attention. The ashlar masonry of the southern facade wall also underscores this point as does the presence of the eagle on the underside of the lintel in the doorway there; and

---

[16] See especially Photos 31, 32, and 33 and Figures 16 and 17.

[17] The legend accompanying Photo 33 on p. 73 is very clear about this. In this photo one can easily compare the five stones in question because they do not appear in Photo 32 on p. 72.

[18] See especially *G* lamp plates A:8, B:2, and D:4.

the southern wall is the only wall that is largely unobscured by buildings built near or up against an exterior wall of the synagogue.

The Western Corridor, South End

In discussing the coin hoard above it should be clear that the north
end of the western corridor is preserved well in the final stages of the
building's history. In that end in addition to the hoard a quantity of
roof tiles were found along with pieces of glass oil lamps, suggesting a
storage function. A cross-wall, 1098, towards the south (Photo 15)
suggests that the space was divided early on in Period I and II. Figure
11 and Photo 28 show how the ashlar southern wall was keyed into
a field-stone wall that connected to the exterior, western wall of
synagogue (L.4008), parts of which may have functioned as a terrace
wall. The complexity of the situation may be observed in Photo 15.
Up against the northern face of this dividing wall at founding level,
homogeneous Middle Roman pottery was found with a third century
coin (L.1100). Examination of section E-E or Figure 10 at the south
end of the western corridor demonstrates that both the inner and
outer walls there go back to Periods I and II. While L.4010.1 is
consistently Byzantine L.4020 is Late Roman and L.4033 Middle
Roman-Late Roman. Other materials that were recovered even
deeper but do not appear on the section drawings go back to Period
I. In other words wherever one looks at "founding" levels of walls—
though because older walls are re-used we might want to call this "re-
founding—that may be associated with the original building we encounter sealed loci of Middle Roman (Period I) or Late Roman
(Period II) debris.

Ceramics and Chronology

Magness' comments on ceramics are always helpful, and I have acknowledged her assistance in that area before.[19] But in the present
instance, pointing out that some lamps or imported wares may actu-

---

[19] For example in my article, "The Torah Shrine in the Ancient Synagogue:
Another Look at the Evidence," in *Jewish Studies Quarterly* 4 (1997), p. 58, I acknowledge her assistance in regard to the dating of late Byzantine-early Arabic-period
black sherds, n. 58.

ally be a bit later is not helpful. Let me explain. It is not enough to go to a lamp plate or pottery plate and pick a sherd or lamp and suggest it may be a little later than the excavators thought. In archaeology what is most important is the full context of an artifact, i.e., its locus in relation to what is around or adjacent to that locus. The possibility that a single sherd might possibly be dated a bit earlier or a bit later is not compelling enough to lower or raise the date of an entire locus. While our expedition did not quantify the sherds it excavated, and saved, and registered, a representative collection was always taken and anomalies always were duly noted. In this regard normally a period was assigned to a locus during the final, writing stage. In the meantime some coin readings may have been revised or many changed, as is the case with Bijovsky's report on the hoard; other coins might have been illegible at the time of the preliminary report. So, for example, the assignment of L.4066 to Period II should be revised to Period III, though the coin may be dated just after the earthquake of 363 C.E. All the associated loci, however, are Roman in date (L.4020 and 4062 and possibly 4071 except for the one coin). In any case, as has already been noted, the north end of the western corridor is primarily preserved in its Period IV use as is demonstrated by the coin hoard. Though Magness' comments are also helpful regarding L.1089, the locus description mentions the possible contamination of it with later Byzantine sherds because of the fact that walls are so close together and that pottery from the interstices could fall in or down into a Roman-period locus. So all of her comments regarding the fills in the northern area of the western corridor should keep this in mind.

Magness, therefore, has tried to revise the chronology of the entire building on the basis of anomalies, most of which are concerned with an area that was preserved best in the synagogue's final phase of use; and while the coin hoard has been re-examined and revised, the new readings do not affect the date suggested as the final use-phase of the building and western corridor. Magness' comments about some of the early Arabic-period pottery should be viewed in the context of post-building use of space. All of the material in question is high up in unsealed materials, some of it near modern surface. It has nothing to do with the last usage of the building as a synagogue, which is recovered from the profile of the coin hoard and from other Byzantine-period loci that are more reliable.

Short Excursus on Magness' Dating of Khirbet Shema[20]

I would like to draw attention to Magness' comments on Khirbet Shema' for several reasons. First, her refusal to consider earthquakes as being relevant to the chronology of sites in the Meiron area of Upper Galilee is pure stubbornness. Surely the circumstances of the collapse at Pella with a human being trapped in a confined area and killed are not required to offer an interpretation that is informed by earthquake![21] Secondly, although the excavators suggested the collapse of the synagogue in 419 C.E. by earthquake was disastrous, they did not mean to suggest that the site was abandoned.[22] Zeev Safrai, however, has recently described the fifth century as a period in which the Jewish settlement of Palestine "regressed greatly," causing a demographic shift that resulted in both settlement decline and "devastation" in trade and the economic sphere.[23] This is precisely the century Magness suggests the Gush Halav synagogue was built and when life at Khirbet Shema' continued to flourish. Magness uses "later" pottery, late Byzantine pottery and early Arabic pottery, to bolster her point, most of which is *ex situ*, or not associated with the synagogue. Magness does invoke an eighth century earthquake to explain the collapse of the Khirbet Shema' building in her conclusion, however, which she argues, brought the synagogue down and signaled the end of the settlement.

The third issue I would like to challenge is her fourth century dating of the synagogue, the only one to have existed in her mind until it was destroyed by earthquake in the eighth century. The case is similar to Gush Halav in that she rejects multiple phases for the *bemas* and hence rejects any multiple phasing of the synagogue. In other words, Magness rejects any hint of the earthquake of 306 C.E. that may be alluded to in Eusebius' *Onomasticon*.[24] No matter that pieces of shattered architectural members were found re-used in the stylobate or found buried in an underground declivity! No matter

---

[20] See above n. 7.

[21] Her reference is to A. McNicoll and R.H. Smith, *Pella in Jordan 1* (Canberra: Australian National Gallery, 1982), p. 138.

[22] See E.M. Meyers, A. Thomas Kraabel, and J.F. Strange, *Ancient Synagogue Excavations at Khirbet Shema'* (Durham, 1976) (hereafter referred to as *Khirbet Shema'*), p. 6.

[23] Z. Safrai, *The Missing Century: Palestine in the Fifth Century, Growth and Decline* (Leuven, 1998), p. 129.

[24] This is discussed in *Khirbet Shema'*, pp. 38-38.

that some of them could actually mend with pieces used to fill the re-built *bema*, some of which were surely parts of an earlier Torah Shrine/*bema* complex.[25] No matter that the capitals of the second synagogue were refashioned after a quake, and some of the earlier, more elaborately decorated pieces of column capitals could mend with the refashioned capitals![26] Magness simply contends there was no earlier structure and only an eighth century earthquake.

One example will suffice to challenge the accuracy of her suggested re-dating. When the excavators dismantled the beautifully preserved *bema*,[27] the first thing they noted was that the bench on the north wall continued behind the it.[28] Secondly, the earthen, rubbly fill dated to the Late Roman period or roughly fourth century C.E.[29] Two coins were found in the rubbly core: one of Alexander Jannaeus (103-76 B.C.E.) and a virtually unworn coin of Constans (337-341 C.E). Magness takes the coin of Constans as a *terminus post quem* for the only synagogue building; the excavators take the Constans coin as providing the date for major renovations of the synagogue or Synagogue II, which included the addition of a *bema*, or as a *terminus ante quem*. The presence of a coin of Gratian (378-383 C.E.) in one of the deep eastern underground declivities suggests that repairs were made throughout the fourth century, or possibly that those declivities were reused for some purpose at that time. In any case, we believe Magness' case for a fourth century dating at Khirbet Shema' does not hold up under scrutiny.

Conclusions

Before summing up a very complex and technical discussion, I would like to thank Professor Magness for taking the time to carefully read the reports upon which she bases her conclusions. Because of the technical data of much of the discussion and material, I fear that

---

[25] This is apparent from Photos 3.8 and 3.11 in *Khirbet Shema'*.

[26] *Khirbet Shema'*, pp.69-70.

[27] Ibid., Photos 3.16 and 3.21.

[28] Ibid., Photos 3.1 and 3.16. That there was a bench on the south wall prior to the building of the *bema* does not prove that there was a synagogue in that earlier stage. The reuse of earlier architectural fragments from a built structure the size of a Torah Shrine, especially the column base in Photo 3.11, however, makes it quite probable.

[29] *Khirbet Shema'*, pp. 71-73.

there are not many individuals apart from archaeologists who will be able independently to make judgments about this important material; and this is surely a shortcoming of the field of archaeology in general. I also believe we must come up with a better way to report the results of our work so that they are accessible to more scholars in biblical and Judaic studies, to mention but a few relevant disciplines. It is then in the spirit of open scholarly exchange that I offer my suggested corrections to Magness' alternative chronology.

In the case of Gush Halav, she is suggesting that there is only one building, one synagogue, which is constructed in the fourth century and used until the early Arab period or eighth century. I have defended a late third century construction that underwent numerous alterations until the synagogue was felled by earthquake in 551 C.E. The coin hoard from the synagogue site itself contains coins that go up until that year and no further. In the case of Khirbet Shema', Magness once again suggests a construction date in the fourth century and a collapse in the eighth century, but admits a decline in the community already in the fifth century. I have defended once again a late third century founding of the Khirbet Shema' synagogue, a major renovation of it in the fourth, and a collapse by earthquake in the fifth century. Though these differences may not strike the reader as all that great, I believe they are very important.

I also believe that the rather substantive differences in assessment of the data originate in part because we know the pottery of the Galilee much better today than when Khirbet Shema' was written (twenty-five years ago) and even when Gush Halav was written (almost ten years ago). But even taking this into account and admitting a willingness to adjust the chronology somewhat on the basis of ceramic typology, the real difference lies in the interpretation of stratigraphic matters, and these are matters not easily resolved. Perhaps face-to-face discussion might help.[30]

If we were to accept Professor Magness' higher chronology, I would expect numerous scholars to question the extent and general well-being of Jewish life at the dawn of the middle ages in Palestine. However much we might like to advocate the construction of new synagogues in the fourth century, we certainly need to take into

---

[30] When Professor Magness first presented her proposed re-dating of the Khirbet Shema' synagogue at a national meeting, I was unable to attend due to a head-on conflict.

account the new legislation against them and the declining status of the Jew in the Holy Land.[31] Hopefully this exchange will find an appropriate forum in which to continue this important dialogue. I will leave the Franciscans to defend their dating of the synagogue at Capernaum.

---

[31] Safrai, op. cit., especially, pp. 129-132. The picture that Safrai paints for the centuries in question, especially the late fourth and fifth is neither one of prosperity nor demographic growth. No doubt Christianity took root more slowly in the rural areas but its rapid spread under official auspices no doubt had a negative impact on Palestinian Jewry.

Figure 1.

Gush Halav synagogue after one year of excavation, looking west.

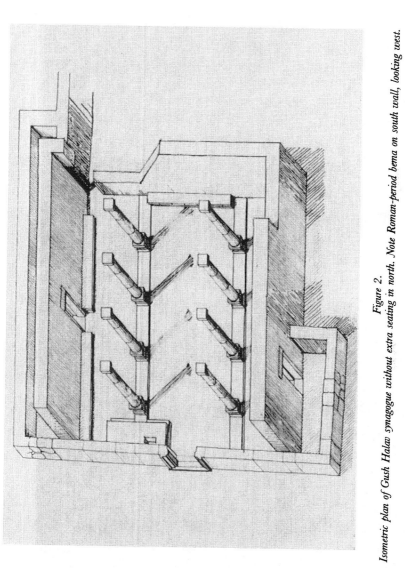

Figure 2.

Isometric plan of Gush Halav synagogue without extra seating in north. Note Roman-period bema on south wall, looking west.

Figure 3.

South entryway to Gush Halaw synagogue with remains of Roman-period bema abutting western doorjamb, looking south.

Figure 4.
Remains of Byzantine-period bema on interior of southern wall, looking south.

Figure 5.
Scattered debris of the destroyed Byzantine-period synagogue at Khirbet Shema', showing evidence of earthquake, looking east.

Figure 6.

Side view of fourth century bema with earlier bench running through it, looking west.

Figure 7.
Reconstructed Synagogue II at Khirbet Shemaʿ, looking east. Note bema at right and reworked capitals on columns.

3. SYNAGOGUE TYPOLOGY AND KHIRBET SHEMAʿ: A RESPONSE TO JODI MAGNESS

James F. Strange
University of South Florida

The typology of synagogues in ancient Palestine has been one of the thorniest issues in synagogue research in this century. Research into the floor plans of around a dozen excavated synagogues in Israel and Jordan resulted in a neat typology that gained wide acceptance in the 1930s, but gained especially wide acknowledgment in the early 1970s.[1] On the other hand, as Dr. Magness points out, the excavations at Khirbet Shema', conducted from 1970-1972, called this neat topology into question, for a broadhouse synagogue seemed to have been constructed at this site before the time that the typology allowed, namely, in mid-third century C.E. or later.[2]

Magness proposes no less than a complete re-interpretation of the published evidence. She claims to re-examine the relevant, "published architectural, stratigraphic, ceramic, and numismatic evidence."[3] It is enough to say that her credentials for this project are formidable, given her amassed publications in archaeology, ancient synagogue research, and allied fields.

Magness first reviews the received typology of synagogues in ancient Palestine from the third to the sixth centuries C.E. In brief, the theory holds that synagogue design and construction occurs in three stages. In stage one, dated to the second and third centuries and confined to the Galilee and the Golan Heights, synagogues are built in basilical plan, with decorated façade, three doors in the façade and the façade facing Jerusalem. The masonry on the outside was richly

---

[1] Eliezer L. Sukenik, *Ancient Synagogues in Palestine and Greece* (Oxford, 1934; reprinted: Munich, 1980); Marilyn Chiat, *Handbook of Synagogue Architecture* (Chico, 1980); Michael Avi-Yonah, "Synagogue Architecture," in *Encyclopedia Judaica* (Jerusalem, 1972), vol. 15, cols. 595-600.

[2] Jodi Magness, "Synagogue Typology and Earthquake Chronology at Khirbet Shema', Israel," in *Journal of Field Archaeology* 24/2 (1997), pp. 211-220. Cf., Eric M. Meyers, A. Thomas Kraabel, and James F. Strange, *Ancient Synagogue Excavations at Khirbet Shemaʿ, 1970-1972* (Annual of the American Schools of Oriental Research 42; Durham, 1976).

[3] Magness, op. cit., p. 211.

carved in relief, and the floors inside were paved with flagstones. There was no set place for the synagogue ark.

In stage two, dated to the fourth century C.E., the so-called transitional group, we find buildings that are broadhouse in plan, with a permanent place for the ark on the long walls, the one facing Jerusalem. Entrances and points of egress are in the short walls. The floors are sometimes paved with flagstones and sometimes with colored mosaics. The prayer hall has no columns at all. There is much less carved relief on the outside.

Stage three, dated to the fifth and sixth centuries C.E., is termed the "Byzantine" group for obvious reasons. These synagogues are basilicas in plan with an apse for the Torah Shrine in the short wall that faces Jerusalem. The floors are uniformly paved with colored mosaics in many styles, from geometric to those with biblical scenes.

The Franciscans launched the first challenge to this typology in the publication of their materials from beneath the floor of the ancient synagogue at Capernaum.[4] In the soil beneath the flagstone floors and beneath the stylobates were simply thousands of coins of the fourth and early fifth centuries. From the point of view of stratigraphy, then, the simplest explanation was that the building was built in the early fifth century, though why all those coins were thrown into the fill was a mystery. On the other hand, Y. Yadin suggested that the stones for the synagogue were cut and prepared in the third century, but the builders simply stacked them to the side for some reason now lost (lack of permission to build?) until they could proceed in the fifth century.[5]

The second major challenge was that of the excavators at Khirbet Shema‘, who proposed that a third century broadhouse appeared in the Galilee a century before it was appropriate, given the chronology of the received typology. The question Jodi Magness is raising is whether this reading of the evidence is fitting, given developments in architectural analysis, stratigraphic analysis, ceramic studies, and numismatics.

The shank of Dr. Magness' argument is as follows: (1) Although the excavators at Khirbet Shema‘ posited the existence of two nearly

---

[4] Virgilio C. Corbo, *Cafarnao*, vol. 1: *Gli Edifici della Citta*. Virgilio C. Corbo (Series ed.). (Jerusalem, 1975); Stanislao Loffreda, *Cafarnao*, vol. *2: La Ceramica* (Jerusalem, 1974); Augusto Spijkerman, *Cafarnao*, vol. 3: *Catalogo delle Monete* (Jerusalem, 1972); Emmanuele Testa, *Cafarnao*, vol. 4: *Graffiti delle Casa di S. Pietro* (Jerusalem, 1972).

[5] Oral communication to the author, summer of 1971, at Khirbet Shema‘.

identical buildings (Synagogue I and II), there is no compelling evidence for Synagogue I. (2) Although it is possible to deduce that certain architectural fragments are in reuse in "Synagogue II", it is not necessary to understand them to be from the hypothetical Synagogue I, only from elsewhere on the site. (3) Although it is clear that the Bema was built over a pre-existing, plastered bench, it is not necessary to interpret the Bema as a part of a second synagogue, only as part of a renovation. (4) The fills beneath the floor contain homogeneous Late Roman pottery, that is, with no Byzantine forms and wares. Furthermore there was an absence of fourth century C.E. coinage in these same fills, suggesting to the excavators a date around 300 C.E. for the construction of Synagogue II. But Magness counters that the absence of fourth century coins is not significant. What is significant, in her view, is that a variety of critical loci from beneath the floor are to be dated to the late fourth century because of latest coins and pottery within them.

Let us now turn to these arguments and counter arguments one at a time and allow their weight to emerge. Is the argument of the excavators as ill-founded as it appears in Dr. Magness' article? Second, we will make some brief comments about the nature of archaeological evidence and the meaning of "explanation" in a final report.

A series of observations by the excavators conspired to suggest that there was a first synagogue, later destroyed and renewed in place. First, architectural fragments of earlier structures were found in the walls and other installations of the existing building. For example, the butt of a column—a fragment—was found built into the top of the "stylobate wall" 80 cm south of the north pedestal. Because it was trimmed for use in the stylobate wall and because of its battered state it was not possible to get exact diameters, but it was about the same size as the other columns in the synagogue, i.e., about 52 cm. in diameter, and it sported a molding called an astragal. Although it was just a fragment, it was possible to deduce that originally it had been cut with more care than most of the cut members of the surviving building. More importantly, one must account for its appearance at all as merely a piece of wall. One cannot launch a large thesis from a single cut stone, but the excavators were alerted to the likelihood that this finely cut column butt came from a building with a colonnade. Second, regular ashlars are visible here and there in the four outer walls of the building. They are often fitted between inferior, only partially cut stones. Most of these ashlars appear west of the north door. Other ashlars, some with drafted margins similar to those of "Herodian" masonry, though smaller, were recovered mixed in soil and rocky debris found within the collapsed structure. The excavators also noticed and recorded that the impressive lintel that had surmounted the two doorposts on the south side of the synagogue was more crudely cut and finished than the doorposts themselves. In other words, the masons who cut and erected the doorposts were not the ones who measured, cut, and finished the lintel with its large menorah. This means little of itself, but it fed the developing hypothesis that the building had undergone important changes in its lifetime. Finally, the cut members that fell to the floor in the last destruction were not of uniform workmanship. In fact, every single capital was cut to a different template and with different quality of workmanship. This was troubling, as inspection of various cut members, especially the doorposts, revealed that the masons were capable of expert stone-cutting. So why were these capitals all different, and why were there so many different degrees of finish in the major stone members?

Perhaps the most important point in this concatenation of such clues is the treatment of the pedestals in the rows of columnation. Generally speaking, the pedestals were well-cut square blocks or ashlars in the north row, simple podiums. In the south row they are a bit more elaborated, decorated with narrow, flat fillets top and bottom, beveled fillets reducing the diameter in the middle, and flat, vertical faces on four sides. The two pedestals in front of the bema were cut with raised stone plinths, the seat of the column.

Two pedestals at the west and east ends of the row appeared at first not to have plinths. Then it was discovered that the western pedestal indeed had a plinth, but the pedestal was emplaced upside down! Inspection of the eastern pedestal to see if it, too, was upside down revealed that it was scarcely a pedestal at all, but simply an ashlar, clumsily chiseled to resemble the other pedestals. Its four vertical edges were battered, particularly on the west side. The workman had cut poor grooves into two opposite, vertical faces to hint at the beveled fillets of the other pedestals, and it never had a stone plinth. Its form is without grace and skill.

But the most telling finds of all had been deposited beneath the synagogue floor. These form part of the argument for a pre-existing set of installations prior to the last synagogue, that is, of Synagogue I, a part of the argument Dr. Magness seems to have missed.

West of the stylobate wall, which the excavators took to be a feature to stabilize the east end of the building after a destruction, two fragments were found of very small column bases. One of these bases appears in Fig. 3.9 on p. 51 of the Khirbet Shema' publication. These bases stood about 20 cm. high and supported a column about 25 cm in diameter. In the same fill beneath the floor were found four fragments of Corinthian capitals of about 22-24 cm in diameter. These and a few other fragments appear most likely to have come from a permanent Torah Shrine that was surely built against or near the south wall. The Torah Shrine as depicted in Jewish art normally has two columns *in antis* supporting a triangular pediment. These elements, then, fit that artistic depiction.

The picture that emerges, then, is the building of a synagogue with re-used cut members, some of which were so badly battered that they were poorly re-cut to serve again. None of the re-cut members were finished with the skill of the surviving members. Therefore we ask ourselves, what process hammers stone like this? The usual answer is fall by deliberate destruction (visualize Vandals pulling down the columns of Roman palaces) or by earthquake. Since such massive, natural destruction, perhaps in which the buildings were shaken to their very foundations, would help explain why the rebuild resulted in workmen overturning one pedestal and cutting a poor ashlar to replace another. It would also explain why the lintel on the south was cut again, this time by workmen of less skill than the original masons. Finally, it would explain what smashed the Torah Shrine to bits, leaving so few fragments for the archaeologists to find.

It is a truism in archaeology that architectural members tend not to "travel" very far at any given site. This simply represents an economy of human effort. It takes more effort to find cut stones, load an animal-drawn sledge, and then move the sledge to the construction site than it does to use those found at the construction site. If no other large building with ashlars is to be found at Khirbet Shema'—and so far none has been found—then it is simpler to reason that the ashlars originated close to their present site in the north wall.

Therefore it seems that Magness' objection that there is no necessary reason to suppose that the architectural members came from ·Synagogue I is technically correct, but it is weakened by the realization that, in general, architectural members tend not to travel far on any given site, and for the specific reason that there does not appear to be any large building anywhere else on the site from which they could have been retrieved. This can be confirmed by examination of Fig. 1.1 on p. 4, which is a stone-for-stone rendition of the entire ruin. Small houses can be detected, and many agricultural terraces, but no large public buildings beside the synagogue. But beyond these considerations, the only cut members that resemble these anomalous, poorly re-cut members in re-use are in the synagogue itself. The column fragment in the stylobate wall resembles the columns within the synagogue. The ashlars resemble in measurement the exterior walls themselves of the synagogue. The pedestals resemble the synagogue pedestals. The fragments from small columns, capitals, and bases fit a synagogue Torah Shrine suitable for a hypothetical Synagogue I.[6]

It may be a matter of debate whether one assigns Synagogue I and Synagogue II the status of two strata, or the status of one stratum with a rebuild. Ordinarily in archaeology, however, we assign complete rebuilds the status of a stratum change even if the orientation of the houses and other architecture does not change. In this case we apparently are dealing with the surviving population, which immediately set about to rebuild its houses, agricultural system, water supply, and finally its place of prayer.

The bema was a troublesome feature from the start, for it seemed to be built upon a pre-existing bench. On the other hand some archaeologists argued with us that, although we could see that the bema overlay two benches, we did not know how far the benches left and right of the *bema* extended into the *bema* proper. The question was whether the *bema* and two benches left and right were built all at once or whether the *bema* was built subsequent to the bench. But there is a second and more penetrating question. Why was the bema built at all? Was this a major architectural change that reflected a major change in social practices, or was it something else?

Dismantling of the *bema* provided most of the answers. The *bema* had a soil and rubble core, i.e., it was not solid masonry. A coin of Constans (337-341) found in the soil indicated that the *bema* could not have been built before this relatively narrow range of dates. The plastered bench that could be seen left and right of the bema was one continuous element beneath the *bema* and had been finished with plaster long before the *bema* was built upon it. The excavators noticed

---

[6] Meyers, Kraabel, and Strange, op. cit., p. 46.

that the lower courses of the perimeter of the *bema* may have been prepared for something else, as they do not precisely fit this purpose.

Was the building of the *bema* part of a renovation, or was it integral to the building of a new synagogue (Synagogue II) on the site of an earlier synagogue (Synagogue I)? It is perfectly possible that it could be either, but in either case it represents a major change in the use of this space against the south wall. The excavators assigned the construction to the building of Synagogue II because there were no other clear indications of renovation. On the other hand the benches against the north wall were made wider by placing ashlar blocks in front of the plastered benches against the wall. It is tempting to classify this widening of the north benches as part of the same work that produced the *bema*, if no other reason than economy in interpretation.

We now turn to the question of dating, which means we consider the fills beneath the floor. It is true that these fills contained what the excavators recognized in the early 1970s as homogeneous Late Roman pottery, that is, with no Byzantine forms and wares. Furthermore there was an absence of fourth century C.E. coinage in these same fills. The latest coin above bedrock just west of the stylobate wall was of the third century C.E. The ceramic wares are recognizable Middle Roman and Late Roman in date. On the east side of the stylobate wall the latest coin is of Trajan (104-107 C.E.?), and all the pottery wares were again Late Roman.

The excavators, then, had to fit a first building into the Late Roman period, and specifically into the third century, in order to accommodate the coin west of the stylobate wall. We all know that Late Roman wares run up into the fourth century C.E., suggesting to the excavators a date around 300 C.E. for the destruction of Synagogue I and the construction of Synagogue II. The excavators looked in the catalog of earthquakes and found a reasonably destructive earthquake in 306 C.E. This is not to say that this is the only possible interpretation, for explanation in archaeology is fundamentally the fitting of the evidence to a plausible and testable hypothesis. The hypothesis that the destruction of 306 C.E. was the most likely destroyer of Khirbet Shema' and its synagogue is still testable.

The pottery wares found within the last, destroyed synagogue were again Late Roman, but also with some easily recognizable early Byzantine wares. It so happens that the coin profile ends about 406 C.E. with Arcadius and Honorius.

Dr. Magness is surely right that some of the ceramic evidence suggests continuation of occupation after the earthquake of 419 C.E. On the other hand, the evidence is so slim that it suggests to me that we should call this the occupation of survivors, but not the majority of the population. The occupation as reflected in the tombs of Khirbet Shema' shows a lack of burials after the first quarter of the fifth century C.E. Therefore, the shattering effect of the earthquake that took out most of the buildings at the site is all the more plausibly connected with the earthquake of 419.

Finally, may I add that explanations, in the nature of the case, are testable hypotheses in archaeology.[7] The team that excavated at Khirbet Shema' turned its attention to other sites in Upper Galilee, and only Meiron seems to be more immune to earthquake destruction than the sites of Khirbet Shema', Gush Halav, and Nabratein.[8] It is also the case that there is a kind of circularity in archaeological interpretation, in that the artifact is interpreted by its context (the "locus"), while the context is to be understood from the vantage of all its artifacts and other data. Thus the architectural fragments within the Khirbet Shema synagogue are to be understood primarily from their context beneath the floor of Synagogue II, while Synagogue II is to be understood in part from those artifacts and architectural fragments deposited beneath the floor. Only more excavation in other such sites or at Khirbet Shema' will tell us whether the destruction of 419 C.E. was as extensive as first thought, and only further excavation of discovered synagogues, especially beneath their floors, will tell us certain irreducibles about these synagogues.

---

[7] Ian Hodder, *Reading the Past: Current Approaches to Interpretation in Archaeology* (second edition: Cambridge, 1991), pp. 146-149, especially p. 149.

[8] Eric M. Meyers, Carol L. Meyers, and James F. Strange, *Excavations at the Ancient Synagogue at Gush Halav* (Meiron Excavation Project 5: Winona Lake, 1990).

4. A RESPONSE TO ERIC M. MEYERS AND
JAMES F. STRANGE

Jodi Magness
Tufts University

I am grateful to Professor Meyers and Professor Strange for their thoughtful comments on this paper and on my earlier article on the synagogue at Khirbet Shemaʿ.[1] Before turning to Gush Halav and Khirbet Shemaʿ, I wish to respond to some of the general points raised by Professor Meyers. Although he claims that the title of my paper "has a ring of anachronism about it," the only real change admitted by advocates of the traditional typology has been to move the construction date of the Galilean type synagogues up from the second and third centuries, to the third and early fourth centuries.[2] Otherwise, the old typological scheme (Galilean type synagogues are early; basilical synagogues with an apse are late) still has many adherents, especially among Israeli archaeologists.

Professor Meyers accuses me of being "content to stay with archaeological minutiae," instead of dealing with the larger historical picture. But the point of my paper is to demonstrate how the misinterpretation and misrepresentation of the "archaeological minutiae" lead to inacccurate and incorrect historical conclusions. For this reason I suggest that we might need to reexamine our assumptions regarding the relationships between Jews and Christians in fifth and

---

[1] See Magness, "Synagogue Typology and Earthquake Chronology."

[2] See, for example, Tsafrir, op. cit., p. 152. On the one hand, Tsafrir acknowledges that, "Since the above typology was proposed, work on synagogues has advanced and many of its points are no longer accepted. The chronological framework has been particularly doubted. It has become clear that difference kinds of synagogues were in use and even being built at about the same time." However, he continues, "...the above-mentioned 'Galilean synagogues' should be dated to the 3rd and first half of the 4th c." Also see Y. Tsafrir, "On the Source of the Architectural Design of the Ancient Synagogues in the Galilee: A New Appraisal," in Urman and Flesher, op. cit., pp. 70-86 (for example, on p. 80: "All this evidence shows that the Galilean synagogue is a third-century C.E. Jewish invention," and on p. 81: "...in the fifth and sixth centuries, ...the Jewish synagogues—those of the "late type"—adopted many features similar to the church structure"). For the same view, see G. Foerster, "Dating Synagogues with a 'Basilical' Plan and an Apse," in Urman and Flesher, op. cit., pp. 87-94.

sixth century Galilee. As an archaeologist and ceramics specialist, I feel that my contribution lies in being able to read and independently evaluate a technical archaeological excavation report (as Professor Meyers notes, "there are not many individuals apart from archaeologists" who can do this), and in presenting the results to the broader scholarly community. On the other hand, I wonder how much information Roman legislation provides specifically about Galilee in the fifth and sixth centuries. It also seems to me that the Roman emperors would not have continued to issue laws prohibiting the construction of new synagogues, unless some Jews were doing exactly that.[3]

Gush Halav

It is not true, as Professor Meyers claims, that I refuse "to consider earthquakes as being relevant to the chronology of sites in the Meiron area of Upper Galilee."[4] Instead, I have pointed to the difficulty of linking a destruction episode to a specific, dated earthquake. Archaeologists working in Palestine often attribute destruction levels to earthquakes, especially when the destruction is believed to have occurred at about the same time as an historically attested earthquake. However, the evidence for earthquake damage is not always convincing, and the chronological correlation is not always secure. In the case of Khirbet Shema', I attempted to demonstrate that even if we accept the existence of an earlier synagogue (the excavators' Synagogue I), its destruction does not have to be attributed to the earthquake of 306 C.E., as the excavators claimed. This is important because Khirbet Shema' was recently listed in the revised catalogue of earthquakes in Palestine in association with the earthquake of 306. The catalogue uncritically lists all archaeological sites where earthquake damage has been claimed by the excavators. Gush Halav is also listed in the revised catalogue in association with the earthquake of 306. The dangers of circular argumentation are apparent from the fact that the final publication of Gush Halav cites both Khirbet

---

[3] See, for example, A. Linder, *The Jews in Roman Imperial Legislation* (Detroit, 1987), pp. 398-402, for a prohibition issued by Justinian in 545.

[4] In fact, readers will note that I accept the excavators' claims that the synagogues at Gush Halav and Khirbet Shema' were eventually brought down by earthquakes, though I propose a different chronology.

Shema' and the earthquake catalogue as evidence for the earthquake of 306![5]

I appreciate the fact that the final reports of the excavations at Gush Halav and Khirbet Shema' provide the reader with enough information to reconstruct the original sequence and remains. I have not, as Professor Meyers claims, based my evaluation of the chronology mainly on section drawings. I chose to begin my discussion of Gush Halav by establishing the original floor level of the synagogue as it appears in the section drawings, since that seemed to be the clearest way to present the data. However, anyone who reads my paper can see that I have carefully read and analyzed the excavation report and have attempted to incorporate and integrate all of the published information.

According to Professor Meyers, the elevations of the southern threshold and stylobate cannot be used to establish founding dates for the associated walls, since the southern facade wall and main entryway remained in use during all of phases postulated by the excavators. As I pointed out in my paper, however, the consistency of the foundation and floor levels, and the lack of evidence for any repeated major reconstructions indicate that there was only one major phase of construction. This consistency can be seen, for example, in the loci flanking Wall 1002. Foundation trench L1033 adjoins the west side of the wall at an approximate elevation of 704.8-703.7 meters. As I noted in my paper, the relatively high level of the top of this trench is apparently due to the fact that the outside of this wall (1002) served as a retaining wall (necessitated by the sloping terrain described by Meyers). It is clear from the section drawing (Fig. 6 in Meyers, Meyers, and Strange) that the foundation trench on the east side of Wall 1002 (L1070) corresponds with L1033 on the other side of the wall. The digging of these foundation trenches obviously exposed the remains of the earlier and lower (Phase I) portion of Wall 1002. The upper part of the wall, which was added when the synagogue was constructed, does not sit squarely on the line of the earlier wall below. L1058, which consisted of the make-up of a plaster floor and fill below it, covered the projecting ledge created when the upper

[5] See Magness, "Synagogue Typology and Earthquake Chronology." For the earthquake catalogue see D.H.K. Amiran, E. Arieh, and T. Turcotte, "Earthquakes in Israel and Adjacent Areas: Macroseismic Observations since 100 B.C.E.," in *Israel Exploration Journal* 44, 1994, pp. 260-305.

part of the wall was added. Locus 1058 lay above foundation trench
L0170, at an approximate elevation of 704.5, and yielded a fifth
century coin.[6]

The western corridor provides a similar picture (see Fig. 9 in
Meyers, Meyers, and Strange). Wall 1098 and adjacent Loci 1100
(which yielded a third century coin), 1101, and 1006 all lay well
below the floor level of the synagogue (including below L1058) and
represent pre-synagogue remains. Photo 15 (in Meyers, Meyers, and
Strange) shows Wall 1098 crossing the western corridor. Wall 1098
can be seen intersecting the lower, earlier portion of Wall 1002 on
the right. The addition of the later wall (or later part of the wall)
above created a step or ledge projecting into the room. This step was
not visible when the synagogue existed, as it was covered by the
plaster floor of L1058. In other words, Photo 15 shows the excavation of the southern part of the western corridor well below the
original floor level of the synagogue. Much of what is visible (especially of the walls) belongs to pre-synagogue structures which were
incorporated into or built upon when the synagogue was constructed.

Professor Meyers fails to provide any new evidence for the chronology and supposed major reconstructions of the synagogue building, instead repeating his published conclusions.[7] As I have attempted

---

[6] See Meyers, Meyers, and Strange, op. cit., p. 266 and Fig. 6.

[7] Not all of the information Meyers provides in his response correlates with the
published report; for example:

1) Meyers's statement that "excavation along its inner face [of Wall 1002] produced early remains of Period II (L.1070)" is contradicted by the presence of eight
coins dated between 341 and 361 and another fourth century coin. The remains
from this locus are from the end, not the early part of the excavators' Period II
(306-363) (see Meyers, Meyers, and Strange, op. cit., p. 267, the "Critical Locus
List").

2) Meyers's claim that the material from the southeast corner associated with the
founding is "uniformly Middle Roman" (L.5029 and 5035)" (in other words, the
excavators' Period I) is contradicted by the presence of Late Roman pottery in
L5029, which is assigned to Period II in the "Critical Locus List" (see Meyers,
Meyers, and Strange, op. cit., p. 282). In addition, L5036, which lay below L5029,
and L5019, at the same level on the other side of Wall 5030, are also assigned to
Period II (see Meyers, Meyers, and Strange, op. cit., pp. 282-283 and Fig. 6).

3) I agree with Meyers that Wall 1002 antedates the synagogue (see my discussion
below). L1071, which lies at the bottom of the section outside Wall 1002, is
misattributed in the "Critical Locus List" to Period III instead of Period I (see
Meyers, Meyers, and Strange, op. cit., p. 267.

4) Although Meyers claims that "L. 2042 and 2043 provide genuine Period I
material, which may be associated with the earliest use of this pre-existing wall as
part of the synagogue," Late Roman pottery is mentioned from L2042 (see

to demonstrate, most of the excavators' Period I fills and occupation deposits antedate the construction of the synagogue, while most of the remains they assigned to Period II should be associated with the synagogue's foundation level. The material from the foundations and from the fill and make-up of the floors (which the excavators assigned to Period III) indicates when the synagogue was constructed. Although the excavators' Period II and III loci obviously contained a great deal of earlier, "survival" material, one of the basic principles of archaeology is that the latest finds provide the date. Therefore, I base my chronology on sound archaeological methodology, not on "anomalies," as Professor Meyers claims. Professor Meyers states that, "The possibility that a single sherd might possibly be dated a bit earlier or a bit later is not compelling enough to lower or raise the date of an entire locus." However, I have not revised the dating of any of the published pottery types (that is, the chronology I propose is not based on my redating of any of the pottery). Instead, the dates

---

Meyers, Meyers, and Strange, op. cit., p. 271; this locus, however, is attributed to Period I in the "Critical Locus List"). In my opinion, L2042 (which contained pieces of plaster) is a foundation trench or fill associated with a pre-synagogue structure represented by Wall 1017/2035. As can be seen in Fig. 6, this locus adjoins the south side of Wall 1017/2035 between about 703-702.5 meters. This means that this locus lies between one and a half to two meters below the floor level of the synagogue. The upper part of Wall 1017/2035 appears to have been added or rebuilt and incorporated into the synagogue.

5) Meyers is "struck by the absence of any Byzantine-period ceramics in L.3022 (with one possible exception in bucket 54), 3032, 3037 on the eastern face of the eastern stylobate and L3022, 3029, and 3033 on the western face. All of the readings [from these loci] were Period I or II." In the "Critical Locus List," however, both L3022 and L3022.1 are identified as Period III, and Late Roman pottery is recorded from two of the three buckets that L3022.1 yielded (in addition to the possible Late Roman pottery from bucket 54, which may have also contained Byzantine I pottery); see Meyers, Meyers, and Strange, op. cit., p. 272. The description in the "Critical Locus List" and Figs. 5 and 6 indicate that L3022 represents the plaster floor of the synagogue, at the same elevation as other preserved sections of the floor.

Meyers has also not provided any new evidence to support the excavators' claim that there were two bemas. Instead, there was apparently only one bema, which consisted of an ashlar frame (their Period I bema) with a fieldstone fill (their Period II bema). Since the floor level at this end of the synagogue lay so close to the modern ground level, it is not surprising that only part of the lowest course of the ashlar frame was preserved, with 1-2 more courses above belonging to the fieldstone fill. As I noted in my paper, the attribution of all of these remains to a single bema is supported by the associated floor and stylobate levels, as there is nearly half a meter discrepancy between the top of the stylobate and the excavators' Period I *bema* (and Period I floor level).

I have provided are those that have been published by others (such as by J.W. Hayes for the Late Roman Red Wares). Similarly, for the coins I relied on the identifications and dates published by the excavators. So, for example, I based the identification of the coin from L4066 (dated 364-367) on the information that the excavators themselves published (see p. 281 in the "Critical Locus List"). Thus, this is not a case of a coin that was illegible at the time of the excavation, the reading of which has since changed, as Professor Meyers suggests. Instead, it is an example of a case where the published archaeological evidence clearly contradicts the excavators' interpretation. If the level in which that coin was found was supposedly destroyed by the earthquake of 363, it does not matter whether the coin is two years or twenty years later (as opposed to what Professor Meyers seems to imply: "though the coin may be dated just after the earthquake of 363"). His reassignment of this locus to Period III (in his response to my paper) does not address these fundamental problems and inconsistencies. I have attempted to show that the latest datable coins and pottery from the relevant loci indicate that the synagogue at Gush Halav was constructed no earlier than the second half of the fifth century. Although the fifth century coins and imported Late Roman Red Wares (which are the most closely datable ceramic types) are not abundant, they are consistent and appear to come mostly if not entirely from secure loci.

Professor Meyers continues to insist that the final destruction of the synagogue at Gush Halav occurred in 551, just after the last coin was deposited in the hoard in the western corridor. I have not, as he suggests, dated the destruction on the basis of material from unsealed loci above the earthquake collapse. Instead, as I noted in my paper, the pottery and coins I discussed come from loci that by the excavators' own definition antedate the collapse of the building. The pottery includes an intact oil lamp, apparently of late seventh to early eighth century date, which comes from a locus described by the excavators as a compact fill buried beneath the collapse of the synagogue (L3012). Another lamp of seventh century date comes from L4015, a dirt and plaster surface associated with the excavators' later bema and with bench L4019. A Cypriot Red Slip Ware bowl dated from ca. 550 to the end of the seventh century is published from L4044 in the western corridor, which is described in the "Critical Locus List" as identical to the locus which contained the coin hoard (L1046). This evidence is complemented by material of the same date (seventh to early eighth centuries) which comes from loci that were not sealed beneath the earthquake collapse. This material suggests that the occupation of the synagogue ended some time in the late seventh or early eighth century.

Professor Meyers has also misrepresented some of my conclusions: "In the case of Gush Halav she is suggesting that there is only one building, one synagogue, which was constructed in the late fourth century and used until the early Arab period or eighth century... In the case of Khirbet Shema' Magness also suggests a construction date in the fourth century and a collapse in the eighth century once again...." I have indeed suggested that there is only one synagogue building at each site—Gush Halav and Khirbet Shema'. However, I propose that the synagogue at Gush Halav was constructed no earlier than the second half of the fifth century (not in the late fourth century) and was occupied without any major destructions and reconstructions until it was abandoned in the late seventh or early eighth century. I believe that the synagogue at Khirbet Shema' was constructed no earlier than the late fourth century, probably in the late fourth to early fifth century. This means that Eusebius' possible allusion to the earthquake of 306 (which Professor Meyers cites) is irrelevant, as there is no evidence that a synagogue existed at Khirbet Shema' at that time. The synagogue may have been abandoned during the fifth century, when there was apparently a decline (but not break) in occupation at Khirbet Shema'. Other evidence suggests that by the second half of the fifth century, Khirbet Shema''s population included Christians. It is not clear whether a Jewish population continued to inhabit the site at this time, and the synagogue was apparently already abandoned when it was destroyed by an earthquake. Coins and pottery associated with a squatter occupation above the ruins of the synagogue provide an eighth to ninth century *terminus ante quem* for the earthquake destruction.[8]

Khirbet Shema'

In their 1970-1972 excavations at Khirbet Shema', Professor Meyers, ·Professor Strange, and A.T. Kraabel identified the remains of two successive and virtually identical synagogues with the same broad-

---

[8] See Magness, "Synagogue Typology and Earthquake Chronology."

house plan.[9] They placed the construction of Synagogue I in the
third century, and the construction of Synagogue II early in the
fourth century. The excavators concluded that both synagogues were
destroyed by earthquakes, the first in 306, and the second in 419.
They also claimed that the second earthquake caused the inhabitants
to abandon the site completely.

As I pointed out in my article, because the buildings are located on
a rocky spur of Mount Meiron, there was almost no accumulated
debris and few sealed loci.[10] There is also little, if any secure archaeological evidence for the dating of Synagogue I. In fact, the chronological and architectural evidence for Synagogue I comes entirely
from Synagogue II. Since the excavators dated the destruction of
Synagogue II to 419 and placed its construction in the first half of the
fourth century, the earthquake that they believe destroyed Synagogue I must have occurred before then. They chose the earthquake
of 306 as the best candidate. I therefore began my analysis by examining the evidence for the dating of Synagogue II. I noted that a coin
of Constans from the fill inside the bema provides a *terminus post quem*
of 337-341 for the construction of Synagogue II, instead of indicating
that the synagogue was built by the time the coin was dropped, as the
excavators concluded.[11] This coin and one of Gratian (367-383)
found deep in the fill of a declivity below the northwest corner of the
synagogue point to a late fourth to early fifth century date for the
construction of Synagogue II.[12] This is important because the de-

---

[9] See E.M. Meyers, A.T. Kraabel, and J.F. Strange, *Ancient Synagogue Excavations at Khirbet Shema', Upper Galilee, Israel, 1970-1972* (Annual of the American Schools of Oriental Research XLII; Durham, 1976).

[10] Magness, "Synagogue Typology and Earthquake Chronology," p. 213.

[11] Ibid., p. 214.

[12] Ibid., p. 215. As I noted, the coin of Constans provides a mid-fourth century *terminus post quem*, not a *terminus ante quem*, for the excavators' Synagogue II. The coin of Gratian comes from the lowest levels of a declivity described by the excavators as "a sealed locus beneath the floor level of the synagogue" (Meyers, Kraabel, and Strange, op. cit., p. 36). Because of the presence of this coin, the excavators suggested that the fill was deposited during a later renovation or remodelling of Synagogue II, perhaps necessitated by heavy winter rains and/or the earthquake of 365. However, this is the only place in the Khirbet Shema' excavation report where such renova-tions or remodelling are mentioned. It seems highly unlikely that damage from an earthquake or even heavy winter rains would have affected only a single locus (and especially one deep below floor level)! I pointed out that the excavators had to associate this fill with a rebuilding in the later fourth century because they used the coin of Constans in the bema to provide a *terminus ante quem* for the construction of the synagogue. If the coin of Constans is used to provide a *terminus post quem* (as it

struction date assigned to Synagogue I is based upon the excavators' assumption that the construction of Synagogue II began immediately after the earthquake of 306. If Synagogue II was, in fact, constructed no earlier than the later fourth century, the destruction of Synagogue I does not have to be attributed to the earthquake of 306. Next I examined the evidence for Synagogue I and the earthquake that destroyed it. There are no sealed loci associated with Synagogue I. All of the evidence for that synagogue described by the excavators is architectural: elements such as walls and doorways that were supposedly left standing after the earthquake of 306, or smashed fragments of architectural members that were built into Synagogue II or incorporated into its fills.[13] It may be reasonable to conclude, as the excavators did, that some of these elements must have come from an earlier building that was located on the site of the present synagogue or very close to it. As Professor Strange notes, "architectural members tend not to 'travel' very far at any given site." There is, however, no evidence to support the excavators' conclusion that these elements originated in a nearly identical synagogue that stood earlier on the same spot. The battered architectural fragments could have come from more than one building, while the fact that the doorposts of Synagogue II appear to be of better workmanship than the rest of the building could simply reflect the hands of different workmen. Other claimed differences between the two synagogues, such as the addition of the bema over the bench on the south wall, may reflect different constructional or occupational phases during the lifetime of the structure identified by the excavators as Synagogue II. I concluded that the battered architectural fragments incorporated into Synagogue II could derive from more than one building and that there is no evidence linking the destruction of the structure or structures from which these elements derive specifically with the earthquake of 306. Any combination of natural or human disasters which occurred before the later fourth century could have destroyed the building(s) to which these elements originally belonged.[14]

---

should), there is no need to attribute the coin of Gratian to any remodelling of the synagogue.

[13] Magness, "Synagogue Typology and Earthquake Chronology, p. 215.

[14] Ibid., pp. 215-216. In my analysis of the Khirbet Shemaʿ report, I deliberately avoided discussing the battered architectural elements (fragments of small columns) built into Synagogue II, which the excavators associated with a Torah Shrine belonging to Synagogue I. The origin of these fragments (as well as others) incorporated into Synagogue II is unknown, and in my opinion their assignment to a Torah

According to Professor Meyers and Professor Strange, these elements must have originated in a virtually identical, earlier synagogue that stood on the same spot, since there does not appear to be any large building elsewhere at Khirbet Shema' from which they could have derived. However, since only limited soundings were conducted in other parts of the site, the building(s) in which these elements originated could have gone undetected in surface surveys. An example of how this can happen is illustrated by the excavations at Khirbet Yattir in southern Judaea, which I currently co-direct. In the summer of 1997, while walking around the site, I noticed the underside of a Corinthian pilaster capital, buried with other stones in a pit. Our excavations in this area (D) have now brought to light a huge Byzantine basilica on a terrace near the top of the tel, whose remains were invisible on the surface of the ground.[15] At Khirbet Shema', earlier (perhaps public) buildings are known to have existed in the vicinity of the synagogue.[16]

Professor Meyers and Professor Strange are disturbed by the differences in form and workmanship of the column capitals and other architectural elements in the synagogue. Such variations, however, can be observed in many monumental buildings of Byzantine Palestine. For example, the bases, column shafts, and capitals in the main hall of the Byzantine church (perhaps the Cathedral) at Pella in Jordan all differ from each other.[17] Although these elements are clearly spolia, some of which are Roman, there is no evidence of any other

---

Shrine is conjectural and problematic. Z.U. Ma'oz has convincingly argued that many of the architectural elements associated by some scholars with Torah Shrines, such as the carved stone pediment from Nabratein, belonged instead to windows (see Ma'oz, *Ancient Synagogues in the Golan*, pp. 23-27; E.M. Meyers, "The Torah Shrine in the Ancient Synagogue: Another Look at the Evidence," in *Jewish Quarterly Studies* 4, 1997, pp. 303-38). In addition, it turns out that the ceramic bowl and oil lamps decorated with possible depictions of Torah Shrines date to the early Islamic period (eighth to tenth centuries). This means that even if these depictions represent Torah Shrines, they are not necessarily relevant to the discussion of much earlier synagogues such as those at Khirbet Shema' and Nabratein (see Magness, "The Dating of the Black Ceramic Bowl").

[15] See H.Eshel, E. Shenhav, and J. Magness, "Khirbet Yattir," in *American Journal of Archaeology* 102, 1998, pp. 797-799.

[16] See Meyers, Kraabel, and Strange, op. cit., pp. 90-98. Only limited soundings in a cistern, the industrial quarter, and a ritual bath were conducted by the excavators outside the area of the synagogue.

[17] See R.H. Smith, and L.P. Day, *Pella of the Decapolis, Volume 2. Final Report on the College of Wooster Excavations in Area IX, The Civic Complex, 1979-1985* (Wooster, 1989), p. 39.

building beneath the church, which was erected ca. 400 (approximately the same date I have proposed for the construction of the synagogue at Khirbet Shema'). They apparently derive from a number of earlier buildings that existed in the vicinity of the church at Pella.[18] Similarly, the colonnade in the hall of a Byzantine monastic church that we have uncovered at Khirbet Yattir incorporated reused Nabataean capitals of the first century C.E., from an otherwise unknown building.[19]

Professor Strange repeatedly states that all of the pottery found in the fills beneath the floors of Synagogue II is "Late Roman," which in the Khirbet Shema' report is defined as the period from 180-306. However, almost no pottery from the "critical loci" in Synagogue II is illustrated and published in the final report.[20] This makes it impossible to evaluate the excavators' claimed Late Roman date for this material. In addition, even if we assume that Synagogue I existed and was destroyed by the earthquake of 306, it seems highly unlikely that such an event would have affected the local ceramic repertoire. This would be especially true if, following the excavators' chronology, there was no break in the occupation at Khirbet Shema' after the earthquake of 306.

Conclusion

In the conclusion to my paper, I noted that the local pottery chronology of Galilee in the fourth to sixth centuries may need to be revised. This means that at least some of the ceramic types identified as Late Roman at Khirbet Shema' could postdate 306. The huge numbers of fourth and early fifth century coins, compared with the much smaller number of later fifth century coins, have led archaeologists and other scholars (such as Z. Safrai, whom Professor Meyers cites) to conclude (I believe erroneously), that Palestine declined dramatically in the fifth century. This has also led to the misdating of the associated levels and remains (such as the local pottery types); a close examina-

---

[18] Ibid., p. 34.

[19] See Eshel, Shenhav, and Magness, op. cit., p. 798.

[20] This was also noted by S. Loffreda, "Review of Ancient Synagogue Excavations at Khirbet Shema' Upper Galilee, Israel, 1970-1972, by E.M. Meyers, A.T. Kraabel, and J.F. Strange (Durham, 1976), in *Bulletin of the American Schools of Oriental Research* 244, 1981, p. 77.

tion of the archaeological evidence indicates that many of the fourth and early fifth century coins actually come from levels dating to the late fifth and early sixth centuries. This phenomenon has been noted by Z.U. Ma'oz in the case of the Golan synagogues (see the discussion in my paper). Similarly, fifth century pottery types in Jerusalem were misdated to the fourth century on the basis of their association with fourth century coins. In footnote 76 in my paper, I cited some examples of how coin evidence can lead to the misdating of associated archaeological remains and to the drawing of incorrect historical conclusions.

Finally, I would like to make it clear that in redating the Galilean type synagogues at Gush Halav and Capernaum (and perhaps others), I am not denying that synagogues existed in Palestine in the second and third centuries (and earlier). I also believe that each synagogue building should be dated independently of typological or historical considerations, on the basis of well-excavated and thoroughly published archaeological evidence. However, I am beginning to suspect that (monumental) synagogue buildings with a distinctive plan and clearly Jewish iconography or decoration (what I would call "archaeologically identifiable synagogues") did not develop in Palestine until the fourth century, especially the later fourth century. It would be interesting to consider whether this may be related to (or in response to) the rise and development of churches.[21]

I would like to close by thanking Professor Meyers and Professor Strange again for their comments on my paper and the Khirbet Shema' article, and for their willingness to engage in a dialogue. I am also grateful to Professor Neusner and Professor Avery-Peck for facilitating this discussion, which illustrates how important it is for the final publication of an excavation to mark the beginning, not the end, of scholarly analysis.

---

[21] The development of monumental synagogue architecture and distinctive Jewish iconography also seems to coincide (according to my chronology) with the strengthening of the priestly class in late Roman and Byzantine Palestine, and may help explain the Temple-oriented nature of much of the Palestinian synagogue iconography. I am grateful to David Amit for bringing this possible relationship to my attention. I heard interesting papers on the subject of the priestly class by O. Irshai, E. Reiner, and R. Elior at a conference on The Spiritual Life of the People of Israel in Late Antiquity in the Byzantine-Christian Context, sponsored by the Dinur Center in Jerusalem, 5-7 July, 1999. The conference papers will be published in a volume edited by L.I. Levine.

Additional references

Amiran, D.H.K., E. Arieh, and T. Turcotte, "Earthquakes in Israel and Adjacent Areas: Macroseismic Observations since 100 B.C.E.," in *Israel Exploration Journal* 44, 1994, pp. 260-305.

Eshel, H., E. Shenhav, and J. Magness, "Khirbet Yattir," in *American Journal of Archaeology* 102, 1998, pp. 797-799.

Foerster, G., "Dating Synagogues with a 'Basilical' Plan and an Apse," in Urman, D., and P.V.M. Flesher, eds., *Ancient Synagogues, Historical Analysis and Archaeological Discovery* (Leiden, 1995), pp. 87-94.

Linder, A., *The Jews in Roman Imperial Legislation* (Detroit, 1987).

Loffreda, S., "Review of Ancient Synagogue Excavations at Khirbet Shemaʿ, Upper Galilee, Israel, 1970-1972, by E.M. Meyers, A.T. Kraabel, and J.F. Strange (Durham, 1976), in *Bulletin of the American Schools of Oriental Research* 244, 1981, pp. 75-79.

Meyers, E.M., "The Torah Shrine in the Ancient Synagogue: Another Look at the Evidence," in *Jewish Quarterly Studies* 4, 1997, pp. 303-338.

Smith, R.H., and L.P. Day, *Pella of the Decapolis, Volume 2. Final Report on The College of Wooster Excavations in Area IX, The Civic Complex, 1979-1985* (Wooster, 1989).

Tsafrir, Y., "On the Source of the Architectural Design of the Ancient Synagogues in the Galilee: A New Appraisal," in Urman, D., and P.V.M. Flesher, eds., *Ancient Synagogues, Historical Analysis and Archaeological Discovery* (Leiden, 1995), pp. 70-86.

5. THE SYNAGOGUE AS METAPHOR

James F. Strange
University of South Florida

The problem of the synagogue in ancient Israel appears to be inexhaustible. At the same time, the subject has been treated so many times that it is becoming rather well worn, if not hackneyed. A new approach is required, and this essay presents a fresh foray into a well-traversed field of encounter.

Jacob Neusner has concluded that a close study of Mishnah Megillah demonstrates that the sages did not consider a synagogue to be required for prayer,[1] for reading of Torah, or for any other public ritual connected with Jewish worship. Rather, "the synagogue represents the occasion at which ten or more Israelite males assemble and embody Israel, and provides for the declamation of the Torah to Israel...."[2] That seems to be a correct conclusion from these brief texts.

On the other hand, the very same text, devoted to the question of the reading of the scroll of Esther, assumes on several occasions that this reading will take place in a specific kind of building: "...The declamation of Scriptures takes place most suitably in the congregation gathered in a particular building erected and set aside for that purpose—not for prayer, not for sacrifice, not for study, but for Torah-declamation."[3] That is, the sages have legislated about Torah reading, recitation of the *Shema*, raising the hands in the priestly benediction, passing before the ark to lead in worship or the *Amidah*, concluding Torah reading by reading from a prophet, and related matters relating to the synagogue. These are understood to take place anywhere, but they take place most appropriately in a synagogue. According to these texts, a synagogue has no specified architectural character.

---

[1] This is a surprise, because in the diaspora the best known Greek name for a synagogue is *euché* (or other words formed on the same root) usually translated "place of prayer."

[2] Jacob Neusner, "Tractate Megillah," in *The Halakhah: An Encyclopaedia of the Law of Judaism* (Leiden, 2000), 5 vols.

[3] Loc. cit.

If one objects that these texts may contain references to traditions earlier than the third, but surely not as early as the first century, then let us turn to Josephus. Josephus uses the term *synagogé* five times to refer to buildings. He understands these to be for Jewish worship and ritual, including Torah reading (*Against Apion* 2.175), and there is hardly reason to accuse Josephus of anachronism, since his audience knew first hand of the First Revolt.[4]

Now we turn to archaeology and to those first century edifices identified as synagogues by their excavators. These are above all the structures at Gamala, Herodium, Masada, and the black basalt structure at Capernaum. Recently, Ehud Netzer has discovered a synagogue at Jericho that seems to be built from the same pattern as the others named (Fig. 1).[5]

I have argued elsewhere that these are indeed synagogues and in fact were intended in the main to be synagogues from the time their columns were erected. The contention rests on the discovery that the signature architecture of these and almost all later buildings identified as synagogues (except Samaritan synagogues and broadhouses) is that the interior floor space is marked by walkways on three or all four walls with benches between the walls and the columniation. The result of such a design is that participants had to look between the columns to see what was going on. Although this feature is known from Nabatean mortuary temples, it is otherwise virtually unknown in the Roman world.[6]

It seems that the simplest explanation of the origin of the nesting of columniation, benches, and walls is the Temple courts in Jerusalem. This is the place where Ezra and later leaders read the Torah (1 Esdras 9:38-41). Therefore, this very idea of declamation of Torah, found to be central to the synagogue according to the sages, was also a characteristic of religious ritual in the forecourts of the Second Temple.

---

[4] Donald D. Binder, *Into the Temple Courts. The Place of the Synagogue in the Second Temple Period* (Atlanta, SBL Dissertation Series, 1999).

[5] See Donald Binder's web page for a plan and several reports of its unearthing http://www.smu.edu/~dbinder/index.html [accessed: 1/1/2000].

[6] James F. Strange, "The Art and Archaeology of Ancient Judaism," in Jacob Neusner, ed., *Judaism in Late Antiquity* (Leiden, 1995), vol. 1, pp. 64-114; James F. Strange, "Ancient Texts, Archaeology as Text, and the Problem of the First Century Synagogue," in Howard Clark Kee and Lynn H. Cohick, eds., *Evolution of the Synagogue: Problems and Progress* (Harrisburg, 1999), pp. 27-45.

Therefore there is potentially less of a disjunction between what Jacob Neusner finds in the Mishnah and what the archaeologists claim are indeed synagogues. That is to say, despite the fact that the documents do not legislate any particular form for the synagogue, those buildings that we do identify as synagogues exhibit a particular architectural signature or perhaps a specified architectural character that is most easily linked to the forecourts of the Second Temple. In other words, although Mishnah Megillah does not legislate the character of the building, it appears that Jews may have already developed a specific type of building for Torah reading.

Yet, it remains to be demonstrated that any of these structures qualify as "a particular building erected and set aside for that purpose" (declamation of Torah). The problem is that we have not demonstrated that those excavated buildings identified as synagogues are not most simply houses of study, schools, or public gathering places for any group whatever. This essay is devoted to attempting to resolve the impasse at which we find ourselves.

Heretofore our task of demonstrating the suitability of a structure for a given purpose has been rendered difficult by a certain looseness in interpretive method. In fact, some archaeologists hardly do more than describe the finds in, for instance, a Canaanite temple, as the lack of unanimity in method in interpretation of religious architecture makes one vulnerable to the critics. This is also true of the attempt to infer religion from material culture in general.

A Recent Development in Interpretation in Archaeology

One promising development in the interpretation of architecture and artifacts is the recent publication of Christopher Tilley, *Metaphor and Material Culture* (Blackwell, 1999). Tilley, Professor of Material Culture in the Department of Anthropology and the Institute of Archaeology at the University College London, is best known for his sorties into theories of archaeology and of material culture, particularly in five books prior to the one under discussion. Two of these books he edited, namely, *Reading Material Culture* (1990) and *Interpretative Archae-ology* (1993). The other three he authored himself: *Material Culture and Text: The Art of Ambiguity* (1991), *A Phenomenology of Landscape* (1994), and *An Ethnography of the Neolithic* (1996). He owes much of his interpretative stance to his studies on the structuralism of Claude Lévi-

Strauss, about whose theory of interpretation he wrote a major article.[7] He has also been in constant dialogue with Daniel Miller, with whom he co-authored an important editorial in the *Journal of Material Culture*.[8]

In the current volume, Tilley boldly appropriates a major linguistic category for interpretation in archaeology, namely, the idea of "metaphor." It is not so much that he is critiquing or making explicit theories of metaphor that lie unarticulated in anthropological and ethnographic interpretations of culture. He certainly accomplishes that in his investigation of the use of the word "megalith" as a controlling metaphor in a century of archaeological investigations in Great Britain and Europe.[9] Rather in the present instance his focus is on artifact as metaphor, or artifact as "solid metaphor" to use his phrase.

The question I wish to address is to what extent understanding artifacts and architecture as "solid metaphors" aids us in understanding the question of the synagogue in the first few centuries C.E. Can we move beyond discussions of the origin of the synagogue, or whether first century synagogues exist at all in ancient Palestine, or whether Jews ever set aside space solely for reading of Torah and worship before the third century C.E. in ancient Palestine? It is possible that "synagogue as metaphor" may move us in a new direction, namely, towards deducing the religion practiced within the structures. If the inferred religious practices are consistent with the stated purpose of the synagogue in Mishnah Megillah, Josephus, and the gospels, then we are on much firmer ground.

"Metaphor and the Constitution of the World"

I borrow Tilley's section title in order to attempt to summarize and re-present his findings on the nature of metaphor, especially on metaphor as used in discussions of material culture and archaeology. I do not wish to be sidetracked into following his discussions of the techni-

---

[7] Christopher Tilley, "Claude Lévi-Strauss: Structuralism and Beyond," in Christopher Tilley, ed., *Reading Material Culture* (Oxford, 1990).

[8] David Miller and Christopher Tilley, "Editorial," in *The Journal of Material Culture*, vol. 1/1 (1996), pp. 5-14.

[9] Christopher Tilley, "Frozen Metaphor: Megaliths in Texts," in *Metaphor and Material Culture* (Oxford, 1999), pp. 82-101.

cal aspects of metaphor and language: trope, metonymy, and synecdoche. He delivers a useful summary of the linguist's understanding
of these terms as a prelude to discussing artifacts as metaphors. For
the purposes of this analysis, it appears more useful to go on to his
analysis of material culture as a system of solid metaphors.

As an aside, we notice that Tilley reports that the experience of
writing about metaphor in archaeology he found to be a transforming and constitutive experience. Rarely do scholars confess such liminal incidents in their works. He goes so far as to confess that, in the
writing of the book, his own understanding of language completely
collapsed.[10] The change he faced was to give up on conventional,
literal theories of language as applied to his own writing. He found
himself using metaphor "to assert the value and significance of metaphor."[11] I take this to mean that he gained a new awareness and
grasp of the fundamental metaphorical nature of language, including
professional archaeological language. This at least rouses the hope
that his analyses may yield propositions that enable us to see and
understand structures and functions of certain artifacts as metaphors
for religion.

Tilley asserts five theses about metaphors that promise to change
our understanding of artifacts:

> 1. "The inexpressibility thesis:" Metaphors give form to ideas and de-
> scriptions of the world that are impossible in a literal language. Meta-
> phors elicit experiences and create meanings in a far richer manner
> than any literal expression. Specifically, metaphors allow emotions, feel-
> ings, and insights to come to expression in a way that stretches our
> imagination. We recognize here a certain affinity with linguistic theories
> of symbol.
> 2. "The compactness thesis:" Metaphors enable communication be-
> tween members of the same culture in the simplest and "most parsimo-
> nious" way possible. It is more succinct to characterize someone as a
> fox than it is to enter into discursive descriptions of his or her character
> and behavior.
> 3. "The vividness thesis:" Metaphors link subjective and objective expe-
> rience. They encode and recall information in a graphic or colorful
> manner that facilitates memory. It is easy to recall that General Sher-
> man engaged in a "scorched earth policy" in Georgia after the Civil
> War but difficult to remember all his tactics. I find this category more
> explicitly helpful in interpretation, for we shall see that a synagogue

---

[10] Op. cit., p. xv.
[11] Loc. cit.

building, for instance, encodes information in a manner that facilitates memory. More on that later.

4. Metaphors facilitate the production of novel understandings and interpretations of the world. For example, by using the metaphor of the human body as a container, it is possible to make comparisons of the human body with pots and baskets. To illustrate, the item that one takes hold of on a basket or pot is a "handle" or "a little hand." Furthermore this aspect of metaphor enables us to see how metaphors mediate between abstract thought and concrete thought about the world. By using the metaphor of the church as the body of Christ, Paul was able to remove the idea of unity from abstract thought and insert it into the realm of concrete thought and experience of the church at Corinth (1 Cor. 12:12-30). Similarly the rabbis could use a *minyan* at prayer as a metaphor for "all Israel" to mediate the abstraction "Israel" into concrete thought and experience (Y. Meg. 4:4).

5. His fifth thesis is not so much about the nature of metaphor as about the nature of interpretation in archaeology. Tilley asserts that thinking about metaphors, especially in the language of archeology, enables us to unmask "factual statements" about archaeology as interpretations. This unmasking has at least two implications. First, when archaeologists learn about metaphors in their own discourse, they learn about the culture of scholarship and the assumptions about language that inform it. Second, when they learn the metaphors in use by ancient peoples of their own world, archaeologists learn the culture and develop the ability to make authoritative statements about the culture of the ancient peoples.

"All social scientific texts," says Tilley, "are motivated by an act of persuasion in which authors employ the powers of metaphor in conjunction with a presentation of empirical materials, or evidence, to convince their readers of the veracity and significance of the statements they are making."[12] At the very least, this statement alerts us to the significance of archaeological reports as rhetorical documents informed by the assumptions of archaeology as a discipline. We are also enabled to see that these reports are replete with the metaphors of interpretation of that discipline.

Tilley also points out that certain theories of culture in anthropology devolve upon certain root metaphors or images of the world. The functionalists think of society as an organism. The structuralists, on the other hand, see culture and society as languages. Cultural evolutionists mediate culture by means of a metaphor of species evolution. The ethnomethodologists conceive of culture as theater or as a game.

---

[12] Op. cit., p. 10.

These metaphors (sometimes called models) are essential to the transmission and preservation of the various forms of the discipline, just as linguistic metaphors and solid metaphors are essential to the transmission and preservation of a society.[13]

Material Metaphors and Rituals

Tilley relies on the analyses of F. Barth to repeat Barth's observation that the material metaphors of a given society are not entirely arbitrary.[14] Thus a given artifact is not merely arbitrary in its form, but it has an origin in the history of the society in question. Tilley asserts (with Barth) that the two questions of the origin and the meaning of a given symbol (sic) are related. Thus I infer that the question about the origin of the synagogue in ancient Israel is related to the question of its meaning. I also infer that the meaning of the synagogue is linked to what this building accomplishes in the mind of ancient Israel. In order to learn that, we must turn to the literature of ancient Israel in the period in question.

Tilley favors an interpretation of a material symbol (sic) as that which bears one or more metaphors, meanings, or ways of seeing. This interpretation suggests that multiple interpretations of the architecture of the synagogue, for example, may be mandated simply by discovering multiple metaphors derived from ancient discussions of the building.

Tilley's few pages devoted to "Metaphor in Architecture" seem potentially fruitful for our analysis of the ancient synagogue.[15] This is especially true of Tilley's appropriation of Bourdieu's idea that the house provides a coherent language with which to organize reality.[16] The same idea has been elaborated elsewhere in the sense that the house is a "structuring structure," that is, the house embodies a metaphorical relationship to the principles of social order.[17] For example, houses are normally variations on a generic theme in terms of size, height, materials, location of doorways (entrance and egress), orienta-

---

[13] Op. cit., p. 17.

[14] Frederik Barth, *Ritual and knowledge among the Baktaman of New Guinea* (Oslo and New Haven, 1975).

[15] Op. cit., pp. 40-49

[16] Pierre Bourdieu, *Outline of a Theory of Practice* (Cambridge, 1977), p. 89.

[17] See the relevant literature cited in Tilley, *Metaphor and Material Culture*, p. 41.

tion, ground plan, and areas devoted to specific activities. By analogy, we might hypothesize that a synagogue was also a variation on
a theme derived from its social order in terms of size, materials,
entrances and exits, orientation, ground plan, and areas devoted to
specific activities, including rituals.

Tilley advances six key ideas about or characteristics of houses,
several of which seem useful in our analysis of synagogues.

> (1) Directional orientation, which has long been noticed of synagogues.
> About half of them are clearly oriented on Jerusalem.
> (2) "Silhouetting, in which an object is identified by its distinctive pro-
> file...."[18] It is arresting to think that the profile or silhouette of a syna-
> gogue is distinctive when compared to Middle Eastern houses.
> (3) Nesting, or the positioning of one element inside another. Nesting is
> observable in the succession of perhaps five (sometimes four) architec-
> tural elements of a synagogue: from outside wall, to walk-around or
> corridor, to benches, to columns, to central floor.
> (4) Skeuomorphs or the substitution for an original material in order to
> represent changes in place, time, or status. If, then, the synagogue rep-
> resents the Temple courts, as is our contention, we should be able to
> find skeuomorphs. For example, we find simple limestone rather than
> the marble of the Temple forecourts.
> (5) "Key ritual actions, architectural elements, or the entire house may
> be used synecdochially to suggest essential features of the cosmos."[19] For
> example, the interior of the synagogue, when well lit by the sun, pro-
> vides a metaphorical experience as well as a literal experience of light.
> The cosmos, as God's creation, declares the glory of God.
> (6) Ideas of transition come to concrete visual expression in certain
> visual metaphors. This invites comparison to one noticeable feature of
> synagogues, namely, that often one enters into the well lit central area
> via a relatively darkened vestibule, as at Gamala. The central area of
> the synagogue would have been bright from the clerestory above, but
> the vestibule would be relatively dark. This also works for entrance into
> other structures via a hall without windows.

Synagogue Space as Metaphor

It has been my contention that the origins of synagogue architecture
are to be found in the forecourts of the Second Temple. If so, some
of Tilley's ideas of architecture as "solid metaphor" surely apply. For

---

[18] Op. cit., p. 43.
[19] Op. cit., p. 44.

example, his idea that metaphors elicit experiences and create meanings in a far richer manner than any literal expression ("the inexpressibility thesis") is potentially fruitful. Specifically, if the first century synagogue is a metaphor for the Temple courts and the activities that took place there, then emotions, feelings, and insights appropriate to that Temple forecourt environment will come to expression in the synagogue environment. These emotions and insights give subjective meaning to "sanctified space" both for the individual and for Israel (the collective) engaged in appropriate activities within the space.

The *"compactness"* thesis suggests that synagogues as metaphors provide the simplest or most parsimonious means of communication between the people of Israel about what it means to be Israel at work declaiming Torah. That is, the builders engaged in a certain economy of effort to produce the most appropriate structure they could to give expression to certain core elements of Israel or of Judaism, that structure which communicates "sanctified space" as efficiently as possible. Our contention is that this is the synagogue as we know it from Gamala, Masada, Herodium, and now from Herodian Jericho. All of these form a template derived from the forecourts of the Second Temple.

"The vividness thesis" tells us that solid metaphors link subjective and objective experience. In Tilley's terms, they encode and recall information in a graphic or colorful manner that facilitates memory. I find this category helpful, for we can see that a synagogue building, if styled after the Second Temple forecourts, therefore encodes and re-presents the visual experience of the Temple forecourts and evokes memories of experiences in that environment, as long as those memories are available. To put it another way, when one participates in reading Torah in the local synagogue, he conjoins his or her subjective experience with the collective experience mediated by and in the architectural space of the synagogue. The synagogue evokes the experience of participation in Torah reading in the forecourts of the Second Temple. Therefore building the synagogue to mimic the Second Temple forecourts guarantees continuity between the experiences *there* with *here*.

If I understand Tilley correctly, synagogues as solid metaphors would actively facilitate the production of novel understandings and interpretations of Israel, God, worship, and so on. In more specific terms, a synagogue as solid metaphor mediates between concrete and abstract thoughts. I may have an abstract concept of worship or

Torah reading as I discuss this idea with my neighbors, but when I enter the synagogue and participate, it is now a concrete experience.

Analysis of Space in the Gamala Synagogue

It now seems appropriate to examine at least one example of a synagogue in use for religious purposes during the first century, bearing in mind the idea that the synagogue building is a "solid metaphor" for synagogue Judaism or even for Israel. Our interest is in discovering how analysis of the material object itself will disclose its metaphorical relationship to Judaism as a religion in the first century. In other words, to what degree is "solid metaphor" a helpful idea in interpreting remains of ancient architecture in terms of the religion they supposedly represent? Secondly, will such an analysis allow us to connect the synagogue as envisioned in Mishnah Megilla with that found in Israel?

Our analysis of space is not so much analytical in the narrow sense. Rather it relies on knowledge of the sources and a certain spatial imagination so that one "sees" the space, complete with human beings in it. This "seeing" helps call to mind or elicit ideas from the observer. Surely this is the kind of seeing implied by Tilley's "inexpressibility" thesis. It is simply that the task at hand is to make explicit what was metaphorical or transfer fully metaphorical architecture to the fully metaphorical language of scholarship.

First we notice that there are some ambiguities and difficulties in establishing the precise plan of the Gamala synagogue. Gutman has reported, for example, that there are "four benches on the east, at the head of which is a basalt-paved platform and behind which is a fifth bench,"[20] but he does not report the dimensions of the platform, nor does he draw it. Yet the platform is visible in the photographs printed

---

[20] Shmaryahu Gutman, "Gamala," in Ephraim Stern, et al., eds., *The New Encyclopedia of Archaeological Excavations in the Holy Land* (Jerusalem, 1993), vol. 2, pp. 459-461, especially p. 460. In an earlier, preliminary publication Gutman noted, "From this floor [the uppermost on the northeast] down to the floor of the hall proper there are four rows of benches, joining up with those on the north and south." See Shmaryahu Gutman, "The Synagogue at Gamla," in Lee I. Levine, ed., *Synagogues Revealed* (Jerusalem, 1981), pp. 30-34, esp. p. 32. In the same volume Zvi Ma'oz reconstructs the Gamala synagogue with "four stepped benches and adjoining paved areas." See his "The Synagogues of Gamla and the Typology of Second-Temple Synagogues," pp. 35-41, esp. p. 38

on pp. 460-461. From the photographs and from visits, it appears that the platform is not centered on the long axis of the building, nor is the fifth bench. If this is original, then the builders more or less centered the fifth bench on the platform. If it is not original, then likely the bench and its platform extended along the northeastern wall. It is even possible that they were symmetric about the long axis.

The putative shift of the platform to the northwest appears to make room for human activity centered on a basin in the platform about three meters from the bench. The builders furnished the basin with a drain that conducted water under the city wall to the northeast.[21]

Gutman observed in 1993 that there are three benches on the northwest and two on the southeast.[22] I take that to mean that there are three benches *extant* on the northwest and two on the southeast. Furthermore he asserts that there are "four raised platforms" surrounding the hall, though his drawing on the same page shows only three, unless one counts the stones at the foot of the lowest bench as a platform.[23] The simplest architectural solution is to show three benches on all sides. The third forms its own platform or walkway next to the walls. The platform on the northeast adds one level, upon which stood the additional bench. On the other hand, whether there were three or four benches all around is not germane to the spatial analysis, as we will see.

There is also a problem in understanding the entrances into the hall. Gutman asserts that there are two entrances, "...a narrow one leading to the northern (sic, northwestern) platform and a wide one leading to the center of the hall."[24] His floor plan on the same page shows *three* entrances.[25] The suggested solution raises more problems than it solves for the putative entrance on the southwest or for the entrance on the southeast shown in his line drawing. The top of the

---

[21] Gutman, op. cit., called the basin a "depression" (p. 32). Ma'oz believes that the "small round plastered basin and water channel" were added by refugees after the sack of Gamla; op. cit., p. 37. If that is the case, the highest platform on the northeast once extended across more of the end of the synagogue.

[22] Loc. cit.

[23] Loc. cit.

[24] Gutman, "Gamala," p. 460.

[25] As does the plan published in Gutman, "The Synagogue at Gamala," p. 31. On the other hand the plan published in 1994 shows only two entrances: Shmaryahu Gutman and Yoel Rapel, *Gamla—A City in Rebellion* (Israel: Ministry of Defense, 1994), p. 101.

third platform on either side of the central doorway would be at least one meter higher than the floor, which requires a staircase or a ladder for entry.[26] On the other hand the central door leading into the center of the hall requires no step up nor down. The floor inside is at the same height as the floor outside. With this difficulty in mind we will not discuss these putative entrances on either side of the main entrance until confirmed in further research.

Gutman further asserts that there is an exedra to the west of the synagogue, "...in front of which an open court forms the southern part of the synagogue." This statement is an odd architectural solution to the problem of entry into the building, particularly as shown in later reconstructions, which favor an enclosed exedra, and which I will assume in this discussion.

We now turn to a discussion of the main features of the plan of the synagogue and of its entire silhouette. Our analysis is informed by the idea that the synagogue stands in a metaphorical relationship to the religion that produced it. The synagogue, then, "stands for" this religious reality. It "provides ways of giving form to" certain abstract, religious ideas. The synagogue "brings to expression" or "presents" the religious system of the congregation or its understanding of the world.

In terms of ancient architecture the building is a species of basilica. That is, it is a public space or roofed hall marked by a rectangle of columns around the central space so as to divide it into a central rectangle surrounded by a corridor or walkway (platform) between the columns and the outside walls (Fig. 2).[27] The corners of the columniation present double columns ("heart-shaped columns"), which inform the eye from inside the columniation that there is a change of direction of the row of columns. One can also think of the corner columns as corner markers.

Sometimes basilicas featured second stories over the corridors and not over the central space. There may be clerestory walls pierced by windows to let in light. The columns support the clerestory walls above. If the citizens used a basilica to hear legal cases, like at Pompeii, there may be a tribunal built at one narrow end where the

---

[26] Ma'oz, op. cit., forthrightly discusses the discrepancy in height between the side entrances and the central entrance without suggesting that stairs were needed, p. 38f.

[27] D.S. Robertson, *Greek and Roman Architecture* (Second Edition: Cambridge, 1943), pp. 267f.

presiding magistrate stood. Sometimes basilicas also had other features, such as an apse at one of the narrow ends or in one of the long sides. Vitruvius directs that they should be built next to the market area or forum so that businessmen could gather out of the weather.[28]

The building at Gamala is surely a basilica, and the unpaved central space strongly suggests that it was roofed. The roof is most easily reconstructed with a clerestory because of the columns, as witness Figures 3 and 4 (the roofing of a basilica, which gives the building a distinctive silhouette). The clerestory roof solves the problem of introducing light into the northwest side of the interior space, since the ground on the outside is roughly at roof height, precluding any use of windows in the northwestern wall. Furthermore the southeastern, outside wall cannot use windows, because the interior floor is too high to leave room for windows higher than the visitor's head, ancient style. The lack of windows in the first story means that we must introduce light from the clerestory. The area within the columns, then, would be relatively more brightly lit by the sun than would the southeastern walking space outside the columns or the exedra, as mentioned above (Fig. 5).

The exedra on the southwest side is not an ordinary feature of Roman basilicas. Its inclusion suggests that the builders added it for some purpose we may deduce in this essay.

The end opposite the exedra is built against the city wall. This bonding or abutment determines the orientation of the building; namely, it points southwest. Some understand this orientation to suggest that the builders were siting the building so that it pointed towards Jerusalem.

It now seems appropriate to discuss the building in detail, but also its siting or emplotment and the organized space within as metaphor. In effect this will be a trial run on Tilley's theses.

The builders did not place the synagogue on the highest point of the city, as legislated by T. Meg. 3:23. On the other hand it is positioned with streets on three sides (or squares on two sides and a narrow street on one side), which isolate the building (Fig. 2). It is also built against the city wall, which ties it to a municipal structure rather than to a domestic building. Crowds of people wishing to use the synagogue could gather on the northwest and southeast with ease, though the street at the narrow end of the building to the

---

[28] Vitruvius, *The Ten Books of Architecture* (New York, 1960), p. 132 (V.1.4).

southwest could only accommodate small crowds. Either or both of these streets or squares on the northwest and southeast conducted crowds to and from the city through the city gates, which suggests that the synagogue occupied a strategic point within the city plan beside the city gate or gates. One may even point out that it is bracketed by city squares.

The siting or emplotment of the building suggests that it was not intended for prosaic or ordinary use. That is, the isolation of the building coheres well with its status as some kind of sanctified space. Furthermore the silhouette of the synagogue (Figs. 3 and 4) signals that it is not a house or domestic space. The siting and the silhouette, then, exclude certain uses, much as is indicated by M. Meg. 3:3, which suggests that people may have taken short cuts through destroyed synagogues, while this is (later) forbidden.

I have made the point that the synagogue building, from its siting, is a public building. M. Meg. 3:1 makes the point that a synagogue exceeds in sanctity a street, if they both belong to the public. The synagogue at Gamala is nested, then, in public space of less sanctity than the space of the synagogue. But the sanctity of the synagogue is of less sanctity than the ark that resides within it. Similarly the ark is of less sanctity than the wrappings for the scrolls within the ark and the wrappings of less sanctity than the Torah scroll itself. The whole of the streets, the edifice, the ark, the wrappings for the Torah scroll, and the Torah scroll itself is an example of nested meanings or values (M. Meg. 3:1):

A. Townsfolk who sold (1) a street of a town buy with its proceeds a synagogue.
B. [If they sold] (2) a synagogue, they buy an ark.
C. [If they sold] (3) an ark, they buy wrappings.
D. [If they sold] (4) wrappings, they buy scrolls [of the prophets or writings].
E. [If they sold] (5) scrolls, they buy a Torah scroll.
F. But if they sold (5) a Torah scroll, they should not buy scrolls.
G. [If they sold] (4) scrolls, they should not buy wrappings.
H. [If they sold] (3) wrappings, they should not buy an ark.
I. [If they sold] (2) an ark, they should not buy a synagogue.
J. [If they sold] (1) a synagogue, they should not buy a street.
K. And so with the surplus [of the proceeds of any of] these.
L. "They do not sell that which belongs to the public to a private person,

M. "Because they thereby diminish its level of sanctity," the words of R. Judah.

N. They said to him, "If so, [they should] not [sell] from a large town to a small one."[29]

We recall that the silhouette of the building is distinctive. One must keep in mind that the buildings around the synagogue would normally include flat roofs, assuming they are consistent with what we know of early Roman urban houses. The gabled roof of the synagogue with its tiles would immediately call attention to itself. The gabled roof of the synagogue appears to function as part of its metaphor as sanctified space. In this case the part stands for the whole, as in synecdoche.

The roof of the exedra or vestibule, since it is not integral to the basilica, is most easily reconstructed with a flat roof. The flat roof would appreciably distinguish the exedra from the basilica. In effect, we would see that the exedra is the standing metaphor for entrance into and exit from the building, an example of an "idea of transition." The center of interest would be the basilica, that is, the synagogue proper. In effect the exedra would stand for some other status than that of the synagogue. In anthropological terms, the exedra or vestibule would be meso-space or the transition from exterior space to interior space, or from public to private, or from less sanctified to more sanctified.

Since the exedra is tall, at least as tall as the interior columniation of the synagogue and the architraves on top the columniation, it is possible that the walls were pierced by windows near the ceiling. This would allow those who enter not to walk immediately into gloom, though the lighting would doubtless be less than that outside, and even less than the light inside the synagogue.

One notices from the outside of the synagogue and its exedra that it is not necessarily obvious to the visitor which entrance is more grand just from examining the doorways. If there were entrances in the northeastern and southwestern walls of the exedra as well as in its long wall, then it is perfectly possible that visitors would immediately grasp by visual inspection that the main entrance was in the exedra because of the number of doorways. On the other hand, if there were only one entrance visible on the southwest (in the exedra) and a

---

[29] Jacob Neusner, *The Mishnah* (New Haven, 1988), p. 320.

second near the east corner with its stairway from the southeast plaza, the architecture of the exedra itself (its height and flat roof) would suggest that this was the preferred entrance. Analysis of the interior space confirms that the entrance in the long, southwest wall of the exedra was the preferred entrance from outside.

If we turn to the hall of the basilica with its columns and benches, we notice that the interior space is more or less symmetric about its long axis but not about the short axis (Fig. 2). The lack of symmetry about the short axis is highlighted by the niche in the west corner and the stairway and exit door in the east corner. The symmetry about the long axis draws attention along an imaginary line from the entrance in the middle of the southwest wall to the platform at least 1.4 m. higher up on the northeast wall.[30]

Curiously, this main entrance is concealed from the street by the vestibule or exedra itself. Thus another function of the exedra, surprisingly enough, is to conceal or hide, perhaps to conceal or hide the entrance to sanctified space from less sanctified space (the street).[31]

It is important to notice that as one enters through the entrance on the long axis and through the southwestern or narrow wall, he or she does not walk the length of the hall on the long axis (Fig. 2). There is an architectural marker or boundary for the central space, namely, the row of columns all around. One also sees that the builders have arranged the entrance so as to cut through the benches and walkways that surround the central space on all four sides. After walking into the narrow rectangle of space between the columns and the benches, one must *ascend* to stand or sit, unless one chooses to keep one's feet on the floor and sit on the first rank of benches. One must make a decision whether to stay on the floor or ascend to a higher bench.

---

[30] Ma'oz is likely right that the fourth platform and its attendant fifth bench were originally centered on the entire end of the hall opposite the entrance. We may not know until further data comes to light from the excavation. In his 1993 article, Gutman says, "At the northern part of the basalt-paved platform, Above the four benches along the eastern wall, the paving was destroyed and show signs of burning. A water channel was discovered here, coming from the east and passing through the wall. It ends in a small basin that may have been used for washing hands." Although it is attractive to interpret this as an architectural remnant that reflects its metaphorical status for hand washing, it seems odd that one would have to crouch or kneel and dip water from *beneath the level of the platform*. Sprinkling or washing with water is not mentioned in M. Megillah, except for use of the Miqveh.

[31] The exedra or vestibule at Jericho also effectively hides the actual entrance into the synagogue space.

One must also decide which one of the four sides is his or her destination. Unfortunately, there is very little to go on to infer what clues the ancients were using to decide where to stand or sit. It is possible, of course, that they simply looked at the people standing here and there and made their choices that way or relied upon tradition.

One sees by simple visual inspection the phenomenon of architectural nesting (Fig. 2), in which the four walkways are nested within the four walls, the benches are nested within the walkways, the columns are nested within the benches, and the central space is nested within the columns. Our eyes are directed to the central space, either at our level or below us, where something of importance takes place.

Furthermore the columniation draws our eyes upward to the clerestory, which contains the most light. The light coming through the windows high up in the clerestory walls on the southeast wall would send shafts of brilliant sunshine through what is otherwise relative darkness, depending on the time of day. As one can see from Fig. 5, and depending on the exact design of the clerestory, the light coming in through the southeastern clerestory wall near noon in the summer would illuminate the central area or, if the sun was low enough, the northwestern wall of the synagogue. A soft, northern light would be coming through the windows in the northwestern clerestory wall.

The benches all around introduce the literal notions of higher and lower, which may in fact operate as metaphors for higher and lower in desirability if not in rank. Of course it is also possible that rank played a role in the seating arrangement, as was the case in Roman theaters. We recall the idea that a house, and therefore a synagogue or other such structure, embodies ideas of the social order. It should not be surprising to find ancient Jewish ideas of rank reflected in the building.

All who sit or stand on the benches have their attention directed to the central space. Yet those participating do not have an unobstructed view of what is going on. On the contrary, the row of columns in front of each observer limits vision, and at Gamala this is a serious problem (see Fig. 7). In fact, if it were crowded, it would be quite difficult to gain a seat that is high enough and not directly behind a column.

Analysis of the line of sight or "viewshed" suggests that the space interior to the four walls is better constructed for hearing or listening than for sight. Let the reader refer to Fig. 7, which is a viewshed analysis of what is visible from the middle of the highest seat near the southeastern wall. One can readily see that more is obscured by the columniation than is revealed by looking between the columns.

Seats that were not situated behind columns and that lay at the topmost bench would be the most desirable. This calls to mind a saying of Jesus in Mark 12:38-39: "Beware of the scribes, who wish to walk about in robes and be greeted in the markets and yearn for the first seats in the synagogues and the first couch in banquets." It is tempting to place these "first seats" at Gamala opposite the main entrance on the long axis and atop the highest bench.

This restricted visual situation supports the ritual of Torah reading, for in the case of Torah declamation, hearing and listening are the issue, not watching someone read. Jacob Neusner has said, "...the synagogue represents the occasion at which ten or more Israelite males assemble and so embody Israel, and provides for the declamation of the Torah to Israel: it is Sinai, no where in particular, to whom it may concern. It is a place made holy by Israel's presence and activity, anywhere Israel assembles, and the presence is for the activity of hearing the Torah proclaimed."[32]

If the building is built so that Torah may be declaimed, and indeed it appears that this architectural arrangement is quite suited to such a holy pursuit, then it follows that there must be at least one Torah scroll present. If there is a Torah scroll, is there an ark for it? Certainly the literary evidence seems to assume the presence of an ark. This is true of M. Meg. 3:1 and following, where the ark is mentioned many times.

Not only does the Mishnah mention the ark, but it mentions the behavior or ritual appropriate to the ark: one "passes before the ark" (to lead in worship or lead the *Amidah*). This is more than likely a stereotyped phrase that has developed in the tradition following the development of conventional behaviors (rituals) associated with the furniture of the ark. Even if one objects that these texts are late (ca. 200 C.E.), it is clear there is a developed ritual behavior and a ritual piece of furniture associated with the synagogue. If the ark exists around 200 C.E., it is because it fulfills a ritual need. If that need exists in the first century, then it seems reasonable that the ark also existed then.

Our reasoning about the presence of an ark is as follows: If one

---

[32] Neusner, op. cit.

sets aside space for reading of Torah, then one needs a Torah scroll at hand. Economy of effort would lead one to suppose that a chest or container of some sort would be present within that space, if it is secure, to hold the Torah scroll. If we are to take seriously the legislation of the sages about ending a Torah reading with a lection from a prophet (M. Meg. 3:4, 3:6), then we expect scrolls of the prophets to be present as well. As our reasoning about the literary evidence progresses, so does the size of the chest or container increase. Furthermore, because of the number of representations of arks on early Roman gold glass, for example, it seems reasonable to hypothesize that a special container called an "ark" would in fact be present. In other words, Jewish art depicts a real object.[33]

In terms of the present analysis, where was the ark? Some have hypothesized that the niche in the wall near the west corner is for an ark. Depictions of the ark and its environment, again in ancient Jewish art, whether on stone, Roman gold glass, on later mosaics, show the ark residing in a central place opposite the main entrance on the long axis. If this applies to the Gamala synagogue (and others), then the ark would reside on the additional platform on the narrow end opposite the main entrance and in front of the fifth bench on that wall. This would help us understand why there was an additional platform of cut stone at the northeastern wall at all. Furthermore, since the ark would define a center of interest, the principle of parsimony or economy of effort would dictate that other ritual actions such as sprinkling or washing would be in the immediate vicinity.[34] That helps us understand the function of the basin or plastered depression northwest of the remains of the platform. That is, there was some provision for water near the ark. We no longer know exactly what that was, but we have found the drain to draw off the water. The builders even made sure that the water was taken completely away from the synagogue, outside the city.

Finally, we may also deduce a simple hypothesis that those involved in Torah reading (as many as seven according to M. Meg. 3:4) sat at the highest rank of the benches, which in the present instance

---

[33] Considering how religion operates with its artifacts, the chances are that any chest for so high a purpose as holding Torah scrolls would exhibit fine workmanship and the finest materials. See Colin Renfrew and Paul Bahn, *Archaeology: Theories, Methods, and Practice* (New York, 1996), p. 391.

[34] Not including ritual immersion. Discussion of the use of *miqva'oth* is reserved for the future.

would be on the fifth bench at the northeastern end of the building.
This would be the evident place also for the translator (M. Meg. 3:6
and more often) and for an attendant (Luke 4:20).

Our analysis has yielded several ways of understanding the synagogue at Gamala that, at least in part, apply to the other early synagogues we have mentioned. First, we see that the synagogue at
Gamala is a public building, as declared by its abutment to the city
wall and by its emplotment between two squares and a street or three
streets. Such placement gives us a building probably intended for
public use.

This building has a distinctive silhouette compared to domestic
structures. It even has a distinctive silhouette compared to its own
vestibule or exedra. Such a silhouette alerts the citizenry to its distinctive status and function.

The vestibule shields or hides the synagogue hall from the street.
That is, the vestibule deadens the sounds of the street and expunges
outside sights. Thus the vestibule functions to ease the visitor into the
environment of the prayer hall without a sudden transition. Even
lighting plays a role, as the brightest area would likely be the street
outside, followed by the synagogue hall, and finally by the vestibule.
Similarly the street would be the loudest, followed by the vestibule,
and finally by the synagogue hall. Thus this flat-roofed structure also
functions as a transition in terms of lighting and of sound.

We discover that the building appears to contain within it the idea
of higher and lower, of higher rank and lower rank, or more desirable
seats and less desirable seats. Such a circumstance suggests that the
society that uses the synagogue is likely stratified in terms of rank. It
also suggests that high-ranking or most desirable space can be reserved for those who play a central role in Torah reading, the central
idea of the synagogue according to Mishnah Megillah, and a situation known by Josephus.

We discover that the presence of a Torah scroll and other scrolls,
as revealed in the ancient literature, suggests that an ark was present,
which makes sense of those representations of arks in Jewish art. We
can even deduce the likely position of the ark at the narrow end of
the building. This position lies on the long axis opposite the main
entrance, and on a special, high platform built for it and the readers,
for the translator, and perhaps even for an attendant, if he is different
from the translator.

Not all of these ideas are equally probably represented, but all of them are best understood as testable hypotheses. That is, we need to examine further examples of possible first century buildings in future archaeology and discover whether they tend to cohere with this pattern. It is certainly true that the buildings at Gamala, Masada, possibly Capernaum (first building), Herodium, and now Jericho exhibit the nesting of walls, walkways, columns, and central space. All four contain the idea of higher and lower, and therefore potentially of rank. The new find at Jericho exhibits a vestibule with apparently the same functions as the one at Gamala. It also has a niche near the corner, as at Gamala.

Conclusions

We are now in a position to suggest that the findings of literary analysis of the role of the synagogue in the Mishnah and the findings of archaeology of synagogues are commensurate with one another. Although some have thought that there was a contradiction between the two, there appears to be none.

We are also in a position to suggest that the idea of synagogue as metaphor aids the analysis materially. We are not engaged in a comparison of literal readings of texts with literal readings of architecture or archaeological remains, but we are instead making reasonable inferences from both types of evidence from the position that the building embodies as "solid metaphor" what the texts assert in linguistic metaphors. Our interpretations give both kinds of evidence a voice, and in this case it is the powerful voice of metaphor.

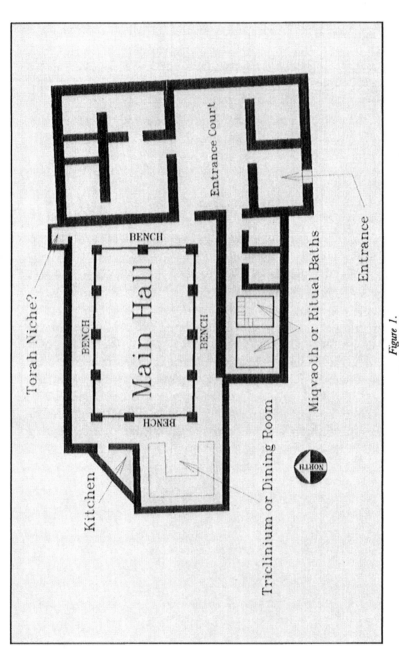

Figure 1.
Jericho Synagogue.
Adapted from Ehud Netzer, "Le Scoperte sotto il Palazzo di Erode," in Archeo, 14, no. 7 (July, 1998) p. 33.

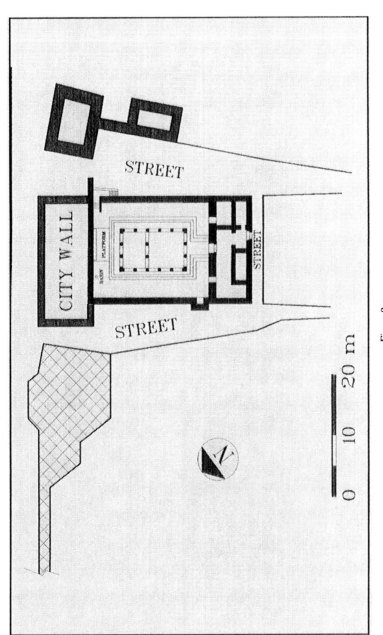

Figure 2.
Plan of the Gamala Synagogue.

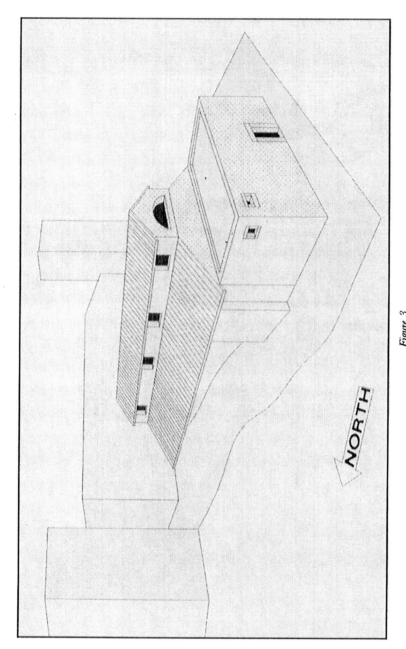

NORTH

Figure 3.
Gamala Synagogue in Perspective from West.

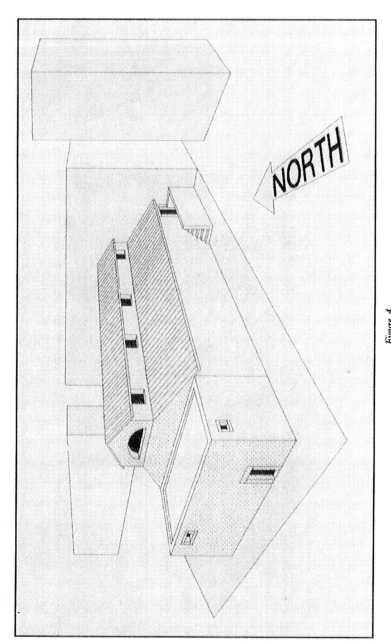

Figure 4.
Gamala Synagogue in Perspective from South.

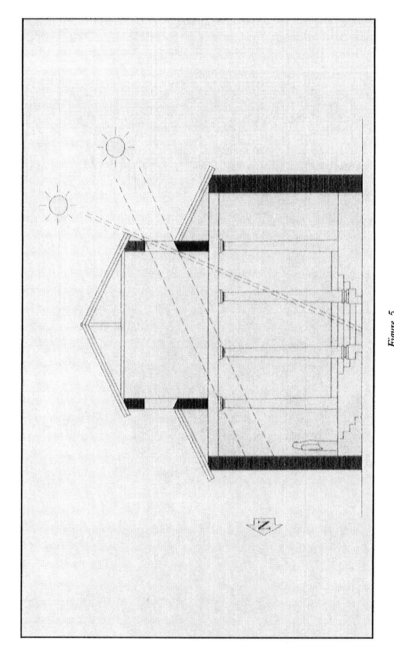

Figure 5.
Interior of the Gamala Synagogue Showing Sunlight Angles.

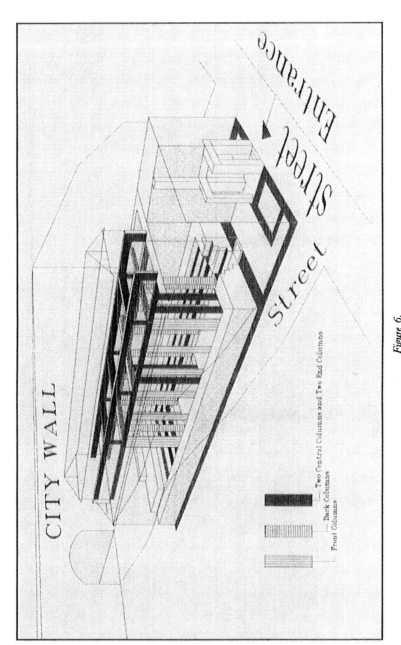

Figure 6.
Gamala Synagogue Showing Calumniation.

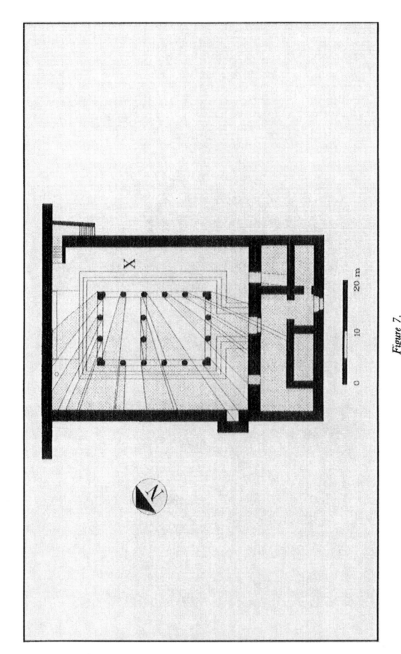

Figure 7.
Viewshed Analysis of the Gamala Synagogue.

6. PROLEGOMENON TO A THEORY OF EARLY SYNAGOGUE DEVELOPMENT

Paul V.M. Flesher
University of Wyoming

The synagogue of medieval and modern times descends from the synagogue formed and shaped in the Galilee and Golan following the destruction of the Jerusalem Temple in 70.[1] The loss of the Temple enabled the synagogue to develop in new directions, which came to fruition in the Rabbinic literature of the third century and later as well as in the synagogue buildings of the fourth century and later. But from where did the synagogue of the Galilee and Golan come? That is where the difficulty arises.

The well-evidenced synagogue of the Rabbinic period is nowhere to be found prior to 70. Scholars know there "must have been" synagogues all over the Galilee and Golan, as the New Testament writings and Gamala synagogue suggest. But apart from those two sources and Josephus, there is little evidence. Judea fares no better. Apart from some general comments about "synagogues in Judea," there may be two synagogues that were built during the war of 68-72 by northern rebels operating in Judea. The book of Acts mentions a Jerusalem synagogue, an undated inscription perhaps indicates another, and Philo suggests that the Essenes worshipped in a synagogue.[2] All-in-all, not much evidence to work with.

---

[1] I treat the Galilee and the Golan together because they are closely related. Galilee in this period was certainly a complex geographical, social and religious area, and adding the Golan to that only increases the complexity. But it is becoming clear that the society based on the western shore of the Sea of Galilee was not limited to one side but extended around to the eastern side of the lake and even into the hills beyond. In addition, the only pre-70 synagogue from a village context known and excavated in Palestine lies in the Golan, not in Galilee. For Galilee, see Meyers, "Regionalism," Meyers, "Response," Horsley, "Dialogue," and Horsley, "Response." See also, Freyne, *Galilee*. For the Golan, see Urman, "Golan Heights." Galilee is such a complex region in this period that researchers are only beginning to understand its intricacies, despite the many recent studies (only a few of which are mentioned here). By comparison, the Golan and its connections to the Galilee has not yet received the attention it deserves.

[2] See Flesher, "Palestinian Synagogues," which discusses the reliability of this evidence. The point here is simpler—there is little available evidence at all.

At this point, scholarship has generally taken its cue from the rabbis and composed explanations of the synagogue's origins that derive it from "biblical Israel," that is, from Jews either living in their Land or on their way to the Land, as recorded in Scripture or Second Temple literature. Just as Rabbinic literature identified the synagogue's origins with different figures and periods described in the Bible, so too scholarly explanations have variously linked the earliest synagogues to the First Temple period, the Exile, the early Persian period under Ezra and Nehemiah, the Hasmoneans, and so on.[3] Unfortunately, these identifications and explanations comprise little more than speculation, since there is no evidence that synagogues actually existed in these periods, let alone originated during them. Now there is nothing wrong with speculation on its own, but it cannot provide support for further research because it itself lacks support. Speculation does not advance scholarly knowledge but constitutes a dead-end. We must take a different approach.

So rather than follow what was originally a theological claim, let us step back and look at the evidence for the early synagogue. What stands out is that Jewish settlers in Egypt used synagogues for worship as early as the third century B.C.E.[4] Over the next three centuries, evidence for synagogues increases throughout the Mediterranean diaspora until, by the first century C.E., it becomes clear that the diaspora synagogue comprised an active, vital Jewish institution. Thus prior to the synagogue's first appearance in the Galilee and Golan, the synagogue underwent more than two centuries of successful development in the Mediterranean world. Indeed, even in the first century, it is in the diaspora that synagogues appear most prominently. While modern scholarship knows of between nine and eleven possible synagogues in all of Palestine that date to the first century C.E. or earlier[5]—despite extensive archaeological exploration—there

---

[3] For further details, see the discussion in Levine, "Nature," pp. 426-427.

[4] This observation is not new; the evidence has been known for decades. For further discussion, see Griffiths, "Egypt."

[5] I here refer to the consensus view. My earlier essay (Flesher, "Palestinian Synagogues") makes it clear that I do not follow the consensus in every detail. There may be archaeological evidence for four Palestinian synagogues: Masada, Herodium, Gamala, and the Theodotus inscription from Jerusalem. Literary evidence suggests also: Capernaum, Chorazin, the Synagogue of the Freedmen in Jerusalem (counting it as one synagogue rather than five), Nazareth, and Tiberias. Dor and Caesaria belong more properly to the diaspora. On the archaeological evidence for pre-70 Palestinian synagogues, see also Chiat, "Synagogue Architecture."

is evidence for thirty-five or more specific pre-70 synagogues in the diaspora.[6] Given this success, the diaspora synagogues played a larger role in the history of the early synagogue than has been recognized.

Could the Palestinian synagogue have developed without influence from the diaspora synagogue? Not likely. Not after two centuries. The first-century synagogues of the Galilee and Golan lie in the shadow of the stature and success of their diaspora counterparts. So any attempt to understand the sources and beginnings of Palestinian synagogues should start by analyzing diaspora synagogues. Although the analysis will not lead back to the synagogue's origins, it will provide a foundation for understanding the synagogues that later appeared in Palestine.

The way to interpret the diaspora synagogue is to analyze its success. Somehow, by 70 C.E., the synagogue had managed to make itself part of the Graeco-Roman world for three centuries. Somehow it had found a place in the Graeco-Roman society where it was accepted by non-Jews. Just what was this place? How did the Graeco-Roman world classify the synagogue prior to 70? The crux of this question is best stated in taxonomic terms: did non-Jews see the synagogue as a *species* within a larger *genus*, or did they understand it as *sui generis*? Did the diaspora synagogue belong to a pre-existing category, or did the Graeco-Romans create a special category in their social organization for the synagogue? To put the question anachronistically, in what category of the telephone Yellow Pages would the synagogue appear? (In my small town, it is listed under "Churches.") The question is thus one of social classification—where does something fit?—and not one of essence—what is it?

The research discussed in this paper reveals that the Graeco-Romans saw the synagogue as belonging to the *genus* of "temple," even though it was not a perfect fit. This should not be surprising, since scholars have long noted similarities between synagogues and Graeco-Roman temples in terms of architecture, artwork, and activi-

---

[6] Leonard V. Rutgers' recent essay ("Diaspora Synagogue") provides a list identifying diaspora synagogues dated to the first century C.E. or earlier in at least twenty eight cities or towns. There are several synagogues for which first-century evidence exists that do not appear on the list: Sardis, Halicarnassus, and Alexandrou-Nesos (a typographical error places it in the Common Era) as well as the Bosporan cities of Gorgippia and Phanagoria (see Harrill, *Manumission*, pp. 174-175, n. 70).

ties practiced in the buildings.[7] These similarities appear in matters we think of as specifically Graeco-Roman as well as in matters we usually associate with Judaism but which were also practiced in Graeco-Roman temples. When analyzed in taxonomic terms, it becomes clear that the similarities between synagogues and Graeco-Roman temples are not random and *ad hoc*, but indicate that the synagogue belonged to the *genus* of "Graeco-Roman temple."

As we discuss this analysis, we will move back and forth between two aspects of the main question. The primary aspect focuses on how the non-Jews of the Graeco-Roman world classified the synagogue. The secondary aspect of the question centers on whether Jews themselves understood that their institution fitted into the Graeco-Roman category of temple. Did they know that the non-Jewish world in which they lived thought that the synagogue was a type of temple, and did they draw upon that classification themselves, and perhaps even promote it? Again, we shall find that the evidence shows they did. In fact, they often act on that classification to defend the synagogues and to further the interests of the Jewish community.

Definitional issues bedevil the study of ancient synagogues, and so I want to take a moment to make clear that this essay defines the synagogue as a building and the set of activities carried out in the building, that is, the synagogue as an institution.[8] It does not refer to the notion of the "synagogue" as only a gathering of the Jewish community.[9] Understanding the Jewish communities of the Mediterranean diaspora is a complicated and difficult matter. Some scholars, such as Tcherikover and Smallwood, have extensively discussed the

---

[7] In a recent article, for example, Lee Levine argued that Hellenistic influence was instrumental in moving the synagogue's fore-runner (the city gate, according to Levine) out of the open air and into a building, which became the synagogue. See Levine, "Nature," p. 443. Levine's recent book-length exploration of the interaction between Judaism and Greek culture provides new insights based on a solid understanding of previous scholarship and includes an extended discussion of the synagogue in this context. See Levine, *Judaism and Hellenism*, esp. pp. 139-179. See also the papers from the first Howard Gilman International Conference, which focused on Hellenic and Jewish Arts, in Ovadiah, *Arts*, including my own contribution, Flesher, "Dura Synagogue Paintings."

[8] I indiscriminately use the term "synagogue" to refer to structures that are called either *proseuche* or *synagoge* in the ancient literature and inscriptions.

[9] This definition is the earliest meaning of the term *synagoge* in a Jewish context—certainly the Septuagint uses it that way. This study analyzes pre-70 occurrences of this term only when they indicate the synagogue institution and not when they simply refer to Jewish assemblies of various kinds.

issue in terms of citizenship and status, showing that these issues were highly involved and problematic in the eastern Mediterranean.[10] Other scholars have recently taken a more localized approach and analyzed the community of each synagogue by likening it to a *collegium*.[11] This is a profitable direction, but it must always be remembered that the term applies to the people who gather together and not to their building.[12] A *collegium* may or may not have owned the building in which it met. Although most *collegia* were involved in worship, only the wealthier ones owned their own shrine. Most simply met and worshipped at a local temple to their deity.[13] This essay focuses not on the status or nature of the Jewish community but on the classification of the building in which they met and worshipped.

This essay's main body discusses how the synagogue fit into Graeco-Roman society as a temple by analyzing its "temple" characteristics. After that, the study's focus takes a more theoretical turn and derives a simple model from the analysis for understanding the interaction between the synagogue's community of worshippers and the Graeco-Roman society around it. The model brings us back to the question of how the diaspora synagogue influenced that of Palestine. Looking briefly at Jerusalem as well as the Galilee and Golan, it explicates how the different religious and cultural circumstances impacted the reception and the formation of the synagogue as an institution.

The Synagogue as a Graeco-Roman Temple

There are two ways in which the surviving evidence shows that pre-70 diaspora synagogues fit into the classification of Graeco-Roman

---

[10] Tcherikover, *Hellenistic Civilization* and Smallwood, *Roman Rule*. Their large-scale focus directs attention away from the synagogue rather than towards it.

[11] Smallwood, *Roman Rule*, pp. 133-138, discusses *collegia* as a useful category for understanding synagogues. Kraabel, "Unity," pp. 24-28, discusses voluntary associations and their place in diaspora Judaism. More recently, a collection of essays on voluntary associations has brought together a number of useful essays on collegia and other types of groups; see Kloppenborg and Wilson. Richardson, "Early Synagogues" is especially helpful. See also Richardson, "Synagogues in Rome."

[12] Unfortunately, after an excellent discussion of the how the idea of the *collegium* fits the synagogue *congregation*, Richardson lets his conclusion become a comment about the synagogue *building*. See Richardson, "Early Synagogues."

[13] Sometimes several *collegia* made use of the same shrine; see MacLean, "Delos," pp. 208 and 211.

temples. First, many of the activities that take place in a synagogue also take place in temples. Even when the Jews thought of their worship and other activities as typically Jewish, the Graeco-Roman world saw the same actions in Graeco-Roman terms. These include practices such as prayer, purification, the holding of council meetings, and even the collection of money. Second, synagogues adopted activities and made statements that were particularly Graeco-Roman, transforming such actions into Jewish activities in the process. Examples of these include the manumission of slaves, the granting of asylum status to a synagogue, and the use of Graeco-Roman temple terminology to describe the synagogue.

This section is organized into four parts.[14] It begins by examining the primary activities of a Graeco-Roman temple to investigate how the synagogue matches them. Next, it analyzes the synagogue in relationship to secondary temple activities. Third, it evaluates the temple terminology used in relationship to synagogues. Finally, it briefly reviews the ways in which synagogues and Graeco-Roman temples are not alike.

Primary Activities of Graeco-Roman Temples and the Synagogue

In his analysis of the Greek temple, Walter Burkert posits that worship consists of three main activities. He states: "The main acts of cult within a [Graeco-Roman temple] sanctuary may also be divided into three categories: prayer (*euchai*), sacrifice (*thysiai*), and the setting up of votives (*anathemata*)."[15] Diaspora synagogues, for their part, provided the locations in which Jews practiced two of the activities, prayer and the display of votive gifts. Additionally, although they did not practice sacrifice, as far as we can tell, the Jews who worshiped in synagogues did perform some activities that may have led those around them to think they did.[16]

---

[14] The following discussion of the diaspora synagogue draws frequently from the Ph.D. thesis of Donald D. Binder, "Into the Temple Courts," soon to be published by Scholars Press. Binder's work constitutes the first monograph-length study of pre-70 synagogues. Although my conclusions are in opposition to his, the study provides an excellent assembly of relevant material.

[15] Burkert, "Temple," p. 36. Brackets mine.

[16] E.P. Sanders discusses many of the functions I describe below in his forthcoming "Texts and Tradition." I want to thank Steven Fine for lending me a prepublication copy of the essay.

Prayer: While it is clear that prayer was a widespread, common, regular part of diaspora Jewish worship, specific evidence indicating praying in the synagogues is rather scarce. Prayer seems to have been so common that it often went unremarked in our sources. But the indications we do have make it clear that the pre-70 diaspora synagogue was a place for prayer. To begin with, the synagogue was called a "prayer house"—*proseuche*—long before the name *synagoge* was attached to it. This designation appears first on inscriptions from third century B.C.E. Egypt—the earliest evidence for synagogues anywhere. It remains the preferred term for the synagogue into the Common Era; Josephus even uses it to describe the synagogue in Tiberias.[17] Since it is hard to imagine that prayer would have been an important Jewish activity but not in the institution called the "prayer-house," this term clearly indicates that Jews used their synagogues for prayer.[18]

Additional information comes from Philo and Josephus. Philo relates a story about what Jews did on one occasion when their synagogues were inaccessible. When Flaccus finally was arrested, after allowing the persecution of the Jews and the destruction of their synagogues, the Jews gathered on the beach, "since their synagogues had been taken from them," and uttered a prayer of thanks to God (*Flaccus* 122-4). If the Jews had possessed their synagogue(s), they would have gone to them to pray. Instead, the community that usually prayed together in their synagogue(s), improvised by praying together on the beach. Josephus relates a decree concerning the synagogue at Sardis that specifies that the synagogue should be a place for "ancestral prayers" (*Ant.* 14:259-61). The use of the term "ancestral" implies that these are fixed liturgical prayers rather than spontaneous supplications. So here again we see that prayer, a Graeco-Roman temple practice as well as a Jewish one, was practiced in the synagogues.[19]

Votive Offerings: Josephus tells of how the successors of Antiochus Epiphanes gave to the synagogue in Antioch the votive offerings he had taken from the Jerusalem Temple. These were "laid up in the

---

[17] Prior to this time, "*synagoge*" indicates a gathering of people rather than a structure. This starts to change by the first century C.E.

[18] This conclusion is accepted by most scholars. See, for example, Levine, "Second Temple," p. 20. See also the discussion in Fine, *Holy Place*, p. 28.

[19] Philo also states that the Jews prayed "with upraised hands"—which was the prayer posture in most Graeco-Roman temples.

synagogue" for display. Later monarchs continued to give gifts, and these "costly offerings formed a splendid ornament to their synagogue" (Josephus, *War* 7:44-5). Since the giving of votives was a central worship activity of the Graeco-Roman temple, as Burkert makes clear, the synagogue's receipt and display of them makes it like a temple. Furthermore, the synagogue displayed these in the proper Graeco-Roman manner. This reveals that the synagogue's Jewish community understood the importance of votives in Graeco-Roman culture and used their synagogue to function as a Graeco-Roman temple in this way.[20]

The original meaning of a "votive offering" was a gift bestowed as the result of a vow.[21] Such a vow was irrevocable and the gift that stemmed from it could never be returned. In the Graeco-Roman period, any offering or gift received the same treatment—the vow was not required. The donation served a two-fold purpose, for it was seen as a self-denying gift to the god, but since it was displayed, the viewers recalled not just the item given, but also the giver. The gift thus continued to bring the giver recognition for years, decades, and even centuries to come. This was particularly evident in monetary donations, especially if the funds were used for building or remodeling purposes, for the benefactor's name would be inscribed in a prominent location identifying him or her. Pre-70 diaspora synagogues were no exception to this practice. Inscriptions are known from Egypt, where "Hermias and his wife Philotera and their children (gave) this *exedra* to the *proseuche*,"[22] as well as from Berenice and Ostia.[23]

Literary passages also reveal that votive offerings dedicated to people and emperors were present in synagogues. Philo, in *Flaccus* 48, refers to the notion that the synagogues are "their means of showing reverence to their benefactors, since [otherwise] they no longer had the sacred precincts in which they could set forth their thankfulness" (brackets mine). Synagogues are the means for showing honor in terms of gifts that are displayed. This treatment of offerings made the synagogue look like a Graeco-Roman temple and constitutes a fur-

---

[20] The Jerusalem Temple also accepted votive offerings.

[21] Burkert, *Greek Religion*, pp. 68-70.

[22] *JIE* 28 (=*CIJ* 2.1444). Cited in Binder, "Into the Temple Courts," p. 194.

[23] For Berenice, see *CJCZ* 72, cited in Binder, "Into the Temple Courts," pp. 207-8. For Ostia, see *JIWE* 1.13, discussed in Binder, "Into the Temple Courts," pp. 260-2. See also White, "Imperial Ostia."

ther reason that the Graeco-Roman world placed the synagogue into that category.

Sacrifice: Although diaspora Jews did not sacrifice in their synagogues, some evidence suggests that they led their non-Jewish compatriots to believe they did. A decree by "the people of Sardis"—the governing council I presume—states that Jews should be given a place to "offer their ancestral prayers and sacrifices to God" (Josephus, *Ant.* 14:259-61). While scholars have usually taken this passage as evidence of synagogue prayer, they have been puzzled about how to interpret the comment about sacrifice, since it seems highly unlikely that blood sacrifices were practiced in any synagogue. Although it could simply be a mistake stemming from the council's understanding of the synagogue as a Graeco-Roman temple, I think another explanation is more probable. The Sardis Jews had been actively involved in defending their rights to build a synagogue for their needs and to worship. They apparently petitioned not only the Sardis Council but also Lucius Antonius, the *proquaestor* (Josephus, *Ant.* 14: 235). Since the decree is written in response to a petition from the Jews, the Jews seem to have led the council to believe that they offered sacrifice, probably by using the term to designate worship activities that did not actually involve animal slaughter. Indeed, D. Binder argues that sacrifice should here be understood more broadly as "ritual" and "may have included prostrations, chanting, and the rendering of votive offerings."[24] Such an approach indicates that the Jews were fairly sophisticated about how the worship activities they carried out in their synagogues were understood by their Graeco-Roman counterparts.

Synagogue activities included another practice that would have sent strong signals to non-Jews that Jews sacrificed, namely, the "common meal." In Graeco-Roman worship, sacrifice and shared meals were intimately linked—the former was followed by the latter. As W. Burkert has observed, "The ritual of animal sacrifice varies... but the fundamental structure is identical and clear: animal sacrifice is ritualized slaughter followed by a meat meal."[25] This strong link between sacrifice and meal would have led the Graeco-Roman world

---

[24] Binder, "Into the Temple Courts," p. 322. He also applies this interpretation to two passages in Philo: *Spec.* 3:171 and *Deus.* 7-9. See Binder, "Into the Temple Courts," pp. 322-323. For Binder's entire discussion of prayer, see pp. 320-328.

[25] Burkert, *Greek Religion*, p. 57.

to think that synagogue worshippers followed some kind of sacrificial activity. While few details exist about common meals in the synagogue, it is clear that they took place. The decree concerning Delos states that the Jews should be allowed to carry out their common meals (Josephus, *Ant.* 14: 214). The decree to Sardis declares that the Jews should be given a place to build a synagogue and to have "suitable food for them brought in" (Josephus, *Ant.* 14:261).

In sum, the synagogue community's performance of two of the three main worship activities for Graeco-Roman temples, prayer and votive offerings, provides strong indication that non-Jews saw the synagogue as belonging to that category. And with regard to the third worship activity, sacrifice, the Jews themselves led those around them to believe they practiced sacrifice, whether through intentional presentation or unintentional performance. The synagogue's conformity to these main forms of Graeco-Roman worship shows that the Graeco-Roman world saw the synagogue as a Graeco-Roman temple.

Secondary Activities of Graeco-Roman Temples and the Synagogue

When we move away from the main foci of Graeco-Roman worship, we find that the pre-70 diaspora synagogue and the activities that took place within it paralleled many of the secondary functions served by the Graeco-Roman temple. Here we find activities that the Jews already performed as well as ones they borrowed from their surroundings and transformed for their own purposes.

Councils and courts: Graeco-Roman temples were well-known as meeting places for political, governmental, and judicial bodies. The Roman Senate itself met in the temples of Mars Ultor, Apollo Patatinus, and Concordia at different times. Even local village councils regularly met in temples.[26] Likewise, courts were usually convened in temples, where the gods were believed to be watching out for any miscarriage of justice.

Jewish councils and courts likewise met in the synagogues. Josephus indicates that the Tiberias council met in the synagogue (Josephus, *Life* 276-303), and the decree concerning the Jews of Sardis

---

[26] Stambaugh, "Roman Temples," pp. 555, 580-582. See also Binder, "Into the Temple Courts," p. 308.

permits them a place to "adjudicate suits among themselves" (Josephus, *Ant.* 14:260).[27] The New Testament also contains remarks reflecting the diaspora synagogues, probably shortly after 70, in which Jesus warns that his followers will be handed over to councils and beaten in synagogues.[28] The "typically Jewish" activity of holding councils and courts in the synagogues thus has strong parallels to the practices of Graeco-Roman temples. Both the temples and the synagogues were public buildings that lent themselves to these activities of governance and judgement.

Taxes and banking: When the Jerusalem Temple stood, all Jews were expected to pay a half-shekel tax to it. The diaspora synagogues served their communities by collecting the payment from individuals and then transporting it to Jerusalem. This activity, while inherently part of Judaism, once again would have looked to non-Jews as similar to what occurred in many Graeco-Roman temples. This is because the synagogue here functioned like a bank, as did many temples. In Rome, for example, the temples of Castor, Mars, and Ops were important places for depositing valuables, as was that of Mars Ultor.[29]

Dedicatory inscriptions: Dedications are the earliest-known features of diaspora synagogues. They show that from the beginning Jews understood their synagogues in light of Graeco-Roman temples. One of the oldest of these dedications comes from Schedia, east of Alexandria. It reads: "On behalf of king Ptolemy and queen Berenice his sister and wife and their children, the Jews (dedicated) the *proseuche.*"[30] This follows a form common not only to many other synagogue dedicatory inscriptions but also to those of non-Jewish temples and shrines. In his comparison of such inscriptions from Egyptian synagogues and temples, Paul Fraser observes, "in most instances the dedication is indistinguishable from a pagan equivalent save for the substitution of the term 'synagogue' for 'the shrine' or 'the temple,' and by the name of the dedicating party."[31] So these inscriptions,

---

[27] This is echoed in Josephus, *Ant.* 235.

[28] Mark 13:9 and the synoptic parallels in Mt. 10:17 and Luke 21:12. See also Luke 12:11 and Acts 26:11. For a fuller discussion, see Binder, "Into the Temple Courts," pp. 352-355.

[29] Stambaugh, "Roman Temples," pp. 585-586.

[30] *JIE* 22 (=*CIJ* 2.1440). See Griffiths, "Egypt," pp. 4-5; and Binder, "Into the Temple Courts," pp. 191-192.

[31] Fraser, *Ptolemaic Alexandria*, vol. 1, p. 283. Cited in Binder, p. 192.

which each Jewish community composed as part of the founding of
their synagogue, placed the synagogue into the classification of
Graeco-Roman temple. And, since these inscriptions provide the earliest evidence of synagogues, they show early on that the Jews themselves conceived of the synagogue in Graeco-Roman terms and recorded that identification in their public records.

Purification: Nearly all religions in the Mediterranean world had
concepts of impurity and rituals of purification. Indeed, the fundamental understanding of impurity was the same across most of the
religions. Most religions in the Graeco-Roman period, including
Judaism, held that impurity derived from the same sources. The most
prominent of these included sexual intercourse, menstruation, childbirth, and death. Further, impurity was so common that nearly all
religions assumed their worshippers lived their daily lives in a state of
(at least) low-level impurity, requiring a minor purification ritual before entering a temple to worship or even just to pray to their god.
The similarities just described would color any member of Graeco-
Roman society's understanding of the purity regulations of the Jerusalem Temple, and vice versa. And, to the extent that purity rituals
were practiced in pre-70 diaspora synagogues, the rites would have
made them seem like temples.

Although there is little direct evidence that diaspora synagogue
worshippers practiced purity, there is a great deal of indirect evidence. The main evidence is that Jews were known to build synagogues in the diaspora near water. If we can take Paul as representative, he expected synagogues to be near the water. Acts 16:13
indicates that when he went into a strange town, he immediately
sought the synagogue near the water. That non-Jews knew about this
tendency as well becomes clear from the decree concerning
Halicarnassus, related by Josephus. It states that the Jews should be
allowed to build their synagogue "near the sea in accordance with
their native custom" (Josephus, *Ant.* 14:258). This evidence indicates
that Jews built their synagogues near the water, which leads to the
conclusion that it was a conscious practice for reasons of purity.

Five of the diaspora synagogues for which we know the location
were constructed near water: Delos, Ostia, Philippi, Halicarnassus,
and Arsinoë-Crocodilopolis.[32] The Delos synagogue was built so close

---

[32] Binder, "Into the Temple Courts," p. 313.

to the sea that the front of the synagogue was washed away long before modern excavators arrived on the scene. The Ostia synagogue was built near the ancient coastline, which has now moved the opposite direction, away from the synagogue. Yet it is clear from the excavation reports by Squarciapino that the first century synagogue provided a purification basin immediately outside, so that worshippers could purify themselves before they entered.[33] It is not a *mikveh*, which we would expect in Palestine,[34] but a well with a basin, which served for washing hands. Although not a biblical form of purification, this is a well-known purity practice in Graeco-Roman religions, in which practitioners would wash their hands before addressing their god or goddess in prayer.[35] Indeed, many Graeco-Roman temples had similar basins outside their entrance for this purpose. While there is no direct evidence for diaspora Jews' requiring purification before praying in the synagogue, Aristeas tells of the Septuagint translators who began their day by washing "their hands in the sea in the course of their prayers to God...following the custom of all Jews."[36] The evidence thus suggests that Jews underwent some purification before worshipping in the synagogue, which would have suggested to non-Jews that Jews followed purity regulations.

Asylum: The concept of asylum was well-known throughout the Graeco-Roman world. Not only was it a common aspect of temples in both the Greek and the Roman periods, but it was also known in pre-Greek Egypt and in biblical Israel. In Israel, it was primarily linked to specific "Cities of Refuge" located across the land.[37] In the Graeco-Roman world, asylum was identified with temples.[38]

Some synagogues in Egypt were given the right of asylum. A papyrus from Alexandrou-Nesos from 218 B.C.E. describes a legal dispute in which one party stole a cloak and then ran to a synagogue for refuge.[39] Another inscription indicates how such a right was given by

---

[33] Binder, "Into the Temple Courts," pp. 265-266.

[34] See Reich, "*Miqweh*."

[35] Stambaugh, "Roman Temples," p. 579.

[36] Aristeas, 305. Josephus's rendering of this story gives a different reason for hand-washing: interaction with the sacred books. He says, "after washing their hands in the sea and purifying themselves, [they] would betake themselves in this state to the translation of the laws" (*Ant.* 12:106).

[37] See Num. 35:9-15, Deut. 4:41-3, Deut. 19:1-13, and Joshua 20.

[38] See Griffiths, "Egypt," p. 12.

[39] Frey, Jean Baptiste, ed., *Corpus Inscriptionum Iudaicarum* 1.129. Cited in Binder, "Into the Temple Courts," p. 345.

the king: "On the orders of the queen and king...King Ptolemy Euergetes [proclaimed] the house of prayer as a refuge."[40] The need to get such authority from the king apparently did not prevent the Jews from seeking such status. This indicates that Jews actively sought this status, one which in a sense served to certify the synagogue as a Graeco-Roman temple.

Manumission: Another indication that synagogues were treated like Graeco-Roman temples stems from fragments of manumission contracts for slaves. While only one region in the pre-70 period is known for this activity, Bospora on the Black Sea, the practice likens it to a prominent Greek temple, the Apollo Temple in Delphi, home of the Delphic oracle.

The moving of an enslaved person to freedom was a complex problem in the Roman legal world, for it involved several contradictions, often seen in economic terms. No one could "purchase" a slave's freedom, because then they themselves would own the slave. Slaves could not purchase their own freedom, because they could not legally possess the necessary money. Rather than confront this legal problem directly, Roman law initially identified three ways around it: to simply have a magistrate declare a slave free by enrolling him or her in on the rolls of free people, to be freed by the will of a dead master, and by a fictive sale to a god. It is the last procedure that the Bosporan synagogues imitated.

In one fragment of a manumission contract from the Bospora region, the obligations of the slave transfer from the master and his heirs to the synagogue. The synagogue then redefines those obligations in ways that impose a light burden on the freed individual. The obligations include "flattery" and attendance in the synagogue. Other contracts simply state that the manumission was carried out in the synagogue.[41] A. Harrill's analysis of these contracts shows that in form they are similar to those of the Apollo sanctuary.[42] The synagogue's participation indicates that the Jewish community was willingly involved in this temple-based activity. Thus it makes clear that

---

[40] Kasher, "Egypt," p. 215. See Binder, "Into the Temple Courts," pp. 345-346.

[41] Harrill, *Manumission*, pp. 174-178. See also Binder, "Into the Temple Courts," pp. 347-352.

[42] Harrill, ibid., pp. 174-175. For an early rabbinic perspective on manumission and the status of the freedman, see Flesher, "Hierarchy," and Flesher, *Slaves in the Mishnah*, pp. 139-158.

they understood it to make the synagogue like a Graeco-Roman temple.

Terminology

The usual terms designating the ancient synagogue are *proseuche* and *synagoge*. The predominance of these terms in the literature and the inscriptions (as well as the scholarly debate about their meaning) has overshadowed the fact that other terms are occasionally used to designate this structure. The most common of these is the Greek word for temple, *hieron*, which appears in several places.[43] Josephus provides the most explicit identification in his discussion of the Antioch synagogue. In the same paragraph, he calls it both a *synagoge* and a *hieron* (*War* 7:44-45).[44] He also speaks of the Jewish "temples" being plundered in the villages of Judea (*War* 4:408) and later of the Palestinian "temples" that the Romans burned during the rebellion (*War* 7:144). Similarly, in *Against Apion* 1:209, Josephus quotes Agatharchides as saying that the Jews pray in "temples."[45] In all three passages, the reference can only be to synagogues, since Judaism has only a single temple. Third Maccabees 2:28 also refers to synagogues as "temples" when Ptolemy announces his punishment against the Jews.

While these passages give some idea of how ancient writers used the term "temple" to designate the synagogue, both Josephus and Philo indicate that the term is also used by Jews with the expectation that Jews will understand what is being said. In *Spec.* 3:171-172, Philo describes the virtuous Jewish woman to his Jewish readers. He indicates that she is modest and does not appear in public, except when going to the "temple" (i.e., an Egyptian synagogue) to pray. Similarly, Josephus tells the story of Onias IV who decided to build a Jewish temple in Egypt to rival the one in Jerusalem. One of his arguments is that the Jewish "temples" that exist throughout Egypt are "ill-disposed" towards each other (*Ant.* 13:65-68). Although the

---

[43] See Binder, "Into the Temple Courts," pp. 95-102.

[44] Steve Fine, *Holy Place*, p. 29, notes this and remarks, "Our author describes this synagogue as having been seen as a 'temple' by Greek and Jew alike.... The synagogue of Antioch, like the 'prayer places' of Egypt and perhaps the *topos* of Sardis Jewry, was seen by non-Jews and apparently by Jews alike as a local temple."

[45] See Shaye Cohen's discussion of this passage in Cohen, "Evidence," pp. 161-162.

meaning of "ill-disposed" is unclear, the reference to temples can only refer to synagogues. In both of these passages, then, we find that Jews are comfortable with the use of the term "temple" to designate the synagogue.

Three other terms indicate that Romans understood the synagogue in terms of their own temples. First, the phrase "sacred precincts" (*hieros peribolos*), usually deployed in connection with Graeco-Roman temples, is used twice in connection with synagogues. The first appears in Philo's *Flaccus* (48) where he describes how the synagogue provides the "sacred precincts" in which the Jews' benefactors (including the emperors) can be recognized. The second is a rather fragmentary dedicatory inscription from Alexandria in the second century B.C.E. in which the synagogue (*proseuche*) is linked to the sacred precincts.[46] This use of the term by Jews in their own synagogue's dedication inscription indicates that they are comfortable describing their synagogue in the terminology of a Graeco-Roman temple. Second, the term *naos*, which designates the inner-most room of a temple where the image of the god resides, is once used of a synagogue. Here the circumstances related by Josephus center on the activities of some hotheads in Dor who put an image of the emperor into the synagogue (*Ant.* 19:301-310, esp. 303-305). The governor of Syria berated them by saying that the image was better suited to the *naos* of a different temple rather than the synagogue's *naos*. Third, in *Ant.* 16:162-165, Josephus gives a decree from Caesar Augustus in which he classifies the stealing of sacred books from a synagogue as temple robbery and puts the thief into the category of a temple robber (*hierosylos*). This is reiterated by Marcus Agrippa (*Ant.* 16:167-60), who enhances the punishment by stating that the temple robber of a synagogue can be taken from a place of asylum for punishment. These decrees thus show that the Roman officials treated the synagogue as belonging to the category of temples.

Given the way that the Roman legal system worked, this decree would have done the Jews good only if they exercised it (when necessary). In other words, individuals brought other individuals to the courts, the government did not charge criminals automatically. Thus, if someone stole a Torah scroll, the Jews would have had to pursue redress themselves before the magistrates and done so in the specific

---

[46] Horbury, William, and David Noy, eds., *Jewish Inscriptions of Graeco-Roman Egypt* 9 (=*CIJ* 2.1433). Cited in Binder, "Into the Temple Courts," pp. 102-103.

terms of the law. Once again, the data indicates that Jews would have known and used the understanding of the synagogue as a Graeco-Roman temple.

How Did Synagogues Differ from Graeco-Roman Temples?

From a Jewish perspective, the main difference between a Graeco-Roman temple and the synagogue was the reading and study of scripture. As Lee Levine has argued, the one practice common to the pre-70 synagogues—both in the diaspora and in Palestine—was the reading and explication of the sacred books.[47] Josephus, Philo, the New Testament, and inscriptions all consistently point to scripture, often specified as the Torah, as the focus of synagogue activity. By contrast, regular public reading of sacred writings, accompanied or not by explication, was almost unknown in Graeco-Roman temples. Some temples had libraries and collections of books, while a few carried on readings of holy writings (nearly always to priests only); none of these approach the devotion synagogue ritual gives to the Jewish scriptures.[48] It is only the synagogues that make scripture reading and explication the focus of worship.

From the Graeco-Roman perspective, there are several obvious differences between diaspora synagogues and Graeco-Roman temples. Of course, the synagogue lacks an altar and carried out no sacrifices.[49] There are no libations and no fire offerings.[50] There is not even an eternal flame, as there was in the Jerusalem Temple and in some Graeco-Roman temples. Nor, even assuming purification rites by water, was there any purification by blood, since the sacrifices necessary for such purification could not be carried out.[51] It is not that these practices did not take place in Judaism, but that they only happened in the Temple in Jerusalem.

The most obvious difference between the Graeco-Roman temple and the synagogue, however, was that the synagogue had no image of its god. The Greek idea of temples was largely to provide houses for the gods—places from which they could look out at the sacrifices

---

[47] Levine, "Second Temple," pp. 15-19.
[48] See Griffiths, "Egypt," pp. 13-14.
[49] Burkert, *Greek Religion*, pp. 55-60, 64-6, 87-88.
[50] Ibid., pp. 60-64, 70-73.
[51] Ibid., pp. 80-82.

being offered and observe the festivals taking place in their honor.[52] The synagogue, by contrast, had no statue and no image of its god. This lack seemed not merely odd to the Graeco-Romans, it was downright disconcerting, even giving rise to accusations that Jews were "atheists."

But even the synagogue's lack of an image of the deity provides evidence that non-Jews considered the synagogue to belong in the category of "temple." Our evidence comes from Philo's description of the disturbances against the Jews during the end of Flaccus' governorship of Egypt. Most of what happened during the troubles could have been directed at any group of people: they were driven out of their homes, raped, had their houses and meeting places destroyed, were killed, tortured, and so on. But the one thing that could be directed only at the Jews was the placing of images into the synagogues. Why would this have been an appropriate act in the eyes of the rioters? They saw synagogues as temples and, as temples, synagogues should contain images—which they themselves consequently provided. The rioters did not understand synagogues as houses or some other kind of non-religious building, but as temples. The synagogue's lack of images appeared "wrong" to the rioters and the placing of images in the synagogues made things "as they should be"—as temples with images. So this attack on the synagogues by placing statues of a "living god" (Gaius no less!) shows that the non-Jewish Alexandrians understood the synagogue in the classification of a Graeco-Roman temple and thus as a place that required a statue of a god.

Summary

This discussion has made clear that the Graeco-Roman world—in both local and empire-wide terms—understood the diaspora synagogue to belong to the category of temple. This classification enabled three centuries of successful development by the first century. It led non-Jews to treat the synagogue with the same respect and rights due to a temple and to assume it had the same features. The prominence of the synagogue in this classification succeeded in giving the Jews a religious, ethnic, and political identity within the empire. They were not just an expatriate community living outside their homeland, but

---

[52] Ibid., pp. 88-92, 99-108; and Stambaugh, "Roman Temples," pp. 568-574.

a distinct group located in many cities and towns across the empire with specific requirements, mostly relating to their religious beliefs and practices. Over the centuries, the synagogue's identifiable character occasionally made Jews and their synagogues a target for trouble, but usually it worked in favor of the Jewish community.

From the Jewish perspective, that of the communities which built the synagogues and worshipped in them, their location within the diaspora meant they always looked in two directions. Their "ancestral customs" always pointed them towards their Jewish past—both biblical and traditional—and compatriots, while the Graeco-Roman world and its understanding of the synagogue as a temple pointed them outward towards the non-Jews around them. Much of what the Graeco-Romans saw in Jewish practices as Graeco-Roman was to the Jews "typically Jewish." The activities came from their history as God's people. These included: prayer, purification, the giving of the half-shekel tax, councils and courts, Torah reading, and even asylum. So while the non-Jews looked at the Jews doing these things and thought "how like us," the Jews practicing them felt they were acting as faithful Jews. In and of themselves, there was nothing Graeco-Roman about these practices, however they were viewed by outsiders.

But of course the synagogue and its worship activities did not exist "in and of themselves;" rather, they took place within the Mediterranean diaspora. And this location brought about some adjustments. Although we remain unable to determine the precise balance of outside influence and internal pressure in these adjustments, it is clear that both were involved. The classification of Graeco-Roman temple imposed expectations on the synagogue from outside while the Jews themselves adopted and used that classification to further their interests. Synagogue councils and Jewish courts, for example, exercised their power in Graeco-Roman terms and within the limits set by the Graeco-Roman authorities. Purification took on a Graeco-Roman veneer, with hand-washing becoming a regularly practiced purification rite. Acquiring the status of asylum for a synagogue took a high-level government dispensation. Common meals took place in comparison to those of pagan temples.[53] And even the synagogue as a meeting place took on a Graeco-Roman cast.

---

[53] Indeed, Philo makes the comparison explicitly—making clear that the Jews were much more sober and responsible about theirs. Compare *Flaccus* 136 with *Legat.* 312-2. See the discussion in Seland, "Associations."

In addition, the Jews themselves brought activities and practices from the Graeco-Roman world into the synagogue. In the process, these were reshaped with Jewish concerns. Most prominently, these include the founding dedications of the synagogues. But the practice of receiving votive and other offerings and displaying them also became important. There is also the use of temple terminology applied to the synagogue and, in the Bosporus, the use of the synagogue as a place of manumission.

So the diaspora synagogue and the activities carried out by the Jewish community within it form a blend of Jewish and Graeco-Roman religious practices and expectations. From the Graeco-Roman perspective, it looks largely like a Graeco-Roman temple. From the Jewish perspective, it looks predominantly Jewish, with a Graeco-Roman veneer. But the Jews know that their Graeco-Roman hosts define the synagogue as a temple and use that definition in their interactions with them.

The blending of the synagogue into Graeco-Roman culture permitted its successful establishment and development for several centuries. But how does the diaspora synagogue shed light on the synagogues of Palestine, especially those of the Galilee and Golan? To answer this question, we need a way of modeling how Graeco-Roman culture influenced the synagogue's development. The model can then be compared with Palestine to see whether it fits and/or how it was modified.

From Historical Analysis to Theoretical Model

Walter Burkert ends his essay, "The Temple in Classical Greece," by arguing that the Greek temple is a monument to the common and collective identity of the community.[54] "A temple is the most prestigious and lasting monument into which the available surplus of society is transformed—a monument of common identity."[55] While in theological respects, then, the temple may honor the god, in sociological respects it symbolizes the community that worships there. The character of the temple displays in a physical way the wealth, creativity, talents and devotion of the god's followers. In the context of a single, uniform community—the *polis* of Burkert's analysis—the people and

---

[54] Burkert, "Temple," pp. 43-45.
[55] Ibid., p. 43.

their temple are not merely linked, but the temple becomes the people's shared symbol.

This characterization has been applied to ancient synagogues. Peter Richardson observes with regard to pre-70 Palestinian synagogues, "Buildings have social meaning, expressing the goals, aspirations, and values of a community or society."[56] A.T. Kraabel follows this reasoning when he argues that the large, prominent synagogue of third-century Sardis "reflects a *self-confident* Judaism"—that is, a self-confident Jewish community of Sardis.[57] There is a direct link, then, between each Jewish community and its synagogue building—the building represents the community; it is a symbolic display created by the group to represent itself, its needs, and its achievements.

But the study undertaken above indicates that the situation is more complicated than these writers suggest. If the synagogue is a display, then the question must be asked, who is looking at the display? In the diaspora, the answer is the Graeco-Roman world. The display communicates to the non-Jewish world in which the diaspora Jews live and becomes their symbolic representation to those around them. It identifies not only where the community is located but also indicates their status and prestige.[58] The synagogue constitutes a symbolic form of communication, informing those who can read the symbolic expression about the community's character.[59] So what we have here is a social model with three key points. First, there is the minority community, in this case the Jewish members of the synagogue. Second, there is the synagogue building itself, established by the community for their worship activities. Third, there is the dominant, majority society and culture within which both the building and its associated community reside—in this case Graeco-Roman culture.

This model is inherently dialectical and represents the interaction between the minority community and the dominant culture. The religious building, in this case the diaspora synagogue, serves as a symbolic mediation point between the two groups. On the one hand

---

[56] Richardson, "Early Synagogues," pp. 102-103.

[57] Kraabel, "Paganism," p. 244 (italics in original).

[58] The rioters in Alexandria knew where to go to get at the Jews: they had to go to their synagogues. See Philo, *Gaius* 132-5, and the comment in Levine, "Nature," pp. 431.

[59] Kraabel moves in this direction in another article, Kraabel, "Unity." On pp. 28-29, he argues that the Jews should be seen as an ethnic minority within Sardis who use the synagogue to communicate their status and prestige within Sardis.

the synagogue and the activities practiced therein express the beliefs, practices, and ideals of the Jewish community that worships there. On the other hand, communication—as opposed to mere display— can only take place in the terms of the dominant culture. The desire and need for communication is not one way. In order to relate to the larger society in which they lived, the Jews could not just display themselves and their religion. Instead they had to bring in the symbols and categories of the surrounding society, and use them to shape their display—i.e., the building and the activities carried out in it.

The synagogue thus becomes a means by which Jews negotiate their place in the Graeco-Roman world. It represents its Jewish community and is controlled and shaped by Jews. But in the Graeco-Roman world—and certainly in each diaspora city, town, and village in which they live—the Jews are a small minority within a dominant Graeco-Roman culture. Since their minority (and essentially powerless) status means that they cannot shape the dominant culture to their view, they must negotiate their position in the Graeco-Roman world by fitting themselves into the pre-existing, Graeco-Roman categories. As we saw, the synagogue becomes classified as a Graeco-Roman temple. But that is not the end of the process. Once the synagogue enters that category, the category begins to redefine the synagogue; the two-way dialectic has begun. The category of Graeco-Roman temple has expectations and characteristics that the synagogue, once it belongs to that category, must attempt to meet in different ways. To continue to fit, then, the synagogue's social group —the Jewish community—adopts that redefinition and incorporates it as part of the institution. Thus over decades and centuries, the characteristics of the diaspora synagogues are shaped not only by Jewish ideals and expectations but also by those of the Graeco-Roman world in which Jews live and the categories and expectations that world applies to the synagogue.

From the perspective of the minority social group, the dominant culture continually exerts pressure on it to conform, to make its building—its symbolic representation—fit the expectations and classification exactly. But the minority community, in this case the Jewish worshippers, do not "sell out" their Jewish beliefs and goals; they do not simply capitulate. As we have seen, the Jews adopted a variety of strategies to continue their symbolic cultural classification without losing what was most important to them. They redefined terms and expectations. They adopted forms but not their content. They allowed and sometimes even encouraged their own practices to be represented in Graeco-Roman terms. And, occasionally, they drew a line in the sand and said, "only this far and no more." For the Jewish communities, this was certainly the case in their reaction against using images and statues in their worship, for instance. And this remained an ongoing, dialectic process. For the expectations and classifications of the dominant cult changed, as did the synagogue's responses to them. As the Graeco-Roman world—whether imperial or local—emphasized different aspects of temples, so the synagogue reacted and shifted to meet those changes.

As we turn from the diaspora to Palestine, we find that although the categories and relationships identified by the model remain the same, the content of the categories changes significantly. These changes reveal areas where the diaspora synagogue did not fit into these new cultural locations, and the alterations it underwent in its attempts to find a place. Rather than start with the Galilee and Golan, however, we will begin with Jerusalem. This approach will provide a second locus of synagogue development that influenced synagogue in the Galilee and Golan and to which we can now compare them.

Jerusalem and Its Earliest Synagogues

Pre-70 Jerusalem provides a radically different religious and cultural context from the diaspora. Jerusalem's population is primarily Jewish, not Graeco-Roman. Its culture is dominated by the Temple and the worship carried out there. Even though Jerusalem has been influenced by Hellenistic and then Roman culture since the third century B.C.E., Temple-based Judaism constitutes the main cultural force. Of course, Jerusalem society is far from unified, even in terms of religion. We know of five different Jewish groups that existed in Jerusalem in the first century C.E. alone: Pharisees, Sadducees, Essenes, Zealots, and Christians. But for the purposes of our discussion, they remain hidden under the umbrella of Temple Judaism.

Our issue concerns how the synagogue, as a Graeco-Roman temple, entered Jerusalem. The historical evidence indicates that it took two centuries for the synagogue to find its way there. The three-part theoretical model makes clear why. Although, for Jerusalem, the model's first two parts remain the same—(1) a Jewish community connected to (2) the synagogue building—the third part has changed significantly. Rather than a non-Jewish dominant society into which the synagogue must fit, Jerusalem provided a Jewish, Temple culture. Thus all the measures the diaspora synagogue took to negotiate its place in the Graeco-Roman world became inappropriate. Many of the features that it developed there were not needed in Jerusalem. So it is not surprising that the synagogue took so long to enter there.

From the perspective of the theoretical model, what should the synagogue have looked like once it appeared in Jerusalem? The expectation would be that a native Jerusalem synagogue would lack its foreign, non-Jewish features. If the diaspora synagogue came into Jerusalem unchanged, it would surely have failed, since it would have communicated to the dominant culture in inappropriate forms. It would also have needed to develop some characteristics that would help it link to Jerusalem's Temple-dominated culture.

The character of Jerusalem's Jewish culture would have determined some of the synagogue's new features. Interestingly, despite the absence of a foreign, unsympathetic dominant culture, Jerusalem does not provide the synagogue and its community with a totally sympathetic context either. Although it guides a Jewish culture in Jerusalem, the Temple is concerned primarily with promoting its own interests and only secondarily with those of the synagogue. Indeed, even more so than Graeco-Roman culture, Jerusalem's Temple culture would expect to control and shape the synagogue from the outside rather than let independent groups of Jewish worshippers make their own decisions and permit them to shape the synagogue in their own way. So the synagogue as it appears in Jerusalem may have existed in a more sympathetic—that is, a more Jewish environment—but that environment at the same time asserted more control over its nature and character.

When we examine the evidence concerning synagogues in pre-70 Jerusalem and ask whether they fit into these theoretical ruminations, we are struck by an odd finding. The only evidence for synagogues in Jerusalem concerns those for Jews from the diaspora; no indication of a system of synagogues for native Jerusalemites appears. Apart from some general remarks implying that there are synagogues in Jerusalem (mostly in John and Acts, and so perhaps anachronistic), the only data about specific synagogues in Jerusalem refers to synagogues of diaspora Jews or for Jewish pilgrims from the diaspora. In fact, there are only two pieces of evidence: Acts 6:9 and the Theodotus inscription.[60]

Acts 6:9 names a synagogue or a number of synagogues, depending on how the passage is interpreted. The name or names all indicate building(s) for Jews from the diaspora. The verse reads, "Then some of those who belonged to the synagogue of the Freedmen (as it was called), and of the Cyrenians, and of the Alexandrians, and of those from Cilicia and Asia, arose and disputed with Stephen." Scholars have debated whether all the terms designate a single synagogue or five of them.[61] If it is one, then it is clearly for Jews from diaspora regions. If it refers to five, then four of them are immediately identifiable as belonging to communities of diaspora Jews. The "Synagogue of the Freedmen" probably also constitutes a synagogue of Jews from foreign lands,[62] since most slaves in this period owned by Jews were foreign, not Jewish. Once freed, they would remain in Jerusalem, and, assuming they had converted, would participate in Jewish worship. So all the synagogues referred to in this verse, whether one or five, belonged to Jews from the diaspora. Unfortunately, there is no other information about their nature. We can suppose that the diaspora Jews who founded them had in their minds their synagogues back in the diaspora, but we have no means for evaluating that supposition. So all we can observe is that this evidence does not indicate any sort of synagogue for native Jews in Jerusalem.

The Theodotus inscription provides more information. Discovered at the bottom of a cistern where it had been thrown as debris, this synagogue inscription was found, as Steve Fine says, only "meters away from the Temple itself." [63] It reads:

---

[60] There are serious problems concerning the date of the Theodotus inscription, which I have discussed in Flesher, "Palestinian Synagogues," p. 33. However, I will use it in this discussion, since it is the best evidence available.

[61] See Riesner's helpful summary and bibliography in his "Synagogues in Jerusalem," pp. 204-206. Smallwood, *Roman Rule*, p. 132, posits that this synagogue consisted of Jewish slaves who were freed in Rome and then returned to Jerusalem.

[62] For a discussion of an early rabbinic understanding of freedmen, see Flesher, *Slaves in the Mishnah*, pp. 139-158.

[63] Fine, *Holy Place*, p. 30. To hold true, my sentence requires the assumption that the inscription is from the pre-70 period and that it belonged to a synagogue near where it was found. Neither assumption can be demonstrated. Even though R. Riesner, "Synagogues in Jerusalem," pp. 195-198, attempts to solidify a first-century date by discussing the surrounding archaeological context, there is no identifiable link between the inscription and the surrounding area. Furthermore, given the meth-

> Theodotus, son of Vettenos the priest and *archisynagogos*, son of a *archisynagogos* and grandson of a *archisynagogos*, who built the synagogue for the purposes of reciting the Law and studying the commandments, and the hostel, chambers and water installations to provide for the needs of itinerants from abroad, and whose father, with the elders and Simonidus, founded the synagogue.[64]

There are several important conclusions we can draw from the inscription. First, the synagogue building was designed and operated as a hostel, that is, a hotel for "itinerants from abroad." It was built specifically for diaspora Jews—pilgrims who came from the diaspora to worship at the Temple. This implies that it had a visiting population rather than a fixed community in Jerusalem.

Second, it seems that the "water installations" refer to private immersion pools to enable guests to attain a state of cultic purity before approaching the Temple complex. Thus the synagogue fits intimately within Jerusalem's Temple culture even as it reaches out to diaspora Jews. The purity expectations here for the visitors are cast in Jewish terms, not in those of the Graeco-Roman temples.

Third, another indication for how well-integrated into the Temple culture this synagogue was comes from the *archisynagogos'* self-identification as a priest. In the diaspora (as well as in post-70 Judaism), there is no expectation that synagogues need be associated with, let alone run by, priests. But the inscription makes clear that the leaders of this synagogue have been priests for three generations. Thus this synagogue's link to Jerusalem's Temple culture was fixed for a long time. In the theoretical terms of our model, the Temple was clearly dominant here and had significant influence on the character of this synagogue.

Fourth, given that influence, I think it is important to note that there is no mention of prayer being conducted here. I think, following other scholars such as Lee Levine, that this is no accident but instead indicates that this synagogue had no need to provide a place

---

ods of the excavators, since the inscription was found at the bottom of a cistern, it was not in a sealed locus and hence could have been placed there at any time over a number of centuries. Riesner also points out that the paleographical analysis suggests the inscription dates most likely to the first century or possibly the second century. But the most recent paleographical analysis is now nearly eighty years old. Given the advances in the field, it would be useful to have it evaluated again. Thus I remain hesitant about assigning the Theodotus Inscription to the first century.

[64] The translation comes from Kloner, "Synagogues in Israel," p. 11.

to pray.[65] With the Temple so close, no need existed to pray in the synagogue.

Fifth, the first item listed here as one of the synagogue's purposes is "the reading of the Torah and study of the commandments." This is significant, for it is the principle way in which diaspora synagogues differed from Graeco-Roman temples. Following scripture's own expectations that Jews should study God's revelation, it shows that this activity was carried out across the Jewish cultures of the Mediterranean. Lee Levine is correct to identify it as perhaps the key common element of synagogues and the worship carried out in them.[66]

On the one hand, the contemporary evidence we have for synagogues in Jerusalem, scant as it is, reveals that the synagogues in Jerusalem are linked to the diaspora through their identification with diaspora Jews, who either were visiting or had settled in Jerusalem. On the other hand, the synagogue described in the Theodotus inscription exhibits a nature different from that of diaspora synagogues. Apart from the reading and studying of Torah, there are few similarities with pre-70 diaspora synagogues. Not only is it a hostel rather than a synagogue for a local population but it is run by a priest—the only pre-70 synagogue for which this is the case.[67] These differences can be explained by the differing cultural and social environments. In Jerusalem the synagogue shaped itself to the dominant Temple culture, while in the diaspora it had to fit into the category of a Graeco-Roman temple. The little evidence we have indicates that, in Jerusalem, the synagogue remained an institution for foreign Jews and never became a native institution.

The Galilee and Golan and Its Earliest Synagogues

The Galilee and Golan present the most complex situation for analyzing the character of the pre-70 synagogues located there. This is because the social and cultural situation brings together several varied and even incompatible cultural elements. First, although the main culture is Jewish, it is mixed with a large Graeco-Roman popu-

---

[65] See Levine, "Second Temple," pp. 20-21, as well as the longer discussion of prayer on pp. 19-20.

[66] Levine, "Second Temple," pp. 15-19.

[67] In other words, it makes up part of the Temple-based, pilgrimage economy that Herod attempted to create. See Goodman, "Pilgrimage Economy."

lation. Second, the region contains both highly urbanized cities, such as in Tiberias and Sepphoris, as well as the rather remote rural locations of Upper Galilee and the Golan. A detailed incorporation of these complexities lies beyond the scope of this essay and must be left for further analysis elsewhere.

For the purposes of our brief discussion, the dominant culture of the Galilee and the Golan was characterized by two features—one that differentiated it from the diaspora and the other that made it like the diaspora. First, the local Jewish culture was dominant enough to pursue its own course relatively unhindered. To be sure, influences were present not only from the local non-Jewish population but also from Jerusalem. But neither of these dominated the social and cultural development in the Galilee and the Golan. Second, Galilean Judaism was not a Temple-based religion. In other words, the Temple did not dominate and control Galilean Judaism the way it did the Judaism practiced in Jerusalem. So the Galilee and Golan was interstitial. On the one hand, it was more like Jerusalem in that the Jews were in a dominant cultural position. On the other hand, it was like the diaspora in that it lacked an immediately accessible Temple. So the dominant Jewish culture of the Galilee and the Golan seems ultimately to have adopted the diaspora synagogue and transformed it into a native cultural and religious institution—although this conclusion probably lies beyond our present evidence.[68]

So in terms of our three-part model, the Galilee and Golan had (1) Jewish communities that were linked to (2) synagogue buildings that interacted with a (3) Jewish culture in which the synagogue was the main institution. So unlike first-century Jerusalem where the dominant Jewish culture was controlled by a different type of institution, the Temple, here in the first-century north the Jewish culture was based on the notion of synagogues as the main religious institution, at least locally.[69] This provides a third scenario for understanding how

---

[68] For a recent attempt to define the Galilean synagogue culture, see Horsley, *Galilee*, pp. 131-153.

[69] To be sure, the Temple and Jerusalem exercised some control in Galilee. Josephus himself was sent to Galilee from Jerusalem to organize the resistance against the Romans. His continuing difficulties with asserting his authority against local contenders, however, provide a good picture of the extent to which the Jews of the Galilee and the Golan considered themselves independent from Jerusalem. Josephus's ultimate failure to bring most of the cities under his control only emphasizes the point.

the synagogue developed in the pre-70 period, namely, a region in which a Jewish synagogue culture could develop without significant interference or control from a dominating Graeco-Roman world or the Jerusalem Temple culture, even though this freedom from control did not mean freedom from influence.

When we ask where the Galilee got its model for the synagogue, the answer is clear. It came from the diaspora, since the evidence we have indicates that Jerusalem did not have a suitable model for native synagogues. The synagogue in Tiberias, for example, is the only Palestinian synagogue that is termed a *proseuche*—the most common diaspora term for synagogue up to the first century—rather than a *synagoge*, the usual Palestinian term. It also provides a venue for both prayer and for meetings of the town council—both features of the diaspora synagogue, and, to the limits of our evidence, probably not features of Jerusalem synagogues.

Of course, since the Galilee lacked the dominance of the Graeco-Roman culture, its Jews were free to develop the synagogue as they saw fit and without having to link it to the Graeco-Roman temple. Thus the rest of the evidence provides our only glimpse of a pre-70 synagogue culture allowed to develop on its own. And it is a mix of things. At Nazareth and elsewhere, there is scripture reading and preaching, as we have seen in both the diaspora and Jerusalem. At Gamala, the synagogue is located next to immersion pools for purification. Since these pools are constructed similarly to those in Jerusalem, this provides some evidence for the Temple's influence.[70]

Unfortunately, we are again prevented by limited evidence from exploring further details. Indeed, for the Galilee and Golan we have a small amount of evidence that at best covers only one hundred years, for the destruction of the Jerusalem Temple in 70, followed by the failure of Bar Kokhba's rebellion in 135, plunges the Galilee into a new stage.

Of Ends and Beginnings

All three of these cultural situations in which the synagogues served to mediate between its community and the dominant culture came to

---

[70] In post-70 Judaism, the importance of purity associated with synagogues seems to disappear. See Reich, "*Miqweh.*"

an end after 70, and all because of radical change in the society in which they were located. One ended immediately, the second over a period of a few decades, while the third managed to last for a couple of centuries.

In Jerusalem, obviously, synagogue development ended forever. Even when centuries later synagogues were once again built in Jerusalem, there was no Temple there to guide them. So the model in which the synagogue was essentially dependent upon and controlled by the Temple was no more.

In the Galilee and Golan, circumstances changed radically, but not quite so fast. The main change followed the defeat of Bar Kokhba's rebellion in 135 and the expulsion of Jews from Judea. In the mid-second century, large numbers of Jews migrated north into this region. This increased the dominance of Jews and Judaism in the region and, since the Romans gave the Jews great latitude to develop their own society under the eye of the Patriarch, there was a new burst of energy in synagogue development. Since many of these Jews came from Jerusalem and Judea, however, the now-destroyed Jerusalem Temple remained important. This importance resulted in a new direction for the synagogue. It was to link the synagogue to the Temple through artistic, architectural, liturgical, and literary means.[71] Indeed, in both the Galilee and the Babylonian diaspora, the synagogue began to take on distinctly Temple-like features. It is this new form of synagogue that became the model on which Judaism of the Moslem and medieval periods built.

In the Graeco-Roman diaspora, by contrast, the destruction of the Temple had less impact. Things continued pretty much as they had been previously, at least with regard to the synagogue's place in Graeco-Roman culture. Synagogues remained in the category of "Graeco-Roman temple" and continued to negotiate their place in Graeco-Roman society through it. The only identifiable change is that the half-shekel Temple tax was replaced by a tax to be paid to the Roman Empire.

It is the rise of Christianity and the ensuing Christianization of the Roman Empire that brings to an end the synagogue as Graeco-Roman temple. It falls because the unthinkable happens—the pagan, Graeco-Roman world disappears under the onslaught of Christian-

---

[71] Some discussions of this trend appear in Neusner, *Symbol*; Branham, "Vicarious Sacrality," and Fine, *Holy Place*.

ity.[72] The synagogue once again finds itself being redefined. It loses its identification as a Graeco-Roman temple, which had enabled it to survive. But at the same time it takes on a negative identification as part of the "rejection front" of Judaism against Christianity. That understanding of synagogues by Christianity derives in part from the Jews themselves, namely, the recasting of the synagogue in imitation of the Jewish Temple.[73] Thus the synagogue defined as a Graeco-Roman temple—the earliest-known formulation of the synagogue institution—comes to an end, and the synagogue as the representative of the Jerusalem Temple rises to historical prominence.

Bibliography

Binder, Donald D., "Into the Temple Courts: The Place of the Synagogues in the Second Temple Period," Ph.D. thesis, Southern Methodist University, 1997. (Forthcoming in book form from Scholars Press, Atlanta, 1999.)

Branham, Joan R., "Vicarious Sacrality: Temple Space in Ancient Synagogues," in Urman and Flesher, vol. 2, pp. 319-345.

Burkert, Walter, "The Meaning and Function of the Temple in Classical Greece," in Fox, Michael V., ed., *Temple in Society* (Winona Lake, 1988), pp. 27-48.

Burkert, Walter, *Greek Religion* (Cambridge, 1985).

Chiat, Marilyn J.S., "First-Century Synagogue Architecture: Methodological Problems," in Gutmann, J., ed., *Ancient Synagogues: The State of the Research* (Chico, 1981), pp. 49-60.

Cohen, Shaye J.D., "Pagan and Christian Evidence on the Ancient Synagogue," in Levine, *SLA*, pp. 159-182.

Edwards, Douglas R., and C. Thomas McCollough, *Archaeology and the Galilee: Texts and Contexts in the Graeco-Roman and Byzantine Periods* (Atlanta, 1997).

Fine, Steven, ed., *Jews, Christians and Polytheists in the Ancient Synagogue: Cultural Interaction During the Greco-Roman Period* (forthcoming, 1999).

Fine, Steven, ed., *Sacred Realm: The Emergence of the Synagogue in the Ancient World* (New York, 1996).

Fine, Steven, *This Holy Place: On the Sanctity of the Synagogue during the Greco-Roman Period* (Notre Dame, 1997).

Flesher, Paul V.M., "Conflict or Cooperation? Non-Jews in the Dura Synagogue Paintings," in Ovadiah, *Arts*, pp. 199-222.

Flesher, Paul V.M., "Hierarchy and Interstitiality: The Bondman and the Freedman in the Mishnah's Caste System," in Neusner, Jacob, ed., *New Perspectives on Ancient Judaism, vol. 1, Religion, Literature, and Society in Ancient Israel, Formative Christianity and Judaism* (Atlanta, 1990), pp. 103-116.

Flesher, Paul V.M., "Palestinian Synagogues before 70 C.E.: A Review of the Evidence," in Urman and Flesher, vol. 1, pp. 27-39.

---

[72] See Rutgers, "Synagogue Archaeology," pp. 93-94.
[73] See Fine, *Holy Place*, pp. 137-156.

Flesher, Paul V.M., *Oxen, Women or Citizens? Slaves in the System of the Mishnah* (Atlanta, 1988).

Fraser, Paul M., *Ptolemaic Alexandria*, 3 vols. (Oxford, 1972).

Frey, Jean Baptiste, ed., *Corpus Inscriptionum Iudaicarum*, 2 vols. (Rome, 1936-1952). Revised edition in one volume (New York, 1975). Cited as *CIJ*.

Freyne, Sean, *Galilee from Alexander the Great to Hadrian 323 B.C.E. to 135 C.E.: A Study of Second Temple Judaism* (Notre Dame, 1980).

Goodman, Martin, "The Pilgrimage Economy of Jerusalem in the Second Temple Period," in Levine, *Jerusalem*, pp. 69-76.

Griffiths, J. Gwyn, "Egypt and the Rise of the Synagogue," in Urman and Flesher, vol. 1, pp. 3-16.

Harrill, J. Albert, *The Manumission of Slaves in Early Christianity* (Tübingen, 1995).

Horbury, William, and David Noy, eds., *Jewish Inscriptions of Graeco-Roman Egypt* (Cambridge, 1992).

Horsley, Richard A., "Archaeology and the Villages of Upper Galilee: A Dialogue with Archaeologists," in *BASOR* 297 (February 1995), pp. 5-16.

Horsley, Richard A., "Response," in *BASOR* 297 (February 1995), pp. 27-28.

Horsley, Richard A., *Archaeology, History and Society in Galilee: The Social Context of Jesus and the Rabbis* (Valley Forge, 1996).

Kasher, A., "Synagogues as 'Houses of Prayer' and 'Holy Places' in the Jewish Communities of Hellenistic and Roman Egypt," in Urman and Flesher, vol. 1, pp. 205-220.

Kloner, A., "Ancient Synagogues in Israel: An Archaeological Survey," in Levine, Lee I., ed., *Ancient Synagogues Revealed* (Detroit, 1982), pp. 11-18.

Kloppenborg, John S., and Stephen G. Wilson, eds., *Voluntary Associations in the Graeco-Roman World* (London, 1996).

Kraabel, A. Thomas, "Paganism and Judaism: The Sardis Evidence," in Overman and MacLennan, pp. 237-256. Reprinted from Benoit, A., M. Philonenko, and C. Vogel, eds., *Paganisme, Judaïsme, Christiansme* (Paris, 1979), pp. 13-33.

Kraabel, A. Thomas, "The Synagogue at Sardis: Jews and Christians," in Overman and MacLennan, pp. 225-236. Reprinted from Eleanor Guralnick, ed., *Sardis: Twenty-Seven Years of Discovery* (Chicago, 1987).

Kraabel, A. Thomas, "Unity and Diversity among Diaspora Synagogues," in Overman and MacLennan, pp. 21-34. Reprinted from Levine, *SLA*, pp. 49-60.

Levine, Lee I., "The Nature and Origin of the Palestinian Synagogue Reconsidered," in *JBL* 115:3 (1996), pp. 425-448.

Levine, Lee I., "The Second Temple Synagogue: The Formative Years," in Levine, *SLA*, pp. 7-32.

Levine, Lee I., ed., *Jerusalem: Its Sanctity and Centrality to Judaism, Christianity, and Islam* (New York, 1999).

Levine, Lee I., ed., *The Galilee in Late Antiquity* (New York, 1992).

Levine, Lee I., ed., *The Synagogue in Late Antiquity* (Philadelphia, 1987).

Levine, Lee I., *Judaism and Hellenism in Antiquity: Conflict or Confluence?* (Seattle, 1998).

Lüderitz, Gert, and Joyce Maire Reynolds, eds., *Corpus jüdischer Zeugnisse aus der Cyrenaika* (Wiesbaden, 1983). Cited as *CJCZ*.

MacLean, B. Hudson, "The Place of Cult in Voluntary Associations and Christian Churches on Delos," in Kloppenborg and Wilson, pp. 186-225.

McKay, Heather A., *Sabbath and Synagogue: The Question of Sabbath Worship in Ancient Judaism* (Leiden, 1994).

Meyers, Eric M., "An Archaeological Response to a New Testament Scholar," in *BASOR* 297 (February 1995), pp. 17-26.

Meyers, Eric M., "Galilean Regionalism as a Factor in Historical Reconstruction," in *BASOR* 221 (February 1976), pp. 93-102.

Modrzejewski, Joseph Mélèze, *The Jews of Egypt: From Rameses II to Emperor Hadrian* (Philadelphia, 1995).

Neusner, Jacob, *Symbol and Theology in Early Judaism* (Minneapolis, 1992).

Noy, David, ed., *Jewish Inscriptions of Western Europe*, 2 vols. (Cambridge, 1993-1995). Cited as *JIWE*.

Ovadiah, Asher, ed., *Hellenic and Jewish Arts: Interaction, Tradition and Renewal* (Tel Aviv, 1998).

Overman, J. Andrew, "The Diaspora in the Modern Study of Ancient Judaism," in Overman and MacLennan, pp. 63-78.

Overman, J. Andrew, and Robert S. Maclennan, eds., *Diaspora Jews and Judaism: Essays in Honor of and in Dialogue with A. Thomas Kraabel* (Atlanta, 1992).

Reich, R., "The Synagogue and the *Miqweh* in Eretz-Israel in the Second-Temple, Mishnaic, and Talmudic Periods," in Urman and Flesher, vol. 1, pp. 289-297.

Richardson, Peter, "Augustan-Era Synagogues in Rome," in *Judaism and Christianity in First-Century Rome*, Karl P. Donfried and Peter Richardson, eds. (Grand Rapids, 1998), pp. 17-29.

Richardson, Peter, "Early Synagogues as Collegia in the Diaspora and Palestine," in Kloppenborg and Wilson, pp. 90-109.

Riesner, R., "Synagogues in Jerusalem," in Bauckham, Richard, ed., *The Book of Acts in Its Palestinian Setting* (Grand Rapids, 1995), pp. 179-212.

Rutgers, Leonard Victor, "Diaspora Synagogues: Synagogue Archaeology in the Greco-Roman World," in Fine, *Sacred Realm*, pp. 67-95. Reprinted in Rutgers, *Diaspora Judaism*, pp. 97-124.

Rutgers, Leonard Victor, "The Diaspora Synagogue: Notes on Distribution and Methodology," in Rutgers, *Diaspora Judaism*, pp. 125-138.

Rutgers, Leonard Victor, *The Hidden Heritage of Diaspora Judaism* (Leuven, 1998).

Seland, Torrey, "Philo and the Clubs and Associations of Alexandria," in Kloppenborg and Wilson, pp. 110-127.

Smallwood, E. Mary, *The Jews under Roman Rule: From Pompey to Diocletian* (Leiden, 1976).

Stambaugh, John E., "The Functions of Roman Temples," in Haase, Wolfgang, ed., *Aufstieg und Niedergang der Römischen Welt* (Berlin, 1978), 2.16.1, pp. 554-608.

Tcherikover, Victor, *Hellenistic Civilization and the Jews* (New York, 1970).

Urman, Dan, "Public Structures and Jewish Communities in the Golan Heights," in Urman and Flesher, vol. 2, pp. 373-618.

Urman, Dan, and Paul V.M. Flesher, eds., *Ancient Synagogues: Historical Analysis and Archaeological Discovery* (Leiden, 1995), 2 vols.

White, L. Michael, "Synagogue and Society in Imperial Ostia: Archaeological and Epigraphic Evidence," in Donfried, Karl P., and Peter Richardson, eds., *Judaism and Christianity in First-Century Rome* (Grand Rapids, 1998), pp. 30-68.

White, L. Michael, *Building God's House in the Roman World: Architectural Adaptation among Pagans, Jews, and Christians* (Baltimore, 1990).

7. THE ANCIENT SYNAGOGUES AT BAR'AM

Mordechai Aviam
University of Rochester
and
Israel Antiquities Authority

In the thirteenth century, a traveler named Rabbi Samuel bar-Samson visited the Arab village of Biri'm in the Upper Galilee and briefly described the remains of one or two ancient synagogues.[1] From that year on, all Jewish travelers to the Galilee mentioned these synagogues: Rabbi Jacob of Paris in the thirteenth century,[2] a student of Maimonides at the beginning of the fourteenth century,[3] Rabbi Moses Bassola in the sixteenth century,[4] Rabbi Moses Yerushalmi in 1769.[5]

Most of the travelers describe the well-preserved, decorated, façade with three doorways of the large synagogue in the center of the village and the complete, decorated doorway of the small synagogue, adorned with a long Hebrew inscription. Two of the travelers mention two standing doorways.

While, in February, 1852, Van DeVelde visited the village and described both synagogues,[6] the first modern description was made by Robinson in 1852,[7] followed by Renan in 1861.[8] In 1865-1866, Wilson surveyed the two synagogues at Bar'am and excavated the small one. His report mainly described the dimensions of the building and its architectural elements.[9] It seems that, as a result of Wilson's

---

[1] J.D.Eisenstein, *Ozar Massaot, Collection of itineraries by Jewish Travelers* (1969), p. 64 (Hebrew).

[2] Ibid, p. 69

[3] A. Ye'ari, *Travels in Eretz Israel* (1976), pp. 90-91.

[4] Ibid, p. 133

[5] Ibid., p. 444.

[6] C.W.M. Van DeVelde, *Narrative of a Journey through Syria an Palestine in 1851 and 1852* (1854).

[7] E. Robinson, *Later Biblical Researches in Palestine and in Adjacent Regions, III: Travels in the Year 1852* (1857), p. 71.

[8] E. Renan, *Mission de Phenicie III* (1874), p.761-783.

[9] C. Wilson, "Notes on Jewish Synagogues in Galilee," in *PEQ* QS II (1869), pp.29-34, 37-41.

excavations, local Arabs started to dismantle ancient buildings such as those at Capernaum and the small synagogue at Bar'am, reusing the stones in their houses and selling some of the architectural remains to antique dealers. V. Guérin visited the site, and while he reported that the site of the synagogue at Capernaum was being dismantled, he still described the small synagogue at Bar'am and its monumental gate *in situ*.[10] Photos taken by the "Survey of Western Palestine" team, conducted by Conder and Kitchener, are the last documentation of the small synagogue. A few photos show the monumental decorated doorway, with its Hebrew inscription, from the north and from the south sides, supplying details of the remains. The threshold is visible, about 30 cm. above the surface, and the first course of foundation stones is visible on the eastern side. A large heap of architectural elements, including pillars, capitals (probably similar to those of the large synagogue, called "Toscanian" style), "heart-shaped" pillars and capitals and ashlar stones, is visible in the inner space of the building.[11]

Kohl and Watzinger contributed the most important study of the ancient synagogues in the Galilee. From 1905 to 1907 they conducted archaeological excavations in eleven ancient synagogues in the Galilee and Golan. When they visited the small synagogue at Bar'am, it was already totally robbed, the doorway had disappeared, and, according to their information, the Arabs had broken the lintel into pieces and sold it. One piece of the Hebrew inscription found its way to the Louvre. Kohl and Watzinger excavated three quarters of the large synagogue, clearing the building down to the floor, but their report does not give any information about finds. On the basis of the architectural design, they dated the building, as did all prior scholars, to the second-third century C.E.[12] In their plan, most of the eastern, northern, and western walls are missing, but there is no doubt about the corners and the exact size of the building. They suggested that there was an eastern doorway in the northern part of the eastern wall.

In 1959, reconstruction began at the large synagogue as the first step in the creation of a national park at the site. The archives of the

---

[10] V. Guérin, *Description de la Palestine-Galilée* (1880).

[11] C. K. Conder and H.H. Kitchener, *The Survey of Western Palestine. Vol. I Galilee* (1881), pp. 230-234.

[12] H. Kohl and C. Watzinger C., *Antike Synagogen in Galilaea* (1916), pp. 89-100

Israel Antiquities Authority contain a short report by G. Foerster about an archaeological check along the western wall of the synagogue. According to this account, there is a large floor, built of large stone pavers "similar to these of the synagogue...." Near the southwest corner of the synagogue, a mouth of a cistern was uncovered, which was full of soil. From the top of the fill, some shards of a cooking pot were found, dated by the excavator to "the first centuries C.E."

The most important find in this archaeological probe was the identification of an original side doorway in the northern part of the west wall. This cancelled Kohl and Watzinger's suggestion of a door in the eastern side.

Between 1907 and 1998, no archaeological excavations were carried out at the site, although the large synagogue is considered to be the most important example of the "Galilean" type. Recently, Ma'oz suggested that the synagogue of Bar'am is the finest example of the "original prototype" of the "original Galilean series" and suggested that this series of synagogues should be dated to the beginning of the third century C.E.[13]

In the summer of 1998, a team from the University of Rochester and the Israel Antiquities Authority excavated at the site. The goals of the dig were: 1) to date the large synagogue by digging under its floors, 2) to check for earlier structures under the floor of the synagogue, 3) to check whether the two large pavers on the southern side of the main hall were built as stylobates for another row of columns, 4) to precisely identify the location of the "small synagogue," 5) to draw a complete plan, and 6) to date this building.

The Excavations

In line with the excavation's goals, two different fields were excavated: one at the large synagogue in the center of the abandoned village and the second at the possible site of the small synagogue, near an Arab Christian cemetery, about 300 m. north of the first. In the large synagogue, early faces of buildings were evident outside and inside the building. It is possible that the segment of walls and floors

---

[13] U.Z. Ma'oz, "When Were the Galilean Synagogues First Built?," in *Eretz Israel* 25 (1998), pp. 416-426. (Hebrew)

found inside the building belonged to an earlier synagogue. Near the modern cemetery, the foundations of the smaller synagogue were completely uncovered along with the remains of the eastern portion of another large building.

The Large Synagogue (fig. A)

Five excavation areas were opened in the synagogue: areas A, B, and D inside the building; E in the eastern side of the *portico*, and F outside the building at the SE corner, along the eastern wall (fig. B, plan 1).

Area A: This area is located between the eastern and the central doorways and is as wide as the first pillar in the eastern row.

The floor of the synagogue is covered with large lime stone tiles that were lifted to enable the excavation below. There is a large area at the center of area A where some pavers where missing (loc. 10). This area was excavated independently to avoid modern contamination. After lifting the pavers in the remaining area, twelve coins were found, but none was found in the area from which pavers were missing. The earliest phase below the floor is a wall (W23), build of rectangular cut stones in the "headers" system (the short side of the stone is shown on both sides of the wall), directly on bedrock. Butting against its western side is another structure (W21) built of large stones, with small stones on the southern and western side creating a kind of a square frame. More to the west, as one part of W21, there is another structure (W22) made of stones that were not built as a wall but rather as a fill behind a southern line of stones. After the small stones from the southern side of W23 were removed and some small stones from the southern edge of W21 were taken, a layer of white plaster was found on the southern face. This suggests that the three architectural elements (W21, W22, and W23) are from the same phase. It is possible that they belong to an early synagogue. A plaster layer covered the surface of W23 but did not cover (and maybe even abuts) both W22 and W23. That could suggest that wall W23 that was covered by the floor was used as a stylobate and that walls W22 and W23 were lifted above the floor level. The floor (loc. 12) covers some parts of the space between W21 and W22 and the existing southern wall of the synagogue. It is built of remains of whitish plaster on yellowish and brown subsoil. To the south, a foundation trench (loc. 14) cut the floor, in which the foundation of the southern, still standing, façade wall is visible. The remains of this possible early synagogue were leveled to erect the new building with its pavers-floor. A layer of brown soil was laid with some plaster upon which the pavers were put, but not before coins were thrown on the soil (fig. C).

The stylobate of the southern pillar of the eastern row was exposed in the northern balk. It is built of two large stones in a L shape, 40 cm thick and based on W23 and W22. In a distance of 90 cm to the west, a paver of 50 X 50 cm was also exposed in the northern balk. It is also 45 cm. thick and is based on W21. It is clear that the southern pillar of the eastern row was a "heart–shaped" pillar. Insofar as the two other stylobates of the northeastern and the northwestern "heart–shaped" pillars are built in the same way, clearly there was a southern row of columns in the synagogue.

Area B: Area B was placed between the central and the western doorways. Here, also, some of the pavers were missing. In most parts of the area, a layer of field-stones on the bedrock served as a fill for the floor of pavers. On the eastern side of the area, remains of the early floor was found. Here it is a thick layer of plaster (5-10 cm) on which the possible impress of pavers is visible (loc. 24). In the southeastern corner of the area, the foundation trench of the southern façade wall (the eastern part of loc. 22, fig. D) cuts the plaster floor. A fill of soil on which the pavers were laid covered the plaster floor and the stone-fill. In this area, with the aid of a metal detector, twenty-five coins were found *in situ* under the floor tiles. They were found only in places that were covered by pavers. In the northeastern corner of the area, sixteen coins of the same size were found as one group (fig. C).

In the northeastern corner of the square, the corner of another stylobate was uncovered, about 40 cm thick. This is the stylobate of the western pillar of the southern row.

Area D: This area lies in the northwest corner, inside the synagogue. This area was chosen for excavation because it had a relatively large number of pavers in a good state of preservation, allowing us to lift them without any damage. After the pavers were removed, thirty-two coins were found *in situ* with the metal detector. All the coins were found under pavers in the dark-brown layer that carried the stone pavement (loc. 42; the small area that had no pavers *in situ*, loc. 40, did not yield any coins). Under some of the pavers were patches of white plaster as part of the base layer. Below this level, there was a thick layer of light soil mixed with stone-chips (that probably came from the chiseling of the pavers and other stones at the site), stones, and pottery (loc. 43). Below this level down to bed rock was a fill layer of soil and pebbles mixed with pottery (loc. 44).

The foundations of both the northern and western walls were uncovered, and they are 10 cm. wider than the walls themselves.

The foundation of the "heart-shaped" pillar was uncovered down to bedrock. Below the pedestal are two large ashlar stones (45 cm thick) arranged in an L shape, used as the *stylobate*. Below these stones are four courses of rough cut stones used as foundations down to the bedrock (fig. E).

A layer of whitish plaster was found on the walls of the synagogue after the pavers were lifted, and it seems that the walls were plastered with the first layer, before the floor was made. This layer survived because the pavers protected it.

Pottery from the two lowest loci dates to the Persian, Hellenistic, Roman, and the Byzantine periods.

Area E: This area was excavated in front of the eastern doorway of the synagogue, covering the whole width of the *portico*.

On bedrock, two or three segments of walls were uncovered. Wall no.W56 is built of large rectangular boulders (0.9 X 1.0 m.), and, along its southern face, a line of small stones was built. It is hard to decide whether those are two different walls or one. The "boulder-wall" ends at the same line as the corner of the synagogue, but no evidence was found for correlation between the building and this wall. In the 10 cm. gap between W56 and the southern wall of the synagogue, a plastered drainage channel was built (loc. 59), probably to lead water to the cistern located on the right side of the main doorway. The drainage was planed with the synagogue as proved by the design of the last stone of the *portico*'s stylobate, where a small square tunnel was especially cut for the drainage.

W60 is a foundation of a wall that runs from west to east, founded on bedrock and built of medium size fieldstones. Since the wall runs below the eastern stylobate of the *portico*, it predates the synagogue. It is possible that this wall cuts another well-built, plastered, drainage channel unearthed south of the wall. If so, the drainage channel is the earliest structure in this area. The latest feature built in this area is wall no. W53. It is probably part of an Ottoman period house. Its southern wall probably reused the southern stylobate of the *portico* and reinforced it with architectural elements from the abandoned synagogue. Two large pieces of the *architrav*, with square (20 X 20 cm.) niches for wooden beams and a broken pillar, were found as building stones in the southern wall. Few other small pieces of architectural elements and some broken clay roof-tiles were also found in this area.

The earlier walls can not be dated because the Ottoman period pottery was found as low as a few cm. above bedrock.

Area F: Three levels were identified in the trench. Level 1 is a sterile natural *terra rosa* above the bed rock, which abuts the foundation courses of the eastern wall with no evidence for a foundation trench. It seems that the builders built the foundation directly on the bedrock and laid a layer of natural *terra rosa* above the rock. Level 2 is a yellowish soil on which a stone-built *tabun* was uncovered. Since a modern object was found in it, this level belongs to the modern Arab village. It seems that the Arab villagers dug, leveled, and used the remains of the synagogue down to its foundation courses. Level 3 is a deep fill of the distraction of the village and the establishment of the national park. This level included pottery from the Hellenistic period (some imported ware and a lot of G.C.W.), Roman period, Byzantine period, Late Arab period, and modern remains.

The foundations themselves were made mainly of large, square, cut stones with small field stones in between, strengthened with mud made with some amount of lime. The last course of foundations was made of ashlars and protruded about 10 cm out of the wall's line. One of the stones of this course is probably a reused architectural element.

The coins (identified by D. Sion)

Seventy-two bronze coins were uncovered in the synagogue, and all but three were found directly under the floor. As a complex, the earliest coins in the three excavated areas are from the beginning of the fourth century C.E. (exceptions are a coin of Macrinus(?) in area B, a Seleucid coin and a coin of Probus in area D). The latest coins sealed under the floor are a coin of mid-fourth century C.E. in area A, two coins of the second half of the fourth century C.E. in area B, and a coin of Theodosius II from the first half of the fifth century C.E. from area D. A group of fifteen coins was found under paver B1 in the northeast corner of area B as a small "hoard;" these were minted 316-329 C.E. Fifty-eight of the sixty-nine coins (84%) found under the floor belong to the fourth century C.E.

Important loci in the large synagogue

Area A:

Loc.13: the fill below the pavers down the head of W21, W22, and W23.

Loc.14: the foundation trench of the southern wall.

L.15: the fill bellow the early floor (loc.12)

L.19

L.20: between the stones of the foundation of the southern wall.

Area B:

Loc.20: the fill below the pavers.

Loc. 23: pottery on bed rock below the fill.

Area D:

Loc.42: below pavers.

Loc.43: first layer of fill.

Loc. 44: second layer off fill to bedrock.

The small synagogue (fig. F; plan 2)

As mentioned earlier, this synagogue was totally ruined below the floor level. Only two excavation squares were opened, and only one of them was completely excavated to bedrock inside the building. The complete plane of the building was achieved by cleaning the surface level.

Area G: The natural rock was cut and straightened to carry the first course of the foundation stones. The foundations of the building were made of ashlar blocks about 70 X 35 cm that were built directly on the bedrock, very different from the foundations of the large synagogue.

The wall uncovered at this square is part of the western *stylobate* (W72). In the northern part of the wall, a drainage channel was uncovered, well built and designed together with the wall. It continues eastwards and its walls are built of small fieldstones. It was probably a covered channel, since a cover-stone is visible in the eastern balk. Between the wall and the western balk, a small area (1 X 1 m.) was uncovered, paved with small flat field-stones that seem like the foundation to a floor. This area was excavated as a sealed locus. The finds from the fill below these stones and down to bedrock included three coins, many shards of many oil lamps, mainly from the type known as "Northern Stamped Oil Lamps,"[14] and pot shards.

On the northern part of the wall, under the corner of a large stone, a rolled bronze amulet was found with an Aramaic inscription.

The Building

This is a rectangular building (16 X 12 m.). The width of the foundation of the western, northern, and eastern walls is 0.60 to 0.80 m, and the width of the southern wall is 1.1 m, probably to support the heavy elements of the façade. There are three walls inside the building that were used as a foundation to the stylobates.

In a secondary use, the northern isle was blocked with a wall that was added to the north-eastern corner of the stylobate (W71). On the northwestern corner of the stylobate a dressed threshold was built and perhaps used as the entrance to the northern room. The stone under which the amulet was found probably belonged to the same construction of the later phase.

Five architectural elements were found in and around the building.

Two small fragments of Corinthian capitals in a Byzantine period style were found inside and outside the building. Another half of a small Corinthian capital of the same style, but smaller (25 cm in diameter), was found on the surface 10 m. west of the synagogue. Insofar as Wilson described the synagogue, hinting that its capitals are of the same style as these of the large synagogue, the Corinthian capitals can be related to the second floor and the small one to the architecture of the Torah Shrine.

Under the southern part of the eastern stylobate, a built tunnel was partially uncovered, oriented in an east-west direction. This element was not excavated more than a meter to each side, and its floor was not unearthed. It is possible that it is part of an underground secret system such as was found under the synagogue at Meroth[15] and near the synagogue at Nabratein.[16]

---

[14] V. Sussman, "Northern Stamped Oil Lamps and Their Typology," in *Michmanim* 4 (1989), pp. 23-58.

[15] Z. Ilan and E. Damati, "The Ancient Synagogue and the Jewish Village at Meroth." (Hebrew)

[16] M. Aviam, "The Secret Hideawys in the Galilee," in *Jews, Pagans and Christians in the Galilee* (forthcoming).

Group of oil lamps fragment from the small synagogue

Loc.88: This locus is the one excavated below the small flat stones between the western wall and the western stylobate. It is likely, mainly because of its level, that it was used as a foundation to the floor. Twenty-four fragments of oil lamps were retained after sorting, and more than fifty were dumped at the site. Out of the twenty-four, eleven are the rear part of oil-lamps with a small low-knob handle. This suggests that, in this small section, at least eleven different oil lamps were dumped (deliberately?) in the fill under the floor. All of the fragments belong the group named "Northern Stamped Oil-Lamps."[17]

Nine more similar oil-lamp handles were uncovered in loci 74, 86, and 82, together with seven large decorated body shards of oil lamps as well as many more small fragments. All came from the built drainage channel that runs below the western stylobate. The design of the oil-lamps, their quality of firing, and their decoration strongly resemble the group of oil lamps found in the rock-cut tombs at Hr. Sugar in the western Galilee.[18]

This group is dated between the end of third-beginning of fourth century C.E. and the seventh century C.E.

Summary

The Large Synagogue: The Early Stage

Built directly on bedrock under a large building identified as a synagogue, the early stage is more likely to be an early synagogue. The only elements that were unearthed are a south-north wall, a rectangular shaped structure, and segments of a floor that has on its eastern side possible paver impression-marks. The latest pottery uncovered in the fill under the floor is from the second or third century C.E. There is no doubt that if this building was in fact an early synagogue, it was smaller than the later stage. No remains of walls or floors were found in area D, excavated in the north-western corner of the large syna-

---

[17] Sussman, ibid..

[18] See detailed discussion and references in M. Aviam and E. Stern, "Burial Caves Near H. Sugar," in Atiqot XXXIII (1997), pp. 92-96 (Hebrew).

gogue. The southern wall (the façade) of the large synagogue was built later to the early building while cutting its floor, leaving a very clear foundation trench. The existence of the foundation trench in both area A and B proves that the plaster floor is not contemporary with any of the large synagogue's walls.

The Synagogue Building

Because there are no remains of another floor (besides the heavy stone tile floor) in area D, because the white, early plaster floor is cut by a foundation trench, and because the tile floor abuts the walls of the building right above the foundation courses in areas A, B and D, at the same point where the wall-plaster begins in area D, there is only one conclusion: the whole synagogue building (the façade, the three side-walls, four rows of columns, and the lime stone tile floor) were erected at the same time, in a single building operation, above the remains of an earlier building (probably a synagogue), at the very end of the fourth or beginning of the fifth century C.E.

The foundation of the southern wall is built of large stones, some of them cut and joined by mortar made of mud, and medium size stones; the foundations are wider than the wall itself, and it is only 40 cm. deep, based on bedrock.

When the new building was erected, the early remains were leveled, covered with a fill, and four corner (heart shape) pillars and fourteen regular pillars, on self-standing stylobates, were built in four rows around the walls. The large synagogue is unique not only for its arrangement of four rows of pillars but also for its *portico*.[19]

The traditional scholarly view is that the arrangement of the prayer hall in the Galilean synagogues is based on three rows of columns (or only two rows in small synagogues) that focus the view of the audience to the southern wall, where the Torah shrine was placed. Tzafrir even points out that in the Gamla synagogue, where there are four rows of columns, the focus of the building is its

---

[19] Foerster already pointed to the uniqueness of the portico, as did scholars years before. It is very unclear to me why Ma'oz designated this one of the typical element of the "original Galilean group" if it exists for certain in only one synagogue. There is almost no evidence for the existence of a portico in the synagogue at Meiron, as was suggested by Meyers and Ma'oz (contrary to Foerster). This is also the case at Meroth, where no substantial proofs were found for the existence of a portico (Ilan, ibid., p. 44).

center.[20] Proving that there was a forth row of two columns in the southern side of the praying hall at Barʿam undermines this conventional view. The shape of the columns at the large synagogue at Barʿam reflects again the large variety in architectural design of synagogues in the Galilee. This variety can be seen at the broad house at Kr. Shema, an eastern doorway at Arbel, east-west direction at Sasa, side staircases leading to five doorways and a large courtyard at Capernaum, peripteral (or only two rows in the north and west sides) building at Qazion, and more.

The major result of the excavation is the dating of both synagogues. In the past twenty-five years, many articles have been written on the problem of dating the "Galilean Group." This is the consequence of the "Capernaum problem" caused after dating trenches excavated by the Franciscan archaeologists under the floors of the synagogue and its courtyard. The results were that both pottery and coins proved that the latest (and the only!!!) archaeological stage of the synagogue should be dated to the fourth or fifth century C.E., or even later (see Magness in this volume).

As a matter of fact, it became more than a question of dating but rather a weighty discussion of two different schools. The first began with Kohel and Watzinger, who dated the Galilean synagogues relying only on architectural style, without using any other finds, such as coins or pottery. Continuing Kohel and Watzinger's dating of the "Galilean" group to the second and third centuries C.E., and supported by modern archaeological evidence from Meiron and Gush-Halav, Foerster, Tzafrir, and others rejected the archaeological dating from Loffreda's probes at Capernaum. Late archaeological data from "Galilean," Roman styled synagogues was uncovered at Capernaum, Chorazim, Meroth, Gush Halav, and now at Barʿam, and, in the case of each of the first four, a different explanation was given to avoid the confrontation of "early architecture" with "late archaeological data."

The second school started with Loffreda, who tried to prove that, in the field of archaeology, the "*terminus post quem*" cannot be ignored or explained through claims of "replacement of *all* the fill below the floor," as was suggested for the finds at Capernaum. Magness is the

---

[20] Tzafrir, *Eretz Israel from the Destruction of the Second Temple to the Muslim Conquest. Vol. II. Archaeology and Art* (Jerusalem, 1984), pp. 185-186.

best representative of this second school. She claims a later date for the synaogue of Kh. Shema' based on her analysis of the pottery. In this volume, she gives a later date to Gush Halav and Capernaum, again focusing on pottery and arguing the methodology of the excavators. In her recent article, for the first time Magness is trying to show that "architectural dating" is not precise enough. She suggests that some architectural fragments from the Byzantine period dated buildings in northern Syria carry a similar design to those of the Roman period. Her summary is that the synagogues at Kh. Shema', Gush Halav, and Capernaum are fifth-sixth century, Byzantine period buildings.

Another recent article discussing the style and dating of Galilean synagogues was published by Z.U. Ma'oz. As a scholar of the first school (concerning Galilean synagogues), he identified a select group of synagogue as "the original series of the Galilean synagogue," and he pointed out that Bar'am should be used as their prototype. He declares that: "there is no doubt that the magnificent Galilean synagogues were built in the days of Rabbi, the days of the Severean dynasty...and it correlates with the architectural style dating."[21] He neglects the debate on the synagogue at Capernaum (this because his suggests that the synagogue was brought from a distance and rebuilt in the center of the Jewish village by Christian authorities as a pilgrimage site), and by this he escapes the confrontation with the dating-evidence excavated below the floor. He is using the results of excavations in the synagogue of Meiron (where problematic dating data came from only one locus out of the synagogue building), the synagogue of Kh. Amudim (where he wishes to look at the only floor that survived, as a second, later, floor level, even though there is no evidence for an earlier floor), and the synagogue at Gush Halav (where he is trying to add "period 0") to prove the founding of the buildings at the beginning of the third century C.E. and to relate the finds to the architectural style and the historical circumstances.

---

[21] Ma'oz, 1996, p. 422.

The Small Synagogue

The Site

The earliest pottery identified at the site is dated to the Persian period. From that time on, there is continuity from the Hellenistic through the Roman period to the end of the Byzantine period. No pottery dated to the Arab period was found. In the open area spread between the hill with the large synagogue and the low hill with the small synagogue, there is no pottery and no traces of walls. The collection of pottery from both sites suggests that both dwellings existed during the same period. This evidence led me to the conclusion that there were two different villages, side by side. Small villages like these two, built a short distance apart and founded in the Hellenistic period (mainly those with the GCW) were identified during our surveys in the Upper Galilee.[22] It is similar to the case of Gischala (Gush Halav), where the main village with a large synagogue was built on the top of the hill, and the small village with a smaller synagogue was built a short distance below.[23] Pottery, coins, building stones, and cisterns were found in a range of more than 50 m. around the synagogue, which yields a site that in size resembles the small village of Kh. Shema'.[24] There is at least one building beside the synagogue that was part of the village, and there is a large number of cooking pots, storage jars, oil lamps, and other potshards that point to private dwellings in the vicinity.

The Small Synagogue Building

Although the synagogue was dismantled below floor level, I do believe that the latest coins and pottery found there date the building stage of the synagogue to the second half of the fourth century C.E.

The plan is of a rectangular building with foundations of stylobates for three rows of pillars. There is no way to prove whether it had one or three entrances. The fifteenth and sixteenth century visitors men-

---

[22] For example, the distance between Har Afaim and Halat Biyar, both in the Meiron Mountains, is 400 m.

[23] E. Meyers, et.al., "Excavatons at Gush Halav," in *Ancient Synagogues Revealed* (1978).

[24] E. Meyers, et. al., "Excavations at Khirbet Shema-Upper Galilee" (1975).

tion two existing doorways, while eighteenth century and later visitors mention only one. According to its size, it is possible that it had only one doorway in the south. There is a possibility that the second door, if it did exist, was at the northern side.

In its second stage, the northern isle was blocked with a wall in the east and probably in the west; a wall was probably built on the northern stylobate (between the pillars or in place of the pillars); and the door was built on the western side of the northern stylobate, leading to a narrow room. To this stage we can correlate the bronze amulet that was placed below the first course of stoned, below the floor level.[25]

The technique of constructing the foundation is much different in the small synagogue from the technique in the large one. In the small synagogue, the foundations are all built of rough ashlars from the first courses down to bedrock. The stylobate's foundation walls are built in the same technique, while the stylobates in the large synagogue are built separately to each pillar in different sizes of cut stones.

As mentioned earlier, an unusual number of oil-lamp fragments were found in loc. 74 and in the built drainage channel. Most of the fragments are of the same "Northern Stamped Oil Lamp" group and probably were thrown into the drainage channel and under the floor at the same time, perhaps as some kind of a custom.

The large number of coins (around seventy) unearthed in the excavated area suggests the same known custom of throwing coins in the fill or under the pavers in ancient synagogues.

Since the synagogue was heavily dismantled, almost no architectural elements were left. The only evidence we have is from the PEF photos, showing a capital similar to those of the large synagogue. In the dig, two small pieces of Corinthian capitals were found, suggesting the decoration of the second story. A small (25 cm in diameter) Corinthian capital was found in the debris heap a short distance from the building, which could be a decoration of the Torah shrine.

---

[25] At the ancient synagogue at Meroth, a bronze amulet with an Aramaic inscription was found under the threshold of the northern entrance. This entrance is one of the latest stages of the building, while it was still being used as a synagogue. See Ilan, ibid.

Conclusion

The Bar'am structures, and especially the large one, add to our knowledge of ancient Galilean synagogues. These buildings challenge the first school of synagogue dating with two more late-dating synagogues; one can no longer defend an early dating by explaining away the "Capernaum problem" with claims of "non-scientific" and "careless" excavations and publications. For the Bar'am evidence comes from modern, careful, scientific excavations, in which every coin was found *in situ* and marked on the spot.

Two directions should be studied and investigated:

A) The suggestion that, in the mountainous Galilee (down to the Jesrael valley), a conservative school of architecture devotionally kept the "Roman style" tradition from earlier synagogues such as Meiron, Kh. Amudim (dated from the end of the third century C.E.), the second level of Nabratein (from the third century C.E.), to the fourth fifth century C.E. synagogues at Bar'am and Capernaum, to the fifth century C.E. synagogue at Chorazin and the fifth-sixth century C.E. synagogue at Meroth.[26] It is no longer possible to reject totally archaeological methods and data (as has been done even by some archaeologists) and to use only architectural design dating. Art and architecture historians will have to re-check their methods and to be more flexible in dating.

B) A change should be made in the traditional ways of thinking. In ancient synagogue research at this point, architectural and the archaeological dating continually clash. A new approach is due.

Until now, no one emphasized that the disagreement between architectural and archaeological dating exists only in ancient synagogues. A few pagan temples from the Early and Late Roman periods have been excavated at Samaria, Caesaria, Beit Shean, Qedesh, Mt. Snaim, Banias, and more, and there were no remains of any disagreement between archaeological and architectural dating. Such is the case with dozens of Byzantine churches that were excavated in the land of Israel. While some of the church's mosaic floors looked very "Late Byzantine," all scholars agreed that they would be dated, according to the archaeological finds, to the Early Arab period.

Should we search for historical or ethnical reasons?

---

[26] Tzafrir carefully hints towards this direction, although he himself does not continue to develop or to support it.

Ma'oz was the first to suggest a different solution to the "Capernaum problem," proposing that the building was moved from another Jewish village to be used at Capernaum as a "holy relict" of Jesus's synagogue, in this important pilgrimage site. Although he did not succeed in proving his theory, it is a new approach to the problem. Building new public buildings by reusing older structures (*spolia*) is well known in the ancient world, but it would still be very hard to prove that most Galilean synagogues were in this category. From the very end of the forth century C.E., Christian emperors legislated against building new synagogues. Is there a chance that rebuilding synagogues out of *spolia* was somehow a trick to avoid the law? Does the later inscription on the Nabratein synagogue provide an example?

Questions and approaches like these should be the next step in research into Galilean synagogues instead of a debate between the architectural and archaeological data.

Figure A.
The large Synagogue at Barᶜam.
Photo by R. Rabinowitz.

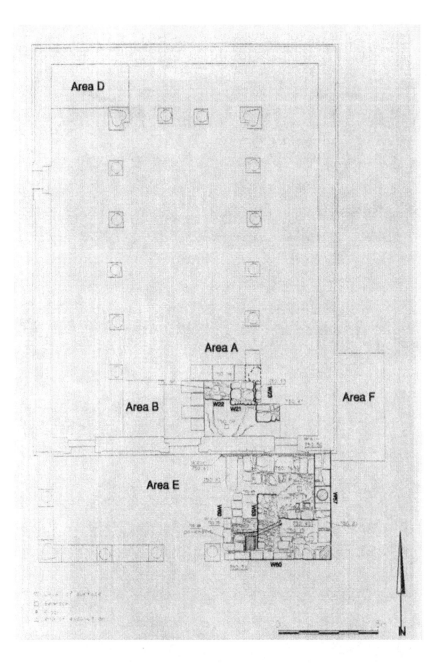

Area D

Area A

Area B

Area F

Area E

N

Figure B.
Plan 1

Figure C.
Coinhoard found at area B, locus 10.
Photo by R. Rabinowitz.

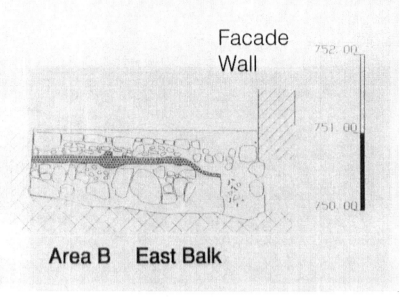

Facade
Wall

752.00

751.00

750.00

Area B   East Balk

Figure D. Area B. East Balk.

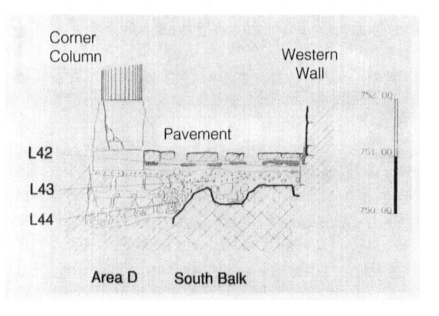

Corner
Column

Western
Wall

752.00

Pavement

751.00

L42

L43

750.00

L44

Area D   South Balk

Figure E. Area D. South Balk.

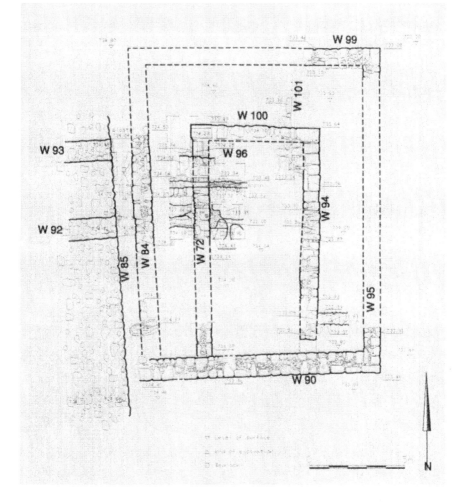

W 99

W 101

W 100

W 93

W 96

W 92

W 94

W 85

W 84

W 72

W 95

W 90

N

Figure F.
Plan 2.

APPENDIX

AN ARAMAIC AMULET FROM BAR'AM

Joseph Naveh
The Hebrew University of Jerusalem

The fragmentary amulet discussed here was found by M. Aviam while excavating the small synagogue at Bar'am. This is an important addition to the seven Jewish Aramaic amulets from the Galilee known to date. Five were published in *AMB* and *MSF*:[1] two from Horvat Kanaf (A2-3) and three others from Horvat Marish (A16), Tiberias (A17) and Horvat Kannah (A19) respectively. Two additional Galilean Aramaic amulets were subsequently published: one was excavated in Sepphoris,[2] and the other is a privately owned amulet inscribed, mostly in Hebrew, on an unbaked piece of clay, said to have been found in a field near Nazareth.[3] Except for the latter, all the incantation texts mentioned above were incised on thin metal sheets.

The reading of the text preserved in the Bar'am bronze amulet (originally c. 6 x 4.5 cm.) is rather difficult. The transliteration and translation below are suggested with a certain amount of reservation:[4]

1. ע[ן   [
2. על לכה דגבריאל בה אשבע[ת]
3. עליך נחמאל מלאכה דתטו[ר]
4. [..]ה דיורדן ברה דנונה ותטר [יתה]

---

[1] See J. Naveh and S. Shaked, *Amulets and Magic Bowls: Aramaic Incantations of Late Antiquity (AMB)* (Jerusalem, 1985); eidem, *Magic Spells and Formulae: Aramaic Incantations of Late Antiquity (MSF)* (Jerusalem, 1993). The numbers of the incantation texts cited below as "Amulet (or A) / Bowl (B) / Geniza (G) X" refer to the numbers of the texts in these books.

[2] C.T. McCollough and Beth Glazier-McDonald, "An Aramaic Amulet from Sepphoris," in *Atiqot* 28 (1996), pp. 161-165.

[3] See G.J. Hamilton, "A New Hebrew-Aramaic Incantation Text from Galilee: 'Rebuking the Sea'," in *Journal of Semitic Studies* 41 (1996), pp. 215-249.

[4] I would like to express my thanks to M. Aviam for entrusting me with the publication of this amulet and to Dr. Ada Yardeni, who produced the attached facsimile drawing and contributed much to the transliteration.

5. ‏[מ]ן ממללה דפמה ומן זמר[תה]‏
6. ‏[   ] ‏[וא פתח]   [‏
7-11. *broken or illegible*
12. ‏[ו] צוריאל כתבת יתך ו[ ]‏
13. ‏[דאלחה יהוה בגינך וס]‏
14. ‏[ד שעת מנה עד שעתה[.].‏על‏]‏
15. ‏[ ] [דיודן ברה דנונה א]‏
16. ‏[ ] ‏[קרע קרע ל]‏
17. *magic characters*
18. ‏[ ] אמן‏

The following translation is rather literal; for the possible meanings of the various Aramaic expressions see the Commentary below:

1.   [...   ]
2.   on the heart of Gabriel. By him [I] adjure
3.   you Naḥamel, the angel, that you should guard
4.   the [...] of Judan son of Nonna and you should guard [him]
5.   from the (evil) speech of the mouth and from [the] evil gaze.
6.   [...   ] open [...   ]
7-11. *broken or illegible*
12.   Ṣuriel. I have written you (the amulet?) [...]
13.   in order that God shall be because of you (?) [...   ]
14.   [...] from it until the time of [...]
15.   [...] that Judan son of Nonna [...]
16.   *magic words*
17.   *magic characters*
18.   [...   ] Amen.

Commentary

Line 1 is missing; only one letter, an *'ayin*, is visible at the beginning. This may perhaps be reconstructed as ‏[על חסדך ועל אמתך]‏ "Fo[r your mercy and for your truth]" (Ps. 115:1; 138:2); see the beginning of Amulet 16, where this phrase is followed by ‏בשם יהוה נעשה ונצליח‏ "In the name YHWH we shall do and succeed."

Line 2. The literal translation of ‏על לבה דגבריאל‏ is "on the heart of Gabriel." In the Babylonian Talmud the words ‏על לבא ד-‏, written ‏אליבא ד-‏, form a prepositional phrase meaning "according to the opinion of." Although ‏לב‏ may also mean "mind," the expression ‏על ליבא/ה ד-‏ is unknown in the Palestinian Talmud in particular and in Palestinian Aramaic in general. However, if one takes ‏לב‏ as an equivalent of Hebrew ‏דעה/דעת‏ "mind, opinion," one may translate ‏על‏

לבה דגבריאל "with the knowledge of Gabriel," and perhaps, in this magical context, even "in the name of Gabriel."[5]

בה "by him" may stand for בשמה "in his name;" see, e.g., Amulet 1:23 עליך בחי האל אלהי ישראל "(I adjure) you by (or: in the name of) the God who lives, God of Israel," which parallels Geniza 5:2-3 משבענה בשם חי האל ובשם צוריאל "I adjure you in the name of the God who lives and in the name of Ṣuriel."

Line 4. At the beginning of the line the amulet is partly broken; there is space for two relatively narrow letters. The remnants before ה דיודן [ ] may perhaps justify the reconstruction ה[רז], but this is somewhat hazardous, because ח is unknown in a similar context. The semantic field of the word רז "secret, mystery" is very broad in the magical texts. The main goal of the magician is to know and utilise the mysteries of the supernatural world,[6] but the word רז may also indicate "invocation, incantation" and even "amulet." A bowl text opens as follows: רזא רזא דנן לשתוקי ולסכורי פומה דכל בני אינשה בישי ותקיפי "Mystery. This mystery is for the the silencing and shutting the mouth of all evil and violent people" (Bowl 6:1-2). In other bowls we read: מזמן הדין רזא לכיבשא ד- "This mystery is designated for the subduing of ..." (Bowl 21:1); דין רזא לאסותא ד- "This mystery is for the healing of ..." (Bowl 19:1). In these examples the word רזא is used exactly as קמיעא "amulet." In Bowl 19:5-6, רז is also used in a negative sense: תוב מומינא ומשבענא וגזרנא ומשמיתנא ובטילנא ית כל רזי חרשין ומיני

---

[5] See B. Yom. 19b: "We adjure you according to our mind and in the mind of the Beit Din" (trans. of I. Epstein, *The Babylonian Talmud, Seder Mo'ed*, III (London, 1938), p. 83); as well as the phrase recited before Kol Nidrei: "With the consent of (trans. of Philip Birnbaum, *High Holiday Prayer Book* (New York, 1951), p. 490) the Lord and with the consent of the Congregation ... we permit to pray with the sinners."

[6] In *The Sword of Moses* we read: "If you wish to use this Sword ... pray three times a day and after each prayer recite the following: 'Blessed are you, O Lord our God, King of the Universe, who opens every day the gates of the East and cleaves the windows of the firmament of the Orient, and gives light to the entire world and to its habitants, with the multitude of His mercies, with His mysteries and secrets, and teaches His people Israel His mysteries and secrets, and reveals to them the Sword used in the world'." Cf. M. Gaster's translation in his *Studies and Texts in Folklore, Magic, Medieval Romance, Hebrew Apocrypha and Samaritan Archaeology*, London 1928 (2nd edition New York: Ktav Publishing House,1971), vol. I, p. 313. For the original Hebrew text see vol. III, p. 70. For a new edition see: יובל הררי, חרבא דמשה, מהדורה חדשה ומחקר, ירושלים: אקדמון, 1997

חרשין "Further, I adjure, invoke, decree, ban and annul all mysteries of sorcerers and kinds of sorceries."

The name of the client's mother, Nonna, occurs in a Palestinian amulet of unknown provenance, where the name of the client is Nonna the daughter of Megale (A25), and in a hardly legible unpublished one, which opens as follows: קמיע לפריגורי בת נונה "An amulet for Paregori daughter of Nonna."

Line 5. [מ]ן ממללה דפמה ומן זמר[תה]. Cf. in a Syriac bowl in *AMB*, Bowl 10:12: מן ממלל פומיה ומן עובדא עדיה "from the speech of his mouth and from the (evil) deeds (or: sorceries) of his hand." There are numerous amulets and recipe fragments in the Geniza written in order that people should not speak evil against the clients. A special recipe משבע אנא "to shut someone's mouth" reads as follows: למסכר פומא ואסרנא ובלימנא ומסכרנא ומטרשנא לבהון דכל בני אנשא וחוה דלא ינזקון יתי אנא פל' בן פל' "I adjure, bind, restrain, shut and obstruct the hearts of all sons of man and Eve, that they may not harm me, I, N. son of N." (G 16, p. 3:8-11). A Geniza amulet begins as follows: על שמך משבענא ואסרנא ובלימנא ומסכרנא ומעינא ומטרשנא לבהון דכל בני אדם וחוה דלא ינזקון יתי אנא סתהם בת סת אלאהל "By your name, I adjure, bind, restrain, bar, investigate and obstruct the hearts of all sons of Adam and Eve, that they should not harm me I, Sitahm daughter of Sitt al-Ahl" (G 19, p. 1:1-8). Then the amulet says: ... ובשם עמיאל ומיכאל ... ועליהם שרים אחרים שהן שליטין על פומא דבני אנשא לאפוקי מלין טבין ולא יכלין לאפוקי מלין בישין ... ויסתכר פמהון דכל בני אנשא ופום מוסי בן גאלא שלא ינזק אותי אני סתחם "and in the name of ʿAmiel and Michael ... and with them other princes ..., who have power over the mouth of people that they may utter good words, and that they should not be able to utter bad words ... and the mouths of all people should be shut as well as the mouth of Musa son of Jala, and he may not harm me, I Sitahm" (p. 1:32, p. 2:10-14). Most instructive is the passage in a Geniza recipe, G15, p. 1:8-10: דלא יקומון ולא יהלכון ולא יאמרון ולא יחשבון ולא ימללון עלי מילה בישה וכל חרשיהון יתבטלון "that they should not stand up, and not walk about and not speak and not think and not utter against me an evil word and all their sorceries be annuled."

The parallel term זמר[תה], must likewise have a negative connotation. In the Syriac bowl cited above "the speech of his mouth" is paralled by "the (evil) deeds of his hand," but such a meaning is difficult to posit for the root זמר. James Nathan Ford pointed out that the collocation of references to evil speech (mouth, tongue) and the

evil eye is known from Mesopotamian and Egyptian incantations.[7]
This suggests a relationship with זמורה, which occurs in a context of
the evil eye in another Jewish Paletinian Aramaic amulet (*AMB*,
A1:16).[8] Both terms would appear to be ultimately related to Syriac
זמרא and its derivatives, which are documented with reference to
eyes. In particular, the mediaeval lexicographer, Bar Bahlūl defines
זמורותא alternately as a color of eyes (rendered "steel-gray," or the
like, by the modern dictionaries[9]) and as an ocular dysfunction
"bulging,"[10] either of which appropriate as an attribute of evil eye.
Although it is difficult to ascertain which of these possible attributes is
intended (here and in *AMB*, A1:16), a translation "evel gaze" seems
suitable in the present context.[11]

Lines 12-13. כתבת יתך ... דאלחא יהוה בגינך "I have written you (the amulet?) ... in order that God will be ...". Cf. A1:12-13: אנה כתבת יי[ן]יאסי
"I have written, Go[d will] heal," as well as two bowl texts, Isbell
1:14-15: אנחנא כתבנא ושמיה יאסיך "we have written, and His name will
heal you;" Isbell 69:8 ... אנא כתבית ואלהא מארי כולא יסי ית "I have written
and God the Lord of all will heal ..."[12]

דאלחה (instead of דאלהה) seems to be a deliberate alteration which is
very common in magical texts.[13]

בגין is generally used as a conjunction "because, since, in order
that," or as a preposition "because of." בגינך "because of you" is
difficult in this context. Can it be a corruption of מגינך "your shield,
your protector"?

---

[7] See M.-L. Thomsen, "The Evil Eye in Mesopotamia," in *JNES* 51 (1992), pp.
21-22, 30-31; I.E.S. Edwards, *Hieratic Papyri in the British Museum. Fourth Series Oracular
Amuletic Decrees of the Late Kingdom*, 2 vols. (London, 1960), pp. 3, 38 (translation); pls.
Ia and XIIIa (text).

[8] Cf. Bereshit Rabba (ed. Theodor-Albeck), p. 1038, line 6: "his eyes were steel-
gray like his mother's" (translation by M. Sokoloff, *A Dictionary of Jewish Palestinian
Aramaic*, Ramat Gan: Bar-Ilan University Press, 1990, p. 178a).

[9] Sokoloff's definition of Jewish Palestinian Aramaic זמוד (above, n. 8) is based on
this interpretation of the Syriac cognate.

[10] See R. Duval, ed., *Lexicon Syriacum auctore Hassano Bar Bahlule, e pluribus codicibus
edidit et notulis instuxit*, Collection Orientale, 15 (Paris 1901), p. 691.

[11] I thank J.N. Ford, who wrote this paragraph, for sharing with me the results of
his unpublished research.

[12] C.D. Isbell, *Corpus of the Aramaic Incantation Bowls* (Missoula, 1975).

[13] See J. Naveh, "Lamp Inscriptions and Inverted writing," in *Israel Exploration
Journal* 38 (1988), pp. 36-43; idem, "Fragments of an Aramaic Magic book from
Qumran," in *Israel Exploration Journal* 48 (1998), p. 259.

Line 14. מנה על[.]. In this fragmentary text על[.] is not clear.

Line 16. קרע seems to belong to the 42-letter combination אבג יתץ קרע ... שטן, consisting of the initials of the prayer of Rabbi Neḥunia ben Haqana: ... אנא בכח גדלת ימינך תתיר צרורה קבל רנת עמך שגבנו טהרנו נורא. If so, this is to the best of my knowledge the earliest allusion to this prayer; the 42-letter combination is known from the Geniza magic texts, but neither from Palestinian amulets nor from Babylonian magic bowls.

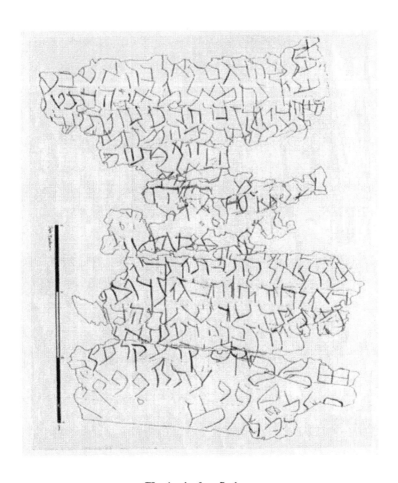

The Amulet from Bar'am.

GENERAL INDEX